自治区社情民意调查中心
（统计咨询服务中心）

自治区社情民意调查中心（统计咨询服务中心）是隶属于自治区统计局的事业法人单位。现有中高级技术人员 11 人，合同制职工 11 人。主要职责是完成国家统计局社情民意调查中心布置的各类全国性社情民意调查工作，组织实施自治区党委、人民政府及有关部门委托的社情民意调查任务；开展统计咨询、相关信息资料、加工处理与咨询服务；组织协调自治区境内信息调查行业相关工作。

中心拥有 60 门国际先进的 GW-CATI(计算机辅助电话访问系统)，40 个访问席位。严格恪守欧洲国际商会和欧洲市场研究于民意测验协会制定的关于市场和社会研究的国际准则 -ESOMAR 规则。与自治区相关部门、研究机构及高等学府有着广泛密切的合作关系。

“听民声、查民情、了解民忧、问政于民”。自治区社情民意调查中心将以更高的标准、科学的管理、严谨认真的工作态度使其成为深入了解民情，充分反映民意，广泛集中民智、切实珍惜民力的一条重要渠道。

PRINT
新疆统计印刷厂
XINJIANGTONGJIYINSHUACHANG
为您的事业
增色添彩
Bestech 40
Akiyama
Akiyama
电话：0991-2626838
手机：18963806118

新疆统计年鉴

XINJIANG STATISTICAL YEARBOOK

2014

新疆维吾尔自治区统计局・编
Compiled by Statistics Bureau of Xinjiang Uygur Autonomous Region

中国统计出版社
China Statistics Press

图书在版编目（CIP）数据

新疆统计年鉴. 2014 ： 汉英对照 / 新疆维吾尔自治区统计局编. -- 北京 ： 中国统计出版社，2014.9
ISBN 978-7-5037-7273-3

Ⅰ. ①新… Ⅱ. ①新… Ⅲ. ①统计资料－新疆－2014－年鉴－汉、英 Ⅳ. ①C832.45-54

中国版本图书馆CIP数据核字（2014）第204367号

新疆统计年鉴—2014

作　　者/新疆维吾尔自治区统计局
责任编辑/佘竞雄
装帧设计/马思蕊
出版发行/中国统计出版社
地　　址/北京市丰台区西三环南路甲6号 邮政编码/100073
电　　话/邮购（010）63376909　书店（010）68783171
网　　址/http://csp.stats.gov.cn
印　　刷/新疆统计印刷厂
经　　销/新华书店
开　　本/890mm×1240mm　1/16
字　　数/1400千字
印　　张/45
版　　别/2014年9月第1版
版　　次/2014年9月第1次印刷
定　　价/460.00元（含光盘）

本书附同版本CD-ROM一张，光盘内容以书面文字为准。
如有印装差错，由本社发行部调换。

《新疆统计年鉴——2014》编辑委员会

XINJIANG STATISTICAL YEARBOOK-2014
NAME LIST OF EDITORIAL BOARD

编者说明

一、《新疆统计年鉴—2014》系统收录了全区和各地、县（市）2013年经济和社会各方面的统计数据，以及重要历史年份和近年全区主要统计数据，并收录了全国及各省市区2013年的主要统计数据，是一部全面反映新疆维吾尔自治区经济和社会发展情况的资料性年刊。

二、全书内容分为：特载（新疆维吾尔自治区2013年国民经济和社会发展统计公报）；综合；国民经济核算；人口与就业；固定资产投资；对外经济贸易和旅游；资源与环境；能源生产和消费；财政；物价；人民生活；城市概况；农业；工业；建筑业；运输和邮电；批发和零售、住宿和餐饮业；金融业；教育、科技和文化；卫生及其他；各地、州、市主要经济指标排序；附录（各省、市、区主要经济指标排序）。各篇前有简要说明，篇末附有《主要统计指标解释》。

三、本《年鉴》的资料来源，大部分来自年度报表，部分来自抽样调查资料。

四、资料中所使用的度量衡单位均采用国家法定计量单位。

五、本《年鉴》总量指标计算所采用的价格均为现行价格。

六、本《年鉴》伊犁哈萨克自治州的数据包括伊犁州直属县（市）、塔城地区和阿勒泰地区。

七、本《年鉴》使用符号说明："#"表示其中项；"..."表示不足小数位的数据；"空"表示没有或未掌握该指标数据。

八、本《年鉴》在编辑过程中得到自治区内外许多单位和同志们的大力支持，在此深表谢意。限于我们的水平，加之时间仓促，不足之处，敬请各级领导、各界人士和统计战线的同仁批评指正。

Editor's Explanatory Notes

Ⅰ.Xinjiang statistical yearbook 2014 systemly included the economic and social aspects of statistical data by region and throughout the county (city) in 2013,and the main statistical data in historically important years and recent years, and included the major statistical data of provinces and regions in 2013.The book is an annual statistic publication of fully reflect the developmen of economic and social in Xinjiang Uygur Autonomous Region.

Ⅱ.The yearbook comprises such sections as: Special Article (Statistical Communique on National Economy and Social Development of Xinjiang Uygur Autonomous Region in the year 2013); general survey; national accounts; population and employment; investment in fixed assets; foreign trade & economic cooperation and tourism; resources and environment; production and consumption of energy; government finance; price; people's livelihood; general survey of cities; agriculture; industry; construction; transport and telecommunication services; wholesale & retail trades, hotels and catering services; financial;education, science & technology and culture; public health and others; ranking of main economic indicators by region of Xinjiang; appendix (ranking of main economic indicators by region),etc. Each section is equipped with Explanatory Notes on Main Statistical Indicators at the end.

Ⅲ. The Yearbook of sources are mostly from the annual statements, in part from the sample survey data.

Ⅳ.The units of measurement used in this yearbook are internationally standard measurement units.

Ⅴ.The computation of all the gross indicators in the yearbook is equipped with current prices.

Ⅵ.The data about Yili Kazak Autonomous Prefecture in the present Xinjiang Statistical Yearbook covers counties (cities) direct under Yili Prefecture, Tacheng Prefecture and Altay Prefecture.

Ⅶ.Description of signs or symbols in the yearbook:

"#"stands for interim item; "..." for data with insufficient decimal place ; "blank" for absence of data indicators or ignorance of them.

Ⅷ.In the course of complication, the yearbook has received great support from many units and comrades in and out of Autonomous Region, we acknowledge their help to the book. Mistakes and faults are inevitable to take place for inadequate proficiency and limited time. Leaders, personnel from all walks of life and colleagues from statistical sector are welcome to make their critical comments and suggestions.

目 录 CONTENTS

第一篇 综 合

CHAPTER 1 GENERAL SURVEY

第 二 篇 国民经济核算

CHAPTER 2 NATIONAL ACCOUNTS

第三篇 人口与就业

CHAPTER 3 POPULATION AND EMPLOYMENT

第 四 篇 固定资产投资

CHAPTER 4 INVESTMENT IN FIXED ASSETS

第 五 篇 对外经济贸易和旅游

CHAPTER 5 FOREIGN TRADE AND ECONOMIC COOPERATION & TOURISM

第 六 篇　资源与环境

CHAPTER 6 NATURAL RESOURCES AND ENVIRONMENT PROTECTION

第 七 篇　能源生产和消费

CHAPTER 7 PRODUCTION AND CONSUMPTION OF ENERGY

第八篇 财 政

CHAPTER 8 GOVERNMENT FINANCE

第九篇 物 价

CHAPTER 9 PRICE

第 十 篇 人民生活

CHAPTER 10 PEOPLE'S LIVELIHOOD AND SOCIAL WELFARE

第 十一 篇 城市概况

CHAPTER 11 GENERAL SURVEY OF CITIES

第十二篇 农 业

CHAPTER 12 AGRICULTURE

第十三篇 工 业

CHAPTER 13 INDUSTRY

第 十四 篇 建筑业

CHAPTER 14 CONSTRUCTION

第 十五 篇 运输和邮电

CHAPTER 15 TRANSPORT, POSTAL AND TELECOMMUNICATION SERVICES

第十六篇 批发和零售业、住宿和餐饮业

CHAPTER 16 WHOLESALE & RETAIL TRADES, HOTELS AND CATERING SERVICES

第十七篇 金融业

CHAPTER 17 FINANCIAL INTERMEDIATION

第十八篇 教育、科技和文化

CHAPTER 18 EDUCATION SCIENCE & TECHNOLOGY AND CULTURE

第 十九 篇　卫生及其他

CHAPTER 19 PUBLIC HEALTH AND OTHERS

第 二十 篇 各地州市主要经济指标排序

CHAPTER 20 RANKING OF MAIN ECONOMIC INDICATORS BY PREFECTURE, AUTONOMOUS PREFECTURE, CITY AND COUNTY OF XINJIANG

附录：各省市区主要经济指标排序

APPENDIX: RANKING OF MAIN ECONOMIC INDICATORS BY REGION

新疆统计年鉴

XINJIANG STATISTICAL YEARBOOK

特载

SPECIAL ARTICLE

新疆维吾尔自治区
2013年国民经济和社会发展
统 计 公 报

2013 年,在党中央、国务院亲切关怀下，自治区党委、人民政府团结带领全区各族人民，认真贯彻落实党的十八大、十八届三中全会和中央新疆工作座谈会精神，按照自治区第八次党代会和自治区党委八届四次全委（扩大）会议部署，始终坚持稳中求进、进中求变总基调，牢牢把握主题主线，在全球经济复杂多变、国内经济下行压力增大的情况下，通过新春好开局、实干促落实等系列活动，沉着应对各种风险挑战，取得经济、文化、社会、生态文明建设新成就。

一、综 合

全年实现地区生产总值（GDP）8360.24 亿元，比上年增长 11.0%。其中，第一产业增加值 1468.30 亿元，增长 6.9%；第二产业增加值 3776.98 亿元，增长 13.1%；第三产业增加值 3114.96 亿元，增长 10.2%。在第二产业中，工业增加值 3035.28 亿元，增长 12.2%;建筑业增加值 741.70 亿元,增长 16.8%。

按常住人口计算，人均地区生产总值 37181 元，增长 9.6%。按当年平均汇率折合 6065 美元。

居民消费价格比上年上涨 3.9%，其中，食品价格上涨 8.5%。

表 1: 2013 年居民消费价格变动情况

指 标	涨跌幅度(%)
居民消费价格	3.9
城 市	3.8
农 村	4.1
食 品	8.5
#粮 食	6.3
肉禽及其制品	14.9
油脂类	3.4
蛋 类	11.0
水产品	7.0
菜 类	5.8
烟酒及用品	1.7
衣 着	-0.2
家庭设备用品及维修服务	1.3
医疗保健和个人用品	1.4
交通和通信	0.1
娱乐教育文化用品及服务	1.1
居 住	3.4

工业生产者出厂价格下降 3.5%，其中，轻工业下降 0.4%，重工业下降 4.0%。工业生产者购进价格下降 2.2%。农业生产资料价格上涨 2.6%。固定资产投资价格上涨 0.5%。

二、农 业

全年实现农林牧渔业总产值 2538.88 亿元，比上年增长 7.2%，其中，农业总产值 1806.11 亿元，增长 7.1%;林业总产值 48.13 亿元，增长 8.1%；畜牧业总产值 604.20 亿元，增长 7.8%；渔业总产值 17.17 亿元，增长 7.8%；农林牧渔服务业总产值 63.27 亿元，增长 5.7%。

农作物播种面积 7818.39 万亩，增长 1.5%。其中，粮食（含薯类）3352.20 万亩，增长 4.9%；棉花 2577.39 万亩，下降 0.2%；油料 332.61 万亩，下降 8.5%；甜菜 98.85 万亩，下降 20.2%；蔬菜 445.02 万亩，下降 3.3%（工业番茄 84.97 万亩，下降 3.0%；工业辣椒 67.12 万亩，下降 18.9%）。特色林果 2210.84 万亩，下降 3.4%。

粮食产量(含薯类)1441.68 万吨，增长 8.8%。棉花 351.80 万吨，下降 0.6%。油料 60.63 万吨，增长 2.7%。甜菜 476.47 万吨，下降 17.5%。蔬菜 1669.92 万吨，增长 0.8%（工业番茄 579.43 万吨，与上年持平；工业辣椒 180.76 万吨，下降 17.3%）。特色林果 1371.03 万吨，增长 9.0%。

表 2：2013 年特色林果产量及变动情况

指　标	产量(万吨)	比上年增长(%)
特色林果	1371.03	9.0
园林水果	782.69	6.2
#红枣	199.37	37.1
香梨	52.14	-13.9
葡萄	223.93	7.1
坚果	44.10	23.2
核桃	40.28	28.4
巴旦木	3.55	57.1
果用瓜	544.24	12.1
甜瓜	239.46	12.2

年末牲畜存栏 4502.86 万头（只），比上年增长 3.9%。全年牲畜出栏 3862.06 万头（只），增长 3.3%。肉类总产量 139.26 万吨，增长 4.1%，其中，羊肉产量 49.71 万吨，增长 3.5%；牛肉产量 37.82 万吨，增长 4.6%；猪肉产量 31.33 万吨，增长 3.9%；禽兔肉产量 11.86 万吨，增长 12.5%。禽蛋产量 28.17 万吨，增长 8.8%。牛奶产量 134.99 万吨，增长 2.1%。羊毛产量 9.68 万吨，增长 5.2%。

年末农业机械总动力 2165.87 万千瓦，增长 10.0%。拥有大中型拖拉机 39.70 万台，增长 15.8%。小型拖拉机 31.85 万台，下降 4.9%。化肥施用量（折纯）203.22 万吨，增长 5.5%。农村用电量 83.92 亿千瓦时，增长 10.7%。

拥有农业产业化经营组织 10210 个。自治区级以上农业产业化重点龙头企业 390 家。农产品加工（流通）企业 10975 个。实现农产品加工（流通）业总产值 1406.87 亿元。

三、工业和建筑业

规模以上工业企业 2224 家，比上年增加 265 家，增长 13.5%，实现工业增加值 2933.87 亿元，增长 12.9%。

在自治区重点监测的十大产业中，有色工业增加值 133.24 亿元，电力工业 237.06 亿元，化学工业 216.41 亿元，钢铁工业 59.25 亿元，煤炭工业 135.93 亿元，纺织工业 45.49 亿元，农副食品加工工业 62.55 亿元，装备制造工业 69.59 亿元，石油工业 1514.47 亿元，汽车工业 0.79 亿元。

规模以上工业出口交货值 68.01 亿元，增长 63.8%。实现利润总额 855.23 亿元，增长 1.6%。

具有资质等级的总承包和专业承包建筑企业总产值 2079.66 亿元，增长 28.2%。

表 3：2013 年工业企业主要产品产量及变动情况

产品名称	单 位	产 量	比上年增长(%)
原 油	万吨	2658.47	3.3
天然气	亿立方米	282.91	11.7
原油加工量	万吨	2510.19	3.3
乙 烯	万吨	131.92	3.8
发电量	亿千瓦时	1613.01	44.0
成品糖	万吨	46.72	-12.9
卷 烟	亿支	180.00	5.9
罐 头	万吨	67.06	-3.4
#番茄酱	万吨	59.99	-4.5
纱	万吨	43.46	8.1
布	万米	7451.00	11.6
机制纸及纸板	万吨	45.74	11.4
化肥(折纯)	万吨	374.77	23.2
粗 钢	万吨	1276.77	12.2
钢 材	万吨	1512.90	17.3
生 铁	万吨	1431.13	7.7
水 泥	万吨	5410.00	25.3
变压器	万千伏安	6036.37	-2.6
塑料制品	万吨	186.66	33.3
服 装	万件	2982.00	5.5
轻 革	万平方米	593.34	14.5

四、固定资产投资

全社会固定资产投资 8148.41 亿元，比上年增长 30.2%。其中，城镇投资 7384.41 亿元，增长 32.0%；农村投资 764.00 亿元，增长 15.0%。

在城镇投资中，第一产业投资 153.17 亿元，增长 38.5%；第二产业投资 3836.05 亿元，增长 24.6%；第三产业投资 3395.20 亿元，增长 41.2%。在第二产业中，工业投资 3764.69 亿元，增长 26.0%。

房地产开发投资 825.69 亿元，增长 36.2%，其中，住宅投资 555.62 亿元，增长 25.1%。房屋施工面积 9459.55 万平方米，增长 37.2%；竣工面积 1722.16 万平方米，下降 0.8%。商品房销售面积 2017.03 万平方米，增长 41.0%；销售额 860.95 亿元，增长 53.6%。

五、国内贸易

社会消费品零售总额 2039.15 亿元，比上年增长 13.4%，扣除价格因素，实际增长 9.8%。

按经营地划分，城镇消费品零售额 1861.36 亿元，增长 13.3%；乡村消费品零售额 177.79 亿元，增长 13.4%。

按行业划分，批发和零售业零售额 1769.33 亿元，增长 13.5%；住宿和餐饮业零售额 269.82 亿元，增长 12.7%。

按商品类别划分，限额以上单位食品类零售额增长 8.8%，服装、鞋帽、针纺织品类增长 4.5%，金银珠宝类增长 19.3%，家用电器和音像制品类增长 3.5%，石油及制品类增长 27.1%，汽车类增长 8.2%。

六、对外经济

货物进出口总额 275.62 亿美元，比上年增长 9.5%。其中，出口 222.70 亿美元，增长 15.1%；进口 52.92 亿美元，下降 9.1%。

拥有 190 个贸易伙伴国家和地区，其中，对哈萨克斯坦进出口总额 122.55 亿美元，增长 9.7%；吉尔吉斯斯坦 41.73 亿美元，增长 3.3%；塔吉克斯坦 15.85 亿美元，增长 12.6%；美国 8.07 亿美元，下降 20.9%；俄罗斯 4.54 亿美元，下降 29.5%。

表 4：2013 年货物进出口总额及变动情况

指　标	绝对数(亿美元)	比上年增长(%)
货物进出口总额	275.62	9.5
货物出口额	222.70	15.1
其中：一般贸易	85.10	21.4
加工贸易	2.12	10.9
边境小额贸易	106.33	19.2
货物进口额	52.92	-9.1
其中：一般贸易	10.02	-30.1
加工贸易	2.98	3.4 倍
边境小额贸易	37.25	-8.8

按登记注册类型划分，国有企业进出口 71.89 亿美元，增长 4.5%；集体企业 1.17 亿美元，下降 52.3%；外商投资企业 2.52 亿美元，下降 8.3%；私营企业 200.04 亿美元，增长 12.6%。

新批准设立外商直接投资企业 45 个，下降 19.6%。合同使用外商直接投资项目 42 个，下降 23.6%；外商直接投资合同金额 3.60 亿美元，下降 41.0%；实际利用外商直接投资 4.81 亿美元，增长 15.7%。

七、交通、邮电和旅游

铁路货运量 7399 万吨，比上年增长 6.7%；公路货运量 68528 万吨，增长 10.8%；机场货物吞吐量 16.88 万吨，增长 18.0%。

铁路客运量 2318 万人，增长 7.2%；公路客运量 56000 万人，增长 6.7%；机场旅客吞吐量 1987.86 万人，增长 15.1%。

年末铁路营业里程 4911 公里，与上年持平；公路里程 17.02 万公里，增长 2.6%。

年末民用汽车保有量 243.3 万辆（包括三轮车和低速货车），增长 15.3%，其中，私人汽车 175.4 万辆，增长 18.9%。

电信业务总量 268.17 亿元，增长 8.7%；邮政业务总量 18.78 亿元，增长 3.4%。年末固定电话用户 544.80 万户，增长 0.9%。固定电话普及率每百人 24.4 部。新增移动电话用户 125.40 万户，年末达到 2133.90 万户，其中，3G 移动电话用户 709.70 万户，增长 78.8%。移动电话普及率每百人 98.6 部。互联网宽带用户 293 万户，增长 15.0%。

全年接待旅游总人数 5205.73 万人次，增长 7.1%，其中，接待入境旅游 156.73 万人次，增长 4.6%；国内旅游 5049 万人次，增长 7.2%。实现旅游总收入 673.29 亿元，增长 16.9%，其中，旅游外汇收入 5.85 亿美元，增长 6.3%；国内旅游收入 637.43 亿元，增长 17.6%。

八、财政和金融

全口径财政收入 2246.6 亿元，比上年增长 16.7%。地方财政收入 1556.55 亿元，增长 24.4%，其中，公共财政预算收入 1128.49 亿元，增长 24.2%；基金预算收入 426.32 亿元，增长 24.4%；国有资本经营预算收入 1.74 亿元，下降 51.0%。

地方财政支出 3519.62 亿元，增长 14.3%。其中，公共财政预算支出 3067.12 亿元，增长 12.8%；基金预算支出 450.33 亿元，增长 25.1%；国有资本经营预算支出 2.17 亿元，下降 30.2%。

年末金融机构（含外资）人民币各项存款余额 14088.83 亿元，比年初增加 1752.82 亿元，比上年增长 14.3%。其中，单位存款余额 7677.24 亿元，增长 16.5%；个人存款余额 6001.74 亿元，增长 13.1%。

年末金融机构（含外资）人民币各项贷款余额 9840.46 亿元，比年初增加 1915.72 亿元，增长 24.3%。其中，短期贷款 3372.94 亿元，增长 22.2%；中长期贷款 5723.23 亿元，增长 23.5%。个人消费贷款 1053.09 亿元，增长 39.9%。

境内上市公司 39 家，与上年持平，总股本 338.61 亿股，增长 27.0%；股票市价总值 2650.78 亿元，增长 5.2%；全年通过发行、配售股票共筹集资金 155.06 亿元，减少 24.1%。

法人证券公司 1 家，证券营业部 62 家，证券交易额 7112.32 亿元，增长 77.8%；期货公司 2 家，期货营业部 9 家，期货交易额 9871.48 亿元，增长 11.5%。

保险公司各项保费收入 273.49 亿元，比上年增长 16.1%。其中，寿险 124.40 亿元，增长 9.4%；财产险 113.23 亿元，增长 20.9%；健康险 25.20 亿元，增长 31.4%；意外伤害险 10.66 亿元，增长 18.2%。

各类保险赔款及给付支出 106.59 亿元，增长 33.0%。其中，财产险赔款 62.35 亿元，增长 23.9%；寿险给付 31.10 亿元，增长 53.0%；健康险赔付 10.37 亿元，增长 43.6%；意外伤害险赔付 2.77 亿元，增长 24.6%。

九、教育和科学技术

年末共有普通高等学校 36 所，比上年增加 2 所。全年研究生教育招生 6222 人，增长 9.1%；在校研究生 16867 人，增长 9.1%；毕业生 4775 人，增长 17.2%。本专科招生 8.34 万人，增长 6.9%；在校生 27.84 万人，增长 3.6%；毕业生 7 万人，增长 8.3%。

中等专业学校 93 所，全年招生 8.39 万人，下降 3.3%；在校生 22.93 万人，下降 2.5%；毕业生 7.49 万人，增长 5.0%。

普通高中 366 所，全年招生 16.36 万人，增长 5.3%；在校生 44.75 万人，增长 1.5%；毕业生 13.98 万人，增长 3.5%。

初中 1102 所，全年招生 31.36 万人，下降 0.3%；在校生 91.85 万人，下降 2.6%；毕业生 31.14 万人，下降 2.5%。

小学 3533 所，全年招生 34.86 万人，增长 5.1%；在校生 189.44 万人，下降 0.3%；毕业生 32.13 万人，增长 0.1%。

特殊教育学校 26 所，全年招生 1473 人，增长 29.6%；在校生 5229 人，增长 6.5%；毕业生 680 人，增长 30.3%。

幼儿园 3864 所，全年招生 37.33 万人，下降 2.0%；在园幼儿 71.90 万人，增长 3.6%；毕业幼儿 31.19 万人，增长 8.3%。

小学学龄儿童净入学率 99.8%；小学毕业生升入初中升学率 97.6%；初中阶段适龄少年净入学率 98.0%；初中毕业升入高中阶段升学率 88.7%。

安排自治区级科技计划项目 2302 项，其中，科技支撑计划 223 项，高技术研究发展计划 149 项，科技兴新项目 152 项，科技成果转化专项资金项目 51 项，科技中小企业技术创新基金项目 136 项。共获得省部级以上科技成果 257 项。

年末拥有县以上政府部门属研究与技术开发机构 111 个。其中，自然科学研究与技术开发机构 97

个，科技信息与文献机构 8 个，社会与人文科学领域研究与技术开发机构 6 个。

重点实验室 33 个，其中，国家重点实验室 1 个。批准成立的工程技术研究中心 20 个，其中，国家级 4 个。组建期内的工程技术中心 87 个。自治区科技成果转化基地 35 个。

国家级高新技术企业 269 个。高新技术工业园区 8 个，其中国家级 2 个。生产力促进中心 64 个，其中，国家级示范中心 9 个。国家级创新型企业 5 个，国家级创新型试点企业 7 个。

全年受理专利申请 8224 项。其中，受理发明专利申请 2081 项，占 25.3%；获得专利授权 4998 项，其中，获得发明专利授权 540 项，占 10.8%。签订技术合同 983 项，技术合同成交金额 2.97 亿元，其中，技术交易额 2.84 亿元。

十、文化和体育

年末共有艺术表演团体 108 个，文化馆 116 个，公共图书馆 106 个，博物馆 76 个，国家综合档案馆 109 个，开放档案室 45.87 万卷。拥有广播电台 6 座，电视台 8 座，广播电视台 88 座，中、短波广播发射台和转播台 66 座。广播综合人口覆盖率 95.7%。电视综合人口覆盖率 96.0%。有线电视用户 199.5 万户，下降 8.0%，其中，有线数字电视用户 186.36 万户，下降 7.0%。广播电视农村直播卫星用户 256.44 万户。

建成 13 个县级全民健身活动中心，36 个乡镇农民体育健身工程，90 个行政村农牧民体育健身工程，10 个社区体育俱乐部和 4 个体育公园。在国际比赛中荣获金牌 2 枚，银牌 2 枚，铜牌 1 枚。在全国比赛中荣获金牌 39 枚，银牌 37 枚，铜牌 51 枚。全年销售体育彩票 15.09 亿元，增长 14.6%；筹集体彩公益金 3.7 亿元，增长 12.1%。

十一、人口与人民生活

年末总人口 2264.30 万人，其中，城镇人口 1006.93 万人，乡村人口 1257.37 万人。城镇化率 44.5%。全年人口出生率 15.84‰，死亡率 4.92‰，自然增长率 10.92‰。

城镇居民人均可支配收入 19874 元，比上年增长 10.9%。人均家庭总收入 22388 元，增长 10.9%，其中，工资性收入 15585 元，增长 8.0%；经营净收入 1803 元，增长 10.4%；财产性收入 153 元，增长 4.9%；转移性收入 4846 元，增长 21.7%。人均消费性支出 15206 元，增长 9.5%。

农村居民人均纯收入 7296 元，比上年增长 14.1%，其中，工资性纯收入 1312 元，增长 30.2%；家庭经营纯收入 4654 元，增长 9.8%；转移性纯收入 1100 元，增长 12.7%；财产性纯收入 230 元，增长 34.8%。人均生活消费支出 6119 元，增长 16.7%。

十二、劳动就业和社会保障

年末就业人员 1096.59 万人，增长 8.5%。全年通过各种途径实现城镇就业再就业 46 万人，其中，就业困难人员实现就业 5.5 万人。全年消除“零就业”家庭 1047 户，帮助实现就业 1114 人。城镇登记失业率 3.4%。

年末参加职工基本养老保险 326.04 万人，增加 13.88 万人。其中，在职人员 239.33 万人，增加 10.47

万人；离退休人员 86.71 万人，增加 3.41 万人。

参加城镇居民社会养老保险 33.42 万人，增加 1.80 万人。

参加新型农村社会养老保险 496.93 万人，下降 0.16 万人。

参加城镇基本医疗保险 650.34 万人，增加 21.18 万人，其中，城镇职工 358.93 万人，增加 16.37 万人；城镇居民 291.41 万人，增加 4.81 万人。

参加失业保险 218.52 万人，增加 9.57 万人。

参加工伤保险 239.87 万人，增加 13.92 万人，其中，参加工伤保险农民工 43.70 万人，增加 3 万人。

参加生育保险 230.22 万人，增加 12.26 万人。

城镇居民中有 82.34 万人得到政府最低生活保障救济。年末各类收养性社会福利单位 600 个，增长 6.2%；拥有床位 5.34 万张，增长 29.0%；收养各类人员 3.26 万人，增长 6.5%。社区服务机构总数 1585 个，增长 10.6%，其中，综合性社区服务中心 237 个，增长 22.8%。全年销售福利彩票 33.95 亿元，增长 22.7%；筹集公益金 9.74 亿元，增长 20.8%；直接接受社会捐赠 292.53 万元。

十三、资源、环境和安全生产

已发现矿种 138 种。查明有资源储量的矿种 98 种，其中，能源矿产 6 种，金属矿产 31 种，非金属矿产 60 种，水气矿产 1 种。新发现大中型矿产地 12 处，其中，能源矿产地 8 处，金属矿产地 4 处。新增查明资源储量中，煤炭储量 211.40 亿吨。

在监测的 19 个城市中，有 10 个城市空气质量达到国家Ⅱ级以上标准；城市空气质量好于Ⅱ级的优良天数占 76.7%。首府乌鲁木齐市空气质量好于Ⅱ级的优良天数占 83.3%，比上年提高 3.5 个百分点。

在监测的 79 条河流 172 个断面中，Ⅰ～Ⅲ类优良水质断面比例为 94.8%，比上年提高 0.1 个百分点；Ⅳ～Ⅴ类轻中度污染水质断面比例为 3.5%，上升 0.5 个百分点；劣Ⅴ类重度污染水质断面比例为 1.7%，下降 0.6 个百分点。

在监测的 32 座湖库中，Ⅰ-Ⅲ类优良水质的湖库比例为 68.8%，下降 3.1 个百分点；劣Ⅴ类重度污染水质的湖库比例为 21.9%，与上年持平。

国家和自治区级自然保护区 28 个，其中，国家级自然保护区 9 个。保护区总面积 1972.56 万公顷，占新疆国土总面积的 11.9%。

共发生各类生产经营性安全事故 6917 起，比上年下降 4.2%。死亡 1073 人，下降 5.0%。亿元 GDP 安全生产事故死亡率 0.26，下降 16.1%；工矿商贸十万从业人员生产安全事故死亡率 5.40，下降 12.9%；道路交通万车死亡率 4.70，下降 8.1%；煤矿百万吨死亡率 0.39，与上年持平。

注释：

[1]本公报中数据为初步统计数。

[2]地区生产总值（GDP）、总产值及各产业增加值绝对数按现价计算，增长速度按可比价格计算。

[3]特色林果含园林水果、坚果和果用瓜。

[4]原煤产量因统计渠道和口径变化，暂不公开发布 2013 年数据。

[5]自 2013 年，基础设施行业范围调整为以下行业：铁路运输业，道路运输业，城市公共交通

业，航空运输业，水上运输业，管道运输业，邮政业，电信、广播电视和卫星传输服务业，互联网和相关服务业，水利管理业，环境管理业，市政公共设施管理业。

[6]科技、文化、劳动就业和社会保障数据不含兵团。

资料来源：

本公报中主要经济指标数据来源于自治区统计局；物价和城乡居民收入和消费性支出数据来源于国家统计局新疆调查总队，其他数据来源于相关部门。其中，农业机械动力来源于自治区农机局；利用外资数据来源于自治区商务厅；货物进出口总额来源于乌鲁木齐海关；铁路客货运量及年末营业里程数据来源于乌鲁木齐铁路局；公路客货运量及公路线路年末营业里程数据来源于自治区交通运输厅；机场客、货运吞吐量来源于新疆（机场）集团有限公司；民用汽车数据来源于自治区公安厅；邮政业务总量数据来源于新疆邮政管理局；电信业务数据来源于自治区通信管理局；国际、国内旅游数据来源于自治区旅游局；财政数据来源于自治区财政厅；金融信贷数据来源于中国人民银行乌鲁木齐中心支行；上市公司数据来源于中国证券监督管理委员会新疆监管局；保险业数据来源于中国保监会新疆监管局；教育数据来源于自治区教育厅；艺术表演团体、博物馆、公共图书馆、文化馆数据来源于自治区文化厅；广播、电视、电影数据来源于自治区广播电视总局；档案数据来源于自治区档案局；体育数据来源于自治区体育局；就业与社会保障数据来源于自治区人力资源和社会保障厅；销售福利彩票及筹集公益金数据来源于自治区福利彩票发行中心；矿产资源数据来源于自治区国土资源厅；环境监测及自然保护区数据来源于自治区环境保护厅；安全生产数据来源于自治区安全监督管理局。

Statistical Communique on the 2013 National Economic & Social Development of the Xinjiang Uygur Autonomous Region

In 2013, in the care of the Party Central Committee and the State Council, the Party committee and the people's Government of the Autonomous Region, united and leaded the people of the region, conscientiously implement the party's eighteen meeting, the Third Plenary Session of the eighteen central and Xinjiang work spirit of the forum, in accordance with the Eighth Party Congress of the autonomous region and autonomous regions (expand) the meeting, always make progress while maintaining stability, the change in tone, and firmly grasp the theme of the main line, in the global economy is complex and changeable, the downtown pressure on the economy of increasing cases, through the new year good opening, work and promote the implementation of a series of activities, to calmly deal with various risks and challenges, made the economic, cultural, social, ecological civilization construction in the new achievements.

I. General Outlook

The gross domestic product (GDP) of Xinjiang was 836.024 billion yuan,up by 11% over the previous year, of which, the added value of the primary industry was 146.830 billion yuan,up by 6.9%; that of the secondary industry was 377.698 billion yuan,up by 13.1%; and that of the tertiary industry was 311.496 billion yuan,up by 10.2% over the previous year. in the secondary industry,the added value of the industry was 303.528 billion yuan,up by 12.2%;the added valur of the construction was 7.4170 billion yuan ,up by 16.8%.

The permanent-population-based per-capita GDP reached 37181 yuan, up by 9.6% over the previous year,equivalent to US$6065 at current exchange rate.

The total consumer price index of the year was up by 3.9% over the previous year, of which,the price of food was up by 8.5%.

The ex-Factory price index of industrial product was down by 3.5%, of which, light industry was down by 0.4%, heavy industry was down by 4.0%. The purchasing price of industrial product was down by 2.2%. The production price of agriculture products increased up by 2.6%. The price of fixed asset investment was up by 0.5%.

Table 1 : Span of rise and decrease on the consumer price indices

unit: %

Items	Span of rise and decrease
Consumer price index	3.9
Rural	3.8
Uban	4.1
Food	8.5
#Grain	6.3
Meal poultry and processed products	14.9
Oil and Fat	3.4
Eggs	11.0
Aquatic products	7.0
Greengrocery	5.8
Tobacco,Liquor and Articles	1.7
Clothing	-0.2
Household Facilities, Articles and Services	1.3
Health Care and Personal Articles	1.4
Transportation and Communication	0.1
Recreation, Education and Culture Articles	1.1
Residence	3.4

II. Agriculture

The gross output value of agriculture,forestry,animal husbandry and fishery was 253.888 billion yuan,up by 7.2%,of which,gross output of agriculture was 18.0611 billion yuan ,up by 7.1%, gross output of frostry was 4.813 billion yuan ,up by 8.1%, gross output of animal husbandry was 60.420 billion yuan ,up by 7.8%, gross output of fishery was 1.717 billion yuan,up by 7.8%,gross output of services of agriculture,forestry,animal husbandry and fishery was 6.327 billion yuan,up by 5.7%.

The total sown areas of farm crops was 78.1839 million mus,up by 1.5% over the previous year.of which, The sown area of grain crops was 33.522 million mus, up by 4.9%; The sown area of cotton crops was 25.7739 million mus, down by 0.2%; The sown area of oil bearing-crops was 3.3261 million mus,down by 8.5%; The sown area of sugar crops was 0.9885 million mus,down by 20.2% over the previous year. The sown area of vegetable crops was4.4502 million mus,down by 3.3% over the previous year. The sown area of fruit crops was22.1084million mus,down by 3.4%.

The total output of grain was 1441.68 ten thousand tons,up by 8.8% over the previous year; The output of cotton was 351.80 ten thousand tons,down by 0.6% over the previous year; The output of oil-bearing crops was 60.63 ten thousand tons, up by 2.7%; The output of sugar was 476.47 ten thousand tons,down by 17.5%. The output of fruit was 1371.03 ten thousand tons, up by 9.0%.

Table 2: The output and changes of Characteristics fruit in 2013

Item	Output (10 000 tons)	Increase by previons year
Characteristics of fruit	1371.03	9.0
Garden fruit	782.69	6.2
#Red dates	199.37	37.1
Pear	52.14	-13.9
Grape	223.93	7.1
Nut	44.10	23.2
Walnut	40.28	28.4
Almond	3.55	57.1
Melon	544.24	12.1
Muslcmelon	239.46	12.2

At the end of the year, livestock (only)were 45.0286 million heads,up by 3.9%.The annual livestock slaughter were 38.6206 million heads, up by 3.3%. Total meat output were 1.3926 million tons, up by 4.1%, of which, the mutton output were 497.1 thousand tons, up by 3.5%; the beef output were 378.2 thousan tons, up by 4.6%; The pork output were 313.3 thousand tons,up by 3.9%. The rabbit meat output was 118.6 thousand tons,up by 12.5%;The production of egg were 281.7 thousand tons, up by 8.8%.The output of Milk were 1349.9thousand tons, up by 2.1%. The output of sheep wool were 96.8 thousand tons, up by 5.2%.

The year-end total agricultural machinery power was 21.6587 million kilowatt,up by 10.0% over the previous year. There were 39.70 ten thousand large and medium-size tractors,up by 15.8%;and 31.85 ten thousand small-size tractors,down by 4.9%. The consumption of chemical fertilizer was 203.22ten thousand tons(100% equivalent),up by 5.5%. Electricity consumed in rural areas was 8.392 billion kwh, up by 10.7%.

III. Industry and Construction

There are 2224 units of added value of enterprise,up by 265,up by 13.5%,The total value-added of the industrial sector was 293.387 billion yuan,up by 12.9% over the previous year.

Table3: Output of Major Industrial Products 2013

Item	Unit	Output	Increase over 2012(%)
Crude oil	10 000 tons	2658.47	3.3
Natural gas	100 million cubic meters	282.91	11.7
Processed oil	10 000 tons	2510.19	3.3
Ethylene	10 000 tons	131.92	3.8
Electricity	100 million kilowatt-hours	1613.01	44.0
Refind sugar	10 000 tons	46.72	-12.9
Cigarettes	100 million pieces	180.00	5.9
Can	10 000 tons	67.06	-3.4
#Tomato	10 000 tons	59.99	-4.5
Yarn	10 000 tons	43.46	8.1
Cloth	10 000meters	7451.00	11.6
Machine-made paper and paperbord	10 000 tons	45.74	11.4
Chemical fertilizers	10 000 tons	374.77	23.2
Crude steel	10 000 tons	1276.77	12.2
Rolled steel	10 000 tons	1512.90	17.3
Pig Iron	10 000 tons	1431.13	7.7
Cement	10 000 tons	5410.00	25.3
Transformer	kilovolt-ampere	6036.37	-2.6
Plastics	10 000 tons	186.66	33.3
Clothing	10 000 sets	2982.00	5.5
Light leather	square meters	593.34	14.5

Among the ten proportion of industrial enterprises above designated,Minging and processing of non-ferrous metal ores was 13.324 billion yuan; Production of electric power was 23.706 billion yuan; Manufacture of chemical products was 21.641 billion yuan;iron and steel industry was 59.25 billion yuan; Minging of coal was 13.593 billion yuan; Manufacture of textile was 4.549 billion yuan; Processing of food from agriculture products was6.255 billion yuan; equipment manufactory industry was 6.959 billion yuan; oil industry was 151.447billion;Manufacture of cars was 0.79 ten million yuan .

The value of delivered exported goods creat by industrial enterprises above designated size was 68.01 billion yuan, up by 63.8%. The profits achieved to 85.523 billion yuan, up by 1.6%.

General contracting and special contracting construction enterprises with qualification grade reaped profits of 207.966 billion yuan, up by 28.2%.

IV. Investment in Fixed Asset

The completed investment in fixed assets was 814.841billion yuan,up by 30.21% over the previous year. In terms of urban and rural areas,that in urban areas was 738.441 billion yuan, up by 32.0%; that in rural areas was 76.400 billion yuan, up by 15.0%.

In terms of three industries, the investment in the primary industry was 15.317 billion yuan,up by 38.5%;the investment in the secondary industry was 383.605 billion yuan,up by 24.6%,The tertiary industry investment was 339.520 billion yuan, up by 41.2%. Among the investment in the secondary industry, the investment in industry was 376.469 billion yuan,up by 26.0%.

The investment in real estate development was 82.569billion yuan,up by 36.2% over the previous year. The investment of residential was 55.562 billion yuan,up by 25.1%The floor space of buildings under construction was 94.5955 million square meters, up by 37.2%. The floor space of building completed was 17.3619 million square meters, down by 0.8%. The total sales area of commercial buildings for the whole year reached 20.1703million square meters,up by 41.0%. The total sales of commercial building was 86.095 billion yuan,up by 53.6%.

V. Domestic Trades

The total retail sales of consumer goods reached 203.915billion yuan,up by13.4% over the previous year. Really up by 9.8%.

In terms of urban and rural areas,the retail sales of consumer goods in urban areas reached 186.136billion yuan,up by13.3%; and the retail sales of consumer goods in rural areas reached 17.779 billion yuan,up by 13.4%.

In terms of different sectors,the sales of the wholesale and retail trade reached 176.933 billion yuan, up by 13.5%; the sales of the accommodation and catering service was 26.982 billion yuan,up by 12.7%.

In the enterprises of wholesale retailsale trade, the volume of food retail sales increased by 8.8%;the volume of clothing,shoses & hat and textiles, up by 4.5%; gold, silver and jewelry, up by 19.3%;household appliance and audiovisual products,up by 3.5%;petroleum product up by 27.1%; automobiles up by4.2%.

VI. Foreign Economic

The total value of import and export reached US$ 27.562billion,up by 9.5% over the previous year. Of which,the value of export was US$ 22.270 billion, up by 15.1%; and the value of import was US$ 5.824 billion,down by 2.8%. The volume of import and export was 529.2 million tons,down by 9.1%.

With 190 trade partner countries and regions, including Kazakhstan, the total import and export value of $12.255 billion, an increase of 9.7%; Kyrgyzstan $4.173,up by 3.3%; Tajikistan $1.585billion, up by 12.6%; America $807 million, down by 20.9%; Russia $454 million, down by 29.5%.

Grouped by registration status, state-owned enterprises import and export were $7.189billion, up by 4.5%; collective enterprises were $117billion, down by 52.3%; enterprises with foreign investment of $25 million, down by 8.3%; private enterprises were $20.004billion, up by12.6%.

Newly approved foreign direct investment enterprises 45, down by 19.6%. Contracts for the use of foreign direct investment projects in 42, down by 23.6%; foreign direct investment in the contract amount of $360million, down by 41%; the actual utilization of foreign direct investment of $481 million, up by 15.7%.

Table4: Total Value of Imports and Exports and Growth Rates

unit: US$ 100 million

Item	2013	Increase over 2012(%)
Total value of imports and exports	275.62	9.5
Total exports	222.70	15.1
#Ordinary trade	85.10	21.4
Processing trade	2.12	10.9
Frontier small trade	106.33	19.2
Total imports	52.92	-9.1
#Ordinary trade	10.02	-30.1
Processing trade	2.98	3.4 倍
Frontier small trade	37.25	-8.8

VII. Transportation,Postal & Telecommunication and Tourism

The freight turnover by railways was 73.99 million tons,up by 6.7% ;that by highways 685.28 million tons,up by 10.8%;that by civil aviation 16.88 ten thousands tons,up by 18.0%.

Passenger traffic by railways was 23.18 million passengers,up by 7.2%;that by highways 560.00million passengers,up by 6.7% ; that by civil aviation 19.8786 million passengers,up by15.1%.

At the end of the year, railway in operation reached 4911kilometers,remained the same from previous year. Total civil aviation routes reached 17.02 ten thousand kilometers,up by 2.6%.

At the end of the year, there were 243.3 ten thousand civilian automobiles, up by 15.3%, of which, there were 175.4ten thousand private automobiles, up by 18.9%.

The total volume of telecommunication was 26.817 billion yuan,up by 8.7% over the previous year. The total volume of post stood at 1.878 billion yuan,up by 3.4%. Number of fixed phone users 5.4480 million,up by 0.9%. The popularization rate of fixed telephone was 24.4 sets/100 persons,The number of newly-increased mobile users was 1.2540 million, Number of mobile phone users 21.3390 million,of which,the number of 3G mobile phone uses was 7.0970 million,up by 78.8%.The popularization rate of mobile telephone was 98.6 sets/100 persons. Year-end Internet customer 2.93 million,up by15.0%.

Tourists through customs to Xinjiang numbered 52.0573 million, up by 7.1%,of which,forien tourists numbered 1.5673 million,up by 4.6%.domesic tourists numbered 5049 ten thousand,up by 7.2%. income from tourism amounted to 67.329 billion, up by 16.9%.of which, Income from foreign tourists amounted 0.585 billion US$, up by 6.3%. Domesitic income amounted 63.743 billion yuan,up by 17.4%.

VIII. Finance and Intermediation

The overall-caliber financial revenue stood at 224.66 billion yuan,up by 16.7%.Local government revenue was 155.655 billion yuan,up by 24.4%,of which,the public financial budget revenue was 112.849billion yuan, up by 24.2%.The fund budget income was 42.632 billion yuan,up by 24.4%;Income of state-owned capital management budget was 0.174 billion yuan,down by 51.0%.

The local government expenditure stood at 351.962 billion yuan,up by 14.3%,of which,the general budgetary expenditure was 306.712 billion yuan,up by 12.8%. The fund budget expenditure was 45.033 billion yuan,up by 25.1%;Expenditure of state-owned capital management budget was 0.217 billion yuan,down by 30.2%.

By the end of 2013,savings deposits of all kinds in financial institutions reached 1408.883 billion yuan,increase by 175.282 billion yuan over the year of beginning, up by 14.3% over the previous year. Of which,units savings deposits were 767.724 billion yuan,up by 16.5%; Personal savings deposits were 600.174 billion yuan, up by 13.1%.

Loans of all kinds in financial institutions were 984.046billion yuan, increase by 191.572 billion yuan over the beginning, up by 24.3%; of which, Loans of short-term were 337.294 billion yuan, up by 22.2%; loan of medium-and long-term were 572.323 billion yuan,up by 23.4%. Individual consumption loans were 105.309 billion yuan, up by 39.9%.

At the end of 2013, there were 39 listed companies, remained over the previous year; total volume issued were 33.861 billion shares, up by 27.0%; Total market capitalization were 265.078billion yuan, up by5.2%. In the year of 2013, the refinancing totaled 15.506 billion yuan,down by 24.1%.

There was 1 Legal person securities companies, 62 securities business department securities ,Transactions of volume were 711.232 billion yuan,up by 77.8%; 2 Futures Company, 9 futures business department, Total futures trading volume were 987.148 billion yuan,up by 11.5%.

The total premium of insurance companies reached 27.349 billion yuan,up by 16.1% over the previous year. of the total,life insurance premium was 11.323 billion yuan,up by 20.9%; Property insurance premium 9.368 billion yuan, up by 19.3%;health and casualty insurance premium were 2.520billion yuan,up by31.4%; that against health and accidental injury were 1.066 billion yuan, up by 18.2%.

Insurance companies paid an indemnity of 10.659 billion yuan as reparation for various property and life insurance programs, up by 33.0%, of which, and that against property was 6.235 billion yuan, up by 23.9%, the indemnity against life insurance was 3.110billion yuan, up by 53.0%; accidental injury were 277million yuan, up by 24.6%.

IX. Education and Scientific Technology

By the end of 2013,there were totally 36 general colleges and universities,an increase by 2.The enrollment of postgraduate students were 6222 new entrants,up by 9.1%; the enrollment of post- graduate students was 16867,up by 9.1%, graduates students were 4775, up by 17.2%. The enrollment of regular under-graduates and college student were 8.34 ten thousand, up by 6.9%; the enrollment of students was 27.84 ten thousand,up by3.6%, graduates students were 7.0 ten thousand,up by8.3%.

There were 93 secondary schools,the recruit students were 8.39 ten thousand,down by 3.3%. enrollment of students were 22.93 ten thousand,down by 2.5%;graduates students were 7.49 ten thousand,up by 5.0%.

There were 1102 regular secondary schools,the recruit students were 31.36 ten thousand,down by 0.3%. enrollment of students were 91.85 ten thousand,down by 2.6%;graduates students were31.14ten thousand,down by 2.5%.

There were 3533 primary schools,the recruit students were 34.86 ten thousand,up by 5.1%;enrollment of student were 18.944 ten thousand,down by 0.3%;graduates students were 32.113 ten thousand,up by 30.3%.

There were 26 special schools,the recruit students were 1473,up by 29.6%;enrollment of student were 5229,up by 6.5%;graduates students were 680 ten thousand,up by 30.3%.

There were 3864 kindergartens, the recruit students were 37.33 ten thousand,down by 2.0%;enrollment of student were 71.90 ten thousand,up by 3.6%; graduated children in kindergartens were 31.19 ten thousand,up by 8.3%.

The enrollment rate of school-age children reached 99.8%. Enrollment rate of junior secondary school-age youth was 97.6%. Junior middle school net enrollment rate of school-age children was 98.0%Promotion rate from junior sendary school to senior secondary school was 88.7%.

In 2013, the autonomous region formulated 2302 sci-tech project plans, of which, science and technology support program 223, high technology research and development program 149, science and technology of new projects 152, scientific and technological achievements into a special fund project 51, tech SME Technology Innovation Fund Project 136. Has won provincial and ministerial level scientific and technological achievements 257.

At the end of the year,There were 111 above the County Department of research and technological development institutions, the natural scientific research and technological development institutions were 97 science and technology information and literature were 8, social sciences and Humanities Research and technological development institutions were 6.

By the end of 2013, there were 33 key laboratories, of which,national key laboratores were 1.founded 20 engineering and technological research centers, of which, 4 national level. 87 engineering and technological centers which are still at the forming stage, and 35 bases for the commercialization of research findings at the level of autonomous region were established.

By the end of 2013, we had 269 high and new tech enterprises, productivity promotion centers were founded, of which, there are 8 state-level demonstration centers, of which,2 nationa level There were 64 productivity Promotion Center,of which, there were 9National innovation enterprises,7 National innovation pilot enterprise.

There are totally 8224 patent applications, of which, there are2081 for a patent for invention taking up 25.3%, and 4998 patent licenses, including 540 invention patent licenses accounting for 10.8%. 983 technology contracts were signed, and the turnover reached 297 million yuan, of which, the volume of technology trade was 284 million yuan.

X. Culture and Sports

At the end of 2013,there were 108performance art guoups,there were 116 cutural centers, 106 public library, 76 museums;109 national comprehensive archives. Open the record rooms were 45.87 ten thousand units. There were 6 radio broadcasting stations, 8 television stations,88 radio and telivision stations. radio broadcasting coverage rate was 95.7%; television coverage rate was 96.0%. Number of users of cable television was 199.5 ten thousand, down by 8.0%, of which, number of Users of digital TV was 186.83ten thousand, down by 7.0%. Number of users of radio and television broadcast statellite 256.44 ten thousands.

There were 13 the rural fitnes centers,the farm fitness projects were 36, 90 administrative village farmer sports fitness project, 10 community sports clubs and 4 sports park. In the international competition Athletes from the Autonomous Region won 2gold medal, 3 silver medal, 1 bronze medal. In the national competition Athletes from the Autonomous Region in matches home and abroad won39gold medals, 37 silver medals,51 bronze medals.;Sales of sports lottery were 1.509 billion yuan, up by 14.6%;raise lottery public welfare fund were 370 million yuan,up by 12.1%.

XI. Populatin and People's Life

By the end of 2013,the population of autonomous region was 22.6430 million, of which, the population in urban areas was10.0693 million, rural areas 12.5737 million; the urbanization rate was 44.5%.The birthrate was 15.84‰; the deathrate was 4.92‰. The natural growth rate of population was 10.92‰.

The per capital disposable income of urban residents

reached 19874 yuan,up by 15.5% over the previous year. The per capital family income reached 22388 yuan,up by 10.9%,Of which, income of salary and wage was 15585 yuan, up by 8.0%, Net operating income were 1803yuan, up by 10.4%, income of property were 153 yuan, up by 4.9%, metastatic income were 4846 yuan, up by 21.7%.per capital annual expenditure was 15206 yuan, up by 9.5%.

The per capital auunal net income of rural households was 7296 yuan, up by 14.1%, of which, income of salaries and wages was 1312yuan, up by 30.2%; income from household operations was 454 yuan, up by 9.8%; Income from transfers was 1100 yuan, up by 12.7%; Income from properties was 230yuan, up by 34.8%. Per capita consumption expenditure of rural households was6119 yuan, up by 16.7% over the previous year, of which.

XII.Employment and Social Security

Number of employed person was 10.9659 million at year-end, up by 8.5%., number of urban employed persons were 46 ten thousand, of which,the reemployment of zero-employment workers was 5.5 ten thousand. The elimination of zero employment family 1047 households, helping to realize the employment of 1114 people.Registered unemployment rate in urban areas was 3.4%.

A total of 3.2604 million people participated in basic social endowment insurance programs,an increase by 13.88ten thousands. Among them, 2.3933 million were employees, an increase by 10.47 ten thousands. 86.71 ten thousand were retirees, an increase of 3.41 ten thousand.

Receive basic social endowment insurance was 33.42 ten thousand, an increase of 1.80ten thousand.

Receive the new type of rural social endowment insrance was 4.9693 million,decrease of 0.16 ten thousands.

The population covered by basic medical insurance programs was 6.5034 million, an increase of 21.18 ten thousand people. Among them, 3.5893 million were urban workers, an increase of 16.37 ten thousands.2.9141 million were urban residents,an increase of 4.81 ten thousands.

A total of 201852 million people participated in unemployment insurance programs,an increase of 9.57 ten thousand.

Receive the industrial injury insurance was 2.3987 million,an incraese of 13.92 ten thousand,among them,migrant of industrial injury insurance received 43.70 ten thousand an increase of 3 ten thousand people.

People participated in the maternity insurance was 2.3022 million,an increase of 12.26 ten thousand.

There were 82.34 ten thousand people recevied basic welfare for urban residents. Number of social welfare institutions were 600 at the end of year,up by 6.2%; Number of beds were 5.34 ten thousand in social welfare institutions at the end of year, up by 29.0%; Number of inmates were 3.26 ten thousand, up by 6.5%.The number of community service equipment was 1585,up by 10.6%.of which, The number of comprehensive community service center were 237,up by 22.8%..Revenue from social welfare lottery tickets were 3.395 billion yuan, up by 22.7%; Social welfare fund were 974 million yuan, up by 20.8%. 2.9253 million yuan of donatioas were received from the general public.

XIII. Resources Environment and Safe production

138 mineral products were found, of which, 98mineral products have resources. Of which, there were 6 energy minerals, 31 metal minerals, 60 non-metal minerals,1 watere mineral. 12 large-medium ore field were discovered, of which, there were 8 energy resouses mines, 4metal mine.An increase of mineral products have resources,of which,coal resources were 21.140 billion tons.

In the 19 monitored cities, 10cities had their air quality reach national standard Grade II. In the Autonomous Region about 76.7% of the year the air quality was better than Grade II. And 83.3% of the year in Urmqi the air quality was better than Grade II ,up by 3.5% over the previous year.

Monitoring of water quality on 172 sections of the 79rivers showed that good quality water of standard Grade I ~III accounted for 94.8%, up by 0.1%. Quality water of standard GradeIV~V accounted for 3.5%, uo by 0.5%, Quality water of standard Grade V accounted for 1.7%, down by 0.6%.

Monitoring of water quality of 32 lakes and reservoirs showed that good quality water of standard Grade I ~III accounted for 68.8%,down by 3.1% Quality water of standard Grade V accounted for 21.9%,equal to previous year..

There were 28national and regional nature reserves.of which,national nature reserves were 9. Area of nature reserves were 1972.56ten thousand sqkm, proportion of nature reserves in total area of territory was 11.9%.

There were 6917 safety accidents occurred, down by4.2%, with 1073person died, decrease of 5.0%. The 100-million-GDP-based death rate in production safety accidents was 0.26, down by 16.1% over the previous year; among every 100 000 employees in trade sectors, 5.40 persons died, down by 12.9%; for every 10 000 vehicles,4.70 persons died, down by8.1%; for every one million tons output of coal mines, 0.39 persons died, equal to previous year.

新疆统计年鉴
XINJIANG STATISTICAL YEARBOOK

1

综 合

COMPREHENSIVE STATISTICS

简要说明

本篇主要内容和资料来源

综合资料主要包括新疆行政区划、国民经济和社会发展综合资料两部分。

行政区划资料由新疆维吾尔自治区民政厅根据国务院批准的、截至到2013年末新疆行政区划变更情况汇总整理并提供；国民经济和社会发展综合资料由新疆维吾尔自治区统计局国民经济综合统计处根据各篇主要指标加工整理而成。

Brief Introduction

Main Content and Source of Data

This chapter mainly covers two parts: the data of division of administrative areas, summary data on the national economy and social development.

Data on division of administrative areas are provided by the Bureau of Civil Affairs of Xinjiang Uygur Autonomous Region. Data on grass-roots units and the national economy and social development are compiled and processed by the Department of Comprehensive statistics of the Xinjiang Bureau of Statistics using relevant .

1-1 行 政 区 划

Divisions of Administrative Areas in Xinjiang Uygur Autonomous Region

单位：个　　(2013 年)　　(unit)

区划名称	Region	地级区划数 Number of Regions at Prefecture Level	县级区划数 Number of Regions at County level	#地州辖市 Cities under the Prefectures	#市辖区 Districts under the Jurisdiction of Cities	#县 Counties	#自治县 Autonomous Counties
总　计	**Total**	**14**	**101**	**16**	**11**	**62**	**6**
乌鲁木齐市	Urumqi City	1	8		7	1	
克拉玛依市	Karamay City	1	4		4		
吐鲁番地区	Turpan Administrative Offices	1	3	1		2	
哈密地区	Hami [Kumul] Administrative Offices	1	3	1		1	1
昌吉回族自治州	Changji Hui Autonomous Prefecture	1	7	2		4	1
伊犁哈萨克自治州	Ili Kazak Autonomous Prefecture	3	24	5		17	2
伊犁州直属县(市)	Counties (Cities) Direct Under Ili Prefecture	1	10	2		7	1
塔城地区	Tacheng [Tarbagatai] Administrative Offices	1	7	2		4	1
阿勒泰地区	Altay Administrative Offices	1	7	1		6	
博尔塔拉自治州	Bortala Mongol Autonomous Prefecture	1	4	2		2	
巴音郭楞自治州	Bayangol Mongol Autonomous Prefecture	1	9	1		7	1
阿克苏地区	Aksu Administrative Offices	1	9	1		8	
克孜勒苏自治州	Kizilsu Kirgiz Autonomous Prefecture	1	4	1		3	
喀什地区	Kashgar [Kaxgar] Administrative Offices	1	12	1		10	1
和田地区	Hotan Administrative Offices	1	8	1		7	
自治区直辖市	Cities under the Autonomous Region		6				
石河子市	Shihezi City		1				
阿拉尔市	Aral City		1				
图木舒克市	Tumxuk City		1				
五家渠市	Wujiaqu City		1				
北屯市	Beitun City		1				
铁门关市	Tiemenguan City		1				

1-1 续表 Continued

单位：个　　(2013 年)　　(unit)

区划名称	Region	乡镇级区划数 Number of Regions at Town-ships Level	#镇 Town	#乡 Township	#民族乡 National Township	#街道办事处 Street Communities
总　计	**Total**	**1035**	**276**	**547**	**42**	**169**
乌鲁木齐市	Urumqi City	93	8	13	1	71
克拉玛依市	Karamay City	14		2		12
吐鲁番地区	Turpan Administrative Offices	30	12	14	1	3
哈密地区	Hami [Kumul] Administrative Offices	42	13	21	3	5
昌吉回族自治州	Changji Hui Autonomous Prefecture	79	40	19	11	9
伊犁哈萨克自治州	Ili Kazak Autonomous Prefecture	243	77	125	17	24
伊犁州直属县(市)	Counties (Cities) Direct Under Ili Prefecture	110	26	61	10	13
塔城地区	Tacheng [Tarbagatai] Administrative Offices	75	33	29	5	8
阿勒泰地区	Altay Administrative Offices	58	18	35	2	3
博尔塔拉自治州	Bortala Mongol Autonomous Prefecture	21	7	9		5
巴音郭楞自治州	Bayangol Mongol Autonomous Prefecture	90	28	56	1	5
阿克苏地区	Aksu Administrative Offices	95	32	51	2	10
克孜勒苏自治州	Kizilsu Kirgiz Autonomous Prefecture	39	6	30	1	2
喀什地区	Kashgar [Kaxgar] Administrative Offices	173	32	133	3	4
和田地区	Hotan Administrative Offices	95	16	73	2	4
自治区直辖市	Cities under the Autonomous Region	21	5	1		15
石河子市	Shihezi City	7	2			5
阿拉尔市	Aral City	6	1	1		4
图木舒克市	Tumxuk City	3				3
五家渠市	Wujiaqu City	5	2			3
北屯市	Beitun City					
铁门关市	Tiemenguan City					

1-2 县级以上行政区划
Divisions of Administrative Areas at and above County Level

(2013 年)

<table>
<tr><th colspan="2">地、州、市名称
Name of Administrative Offices, Autonomous Prefectures, Cities</th><th>市、县(市辖区)名称
Names of Cities and Counties (Districts under Cities)</th></tr>
<tr><td colspan="2">乌鲁木齐市
Urumqi City</td><td>天山区、沙依巴克区、高新区(新市区)、水磨沟区、经济技术开发区(头屯河区)、达坂城区、米东区、乌鲁木齐县
Tianshan District, Shayibak District, Gaoxin District(Xinshi District), Shui Mogou District, Economic and Technological Development Zone(Tou Tunhe District), Da Bancheng District, Midong District, Urumqi County</td></tr>
<tr><td colspan="2">克拉玛依市
Karamay City</td><td>克拉玛依区、独山子区、白碱滩区、乌尔禾区
Karamay District, Dushanzi District, Bai Jiantan District, Urhe District</td></tr>
<tr><td colspan="2">吐鲁番地区
Turpan Administrative Offices</td><td>吐鲁番市、鄯善县、托克逊县
Turpan City, Shanshan [Piqan] County, Toksun County</td></tr>
<tr><td colspan="2">哈密地区
Hami [Kumul] Administrative Offices</td><td>哈密市、巴里坤哈萨克自治县、伊吾县
Hami [Kumul] City, Barkol Kazak Autonomous County, Yiwu[Araturuk] County</td></tr>
<tr><td colspan="2">昌吉回族自治州
Changji Hui Autonomous Prefecture</td><td>昌吉市、阜康市、呼图壁县、玛纳斯县、奇台县、吉木萨尔县、木垒哈萨克自治县
Changji City, Fukang City, Hutubi County, Manas County, Qitai County, Jimsar County, Mori Kazak Autonomous County</td></tr>
<tr><td rowspan="3">伊犁哈萨克自治州
Ili Kazak Auto-nomous Prefecture</td><td>伊犁州直属县(市)
Counties (Cities) Direct Under Ili Prefecture</td><td>伊宁市、奎屯市、伊宁县、察布查尔锡伯自治县、霍城县、巩留县、新源县、昭苏县、特克斯县、尼勒克县
Yining [Gulja] City, Kuytun City , Yining [Gulja] County, Qapqal Xibe AutonomousCounty, Huocheng [Korgas] County, Gongliu [Tokkuzlara] County, Xinyuan [Kunes] County, Zhaosu [Mongolkure] County, Tekes County, Nilka County</td></tr>
<tr><td>塔城地区
Tacheng [Tarbagatai] Administrative Offices</td><td>塔城市、乌苏市、额敏县、沙湾县、托里县、裕民县、和布克赛尔蒙古自治县
Tacheng [Qoqek] City, Usu City, Emin [Dorbiljin] County, Shawan County, Toli County, Yumin [Qagantokay] County, Hoboksar Mongol Autonomous County</td></tr>
<tr><td>阿勒泰地区
Altay Administrative Offices</td><td>阿勒泰市、布尔津县、富蕴县、福海县、哈巴河县、青河县、吉木乃县
Altay City, Burqin County, Fuyun [Koktokay] County, Fuhai [Burultokay] County, Habahe [Kaba] County, Qinghe [Qinggil] County, Jeminay county</td></tr>
<tr><td colspan="2">博尔塔拉蒙古自治州
Bortala Mongol Autonomous Prefecture</td><td>博乐市、精河县、温泉县、阿拉山口市
Bole [Bortala] City, Jinghe [Jing] County, Wenquan [Arxang] County，Alashankou City</td></tr>
<tr><td colspan="2">巴音郭楞蒙古自治州
Bayangol Mongol Autonomous Prefecture</td><td>库尔勒市、轮台县、尉犁县、若羌县、且末县、焉耆回族自治县、和静县、和硕县、博湖县
Korla City, Luntai [Bugur] County, Yuli [Lopnur] County, Ruoqiang [Qarkilik] County, Qiemo [Qarqan] County, Yanqi Hui Autonomous County, Hejing County, Bohu [Bagrax] County</td></tr>
<tr><td colspan="2">阿克苏地区
Aksu Administrative Offices</td><td>阿克苏市、温宿县、库车县、沙雅县、新和县、拜城县、乌什县、阿瓦提县、柯坪县
Aksu City, Wensu [Onsu] County, Kuqa County, Xayar County, Xinhe [Toksu] County, Baicheng [Bay] County, Wushi [Uqturpan] County, Awat County, Kalpin County</td></tr>
<tr><td colspan="2">克孜勒苏柯尔克孜自治州
Kizilsu Kirgiz Autonomous Prefecture</td><td>阿图什市、阿克陶县、阿合奇县、乌恰县
Artux City, Akto County, Akqi County, Wuqia [Ulugqat] County</td></tr>
<tr><td colspan="2">喀什地区
Kashgar [Kaxgar] Administrative Offices</td><td>喀什市、疏附县、疏勒县、英吉沙县、泽普县、莎车县、叶城县、麦盖提县、岳普湖县、伽师县、巴楚县、塔什库尔干塔吉克自治县
Kashgar [Kaxgar] City, Shufu County, Shule County, Yengisar County, Zepu [Poskam] County, Shache [Yarkant] County, Yecheng [Kagilik] County, Makit County, Yopurga County, Jiashi [Payzawat] County, Bachu [Maralbexi] County, Taxkorgan Tajik Aotonomous County</td></tr>
<tr><td colspan="2">和田地区
Hotan Administrative Offices</td><td>和田市、和田县、墨玉县、皮山县、洛浦县、策勒县、于田县、民丰县
Hotan City, Hotan County, Moyu [Karakax] County, Pishan [Guma] County, Lop County, Qira County, Yutian [Keriya] County, Minfeng [niya] County</td></tr>
<tr><td colspan="2">自治区直辖县级市
Municpality Countrylevel City directly under the Central Government</td><td>石河子市、 阿拉尔市、图木舒克市、五家渠市、北屯市、铁门关市
Shihezi City,Aral City,Tumxuk City,Wujiaqu City,Beitun City,Tiemenguan City</td></tr>
</table>

1-3 主要年份国民经济和社会发展总量与速度指标

指　　标	Item	1978
人口与就业	**Population and Employment**	
人口(万人)	**Population (10 000 persons)**	
年末总人口	Population at the Year-end	1233.01
男　性	Male	630.18
女　性	Female	602.83
就业(万人)	**Employment (10 000 persons)**	
就业人员数	Employment	491.25
#在岗职工人数	Staff and Workers	226.69
城镇登记失业人数	Urban Registeration Unemployment	
宏观经济	**Macro Economy**	
国民经济核算(亿元)	**National Accounting (100 million yuan)**	
新疆生产总值	Gross Domestic Product	39.07
第一产业	Primary Industry	13.97
第二产业	Secondary Industry	18.35
第三产业	Tertiary Industry	6.75
支出法新疆生产总值	Gross Domestic Product by Expenditure Approach	
#最终消费	Final Consumption Expenditure	27.64
居民消费	Houshold Consumption Expenditure	22.61
政府消费	Government Consumption Expenditure	5.03
资本形成总额	Gross Capital Formation	18.43
固定资本形成	Gross Fixed Capital Formation	13.25
存货增加	Changes in Inventories	5.18
货物和服务净出口	Net Export of Goods and Services	-7.00
固定资产投资(亿元)	**Investment in Fixed Assets (100 million yuan)**	
全社会固定资产投资总额	Total Investment in Fixed Assets	13.00
城　镇	Urban	13.00
#房地产	Real Estate Development	
农　村	Rural	
全社会施工房屋建筑面积(万平方米)	Floor Space of Buildings under Construction (10 000 sq.m)	
全社会竣工房屋建筑面积(万平方米)	Floor Space of Building Completed (10 000 sq.m)	
消　费	**Consumption**	
社会消费品零售总额(亿元)	Total Retail Sales of Consumer Goods (100 million yuan)	21.89
对外贸易	**Foreign Trade**	
进出口总额(亿美元)	Total Value of Imports and Exports	0.23
出口额	Exports	0.09
进口额	Imports	0.14
利用外资(万美元)	**Utilization of Foreign Capital (USD 10 000)**	
签订利用外资协议额	Amount of Foreign Capital for Utilization through Signed Contracts or Agreements	
实际利用外资额	Amount of Foreign Capital Actually Utilized	
财政(亿元)	**Public Finance (100 million yuan)**	
公共财政预算收入	Local Financial Governments Intrabudgetary Ordinary Revenue	7.14
#税收收入	Various Taxes	4.34

Principal Aggregate Indicators on National Economic and Social Development and Growth Rates in Main Years

总量指标 Aggregate Data				速度指标(%) Indices and Growth Rates						
				指数(2013 年比以下各年) Index (2013 as percentuage of the following years)				平均增长速度 Average Annual Growth Rate		
2000	2010	2012	2013	1978	2000	2010	2012	1979-2013	2001-2013	2011-2013
1849.41	2181.58	2232.78	2264.30	183.6	122.4	103.8	101.4	1.8	1.6	1.2
957.07	1127.01	1145.21	1151.77	182.8	120.3	102.2	100.6	1.7	1.4	0.7
892.34	1054.57	1087.57	1112.53	184.6	124.7	105.5	102.3	1.8	1.7	1.8
672.50	894.65	1010.44	1096.59	223.2	163.1	122.6	108.5	2.3	3.8	7.0
255.75	245.48	280.33	298.93	131.9	116.9	121.8	106.6	0.8	1.2	6.8
11.00	10.99	11.85	11.90		108.2	108.3	100.4		0.6	2.7
1363.56	5437.47	7505.31	8360.24	3263.1	371.5	139.2	111.0	10.5	10.6	11.7
288.18	1078.63	1320.57	1468.30	1208.7	210.6	121.8	106.9	7.4	5.9	6.8
537.58	2592.15	3481.56	3776.98	3111.4	425.9	144.0	113.1	10.3	11.8	12.9
537.80	1766.69	2703.18	3114.96	8586.8	414.6	142.6	110.2	13.6	11.6	12.5
760.20	2865.56	4262.51	4599.24							
492.32	1578.93	2370.67	2563.54							
267.88	1286.63	1891.84	2035.70							
618.12	3371.22	5792.16	7192.45							
648.12	3233.00	5477.61	6943.72							
-30.00	138.22	314.55	248.73							
-14.76	-799.31	-2549.36	-3431.45							
610.38	3539.69	6258.38	8148.41	62680.1	1335.0	230.2	130.2	20.2	22.1	32.0
556.85	3181.58	5593.81	7384.41	56803.2	1326.1	232.1	132.0	19.9	22.0	32.4
57.43	347.72	606.09	825.69		1437.7	237.5	136.2		22.8	33.4
53.53	358.11	664.58	764.00		1427.2	213.3	115.0		22.7	28.7
4485.77	11361.96	21626.33	25595.40		570.6	225.3	118.4		14.3	31.1
2633.23	4649.89	7821.44	6085.61		231.1	130.9	77.8		6.7	9.4
374.50	1324.48	1798.99	2039.15	9315.4	544.5	154.0	113.3	13.8	13.9	15.5
22.64	171.28	251.71	275.62	119834.8	1217.4	160.9	109.5	22.5	21.2	17.2
12.04	129.70	193.47	222.70	247444.4	1849.7	171.7	115.1	25.0	25.2	19.7
10.60	41.58	58.24	52.92	37800.0	499.2	127.3	90.9	18.5	13.2	8.4
9212	30091	61056	36034		391.2	119.8	59.0		11.1	6.2
1923	23742	40795	48102		2501.4	202.6	117.9		28.1	26.5
79.07	500.58	908.97	1128.49	15805.2	1427.2	225.4	124.2	15.6	22.7	31.1
64.53	416.23	698.93	826.34	19040.1	1280.6	198.5	118.2	16.2	21.7	25.7

1-3 续表 1

指　标	Item	1978
公共财政预算支出	Local Financial Governments Intrabudgetary Ordinary Expenditures	17.02
#一般公共服务	General Common Service	
教育与科学技术	Operating Expenses for Education and Operating Expenses for Science and Technology	
社会保障和就业	Operating Expenses for Medical Treatment and Sanitation	
节能环保	Energy Saving and Environmental Protection	
城乡社区事务	Expenses of Community	
农林水事务	Expenses of Agriculture, Forest and Irrigation	
物价总指数(上年=100)	**Price Indices (preceding year=100)**	
居民消费价格总指数	Consumer Price Index	101.2
商品零售价格总指数	Retail Price Index	101.4
工业生产者出厂价格指数	Producer Price Indices for Manufacture Goods	
工业生产者购进价格指数	Purchasing Price Indices of Industrial Products	
固定资产投资价格指数	Investment in Fixed Assets Price Indices	
能源生产与消费(万吨标准煤)	**Production and Consumption of Energy (10 000 tons of SCE)**	
能源生产总量	Total Energy Production	1410.75
能源消费总量	Total Energy Consumption	979.27
产　业	**Industry**	
农　业	**Agriculture**	
农林牧渔业总产值(亿元)	Gross Output Value of Farming, Forestry, Animal Husbandry and Fishery (100 million yuan)	19.12
主要农产品产量(万吨)	Output of Major Farm Products (10 000 tons)	
粮　食	Grain	370.01
棉　花	Cotton	5.50
油　料	Oil-bearing Crops	10.33
甜　菜	Beet Roots	16.37
水　果	Fruits	13.98
肉　类	Meat	9.65
奶　类	Milk	5.25
水产品	Aquatic Products	0.57
工　业	**Industry**	
主要工业产品产量	Output of Major Industrial Products	
纱(万吨)	Yarn (10 000 tons)	2.80
布(亿米)	Cloth (100 million meter)	1.56
绒线(吨)	Knitting Wool (ton)	1239
呢绒(万米)	Woolen Goods (10 000 meter)	189
原盐(万吨)	Crude Salt (10 000 tons)	51.71
机制纸及纸板(万吨)	Machine-Made Paper and Paperboards (10 000 tons)	1.99
成品糖(万吨)	Refined Sugar (10 000 tons)	2.08
原油(万吨)	Crude Oil (10 000 tons)	353.05
天然气(亿立方米)	Natural Gas (100 million cu.m)	2.51
发电量(亿千瓦小时)	ElectriCity (100 million kwh)	21.17

Continued

总量指标 Aggregate Data				速度指标(%) Indices and Growth Rates						
				指数(2013 年比以下各年) Index (2013 as percentuage of the following years)				平均增长速度 Average Annual Growth Rate		
2000	2010	2012	2013	1978	2000	2010	2012	1979-2013	2001-2013	2011-2013
190.95	1698.91	2720.07	3067.12	18020.7	1606.2	180.5	112.8	16.0	23.8	21.8
	195.57	303.67	337.37			172.5	111.1			19.9
	334.02	506.87	572.52			171.4	113.0			19.7
	166.40	227.79	263.17			158.2	115.5			16.5
	51.02	64.12	68.99			135.2	107.6			10.6
	95.28	183.49	243.05			255.1	132.5			36.6
	220.50	365.39	387.42			175.7	106.0			20.7
99.4	104.3	103.8	103.9							
98.3	104.6	103.3	103.3							
129.4	125.3	96.9	96.5							
115.2	123.9	97.9	97.8							
103.6	104.6	100.6	100.5							
5419.77	14696.76	17744.42								
3316.03	8290.20	11831.62								
487.20	1846.18	2275.67	2538.88	1319.0	225.0	123.1	107.2	7.6	6.4	7.2
808.60	1150.20	1259.83	1360.83	367.8	168.3	118.3	108.0	3.8	4.1	5.8
150.00	247.90	353.95	351.80	6396.4	234.5	141.9	99.4	12.6	6.8	12.4
60.14	66.62	59.04	60.63	586.9	100.8	91.0	102.7	5.2	0.1	-3.1
292.65	486.97	577.19	476.47	2910.6	162.8	97.8	82.5	10.1	3.8	-0.7
151.87	593.85	736.74	782.69	5598.6	515.4	131.8	106.2	12.2	13.4	9.6
90.00	121.74	134.23	139.26	1443.1	154.7	114.4	103.7	7.9	3.4	4.6
78.23	132.82	136.32	139.19	2651.2	177.9	104.8	102.1	9.8	4.5	1.6
6.01	10.11	12.53	13.17	2310.5	219.1	130.3	105.1	9.4	6.2	9.2
33.43	41.58	40.22	43.46	1552.1	130.0	104.5	108.1	8.2	2.0	1.5
2.81	1.51	0.67	0.75	48.1	26.7	49.7	111.9	-2.1	-9.7	-20.8
1184	741	545	323	26.1	27.3	43.6	59.3	-3.8	-9.5	-24.2
754	326	332	259	137.0	34.4	79.4	78.0	0.9	-7.9	-7.4
31.78	174.67	301.40	318.63	616.2	1002.6	182.4	105.7	5.3	19.4	22.2
17.65	37.10	41.05	45.74	2298.5	259.2	123.3	111.4	9.4	7.6	7.2
30.76	45.10	53.64	46.72	2246.2	151.9	103.6	87.1	9.3	3.3	1.2
1848.43	2558.16	2670.68	2658.47	753.0	143.8	103.9	99.5	5.9	2.8	1.3
35.39	249.91	253.01	282.91	11271.3	799.4	113.2	111.8	14.5	17.3	4.2
182.98	679.33	1187.48	1613.01	7619.3	881.5	237.4	135.8	13.2	18.2	33.4

1-3 续表 2

指 标	Item	1978
粗钢(万吨)	Crude Steel (10 000 tons)	8.46
钢材(万吨)	Steel Products (10 000 tons)	6.83
水泥(万吨)	Cement (10 000 tons)	78.15
全部工业总产值(亿元)	Gross industrial Output Value (100 million yuan)	33.91
规模以上工业企业主要经济指标	Principal Financial Indicators of Industrial Enterprises Above Designated Size	
工业总产值	Gross Industrial Output Value	28.43
资产总计	Origninal Value of fixed Assets	
主营业务收入	Revenue from Principal Business	
利润总额(亿元)	Profits (100 million yuan)	4.28
建筑业	**Construction**	
建筑业企业从业人员(万人)	Number of Employed Persons (10 000 persons)	
建筑业企业总产值(亿元)	Gross Output Value (100 million yuan)	
施工房屋面积(万平方米)	Floor Space of Buildings under Construction (10 000 sq.m)	
竣工房屋面积(万平方米)	Floor Space of Buildings Completed (10 000 sq.m)	
交通运输	**Transportation**	
货运量(万吨)	Freight Traffic (10 000 tons)	6064
铁 路	Railways	923
公 路	Highways	4843
管 道	Pipelines	298
航 空	Civil Aviation	0.12
客运量(万人)	Passenger Traffic Volume (10 000 persons)	941
铁 路	Railways	148
公 路	Highways	786
航 空	Civil Aviation	7
邮电通信业	**Postal and Telecommunication Services**	
邮政业务总量(亿元)	Business Volume of Postal Services (100 million yuan)	
电信业务总量(亿元)	Business Volume of Telecommunication Services (100 million yuan)	
函 件(万件)	Number of Letters Delivered (10 000 pieces)	4843
报刊期发数(万份)	Number of Newspapers and Magazines Distributed (10 000 copies)	224
局用交换机容量(万门)	CapaCity of Office Telephone Exchanges (10 000 lines)	
固定电话年末用户(万部)	Local Telephone Subscribers at Year-end (10 000 subscribers)	2.90
移动电话用户(万户)	Number of Mobile Telephone Subscribers (10 000 subscribers)	
旅 游	**Tourism**	
入境旅游过夜者人数(万人)	Number of Tourists (10 000 person-times)	0.01
入境旅游收入(万美元)	Foreign Exchange Eearnings from International Tourism (100 million yuan)	5
金 融	**Finance and Insurance**	
金融机构各项存款(亿元)	Deposits of National Banking System (100 million yuan)	32.07
金融机构各项贷款(亿元)	Loans of National Banking System (100 million yuan)	18.26
教育、科技、文化	**Education, Science & Technology and Culture**	
教 育	**Education**	
专任教师数(人)	Full-time Teachers (person)	
普通高等学校	Regular Institutions of Higher Education	2458

Continued

总量指标 Aggregate Data				速度指标(%) Indices and Growth Rates						
				指数(2013 年比以下各年) Index (2013as percentuage of the following years)				平均增长速度 Average Annual Growth Rate		
2000	2010	2012	2013	1978	2000	2010	2012	1979-2013	2001-2013	2011-2013
109.70	825.54	1138.23	1276.77	15091.8	1163.9	154.7	112.2	15.4	20.8	15.6
131.26	891.70	1289.84	1512.90	22150.8	1152.6	169.7	117.3	16.7	20.7	19.3
895.67	2400.96	4315.93	5410.34	6923.0	604.1	225.3	125.4	12.9	14.8	31.1
1061.29	5766.51	7886.25	9121.22	5152.3	515.0	154.6	120.6	11.9	13.4	15.6
852.01	5341.90	7532.67	8679.63	30529.8	1018.7	162.5	115.23	17.8	19.5	17.6
1708.81	7911.97	11669.17	14331.25		838.7	181.1	122.8		17.8	21.9
821.26	5492.61	7510.67	8718.71		1061.6	158.7	116.1		19.9	16.7
90.49	852.43	888.64	855.23	19982.0	945.1	100.3	96.2	16.3	18.9	0.1
26.16	56.48	63.81	79.11		302.4	140.1	124.0		8.9	11.9
234.95	969.47	1633.11	2098.89		893.3	216.5	128.5		18.3	29.4
2241.48	6620.14	11026.49	13096.18		584.3	197.8	118.8		14.5	25.5
1261.42	2891.45	4553.97	5775.14		457.8	199.7	126.8		12.4	25.9
33091	64597	78249	83717	1380.6	253.0	129.6	107.0	7.8	7.4	9.0
4199	6853	6933	7399	801.6	176.2	108.0	106.7	6.1	4.5	2.6
27048	50448	61850	68528	1415.0	253.4	135.8	110.8	7.9	7.4	10.7
1840	7292	9460	7783	2611.7	423.0	106.7	82.3	9.8	11.7	2.2
3.50	3.70	5.80	6.66	5550.0	190.3	180.0	114.8	12.2	5.1	21.6
23191	46346	55298	59024	6272.5	254.5	127.4	106.7	12.6	7.5	8.4
1147	1523	2162	2318	1566.2	202.1	152.2	107.2	8.2	5.6	15.0
21877	44333	52473	56000	7124.7	256.0	126.3	106.7	13.0	7.5	8.1
167	490	663	706	10085.7	422.8	144.1	106.5	14.1	11.7	12.9
5.94	16.58	18.17	18.78		316.2	113.3	103.4		9.3	4.2
41.36	565.47	246.67	268.17		648.4	47.4	108.7		15.5	-22.0
7148	2926	2529	2041	42.1	28.6	69.8	80.7	-2.4	-9.2	-11.3
535	307	310	353	157.6	66.0	115.0	113.9	1.3	-3.1	4.8
241.67	928.20	623.60	832.30		344.4	89.7	133.5		10.0	-3.6
191.03	547.50	540.10	544.80	18786.2	285.2	99.5	100.9	16.1	8.4	-0.2
78.00	1359.80	2008.50	2133.90		2735.8	156.9	106.2		29.0	16.2
25.61	101.03	149.80	156.73	1567300.0	612.0	155.1	104.6	31.8	15.0	15.8
9494	36844	55057	58502	1170040.0	616.2	158.8	106.3	30.7	15.0	16.7
1863.48	8870.72	12330.89	14088.83	43931.5	756.0	158.8	114.3	19.0	16.8	16.7
1403.13	4973.16	7914.00	9840.46	53890.8	701.3	197.9	124.3	19.7	16.2	25.5
7924	16506	17570	18327	745.6	231.3	111.0	104.3	5.9	6.7	3.5

1-3 续表 3

指　　标	Item	1978
中等学校	Regular Secondary Schools	44417
小　学	Regular Primary Schools	82616
在校学生数(万人)	Students Enrollment (10 000 persons)	
普通高等学校	Regular Institutions of Higher Education	1.02
中等学校	Regular Secondary Schools	83.86
小　学	Regular Primary Schools	202.88
科　技	**Science and Technology**	
研究与发展经费支出(万元)	Expenditures on Research and Development (10 000 yuan)	
技术市场交易额(万元)	Volume of Transaction in Technical Markets (10 000 yuan)	
文　化	**Culture**	
电视节目制作时间(小时)	Time for TV Programs Production (hour)	
家庭、生活、环境	**Family, People's Livelihood and Environment**	
家　庭	**Family**	
家庭总户数(万户)	Total Number of Households (10 000 households)	
婚　姻	**Marriages and Divorces**	
结婚数(万对)	Number of Marriages (10 000 couples)	
离婚数(万对)	Number of Divorces (10 000 couples)	
居　住	**Housing**	
城镇居民人均住房建筑面积(平方米)	Per capita Gross Floor Space of Urban Residents (sq.m)	
农村居民人均住房面积(平方米)	Per capita Net Floor Space of Rural Residents (sq.m)	
生　活	**People's Livelihood**	
城镇居民人均可支配收入(元)	Per Capita Annual Disposable Income of Urban Households (yuan)	319
农村居民人均纯收入(元)	Per Capita Net Income of Rural Residents (yuan)	119
城乡居民储蓄存款余额(亿元)	Outstanding Amount of Saving Deposits in Urban and Rural Areas (100 million yuan)	6.42
卫　生	**Health Care**	
医院、卫生院(个)	Number of Hospitals (unit)	806
医生(人)	Number of Doctors (person)	16898
医院、卫生院床位数(张)	Number of Hospital Beds (unit)	39179
市政建设	**Municipal Works**	
自来水供应量(亿立方米)	Volume of Tapping Water Supply(100 million cu.m)	
下水道长度(公里)	Length of Sewer Pipelines (km)	
铺装道路长度(公里)	Length of Paved Roads (km)	
环境、灾害	**Environment and Disaster**	
化学需氧量排放量(万吨)	COD Discharge (10 000 tons)	
二氧化硫排放量(万吨)	Sulphur Dioxide Emission (10 000 tons)	
火灾发生数(起)	Number of Fire Disasters (times)	
火灾损失(万元)	Fire Loss (10 000 yuan)	
交通事故发生数(起)	Number of Traffic Accidents (times)	
交通事故损失(万元)	Loss of Traffic Accidents (10 000 yuan)	

Continued

总量指标 Aggregate Data				速度指标(%) Indices and Growth Rates						
				指数(2013 年比以下各年) Index (2013 as percentuage of the following years)				平均增长速度 Average Annual Growth Rate		
2000	2010	2012	2013	1978	2000	2010	2012	1979-2013	2001-2013	2011-2013
89211	128306	134900	137901	310.5	154.6	107.5	102.2	3.3	3.4	2.4
131259	133963	136130	140561	170.1	107.1	104.9	103.3	1.5	0.5	1.6
7.41	26.38	28.42	29.53	2895.1	398.5	111.9	103.9	10.1	11.2	3.8
131.18	168.40	165.16	163.29	194.7	124.5	97.0	98.9	1.9	1.7	-1.0
247.74	193.58	190.08	189.44	93.4	76.5	97.9	99.7	-0.2	-2.0	-0.7
32381	266545	397289	454598		1403.9	170.6	114.4		22.5	19.5
66168	43146	54910	29653		44.8	68.7	54.0		-6.0	-11.8
29261	76467	92503	93097		318.2	121.7	100.6		9.3	6.8
481.91	639.86	675.17	682.18		141.6	106.6	101.0		2.7	2.2
16.25	26.40	26.29	26.07			98.8	99.2			-0.4
5.90	9.78	10.43	10.91			111.6	104.6			3.7
26.75	27.25	29.03	30.61		114.4	112.3	105.4		1.0	4.0
17.25	24.00	27.18	24.57		142.4	102.4	90.4		2.8	0.8
5645	13644	17921	19874	6230.1	392.0	151.2	110.9	12.5	11.1	14.8
1618	4643	6394	7296	6131.1	451.1	157.1	114.1	12.5	12.3	16.3
908.55	3713.47	5281.83	5884.50	91658.9	647.7	158.5	111.4	21.5	15.5	16.6
1352	1712	1759	1784	221.3	132.0	104.2	101.4	2.3	2.2	1.4
45402	48166	49558	51959	307.5	114.4	107.9	104.8	3.3	1.0	2.6
65916	109851	125064	137325	350.5	208.3	125.0	109.8	3.6	5.8	7.7
5.00	7.73	8.59	8.80		176.0	113.8	102.4		4.4	4.4
2008	4372	4956	5660		281.9	129.5	114.2		8.3	9.0
2809	5178	5813	6527		232.4	126.1	112.3		6.7	8.0
	29.60	67.92	67.23			227.1	99.0			31.4
31.10	58.85	79.61	82.94		266.7	140.9	104.2		7.8	12.1
3050	5209	7201	11909		390.5	228.6	165.4		11.0	31.7
2329	3041	8589	8686		372.9	285.6	101.1		10.7	41.9
10048	4949	4942	8923		88.8	180.3	180.6		-0.9	21.7
4443	864	1233	1316		29.6	152.3	106.7		-8.9	15.1

1-4 主要年份国民经济和社会发展结构指标
Composition Indicators on National Economic and Social Development in Main Years

单位: % (%)

指　标	Item	1978	2000	2010	2012	2013
人口与就业	**Population and Employment**					
人　口	**Population**					
性别结构	Sexual Composition					
男	Male	51.1	51.8	51.3	51.3	50.9
女	Female	48.9	48.2	48.7	48.7	49.1
就　业	**Employment**					
产业结构	Industrial Composition					
第一产业	Primary Industry	72.1	57.7	49	48.7	46.2
第二产业	Secondary Industry	14.3	13.8	14.8	15.6	16.3
第三产业	Tertiary Industry	13.6	28.5	36.2	35.7	37.5
宏观经济	**Macro Economy**					
国民核算	**National Accounting**					
新疆生产总值产业结构	Industrial Composition					
第一产业	Primary Industry	35.8	21.1	19.8	17.6	17.6
第二产业	Secondary Industry	47.0	39.4	47.7	46.4	45.2
#工　业	Industry	37.1	30.7	39.8	38.0	36.3
第三产业	Tertiary Industry	17.2	39.5	32.5	36.0	37.2
固定资产投资	**Investment**					
全社会固定资产投资结构	Composition of Total Investment in Fixed Assets					
城　镇	Urban	100.0	91.2	89.9	89.4	90.6
#房地产	Real Estate Development		10.3	9.8	9.7	10.1
农　村	Rural		8.8	10.1	10.6	9.4
资金来源结构	Composition of Funded Sources					
国家预算内资金	State Budgetary Appropriation	79.0	8.3	16.8	13.0	13.5
国内贷款	Domestic Loans		22.1	15.2	13.3	12.1
利用外资	Foreign Investment		1.6	0.3	0.3	…
自筹和其他投资	Fundraising and Other Investment	21.0	68.0	67.7	73.4	74.4
对外经济贸易	**Foreign Economic Trade**					
进出口总额结构	Composition of total Value of Exports and Imports					
出口额	Exports	39.9	53.2	75.7	76.9	80.8
进口额	Imports	60.1	46.8	24.3	23.1	19.2
财　政	**Government Finance**					
公共财政预算收入结构	Composition of Government Revenue					
税收收入	Various Taxes	60.8	81.6	83.2	76.9	73.2
非税收入	Nontax Revenues	39.2	18.4	16.8	23.1	26.8
公共财政预算支出结构	Composition of Government Expenditures					
一般公共服务	General Common Service			11.5	11.2	11.0
教育与科学技术	Operating Expenses for Education and Operating Expenses for Science and Technology			19.7	18.6	18.7
社会保障和就业	Operating Expenses for Medical Treatment and Sanitation			9.8	8.4	8.6
环境保护	Operating Expenses for Environmental Conservation			3.0	2.4	2.2
城乡社区事务	Expenses of Community			5.6	6.7	7.9
农林水事务	Expenses of Agriculture, Forest and Irrigation			13.0	13.4	12.6
其他各项支出	Other Expense			37.4	39.3	39.0
能源生产与消费	**Energy Production and Consumption**					
能源生产总量结构	Composition of Total Energy Production					
原　煤	Coal	60.0	40.6	49.2	55.7	
原　油	Petroleum Crude Oil	35.8	48.7	24.9	21.5	
天然气	Natural Gas	2.4	7.9	22.6	19.0	
水风电	Water, Wind and Electricity	1.8	2.8	3.3	3.8	

1-4 续表 1 Continued

单位: % (%)

指　标	Item	1978	2000	2010	2012	2013
能源消费总量结构	Composition of Total Energy Consumption					
煤　炭	Coal	72.5	63.6	65.8	68.4	
石　油	Petroleum Oil	21.5	23.3	15.8	14.4	
天然气	Natural Gas	3.4	8.6	12.4	11.5	
水电、风电	Hydro-power, Wind Power	2.6	4.5	5.6	5.7	
产　业	**Industrial**					
农　业	**Agriculture**					
农林牧渔业产值结构	Composition of Gross Output Value of Agriculture, Forestry, Animal Husbandry, Fishery					
农　业	Farming	74.5	74.0	74.6	73.6	71.1
林　业	Forestry	1.8	1.7	1.9	1.9	1.9
牧　业	Animal Husbandry	23.5	23.5	20.4	21.3	23.8
渔　业	Fishery	0.2	0.8	0.7	0.7	0.7
农林牧渔服务业	Agricultural, Forestry, Animal Husbandry, Fishery and Their Services			2.4	2.5	2.5
工　业	**Industry**					
工业总产值规模结构	Composition of Gross Output Value of Industry					
大型企业	Large Enterprises		53.7	55.2	64.6	63.0
中型企业	Medium-sized Enterprises		10.1	24.4	15.6	15.2
小型企业	Small Enterprises		36.2	20.4	18.9	21.0
微型企业	Min Enterprises				0.9	0.8
建筑业	**Construction**					
建筑业总产值结构	Composition of Gross Output Value of Construction Industry					
建筑工程	Construction Projects		88.3	87.2	89.1	90.0
安装工程	Installation Projects		9.1	11.4	8.7	8.1
其　他	Others		2.6	1.4	2.2	1.9
交通运输业	**Transportation**					
货运量结构按运输方式分	By Means of Transportation					
铁　路	Railways	15.2	12.7	10.6	8.9	8.8
公　路	Highways	79.9	81.7	78.1	79.0	81.9
民用航空	Civil Aviation	…	…	…	…	…
管道输油(气)	Pipelines	4.9	5.6	11.3	12.1	9.3
旅游业	**International Tourism**					
来华旅游人数结构	Composition of Tourists					
外国人	Foreigners	100.0	81.4	94.8	91.0	94.4
港澳台同胞	Compatriots form Hong Kong, Macao and Taiwan		18.6	5.2	9.0	5.6
金　融	**Finance**					
金融机构资金来源结构	Composition of Sources of Funds in State Banks					
各项存款	Various Deposits		122.8	110.1	101.8	99.9
应付及暂收款	Payable and Temporary Collection		…	1.5	1.6	1.9
所有者权益	Owner's Right and Interest		0.1	3.6	4.5	4.9
其　他	Others		-22.9	-15.3	-7.9	-6.7
金融机构资金运用结构	Composition of Fund Uses in State Banks					
各项贷款	Loans		92.5	61.8	65.3	69.8
有价证券及投资	Securities and Investment		4.4	5.6	5.5	5.6
系统内资金往来	Funds Tranfer inward Banks		1.6	29.1	22.7	16.6
库存现金	Cash in Stock		1.1	0.7	0.8	0.8
其　他	Others		0.4	2.8	5.7	7.2
教育、科技	**Education and Science**					
教　育	**Education**					
在校学生结构	Composition of Student Enrollment					
大学生	College and University Students	0.4	2.0	6.8	7.4	7.7
中学生	Secondary School Students	29.1	30.8	43.4	43.0	42.7

1-4 续表 2 Continued

单位: % (%)

指　　标	Item	1978	2000	2010	2012	2013
小学生	Primary School Students	70.5	67.2	49.8	49.6	49.6
专任教师结构	Full-time Teachers by Type					
大　学	Colleges and Universities	1.9	3.5	5.9	6.1	6.2
中　学	Secondary Schools	34.3	39.1	46.0	46.7	46.5
小　学	Primary Schools	63.8	57.4	48.1	47.2	47.3
科　技	**Science and Technology**					
科学研究与试验发展经费支出结构	Composition of Expenditure on Research and Development					
基础研究	Basic Research		4.7	5.4	8.0	
应用研究	Supplied Research		27.4	23.6	18.8	
实验发展	Experimental Development		67.9	71.0	73.2	
卫　生	**Health Care**					
卫生技术人员结构	Medical Technical Personnel by Types					
执业医师(西医师)	Licensed Doctors (Western Medicine)	14.4	76.9	32.0	30.3	29.9
执业助理医师(西医士)	Licensed Assistant Doctor (Western Medicine)	18.7	23.1	7.2	6.7	6.5
注册护士	Registered Nurses	21.1		36.0	38.4	38.8
药剂人员	Pharmacist			5.2	4.8	4.7
技师(士)	Laboratory Technician			6.3	5.8	5.9
其他	Others			13.3	14.0	14.2
人民生活	**People's Livelihood**					
城镇居民消费结构	**Consumption Composition of Urban Residents**					
食品类	Food		36.4	36.2	37.7	35.0
衣着类	Clothing		13.1	14.8	14.6	13.4
家庭设备、用品及服务	Articles for Daily Use and Others		7.6	6.6	6.8	8.4
医疗保健	Health Care and Medical Services		7.5	6.9	7.4	6.4
交通通讯	Transport and Communication		7.5	12.3	12.0	7.8
教育文化娱乐服务	Education,Cultral and Recreation Services		15.1	9.9	9.2	14.5
居　住	Residence		9.4	8.8	8.4	10.5
杂项商品和服务	Miscellaneous Goods and Services		3.4	4.5	3.9	4.0
农村居民消费结构	**Consumption Composition of Rural Residents**					
食品类	Food		50.0	40.3	36.1	33.9
衣着类	Clothing		9.2	8.8	8.2	7.9
家庭设备、用品及服务	Articles for Daily Use and Others		3.7	4.0	4.2	4.2
医疗保健	Health Care and Medical Services		6.0	9.1	8.5	9.7
交通和通讯	Transport and Communication		4.9	11.1	12.3	11.4
文教娱乐用品及服务	Education,Cultural and Recreation Services		8.6	4.9	3.9	4.6
居　住	Residence		13.8	20.1	24.7	26.5
其他商品和服务	Other Goods and Services		3.8	1.7	2.1	1.8
环境、灾害	**Environment and Disasters**					
工业污染治理投资结构	**Composition of Investment in the Treatment of Industrial Pollution**					
治理废水	Waste Water Treatment		38.2	29.5	47.9	17.3
治理废气	Waste Gas Treatment		40.9	69.3	51.2	74.8
治理固体废物	Solid Wastes Treatment		1.6	1.2		3.6
治理噪声	Noise Abatement		18.4			...
其　他	Others		0.9	...	0.9	4.3
火灾事故损失额结构	**Composition of Fire Losses Converted into Cash**					
特　大	Extraordinarily Serious Fires		15.7			
重　大	Serious Fires		14.3	...		
较　大	Big Fires			0.1	27.6	
一　般	Ordinary Fires		70.0	99.9	72.4	100.0

1-5 主要年份国民经济和社会发展比例和效益指标
Indicators on Proportions and Efficiency in National Economic and Social Development in Main Years

指　标	Item	1978	2000	2010	2012	2013
人口与就业	**Population and Employment**					
出生率(‰)	Birth Rate(‰)	22.55	17.57	14.85	15.32	15.84
死亡率(‰)	Death Rate(‰)	7.69	5.40	4.14	4.48	4.92
自然增长率(‰)	Natural Growth Rate(‰)	14.86	12.17	10.71	10.84	10.92
城镇登记失业率(%)	Unemployment Rate in Urban Areas (%)		3.8	3.2	3.7	3.4
国民经济核算	**National Accounting**					
人均生产总值(元/人)	Per Capita GDP (yuan/person)	313	7372	25034	33796	37181
固定资产投资	**Investment in Fixed Assets**					
全社会固定资产投资相当于新疆生产总值比例(%)	Proportion of Investment in Fixed Assets to GDP of Xinjiang (%)	33.3	44.8	65.1	83.4	97.5
全社会房屋建筑面积竣工率(%)	Rate of Total Floor Space of Buildings Completed in Construction (%)		58.7	40.9	36.2	23.8
消　费	**Consumption**					
人均社会消费品零售额(元)	Per Capita Retail Sales of Consumer Goods(yuan)	179	2066	6104	8101	9069
对外贸易	**Foreign Trade**					
进出口总额相当于新疆生产总值比例(%)	Proportion of Total Value of Imports & Exports to GDP	1.01	13.74	21.32	21.17	20.42
财　政	**Finance**					
公共财政预算收入相当于新疆生产总值比例(%)	Proportion of Local Financial Revenue to GDP of Xinjiang (%)	18.3	5.8	9.2	12.1	13.5
公共财政预算支出相当于新疆生产总值比例(%)	Proportion of Local Financial Expenditure to GDP of Xinjiang (%)	43.6	14.0	31.2	36.2	36.7
利用外资	**Utilization of Foreign Capital**					
实际利用外资额相当于签订利用外资额比例(%)	Proportion of Actually Foreign Direct Investment for Foreign Direct Investment (%)		20.87	78.90	66.80	133.50
能　源	**Energy**					
能源生产弹性系数	Elasticity Ratio of Energy Production	1.20	0.40	0.80	0.84	
电力生产弹性系数	Elasticity Ratio of Electricety Production		0.99	2.02	2.98	
能源消费弹性系数	Elasticity Ratio of Energy Consumption	0.74	0.38	0.92	1.60	
电力消费弹性系数	Elasticity Ratio of Electricity Consumption		0.99	2.20	3.10	

1-5 续表 1 Continued

指　　标	Item	1978	2000	2010	2012	2013
农　业	**Agriculture**					
每公顷播种面积农产品产量(公斤)	Output of Farm Crops per Hectare of Sown Area (kg)					
粮　食	Grain	1650	5595	5771	5990	6174
棉　花	Cotton	375	1485	1697	2057	2047
油　料	Oil-bearing Crops	510	1935	2437	2436	2734
工　业(规模以上)	**Industry(Aboue Designated Size)**					
总资产贡献率(%)	Rate of Total Assets to Industrial Output Value (%)		11.2	18.2	14.5	12.2
资产负债率(%)	Assets-Liability Ratio (%)		62.7	50.8	57.2	61.3
成本费用利润率(%)	Rate of Profits to Industrial Cost (%)		12.8	19.3	14.0	11.3
流动资产周转次数(次/年)	Number of Times of Annual of Turnover Circulating Funds (times/year)		1.6	2.2	2.0	2.0
建筑业	**Construction**					
技术装备率(元/人)	Value of Machinery per Laborer (yuan/person)		8582	7145	6568	5533
动力装备率(千瓦/人)	Power of Machines Per Laborer (kw/person)		7	4	4	3
全员劳动生产率(按总产值计算) (元/人)	Overall Labor Productivity (yuan/person) (in terms of gross output value per employee)		74994	176404	249202	265325
交通运输业	**Transportation**					
铁路网密度(公里/万平方公里)	Railway Density (km/10 000 sq.km)	6.19	18.08	26.39	29.52	29.43
公路网密度(公里/万平方公里)	Highway Density (km/10 000 sq.km)	143	208	918	997	1022
邮电通信业	**Post and Communications**					
固定电话普及率(部/百人)	PopularizationRate of Telephones (set/100 persons)		15.0	25.4	24.5	24.4
移动电话普及率(部/百人)	Popularization Rate of Mobile Telephones (set/100 persons)			63.0	90.9	98.6
旅游业	**International Tourism**					
每一来华游客花费(美元)	Expenditure per International Tourist in China (USD)		371	346	368	373
国内旅游人均花费(元)	Expenditure per Domestic Tourism		827	925	1150	1263

1-5 续表 2 Continued

指　标	Item	1978	2000	2010	2012	2013
金融业	**Finance**					
金融机构存款相当于新疆生产总值比例(%)	Bank Deposits as Percentage of GDP in Xinjiang (%)	82.08	136.62	163.13	164.30	168.52
金融机构贷款相当于新疆生产总值比例(%)	Bank Loans as Percentage of GDP in Xinjiang (%)	46.74	102.87	91.46	105.45	117.70
教　育	**Education**					
学龄儿童入学率(%)	Rate of School-age Children Enrollment (%)	96.00	97.03	99.78	99.79	99.81
小学升学率(%)	Rate of Graduates of Primary Schools Entering Junior Secondary Schools (%)	88.67	92.01	100.53	97.94	97.60
初中升学率(%)	Rate of Graduates of Junior Secondary Schools Entering Senior Secondary Schools (%)	48.22	30.30	45.40	48.60	52.53
学校教师负担系数(%)	Student-teacher Ratio (in percentage) (%)					
高等学校	Colleges and Universities	4.16	9.34	15.22	15.29	15.19
普通中等	Secondary Schools	19.36	14.92	12.48	11.70	11.28
小学学校	Primary Schools	24.56	18.87	14.45	13.96	13.48
科　技	**Science and Technology**					
研究与开发经费支出相当于新疆生产总值比例(%)	R&D Expenditures as Percentage of GDP (%)		0.38	0.49	0.53	0.54
文　化	**Culture**					
每百万人有艺术表演团体(个)	Number of Troupes per Million Persons(unit)	5.24	4.76	6.08	4.88	4.77
每百万人有公共图书馆(个)	Number of Public Libraries per Million Persons(unit)	0.41	4.33	4.75	4.70	4.68
每百万人有博物馆(个)	Number of Museums per Million Persons(unit)	0.08	1.24	3.27	3.22	3.36
卫　生	**Health Care**					
每万人医院、卫生院数(个)	Number of Hospitals and Health Centers per 10 000 Persons (unit)	0.66	0.73	0.79	0.79	0.79
每万人医生数(人)	Number of Doctors per 10 000 Persons (person)	13.70	24.55	22.25	22.20	23.39
每万人医院、卫生院床位数(张)	Number of Hospital and Health Centers Beds per 10 000 Persons (unit)	31.78	35. 64	50.36	56.01	57.75
医院病床使用率(%)	Utilization Rate of Hospital Beds (%)		66.31	89.19	86.35	88.41
市政建设	**City Construction**					
城市自来水普及率(%)	Percentage of Households with Access to Tap Water (%)	59.0	98.8	99.2	99.1	98.1
城市燃气普及率(%)	Percentage of Households with Access to Tap Gas (%)	11.0	92.8	95.8	96.6	96.5
建成区绿化覆盖率(%)	Green Covrage Rate in Completed Area(%)		29.1	36.4	35.9	36.4
灾　害	**Disasters**					
平均每起火灾损失(元)	Average Loss of per Fire Disaster (yuan)		7635	5422	11928	7293
平均每起交通事故损失(元)	Average Loss of per Traffic Accident (yuan)		4775	1746	2494	2673

1-6 主要年份人均主要工农业产品产量

Per Capita Output of Major Industrial and Agricultural Products in Main Years

年 份 Year	粮 食 (公斤) Grain (kg)	棉 花 (公斤) Cotton (kg)	油 料 (公斤) Oil-bearing Crops (kg)	甜 菜 (公斤) Sugar Crops (kg)	水 果 (公斤) Fruits (kg)	猪牛羊肉 (公斤) Pork, Beef and Mutton (kg)	水产品 (公斤) Aquatic Products (kg)
1978	303.0	4.5	8.5	13.4	11.4	7.9	0.5
1980	304.1	6.2	13.9	30.3	12.3	9.4	0.5
1985	367.2	13.9	25.3	30.1	36.4	12.8	0.7
1990	453.8	31.4	26.1	150.4	53.6	18.6	1.6
1995	443.3	56.8	30.0	174.9	69.4	27.9	2.7
2000	446.2	82.8	33.2	161.5	83.8	42.4	3.3
2001	427.3	84.3	22.9	244.3	82.8	44.5	3.3
2002	463.3	79.3	23.5	246.9	104.8	46.9	3.4
2003	417.6	83.4	26.1	198.8	113.7	50.4	3.5
2004	425.2	89.9	22.9	176.7	135.6	55.2	3.8
2005	441.5	98.5	19.6	211.0	146.6	60.5	4.0
2006	441.0	131.8	16.2	273.6	169.0	66.5	4.1
2007	418.3	139.9	19.4	283.2	214.7	67.1	4.3
2008	430.2	142.7	26.9	207.7	213.4	47.4	4.4
2009	537.1	117.7	29.8	195.1	263.5	46.5	4.5
2010	530.1	114.2	30.7	224.4	275.1	48.6	4.7
2011	547.0	132.0	30.4	236.4	274.1	50.1	5.3
2012	567.3	159.4	26.6	259.9	331.8	51.5	5.6
2013	605.2	156.5	27.0	211.9	348.1	52.9	5.9

年 份 Year	布 (米) Cloth (m)	机制纸及纸板 (公斤) Machine-made Paper and Paperboard (kg)	纱 (公斤) Yarn (kg)	原 油 (公斤) Crude Oil (kg)	发 电 量 (千瓦小时) Electricity (kwh)	粗钢 (公斤) Steel (kg)	水 泥 (公斤) Cement (kg)
1978	13.0	1.6	2.3	289	173	7	64
1980	13.0	1.9	2.5	308	186	8	72
1985	16.0	3.1	2.9	369	282	15	149
1990	20.0	6.1	6.8	466	468	23	191
1995	18.0	11.0	14.9	770	731	43	297
2000	15.0	9.7	18.5	1021	1011	61	495
2001	14.0	10.4	16.3	1045	1061	72	527
2002	11.0	12.0	16.7	1077	1123	93	545
2003	8.0	12.2	15.3	1116	1222	106	588
2004	7.0	13.5	15.0	1156	1367	128	623
2005	7.0	14.6	17.2	1212	1545	154	625
2006	8.0	14.5	17.6	1219	1759	194	657
2007	8.0	12.2	19.7	1257	2011	216	742
2008	7.2	14.3	18.8	1285	2315	254	792
2009	7.1	16.6	18.0	1171	2664	305	956
2010	7.0	17.1	19.2	1179	3131	380	1106
2011	2.0	19.3	18.2	1146	3987	407	1445
2012	3.0	18.5	18.1	1203	5351	513	1943
2013	3.0	20.3	19.3	1182	7174	568	2406

1-7 主要年份人均国民经济主要指标
Per Capita Main Indicators on National Economy in Main Years

指 标	Item	1978	2000	2010	2012	2013
新疆生产总值(元)	Gross Domestic Product of Xinjiang (yuan)	313	7372	25034	33796	37181
工农业总产值(元)	Gross Output Value of Industry and Agriculture (yuan)	450	8544	35082	45759	51856
工业总产值	Gross Industrial Output Value	278	5856	26574	35512	40565
农林牧渔业总产值	Gross Output Value of Agriculture, Forestry, Animal Husbandry and Fishery	172	2688	8508	10247	11291
固定资产投资总额(元)	Total Investment in Fixed Assets (yuan)	106	3368	16312	28181	36239
公共财政预算收入(元)	General Budgetary Revenue in Local Finance (yuan)	58	436	2307	4093	5019
公共财政预算支出(元)	General Budgetary Expenditure in Local Finance (yuan)	139	1054	7829	12248	13641
主要工农业产品产量	Output of Major Industrial and Agriculturd Produts					
粮食(公斤)	Grain Yield (kg)	303.0	446.2	530.1	567.3	605.2
棉花(公斤)	Cotton Yield (kg)	4.5	82.8	114.2	159.4	156.5
油料(公斤)	Oil-bearing Crops Yield (kg)	8.5	33.2	30.7	26.6	27.0
甜菜(公斤)	Beet Roots Yield (kg)	13.4	161.5	224.4	259.9	211.9
猪牛羊肉(公斤)	Pork, Beef and Mutton Yield (kg)	7.9	42.4	48.6	51.5	52.9
水产品(公斤)	Aquatic Products Yield (kg)	0.5	3.3	4.7	5.6	5.9
水果(公斤)	Fruits Yield (kg)	11.4	83.8	275.1	331.8	348.1
果用瓜(公斤)	Fruit Melon Yield (kg)	36.1	83.3	200.5	218.6	242.0
布(米)	Cloth (m)	13.0	15.0	7.0	3.0	3.0
机制纸和纸板(公斤)	Machine-made Paper and Paperboard (kg)	1.6	9.7	17.1	18.5	20.3
纱(公斤)	Yarn (kg)	2.3	18.5	19.2	18.1	19.3
原油(公斤)	Crude Oil Output (kg)	289	1021	1179	1203	1182
发电量(千瓦小时)	Electric Power (kwh)	173	1011	3131	5351	7174
水泥(公斤)	Cement (kg)	64	495	1106	1943	2406
社会消费品零售总额(元)	Total Retail Sales of Consumer Goods (yuan)	179	2066	6104	8101	9069
海关出口总额(美元)	Value of Exports (USD)	0.8	66.5	789.3	871.2	1225.8
高等学校在校学生数(人/万人)	Students Enrollment in Institions of Higher Education (person/10 000 persons)	8.3	41.1	115.1	120.3	123.0
中等专业学校在校学生数(人/万人)	Students Enrollment in Specialized Secondary Schools (person/10 000 persons)	19.2	56.9	69.8	71.2	70.8
普通中学在校学生数(人/万人)	Students Enrollment in Regular Secondary Schools (person/10 000 persons)	654.0	638.0	652.1	619.8	603.3
医院、卫生院床位数(张/万人)	Beds of Medical and Health Centers (unit/10 000 persons)	31.8	35.6	50.4	56.3	57.8
卫生技术人员数(人/万人)	Medical Technical Personnel (person/10 000 persons)	41.4	53.0	56.3	61.2	64.9
#医 生	Doctors	13.7	24.6	22.3	22.6	23.4
城乡居民储蓄存款余额(元)	Urban and Rural Savings Deposits (yuan)	57	4913	17113	23783	25988

1-8 新疆建区以来主要年份国民经济主要指标

年份 Year	年末总人口(万人) Year-end Population (10 000 persons)	就业人员(万人) Employed Persons (10 000 persons)	新疆生产总值(亿元) Gross Domestic Product of Xinjiang (100 million yuan)	第一产业 Primary Industry	第二产业 Secondary Industry	#工业 Industry	第三产业 Tertiary Industry	人均新疆生产总值(元) Per Capita GDP (yuan)
1955	511.78	254.58	12.31	6.69	3.22	2.10	2.40	241
1960	686.33	338.32	25.20	9.27	11.06	8.12	4.87	374
1965	789.10	350.25	24.20	12.48	7.32	5.03	4.40	312
1970	976.58	410.33	23.08	10.35	8.67	6.19	4.06	236
1975	1154.53	466.43	28.12	11.21	12.20	8.86	4.71	240
1978	1233.01	491.25	39.07	13.97	18.35	14.48	6.75	313
1980	1283.24	506.35	53.24	21.53	21.44	17.48	10.27	410
1985	1361.14	565.81	112.24	42.89	40.50	32.14	28.85	820
1990	1529.16	617.70	261.44	104.09	83.18	71.50	74.17	1713
1991	1554.57	638.49	335.91	111.86	107.99	84.07	116.06	2101
1992	1580.63	646.94	402.31	114.50	147.64	106.29	140.17	2477
1993	1605.26	655.98	495.25	126.85	205.07	155.92	163.33	2964
1994	1632.70	657.54	662.32	187.69	249.11	190.00	225.52	3888
1995	1661.35	676.00	814.85	240.71	283.97	219.01	290.17	4701
1996	1689.29	684.00	900.93	249.31	313.70	239.07	337.92	5102
1997	1718.08	715.40	1039.85	279.73	385.37	302.50	374.75	5848
1998	1747.35	680.92	1106.95	291.05	395.75	298.53	420.15	6174
1999	1775.00	694.34	1163.17	268.51	420.48	315.86	474.18	6443
2000	1849.41	672.50	1363.56	288.18	537.58	418.63	537.80	7372
2001	1876.19	685.38	1491.60	288.12	573.91	445.60	629.57	7945
2002	1905.19	701.49	1612.65	305.00	603.15	463.59	704.50	8457
2003	1933.95	721.27	1886.35	412.90	719.54	563.57	753.91	9828
2004	1963.11	744.49	2209.09	446.13	914.47	734.10	848.49	11337
2005	2010.35	791.62	2604.14	510.00	1164.80	961.62	929.34	13108
2006	2050.00	811.75	3045.26	527.80	1459.30	1241.33	1058.16	15000
2007	2095.19	830.42	3523.16	628.72	1647.55	1405.11	1246.89	16999
2008	2130.81	847.58	4183.21	691.07	2070.76	1755.35	1421.38	19797
2009	2158.63	866.15	4277.05	759.74	1929.59	1555.84	1587.72	19942
2010	2181.58	894.65	5437.47	1078.63	2592.15	2161.39	1766.69	25034
2011	2208.71	953.34	6610.05	1139.03	3225.90	2700.20	2245.12	30087
2012	2232.78	1010.44	7505.31	1320.57	3481.56	2850.06	2703.18	33796
2013	2264.30	1096.60	8360.24	1468.30	3776.98	3035.28	3114.96	37181
平均增长速度(%)								
1956-2013	2.6	2.5	8.4	5.8	9.4	9.8	9.7	5.5
1979-2013	1.8	2.3	10.5	7.4	10.3	10.2	13.6	8.6
2001-2013	1.6	3.8	10.6	5.9	11.8	11.9	11.6	9.0

Main Indicators of National Economic since Xinjing Established in Main Years

全社会固定资产投资总额(亿元) Total Investment in Fixed Assets (100 million yuan)	社会消费品零售总额(亿元) Total Retail Sales of Consumer Goods (100 million yuan)	公共财政预算收入(亿元) General Budgetary Revenue in Local Finance (100 million yuan)	公共财政预算支出(亿元) General Budgetary Expenditure in Local Finance (100 million yuan)	金融机构存款余额(亿元) Deposits of National Banking System (100 million yuan)	金融机构贷款余额(亿元) Loans of National Banking System (100 million yuan)	进出口总额(亿美元) Total Imports And Exports (USD 100 million)	#出口额 Exports	农村居民人均纯收入(元) Annual Per capita Net Income of Rural Residents (yuan)	城镇居民人均可支配收入(元) Annual Per capita Disposable Income of Urban Residents (yuan)
2.62	6.14	1.73	1.83	2.72	3.41	0.51	0.20		
10.59	11.91	6.36	9.58	6.89	15.50	0.73	0.48		
4.03	11.30	4.53	4.89	11.52	9.70	0.14	0.13		
4.50	13.23	3.57	6.05	17.25	14.35	0.02	…		
6.11	16.85	1.01	8.85	26.88	14.71	0.09	0.04		
13.00	21.89	7.14	17.02	32.07	18.26	0.23	0.09	119	319
20.47	29.36	4.03	16.22	38.56	24.74	0.32	0.17	201	427
44.48	57.38	8.47	28.60	82.96	72.68	2.92	1.80	394	735
88.78	104.30	21.78	47.62	221.80	233.72	4.10	3.35	684	1314
124.93	121.52	26.47	50.34	282.21	299.59	4.59	3.63	703	1476
170.03	138.25	26.07	56.09	336.58	380.26	7.50	4.54	740	1952
248.44	168.37	35.13	64.71	397.39	467.81	9.22	4.95	778	2423
285.48	197.11	28.70	71.10	634.44	632.32	10.41	5.76	936	3170
333.34	253.65	38.28	96.40	838.42	843.38	14.28	7.69	1137	4163
387.85	295.36	48.31	114.88	1012.47	1016.20	14.04	5.50	1290	4650
446.81	310.42	54.52	123.35	1180.78	1215.39	14.47	6.65	1500	4845
519.77	327.52	65.39	145.99	1336.58	1318.41	15.32	8.08	1600	5001
534.65	347.40	71.31	166.28	1548.72	1386.78	17.65	10.27	1473	5320
610.38	374.50	79.07	190.95	1863.48	1403.13	22.64	12.04	1618	5645
706.00	406.35	95.09	263.32	1972.55	1584.73	17.71	6.68	1710	6215
813.02	442.88	116.47	361.17	2225.31	1801.15	26.92	13.08	1863	6554
1002.13	421.16	128.22	368.47	2661.65	2099.09	47.72	25.42	2106	7006
1161.52	563.41	155.70	421.04	2959.78	2214.66	56.36	30.47	2245	7503
1352.27	637.78	180.32	519.02	3427.48	2272.08	79.42	50.40	2482	7990
1567.05	727.59	219.46	678.47	4040.78	2412.69	91.03	71.39	2737	8871
1850.84	847.70	285.86	795.15	4614.62	2685.00	137.16	115.03	3183	10313
2259.97	1025.72	361.06	1059.36	5399.34	2826.53	222.17	192.99	3503	11432
2827.24	1177.53	388.78	1346.91	6845.07	3782.92	138.28	108.23	3883	12258
3539.69	1324.48	500.58	1698.91	8870.02	4973.16	171.28	129.70	4643	13644
4712.77	1557.09	720.43	2284.49	10387.00	6270.21	228.22	168.29	5442	15514
6258.38	1798.99	908.97	2720.27	12330.89	7914.00	251.71	193.47	6394	17921
8148.41	2039.15	1128.49	3067.12	14088.83	9840.46	275.62	222.70	7296	19874
Average Annual Growth Rate (%)									
14.9	10.5	11.8	13.7	15.9	14.7	11.5	12.9		
20.2	13.8	15.6	16.0	19.0	19.7	22.5	25.0	12.5	12.5
23.3	14.6	23.7	25.1	18.5	16.3	23.5	26.7	13.1	10.7

1-8 续表

年 份 Year	主要农产品产量(万吨) Output of Major Farm(10 000 tons)					年末牲畜存栏数(万头(只)) The Year-end Domesticated Animals in Stock (10 000 heads)	
	粮食 Grain	棉花 Cotton	油料 Oil-bearing Crops	甜菜 Beet	水果 Fruit		#羊 Sheep and Goats
1955	147.02	2.51	6.84	0.10	12.33	1640.07	1224.33
1960	197.98	3.19	5.88	7.09	16.10	1911.59	1529.89
1965	261.74	7.59	6.97	15.97	22.35	2697.53	2192.31
1970	303.21	6.46	6.84	21.06	13.70	2431.32	1949.67
1975	310.96	4.67	9.04	15.12	14.25	2436.08	1916.15
1978	370.01	5.50	10.33	16.37	13.98	2476.98	1927.54
1980	386.13	7.92	17.59	38.52	15.62	2672.60	2105.43
1985	496.65	18.78	34.25	40.69	49.25	3016.04	2431.91
1990	676.89	46.88	38.96	224.37	79.88	3496.40	2830.81
1991	672.52	63.95	40.49	256.85	81.10	3494.00	2830.65
1992	706.27	66.76	35.62	329.07	91.89	3495.41	2830.36
1993	720.37	68.00	37.02	236.91	99.82	3514.72	2842.83
1994	666.17	88.21	50.76	299.24	107.52	3599.01	2905.80
1995	730.16	93.50	49.41	288.14	114.43	3724.32	3009.02
1996	818.20	94.04	30.95	354.52	115.99	3863.80	3136.21
1997	825.34	115.00	29.95	388.71	123.67	4007.66	3261.81
1998	830.00	140.00	37.52	513.12	121.48	4223.99	3447.38
1999	838.78	140.75	60.46	354.24	136.42	4396.54	3592.29
2000	808.60	150.00	60.14	292.65	151.87	4524.67	3690.21
2001	796.00	157.00	42.64	455.12	154.25	4603.78	3764.88
2002	875.87	150.00	44.37	466.81	198.20	4781.77	3908.23
2003	801.64	160.00	50.13	381.65	218.34	5026.54	4104.30
2004	828.53	175.25	44.54	344.21	264.22	5206.37	4266.73
2005	877.21	195.70	38.94	419.12	291.26	5333.60	4355.50
2006	895.22	267.53	32.82	555.53	343.14	5339.71	4359.50
2007	867.04	290.00	40.30	586.93	411.98	5023.37	4083.44
2008	909.00	301.55	56.85	438.88	450.87	3746.11	3025.70
2009	1152.00	252.40	63.91	418.41	565.15	3844.75	3127.50
2010	1150.20	247.90	66.62	486.97	593.85	3722.15	3013.37
2011	1200.75	289.77	66.76	518.95	601.65	3697.60	3016.40
2012	1259.83	353.95	59.04	577.19	736.74	4333.25	3502.05
2013	1360.83	351.80	60.63	476.47	782.69	4502.86	3663.22
			平均增长速度(%)				
1956-2013	3.9	8.9	3.8	15.7	7.4	1.8	1.9
1979-2013	3.8	12.6	5.2	10.1	12.2	1.7	1.9
2001-2013	3.8	7.3	…	2.3	14.4	0.2	0.2

Continued

主要畜产品产量(万吨) Output of Major Livestock Products(10 000 tons)			水产品产量(万吨) Output of Aquatic Products (10 000 tons)	主要工业产品产量 Output of Major Industrial Products			
肉类 Meat	羊毛 Wool	奶类 Milk		原油(万吨) Crude Oil (10 000 tons)	天然气(亿立方米) Natural Gas (100 million cu.m)	发电量(亿千瓦时) Volume of Electric Generation (100 million kwh)	钢材(万吨) Steel Rolled (10 000 tons)
6.69			0.07	3.29	0.01	0.55	0.66
6.08			0.57	166.23	0.06	3.44	3.63
9.17			0.46	97.31	0.01	4.46	3.94
8.84		8.53	0.65	153.60	0.66	7.95	4.21
9.16	3.16	6.35	0.50	300.19	3.76	13.23	2.20
9.65	3.08	5.25	0.57	353.05	2.51	21.17	6.83
12.70	3.31	7.28	0.66	390.58	3.53	23.58	8.59
18.37	7.07	19.70	0.90	499.00	5.46	38.11	16.73
30.46	5.09	35.64	2.32	695.00	5.02	69.79	28.48
32.94	5.19	37.49	2.52	762.00	5.54	78.04	33.80
36.02	5.20	39.79	2.66	831.66	6.75	86.80	40.30
38.30	5.28	40.85	2.88	1065.50	8.43	95.78	45.98
42.81	5.46	44.83	3.53	1156.62	9.06	106.17	57.71
52.38	5.66	49.81	4.44	1267.83	11.48	120.43	66.55
60.31	5.99	54.22	4.79	1457.10	14.06	136.03	86.70
64.40	6.25	58.78	5.24	1629.25	21.30	150.58	99.89
75.19	6.48	65.02	5.34	1628.38	23.78	157.76	116.19
81.36	6.76	70.43	5.58	1739.65	31.06	169.30	117.30
90.00	6.98	78.23	6.01	1848.43	35.39	182.98	131.25
97.00	7.30	87.85	6.09	1946.95	41.74	197.62	134.42
105.44	7.78	100.71	6.39	2036.19	48.52	212.24	173.07
115.00	8.21	119.21	6.73	2141.40	50.29	234.62	203.10
128.13	8.91	139.73	7.33	2253.02	57.48	266.30	238.52
141.46	9.38	157.84	7.93	2408.32	106.64	306.92	326.96
158.21	9.62	185.41	8.45	2474.74	164.21	357.15	411.45
160.58	9.34	201.77	8.89	2604.31	210.33	416.87	470.94
114.74	9.03	137.40	9.26	2715.13	235.89	489.17	576.62
115.31	7.60	125.15	9.70	2512.86	245.39	571.31	690.81
121.74	8.69	132.82	10.11	2558.16	249.91	679.32	891.70
127.28	9.01	133.91	11.69	2615.63	235.38	875.19	985.14
134.23	9.20	136.32	12.53	2670.68	253.01	1187.48	1289.84
139.26	9.68	139.19	13.17	2658.47	282.91	1613.01	1512.90
Average Annual Growth Rate (%)							
5.4			9.4	12.2	19.3	14.8	14.3
7.9	3.3	9.8	9.4	5.9	14.5	13.2	16.7
4.2	2.8	5.4	6.8	3.3	18.5	18.9	21.7

1-9 各时期经济发展主要指标
Major Economic Development Indicators of Each Period

时　期	Period	新疆生产总值(亿元) Gross Domestic Product of Xinjiang (100 million yuan)	第一产业 Primary Industry	第二产业 Secondary Industry	#工业 Industry	第三产业 Tertiary Industry	全社会固定资产投资总额(亿元) Total Investment in Fixed Assets (100 million yuan)
"一五" 时期	"First Five-year Plan" Period	60.35	33.86	15.54	8.82	10.95	
"二五" 时期	"Second Five-year Plan" Period	102.65	43.27	39.48	28.37	19.90	31.42
	1963—1965	64.76	33.56	19.27	13.64	11.93	10.43
"三五" 时期	"Third Five-year Plan" Period	111.94	53.53	38.02	27.84	20.39	18.82
"四五" 时期	"Fourth Five-year Plan" Period	128.37	54.38	50.55	36.84	23.44	24.72
"五五" 时期	"Fifth Five-year Plan" Period	205.39	77.27	91.75	72.34	36.37	69.12
"六五" 时期	"Sixth Five-year Plan" Period	405.19	165.70	146.99	117.51	92.50	149.13
"七五" 时期	"Seventh Five-year Plan" Period	948.99	356.55	318.96	263.20	273.48	331.97
"八五" 时期	"Eighth Five-year Plan" Period	2710.64	781.61	993.78	755.30	935.25	1162.22
"九五" 时期	"Ninth Five-year Plan" Period	5574.46	1376.78	2052.88	1574.58	2144.80	2499.46
"十五" 时期	"Tenth Five-year Plan" Period	9803.83	1962.15	3975.87	3168.48	3865.81	5034.95
"十一五" 时期	"Eleventh Five-year Plan " Period	20466.15	3685.96	9699.35	8119.02	7080.84	12044.80
"十二五" 时期	"Twelfth Five-year Plan " Period						
	2011	6610.05	1139.03	3225.90	2700.20	2245.12	4712.77
	2012	7505.31	1320.57	3481.56	2850.06	2703.18	6258.38
	2013	8360.24	1468.30	3776.98	3035.28	3114.96	8148.41

时　期	Period	住宅竣工建筑面积(万平方米) Floor Space of Building Completed (10 000 sq.m)	公共财政预算收入(亿元) General Budgetary Revenue in Local Finance (100 million yuan)	公共财政预算支出(亿元) General Budgetary Expenditure in Local Finance (100 million yuan)	进出口总额(万美元) Total Imports And Exports (USD 10 000)	#出口额 Exports	社会消费品零售总额(亿元) Total Retail Sales of Consumer Goods (100 million yuan)
"一五" 时期	"First Five-year Plan" Period		8.65	9.50	20819	10945	31.38
"二五" 时期	"Second Five-year Plan" Period		21.39	27.16	26197	17976	53.43
	1963—1965		12.20	11.61	4806	4632	31.92
"三五" 时期	"Third Five-year Plan" Period		15.38	21.78	1243	633	63.75
"四五" 时期	"Fourth Five-year Plan" Period		11.11	39.78	2922	1217	76.26
"五五" 时期	"Fifth Five-year Plan" Period		18.24	54.80	10255	4310	113.51
"六五" 时期	"Sixth Five-year Plan" Period	3279.57	27.35	100.30	81536	57445	215.35
"七五" 时期	"Seventh Five-year Plan" Period	4175.39	75.48	197.04	190173	142124	323.14
"八五" 时期	"Eighth Five-year Plan" Period	4928.74	155.63	338.64	460033	265704	878.89
"九五" 时期	"Ninth Five-year Plan" Period	8341.78	318.60	741.45	841181	425462	1655.20
"十五" 时期	"Tenth Five-year Plan" Period	12466.98	675.80	1933.02	2281284	1260601	2471.83
"十一五" 时期	"Eleventh Five-year Plan " Period	19074.22	1755.75	5578.82	7599235	6173465	5134.21
"十二五" 时期	"Twelfth Five-year Plan " Period						
	2011	4504.94	720.43	2284.49	2282225	1682886	1557.09
	2012	6152.03	908.97	2720.07	2517075	1934686	1798.99
	2013	4228.72	1128.49	3067.12	2756191	2226980	2039.15

1-10 各时期经济发展主要指标平均增长率
Growth Rate of Major Economic Development Indicators of Each Period

单位：% (%)

时 期	Period	新疆生产总值 Gross Domestic Product of Xinjiang	第一产业 Primary Industry	第二产业 Secondary Industry	#工 业 Industry	第三产业 Tertiary Industry	全社会固定资产投资总额 Total Investment in Fixed Assets
"一五" 时期	"First Five-year Plan" Period	9.0	5.1	12.6	8.8	18.8	
"二五" 时期	"Second Five-year Plan" Period	4.5	2.8	11.0	24.5	-1.3	-14.8
	1963—1965	12.9	17.9	8.4	3.3	5.4	28.4
"三五" 时期	"Third Five-year Plan" Period	0.3	-3.1	3.8	4.3	4.8	2.2
"四五" 时期	"Fourth Five-year Plan" Period	2.9	…	7.2	7.3	-0.5	6.3
"五五" 时期	"Fifth Five-year Plan" Period	10.5	7.4	11.6	14.3	14.5	34.1
"六五" 时期	"Sixth Five-year Plan" Period	12.5	13.0	9.2	9.3	17.6	10.9
"七五" 时期	"Seventh Five-year Plan" Period	9.8	7.9	8.2	9.2	14.7	14.8
"八五" 时期	"Eighth Five-year Plan" Period	11.8	6.7	14.2	13.5	15.0	30.3
"九五" 时期	"Ninth Five-year Plan" Period	7.7	5.8	6.8	5.9	10.3	12.9
"十五" 时期	"Tenth Five-year Plan" Period	10.0	5.6	10.6	11.3	11.2	17.2
"十一五"时期	"Eleventh Five-year Plan " Period	10.6	5.6	11.8	12.1	11.4	21.2
"十二五" 时期	"Twelfth Five-year Plan " Period						
	2011	12.0	6.5	12.0	11.4	15.2	33.1
	2012	12.0	7.0	13.7	12.7	12.3	32.8
	2013	11.0	6.9	13.1	12.2	10.2	30.2

时 期	Period	住宅竣工建筑面积 Floor Space of Building Completed	公共财政预算收入 General Budgetary Revenue in Local Finance	公共财政预算支出 General Budgetary Expenditure in Local Finance	进出口总 额 Total Imports And Exports	#出口额 Exports	社会消费品零售总额 Total Retail Sales of Consumer Goods
"一五" 时期	"First Five-year Plan" Period		25.0	30.7	17.8	17.8	18.5
"二五" 时期	"Second Five-year Plan" Period		4.7	-0.4	-12.5	-9.6	4.3
	1963—1965		16.8	30.5	-20.4	-13.8	2.3
"三五" 时期	"Third Five-year Plan" Period		-4.7	4.3	-34.4	-50.3	3.2
"四五" 时期	"Fourth Five-year Plan" Period		-22.3	7.9	40.6	58.0	5.0
"五五" 时期	"Fifth Five-year Plan" Period		31.9	12.9	28.4	35.5	11.7
"六五" 时期	"Sixth Five-year Plan" Period		16.0	12.0	56.0	60.2	14.3
"七五" 时期	"Seventh Five-year Plan" Period	2.3	20.8	10.7	7.0	13.2	12.7
"八五" 时期	"Eighth Five-year Plan" Period	3.1	11.9	15.1	28.3	18.1	19.4
"九五" 时期	"Ninth Five-year Plan" Period	12.1	15.6	14.6	9.7	9.4	8.1
"十五" 时期	"Tenth Five-year Plan" Period	14.0	17.9	22.1	28.5	33.2	11.2
"十一五" 时期	"Eleventh Five-year Plan " Period	-1.9	22.7	26.8	16.6	20.8	15.7
"十二五" 时期	"Twelfth Five-year Plan " Period						
	2011	36.8	43.9	34.5	33.2	29.8	17.6
	2012	36.6	26.2	19.1	10.3	15.0	15.5
	2013	-31.2	24.2	12.8	9.5	15.1	13.3

1-11 天山北坡经济带主要经济指标

(2013 年)

指 标	Item	全区合计 Total of the whole region	北坡经济带合计 Total of the economic belt	北坡经济带占全区比重(%) ratio of the economic belt (%)	乌昌合计 Total of Urmqi and Changji	乌昌占全区比重(%) Pencent-age of Urmqi and Changji to total(%)	乌鲁木齐市 Urumqi City
人 口	**Population**						
年末总人口	Total Population at Year-end	2264.30	883.31	39.0	403.43	17.8	262.93
#少数民族人口	Minority Nationalities Population	1406.57	321.9	22.9	109.71	7.8	71.55
城镇人口	Urban Population	1006.93	767.08	76.2	377.92	37.5	256.68
乡村人口	Rural Population	1257.37	116.23	9.2	25.51	2.0	6.25
综 合	**General**						
新疆生产总值(亿元)	Gross Domestic Produc in Xinjiang (100 million yuan)	8360.24	5803.52	69.4	3140.16	37.6	2202.85
第一产业	First Industry	1468.30	613.37	41.8	265.09	18.1	26.31
第二产业	Second Industry	3776.98	2837.18	75.1	1326.56	35.1	875.10
#工 业	Industry	3035.28	2416.12	79.6	1111.91	36.6	746.75
第三产业	Tertiary Industry	3114.96	2352.98	75.5	1548.51	49.7	1301.44
新疆生产总值构成(%)	Composition of Gross Domestic Produc in Xinjiang (%)						
第一产业	First Industry	17.6	10.6		8.4		1.2
第二产业	Second Industry	45.2	48.9		42.2		39.7
#工 业	Industry	36.3	41.6		35.4		33.9
第三产业	Tertiary Industry	37.2	40.5		49.3		59.1
财政收入相当于新疆生产总值比重(%)	Ratio of GDP covered by financial Expenditure (%)	13.5	10.4		12.2		13.7
财政支出相当于新疆生产总值比重(%)	Ratio of GDP covered by financial Expenditure (%)	36.7	15.3		16.6		16.0
固定资产投资(亿元)	**Fixed Asset Investment (100 million yuan)**						
城镇固定资产投资总额	Fixed Asset Value of the town	6558.73	3647.54	55.6	1687.62	25.7	759.25
财政、金融(亿元)	**Finance and Public Money(100 million yuan)**						
公共财政预算收入	Local Financial Income	1128.49	604.49	53.6	383.24	34.0	301.90
#各项税收	Various Tax Incomes	826.34	519.09	62.8	332.37	40.2	265.89
公共财政预算支出	Expenditure of Local Finance	3067.12	886.24	28.9	522.01	17.0	353.20
#一般公共服务	General Common Service	337.37	91.60	27.2	50.85	15.1	30.74
教 育	Operating Expenses for Education	532.67	173.47	32.6	90.29	17.0	59.05
社保和就业	Operating Expenses for Medical Treatment and Sanitation	263.17	70.78	26.9	40.50	15.4	30.74
金融机构年末存款余额	Year-end Loan Balance of Finance	14088.83	9785.47	69.5	6516.72	46.3	5590.19
金融机构年末贷款余额	Year-end Deposit Balance of Finance	9840.46	6234.90	63.4	4581.71	46.6	3922.02
物价(上年=100)	**Commodity Price (Preceding year=100)**						
商品零售价格指数	Index of Commodity Retail Price	103.3					103.5
居民消费价格指数	Index of Price for Residents' Consumption	103.9					103.5
人民生活	**People's life**						
在岗职工平均货币工资(元)	Average Staff''s Money Wage (yuan)	49843					57392
农村居民家庭人均纯收入(元)	Annual Per capita Net Income of Rural Residents (yuan)	7296					12065
城乡居民储蓄存款余额(亿元)	Balance of Both Urban and Rural Deposit(100 million yuan)	5884.50	3823.61	65.0	2375.26	40.4	1894.47
建成区绿化覆盖率(%)	Ratio of Green Coverage in Completed Areas(%)	36.40					37.93

Main Economic Indicators for Economic Belt on the Northern Scope of the Tianshan Mountains

克拉玛依市 Karamay City	石河子市 Shihezi City	五家渠市 Wujiaqu City	哈密市 Hami [Kumul] City	吐鲁番市 Turpan City	鄯善县 Shanshan [Piqan] County	托克逊县 Toksun County	伊宁市 Yining [Gulja] City	奎屯市 Kuytun City	伊宁县 Yining [Gulja] County	察布查尔锡伯自治县 Qapqal Xibe Autonomous county	霍城县 Huocheng [Korgas] County	乌苏市 Usu City	沙湾县 Shawan County
29.02	62.26	9.10	48.02	28.40	23.86	12.03	53.57	30.15	44.85	19.79	41.29	23.14	21.88
7.35	3.80	0.32	13.82	23.17	16.85	10.12	34.28	1.61	37.49	13.09	24.24	8.50	7.15
29.02	62.26	9.10	48.02	28.4	15.42	2.56	53.57	30.15	9.38	6.58	21.84	23.14	18.73
					8.44	9.47			35.47	13.21	19.45		3.15
853.11	255.33	104.67	263.54	61.52	147.40	51.19	162.66	122.58	60.10	39.89	89.77	169.83	155.35
5.01	11.58	7.34	23.31	16.48	15.06	8.24	6.93	6.19	25.51	19.30	29.66	52.71	78.91
739.03	147.65	62.81	134.50	12.96	110.67	34.19	44.83	64.48	16.42	9.84	23.11	85.38	34.94
715.72	112.80	59.50	87.37	8.40	96.48	28.84	23.36	51.34	12.55	7.27	18.96	70.94	26.00
109.07	96.11	34.52	105.73	32.07	21.67	8.76	110.90	51.92	18.17	10.74	36.99	31.75	41.51
0.6	4.5	7.0	8.8	26.8	10.2	16.1	4.3	5.0	42.4	48.4	33.0	31.0	50.8
86.6	57.8	60.0	51.0	21.1	75.1	66.8	27.6	52.6	27.3	24.7	25.7	50.3	22.5
83.9	44.2	56.8	33.2	13.7	65.5	56.3	14.4	41.9	20.9	18.2	21.1	41.8	16.7
12.8	37.7	33.0	40.2	52.1	14.7	17.1	68.1	42.4	30.3	26.9	41.3	18.7	26.7
7.7	11.1	8.9	11.0	10.1	8.4	12.7	12.9	13.4	8.2	8.1	4.3	5.9	3.9
9.4	13.0	11.0	14.4	29.0	14.6	28.4	22.7	17.1	40.4	41.0	22.2	13.2	11.2
411.37	179.56	177.04	265.09	52.29	117.66	60.13	152.91	85.76	63.40	36.37	87.54	78.32	65.19
65.83	28.31	9.29	28.91	6.19	12.32	6.52	21.06	16.45	4.95	3.25	3.86	10.01	6.12
58.36	23.46	8.98	23.51	4.34	8.37	4.06	19.80	13.20	4.39	2.06	3.08	7.56	4.93
79.81	33.18	11.48	38.04	17.82	21.51	14.53	36.92	20.90	24.26	16.36	19.89	22.46	17.39
9.91	1.81	0.72	4.60	2.11	3.93	1.84	4.37	2.04	2.69	1.74	1.98	2.73	2.25
17.70	4.99	1.27	5.81	4.08	3.64	3.16	9.90	5.27	7.56	3.67	5.60	4.62	4.46
6.09	2.24	0.85	3.1	1.24	1.53	1.04	4.28	1.21	1.90	1.65	2.16	1.89	1.38
1108.40	459.65	93.52	392.31	84.58	87.36	32.01	390.98	220.94	41.29	36.82	66.01	106.07	81.24
323.80	293.86	86.12	258.86	46.93	42.93	22.93	229.37	109.01	54.09	18.78	26.60	73.76	55.74
103.7	103.0		103.0	102.7			103.5	103.2					102.7
104.4	103.0		103.6	104.0			103.5	103.8					103.6
78964	50500	53086	50029	47944	64014	55902	43280	45394	32800	38858	36593	31970	41451
15596	13877	14317	10852	8694	8614	7953	11369	11230	10179	9992	10994	14465	17100
236.32	304.38	45.67	209.67	46.25	50.76	18.68	174.94	123.30	23.02	18.62	40.93	64.67	57.75
42.93	42.10	37.29	43.32	37.61	30.26	35.20	39.20	44.10	31.70	32.58	45.63	30.86	33.44

1-11 续表 1

指标	Item	全区合计 Total of the whole region	北坡经济带合计 Total of the economic belt	北坡经济带占全区比重(%) ratio of the economic belt (%)	乌昌合计 Total of Urmqi and Changji	乌昌占全区比重(%) Pencent-age of Urmqi and Changji to total(%)	乌鲁木齐市 Urumqi City
农　业	**Agriculture**						
农林牧渔业总产值(亿元)	Value of Farm, Forestry, Herding and Fishery (100 million yuan)	2538.88	1243.23	49.0	345.10	13.6	36.94
农　业	Farming	1806.11	782.58	43.3	155.85	8.6	16.32
林　业	Forestry	48.13	19.94	41.4	3.65	7.6	0.88
牧　业	Animal Husbandry	604.20	377.78	62.5	179.84	29.8	18.86
渔　业	Fishery	17.17	9.01	52.5	2.65	15.4	0.72
农林牧渔服务业	Services for Farming, Forestry, Animal Husbandary and Fishery	63.27	53.91	85.2	3.11	4.9	0.16
主要农产品产量(万吨)	Main Rural Products Output (10 000 tons)						
粮　食	Grain	1360.83	609.86	44.8	222.59	16.4	14.69
棉　花	Cotton	351.80	161.99	46.0	21.97	6.2	0.15
油　料	Oil-bearing Crops	60.63	25.82	42.6	9.67	15.9	0.91
甜　菜	Beet	476.47	219.31	46.0	64.99	13.6	0.33
水　果	Fruit	782.69	221.80	28.3	14.76	1.9	0.79
肉　类	Meat	139.26	111.83	80.3	56.73	40.7	6.47
工　业	**Industry**						
工业总产值(规模以上)(亿元)	Total Value of Industrial Products (100 million yuan)	8679.63	6672.51	76.9	3334.51	38.4	2427.01
轻工业	Light Industry	1061.81	731.63	68.9	395.60	37.3	189.53
重工业	Heavy Industry	7617.82	5940.89	78.0	2938.91	38.6	2237.48
主要工业产品产量	Output of Main Industrial Products						
纱(万吨)	Cotton Yarn (10 000 tons)	43.46	24.54	56.5	4.01	9.2	0.99
布(万米)	Cloth (10 000 m)	7451.42	3563.92	47.8	518.50	7.0	358.50
绒线(吨)	Woolen knitting wool (ton)	323.11	185.11	57.3	185.11	57.3	185.11
呢绒(万米)	Woolen Goods (10 000 m)	259.00	259.00	100.0			
原盐(万吨)	Crude Salt (10 000 tons)	318.63	121.07	38.0	10.31	3.2	10.31
成品糖(万吨)	Sugar (10 000 tons)	46.72	27.27	58.4	6.48	13.9	
原油(万吨)	Crude Oil (10 000 tons)	2658.47	2068.03	77.8	737.00	27.7	737.00
发电量(亿千瓦小时)	Volume of Electric Generation (100 million kwh)	1613.01	1122.42	69.6	597.17	37.0	255.40
粗钢(万吨)	Grude steel (10 000 tons)	1276.77	844.57	66.1	740.67	58.0	727.64
钢材(万吨)	Steel Rolled (10 000 tons)	1512.90	1013.44	67.0	906.53	59.9	894.82
水泥(万吨)	Cement (10 000 tons)	5410.34	2532.79	46.8	1113.84	20.6	435.31
运输邮电业	**Traffic and Telecommunication Sector**						
公路客运量(万人)	Highway Passenger Volume (10 000 persons)	56000	17144	30.6	10527	18.8	3481
公路货运量(万吨)	Highway Cargo Volume (10 000 tons)	68528	42881	62.6	27412	40.0	17853
公路货物周转量(亿吨公里)	Turnover of Highway Cargo (100million tons-km)	1055.20	562.58	53.3	390.13	37.0	253.48
邮电业务总量(亿元)	Volume of Postal-Telecommunication (100 million yuan)	286.95	107.21	37.4	84.38	29.4	65.53
国内商业	**Domestic Trades**						
社会消费品零售总额(亿元)	Retail Volume of Social Commodities (100 million yuan)	2039.15	1665.19	81.7	993.74	48.7	811.47
教育、卫生	**Education and Health**						
在校学生数(人)	Number of Registered Students (person)						
高等学校	Institutions of Higher Education	278425	252093	90.5	187914	67.5	165090
中等职业学校	Specialized Secondary School	229294	144496	63.0	82873	36.1	69623
普通中学	Ordinary Middle School	1366013	566027	41.4	230548	16.9	153059
小　学	Elementary School	1894401	658620	34.8	264649	14.0	186289
毕业生数(人)	Number of Graduates (person)						
高等学校	Institutions of Higher Education	69983	59018	84.3	47105	67.3	40782
中等职业学校	Specialized Secondary School	74860	45078	60.2	26504	35.4	22676
普通中学	Ordinary Middle School	451275	186865	41.4	74838	16.6	47710
小　学	Elementary School	321294	114480	35.6	44569	13.9	30367
医院、卫生院床位数(张)	Number of Sick Beds (unit)	130889	70350	53.7	36859	28.2	26989
卫生技术人员数(人)	Number of Hygiene Technicians (person)	145851	90285	61.9	45726	31.4	34303

Continued

克拉玛依市 Karamay City	石河子市 Shihezi City	五家渠市 Wujiaqu City	哈密市 Hami [Kumul] City	吐鲁番市 Turpan City	鄯善县 Shanshan [Piqan] County	托克逊县 Toksun County	伊宁市 Yining [Gulja] City	奎屯市 Kuytun City	伊宁县 Yining [Gulja] County	察布查尔锡伯自治县 Qapqal Xibe Autonomous county	霍城县 Huocheng [Korgas] County	乌苏市 Usu City	沙湾县 Shawan County
11.48	25.08	15.89	23.50	27.71	25.39	13.71	12.32	1.86	42.56	24.91	28.00	53.71	69.41
3.78	15.02	10.88	16.28	23.21	21.56	10.23	7.02	0.95	21.93	14.86	14.89	39.32	46.96
2.46	0.32	0.12	0.52	0.21	0.12	0.11	0.09	0.01	0.29	1.53	0.36	0.47	0.27
4.02	6.61	3.53	6.24	3.78	3.54	3.17	4.70	0.76	18.89	8.02	12.08	13.31	20.72
0.11	0.34	0.15	0.21	0.05	0.01		0.21		0.82	0.12	0.05	0.10	0.24
1.11	2.79	1.21	0.25	0.46	0.16	0.20	0.30	0.14	0.63	0.38	0.62	0.51	1.22
1.25	1.67	2.49	3.84	0.57	0.30	2.66	11.54	1.40	75.10	47.97	32.60	23.58	27.25
0.99	3.89	1.81	3.68	0.67	1.01	1.35		0.25	0.01	0.04	0.29	11.43	13.27
0.04	0.05	0.13	0.12			0.12	0.15	0.01	0.97	0.97	1.13	0.16	0.75
0.81	0.25						1.15		5.68	5.77	23.09	0.24	3.64
	3.88	0.74	13.00	44.19	41.29	5.66	2.28		7.66	1.72	11.16	0.18	1.87
1.08	1.97	1.27	2.77	2.10	1.07	0.94	1.37	0.46	4.87	1.95	3.83	3.77	5.20
1776.77	387.23	225.11	230.96	27.95	184.74	65.26	52.53	143.81	38.69	21.11	40.33	43.55	58.68
3.26	80.12	45.11	13.79	4.81	0.49	0.52	17.45	60.39	10.50	8.30	22.66	11.37	37.41
1773.51	307.11	180.00	217.17	23.14	184.25	64.73	35.08	83.42	28.19	12.81	17.67	32.18	21.28
	10.76	1.35	0.87	0.24				3.83				0.59	0.44
1.00	2539.50												371.00
	259.00												
0.08			4.33			100.00							
								3.14	3.84		10.18		
1160.02					171.01								
47.18	168.28	144.89	53.37	3.43	0.84	54.02	37.44	23.91	4.11		4.19		0.39
		38.47			0.67		0.13	58.70					5.92
11.70	4.60	34.49					0.82	46.76			2.71		5.82
	353.08			161.52		159.06			174.21	287.29		75.00	102.01
696	1214	1603	365				1573	680	440	181	685	1961	1300
3147	4419	5705	1229				1805	524	931	172	620	592	1500
68.40	83.74	37.59	21.16					10.47	1.41	1.15	3.08	10.40	9.00
0.53	8.90	0.49	6.95	2.26	2.05	0.73	0.50	0.48	0.10	0.08	0.26	1.70	0.52
53.54	63.27	37.88	58.08	17.77	10.72	3.86	58.76	21.15	12.10	2.62	16.96	12.23	13.58
4488	6355	3081	3701				29393						
688	2005	2059	3766	2640	629	452	9928						580
25239	19425	10231	27884	14231	11981	5785	36268	14499	21905	8416	14935	13235	7973
22726	11959	3158	26409	21921	20443	9140	49000	10135	38235	12745	24495	16529	14047
1288	2043	751	684				4163						
245	774	316	1005	601	22	103	2140						174
8116	6223	2627	9094	4594	3918	2080	11673	4616	7149	2867	4678	4874	2666
4094	2278	1911	4806	3705	3277	1475	7131	1829	5849	1938	3728	2860	2470
1799	3423	795	2295	1187	1066	631	4066	850	653	280	713	1368	733
3057	6496	1022	3029	1540	1351	727	5154	1150	1580	600	1105	1556	1238

1-11 续表 2

指　　标	Item	昌吉市 Changji City	阜康市 Fukang City	呼图壁县 Hu Tubi County	玛纳斯县 Manas County	奇台县 Qitai County	吉木萨尔县 Jimsar County
人　口	**Population**						
年末总人口	Total Population at Year-end	36.76	16.92	21.87	17.58	24.20	14.18
#少数民族人口	Minority Nationalities Population	10.10	4.96	5.29	3.47	6.56	4.52
城镇人口	Urban Population	36.76	16.92	20.34	15.23	16.33	11.72
乡村人口	Rural Population			1.53	2.35	7.87	2.46
综　合	**General**						
新疆生产总值(亿元)	Gross Domestic Produc in Xinjiang (100 million yuan)	292.13	126.52	119.05	148.66	97.69	75.13
第一产业	First Industry	36.99	23.44	44.19	62.92	41.19	17.54
第二产业	Second Industry	141.96	74.93	42.05	52.23	32.93	43.93
#工　业	Industry	118.97	65.84	23.12	42.68	25.33	40.24
第三产业	Tertiary Industry	113.19	28.15	32.81	33.50	23.56	13.66
新疆生产总值构成(%)	Composition of Gross Domestic Produc in Xinjiang (%)						
第一产业	First Industry	12.7	18.5	37.1	42.3	42.2	23.3
第二产业	Second Industry	48.6	59.2	35.3	35.1	33.7	58.5
#工　业	Industry	40.7	52.0	19.4	28.7	25.9	53.6
第三产业	Tertiary Industry	38.7	22.3	27.6	22.6	24.1	18.2
财政收入相当于新疆生产总值比重(%)	Ratio of GDP covered by financial Expenditure (%)	8.9	11.6	6.0	4.8	6.3	11.8
财政支出相当于新疆生产总值比重(%)	Ratio of GDP covered by financial Expenditure (%)	12.3	16.2	14.5	11.4	19.6	22.7
固定资产投资(亿元)	**Fixed Asset Investment (100 million yuan)**						
城镇固定资产投资总额	Fixed Asset Value of the town	151.22	168.27	69.27	132.07	146.44	242.61
财政、金融(亿元)	**Finance and Public Money(100 million yuan)**						
公共财政预算收入	Local Financial Income	25.90	14.62	7.13	7.19	6.17	8.85
#各项税收	Various Tax Incomes	21.23	11.30	6.02	6.35	5.51	8.12
公共财政预算支出	Expenditure of Local Finance	36.07	20.55	17.25	17.00	19.13	17.04
#一般公共服务	General Common Service	5.36	1.91	1.58	1.81	2.01	2.01
教　育	Operating Expenses for Education	6.30	3.94	4.02	3.59	4.15	2.85
社保和就业	Operating Expenses for Medical Treatment and Sanitation	1.57	1.07	1.08	0.94	1.29	1.14
金融机构年末存款余额	Year-end Loan Balance of Finance	412.00	96.90	91.80	78.50	86.70	49.60
金融机构年末贷款余额	Year-end Deposit Balance of Finance	289.00	73.10	65.10	52.70	48.00	29.10
物价(上年=100)	**Commodity Price (Preceding year=100)**						
商品零售价格指数	Index of Commodity Retail Price	103.7					
居民消费价格指数	Index of Price for Residents' Consumption	104.1					
人民生活	**People's life**						
在岗职工平均货币工资(元)	Average Staff"s Money Wage (yuan)	50287	49843	43887	45196	46472	53749
农村居民家庭人均纯收入(元)	Annual Per capita Net Income of Rural Residents (yuan)	14344	13971	15062	16750	13188	12918
城乡居民储蓄存款余额(亿元)	Balance of Both Urban and Rural Deposit(100 million yuan)	187.00	58.70	56.70	49.10	47.50	26.90
建成区绿化覆盖率(%)	Ratio of Green Coverage in Completed Areas(%)	39.12	36.18	40.18	40.46	20.27	25.83

Continued

博乐市 Bole [Bortala] City	精河县 Jinghe [Jing] County	农四师 XJPCC No.4 Division	农五师 XJPCC No.5 Division	农六师 XJPCC No.6 Division	农七师 XJPCC No.7 Division	农八师 XJPCC No.8 Division	建工师 XJPCC architectu-ral engineer Division	农十二师 XJPCC No.12 Division	农十三师 XJPCC No.13 Division	兵团直属 Directly under XPCG
27.13	14.38									
9.03	4.63									
27.13	7.80									
	6.58									
151.56	52.99									
31.05	23.51									
39.73	13.51									
25.95	7.71									
80.79	15.97									
20.5	44.4									
26.2	25.5									
17.1	14.5									
53.3	30.1									
4.8	4.6									
12.8	22.9									
104.24	41.54									
7.23	2.43									
6.52	2.05									
19.34	12.11									
2.28	1.18									
4.33	3.51									
1.62	0.77									
134.39	44.21									
82.50	30.60									
103.3										
104.3										
40360	34432									
11298	11206									
60.26	28.02									
37.20	37.20									

1-11 续表 3

指　标	Item	昌吉市 Changji City	阜康市 Fukang City	呼图壁县 Hu Tubi County	玛纳斯县 Manas County	奇台县 Qitai County	吉木萨尔县 Jimsar County
农　业	**Agriculture**						
农林牧渔业总产值(亿元)	Value of Farm, Forestry, Herding and Fishery (100 million yuan)	45.26	36.78	52.67	59.57	65.98	26.39
农　业	Farming	17.78	16.48	18.85	34.61	29.15	11.53
林　业	Forestry	0.43	0.23	0.41	0.34	0.59	0.58
牧　业	Animal Husbandry	25.64	19.84	31.75	23.44	36.21	13.99
渔　业	Fishery	1.03	0.06	0.40	0.28		0.17
农林牧渔服务业	Services for Farming, Forestry, Animal Husbandary and Fishery	0.38	0.17	1.26	0.90	0.03	0.12
主要农产品产量(万吨)	Main Rural Products Output (10 000 tons)						
粮　食	Grain	29.31	20.61	20.36	17.80	73.66	25.10
棉　花	Cotton	6.66	0.13	5.78	9.19		0.06
油　料	Oil-bearing Crops	0.90	1.61	0.16	0.89	3.07	1.67
甜　菜	Beet	11.27	11.61	4.67	1.34	33.38	2.36
水　果	Fruit	6.49	0.51	0.48	4.69	0.07	1.62
肉　类	Meat	10.15	5.39	8.89	6.86	12.64	4.74
工　业	**Industry**						
工业总产值(规模以上)(亿元)	Total Value of Industrial Products (100 million yuan)	304.19	187.74	66.57	136.67	55.20	150.16
轻工业	Light Industry	93.40	1.33	28.83	59.01	18.20	5.29
重工业	Heavy Industry	210.79	186.41	37.74	77.66	37.00	144.88
主要工业产品产量	Output of Main Industrial Products						
纱(万吨)	Cotton Yarn (10 000 tons)	0.31		1.14	1.52		
布(万米)	Cloth (10 000 m)			160.00			
绒线(吨)	Woolen knitting wool (ton)						
呢绒(万米)	Woolen Goods (10 000 m)						
原盐(万吨)	Crude Salt (10 000 tons)						
成品糖(万吨)	Sugar (10 000 tons)	2.70				3.78	
原油(万吨)	Crude Oil (10 000 tons)						
发电量(亿千瓦小时)	Volume of Electric Generation (100 million kwh)	50.85	110.82		70.28	0.13	86.97
粗钢(万吨)	Grude steel (10 000 tons)		10.35	2.68			
钢材(万吨)	Steel Rolled (10 000 tons)		9.03	2.68			
水泥(万吨)	Cement (10 000 tons)	126.05	137.44			345.63	12.77
运输邮电业	**Traffic and Telecommunication Sector**						
公路客运量(万人)	Highway Passenger Volume (10 000 persons)	2965					
公路货运量(万吨)	Highway Cargo Volume (10 000 tons)	4384					
公路货物周转量(亿吨公里)	Turnover of Highway Cargo (100million tons-km)	62.70					
邮电业务总量(亿元)	Volume of Postal-Telecommunication (100 million yuan)	7.60	1.94	1.68	1.72	1.86	1.21
国内商业	**Domestic Trades**						
社会消费品零售总额(亿元)	Retail Volume of Social Commodities (100 million yuan)	75.81	25.13	21.36	23.48	20.60	9.88
教育、文化、卫生	**Education, Culture and Health**						
在校学生数(人)	Number of Registered Students (person)						
高等学校	Institutions of Higher Education	39985					
中等职业学校	Specialized Secondary School	15242	1462	907	752	1431	762
普通中学	Ordinary Middle School	30696	8334	9187	7307	12454	6125
小　学	Elementary School	28040	8107	10932	8588	11475	6718
毕业生数(人)	Number of Graduates (person)						
高等学校	Institutions of Higher Education	9307					
中等职业学校	Specialized Secondary School	4312	638	256	211	230	71
普通中学	Ordinary Middle School	11249	2788	2984	2311	4480	2129
小　学	Elementary School	4949	1367	1785	1573	2150	1225
医院床位数(张)	Number of Sick Beds (unit)	4504	570	849	733	927	522
卫生技术人员数(人)	Number of Hygiene Technicians (person)	4024	664	809	725	941	415

Continued

博尔市 Bole [Bortala] City	精河县 Jinghe [Jing] County	农四师 XJPCC No.4 Division	农五师 XJPCC No.5 Division	农六师 XJPCC No.6 Division	农七师 XJPCC No.7 Division	农八师 XJPCC No.8 Division	建工师 XJPCC architectural engineer Division	农十二师 XJPCC No.12 Division	农十三师 XJPCC No.13 Division	兵团直属 Directly under XPCG
30.67	30.32	68.24	39.15	97.86	75.24	153.99	0.09	19.33	26.73	2.50
21.84	25.40	45.77	30.98	65.89	57.81	113.63	0.09	11.66	17.73	0.18
0.19	0.30	0.81	0.26	0.88	0.87	4.79		1.27	0.23	
6.07	3.02	18.04	4.94	21.52	12.37	20.55		3.82	6.37	1.98
1.37	0.09	0.89	0.12	0.32	0.36	0.53		0.24	0.03	
1.20	1.51	2.73	2.85	9.25	3.83	14.49		2.33	2.38	0.34
33.67	1.57	66.14	8.18	40.97	10.22	9.55	0.01	2.72	3.08	
5.74	8.69	2.46	9.37	15.89	15.93	40.42	0.03	0.10	2.69	
		6.25	0.75	1.96	0.85	1.38	0.01	0.76	0.04	
3.28	1.19	48.09	25.62	3.63	31.23	0.53	0.15	0.00		
0.35	0.28	26.08	6.29	3.06	3.78	11.34		8.86	13.49	
1.05	0.57	4.18	1.50	5.93	2.39	5.33		0.81	1.46	0.82
38.17	10.08									
15.75	4.11									
22.42	5.97									
1.29	1.19									
133.92										
	6.34									
3.64										
5.80	0.12									
103.17	60.25									
	0.12									
22.33	5.09	15.75	12.21	55.92	28.27	70.10	1.14	31.86	8.07	44.20
		2828	269	2212	537	4324	1573	377	490	18960
10524	6030	14087	8930	15769	9664	20341	4639	5235	4842	6797
13723	9356	15710	9397	17629	9727	23119	3929	6103	6718	2118
		1009	70	626	287	1295	767	150	78	7022
3520	2140	5352	3354	5872	3212	7078	1879	1597	1652	2383
2330	1542	3490	1813	3389	2294	4847	1182	1081	1260	485
1225	508	1494	836	1927	1906	5318	88	318	1000	777
1499	623	1562	1055	2644	2145	6470	138	329	1280	1054

主要统计指标解释

行政区划 指国家对行政区域的划分。根据有关法规规定，我国的行政区域划分如下：(1)全国分为省、自治区、直辖市；(2)省、自治区分为自治州、县、自治县、市；(3)自治州分为县、自治县、市；(4)县、自治县分为乡、民族乡、镇；(5)直辖市和较大的市分为区、县；(6)国家在必要时设立的特别行政区。

平均增长速度 平均增长速度表明社会经济现象在一个较长的时期内逐期平均增长变化的程度，它不能根据各个环比增长速度直接求得，但与平均发展速度之间存在着一定的数量关系：平均增长速度=平均发展速度-1

平均发展速度是一种根据环比发展速度计算的序时平均数，由于各时期对比的基础不同，所以计算平均发展速度不能采用一般的序时平均数的计算方法，计算方法分为水平法和累计法。水平法，又称几何平均法，即将环比发展速度按连乘法用几何平均数公式计算。累计法，也称方程法，根据一段时期内各年发展水平总和与基期水平的关系，列出方程式计算平均发展速度。水平法着重考虑最后一年所达到的发展水平；累计法着重考虑整个时期累计发展水平的总量。

本《年鉴》内所列的平均增长速度，均用"水平法"计算。从某年到某年平均增长速度的年份，均不包括基期年在内。如建国四十三年的平均增长速度是以1949年为基期计算的，则写为1950-1992年平均增长速度，其余类推。

国民经济行业分类 自 2012 年定期报表开始使用新的《国民经济行业分类》(GB/T4754-2011)，该分类是由国家统计局组织修订，经国家检验检疫总局和国家标准化委员会批准，于 2011 年 4 月 29 日发布实施。这次修订是在 2002 年分类标准的基础上，参照联合国《全部经济活动的国际标准产业分类》(ISIC/Rev.4)进行的。修订后的《国民经济行业分类》(GB/T4754-2011)共有门类 20 个，大类 96 个，中类 432 个，小类 1094 个。

企业(单位)登记注册类型 是以在工商行政管理机关登记注册的各类企业为划分对象，以工商行政管理部门对企业登记注册的类型为依据，将企业登记注册类型分为内资企业、港澳台商投资企业和外商投资企业三大类。内资企业包括国有企业、集体企业、股份合作企业、联营企业、有限责任公司、股份有限公司、私营公司和其他企业；港澳台商投资企业和外商投资企业分别包括合资经营企业、合作经营企业、独资经营企业和股份有限公司。对不在工商行政管理部门进行登记注册的行政机关、事业单位和社会团体，主要按其经费来源和管理方式进行划分。

国有企业 指企业全部资产归国家所有，并按《中华人民共和国企业法人登记管理条例》规定登记注册的非公司制的经济组织。不包括有限责任公司中的国有独资公司。

集体企业 指企业资产归集体所有，并按《中华人民共和国企业法人登记管理条例》规定登记注册的经济组织。

股份合作企业 指以合作制为基础，由企业职工共同出资入股，吸收一定比例的社会资产投资组建，实行自主经营，自负盈亏，共同劳动，民主管理，按劳分配与按股分红相结合的一种集体经济组织。

联营企业 指两个及两个以上相同或不同所有制性质的企业法人或事业单位法人，按自愿、平等、互利的原则，共同投资组成的经济组织。联营企业包括国有联营企业、集体联营企业、国有与集体联营企业和其他联营企业。

有限责任公司 指根据《中华人民共和国公司登记管理条例》规定登记注册，由两个以上、五十个以下的股东共同出资，每个股东以其所认缴的出资额对公司承担有限责任，公司以其全部资产对其债务承担责任的经济组织。有限责任公司包括国有独资公司以及其他有限责任公司。

股份有限公司 指根据《中华人民共和国公司登记管理条例》规定登记注册，其全部注册资本由等额股份构成并通过发行股票筹集资本，股东以其认购的股份对公司承担有限责任，公司以其全部资产对其债务承担责任的经济组织。

私营企业 指由自然人投资设立或由自然人控股，以雇佣劳动为基础的营利性经济组织。包括按照《公司法》、《合伙企业法》、《私营企业暂行条例》规定登记注册的私营有限责任公司、私营股份有限公司、私营合伙企业和私营独资企业。

其他企业 指上述企业之外的其他内资经济组织。

合资经营企业(港或澳、台商) 指港澳台地区投资者与内地的企业依照《中华人民共和国中外合资经营企业法》及有关法律的规定，按合同规定的比例投资设立、分享利润和分担风险的企业。

合作经营企业(港或澳、台商) 指港澳台地区投资者与内地企业依照《中华人民共和国中外合作经营企业法》及有关法律的规定，依照合作合同的约定进行投资或提供条件设立、分配利润和分担风险的企业。

港澳台商独资经营企业 指依照《中华人民共和国外资企业法》及有关法律的规定，在内地由港澳台地区投资者全额投资设立的企业。

港澳台商投资股份有限公司 指根据国家有关规定，经商务部批准设立，其中港、澳、台商的股本占公司注册资本的比例达 25% 以上的股份有限公司。凡其中港、澳、台商的股本占公司注册资本的比例小于 25%的，属于内资企业中的股份有限公司。

其他港澳台商投资企业 指在中国境内参照《外国企业或个人在中国境内设立合伙企业管理办法》和《外商投资合伙企业登记管理规定》，依法设立的港、澳、台商投资合伙企业等。

中外合资经营企业 指外国企业或外国人与中国内地企业依照《中华人民共和国中外合资经营企业法》及有关法律的规定，按合同规定的比例投资设立、分享利润和分担风险的企业。

中外合作经营企业 指外国企业或外国人与中国内地企业依照《中华人民共和国中外合作经营企业法》及有关法律的规定，依照合作合同的约定进行投资或提供条件设立、分配利润和分担风险的企业。

外资企业 指依照《中华人民共和国外资企业法》及有关法律的规定，在中国内地由外国投资者全额投资设立的企业。

外商投资股份有限公司 指根据国家有关规定，经商务部批准设立，并且其中外资的股本占公司注册资本的比例达25% 以上的股份有限公司。凡其中外资股本占公司注册资本的比例小于25%的，属于内资中的股份有限公司。

其他外商投资企业 指在中国境内依照《外国企业或个人在中国境内设立合伙企业管理办法》和《外商投资合伙企业登记管理规定》，依法设立的外商投资合伙企业等。

行政机关、事业单位和社会团体 参照企业登记注册类型，主要按其经费来源和管理方式划分。具体规定如下：

(1)行政机关：包括国家机关和政党机关，原则上均列为“国有”。但有特殊规定的，如供销社等，则列为“集体”。

(2)事业单位：包括经国家机构编制部门和有关业务主管部门批准成立的各类事业单位，不包括实行企业化管理的事业单位。事业单位的划分办法如下：

①由国家财政预算拨款或列入财政预算外资金管理以及经费主要来源于国有主管部门或国有上级单位的事业单位，列为“国有”。

②经费主要来源于集体单位的事业单位，列为“集体”。

③公民个人(或个人合伙)开办的事业单位，列为“私营”。

④上述以外的其他事业单位，如果其经费来源不明确，按管理方式进行归类。

(3)社会团体：包括经民政部门批准成立以及未纳入社会团体管理条例范围的工会、妇联等各类社会团体。社会团体的划分办法如下：

①未纳入民政部社会团体管理条例范围的工会、妇联、共青团、青联、工商联、科协、侨联等社会团体，国家拨款设立的基金会或基金管理组织以及经费主要来源于国有业务主管部门或国有上级单位的社会团体，列为“国有”。

②经费主要来源于集体单位的社会团体，列为“集体”。

③公民个人(或个人合伙)开办的社会团体，划为“私营”。

④上述以外的其他社会团体，如果其经费来源不明确，改按管理方式进行归类。

各个计划时期 表内所用各个“时期”代表的年份如下：恢复时期为 1950 到 1952 年；第一个五年计划时期(简称“一五”时期)为 1953 到 1957 年；第二个五年计划时期(简称“二五”时期)为 1958 到 1962 年；第三个五年计划时期(简称“三五”时期)为 1966 到 1970 年；第四个五年计划时期(简称“四五”时期)为 1971 到 1975 年；第五个五年计划时期(简称“五五”时期)为 1976 到 1980 年；第六个五年计划时期(简称“六五”时期)为 1981 到 1985 年；第七个五年计划时期(简称“七五”时期)为 1986 到 1990 年；第八个五年计划时期(简称“八五”时期)为 1991 到 1995 年；第九个五年计划时期(简称“九五”时期)为 1996 到 2000 年；第十个五年计划时期(简称“十五”时期)为 2001 到 2005 年；第十一个五年计划时期(简称“十一五”时期)为 2006 到 2010 年。第十二个五年计划时期（简称“十二五”时期）为 2011 到 2015 年。

法人单位 指具备：

(1)依法成立、有自己的名称、组织机构和场所、能够独立承担民事责任；

(2)独立拥有和使用（或授权使用）资产、承担负债、有权与其它单位签订合同；

(3)会计上独立核算、能够编制资产负债表。法人单位包括企业法人、事业单位法人、机关法人、社会团体法人和其他法人。

单产业法人 指只在一个地点，主要从事一种生产经营活动的法人单位。

多产业法人 指坐落于两个及两个以上地点、或主要从事两种及两种以上生产经营活动的，按照单位划分规定可以划分为两个或两个以上产业活动单位的法人单位。

产业活动单位 是法人单位的附属单位。产业活动单位应具备下列条件：

(1)在一个场所从事一种或主要从事一种社会经济活动；

(2)相对独立组织生产经营和业务活动；

(3)能够掌握收入和支出等业务核算资料。

服务业 指生产和销售产品的生产部门和企业的集合。在国民经济核算中，将服务业视同为第三产业，即除农业、工业、建筑业以外的其它所有产业部门。

Explanatory Notes on Main Statistical Indicators

Divisions of Administrative Areas refer to the division of administrative areas by the State. The relative laws stipulate that 1) the whole country is divided into provinces, autonomous regions and municipalities directly under the Central Government; 2) provinces and autonomous regions are further divided into autonomous prefectures, counties, autonomous counties and cities; 3) autonomous prefectures are further divided into counties, autonomous counties and cities; 4) counties and autonomous counties are further divided into townships, ethnic townships and towns; 5) municipalities directly under the Central Government and large cities are divided into districts and counties; 6) the State shall, when necessary, establish special administrative regions.

Average Annual Growth Rate shows the average growth rate of social and economic development during a longer period. It can not be directly calculated by chain based growth rate. The relation is:

Average Annual Growth Rate = Average Speed of Development-1

Average speed of development is the time series average of speed which calculated by chain based. Because the reference bases during the different periods are not same, average speed of development can not be calculated by the general method. Level approach and accumulative approach for calculating average speed of development rate are applied. The "level approach", or the method of calculating the geometric average, is derived by the formula of geometric average of the chain-based speeds of development, or comparing the level of the last year of the interval with that of the beginning year; the other is called the "accumulative approach" or the "algebraic average", "equation" method, which is derived by the summation of the actual figure of each year in the interval divided by the figure in the base year. The level approach focuses on the level of the last year, while the accumulative approach emphasizes the aggregate development in the duration.

The average annual growth rates listed in this statistical yearbook are calculated by level approach except for the growth rate of investment in fixed assets. The base years are not listed when the years are listed for average annual growth rates. For instance,the average annual growth rate of 43 years since 1949 is listed as average annual growth rate of 1950-1992 without listing the base year 1949.

Industrial Classification of the National Economy *The new Industrial Classification of the National Economy* (GB/T 4754-2011) is introduced starting from the compilation of 2012 annual statistics. The revision, based on the 2002 classification, was organized by the National Bureau of Statistics taking into consideration of *the International Standards of the Industrial Classification of All Economic Activities* (ISIC/Rev.4) of the United Nations. The new Classification was promulgated by the National Administration of Quality Supervision, Inspection and Quarantine and the Standardization Administration of the People's Republic of China on April 29, 2011. The revised version of *the Industrial Classification of the National Economy* (GB/T 4754-2012) is composed of 20 sections, 96 divisions, 432 groups and 1094 classes.

Registration Status of Enterprises (Units) Enterprises are classified into 3 categories, namely domestic-funded enterprises, enterprises with investment from Hong Kong, Macao and Taiwan, and enterprises with foreign investment, according to the registration status of an enterprise in industrial and commercial administration agencies. Domestic-funded enterprises include State-owned enterprises, collective-owned enterprises, cooperative enterprises, joint ownership enterprises, limited liability corporations, share-holding corporations Ltd., private enterprises and other enterprises. Included in the enterprises with investment from Hong Kong, Macao and Taiwan and enterprises with foreign investment are joint-venture enterprises, cooperative enterprises, sole investment enterprises and share-holding corporations Ltd. For government agencies, institutions and social organizations which are not registered in industrial and commercial administration agencies, they are classified mainly by their sources of funding and manner of management.

State-owned Enterprises refer to non-corporation economic units where the entire assets are owned by the state and which have been registered in accordance with *the Regulation of the People's Republic of China on the Management of Registration of Corporate Enterprises*. Not included from this category are solely state-funded corporations in the limited liability corporations.

Collective-owned Enterprises refer to economic units where the assets are owned collectively and which have been registered in accordance with *the Regulation of the People's Republic of China on the Management of Registration of Corporate Enterprises*.

Cooperative Enterprises refer to a form of collective economic units (enterprises) where capitals come mainly from employees as their shares, with certain proportion of capital from the outside, where production is organized on the basis of independent operation, independent accounting for profits and losses, joint work, democratic management, and a distribution system that integrates remuneration according to work with dividend according to capital share.

Joint Ownership Enterprises refer to economic units established by two or more corporate enterprises or corporate institutions of the same or different ownership, through joint investment on the basis of voluntary participation , equality, and mutual benefits. They include State joint ownership enterprises; collective joint ownership enterprises; joint State-collective enterprises; and other joint ownership enterprises.

Limited Liability Corporations refer to economic units established with investment from 2-50 investors and registered in accordance with *the Regulation of the People's Republic of China on the Management of Registration of Corporations*, each investor bearing limited liability to the corporation depending on its share of investment, and the corporation bearing liability to its debt to the maximum of its total assets. Limited liability corporations include exclusive state-funded limited liability corporations and other limited liability corporations.

Share-holding Corporations Ltd. refer to economic units registered in accordance with the *Regulation of the People's Republic of China on the Management of Registration of Corporations*, with total registered capitals divided into equal shares and raised through issuing stocks. Each investor bears limited liability to the corporation depending on the holding of shares, and the corporation bears liability to its debt to the maximum of its total assets.

Private Enterprises refer to profit-making economic units invested and established by natural persons, or controlled by natural persons using employed labour. Included in this category are private limited liability corporations, private share-holding corporations Ltd., private partnership enterprises and private-funded enterprises registered in accordance with the Company Law, the Law on Partnership Business and Interim Regulations on Private Enterprises.

Other Domestic-funded Enterprises refer to domestic-funded economic units other than those mentioned above.

Joint Venture Enterprises(Funds are from Hong Kong, Macao or Taiwan) are enterprises established by investors from Hong Kong, Macao and Taiwan with enterprises in the mainland of China in accordance with *the Law of the People's Republic of China on Sino-foreign Equity Joint Ventures* and other relevant laws, where the establishment of the investment and the sharing of profits and risks are stipulated under joint venture contracts.

Cooperative Enterprises(Funds are from Hong Kong ,Macao orTaiwan) established by investors from Hong Kong, Macao and Taiwan with enterprises in the mainland of China in accordance with *the Law of the People's Republic of China on Sino-foreign Contractual Joint Venture* and other relevant laws, where the investment or provision of facilities and the sharing of profits and risks are stipulated under cooperative contracts.

Enterprises with Sole (exclusive) Investment from Hong Kong, Macao and Taiwan refer to enterprises established in the mainland of China with exclusive investment from investors from Hong Kong, Macao and Taiwan in accordance with *the Law of the People's Republic of China on Wholly Foreign-owned Enterprises* and other relevant laws.

Share-holding Corporations Ltd. with Investment from Hong Kong, Macao and Taiwan refer to share-holding corporations Ltd. established with the approval from the former Ministry of Foreign Trade and Economic Relations in line with relevant State regulations, where the share of investment from Hong Kong, Macao or Taiwan businessmen exceeds 25% of the total registered capital of the corporation. In case the share of investment from Hong Kong, Macao or Taiwan is less than 25% of the total registered capital, the enterprise is to be classified as domestic-funded share-holding corporation Ltd.

Joint Venture Enterprises with Foreign Investment refer to enterprises jointly established by foreign enterprises or foreigners with enterprises in the mainland of China in accordance with the Law of the People's Republic of China on Sino-foreign Equity Joint Ventures and other relevant laws, where the sharing of investment, profits and risks is stipulated under contract.

Cooperative Enterprises with Foreign Investment refer to enterprises jointly established by foreign enterprises or foreigners with enterprises in the mainland of China in accordance with the Law of the People's Republic of China on Sino-foreign Contractual Joint Venture and other relevant laws, where the investment or provision of facilities and the sharing of profits and risks are stipulated under cooperative contract

Enterprises with Sole (exclusive) Foreign Investment refer to enterprises established in the mainland of China with exclusive investment from foreign investors in accordance with the Law of the People's Republic of China on Wholly Foreign-owned Enterprises and other relevant laws.

Share-holding Corporations Ltd. with Foreign Investment refer to share-holding corporations Ltd. established with the approval from the former Ministry of Foreign Trade and Economic Relations in line with relevant State regulations, where the share of investment from foreign investors exceeds 25% of the total registered capital of the corporation. In case the share of foreign investment is less than 25% of the total registered capital, the enterprise is to be classified as domestic-funded share-holding corporation Ltd.

Other Enterprises with Foreign Funds refer to partnership enterprises established within the territory of China in accordance with Administrative Measures on the Establishment of Partnership

Enterprises in China by Foreign Enterprises or Foreign Individuals and Regulations for the Administration of the Registration of Foreign-invested Partnership Enterprises.

Government Agencies, Institutions and Social Organizations are classified into the following categories by source of funds and manner of management taking reference of the registration status of enterprises:

(1) Government agencies: include State and party agencies, classified in principle as State-owned. There are exceptions, such as supply and marketing cooperatives which are classified as collective-owned.

(2) Institutions: include institutions of various types established with the approval by organization and staffing departments of the government, but exclude institutions where enterprise management system is introduced. Institutions are further classified as follows:

(a) Institutions for which their main budgets are from government budget appropriations or extra-budget funds, or allocated from the budget of their competent government agencies. Such institutions are classified as state-owned.

(b) Institutions for which their budget mainly come from collective units. Such institutions are classified as collective-owned.

(c) Social institutions established by individual or a group of citizens, which are classified as private.

(d) Institutions other than those mentioned above for which their sources of budget are not clear. Such institutions are classified by the manner of management.

(3) Social organizations: include social organizations established with the approval from the Ministry of Civil Affairs, and organizations that are not covered by social organization management regulations such as trades unions, women's federations etc.. Social organizations are further classified as follows:

(a) Social organizations that are not covered by social organization management regulations of the Ministry of Civil Affairs such as trades unions, women federations, communist youth leagues, youth associations, industrial and commerce associations, scientists associations, overseas Chinese associations, etc.foundations and fund management organizations established with funds from the state, and social organizations whose funds mainly come from the budget of their competent government agencies. Such institutions are classified as state-owned.

(b) Social organizations for whose their budget mainly comes from collective units. Such institutions are classified as collective-owned.

(c) Social organizations established by individual or a group of citizens, which are classified as private.

(d) Social organizations other than those mentioned above for whose their source of budget is not clear. Such organizations are classified by the manner of management.

Each Plan Period recovery period refer to 1950-1952;the first five-year plan refer to 1953-1957;the second five-year plan refer to 1958-1962;the third five-year plan refer to 1966-1970;the fourth five-year plan refer to 1971-1975; the fifth five-yaer plan refer to 1976-1980;the sixth five-year plan refer to 1981-1985;the seventh five-yaer plan refer to 1986-1990;the eighth five-yaer plan refer to 1991-1995;the ninth five-year plan refer to 1996-2000;the tenth five-year plan refer to 2001-2005;the eleventh five-year plan refer to 2006-2010;the twelvth five-yaer plan refer to 2011-2015.

Legal person units refer to unit that have following conditions:

(1) legally Estabilished,have own name,organization,location and can undertake a civil case responsibility independently by law.

(2) independently own and use (or authorizable usage)a property,undertake liabilities and can make a bargain with other units.

(3) can independently account and workout balance sheet.artificial person unit Includes business artificial person,artifial person organization,artifial person,meeting group artificial person and other.

Single sector legal person refer to the unit that have only one location and be engaged in one kind of production mangement activity.

Multi-sector legal person refer to the unit that have 2 or above 2 locations,or mainly be engaged in 2 kinds or above 2 kinds of production management activity,and who can be diviede 2 or above 2 establishment units.

Industrial activity unit refer to the subsidiary unit of legal person unit.It should have following conditions:

(1) Be engaged in only one kind of social economic activities in excusive conditon.

(2) Opposite independtly organize management and business activity.

(3) Predominate data of business,such as income and expenditure ect.

Service refer to the enterprises and prodution department for production and selling the products.In the national economy accounting,services for the third industry,other said that refers to all sectors except agriculture,industry and construction.

2

国民经济核算

NATIONAL ACCOUNTS

简要说明

本篇主要内容和资料来源

国民经济核算篇资料主要包括新疆维吾尔自治区主要年份生产总值的绝对值、构成和指数，居民消费水平，各地、州、市、县生产总值、构成和指数等资料。以上资料是由新疆维吾尔自治区统计局国民经济核算处根据不同产业部门、不同支出构成的特点和资料来源，严格按照国家国民经济核算制度计算的。

本篇所列分地、州(市)、县的数据来自各地、州(市)、县统计局的国民经济核算资料。由于采用分级核算，各地区数据相加不等于全疆总计，地区所辖县、市数据相加不等于地区合计。

本篇中人均地区生产总值按年平均常住人口计算。

Brief Introduction

Main Content and Source of Data

Statistics on national accounts include mainly gross domestic product of Xinjiang Bureau of Statistics, it's composition and indices of gross domestic product, household consumption level, composition and indices of gross domestic product by prefecture, autonomous prefecture, city and county. Data on GDP are calculated by the Department of National Accounts Statistics of the Xinjiang Bureau of Statistics with various approaches in the light of the features of various sectors, various expenditure structures and the data sources and National Accounts system.

Data on the table come from national accounts statistics by prefecture, autonomous prefecture, city and county. Due to the adoption of hierarchical accounting, regional data do not add up to a total area of Xinjiang, under the jurisdiction of county, city is not equal to the sum of the data region total.

Per-capita Gross Domestic Product are calculated at annual permanent population.

2-1 1978-2013 年历年新疆生产总值
Gross Domestic Product in Xinjiang(1978-2013)

单位：亿元 (100 million yuan)

年 份 Year	新疆生产总值 Gross Domestic Product	第一产业 Primary Industry	第二产业 Secondary Industry			第三产业 Tertiary Industry			人均新疆生产总值(元) Per Capita GDP (yuan)
				工 业 Industry	建筑业 Construction		#交通运输仓储和邮政业 Transport, Storage and Post	#批发和零售业 Wholesale, and Retail Trades	
1978	39.07	13.97	18.35	14.48	3.87	6.75	1.19	2.07	313
1979	45.63	16.32	21.43	17.16	4.27	7.88	1.52	2.34	359
1980	53.24	21.53	21.44	17.48	3.96	10.27	1.91	2.91	410
1981	59.41	25.18	22.39	17.93	4.46	11.84	2.25	3.41	450
1982	65.24	28.11	23.35	18.66	4.69	13.78	2.53	3.84	488
1983	78.55	32.84	29.10	23.33	5.77	16.61	3.01	4.75	583
1984	89.75	36.68	31.65	25.45	6.20	21.42	4.01	6.29	661
1985	112.24	42.89	40.50	32.14	8.36	28.85	4.59	8.97	820
1986	129.04	46.00	45.63	36.79	8.84	37.41	5.98	10.48	924
1987	148.50	56.18	50.30	41.16	9.14	42.02	7.73	12.45	1053
1988	192.72	72.27	66.02	53.53	12.49	54.43	11.60	16.11	1347
1989	217.29	78.01	73.83	60.21	13.62	65.45	12.90	17.59	1493
1990	261.44	104.09	83.18	71.50	11.68	74.17	14.63	20.48	1713
1991	335.91	111.86	107.99	84.07	23.92	116.06	22.63	36.88	2101
1992	402.31	114.50	147.64	106.29	41.35	140.17	28.32	39.85	2477
1993	495.25	126.85	205.07	155.92	49.15	163.33	32.58	43.46	2964
1994	662.32	187.69	249.11	190.00	59.11	225.52	44.40	57.67	3888
1995	814.85	240.71	283.97	219.01	64.96	290.17	59.63	73.78	4701
1996	900.93	249.31	313.70	239.07	74.63	337.92	73.74	87.25	5102
1997	1039.85	279.73	385.37	302.50	82.87	374.75	85.70	94.23	5848
1998	1106.95	291.05	395.75	298.53	97.22	420.15	106.87	98.06	6174
1999	1163.17	268.51	420.48	315.86	104.62	474.18	129.60	102.26	6443
2000	1363.56	288.18	537.58	418.63	118.95	537.80	148.63	110.10	7372
2001	1491.60	288.12	573.91	445.60	128.31	629.57	148.38	118.45	7945
2002	1612.65	305.00	603.15	463.59	139.56	704.50	168.58	123.88	8457
2003	1886.35	412.90	719.54	563.57	155.97	753.91	159.43	141.32	9828
2004	2209.09	446.13	914.47	734.10	180.37	848.49	186.70	160.30	11337
2005	2604.14	510.00	1164.80	961.62	203.18	929.34	149.61	145.10	13108
2006	3045.26	527.80	1459.30	1241.33	217.97	1058.16	165.60	163.15	15000
2007	3523.16	628.72	1647.55	1405.11	242.44	1246.89	177.28	187.10	16999
2008	4183.21	691.07	2070.76	1755.35	315.41	1421.38	191.84	222.74	19797
2009	4277.05	759.74	1929.59	1555.84	373.75	1587.72	209.10	253.60	19942
2010	5437.47	1078.63	2592.15	2161.39	430.76	1766.69	222.47	276.28	25034
2011	6610.05	1139.03	3225.90	2700.20	525.70	2245.12	256.72	371.90	30087
2012	7505.31	1320.57	3481.56	2850.06	631.50	2703.18	357.90	426.65	33796
2013	8360.24	1468.30	3776.98	3035.28	741.70	3114.96	391.97	480.94	37181

注：根据自治区第三次全国人口普查结果,对 2010 年人均新疆生产总值数据进行了调整。
Note: According to the results of the third national census of 2010,per capita GDP of Xinjiang data were adjusted.

2-2 1978-2013 年历年新疆生产总值构成
Composition of Gross Domestic Product in Xinjiang(1978-2013)

单位：% (%)

年 份 Year	新疆生产总值构成 Composition of Gross Domestic Product	第一产业 Primary Industry	第二产业 Secondary Industry	工 业 Industry	建筑业 Construction	第三产业 Tertiary Industry	#交通运输仓储和邮政业 Transport, Storage and Post	#批发和零售业 Wholesale, and Retail Trades
1978	100	35.8	47.0	37.1	9.9	17.2	3.0	5.3
1979	100	35.7	47.0	37.6	9.4	17.3	3.3	5.1
1980	100	40.4	40.3	32.9	7.4	19.3	3.6	5.5
1981	100	42.4	37.7	30.2	7.5	19.9	3.8	5.7
1982	100	43.1	35.8	28.6	7.2	21.1	3.9	5.9
1983	100	41.8	37.1	29.8	7.3	21.1	3.8	6.0
1984	100	40.9	35.2	28.3	6.9	23.9	4.5	7.0
1985	100	38.2	36.1	28.7	7.4	25.7	4.1	8.0
1986	100	35.6	35.4	28.5	6.9	29.0	4.6	8.1
1987	100	37.8	33.9	27.7	6.2	28.3	5.2	8.4
1988	100	37.5	34.3	27.8	6.5	28.2	6.0	8.4
1989	100	35.9	34.0	27.7	6.3	30.1	5.9	8.1
1990	100	39.8	31.8	27.3	4.5	28.4	5.6	7.8
1991	100	33.3	32.1	25.0	7.1	34.6	6.7	11.0
1992	100	28.5	36.7	26.4	10.3	34.8	7.0	9.9
1993	100	25.6	41.4	31.5	9.9	33.0	6.6	8.8
1994	100	28.3	37.6	28.7	8.9	34.1	6.7	8.7
1995	100	29.5	34.9	26.9	8.0	35.6	7.3	9.1
1996	100	27.7	34.8	26.5	8.3	37.5	8.2	9.7
1997	100	26.9	37.1	29.1	8.0	36.0	8.2	9.1
1998	100	26.3	35.7	27.0	8.7	38.0	9.7	8.9
1999	100	23.1	36.1	27.1	9.0	40.8	11.1	8.8
2000	100	21.1	39.4	30.7	8.7	39.5	10.9	8.1
2001	100	19.3	38.5	29.9	8.6	42.2	9.9	7.9
2002	100	18.9	37.4	28.7	8.7	43.7	10.5	7.7
2003	100	21.9	38.1	29.8	8.3	40.0	8.5	7.5
2004	100	20.2	41.4	33.2	8.2	38.4	8.5	7.3
2005	100	19.6	44.7	36.9	7.8	35.7	5.7	5.6
2006	100	17.3	47.9	40.7	7.2	34.8	5.4	5.4
2007	100	17.8	46.8	39.9	6.9	35.4	5.0	5.3
2008	100	16.5	49.5	42.0	7.5	34.0	4.6	5.3
2009	100	17.8	45.1	36.4	8.7	37.1	4.9	5.9
2010	100	19.8	47.7	39.8	7.9	32.5	4.1	5.1
2011	100	17.2	48.8	40.8	8.0	34.0	3.9	5.6
2012	100	17.6	46.4	38.0	8.4	36.0	4.8	5.7
2013	100	17.6	45.2	36.3	8.9	37.2	4.7	5.8

注：本表按当年价格计算。
Note: Data in value terms in this table are calculated at current prices.

2-3 1978-2013 年历年新疆生产总值指数
Indices of Gross Domestic Product in Xinjiang(1978-2013)

(上年=100) (preceding year=100)

年份 Year	新疆生产总值 Gross Domestic Product	第一产业 Primary Industry	第二产业 Secondary Industry	工业 Industry	建筑业 Construction	第三产业 Tertiary Industry	#交通运输仓储和邮政业 Transport, Storage and Post	#批发和零售业 Wholesale, and Retail Trades	人均新疆生产总值 Per Capita GDP
1978	109.8	110.2	110.3	112.8	101.8	107.2	102.1	109.3	106.9
1979	112.4	109.8	111.5	111.2	112.6	120.8	121.6	117.5	110.2
1980	107.3	106.0	105.2	108.5	93.1	116.6	115.6	125.5	105.0
1981	108.5	115.2	99.3	99.1	100.3	113.4	119.4	117.9	106.6
1982	109.9	111.2	104.3	104.6	102.8	117.1	118.9	119.8	108.5
1983	113.5	112.1	111.9	112.4	109.8	118.7	113.3	108.8	112.5
1984	114.1	113.6	114.7	115.1	112.9	114.0	100.0	109.2	113.2
1985	116.9	112.9	116.6	116.1	119.0	125.0	100.3	126.6	115.9
1986	111.7	108.3	109.5	111.0	102.5	120.7	124.7	110.0	109.2
1987	110.0	110.7	105.6	108.5	91.4	114.7	119.3	111.0	108.7
1988	109.6	103.3	114.6	113.6	120.2	112.9	118.8	114.7	108.0
1989	106.1	101.8	105.0	106.9	94.5	113.5	112.7	107.5	104.1
1990	111.7	116.0	106.7	106.4	108.6	112.0	106.7	104.5	106.8
1991	114.4	111.2	117.0	113.1	140.6	115.7	128.8	101.6	109.0
1992	113.1	105.5	119.4	112.6	152.8	115.7	124.6	112.6	111.3
1993	110.2	101.1	113.3	111.4	120.3	117.7	118.3	121.3	106.9
1994	112.1	111.2	110.2	111.3	106.3	115.3	109.7	105.6	110.2
1995	109.1	104.9	111.5	113.3	105.0	110.9	119.5	108.9	107.4
1996	106.5	103.5	107.8	107.4	109.5	108.0	113.0	109.6	104.5
1997	108.4	110.8	105.2	103.4	112.0	109.7	119.6	105.8	107.6
1998	107.5	107.2	105.7	103.0	115.0	109.6	117.5	104.9	106.6
1999	107.4	102.7	106.8	106.5	107.7	112.3	114.7	107.9	106.6
2000	108.7	104.8	108.6	109.1	107.3	112.1	114.4	109.6	106.2
2001	108.6	102.8	108.1	107.8	109.0	112.1	109.5	105.0	107.0
2002	108.2	105.0	107.4	107.7	106.3	110.4	114.3	110.3	106.5
2003	111.2	108.2	111.6	111.2	112.8	112.3	115.1	110.9	110.5
2004	111.4	105.7	114.0	114.5	112.2	111.5	115.1	112.6	109.7
2005	110.9	106.5	114.4	115.7	109.7	109.4	109.0	111.9	108.8
2006	111.0	105.7	111.2	112.5	105.0	113.6	107.2	110.5	108.7
2007	112.2	107.1	112.7	114.1	105.4	114.3	106.1	109.1	109.9
2008	111.0	106.4	114.3	114.3	114.1	109.2	108.7	110.3	108.9
2009	108.1	104.5	108.5	106.2	120.9	109.2	107.0	113.4	106.5
2010	110.6	104.5	112.6	113.5	108.3	110.8	107.9	108.3	109.3
2011	112.0	106.5	112.0	111.4	115.0	115.2	117.3	116.6	110.7
2012	112.0	107.0	113.7	112.7	118.2	112.3	124.1	107.8	110.8
2013	111.0	106.9	113.1	112.2	116.8	110.2	112.0	109.1	109.6

注：本表按可比价计算。
Note: Data in this table are calculated at constant prices.

2-4 1978-2013 年历年新疆生产总值指数
Indices of Gross Domestic Product in Xinjiang(1978-2013)

(1978 年=100)

年份 Year	新疆生产总值 Gross Domestic Product	第一产业 Primary Industry	第二产业 Secondary Industry	工业 Industry	建筑业 Construction	第三产业 Tertiary Industry	#交通运输仓储和邮政业 Transport, Storage and Post	#批发和零售业 Wholesale, and Retail Trades	人均新疆生产总值 Per Capita GDP
1978	100	100	100	100	100	100	100	100	100
1979	112.4	109.8	111.5	111.2	112.6	120.8	121.6	117.5	110.2
1980	120.6	116.4	117.3	120.7	104.8	140.9	140.6	147.5	115.7
1981	130.9	134.1	116.5	119.6	105.1	159.8	167.9	173.9	123.3
1982	143.9	149.1	121.5	125.1	108.0	187.1	199.6	208.3	133.8
1983	163.3	167.1	136.0	140.6	118.6	222.1	226.1	226.6	150.6
1984	186.3	189.8	156.0	161.8	133.9	253.2	226.1	247.4	170.4
1985	217.8	214.3	181.9	187.8	159.3	316.5	226.8	313.2	197.5
1986	243.3	232.1	199.2	208.5	163.3	382.0	282.8	344.5	215.7
1987	267.6	256.9	210.4	226.2	149.3	438.2	337.4	382.4	234.5
1988	293.3	265.4	241.1	257.0	179.5	494.7	400.8	438.6	253.2
1989	311.2	270.2	253.2	274.7	169.6	561.5	451.7	471.5	263.6
1990	347.6	313.4	270.2	292.3	184.2	628.9	482.0	492.7	281.5
1991	397.7	348.5	316.1	330.6	259.0	727.6	620.8	500.6	306.9
1992	449.8	367.7	377.4	372.3	395.8	841.8	773.5	563.7	341.6
1993	495.7	371.7	427.6	414.7	476.1	990.8	915.1	683.8	365.1
1994	555.7	413.3	471.2	461.6	506.1	1142.4	1003.9	722.1	402.4
1995	606.3	433.6	525.4	523.0	531.4	1266.9	1199.7	786.4	432.1
1996	645.7	448.8	566.4	561.7	581.9	1368.3	1355.7	861.9	451.6
1997	699.9	497.3	595.9	580.8	651.7	1501.0	1621.4	911.9	485.9
1998	752.4	533.1	629.9	598.2	749.5	1645.1	1905.1	956.6	518.0
1999	808.1	547.5	672.7	637.1	807.2	1847.4	2185.1	1032.2	552.2
2000	878.4	573.8	730.6	695.1	866.1	2070.9	2499.8	1131.3	586.4
2001	953.9	589.9	789.8	749.3	944.0	2321.5	2737.3	1187.9	627.4
2002	1032.1	619.4	848.2	807.0	1003.5	2562.9	3128.7	1310.3	668.2
2003	1147.7	670.2	946.6	897.4	1131.9	2878.1	3601.1	1453.1	738.4
2004	1278.5	708.4	1079.1	1027.5	1270.0	3209.1	4144.9	1636.2	810.0
2005	1417.9	754.4	1234.5	1188.8	1393.2	3510.8	4517.9	1830.9	881.3
2006	1573.9	797.4	1372.8	1337.4	1462.9	3988.3	4843.2	2023.1	958.0
2007	1765.9	854.0	1547.1	1526.0	1541.9	4558.6	5138.6	2207.2	1052.8
2008	1960.1	908.7	1768.3	1744.2	1759.3	4978.0	5585.7	2434.5	1146.5
2009	2118.9	949.5	1918.6	1852.4	2127.0	5436.0	5976.7	2760.8	1221.0
2010	2343.5	992.2	2160.3	2102.5	2303.5	6023.1	6448.9	2989.9	1334.6
2011	2624.7	1056.7	2419.5	2342.2	2649.0	6938.6	7564.6	3486.2	1477.4
2012	2939.7	1130.7	2751.0	2639.7	3131.1	7792.0	9387.7	3758.1	1637.0
2013	3263.1	1208.7	3111.4	2961.7	3657.1	8586.8	10514.2	4100.1	1794.2

注：本表按可比价计算。
Note: Data in this table are calculated at constant prices.

2-5 分行业新疆生产总值
Gross Domestic Product by Sector in Xinjiang

指　标	Item	增加值(亿元) Added Value (100 million yuan)		构　成(%) Composition (%)		指数(上年=100) Indices (preceding year=100)	
		2012	2013	2012	2013	2012	2013
新疆生产总值	**Gross Domestic Product**	**7505.31**	**8360.24**	**100.0**	**100.0**	**112.0**	**111.0**
第一产业	Primary Industry	1320.57	1468.30	17.6	17.6	107.0	106.9
第二产业	Secondary Industry	3481.56	3776.98	46.4	45.2	113.7	113.1
工　业	Industry	2850.06	3035.28	38.0	36.3	112.7	112.2
建筑业	Construction	631.50	741.70	8.4	8.9	118.2	116.8
第三产业	Tertiary Industry	2703.18	3114.96	36.0	37.2	112.3	110.2
交通运输、仓储和邮政业	Transport, storage and Post	357.90	391.97	4.8	4.7	124.1	112.0
批发和零售业	Wholesale and Retail Trades	426.65	480.94	5.7	5.8	107.8	109.1
住宿和餐饮业	Hotels and Catering Services	108.39	105.76	1.4	1.3	105.9	90.6
金融业	Financial Intermediation	360.40	420.29	4.8	5.0	123.9	115.2
房地产业	Real Estate	194.38	242.63	2.6	2.9	96.7	114.6
其他服务业	Others	1255.46	1473.37	16.7	17.6	110.6	109.4

注：本表按当年价格计算，指数按不变价格计算，采用 GB/T4754-2002 国民经济行业分类标准。
Note: Data in value terms in this table are calculated at current prices, indices in this table are caculated at constant prices, adopted the new Industrial Classification of National Economy (GB/T4754-2002).

2-6 新疆生产总值项目结构
Components of Gross Domestic Product in Xinjiang

(2013 年)

指　　标	Item	新疆生产总值 Gross Domestic Product	劳动者报酬 Compensation of Employees	生产税净额 Net Taxes on Production	固定资产折旧 Depreciation of Fixed Assets	营业盈余 Operating Surplus
新疆生产总值(亿元)	**Gross Domestic Product (100 million yuan)**	**8360.24**	**4543.93**	**1181.42**	**1237.07**	**1397.82**
第一产业	Primary Industry	1468.30	1378.92		89.38	
第二产业	Secondary Industry	3776.98	1271.03	833.12	761.31	911.52
工　业	Industry	3035.28	768.13	714.07	705.91	847.17
建筑业	Construction	741.70	502.90	119.05	55.40	64.35
第三产业	Tertiary Industry	3114.96	1893.98	348.30	386.39	486.29
交通运输、仓储和邮政业	Transport, storage and Post	391.97	211.69	24.33	70.36	85.59
信息传输、计算机服务和软件业	Information Transmission, Computer Service and Software	118.21	35.46	22.98	40.77	19.00
批发和零售业	Wholesale and Retail Trades	480.94	188.71	185.21	31.84	75.18
住宿和餐饮业	Hotels and Catering Services	105.76	94.94	6.36	8.68	-4.22
金融业	Financial Intermediation	420.29	130.53	38.78	15.84	235.14
房地产业	Real Estate	242.63	32.56	50.16	110.22	49.69
租赁和商务服务业	Leasing and Business Service	62.54	41.82	6.32	10.47	3.93
科学研究、技术服务和地质勘查业	Scientific Research, Technology Service and Geological Prospecting	71.35	51.03	4.86	6.34	9.12
水利、环境和公共设施管理业	Water Conservancy, Environment and Public Facility Management	51.63	23.99	1.17	25.62	0.85
居民服务和其他服务业	Community Service and Other Services	64.80	56.95	5.33	1.78	0.74
教　育	Education	317.00	298.51	0.68	20.34	-2.53
卫生、社会保障和社会福利业	Health, Social Security and Social Welfare	137.43	110.45	0.78	9.61	16.59
文化、体育和娱乐业	Culture, Sports and Entertainment	32.17	28.71	1.03	4.68	-2.25
公共管理和社会组织	Public Management and Social Organizations	618.24	588.63	0.31	29.84	-0.54

注：本表按当年价格计算。
Note: Data in value terms in this table are calculated at current prices.

2-7 主要年份支出法新疆生产总值
Gross Domestic Product by Expenditure Approach in Xinjiang in Main Years

单位：亿元 (100 million yuan)

年 份 Year	支出法新疆生产总值 Gross Domestic Product by Expenditure	最终消费 Final Consumption Expenditures	资本形成总额 Gross Capital Formation	货物和服务净出口 Net Export of Goods and Services	最终消费率(消费率)(%) Final Consumption Rate (%)	资本形成率(投资率)(%) Capital Formation Rate (%)
1978	39.07	27.64	18.43	-7.00	70.7	47.2
1980	53.24	39.82	23.15	-9.73	74.8	43.5
1985	112.24	78.04	58.43	-24.23	69.5	52.1
1986	129.04	92.38	60.26	-23.60	71.6	46.7
1987	148.51	103.77	69.94	-25.20	69.9	47.1
1988	192.72	126.09	98.31	-31.67	65.4	51.0
1989	217.29	137.50	117.84	-38.05	63.3	54.2
1990	261.44	166.77	141.17	-46.50	63.8	54.0
1991	335.91	196.58	169.15	-29.81	58.5	50.4
1992	402.31	221.57	249.26	-68.52	55.1	61.9
1993	495.25	269.92	356.16	-130.83	54.5	71.9
1994	662.32	336.94	487.55	-162.17	50.9	73.6
1995	814.85	444.62	473.71	-103.48	54.6	58.1
1996	900.93	553.90	456.96	-109.93	61.5	50.7
1997	1039.85	611.81	564.92	-136.89	58.8	54.3
1998	1106.95	642.48	685.85	-221.37	58.0	62.0
1999	1163.17	690.57	581.59	-108.99	59.4	50.0
2000	1363.56	760.20	618.12	-14.76	55.8	45.3
2001	1491.60	859.00	771.42	-138.82	57.6	51.7
2002	1612.65	963.71	864.27	-215.33	59.8	53.6
2003	1886.35	1027.22	1119.21	-260.08	54.5	59.3
2004	2209.09	1125.11	1350.47	-266.50	50.9	61.1
2005	2604.14	1266.52	1505.97	-168.35	48.6	57.8
2006	3045.26	1464.53	1654.70	-73.97	48.1	54.3
2007	3513.16	1740.56	1970.06	-197.46	49.5	56.1
2008	4183.21	2073.05	2301.50	-191.34	49.6	55.0
2009	4277.05	2266.20	2549.75	-538.90	53.0	59.6
2010	5437.47	2865.56	3371.22	-799.31	52.7	62.0
2011	6610.05	3518.82	4162.32	-1071.09	53.2	63.0
2012	7505.31	4262.51	5792.16	-2549.36	56.8	77.2
2013	8360.24	4599.24	7192.45	-3431.45	55.0	86.0

注：2005 年以后数据依据 2008 年经济普查资料已修订。
Note: Since 2005 the data has adjusted according to the economic census in 2008.

2-8 主要年份资本形成总额及其构成
Gross Capital Formation and Its Composition in Main Years

年 份	Year	资本形成总额(亿元) Gross Capital Formation (100 million yuan)	固定资本形成 Gross Fixed Capital Formation	存货增加 Change in Inventories	以资本形成总额为100 Gross Capital Formation=100 固定资本形成(%) Gross Fixed Capital Formation (%)	存货增加(%) Change in Inventories (%)
	1978	18.43	13.25	5.18	71.9	28.1
	1980	23.15	18.14	5.01	78.3	21.7
	1985	58.43	46.78	11.65	80.1	19.9
	1990	141.17	91.50	49.67	64.8	35.2
	1991	169.15	124.77	44.38	73.8	26.2
	1992	249.26	181.17	68.09	72.7	27.3
	1993	356.16	264.90	91.26	74.4	25.6
	1994	487.55	376.95	110.60	77.3	22.7
	1995	473.71	377.91	95.80	79.8	20.2
	1996	456.96	422.87	34.09	92.5	7.5
	1997	564.92	461.41	103.51	81.7	18.3
	1998	685.85	543.78	142.06	79.3	20.7
	1999	581.59	551.72	29.87	94.9	5.1
	2000	618.12	648.12	-30.00	104.9	-4.9
	2001	771.42	720.12	51.30	93.3	6.7
	2002	864.27	856.70	7.57	99.1	0.9
	2003	1119.21	1079.24	39.98	96.4	3.6
	2004	1350.47	1239.50	110.97	91.8	8.2
	2005	1505.97	1384.33	121.63	91.9	8.1
	2006	1654.70	1596.16	58.54	96.5	3.5
	2007	1970.06	1885.24	84.83	95.7	4.3
	2008	2301.50	2285.60	15.90	99.3	0.7
	2009	2549.75	2473.24	76.51	97.0	3.0
	2010	3371.22	3233.00	138.22	95.9	4.1
	2011	4162.32	3948.87	213.45	94.9	5.1
	2012	5792.16	5477.61	314.55	94.6	5.4
	2013	7192.45	6943.72	248.73	96.5	3.5
"一五" 时期	"First Five-year Plan" Period	16.26	14.33	1.94	88.1	11.9
"二五" 时期	"Second Five-year Plan" Period	36.39	26.69	9.70	73.3	26.7
	1963—1965	19.40	14.34	5.06	73.9	26.1
"三五" 时期	"Third Five-year Plan" Period	30.65	20.96	9.68	68.4	31.6
"四五" 时期	"Fourth Five-year Plan" Period	51.70	32.13	19.57	62.1	37.9
"五五" 时期	"Fifth Five-year Plan" Period	87.76	62.50	25.26	71.2	28.8
"六五" 时期	"Sixth Five-year Plan" Period	191.38	158.48	32.91	82.8	17.2
"七五" 时期	"Seventh Five-year Plan" Period	487.52	361.64	125.88	74.2	25.8
"八五" 时期	"Eighth Five-year Plan" Period	1735.83	1325.70	410.12	76.4	23.6
"九五" 时期	"Ninth Five-year Plan" Period	2907.43	2627.90	279.53	90.4	9.6
"十五" 时期	"Tenth Five-year Plan" Period	5611.34	5279.89	331.45	94.1	5.9
"十一五"时期	"Eleventh Five-year Plan " Period	11847.23	11473.23	374.00	96.8	3.2

注：本表按当年价格计算。
Note: Data in value terms in this table are calculated at current prices.

2-9 主要年份最终消费及其构成
Final Consumption Expenditure and Its Composition in Main Years

单位：% (%)

年 份	Year	最终消费(亿元) Final Consumption Expenditures (100 million yuan)	居民消费 Household Consumption	农村居民 Rural Household	城镇居民 Urban Household	政府消费 Government Consumption	最终消费=100 Final Consumption Expenditure=100: 居民消费 Household Consumption	最终消费=100: 政府消费 Government Consumption	居民消费=100 Houshold Consumption=100: 农村居民 Rural Household	居民消费=100: 城镇居民 Urban Household
	1978	27.64	22.61	12.08	10.53	5.03	81.8	18.2	53.4	46.6
	1980	39.82	32.78	16.20	16.58	7.04	82.3	17.7	49.4	50.6
	1985	78.04	58.51	26.41	32.10	19.53	75.0	25.0	45.1	54.9
	1990	166.77	121.12	45.67	75.46	45.65	72.6	27.4	37.7	62.3
	1991	196.58	145.55	52.30	93.26	51.02	74.0	26.0	35.9	64.1
	1992	221.57	159.20	55.18	104.02	62.37	71.9	28.1	34.7	65.3
	1993	269.92	197.78	63.96	133.82	72.14	73.3	26.7	32.3	67.7
	1994	336.94	242.79	83.04	159.75	94.15	72.1	27.9	34.2	65.8
	1995	444.62	320.70	108.43	212.27	123.93	72.1	27.9	33.8	66.2
	1996	553.90	397.61	156.07	241.54	156.29	71.8	28.2	39.3	60.7
	1997	611.81	436.67	164.84	271.84	175.14	71.4	28.6	37.7	62.3
	1998	642.48	457.38	175.72	281.66	185.10	71.2	28.8	38.4	61.6
	1999	690.57	475.74	158.98	316.76	214.83	68.9	31.1	33.4	66.6
	2000	760.20	492.32	159.97	332.34	267.88	64.8	35.2	32.5	67.5
	2001	859.00	545.49	176.00	369.49	313.51	63.5	36.5	32.3	67.7
	2002	963.71	615.47	190.85	424.62	348.25	63.9	36.1	31.0	69.0
	2003	1027.22	623.61	202.67	420.94	403.61	60.7	39.3	32.5	67.5
	2004	1125.11	671.28	209.99	461.29	453.84	59.7	40.3	31.3	68.7
	2005	1266.52	764.26	238.98	525.28	502.26	60.3	39.7	31.3	68.7
	2006	1464.53	853.88	253.58	600.31	610.65	58.3	41.7	29.7	70.3
	2007	1740.56	1013.48	295.52	717.96	727.09	58.2	41.8	29.2	70.8
	2008	2073.05	1171.05	340.69	830.36	902.00	56.5	43.5	29.1	70.9
	2009	2266.20	1284.66	385.66	898.99	981.54	56.7	43.3	30.0	70.0
	2010	2865.56	1578.93	456.31	1122.62	1286.63	55.1	44.9	28.9	71.1
	2011	3518.82	1954.33	560.30	1394.03	1564.49	55.5	44.5	28.7	71.3
	2012	4262.51	2370.67	675.64	1695.03	1891.84	55.6	44.4	28.5	71.5
	2013	4599.24	2563.54	745.18	1818.36	2035.70	55.7	44.3	29.1	70.9
“一五”时期	"First Five-year Plan" Period	42.97	38.62	23.89	14.73	4.35	89.9	10.1	61.9	38.1
“二五”时期	"Second Five-year Plan" Period	71.40	64.02	39.30	24.72	7.38	89.7	10.3	61.4	38.6
	1963—1965	47.00	42.42	30.93	11.49	4.58	90.3	9.7	72.9	27.1
“三五”时期	"Third Five-year Plan" Period	80.09	72.97	49.13	23.84	7.12	91.1	8.9	67.3	32.7
“四五”时期	"Forth Five-year Plan" Period	97.46	83.75	51.78	31.97	13.71	85.9	14.1	61.8	38.2
“五五”时期	"Fifth Five-year Plan" Period	149.77	123.11	65.02	58.09	26.66	82.2	17.8	52.8	47.2
“六五”时期	"Sixth Five-year Plan" Period	289.27	227.00	107.93	119.06	62.28	78.5	21.5	47.5	52.5
“七五”时期	"Seventh Five-year Plan" Period	626.51	464.17	186.47	277.70	162.34	74.1	25.9	40.2	59.8
“八五”时期	"Eighth Five-year Plan" Period	1469.63	1066.03	362.91	703.12	403.60	72.5	27.5	34.0	66.0
“九五”时期	"Ninth Five-year Plan" Period	3258.96	2259.72	815.58	1444.14	999.24	69.3	30.7	36.1	63.9
“十五”时期	"Tenth Five-year Plan" Period	5241.57	3220.11	1018.50	2201.61	2021.46	61.4	38.6	31.6	68.4
“十一五”时期	"Eleventh Five-year Plan " Period	10409.90	5902.00	1731.76	4170.24	4507.90	56.7	43.3	29.3	70.7

注：本表按当年价格计算。
Note: Data in value terms in this table are calculated at current prices.

2-10 各地、州、市、县(市)地区生产总值

单位：万元 (2013 年)

地　区	Region	地区生产总值 Gross Regional Product	第一产业 Primary Industry
乌鲁木齐市	**Urumqi City**	**22028545**	**263065**
#乌鲁木齐县	Urumqi County	191871	64422
克拉玛依市	**Karamay City**	**8531091**	**50093**
石河子市	**Shihezi City**	**2553304**	**115764**
吐鲁番地区	**Turpan Administrative Offices**	**2608927**	**397772**
吐鲁番市	Turpan City	615190	164817
鄯善县	Shanshan [Piqan] County	1473952	150602
托克逊县	Toksun County	511915	82354
哈密地区	**Hami [Kumul] Administrative Offices**	**3339310**	**373130**
哈密市	Hami [Kumul] City	2635379	233131
巴里坤哈萨克自治县	Barkol Kazak Autonomous County	391898	96067
伊吾县	Yiwu [Araturuk] County	312131	43932
昌吉回族自治州	**Changji Hui Autonomous Prefecture**	**9373116**	**2387831**
昌吉市	Changji City	2921346	369879
阜康市	Fukang City	1265151	234357
呼图壁县	Hutubi County	1190516	441863
玛纳斯县	Manas County	1486571	629242
奇台县	Qitai County	976851	411943
吉木萨尔县	Jimsar County	751306	175393
木垒哈萨克自治县	Mori Kazak Autonomous County	237802	112520
伊犁哈萨克自治州	**Ili Kazak Autonomous Prefecture**	**14350077**	**3914568**
伊犁州直属县(市)	**Counties (Cities) Direct Under Ili Prefecture**	**6811619**	**1616612**
伊宁市	Yining [Gulja] City	1626561	69324
奎屯市	Kuytun City	1225782	61860
伊宁县	Yining [Gulja] County	600981	255110
察布查尔锡伯自治县	Qapqal Xibe Autonomous County	398880	193037
霍城县	Huocheng [Korgas] County	897652	296631
巩留县	Gongliu [Tokkuztara] County	339712	126513
新源县	Xinyuan [Kunes] County	751882	231586
昭苏县	Zhaosu [Mongolkure] County	364019	169358
特克斯县	Tekes County	200981	89203
尼勒克县	Nilka County	409569	123990

Gross Regional Product by Prefecture, Autonomous Prefecture, City and County

(10 000 yuan)

第二产业 Secondary Industry	工业 Industry	建筑业 Construction	第三产业 Tertiary Industry	#交通运输、仓储和邮政业 Transport,storage And Post	#批发和零售业 Wholesale, and Retail Trades	人均地区生产总值(元) Per Capita GDP (yuan)
8751032	**7467517**	**1283515**	**13014448**	**2853747**	**1912122**	**64695**
59000	52000	7000	68449	5825	8136	31097
7390278	**7157178**	**233100**	**1090720**	**156859**	**123282**	**149127**
1476482	**1127974**	**348508**	**961058**	**84623**	**96753**	**73695**
1585763	**1344763**	**241000**	**625392**	**171445**	**48302**	**41473**
129640	84040	45600	320733	80869	28579	22553
1106684	964782	141901	216666	75378	13312	62721
341944	288444	53500	87617	11120	6694	42305
1722402	**1142402**	**580000**	**1243778**	**340595**	**201943**	**55622**
1344983	873661	471322	1057265	302759	172299	55734
174853	122786	52067	120978	22774	18887	37472
203758	147147	56611	64441	14356	11038	136290
4514582	**3651618**	**862964**	**2470703**	**357426**	**378960**	**58479**
1419578	1189736	229842	1131889	193603	122928	60609
749255	658358	90897	281539	31366	47654	75712
420527	231169	189358	328126	45044	85753	53627
522324	426788	95536	335005	30918	63805	58411
329303	253350	75953	235605	25441	46578	45498
439329	402357	36972	136584	8753	19017	58241
44417	29374	15043	80865	3703	11551	26867
5272107	**3860685**	**1411422**	**5163402**	**526986**	**821199**	**30328**
2319909	**1665908**	**654001**	**2875098**	**274058**	**401715**	**24567**
448254	233586	214668	1108983	78548	189630	31554
644768	513356	131412	519154	88012	43948	79236
164190	125488	38702	181681	20571	7033	13951
98443	72678	25765	107400	6564	10512	20414
231104	189608	41496	369917	38531	113205	21883
117365	79464	37901	95834	9097	1778	16868
331970	249753	82217	188326	20205	10411	23489
72152	51613	20539	122509	7821	9534	19199
30440	18441	11999	81338	4569	1754	11604
208434	159132	49302	77145	2626	4711	21797

2-10 续表 1

单位：万元

地区	Region	地区生产总值 Gross Regional Product	第一产业 Primary Industry
塔城地区	**Tacheng [Tarbagatai] Administrative Offices**	**5429094**	**1885001**
塔城市	Tacheng [Qoqek] City	646389	160603
乌苏市	Usu City	1698312	527053
额敏县	Emin [Dorbiljin] County	624936	212158
沙湾县	Shawan County	1553490	789062
托里县	Toli County	417810	54017
裕民县	Yumin [Qagantokay] County	139372	55498
和布克赛尔蒙古自治县	Hoboksar Mongol Autonomous County	401848	65803
阿勒泰地区	**Altay Administrative Offices**	**2109364**	**412955**
阿勒泰市	Altay City	519316	79354
布尔津县	Burqin County	166740	31621
富蕴县	Fuyun [Koktokay] County	483733	64446
福海县	Fuhai [Burultokay] County	326442	121285
哈巴河县	Habahe [Kaba] County	369818	69475
青河县	Qinghe [Qinggil] County	123947	33346
吉木乃县	Jeminay County	73401	13990
博尔塔拉蒙古自治州	**Bortala Mongolian Autonomous Prefecture**	**2221707**	**602552**
博乐市	Bole [Bortala] City	1515599	310472
精河县	Jinghe [Jing] County	529898	235116
温泉县	Wenquan [Araxang] County	184869	78977
巴音郭楞蒙古自治州	**Bayangol Mongol ian Autonomous Prefecture**	**10169959**	**1766244**
库尔勒市	Korla City	6534087	379567
轮台县	Luntai [Bugur] County	602491	197133
尉犁县	Yuli [Lopnur] County	405371	251979
若羌县	Ruoqiang [Qarkilik] County	626147	182500
且末县	Qiemo [Qarqan] County	225492	101325
焉耆回族自治县	Yanqi Hui Autonomous County	536007	145000
和静县	Hejing County	756049	200049
和硕县	Hoxud County	275150	177466
博湖县	Bohu [Bagrax] County	210200	89487
阿克苏地区	**Aksu Administrative Offices**	**6926045**	**2202847**
阿克苏市	Aksu City	1453838	118762
温宿县	Wensu [Onsu] County	510156	228247
库车县	Kuqa County	1405396	193131

Continued

(10 000 yuan)

第二产业 Secondary Industry	工　业 Industry	建筑业 Construction	第三产业 Tertiary Industry	#交通运输、仓储和邮政业 Transport,storage And Post	#批发和零售业 Wholesale, and Retail Trades	人均地区生产总值(元) Per Capita GDP (yuan)
1980362	**1461276**	**519086**	**1563731**	**159805**	**352280**	**40587**
150438	70318	80120	335348	39384	92977	38939
853753	709352	144401	317505	34368	84312	50666
191831	130953	60878	220947	20362	44203	28516
349358	259975	89383	415070	47025	103927	39691
287241	222323	64918	76552	12302	10248	41347
29553	6814	22739	54321	2113	6753	23379
257784	116703	141081	78261	10425	9860	62302
971836	**733501**	**238335**	**724573**	**93123**	**67204**	**33945**
110050	61450	48600	329912	32041	39826	27147
65359	40759	24600	69760	5919	6538	24342
332459	271459	61000	86828	21070	7884	52295
111858	82258	29600	93299	11663	10870	41479
229538	190338	39200	70805	13559	5095	43187
40006	19500	20506	50595	2845	4498	18583
33764	22164	11600	25647	2033	1687	19265
575415	**368196**	**207219**	**1043740**	**153886**	**316038**	**45579**
397272	259462	137810	807855	110490	272068	56455
135097	77051	58046	159685	27584	24752	36786
37507	17136	20371	68385	5119	3898	24663
6402135	**5667135**	**735000**	**2001580**	**244457**	**248969**	**72492**
5154560	4624153	530407	999960	117992	164013	110980
205120	185120	20000	200238	38900	17873	50460
45706	11642	34064	107686	11730	15102	34916
389600	372000	17600	54047	7391	2400	100659
44675	28571	16104	79492	4259	532	34171
156000	98000	58000	235007	44000	23735	38841
346000	316000	30000	210000	75700	11050	37781
36645	23795	12850	61039	8598	6487	35497
40072	19826	20246	80641	6838	9886	33997
2183366	**1612720**	**570646**	**2539832**	**258837**	**320586**	**28535**
378130	345132	32997	956946	92457	144030	28954
145377	75014	70364	136532	6419	15970	20337
820871	633548	187322	391394	91402	40156	29524

2-10 续表 2

单位：万元

地　　区	Region	地区生产总值 Gross Regional Product	第一产业 Primary Industry
沙雅县	Xayar County	438805	138500
新和县	Xinhe [Toksu] County	281439	113652
拜城县	Baicheng [Bay] County	479597	100684
乌什县	Wushi [Uxturpan] County	237163	92695
阿瓦提县	Awat County	481319	240143
柯坪县	Kalpin County	75664	20403
克孜勒苏柯尔克孜自治州	**Kizilsu Kirgiz Autonomous Prefecture**	**778395**	**123806**
阿图什市	Artux City	343956	53925
阿克陶县	Akto County	205669	51082
阿合奇县	Akqi County	68625	9703
乌恰县	Wuqia [Ulugqat] County	156513	9078
喀什地区	**Kashgar [Kaxgar] Administrative Offices**	**6173033**	**1913001**
喀什市	Kashgar [Kaxgar] City	1609523	56517
疏附县	Shufu County	390678	191001
疏勒县	Shule County	643911	182001
英吉沙县	Yengisar County	253100	100092
泽普县	Zepu [Poskam] County	371168	120187
莎车县	Shache [Yarkant] County	702071	358237
叶城县	Yecheng [Kagilik] County	600698	292969
麦盖提县	Makit County	304180	160004
岳普湖县	Yopurga County	267185	80150
伽师县	Jiashi [Payzawat] County	496740	207000
巴楚县	Bachu [Maralbexi] County	546670	190128
塔什库尔干塔吉克自治县	Taxkorgan Tajik Autonomous County	78490	11004
和田地区	**Hotan Administrative Offices**	**1716493**	**531147**
和田市	Hotan City	462375	35235
和田县	Hotan County	220923	81366
墨玉县	Moyu [Karakax] County	292287	120670
皮山县	Pishan [Guma] County	170024	80112
洛浦县	Lop County	184374	54354
策勒县	Qira County	128683	47740
于田县	Yutian [Keriya] County	180361	61916
民丰县	Minfeng [Niya] County	67849	13484

Continued

(10 000 yuan)

第二产业 Secondary Industry	工　业 Industry	建筑业 Construction	第三产业 Tertiary Industry	#交通运输、仓储和邮政业 Transport,storage And Post	#批发和零售业 Wholesale, and Retail Trades	人均地区生产总值(元) Per Capita GDP (yuan)
97605	65238	32367	202700	11061	28687	16475
55746	39941	15805	112041	11298	11586	16011
225390	191157	34233	153523	18407	12225	20410
29874	14092	15781	114594	3553	3026	10813
70398	35303	35095	170778	8124	16447	19285
13139	4847	8292	42122	2774	89	14492
253804	**162804**	**91000**	**400785**	**27939**	**22271**	**13694**
85219	57845	27374	204812	20711	10377	13292
74249	42651	31598	80338	2190	2804	9926
18186	12586	5600	40736	1876	1591	15933
77301	50686	26615	70134	4246	4259	26384
1850058	**1049001**	**801057**	**2409974**	**181054**	**706782**	**16076**
565813	412039	153774	987193	106031	399706	27936
59600	19748	39852	140077	6310	9701	11367
351490	201107	150383	110420	4177	9544	18492
70000	20091	49909	83008	5491	12847	8762
85140	40048	45092	165841	7271	60865	17248
108046	55060	52986	235788	7856	22816	8812
137509	81678	55831	170220	10680	23702	12574
57706	25000	32706	86470	4603	20804	13276
101032	36029	65003	86003	6267	8715	16682
151707	100168	51539	138033	22174	33610	12124
99318	40149	59169	257224	10421	139564	15731
39285	15332	23953	28201	1020	2223	19790
337711	**127847**	**209864**	**847635**	**33973**	**36611**	**8025**
166291	74749	91542	260849	17424	20263	7840
49618	23273	26345	89939	949	1399	7730
26123	6925	19198	145494	13665	4787	5404
16120	5047	11073	73792	1751	1260	6347
33587	10427	23160	96433	2820	2193	7135
17434	2586	14848	63509	1830	1425	8150
21292	3620	17672	97153	3975	4506	6876
11568	5569	5999	42797	1414	1408	17703

2-11 各地、州、市、县(市)地区生产总值构成

单位：%　　(2013 年)

地　　区	Region	地区生产总值 Gross Regional Product	第一产业 Primary Industry
乌鲁木齐市	**Urumqi City**	**100.0**	**1.2**
#乌鲁木齐县	Urumqi County	100.0	33.6
克拉玛依市	**Karamay City**	**100.0**	**0.6**
石河子市	**Shihezi City**	**100.0**	**4.5**
吐鲁番地区	**Turpan Administrative Offices**	**100.0**	**15.3**
吐鲁番市	Turpan City	100.0	26.8
鄯善县	Shanshan [Piqan] County	100.0	10.2
托克逊县	Toksun County	100.0	16.1
哈密地区	**Hami [Kumul] Administrative Offices**	**100.0**	**11.2**
哈密市	Hami [Kumul] City	100.0	8.8
巴里坤哈萨克自治县	Barkol Kazak Autonomous County	100.0	24.5
伊吾县	Yiwu [Araturuk] County	100.0	14.1
昌吉回族自治州	**Changji Hui Autonomous Prefecture**	**100.0**	**25.5**
昌吉市	Changji City	100.0	12.7
阜康市	Fukang City	100.0	18.5
呼图壁县	Hutubi County	100.0	37.1
玛纳斯县	Manas County	100.0	42.3
奇台县	Qitai County	100.0	42.2
吉木萨尔县	Jimsar County	100.0	23.3
木垒哈萨克自治县	Mori Kazak Autonomous County	100.0	47.3
伊犁哈萨克自治州	**Ili Kazak Autonomous Prefecture**	**100.0**	**27.3**
伊犁州直属县(市)	**Counties (Cities) Direct Under Ili Prefecture**	**100.0**	**23.7**
伊宁市	Yining [Gulja] City	100.0	4.3
奎屯市	Kuytun City	100.0	5.0
伊宁县	Yining [Gulja] County	100.0	42.4
察布查尔锡伯自治县	Qapqal Xibe Autonomous County	100.0	48.4
霍城县	Huocheng [Korgas] County	100.0	33.0
巩留县	Gongliu [Tokkuztara] County	100.0	37.2
新源县	Xinyuan [Kunes] County	100.0	30.8
昭苏县	Zhaosu [Mongolkure] County	100.0	46.5
特克斯县	Tekes County	100.0	44.4
尼勒克县	Nilka County	100.0	30.3

Composition of Gross Domestic Product by Prefecture, Autonomous Prefecture, City and County

(%)

第二产业 Secondary Industry	工　业 Industry	建筑业 Construction	第三产业 Tertiary Industry	#交通运输、仓储和邮政业 Transport,storage And Post	#批发和零售业 Wholesale, and Retail Trades
39.7	**33.9**	**5.8**	**59.1**	**13.0**	**8.7**
30.7	27.1	3.6	35.7	3.0	4.2
86.6	**83.9**	**2.7**	**12.8**	**1.8**	**1.4**
57.8	**44.2**	**13.6**	**37.7**	**3.3**	**3.8**
60.8	**51.6**	**9.2**	**23.9**	**6.6**	**1.9**
21.1	13.7	7.4	52.1	13.1	4.6
75.1	65.5	9.6	14.7	5.1	0.9
66.8	56.3	10.5	17.1	2.2	1.3
51.6	**34.2**	**17.4**	**37.2**	**10.2**	**6.0**
51.0	33.2	17.9	40.2	11.5	6.5
44.6	31.3	13.3	30.9	5.8	4.8
65.3	47.1	18.1	20.6	4.6	3.5
48.2	**39.0**	**9.2**	**26.3**	**3.8**	**4.0**
48.6	40.7	7.9	38.7	6.6	4.2
59.2	52.0	7.2	22.3	2.5	3.8
35.3	19.4	15.9	27.6	3.8	7.2
35.1	28.7	6.4	22.6	2.1	4.3
33.7	25.9	7.8	24.1	2.6	4.8
58.5	53.6	4.9	18.2	1.2	2.5
18.7	12.4	6.3	34.0	1.6	4.9
36.7	**26.9**	**9.8**	**36.0**	**3.7**	**5.7**
34.1	**24.5**	**9.6**	**42.2**	**4.0**	**5.9**
27.6	14.4	13.2	68.1	4.8	11.7
52.6	41.9	10.7	42.4	7.2	3.6
27.3	20.9	6.4	30.3	3.4	1.2
24.7	18.2	6.5	26.9	1.6	2.6
25.7	21.1	4.6	41.3	4.3	12.6
34.5	23.4	11.2	28.3	2.7	0.5
44.2	33.2	10.9	25.0	2.7	1.4
19.8	14.2	5.6	33.7	2.1	2.6
15.1	9.2	6.0	40.5	2.3	0.9
50.9	38.9	12.0	18.8	0.6	1.2

2-11 续表 1

单位：%

地　　区	Region	地区生产总值 Gross Regional Product	第一产业 Primary Industry
塔城地区	**Tacheng [Tarbagatai] Administrative Offices**	**100.0**	**34.7**
塔城市	Tacheng [Qoqek] City	100.0	24.8
乌苏市	Usu City	100.0	31.0
额敏县	Emin [Dorbiljin] County	100.0	33.9
沙湾县	Shawan County	100.0	50.8
托里县	Toli County	100.0	12.9
裕民县	Yumin [Qagantokay] County	100.0	39.8
和布克赛尔蒙古自治县	Hoboksar Mongol Autonomous County	100.0	16.4
阿勒泰地区	**Altay Administrative Offices**	**100.0**	**19.6**
阿勒泰市	Altay City	100.0	15.3
布尔津县	Burqin County	100.0	19.0
富蕴县	Fuyun [Koktokay] County	100.0	13.3
福海县	Fuhai [Burultokay] County	100.0	37.2
哈巴河县	Habahe [Kaba] County	100.0	18.8
青河县	Qinghe [Qinggil] County	100.0	26.9
吉木乃县	Jeminay County	100.0	19.1
博尔塔拉蒙古自治州	**Bortala Mongolian Autonomous Prefecture**	**100.0**	**27.1**
博乐市	Bole [Bortala] City	100.0	20.5
精河县	Jinghe [Jing] County	100.0	44.4
温泉县	Wenquan [Araxang] County	100.0	42.7
巴音郭楞蒙古自治州	**Bayangol Mongol ian Autonomous Prefecture**	**100.0**	**17.4**
库尔勒市	Korla City	100.0	5.8
轮台县	Luntai [Bugur] County	100.0	32.7
尉犁县	Yuli [Lopnur] County	100.0	62.2
若羌县	Ruoqiang [Qarkilik] County	100.0	29.1
且末县	Qiemo [Qarqan] County	100.0	44.9
焉耆回族自治县	Yanqi Hui Autonomous County	100.0	27.1
和静县	Hejing County	100.0	26.5
和硕县	Hoxud County	100.0	64.5
博湖县	Bohu [Bagrax] County	100.0	42.6
阿克苏地区	**Aksu Administrative Offices**	**100.0**	**31.8**
阿克苏市	Aksu City	100.0	8.2
温宿县	Wensu [Onsu] County	100.0	44.7
库车县	Kuqa County	100.0	13.7

Continued

(%)

第二产业 Secondary Industry	工 业 Industry	建筑业 Construction	第三产业 Tertiary Industry	#交通运输、仓储和邮政业 Transport,storage And Post	#批发和零售业 Wholesale, and Retail Trades
36.5	**26.9**	**9.6**	**28.8**	**2.9**	**6.5**
23.3	10.9	12.4	51.9	6.1	14.4
50.3	41.8	8.5	18.7	2.0	5.0
30.7	21.0	9.7	35.4	3.3	7.1
22.5	16.7	5.8	26.7	3.0	6.7
68.7	53.2	15.5	18.4	2.9	2.5
21.2	4.9	16.3	39.0	1.5	4.8
64.1	29.0	35.1	19.5	2.6	2.5
46.1	**34.8**	**11.3**	**34.3**	**4.4**	**3.2**
21.2	11.8	9.4	63.5	6.2	7.7
39.2	24.4	14.8	41.8	3.5	3.9
68.7	56.1	12.6	18.0	4.4	1.6
34.3	25.2	9.1	28.5	3.6	3.3
62.1	51.5	10.6	19.1	3.7	1.4
32.3	15.7	16.5	40.8	2.3	3.6
46.0	30.2	15.8	34.9	2.8	2.3
25.9	**16.6**	**9.3**	**47.0**	**6.9**	**14.2**
26.2	17.1	9.1	53.3	7.3	18.0
25.5	14.5	11.0	30.1	5.2	4.7
20.3	9.3	11.0	37.0	2.8	2.1
63.0	**55.7**	**7.2**	**19.6**	**2.4**	**2.4**
78.9	70.8	8.1	15.3	1.8	2.5
34.0	30.7	3.3	33.3	6.5	3.0
11.3	2.9	8.4	26.5	2.9	3.7
62.2	59.4	2.8	8.7	1.2	0.4
19.8	12.7	7.1	35.3	1.9	0.2
29.1	18.3	10.8	43.8	8.2	4.4
45.8	41.8	4.0	27.7	10.0	1.5
13.3	8.6	4.7	22.2	3.1	2.4
19.1	9.4	9.6	38.3	3.3	4.7
31.5	**23.3**	**8.2**	**36.7**	**3.7**	**4.6**
26.0	23.7	2.3	65.8	6.4	9.9
28.5	14.7	13.8	26.8	1.3	3.1
58.4	45.1	13.3	27.9	6.5	2.9

2-11 续表 2

单位：%

地　区	Region	地区生产总值 Gross Regional Product	第一产业 Primary Industry
沙雅县	Xayar County	100.0	31.6
新和县	Xinhe [Toksu] County	100.0	40.4
拜城县	Baicheng [Bay] County	100.0	21.0
乌什县	Wushi [Uxturpan] County	100.0	39.1
阿瓦提县	Awat County	100.0	49.9
柯坪县	Kalpin County	100.0	27.0
克孜勒苏柯尔克孜自治州	**Kizilsu Kirgiz Autonomous Prefecture**	**100.0**	**15.9**
阿图什市	Artux City	100.0	15.7
阿克陶县	Akto County	100.0	24.8
阿合奇县	Akqi County	100.0	14.1
乌恰县	Wuqia [Ulugqat] County	100.0	5.8
喀什地区	**Kashgar [Kaxgar] Administrative Offices**	**100.0**	**31.0**
喀什市	Kashgar [Kaxgar] City	100.0	3.5
疏附县	Shufu County	100.0	48.9
疏勒县	Shule County	100.0	28.3
英吉沙县	Yengisar County	100.0	39.5
泽普县	Zepu [Poskam] County	100.0	32.4
莎车县	Shache [Yarkant] County	100.0	51.0
叶城县	Yecheng [Kagilik] County	100.0	48.8
麦盖提县	Makit County	100.0	52.6
岳普湖县	Yopurga County	100.0	30.0
伽师县	Jiashi [Payzawat] County	100.0	41.7
巴楚县	Bachu [Maralbexi] County	100.0	34.8
塔什库尔干县	Taxkorgan Tajik Autonomous County	100.0	14.0
和田地区	**Hotan Administrative Offices**	**100.0**	**30.9**
和田市	Hotan City	100.0	7.6
和田县	Hotan County	100.0	36.8
墨玉县	Moyu [Karakax] County	100.0	41.3
皮山县	Pishan [Guma] County	100.0	47.1
洛浦县	Lop County	100.0	29.5
策勒县	Qira County	100.0	37.1
于田县	Yutian [Keriya] County	100.0	34.3
民丰县	Minfeng [Niya] County	100.0	19.9

Continued

(%)

第二产业 Secondary Industry	工　业 Industry	建筑业 Construction	第三产业 Tertiary Industry	#交通运输、仓储和邮政业 Transport,storage And Post	#批发和零售业 Wholesale, and Retail Trades
22.2	14.9	7.4	46.2	2.5	6.5
19.8	14.2	5.6	39.8	4.0	4.1
47.0	39.9	7.1	32.0	3.8	2.5
12.6	5.9	6.7	48.3	1.5	1.3
14.6	7.3	7.3	35.5	1.7	3.4
17.4	6.4	11.0	55.6	3.7	0.1
32.6	**20.9**	**11.7**	**51.5**	**3.6**	**2.9**
24.8	16.8	8.0	59.5	6.0	3.0
36.1	20.7	15.4	39.1	1.1	1.4
26.5	18.3	8.2	59.4	2.7	2.3
49.4	32.4	17.0	44.8	2.7	2.7
30.0	**17.0**	**13.0**	**39.0**	**2.9**	**11.4**
35.2	25.6	9.6	61.3	6.6	24.8
15.3	5.1	10.2	35.8	1.6	2.5
54.6	31.2	23.4	17.1	0.6	1.5
27.7	7.9	19.7	32.8	2.2	5.1
22.9	10.8	12.1	44.7	2.0	16.4
15.4	7.8	7.5	33.6	1.1	3.2
22.9	13.6	9.3	28.3	1.8	3.9
19.0	8.2	10.8	28.4	1.5	6.8
37.8	13.5	24.3	32.2	2.3	3.3
30.5	20.2	10.4	27.8	4.5	6.8
18.2	7.3	10.8	47.0	1.9	25.5
50.1	19.5	30.5	35.9	1.3	2.8
19.7	**7.4**	**12.2**	**49.4**	**2.0**	**2.1**
36.0	16.2	19.8	56.4	3.8	4.4
22.5	10.5	11.9	40.7	0.4	0.6
8.9	2.4	6.6	49.8	4.7	1.6
9.5	3.0	6.5	43.4	1.0	0.7
18.2	5.7	12.6	52.3	1.5	1.2
13.5	2.0	11.5	49.4	1.4	1.1
11.8	2.0	9.8	53.9	2.2	2.5
17.0	8.2	8.8	63.1	2.1	2.1

2-12 各地、州、市、县(市)地区生产总值指数

(上年=100) (2013 年)

地区	Region	地区生产总值 Gross Regional Product	第一产业 Primary Industry
乌鲁木齐市	**Urumqi City**	**115.0**	**109.0**
#乌鲁木齐县	Urumqi County	114.5	106.5
克拉玛依市	**Karamay City**	**106.8**	**103.8**
石河子市	**Shihezi City**	**122.3**	**110.6**
吐鲁番地区	**Turpan Administrative Offices**	**105.5**	**106.4**
吐鲁番市	Turpan City	98.5	105.7
鄯善县	Shanshan [Piqan] County	102.5	106.8
托克逊县	Toksun County	116.6	106.7
哈密地区	**Hami [Kumul] Administrative Offices**	**122.2**	**106.8**
哈密市	Hami [Kumul] City	120.9	107.9
巴里坤哈萨克自治县	Barkol Kazak Autonomous County	114.5	104.9
伊吾县	Yiwu [Araturuk] County	143.5	102.4
昌吉回族自治州	**Changji Hui Autonomous Prefecture**	**116.9**	**106.0**
昌吉市	Changji City	116.5	106.4
阜康市	Fukang City	114.8	105.7
呼图壁县	Hutubi County	114.3	105.6
玛纳斯县	Manas County	117.4	105.4
奇台县	Qitai County	114.0	108.0
吉木萨尔县	Jimsar County	163.1	107.9
木垒哈萨克自治县	Mori Kazak Autonomous County	113.6	106.3
伊犁哈萨克自治州	**Ili Kazak Autonomous Prefecture**	**113.3**	**106.8**
伊犁州直属县(市)	**Counties (Cities) Direct Under Ili Prefecture**	**114.3**	**107.9**
伊宁市	Yining [Gulja] City	116.0	98.9
奎屯市	Kuytun City	116.6	109.7
伊宁县	Yining [Gulja] County	110.0	107.8
察布查尔锡伯自治县	Qapqal Xibe Autonomous County	113.2	112.8
霍城县	Huocheng [Korgas] County	116.1	108.9
巩留县	Gongliu [Tokkuztara] County	111.4	109.3
新源县	Xinyuan [Kunes] County	107.2	105.1
昭苏县	Zhaosu [Mongolkure] County	114.0	112.2
特克斯县	Tekes County	114.6	105.2
尼勒克县	Nilka County	113.0	108.1

Indices of Gross Domestic Product by Prefecture, Autonomous Prefecture, City and County

(preceding year=100)

第二产业 Secondary Industry	工业 Industry	建筑业 Construction	第三产业 Tertiary Industry	#交通运输、仓储和邮政业 Transport,storage And Post	#批发和零售业 Wholesale, and Retail Trades
115.4	**116.3**	**109.6**	**114.8**	**118.3**	**108.6**
120.9	126.1	114.0	114.5	109.9	116.0
105.9	**105.8**	**110.4**	**114.8**	**108.0**	**111.5**
121.7	**121.2**	**123.4**	**124.9**	**121.0**	**128.1**
104.4	**103.8**	**107.4**	**108.0**	**107.9**	**125.8**
82.2	75.9	109.3	106.6	108.6	118.7
101.1	100.6	103.5	107.3	105.6	164.1
121.0	121.6	117.4	109.1	109.6	124.8
131.9	**133.1**	**129.2**	**113.0**	**112.2**	**118.1**
129.0	128.9	129.2	113.1	112.5	118.8
120.3	119.3	123.4	112.2	112.0	113.8
165.4	180.3	134.6	113.8	124.1	112.4
125.7	**129.1**	**112.4**	**112.3**	**111.4**	**109.2**
120.2	120.5	118.6	114.8	108.6	107.4
117.4	117.8	114.6	113.8	99.7	110.7
124.6	132.6	114.9	113.6	112.0	114.7
135.3	140.6	113.0	113.0	115.5	115.9
120.3	117.6	132.7	114.7	111.6	113.0
223.4	238.1	123.2	112.8	110.8	112.9
134.8	129.0	150.5	110.5	110.9	112.4
118.2	**119.8**	**113.3**	**112.2**	**113.2**	**104.6**
118.2	**118.5**	**117.3**	**113.6**	**110.5**	**108.5**
122.6	125.0	119.1	114.0	109.4	115.1
117.6	117.8	116.3	116.0	107.6	103.4
109.8	108.2	120.0	113.5	115.9	108.1
113.0	112.7	114.2	114.1	119.4	116.0
134.5	137.4	121.6	110.5	116.5	106.2
111.9	110.6	114.8	113.2	115.5	121.7
105.6	104.0	113.3	113.7	112.3	114.1
124.9	127.4	117.9	109.3	115.0	120.2
138.5	149.8	114.5	113.6	111.0	109.8
115.7	115.3	117.3	111.2	111.4	111.8

2-12 续表 1

(上年=100)

地　　区	Region	地区生产总值 Gross Regional Product	第一产业 Primary Industry
塔城地区	**Tacheng [Tarbagatai] Administrative Offices**	**112.5**	**106.4**
塔城市	Tacheng [Qoqek] City	113.5	108.2
乌苏市	Usu City	115.9	108.8
额敏县	Emin [Dorbiljin] County	113.0	112.5
沙湾县	Shawan County	113.3	103.2
托里县	Toli County	116.4	106.0
裕民县	Yumin [Qagantokay] County	113.8	111.4
和布克赛尔蒙古自治县	Hoboksar Mongol Autonomous County	116.3	108.8
阿勒泰地区	**Altay Administrative Offices**	**112.2**	**107.1**
阿勒泰市	Altay City	111.3	104.2
布尔津县	Burqin County	108.9	103.5
富蕴县	Fuyun [Koktokay] County	111.7	104.0
福海县	Fuhai [Burultokay] County	114.3	109.8
哈巴河县	Habahe [Kaba] County	107.8	111.2
青河县	Qinghe [Qinggil] County	114.6	110.3
吉木乃县	Jeminay County	118.6	107.9
博尔塔拉蒙古自治州	**Bortala Mongolian Autonomous Prefecture**	**118.0**	**107.6**
博乐市	Bole [Bortala] City	117.7	106.4
精河县	Jinghe [Jing] County	117.5	106.8
温泉县	Wenquan [Araxang] County	110.4	104.4
巴音郭楞蒙古自治州	**Bayangol Mongol ian Autonomous Prefecture**	**110.0**	**105.9**
库尔勒市	Korla City	108.8	104.0
轮台县	Luntai [Bugur] County	117.0	110.2
尉犁县	Yuli [Lopnur] County	113.7	111.7
若羌县	Ruoqiang [Qarkilik] County	107.0	108.0
且末县	Qiemo [Qarqan] County	115.5	115.7
焉耆回族自治县	Yanqi Hui Autonomous County	113.0	107.4
和静县	Hejing County	113.1	101.2
和硕县	Hoxud County	111.2	105.7
博湖县	Bohu [Bagrax] County	115.0	105.2
阿克苏地区	**Aksu Administrative Offices**	**112.8**	**111.6**
阿克苏市	Aksu City	92.0	44.7
温宿县	Wensu [Onsu] County	104.8	98.9
库车县	Kuqa County	109.3	107.0

Continued

(preceding year=100)

第二产业 Secondary Industry	工　业 Industry	建筑业 Construction	第三产业 Tertiary Industry	#交通运输、仓储和邮政业 Transport,storage And Post	#批发和零售业 Wholesale, and Retail Trades
119.4	**123.0**	**108.5**	**110.7**	**116.5**	**101.1**
103.2	89.3	117.2	121.4	116.1	117.7
119.8	123.4	105.4	118.3	113.2	117.1
111.0	109.1	115.4	115.3	110.7	112.2
129.0	138.9	100.5	115.4	120.5	112.4
119.2	119.4	118.0	113.1	113.5	111.1
104.4	95.5	107.3	122.5	113.6	116.4
121.7	112.4	130.3	107.6	108.0	121.1
115.9	**116.7**	**113.3**	**110.3**	**115.5**	**105.4**
121.7	123.8	118.6	109.0	118.5	109.2
102.7	123.9	117.1	102.5	112.0	99.6
111.9	110.0	121.4	117.3	111.0	118.4
123.8	124.9	120.7	109.7	108.8	114.7
105.7	105.4	107.7	112.8	113.2	107.7
128.1	189.8	104.4	104.8	84.0	107.6
129.3	183.1	102.3	116.2	138.8	111.5
133.9	**133.4**	**134.7**	**117.4**	**109.6**	**120.3**
138.4	133.3	150.3	113.4	111.6	108.8
141.5	140.0	144.0	119.8	108.4	144.2
113.2	108.7	117.3	115.6	130.0	114.8
109.5	**109.7**	**108.1**	**115.1**	**106.3**	**118.6**
108.3	108.0	110.0	113.5	110.2	112.5
123.2	124.4	111.3	117.1	117.5	116.0
124.6	157.2	115.3	114.3	111.2	114.8
104.2	103.0	135.8	124.5	126.2	121.4
126.4	141.2	107.1	110.0	116.0	116.0
114.8	115.4	113.4	115.6	119.3	118.5
118.1	119.8	103.1	115.2	116.7	146.3
120.7	123.2	115.5	116.4	111.6	114.2
122.5	115.0	131.5	122.6	117.7	119.1
115.2	**118.6**	**105.7**	**111.6**	**108.2**	**111.7**
89.6	107.0	33.1	110.8	98.1	98.5
116.0	117.2	114.7	104.0	100.9	95.6
109.9	107.9	116.9	109.2	112.9	100.6

2-12 续表 2

(上年=100)

地　　区	Region	地区生产总值 Gross Regional Product	第一产业 Primary Industry
沙雅县	Xayar County	111.2	108.0
新和县	Xinhe [Toksu] County	110.6	108.7
拜城县	Baicheng [Bay] County	117.1	105.1
乌什县	Wushi [Uxturpan] County	109.8	108.8
阿瓦提县	Awat County	112.7	109.1
柯坪县	Kalpin County	110.3	111.7
克孜勒苏柯尔克孜自治州	**Kizilsu Kirgiz Autonomous Prefecture**	**118.5**	**104.9**
阿图什市	Artux City	114.3	106.4
阿克陶县	Akto County	119.5	103.5
阿合奇县	Akqi County	114.8	109.2
乌恰县	Wuqia [Ulugqat] County	139.9	105.5
喀什地区	**Kashgar [Kaxgar] Administrative Offices**	**115.5**	**106.1**
喀什市	Kashgar [Kaxgar] City	117.8	106.7
疏附县	Shufu County	113.2	96.7
疏勒县	Shule County	119.1	105.7
英吉沙县	Yengisar County	116.4	105.3
泽普县	Zepu [Poskam] County	117.5	115.2
莎车县	Shache [Yarkant] County	117.3	112.1
叶城县	Yecheng [Kagilik] County	118.0	112.2
麦盖提县	Makit County	113.3	106.1
岳普湖县	Yopurga County	116.1	106.1
伽师县	Jiashi [Payzawat] County	106.5	103.3
巴楚县	Bachu [Maralbexi] County	115.7	108.9
塔什库尔干县	Taxkorgan Tajik Autonomous County	107.2	105.8
和田地区	**Hotan Administrative Offices**	**111.1**	**104.9**
和田市	Hotan City	113.8	103.5
和田县	Hotan County	110.5	104.1
墨玉县	Moyu [Karakax] County	110.4	104.0
皮山县	Pishan [Guma] County	110.3	105.0
洛浦县	Lop County	110.4	103.3
策勒县	Qira County	110.8	104.6
于田县	Yutian [Keriya] County	109.9	104.3
民丰县	Minfeng [Niya] County	111.2	105.5

Continued

(preceding year=100)

第二产业 Secondary Industry	工业 Industry	建筑业 Construction	第三产业 Tertiary Industry	#交通运输、仓储和邮政业 Transport,storage And Post	#批发和零售业 Wholesale, and Retail Trades
120.9	124.4	113.7	108.9	108.4	99.6
118.4	120.7	111.4	108.2	92.5	102.9
122.7	124.1	113.4	114.7	106.4	124.3
119.1	115.6	122.0	108.6	109.2	105.5
116.3	117.8	115.1	116.9	120.9	120.1
114.4	114.7	113.9	107.2	107.8	100.0
131.7	**139.9**	**123.3**	**116.7**	**110.6**	**134.0**
117.0	115.6	118.8	115.5	112.2	132.8
133.7	147.8	122.6	120.3	111.7	126.1
115.3	128.4	92.7	115.6	113.9	118.6
179.0	231.0	128.7	116.3	126.4	122.7
125.3	**126.0**	**124.4**	**116.9**	**111.0**	**117.4**
120.8	122.9	115.2	116.8	116.9	120.7
120.5	153.3	109.1	140.7	136.8	139.2
136.4	147.3	128.4	119.1	113.9	122.4
125.3	159.0	115.9	126.3	176.6	153.1
115.5	92.0	147.6	120.3	103.8	125.3
123.3	128.5	118.9	122.8	124.0	123.2
134.9	148.0	119.5	117.6	115.2	116.7
121.0	120.8	121.1	118.5	124.5	118.1
125.0	130.0	122.6	115.7	117.4	112.2
101.4	100.2	103.7	117.8	113.1	129.6
116.4	118.1	115.3	123.3	112.7	124.8
100.7	83.1	114.2	117.4	119.5	121.8
112.5	**112.9**	**112.1**	**114.6**	**106.8**	**107.3**
114.2	111.2	116.6	114.9	102.4	113.5
114.4	111.9	116.3	114.4	109.8	114.8
114.9	111.5	116.2	114.7	110.9	112.5
115.1	114.4	115.5	115.2	97.9	106.6
113.3	113.1	113.4	113.5	97.9	112.6
119.6	145.9	116.0	112.9	116.7	112.8
128.3	247.2	116.3	110.1	119.0	119.5
114.9	115.9	114.2	112.4	112.8	112.8

2-13 三次产业贡献率
Share of the Contributions of Three Strata of Industry to the Increase of the GDP

单位：%　　(%)

年 份 Year	新疆生产总值构成 Composition of Gross Domestic Product	第一产业 Primary Industry	第二产业 Secondary Industry	工 业 Industry	建筑业 Construction	第三产业 Tertiary Industry
2001	100.0	12.9	44.0	34.3	9.7	43.1
2002	100.0	12.0	38.2	28.2	10.0	49.8
2003	100.0	13.8	42.7	29.5	13.2	43.5
2004	100.0	9.2	50.5	37.7	12.8	40.3
2005	100.0	11.1	52.9	45.1	7.8	36.0
2006	100.0	10.1	45.8	41.9	3.9	44.1
2007	100.0	10.9	46.2	43.2	2.9	42.9
2008	100.0	10.3	58.5	49.6	8.9	31.2
2009	100.0	9.5	48.6	30.2	18.5	41.8
2010	100.0	7.0	55.4	49.2	6.3	37.6
2011	100.0	10.8	47.8	37.9	9.9	41.4
2012	100.0	11.1	54.4	42.0	12.4	34.5
2013	100.0	11.3	57.7	44.5	13.2	31.0

注：1.三次产业贡献率指各产业增加值增量与 GDP 增量之比。2.本表按不变价格计算。
Note:a) Share of the contributions of the three strata of industry to the increase of the GDP refers to the proportion of the increment of the value-added of each industry to the increment of GDP.　b) Data in this table are calculated at constant prices.

2-14 三次产业对地区生产总值增长的拉动
Contribution of the Three Strata of Industry to GDP Growth

单位：百分点　　(percentage points)

年 份 Year	新疆生产总值指数 Indices of Gross Domestic Product	第一产业 Primary Industry	第二产业 Secondary Industry	工 业 Industry	建筑业 Construction	第三产业 Tertiary Industry
2001	8.6	1.1	3.8	2.9	0.8	3.7
2002	8.2	1.0	3.1	2.3	0.8	4.1
2003	11.2	1.5	4.8	3.3	1.5	4.9
2004	11.4	1.1	5.8	4.3	1.5	4.6
2005	10.9	1.2	5.8	4.9	0.9	3.9
2006	11.0	1.1	5.0	4.6	0.4	4.9
2007	12.2	1.3	5.7	5.3	0.4	5.2
2008	11.0	1.1	6.5	5.5	1.0	3.4
2009	8.1	0.8	3.9	2.4	1.5	3.4
2010	10.6	0.7	5.9	5.2	0.7	4.0
2011	12.0	1.3	5.7	4.5	1.2	5.0
2012	12.0	1.3	6.5	5.0	1.5	4.2
2013	11.0	1.3	6.3	4.9	1.4	3.4

注：1.三次产业拉动指 GDP 增长速度与各产业贡献率之乘积。2.本表按不变价格计算。
Note: a) Contribution of the three strata of industry to GDP growth refers to the growth rate of GDP multiplied by the contribution share of every industry.　b) Data in this table are calculated at constant prices.

2-15 主要年份居民消费水平及指数
Household Consumption Expenditure and Its Indices in Main Years

年 份 Year	居民消费水平(元) Household Consumption (yuan)	农村居民 Rural Households	城镇居民 Urban Households	居民消费水平指数(1952 年=100) Index of Residents' Consumption Level (1952=100)	农村居民 Rural Households
1978	181	131	323	140.5	144.5
1980	252	180	417	182.4	184.4
1990	796	447	1508	299.5	236.3
1995	1852	977	3414	344.1	246.5
1996	2266	1387	3836	377.1	312.6
1997	2455	1445	4261	384.6	313.9
1998	2539	1520	4364	396.1	339.3
1999	2606	1358	4841	413.1	319.3
2000	2662	1308	5131	415.2	299.2
2001	2905	1427	5743	434.3	307.6
2002	3228	1525	6483	484.7	325.4
2003	3249	1603	6427	488.6	338.1
2004	3445	1652	6808	502.3	339.8
2005	3814	1884	7221	556.0	385.7
2006	4151	2000	7728	596.2	400.6
2007	4831	2320	8833	661.4	432.7
2008	5521	2686	9882	700.1	452.7
2009	5945	3029	10366	753.6	503.9
2010	7400	3674	12665	894.8	587.6
2011	8895	4495	14663	991.5	644.6
2012	10675	5410	17442	1149.1	749.0
2013	11401	5942	18285	1227.2	822.4

年 份 Year	城镇居民 Urban Households	居民消费水平指数(上年=100) Index of Residents' Consumption Level (preceding year=100)	农村居民 Rural Households	城镇居民 Urban Households
1978	99.0	104.7	102.3	102.8
1980	119.3	111.9	107.6	113.1
1990	226.4	103.8	98.8	105.0
1995	257.4	109.0	102.3	112.3
1996	260.7	109.6	126.8	101.3
1997	268.5	102.0	100.4	103.0
1998	268.5	103.0	108.1	100.0
1999	297.8	104.3	94.1	110.9
2000	315.7	100.5	93.7	106.0
2001	338.7	104.6	102.8	107.3
2002	386.8	111.6	105.8	114.2
2003	386.8	100.8	103.9	100.0
2004	396.1	102.8	100.5	102.4
2005	421.1	110.7	113.5	106.3
2006	445.3	107.2	103.9	105.7
2007	489.7	110.9	108.0	110.0
2008	512.3	105.9	104.6	104.6
2009	540.7	107.6	111.3	105.5
2010	627.2	118.7	116.6	116.0
2011	676.7	110.8	109.7	107.9
2012	776.9	115.9	116.2	114.8
2013	814.2	106.8	109.8	104.8

2-16 居民消费支出
Household Consumption Expenditure

单位：亿元 (100 million yuan)

项　目	Item	2012	2013
居民消费支出	**Household Consumption Expenditure**	**2370.67**	**2563.54**
食品类支出	Foods	745.30	732.56
衣着类支出	Clothes	251.08	263.08
居住类支出	Residence	142.63	182.88
家庭设备、用品及服务类支出	Family Facilities and Servises	119.70	129.40
医疗保健类支出	Medical and Hygiencic Expenditure	265.92	220.52
交通和通信类支出	Traffic and Telecommunications	243.08	307.60
文教娱乐用品及服务类支出	Teathing, Entertainment and Services	150.22	194.11
金融中介服务虚拟支出	Imaginary Expenditure of Middle Finance Services	199.63	250.44
自有住房服务虚拟支出	Imaginary Expenditure of Freeform Resident Services	170.88	202.09
实物消费支出	Reality Consumption	16.36	7.19
其他商品和服务类支出	Other Goods and Services	65.87	73.67
按城乡分	**By Residence**		
农村居民支出	Rural Households Expenditure	675.64	745.18
食品类支出	Foods	236.17	203.16
衣着类支出	Clothes	53.69	60.52
居住类支出	Residence	58.99	85.56
家庭设备、用品及服务类支出	Family Facilities and Servises	27.36	32.16
医疗保健类支出	Medical and Hygiencic Expenditure	70.71	92.39
交通和通信类支出	Traffic and Telecommunications	81.73	87.80
文教娱乐用品及服务类支出	Teathing, Entertainment and Services	25.75	35.20
金融中介服务虚拟支出	Imaginary Expenditure of Middle Finance Services	53.69	64.25
自有住房服务虚拟支出	Imaginary Expenditure of Freeform Resident Services	53.79	70.59
其他商品和服务类支出	Other Goods and Services	13.76	13.55
城镇居民支出	Urban Households Expenditure	1695.03	1818.36
食品类支出	Foods	509.13	529.40
衣着类支出	Clothes	197.39	202.56
居住类支出	Residence	83.64	97.32
家庭设备、用品及服务类支出	Family Facilities and Servises	92.34	97.24
医疗保健类支出	Medical and Hygiencic Expenditure	195.21	128.13
交通和通信类支出	Traffic and Telecommunications	161.35	219.80
文教娱乐用品及服务类支出	Teathing, Entertainment and Services	124.47	158.91
金融中介服务虚拟支出	Imaginary Expenditure of Middle Finance Services	145.94	186.19
自由住房服务虚拟支出	Imaginary Expenditure of Freeform Resident Services	117.09	131.50
实物消费支出	Reality Consumption	16.36	7.19
其他商品和服务类支出	Other Goods and Services	52.11	60.12

主要统计指标解释

国内生产总值(GDP)　指按市场价格计算的一个国家(或地区)所有常住单位在一定时期内生产活动的最终成果。国内生产总值有三种表现形态，即价值形态、收入形态和产品形态。从价值形态看，它是所有常住单位在一定时期内生产的全部货物和服务价值与同期投入的全部非固定资产货物和服务价值的差额，即所有常住单位的增加值之和；从收入形态看，它是所有常住单位在一定时期内创造并分配给常住单位和非常住单位的初次收入之和；从产品形态看，它是所有常住单位在一定时期内最终使用的货物和服务价值与货物和服务净出口价值之和。在实际核算中，国内生产总值有三种计算方法，即生产法、收入法和支出法。三种方法分别从不同的方面反映国内生产总值及其构成。

对于一个地区来说，称为地区生产总值或地区GDP。

三次产业　三次产业的划分是世界上较为常用的产业结构分类，但各国的划分不尽一致。我国的三次产业划分是：

第一产业是指农、林、牧、渔业 (不含农、林、牧、渔服务业) 。

第二产业是指采矿业(不含开采辅助活动)，制造业 (不含金属制品、机械和设备修理业)，电力、煤气及水的生产和供应业，建筑业。

第三产业是指除第一、二产业以外的其他行业。

劳动者报酬　指劳动者因从事生产活动所获得的全部报酬。包括劳动者获得的各种形式的工资、奖金和津贴，既包括货币形式的，也包括实物形式的，还包括劳动者所享受的公费医疗和医药卫生费、上下班交通补贴、单位支付的社会保险费、住房公积金等。

生产税净额　指生产税减生产补贴后的余额。生产税指政府对生产单位从事生产、销售和经营活动以及因从事生产活动使用某些生产要素(如固定资产、土地、劳动力)所征收的各种税、附加费和规费。生产补贴与生产税相反，指政府对生产单位的单方面转移支出，因此视为负生产税，包括政策亏损补贴、价格补贴等。

固定资产折旧　指一定时期内为弥补固定资产损耗按照规定的固定资产折旧率提取的固定资产折旧，或按国民经济核算统一规定的折旧率虚拟计算的固定资产折旧。它反映了固定资产在当期生产中的转移价值。各类企业和企业化管理的事业单位的固定资产折旧是指实际计提的折旧费；不计提折旧的政府机关、非企业化管理的事业单位和居民住房的固定资产折旧是按照统一规定的折旧率和固定资产原值计算的虚拟折旧。原则上，固定资产折旧应按固定资产的重置价值计算，但是目前我国尚不具备对全社会固定资产进行重估价的基础，所以暂时只能采用上述办法。

营业盈余　指常住单位创造的增加值扣除劳动者报酬、生产税净额和固定资产折旧后的余额。它相当于企业的营业利润加上生产补贴，但要扣除从利润中开支的工资和福利等。

支出法国内生产总值　是从最终使用的角度反映一个国家(或地区)一定时期内生产活动最终成果的一种方法，包括最终消费支出、资本形成总额及货物和服务净出口三部分。计算公式为：

支出法国内生产总值=最终消费支出+资本形成总额+货物和服务净出口

最终消费支出　指常住单位为满足物质、文化和精神生活的需要，从本国经济领土和国外购买的货物和服务的支出。它不包括非常住单位在本国经济领土内的消费支出。最终消费支出分为居民消费支出和政府消费支出。

居民消费支出　指常住住户在一定时期内对于货物和服务的全部最终消费支出。居民消费支出除了直接以货币形式购买的货物和服务的消费支出外，还包括以其他方式获得的货物和服务的消费支出，即所谓的虚拟消费支出。居民虚拟消费支出包括如下几种类型：单位以实物报酬及实物转移的形式提供给劳动者的货物和服务；住户生产并由本住户消费了的货物和服务，其中的服务仅指住户的自有住房服务和付酬的家庭雇员提供的家庭和个人服务；金融机构提供的金融媒介服务。

政府消费支出　指政府部门为全社会提供的公共服务的消费支出和免费或以较低的价格向居民住户提供的货物和服务的净支出，前者等于政府服务的产出价值减去政府单位所获得的经营收入的价值，后者等于政府部门免费或以较低价格向居民住户提供的货物和服务的市场价值减去向住户收取的价值。

资本形成总额　指常住单位在一定时期内获得减去处置的固定资产和存货的净额，包括固定资本形成总额和存货变动两部分。

固定资本形成总额 指常住单位在一定时期内获得的固定资产减处置的固定资产的价值总额。固定资产是通过生产活动生产出来的，且其使用年限在一年以上、单位价值在规定标准以上的资产，不包括自然资产。可分为有形固定资本形成总额和无形固定资本形成总额。有形固定资本形成总额包括一定时期内完成的建筑工程、安装工程和设备工器具购置(减处置)价值，以及土地改良、新增役、种、奶、毛、娱乐用牲畜和新增经济林木价值。无形固定资本形成总额包括矿藏的勘探、计算机软件等获得减处置。

存货变动 指常住单位在一定时期内存货实物量变动的市场价值，即期末价值减期初价值的差额，再扣除当期由于价格变动而产生的持有收益。存货变动可以是正值，也可以是负值，正值表示存货上升，负值表示存货下降。存货包括生产单位购进的原材料、燃料和储备物资等存货，以及生产单位生产的产成品、在制品和半成品等存货。

货物和服务净出口 指货物和服务出口减货物和服务进口的差额。出口包括常住单位向非常住单位出售或无偿转让的各种货物和服务的价值；进口包括常住单位从非常住单位购买或无偿得到的各种货物和服务的价值。由于服务活动的提供与使用同时发生，一般把常住单位从非常住单位得到的服务作为进口，非常住单位从常住单位得到的服务作为出口。货物的出口和进口都按离岸价格计算。

Explanatory Notes on Main Statistical Indicators

Gross Domestic Product (GDP) refers to the final products at market prices produced by all resident units in a country during a certain period of time. Gross domestic product is expressed in three different perspectives, namely value, income, and products respectively. GDP in its value perspective refers to the balance of total value of all goods and services produced by all resident units during a certain period of time, minus the total value of input of goods and services of the nature of non-fixed assets; in other words, it is the sum of the value-added of all resident units. GDP from the perspective of income includes the primary income created by all resident units and distributed to resident and non-resident units. GDP from the perspective of products refers to the value of all goods and services for final demand by all resident units plus the net exports of goods and services during a given period of time. In the practice of national accounting, gross domestic product is calculated from three approaches, namely production approach, income approach and expenditure approach, which reflect gross domestic product and its composition from different angles.

For a region, it is called as Gross Regional Product(GRP) or regional GDP.

Three Strata of Industry Classification of economic activities into three strata of industry is a common practice in the world, although the grouping varies to some extent from country to country. In China economic activities are categorized into the following three strata of industry:

Primary industry refers to agriculture, forestry, animal husbandry and fishery industries.

Secondary industry refers to mining and quarrying, manufacturing, production and supply of electricity, water and gas, and construction.

Tertiary industry refers to all other economic activities not included in the primary or secondary industries.

Compensation of Employees refers to the total payment of various forms to employees for the productive activities they are engaged in. It includes wages, bonuses and allowances, which the employees earn in cash or in kind. It also includes the free medical services provided to the employees and the medicine expenses, transport subsidies and social insurance, and housing fund paid by the employers.

Net Taxes on Production refers to taxes on production less subsidies on production. The taxes on production refers to the various taxes, extra charges and fees levied on the production units on their production, sale and business activities as well as on the use of some factors of production, such as fixed assets, land and labour in the production activities they are engaged in. In contrast to taxes on production, subsidies on production refer to the unilateral government transfer to the production units and are therefore regarded as negative taxes on production. They include subsidies on the loss due to implementation of government policies, price subsidies, etc.

Depreciation of Fixed Assets refers to the depreciation of fixed assets in a given period, drawn in accordance with the stipulated depreciation rate for the purpose of compensating the wear-and-tear loss of the fixed assets or the depreciation of fixed assets imputed in accordance with the stipulated unified depreciation rate in the national economic accounting system. It reflects the value of transfer of the fixed assets in the production of the current period. The depreciation of fixed assets in various enterprises and institutions managed as enterprises refers to the depreciation expenses actually drawn. In government agencies and institutions not managed as enterprises which do not draw the depreciation expenses, as well as for the houses of residents, the depreciation of fixed assets is the imputed depreciation, which is calculated in accordance with the stipulated unified depreciation rate. In principle, the depreciation of fixed assets should be calculated on the basis of the re-purchased value of the fixed assets. However, currently the conditions in China do not facilitate the revaluation of all the fixed assets. Therefore, only the above-mentioned methods can be adopted at present.

Operating Surplus refers to the balance of the value added created by the resident units after deducting the labourers remuneration, net taxes on production and the depreciation of fixed assets. It is equivalent to the business profit of the enterprises plus subsidies to production, but the wages and welfare expenses paid from the profits should be deducted.

GDP by Expenditure Approach refers to the method of measuring the final results of production activities of a country (region) during a given period from the perspective of final uses. It includes final consumption expenditure, gross capital formation and net export of goods and services. The formula for computation is.:

GDP by expenditure approach = final consumption expenditure + gross capital formation + net export of goods and services

Final Consumption Expenditure refers to the total expenditure of resident units for purchases of goods and services from both the domestic economic territory and abroad to meet the needs of material, cultural and spiritual life. It does not include the expenditure of non-resident units on consumption in the economic territory of the country. The final consumption expenditure is broken down into household consumption expenditure and government consumption expenditure.

Households Consumption Expenditure refers to the total expenditure of resident households on the final consumption of goods and services. In addition to the consumption of goods and services bought by the households directly with money, the households consumption expenditure also includes expenditure on goods and services obtained by the households in other ways, i.e. the so-called imputed consumption expenditure, which includes the following: (a) the goods and services provided to households by employer in the form of payment in kind and transfer in kind; (b) goods and services produced and consumed by the households themselves, in which the services refer to the owner-occupied housing and services offered by paid family employees; (c) financial intermediate services provided by financial institutions.

Government Consumption Expenditure refers to the consumption expenditure spent for the provision of public services provided by the government to the whole country and the net expenditure on the goods and services provided by the government to households free of charge or at reduced prices. The former equals to the output value of the government services minus the value of operating income obtained by the government departments. The latter equals to the market value of the goods and services provided by the government free of charge or at reduced prices to the households minus the value received by the government from the households.

Gross Capital Formation refers to the fixed assets acquired less disposals and the net value of inventory, thus including gross fixed capital formation and changes in inventories.

Gross Fixed Capital Formation refers to the value of acquisitions less those disposals of fixed assets during a given period. Fixed assets are the assets produced through production activities with unit value above a specified amount and which could be used for over one year. Natural assets are not included. Gross fixed capital formation can be categorized into total tangible fixed capital formation and total intangible fixed capital formation. Total tangible fixed capital formation includes the value of the construction projects and installation projects completed and the equipment, apparatus and instruments purchased (less those disposed) as well as the value of land improved, the value of draught animals, breeding stock and animals for milk, for wool and for recreational purposes and the newly increased forest with economic value. Total intangible fixed capital formation includes the prospecting of minerals and the acquisition of computer software minus the disposal of them.

Changes in Inventories refers to the market value of the change in the physical volume of inventory of resident units during a given period, i.e. the difference between the values at the beginning and at the end of the period minus the gains due to the change in prices. The changes in inventories can have a positive or a negative value. A positive value indicates an increase in inventory while a negative value indicates a decrease in inventory. The inventory includes raw materials, fuels and reserve materials purchased by the production units as well as the inventory of finished products, semi-finished products and work-in-progress.

Net Export of Goods and Services refers to the exports of goods and services subtracting the imports of goods and services. Exports include the value of various goods and services sold or gratuitously transferred by resident units to non-resident units. Imports include the value of various goods and services purchased or gratuitously acquired resident units from non-resident units. Because the provision of services and the use of them happen simultaneously, the acquisition of services by resident units from abroad is usually treated as import while the acquisition of services by non-resident units in this country is usually treated as export. The exports and imports of goods are calculated at FOB.

新疆统计年鉴
XINJIANG STATISTICAL YEARBOOK

3

人口与就业

POPULATION AND EMPLOYMENT

简要说明

本篇主要内容和资料来源

本篇内容主要包括人口、计划生育、就业、工资等资料。人口资料包括全区、各地、州、市、县及兵团人口情况、人口普查的主要数据等。

本篇人口及相关分组数据，除3-1、3-2表是由新疆维吾尔自治区统计局人口与就业统计处根据2013年人口变动调查数据推算外，其他人口资料取自新疆维吾尔自治区公安厅户籍处所提供的公安户籍年报；计划生育资料由新疆维吾尔自治区计划生育委员会提供；失业资料由新疆维吾尔自治区人力资源和社会保障厅提供；就业和劳动报酬资料由新疆维吾尔自治区统计局人口与就业统计处提供。

Brief Introduction

Main Content and Source of Data

Data in this chapter show the basic condition of population, employment, wages of staff and workers, family planning. Data of population mainly include the condition of population by whole region, prefecture, autonomous prefecture, city, country and Xinjiang Production and Construction Group, and the data of 5 national population censuses.

The data on household registered population are provided by Municipal Bureau of Public Security of Xinjiang Uygur Autonomous Region,except the data of 3-1,3-2 are estimated from the 2013 national sample survey on population changes by the Department of Population and Social Science and Technology Statistic of the Xinjiang Bureau of Statistics;Data on family planning come from Municipal Family Planning Commission. Data on unemployment are provided by Bureau of Labor and Social Security; The data of population census, employment and wages are provided by the Department of Population and Social Science and Technology Statistic of the Xinjiang Bureau of Statistics.

3-1 主要年份人口数及构成
Population and Its Composition in Main Years

单位：万人、%　　(10 000 persons,%)

年份 Year	年末总人口 Total Population (Year-end)	按性别分 By Sex 男 Male 人口数 Population	比重 Proportion	女 Female 人口数 Population	比重 Proportion	按城乡分 By Residence 城镇人口 Urban 人口数 Population	比重 Proportion	乡村人口 Rural 人口数 Population	比重 Proportion
1978	1233.01	630.18	51.11	602.83	48.89	321.40	26.07	911.61	73.93
1980	1283.24	654.90	51.03	628.34	48.97	372.74	29.05	910.50	70.95
1985	1361.14	696.81	51.19	664.33	48.81	582.24	42.78	778.90	57.22
1990	1529.16	785.06	51.34	744.10	48.66	685.96	44.86	843.20	55.14
1995	1661.35	848.12	51.05	813.23	48.95	822.53	49.51	838.82	50.49
1996	1689.29	869.59	51.48	819.70	48.52	846.17	50.09	843.12	49.91
1997	1718.08	883.03	51.40	835.05	48.60	860.76	50.10	857.32	49.90
1998	1747.35	897.90	51.39	849.45	48.61	875.42	50.10	871.93	49.90
1999	1775.00	910.98	51.32	864.02	48.68	929.00	52.34	846.00	47.66
2000	1849.41	957.07	51.75	892.34	48.25	624.18	33.75	1225.23	66.25
2001	1876.19	954.23	50.86	921.96	49.14	633.21	33.75	1242.98	66.25
2002	1905.19	975.46	51.20	929.73	48.80	644.72	33.84	1260.47	66.16
2003	1933.95	994.24	51.41	939.71	48.59	665.11	34.39	1268.84	65.61
2004	1963.11	1008.02	51.30	955.09	48.70	690.11	35.15	1273.00	64.85
2005	2010.35	1029.70	51.22	980.65	48.78	746.85	37.15	1263.50	62.85
2006	2050.00	1050.01	51.22	999.99	48.78	777.77	37.94	1272.23	62.06
2007	2095.19	1072.53	51.19	1022.66	48.81	820.27	39.15	1274.92	60.85
2008	2130.81	1083.94	50.87	1046.87	49.13	844.65	39.64	1286.16	60.36
2009	2158.63	1098.31	50.88	1060.32	49.12	860.21	39.85	1298.42	60.15
2010	2181.58	1127.01	51.66	1054.57	48.34	933.58	42.79	1248.01	57.21
2011	2208.71	1128.75	51.10	1079.96	48.90	961.67	43.54	1247.04	56.46
2012	2232.78	1145.21	51.29	1087.57	48.71	981.98	44.00	1250.80	56.00
2013	2264.30	1151.77	50.87	1112.53	49.13	1006.93	44.47	1257.37	55.53

3-2 主要年份人口出生率、死亡率、自然增长率
Birth Rate,Death Rate and Natural Growth Rate of Population in Main Years

单位：‰　　(‰)

年份 Year	出生率 Birth Rate	死亡率 Death Rate	自然增长率 Natural Growth Rate	年份 Year	出生率 Birth Rate	死亡率 Death Rate	自然增长率 Natural Growth Rate
1978	22.55	7.69	14.86	1999	18.76	6.96	11.80
1980	21.28	7.62	13.66	2000	17.57	5.40	12.17
1985	19.80	6.39	13.41	2001	16.82	5.69	11.13
1986	20.54	6.13	14.41	2002	16.30	5.43	10.87
1987	21.03	5.96	15.07	2003	16.01	5.23	10.78
1988	19.72	5.99	13.73	2004	16.00	5.09	10.91
1989	21.15	5.77	15.38	2005	16.42	5.04	11.38
1990	26.41	7.81	18.60	2006	15.97	5.03	10.94
1991	24.45	7.86	16.59	2007	16.79	5.01	11.78
1992	22.80	7.84	14.96	2008	16.05	4.88	11.17
1993	21.53	7.68	13.85	2009	15.99	5.43	10.56
1994	20.82	7.43	13.39	2010	14.85	4.14	10.71
1995	18.90	6.45	12.45	2011	14.99	4.42	10.57
1996	19.45	6.60	12.85	2012	15.32	4.48	10.84
1997	19.66	6.55	13.11	2013	15.84	4.92	10.92
1998	19.74	6.93	12.81				

3-3 新疆人口普查基本情况
Basic Statistics on National Population Census in Xinjiang

单位：万人 (10 000 persons)

指　　标	Items	第二次普查 (1964 年) 1964 Census	第三次普查 (1982 年) 1982 Census	第四次普查 (1990 年) 1990 Census	第五次普查 (2000 年) 2000 Census	第六次普查 (2010 年) 2010 Census
总人口	**Total Population**	**727.01**	**1308.15**	**1515.69**	**1845.95**	**2181.58**
男	Male	389.47	673.22	782.32	955.22	1127.01
女	Female	337.54	634.93	733.37	890.73	1054.57
总户数(万户)	**Total Household (10 000 household)**	**178.00**	**293.79**	**337.41**	**491.66**	**690.29**
家 庭 户	Family Households		292.70	334.89	479.38	670.56
集 体 户	Collective Households		1.09	2.52	12.28	19.73
各年龄组人口	Population by Age Group					
0-5　岁	Age 0-5	121.86	186.70	218.85	165.12	185.03
6-14　岁	Age 6-14	146.77	330.85	282.12	338.18	261.15
15-64 岁	Age 15-64	428.73	742.42	955.49	1256.40	1593.99
65 岁及以上	Aged 65 and Over	29.65	48.18	59.23	86.25	141.41
民族人口	**Nationality Population**					
汉 族	Han Nationality	232.12	528.40	569.54	748.99	882.99
少数民族	Minority Nationalities	494.89	779.75	946.15	1096.96	1298.59
各种文化程度人口	**Population by Educational Level**					
大专及以上	College and Above	4.10	8.37	27.98	94.65	231.53
高中和中专	Senior Secondary School and Specialized Secondary School	15.51	84.28	157.42	224.79	254.56
初 中	Junior Secondary School	50.37	228.63	313.51	508.59	790.62
小 学	Primary School	197.34	442.57	552.55	699.78	656.32
不识字或识字很少	Illiterate and Semi-iliterate	249.03	265.39	198.11	103.68	63.52

注：不识字或识字很少除 1964 年包含 12-14 岁人口外，其他均为 15 岁及以上人口。
Note：Illiterate or semi-illiterate population refers to the population aged above 15 except for the population aged between 12 and 14 in 1964.

3-4 主要年份婚姻登记情况
Number of Marriages Registry in Main Years

指　　标	Item	2005	2010	2013
登记结婚(对)	**Registered Marriages (couple)**	**184714**	**264013**	**260713**
初婚(人)	First Marriage (person)	275752	389342	480231
再婚(人)	Remarriage (person)	93676	138684	41195
#男	Male	42576	73863	22470
#再婚中恢复结婚(对)	Resumed Marriages (couple)	6815	11108	6668
登记离婚(对)	**Registered Divorces (couple)**	**74342**	**97817**	**109120**
民政部门批准	Approved by the Civil Administration	47917	69137	78875
法院调判	Mediated by the court	26425	28680	30245
涉外及华侨港澳台居民婚姻	**Marital status of OverseasChinese ,Foreigner and Hong Kong, Macao and Taiwan Compatriots**			
登记结婚(对)	Registered Marriages (couple)	223	235	319
国内公民(人)	Citizen (person)	223	235	312
港澳台居民(人)	Compatriots of Hong Kong, Macao and Taiwan (person)	57	31	59
华　侨(人)	Overseas Chinese (person)	12	13	2
外国人(人)	Foreigner (person)	154	191	265
登记离婚(对)	Registered Divorces (couple)	6	26	31

3-5 各地、州、市、县(市)户数、人口数、土地面积

Household, Population, Land Area by Prefecture, Autonomous Prefecture,City and County

(2013 年)

地　区	Region	户 数 (万户) Number of Households (10 000 households)	年末人口 (万人) Population at Year-end (10 000 persons)	#男 Male	平均每户人口 (人) Average Persons Per Household (person)	土地面积 (平方公里) Land Area (sq.km)
总　计	**Total**	**682.18**	**2266.63**	**1155.22**	**3.32**	**1664897.17**
乌鲁木齐市	**Urumqi City**	**84.12**	**262.93**	**136.11**	**3.13**	**14875.50**
天山区	Tianshan District	17.78	58.61	29.36	3.30	47.31
沙依巴克区	Shayibak District	17.05	55.05	28.92	3.23	38.60
新市区	Xinshi District	18.30	59.69	31.16	3.26	57.07
水磨沟区	Shui Mogou Distric	9.36	28.47	14.91	3.04	10.76
头屯河区	Tou Tunhe District	8.21	23.06	12.16	2.81	20.11
达坂城区	Da Bancheng District	1.44	4.21	2.26	2.92	1111.85
米东区	Midong District	9.77	27.67	14.29	2.83	3789.22
乌鲁木齐县	Urumqi County	2.21	6.17	3.05	2.79	9800.58
克拉玛依市	**Karamay City**	**10.81**	**29.02**	**14.71**	**2.68**	**8654.08**
独山子区	Dushanzi District	2.19	5.72	2.93	2.61	379.11
克拉玛依区	Karamay District	7.06	19.00	9.57	2.69	4231.56
白碱滩区	Bai Jiantan District	1.47	4.07	2.09	2.77	2618.76
乌尔河区	Urhe District	0.09	0.23	0.12	2.56	1424.65
吐鲁番地区	**Turpan Administrative Offices**	**19.55**	**64.29**	**32.48**	**3.29**	**67562.91**
吐鲁番市	Turpan City	7.81	28.40	14.29	3.64	13589.22
鄯善县	Shanshan [Piqan] County	7.98	23.86	12.08	2.99	38281.46
托克逊县	Toksun County	3.76	12.03	6.11	3.20	15692.23
哈密地区	**Hami [Kumul] Administrative Offices**	**21.51**	**60.84**	**31.35**	**2.83**	**142094.88**
哈密市	Hami [Kumul] City	16.82	48.02	24.84	2.85	85587.23
巴里坤哈萨克自治县	Barkol Kazak Autonomous County	3.85	10.51	5.33	2.73	36988.55
伊吾县	Yiwu [Araturuk] County	0.84	2.31	1.18	2.75	19519.10

注：1.全区年末人口数、各地、州、市、县、区人口数据为 2013 年公安年报数据。
2.全疆各地州市土地面积为国土资源厅 2008 年数据。

Note：a) The data of population by prefecture,antonomous prefecture,city and county come from the annual data of public security.
b) The land area of different prefectures and cities come from the Burean of State Land.

3-5 续表 1 Continued

地　区	Region	户数 (万户) Number of Households (10 000 households)	年末人口 (万人) Population at Year-end (10 000 persons)	#男 Male	平均每户人口 (人) Average Persons Per Household (person)	土地面积 (平方公里) Land Area (sq.km)
昌吉回族自治州	**Changji Hui Autonomous Prefecture**	**48.23**	**140.5**	**71.25**	**2.91**	**73139.75**
昌吉市	Changji City	12.61	36.76	18.46	2.92	7505.12
阜康市	Fukang City	5.78	16.92	8.57	2.93	8534.97
呼图壁县	Hutubi County	7.79	21.87	11.13	2.81	9421.03
玛纳斯县	Manas County	6.44	17.58	8.86	2.73	9597.27
奇台县	Qitai County	7.75	24.20	12.32	3.12	16635.92
吉木萨尔县	Jimsar County	4.93	14.18	7.28	2.88	8144.58
木垒哈萨克自治县	Mori Kazak Autonomous County	2.93	8.99	4.63	3.07	13300.86
伊犁哈萨克自治州	**Ili Kazak Autonomous Prefecture**	**153.55**	**471.57**	**239.27**	**3.07**	**268778.72**
伊犁州直属县(市)	**Counties (Cities) Direct Under Ili Prefecture**	**95.58**	**298.53**	**151.84**	**3.12**	**56381.53**
伊宁市	Yining [Gulja] City	17.29	53.57	26.80	3.10	524.94
奎屯市	Kuytun City	11.08	30.15	15.18	2.72	1109.89
伊宁县	Yining [Gulja] County	11.81	44.85	23.15	3.80	4681.90
察布查尔锡伯自治县	Qapqal Xibe Autonomous County	6.71	19.79	10.08	2.95	4471.95
霍城县	Huocheng [Korgas] County	14.10	41.29	21.09	2.93	5429.83
巩留县	Gongliu [Tokkuztara] County	6.42	20.80	10.63	3.24	4326.90
新源县	Xinyuan [Kunes] County	10.45	32.52	16.64	3.11	6813.74
昭苏县	Zhaosu [Mongolkure] County	6.64	19.12	9.68	2.88	11127.91
特克斯县	Tekes County	5.66	17.45	8.90	3.08	7764.10
尼勒克县	Nilka County	5.42	18.99	9.69	3.50	10130.37
塔城地区	**Tacheng [Tarbagatai] Administrative Offices**	**36.42**	**105.99**	**53.62**	**2.91**	**94698.18**
塔城市	Tacheng [Qoqek] City	5.86	17.19	8.64	2.93	3991.25
乌苏市	Usu City	7.47	23.14	11.76	3.10	14299.86
额敏县	Emin [Dorbiljin] County	8.33	22.14	11.25	2.66	9448.37
沙湾县	Shawan County	7.55	21.88	11.06	2.90	12676.58
托里县	Toli County	3.05	10.19	5.14	3.34	28192.65
裕民县	Yumin [Qagantokay] County	2.14	5.98	3.02	2.79	6112.13
和布克赛尔蒙古自治县	Hoboksar Mongol Autonomous County	2.02	5.47	2.75	2.71	19977.34

3-5 续表 2 Continued

地　区	Region	户 数 (万户) Number of Households (10 000 households)	年末人口 (万人) Population at Year-end (10 000 persons)	#男 Male	平均每户人口 (人) Average Persons Per Household (person)	土地面积 (平方公里) Land Area (sq.km)
阿勒泰地区	**Altay Administrative Offices**	**21.55**	**67.05**	**33.81**	**3.11**	**117699.01**
阿勒泰市	Altay City	7.68	23.42	11.82	3.05	10829.06
布尔津县	Burqin County	2.51	7.22	3.64	2.88	10357.35
富蕴县	Fuyun [Koktokay] County	2.83	9.67	4.87	3.42	32186.11
福海县	Fuhai [Burultokay] County	2.39	7.57	3.84	3.17	33250.74
哈巴河县	Habahe [Kaba] County	2.73	8.81	4.46	3.23	8166.58
青河县	Qinghe [Qinggil] County	1.91	6.45	3.24	3.38	15756.87
吉木乃县	Jemnay County	1.50	3.91	1.94	2.61	7152.30
博尔塔拉蒙古自治州	**Bortala Mongol Autonomous Prefecture**	**17.52**	**49.04**	**25.00**	**2.80**	**24934.33**
博乐市	Bole [Bortala] City	9.62	27.13	13.82	2.82	7877.34
精河县	Jinghe [Jing] County	4.97	14.38	7.35	2.89	11175.25
温泉县	Wenquan [Araxang] County	2.93	7.53	3.83	2.57	5881.74
巴音郭楞蒙古自治州	**Bayangol Mongol Autonomous Prefecture**	**43.54**	**140.42**	**73.40**	**3.23**	**470954.25**
库尔勒市	Korla City	17.08	56.86	30.15	3.33	7215.90
轮台县	Luntai [Bugur] County	3.48	11.95	6.15	3.43	14156.61
尉犁县	Yuli [Lopnur] County	3.74	11.13	5.81	2.98	59234.48
若羌县	Ruoqiang [Qarkilik] County	1.15	3.50	1.81	3.04	198793.52
且末县	Qiemo [Qarqan] County	2.01	7.10	3.68	3.53	137831.05
焉耆回族自治县	Yanji Hui Autonomous County	4.65	16.10	8.35	3.46	2440.73
和静县	Hejing County	6.81	19.85	10.29	2.91	34886.74
和硕县	Hoxud County	2.64	7.75	3.99	2.94	12816.49
博湖县	Bohu [Bagrax] County	1.98	6.18	3.17	3.12	3578.73
阿克苏地区	**Aksu Administrative Offices**	**63.92**	**245.76**	**124.78**	**3.84**	**127144.91**
阿克苏市	Aksu City	14.48	50.92	25.81	3.52	13987.61
温宿县	Wensu [Onsu] County	6.65	25.41	12.92	3.82	14202.46
库车县	Kuqa County	11.46	48.14	24.36	4.20	14602.95
沙雅县	Xayar County	7.05	26.88	13.65	3.81	31955.15
新和县	Xinhe [Toksu] County	4.84	17.85	8.96	3.69	5817.82
拜城县	Baicheng [Bay] County	7.08	23.81	12.16	3.36	15553.70
乌什县	Wushi [Uxturpan] County	5.52	22.11	11.32	4.01	9082.00
阿瓦提县	Awat County	5.59	25.33	12.88	4.53	13233.57
柯坪县	Kalpin County	1.25	5.31	2.72	4.25	8709.65

3-5 续表 3 Continued

地　区	Region	户数 (万户) Number of Households (10 000 households)	年末人口 (万人) Population at Year-end (10 000 persons)	#男 Male	平均每户人口 (人) Average Persons Per Household (person)	土地面积 (平方公里) Land Area (sq.km)
克孜勒苏柯尔克孜自治州	**Kizilsu Kirgiz Autonomous Prefecture**	**14.81**	**57.62**	**29.29**	**3.89**	**72468.08**
阿图什市	Artux City	6.17	26.32	13.39	4.27	16151.17
阿克陶县	Akto County	5.49	20.95	10.68	3.82	24539.86
阿合奇县	Akqi County	1.19	4.36	2.18	3.66	12737.09
乌恰县	Wuqia [Ulugqat] County	1.96	5.99	3.04	3.06	19039.96
喀什地区	**Kashgar [Kaxgar] Administrative Offices**	**107.66**	**422.82**	**213.39**	**3.93**	**137578.51**
喀什市	Kashgar [Kaxgar] City	15.79	57.11	28.51	3.62	199.38
疏附县	Shufu County	6.59	27.06	13.83	4.11	3323.12
疏勒县	Shule County	8.86	35.16	17.74	3.97	2485.31
英吉沙县	Yengisar County	6.57	29.52	14.86	4.49	3223.87
泽普县	Zepu [Poskam] County	6.61	21.53	10.79	3.26	826.90
莎车县	Shache [Yarkant] County	18.75	79.87	40.31	4.26	9066.86
叶城县	Yecheng [Kagilik] County	11.76	48.11	24.36	4.09	29359.29
麦盖提县	Makit County	7.08	26.58	13.48	3.75	10276.57
岳普湖县	Yopurga County	4.49	16.49	8.48	3.67	2700.48
伽师县	Jiashi [Payzawat] County	10.32	42.25	21.39	4.09	6668.59
巴楚县	Bachu [Maralbexi] County	9.56	35.18	17.65	3.68	18903.70
塔什库尔干塔吉克自治县	Taxkorgan Tajik Autonomous County	1.28	3.96	1.99	3.09	50544.44
和田地区	**Hotan Administrative Offices**	**57.36**	**215.45**	**109.98**	**3.76**	**249146.59**
和田市	Hotan City	8.78	33.15	16.89	3.78	495.84
和田县	Hotan County	6.58	28.58	14.62	4.34	40876.80
墨玉县	Moyu [Karakax] County	14.05	54.33	27.89	3.87	25624.02
皮山县	Pishan [Guma] County	7.36	27.53	13.99	3.74	39819.75
洛浦县	Lop County	6.37	25.84	13.16	4.06	14286.97
策勒县	Qira County	5.06	15.96	8.13	3.15	31342.58
于田县	Yutian [Keriya] County	7.84	26.23	13.36	3.35	39126.14
民丰县	Minfeng [Niya] County	1.32	3.83	1.94	2.90	57574.49
自治区直辖县级市	**Municpality Country-LevelCity directly under the Central Govern-ment**	**39.62**	**106.38**	**54.25**	**2.69**	**7267.04**
石河子市	Shihezi City	23.68	62.26	31.22	2.63	459.94
阿拉尔市	Aral City	7.43	18.61	10.04	2.50	4196.00
图木舒克市	Tumxuk City	4.90	16.41	8.41	3.35	1901.10
五家渠市	Wujiaqu City	3.61	9.10	4.58	2.52	710.00

3-6 各地、州、市、县(市)人口自然变动情况

Population Natural Changes by Prefecture, Autonomous Prefecture, City and County

单位：‰　　(2013 年)　　(‰)

地　区	Region	出生率 Birth Rate	#少数民族 Minority Nationalities	死亡率 Death Rate	#少数民族 Minority Nationalities	自然增长率 Natural Growth Rate	#少数民族 Minority Nationalities
乌鲁木齐市	**Urumqi City**	**9.59**	**15.15**	**2.70**	**3.12**	**6.89**	**12.03**
天山区	Tianshan District	9.12	14.28	2.61	2.54	6.51	11.74
沙依巴克区	Shayibak District	9.23	14.47	2.88	3.17	6.35	11.30
新市区	Xinshi District	9.58	13.74	1.95	2.20	7.63	11.54
水磨沟区	Shui Mogou Distric	8.54	19.09	2.54	5.03	6.00	14.06
头屯河区	Tou Tunhe District	8.63	13.76	3.68	4.77	4.95	8.99
达坂城区	Da Bancheng District	9.73	14.99	3.58	3.88	6.15	11.11
米东区	Midong District	11.98	16.85	3.10	2.96	8.88	13.89
乌鲁木齐县	Urumqi County	15.17	19.52	3.60	4.32	11.57	15.20
克拉玛依市	**Karamay City**	**10.51**	**16.58**	**3.72**	**4.35**	**6.79**	**12.23**
独山子区	Dushanzi District	14.21	17.04	4.30	4.73	9.91	12.31
克拉玛依区	Karamay District	9.82	16.44	3.65	4.48	6.17	11.96
白碱滩区	Bai Jiantan District	8.46	16.20	3.31	3.33	5.15	12.87
乌尔河区	Urhe District	12.20	19.86	3.05	4.73	9.15	15.13
吐鲁番地区	**Turpan Administrative Offices**	**23.38**	**27.62**	**4.21**	**4.41**	**19.17**	**23.21**
吐鲁番市	Turpan City	27.58	31.86	4.01	3.88	23.57	27.98
鄯善县	Shanshan [Piqan] County	21.61	27.39	3.80	4.41	17.81	22.98
托克逊县	Toksun County	17.01	18.41	5.50	5.61	11.51	12.80
哈密地区	**Hami [Kumul] Administrative Offices**	**10.26**	**18.63**	**3.78**	**3.82**	**6.48**	**14.81**
哈密市	Hami [Kumul] City	9.66	18.20	3.55	3.90	6.11	14.30
巴里坤哈萨克自治县	Barkol Kazak Autonomous County	12.28	20.82	4.86	3.39	7.42	17.43
伊吾县	Yiwu [Araturuk] County	13.32	16.67	3.54	4.18	9.78	12.49
昌吉回族自治州	**Changji Hui Autonomous Prefecture**	**22.09**	**37.43**	**7.71**	**7.00**	**14.38**	**30.43**
昌吉市	Changji City	22.04	33.99	6.76	7.40	15.28	26.59
阜康市	Fukang City	22.69	37.70	8.45	7.38	14.01	30.32
呼图壁县	Hutubi County	22.46	39.82	8.44	6.76	14.04	33.06
玛纳斯县	Manas County	19.47	37.14	7.25	6.80	12.22	30.34
奇台县	Qitai County	22.73	40.72	8.46	6.28	14.27	34.44
吉木萨尔县	Jimsar County	22.54	36.89	7.42	6.42	15.12	30.47
木垒哈萨克自治县	Mori Kazak Autonomous County	22.96	38.21	7.70	8.05	15.26	30.16

3-6 续表 1 Continued

单位：‰ (‰)

地　区	Region	出生率 Birth Rate	#少数民族 Minority Nationalities	死亡率 Death Rate	#少数民族 Minority Nationalities	自然增长率 Natural Growth Rate	#少数民族 Minority Nationalities
伊犁哈萨克自治州	**Ili Kazak Autonomous Prefecture**	**16.50**	**22.42**	**4.13**	**4.17**	**12.37**	**18.25**
伊犁州直属县(市)	**Counties (Cities) Direct Under Ili Prefecture**	**18.36**	**24.20**	**3.99**	**3.74**	**14.37**	**20.46**
伊宁市	Yining [Gulja] City	19.18	24.70	3.76	3.79	15.42	20.91
奎屯市	Kuytun City	6.04	11.53	5.41	4.95	0.63	6.58
伊宁县	Yining [Gulja] County	21.81	24.40	3.04	2.57	18.77	21.83
察布查尔锡伯自治县	Qapqal Xibe Autonomous County	17.94	22.50	3.94	4.15	14.00	18.35
霍城县	Huocheng [Korgas] County	17.20	23.35	4.04	3.89	13.16	19.46
巩留县	Gongliu [Tokkuztara] County	21.48	23.81	3.49	3.29	17.99	20.52
新源县	Xinyuan [Kunes] County	20.23	26.74	4.74	5.06	15.49	21.68
昭苏县	Zhaosu [Mongolkure] County	19.23	23.17	4.03	4.32	15.20	18.85
特克斯县	Tekes County	20.36	23.41	3.17	3.22	17.19	20.19
尼勒克县	Nilka County	21.51	25.43	4.53	4.43	16.98	21.00
塔城地区	**Tacheng [Tarbagatai] Administrative Offices**	**12.28**	**17.66**	**4.41**	**5.56**	**7.87**	**12.10**
塔城市	Tacheng [Qoqek] City	10.27	14.50	3.71	4.08	6.56	10.42
乌苏市	Usu City	11.39	15.87	3.53	4.37	7.86	11.50
额敏县	Emin [Dorbiljin] County	13.45	19.36	4.27	4.92	9.18	14.44
沙湾县	Shawan County	11.06	19.51	2.99	3.64	8.07	15.87
托里县	Toli County	16.47	19.48	8.24	8.80	8.23	10.68
裕民县	Yumin [Qagantokay] County	13.55	18.47	9.04	13.20	4.51	5.27
和布克赛尔蒙古自治县	Hoboksar Mongol Autonomous County	13.34	14.56	4.46	4.77	8.87	9.79
阿勒泰地区	**Altay Administrative Offices**	**15.29**	**19.73**	**4.41**	**4.61**	**10.88**	**15.13**
阿勒泰市	Altay City	11.58	17.41	4.29	4.46	7.29	12.95
布尔津县	Burqin County	15.68	18.22	4.37	4.56	11.31	13.66
富蕴县	Fuyun [Koktokay] County	20.75	23.72	4.32	4.54	16.43	19.18
福海县	Fuhai [Burultokay] County	19.14	25.83	4.98	5.25	14.16	20.58
哈巴河县	Habahe [Kaba] County	15.20	18.39	4.31	4.57	10.89	13.82
青河县	Qinghe [Qinggil] County	19.90	22.11	4.38	4.25	15.52	17.86
吉木乃县	Jemnay County	10.21	11.05	4.81	5.49	5.40	5.56
博尔塔拉蒙古自治州	**Bortala Mongol Autonomous Prefecture**	**11.62**	**19.33**	**3.45**	**4.34**	**8.17**	**14.99**
博乐市	Bole [Bortala] City	11.26	18.10	2.66	2.99	8.60	15.11
精河县	Jinghe [Jing] County	12.10	21.89	4.57	5.59	7.53	16.30
温泉县	Wenquan [Araxang] County	12.01	18.97	4.23	6.86	7.78	12.11
巴音郭楞蒙古自治州	**Bayangol Mongol Autonomous Prefecture**	**13.70**	**18.32**	**4.16**	**4.37**	**9.54**	**13.95**
库尔勒市	Korla City	13.07	22.82	3.84	4.91	9.23	17.91
轮台县	Luntai [Bugur] County	22.32	24.01	6.19	7.07	16.13	16.94
尉犁县	Yuli [Lopnur] County	12.40	18.65	5.42	4.87	6.98	13.78
若羌县	Ruoqiang [Qarkilik] County	15.39	21.54	5.38	6.75	10.01	14.79
且末县	Qiemo [Qarqan] County	9.97	8.57	2.10	2.08	7.87	6.49
焉耆回族自治县	Yanji Hui Autonomous County	14.06	16.95	3.67	3.40	10.39	13.55
和静县	Hejing County	14.44	20.60	4.83	4.51	9.61	16.09
和硕县	Hoxud County	10.42	14.40	4.39	4.54	6.03	9.86
博湖县	Bohu [Bagrax] County	13.34	18.10	3.64	3.37	9.70	14.73

3-6 续表 2 Continued

单位：‰ (‰)

地　区	Region	出生率 Birth Rate	#少数民族 Minority Nationalities	死亡率 Death Rate	#少数民族 Minority Nationalities	自然增长率 Natural Growth Rate	#少数民族 Minority Nationalities
阿克苏地区	**Aksu Administrative Offices**	**19.12**	**20.95**	**5.69**	**6.29**	**12.43**	**14.66**
阿克苏市	Aksu City	16.18	20.37	4.41	5.77	11.77	14.60
温宿县	Wensu [Onsu] County	16.99	18.86	0.83	0.91	16.16	17.95
库车县	Kuqa County	16.92	17.29	7.11	7.49	9.81	9.80
沙雅县	Xayar County	36.10	39.95	12.45	13.31	23.65	26.64
新和县	Xinhe [Toksu] County	17.20	17.74	4.42	4.60	12.78	13.14
拜城县	Baicheng [Bay] County	19.85	20.82	8.24	8.92	11.61	11.90
乌什县	Wushi [Uxturpan] County	17.10	17.50	5.37	5.35	11.73	12.15
阿瓦提县	Awat County	16.78	18.41	2.62	2.51	14.16	15.90
柯坪县	Kalpin County	14.10	14.13	2.66	2.68	11.44	11.45
克孜勒苏柯尔克孜自治州	**Kizilsu Kirgiz Autonomous Prefecture**	**28.11**	**28.75**	**4.43**	**4.62**	**23.68**	**24.13**
阿图什市	Artux City	33.44	34.55	4.37	4.62	29.07	29.93
阿克陶县	Akto County	24.30	24.58	4.10	4.19	20.20	20.39
阿合奇县	Akqi County	21.91	22.40	4.97	5.24	16.94	17.16
乌恰县	Wuqia [Ulugqat] County	23.02	23.46	5.57	5.90	17.45	17.56
喀什地区	**Kashgar [Kaxgar] Administrative Offices**	**22.97**	**23.40**	**4.86**	**4.92**	**18.11**	**18.48**
喀什市	Kashgar [Kaxgar] City	26.19	28.49	5.37	5.32	20.82	23.17
疏附县	Shufu County	24.18	24.31	3.52	3.52	20.66	20.79
疏勒县	Shule County	23.66	24.67	4.60	4.71	19.06	19.96
英吉沙县	Yengisar County	36.74	37.05	3.50	3.53	33.24	33.52
泽普县	Zepu [Poskam] County	29.25	31.61	6.37	7.07	22.88	24.54
莎车县	Shache [Yarkant] County	13.41	13.33	5.18	5.24	8.23	8.09
叶城县	Yecheng [Kagilik] County	17.34	17.70	5.40	5.48	11.94	12.22
麦盖提县	Makit County	22.91	26.22	4.78	5.10	18.13	21.12
岳普湖县	Yopurga County	23.05	17.10	4.50	4.29	18.55	12.81
伽师县	Jiashi [Payzawat] County	25.26	25.45	4.37	4.40	20.89	21.05
巴楚县	Bachu [Maralbexi] County	28.38	28.69	5.21	5.33	23.17	23.36
塔什库尔干塔吉克自治县	Taxkorgan Tajik Autonomous County	18.46	18.98	3.74	3.95	14.72	15.03
和田地区	**Hotan Administrative Offices**	**23.52**	**24.16**	**4.45**	**4.57**	**19.07**	**19.59**
和田市	Hotan City	14.56	15.98	2.30	2.50	12.26	13.48
和田县	Hotan County	22.83	22.98	4.09	4.12	18.74	18.86
墨玉县	Moyu [Karakax] County	20.31	20.70	3.37	3.40	16.94	17.30
皮山县	Pishan [Guma] County	25.44	25.73	4.86	4.91	20.58	20.82
洛浦县	Lop County	28.69	29.07	4.57	4.64	24.12	24.43
策勒县	Qira County	28.32	28.52	8.30	8.43	20.02	20.09
于田县	Yutian [Keriya] County	32.48	32.75	6.64	6.77	25.84	25.98
民丰县	Minfeng [Niya] County	22.48	24.75	6.33	6.67	16.15	18.08
自治区直辖县级市	**Municpality Country-LevelCity dire-ctlyunder the Central overn-ment**						
石河子市	Shihezi City	5.73	12.43	4.66	4.13	1.07	8.30
阿拉尔市	Aral City	8.62	11.23	2.95	1.60	5.67	9.63
图木舒克市	Tumxuk City	10.79	10.64	4.60	6.03	6.19	4.61
五家渠市	Wujiaqu City	7.00	15.90	5.90	4.00	1.10	11.90

3-7 各地、州、市、县(市)分民族人口数

单位：人 (2013 年)

地 区	Region	合 计 Total	#少数民族 Minority Nationalities	维吾尔族 Uygur	汉 族 Han	哈萨克族 Kazak
乌鲁木齐市	**Urumqi City**	**2629300**	**715497**	**332734**	**1913803**	**68045**
天山区	Tianshan District	586068	225928	149775	360140	14448
沙依巴克区	Shayibak District	550533	128492	69911	422041	8457
新市区	Xinshi District	596875	106023	44938	490852	4920
水磨沟区	Shui Mogou Distric	284745	47379	28984	237366	2956
头屯河区	Tou Tunhe District	230600	52136	25044	178464	2410
达坂城区	Da Bancheng District	42075	23225	2757	18850	6638
米东区	Midong District	276712	93042	10447	183670	4553
乌鲁木齐县	Urumqi County	61692	39272	878	22420	23663
克拉玛依市	**Karamay City**	**290144**	**73471**	**45307**	**216673**	**11944**
独山子区	Dushanzi District	57225	15168	9291	42057	2583
克拉玛依区	Karamay District	189978	45805	27920	144173	7552
白碱滩区	Bai Jiantan District	40642	11432	7724	29210	1740
乌尔河区	Urhe District	2299	1066	372	1233	69
吐鲁番地区	**Turpan Administrative Offices**	**642910**	**501392**	**461000**	**141518**	**307**
吐鲁番市	Turpan City	283979	231722	211156	52257	25
鄯善县	Shanshan [Piqan] County	238588	168480	156744	70108	37
托克逊县	Toksun County	120343	101190	93100	19153	245
哈密地区	**Hami [Kumul] Administrative Offices**	**608369**	**193067**	**110278**	**415302**	**56739**
哈密市	Hami [Kumul] City	480229	138173	100536	342056	14720
巴里坤哈萨克自治县	Barkol Kazak Autonomous County	105063	39925	153	65138	37573
伊吾县	Yiwu [Araturuk] County	23077	14969	9589	8108	4446
昌吉回族自治州	**Changji Hui Autonomous Prefecture**	**1405038**	**381606**	**67047**	**1023432**	**145042**
昌吉市	Changji City	367638	101038	11267	266600	19707
阜康市	Fukang City	169227	49607	10596	119620	14945
呼图壁县	Hutubi County	218722	52938	6418	165784	26574
玛纳斯县	Manas County	175759	34681	6060	141078	19478
奇台县	Qitai County	242002	65624	19845	176378	27183
吉木萨尔县	Jimsar County	141789	45163	7768	96626	12084
木垒哈萨克自治县	Mori Kazak Autonomous County	89901	32555	5093	57346	25071

Population of Major Nationalities by Prefecture, Autonomous Prefecture, City and County

(person)

回　族 Hui	柯尔克孜族 Kirgiz	蒙古族 Mongolian	锡伯族 Xibo	俄罗斯族 Russion	塔吉克族 Tajik	乌孜别克族 Uzbek	塔塔尔族 Tatar	满　族 Manchu	达斡尔族 Daur	其　它 Others
267943	**2320**	**10582**	**5720**	**3708**	**257**	**2151**	**1084**	**10919**	**629**	**9405**
47582	1214	3340	1848	1195	120	1287	621	2532	190	1776
39078	447	2632	1353	979	45	410	188	2664	153	2175
45939	396	2187	1364	805	52	250	126	2887	169	1990
11458	111	982	513	319	16	94	35	1057	44	810
21102	65	662	496	178	19	46	14	1009	32	1059
13547	15	31	4	10	2	1	5	88	2	125
74933	34	621	135	221	3	11	24	665	35	1360
14304	38	127	7	1		52	71	17	4	110
7101	**145**	**2716**	**966**	**630**	**30**	**317**	**97**	**1275**	**148**	**2795**
1601	11	494	149	156	3	78	8	292	26	476
4637	93	1355	702	422	23	202	61	818	108	1912
847	41	267	110	52	4	37	27	165	14	404
16		600	5				1			3
38360	**1**	**223**	**27**	**57**		**23**	**5**	**295**	**5**	**1089**
19555		118	19	39		5	2	146	5	652
11122		88	4	15		18	3	113		336
7683	1	17	4	3				36		101
18983	**30**	**2786**	**176**	**103**		**11**	**30**	**1830**	**12**	**2089**
17788	27	1181	167	84		8	5	1771	12	1874
342	3	1595	9	19		1	25	54		151
853		10				2		5		64
145600	**176**	**6926**	**641**	**747**	**4**	**2405**	**911**	**3262**	**67**	**8778**
63247	105	1601	398	321	4	156	100	1342	36	2754
21578	16	421	70	109		41	57	222	9	1543
17346	3	329	42	100		3	31	176	2	1914
7732	35	129	28	109		20	8	168	12	902
13604	8	1788	74	75		658	458	1193	5	733
21151	6	2630	21	21		493	165	119	3	702
942	3	28	8	12		1034	92	42		230

3-7 续表 1

单位：人

地 区	Region	合 计 Total	#少数民族 Minority Nationalities	维吾尔族 Uygur	汉 族 Han	哈萨克族 Kazak
伊犁哈萨克自治州	**Ili Kazak Autonomous Prefecture**	**4715666**	**2737118**	**807433**	**1978548**	**1247831**
伊犁州直属县(市)	**Counties (Cities) Direct Under Ili Prefecture**	**2985294**	**1883148**	**755043**	**1102146**	**628718**
伊宁市	Yining [Gulja] City	535668	342797	258913	192871	25375
奎屯市	Kuytun City	301498	16053	977	285445	5249
伊宁县	Yining [Gulja] County	448498	374914	207495	73584	55728
察布查尔锡伯自治县	Qapqal Xibe Autonomous County	197890	130857	55767	67033	40305
霍城县	Huocheng [Korgas] County	412888	242355	92175	170533	36909
巩留县	Gongliu [Tokkuztara] County	208072	149431	45422	58641	62066
新源县	Xinyuan [Kunes] County	325212	208111	33157	117101	147707
昭苏县	Zhaosu [Mongolkure] County	191161	139402	18949	51759	93638
特克斯县	Tekes County	174528	137984	19856	36544	74752
尼勒克县	Nilka County	189879	141244	22332	48635	86989
塔城地区	**Tacheng [Tarbagatai] Administrative Offices**	**1059881**	**457583**	**42767**	**602298**	**270687**
塔城市	Tacheng [Qoqek] City	171917	64478	5226	107439	27809
乌苏市	Usu City	231401	84989	17227	146412	22937
额敏县	Emin [Dorbiljin] County	221342	103758	8266	117584	78027
沙湾县	Shawan County	218785	71530	9530	147255	37457
托里县	Toli County	101960	73847	1237	28113	70643
裕民县	Yumin [Qagantokay] County	59759	24175	179	35584	18539
和布克赛尔蒙古自治县	Hoboksar Mongol Autonomous County	54717	34806	1102	19911	15275
阿勒泰地区	**Altay Administrative Offices**	**670491**	**396387**	**9623**	**274104**	**348426**
阿勒泰市	Altay City	234233	96166	5000	138067	78868
布尔津县	Burqin County	72225	50538	1014	21687	41414
富蕴县	Fuyun [Koktokay] County	96675	75455	1956	21220	70531
福海县	Fuhai [Burultokay] County	75651	34796	530	40855	30734
哈巴河县	Habahe [Kaba] County	88074	61701	349	26373	53571
青河县	Qinghe [Qinggil] County	64495	52506	576	11989	49199
吉木乃县	Jemnay County	39138	25225	198	13913	24109
博尔塔拉蒙古自治州	**Bortala Mongol Autonomous Prefecture**	**490392**	**168848**	**66348**	**321544**	**48911**
博乐市	Bole [Bortala] City	271315	90292	43777	181023	20696
精河县	Jinghe [Jing] County	143763	46302	19033	97461	13845
温泉县	Wenquan [Araxang] County	75314	32254	3538	43060	14370
巴音郭楞蒙古自治州	**Bayangol Mongol Autonomous Prefecture**	**1404151**	**607246**	**470650**	**796905**	**1397**
库尔勒市	Korla City	568571	166908	143461	401663	177
轮台县	Luntai [Bugur] County	119449	97478	96842	21971	7
尉犁县	Yuli [Lopnur] County	111327	36625	35510	74702	15
若羌县	Ruoqiang [Qarkilik] County	35030	14972	13268	20058	5
且末县	Qiemo [Qarqan] County	70965	50549	50167	20416	3
焉耆回族自治县	Yanji Hui Autonomous County	160976	95007	54278	65969	38
和静县	Hejing County	198493	96126	54003	102367	1098
和硕县	Hoxud County	77510	27502	12909	50008	37
博湖县	Bohu [Bagrax] County	61830	22079	10212	39751	17

Continued

(person)

回 族 Hui	柯尔克孜族 Kirgiz	蒙古族 Mongolian	锡伯族 Xibo	俄罗斯族 Russion	塔吉克族 Tajik	乌孜别克族 Uzbek	塔塔尔族 Tatar	满 族 Manchu	达斡尔族 Daur	其 它 Others
431155	**22088**	**76733**	**34723**	**5505**	**147**	**8014**	**2833**	**5198**	**5899**	**89559**
322896	**19842**	**35414**	**32633**	**1582**	**141**	**7427**	**1288**	**4006**	**518**	**73640**
38893	671	2029	5058	805	87	4474	525	2106	61	3800
6637	27	1082	267	93	3	15	5	438	36	1224
74868	370	298	266	29	10	744	63	364	6	34673
10835	309	177	20697	101		136	11	108	17	2394
87123	308	786	3280	246	4	221	119	343	340	20501
32181	472	2790	1605	117	1	174	113	289	6	4195
23044	468	176	422	95	6	720	145	151	6	2014
5363	5622	14254	90	40	4	395	281	38	1	727
24455	10874	4708	264	5	19	286	19	79	3	2664
19497	721	9114	684	51	7	262	7	90	42	1448
83629	**2189**	**34842**	**2000**	**3502**	**5**	**405**	**500**	**837**	**5365**	**10855**
13642	1822	1819	1550	2391	1	163	249	242	5177	4387
34732	5	8169	150	136	1	55	29	134	32	1382
7596	306	6251	88	564		121	63	155	62	2259
22156	11	494	41	123	2	21	20	190	23	1462
1095	19	520	59	17	1	23	43	50	6	134
3895	6	155	56	236			9	27	42	1031
513	20	17434	56	35		22	87	39	23	200
24630	**57**	**6477**	**90**	**421**	**1**	**182**	**1045**	**355**	**16**	**5064**
6989	31	2889	41	191	1	124	316	189	5	1522
4687	5	1681	12	141		4	336	45	2	1197
2003	13	308	11	38		14	89	39	4	449
2656		212	8	33			51	34	3	535
6254	5	455	7			11	48	8		993
1322		903	9	11		29	195	10		252
719	3	29	2	7			10	30	2	116
20149	**86**	**28580**	**416**	**198**	**4**	**171**	**19**	**375**	**29**	**3562**
10458	32	13151	296	155	4	103	14	279	13	1314
6504	26	5149	62	40		41	4	66		1532
3187	28	10280	58	3		27	1	30	16	716
71910	**238**	**52145**	**218**	**264**	**5**	**144**	**3**	**1374**	**28**	**8870**
12635	10	5689	187	231	4	80	2	1068	19	3345
383	1	51	5	3		5		24		157
558		36	2	9		15		38	5	437
1198		28	2					7		464
196		23	2		1	10		4		143
35758	104	3803	3	1		26	1	75	1	919
7319	110	31411	12	12		8		100	3	2050
7152	2	6620	3	8				28		743
6711	11	4484	2					30		612

3-7 续表 2

单位：人

地　　区	Region	合　计 Total	#少数民族 Minority Nationalities	维吾尔族 Uygur	汉　族 Han	哈萨克族 Kazak
阿克苏地区	**Aksu Administrative Offices**	**2457547**	**1980573**	**1946752**	**476974**	**168**
阿克苏市	Aksu City	509235	273915	265196	235320	44
温宿县	Wensu [Onsu] County	254080	199414	192958	54666	12
库车县	Kuqa County	481427	432198	428853	49229	57
沙雅县	Xayar County	268749	227708	224855	41041	6
新和县	Xinhe [Toksu] County	178452	167441	166850	11011	11
拜城县	Baicheng [Bay] County	238061	209614	207319	28447	20
乌什县	Wushi [Uxturpan] County	221088	209039	201722	12049	10
阿瓦提县	Awat County	253336	209667	207532	43669	7
柯坪县	Kalpin County	53119	51577	51467	1542	1
克孜勒苏柯尔克孜自治州	**Kizilsu Kirgiz Autonomous Prefecture**	**576168**	**533295**	**371716**	**42873**	**160**
阿图什市	Artux City	236144	213161	209369	22983	62
阿克陶县	Akto County	209526	201128	151217	8398	23
阿合奇县	Akqi County	43550	39175	1189	4375	37
乌恰县	Wuqia [Ulugqat] County	59948	52831	9941	7117	38
喀什地区	**Kashgar [Kaxgar] Administrative Offices**	**4228237**	**3934033**	**3869801**	**294204**	**278**
喀什市	Kashgar [Kaxgar] City	571045	484998	480216	86047	148
疏附县	Shufu County	270631	265207	264374	5424	7
疏勒县	Shule County	351633	326905	325922	24728	2
英吉沙县	Yengisar County	295209	290343	289524	4866	20
泽普县	Zepu [Poskam] County	215268	178810	172473	36458	12
莎车县	Shache [Yarkant] County	798650	770859	763511	27791	12
叶城县	Yecheng [Kagilik] County	481060	457664	451991	23396	34
麦盖提县	Makit County	265775	217932	216692	47843	5
岳普湖县	Yopurga County	164984	157093	156827	7891	3
伽师县	Jiashi [Payzawat] County	422532	412883	412419	9649	17
巴楚县	Bachu [Maralbexi] County	351821	334501	333704	17320	4
塔什库尔干塔吉克自治县	Taxkorgan Tajik Autonomous County	39629	36838	2148	2791	14
和田地区	**Hotan Administrative Offices**	**2154462**	**2071360**	**2066215**	**83102**	**94**
和田市	Hotan City	331499	290376	288669	41123	36
和田县	Hotan County	285809	283882	283543	1927	1
墨玉县	Moyu [Karakax] County	543268	524018	523751	19250	3
皮山县	Pishan [Guma] County	275267	271224	269064	4043	1
洛浦县	Lop County	258391	253247	253063	5144	31
策勒县	Qira County	159622	156576	156576	2936	2
于田县	Yutian [Keriya] County	262281	257284	256984	4997	18
民丰县	Minfeng [Niya] County	38325	34643	34565	3682	2
自治区直辖县级市	**Municpality Country-LevelCity directly under the Central Govern-ment**	**1063882**	**168164**	**128796**	**895718**	**4449**
石河子市	Shihezi City	622594	37977	8453	584617	4225
阿拉尔市	Aral City	186144	18301	12756	167843	118
图木舒克市	Tumxuk City	164138	108643	107510	55495	1
五家渠市	Wujiaqu City	91006	3243	77	87763	105

Continued

(person)

回 族 Hui	柯尔克孜族 Kirgiz	蒙古族 Mongolian	锡伯族 Xibo	俄罗斯族 Russion	塔吉克族 Tajik	乌孜别克族 Uzbek	塔塔尔族 Tatar	满 族 Manchu	达斡尔族 Daur	其 它 Others
14458	**11315**	**889**	**150**	**130**	**7**	**202**	**10**	**600**	**1**	**5891**
4938	223	612	78	63		40		352		2369
832	4155	41	6	2	3	2		14		1389
2477	150	86	31	25	2	44	1	110	1	361
2258	11	25	7	21		6		35		484
338	7	14	5	12			2	43		159
908	1165	33	12		2	12	1	24		118
1454	5558	13	8			76	2	6		190
1229	17	56	2	7		22	4	16		775
24	29	9	1							46
721	**154141**	**94**	**33**	**6**	**5667**	**175**	**29**	**96**		**457**
304	29954	54	15	6	27	17	1	78		274
202	43847	22	6		5599	103	28	2		79
87	37820	3	2		3			5		29
128	42520	15	10		38	55		11		75
6466	**6875**	**774**	**152**	**123**	**41842**	**4491**	**78**	**595**	**14**	**2544**
1593	346	176	64	88	176	1272	33	282	8	596
71	632	8	2		5	10		1	1	96
335	364	108	4	2	1	13	2	32		120
89	603	21	4	4	21	23		24	2	8
1051	148	134	10	11	4351	149	1	65		405
1005	1198	97	39	6	2832	1788	36	47	1	287
838	1230	53	8	7	2160	1083	2	42		216
710	5	43	1	1	6	50	1	29		389
106		57	2		2			4		92
72	46	42	6	1		67	3	36		174
572	4	28	6	2	1	36		25	2	117
24	2299	7	6	1	32287			8		44
2053	**943**	**213**	**58**	**8**	**1035**	**50**	**10**	**83**	**1**	**597**
1185	23	113	26	8	7	33	5	42		229
332		1								5
148	1	8	3			6		10		88
102	914	21	12		1023	7			1	79
55		27	2					6		63
50		6	3		1	1		2		45
149	4	28	12		4			23		62
32	1	9				3	5			26
20842	**185**	**1631**	**187**	**313**	**24**	**48**	**1**	**1216**	**13**	**10459**
17540	132	848	156	241	20	17	1	926	11	5407
956	52	250	8	16	4	1		63		4077
513		57	2	5		29		33		493
1833	1	476	21	51		1		194	2	482

3-8 主要年份分民族人口数
Population by Nationality in Main Years

单位：万人 (10 000 persons)

年 份 Year	维吾尔族 Uygur	汉 族 Han	哈萨克族 Kazak	回 族 Hui	柯尔克孜族 Kirgiz	蒙古族 Mongolian	锡伯族 Xibo
1978	555.53	512.90	82.10	53.12	10.40	10.74	2.55
1980	576.46	531.03	87.68	56.56	10.89	11.32	2.59
1985	629.44	534.92	98.72	59.96	12.35	12.33	2.93
1990	724.95	574.66	113.92	68.89	14.44	14.28	3.42
1995	780.00	631.81	123.77	74.76	15.78	15.28	3.82
1996	791.60	643.28	125.70	76.02	16.05	15.54	3.89
1997	802.00	660.13	127.08	77.06	16.27	15.75	3.90
1998	813.95	674.11	128.70	78.20	16.41	15.91	3.95
1999	825.03	687.15	130.45	79.26	16.64	16.13	4.00
2000	852.33	725.08	131.87	83.93	16.47	16.20	4.05
2001	860.56	742.20	131.92	84.42	17.01	16.19	4.13
2002	869.23	759.57	133.35	85.46	17.13	16.38	4.10
2003	882.35	771.10	135.21	86.67	17.37	16.69	4.03
2004	897.67	780.25	138.16	87.63	17.12	16.96	4.08
2005	923.50	795.66	141.39	89.35	17.15	17.17	4.15
2006	941.38	812.16	143.50	90.96	17.59	17.46	4.19
2007	965.06	823.93	148.39	94.30	18.19	17.71	4.24
2008	983.18	836.33	151.05	95.30	18.64	18.10	4.32
2009	1001.98	841.69	151.48	98.04	18.93	17.96	4.28
2010	1017.15	832.29	151.16	98.40	18.92	17.74	4.23
2011	1037.04	844.42	154.26	100.34	19.40	17.89	4.27
2012	1052.86	847.29	155.75	102.31	19.44	18.08	4.29
2013	1074.41	860.06	158.54	104.57	19.85	18.43	4.35

年 份 Year	俄罗斯族 Russian	塔吉克族 Tajik	乌孜别克族 Uzbek	塔塔尔族 Tatar	满 族 Manchu	达斡尔族 Daur	其他民族 Others
1978	0.06	2.28	0.77	0.31	0.42	0.41	1.42
1980	0.06	2.41	0.79	0.31	0.50	0.40	2.24
1985	0.43	2.89	0.93	0.33	0.95	0.48	4.49
1990	0.75	3.44	1.14	0.40	1.66	0.56	6.65
1995	0.90	3.82	1.33	0.47	1.99	0.62	7.00
1996	0.92	3.89	1.35	0.47	2.05	0.63	7.90
1997	0.92	3.90	1.35	0.46	2.06	0.63	6.56
1998	0.93	3.96	1.37	0.47	2.09	0.64	6.66
1999	0.94	4.01	1.39	0.48	2.12	0.65	6.75
2000	1.09	4.09	1.36	0.48	2.31	0.66	9.48
2001	1.08	4.12	1.37	0.47	2.30	0.67	9.75
2002	1.12	4.07	1.39	0.48	2.35	0.67	9.89
2003	1.11	4.09	1.46	0.49	2.39	0.67	10.32
2004	1.13	4.35	1.42	0.47	2.41	0.67	10.79
2005	1.12	4.40	1.51	0.47	2.46	0.65	11.37
2006	1.14	4.47	1.60	0.47	2.52	0.66	11.91
2007	1.16	4.48	1.61	0.47	2.56	0.67	12.42
2008	1.16	4.54	1.69	0.49	2.59	0.68	12.74
2009	1.17	4.72	1.67	0.49	2.62	0.69	12.91
2010	1.16	4.69	1.70	0.49	2.61	0.67	13.23
2011	1.16	4.73	1.74	0.49	2.64	0.69	13.59
2012	1.17	4.86	1.77	0.50	2.66	0.68	14.39
2013	1.18	4.90	1.82	0.51	2.71	0.68	14.61

3-9 各地、州、市、县(市)按城镇、乡村和农业、非农业分人口数

Population of Urban and Rural, Agriculture and Non-Agriculture by Prefecture, Autonomous Prefecture, City and County

单位：万人 (2013 年) (10 000 persons)

地　区	Region	城镇人口 Urban Population	#非农业人口 Non-agri-cultural Population	乡村人口 Rural Population	农业人口 Agricul-tural Population	非农业人口 Non-agri-cultural Population
乌鲁木齐市	**Urumqi City**	**256.68**	**189.54**	**6.25**	**72.42**	**190.51**
天山区	Tianshan District	58.61	47.47		11.14	47.47
沙依巴克区	Shayibak District	55.05	46.52		8.53	46.52
新市区	Xinshi District	59.69	39.57		20.12	39.57
水磨沟区	Shui Mogou Distric	28.47	20.25		8.22	20.25
头屯河区	Tou Tunhe District	23.06	18.45		4.61	18.45
达坂城区	Da Bancheng District	3.21	1.65	1.00	2.45	1.76
米东区	Midong District	27.16	15.10	0.51	12.49	15.18
乌鲁木齐县	Urumqi County	1.43	0.53	4.74	4.86	1.31
克拉玛依市	**Karamay City**	**29.02**	**28.65**		**0.37**	**28.65**
独山子区	Dushanzi District	5.72	5.72			5.72
克拉玛依区	Karamay District	19.00	18.81		0.19	18.81
白碱滩区	Bai Jiantan District	4.07	4.05		0.02	4.05
乌尔河区	Urhe District	0.23	0.07		0.16	0.07
吐鲁番地区	**Turpan Administrative Offices**	**46.38**	**15.94**	**17.91**	**46.14**	**18.15**
吐鲁番市	Turpan City	28.40	8.44		19.96	8.44
鄯善县	Shanshan [Piqan] County	15.42	5.18	8.44	17.76	6.10
托克逊县	Toksun County	2.56	2.32	9.47	8.42	3.61
哈密地区	**Hami [Kumul] Administrative Offices**	**53.89**	**32.29**	**6.95**	**26.57**	**34.27**
哈密市	Hami [Kumul] City	48.02	29.98		18.04	29.98
巴里坤哈萨克自治县	Barkol Kazak Autonomous County	4.81	1.62	5.70	7.17	3.34
伊吾县	Yiwu [Araturuk] County	1.06	0.69	1.25	1.36	0.95
昌吉回族自治州	**Changji Hui Autonomous Prefecture**	**121.24**	**67.33**	**19.26**	**71.32**	**69.18**
昌吉市	Changji City	36.76	23.65		13.11	23.65
阜康市	Fukang City	16.92	9.65		7.27	9.65
呼图壁县	Hutubi County	20.34	11.75	1.53	9.43	12.44
玛纳斯县	Manas County	15.23	7.25	2.35	10.06	7.52
奇台县	Qitai County	16.33	8.57	7.87	15.28	8.92
吉木萨尔县	Jimsar County	11.72	4.54	2.46	9.52	4.66
木垒哈萨克自治县	Mori Kazak Autonomous County	3.94	1.92	5.05	6.65	2.34

注：1.各地、州、市城镇人口、乡村人口为 2013 年公安年报按行政建制划分的人口数。
　　2.各地、州、市农业人口数均含未落常住户口人员。

Note: a) Population of urban and rural by prefecture,Autonomous prefecture,city and county come from Annual Report on Public Security in 2013
　　b) Population of agriculture by Prefecture,Autonomous prefecture,city and county included population of without habitual residence.

3-9 续表 1 Continued

单位：万人 (10 000 persons)

地 区	Region	城镇人口 Urban Population	#非农业人口 Non-agri-cultural Population	乡村人口 Rural Population	农业人口 Agricul-tural Population	非农业人口 Non-agri-cultural Population
伊犁哈萨克自治州	**Ili Kazak Autonomous Prefecture**	**284.34**	**176.41**	**187.23**	**260.70**	**210.87**
伊犁州直属县(市)	**Counties (Cities) Direct Under Ili Prefecture**	**166.25**	**100.57**	**132.28**	**176.61**	**121.92**
伊宁市	Yining [Gulja] City	53.57	35.45		18.12	35.45
奎屯市	Kuytun City	30.15	27.26		2.89	27.26
伊宁县	Yining [Gulja] County	9.38	4.75	35.47	37.85	7.00
察布查尔锡伯自治县	Qapqal Xibe Autonomous County	6.58	4.88	13.21	13.23	6.56
霍城县	Huocheng [Korgas] County	21.84	5.88	19.45	26.11	15.18
巩留县	Gongliu [Tokkuztara] County	4.01	3.08	16.79	16.46	4.34
新源县	Xinyuan [Kunes] County	27.51	7.95	5.01	23.55	8.97
昭苏县	Zhaosu [Mongolkure] County	4.78	4.92	14.34	11.93	7.19
特克斯县	Tekes County	4.26	3.14	13.19	12.55	4.90
尼勒克县	Nilka County	4.17	3.26	14.82	13.92	5.07
塔城地区	**Tacheng [Tarbagatai] Administrative Offices**	**79.84**	**48.27**	**26.15**	**50.25**	**55.74**
塔城市	Tacheng [Qoqek] City	17.19	10.86		6.33	10.86
乌苏市	Usu City	23.14	8.14		15.00	8.14
额敏县	Emin [Dorbiljin] County	11.72	9.39	10.42	8.93	13.21
沙湾县	Shawan County	18.73	12.44	3.15	8.34	13.54
托里县	Toli County	4.53	3.44	5.66	6.19	4.00
裕民县	Yumin [Qagantokay] County	2.03	1.97	3.95	3.03	2.95
和布克赛尔蒙古自治县	Hoboksar Mongol Autonomous County	2.50	2.03	2.97	2.43	3.04
阿勒泰地区	**Altay Administrative Offices**	**38.25**	**27.57**	**28.80**	**33.84**	**33.21**
阿勒泰市	Altay City	23.42	15.14		8.28	15.14
布尔津县	Burqin County	3.31	2.18	3.91	4.47	2.75
富蕴县	Fuyun [Koktokay] County	3.29	2.89	6.38	5.71	3.96
福海县	Fuhai [Burultokay] County	2.93	2.80	4.64	3.65	3.92
哈巴河县	Habahe [Kaba] County	1.93	1.80	6.88	5.74	3.07
青河县	Qinghe [Qinggil] County	1.98	1.56	4.47	4.08	2.37
吉木乃县	Jemnay County	1.39	1.20	2.52	1.91	2.00
博尔塔拉蒙古自治州	**Bortala Mongol Autonomous Prefecture**	**39.38**	**24.37**	**9.66**	**22.15**	**26.89**
博乐市	Bole [Bortala] City	27.13	16.73		10.40	16.73
精河县	Jinghe [Jing] County	7.80	4.49	6.58	7.99	6.39
温泉县	Wenquan [Araxang] County	4.45	3.15	3.08	3.76	3.77
巴音郭楞蒙古自治州	**Bayangol Mongol Autonomous Prefecture**	**110.77**	**64.02**	**29.65**	**72.78**	**67.64**
库尔勒市	Korla City	56.86	35.41		21.45	35.41
轮台县	Luntai [Bugur] County	7.23	2.48	4.72	9.01	2.94
尉犁县	Yuli [Lopnur] County	6.23	4.90	4.90	5.61	5.52
若羌县	Ruoqiang [Qarkilik] County	2.42	1.46	1.08	1.81	1.69
且末县	Qiemo [Qarqan] County	1.93	1.62	5.17	4.79	2.31
焉耆回族自治县	Yanji Hui Autonomous County	11.18	5.73	4.92	9.77	6.33
和静县	Hejing County	17.56	8.02	2.29	11.47	8.38
和硕县	Hoxud County	4.15	2.72	3.60	4.59	3.16
博湖县	Bohu [Bagrax] County	3.21	1.68	2.97	4.28	1.90

3-9 续表 2 Continued

单位：万人 (10 000 persons)

地　　区	Region	城　镇人　口 Urban Population	#非农业人　口 Non-agri-cultural Population	乡　村人　口 Rural Population	农　业人　口 Agricul-tural Population	非农业人　口 Non-agri-cultural Population
阿克苏地区	**Aksu Administrative Offices**	**157.65**	**71.11**	**88.11**	**167.59**	**78.17**
阿克苏市	Aksu City	50.92	27.75		23.17	27.75
温宿县	Wensu [Onsu] County	16.87	6.28	8.54	18.04	7.37
库车县	Kuqa County	34.49	15.67	13.65	31.00	17.14
沙雅县	Xayar County	18.55	5.50	8.33	21.03	5.85
新和县	Xinhe [Toksu] County	5.51	2.79	12.34	14.26	3.59
拜城县	Baicheng [Bay] County	8.48	4.40	15.33	18.42	5.39
乌什县	Wushi [Uxturpan] County	7.81	3.16	14.30	18.36	3.75
阿瓦提县	Awat County	14.04	4.74	11.29	19.64	5.69
柯坪县	Kalpin County	0.98	0.82	4.33	3.67	1.64
克孜勒苏柯尔克孜自治州	**Kizilsu Kirgiz Autonomous Prefecture**	**33.98**	**14.86**	**23.64**	**39.98**	**17.64**
阿图什市	Artux City	26.32	9.23		17.09	9.23
阿克陶县	Akto County	4.43	2.42	16.52	17.23	3.72
阿合奇县	Akqi County	1.29	1.27	3.07	2.43	1.93
乌恰县	Wuqia [Ulugqat] County	1.94	1.94	4.05	3.23	2.76
喀什地区	**Kashgar [Kaxgar] Administrative Offices**	**160.31**	**82.22**	**262.51**	**326.57**	**96.25**
喀什市	Kashgar [Kaxgar] City	57.11	30.19		26.92	30.19
疏附县	Shufu County	3.21	2.03	23.85	23.87	3.19
疏勒县	Shule County	10.69	3.11	24.47	30.76	4.40
英吉沙县	Yengisar County	4.17	3.20	25.35	25.16	4.36
泽普县	Zepu [Poskam] County	5.95	4.97	15.58	15.22	6.31
莎车县	Shache [Yarkant] County	33.42	11.24	46.45	66.54	13.33
叶城县	Yecheng [Kagilik] County	12.30	7.85	35.81	38.93	9.18
麦盖提县	Makit County	7.20	6.63	19.38	18.43	8.15
岳普湖县	Yopurga County	6.46	2.72	10.03	12.93	3.56
伽师县	Jiashi [Payzawat] County	4.92	3.24	37.33	37.40	4.85
巴楚县	Bachu [Maralbexi] County	13.35	5.83	21.83	27.66	7.52
塔什库尔干塔吉克自治县	Taxkorgan Tajik Autonomous County	1.53	1.21	2.43	2.75	1.21
和田地区	**Hotan Administrative Offices**	**75.74**	**29.17**	**139.71**	**178.19**	**37.26**
和田市	Hotan City	33.15	14.34		18.81	14.34
和田县	Hotan County	5.94	0.42	22.64	27.13	1.45
墨玉县	Moyu [Karakax] County	12.95	3.54	41.38	49.06	5.27
皮山县	Pishan [Guma] County	7.78	4.28	19.75	21.52	6.01
洛浦县	Lop County	4.31	1.94	21.53	22.74	3.10
策勒县	Qira County	3.01	1.53	12.95	13.53	2.43
于田县	Yutian [Keriya] County	7.05	2.29	19.18	22.71	3.52
民丰县	Minfeng [Niya] County	1.55	0.83	2.28	2.69	1.14
自治区直辖县级市	**Municpality Country-LevelCity directly under the Central Govern-ment**	**106.38**	**89.94**		**16.44**	**89.94**
石河子市	Shihezi City	62.26	58.01		4.25	58.01
阿拉尔市	Aral City	18.61	9.68		8.93	9.68
图木舒克市	Tumxuk City	16.41	13.65		2.76	13.65
五家渠市	Wujiaqu City	9.10	8.60		0.50	8.60

3-10 各地、州、市采取各种避孕措施情况

Condition of Adopting Various Contraceptives by Prefecture, Autonomous Prefecture, City and County

单位：% (2013 年) (%)

地 区	Region	男性绝育 Masculine Sterilization	女性绝育 Female Sterilization	宫内节育器 IUD Intrauterine Device	皮下埋植 Subdermal Implant
总 计	**Total**	**0.15**	**4.58**	**79.70**	**0.27**
城 镇	Urban	0.12	2.57	75.30	0.19
农 村	Rural	0.17	5.66	82.05	0.31
乌鲁木齐市	Urumqi City	0.12	2.53	51.52	0.25
克拉玛依市	Karamay City	0.37	4.50	59.87	0.39
吐鲁番地区	Turpan Administrative Offices	0.05	1.74	88.06	0.36
哈密地区	Hami [Kumul] Administrative Offices	0.07	3.66	75.41	0.45
昌吉回族自治州	Changji Hui Autonomous Prefecture	0.14	5.12	77.99	0.33
伊犁州直属县(市)	Counties (Cities) Direct Under Ili Prefecture	0.13	3.73	79.15	0.15
塔城地区	Tacheng [Tarbagatai] Administrative Offices	0.23	6.30	79.36	0.93
阿勒泰地区	Altay Administrative Offices	0.09	2.72	77.11	0.41
博尔塔拉蒙古自治州	Bortala Mongol Autonomous Prefecture	0.41	6.94	72.41	0.56
巴音郭楞蒙古自治州	Bayangol Mongol Autonomous Prefecture	0.59	6.25	81.67	0.10
阿克苏地区	Aksu Administrative Offices	0.16	6.29	86.43	0.49
克孜勒苏柯尔克孜自治州	Kizilsu Kirgiz Autonomous Prefecture		2.12	90.98	0.11
喀什地区	Kashgar [Kaxgar] Administrative Offices	0.05	3.34	92.84	0.15
和田地区	Hotan Administrative Offices	0.04	8.39	87.99	0.01

地 区	Region	口服药及注射针 Medicine and Entry Needle	避孕套 Contraceptives	外用药 Drug for Exterior Use	其 他 Other
总 计	**Total**	**0.36**	**14.26**	**0.64**	**0.03**
城 镇	Urban	0.41	21.09	0.27	0.05
农 村	Rural	0.33	10.61	0.84	0.02
乌鲁木齐市	Urumqi City	0.67	44.63	0.19	0.10
克拉玛依市	Karamay City	0.49	34.04	0.34	
吐鲁番地区	Turpan Administrative Offices	0.50	8.99	0.29	0.01
哈密地区	Hami [Kumul] Administrative Offices	0.30	20.02	0.07	0.01
昌吉回族自治州	Changji Hui Autonomous Prefecture	0.30	16.00	0.11	0.02
伊犁州直属县(市)	Counties (Cities) Direct Under Ili Prefecture	0.28	16.31	0.15	0.08
塔城地区	Tacheng [Tarbagatai] Administrative Offices	0.25	12.88	0.06	
阿勒泰地区	Altay Administrative Offices	0.20	19.39	0.08	
博尔塔拉蒙古自治州	Bortala Mongol Autonomous Prefecture	0.32	19.16	0.20	
巴音郭楞蒙古自治州	Bayangol Mongol Autonomous Prefecture	0.14	11.14	0.09	0.02
阿克苏地区	Aksu Administrative Offices	0.55	4.90	1.19	
克孜勒苏柯尔克孜自治州	Kizilsu Kirgiz Autonomous Prefecture	1.14	3.91	1.64	0.09
喀什地区	Kashgar [Kaxgar] Administrative Offices	0.26	1.56	1.80	0.01
和田地区	Hotan Administrative Offices	0.02	3.07	0.47	

注：表 3-10、3-11 根据自治区计生委 2013 年计划生育统计年报整理，不包括兵团。

Note: In table 3-10 and 3-11,data are compiled on statistic annals of the family planning in Xinjiang Uygur Autonomous Region in 2013, exclusive of the Xinjiang Production and Construction Group.

3-11 各地、州、市计划生育及领证情况

Family Planning and Certificate Receiving by Prefecture, Autonomous Prefecture and City

(2013 年)

地　区	Region	计划生育率 (%) Family Planning Rate (%)	领证率 (%) Coverage of One-child Certificate (%)	领取计划生育证人数 (人) Number of Persons Receiving Certificates of Honor (person)	领取独生子女证人数 (人) Number of Married Couples with One-child Certificate (person)
总　计	**Total**	**99.71**	**36.81**	**722825**	**832146**
城　镇	Urban	99.64	51.23	214282	518365
农　村	Rural	99.73	29.42	508543	313781
乌鲁木齐市	Urumqi City	99.79	45.48	51025	193704
克拉玛依市	Karamay City	99.84	68.29	10268	44322
吐鲁番地区	Turpan Administrative Offices	99.55	37.26	31680	20052
哈密地区	Hami [Kumul] Administrative Offices	99.74	63.04	13499	47306
昌吉回族自治州	Changji Hui Autonomous Prefecture	99.68	46.73	23664	101851
伊犁州直属县(市)	Counties (Cities) Direct Under Ili Prefecture	99.78	37.72	119176	80095
塔城地区	Tacheng [Tarbagatai] Administrative Offices	99.73	40.81	29192	49055
阿勒泰地区	Altay Administrative Offices	99.68	47.05	32931	23573
博尔塔拉蒙古自治州	Bortala Mongol Autonomous Prefecture	98.88	45.29	13028	20746
巴音郭楞蒙古自治州	Bayangol Mongol Autonomous Prefecture	99.42	33.33	42720	59928
阿克苏地区	Aksu Administrative Offices	99.87	30.74	103365	52088
克孜勒苏柯尔克孜自治州	Kizilsu Kirgiz Autonomous Prefecture	99.92	39.57	33139	9689
喀什地区	Kashgar [Kaxgar] Administrative Offices	99.62	25.72	136895	79870
和田地区	Hotan Administrative Offices	99.80	31.21	82243	49867

3-12 主要年份新疆生产建设兵团人口情况

Population of Xinjiang Production and Construction Group in Main Years

单位：人　　(person)

年　份 Year	总人口 Total Population	男 Male	女 Female	农业人口 Agricultural Population	非农业人口 Non-Agricultural Population	出生人口 Birth Population	死亡人口 Death Population	出生率 (‰) Birth Rate (‰)	死亡率 (‰) Death Rate (‰)	自然增长率 (‰) Natural Growth Rate (‰)
1978	2119835	1090674	1029161			32749	6203	16.56	3.14	13.42
1980	2200755	1127050	1073705			26972	7162	12.27	3.26	9.01
1990	2143528	1110475	1033053	1132435	1044093	24589	9305	11.48	4.35	7.13
1995	2287896	1194166	1093730	1230151	1057745	22519	10044	9.98	4.45	5.53
2000	2427920	1272719	1155201	1379913	1048007	22674	12525	9.40	5.20	4.20
2001	2453575	1289954	1163621	1325998	1127577	19061	9014	7.80	3.70	4.10
2002	2501189	1311750	1189439	1355526	1145663	18179	9842	7.37	3.99	3.38
2003	2542170	1330666	1211504	1377224	1164946	17218	9914	6.84	3.94	2.90
2004	2563837	1341213	1222624	1413197	1150640	15860	9864	6.21	3.86	2.35
2005	2569756	1346901	1222855	1332458	1237298	16381	11934	6.38	4.65	1.73
2006	2579435	1352541	1226894	1312908	1266527	14687	11858	5.71	4.61	1.10
2007	2584732	1353053	1231679	1316590	1268142	13289	10131	5.15	3.92	1.23
2008	2573077	1344445	1228632	1289450	1283627	14612	11183	5.67	4.34	1.33
2009	2573145	1346229	1226918	1296755	1276390	14447	11285	5.61	4.39	1.22
2010	2607184	1376580	1230604			19205	10572	6.30	4.08	2.22
2011	2613724	1372606	1241118	1244796	1368928	13838	12198	5.33	4.70	0.63
2012	2648636	1390548	1258088	1192468	1456168	14916	14794	5.67	5.62	0.05
2013	2701427	1423075	1278352	1075898	1625529	15305	13203	5.72	4.94	0.79

3-13 按县、市分列的团场户数、人口数
Household and Population of Regiment Farms by City and County

(2013 年)

团　场	Regiment Farm	户数(户) Number of Households (household)	人口数(人) Population (person)	团　场	Regiment Farm	户数(户) Number of Households (household)	人口数(人) Population (person)
总　计	**Total**	**636974**	**1791188**	共青团农场	Communist League Farm	3223	11020
乌鲁木齐市	**Urumqi City**	**22994**	**61023**	军户农场	Junhu Farm	5574	14443
沙依巴克区	Shayibake District	9899	27007	呼图壁县	Hutubi County	30535	77863
104 团	No.104 Regiment Farm	7889	21054	105 团	No.105 Regiment Farm	4616	13571
西山农场	Xishan Farm	2010	5953	106 团	No.106 Regiment Farm	2726	6026
头屯河区	Tou Tunhe District	13095	34016	芳草湖农场	Fang Caohu Farm	23193	58266
三平农场	Sanping Farm	3571	11272	玛纳斯县	Manas County	42699	107462
五一农场	MayIst Farm	3953	11332	147 团	No.147 Regiment Farm	6225	14702
头屯河农场	Tou Tunhe Farm	5571	11412	148 团	No.148 Regiment Farm	9697	25185
克拉玛依市	**Karamay City**	**6826**	**19020**	149 团	No.149 Regiment Farm	5921	16578
136 团	No.136 Regiment Farm	3538	10102	150 团	No.150 Regiment Farm	7166	14033
137 团	No.137 Regiment Farm	3288	8918	新湖农场	Xinhu Farm	13690	36964
石河子市	**Shihezi City**	**21011**	**53824**	奇台县	Qitai County	11559	31306
152 团	No.152 Regiment Farm	2387	7096	奇台农场	Qitai Farm	10653	27699
石河子总场	General Shihezi Farm	18624	46728	北塔山牧场	Bei Tashan Ranch	906	3607
吐鲁番地区	**Turpan Administrative Offices**	**1736**	**5407**	阜康市	Fukang City	9183	21791
吐鲁番市	Turpan City	1736	5407	222 团	No.222 Regiment Farm	4234	10786
221 团	No.221 Regiment Farm	1736	5407	土墩子农场	Tu Dunzi Farm	2053	5256
哈密地区	**Hami [Kumul] Administrative Offices**	**26017**	**77901**	六运湖农场	Liu Yunhu Farm	2896	5749
哈密市	Hami [Kumul] City	21362	63805	吉木萨尔县	Jimsar County	5138	12982
红星一场	Red Star No.1 Farm	3392	8628	红旗农场	Red Flag Farm	5138	12982
红星二场	Red Star No.2 Farm	2934	6639	**伊犁哈萨克自治州**	**Ili Kazak Autonomous Prefecture**	**226164**	**592910**
红星四场	Red Star No.4 Farm	2936	7838	**伊犁州直属县(市)**	**Counties (Cities) Direct Under Ili Prefecture**	**72268**	**194946**
黄田农场	Huangtian Farm	3299	10924	奎屯市	Kuytun City	8468	19038
火箭农场	Huojian Farm	5408	18835	131 团	No.131 Regiment Farm	8468	19038
柳树泉农场	Liu Shuquan Farm	3393	10941	伊宁县	Yining [Gulja] County	3737	9978
巴里坤哈萨克自治县	Barkol Kazak AutonomousCounty	3654	11582	70 团	No.70 Regiment Farm	3737	9978
红山农场	Hongshan Farm	3654	11582	察布查尔锡伯自治县	Qapqal Xibe Autonomous County	9122	26337
伊吾县	Yiwu [Araturuk] County	1001	2514	67 团	No.67 Regiment Farm	3788	11936
淖毛湖农场	Zhuo Maohu Farm	1001	2514	68 团	No.68 Regiment Farm	3203	8171
昌吉回族自治州	**Changji Hui Autonomous Prefecture**	**123739**	**318590**	69 团	No.69 Regiment Farm	2131	6230
五家渠市	Wujiaqu City	15828	41723	霍城县	Huocheng [Korgas] County	28727	81069
101 团	No.101 Regiment Farm	2866	8461	61 团	No.61 Regiment Farm	4085	11436
102 团	No.102 Regiment Farm	6267	17620	62 团	No.62 Regiment Farm	5035	15556
103 团	No.103 Regiment Farm	6695	15642	63 团	No.63 Regiment Farm	3346	8494
昌吉市	Changji City	8797	25463	64 团	No.64 Regiment Farm	7416	21019

注：总计中包括农一师的阿拉尔农场和幸福城农场，两个农场共计 3612 户、11638 人。
Note: Total in this table includes Alaer and Xinfu farms of division 1,there are 3612 households and 11638 persons in this two farms.

3-13 续表 1 Continued

团　场	Regiment Farm	户数(户) Number of House-holds (house-hold)	人口数(人) Popula-Tion (person)	团　场	Regiment Farm	户数(户) Number of House-holds (house-hold)	人口数(人) Popula-Tion (person)
66 团	No.66 Regiment Farm	8845	24564	134 团	No.134 Regiment Farm	8538	18870
巩留县	Gongliu [Tokkuztara] County	2617	7211	141 团	No.141 Regiment Farm	3726	9116
73 团	No.73 Regiment Farm	2617	7211	142 团	No.142 Regiment Farm	9395	25428
新源县	Xinyuan [Kunes] County	8622	20516	143 团	No.143 Regiment Farm	13603	31556
71 团	No.71 Regiment Farm	4187	10190	144 团	No.144 Regiment Farm	4988	11724
72 团	No.72 Regiment Farm	4435	10326	托里县	Toli County	1068	3007
昭苏县	Zhaosu [Mongolkure] County	7809	21841	170 团	No.170 Regiment Farm	1068	3007
74 团	No.74 Regiment Farm	1179	3119	裕民县	Yumin [Qagantokay] County	1948	5186
75 团	No.75 Regiment Farm	1076	2783	161 团	No.161 Regiment Farm	1948	5186
76 团	No.76 Regiment Farm	3342	9211	和布克赛尔蒙古自治县	Hoboksar Mongol Autonomous County	2379	6778
77 团	No.77 Regiment Farm	2212	6728	184 团	No.184 Regiment Farm	2379	6778
特克斯县	Tekes County	1637	4424	**阿勒泰地区**	**Altay Administrative Offices**	**16300**	**43462**
78 团	No.78 Regiment Farm	1637	4424	阿勒泰市	Altay City	3292	9503
尼勒克县	Nilka County	1529	4532	181 团	No.181 Regiment Farm	3292	9503
79 团	No.79 Regiment Farm	1529	4532	福海县	Fuhai [Burultokay] County	1639	4711
塔城地区	**Tacheng [Tarbagatai] Administrative Offices**	**137596**	**354502**	182 团	No.182 Regiment Farm	1639	4711
塔城市	Tacheng City	5388	15296	北屯市	Beitun City	9403	23769
163 团	No.163 Regiment Farm	3376	9662	183 团	No.183 Regiment Farm	3124	8046
164 团	No.164 Regiment Farm	2012	5634	187 团	No.187 Regiment Farm	2310	6122
额敏县	Emin [Dorbiljin] County	11217	30442	188 团	No.188 Regiment Farm	3969	9601
165 团	No.165 Regiment Farm	1674	5247	哈巴河县	Habahe [Kaba] County	1098	3108
166 团	No.166 Regiment Farm	2393	7607	185 团	No.185 Regiment Farm	1098	3108
167 团	No.167 Regiment Farm	1967	5493	吉木乃县	Jeminay County	868	2371
168 团	No.168 Regiment Farm	3895	8785	186 团	No.186 Regiment Farm	868	2371
团结农场	Tuanjie Farm	1288	3310	**博尔塔拉蒙古自治州**	**Bortala Mongol Autonomous Prefecture**	**30439**	**91235**
乌苏市	Usu City	51663	136725	博乐市	Bole [Bortala] City	18670	57633
123 团	No.123 Regiment Farm	9256	22936	81 团	No.81 Regiment Farm	3497	10933
124 团	No.124 Regiment Farm	6844	17936	84 团	No.84 Regiment Farm	2236	7362
125 团	No.125 Regiment Farm	7127	18563	86 团	No.86 Regiment Farm	4853	15129
126 团	No.126 Regiment Farm	3881	11929	89 团	No.89 Regiment Farm	5233	15109
127 团	No.127 Regiment Farm	5496	14588	90 团	No.90 Regiment Farm	2851	9100
128 团	No.128 Regiment Farm	5374	15069	精河县	Jinghe [Jing] County	8663	25087
129 团	No.129 Regiment Farm	6107	16202	83 团	No.83 Regiment Farm	7233	21325
130 团	No.130 Regiment Farm	7578	19502	91 团	No.91 Regiment Farm	1430	3762
沙湾县	Shawan County	63933	157068	温泉县	Wenquan [Araxang] County	3106	8515
121 团	No.121 Regiment Farm	14867	38059	87 团	No.87 Regiment Farm	1597	4301
133 团	No.133 Regiment Farm	8816	22315	88 团	No.88 Regiment Farm	1509	4214

3-13 续表 2 Continued

团 场	Regiment Farm	户数（户）Number of House-holds (house-hold)	人口数（人）Popula-Tion (person)
巴音郭楞蒙古自治州	**Bayangol Mongol Autonomous Prefecture**	**51039**	**142110**
铁门关市	Tiememguan city	12565	35864
29 团	No.29 Regiment Farm	9607	26974
30 团	No.30 Regiment Farm	2958	8890
尉犁县	Yuli [Lopnur] County	10656	30954
31 团	No.31 Regiment Farm	3215	8686
33 团	No.33 Regiment Farm	4107	11947
34 团	No.34 Regiment Farm	3334	10321
若羌县	Ruoqiang [Qarkilik] County	2527	6901
36 团	No.36 Regiment Farm	2527	6901
焉耆回族自治县	Yanji Hui Autonomous County	4531	10605
27 团	No.27 Regiment Farm	4531	10605
和静县	Hejing County	13346	35474
21 团	No.21 Regiment Farm	3816	10301
22 团	No.22 Regiment Farm	6541	17397
223 团	No.223 Regiment Farm	2989	7776
和硕县	Hoxud County	4176	11533
24 团	No.24 Regiment Farm	4176	11533
博湖县	Bohu [Bagrax] County	1811	5283
25 团	No.25 Regiment Farm	1811	5283
且末县	Qiemo County	1427	5496
37 团	No.37 Regiment Farm	572	1958
38 团	No.38 Regiment Farm	855	3538
阿克苏地区	**Aksu Administrative Offices**	**60992**	**191297**
阿克苏市	Aksu City	9602	32189
1 团	No.1 Regiment Farm	6037	21055
2 团	No.2 Regiment Farm	3565	11134
阿拉尔市	Alar City	35323	109920
7 团	No.7 Regiment Farm	4190	11805
8 团	No.8 Regiment Farm	3347	10009
10 团	No.10 Regiment Farm	5300	16100
11 团	No.11 Regiment Farm	3295	9955
12 团	No.12 Regiment Farm	6145	19008
13 团	No.13 Regiment Farm	5540	20159
14 团	No.14 Regiment Farm	2662	7878
16 团	No.16 Regiment Farm	4844	15006
温宿县	Wensu [Onsu] County	8608	27527
5 团	No.5 Regiment Farm	5725	17718
6 团	No.6 Regiment Farm	2883	9809
乌什县	Wushi [Uxturpan] County	2410	7079
4 团	No.4 Regiment Farm	2410	7079
阿瓦提县	Awat County	5049	14582
3 团	No.3 Regiment Farm	5049	14582
克孜勒苏柯尔克孜自治州	**Kizilsu Kirgiz Autonomous Prefecture**	**1215**	**4558**
阿图什市	Artux City	939	3682
红旗农场	Red Flag Farm	939	3682
乌恰县	Wuqia [Ulugqat] County	276	876
托云牧场	Tuoyun Ranch	276	876
喀什地区	**Kashgar [Kaxgar] Administrative Offices**	**49347**	**181396**
疏勒县	Shule County	2239	6386
41 团	No.41 Regiment Farm	2239	6386
英吉莎县	Yengisar County	421	1512
东风农场	Dong Feng Farm	421	1512
叶城县	Yecheng [Kagilik] County	358	1328
叶城牧场	Yechen Ranch	358	1328
麦盖提县	Makit County	8013	25908
45 团	No.45 Regiment Farm	6770	22341
46 团	No.46 Regiment Farm	1243	3567
岳普湖县	Yopurga County	1270	3181
42 团	No.42 Regiment Farm	1270	3181
伽师县	Jiashi [Payzawat] County	3598	11612
伽师总场	General Jiashi Farm	3598	11612
巴楚县	Bachu [Maralbexi] County	2042	6578
48 团	No.48 Regiment Farm	2042	6578
图木舒克市	Tumxuk City	31406	124891
44 团	No.44 Regiment Farm	7124	25734
49 团	No.49 Regiment Farm	4168	14893
50 团	No.50 Regiment Farm	5560	18436
51 团	No.51 Regiment Farm	9568	44968
53 团	No.53 Regiment Farm	4986	20860
和田地区	**Hotan Administrative Offices**	**11843**	**40279**
墨玉县	Moyu [Karakax] County	4366	13612
47 团	No.47 Regiment Farm	1471	4061
224 团	No.224 Regiment Farm	2895	9551
皮山县	Pishan [Guma] County	6586	24422
皮山农场	Pishan Farm	6586	24422
策勒县	Qira County	891	2245
一牧场	No.1Ranch	891	2245

3-14 主要年份按三次产业分的就业人员
Number of Employed Persons by Three Strata of Industry in Main Years

单位：万人 (10 000 persons)

年份 Year	经济活动人口 Economically Active Population	就业人员合计 Total Number of Employed persons	第一产业 Primary Industry	第二产业 Secondary Industry
1978		491.25	353.99	70.42
1980		506.35	354.49	75.12
1985		565.81	363.24	89.64
1990		617.70	378.47	107.42
1995		676.00	388.16	124.21
1996		684.00	390.98	119.39
1997		715.40	421.30	105.40
1998		680.92	387.80	106.22
1999		694.34	385.57	104.51
2000		672.50	387.90	92.70
2001	697.45	685.38	388.19	92.19
2002	714.17	701.49	391.84	95.82
2003	734.02	721.27	397.20	95.69
2004	755.36	744.49	403.31	98.49
2005	802.75	791.62	408.00	122.81
2006	823.73	811.75	414.45	111.28
2007	842.12	830.42	417.73	118.34
2008	859.35	847.58	421.32	120.05
2009	878.01	866.15	427.48	127.28
2010	905.64	894.65	438.13	132.75
2011	964.46	953.34	463.91	149.04
2012	1022.29	1010.44	492.36	157.71
2013	1108.50	1096.59	506.35	178.79

年份 Year	第三产业 Tertiary Industry	构成(合计=100) (%) Composition in Percentage (total=100)(%)		
		第一产业 Primary Industry	第二产业 Secondary Industry	第三产业 Tertiary Industry
1978	66.84	72.06	14.33	13.61
1980	76.74	70.01	14.84	15.15
1985	112.93	64.20	15.84	19.96
1990	131.81	61.27	17.39	21.34
1995	163.63	57.42	18.37	24.21
1996	173.63	57.16	17.45	25.39
1997	188.70	58.89	14.73	26.38
1998	186.90	56.95	15.60	27.45
1999	204.26	55.53	15.05	29.42
2000	191.90	57.68	13.78	28.54
2001	205.00	56.64	13.45	29.91
2002	213.83	55.86	13.66	30.48
2003	228.38	55.07	13.27	31.66
2004	242.69	54.17	13.23	32.60
2005	260.81	51.54	15.51	32.95
2006	286.02	51.06	13.71	35.23
2007	294.35	50.30	14.25	35.45
2008	306.21	49.71	14.16	36.13
2009	311.39	49.35	14.70	35.95
2010	323.77	48.97	14.84	36.19
2011	340.39	48.66	15.63	35.71
2012	360.37	48.73	15.61	35.66
2013	411.46	46.17	16.31	37.52

3-15 主要年份城镇登记失业人数及失业率

Number of Registered Unemployed Persons in Urban Areas and Unemployment Rate in Main Years

单位：万人 (10 000 persons)

年份 Year	城镇登记失业人数 Number of Registered Unemployment Persons in Urban Area	城镇登记失业率(%) Registered Unemployment Rate in Urban Areas (%)	年份 Year	城镇登记失业人数 Number of Registered Unemployment Persons in Urban Area	城镇登记失业率(%) Registered Unemployment Rate in Urban Areas (%)
1980	13.55	7.5	2001	12.07	3.7
1985	4.04	1.9	2002	12.68	3.6
1990	9.60	3.8	2003	12.75	3.8
1991	9.95	3.8	2004	10.87	3.8
1992	9.81	3.7	2005	11.13	3.9
1993	9.50	3.6	2006	11.98	3.9
1994	10.00	3.8	2007	11.70	3.9
1995	10.24	3.9	2008	11.77	3.7
1996	9.81	3.8	2009	11.86	3.8
1997	10.20	3.8	2010	10.99	3.2
1998	11.06	3.9	2011	11.12	3.2
1999	10.30	3.7	2012	11.85	3.4
2000	11.00	3.8	2013	11.90	3.4

3-16 各地、州、市城镇登记失业率

Registered Unemployment Rate in Urban Area by Prefecture, Autonomous Prefecture and City

单位：% (%)

地区	Region	2012	2013
总计	**Total**	**3.39**	**3.40**
乌鲁木齐市	Urumqi City	3.48	3.50
克拉玛依市	Karamay City	0.69	2.00
吐鲁番地区	Turpan Administrative Offices	3.19	2.83
哈密地区	Hami [Kumul] Administrative Offices	2.70	2.74
昌吉回族自治州	Changji Hui Autonomous Prefecture	2.75	2.33
伊犁州直属县(市)	Counties (Cities) Direct Under Ili Prefecture	2.76	3.49
塔城地区	Tacheng [Tarbagatai] Administrative Offices	0.99	1.08
阿勒泰地区	Altay Administrative Offices	2.70	2.81
博尔塔拉蒙古自治州	Bortala Mongol Autonomous Prefecture	3.72	3.68
巴音郭楞蒙古自治州	Bayangol Mongol Autonomous Prefecture	2.89	2.62
阿克苏地区	Aksu Administrative Offices	2.42	2.25
克孜勒苏柯尔克孜自治州	Kizilsu Kirgiz Autonomous Prefecture	2.09	2.23
喀什地区	Kashgar [Kaxgar] Administrative Offices	3.98	3.78
和田地区	Hotan Administrative Offices	2.35	2.65

3-17 各地区按行业分城镇非私营单位就业人员(年末数)
Number of Employed Persons in Urban Non-Private Units at Year-end by Sectors and Region

单位：人 (2013 年) (person)

项 目	Item	合 计 Total	国有单位 State-owned Units	城镇集体 Urban Collective-Owned Units	其他单位 Units of Other Types Of Ownership
总 计	**Total**	**3095086**	**2018363**	**29123**	**1047600**
按国民经济行业分组	**Grouped by Sectors**				
农林牧渔业	Farming, Forestry, Animal Husbandry and Fishery	548887	534491	66	14330
采 矿 业	Mining	197095	16406	225	180464
制 造 业	Manufacturing	336979	12199	3312	321468
电力、热力、燃气及水生产和供应业	Production and Distribution of Electricity, Gas and Water	83170	28709	296	54165
建 筑 业	Construction	262547	48735	3158	210654
批发和零售业	Wholesale and Retail Trades	82738	16224	3560	62954
交通运输、仓储和邮政业	Traffic Transport, Storage and Post	174866	141202	754	32910
住宿和餐饮业	Hotels and Catering Services	27791	11999	784	15008
信息传输、软件和信息技术服务业	Information Transmission, Computer Services and Software	28804	8879	7	19918
金 融 业	Financial Intermediation	87380	31271	10498	45611
房地产业	Real Estate	39761	3770	547	35444
租赁和商务服务业	Leasing and Business Services	59422	24118	3824	31480
科学研究和技术服务业	Scientific Research and Technical Service	64736	52352	211	12173
水利、环境和公共设施管理业	Management of Water Conservancy, Environment and PublicFacility	54409	50297	2	4110
居民服务、修理和其他服务业	Services to households and Other Services	6916	4557	290	2069
教 育	Education	370442	367635	117	2690
卫生和社会工作	Health and Social Security	167208	164451	1472	1285
文化、体育和娱乐业	Culture, Sports and Entertainment	29594	28747		847
公共管理、社会保障和社会组织	Public Management and Social Organization	472341	472321		20
按地区分	**By Region**				
乌鲁木齐市	Urumqi City	725940	427913	8402	289625
克拉玛依市	Karamay City	180316	35843	1728	142745
吐鲁番地区	Turpan Administrative Offices	79861	52475	770	26616
哈密地区	Hami [Kumul] Administrative Offices	101088	61691	620	38777
昌吉回族自治州	Changji Hui Autonomous Prefecture	235285	128013	2871	104401
伊犁哈萨克自治州	Ili Kazak Autonomous Prefecture	635958	498333	5398	132227
伊犁州直属县(市)	Counties (Cities) Direct Under Ili Prefecture	290841	209940	2802	78099
塔城地区	Tacheng [Tarbagatai] Administrative Offices	227371	190058	1801	35512
阿勒泰地区	Altay Administrative Offices	117746	98335	795	18616
博尔塔拉蒙古自治州	Bortala Mongol Autonomous Prefecture	97811	83892	678	13241
巴音郭楞蒙古自治州	Bayangol Mongol Autonomous Prefecture	220242	144914	2490	72838
阿克苏地区	Aksu Administrative Offices	221989	152354	2186	67449
克孜勒苏柯尔克孜自治州	Kizilsu Kirgiz Autonomous Prefecture	49583	42172	389	7022
喀什地区	Kashgar [Kaxgar] Administrative Offices	239292	183551	2668	53073
和田地区	Hotan Administrative Offices	106296	94378	618	11300
石河子市	Shihezi City	101550	45043	305	56202
阿拉尔市	Aral City	42865	36777		6088
图木舒克市	Tumxuk City	20426	14560		5866
五家渠市	Wujiaqu City	36584	16454		20130

3-18 各地区城镇非私营单位在岗职工（含劳务派遣工）人数
Number of Employed Persons (including the dispatched employees) in Urban Non-Private Units at Year-end by Region

单位：万人 (10 000 persons)

年份 Year	地区 Region	合计 Total	国有单位 State-owned Units	城镇集体 Urban Collective-owned Units	其他单位 Units of Other Types of Ownership
	2002	242.26	189.26	9.31	43.69
	2003	237.94	184.02	7.55	46.37
	2004	235.97	182.80	6.43	46.74
	2005	237.84	181.92	5.96	49.96
	2006	238.95	182.91	5.19	50.85
	2007	239.45	181.46	4.58	53.41
	2008	239.16	180.29	3.64	55.23
	2009	239.54	175.90	3.54	60.10
	2010	245.48	178.40	3.00	64.08
	2011	270.77	187.78	3.00	79.99
	2012	280.33	195.47	3.26	81.60
	2013	298.93	196.42	2.79	99.72
乌鲁木齐市	Urumqi City	70.93	42.23	0.81	27.89
克拉玛依市	Karamay City	17.18	3.47	0.16	13.55
吐鲁番地区	Turpan Administrative Offices	7.51	4.93	0.07	2.51
哈密地区	Hami [Kumul] Administrative Offices	9.66	6.04	0.06	3.56
昌吉回族自治州	Changji Hui Autonomous Prefecture	22.74	12.56	0.27	9.91
伊犁哈萨克自治州	Ili Kazak Autonomous Prefecture	62.37	49.12	0.53	12.72
伊犁州直属县(市)	Counties (Cities) Direct Under Ili Prefecture	28.72	20.84	0.28	7.60
塔城地区	Tacheng [Tarbagatai] Administrative Offices	22.25	18.76	0.17	3.32
阿勒泰地区	Altay Administrative Offices	11.40	9.52	0.08	1.80
博尔塔拉蒙古自治州	Bortala Mongol Autonomous Prefecture	9.45	8.10	0.06	1.29
巴音郭楞蒙古自治州	Bayangol Mongol Autonomous Prefecture	20.64	13.49	0.24	6.91
阿克苏地区	Aksu Administrative Offices	22.03	15.19	0.22	6.62
克孜勒苏柯尔克孜自治州	Kizilsu Kirgiz Autonomous Prefecture	4.49	3.91	0.04	0.54
喀什地区	Kashgar [Kaxgar] Administrative Offices	22.61	17.75	0.24	4.62
和田地区	Hotan Administrative Offices	9.49	8.44	0.06	0.99
石河子市	Shihezi City	10.06	4.48	0.03	5.55
阿拉尔市	Aral City	4.29	3.68		0.61
图木舒克市	Tumxuk City	1.89	1.43		0.46
五家渠市	Wujiaqu City	3.59	1.60		1.99

3-19 分行业城镇非私营单位在岗职工(含劳务派遣工)人数
Number of Employed Persons (including the dispatched employees) in Urban Non-Private Units at Year-end by Sectors

单位：人 (2013 年) (person)

项目	Item	合计 Total	国有单位 State-owned Units	城镇集体单位 Urban Collective-owned Units	其他单位 Units of Other Types of Ownership
总计	**Total**	**2989337**	**1964185**	**27906**	**997246**
农林牧渔业	**Farming, Forestry, Animal Husbandry and Fishery**	**536779**	**522656**	**66**	**14057**
农业	Farming	442192	434517	39	7636
林业	Forestry	7910	6568		1342
畜牧业	Animal Husbandry	67895	64387	19	3489
渔业	Fishery	230	163		67
农林牧渔服务业	Services in Support of Agriculture	18552	17021	8	1523
采矿业	**Mining**	**194070**	**16390**	**225**	**177455**
#煤炭开采和洗选业	Mining and Washing of Coal	58537	2315	168	56054
石油和天然气开采业	Extraction of Petroleum and Natural Gas	71776			71776
黑色金属矿采选业	Mining and Processing of Ferrous Metal Ores	9680	220		9460
有色金属矿采选业	Mining and Processing of Non-Ferrous Metal Ores	7150	18		7132
非金属矿采选业	Mining and Processing of Nonmetal Ores	3170	590	54	2526
开采辅助活动	Mining Activities	43736	13231	3	30502
其他采矿业	Mining of Other Ores	21	16		5
制造业	**Manufacturing**	**330803**	**12013**	**3278**	**315512**
#农副食品加工业	Processing of Food from Agriculture Products	24111	608	11	23492
食品制造业	Manufacture of Food	19281	80	80	19121
酒、饮料和精制茶制造业	Manufacture of Beverage	11097	289	7	10801
烟草制品业	Manufacture of Tobacco	1015	1015		
纺织业	Manufacture of Textile	22295	552	29	21714
纺织服装、服饰业	Manufacture of Textile Wearing Apparel, Footware and Caps	2414	186	58	2170
皮革、毛皮、羽毛及其制品和制鞋业	Manufacture of Leather, Fur, Feather and Related Products	344		5	339
木材加工和木、竹、藤、棕、草制品业	Processing of Timber, Manufacture of Wood, Bamboo, Rattan, Palm and Straw Products	618	4	10	604
家具制造业	Manufacture of Furniture	180	47	13	120
造纸及纸制品业	Manufacture of Paper and Paper Products	4605		109	4496
印刷业和记录媒介的复制业	Printing and Record Medium Reproduction	2986	1812	50	1124
文教、工美、体育和娱乐用品制造业	Manufacture of Articles For Culture, Education and Sport Activities	281		56	225
石油加工、炼焦及核燃料加工业	Oil processing, Refining and Nuclear-fuel processing	38743		4	38739
化学原料及化学制品制造业	Raw Chemical Materials and Chemical Products	59568	1165	512	57891
医药制造业	Manufacture of Medicines	3449	51		3398
化学纤维制造业	Manufacture of Chemical Fibers	4300			4300
橡胶和塑料制品业	Plastic Products	9504	631	295	8578
非金属矿物制品业	Manufacture of Non-metal Mineral Products	43086	2024	851	40211
黑色金属冶炼及压延加工业	Smelting and Pressing of Ferrous Metals	37296	367	639	36290
有色金属冶炼及压延加工业	Smelting and Pressing of Nonferrous Metals	21343	97	92	21154
金属制品业	Smelting and Pressing of Ferrous Metals	5975	192	101	5682
通用设备制造业	Manufacturing of Equipment for General Purpose	2160	120		2040
专用设备制造业	Manufacture of Special Purpose Machinery	4107	1012	44	3051

3-19 续表 1 Continued

单位：人 (person)

项目	Item	合计 Total	国有单位 State-owned Units	城镇集体单位 Urban Collective-owned Units	其他单位 Units of Other Types of Ownership
汽车制造业	Manufacture of Metal Car	2668			2668
铁路、船舶、航空航天和其他运输设备制造业	Manufacture of Transport Equipment	1797	1561		236
电气机械和器材制造业	Manufacture of Electrical Machinery and Equipment	6404	80	25	6299
计算机、通信和其他电子设备制造业	Manufacture of Communication Equipment, Computers and Other Electronic Equipment	45			45
仪器仪表制造业	Manufacture of Measuring Instruments	138			138
其他制造业	Other Electronic Equipment	9			9
废弃资源综合利用业	Recycling and Disposal of Waste	197	25		172
金属制品、机械和设备修理业	Manufacture of Electrical Machinery and Equipment	787	95	287	405
电力、热力、燃气及水的生产和供应业	**Production and Distribution of Electricity, Gas and Water**	**82494**	**28489**	**281**	**53724**
电力、热力的生产和供应业	Production and Distribution of Electric Power, Thermal Power	70166	24369	37	45760
燃气生产和供应业	Production and Distribution of Gas	4253	54		4199
水的生产和供应业	Production and Distribution of Water	8075	4066	244	3765
建 筑 业	**Construction**	**246986**	**47892**	**2791**	**196303**
房屋建筑业	Construction of Buildings	153134	26529	469	126136
土木工程建筑业	Construction of Civil Engineering	71115	14362	1920	54833
建筑安装业	Building Installation	12774	811	379	11584
建筑装饰和其他建筑业	Other Construction	9963	6190	23	3750
批发和零售业	**Wholesale and Retail Trades**	**80702**	**15802**	**3174**	**61726**
批发业	Wholesale Trades	52189	12826	2787	36576
零售业	Retail Trades	28513	2976	387	25150
交通运输、仓储和邮政业	**Transport, Storage and Post**	**172348**	**139224**	**750**	**32374**
铁路运输业	Railway Transport	55320	55304		16
道路运输业	Road Transport	82449	61149	64	21236
航空运输业	Air Transport	11202	6507		4695
管道运输业	Via Pipe Transport	3347			3347
装卸搬运和运输代理业	Loading and Discharging; Other Transportation Service	2876	1289	686	901
仓储业	Storage	2865	2475		390
邮政业	Post	14289	12500		1789
住宿和餐饮业	**Hotels and Catering Services**	**26828**	**11423**	**776**	**14629**
住宿业	Hotels	20953	8787	769	11397
餐饮业	Catering Services	5875	2636	7	3232
信息传输、软件和信息技术服务业	**Information Transmission, Computer Service and Software**	**28379**	**8842**	**7**	**19530**
电信、广播电视和卫星传输服务	Telecommunication and Other I.T Transmission Service	26624	8426	7	18191
互联网和相关服务	Computer Service	431	227		204
软件和信息技术服务业	Software	1324	189		1135
金 融 业	**Financial Intermediation**	**68460**	**29571**	**10313**	**28576**
货币金融服务业	Banking	52449	25850	10260	16339
资本市场服务业	Security Activities	941	224		717
保险业	Insurance	14630	3388	53	11189

3-19 续表 2 Continued

单位：人 (person)

项　目	Item	合 计 Total	国有单位 State-owned Units	城镇集体单位 Urban Collective-owned Units	其他单位 Units of Other Types of Ownership
其他金融活动	Other Finance Activities	440	109		331
房地产业	**Real Estate**	**38238**	**3734**	**466**	**34038**
#房地产开发经营	Development and Management of Real Estate	18411	445	39	17927
物业管理	Real Estate Management	17176	2190	192	14794
房地产中介服务	Agency Service for Real Estate	453	188	5	260
租赁和商务服务业	**Leasing and Business Service**	**53494**	**22250**	**3791**	**27453**
租赁业	Leasing	908	164		744
商务服务业	Business Service	52586	22086	3791	26709
科学研究、技术服务和地质勘查业	**Scientific Research, Technology Service and Geological Prospecting**	**62592**	**51133**	**211**	**11248**
研究与试验发展	Research and Experiment Development	7308	7077		231
专业技术服务业	Professional Technique Service	45422	34242	211	10969
科技推广和应用服务业	Science and Technology Popularization and Application Services	9862	9814		48
水利、环境和公共设施管理业	**Management of Water Conservancy, Environment and Public Facility**	**51486**	**47427**	**2**	**4057**
水利管理业	Management of Water Conservance	20306	20125		181
生态保护和环境治理业	Environmental Management	2609	2417		192
公共设施管理业	Management of Public Facilities	28571	24885	2	3684
居民服务、修理和其他服务业	**Service to Households and Other Services**	**6698**	**4521**	**289**	**1888**
居民服务业	Services to Households	2682	1622	95	965
机动车、电子产品和日用产品修理业	Repair of motor car,electruical products	607	403	4	200
其他服务业	Other Services	3409	2496	190	723
教　育	**Education**	**366984**	**364284**	**117**	**2583**
#初等教育	Junior Education	135691	135452		239
中等教育	Secondary Education	179153	178681	15	457
高等教育	Senior Education	29296	29296		
卫生和社会工作	**Health, Social Security and Social Welfare**	**160767**	**158168**	**1369**	**1230**
卫　生	Health	155926	153371	1369	1186
社会工作	Social Security	4841	4797		44
文化、体育和娱乐业	**Culture, Sports and Entertainment**	**29023**	**28180**		**843**
新闻和出版业	Journalism and Publishing Activities	6227	5570		657
广播、电视、电影和影视录音制作业	Broadcasting, Movies, Televisions and Audiovisual Activities	10355	10348		7
文化艺术业	Culture and Art Activities	11122	11018		104
体　育	Sports	881	868		13
娱乐业	Entertainment	438	376		62
公共管理、社会保障和社会组织	**Public Management and Social Organization**	**452206**	**452186**		**20**
#中国共产党机关	Organs of Communist Party of China	24640	24640		
国家机构	Government Agencies	416048	416042		6
人民政协和民主党派	People's Political Consultative Conference and Democratic Parties	2701	2701		
社会保障	Social Security	3830	3830		
群众社团、社会团体和其他成员组织	Non-Governmental Organizations, Social Organizations and Religion Organizations	4987	4973		14

3-20 各地、州、市分行业城镇非私营单位在岗职工(含劳务派遣工)人数

Number of Employed Persons in Urban Non-Private Units at Year-end by Sector and Prefecture, Autonomous Prefecture and City(including the dispatched employees)

单位：人 (2013 年) (person)

年 份 Year	地 区 Region	合 计 Total	农林牧渔业 Farming, Forestry, Animal Husbandry and Fishery	采 矿 业 Mining	制 造 业 Manufacturing	电力、热力、燃气及水的生产和供应业 Production and Distribution of Power, Gas and Water
总　计	**Total**	**2989337**	**536779**	**194070**	**330803**	**82494**
乌鲁木齐市	Urumqi City	709257	10534	21117	84369	20472
克拉玛依市	Karamay City	171830	8349	74975	30011	64
吐鲁番地区	Turpan Administrative Offices	75054	3223	23448	9100	2256
哈密地区	Hami [Kumul] Administrative Offices	96600	18660	16203	6298	2832
昌吉回族自治州	Changji Hui Autonomous Prefecture	227422	54263	9155	51972	7548
伊犁哈萨克自治州	Ili Kazak Autonomous Prefecture	623677	230852	17262	45930	15967
伊犁州直属县(市)	Counties (Cities) Direct Under Ili Prefecture	287191	66959	4149	30440	8750
塔城地区	Tacheng [Tarbagatai] Administrative Offices	222479	119429	7528	13351	3771
阿勒泰地区	Altay Administrative Offices	114007	44464	5585	2139	3446
博尔塔拉蒙古自治州	Bortala Mongol Autonomous Prefecture	94469	38201	23	4097	2492
巴音郭楞蒙古自治州	Bayangol Mongol Autonomous Prefecture	206447	45678	20899	21157	5250
阿克苏地区	Aksu Administrative Offices	220276	36919	9225	19720	6503
克孜勒苏柯尔克孜自治州	Kizilsu Kirgiz Autonomous Prefecture	44865	2171	915	1410	694
喀什地区	Kashgar [Kaxgar] Administrative Offices	226129	16216	734	9253	6535
和田地区	Hotan Administrative Offices	94941	14249	114	1436	2566
石河子市	Shihezi City	100636	10535		27284	6666
阿拉尔市	Aral City	42859	30755		3021	501
图木舒克市	Tumxuk City	18916	8849		1612	558
五家渠市	Wujiaqu City	35959	7325		14133	1590

年 份 Year	地 区 Region	建 筑 业 Construction	批发和零售业 Wholesale and Retail Trades	交通运输、仓储和邮政业 Transport, Storage and Post	住宿和餐饮业 Hotels and Catering Services	信息传输、软件和信息技术服务业 Information Transmission, Computer Servcie and Software
总　计	**Total**	**246986**	**80702**	**172348**	**26828**	**28379**
乌鲁木齐市	Urumqi City	114123	30143	133156	12463	9368
克拉玛依市	Karamay City	14641	2179	2805	1167	749
吐鲁番地区	Turpan Administrative Offices	1652	1506	1486	354	634
哈密地区	Hami [Kumul] Administrative Offices	4912	2277	1479	1199	955
昌吉回族自治州	Changji Hui Autonomous Prefecture	13684	4404	3270	375	1885
伊犁哈萨克自治州	Ili Kazak Autonomous Prefecture	20622	11461	11312	5777	6187
伊犁州直属县(市)	Counties (Cities) Direct Under Ili Prefecture	12962	7576	6300	3227	2954
塔城地区	Tacheng [Tarbagatai] Administrative Offices	6109	2136	2227	708	1370
阿勒泰地区	Altay Administrative Offices	1551	1749	2785	1842	1863
博尔塔拉蒙古自治州	Bortala Mongol Autonomous Prefecture	4890	2010	1850	434	614
巴音郭楞蒙古自治州	Bayangol Mongol Autonomous Prefecture	11031	6229	4704	1129	1508
阿克苏地区	Aksu Administrative Offices	13929	7607	3162	837	2117
克孜勒苏柯尔克孜自治州	Kizilsu Kirgiz Autonomous Prefecture	1375	583	1078	203	509
喀什地区	Kashgar [Kaxgar] Administrative Offices	17946	7458	4662	1874	1641
和田地区	Hotan Administrative Offices	2861	1226	1943	407	1012
石河子市	Shihezi City	20269	1690	1138	450	1155
阿拉尔市	Aral City	1228	1198	12		
图木舒克市	Tumxuk City	2658	50		23	
五家渠市	Wujiaqu City	1165	681	291	136	45

3-20 续表 Continued

单位：人 (person)

年份 Year	地区 Region	金融业 Financial Intermediation	房地产业 Real Estate	租赁和商务服务业 Leasing and Business Services	科学研究、技术服务业 Scientific Research, Technology Service and Geological Prospecting	水利、环境和公共设施管理业 Management of Water Conservancy, Environment and Public Facility
总　计	**Total**	**68460**	**38238**	**53494**	**62592**	**51486**
乌鲁木齐市	Urumqi City	19356	15785	19641	24360	5876
克拉玛依市	Karamay City	2791	3394	4437	1678	1175
吐鲁番地区	Turpan Administrative Offices	1800	415	655	1488	861
哈密地区	Hami [Kumul] Administrative Offices	2505	437	724	2883	3953
昌吉回族自治州	Changji Hui Autonomous Prefecture	5046	4378	3109	4904	5416
伊犁哈萨克自治州	Ili Kazak Autonomous Prefecture	12237	4921	3910	10444	10804
伊犁州直属县(市)	Counties (Cities) Direct Under Ili Prefecture	6565	3968	2622	4944	5025
塔城地区	Tacheng [Tarbagatai] Administrative Offices	3277	584	518	2560	3551
阿勒泰地区	Altay Administrative Offices	2395	369	770	2940	2228
博尔塔拉蒙古自治州	Bortala Mongol Autonomous Prefecture	1679	450	6795	1376	1405
巴音郭楞蒙古自治州	Bayangol Mongol Autonomous Prefecture	4216	1670	3497	4084	5478
阿克苏地区	Aksu Administrative Offices	4437	2093	2695	3217	7002
克孜勒苏柯尔克孜自治州	Kizilsu Kirgiz Autonomous Prefecture	920	160	968	2101	544
喀什地区	Kashgar [Kaxgar] Administrative Offices	6402	2576	1574	2977	3955
和田地区	Hotan Administrative Offices	2338	194	723	1378	1594
石河子市	Shihezi City	3685	427	4384	1026	1880
阿拉尔市	Aral City		126	30	77	529
图木舒克市	Tumxuk City			133	19	254
五家渠市	Wujiaqu City	1048	1212	219	580	760

年份 Year	地区 Region	居民服务、修理和其他服务业 Service to Households and Other Services	教　育 Education	卫生社会工作 Health, Social Security and Social Welfare	文化、体育和娱乐业 Culture, Sports and Entertainment	公共管理、社会保障和社会组织 Public Management and Social Organizations
总　计	**Total**	**6698**	**366984**	**160767**	**29023**	**452206**
乌鲁木齐市	Urumqi City	1525	51244	34895	12360	88470
克拉玛依市	Karamay City	1160	7277	3068	455	11455
吐鲁番地区	Turpan Administrative Offices		9250	3252	515	13159
哈密地区	Hami [Kumul] Administrative Offices	277	10507	5268	1088	14143
昌吉回族自治州	Changji Hui Autonomous Prefecture	120	21500	11742	969	23682
伊犁哈萨克自治州	Ili Kazak Autonomous Prefecture	690	80453	33402	4313	97133
伊犁州直属县(市)	Counties (Cities) Direct Under Ili Prefecture	553	46705	19602	2353	51537
塔城地区	Tacheng [Tarbagatai] Administrative Offices	72	21565	8313	1003	24407
阿勒泰地区	Altay Administrative Offices	65	12183	5487	957	21189
博尔塔拉蒙古自治州	Bortala Mongol Autonomous Prefecture	7	9882	4333	822	13109
巴音郭楞蒙古自治州	Bayangol Mongol Autonomous Prefecture	137	22798	11704	920	34358
阿克苏地区	Aksu Administrative Offices	143	35159	13733	1975	49803
克孜勒苏柯尔克孜自治州	Kizilsu Kirgiz Autonomous Prefecture	2287	11108	5599	995	11245
喀什地区	Kashgar [Kaxgar] Administrative Offices	211	66109	18434	2547	55025
和田地区	Hotan Administrative Offices	97	26517	7244	1224	27818
石河子市	Shihezi City	42	8005	5127	579	6294
阿拉尔市	Aral City		2899	1169	131	1183
图木舒克市	Tumxuk City		2073	624		2063
五家渠市	Wujiaqu City	2	2203	1173	130	3266

3-21 分行业城镇非私营单位女性就业人员（年末数）

Number of Female Employed Persons in Urban Non-Private Units at Year-end by Sectors

单位：人 (2013 年) (person)

项　目	Item	合 计 Total	国有单位 State-owned Units	城镇集体单位 Urban Collective-owned Units	其他单位 Units of Other Types of Ownership
总　计	**Total**	**1219635**	**899856**	**11443**	**308336**
农林牧渔业	Farming, Forestry, Animal Husbandry and Fishery	247300	241254	17	6029
采 矿 业	Mining	51239	4589	19	46631
制 造 业	Manufacturing	103177	3952	1037	98188
电力、热力、燃气及水生产和供应业	Production and Distribution of Electricity, Gas and Water	23242	8026	124	15092
建 筑 业	Construction	34251	5579	589	28083
批发和零售业	Wholesale and Retail Trades	34151	6078	1151	26922
交通运输、仓储和邮政业	Transport, Storage and Post	43870	34524	455	8891
住宿和餐饮业	Hotels and Catering Services	15683	6927	420	8336
信息传输、软件和信息技术服务业	Information Transmission, Computer Servcie and Software Industries	14553	4610	2	9941
金 融 业	Financial Intermediation	44956	16261	4887	23808
房地产业	Real Estate	16612	1806	235	14571
租赁和商务服务业	Leasing and Business Services	23018	9002	1093	12923
科学研究、技术服务业	Scientific Research, Technology Service and Geological Prospecting	21316	18199	54	3063
水利、环境和公共设施管理业	Management of Water Conservancy, Environment and Public Facility	23355	21195	1	2159
居民服务、修理和其他服务业	Services to households and Other Services	3881	2504	258	1119
教　育	Education	228137	226756	66	1315
卫生和社会工作	Health, Social Security and Social Welfare	114944	113048	1035	861
文化、体育和娱乐业	Culture, Sports and Entertainment	13826	13429		397
公共管理、社会保障和社会组织	Public Management and Social Organizations	162124	162117		7

3-22 城镇非私营单位在岗职工工资总额及构成
Total Wages of Employed Persons and Its Composition in Urban Non-Private Units

年份 Year	地区 Region	工资总额（万元）Total wages Bill(10 000 yuan) 合计 Total	国有单位 State-owned Units	城镇集体单位 Urban Collective-owned Units	其他单位 Units of Other Types of Ownership
	1978	159409	148278	11131	
	1980	212446	196711	15735	
	1985	339110	304999	33789	322
	1990	668808	601300	65858	1650
	1995	1677257	1521670	135990	19597
	2000	2344694	2007823	125510	211361
	2001	2677431	2092155	105861	479415
	2002	2915398	2211411	93605	610382
	2003	3315399	2497369	77460	740570
	2004	3563312	2691462	78224	793626
	2005	3874068	2871542	75971	926555
	2006	4429959	3318694	77978	1033287
	2007	5332395	3951882	82215	1298298
	2008	6198976	4428784	84187	1686005
	2009	6912058	4796811	91488	2023759
	2010	8286857	5669760	105413	2511684
	2011	11034557	7021538	140410	3872609
	2012	13662181	8543738	174136	4944307
	2013	16395372	9173367	167510	7054495
乌鲁木齐市	Urumqi City	4649082	2517286	43159	2088637
克拉玛依市	Karamay City	1364369	227966	5768	1130635
吐鲁番地区	Turpan Administrative Offices	435435	277091	2804	155540
哈密地区	Hami [Kumul] Administrative Offices	470778	262566	3678	204534
昌吉回族自治州	Changji Hui Autonomous Prefecture	1221230	609811	20893	590526
伊犁哈萨克自治州	Ili Kazak Autonomous Prefecture	2655092	1798348	31601	825143
伊犁州直属县(市)	Counties (Cities) Direct Under Ili Prefecture	1362855	832499	15726	514630
塔城地区	Tacheng [Tarbagatai] Administrative Offices	874833	663064	9760	202009
阿勒泰地区	Altay Administrative Offices	417404	302785	6115	108504
博尔塔拉蒙古自治州	Bortala Mongol Autonomous Prefecture	385834	308680	11260	65894
巴音郭楞蒙古自治州	Bayangol Mongol Autonomous Prefecture	1194435	567325	16065	611045
阿克苏地区	Aksu Administrative Offices	996144	597383	11291	387470
克孜勒苏柯尔克孜自治州	Kizilsu Kirgiz Autonomous Prefecture	203798	174528	1262	28008
喀什地区	Kashgar [Kaxgar] Administrative Offices	1100631	821024	11155	268452
和田地区	Hotan Administrative Offices	491064	427102	4780	59182
石河子市	Shihezi City	769626	326595	3794	439237
阿拉尔市	Aral City	160260	117368		42892
图木舒克市	Tumxuk City	107004	63121		43883
五家渠市	Wujiaqu City	190590	77173		113417

注：含劳务派遣工.
Note: Including the dispatched workers.

3-23 主要年份城镇非私营单位在岗职工工资总额指数

Indices of Total Wages of Employed Persons in Urban Non-Private Units in Main Years

年份 Year	指数(上年=100) Indices (preceding year=100)				指数(1978年=100) Indices (1978=100)			
	合计 Total	国有单位 State-owned Units	城镇集体单位 Urban Collective-owned Units	其他单位 Units of Other Types of Ownership	合计 Total	国有单位 State-owned Units	城镇集体单位 Urban Collective-owned Units	其他单位 Units of Other Types of Ownership
1978	114.2	114.5	109.6		100.0	100.0	100.0	
1980	120.5	120.1	125.2		133.3	132.7	141.4	
1985	117.4	117.5	116.0	167.5	212.7	205.7	303.6	100.0
1990	116.6	116.3	126.9	132.6	419.6	405.5	591.7	513.4
1995	126.3	126.8	119.3	146.6	1052.2	1026.2	1221.7	6097.7
2000	110.7	108.1	91.4	171.0	1470.9	1354.1	1127.6	65762.7
2001	114.2	104.2	84.3	226.8	1679.6	1411.0	951.0	149164.7
2002	108.9	105.7	88.4	127.3	1828.9	1491.4	840.9	189913.4
2003	113.7	112.9	82.8	121.3	2079.8	1684.2	695.9	230420.0
2004	107.5	107.8	101.0	107.2	2235.3	1815.1	702.8	246927.8
2005	108.7	106.7	97.1	116.7	2430.3	1936.6	682.5	288287.3
2006	114.3	115.6	102.6	111.5	2779.0	2238.2	700.5	321896.3
2007	120.4	119.1	105.4	125.6	3345.1	2665.2	738.6	403198.1
2008	116.3	112.1	102.4	129.9	3888.7	2986.8	756.3	523604.0
2009	111.5	108.3	108.7	120.0	4336.1	3235.0	821.9	628496.6
2010	119.9	118.2	115.2	124.1	5198.5	3823.7	947.0	780026.1
2011	133.2	123.8	133.2	154.2	6922.2	4735.4	1261.4	1202673.7
2012	123.8	121.7	124.0	127.7	8570.5	5762.0	1564.4	1535499.1
2013	120.0	107.4	96.2	142.7	10285.1	6186.6	1504.9	2190837.0

注：2000 年起职工工资总额指数由在岗职工工资总额计算而得。
Note: Since 2000,total wages of staff and worders were caculated by indices of total wages of stuff and workers.

3-24 主要年份城镇非私营单位在岗职工工资情况

Wages of Full-Employed Employed Persons in Urban Non-Private Units in Main Years

年份 Year	在岗职工工资总额(亿元) Total Wages of staff and workers (100 million yuan)	国有单位 State-owned Units	城镇集体单位 Urban Collective-owned Units	其他单位 Units of Other Types of Ownership	在岗职工平均工资(元) Average Wage of Staff and Workers (yuan)	国有单位 State-owned Units	城镇集体单位 Urban Collective-owned Units	其他单位 Units of Other Types of Ownership
1999	211.86	185.77	13.73	12.36	7611	7614	6815	8681
2000	234.47	200.78	12.55	21.14	8717	8731	7489	9498
2001	267.74	209.22	10.59	47.94	10278	10145	8197	11594
2002	291.54	221.14	9.36	61.04	11605	11435	9353	12767
2003	331.54	249.74	7.75	74.06	13255	13199	9966	13937
2004	356.33	269.15	7.82	79.36	14484	14477	11594	14870
2005	387.41	287.15	7.60	92.66	15558	15364	12738	16503
2006	443.00	331.87	7.80	103.33	17819	17704	14209	18566
2007	533.24	395.19	8.22	129.83	21434	21369	17780	21921
2008	619.90	442.88	8.42	168.60	24687	24016	22060	26815
2009	691.21	479.68	9.15	202.38	27753	26872	22862	30409
2010	828.69	566.98	10.54	251.17	32361	31390	31997	34807
2011	1103.46	702.15	14.04	387.26	38820	36752	40102	43177
2012	1366.22	854.37	17.41	494.43	45243	43115	47248	49380
2013	1639.54	917.34	16.75	705.45	49843	46523	57518	54749

3-25 各地区按行业分城镇非私营单位就业人员平均工资
Average Wage of Employed Persons in Urban Non-Private Units by Sector in Detail

单位：元 (2013 年) (yuan)

项　目	Item	2012	2013
总　计	**Total**	**44576**	**49064**
按行业分	**Grouped by Industrial Sector**		
农、林、牧、渔业	Farming, Forestry, Animal Husbandry and Fishery	26323	30194
采 矿 业	Mining	76486	79421
制 造 业	Manufacturing	47371	51672
电力、热力、燃气及水生产和供应业	Production and Distribution of Electricity, Gas and Water	53796	62704
建筑业	Construction	41232	45940
批发和零售业	Mining	45733	49633
交通运输、仓储和邮政业	Mining and Washing of Coal	62427	64999
住宿和餐饮业	Extraction of Petroleum and Natural Gas	32468	37072
信息传输、软件和信息技术服务业	Information Transmission, Computer Services and Software	54862	64201
金融业	Financial Intermediation	69445	74551
房地产业	Real Estate	36266	42125
租赁和商务服务业	Leasing and Business Services	35016	39137
科学研究、技术服务业	Scientific Research, Technology Service	50555	60850
水利、环境和公共设施管理业	Management of Water Conservancy, Environment and Public Facilities	32060	36318
居民服务、修理和其他服务业	Services to households and Other Services	27376	32078
教育	Education	47187	50808
卫生和社会工作	Health and Social Security	44864	49698
文化、体育和娱乐业	Culture, Sports and Entertainment	45049	50969
公共管理、社会保障和社会组织	Public Management and Social Organization	45071	46626
按地区分	**By Region**		
乌鲁木齐市	Urumqi City	51906	56783
克拉玛依市	Karamay City	71896	75743
吐鲁番地区	Turpan Administrative Offices	49659	54377
哈密地区	Hami [Kumul] Administrative Offices	43990	48594
昌吉回族自治州	Changji Hui Autonomous Prefecture	42217	47693
伊犁哈萨克自治州	Ili Kazak Autonomous Prefecture	34149	38549
伊犁州直属县(市)	Counties (Cities) Direct Under Ili Prefecture	36391	41547
塔城地区	Tacheng [Tarbagatai] Administrative Offices	32594	36365
阿勒泰地区	Altay Administrative Offices	31636	34878
博尔塔拉蒙古自治州	Bortala Mongol Autonomous Prefecture	33516	36922
巴音郭楞蒙　自治州	Bayangol Mongol Autonomous Prefecture	44130	47585
阿克苏地区	Aksu Administrative Offices	41728	44584
克孜勒苏柯尔克孜自治州	Kizilsu Kirgiz Autonomous Prefecture	38589	42741
喀什地区	Kashgar [Kaxgar] Administrative Offices	40719	45342
和田地区	Hotan Administrative Offices	45529	47625
石河子市	Shihezi City	44194	50407
阿拉尔市	Aral City	38145	43792
图木舒克市	Tumxuk City	36937	46641
五家渠市	Wujiaqu City	45807	52564

3-26 分地区分行业城镇私营单位就业人员平均工资

Average Wage of Employed Persons in Urban Private Unites by Sector and Region

单位：元 (yuan)

项 目	Item	2012	2013
总 计	**Total**	**29486**	**33409**
农、林、牧、渔业	Farming, Forestry, Animal Husbandry and Fishery	23683	30308
采矿业	Mining	40581	44315
制造业	Manufacturing	28876	32990
电力、煤气及水的生产和供应	Production and Distribution of Electricity, Gas and Water	28189	33911
建筑业	Construction	37844	41001
批发和零售业	Wholesale and Retail Trades	24048	27373
交通运输、仓储和邮政业	Transport, Storage and Post	28966	37746
住宿和餐饮业	Hotels and Catering Services	23806	24646
信息传输、计算机服务和软件	Information Transmission, Computer Servcie and Software Industries	25610	31279
金融业	Financial Intermediation	28851	36275
房地产业	Real Estate	31252	34108
租赁和商务服务业	Leasing and Business Services	23595	27265
科学研究、技术服务和地质勘查业	Scientific Research, Technology Service and Geological Prospecting	30500	32319
水利、环境和公共设施管理	Management of Water Conservancy, Environment and Public Facility	22446	27346
居民服务和其他服务业	Services to households and Other Services	21843	27320
教 育	Education	23493	29960
卫生、社会保障和社会福利	Health, Social Security and Social Welfare	26461	32130
文化、体育和娱乐业	Culture, Sports and Entertainment	18168	22839
按地区分	**By Region**		
乌鲁木齐市	Urumqi City	26485	28896
克拉玛依市	Karamay City	28404	42558
吐鲁番地区	Turpan Administrative Offices	22152	30775
哈密地区	Hami [Kumul] Administrative Offices	26144	37123
昌吉回族自治州	Changji Hui Autonomous Prefecture	27225	35715
伊犁州直属县(市)	Counties (Cities) Direct Under Ili Prefecture	25788	38330
塔城地区	Tacheng [Tarbagatai] Administrative Offices	15279	27458
阿勒泰地区	Altay Administrative Offices	26361	33520
博尔塔拉蒙古自治州	Bortala Mongol Autonomous Prefecture	23856	33458
巴音郭楞蒙古自治州	Bayangol Mongol Autonomous Prefecture	22678	29484
阿克苏地区	Aksu Administrative Offices	26056	37371
克孜勒苏柯尔克孜自治州	Kizilsu Kirgiz Autonomous Prefecture	21197	35300
喀什地区	Kashgar [Kaxgar] Administrative Offices	18490	27148
和田地区	Hotan Administrative Offices	24381	33391
生产建设兵团	Xinjiang Production and Construction Group	26359	39908

3-27 主要年份城镇非私营单位在岗职工平均货币工资
Average Money Wage of Employed Persons in Urban Non-Private Units in Main Years

单位：元 (yuan)

年份 Year	全部职工 Full Staff and Workers	国有单位 State-owned Units	城镇集体单位 Urban Collective-owned Units	其他单位 Units of Other Types of Ownership
1978	717	726	614	
1980	882	904	676	
1985	1277	1310	1038	1707
1990	2272	2345	1765	2498
1995	5348	5431	4509	5973
2000	8717	8731	7489	9498
2001	10278	10145	8197	11594
2002	11605	11435	9353	12767
2003	13255	13199	9966	13937
2004	14484	14477	11594	14870
2005	15558	15364	12738	16503
2006	17819	17704	14209	18566
2007	21434	21369	17780	21921
2008	24687	24016	22060	26815
2009	27753	26872	22862	30409
2010	32361	31390	31997	34807
2011	38820	36752	40102	43177
2012	45243	43115	47248	49380
2013	49843	46523	57518	54749

3-28 主要年份城镇非私营单位在岗职工平均工资指数
Indices of Average Wage of Employed Persons in Urban Non-Private Units in Main Years

(上年=100) (preceding year=100)

年份 Year	货币工资 Money Wage				实际工资 Real Wage			
	合计 Total	国有单位 State-owned Units	城镇集体单位 Urban Collective-owned Units	其他单位 Units of Other Types of Ownership	合计 Total	国有单位 State-owned Units	城镇集体单位 Urban Collective-owned Units	其他单位 Units of Other Types of Ownership
1978		105.2				103.9		
1980	114.5	115.3	108.3		109.3	110.0	103.4	
1985	115.7	116.0	112.5	124.6	105.9	106.0	102.7	113.7
1990	113.2	113.3	113.6	96.5	108.3	108.4	108.7	92.3
1995	125.8	125.7	125.8	120.9	105.7	105.6	105.7	101.6
2000	114.5	114.7	109.9	109.4	115.2	115.4	110.6	110.1
2001	117.9	116.2	109.5	122.1	113.4	111.7	105.3	117.4
2002	112.9	112.7	114.1	110.1	113.6	113.4	114.8	110.8
2003	114.2	115.4	106.6	109.2	113.6	114.8	106.1	108.7
2004	109.3	109.7	116.3	106.7	107.0	107.4	113.9	104.5
2005	107.4	106.1	109.9	111.0	106.7	105.4	109.1	110.2
2006	114.5	115.2	111.5	112.5	113.7	114.4	110.7	111.7
2007	120.3	120.7	125.1	118.1	114.0	114.4	118.6	111.9
2008	115.2	112.4	124.1	122.3	106.6	104.0	114.8	113.1
2009	112.4	111.9	103.6	113.4	111.6	111.1	102.9	112.6
2010	116.6	116.8	140.0	114.5	111.8	112.0	134.2	109.7
2011	120.0	117.1	125.3	124.0	113.3	110.6	118.3	117.1
2012	116.5	117.3	117.8	114.4	112.2	113.0	113.5	110.2
2013	110.2	107.9	121.7	110.9	106.0	103.8	117.2	106.7

3-29 各地、州、市分行业城镇非私营单位在岗职工(含劳务派遣工)平均货币工资
Average Wage of Employed Persons in Urban Non-Private Unites (including the dispatched employees) by Sector and Prefecture, Autonomous Prefecture and City

单位：元 (2013 年) (yuan)

年 份 Year	地 区 Region	合 计 Total	农林牧渔业 Farming, Forestry, Animal Husbandry and Fishery	采 矿 业 Mining	制 造 业 Manufacturing	电力、热力、燃气及水的生产和供应业 Production and Distribution of Power, Gas and Water
总　　计	**Total**	**49843**	**30444**	**80054**	**52007**	**62962**
乌鲁木齐市	Urumqi City	57392	36215	82912	56014	71886
克拉玛依市	Karamay City	78964	39720	95783	76511	70560
吐鲁番地区	Turpan Administrative Offices	56683	33033	71329	51044	74584
哈密地区	Hami [Kumul] Administrative Offices	48894	30850	61366	48810	69194
昌吉回族自治州	Changji Hui Autonomous Prefecture	48164	39163	62804	46959	62550
伊犁哈萨克自治州	Ili Kazak Autonomous Prefecture	38785	24813	51134	45465	66462
伊犁州直属县(市)	Counties (Cities) Direct Under Ili Prefecture	41658	28495	61455	47669	65525
塔城地区	Tacheng [Tarbagatai] Administrative Offices	36764	27118	46416	41707	66721
阿勒泰地区	Altay Administrative Offices	34940	12798	49784	38468	68535
博尔塔拉蒙古自治州	Bortala Mongol Autonomous Prefecture	37605	31974	34577	34965	52750
巴音郭楞蒙古自治州	Bayangol Mongol Autonomous Prefecture	49049	31089	81878	49264	53355
阿克苏地区	Aksu Administrative Offices	44683	26582	75064	48387	61194
克孜勒苏柯尔克孜自治州	Kizilsu Kirgiz Autonomous Prefecture	45202	37740	53426	59663	60701
喀什地区	Kashgar [Kaxgar] Administrative Offices	46390	36071	44583	34413	49319
和田地区	Hotan Administrative Offices	51059	30519	66464	49945	52142
石河子市	Shihezi City	50500	54519		48599	52101
阿拉尔市	Aral City	43793	39453		42517	48186
图木舒克市	Tumxuk City	46767	36611		54270	82686
五家渠市	Wujiaqu City	53086	34070		54044	59721

年 份 Year	地 区 Region	建 筑 业 Construction	批发和零售业 Wholesale and Retail Trades	交通运输、仓储和邮政业 Transport, Storage and Post	住宿和餐饮业 Hotels and Catering Services	信息传输、软件和信息技术服务业 Information Transmission, Computer Servcie and Software
总　　计	**Total**	**46429**	**50140**	**65649**	**37413**	**64603**
乌鲁木齐市	Urumqi City	46434	55170	71521	44129	74660
克拉玛依市	Karamay City	60810	64034	54963	33003	66884
吐鲁番地区	Turpan Administrative Offices	57273	60694	33801	31804	64210
哈密地区	Hami [Kumul] Administrative Offices	55606	60820	40889	40676	65704
昌吉回族自治州	Changji Hui Autonomous Prefecture	46508	52787	47236	30507	59263
伊犁哈萨克自治州	Ili Kazak Autonomous Prefecture	41596	41146	43316	28394	53327
伊犁州直属县(市)	Counties (Cities) Direct Under Ili Prefecture	44353	39646	40341	28652	58372
塔城地区	Tacheng [Tarbagatai] Administrative Offices	37008	36757	46264	23652	52149
阿勒泰地区	Altay Administrative Offices	34680	52887	47756	29612	46076
博尔塔拉蒙古自治州	Bortala Mongol Autonomous Prefecture	29622	50007	52955	32082	64124
巴音郭楞蒙古自治州	Bayangol Mongol Autonomous Prefecture	50284	49374	39603	29382	73294
阿克苏地区	Aksu Administrative Offices	56297	40471	42233	34030	61530
克孜勒苏柯尔克孜自治州	Kizilsu Kirgiz Autonomous Prefecture	43860	34329	46522	32866	47400
喀什地区	Kashgar [Kaxgar] Administrative Offices	46522	42384	50191	32938	63662
和田地区	Hotan Administrative Offices	51692	54565	44153	32758	52654
石河子市	Shihezi City	44006	50749	65192	41427	64685
阿拉尔市	Aral City	48655	46397	41583		
图木舒克市	Tumxuk City	49176	93500		27765	
五家渠市	Wujiaqu City	62475	51874	42934	39916	39778

3-29 续表 Continued

单位：元 (yuan)

年 份 Year	地 区 Region	金融业 Financial Intermedition	房地产业 Real Estate	租赁和商务服务业 Leasing and Business Services	科学研究、技术服务 Scientific Research, Technology Service	水利、环境和公共设施管理业 Management of Water Conservancy, Environment and Public Facility
总 计	**Total**	**87175**	**42805**	**40310**	**61462**	**37631**
乌鲁木齐市	Urumqi City	119185	49576	55496	74575	44523
克拉玛依市	Karamay City	88536	35006	44184	81832	43466
吐鲁番地区	Turpan Administrative Offices	67555	30469	31745	45609	38160
哈密地区	Hami [Kumul] Administrative Offices	85185	36850	43300	57256	26686
昌吉回族自治州	Changji Hui Autonomous Prefecture	90959	40679	30499	49986	40649
伊犁哈萨克自治州	Ili Kazak Autonomous Prefecture	68756	34196	29771	47997	33885
伊犁州直属县(市)	Counties (Cities) Direct Under Ili Prefecture	67953	34663	28826	47360	27315
塔城地区	Tacheng [Tarbagatai] Administrative Offices	71661	33392	35725	49023	42798
阿勒泰地区	Altay Administrative Offices	67009	30955	29464	48168	34654
博尔塔拉蒙古自治州	Bortala Mongol Autonomous Prefecture	86838	36247	14284	60991	40525
巴音郭楞蒙古自治州	Bayangol Mongol Autonomous Prefecture	86566	32691	49980	53762	28408
阿克苏地区	Aksu Administrative Offices	68849	37182	27865	49377	33098
克孜勒苏柯尔克孜自治州	Kizilsu Kirgiz Autonomous Prefecture	44234	37088	19520	44694	52006
喀什地区	Kashgar [Kaxgar] Administrative Offices	64748	36491	27412	53350	43040
和田地区	Hotan Administrative Offices	73061	41985	28861	52992	38354
石河子市	Shihezi City	67633	71664	35746	71343	57212
阿拉尔市	Aral City		33445	55357	61471	59043
图木舒克市	Tumxuk City			50698	48000	39173
五家渠市	Wujiaqu City	80271	59111	55084	64887	62409

年 份 Year	地 区 Region	居民服务、修理和其他服务业 Services to households and Other Services	教 育 Education	卫生和社会事业 Health, Social Security and Social Welfare	文化、体育和娱乐业 Culture, Sports and Entertainment	公共管理、社会保障和社会组织 Public Administration and Social Organizations
总 计	**Total**	**32454**	**51084**	**50795**	**51336**	**47875**
乌鲁木齐市	Urumqi City	45060	50447	61411	56420	45252
克拉玛依市	Karamay City	28694	79801	93028	90797	66967
吐鲁番地区	Turpan Administrative Offices		47843	58413	47596	47708
哈密地区	Hami [Kumul] Administrative Offices	36048	52533	47877	38312	48076
昌吉回族自治州	Changji Hui Autonomous Prefecture	53664	55849	49371	50684	52498
伊犁哈萨克自治州	Ili Kazak Autonomous Prefecture	26211	47324	44352	43545	46184
伊犁州直属县(市)	Counties (Cities) Direct Under Ili Prefecture	26030	45179	42701	42016	42709
塔城地区	Tacheng [Tarbagatai] Administrative Offices	25384	51129	47233	43763	49256
阿勒泰地区	Altay Administrative Offices	28754	48761	45805	47205	51003
博尔塔拉蒙古自治州	Bortala Mongol Autonomous Prefecture	39143	50570	49722	47325	44212
巴音郭楞蒙古自治州	Bayangol Mongol Autonomous Prefecture	32797	50280	46264	46978	47833
阿克苏地区	Aksu Administrative Offices	32590	45741	41826	42690	42373
克孜勒苏柯尔克孜自治州	Kizilsu Kirgiz Autonomous Prefecture	23197	48601	38642	45660	50426
喀什地区	Kashgar [Kaxgar] Administrative Offices	49903	50576	42670	48101	46145
和田地区	Hotan Administrative Offices	52526	55570	51153	53499	56376
石河子市	Shihezi City	42262	71819	71865	56690	69461
阿拉尔市	Aral City		54924	52813	58421	54784
图木舒克市	Tumxuk City		47980	52055		65044
五家渠市	Wujiaqu City	64000	61582	60081	53397	61484

3-30 各地、州、市、县(市)城镇非私营单位在岗职工(含劳务派遣工)平均货币工资
Average Wages of Fully Employed Persons in Urban Non-Private Units (including the dispatched employees)by Prefecture, Autonomous Prefecture, City and County

单位：元 (2013 年) (yuan)

地　区	Region	合 计 Total	国有单位 State-owned Units	城镇集体单位 Urban Collective-owned Units	其他单位 Units of Other Types of Ownership
总　计	**Total**	**49843**	**46523**	**57518**	**54749**
乌鲁木齐市	**Urumqi City**	**57392**	**59223**	**53434**	**55413**
天山区	Tianshan District	54895	58496	52013	50312
沙依巴克区	Shayibak District	53351	54641	55406	52217
新市区	Xinshi District	56553	54953	55952	57814
水磨沟区	Shui Mogou Distric	51617	52904	23866	50028
头屯河区	Tou Tunhe District	48890	41092	56108	55165
达坂城区	Da Bancheng District	57481	46829	41882	60963
米东区	Midong District	63087	52672	50231	69907
乌鲁木齐县	Urumqi County	60386	59219	80995	55859
克拉玛依市	**Karamay City**	**78964**	**65928**	**36390**	**82758**
独山子区	Dushanzi District	77367	76817	37736	79271
克拉玛依区	Karamay District	81895	66253	34476	85734
白碱滩区	Bai Jiantan District	53518	69358	34000	47373
乌尔河区	Urhe District	43841	38568		67766
吐鲁番地区	**Turpan Administrative Offices**	**56683**	**55950**	**39776**	**58496**
吐鲁番市	Turpan City	47944	49526	35660	44348
鄯善县	Shanshan [Piqan] County	64014	63081	57583	65747
托克逊县	Toksun County	55902	50898	40538	60550
哈密地区	**Hami [Kumul] Administrative Offices**	**48894**	**43585**	**60493**	**57721**
哈密市	Hami [Kumul] City	50029	44753	56183	57362
巴里坤哈萨克自治县	Barkol Kazak Autonomous County	39960	37554	71983	59408
伊吾县	Yiwu [Araturuk] County	54401	49373	37583	62066
昌吉回族自治州	**Changji Hui Autonomous Prefecture**	**48164**	**46552**	**77524**	**49267**
昌吉市	Changji City	50287	51376	108721	48553
阜康市	Fukang City	49843	46471	118673	50272
呼图壁县	Hutubi County	43887	41208	105447	47108
玛纳斯县	Manas County	45196	44337	24310	48010
奇台县	Qitai County	46472	44932	65927	47911
吉木萨尔县	Jimsar County	53749	51310	106474	54392
木垒哈萨克自治县	Mori Kazak Autonomous County	54694	53751	89673	55197
伊犁哈萨克自治州	**Ili Kazak Autonomous Prefecture**	**38785**	**36227**	**58729**	**45144**
伊犁州直属县(市)	**Counties (Cities) Direct Under Ili Prefecture**	**41658**	**39135**	**52810**	**46176**
伊宁市	Yining [Gulja] City	43280	42067	66409	44535
奎屯市	Kuytun City	45394	45932	36957	45283
伊宁县	Yining [Gulja] County	32800	28776	23950	44080
察布查尔锡伯自治县	Qapqal Xibe Autonomous County	38858	37098	57550	47886
霍城县	Huocheng [Korgas] County	36593	35150	35424	46631
巩留县	Gongliu [Tokkuztara] County	44004	43775	66929	

3-30 续表 1 Continued

单位：元　　(2013 年)　　(yuan)

地　区	Region	合 计 Total	国有单位 State-owned Units	城镇集体单位 Urban Collective-owned Units	其他单位 Units of Other Types of Ownership
新源县	Xinyuan [Kunes] County	48425	44356	45829	53567
昭苏县	Zhaosu [Mongolkure] County	37794	37703	71116	31628
特克斯县	Tekes County	41018	40832	69888	40101
尼勒克县	Nilka County	40957	36092	103855	49515
塔城地区	**Tacheng [Tarbagatai] Administrative Offices**	**36764**	**35155**	**59584**	**42343**
塔城市	Tacheng [Qoqek] City	42645	39778	52381	55013
乌苏市	Usu City	31970	29010	55867	46211
额敏县	Emin [Dorbiljin] County	26557	25512	91512	33853
沙湾县	Shawan County	41451	43465	75217	35402
托里县	Toli County	48937	49248	23767	48973
裕民县	Yumin [Qagantokay] County	35406	35424	45911	23619
和布克赛尔蒙古自治县	Hoboksar Mongol Autonomous County	36506	29181	70672	54242
阿勒泰地区	**Altay Administrative Offices**	**34940**	**31847**	**79936**	**45930**
阿勒泰市	Altay City	38294	35408	87480	47088
布尔津县	Burqin County	33519	31709	71471	37279
富蕴县	Fuyun [Koktokay] County	28371	20723	114748	50866
福海县	Fuhai [Burultokay] County	32466	30642	96278	49194
哈巴河县	Habahe [Kaba] County	35604	32865	39472	44501
青河县	Qinghe [Qinggil] County	40274	40451	78747	35310
吉木乃县	Jemnay County	35289	34512	50217	43066
博尔塔拉蒙古自治州	**Bortala Mongol Autonomous Prefecture**	**37605**	**37936**	**53848**	**34426**
博乐市	Bole [Bortala] City	40360	40921	43982	37139
阿拉山口市	Alashankou City	87218	77605		88346
精河县	Jinghe [Jing] County	34432	32940	52122	34762
温泉县	Wenquan [Araxang] County	31057	34100	120397	22284
巴音郭楞蒙古自治州	**Bayangol Mongol Autonomous Prefecture**	**49049**	**42602**	**71721**	**56520**
库尔勒市	Korla City	54002	47235	61969	58596
轮台县	Luntai [Bugur] County	51096	42091	138752	63122
尉犁县	Yuli [Lopnur] County	37320	40732	62518	24964
若羌县	Ruoqiang [Qarkilik] County	69878	48857	125135	100078
且末县	Qiemo [Qarqan] County	39833	39589	45845	41812
焉耆回族自治县	Yanji Hui Autonomous County	41896	40566	92106	45815
和静县	Hejing County	39097	36586	40263	43400
和硕县	Hoxud County	34727	33281	99977	42654
博湖县	Bohu [Bagrax] County	39996	39832	88411	31394
阿克苏地区	**Aksu Administrative Offices**	**44683**	**41079**	**52419**	**51417**
阿克苏市	Aksu City	49210	46624	42679	53211
温宿县	Wensu [Onsu] County	32882	31963	40285	34972
库车县	Kuqa County	46005	38016	45196	56407
沙雅县	Xayar County	40860	38583	77847	43854

3-30 续表 2 Continued

单位：元 (2013 年) (yuan)

地　　区	Region	合 计 Total	国有单位 State-owned Units	城镇集体单　位 Urban Collective-owned Units	其他单位 Units of Other Types of Ownership
新和县	Xinhe [Toksu] County	42018	41478	77178	41204
拜城县	Baicheng [Bay] County	53312	43315	92401	65318
乌什县	Wushi [Uxturpan] County	40656	40762	46849	38027
阿瓦提县	Awat County	39749	39696	34189	40407
柯坪县	Kalpin County	43761	43781	37320	46520
克孜勒苏柯尔克孜自治州	**Kizilsu Kirgiz Autonomous Prefecture**	**45202**	**44801**	**30995**	**48940**
阿图什市	Artux City	42789	43152	30377	41664
阿克陶县	Akto County	52541	53274	30497	41861
阿合奇县	Akqi County	41405	35551	39179	99203
乌恰县	Wuqia [Ulugqat] County	46440	45366	30023	56161
喀什地区	**Kashgar [Kaxgar] Administrative Offices**	**46390**	**46978**	**48290**	**44610**
喀什市	Kashgar [Kaxgar] City	48134	48426	37556	47990
疏附县	Shufu County	48438	49231	44639	25769
疏勒县	Shule County	40388	43121	30676	29421
英吉沙县	Yengisar County	42840	42499	22288	47367
泽普县	Zepu [Poskam] County	45348	47020	37800	24603
莎车县	Shache [Yarkant] County	50161	52125	77798	29979
叶城县	Yecheng [Kagilik] County	49276	52643	51907	36925
麦盖提县	Makit County	43012	42758	54833	44133
岳普湖县	Yopurga County	39617	40128	43667	32882
伽师县	Jiashi [Payzawat] County	40219	40412		36227
巴楚县	Bachu [Maralbexi] County	45039	45865	45036	36773
塔什库尔干塔吉克自治县	Taxkorgan Tajik Autonomous County	57491	56397		66742
和田地区	**Hotan Administrative Offices**	**51059**	**51077**	**82279**	**49421**
和田市	Hotan City	53835	55833	59876	48151
和田县	Hotan County	55948	54116		77235
墨玉县	Moyu [Karakax] County	49713	50028		44583
皮山县	Pishan [Guma] County	40485	39810	129451	33845
洛浦县	Lop County	54165	55447	46875	37141
策勒县	Qira County	51651	49118	119071	61367
于田县	Yutian [Keriya] County	53804	53251		70906
民丰县	Minfeng [Niya] County	55935	55981	52594	46000
自治区直辖县级市	**Municpality Country-LevelCity dire-ctlyunder the Central overn-ment**	**49539**	**49654**	**131284**	**49253**
石河子市	Shihezi City	50500	54544	131284	47621
阿拉尔市	Aral City	43793	42930		46340
图木舒克市	Tumxuk City	46767	44005		51409
五家渠市	Wujiaqu City	53086	47919		57290

主要统计指标解释

人口数　指一定时点、一定地区范围内的有生命的个人的总和。

年度统计的年末人口数指每年 12 月 31 日 24 时的人口数。

户籍人口　指公民依照《中华人民共和国户口登记条例》已在其经常居住地的公安户籍管理机关登记了常住户口的人。

常住人口　指在某地区实际居住半年以上的人口。

城镇人口和乡村人口　城镇人口是指居住在城镇范围内的全部常住人口；乡村人口是除上述人口以外的全部人口。

出生率(又称粗出生率)　指在一定时期内(通常为一年)一定地区的出生人数与同期内平均人数(或期中人数)之比，用千分率表示。本资料中的出生率指年出生率，其计算公式为：

出生率＝年出生人数／年平均人数×1000‰

式中：出生人数指活产婴儿，即胎儿脱离母体时(不管怀孕月数)，有过呼吸或其他生命现象。年平均人数指年初、年底人口数的平均数，也可用年中人口数代替。

死亡率(又称粗死亡率)　指在一定时期内(通常为一年)一定地区的死亡人数与同期内平均人数(或期中人数)之比，用千分率表示。本资料中的死亡率指年死亡率，其计算公式为：

死亡率＝年死亡人数／年平均人数×1000‰

人口自然增长率　指在一定时期内(通常为一年)人口自然增加数(出生人数减死亡人数)与该时期内平均人数(或期中人数)之比，用千分率表示。计算公式为：

人口自然增长率＝(本年出生人数－本年死亡人数)／年平均人数×1000‰＝人口出生率－人口死亡率

经济活动人口　指在 16 周岁及以上，有劳动能力，参加或要求参加社会经济活动的人口；包括就业人员和失业人员。

就业人员　指 16 周岁及以上，从事一定的社会劳动并取得劳动报酬或经营收入的人员。这一指标反映了一定时期内全部劳动力资源的实际利用情况，是研究我国基本国情国力的重要指标。

单位就业人员　指报告期末最后一日 24 时在本单位中工作，并取得工资或其他形式劳动报酬的人员数。该指标为时点指标，不包括最后一日当天及以前已经与单位解除劳动合同关系的人员，是在岗职工、劳务派遣人员及其他就业人员之和。就业人员不包括：

(1)离开本单位仍保留劳动关系，并定期领取生活费的人员；

(2)利用课余时间打工的学生及在本单位实习的各类在校学生；

(3)本单位因劳务外包而使用的人员。

国有单位　指资产归国家所有的经济组织。包括按《中华人民共和国企业法人登记管理条例》规定登记注册的非公司制的经济组织，以及中央、地方各级国家机关、事业单位和社会团体。

集体单位　指生产资料归集体所有，并按《中华人民共和国企业法人登记管理条例》规定登记注册的经济组织。

其他单位　包括股份合作单位、联营单位、有限责任公司、股份有限公司、港澳台商投资单位以及外商投资单位等其他登记注册类型单位。

城镇私营和个体就业人员　城镇私营就业人员指在工商管理部门注册登记，其经营地址设在县城关镇(含县城关镇)以上的私营企业就业人员，包括私营企业投资者和雇工。城镇个体就业人员指在工商管理部门注册登记，并持有城镇户口或在城镇长期居住，经批准从事个体工商经营的就业人员，包括个体经营者和在个体工商户劳动的家庭帮工和雇工。

在岗职工　指在本单位工作且与本单位签订劳动合同，并由单位支付各项工资和社会保险、住房公积金的人员，以及上述人员中由于学习、病伤、产假等原因暂未工作仍由单位支付工资的人员。在岗职工还包括：

(1)应订立劳动合同而未订立劳动合同人员(如使用的农村户籍人员)；

(2)处于试用期人员；

(3)编制外招用的人员；

(4)派往外单位工作，但工资仍由本单位发放的人员(如挂职锻炼、外派工作等情况)。

工资总额　指根据《关于工资总额组成的规定》(1990 年 1 月 1 日国家统计局发布的一号令)进行修订，在报告期内(季度或年度)直接支付给本单位全部就业人员的劳动报酬总额。包括计时工资、计件工资、奖金、津贴和补贴、加班加点工资、特殊情况下支付的工资，是在岗职工工资总额、劳务派遣人员工资总额和其他就业人员工资总额之和。

工资总额是税前工资，包括单位从个人工资中直接为其代扣或代缴的房费、水费、电费、住房公积金和社会保险基金个人缴纳部分等。

工资总额不论是计入成本的还是不计入成本的，不论是以货币形式支付的还是以实物形式支付的，均应列入工资总额的计算范围。

平均工资　指单位就业人员在一定时期内平均每人所得的货币工资额。它表明一定时期职工工资收入的高低程

度，是反映就业人员工资水平的主要指标。计算公式为:

平均工资＝报告期实际支付的全部就业人员工资总额／报告期全部就业人员平均人数

平均工资指数 指报告期就业人员平均工资与基期就业人员平均工资的比率，是反映不同时期就业人员货币工资水平变动情况的相对数。计算公式为：

平均工资指数＝报告期就业人员平均工资／基期就业人员平均工资

平均实际工资指数 就业人员平均实际工资指扣除物价变动因素后的就业人员平均工资。就业人员平均实际工资指数是反映实际工资变动情况的相对数，表明就业人员实际工资水平提高或降低的程度。计算公式为：

平均实际工资指数＝报告期就业人员平均工资指数／报告期城镇居民消费价格指数×100%

城镇登记失业人员 指有非农业户口，在一定的劳动年龄内（16 周岁至退休年龄），有劳动能力，无业而要求就业，并在当地劳动保障部门进行失业登记的人员。

城镇登记失业率 城镇登记失业人员与城镇单位就业人员（扣除使用的农村劳动力、聘用的离退休人员、港澳台及外方人员）、城镇单位中不在岗职工、城镇私营业主、个体户主、城镇私营企业和个体就业人员、城镇登记失业人数之和的比。

Explanatory Notes on Main Statistical Indicators

Total Population refers to the total number of people alive at a certain point of time within a given area.

The annual statistics on total population is taken at midnight, the 31st of December.

The household register population refers to citizens in accordance with the "people's Republic of Household Registration Ordinance" has been registered permanent residence.

The resident population refers to the practical living more than half year of the population.

Urban Population and Rural Population Urban population refers to all people residing in cities and towns, while rural population refers to population other than urban population.

Birth Rate(or Crude Birth Rate) refers to the ratio of the number of births to the average population (or mid-period population) during a certain period of time (usually a year), expressed in ‰. Birth rate in the chapter refers to annual birth rate. The following formula is used:

Brith Rate= Number of Births/Annual Average Number of Population*1000

Number of births in the formula refers to live births, i.e. when a baby has breathed or showed any vital phenomena regardless of the length of pregnancy.

Annual average population is the average of the number of population at the beginning of the year and that at the end of the year. Sometimes it is substituted by the mid-year population.

Death Rate(or Crude Death Rate) refers to the ratio of the number of deaths to the average population (or mid- period population) during a certain period of time (usually a year), expressed in‰. Death rate in the chapter refers to annual death rate. The following formula is used:

Death Rate =Number of Deaths/ Annual Average Number of Population*1000

Natural Growth Rate of Population refers to the ratio of natural increase in population(number of births minus number of deaths)in a certain period of time(usually a year)to the average population(or mid-period population)of the same period , expressed in‰. The following formula is applied:

Natural Growth Rate of Population= Number of Births-Number of Deaths / Annual Average Number of Population *1000

Natural Growth Rate of Population=Birth Rate-Death Rate

Economically Active Population refers to the population aged 16 and over who are capable of working, are participating in or willing to participate in economic activities, including employed persons and unemployed persons.

Employed Persons refer to persons aged 16 and over who are engaged in gainful employment and thus receive remuneration payment or earn business income. This indicator reflects the actual utilization of total labour force during a certain period of time and is often used for the research on China's economic situation and national power.

Persons Employed in Various Units refer to the total number of employees who work at his unit and obtain wages or other forms of payment at the end of the reporting period. This indicator is a kind of time point index and it equals to the sum of the number of employed staff and workers, labor dispatch personnel and other employed persons. Employed persons do not include:

、 1)persons who have left their working units while keeping their labour contract (employment relation) unchanged and receiving regular alimony;

2)students who do part-time jobs in spare time and all kinds of enrolled students who do internship in various units;

3)persons employed due to labor outsourcing;

4)persons who dissolve labor contracts with their units on the last day of reporting period or before.

State-owned Units refer to economic units whose assets are owned by the state.Included are non-corporation units registered according to Regulation of the People's Republic of China on the Registration of Enterprises and Corporation ,state argans,institutions and social organizations at the central and local levels.

Collective-owned Units refer to economic units registered according to Regulation of the People's Republic of China on the Registration of Enterprises and Corporations where the means of production are collectively owned.

Units of Other Types of Ownership refer to units registered with other types of ownership,including cooperative units,joint ownership units,limited companies,share holding corporation,units invested by entrepreneurs from Hong Kong, Macao,and Taiwan,and foreign-invested units.

Persons Employed in Private Enterprises and Self-Employed Individuals in Urban Areas Persons employed in private enterprises refer to the persons employed in the private enterprises which have been registered at the departments of industrial and commercial administration for which the business operation are situated at a county town (i.e. a town where the county government is located), or at urban areas with administrative hierarchy higher than a county town. The self-employed individuals in urban areas refer to persons who hold the certificates of residence in urban areas or have resided in the urban areas for a long time and have been registered at the departments of industrial and commercial administration and approved to be engaged in individual industrial or commercial business, including self-employed persons as well as helpers and hired laborers who work in individual households.

Employed Staff and Workers refer to persons who signed labor contracts with working units and working units would pay wages, social insurance and housing funds for them. Persons who have their work posts but are temporarily absent from work for reasons of study or on sick, injury or maternal leave and still receive wages from their working units are also included. Employed staff and workers also include:

1)Persons who should have signed the labor contracts but not (like people with rural household registration);

2)Employees on probation;

3)Employees beyond the staffing quota;

4)Employees who are sent to other working units but still obtain wages from their original units (situations like on-the-job placement, expatriated assignment, etc.)

1)Employed Staff and Workers do not include: Dispatched personnel who work and are paid directly by the working units; they shall be counted into "labour dispatch personnel" of the working units;

2)Personnel through labor outsourcing, they shall be counted into "employed staff and workers" of the units which contracted them.

Total Wage Bill It is revised according to the "Provision of Composition of Total Wages" (Order No.1 by National Bureau of Statistics on January, 1st, 1990), total wage bill refers to the total remuneration payment to all employed persons in various units during the reporting period (by quarter or by year), including hourly-paid wages, piece-rate wages, bonuses, allowance and subsidies, overtime wages and wages paid under special circumstances. It equals to the sum of total wages of employed staff and workers, dispatch labors and other employed persons.

Total wage bill is pre-tax wages, including the room charges, utility bills, housing funds and social insurance paid or withheld by employee's units.

Total wage bill, whether or not included in cost, whether or not paid in money or in kind, shall be included in the calculation of total wage.

Average Wage refers to the average per capita wage in money terms during a certain period of time for employed persons. It shows the general level of wage income of staff and worker during a certain period of time, one major indicator to reflect the wage level. It is calculated as follows:

Average Wage =Total Wage Bill of Empioyed Perons at Reference Time /Average Number of Persons Employed at Reference Time

Average Wage Indices refers to the ratio of average wage of employed persons the reference period to that at the base period, which reflects the change of wage of employed persons at the different period. It is calculated as follows:

Average Wage Indices = Average Wage of Employed Persons at Reference Time / Average Wage of Persons Employeds at Base Period *100%

Average Real Wage Indices average real wage of employed persons refers to the average wage of employed persons after removing the effects of the price changes and average real wage indices of employed persons refers to the change of real wage, which reflects the relative increasing or decreasing level of real wage of employed persons ,which is calculated as follows:

Average Real Wage Indices =Average Wage Indices of Employed Persons at the Reference Time / Urban Consumer Price Indices at Reference Time *100%

Registered Unemployed Persons in Urban Areas refer to the persons with non-agricultural household registration at certain working ages (16 years old to retirement age), who are capable of working, unemployed and willing to work, and have been registered at the local employment service agencies to apply for a job.

Registered Unemployment Rate in Urban Areas refers to the ratio of the number of the registered unemployed persons to the sum of the number of persons employed in various units (minus the employed rural labour force, re-employed retirees, and Hong Kong, Macao, Taiwan or foreign employees), laid-off staff and workers in urban units, owners of private enterprises in urban areas, owners of self-employed individuals in urban areas, employees of private enterprises in urban areas, employee of self-employed individuals in urban areas, and the registered unemployed persons in urban areas.

新疆统计年鉴

XINJIANG STATISTICAL YEARBOOK

4

固定资产投资

INVESTMENT IN FIXED ASSETS

简要说明

本篇主要内容和资料来源

本篇资料包括主要年份全社会固定资产投资及其主要分组；2013年及同期的全区固定资产投资及其细化分组；2013年新增主要产品生产能力(或效益)；房地产开发企业基本情况；农村非农户固定资产投资情况。

本篇资料来自新疆维吾尔自治区统计局固定资产投资统计处。

本篇资料的统计范围，2011年及以前年份，固定资产投资统计起点为50及50万元以上；2012年开始，按照国家统计局相关规定，固定资产投资统计起点调整为500万元及以上。

本篇的统计调查方法为全面调查。

Brief Introduction

Main Content and Source of Data

Statistics in this chapter cover the total investment in fixed assets of the whole society and its composition, total investment in fixed assets and its refining grouping by region in 2013;newly increased production capacity of major production in 2013; basic condition of enterprises for real estate development, basic condition of individual investment in fixed assets of farm households and non-farm households.

The data of investment in fixed assets in rural areas come from the Division of Investment in Fixed Assets, Xinjiang Bureau of Statistics.

Scope of statistics: Before and in 2011,the starting point of fixed assets is changed from RMB 500,000 and above; From 2012,the stating point of fixed assets is changed to RMB 5 million according to relevant regulations of National Bureau of Statistics.

All data on the investment in fixed assets are collected by the statistical reporting system with complete enumeration.

4-1 1978-2013 年历年全社会固定资产投资
Total Investment in Fixed Assets in the Whole Country by Period (1978-2013)

单位：万元 (10 000 yuan)

年 份 Year	合 计 Total	城 镇 Urban Area	#房地产 Real Estate Development	农 村 Rural Area	非农户 Non-Farm Households	农村个人 Farm Individuals
1978	129999	129999				
1979	138253	138253				
1980	204652	203489		1163		1163
1981	183986	171706		12280	10000	2280
1982	247382	233668		13714	9693	4021
1983	277923	262027		15896	8804	7092
1984	337250	305713		31537	11089	20448
1985	444758	408435		36323	11528	24795
1986	484658	443631		41027	13934	27093
1987	512479	469898		42581	14714	27867
1988	684119	622041		62078	16848	45230
1989	750698	664243		86455	18841	67614
1990	887775	791555	9456	96220	20578	75642
1991	1249325	1130155	16886	119170	26946	92224
1992	1700326	1571456	23941	128870	33202	95668
1993	2484352	2336810	53616	147542	40738	106804
1994	2854786	2614211	86244	240575	70349	170226
1995	3333404	3035386	171238	298018	92118	205900
1996	3878472	3495942	156232	382530	111936	270594
1997	4468148	3987127	169906	481021	131063	349958
1998	5197673	4709794	148577	487879	136402	351477
1999	5346468	4847597	234481	498871	150744	348127
2000	6103843	5568492	574347	535351	171862	363489
2001	7059970	6469753	979184	590217	210040	380177
2002	8130223	7474024	877060	656199	252891	403308
2003	10021256	9213289	1024908	807967	327137	480830
2004	11615245	10608048	1125577	1007197	463358	543839
2005	13522757	12232255	1016618	1290502	573585	716917
2006	15670521	14180110	1208786	1490411	699084	791327
2007	18508415	16591894	1683160	1916521	1080611	835910
2008	22599746	20256393	2286267	2343353	1412796	930557
2009	28272359	25358648	2358805	2913711	1874325	1039386
2010	35396941	31815829	3477185	3581112	2395698	1185414
2011	47127699	42044959	5163895	5082740	3211176	1871564
2012	62583830	55938065	6060939	6645765	3637772	3007993
2013	81484141	73844121	8256855	7640020	4030020	3610000

4-2 全社会固定资产投资
Total Investment in Fixed Assets in the Whole Country

单位：万元 (2013 年) (10 000 yuan)

项　目	Item	合 计 Total	城 镇 Urban	#房地产 Real Estate Development
投资总额	**Total Investment**	**81484141**	**73844121**	**8256855**
#住 宅	Residential Buildings	11362478	10890654	5556183
#国有经济控股	State-holding	45105309	42530959	1425934
按构成分	**Grouped by Use of Funds**			
建筑工程	Construction	50280291	47163528	6428567
安装工程	Installation	6153338	5956791	653940
设备工器具购置	Purchase of Equipment and Instruments	16516828	15968939	138890
其他费用	Other Expenses	4923684	4754863	1035458
按三次产业分	**Grouped by Three Strata of Industry**			
第一产业	Primary Industry	2355032	1531678	
第二产业	Secondary Industry	39793641	38360470	
第三产业	Tertiary Industry	35725468	33951973	8256855
按登记注册类型分	**Grouped by Types of Registration**			
内资企业	Domestic Fund Enterprises	77114921	73160734	8237055
国 有	State-owned	34093427	31831043	258543
集 体	Collective-owned	227024	109038	50
股份合作	Share-holding Cooperative	111437	100837	300
联营企业	Joint Ownership Enterprises	158878	144028	
国有联营企业	State Joint Ownership Enterprises	101152	92102	
集体联营企业	Collective-owned Joint Ownership Enterprises	17303	11503	
国有与集体联营企业	State and Collective-owned Joint Ownership Enterprises	2170	2170	
其他联营企业	Others	38253	38253	
有限责任公司	Limited Liability Corporations	21919180	21209863	4112577
国有独资公司	State-funded Corporations	1913033	1890068	316540
其他有限责任公司	Other Limited Liability Corporations	20006147	19319795	3796037
股份有限公司	Share-holding Corporations Ltd	5666663	5442415	73712
私营企业	Private Enterprises	13863917	13429288	3769503
其他企业	Others	1074395	894222	22370
港澳台商投资企业	Funds from Hongkong,Macao and Taiwan	141440	140050	19800

4-2 续表 1 Continued

单位：万元 (10 000 yuan)

项　目	Item	农　村 Rural	#非农户 Non-Rural Households
投资总额	**Total Investment**	**7640020**	**4030020**
#住 宅	Residential Buildings	471824	471824
#国有经济控股	State-holding	2574350	2574350
按构成分	**Grouped by Use of Funds**		
建筑工程	Construction	3116763	3116763
安装工程	Installation	196547	196547
设备工器具购置	Purchase of Equipment and Instruments	547889	547889
其他费用	Other Expenses	168821	168821
按三次产业分	**Grouped by Three Strata of Industry**		
第一产业	Primary Industry	823354	823354
第二产业	Secondary Industry	1433171	1433171
第三产业	Tertiary Industry	1773495	1773495
按登记注册类型分	**Grouped by Types of Registration**		
内资企业	Domestic Fund Enterprises	3954187	3954187
国 有	State-owned	2262384	2262384
集 体	Collective-owned	117986	117986
股份合作	Share-holding Cooperative	10600	10600
联营企业	Joint Ownership Enterprises	14850	14850
国有联营企业	State Joint Ownership Enterprises	9050	9050
集体联营企业	Collective-owned Joint Ownership Enterprises	5800	5800
国有与集体联营企业	State and Collective-owned Joint Enterprises		
其他联营企业	Others		
有限责任公司	Limited Liability Corporations	709317	709317
国有独资公司	State-funded Corporations	22965	22965
其他有限责任公司	Other Limited Liability Corporations	686352	686352
股份有限公司	Share-holding Corporations Ltd	224248	224248
私营企业	Private Enterprises	434629	434629
其他企业	Others	180173	180173
港澳台商投资企业	Enterprises With Funds from Hong Kong, Macao and Taiwan	1390	1390

注：该表各分组指标均不含农村个人投资。
Note:Grouped data in this table do not include rural individual investment.

4-2 续表 2 Continued

单位：万元 (10 000 yuan)

项 目	Item	合 计 Total	城 镇 Urban	#房地产 Real Estate Development
合资经营企业(港或澳、台资)	Joint-venture Enterprises (Hongkong,Macao and Taiwan)	58229	58229	17223
合作经营企业(港或澳、台资)	Cooperation Enterprises (Hongkon,Macao and Taiwan)			
港、澳、台商独资经营企业	Enterprises With Sole Investment	58040	58040	2577
港、澳、台商投资股份有限公司	Share-holding Corporation Ltd.	25171	23781	
其他港、澳、台商投资企业	Others			
外商投资企业	Foreign Funded Enterprises	457438	455109	
中外合资经营企业(港或澳、台资)	Joint-venture Enterprises (Hongkong,Macao and Taiwan)	59451	59451	
中外合作经营企业(港或澳、台资)	Cooperation Enterprises (Hongkon,Macao and Taiwan)	30941	30941	
外资企业	Enterprises With Sole Funds	142860	142860	
外商投资股份有限公司	Share-holding Corporations Ltd.	207587	207587	
其他外商投资企业	Others	16599	14270	
个体经营	Individual Operate	160342	88228	
#个 体 户	Self-employed Personel	105072	59749	
个人合伙	Individual Partnership	55270	28479	
按隶属关系分	**By Administrative Relationship**			
中 央	Central Government	17472967	16393541	548612
地 方	Local	60401174	57450580	7708243
资金来源小计	**All Sources**	**82681763**	**78282122**	**11131481**
国家预算内资金	State Budget Funds	11177239	9889698	
国内贷款	Domestic Loans	10013972	9662990	1066046
债 券	Bonds	211314	210899	
利用外资	Foreign Investment	37902	37292	
自筹资金	Self-raising Funds	51398798	48854897	4121799
其他资金来源	Others	9842538	9626346	5943636
本年新增固定资产	**Newly Increased Fixed Assets**	**49084751**	**45915506**	**4301213**
房屋施工面积(万平方米)	**Floor Space of Buildings (10 000 sq.m)**	**25595.40**	**22613.27**	**9459.55**
#住 宅	Residential Buildings	13455.29	12756.92	6982.70
房屋竣工面积(万平方米)	**Floor Space of Buildings Completed (10 000 sq.m)**	**6085.61**	**5708.43**	**1722.16**
#住 宅	Residential Buildings	4228.72	3996.06	1394.08

4-2 续表 3 Continued

单位：万元 (10 000 yuan)

项　目	Item	农　村 Rural	#非农户 Non-Rural Households
合资经营企业(港或澳、台资)	Joint-venture Enterprises (Hongkong,Macao and Taiwan)		
合作经营企业(港或澳、台资)	Cooperation Enterprises (Hongkon,Macao and Taiwan)		
港、澳、台商独资经营企业	Enterprises With Sole Investment		
港、澳、台商投资股份有限公司	Share-holding Corporation Ltd.	1390	1390
其他港、澳、台商投资企业	Others		
外商投资企业	Foreign Funded Enterprises	2329	2329
中外合资经营企业(港或澳、台资)	Joint-venture Enterprises (Hongkong,Macao and Taiwan)		
中外合作经营企业(港或澳、台资)	Cooperation Enterprises (Hongkon,Macao and Taiwan)		
外资企业	Enterprises With Sole Funds		
外商投资股份有限公司	Share-holding Corporations Ltd.		
其他外商投资企业	Others	2329	2329
个体经营	Individual Operate	72114	72114
#个 体 户	Self-employed Personel	45323	45323
个人合伙	Individual Partnership	26791	26791
按隶属关系分	**By Administrative Relationship**		
中 央	Central Government	1079426	1079426
地 方	Local	2950594	2950594
资金来源小计	**All Sources**	**4399641**	**4399641**
国家预算内资金	State Budget Funds	1287541	1287541
国内贷款	Domestic Loans	350982	350982
债　券	Bonds	415	415
利用外资	Foreign Investment	610	610
自筹资金	Self-raising Funds	2543901	2543901
其他资金来源	Others	216192	216192
本年新增固定资产	**Newly Increased Fixed Assets**	**3169245**	**3169245**
房屋施工面积(万平方米)	**Floor Space of Buildings (10 000 sq.m)**	**2982.13**	**2982.13**
#住 宅	Residential Buildings	698.37	698.37
房屋竣工面积(万平方米)	**Floor Space of Buildings Completed (10 000 sq.m)**	**377.18**	**377.18**
#住 宅	Residential Buildings	232.66	232.66

4-3 按构成分全社会固定资产投资

Structure of Total Investment in Fixed Assets in the whole Country

单位：万元 (10 000 yuan)

年 份 Year	地 区 Region	合计 Total	建筑工程 Construction Works	安装工程 Installation Works	设备工具器具购置 Purchase of Equipment and Instruments	其他费用 Others
	1978	129999	86667		35686	7646
	1985	444758	323395		93254	28109
	1990	887775	571461		274647	41667
	1995	3333404	2145762		810995	376647
	1996	3878472	2245924	278445	929463	424640
	1997	4468148	2725428	310687	988070	443963
	1998	5197673	3435120	278895	920992	562666
	1999	5346468	3245779	344130	1039617	716942
	2000	6103843	3833328	416759	1254077	599679
	2001	7059970	4232768	454765	1616907	755530
	2002	8130223	4815707	593242	1787899	933375
	2003	10021256	6075091	690459	2030335	1225371
	2004	11615245	7133323	806705	2304931	1370286
	2005	13522757	8499303	993311	2637777	1392366
	2006	15670521	9776613	1014851	3166617	1712440
	2007	18508415	10667717	1517359	4312525	2010814
	2008	22599746	13071829	1773200	5488261	2266456
	2009	28272359	17511739	1938944	5855684	2965992
	2010	35396941	22224487	1943535	7960420	3268499
	2011	47127699	29541315	3362813	10626129	3597442
	2012	62583830	39278692	4507946	14260205	4536987
	2013	77874141	50280291	6153338	16516828	4923684
乌鲁木齐市	Urumqi City	10559221	6902877	846418	1827040	982886
克拉玛依市	Karamay City	4564651	2882900	533025	679572	469154
吐鲁番地区	Turpan Administrative Offices	2360493	1211391	177471	846343	125288
哈密地区	Hami [Kumul] Administrative Offices	4435424	2206865	381867	1681873	164819
昌吉回族自治州	Changji Hui Autonomous Prefecture	10400162	5213037	919606	3755896	511623
伊犁哈萨克自治州	Ili Kazak Autonomous Prefecture	13314554	8830544	880943	2391559	1211508
伊犁州直属县(市)	Counties (Cities) Direct Under Ili Prefecture	7062821	4417606	603152	1227843	814220
塔城地区	Tacheng [Tarbagatai] Administrative Offices	3584137	2650733	190922	503680	238802
阿勒泰地区	Altay Administrative Offices	2667596	1762205	86869	660036	158486
博尔塔拉蒙古自治州	Bortala Mongol Autonomous Prefecture	2050059	1449072	75846	412616	112525
巴音郭楞蒙古自治州	Bayangol Mongol Autonomous Prefecture	7238110	5440503	494854	1062566	240187
阿克苏地区	Aksu Administrative Offices	4903854	3116544	604761	911524	271025
克孜勒苏柯尔克孜自治州	Kizilsu Kirgiz Autonomous Prefecture	911218	729503	49675	121009	11031
喀什地区	Kashgar [Kaxgar] Administrative Offices	6582883	5226558	481896	677882	196547
和田地区	Hotan Administrative Offices	1890891	1758518	41643	42612	48118
石河子市	Shihezi City	2088010	843268	230255	812408	202079
阿拉尔市	Aral City	1086972	721147	60573	258589	46663
图木舒克市	Tumxuk City	569900	412330	14911	120724	21935
五家渠市	Wujiaqu City	2406783	1073389	349829	874651	108914
跨地区投资	Trans-regional Investment	2510956	2261845	9765	39964	199382

注：该表中不包括农村个人投资。
Note: Total investment in this table do not include rural individual investment.

4-4 全社会固定资产投资资金来源情况
Sources of Funds of Total Investment in Fixed Assets in the Whole Country

单位：万元 (10 000 yuan)

年 份 Year	地 区 Region	合 计 Total	国家预算内资金 State Budget	国内贷款 Domestic Loans	债 券 Bonds	利用外资 Foreign Investment	自筹及其他资金 Self-raising Fund And Others
	1978	129999	102693				27306
	1985	444758	117439	72227		7708	247384
	1990	887775	105423	294985		40927	446440
	1995	3333404	98004	818914		307619	2108867
	1996	3878472	128725	756412		324532	2668803
	1997	4468148	269106	749345		109629	3340068
	1998	5197673	384195	1116497		133936	3563045
	1999	5346468	512364	1097949	12376	93895	3629884
	2000	6103843	506867	1346175	19429	99942	4131430
	2001	7059970	545176	1321317	8340	64834	5120303
	2002	8130223	1323660	1607535	30504	62992	5105532
	2003	10021256	1626261	1896104	21586	95287	6382018
	2004	11490824	1799593	1555105	46095	87388	8002643
	2005	13543432	2093022	1677020	15428	109968	9647994
	2006	15773966	2119253	1854512	8193	88675	11703333
	2007	19070184	2258779	2480410	5526	110034	14215435
	2008	22725814	3388141	3020001	3410	90233	16224029
	2009	30345365	5813486	5246186	54636	94000	19137057
	2010	37844438	6347565	5750361	11544	120367	25614601
	2011	51265602	6266348	6679368	22559	137967	38159360
	2012	66725427	8684685	8897975	59736	91197	48991834
	2013	82681763	11177239	10013972	211314	37902	61241336
乌鲁木齐市	Urumqi City	12250168	777072	2299072		500	9173524
克拉玛依市	Karamay City	4681598	241611	539012			3900975
吐鲁番地区	Turpan Administrative Offices	2536991	197373	434774		5978	1898866
哈密地区	Hami [Kumul] Administrative Offices	4325746	265859	1074490	810	1128	2983459
昌吉回族自治州	Changji Hui Autonomous Prefecture	11744376	915459	671624	5000	150	10152143
伊犁哈萨克自治州	Ili Kazak Autonomous Prefecture	13385893	2419418	1134252	3699	29338	9799186
伊犁州直属县(市)	Counties (Cities) Direct Under Ili Prefecture	7229457	916366	603519	3549	13087	5692936
塔城地区	Tacheng [Tarbagatai] Administrative Offices	3750426	897347	147234			2705845
阿勒泰地区	Altay Administrative Offices	2406010	605705	383499	150	16251	1400405
博尔塔拉蒙古自治州	Bortala Mongol Autonomous Prefecture	2012159	310538	113720	900		1587001
巴音郭楞蒙古自治州	Bayangol Mongol Autonomous Prefecture	7026889	581427	454803	375		5990284
阿克苏地区	Aksu Administrative Offices	4952791	770533	434308		500	3747450
克孜勒苏柯尔克孜自治州	Kizilsu Kirgiz Autonomous Prefecture	844433	347073	103464	415	308	393173
喀什地区	Kashgar [Kaxgar] Administrative Offices	8138844	2394743	192714	115		5551272
和田地区	Hotan Administrative Offices	2229232	1159592	98746			970894
石河子市	Shihezi City	2148899	77987	602263			1468649
阿拉尔市	Aral City	956297	295705	130545			530047
图木舒克市	Tumxuk City	525471	176831	18174			330466
五家渠市	Wujiaqu City	2434670	47438	138939			2248293
跨地区投资	Trans-regional Investment	2487306	198580	1573072	200000		515654

注：1.自 2004 年起资金来源为本年实际到位资金。2.该表资金来源不包括农村个人资金。
Note: a) Sources of capital caculated on actual arrived investment from 2004. b) Sources of Capital in this table do not include rural individual fund.

4-5 按行业分全社会固定资产投资
Total Investment in Fixed Assets in the Whole Country by Sector

单位：万元 (10 000 yuan)

行　业	Sector	2012	2013
总　计	**Total**	**62583830**	**81484141**
农、林、牧、渔业	**Agriculture, Forestry, Animal Husbandry and Fishery**	**2939876**	**2355032**
农　业	Agriculture	316170	350811
林　业	Forestry	153960	186359
畜牧业	Animal Husbandry	268860	560465
渔　业	Fishery	2275	11510
农、林、牧、渔服务业	Services in Support of Agriculture	971928	1245887
采矿业	**Mining**	**7487174**	**9077629**
#煤炭开采和洗选业	Mining and Washing of Coal	1719835	2040867
石油和天然气开采业	Extraction of Petroleum and Natural Gas	4405085	5257066
黑色金属矿采选业	Mining and Processing of Ferrous Metals Ores	309489	578974
#铁矿采选	Mining and Processing of Iron Ore	291779	568274
有色金属矿采选业	Mining and Processing of Non-ferrous Metals Ores	604555	531121
#常用有色金属矿采选	Mining and Processing of Common Non-ferrous Metal	489263	339541
非金属矿采选业	Mining and Processing of Nonmetal Ores	147654	239307
#土砂石开采	Mining of Earth and Gravel	90997	155027
化学矿采选	Extracting of Chemical Ore	6280	9400
制造业	**Manufacturing**	**15901587**	**17318300**
#农副食品加工业	Processing of Food from Agricultural Products	690933	772494
食品制造业	Manufacture of Food	544558	456364
烟草制品业	Manufacture of Tobacco	54155	27668
纺织业	Manufacture of Textile	435812	504723
皮革、毛皮、羽绒及其制品业	Leather, Fur, Feather and Related Products Manufacturing	859	3836
木材加工和木、竹、藤、棕、草制品业	Processing of Timber, Wood, Bamboo, Cane, Grass Products	58514	72104
家具制造业	Furniture Manufacturing	21183	12929
造纸及纸制品业	Paper and Paper Products Manufacturing	116885	88668
印刷和记录媒介复制业	Printing and Copying of Medium for Record	35451	28550
石油加工及炼焦业	Oil Processing, Coking and Nuclear Fuel Processing	1447755	2127463
#精炼石油产品制造	Manufacture of Oil Products	791839	1079289
炼　焦	Coking	655916	1048174
化学原料及化学制品制造业	Raw Chemical Material and Chemical Products	2888806	3321618
#基础化学原料制造	Basic Chemical Material	1208988	1125579
肥料制造	Fertilizer Making	561291	843704
医药制造业	Medicine Manufacturing	295711	204418
#中药饮片加工	Processing of Chinese Herbs and Tablet	10403	19837
中成药制造	Manufacture of Chinese Herbs and Patent Medicine	18972	21455
化学纤维制造业	Chemical Fiber Manufacturing	89202	32979
橡胶和塑料制品业	Manufacture of Rubber and Plastics	339221	515137
橡胶制品业	Manufacture of Rubber	38273	31173
塑料制品业	Manufacture of Plastic	300948	483964

注：分行业不包括农村个人投资。
Note: The major category in this table do not include rural individual investment.

4-5 续表 1 Continued

单位：万元 (10 000 yuan)

行 业	Sector	2012	2013
非金属矿物制品业	Manufacture of Non-metallic Mineral Products	2796123	2415745
#水泥、石灰和石膏的制造	Cement Manufacturing	1288059	806005
黑色金属冶炼及压延加工业	Smelting and Pressing of Non-Ferrous Metals	2209612	1454527
#钢压延加工	Steel Rolling	424172	172681
有色金属冶炼及压延加工业	Smelting and Pressing of Nonferrous Metals	2055339	3063740
#常用有色金属冶炼	Smeltering of Common Non-ferrous Metal	1710794	2289035
金属制品业	Manufacture of Metal Products	332819	298091
通用设备制造业	Manufacture of General Purpose Machinery	188365	316810
专用设备制造业	Manufacture of Special Purpose Machinery	198432	209227
汽车制造	Manufacture of Car	218202	181006
电气机械及器材制造业	Manufacture of Electricial Equipment and Machinery	160224	183391
电力、热力、燃气及水的生产和供应业	**Production and Supply of Electricity Gas and Water**	**7815608**	**12612328**
电力、热力的生产和供应业	Production and Supply of Electric Power and Heat Power	6534845	10417428
电力生产	Production of Electric Power	5025890	8457942
电力供应	Distribution of Electric Power	865387	1066271
热力生产和供应	Production and Supply of Heat Power	643568	893215
燃气生产和供应业	Production and Supply of Gas	852032	1429890
水的生产和供应业	Production and Supply of Water	428731	765010
#自来水的生产和供应	Production and Distribution of Running Water	325050	527808
污水处理及其再生利用	Treatment and Recycle of Waste Water	82826	190562
建筑业	**Construction**	**2396028**	**785384**
#房屋和土木工程建筑业	Construction of Buildings and Givil Engineering	910907	749025
建筑安装业	Building Installation	16641	8969
交通运输、仓储和邮政业	**Transport, Storage and Post**	**4421504**	**5715253**
铁路运输业	Railway Transport	930826	1094154
道路运输业	Road Transport	2384540	3403575
#城市公共交通业	Urban Public Transport	82673	158947
航空运输业	Air Transport	53335	59454
管道运输业	Via Pipeline Transport	50908	249388
装卸搬运和其他运输服务业	Loading, Unloading and Other Transport Services	18919	10106
仓储业	Storage	638585	892123
邮政业	Post	5246	6323
信息传输、软件和信息技术服务业	**Information Transmission, Computer Services and Software**	**444177**	**530725**
#电信、广播电视和卫星传输服务	Telecommunication and Other Information Transmission Services	404589	452328
#电 信	Telecommunication	384433	429702
批发和零售业	**Wholesal and Retail Trades**	**865063**	**1493666**
批发业	Wholesale Trade	458366	665300
零售业	Retail Trade	406697	828366
住宿和餐饮业	**Hotels and Catering Services**	**394495**	**710684**
住宿业	Hotels	309975	527435
#旅游饭店	Tourist Restaurant	248567	363051
餐饮业	Catering Service	77124	183249
金融业	**Financial Intermediation**	**32070**	**41608**

4-5 续表 2 Continued

单位：万元 (10 000 yuan)

行业	Sector	2012	2013
#银行业	Banks	26082	35013
保险业	Insurance	758	2235
其他金融活动	Other Financial Activities	1230	3010
房地产业	**Real Estate**	**12779833**	**16509991**
#房地产开发与经营业	Real Estate Development and Operation	6671772	8433071
物业管理	Real Estate Management	42259	4365
租赁和商务服务业	**Leasing and Business Services**	**197044**	**365755**
租赁业	Leasing	20216	4096
商务服务业	Business Service	176828	361659
科学研究和技术服务业	**Scientific Research, Technical Service and Geological Prospecting**	**188774**	**118327**
研究与试验发展	Research and Experimental Development	13182	25397
专业技术服务业	Professional Technical Service	145696	59395
科技推广和应用服务业	Services of Science and Technology Exchanges and Promotion	29896	33535
水利、环境和公共设施管理业	**Management of Water Conservancy, Environment and Public Facilities**	**3425828**	**6015289**
水利管理业	Management of Water Conservancy	1046318	1487745
生态保护和环境治理业	Environmental Management	150328	150392
公共设施管理业	Management of Public Facilities	2229182	4377152
#市政设施管理	Management of Public Facilities	1732498	3559447
绿化管理	Urban Greening Management	139553	270701
公园和游览景区管理	Scenic-Spot Management	213676	363614
居民服务、修理和其他服务业	**Services to Households and Other Services**	**108870**	**174446**
教　育	**Education**	**974774**	**1294710**
#初等教育	Junion Education	155797	197500
中等教育	Secondary Education	553117	722944
高等教育	Senior Education	84042	173937
卫生和社会工作	**Health, Social Security and Social Welfare**	**400699**	**592616**
卫　生	Health Care	320524	456192
#医　院	Hospital	234936	374097
社会工作	Social Services	80175	136424
文化、体育和娱乐业	**Culture, Sports and Entertainment**	**351896**	**700455**
新闻和出版业	Journalism and Publishing Activities	7000	8418
广播、电视、电影和影视录音制作	Broadcasting,Movies,Televisions and Audiovisual Activites	27722	27768
文化艺术业	Culture and Art Activities	202491	404792
体　育	Sports	104391	212146
娱乐业	Entertainment	10292	47331
公共管理、社会保障和社会组织	**Public Management and Social Organization**	**1458530**	**1461943**
中国共产党机关	Orgars of Communist Party of China	18538	50163
国家机构	Government Agencies	1310277	1262400
人民政协、民主党派	People's Political Consultative Conference and Democratic Parties	550	130
社会保障	Social Security	13873	35814
群众团体、社会团体和其他成员组织	Non-Governmental Institutions,Social Organizations and Religion Organizations	91446	48184
基层群众自治组织	Grass Roots Self-governing Organizations	23846	65252

4-6 全社会房屋施工面积、竣工面积
Floor Space of Buildings under Construction and Completed in Whole Country

单位：万平方米 (10 000 sq.m)

年 份 Year	地 区 Region	施工面积 Floor Space of Buildings under Construction	#住 宅 Residential Buildings	竣工面积 Floor Space of Buildings Completed	#住 宅 Residential Buildings	房屋建筑面积竣工率(%) Rate of Floor Space of Building Completed (%)	#住 宅 Residential Buildings
	1985	1670.30	945.76	1327.69	816.26	79.5	86.3
	1990	1740.94	1074.98	1337.06	912.57	76.8	84.9
	1995	2420.38	1368.84	1634.33	1064.14	67.5	77.7
	1996	2952.02	1901.01	2095.58	1441.22	71.0	75.8
	1997	2574.79	1732.19	1903.96	1393.11	73.9	80.4
	1998	2946.76	2057.08	2148.75	1604.68	72.9	78.0
	1999	3439.11	2470.41	2618.98	2020.89	76.2	81.8
	2000	4485.77	2509.17	2633.23	1881.88	58.7	75.0
	2001	4940.70	3282.51	3386.60	2411.78	68.5	73.5
	2002	3986.81	2358.04	2706.44	1790.82	67.9	75.9
	2003	5004.13	2863.92	3599.74	2347.04	71.9	82.0
	2004	5290.77	2999.85	4273.02	2298.56	80.8	76.6
	2005	6677.06	4522.20	4705.07	3618.78	70.5	80.0
	2006	7854.43	5694.75	4773.93	3785.46	60.8	66.5
	2007	8028.32	5915.83	5441.23	4458.77	67.8	75.4
	2008	8317.15	5938.78	5184.01	4125.67	62.3	69.5
	2009	9511.02	6344.39	4598.79	3412.43	48.4	53.8
	2010	11361.96	7640.58	4649.89	3291.89	40.9	43.1
	2011	16804.88	11357.36	5899.06	4504.94	35.1	39.7
	2012	21626.33	14159.68	7821.44	6152.03	36.2	43.4
	2013	25595.40	13455.29	6085.61	4228.72	23.8	31.4
乌鲁木齐市	Urumqi City	5253.82	3499.66	622.70	449.10	11.9	12.8
克拉玛依市	Karamay City	697.02	369.11	152.22	91.62	21.8	24.8
吐鲁番地区	Turpan Administrative Offices	233.37	153.98	54.50	44.33	23.4	28.8
哈密地区	Hami [Kumul] Administrative Offices	783.14	516.61	226.53	179.68	28.9	34.8
昌吉回族自治州	Changji Hui Autonomous Prefecture	2918.60	707.59	315.55	233.11	10.8	32.9
伊犁哈萨克自治州	Ili Kazak Autonomous Prefecture	4539.34	2513.55	1696.60	1175.21	37.4	46.8
伊犁州直属县(市)	Counties (Cities) Direct Under Ili Prefecture	2533.21	1355.60	722.31	507.72	28.5	37.5
塔城地区	Tacheng [Tarbagatai] Administrative Offices	1308.81	680.51	608.82	409.15	46.5	60.1
阿勒泰地区	Altay Administrative Offices	694.32	477.44	365.47	258.34	52.6	54.1
博尔塔拉蒙古自治州	Bortala Mongol Autonomous Prefecture	754.01	485.73	232.97	184.58	30.9	38.0
巴音郭楞蒙古自治州	Bayangol Mongol Autonomous Prefecture	2324.34	1525.39	696.50	541.55	30.0	35.5
阿克苏地区	Aksu Administrative Offices	1936.50	901.63	342.03	270.05	17.7	30.0
克孜勒苏柯尔克孜自治州	Kizilsu Kirgiz Autonomous Prefecture	404.26	219.13	115.21	73.70	28.5	33.6
喀什地区	Kashgar [Kaxgar] Administrative Offices	2613.83	805.76	402.68	169.41	15.4	21.0
和田地区	Hotan Administrative Offices	1240.80	805.52	732.03	507.45	59.0	63.0
石河子市	Shihezi City	718.12	364.81	79.02	59.93	11.0	16.4
阿拉尔市	Aral City	367.10	146.67	115.12	62.67	31.4	42.7
图木舒克市	Tumxuk City	264.65	192.00	133.42	110.86	50.4	57.7
五家渠市	Wujiaqu City	546.50	248.15	168.53	75.47	30.8	30.4

注：该表房屋施工面积、竣工面积未包括农村个人。
Note: Floor space under construction and completed floor space in this table do not include rural individual.

4-7 按构成及建设性质分城镇固定资产投资
Investment in Fixed Assets in Urban Area by Composition of Funds and Type of Construction

单位：万元 (10 000 yuan)

年 份 Year	地 区 Region	合 计 Total	按构成分 By Composition of Funds			
			建筑安装工程 Construction and Installation	设备工具器具购置 Purchase of Equipment and Instruments	#用于更新的设备 Update Equipment	其他费用 Others
	1978	129999	86667	35686		7646
	1985	408435	314651	67295	5499	26489
	1990	782099	516443	224673	25153	40983
	1995	2864148	1817364	754369	64612	292415
	1996	3339710	2167304	825067	66119	347339
	1997	3817221	2600884	858958	61094	357379
	1998	4561217	3333948	792449	71986	434820
	1999	4613116	3294346	831951	82363	486819
	2000	4994145	3531280	1103399	104850	359466
	2001	5490569	3638754	1392920	186605	458895
	2002	6596964	4379556	1558818	181920	658590
	2003	8188381	5599787	1718853	105728	869741
	2004	9482471	6451184	2047000	232343	984287
	2005	11215637	7926905	2230165	145514	1058567
	2006	12971324	8943879	2686125	188170	1341320
	2007	14908734	9646247	3746476	177062	1516011
	2008	17970126	11542024	4772937	311014	1655165
	2009	22999843	15632380	5026513	552733	2340950
	2010	28338644	18973774	6938417	346525	2426453
	2011	36881064	25313983	9102251	726850	2464830
	2012	49877126	34176800	12344316	1048785	3356010
	2013	65587266	46037812	15830049	2022503	3719405
乌鲁木齐市	Urumqi City	7592505	5182796	1793759	480316	615950
克拉玛依市	Karamay City	4113706	3002555	678395	114306	432756
吐鲁番地区	Turpan Administrative Offices	2300868	1340810	846023	13868	114035
哈密地区	Hami [Kumul] Administrative Offices	4030059	2256457	1650916	10264	122686
昌吉回族自治州	Changji Hui Autonomous Prefecture	9283655	5213670	3624830	955703	445155
伊犁哈萨克自治州	Ili Kazak Autonomous Prefecture	10534222	7404456	2226187	275266	903579
伊犁州直属县(市)	Counties (Cities) Direct Under Ili Prefecture	5072791	3359069	1124978	124277	588744
塔城地区	Tacheng [Tarbagatai] Administrative Offices	3037553	2396289	454768	120929	186496
阿勒泰地区	Altay Administrative Offices	2423878	1649098	646441	30060	128339
博尔塔拉蒙古自治州	Bortala Mongol Autonomous Prefecture	1574822	1120213	378541	34648	76068
巴音郭楞蒙古自治州	Bayangol Mongol Autonomous Prefecture	6576763	5322956	1048181	17378	205626
阿克苏地区	Aksu Administrative Offices	3710672	2709186	809286	11954	192200
克孜勒苏柯尔克孜自治州	Kizilsu Kirgiz Autonomous Prefecture	758417	641343	113736	52828	3338
喀什地区	Kashgar [Kaxgar] Administrative Offices	5813747	5071281	601064	32416	141402
和田地区	Hotan Administrative Offices	1838165	1756951	38461	2699	42753
石河子市	Shihezi City	1795613	854047	809288	3897	132278
阿拉尔市	Aral City	890688	613082	237983	11243	39623
图木舒克市	Tumxuk City	491992	361768	113870	300	16354
五家渠市	Wujiaqu City	1770416	914631	819565	417	36220
跨地区投资	Trans-regional Investment	2510956	2271610	39964	5000	199382

注：城镇投资额未含房地产投资，以下同。
Note: Urban Investment exclude real estate, the following the same as follows.

4-7 续表 Continued

单位：万元 (10 000 yuan)

年份 Year	地区 Region	按建设性质分 By Type of Construction 新建 New Construction	扩建 Expansion	改建 Reconstruction	其他 Others
	1978	93462	34399		2138
	1985	110236	160639	116006	21554
	1990	299356	148222	277007	57514
	1995	1067281	886882	646081	263904
	1996	1240585	820966	967022	311137
	1997	1405259	911902	1155121	344939
	1998	1648622	1017786	1338994	555815
	1999	1381764	1226797	1326775	677780
	2000	1410065	1424339	1558514	601227
	2001	891146	2373927	1614961	610535
	2002	1429874	2687996	1984657	494437
	2003	2207269	3128374	2237752	614986
	2004	2358662	3595847	2781101	746861
	2005	3397472	3657464	3063457	1097244
	2006	3633284	5436397	2430373	1471270
	2007	3759028	7439715	2386806	1323185
	2008	5350574	8078708	2759536	1781308
	2009	9465044	7634515	4113649	1786635
	2010	13612835	8408038	4177527	2140244
	2011	19799225	9910989	4216233	2954617
	2012	29842768	12229771	4387038	3417549
	2013	43552033	13405908	5259439	3369886
乌鲁木齐市	Urumqi City	3200683	3324573	573624	493625
克拉玛依市	Karamay City	3660289	50221	325040	78156
吐鲁番地区	Turpan Administrative Offices	1577950	603634	78011	41273
哈密地区	Hami [Kumul] Administrative Offices	2345677	1493892	97115	93375
昌吉回族自治州	Changji Hui Autonomous Prefecture	7657764	599149	831636	195106
伊犁哈萨克自治州	Ili Kazak Autonomous Prefecture	5994577	2919393	693779	926473
伊犁州直属县(市)	Counties (Cities) Direct Under Ili Prefecture	3301847	1200253	197602	373089
塔城地区	Tacheng [Tarbagatai] Administrative Offices	1836795	548840	350829	301089
阿勒泰地区	Altay Administrative Offices	855935	1170300	145348	252295
博尔塔拉蒙古自治州	Bortala Mongol Autonomous Prefecture	788004	460191	121632	204995
巴音郭楞蒙古自治州	Bayangol Mongol Autonomous Prefecture	5442577	735452	107132	291602
阿克苏地区	Aksu Administrative Offices	2908564	497087	150002	155019
克孜勒苏柯尔克孜自治州	Kizilsu Kirgiz Autonomous Prefecture	692096	27686	23990	14645
喀什地区	Kashgar [Kaxgar] Administrative Offices	4977458	481824	136039	218426
和田地区	Hotan Administrative Offices	894040	719407	54397	170321
石河子市	Shihezi City	1111838	439309	95812	148654
阿拉尔市	Aral City	635782	39257	65142	150507
图木舒克市	Tumxuk City	243116	69701	11372	167803
五家渠市	Wujiaqu City	842553	860132	47825	19906
跨地区投资	Trans-regional Investment	579065	85000	1846891	

4-8 分行业城镇固定资产投资主要指标
Main Indicators of Investment in Fixed Assets in Urban Area by Sector

(2013 年)

行业	Sector	投资额(万元) Total Investment (10 000 yuan)	#地方 Local	施工项目个数(个) Number of Projects under Construction (unit)	竣工项目个数(个) Number of Projects Completed (unit)	本年新增固定资产(万元) Newly Increased Fixed Assets (10 000 yuan)
总　计	**Total**	**65587266**	**49742337**	**11814**	**7097**	**41614293**
农、林、牧、渔业	**Agriculture, Forestry, Animal Husbandry and Fishery**	**1531678**	**1215222**	**827**	**630**	**1249250**
农　业	Agriculture	236666	196450	117	75	194337
林　业	Forestry	140036	124002	80	69	104107
畜牧业	Animal Husbandry	300471	278201	141	100	195070
渔　业	Fishery	5200	5200	3	2	3200
农、林、牧、渔服务业	Service in Support of Agriculture	849305	611369	486	384	752536
采矿业	**Mining**	**8781023**	**3119190**	**407**	**226**	**6013457**
#煤炭开采和洗选业	Mining and Washing of Coal	1818836	1655935	129	44	1184628
石油和天然气开采业	Extraction of Petroleum and Natural Gas	5254166	4432	15	11	3632152
黑色金属矿采选业	Mining and Processing of Ferrous Metals Ores	550249	527272	80	53	376373
#铁矿采选	Mining and Processing of Iron Ore	539549	516572	77	52	373073
有色金属矿采选业	Mining and Processing of Non-ferrous Metals Ores	500089	487516	88	55	306040
#常用有色金属矿采选	Mining and Processing of Common Non-ferrous Metal	312432	299859	57	32	199020
非金属矿采选业	Mining and Processing of Nonmetal Ores	227389	226389	55	42	163317
#土砂石开采	Mining of Earth and Gravel	146809	146809	27	18	81837
制造业	**Manufacturing**	**16840187**	**16050836**	**1993**	**1010**	**11077282**
#农副食品加工业	Processing of Food from Agricultural Products	731235	700867	259	170	655322
食品制造业	Manufacture of Foods	441458	430378	52	21	831767
酒、饮料和精制茶制造业	Manufacture of Tobacco,Wine and Tea	254676	236993	84	47	177206
烟草制品业	Manufacture of Tobacco	27668	27668	2		
纺织业	Manufacture of Textile	483263	475036	65	35	247358
纺织服装、服饰业	Manufacture of Textile Wearing Apparel, Footware and Caps	7426	6896	6	2	2700
皮革、毛皮、羽毛及其制品和制鞋业	Manufacture of Leather,Fur,Feather and Related Products	2135	2135	2	1	1130
木材加工和木、竹、藤、棕、草制品业	Processing of Timber, Wood, Bamboo, Cane, Grass Products	67348	67348	21	10	48088
造纸和纸制品业	Manufacture of Paper and Paper Products	88668	80996	27	20	147009
印刷和记录媒介复制业	Printing,Reproduction,of Recording Media	28550	27500	17	10	16598
石油加工、炼焦和核燃料加工业	Processing of Petroleum,Coking	2109500	1884720	107	35	792822
#精炼石油产品制造	Manufacture of Oil Products	1079289	911693	60	19	492524
炼　焦	Coking	1030211	973027	47	16	300298
化学原料和化学制品制造业	Manufacture of Raw Chemical Material and Chemical Products	3296215	3001442	202	75	2245986

4-8 续表 1 Continued

行业	Sector	投资额（万元）Total Investment (10 000 yuan)	#地方 Local	施工项目个数（个）Number of Projects under Construction (unit)	竣工项目个数（个）Number of Projects Completed (unit)	本年新增固定资产（万元）Newly Increased Fixed Assets (10 000 yuan)
医药制造业	Manufacture of Medicine	196851	180543	36	20	91937
化学纤维制造业	Manufacture of Chemical Fibers	31989	26989	7	5	24093
橡胶和塑料制品业	Manufacture of Rubber and Plastic Products	505212	504702	133	75	422121
非金属矿物制品业	Manufactureof Non-metallicMineral Products	2202920	2113415	467	260	1723329
#水泥、石灰和石膏制造	Cement Manufacturing	730541	668515	66	31	563569
玻璃制造	Manufacture of Glasses	48546	48546	12	9	48548
黑色金属冶炼和压延加工业	Smelting and Pressing of Ferrous Metals	1431339	1372614	88	36	681326
#炼　铁	Iron Making	457760	403135	21	7	51120
炼　钢	Steel Making	650996	646896	20	7	428714
有色金属冶炼和压延加工业	Smelting and Pressing of Nonferrous Metals	3063740	3063740	44	16	2024798
金属制品业	Manufacture of Metal Products	288042	288042	84	44	179947
通用设备制造业	Manufacture of General Purpose Machinery	282749	269149	70	29	116896
专用设备制造业	Manufacture of Special Purpose Machinery	204607	204607	59	23	123254
汽车制造业	Manufacture of Car	174211	171535	13	1	17304
计算机、通信和其他电子设备制造业	Manufacture of Communication Equipment, Comuputer and othe Elctronic Equipment	107802	104509	13	6	195038
电力、热力、燃气及水生产和供应业	**Production and Supply of Electricity,Gas and Water**	**12025697**	**8958046**	**1286**	**734**	**5684455**
电力、热力生产和供应业	Production and Supply of Electricity Power and Heat Power	9903887	7050565	879	497	5049186
电力生产	Production of Electric Power	8057144	5978689	334	127	3743591
电力供应	Supply of Electric Power	986823	470853	301	209	752322
热力生产和供应	Production and Supply of Heat Power	859920	601023	244	161	553273
燃气生产和供应业	Production and Supply of Gas	1398968	1327070	132	79	299715
水的生产和供应业	Production and Supply of Water	722842	580411	275	158	335554
#自来水生产和供应	Production and Distribution of Running Water	494568	387893	189	118	225458
污水处理及其再生利用	Treatment and Recycle of Waste Water	183377	147621	66	26	69591
建筑业	**Construction**	**713563**	**437119**	**230**	**150**	**744514**
#房屋建筑业	Construction of Buildings	136078	102880	76	40	86313
土木工程建筑业	Buildings and Givil Engineering Construction	542169	299092	140	100	628287
建筑安装业	Building Installation	7926	7926	4	2	4670
批发和零售业	**Wholesale&Retail Trades**	**1466200**	**1246651**	**371**	**235**	**885496**
批发业	Wholesale Trades	657546	516413	158	99	426401

4-8 续表 2 Continued

行　业	Sector	投资额（万元）Total Investment (10 000 yuan)	#地　方 Local	施工项目个数（个）Number of Projects under Construction (unit)	竣工项目个数（个）Number of Projects Completed (unit)	本年新增固定资产（万元）Newly Increased Fixed Assets (10 000 yuan)
零售业	Retail Trades	808654	730238	213	136	459095
交通运输、仓储和邮政业	**Transport, Storage and Post**	**5456501**	**4020503**	**633**	**344**	**2850875**
#铁路运输业	Railway Transport	1094154	427239	28	5	154945
道路运输业	Road Transport	3200757	2694742	428	260	1830207
航空运输业	Air Transport	59454	24879	15	7	29053
管道运输业	Via Pipelines Transport	249388	87141	6	4	397474
仓储业	Storage	836189	770630	148	64	428793
邮政业	Post	6323	6323	2		2897
住宿和餐饮业	**Hotels and Catering Services**	**676159**	**628007**	**157**	**70**	**380403**
住宿业	Hotels	495785	454109	124	58	282489
#旅游饭店	Tourist Restaurant	335021	296321	73	27	206980
餐饮业	Catering Services	180374	173898	33	12	97914
信息传输、软件和信息技术服务业	**Information Transmission, Computer Services and Software**	**529250**	**256670**	**73**	**54**	**453509**
#电信、广播电视和卫星传输服务	Telecommunication and Other Information Transmission Services	450853	201613	64	51	444877
电　信	Telecommunication	428427	179967	46	42	431248
金融业	**Financial Intermediation**	**40108**	**32658**	**31**	**19**	**26725**
#货币金融服务	Services of Intermediation	33513	28723	25	15	23290
资本市场服务	Services of Capital Market	1350	1350	1		
保险业	**Insurance**	**2235**	**435**	**2**	**1**	**435**
房地产业	**Real Estate**	**7514900**	**5314470**	**1689**	**1016**	**5246740**
#房地产开发经营	Real Estate Development and Operation	166713	163741	47	29	98606
物业管理	Management of Real Estate	2065		1	1	2065
其他房地产业	Other Real Estate	7319837	5124444	1625	978	5118312
租赁和商务服务业	**Leasing and Business Services**	**353855**	**351872**	**99**	**66**	**151193**
租赁业	Leasing	4096	4096	5	4	3734
商务服务业	Business Service	349759	347776	94	62	147459
科学研究和技术服务业	**Scientific Research, Technical Service and Geological Prospecting**	**114727**	**101747**	**83**	**54**	**76108**
研究和试验发展	Research and Experiment Development	25397	18971	8	2	11199
专业技术服务业	Professional Technical Service	57395	52137	53	37	40099
科技推广和应用服务业	Services of Science and Technology Exchanges and Difussion	31935	30639	22	15	24810

4-8 续表 3 Continued

行　　业	Sector	投资额 (万元) Total Investment (10 000 yuan)	#地　方 Local	施工项目个数 (个) Number of Projects under Construction (unit)	竣工项目个数 (个) Number of Projects Completed (unit)	本年新增固定资产 (万元) Newly Increased Fixed Assets (10 000 yuan)
水利、环境和公共设施管理业	**Management of Water Conservancy, Environment and Public Facilities**	**5542753**	**4489137**	**1861**	**1196**	**3830751**
水利管理业	Management of Water Conservancy	1182448	1031305	489	351	763066
生态保护和环境治理业	Environmental Management	134028	131988	44	27	68538
公共设施管理业	Management of Public Facilities	4226277	3325844	1328	818	2999147
市政设施管理	Management of Public Facilities	3435771	2596541	1043	634	2347367
环境卫生管理	Management of Enviroment	86556	80405	54	38	81528
城乡市容管理	Management of Apperance City	88969	74086	48	36	82669
绿化管理	Management of Urban Greening	267102	248186	65	45	217619
公园和游览景区管理	Scenic-Spot Management	347879	326626	118	65	269964
居民服务、修理和其他服务业	**Resident Service and Other Services**	**168431**	**143819**	**88**	**61**	**118496**
教　育	**Education**	**1244939**	**1115888**	**748**	**469**	**917435**
#初等教育	Elementary Education	188752	179655	149	111	175552
中等教育	Secondary Education	700595	617264	402	267	545093
高等教育	Higher Education	173937	158216	38	8	54141
卫生和社会工作	**Health, Social Security and Social Welfare**	**586712**	**528911**	**279**	**180**	**452539**
卫　生	Health Care	452031	406455	190	121	336391
#医　院	Hospital	374097	332612	126	77	269406
社会工作	Mangement of　Social	134681	122456	89	59	116148
文化、体育和娱乐业	**Culture, Sports and Entertainment**	**683799**	**591647**	**244**	**136**	**423676**
新闻和出版业	Journalism and Publishing Activities	8418	5618	3	2	5618
广播、电视、电影和影视录音制作业	Broadcasting,Movies,Televisions and Audiovisual Activites	27768	27768	18	13	21111
文化艺术业	Cultural and Art Activities	396597	339857	153	86	260130
体　育	Sports	204237	171625	57	28	118821
娱乐业	Entertainment	46779	46779	13	7	17996
公共管理、社会保障和社会组织	**Public Management and Social Organization**	**1316784**	**1139944**	**715**	**447**	**1031389**
中国共产党机关	Organ of Communist Party of China	32479	31409	11	7	22538
国家机构	Government Agencies	1155649	991213	630	391	891033
人民政协、民主党派	People's Political Consultative Conference and Democratic Parties	130	130	1	1	130
社会保障	Social Security	32852	31997	20	11	28637
群众团体、社会团体和其他成员组织	Non-Governmental Institutions,Social Organizations and Religion Organizations	32529	22700	22	13	29080
基层群众自治组织	Grass Roots Self-governing Organizations	63145	62495	31	24	59971

4-9 分行业城镇固定资产投资资金来源情况

单位：万元 (2013 年)

行　业	Sector	本年资金来源小计 Sub-total Funds This Year
总　计	**Total**	**67150641**
农、林、牧、渔业	**Agriculture, Forestry, Animal Husbandry and Fishery**	**1499824**
农　业	Agriculture	224717
林　业	Forestry	107171
畜牧业	Animal Husbandry	317934
渔　业	Fishery	5200
农、林、牧、渔服务业	Service in Support of Agriculture	844802
采矿业	**Mining**	**9498761**
#煤炭开采和洗选业	Mining and Washing of Coal	1869748
石油和天然气开采业	Extraction of Petroleum and Natural Gas	5251920
黑色金属矿采选业	Mining and Processing of Ferrous Metals Ores	1193023
#铁矿采选	Mining and Processing of Iron Ore	1182173
有色金属矿采选业	Mining and Processing of Non-ferrous Metals Ores	530102
#常用有色金属矿采选	Mining and Processing of Common Non-ferrous Metal	319989
非金属矿采选业	Mining and Processing of Nonmetal Ores	208870
#土砂石开采	Mining of Earth and Gravel	130448
制造业	**Manufacturing**	**17185900**
#农副食品加工业	Processing of Food from Agricultural Products	784660
食品制造业	Manufacture of Foods	445803
酒、饮料和精制茶制造业	Manufacture of Tobacco,Wine and Tea	256525
烟草制品业	Manufacture of Tobacco	27670
纺织业	Manufacture of Textile	454005
纺织服装、服饰业	Manufacture of Textile Wearing Apparel,Footware and Caps	7051
皮革、毛皮、羽毛及其制品和制鞋业	Manufacture of Leather,Fur,Feather and Related Products	2135
木材加工和木、竹、藤、棕、草制品业	Processing of Timber, Wood, Bamboo, Cane, Grass Products	87147
造纸和纸制品业	Manufacture of Paper and Paper Products	96243
印刷和记录媒介复制业	Printing,Reproduction,of Recording Media	28640
石油加工、炼焦和核燃料加工业	Processing of Petroleum,Coking	2001433
#精炼石油产品制造	Manufacture of Oil Products	1016995
炼　焦	Coking	984438

Sources of Funds of Investment in Fixed Assets in Urban Area by Sector

(10 000 yuan)

国家预算内资金 State Budget	国内贷款 Domestic Loans	债券 Bonds	利用外资 Foreign Investment	自筹资金 Self-raising Funds	其他资金来源 Others
9889698	**8596944**	**210899**	**37292**	**44733098**	**3682710**
403829	**28250**		**1278**	**926325**	**140142**
41837	1838			153202	27840
35972			1128	60411	9660
41314	4350			242573	29697
2000				3200	
282706	22062		150	466939	72945
5680	**242326**			**9208381**	**42374**
2970	120690			1730695	15393
210				5251415	295
	86845			1102278	3900
	86845			1091428	3900
	23891			503081	3130
	23441			293418	3130
2500	2900			188934	14536
2500	2900			125042	6
82719	**1268944**		**500**	**15447273**	**386464**
4552	54041		500	687360	38207
8810	783			436210	
2306	3288			234359	16572
				27670	
5924	35590			410676	1815
260	500			6291	
				2135	
	4269			81878	1000
	20001			74242	2000
2337	1580			24723	
25015	128052			1735576	112790
25015	66852			812338	112790
	61200			923238	

4-9 续表 1

单位：万元

行　业	Sector	本年资金来源小计 Sub-total Funds This Year
化学原料和化学制品制造业	Manufacture of Raw Chemical Material and Chemical Products	3400317
医药制造业	Manufacture of Medicine	210812
化学纤维制造业	Manufacture of Chemical Fibers	26341
橡胶和塑料制品业	Manufacture of Rubber and Plastic Products	529927
非金属矿物制品业	Manufacture of Non-metallic Mineral Products	2291945
#水泥、石灰和石膏制造	Cement Manufacturing	764004
玻璃制造	Manufacture of Glasses	44238
黑色金属冶炼和压延加工业	Smelting and Pressing of Ferrous Metals	1339483
#炼 铁	Iron Making	520519
炼 钢	Steel Making	436129
有色金属冶炼和压延加工业	Smelting and Pressing of Nonferrous Metals	3173490
金属制品业	Manufacture of Metal Products	288881
通用设备制造业	Manufacture of General Purpose Machinery	346435
专用设备制造业	Manufacture of Special Purpose Machinery	239817
汽车制造业	Manufacture of Car	218995
电气机械和器材制造业	Manufacture of Electric Equipment and Machinery	177188
计算机、通信和其他电子设备制造业	Manufacture of Communication Equipment,Comuputer and othe Elctronic	111800
电力、热力、燃气及水生产和供应业	**Production and Supply of Electricity,Gas and Water**	**11935421**
电力、热力生产和供应业	Production and Supply of Electricity Power and Heat Power	9867713
电力生产	Production of Electric Power	8229171
电力供应	Supply of Electric Power	928832
热力生产和供应	Production and Supply of Heat Power	709710
燃气生产和供应业	Production and Supply of Gas	1313051
水的生产和供应业	Production and Supply of Water	754657
#自来水生产和供应	Production and Distribution of Running Water	501674
污水处理及其再生利用	Treatment and Recycle of Waste Water	205910
建筑业	**Construction**	**698667**
#房屋建筑业	Consturction of Buildings	146040
土木工程建筑业	Buildings and Givil Engineering Construction	516117
建筑安装业	Building Installation	8517
批发和零售业	**Wholesale&Retail Trades**	**1514468**
批发业	Wholesale Trades	640875

Continued

(10 000 yuan)

国家预算内资金 State Budget	国内贷款 Domestic Loans	债券 Bonds	利用外资 Foreign Investment	自筹资金 Self-raising Funds	其他资金来源 Others
2716	457581			2856118	83902
50	7950			199892	2920
	1500			24841	
	7325			513395	9207
5248	72380			2129975	84342
1600	38250			686227	37927
	2500			41738	
	213433			1118588	7462
	82080			438389	50
	104853			327464	3812
	125100			3042390	6000
	3580			284801	500
17000	14592			313743	1100
2875	15700			216112	5130
	33699			185296	
500	23000			152171	1517
	23400			86832	1568
821728	**3572188**	**1359**	**11506**	**7297385**	**231255**
560217	3471412	849	8643	5706415	120177
91068	3031206			5056702	50195
234311	334503	849		320460	38709
234838	105703		8643	329253	31273
13997	73724			1181691	43639
247514	27052	510	2863	409279	67439
167951	3709	510	612	282851	46041
70321	16543		2251	97657	19138
179371	**196523**	**900**		**290108**	**31765**
67428	1000	900		67850	8862
99547	193554			200113	22903
1000	1800			5717	
42134	**49895**			**1349360**	**73079**
1250	14270			605082	20273

4-9 续表 2

单位：万元

行业	Sector	本年资金来源小计 Sub-total Funds This Year
零售业	Retail Trades	873593
交通运输、仓储和邮政业	**Transport Storage and Post**	**5697245**
#铁路运输业	Railway Transport	942148
道路运输业	Road Transport	3389289
航空运输业	Air Transport	146135
管道运输业	Via Pipelines Transport	251045
仓储业	Storage	950728
邮政业	Post	7664
住宿和餐饮业	**Hotels and Catering Services**	**709134**
住宿业	Hotels	480378
#旅游饭店	Tourist Restaurant	330187
餐饮业	Catering Services	228756
信息传输、软件和信息技术服务业	**Information Transmission, Computer Services and Software**	**516700**
#电信、广播电视和卫星传输服务	Telecommunication and Other Information Transmission Services	439888
#电 信	Telecommunication	415052
金融业	**Financial Intermediation**	**40586**
#货币金融服务	Services of Intermediation	34250
资本市场服务	Services of Capital Market	1350
保险业	**Insurance**	**2236**
房地产业	**Real Estate**	**7776506**
#房地产开发经营	Real Estate Development and Operation	218651
物业管理	Management of Real Estate	2065
其他房地产业	Other Real Estate	7528128
租赁和商务服务业	**Leasing and Business Services**	**382238**
租赁业	Leasing	4069
商务服务业	Business Service	378169
科学研究和技术服务业	**Scientific Research, Technical Service and Geological Prospecting**	**113393**
研究和试验发展	Research and Experiment Development	27627
专业技术服务业	Professional Technical Service	54662
科技推广和应用服务业	Services of Science and Technology Exchanges and Difussion	31104

Continued

(10 000 yuan)

国家预算内资金 State Budget	国内贷款 Domestic Loans	债券 Bonds	利用外资 Foreign Investment	自筹资金 Self-raising Funds	其他资金来源 Others
40884	35625			744278	52806
1270404	**1853893**	**205000**		**1795958**	**571990**
109417	222700	150000		439531	20500
813328	1457900	50000		529574	538487
23730				122405	
2700	112304			136041	
321229	59989	5000		551507	13003
				7664	
121661	**40544**		**2770**	**513983**	**30176**
37399	36200		2770	397714	6295
9455	7600		2770	307677	2685
84262	4344			116269	23881
61760	**6500**			**440140**	**8300**
20760				410828	8300
8006				407046	
632				**38324**	**1630**
632				32848	770
				1350	
				2236	
2564063	**220891**	**525**	**1250**	**3546592**	**1443185**
15484	60197			135487	7483
				2065	
2543428	160094	525	1250	3398767	1424064
91741	**7816**			**255498**	**27183**
1627				2442	
90114	7816			253056	27183
54654	**2000**			**49048**	**7691**
18362				9265	
29918				19681	5063
6374	2000			20102	2628

4-9 续表 3

单位：万元

行　业	Sector	本年资金来源小计 Sub-total Funds This Year
水利、环境和公共设施管理业	**Management of Water Conservancy, Environment and Public Facilities**	**5567844**
水利管理业	Management of Water Conservancy	1238010
生态保护和环境治理业	Environmental Management	142509
公共设施管理业	Management of Public Facilities	4187325
市政设施管理	Management of Public Facilities	3337652
环境卫生管理	Management of Enviroment	82061
城乡市容管理	Management of Apperance City	89750
绿化管理	Management of Urban Greening	260453
公园和游览景区管理	Scenic-Spot Management	417409
居民服务、修理和其他服务业	**Resident Service and Other Services**	**179795**
教　育	**Education**	**1280884**
#初等教育	Elementary Education	186012
中等教育	Secondary Education	707925
高等教育	Higher Education	188516
卫生和社会工作	**Health, Social Security and Social Welfare**	**586808**
卫　生	Health Care	447641
#医　院	Hospital	366637
社会工作	Mangement of Social	139167
文化、体育和娱乐业	**Culture, Sports and Entertainment**	**677357**
新闻和出版业	Journalism and Publishing Activities	8518
广播、电视、电影和影视录音制作业	Broadcasting,Movies,Televisions and Audiovisual Activites	23147
文化艺术业	Cultural and Art Activities	409528
体　育	Sports	199489
娱乐业	Entertainment	36675
公共管理、社会保障和社会组织	**Public Management and Social Organization**	**1289110**
中国共产党机关	Organ of Communist Party of China	28832
国家机构	Government Agencies	1132198
人民政协、民主党派	People's Political Consultative Conference and Democratic Parties	130
社会保障	Social Security	35089
群众团体、社会团体和其他成员组织	Non-Governmental Institutions,Social Organizations and Religion Organizations	32132
基层群众自治组织	Grass Roots Self-governing Organizations	60729

Continued

(10 000 yuan)

国家预算内资金 State Budget	国内贷款 Domestic Loans	债券 Bonds	利用外资 Foreign Investment	自筹资金 Self-raising Funds	其他资金来源 Others
2114724	**909483**		**19988**	**2200959**	**322690**
743279	110884		5978	338497	39372
45201	61938			26501	8869
1326244	736661		14010	1835961	274449
992019	720688		14010	1388380	222555
61731	500			16552	3278
19416				68859	1475
132678	1000			122970	3805
120400	14473			239200	43336
77250	**4160**			**87593**	**10792**
836015	**55350**	**3000**		**291832**	**94687**
141821	4350	3000		29117	7724
510648	31700			98832	66745
55558	13230			118523	1205
225601	**24523**	**115**		**289208**	**47361**
176696	15563	115		223910	31357
140356	15563			189951	20767
48905	8960			65298	16004
237584	**100415**			**307579**	**31779**
2900				5618	
12013				5957	5177
155161	75659			157558	21150
66810	24756			106071	1852
700				32375	3600
698148	**13243**			**397552**	**180167**
7940				13295	7597
624893	13243			330765	163297
130					
7946				20775	6368
10909				20731	492
46330				11986	2413

4-10 各地、州、市、县(市)城镇固定资产投资和新增固定资产
Total Investment and Newly Increased Fixed Assets in Urban Area by Prefecture, Autonomous Prefecture, City and County

单位：万元 (2013 年) (10 000 yuan)

地区 Region	投资总额 Total Investment	第一产业 Primary Industry	第二产业 Secondary Industry	第三产业 Tertiary Industry	新增固定资产 Newly Increased Fixed Assets	房屋建筑面积(万平方米) Floor Space of Buildings (10 000 sq.m) 施工面积 Floor Space Under Construction	竣工面积 Floor Space Completed
总计 Total	**65587266**	**1531678**	**38360470**	**25695118**	**41614293**	**13153.72**	**3986.27**
按隶属关系分 By Administrative Relationship							
中央 Central Government	15844929	316456	9795279	5733194	10623496	2702.06	1289.54
地方 Local	49742337	1215222	28565191	19961924	30990797	10451.66	2696.73
按区域分 Grouped by Region							
乌鲁木齐市 Urumqi City	**7592505**	**46155**	**3334200**	**4212150**	**4695412**	**1622.17**	**192.97**
#乌鲁木齐县 Urumqi County	272822	5705	84557	182560	110814	65.87	8.72
克拉玛依市 Karamay City	**4113706**	**16735**	**3180083**	**916888**	**3051189**	**288.62**	**62.99**
吐鲁番地区 Turpan Administrative Offices	**2300868**	**15187**	**1995957**	**289724**	**1337222**	**158.15**	**47.34**
吐鲁番市 Turpan City	522908	3873	406379	112656	387436	86.92	14.60
鄯善县 Shanshan [Piqan] County	1176628	7760	1071890	96978	718903	30.44	5.84
托克逊县 Toksun County	601332	3554	517688	80090	230883	40.79	26.90
哈密地区 Hami [Kumul] Administrative Offices	**4030059**	**50767**	**3227629**	**751663**	**949575**	**436.31**	**163.35**
哈密市 Hami [Kumul] City	2650881	34459	2172915	443507	717943	394.39	158.49
巴里坤哈萨克自治县 Barkol Kazak Autonomous County	569887	5365	494377	70145	130257	30.36	3.36
伊吾县 Yiwu [Araturuk] County	809291	10943	560337	238011	101375	11.56	1.50
昌吉回族自治州 Changji Hui Autonomous Prefecture	**9283655**	**193668**	**7327542**	**1762445**	**9176327**	**525.69**	**147.95**
昌吉市 Changji City	1512172	72411	554690	885071	1512011	104.83	6.00
阜康市 Fukang City	1682684	56297	1402334	224053	1648063	142.91	49.46
呼图壁县 Hutubi County	692711	24252	522265	146194	717732	69.18	28.27
玛纳斯县 Manas County	1320674	15392	1179036	126246	1265953	120.16	25.86
奇台县 Qitai County	1464402	23816	1140424	300162	1424156	68.00	34.13
吉木萨尔县 Jimsar County	2426134	1500	2373003	51631	2423534	14.76	4.23
木垒哈萨克自治县 Mori Kazak Autonomous County	184878		155790	29088	184878	5.85	
伊犁哈萨克自治州 Ili Kazak Autonomous Prefecture	**10534222**	**367042**	**5639232**	**4527948**	**6050120**	**2564.93**	**1088.69**
伊犁州直属县(市) Counties (Cities) Direct Under Ili Prefecture	**5072791**	**69867**	**2892178**	**2110746**	**2578857**	**1117.23**	**342.90**
伊宁市 Yining [Gulja] City	1529137	19753	1003751	505633	223603	210.13	12.74

4-10 续表 1 Continued

单位：万元 (10 000 yuan)

地区 Region	投资总额 Total Investment	第一产业 Primary Industry	第二产业 Secondary Industry	第三产业 Tertiary Industry	新增固定资产 Newly Increased Fixed Assets	房屋建筑面积(万平方米) Floor Space of Buildings (10 000 sq.m)	
						施工面积 Floor Space Under Construction	竣工面积 Floor Space Completed
奎屯市 Kuytun City	857637	12800	329123	515714	468961	206.52	67.85
伊宁县 Yining [Gulja] County	633986	6487	540863	86636	570721	116.22	37.98
察布查尔锡伯自治县 Qapqal Xibe Autonomous County	363674	8171	252689	102814	296150	62.17	36.74
霍城县 Huocheng [Korgas] County	875394	6483	395662	473249	506769	318.02	120.18
巩留县 Gongliu [Tokkuztara] County	161177	5152	80091	75934	126329	38.85	28.14
新源县 Xinyuan [Kunes] County	224083	9100	101872	113111	143810	61.30	11.86
昭苏县 Zhaosu [Mongolkure] County	121991	1050	16811	104130	82579	51.65	15.08
特克斯县 Tekes County	103447		66197	37250	57482	10.29	6.93
尼勒克县 Nilka County	202265	871	105119	96275	102453	42.08	5.40
塔城地区 Tacheng [Tarbagatai] Administrative Offices	**3037553**	**198895**	**1329146**	**1509512**	**2015159**	**1046.09**	**499.99**
塔城市 Tacheng [Qoqek] City	276639	18980	88150	169509	195464	75.30	31.83
乌苏市 Usu City	783157	54661	358868	369628	451033	396.70	107.35
额敏县 Emin Ciunty	388872	55223	111471	222178	423396	109.31	79.87
沙湾县 Shawan County	651905	50517	136946	464442	523916	386.47	241.16
托里县 Toli County	274386	12337	180154	81895	167653	29.66	22.96
裕民县 Yumin [Qagantokay] County	56973	4854	14121	37998	34577	13.62	5.41
和布克赛尔蒙古自治县 Hoboksar Mongol Autonomous County	605621	2323	439436	163862	219120	35.03	11.41
阿勒泰地区 Altay Administrative Offices	**2423878**	**98280**	**1417908**	**907690**	**1456104**	**401.61**	**245.80**
阿勒泰市 Altay City	577168	19350	185553	372265	306110	197.42	98.79
布尔津县 Burqin County	305185	26733	209813	68639	257545	40.21	38.01
富蕴县 Fuyun [Koktokay] County	583084		480115	102969	96819	29.39	19.56
福海县 Fuhai [Burultokay] County	183301	26115	51847	105339	119787	60.45	34.43
哈巴河县 Habahe [Kaba] County	332783	15785	188227	128771	387092	27.36	27.21
青河县 Qinghe [Qinggil] County	272485	3977	194499	74009	155927	31.74	17.04
吉木乃县 Jeminay County	169872	6320	107854	55698	132824	15.04	10.76
博尔塔拉蒙古自治州 Bortala Mongol Autonomous Prefecture	**1574822**	**65966**	**605234**	**903622**	**1327208**	**482.90**	**191.43**
博乐市 Bole [Bortala] City	1042393	22503	348855	671035	846455	307.13	105.63

4-10 续表 2 Continued

单位：万元 (10 000 yuan)

地区 Region	投资总额 Total Investment	第一产业 Primary Industry	第二产业 Secondary Industry	第三产业 Tertiary Industry	新增固定资产 Newly Increased Fixed Assets	房屋建筑面积(万平方米) Floor Space of Buildings (10 000 sq.m) 施工面积 Floor Space Under Construction	竣工面积 Floor Space Completed
精河县 Jinghe [Jing] County	415402	33393	234080	147929	370832	158.05	80.81
温泉县 Wenquan [Araxang] County	117027	10070	22299	84658	109921	17.72	4.99
巴音郭楞蒙古自治州 Bayangol Mongol Autonomous Prefecture	**6576763**	**207284**	**4805199**	**1564280**	**3694590**	**1358.58**	**437.59**
库尔勒市 Korla City	3518861	22665	2981370	514826	1829326	381.49	163.24
轮台县 Luntai [Bugur] County	388117	25860	285533	76724	300631	167.22	58.39
尉犁县 Yuli [Lopnur] County	226022	10522	109348	106152	219939	56.92	35.83
若羌县 Ruoqiang [Qarkilik] County	573824	22896	456649	94279	389368	52.24	11.76
且末县 Qiemo [Qarqan] County	300991	37048	129978	133965	172077	219.75	14.70
焉耆回族自治县 Yanqi Hui Autonomous County	267915	22665	107356	137894	76118	76.73	35.40
和静县 Hejing County	985799	34761	604511	346527	534675	209.08	68.87
和硕县 Hoxud County	192127	19777	85429	86921	77532	126.40	25.30
博湖县 Bohu [Bagrax] County	123107	11090	45025	66992	94924	68.75	24.10
阿克苏地区 Aksu Administrative Offices	**3710672**	**81374**	**2033887**	**1595411**	**1788719**	**979.36**	**162.57**
阿克苏市 Aksu City	925056	20906	380260	523890	323499	534.30	22.64
温宿县 Wensu [Onsu] County	422564	8857	225455	188252	197795	50.36	12.78
库车县 Kuqa County	1075712	8274	654084	413354	323633	78.60	53.72
沙雅县 Xayar County	304381	8452	199519	96410	112872	54.88	18.03
新和县 Xinhe [Toksu] County	170669	12073	99720	58876	171313	38.37	33.48
拜城县 Baicheng [Bay] County	408749		282004	126745	272320	16.05	
乌什县 Wushi [Uxturpan] County	134648	8996	33420	92232	127822	87.62	5.20
阿瓦提县 Awat County	194739	11336	97094	86309	209065	35.07	16.72
柯坪县 Kalpin County	74154	2480	62331	9343	50400	84.11	
克孜勒苏柯尔克孜自治州 Kizilsu Kirgiz Autonomous Prefecture	**758417**	**37106**	**432640**	**288671**	**486540**	**250.18**	**83.88**
阿图什市 Artux City	240590	4407	119804	116379	240926	77.98	19.62
阿克陶县 Akto County	291513	23162	187476	80875	107620	57.95	30.20
阿合奇县 Akqi County	49412		42239	7173	10721	10.21	2.19
乌恰县 Wuqia [Ulugqat] County	176902	9537	83121	84244	127273	104.04	31.87

4-10 续表 3 Continued

单位：万元 (10 000 yuan)

地 区 Region	投资总额 Total Investment	第一产业 Primary Industry	第二产业 Secondary Industry	第三产业 Tertiary Industry	新增固定资产 Newly Increased Fixed Assets	房屋建筑面积(万平方米) Floor Space of Buildings (10 000 sq.m)	
						施工面积 Floor Space Under Construction	竣工面积 Floor Space Completed
喀什地区 Kashgar [Kaxgar] Administrative Offices	**5813747**	**235416**	**1768819**	**3809512**	**3833435**	**2136.52**	**323.16**
喀什市 Kashgar [Kaxgar] City	1155666	2500	307921	845245	106775	167.67	5.13
疏附县 Shufu County	370112	4050	81406	284656	161648	217.03	98.85
疏勒县 Shule County	993317	98092	337366	557859	850737	264.37	9.81
英吉沙县 Yengisar County	322777	22588	63717	236472	349061	72.05	1.11
泽普县 Zepu [Poskam] County	306095	1900	40640	263555	240365	171.84	
莎车县 Shache [Yarkant] County	385518	4050	137313	244155	75273	284.74	
叶城县 Yecheng [Kagilik] County	443520	2753	133654	307113	446815	108.80	2.30
麦盖提县 Makit County	324162	32255	75716	216191	298915	68.72	20.19
岳普湖县 Yopurga County	411701	32709	182671	196321	398007	133.60	1.52
伽师县 Jiashi [Payzawat] County	481092	17634	151425	312033	348937	157.90	17.56
巴楚县 Bachu [Maralbexi] County	400265	16294	119390	264581	331358	480.46	166.69
塔什库尔干塔吉克自治县 Taxkorgan Tajik Autonomous County	219522	591	137600	81331	225544	9.34	
和田地区 Hotan Administrative Offices	**1838165**	**120149**	**375493**	**1342523**	**1519859**	**1198.92**	**709.42**
和田市 Hotan City	510472	23177	19817	467478	419889	341.78	142.10
和田县 Hotan County	246223	23043	92149	131031	199865	73.93	44.49
墨玉县 Moyu [Karakax] County	307117	9648	66280	231189	233695	214.28	153.62
皮山县 Pishan [Guma] County	191365	4220	46520	140625	156800	138.89	108.77
洛浦县 Lop County	180718	8150	45835	126733	171928	174.02	96.79
策勒县 Qira County	134263	19852	36606	77805	159316	99.50	86.23
于田县 Yutian [Keriya] County	200519	24469	50161	125889	126002	122.04	63.35
民丰县 Minfeng [Niya] County	67488	7590	18125	41773	52364	34.48	14.07
自治区直辖县级市 Municpality Country-LevelCity directly under the Central Government	**4948709**	**94829**	**3634555**	**1219325**	**2731662**	**1151.39**	**374.93**
石河子市 Shihezi City	1795613	37992	1471899	285722	271385	362.03	38.58
阿拉尔市 Aral City	890688	22855	411548	456285	771825	307.74	83.39
图木舒克市 Tumxuk City	491992	6482	208652	276858	303301	222.33	122.89
五家渠市 Wujiaqu City	1770416	27500	1542456	200460	1385151	259.29	130.07
跨地区投资 Trans-regional Investment	**2510956**			**2510956**	**972435**		

4-11 各地、州、市分行业城镇固定资产投资

单位：万元 (2013 年)

行业 Sector	合计 Total	乌鲁木齐市 Urumqi City	克拉玛依市 Karamay City	吐鲁番地区 Turpan Administrative Offices	哈密地区 Hami [Kumul] Administrative Offices	昌吉回族自治州 Changji Hui Autonomous Prefecture	伊犁哈萨克自治州 Ili Kazak Autonomous Prefecture	伊犁州直属县(市) Counties (Cities) Direct Under Ili Prefecture
总计 Total	**65587266**	**7592505**	**4113706**	**2300868**	**4030059**	**9283655**	**10534222**	**5072791**
农、林、牧、渔业 Farming, Forestry, Animal Husbandry and Fishery	1531678	46155	16735	15187	50767	193668	367042	69867
采矿业 Mining	8781023	86160	2435071	810600	423430	891733	702059	381846
制造业 Manufacturing	16840187	1935340	432350	426195	637694	5521667	2004467	1284378
电力、热力、燃气及水生产和供应业 Production and Supply of Electricity, Gas and Water	12025697	1052832	217131	759162	2166505	912342	2877620	1175916
建筑业 Construction	713563	259868	95531			1800	55086	50038
交通运输、仓储及邮政业 Transport, Storage, Postal and Telecommunications Services	676159	56378	35974	22365	4131	149500	125180	52648
信息传输、软件和信息技术服务业 Information Transmission, Computer Services and Software	1466200	202771	121754	5568	41226	124575	380183	224955
批发和零售业 Wholesale&Retail Trades	529250	369366	44117		4234	2800	28263	6446
住宿和餐饮业 Hotels and Catering Services	5456501	536913	23153	60357	271140	441641	728294	387378
金融业 Financial Intermediation	40108	1676				6800	10302	
房地产业 Real Estate	7514900	970317	104967	53015	237696	356564	1494831	634723
租赁和商务服务业 Leasing and Business Services	353855	10561	131067	1516	9700	19157	42648	40698
科学研究和技术服务业 Scientific Research, Technical Service and Geological Prospection	114727	21722	5003	1645	1062	5119	4324	2802
水利、环境和公共设施管理业 Management of Water Conservancy, Environment and Public Facilities	5542753	1524506	205690	84027	97035	401313	1041116	417209
居民服务、修理和其他服务业 Service to Households and Others Services	168431	900	12706	600	3168	10564	16371	6400
教育 Education	1244939	173496	84263	28103	28577	55543	216015	97254
卫生和社会工作 Health, Social Securities and Social Welfare	586712	111602	16714	11998	8713	40677	73842	41721
文化、体育和娱乐业 Culture, Sports and Entertainment	683799	63898	104956	1570	7178	116944	123242	51823
公共管理、社会保障和社会组织 Public Management and Social Organization	1316784	168044	26524	18960	37803	31248	243337	146689

Investment in Fixed Assets in Urban Area by Sectors in Prefecture, Autonomous Prefecture and City

(10 000 yuan)

塔城地区 Tacheng [Tarbagatai] Administra -tive Offices	阿勒泰地区 Altay Administra -tive Offices	博尔塔拉蒙古自治州 Bortala Mongol Autono -mous Prefecture	巴音郭楞蒙古自治州 Bayangol Mongol Autono -mous Prefecture	阿克苏地区 Aksu Administra -tive Offices	克孜勒苏柯尔克孜自治州 Kizilsu Kirgiz Autono -mous Prefecture	喀什地区 Kashgar [Kaxgar] Administra -tive Offices	和田地区 Hotan Administra -tive Offices	石河子市 Shihezi City	阿拉尔市 Aral City	图木舒克市 Tumxuk City	五家渠市 Wujiaqu City	跨地区投资 Trans-regional Investment
3037553	**2423878**	**1574822**	**6576763**	**3710672**	**758417**	**5813747**	**1838165**	**1795613**	**890688**	**491992**	**1770416**	**2510956**
198895	98280	65966	207284	81374	37106	235416	120149	37992	22855	6482	27500	
208305	111908	42890	3048075	76846	52860	192854	18445					
432432	287657	226302	1099461	1226917	137143	944365	137364	822072	154033	56349	1078468	
683539	1018165	328787	657663	523233	165173	625857	219684	648902	257515	149303	463988	
4870	178	7255		206891	77464	5743		925		3000		
53038	19494	11225	31354	48670	980	143254	21471	8546	10291	6840		
115662	39566	11749	74931	111974	3293	272828	13766	5970	47017	5735	42860	
17802	4015	16487		1050	676	43650	12740	5867				
206217	134699	75056	164138	177947	20553	323894	72793	18007	3567	15698	12394	2510956
1814	8488	970	5819	6755		6956	830					
615966	244142	285116	620093	620237	95260	1544075	668938	131612	148253	164020	19906	
350	1600	6046	22837	7800		82423	20100					
1362	160	6101	11792	16569	3200	29696	7244	1250				
285229	338678	253995	413560	436729	64951	469047	143730	75116	181346	58694	91898	
4533	5438	4925	950	9331	4255	92236	6605	4180	1110		530	
73837	44924	34177	74503	57577	15444	237204	191112	2751	33112	5692	7370	
24383	7738	18276	24894	27978	5220	149966	70970	4685	5827	2719	12631	
56204	15215	33196	18914	32172	25369	92254	34268	8773	10704	5990	4371	
53115	43533	146303	100495	40622	49470	322029	77956	18965	15058	11470	8500	

4-12 城镇固定资产投资效果指标
Investment Result of Urban Investment

指　标	Item	2012	2013
建设周期(年)	Construction Cycle (year)	4	3
计划总投资(万元)	Total Planned Investment (10 000 yuan)	180099700	220183646
本年完成投资(万元)	Completed Invetsment for the Current Year (10 000 yuan)	49877126	65587266
本年新增固定资产(万元)	Newly Increased Fixed Assets for the Current Year (10 000 yuan)	29218800	41614293
固定资产交付使用率(%)	Rate of Projects of Fixed Assets Completed and Put into Operation (%)	58.6	63.4
施工项目个数(个)	Number of Projects under Construction (unit)	9879	11814
竣工项目个数(个)	Number of Projects Completed (unit)	5799	7097
建设项目投产率(%)	Rate of Projects Completed&Put into Use (%)	58.7	60.1

4-13 全社会基础设施投资
Investment of Basic Facilities in the Whole County

单位：万元　　(10 000 yuan)

指　标	Item	2012	2013
总　计	**Total**	**16107117**	**24873595**
电力、燃气及水的生产和供应业	Production and Supply of Electricity, Gas and Water	7815608	12612328
交通运输、仓储和邮政业	Transport, Storage, Postal and Telecommunications Services	4421504	5715253
信息传输、计算机服务和软件业	Information Transmission,Computer and Software Technology	444177	530725
水利、环境和公共设施管理业	Management of Water Conservancy, Environment and Public Facilities	3425828	6015289

4-14 主要年份房地产开发企业基本情况
Basic Condition of Enterprises for Real Estate Development in Main Years

指　标	Item	2005	2010	2013
企业单位数(个)	**Number of Enterprises (unit)**	**756**	**1233**	**1634**
#亏损企业	Loss- Suffering Enterprises	410	606	969
主要财务指标（万元）	**Main Financial Indices (10 000 yuan)**			
年末资产负债情况	Situation of Year-end Liabilities			
资产总计	Total Assets	4861415	12591584	31005187
固定资产累计折旧	Accumulated Depreciation of Fixed Assets	81096	156739	316889
#本年折旧	Depreciation for the Current Year	17981	34814	75775
负债总计	Total Liabilities	2932694	9422446	24385879
所有者权益合计	Total of Owner's Right and Interest	1928721	3169138	6619308
实收资本	Total of Actual Capital	970103	2109245	3726602
损益情况	Situation of Profit and Loss			
经营收入总计	Total Income of Business	1084796	4119413	7367305
#土地转让收入	Income of Land Transfer	11295	19029	17325
商品房销售收入	Sales Income of Commercial Flat	1047965	4022490	7129796
房屋出租收入	Income of Renting House	15773	39343	85274
其他收入	Others	9763	38550	134911
经营成本	Operating Cost	871320	3040741	5313902
经营税金及附加	Operating Tax and Extra Charges	63562	295011	583407
销售费用	Expenses of sales	27319	100896	239804
其他业务利润	Other Business Profits	9161	28592	43977
管理费用及财务费用	Expenses of Both Management and Finance	80949	257405	542372
投资收益及营业外收入	Income of Investment earnings and Extra-business	7829	14881	120557
营业外支出	Expenditure of Extra-business	3456	14909	25520
利润总额	Total Profits	34320	454814	834862

注：2004 年以后，企业个数包括了没有开发量的企业数，而往年未包括。
Note: Urban Investment exclude real estate, the following the same as follows.

4-15 主要年份房地产投资主要指标
Main Indicators of Real Estate Investment in Main Years

指 标	Item	2005	2010	2013
本年购置土地面积(万平方米)	**Land Area Purchased for the Current Year (10 000 sq. m)**	**447.30**	**557.69**	**976.24**
房地产开发投资额(万元)	**Total Investment of Real-Estate Development (10 000 yuan)**	**1016618**	**3477185**	**8256855**
按中央和地方分	Grouped by Central and Local			
中央企业	Central Enterprises	54128	175564	548612
地方企业	Local Enterprises	962490	3301621	7708243
按投资构成分	Classified by Use of Funds			
建筑工程	Construction Works	810003	2742491	6428567
安装工程	Works of Installation	49559	161703	653940
设备工器具购置	Purchase of Equipment and Instruments	14135	51777	138890
其他费用	Other Expenses	142921	521214	1035458
#土地购置费	Expenses of Land Purchase	94230	313568	595300
按工程用途分	Grouped by Purpose of Projects			
住 宅	Residential buildings	679521	2815620	5556183
办公楼	Office Building	40977	102895	249894
商业营业用房	Houses for Commercial and Business Purpose	247033	380275	1628450
其 他	Others	49087	178395	822328
本年资金来源小计（万元）	**Sub-total of Capital Sources for the Current Year (10 000 yuan)**	**1137693**	**5380739**	**11131481**
国内贷款	Domestic Loans	113887	684191	1066046
利用外资	Foreign Investment	160		
自筹资金	Self-raising Funds	479948	1397982	4121799
其它资金	Others	543698	3298566	5943636

4-16 按用途分房地产开发企业（单位）投资完成额
Investment Actually Completed by Enterprises for Real Estate Development by Use

单位：万元 (10 000 yuan)

年份 Year	地区 Region	企业个数（个） Number of Enterprises (unit)	本年完成投资 Investment Completed This Year	住宅 Residential Buildings	#别墅、高档公寓 Villas, High-grade Apartments
	1996	139	156232	80728	
	1997		169906	81886	1668
	1998		148577	95225	1000
	1999	165	234481	174446	2994
	2000	209	574347	500381	2390
	2001	293	979184	757490	3126
	2002	335	877060	570643	11001
	2003	492	1024908	547770	20212
	2004	709	1125577	599276	29585
	2005	756	1016618	679521	26634
	2006	824	1208786	899482	48542
	2007	909	1683160	1390360	57776
	2008	1130	2286267	1937460	94256
	2009	1159	2358805	1882530	148916
	2010	1233	3477185	2815620	194136
	2011	1421	5163895	4163926	258846
	2012	1509	6060939	4442667	368122
	2013	1634	8256855	5556183	475062
乌鲁木齐市	Urumqi City	401	2875305	2099155	174829
克拉玛依市	Karamay City	36	427468	325739	21708
吐鲁番地区	Turpan Administrative Offices	26	56347	29305	
哈密地区	Hami [Kumul] Administrative Offices	87	320707	205656	1526
昌吉回族自治州	Changji Hui Autonomous Prefecture	145	486649	363292	2629
伊犁哈萨克自治州	Ili Kazak Autonomous Prefecture	327	1282839	828192	9970
伊犁州直属县(市)	Counties (Cities) Direct Under Ili Prefecture	190	972653	625752	3576
塔城地区	Tacheng [Tarbagatai] Administrative Offices	55	146735	114133	475
阿勒泰地区	Altay Administrative Offices	82	163451	88307	5919
博尔塔拉蒙古自治州	Bortala Mongol Autonomous Prefecture	57	269690	145366	5918
巴音郭楞蒙古自治州	Bayangol Mongol Autonomous Prefecture	159	616271	452588	135581
阿克苏地区	Aksu Administrative Offices	147	597004	385265	3799
克孜勒苏柯尔克孜自治州	Kizilsu Kirgiz Autonomous Prefecture	15	42809	20670	
喀什地区	Kashgar [Kaxgar] Administrative Offices	109	274823	121947	2400
和田地区	Hotan Administrative Offices	4	9466	4233	
石河子市	Shihezi City	61	291526	193347	
阿拉尔市	Aral City	14	42052	28205	
图木舒克市	Tumxuk City	11	39996	16806	
五家渠市	Wujiaqu City	35	623903	336417	116702

4-16 续表 Continued

单位：万元 (10 000 yuan)

年 份 Year	地 区 Region	办公楼 Office buildings	商业营业用房 Houses for Business Use	其 他 Other
	1996	18108	42562	14834
	1997	25347	41935	20738
	1998	17394	22027	13931
	1999	9133	27068	23834
	2000	13171	42601	18194
	2001	41911	111028	68755
	2002	81119	153498	71800
	2003	81497	286896	108745
	2004	77843	390566	57892
	2005	40977	247033	49087
	2006	28233	236945	44126
	2007	27629	205590	59581
	2008	56358	221418	71031
	2009	81926	281946	112403
	2010	102895	380275	178395
	2011	155400	572602	271967
	2012	120840	976135	521297
	2013	249894	1628450	822328
乌鲁木齐市	Urumqi City	139917	344190	292043
克拉玛依市	Karamay City	8132	63123	30474
吐鲁番地区	Turpan Administrative Offices	360	25428	1254
哈密地区	Hami [Kumul] Administrative Offices	8565	47000	59486
昌吉回族自治州	Changji Hui Autonomous Prefecture	9018	81645	32694
伊犁哈萨克自治州	Ili Kazak Autonomous Prefecture	26813	347662	80172
伊犁州直属县(市)	Counties (Cities) Direct Under Ili Prefecture	24586	270172	52143
塔城地区	Tacheng [Tarbagatai] Administrative Offices	240	29327	3035
阿勒泰地区	Altay Administrative Offices	1987	48163	24994
博尔塔拉蒙古自治州	Bortala Mongol Autonomous Prefecture	6932	108423	8969
巴音郭楞蒙古自治州	Bayangol Mongol Autonomous Prefecture	9931	114424	39328
阿克苏地区	Aksu Administrative Offices	9521	176680	25538
克孜勒苏柯尔克孜自治州	Kizilsu Kirgiz Autonomous Prefecture	450	11806	9883
喀什地区	Kashgar [Kaxgar] Administrative Offices	24771	109462	18643
和田地区	Hotan Administrative Offices		2462	2771
石河子市	Shihezi City	5384	59547	33248
阿拉尔市	Aral City		13847	
图木舒克市	Tumxuk City		22576	614
五家渠市	Wujiaqu City	100	100175	187211

4-17 房地产开发企业（单位）资金来源
Sources of Funds of Enterprises for Real Estate Development

单位：万元 (10 000 yuan)

年份 Year	地区 Region	合计 Total	国内贷款 Domestic Loans	利用外资 Foreign Investment	自筹资金 Self-raising Funds	其他资金来源 Others
	1996	154995	51048	742	45104	58101
	1997	161399	51443	500	60573	48883
	1998	151094	22419	500	49427	78748
	1999	244252	29665	5770	73899	134918
	2000	701332	113823	600	232768	354141
	2001	890102	106794	1278	303975	478055
	2002	1064031	158511		455707	449813
	2003	1117659	208348		448441	460870
	2004	1215850	125553		546282	544015
	2005	1137693	113887	160	479948	543698
	2006	1446593	145340		478871	822382
	2007	2243755	217380		766344	1260031
	2008	2427323	253427		961343	1212553
	2009	3683795	453692	50	915219	2314834
	2010	5380739	684191		1397982	3298566
	2011	6843313	731550	1666	2314233	3795864
	2012	7979461	908749		2976896	4093816
	2013	11131481	1066046		4121799	5943636
乌鲁木齐市	Urumqi City	4269133	497454		1003527	2768152
克拉玛依市	Karamay City	625844	54221		167207	404416
吐鲁番地区	Turpan Administrative Offices	61616	2000		49233	10383
哈密地区	Hami [Kumul] Administrative Offices	424723	29703		159122	235898
昌吉回族自治州	Changji Hui Autonomous Prefecture	953079	130730		241265	581084
伊犁哈萨克自治州	Ili Kazak Autonomous Prefecture	1660734	119138		731891	809705
伊犁州直属县(市)	Counties (Cities) Direct Under Ili Prefecture	1342334	111888		515428	715018
塔城地区	Tacheng [Tarbagatai] Administrative Offices	166275	2700		124700	38875
阿勒泰地区	Altay Administrative Offices	152125	4550		91763	55812
博尔塔拉蒙古自治州	Bortala Mongol Autonomous Prefecture	236864	1850		125729	109285
巴音郭楞蒙古自治州	Bayangol Mongol Autonomous Prefecture	752662	60672		358413	333577
阿克苏地区	Aksu Administrative Offices	710652	47970		415726	246956
克孜勒苏柯尔克孜自治州	Kizilsu Kirgiz Autonomous Prefecture	46280	630		34703	10947
喀什地区	Kashgar [Kaxgar] Administrative Offices	279837	68478		112870	98489
和田地区	Hotan Administrative Offices	7889			7889	
石河子市	Shihezi City	321360	16200		86008	219152
阿拉尔市	Aral City	51547	500		34000	17047
图木舒克市	Tumxuk City	35754			27606	8148
五家渠市	Wujiaqu City	693507	36500		566610	90397

4-18 房地产开发企业（单位）施工、销售和待售情况

单位：万平方米

年 份 Year	地 区 Region	本年施工房屋面积 Floor Space of Building under Construction This Year	#住宅 Residential Buildings	#商业营业用房 Houses for Business Use	本年新开工房屋面积 Floor Space Started This Year	#住宅 Residential Buildings	#商业营业用房 Houses for Business Use
	1996	224.90	150.80	41.67	103.87	69.84	19.52
	1997	222.20	144.50	47.68	90.24	70.08	12.81
	1998	252.61	188.38	40.72	133.26	120.95	6.35
	1999	343.38	295.62	34.33	212.73	194.77	12.48
	2000	771.86	665.30	74.20	453.63	397.77	43.00
	2001	1433.54	1207.89	150.63	912.06	778.55	97.24
	2002	1246.89	946.11	204.52	577.04	433.57	98.13
	2003	1382.14	962.89	298.51	782.78	557.28	175.73
	2004	1333.03	863.19	357.53	771.47	550.66	178.43
	2005	1371.15	941.58	340.63	793.55	639.98	130.90
	2006	1567.70	1188.61	307.19	1035.59	875.99	131.90
	2007	2053.76	1715.00	271.52	1347.11	1216.39	101.82
	2008	2639.06	2247.80	259.78	1703.86	1500.75	129.11
	2009	3064.41	2560.67	305.81	1718.17	1482.86	158.07
	2010	3980.80	3317.68	410.96	2177.24	1852.88	214.50
	2011	5481.44	4574.72	543.12	2974.51	2510.68	304.46
	2012	6896.54	5482.59	841.24	2823.64	2149.35	421.32
	2013	9459.55	6982.71	1545.44	3729.88	2499.16	838.51
乌鲁木齐市	Urumqi City	3507.76	2690.46	317.29	1000.14	683.71	146.07
克拉玛依市	Karamay City	408.40	341.28	40.38	151.66	119.74	19.05
吐鲁番地区	Turpan Administrative Offices	75.22	40.64	29.78	34.70	19.86	14.06
哈密地区	Hami [Kumul] Administrative Offices	341.26	248.35	51.69	197.25	139.89	29.04
昌吉回族自治州	Changji Hui Autonomous Prefecture	630.61	528.86	66.08	305.20	251.15	41.61
伊犁哈萨克自治州	Ili Kazak Autonomous Prefecture	1506.03	1024.10	385.20	697.10	438.10	198.16
伊犁州直属县(市)	Counties (Cities) Direct Under Ili Prefecture	1061.84	684.50	297.86	524.67	320.65	152.74
塔城地区	Tacheng [Tarbagatai] Administrative Offices	174.96	144.57	27.51	83.29	63.05	18.60
阿勒泰地区	Altay Administrative Offices	269.23	195.03	59.83	89.14	54.40	26.82
博尔塔拉蒙古自治州	Bortala Mongol Autonomous Prefecture	235.31	141.82	76.25	128.50	69.34	46.80
巴音郭楞蒙古自治州	Bayangol Mongol Autonomous Prefecture	952.27	746.49	139.60	335.54	248.34	61.33
阿克苏地区	Aksu Administrative Offices	642.79	457.58	159.76	375.72	245.44	114.51
克孜勒苏柯尔克孜自治州	Kizilsu Kirgiz Autonomous Prefecture	80.87	55.36	23.50	49.63	29.12	19.27
喀什地区	Kashgar [Kaxgar] Administrative Offices	338.86	186.11	111.23	151.17	66.04	59.90
和田地区	Hotan Administrative Offices	14.38	10.97	1.89	6.38	5.08	1.28
石河子市	Shihezi City	356.09	253.61	57.16	133.63	83.86	30.93
阿拉尔市	Aral City	47.08	35.79	11.29	43.75	32.46	11.29
图木舒克市	Tumxuk City	36.68	18.87	17.34	15.51	5.78	9.58
五家渠市	Wujiaqu City	285.94	202.42	57.00	104.00	61.25	35.63

Condition of Under Construction, Sale and Idle of Enterprises for Real Estate Development

(10 000 sq.m)

本年竣工房屋面积 Floor Space of Buindings Completed This Year	#住宅 Residential Buildings	#商业营业用房 Houses for Business Use	本年房屋销售面积 Floor Space of Building Sold This Year	#住宅 Residential Buildings	#商业营业用房 Houses for Business Use	房屋销售额（万元） Sales Value of Buildings (10 000 yuan)	#住宅 Residential Buildings	#商业营业用房 Houses for Business Use
81.19	64.51	8.14	45.60	41.29	2.91	67514	57024	5883
93.56	73.32	6.93	55.43	52.48	0.98	75110	67585	1569
94.28	79.92	6.23	83.29	75.97	3.46	118386	98803	8544
159.99	143.93	13.52	127.48	120.44	4.67	177683	158304	12599
330.11	298.79	23.07	262.52	250.95	9.82	373801	333166	35153
633.25	559.91	57.01	419.87	381.67	31.77	643814	537818	90441
727.21	616.12	85.03	506.66	455.68	46.34	879287	658157	208821
791.14	626.50	126.42	587.02	516.48	53.44	1066640	768012	224579
704.25	511.61	156.54	635.53	538.33	81.27	1106143	784408	281856
717.43	553.48	121.37	687.20	606.48	68.16	1235410	915191	288747
679.06	551.63	104.13	892.41	806.46	73.96	1658176	1358136	265450
890.55	798.12	72.07	1144.34	1078.28	51.57	2381520	2113425	211508
1049.29	943.40	67.30	954.35	886.35	51.22	2137859	1861169	212861
1032.72	900.87	76.28	1406.55	1326.67	65.81	3662638	3271682	317310
1012.90	859.92	98.40	1564.90	1450.02	94.42	4830392	4164140	523153
1270.48	1108.02	109.66	1728.23	1570.56	123.12	6133128	5162366	779898
1736.19	1438.43	177.43	1430.30	1274.79	116.33	5604508	4581386	759812
1722.16	1394.08	220.40	2017.03	1799.94	172.46	8609530	7107384	1231744
429.58	354.55	26.61	566.25	515.31	20.58	3397692	2959181	244275
89.23	74.58	5.98	191.66	186.98	3.57	606769	568895	34623
7.16	6.41	0.75	15.39	12.84	2.55	45304	33593	11711
60.56	46.87	7.27	62.13	55.43	4.61	232208	190671	31421
163.89	148.75	11.75	234.33	214.47	15.56	914137	775324	108305
363.09	298.92	53.01	368.43	324.86	40.12	1312032	1020874	273782
210.56	170.04	34.44	266.18	235.11	28.41	1004201	783667	204940
48.40	41.76	6.16	44.24	38.73	5.30	156727	117481	39109
104.13	87.12	12.41	58.01	51.02	6.41	151104	119726	29733
31.90	26.23	4.83	56.68	41.03	14.96	212225	119119	90919
250.31	222.79	20.48	148.90	137.07	11.35	493234	409401	82564
134.14	89.99	38.29	126.28	101.39	24.28	432364	301812	127886
4.96	3.89	0.67	12.05	10.40	1.65	25517	17014	8503
79.29	34.24	32.19	46.71	38.34	7.30	165169	111496	47467
1.22		1.22	3.32	2.96	0.37	11567	8501	3066
40.44	35.50	3.60	74.38	62.25	11.78	360467	277015	81141
21.80	17.06	4.74	27.04	22.18	4.86	92131	67499	24632
7.40	4.56	2.84	7.38	4.91	2.45	25870	9054	16722
37.19	29.74	6.17	76.10	69.52	6.47	282844	237935	44727

4-18 续表 Continued

单位：万平方米 (10 000 sq.m)

年 份 Year	地 区 Region	房屋待售面积 Floor Space At Idle	#住宅 Residential Buildings	#商业营业用房 Houses for Business Use
	1996	33.20	27.41	4.44
	1997	36.33	25.58	3.76
	1998	27.20	20.33	2.78
	1999	63.01	49.00	8.91
	2000	69.75	58.92	6.35
	2001	200.46	169.78	20.26
	2002	353.23	285.87	51.33
	2003	422.11	313.93	84.81
	2004	400.40	248.38	125.31
	2005	460.99	269.07	151.02
	2006	406.25	208.02	157.83
	2007	289.22	115.39	150.68
	2008	389.70	245.81	119.10
	2009	419.83	254.36	121.41
	2010	348.98	195.47	106.55
	2011	367.02	220.45	92.77
	2012	459.21	277.72	93.42
	2013	731.88	472.59	155.43
乌鲁木齐市	Urumqi City	173.41	69.92	35.59
克拉玛依市	Karamay City	2.90	0.46	1.65
吐鲁番地区	Turpan Administrative Offices	17.05	13.19	3.86
哈密地区	Hami [Kumul] Administrative Offices	15.44	10.62	3.40
昌吉回族自治州	Changji Hui Autonomous Prefecture	44.69	35.82	4.37
伊犁哈萨克自治州	Ili Kazak Autonomous Prefecture	146.42	97.93	41.05
伊犁州直属县(市)	Counties (Cities) Direct Under Ili Prefecture	83.46	47.37	32.57
塔城地区	Tacheng [Tarbagatai] Administrative Offices	27.51	23.17	3.60
阿勒泰地区	Altay Administrative Offices	35.45	27.39	4.88
博尔塔拉蒙古自治州	Bortala Mongol Autonomous Prefecture	9.62	6.01	3.53
巴音郭楞蒙古自治州	Bayangol Mongol Autonomous Prefecture	123.92	97.27	21.38
阿克苏地区	Aksu Administrative Offices	92.28	74.78	14.20
克孜勒苏柯尔克孜自治州	Kizilsu Kirgiz Autonomous Prefecture	22.87	19.08	3.79
喀什地区	Kashgar [Kaxgar] Administrative Offices	33.05	18.45	5.56
和田地区	Hotan Administrative Offices	2.22	0.99	1.23
石河子市	Shihezi City	13.51	8.98	2.74
阿拉尔市	Aral City	11.92	7.70	4.23
图木舒克市	Tumxuk City	4.74	2.55	2.20
五家渠市	Wujiaqu City	17.84	8.84	6.65

4-19 新增主要产品生产能力
Newly Increased Production Capacity of Major Products

项　目	Item	2012	2013
原煤开采(万吨/年)	Coal Mining (10 000 tons/year)	1356.60	1786.12
焦炭(万吨/年)	Coke (10 000 tons/year)	697.50	748.80
天然原油开采(万吨/年)	Petroleum Extractin (10 000 tons/year)	243.46	273.25
天然气开采(亿立方米/年)	Natural Gas Extraction (100 million cu.m/year)	16.00	8.70
裂化设备能力(处理万吨/年)	Cracking Equipment Capabillity(handle 10 000 tons/year)	10.30	9.30
铁矿石开采(原矿) (万吨/年)	Iron-Ore Mining (10 000 tons/year)	226.90	819.80
铁矿选矿处理原矿量(万吨/年)	Iron-ore Dressing (10 000 tons/year)	428.20	315.00
生铁(万吨/年)	Pig Iron(10 000 tons/year)	356.80	153.00
粗钢(万吨/年)	Crude Steel(10 000 tons/year)	311.50	328.00
铜采矿(原矿)(万吨/年)	Copper Ore Mining (10 000 tons/year)	60.51	439.57
处理原矿(万吨/年)	Raw Ore Treatment (10 000 tons/year)	50.70	2.00
铅锌采矿(原矿) (万吨/年)	Plumbum/Zinc Ore Mining (10 000 tons/year)	95.00	20.00
铝加工(吨/年)	Aluminium Processing (ton/year)	112193	866400
黄金(公斤/年)	Gold (kg/year)	335.34	2005.40
发电机组容量(万千瓦)	Capacity of Generating Setes (10 000 kw/year)		
水力发电	Hydropower	91.15	82.12
火力发电	Thermal Power	400.20	737.00
其他发电	Others	0.80	3.72
输电线路长度(11 万伏及以上)(公里)	Transmission Line (110 000V)(km)	5460.46	4748.80
水泥(万吨/年)	Cement (10 000 tons/year)	2685.30	1577.45

4-19 续表 Continued

项　目	Item	2012	2013
农用氮、磷、钾化学肥料(吨/年)	Farm-use Nitrogen, Phosphorus and Potassium Fertilizer (ton/year)		
氮肥	Nitrogen Fertilizer	591320	380750
磷肥	Phoshate Fertilizer	10526	49002
钾肥	Potash Fertilizer	1000	200
塑料树脂及共聚物(吨/年)	Plastic Colophony and Polymer (ton/year)	600000	738500
棉纺锭(锭)	Cotton Spindle (spindle)	305720	194000
酒(万吨/年)	Liquors (10 000 tons/year)	10.40	13.13
其他酒	Others	5.70	6.75
新建公路(公里)	Length of New Highways (km)	1473.11	1933.06
二级公路	Second Class highways	52.08	68.47
改建公路(公里)	Length of Reconstructed Highways(km)	7239.27	4194.31
二级公路	Second Class highways	598.80	1045.20
新建独立公路桥梁(延长米)	New-Built Separate Highway and Bridge (Extended Length m)	5294.69	4496.00
(座)	(unit)	9	11
新(扩)建客、货运站(个)	Number of newly-Built or Expanded Passenger and Freight Stations (unit)	9	13
(平方米)	(sq.m)	45863	41163
城市自来水供水能力(万吨/日)	Capacity of City Tap Water Supply (10 000 tons/day)	27.19	61.34
城市污水处理能力(万吨/日)	Disposal Capacity of Sewer (10 000 tons/day)	19.75	57.70

4-20 农村非农户固定资产投资情况
Investment in Fixed Assets of Non-Rural Households in Rural Areas

单位：万元 (10 000 yuan)

指 标	Item	2012	2013
新增固定资产	**Newly Increased Investment in Fixed Assets**	**2918075**	**3169245**
固定资产投资完成额	**Completed Investment in Fixed Assets**	**3637772**	**4030020**
按投资构成分	By Use of Funds		
建筑工程	Construction Works	2681289	3116763
安装工程	Installation Works	215391	196547
设备工器具购置	Purchase of Equipment and Instruments	576768	547889
#用于更新的设备	Renew of Equipment and Instruments	82003	39823
其 他	Others	164324	168821
按投资方向分	By Sector of Investment		
农、林、牧、渔业	Agriculture, Forestry, Animal Husbandry and Fishing	607559	824354
采矿业	Mining	162953	296606
制造业	Manufacturing	664789	478113
电力、热力、燃气及水的生产及供应业	Production and Supply of Electricity Gas and Water	442628	587106
建筑业	Construction	110171	71821
交通运输、仓储和邮政业	Transport, Storage and Post	280179	258752
批发和零售业	Wholesale and Retail Trades	33200	27466
住宿和餐饮业	Hotel and Catering Service	15384	34525
金融业	Financial Intermediation	1700	1500
房地产业	Real Estate	725465	738236
租赁和商务服务业	Leasing and Business Service Industries	2211	11900
科学研究和技术服务业	Scientific Research, Technology Service and Geological Prospecting	2057	3600
水利、环境和公共设施管理业	Water Conservancy, Environment and Public Facility Management	316409	472536
居民服务、修理和其他服务业	Community Service and Other Services	15236	6015
教 育	Education	35130	49771
卫生和社会工作	Health, Social Security and Social Welfare	8294	5904
文化、体育和娱乐业	Culture, Sports and Entertainment	13332	16656
公共管理、社会保障和社会组织	Public Management and Social Organizations	201075	145159
资金来源	**Sub-total Funds**	**3892244**	**4399641**
国家预算内资金	State Budgetary Funds	1032231	1287541
国内贷款	Domestic Loans	406590	350982
债 券	Bonds	432	415
利用外资	Foreign Investment	9600	610
自筹资金	Self-raising Funds	2135673	2543901
其他资金	Others	307718	216192
本年施工房屋面积(万平方米)	**Floor Space of Buildings Under Construction (10 000 sq.m)**	**1384.06**	**2982.13**
#住 宅	Residential Building	859.91	698.37
本年竣工房屋面积(万平方米)	**Floor Space of Completed Building (10 000 sq.m)**	**881.48**	**377.18**
#住 宅	Residential Building	544.29	232.66

主要统计指标解释

全社会固定资产投资 以货币形式表现的在一定时期内全社会建造和购置固定资产的工作量以及与此有关的费用的总称。该指标是反映固定资产投资规模、结构和发展速度的综合性指标,又是观察工程进度和考核投资效果的重要依据。全社会固定资产投资按登记注册类型可分为国有、集体、联营、股份制、私营和个体、港澳台商、外商、其他等。

固定资产投资(不含农户) 指城镇和农村各种登记注册类型的企业、事业、行政单位及城镇个体户进行的计划总投资500万元及500万元以上的建设项目投资和房地产开发投资,包含原口径的城镇固定资产投资加上农村企事业组织项目投资，该口径自2011年起开始使用。

房地产开发投资 指各种登记注册类型的房地产开发法人单位统一开发的包括统代建、拆迁还建的住宅、厂房、仓库、饭店、宾馆、度假村、写字楼、办公楼等房屋建筑物,配套的服务设施，土地开发工程（如道路、给水、排水、供电、供热、通讯、平整场地等基础设施工程）和土地购置的投资；不包括单纯的土地开发和交易活动。

建设总规模 是指在报告期内所有施工项目的计划总投资。

在建总规模 是指在报告期末所有在建项目的计划总投资。

在建净规模 是指报告期末所有在建项目建成投产尚需的投资总量。

在建净规模=在建总规模-未投产项目（期末在建）累计完成投资。

固定资产投资的实际到位资金 根据固定资产投资的资金来源不同，分为国家预算资金、国内贷款、利用外资、自筹资金和其他资金。

(1)国家预算资金: 国家预算包括一般预算、政府性基金预算、国有资本经营预算和社保基金预算。各类预算中用于固定资产投资的资金全部作为国家预算资金填报,其中一般预算中用于固定资产投资的部分包括基建投资、车购税、灾后恢复重建基金和其他财政投资。各级政府债券也应归入国家预算资金。

(2)国内贷款: 指报告期固定资产项目投资单位向银行及非银行金融机构借入的用于固定资产投资各种国内借款,包括银行利用自有资金及吸收存款发放的贷款、上级主管部门拨入的国内贷款、国家专项贷款（包括煤代油贷款、劳改煤矿专项贷款等），地方财政专项资金安排的贷款、国内储备贷款、周转贷款等。

(3)利用外资: 指报告期收到的境外（包括外国及港澳台地区）资金(包括设备、材料、技术在内)。包括对外借款(外国政府贷款、国际金融组织贷款、出口信贷、外国银行商业贷款、对外发行债券和股票)、外商直接投资、外商其他投资(包括利用外商投资收益在国内进行固定资产再投资活动的资金)。不包括我国自有外汇资金(国家外汇、地方外汇、留成外汇、调剂外汇和国内银行自有资金发放的外汇贷款等)。各类外资按报告期末的外汇牌价(中间价)折成人民币计算。

(4)自筹资金: 指固定资产投资单位在报告期收到的，由各企、事业单位筹集用于固定资产投资的资金，包括各类企事业单位的自有资金和从其他单位筹集的用于固定资产投资的资金，但不包括各类财政性资金、从各类金融机构借入资金和国外资金。

(5)其他资金: 指在报告期收到的除以上各种资金之外的用于固定资产投资的资金，包括社会集资、个人资金、无偿捐赠的资金及其他单位拨入的资金等。

固定资产投资按国民经济行业分 指根据其从事的社会经济活动性质对各类单位进行的分类。应根据建设项目建成投产后的主要产品种类或主要用途及社会经济活动种类来划分，不能根据项目单位本身的行业类别来划分。如果项目投产后有几种产品，应根据主要产品来确定行业类别。一般情况下，一个建设项目只能属于一种国民经济行业。

固定资产投资按隶属关系分 是按建设单位或企业、事业、行政单位的主管上级机关确定的。

(1)中央 是指中共中央、人大常委会和国务院各部、委、局、总公司以及直属机构直接领导的建设项目和企业、事业、行政单位。这些单位的固定资产投资计划由国务院各部门直接编制和下达，统一组织或委托下级实施。包括有中央垂直管理的部门（如国家统计局各级调查队）和中央直属企业、事业单位（如工商银行、中国电信、中国石油）等。

(2)地方 是由省（自治区、直辖市）、地（区、市、州、盟）、县（区、市、旗）三级政府及业务主管部门直接领导和管理的建设项目、企业、事业、行政单位。地方项目还包括不隶属以上各级政府及主管部门的建设项目和企业、事业单位，如外商投资企业和无主管部门的企业等。

固定资产投资按建设性质分 按整个建设项目情况来确定。建设项目的性质一般分为新建、扩建、改建和技术改造、单纯建造生活设施、迁建、恢复、单纯购置。房地产开发单位、农户投资不划分建设性质。

(1)新建 指从无到有“平地起家”开始建设的项目。现有企业、事业、行政单位投资的项目一般不属于新建。但如有的单位原有基础很小，经过建设后新增的固定资产价值超过该企业、事业、行政单位原有固定资产价值（原值）三倍以上的，也应作为新建。

(2)扩建 指在厂内或其他地点，为扩大原有产品的生产能力(或效益)或增加新的产品生产能力，而增建的生产车间(或主要工程)、分厂、独立的生产线的企业、事业单位。行政、事业单位在原单位增建业务性用房(如学校增建教学用房、医院增建门诊部、病房等)也作为扩建。

现有企、事业单位为扩大原有主要产品生产能力或增加新的产品生产能力，增建一个或几个主要生产车间(或主要工程)、分厂，同时进行一些更新改造工程的，也应作为扩建。

(3)改建和技术改造　指现有企业、事业单位对原有设施进行技术改造或更新(包括相应配套的辅助性生产、生活福利设施) 的建设项目。改建项目包括现有企业、事业单位为适应市场变化的需要，而改变企业的主要产品种类(如军工企业转民产品等) 的建设项目，原有产品生产作业线由于各工序(车间)之间能力不平衡，为填平补齐充分发挥原有生产能力而增建不增加本企业主要产品设计能力的车间的建设项目。技术改造是指企业、事业单位在现有基础上，用先进的技术代替落后的技术，用先进的工艺和装备代替落后的工艺和装备，以改变企业落后的技术经济面貌，实现以内涵为主的扩大再生产，达到提高产品质量、促进产品更新换代、节约能源、降低消耗、扩大生产规模、全面提高社会经济效益的目的。技术改造具体包括以下内容：机器设备和工具的更新改造；生产工艺改革、节约能源和原材料的改造；厂房建筑和公共设施的改造；保护环境进行的“三废”治理改造；劳动条件和生产环境的改造等。

固定资产投资按构成分

(1)建筑工程　指各种房屋、建筑物的建造工程，又称建筑工作量。这部分投资额必须兴工动料，通过施工活动才能实现，是固定资产投资额的重要组成部分。

(2)安装工程　指各种设备、装置的安装工程，又称安装工作量。

在安装工程中，不包括被安装设备本身价值。

(3)设备工具器具购置　指建设单位或企、事业单位购置或自制的，达到固定资产标准的设备、工具、器具的价值。新建单位及扩建单位的新建车间，按照设计或计划要求购置或自制的全部设备、工具、器具，不论是否达到固定资产标准均计入“设备工具器具购置”中。

(4)其他费用　指在固定资产建造和购置过程中发生的，除建筑安装工程和设备、工器具购置投资完成额以外的应当分摊计入固定资产投资的费用，不指经营中财务上的其他费用。

施工项目个数　是指本年正式进行过建筑或安装施工活动的建设项目个数。包括本年新开工项目，以前年度开工跨入本年继续施工项目，本年全部建成投产项目、以前年度全部停缓建在本年恢复施工的项目，本年进行过施工又在本年内全部停缓建的项目。施工项目个数可以反映一定时期固定资产投资的实际规模，与同期全部建成投产项目个数相比，可以从建设速度的角度反映固定资产投资的效果。

本年投产项目个数　指报告期内按设计文件规定建成主体工程和相应配套的辅助设施，形成生产能力或工程效益，经过验收合格，并且已正式投入生产或交付使用的建设项目。

新增生产能力(或工程效益)　指通过固定资产投资活动而增加的设计能力(或工程效益)，主要指标包括建设规模、本年施工规模、自开始建设累计新增生产能力（或工程效益）、本年新增生产能力（或工程效益）等。

房屋施工面积　指报告期内施工的全部房屋建筑面积。包括本期新开工的面积、上期跨入本期继续施工的房屋建筑面积、上期停缓建在本期恢复施工的房屋建筑面积、本期竣工的房屋建筑面积以及本期施工后又停缓建的房屋建筑面积。多层建筑应填各层建筑面积之和。

房屋竣工面积　指在报告期内房屋建筑按照设计要求已经全部完工，达到住人和使用条件，经验收鉴定合格或达到竣工验收标准，可正式移交使用的各栋房屋建筑面积的总和。

新增固定资产　是指已经完成建造和购置过程，并已交付生产或使用单位的固定资产的价值，包括已经建成投入生产或交付使用的工程投资和达到固定资产标准的设备、工具、器具的投资及有关应摊入的费用。该指标是表示固定资产投资成果的价值指标，也是反映建设进度，计算固定资产投资效果的重要指标。

项目建成投产率　指一定时期内全部建成投产项目个数与同期施工项目个数的比率。该指标从建设单位建设速度的角度反映投资效果。

固定资产交付使用率　指一定时期新增固定资产与同期完成投资额的比率。该指标是反映固定资产动用速度，衡量建设过程中宏观投资效果的综合指标。由于新增固定资产是较长时期内形成的结果，而投资额则是当年完成的，因此，该指标一般适宜于反映较长时期内固定资产的动用情况。

商品房销售面积　指报告期内出售商品房屋的合同总面积（即双方签署的正式买卖合同中所确定的建筑面积）。由现房销售面积和期房销售面积两部分组成。

商品房销售额　指报告期内出售商品房屋的合同总价款（即双方签署的正式买卖合同中所确定的合同总价）。该指标与商品房销售面积同口径，由现房销售额和期房销售额两部分组成。

Explanatory Notes on Main Statistical Indicators

Total Investment in Fixed Assets in the Whole Country refers to the volume of activities in construction and purchases of fixed assets of the whole country and related fees, expressed in monetary terms during the reference period. It is a comprehensive indicator which shows the size, structure and growth of the investment in fixed assets, providing a basis for observing the progress of construction projects and evaluating results of investment. Total investment in fixed assets in the whole country includes, by type of ownership, the investment by State-owned units, collective-owned units, joint ownership units, share-holding units, private units, individuals as well as investments by entrepreneurs from Hong Kong, Macao and Taiwan, foreign investors and others.

Investment in Fixed Assets (Excluding Rural Households) refers to the investment in construction projects with a total planned investment of 5 million yuan and over by enterprises of various ownerships, institutions, administrative units and urban self-employed individuals, and the investment in real estate development in both urban and rural areas. Since 2011, it covers the urban investment in fixed assets under the previous statistical coverage plus project investments by rural enterprises and institutions.

Investment in Real Estate Development refers to investment by real estate development companies, commercialized buildings construction companies and other real estate development units of various types of ownership in the construction of buildings, such as residential buildings, factory buildings, warehouses, hotels, guesthouses, holiday villages, office buildings, the complementary service facilities and land development projects, such as roads, water supply, water drainage, power supply, heating supply, telecommunications, land leveling and other infrastructural projects. It does not include activities in pure land transactions.

Total Size of Construction refers to the planned total investment for all construction projects during the reference period.

Total Size of Investment in Projects under Construction refers to the planned total investment of all projects under construction at the end of the reference period.

Net Size of Investment in Projects under Construction refers to the outstanding requirement of investment of all projects under construction at the end of the reference period.

Net size of investment in projects under construction= Total size of investment–Accumulated completed investment of projects under construction

Actual Funds in Place for Investment in Fixed Assets are categorized as funds from the State budget, domestic loans, foreign investment, self-raised funds, and others, depending on the sources of investment.

(1) Fund from the State budget: State budget consists of general budget, government fund budget, operation budget of state-owned assets and social security fund budget. Funds for investment in fixed assets from various budgets are reported as fund from the state budget, of which, the general budget utilized on fixed assets investment includes investment on infrastructure construction, vehicle purchase tax, post-disaster restoration and reconstruction funds and other financial investment. Government bonds at all levels should also be included.

(2) Domestic loans refer to loans of various forms borrowed by investing units from banks and non-bank financial institutions during the reference period for the purpose of investment in fixed assets, including loans issued by banks from their self-owned funds and deposit, loans appropriated by higher responsible authorities, special loans by government (including loan for substituting petroleum with coal, special loans for reform-through-labour coal mines), loans arranged by local government from special funds, domestic reserve loan, and revolving loan, etc.

(3) Foreign investment refers to overseas (including foreign countries, Hongkong, Macao and Taiwan) funds received during the reference period (covering equipment, materials and technology), including foreign borrowings (loans from foreign governments and international financial institutions, export credit, commercial loans from foreign banks, issue of bonds and stocks overseas), foreign direct investment and other foreign investments (including funds from foreign direct investment income that are reinvested in fixed assets domestically). Excluded from this category is capital in foreign exchanges owned by China (foreign exchanges owned by the central and local governments, foreign exchanges retained by enterprises, foreign exchanges by enterprises through the regulating mechanism, loans in foreign exchanges issued by the Bank of China with its own fund, etc.). In calculating the utilization of foreign capital, foreign currencies are converted into Chinese Renminbi applying the exchange rate (central parity rate) at the end of the reference period.

(4) Self-raised funds refer to funds for investment in fixed assets received during the reference period by investing units, including investment in fixed assets using own funds of various enterprises and institutions or funds raised from other units other than financial funds, funds borrowed from financial

institutions and overseas funds.

(5) Others refer to funds for investment in fixed assets received from sources other than those listed above, including funds raised from individuals and through donations, and funds transferred from other units.

Investment in Fixed Assets by Sector refers to the classification of investment by the nature of social economic activities the investing units are engaged in. The classification of construction projects by sector is determined by the major products or the purpose of the projects when they are put into production or use, and by the nature of their social economic activities, instead of being determined by industrial classification of the project enterprises. The project will be classified according to major product if there are several kinds of products yielded. In general, one project can only be classified into one sector.

Investment in Fixed Assets by Jurisdiction of Management refers to the classification of investment by the competent authorities under which investment is made by construction units, enterprises, institutions or administrative units.

(1) Central investment refers to the investment in projects or by enterprises, institutions or administrative units which are under the direct leadership and management of the State Council and of the national commissions, ministries, agencies and State-owned large corporations. Various ministries and departments of the State Council prepare and implement plans through unified organization or lower-level commissions, which include departments direct under central government (i.e. survey offices at all level of the National Bureau of Statistics) and enterprises and institutions directly under central government (like the Industrial and Commercial Bank of China, China Telecom and China National Petroleum Corporation).

(2) Local investment refers to the investment in projects or by enterprises, institutions or administrative units which are under the direct leadership and management of competent departments and governments at the level of province (autonomous regions and municipalities directly under the Central Government), prefecture (prefectures, cities and leagues) and county (districts, cities and banners). Also included are projects by foreign-invested enterprises and enterprises without competent managing authorities.

Investment in Fixed Assets by Type of Construction Construction projects in general can be classified, by the type of construction, into new construction, expansion, reconstruction and technical transformation, purely construction of living facilities, moving, restoration and purely purchasing. However, investment by type of construction is not applied to investment by real-estate development units and investment by rural households.

(1) New construction in general refers to construction projects, which start from scratch. The existing projects invested by enterprises, institutions and administrative agencies cannot be classified as new construction. In case the size of the existing unit is quite small, and the value of newly added fixed assets is more than three times of the original value, the expansion will be considered as new construction.

(2) Expansion refers to construction of new production workshop, branch factory or independent production line within a factory or in other locations, for the purpose of increasing the production capacity (or improving efficiency) or adding new production capacity by enterprises and institutions. Newly constructed accommodation for the operation of institutions and administrative organizations (such as newly constructed buildings for teaching in schools, buildings for clinics or wards in hospitals, etc.) are also classified as expansion.

Also included in expansion are investments by existing enterprises or institutions in building major production line(s) or branch factory (ies) along with some work on innovation, for the purpose of expanding the production capacity of original products or producing new products.

(3) Reconstruction and technical transformation refers to construction projects by existing enterprises or institutions in innovation or technical transformation of the old facilities (including auxiliary production equipment and welfare facilities). Also considered as reconstruction is the construction of new workshops by the existing enterprises or institutions to change the variety of products to meet the market demand (such as the production of civil products by defence industries), or to bring the designed production capacity into full play through a more balanced production process on production lines. Technical transformation refers to replacement of old technology or equipment by new technology or equipment, in order to expand the reproduction through improvement of technology contents in production, to improve product quality, to promote new products, to save energy, to reduce consumption, to expand the production scale and to improve overall social-economic efficiency. Contents of technical transformation include: updating of machinery, equipment and tools; reforming production process by using energy or materials saving technology; construction of factory workshops and transformation of public facilities; treatment transformation of “three wastes” (waste gas, waste water and industrial residue) aiming at environmental protection; improvement of working conditions and environment, etc.

Investment in Fixed Assets by Structure

(1) Construction refers to the construction of houses and buildings, also known as work volume of construction. This part of investment can only be achieved through construction

activities, it is the major component of the total investment in fixed assets.

(2) Installation refers to the installation of various kinds of equipment and instruments, also known as work volume of installation.

The value of equipment installed itself is not included in the value of installation projects.

(3) Purchase of equipment and instruments refers to the total value of equipment, tools, and instruments purchased or self-produced which come up to the cut-off point for fixed assets during the reference period. Equipment, tools and instruments purchased or self-produced for new workshops by newly established or expanded units are categorized as "purchase of equipment and instruments" no matter whether they come up to the cut-off point for fixed assets.

(4) Other expenses refer to expenses arising during the construction or purchase of fixed assets other than those expenses on construction, installation and purchase of equipment and instruments. Other financial expenses arising in operation are not included.

Number of Projects under Construction refers to number of all projects with actual construction or installation activities in current year, including newly started projects, projects started previously and extended into the current year, projects completed and put into operation in current year, projects suspended previously and resumed in current year, and projects started this year but suspended or postponed in current year. The number of projects under construction can reflect the actual size of investment in fixed assets during a given period, and when compared with the number of projects completed and put into use during the same period, it demonstrates the results of investment in fixed assets from the angle of the speed of the construction.

Number of Projects Put into Use This Year refer to projects have completed the main construction and correspondent auxiliary facilities in accordance with the design documents, resulting in forming production capacity (efficiency) and have been checked and accepted after relevant tests, and have been formally delivered for use.

Newly Increased Production Capacity (or Project Efficiency) refers to the increase in design capacity (or project efficiency) through investment in fixed assets. The main indicators include: construction scale, scale of projects under construction in current year, the accumulated newly increased production capacity (project efficiency) since the start of the projects and the newly increased production capacity (project efficiency) of current year.

Floor Space of Buildings under Construction refers to total floor space of the horizontal section of outer walls above the plinth of the building, including the effective area and the area occupied by the structure. This indicator is one of the important indicators in physical terms to reflect the scale and accomplishment of the construction industry, and important basis for monitoring the pr ogress, calculating the cost, analyzing the efficiency and studying the sup ply of building materials in relation with the construction projects.

Floor Space of Residential Buildings refers to the floor space of the residential buildings among the total space of buildings under construction or completed.

Newly Increased Fixed Assets refer to the value of fixed assets that has completed the construction and purchase, and has been delivered to the production or owner units, including investment in projects that have been completed and put into operation in current year and the investment in equipment, tools and appliance that meet the standard of fixed assets and fees that should be apportioned. This is an indicator that demonstrates the results of investment in fixed assets in monetary terms, and an important indicator to reflect the speed of construction and to calculate the efficiency of investment.

Rate of Construction Projects Completed and Put into Use refers to the ratio of the number of construction projects completed and put into use in a certain period of time to the number of projects under construction in the same period. This reflects the investment efficiency from the perspective of the speed of projects construction.

Rate of Projects of Fixed Assets Completed and Put into Operation refers to the ratio of the newly increased fixed assets to the total investment made in the same period. This is a comprehensive indicator reflecting the speed of the employment of fixed assets and the investment efficiency at the macro-level. As the newly increase fixed assets is the result of a long period while the investment is completed in the current year, this indicator is expected to be used to reflect the employment of fixed assets over a long period of time.

Area of Commercialized Housing Sold refers to total contracted area of commercialized housing (i.e. area of floor space as designated in the formal contracts signed by both sides) during the reference time. It constitutes floor space of completed housing and floor space of future housing.

Value of Commercialized Housing Sold refers to the total contracted value (i.e. value of sales/purchase for selling/purchase of commercialized housing as designated in the contract signed by both sides) during the reference time. This indicator has the same coverage as the area of commercialized housing sold, which constitutes floor space of completed housing and floor space of housing yet to be completed.

5

对外经济贸易和旅游

FOREIGN TRADE AND ECONOMIC COOPERATION & TOURISM

简要说明

本篇主要内容和资料来源

本篇内容包括海关进出口额、主要进出口商品数量及金额、对外承包工程和劳务合作、利用外资、外国和港澳台地区在新疆直接投资情况、新疆在国外和港澳台地区直接投资、经济技术开发(合作)主要情况、旅游情况等。

海关进出口额、利用外资、旅游资料由新疆维吾尔自治区统计局贸易外经统计处分别根据乌鲁木齐海关、新疆维吾尔自治区对外经济贸易厅、新疆维吾尔自治区工商管理局和新疆维吾尔自治区旅游局的有关资料加工整理。

Brief Introduction

Main Content and Source of Data

Data in this chapter cover mainly total imports and exports at customs, main imports and exports in volume and value, contracted projects and labor services cooperation, utilization of foreign capital, basic condition of direct investment in Xinjiang by foreign countries and compatriots from Hong Kong, Macao and Taiwan, main condition of economic and technological development and cooperation zones, condition of tourism.

Data on imports and exports, utilization of foreign capitals, tourism are collected and processed by the Department of Trade Statistics, the Xinjiang Bureau of Statistics in accordance with the data from custom of Urumqi, Foreign Economic and Trade Commission of Xinjiang, Xinjiang Administration for Industry and Commerce, Tourist Bureau of Xinjiang.

5-1 进出口贸易总额
Total Value of Imports and Exports

单位：万美元 (USD 10 000)

年份 Year	地区 Region	进出口总额 Total Imports and Exports	出口额 Exports	#一般贸易 Ordinary Trade	#边境贸易 Border Trade	进口额 Imports	#一般贸易 Ordinary Trade	#边境贸易 Border Trade
	1978	2346	937			1409		
	1985	29197	18020			11177		
	1990	41025	33530		3506	7495		3416
	1995	142798	76880	44550	27562	65918	17640	41888
	1996	140367	54975	30281	18647	85392	25982	54484
	1997	144667	66547	36061	22962	78120	24061	52031
	1998	153214	80789	32268	37599	72425	20972	49354
	1999	176534	102743	37120	57329	73791	25723	44976
	2000	226399	120408	55060	58020	105991	28020	73950
	2001	177148	66849	29523	18418	110299	24895	79661
	2002	269186	130849	54404	47218	138337	26028	107152
	2003	477198	254221	71115	160411	222977	72510	143504
	2004	563563	304658	50194	223782	258905	101540	147058
	2005	794189	504024	88036	386237	290165	108894	167648
	2006	910327	713923	158842	522038	196404	61915	126429
	2007	1371623	1150311	294000	806885	221312	75418	134778
	2008	2221680	1929925	290237	1576911	291755	92279	187279
	2009	1382771	1082325	168078	754206	300446	128702	157390
	2010	1712834	1296981	208909	767478	415853	154567	236745
	2011	2282225	1682886	476788	881882	599339	170863	401754
	2012	2517075	1934686	700915	891987	582389	144347	408382
	2013	2756191	2226980	850994	1063308	529211	100235	372450
乌鲁木齐市	Urumqi City	779766	639936			139830		
克拉玛依市	Karamay City	77846	21346			56500		
石河子市	Shihezi City	149700	146005			3695		
吐鲁番地区	Turpan Administrative Offices	9274	8339			935		
哈密地区	Hami [Kumul] Administrative Offices	8159	2685			5474		
昌吉回族自治洲	Changji Hui Autonomous Prefecture	157655	145737			11918		
伊犁哈萨克自治州	Ili Kazak Autonomous Prefecture	981094	792749			188345		
伊犁州直属县(市)	Counties (Cities) Direct Under Ili Prefecture	750372	568855			181517		
塔城地区	Tacheng [Tarbagatai] Administrative Offices	119832	116040			3792		
阿勒泰地区	Altay Administrative Offices	110890	107854			3036		
博尔塔拉蒙古自治州	Bortala Mongol Autonomous Prefecture	269842	156315			113527		
巴音郭楞蒙古自治州	Bayangol Mongol Autonomous Prefecture	19023	16101			2922		
阿克苏地区	Aksu Administrative Offices	58448	57184			1264		
克孜勒苏柯尔克孜自治州	Kizilsu Kirgiz Autonomous Prefecture	43180	40364			2816		
喀什地区	Kashgar [Kaxgar] Administrative Offices	200939	199171			1768		
和田地区	Hotan Administrative Offices	1265	1048			217		

注：1998 年以前的资料由外经贸厅提供，1998 年以后资料由乌鲁木齐海关提供(5-2、5-3、5-4 表相同)。
Note: The data prior to 1998 is offered by the Bureau of Foreign Economic and Trades , data after 1998 is offered by Urumqi Customs (The same in the 5-2, 5-3, 5-4 tables).

5-2 主要进出口商品数量和金额
Main Imports and Exports in Volume and Value

项 目	Item	2012		2013	
		数 量 Volume	金 额 (万美元) Value (USD 10 000)	数 量 Volume	金 额 (万美元) Value (USD 10 000)
主要出口商品	**Main Export Commodities**				
棉纱(吨)	Cotton Yarn (ton)	2750	1268	3812	1833
棉机织物(万米)	Cotton Woven Fabrics(10 000 m)	18315	26287	15722	26182
肠衣(吨)	Casings (ton)	458	2603	390	2242
番茄酱(万吨)	Tomato Jam (10 000 tons)	58	44179	47	43136
电视机(万台)	TV Sets (10 000 sets)	31	471	57	1813
地毯(吨)	Carpets (ton)	2552	1418	3552	2178
药材(吨)	Medical Materials (ton)	287	96	7015	947
鞋 类	Shoes		213716		173931
主要进口商品	**Main Import Commodities**				
羊毛及条(吨)	Wool and Wool Tops (ton)	5535	620	6650	1292
钢材(万吨)	Rolled Steel (10 000 tons)	21	16875	14	8881
纸及纸板(未切成型的)(吨)	Paper and Paperboard in Rolls (ton)	10	8.6	175	67
原木(万立方米)	Logs (10 000 cu.m)	0.7	107	1	104
医疗仪器及器械	Medical Equipment and Apparatus		4184		5546
肥料(万吨)	Fertilizers (10 000 tons)	2	662	4	1427
原油(万吨)	Crude Oil (10 000 tons)	371	307388	368	291462
成品油(万吨)	Oil Product (10 000 tons)	34	22220	21	13171
牛皮革及马皮革(吨)	Cattle and Horse Leather (ton)	23651	2681	34975	3908

5-3 新疆同各国(地区)海关进出口总额

Value of Xinjiang's Imports and Exports by Countries(Region) of Destination

单位：万美元 (USD 10 000)

国别（地区）	Country (Region)	2012			2013		
		进出口总额 Total Value of Imports and Exports	出口额 Exports	进口额 Imports	进出口总额 Total Value of Imports and Exports	出口额 Exports	进口额 Imports
合　计	**Total**	**2517075**	**1934686**	**582389**	**2756191**	**2226980**	**529211**
亚　洲	**Asia**	**2022402**	**1526269**	**496133**	**2329481**	**1864309**	**465172**
阿富汗	Afghanistan	262	254	8	1040	1022	18
巴　林	Bahrain	963	511	452	1157	1157	
孟加拉国	Bangladesh	1670	1670		2986	2986	
不　丹	Bhutan	50	50		24	24	
文　莱	Brunei	946	946		1497	1497	
缅　甸	Myanmar	374	374		1215	1215	
柬埔寨	Cambodia	832	832		369	369	
塞浦路斯	Cyprus	117	117		299	299	
朝　鲜	Korea DPR	628	236	392	2034	885	1149
香　港	Hong Kong, China	9075	8949	126	15976	15946	30
印　度	India	19460	16016	3444	34311	29141	5170
印度尼西亚	Indonesia	20116	19915	201	21850	21740	110
伊　朗	Iran	4139	4052	87	104504	104023	481
伊拉克	Iraq	1149	1071	78	869	816	53
以色列	Israel	3449	3035	414	3903	3792	111
日　本	Japan	22871	10993	11878	15696	10549	5147
约　旦	Jordan	1510	1510		2247	2247	
科威特	Kuwait	623	623		731	729	2
老　挝	Laos	136	136		95	95	
黎巴嫩	Lebanon	714	714		1996	1996	
澳　门	Macao				134	134	
马来西亚	Malaysia	35437	33847	1590	44711	43817	894
马尔代夫	Maldives	53	53		44	44	
蒙　古	Mongolia	34356	25474	8882	37338	27033	10305
尼泊尔联邦民主共和国	Nepal	86	85	1	12	12	
阿　曼	Aman	852	849	3	1395	1373	22
巴基斯坦	Pakistan	13965	13696	269	14716	13315	1401
巴勒斯坦	Palestine	18	18		198	198	
菲律宾	Philppines	4066	3799	267	5152	5098	54
卡塔尔	Qatar	589	589		876	876	
沙特阿拉伯	Saudi Arbia	9512	9397	115	13244	13001	243
新加坡	Singapore	11429	9675	1754	25180	23903	1277
韩　国	Korea Rep.	24693	19793	4900	18620	16261	2359
斯里兰卡	Sri Lanka	830	787	43	1419	1358	61
叙利亚	Syria	186	183	3	125	125	
泰　国	Thailand	10249	10094	155	10486	10345	141
土耳其	Turkey	4798	2299	2499	10605	7370	3235
阿联酋	United Arad Emirates	11046	11007	39	14611	14424	187
也　门	Yemen	1902	1902		2026	2026	
越　南	Vietnam	6113	6049	64	7769	7386	383
中华人民共和国	P.R.China	1178		1178	147		147
台湾省	Taiwan,China	3603	3214	389	4172	3769	403
东帝汶	Timor Lestor	24	24		31	31	
哈萨克斯坦	Kazakhstan	1116736	713941	402795	1225493	836941	388552
吉尔吉斯斯坦	Kirghizia	403899	398808	5091	417290	413392	3898
塔吉克斯坦	Tadzhikistan	140738	136722	4016	158502	157579	923
土库曼斯坦	Turkmenistan	13849	13488	361	15192	14795	397
乌兹别克斯坦	Uzbekistan	83111	38472	44639	87194	49175	38019
非　洲	**Africa**	**90661**	**85697**	**4964**	**54556**	**54241**	**315**
阿尔及利亚	Algeria	2087	2087		4362	4362	

5-3 续表 1 Continued

单位：万美元 (USD 10 000)

国别（地区）	Country (Region)	2012 进出口总额 Total Value of Imports and Exports	2012 出口额 Exports	2012 进口额 Imports	2013 进出口总额 Total Value of Imports and Exports	2013 出口额 Exports	2013 进口额 Imports
安哥拉	Angola	6096	6091	5	4553	4540	13
贝 宁	Benin	5571	1202	4369	2489	2489	
博茨瓦纳	Botswana	41	41		56	56	
布隆迪	Burundi	5	5		138	138	
喀麦隆	Cameroon	1120	1120		1432	1432	
佛得角	Cape Verde	81	81		36	36	
中 非	Central African				2	2	
科摩罗	Comoros	51	51		58	58	
刚果(布)	Congo	180	180		185	184	1
吉布提	Djibouti	551	551		836	836	
埃及	Egypt	2274	2273	1	1998	1894	104
赤道几内亚	Eq. Guinea	59	59		1	1	
埃塞俄比亚	Ethiopia	4977	4977		52	52	
加 纳	Ghana	13293	13293		1962	1962	
冈比亚	Gambia	94	94		63	63	
加 蓬	Gabon	239	239		82	82	
几内亚	Guinea	1933	1933		654	654	
科特迪瓦	Cote d'lvoire	1108	1108		578	578	
肯尼亚	Kenya	2696	2696		1373	1373	
利比里亚	Liberia	74	74		109	109	
利比亚	Libya	426	426		295	295	
马达加斯加	Madagascar	123	123		304	304	
马拉维	Malawi	230	230		371	371	
马 里	Mali	690	175	515	70	70	
毛里塔尼亚	Mauritania	185	185		57	57	
毛里求斯	Mauritius	672	672		398	398	
摩洛哥	Morocco	1946	1946		1639	1639	
莫桑比克	Mozambique	944	939	5	454	451	3
纳米比亚	Namibia	260	260		287	280	7
尼日尔	Niger	297	297		131	131	
尼日利亚	Nigeria	7493	7479	14	6575	6512	63
留尼汪	Reunion	55	55		10	10	
卢旺达	Rwanda	21	21				
圣多美和普林西比	Sao Tome & Principe	3	3		10	10	
塞内加尔	Senegal	1873	1873		788	788	
塞拉利昂	Sierra Leone	278	278		174	174	
塞舌尔	Seychelles				69	69	
索马里	Somalia	40	40		15	15	
南 非	South Africa	13568	13517	51	10814	10694	120
苏 丹	Sudan	4319	4319		2133	2133	
坦桑尼亚	Tanzania	1684	1684		1410	1410	
多 哥	Togo	10689	10689		2225	2225	
突尼斯	Tunisia	946	942	4	409	405	4
乌干达	Uganda	389	389		518	518	
布基纳法索	Burkina Faso	3	3		8	8	
刚果(金)	Congo DR	408	408		59	59	
赞比亚	Zambia	295	295		3970	3970	
莱索托	Lesotho	10	10		34	34	
津巴布韦	Zimbabwe	131	131		48	48	
厄立特里亚	Eritrea				3	3	
马约特	Mayotte	111	111		231	231	
梅利利亚	Melilla	10	10		28	28	
斯威士兰	Swaziland	1	1				
厄立特里亚	Eritrea	31	31				

5-3 续表 2 Continued

单位：万美元 (USD 10 000)

国 别 (地 区)	Country (Region)	2012 进出口总额 Total Value of Imports and Exports	2012 出口额 Exports	2012 进口额 Imports	2013 进出口总额 Total Value of Imports and Exports	2013 出口额 Exports	2013 进口额 Imports
欧 洲	**Europe**	**234045**	**179937**	**54108**	**218642**	**179391**	**39251**
比利时	Belgium	5768	5603	165	4472	3894	578
丹 麦	Denmark	1353	628	725	1262	577	685
英 国	United Kingdom	16642	15687	955	15577	14497	1080
德 国	Germany	31451	19868	11583	28163	16507	11656
法 国	France	7282	5512	1770	7230	5918	1312
爱尔兰	Ireland	585	292	293	597	269	328
意大利	Italy	10810	8094	2716	9418	6845	2573
卢森堡	Luxembourg	84	79	5	118	90	28
荷 兰	Netherlands	13631	13064	567	12310	11869	441
希 腊	Greece	932	928	4	1067	1046	21
葡萄牙	Portugal	730	729	1	894	882	12
西班牙	Spain	8364	8263	101	7041	6894	147
阿尔巴尼亚	Albania	61	61		37	37	
安道尔	Andorra	919	919				
奥地利	Austria	695	416	279	1184	547	637
保加利亚	Bulgaria	437	437		278	278	
芬 兰	Finland	3254	898	2356	5208	812	4396
直布罗陀	Gibraltar	10	10		10	10	
匈牙利	Hungary	72	72		127	127	
马耳他	Malta	2060	2060		2357	2357	
摩纳哥	Monaco	336	336		39	39	
挪 威	Norway	830	688	142	742	523	219
波 兰	Poland	6812	6560	252	5270	5254	16
罗马尼亚	Romania	1719	1602	117	3946	3830	116
瑞 典	Sweden	2454	651	1803	2804	1044	1760
瑞 士	Switzerland	4712	1004	3708	3557	1253	2304
爱沙尼亚	Estonia	51	42	9	93	27	66
拉脱维亚	Latvia	202	202		217	217	
立陶宛	Lithuania	512	512		661	661	
格鲁吉亚	Georgia	1141	1107	34	1054	990	64
亚美尼亚	Armenia	328	328		11	11	
阿塞拜疆	Azerbaijan	26057	25905	152	24105	22920	1185
白俄罗斯	Byelorussia	276	30	246	519	70	449
摩尔多瓦	Moldavia	191	191		187	187	
俄罗斯联邦	Russia	64442	38491	25951	45420	36688	8732
乌克兰	Ukraine	17139	17076	63	30120	29842	278
斯洛文尼亚	Slovenia	436	436		369	360	9
克罗地亚	Croatia	209	209		338	338	
捷 克	Czech	742	631	111	1622	1500	122
斯洛伐克	Slovak	73	73		87	50	37
前南马其顿	Macedonia	4	4				
波 黑	Bosnia & Herzegovina	20	20				
塞尔维亚	Serbia	197	197		125	125	
黑 山	Montenegro	22	22		6	6	
拉丁美洲	**Latin America**	**42529**	**41901**	**628**	**37718**	**34842**	**2876**
阿根廷	Argentina	3023	3014	9	2969	2147	822
阿鲁巴	Aruba	21	21		139	139	
巴哈马	Bahamas	319	319				
巴巴多斯	Barbados	97	97		1	1	

5-3 续表 3 Continued

单位：万美元　　　　(USD 10 000)

国别（地区）	Country (Region)	2012			2013		
		进出口总额 Total Value of Imports and Exports	出口额 Exports	进口额 Imports	进出口总额 Total Value of Imports and Exports	出口额 Exports	进口额 Imports
伯利兹	Belize	16	16		5	5	
多民族玻利维亚国	Bolivia	2	2				
巴　西	Brazil	12305	11897	408	11183	9323	1860
智　利	Chile	2708	2682	26	4299	4255	44
开曼群岛	Cayman Islands				7		7
哥伦比亚	Colombia	1077	1077		951	951	
多米尼克	Dominica	36	36		59	59	
哥斯达黎加	Costa Rica	165	165		91	91	
古　巴	Cuba	714	714		686	686	
库腊索岛	Curacao	29	29				
多米尼加共和国	Dominica Rep	127	119	8	81	71	10
厄瓜多尔	Ecuador	1605	1605		312	312	
法属圭亚那	French Guyana	6	6		15	15	
格林纳达	Granada	44	44		20	20	
瓜德罗普	Guadeloupe				5	5	
危地马拉	Guatemala	261	260	1	70	70	
圭亚那	Guyana	177	177		88	88	
海　地	Haiti	155	155		80	80	
洪都拉斯	Honduras	896	896		119	119	
牙买加	Jamaica	2949	2949		824	824	
马提尼克	Martinique	10	10		20	20	
墨西哥	Mexico	3902	3726	176	3360	3227	133
尼加拉瓜	Nicaragua	10	10		8	8	
巴拿马	Panama	6255	6255		8756	8756	
巴拉圭	Paraguay	726	726		205	205	
秘　鲁	Peru	974	974		1849	1849	
波多黎各	Puerto Rico	55	55		95	95	
圣卢西亚	Saint Lucia	63	63		26	26	
圣马丁岛	Saint Martin Islands	5	5				
萨尔瓦多	EL Salvador	500	500		103	103	
苏里南	Surinam	79	79		124	124	
特立尼达和多巴哥	Trinidad and Tobago	68	68		16	16	
乌拉圭	Uruguay	1400	1400		640	640	
委内瑞拉	Venezuela	1740	1740		512	512	
荷属安的列斯群岛	Andreas Islands (N)	10	10				
北美洲	**North America**	**111901**	**88853**	**23048**	**90916**	**71211**	**19705**
加拿大	Canada	9894	9167	727	10227	9181	1046
美　国	United States	102007	79686	22321	80689	62030	18659
大洋洲	**Oceanic**	**15537**	**12029**	**3508**	**24874**	**22986**	**1888**
澳大利亚	Australia	13412	10089	3323	23436	21664	1772
斐　济	Fiji	123	123		100	100	
新喀里多尼亚	New Caledonia (Fr)	41	41		16	16	
瓦努阿图	Vanuatu	20	20		10	10	
新西兰	New Zealand	1079	894	185	1196	1081	115
巴布亚新几内亚	Papua New Guinea	177	177		45	45	
社会群岛	Society Islands	10	10				
所罗门群岛	Solomon Islands	5	5		17	17	
汤　加	Tonga	64	64		36	36	
萨摩亚	Samoa	246	246		1		1
马绍尔群岛	Marshall Islands	339	339		15	15	
瓦利斯和浮图纳群岛	Wallis and Futuna Islands	16	16		2	2	
其　他	**Others**	**5**	**5**		**4**		**4**

5-4 按贸易方式和登记注册类型分的海关进出口额

Total Value of Imports and Exports by Customs Regime and Registration (Customs Statiatics)

单位：万美元 (USD 10 000)

项　目	Item	2012			2013		
		进出口总额 Total Imports and Exports	出口额 Exports	进口额 Imports	进出口总额 Total Imports and Exports	出口额 Exports	进口额 Imports
总　计	**Total**	**2517075**	**1934686**	**582389**	**2756191**	**2226980**	**529211**
按贸易方式分	**By Customs Regime**						
一般贸易	Ordinary Trades	845263	700915	144347	951229	850994	100235
加工贸易	Processing Trades	25911	19120	6791	50993	21195	29798
边境小额贸易	Petty-volume Border Trades	1300369	891987	408382	1435758	1063308	372450
其它贸易	Other Trades	345532	322664	22869	318211	291483	26728
按登记注册类型分	**By Registration Status**						
国有经济	State-owned Units	688244	194449	493795	718913	280554	438359
集体经济	Collective-owned Units	27439	15651	11788	11656	6199	5457
私营经济	Private-owned Units	1776970	1706386	70584	2000444	1928005	72439
三资企业	Three Kinds of Ventures	24422	18200	6222	25163	12210	12953
其它经济	Other Types of Ownership				15	12	3

5-5 主要年份人民币对主要外币年平均汇价(中间价)

Average Exchange Rate of RMB Yuan Against Main Convertible Currences in Main Years (Medium Rate)

单位：人民币元 (RMB yuan)

年 份 Year	100 美元 100 US Dollars	100 日元 100 JapaneseYen	100 港元 100 Hong Kong Dollars	100 欧元 100 Euros
1985	293.66	1.25	37.57	
1990	478.32	3.32	61.39	
1995	835.10	8.92	107.96	
1996	831.42	7.64	107.51	
1997	828.98	6.86	107.09	
1998	827.91	6.35	106.88	
1999	827.83	7.29	106.66	
2000	827.84	7.69	106.18	
2001	827.70	6.81	106.08	
2002	827.70	6.62	106.07	800.58
2003	827.70	7.15	106.24	936.13
2004	827.68	7.66	106.23	1029.00
2005	819.17	7.45	105.30	1019.53
2006	797.18	6.86	102.62	1001.90
2007	760.40	6.46	97.46	1041.75
2008	694.51	6.74	89.19	1022.27
2009	683.10	7.29	88.12	952.70
2010	676.95	7.73	87.13	897.25
2011	645.88	8.11	82.97	900.11
2012	631.25	7.90	81.38	810.67
2013	619.32	6.30	79.80	822.19

5-6 对外承包工程和劳务合作
Contracted Projects in Foreign Countries or Territories

单位：个、万美元 (unit,USD 10 000)

项　目	Item	2012	2013
承包工程	**Contracted Projects**		
新签合同数	Number of Newly Signed Contracts	154	
新签合同金额	Newly Signed Contracted Value	224107	149662
实际营业额	Actual Business Volume	147047	199012

5-7 外商直接投资
Direct Foreign Investments

单位：个、万美元 (unit, USD 10 000)

指　标	Item	2012			2013		
		项 目 Number of Projects	合同金额 Contract Value	实际使用金额 Used Value	项 目 Number of Projects	合同金额 Contract Value	实际使用金额 Used Value
总　计	**Total**	**55**	**61056**	**40795**	**42**	**36034**	**48102**
独资经营企业	Foreign Investment Enterprises	32	22841	13536	30	2941	26446
合资经营企业	Joint Ventures Enterprises	22	23419	12413	12	12094	12221
合作经营企业	Cooperative Operation Enterprises	1	2734	13		7340	109
股份制企业	Share-holding Corporations Ltd.		12062	14833		13659	9326

5-8 外国和港澳台地区在华直接投资情况

Basic Conditions of Direct Investment in China by Foreign Countries and Compatriots from Hongkong， Macao and Taiwan

单位：个、万美元 (2013 年) (unit, USD 10 000)

项 目	Item	签订协议情况 Signed Agreements 合同数 Number of Contracts	客商投资额 Actually Used Amount of Region Investment	客商实际投资额 Used Amount of Foreign Investment	年末实有企业个数 Number of Enterprises at Year-end
总 计	**Total**	**42**	**36034**	**48102**	**512**
按投资方式分	**Grouped by Investment Mode**				
独资经营企业	Foreign Investment Enterprises	30	2941	26446	275
合资经营企业	Joint Ventures Enterprises	12	12094	12221	206
合作经营企业	Cooperative Operation Enterprises		7340	109	23
外商投资股份制企业	Foreign Investment Share Enterprises		13659	9326	8
按国民经济行业分	**Grouped by Economic Sector**				
农、林、牧、渔业	Farming, Forestry, Animal Husbandry and Fishery	1	112	1108	26
采矿业	Mining and Quarrying		4099	8677	26
制造业	Manufacturing	7	9518	9699	165
电力、煤气及水的生产和供应业	Production and Distribution of Electricity, Gas and Water			564	9
建筑业	Construction		-353		7
交通运输、仓储及邮电通讯业	Transport, Storage, Post and Telecommunications	2	14117	9326	11
信息传输、计算机服务和软件业	Information Transmission, Computer Service and Software			30	3
批发和零售业	Wholesale and Retail Trades	26	4554	10667	161
住宿和餐饮业	Accommodation and Catering Service	1	-36	9	25
金融业	Financial Intermediation			1112	2
房地产业	Real Estate		106	634	11
租赁和商务服务业	Leasing and Business Services	3	1565	5827	34
科学研究、技术服务和地质勘察业	Scientific Research, Technical Service and Geological Prospecting	1	2303	449	21
水利、环境和公共设施管理业	Water Conservancy, Environment and Public Facility Management				5
居民服务和其他服务业	Services to Households and Other Services	1	49		3
教 育	Education				2
文化、体育和娱乐业	Culture,Sports and Entertainment				1
按国别、地区分	**By Country or Territory**				
中国香港	Hong Kong,China	7	3382	26645	195
中国台湾	Taiwan,China		-362	189	21
日 本	Japan		181		10
美 国	United States	1	9	376	26
加拿大	Canada	1	8		8
德 国	Federal Republic of Germany			167	5
土耳其	Turkey	3	16	83	
英 国	United Kingdom	2	65	106	6
新加坡	Singapore	1	4550	903	
澳大利亚	Australia		245	11	13
独联体	Commonwealth of Independent States	18	890	378	26
马来西亚	Malaysia	1	997		
韩 国	Republic of Korea	1	-244	11	22

5-9 各地、州、市利用外商直接投资情况
Conditions of Foreign Direct Investment Used by Prefecture, Autonomous Prefecture and City

单位：个、万美元　　　　(unit, USD 10 000)

地　区	Region	2012			2013		
		签　订合同数 Number of Contracts	合同金额 Contract Value	实际使用投资 Amount of Foreingn Capital Actually Used	签　订合同数 Number of Contracts	合同金额 Contract Value	实际使用投资 Amount of Foreign Capital Actually Used
总　计	**Total**	**55**	**61056**	**40795**	**42**	**36035**	**48102**
乌鲁木齐市	Urumqi City	35	24166	17572	25	20015	17792
克拉玛依市	Karamay City	1	52	1720		-5	1741
石河子市	Shihezi City	5	14393	4406	3	-370	11635
吐鲁番地区	Turpan Administrative Offices	1	545	300	1	8	345
哈密地区	Hami [Kumul] Administrative Offices		583	2333		2877	1648
昌吉回族自治州	Changji Hui Autonomous Prefecture	4	7850	4174	3	5905	4477
伊犁哈萨克自治州	Ili Kazak Autonomous Prefecture	3	2525	3819	3	2830	3616
伊犁州直属县(市)	Counties (Cities) Direct Under Ili Prefecture	3	2736	1873	2	1622	1813
塔城地区	Tacheng [Tarbagatai] Administrative Offices		-211	675			387
阿勒泰地区	Altay Administrative Offices			1271	1	1208	1416
博尔塔拉蒙古自治州	Bortala Mongol Autonomous Prefecture	1	2393			20	
巴音郭楞蒙古自治州	BayangolMongol Autonomous Prefecture	2	4784	2858	2	-289	3160
阿克苏地区	Aksu Administrative Offices	2	1273	2922	3	4332	3404
克孜勒苏柯尔克孜自治州	Kizilsu Kirgiz Autonomous Prefecture		2323	11			
喀什地区	Kashgar [Kaxgar] Administrative Offices	1	169	680	2	712	284
和田地区	Hotan Administrative Offices						

5-10 新疆在外国和港澳台地区直接投资
Direct Investment in Foreign Countries and Hong Kong, Macao and Taiwan Made by Xinjiang Partner

单位：个、万美元　　　　(unit, USD 10 000)

年　份 Year	投资额 Investment	年　份 Year	投资额 Investment
2005	5280	2011	41803
2009	28619	2012	25920
2010	47809	2013	39968

5-11 主要年份旅游事业发展情况
Development of Tourism in Main Years

项 目	Item	1995	2000	2013
旅行社总数(个)	**Total Number of Travel Agencies (unit)**	**79**	**130**	**321**
入境旅游人数(人)	**Total Number of Overseas Vistor Arrivals (person)**	**203579**	**256082**	**1567283**
外国人	Foreigners	185514	208374	1479467
#日 本	Japan	43983	51974	24940
新加坡	Singapore	2048	5137	10452
美 国	United States	5595	10231	29746
英 国	United Kingdom	2422	3702	10256
法 国	France	3062	5218	12321
德 国	Federal Republic of Germany	4892	6310	11236
独联体	Commonwealth of Independent States	93578	76966	1170416
香港同胞	Compatriots from Hong Kong		12710	21133
澳门同胞	Compatriots from Macao		1387	6336
台湾同胞	Compatriots from Taiwan	8816	33611	60347
按地区分	**By Regions**			
乌鲁木齐市	Urumqi City	63275	144830	350330
克拉玛依市	Karamay City		505	4105
石河子市	Shihezi City		532	114
吐鲁番地区	Turpan Administrative Offices	27230	43641	22000
哈密地区	Hami [Kumul] Administrative Offices	1220	624	24079
昌吉回族自治州	Changji Hui Autonomous Prefecture	224	213	14539
伊犁哈萨克自治州	Ili Kazak Autonomous Prefecture	68948	18204	1024369
伊犁州直属县(市)	Counties (Cities) Direct Under Ili Prefecture	67651	15356	850124
塔城地区	Tacheng [Tarbagatai] Administrative Offices	1297	298	35155
阿勒泰地区	Altay Administrative Offices		2550	139090
博尔塔拉蒙古自治州	Bortala Mongol Autonomous Prefecture	354	672	48000
巴音郭楞蒙古自治州	BayangolMongol Autonomous Prefecture	1738	7313	17793
阿克苏地区	Aksu Administrative Offices	5737	6028	5643
克孜勒苏柯尔克孜自治州	Kizilsu Kirgiz Autonomous Prefecture	2485	2100	22254
喀什地区	Kashgar [Kaxgar] Administrative Offices	31102	27510	28334
和田地区	Hotan Administrative Offices	1266	3910	5723
国内旅游人数(万人)	**Number of Domestic Visitors (10 000 persons)**	**514**	**758**	**5049**
疆内居民出境游(人)	**Number of Domestic Resident Outbound Visitors (person)**	**591**	**4535**	**26350**
旅游收入	**Income of Tourism**			
入境旅游收入(万美元)	Foreign Exchange Earnings from International Tourism (USD 10 000)	5268	9494	58502
国内旅游收入(亿元)	Earnings from Domestic Tourism (100 million yuan)	7.10	62.67	637.43

5-12 各地、州、市旅行社及旅游宾馆(酒店)基本情况
Accommodation of Travel Agencies and Tourist Hotels by Prefecture, Autonomous Prefecture and City

(2013 年)

地区	Region	旅行社(个) Number of Travel Agencies (unit)	星级宾馆(个) Number of Star-rated Hotels (unit)	客房(间) Number of Rooms (unit)	床位(张) Number of Beds (unit)
总计	**Total**	**321**	**417**	**44141**	**81077**
乌鲁木齐市	Urumqi City	161	64	10861	19371
克拉玛依市	Karamay City	14	16	1400	2418
吐鲁番地区	Turpan Administrative Offices	8	28	2526	4817
哈密地区	Hami [Kumul] Administrative Offices	7	15	1825	3328
昌吉回族自治州	Changji Hui Autonomous Prefecture	11	36	2619	4790
伊犁哈萨克自治州	Ili Kazak Autonomous Prefecture	60	116	10629	20210
伊犁州直属县(市)	Counties (Cities) Direct Under Ili Prefecture	29	54	4413	8479
塔城地区	Tacheng [Tarbagatai] Administrative Offices	4	14	1037	1948
阿勒泰地区	Altay Administrative Offices	27	48	5179	9783
博尔塔拉蒙古自治州	Bortala Mongol Autonomous Prefecture	4	11	830	1562
巴音郭楞蒙古自治州	Bayangol Mongol Autonomous Prefecture	17	38	4324	7929
阿克苏地区	Aksu Administrative Offices	8	35	3655	6805
克孜勒苏柯尔克孜自治州	Kizilsu Kirgiz Autonomous Prefecture	2	5	472	850
喀什地区	Kashgar [Kaxgar] Administrative Offices	26	34	3556	6427
和田地区	Hotan Administrative Offices	3	19	1444	2570

注：本表数据不含兵团数据。
Note:The date of this table don’t cover the date of XJPCC.

5-13 各地、州、市旅游收入情况

Income of Tourism by Prefecture, Autonomous Prefecture and City

(2013 年)

地　区	Region	入境旅游收入 (万美元) Foreign Exchange Earnings from International Tourism (USD 10 000)	国内旅游收入 (万元) Earnings from Domestic Tourism (10 000 yuan)
总　计	**Total**	**58502**	**6374300**
乌鲁木齐市	Urumqi City	21013	2600000
克拉玛依市	Karamay City	163	230000
石河子市	Shihezi City	5	230000
吐鲁番地区	Turpan Administrative Offices	1452	450000
哈密地区	Hami [Kumul] Administrative Offices	1084	230000
昌吉回族自治州	Changji Hui Autonomous Prefecture	478	410000
伊犁哈萨克自治州	Ili Kazak Autonomous Prefecture	28493	1296000
伊犁州直属县(市)	Counties (Cities) Direct Under Ili Prefecture	23950	550000
塔城地区	Tacheng [Tarbagatai] Administrative Offices	943	156000
阿勒泰地区	Altay Administrative Offices	3600	590000
博尔塔拉蒙古自治州	Bortala Mongol Autonomous Prefecture	924	92000
巴音郭楞蒙古自治州	BayangolMongol Autonomous Prefecture	1125	360000
阿克苏地区	Aksu Administrative Offices	339	210000
克孜勒苏柯尔克孜自治州	Kizilsu Kirgiz Autonomous Prefecture	1082	21000
喀什地区	Kashgar [Kaxgar] Administrative Offices	2021	200000
和田地区	Hotan Administrative Offices	323	45300

5-14 入境旅游收入及构成
Foreign Exchange Earnings from International Tourism and Composition

单位：万美元、% (USD 10 000,%)

指标	Item	2012 金额 Value	2012 比重 Percentage	2013 金额 Value	2013 比重 Percentage
总计	**Total**	**55057**	**100**	**58502**	**100**
长途交通费	Long Distance Transportation	21087	38.3	21002	35.9
民航	Air	12828	23.3	10764	18.4
铁路	Railway	2533	4.6	5675	9.7
汽车	Highway	5726	10.4	4563	7.8
游览	Visiting	2973	5.4	3744	6.4
住宿	Accommodation	6717	12.2	7196	12.3
餐饮	Catering	2753	5.0	3569	6.1
商品销售	Commodity Sales	11011	20.0	11583	19.8
娱乐	Entertainment	3909	7.1	3627	6.2
邮电通信	Post and Communication Services	1376	2.5	1638	2.8
市内交通	Local Transportation	1817	3.3	1346	2.3
其他服务	Other Services	3414	6.2	4797	8.2

5-15 接待外国旅游人数(按国别分)
Number of Foreign Tourists Received by Country

单位：人 (person)

国别	Country	2012	2013	国别	Country	2012	2013
总计	**Total**	**1363266**	**1479467**	德国	Federal Republic of Germany	9098	11236
亚洲	**Asia**	**1041182**	**1137828**	法国	France	12671	12321
印度	India	1230	1483	意大利	Italy	4028	3618
印度尼西亚	Indonesia	1714	1746	西班牙	Spain	1885	1840
日本	Japan	26992	24940	瑞典	Sweden	1599	2483
马来西亚	Malaysia	11930	12576	瑞士	Switzerland	2750	2792
蒙古	Mongolia	62303	70743	独联体(欧洲部分)	Commonwealth of Independent States (Europe)	212420	228291
菲律宾	The Philppines	536	733	其他	Others	5896	5928
新加坡	Singapore	10331	10452	**北美洲**	**North America**	**41279**	**42101**
韩国	Republic of Korea	23768	25292	加拿大	Canada	9185	9352
泰国	Thailand	3539	3605	美国	United States	29235	29746
巴基斯坦	Pakistan	43997	44133	其他	Others	2859	3003
哈萨克斯坦	Haskistan	813385	895513	**大洋洲**	**Oceania**	**14402**	**15479**
其他	Others	41457	46612	澳大利亚	Australia	9730	10482
非洲	**Africa**	**816**	**854**	新西兰	New Zealand	3931	4288
欧洲	**Europe**	**260695**	**278765**	其他	Others	741	709
英国	United Kingdom	10348	10256	**其他小计**	**Other sub-total**	**4892**	**4440**

注：表中独联体仅指独联体在欧洲部分的国家。
Note: Commonwealth of Independent State in the table only refer to the part of the countries in Europe.

主要统计指标解释

货物进出口总额　指实际进出我国国境的货物总金额。包括对外贸易实际进出口货物，来料加工装配进出口货物，国家间、联合国及国际组织无偿援助物资和赠送品，华侨、港澳台同胞和外籍华人捐赠品，租赁期满归承租人所有的租赁货物，进料加工进出口货物，边境地方贸易及边境地区小额贸易进出口货物(边民互市贸易除外)，中外合资企业、中外合作经营企业、外商独资经营企业进出口货物和公用物品，到、离岸价格在规定限额以上的进出口货样和广告品(无商业价值、无使用价值和免费提供出口的除外)，从保税仓库提取在中国境内销售的进口货物，以及其他进出口货物。该指标可以观察一个国家在对外贸易方面的总规模。我国规定出口货物按离岸价格统计，进口货物按到岸价格统计。

外商直接投资　是指外国投资者在我国境内通过设立外商投资企业、合伙企业、与中方投资者共同进行石油资源的合作勘探开发以及设立外国公司分支机构等方式进行投资。外国投资者可以用现金、实物、无形资产、股权等投资，还可以用从外商投资企业获得的利润进行再投资。

对外承包工程　根据《对外承包工程管理条例》，对外承包工程是指中国的企业或者其他单位承包境外建设工程项目的活动。

对外劳务合作　指组织劳务人员赴其他国家或地区为国外的企业或机构工作的经营性活动。

入境游客　指报告期内来中国（大陆）观光、度假、探亲访友、就医疗养、购物、参加会议或从事经济、文化、体育、宗教活动的外国人、港澳台同胞等游客（即入境旅游人数）。统计时，入境游客按每入境一次统计 1 人次。入境旅游人数包括入境过夜游客和入境一日游游客。

出境人数　指中国（大陆）居民因公或因私出境前往其他国家、中国香港特别行政区、澳门特别行政区和台湾省观光、度假、探亲访友、就医疗养、购物、参加会议或从事经济、文化、体育、宗教活动的人数（即出境游客）。统计时，出境游客按每出境一次统计 1 人次。

国内游客　指在报告期内在中国（大陆）观光游览、度假、探亲访友、就医疗养、购物、参加会议或从事经济、文化、体育、宗教活动的中国（大陆）居民人数，其出游的目的不是通过所从事的活动谋取报酬。统计时，国内游客按每出游一次统计 1 人次。

国际旅游(外汇)收入　指入境游客在中国（大陆）境内旅行、游览过程中用于交通、参观游览、住宿、餐饮、购物、娱乐等全部花费。

国内旅游收入　指国内游客在国内旅行、游览过程中用于交通、参观游览、住宿、餐饮、购物、娱乐等全部花费。

星级饭店　指设备、设施、服务符合《旅游饭店星级的划分与评定》(GB/T14308-2003)，通过相关旅游管理部门评定，并取得星级饭店称号的饭店（含预备星级饭店）。

Explanatory Notes on Main Statistical Indicators

Total Import and Export of Goods refer to the real value of commodities imported and exported across the border of China. They include the actual imports and exports through foreign trade, imported and exported goods under the processing and assembling trades and materials, supplies and gifts as aid given gratis between governments and by the United Nations and other international organizations, and contributions donated by overseas Chinese, compatriots in Hong Kong and Macao and Chinese with foreign citizenship, leasing commodities owned by tenant at the expiration of leasing period, the imported and exported commodities processed with imported materials, commodities trading in border areas (excluding mutual exchange goods), the imported and exported commodities and articles for public use of the Sino-foreign joint ventures, cooperative enterprises and ventures with sole foreign investment. Also included is import or export of samples and advertising goods for which CIF or FOB value are beyond the permitted ceiling (excluding goods of no trading or use value and free commodities for export), imported goods sold in China from bonded warehouses and other imported or exported goods. The indicator of the total imports and exports at customs can be used to observe the total size of external trade in a country. In accordance with the stipulation of the Chinese government, imports are calculated at CIF, while exports are calculated at FOB.

Foreign Direct Investment refers to foreign investment in China through the establishment of foreign invested enterprises, cooperative exploration and development of petroleum resources with domestic investors and the establishment of branch organizations of foreign enterprises. Foreign investment can be made in forms of cash, physical investment, intangible assets and equity, in addition with reinvestment of the foreign enterprises with the profits gained from the investment.

Overseas Contracted Projects refer to activities of contracting overseas construction projects by Chinese enterprises or any other units, which are stipulated in the Regulations on Administration of Foreign Contracted Project.

Overseas Labour Services refer to operational activities of organizing labour force to go abroad providing services to foreign enterprises or agencies.

Overseas Visitor Arrivals refer to the number of tourists of foreigners, Chinese compatriots from Hong Kong, Macao and Taiwan who come to China (mainland) within the reference period for sight-seeing, vacation, visiting relatives, medical treatment, shopping, attending conference, or to engage in economic, cultural, sports and religious activities (namely the number of overseas visitor arrivals). In compiling statistics, each arrival is counted as one person-time. The number of overseas visitor arrivals includes inbound overnight tourists and one-day tourists.

Number of Chinese Residents Going Abroad (Chinese Outbound Visitors) refers to the number of Chinese (mainland) residents going to other countries, Hong Kong Special Administrative region, Macao Special Administrative region and Taiwan for on official or private purposes, for sight-seeing, vacation, visiting relatives, medical treatment, shopping, attending conference, or to engage in economic, cultural, sports and religious activities (namely the Chinese outbound visitors). In compiling statistics, each time of leaving is counted as one person-time.

Number of Domestic Tourists refers to the number of Chinese (mainland) residents who travel within China (mainland) for sight-seeing, vacation, visiting relatives, medical treatment, shopping, attending conference, or to engage in economic, cultural, sports and religious activities. In compiling statistics, each time of travelling is counted as one person-time.

Foreign Exchange Earnings from International Tourism refer to the total expenditure of foreigners, overseas Chinese, Chinese compatriots from Hong Kong, Macao and Taiwan during their stay in the mainland of China on transportation, sighting, accommodation, food, shopping and entertainment.

Income from Domestic Tourism refer to expenditure of domestic tourists on transportation, sighting, accommodation, food, shopping and entertainment while they travel.

Star-rated Hotels refer to hotels rated with stars as assessed by the relevant tourism authorities according to GB/T14308-2003 standard with reference to their infrastructure, facilities and service levels.

新疆统计年鉴

XINJIANG STATISTICAL YEARBOOK

6

资源与环境

NATURAL RESOURCES AND ENVIRONMENT PROTECTION

简要说明

本篇主要内容和资料来源

本篇主要反映新疆维吾尔自治区资源及环境保护事业发展情况等资料。主要内容包括自然资源储量和自然状况及水环境、大气环境、固体废物、声环境、生态环境、环境污染治理投资等内容。

水资源、城市生活垃圾清运及处理、地质灾害、矿产资源资料、土地资源情况、林木资源等资料分别由新疆维吾尔自治区水利厅、建设厅、地震局、国土资源厅、林业厅提供；气象资料由新疆维吾尔自治区气象局提供。环境污染与治理、声环境、工业污染治理投资等情况由新疆维吾尔自治区环境保护厅依据年报资料整理提供。

土地资源仍沿用2008年数据。

Brief Introduction

Main Content and Source of Data

This chapter contain information that reflect the natural conditions and natural resources and data on development of environment protection in Xinjiang Uygur Autonomous Region, including natural resources and natural condition,total water resources, atmosphere environment, solid wastes, environmental noise, eco-environment protection, natural disaster and investments in the treatment of environmental pollution etc.

Data on water resource, collection and disposal of urban consumption wastes, geological disasters, land use, forest resource, etc. are provided respectively by Bureau of Water Conservancy, Bureau of Construction, Seismological Bureau, Bureau of Land and Resources, Forestry Bureau in Xinjiang Uygur Autonomous Region; Meteorological data are provided by the Xinjiang Uygur Autonomous Region Meteorological Bureau. Data on environment pollution and treatment, noise monitoring and on investment in the treatment of industrial pollution are provided by the Xinjiang Environmental Protection Bureau.

Data of land resources still followed 2008 annual data.

6-1 自然资源
Natural Resources

指　标	Item	2013
自然状况	**State of the Nature**	
经纬度	Longitude and Latitude	
东　经	East Longitude	73°40′～96°23′
北　纬	North Latitude	34°25′～49°10′
气　候	Climate	
年平均气温(摄氏度)	Annual Average Temperature (℃)	10.6
北　疆	North Xinjiang	8.4
南　疆	South Xinjiang	13.5
东　疆	East Xinjiang	13.4
年平均降水量(毫米)	Annual Average Precipitation (mm)	176.8
北　疆	North Xinjiang	262.9
南　疆	South Xinjiang	87.0
东　疆	East Xinjiang	14.0
平均日照时数(小时)	Average Sunny Hours (hour)	2842.3
北　疆	North Xinjiang	2775.1
南　疆	South Xinjiang	2888.1
东　疆	East Xinjiang	3030.3
自然资源	**Natural Resources**	
土地资源(万公顷)	Land Resources (10 000 hectares)	
土地总面积	Total Land Area	16648.97
农用地	Land for Farm Use	6308.48
耕地面积	Area of Cultivated Land	412.46
园地面积	Garden Area	36.42
林地面积	Woodland Area	676.48
牧草地面积	Pastureland Area	5111.38
其他农用地	Other Land for Agriculture	71.75
建设用地	Land for Construction	123.98
未利用地	Land yet to be Used	10216.51
土地利用率(%)	Land Utilization Rate (%)	38.64
林木资源	Forest Resources	
活立木总蓄积量(万立方米)	Total Standing Stock Volume (10 000 cu.m)	38679
森林蓄积量(万立方米)	Woodland Stock Volume (10 000 cu.m)	33654

6-1 续表 Continued

指　标	Item	2013
有林地面积(万公顷)	Woodland Area (10 000 hectares)	236
灌木林地面积(万公顷)	Bush Woodland Area (10 000 hectares)	466
四旁树(万株)	Surrounding Woods (10 000 trees)	25095
森林覆盖率(%)	Forest Coverage Rate (%)	4.24
水资源(亿立方米)	Water Resources (100 million cu.m)	
水资源总量	Total Water Resources Volume	588.58
地表水水资源量	Surface Water Volume	472.47
地下水水资源量	Underground Water Volume	114.94
重复计算量	Volume of Repeated Computation	1.17
主要矿产资源保有储量	**Reserve of Main Mineral Resources**	
铁矿(亿吨)	Iron Ore (100 million tons)	20.06
铬矿(万吨)	Chromium Ore (10 000 tons)	88.86
铜矿(金属)(万吨)	Copper Ore (10 000 tons)	652.52
铅矿(金属)(万吨)	Lead Ore (10 000 tons)	372.54
锌矿(金属)(万吨)	Zinc Ore (10 000 tons)	1002.35
铝土矿(万吨)	Bauxite(10 000 tons)	55.26
镍矿(金属)(万吨)	Nickel Ore (10 000 tons)	149.56
煤(亿吨)	Coal (100 million tons)	3502.17
耐火粘土(万吨)	Fire-proof Clay (10 000 tons)	698.10
钠硝石(万吨)	Nitratite (10 000 tons)	49946.93
芒硝(Na2SO4) (亿吨)	Mirabilite(Na2SO4) (100 million tons)	859.34
盐矿(NaCl) (亿吨)	Solidum Salt(NaCI) (100 million tons)	119.06
钾盐(KCl) (万吨)	Potassium(KCI) (10 000 tons)	15800.45
石棉(万吨)	Asbest (10 000 tons)	844.44
云母(工业原料) (吨)	Mica(Industrial raw materials) (ton)	54416.75
蛭石(万吨)	Roseite (10 000 tons)	1650.31
水泥用灰岩(亿吨)	Limestone Used for Cement (100 million tons)	38.29
膨润土(万吨)	Bentonite (10 000 tons)	36536.87
饰面用花岗岩(万立方米)	Granite as Veneer (10 000 cu.m)	16471.77

注：1.林木资源为 2011 年第八次全国森林资源清查、自治区森林资源第六次复查数据（2012 年公布）。2.土地资源仍沿用 2008 年度数据。
Note: a) Figures of 2011 forest resources were form the fifth Autonomous Region Forest Survey(2012 announced).b) Data of land resources followed in 2008.

6-2 主要城市平均气温
Monthly Average Temperature of Major Cities

单位：摄氏度 (2013 年) (℃)

城　市	City	一月 Jan.	二月 Feb.	三月 Mar.	四月 Apr.	五月 May	六月 June	七月 July
乌鲁木齐市	Urumqi City	-10.3	-10.1	5.5	12.4	16.6	21.5	23.6
克拉玛依市	Karamay City	-15.3	-12.2	6.5	14.7	19.0	24.1	25.8
石河子市	Shihezi City	-18.4	-12.7	1.2	16.5	21.1	26.0	26.1
阜康市	Fukang City	-15.8	-12.7	4.9	13.7	18.2	23.5	25.5
米泉市	Miquan City	-12.8	-10.2	6.1	14.3	18.9	24.1	26.3
伊宁市	Yining [Gulja] City	-10.8	-7.9	2.8	16.4	19.7	23.2	24.5
塔城市	Tacheng [Qoqek] City	-7.5	-10.0	6.3	12.5	15.8	20.2	22.0
阿勒泰市	Altay City	-13.8	-14.8	2.1	10.6	13.6	18.9	20.5
博乐市	Bole [Bor tala] City	-14.5	-12.3	5.2	13.0	17.8	21.8	23.6
库尔勒市	Korla City	-7.7	0.7	12.3	18.2	21.9	24.5	27.0
阿克苏市	Aksu City	-7.2	0.0	10.9	17.4	20.3	23.4	24.5
阿图什市	Artux City	-4.6	1.8	13.1	18.5	20.6	25.8	26.5
喀什市	Kashgar [Kaxgar] City	-4.7	1.7	12.8	17.9	20.0	25.2	26.2
和田市	Hotan City	-3.4	3.4	14.0	19.0	20.9	25.8	26.7
吐鲁番市	Turpan City	-10.8	1.1	15.6	21.5	26.6	31.1	32.8
哈密市	Hami [Kumul] City	-12.5	-4.3	9.2	15.9	21.0	24.7	26.9

城　市	City	八月 Aug.	九月 Sept.	十月 Oct.	十一月 Nov.	十二月 Dec.	全年平均 Annual Average
乌鲁木齐市	Urumqi City	22.8	17.5	11.4	0.2	-6.8	8.7
克拉玛依市	Karamay City	25.0	19.4	12.2	0.7	-8.6	9.3
石河子市	Shi Hezi City	24.4	18.4	9.1	-3.9	-16.1	7.6
阜康市	Fukang City	23.8	17.5	10.8	-0.5	-8.2	8.4
米泉市	Miquan City	25.0	19.1	12.4	0.9	-6.3	9.8
伊宁市	Yining [Gulja] City	23.6	18.2	9.1	0.8	-9.6	9.2
塔城市	Tacheng [Qoqek] City	21.4	16.8	11.0	1.8	-4.3	8.8
阿勒泰市	Altay City	19.2	14.3	8.1	-0.8	-9.5	5.7
博乐市	Bole [Bor tala] City	22.6	17.3	10.6	-0.8	-7.0	8.1
库尔勒市	Korla City	27.7	21.4	15.1	2.3	-3.9	13.3
阿克苏市	Aksu City	25.0	19.5	13.6	1.5	-3.8	12.1
阿图什市	Artux City	26.9	21.7	16.0	3.8	-2.1	14.0
喀什市	Kashgar [Kaxgar] City	25.9	20.8	15.4	3.8	-2.1	13.6
和田市	Hotan City	26.9	22.2	16.4	4.2	-1.4	14.6
吐鲁番市	Turpan City	31.8	24.3	16.2	4.6	-2.5	16.0
哈密市	Hami [Kumul] City	25.3	17.8	11.5	-0.1	-7.0	10.7

6-3 主要城市降水量
Monthly Precipitation of Major Cities

单位：毫米 (2013 年) (millimeter)

城市	City	一月 Jan.	二月 Feb.	三月 Mar.	四月 Apr.	五月 May	六月 June	七月 July
乌鲁木齐市	Urumqi City	7.1	11.7	13.2	69.2	27.1	31.3	23.3
克拉玛依市	Karamay City	1.1	1.8	1.3	14.0	14.3	37.4	53.2
石河子市	Shi Hezi City	6.8	5.0	4.9	39.2	26.0	29.1	32.0
阜康市	Fukang City	5.7	9.3	9.2	58.0	18.7	33.0	17.9
米泉市	Miquan City	7.3	9.1	11.3	53.4	28.3	25.1	23.1
伊宁市	Yining [Gulja] City	17.7	23.7	20.6	8.0	11.8	9.8	11.9
塔城市	Tacheng [Qoqek] City	35.7	10.4	11.9	17.3	50.8	60.0	79.4
阿勒泰市	Altay City	19.6	8.6	7.0	12.2	18.8	57.3	30.0
博乐市	Bole [Bortala] City	6.8	6.7	2.1	85.2	16.5	32.4	55.6
库尔勒市	Korla City		1.4		6.5	3.6	22.5	16.7
阿克苏市	Aksu City	0.5				27.8	93.2	12.0
阿图什市	Artux City		7.8		4.3	25.6	12.0	14.0
喀什市	Kashgar [Kaxgar] City	0.3	4.0		1.9	18.1	11.8	9.2
和田市	Hotan City					22.4	9.9	11.5
吐鲁番市	Turpan City				3.9	0.2	1.2	0.3
哈密市	Hami [Kumul] City		4.1			1.5	3.4	4.4

城市	City	八月 Aug.	九月 Sept.	十月 Oct.	十一月 Nov.	十二月 Dec.	全年合计 Annual Total
乌鲁木齐市	Urumqi City	29.2	12.7	16.6	44.5	15.0	300.9
克拉玛依市	Karamay City	37.7	28.8	1.0	5.3	6.9	202.8
石河子市	Shihezi City	19.5	7.4	13.3	15.0	12.9	211.1
阜康市	Fukang City	33.2	7.0	13.5	16.9	9.1	231.5
米泉市	Miquan City	40.4	15.0	16.8	22.1	10.6	262.5
伊宁市	Yining [Gulja] City	12.7	4.2	23.2	31.4	60.0	235.0
塔城市	Tacheng [Qoqek] City	74.7	3.8	8.2	13.4	14.7	380.3
阿勒泰市	Altay City	18.0	20.7	22.9	10.1	3.8	229.0
博乐市	Bole [Bortala] City	36.0	24.2	18.6	17.9	11.2	313.2
库尔勒市	Korla City	3.8	0.3		0.4	0.7	55.9
阿克苏市	Aksu City	10.0	15.5	6.0	11.2		176.2
阿图什市	Artux City	17.6	1.9		6.0	0.2	89.4
喀什市	Kashgar [Kaxgar] City	14.9	0.4		7.6	0.9	69.1
和田市	Hotan City	0.3	0.3			0.1	44.5
吐鲁番市	Turpan City	2.9	0.2				8.7
哈密市	Hami [Kumul] City	0.5	5.1	0.2	0.1		19.3

6-4 主要城市日照时数
Monthly Sunshine Hours of Major Cities

单位：小时 (2013 年) (hour)

城　　市	City	一月 Jan.	二月 Feb.	三月 Mar.	四月 Apr.	五月 May	六月 June	七月 July
乌鲁木齐市	Urumqi City	165.8	157.7	259.1	270.7	329.8	325.0	354.8
克拉玛依市	Karamay City	124.2	136.0	243.7	256.2	315.1	253.5	271.4
石河子市	Shi Hezi City	49.0	102.7	237.8	274.8	338.2	317.3	337.0
阜康市	Fukang City	59.0	128.7	242.6	278.3	348.7	317.9	348.7
米泉市	Miquan City	12.7	56.1	192.3	260.6	344.3	326.2	342.4
伊宁市	Yining [Gulja] City	161.4	142.0	252.3	265.0	321.7	320.5	345.6
塔城市	Tacheng [Qoqek] City	119.0	159.0	231.7	252.7	337.5	288.1	322.6
阿勒泰市	Altay City	147.2	161.0	228.7	289.1	313.3	296.9	324.9
博乐市	Bole [Bortala] City	132.5	155.8	191.3	232.8	306.0	266.2	303.0
库尔勒市	Korla City	202.1	213.2	271.8	294.4	275.0	233.6	318.4
阿克苏市	Aksu City	191.4	189.2	219.0	263.7	299.2	347.2	360.2
阿图什市	Artux City	158.9	147.6	191.2	196.5	240.6	310.1	325.8
喀什市	Kashgar [Kaxgar] City	189.6	180.8	244.2	248.7	282.3	348.7	364.9
和田市	Hotan City	194.1	160.8	222.4	250.7	248.1	274.3	263.2
吐鲁番市	Turpan City	45.2	131.0	218.0	292.7	304.8	279.2	319.0
哈密市	Hami [Kumul] City	226.1	237.6	311.3	329.0	366.9	329.1	378.2

城　　市	City	八月 Aug.	九月 Sept.	十月 Oct.	十一月 Nov.	十二月 Dec.	全年合计 Annual Total
乌鲁木齐市	Urumqi City	317.4	306.6	281.0	195.3	105.4	3068.6
克拉玛依市	Karamay City	272.1	281.1	222.9	168.0	46.0	2590.2
石河子市	Shi Hezi City	306.9	296.9	271.5	142.3	37.5	2711.9
阜康市	Fukang City	292.9	284.7	261.0	137.0	54.3	2753.8
米泉市	Miquan City	309.3	293.3	259.5	120.7	29.8	2547.2
伊宁市	Yining [Gulja] City	316.8	299.6	265.7	189.1	162.0	3041.7
塔城市	Tacheng [Qoqek] City	291.2	286.2	206.6	162.7	134.2	2791.5
阿勒泰市	Altay City	319.8	291.7	220.6	170.7	156.5	2920.4
博乐市	Bole [Bortala] City	272.9	274.1	220.6	128.2	66.7	2550.1
库尔勒市	Korla City	290.2	270.8	277.8	180.7	142.5	2970.5
阿克苏市	Aksu City	281.5	286.8	282.8	168.0	161.7	3050.7
阿图什市	Artux City	253.5	261.9	240.9	177.7	119.4	2632.2
喀什市	Kashgar [Kaxgar] City	274.3	299.7	278.6	198.6	146.5	3056.9
和田市	Hotan City	212.6	238.4	279.4	204.4	181.8	2730.2
吐鲁番市	Turpan City	307.1	263.8	194.9	116.7	29.9	2502.3
哈密市	Hami [Kumul] City	351.8	324.8	282.1	213.8	207.6	3558.3

6-5 环境保护基本情况
Basic Statistics on Environmental Protection

项　　目	Item	2012	2013
水环境	**Water Environment**		
废水排放总量(亿吨)	Volume of Waste Water Discharged (100 million tons)	9.37	10.07
#工业废水排放量	Volume of Industrial Waste Water Discharged	2.97	3.47
城镇生活废水排放量	Volume of Non-industrial Waste Water Discharged	6.40	6.59
集中式治理设施废水排放量	Volume of Centralized Treatment for Waste Water Facilities	…	0.01
化学需氧量排放量(万吨)	Amount of COD Discharged (10 000 tons)	67.92	67.23
#工业化学需氧量排放量	Amount of COD Discharged by industry	18.63	18.59
城镇生活化学需氧量排放量	Amount of COD Discharged by Non-industry	12.12	11.81
农业化学需氧量排放量	Amount of COD Discharged by Agricutral	36.72	36.39
集中式治理设施化学需氧量排放量	Amount of Centralized Treatment for COD Facilities	0.45	0.45
氨氮排放量(万吨)	Ammonia Nitrogen Discharged (10 000 tons)	4.73	4.65
#工业氨氮排放量	Industrial Ammonia Nitrogen Discharged	1.18	1.18
城镇生活氨氮排放量	Non-industrial Ammonia Nitrogen Discharged	2.24	2.18
农业氨氮排放量	Agricultural Ammonia Nitrogen Discharged	1.28	1.26
集中式治理设施氨氮排放量	Amount of Centralized Treatment for Ammonia Nitrogen Facilities	0.03	0.03
大气环境	**Atmosphere Environment**		
工业废气排放量(亿标立方米)	Industrial Waste Air Emission (100 million cu.m)	15869.86	19970.87
二氧化硫排放量(万吨)	Volume of Sulphur Dioxide Emission (10 000 tons)	79.61	82.94
#工业二氧化硫排放量	Volume of Sulphur Dioxide Emission by Industry	70.47	73.86
城镇生活二氧化硫排放量	Volume of Sulphur Dioxide Emission by Consumption	9.14	9.09
氮氧化物排放量(万吨)	Ammonia Nitrogen Discharged (10 000 tons)	81.95	88.67

注：2011 年、2012 年、2013 年自然保护区只包含自治区及国家级自然保护区。
Note: The nature reserves contain the municipality and state leuel nature protection area.

6-5 续表 1 Continued

项　目	Item	2012	2013
#工业氮氧化物排放量	Industrial Ammonia Nitrogen Discharged	50.57	57.30
城镇生活氮氧化物排放量	Non-industrial Ammonia Nitrogen Discharged	1.58	1.66
机动车氮氧化物排放量	Agricultural Ammonia Nitrogen Discharged	29.80	29.71
烟(粉)尘排放量(万吨)	Volume of Soot Emission (10 000 tons)	69.61	75.59
#工业烟(粉)尘排放量	Volume of Industrial Soot Emission	60.60	66.33
城镇生活烟(粉)尘排放量	Volume of Soot Emission by Consumption	6.74	7.04
机动车烟(粉)尘排放量(总颗粒物排放量)	Volume of Soot Emission by Consumption	2.26	2.22
固体废物	**Solid Wastes**		
一般工业固体废物产生量(万吨)	Industrial Solid Wastes Produced (10 000 tons)	7881.15	9283.05
一般工业固体废物综合利用量(万吨)	Industrial Solid Wastes Utilized (10 000 tons)	4064.14	4814.37
一般工业固体废物处置量(万吨)	Ratio of Industrial Solid Wastes Utilized (%)	532.65	886.48
一般工业固体废物储存量(万吨)	Industrial Solid Wastes Discharged (10 000 tons)	3250.56	3561.56
一般工业固体废物倾倒丢弃量(万吨)	General volume of industrial solid wastes dumping of discarded (10 000 tons)	34.86	26.50
危险废物产生量（万吨）	Amount of hazardous waste generated (10 000 tons)	444.18	302.67
生态环境	**Eco-Environment**		
当年造林面积(万公顷)	Area of Reforestation of the Year (10 000 hectares)	18.73	14.74
自然保护区数(个)	Number of Nature Reserves (unit)	28	28
#国家级	National Level	9	9
自然保护区面积(万公顷)	Area of Nature Reserves (10 000 hectares)	2140.56	1972.56
#国家级	National Level	1365.53	1196.30

6-5 续表 2 Continued

项　　目	Item	2012	2013
自然保护区面积占辖区面积比重(%)	Area of Nature Reserves in Regions (%)	12.86	11.89
农村生态示范建设个数(个)	Number of Demonstration Zones of Ecology (unit)	151	523
国家级生态乡镇数(个)	Number of National Eco-towns (unit)	24	24
国家级生态村数(个)	Number of National Eco-village (unit)	7	7
自然灾害	**Natural Disaster**		
发生地质灾害起数(次)	Geological Disaster(case)	44	36
发生地震灾害次数(次)	Seismic Disaster(case)	11	5
#5.0 级以上	Magnitude above 5 Richter Scale	11	5
森林火灾次数(次)	Forest Fire (case)	41	31
森林火灾受灾面积（公顷)	Fire-Affected Forest Area (hectare)	17.35	12.79
森林病虫害发生面积(万公顷)	Forest Area Affected by Disease and Pests (10 000 hectares)	126.14	140.30
森林病虫害防治面积(万公顷)	Forest Area Provented and Cured from Disease and Pests (10 000 hectares)	53.90	53.75
森林病虫害防治率(%)	Rate of Prevention and Cure (%)	42.7	38.3
环境污染治理投资	**Investment in the Treaiment of Environmental Pollution**		
环境污染治理投资总额(亿元)	Total Investment in Pollution Treatment (10 000 yuan)	237.09	281.15
城镇环境基础设施建设投资额	Investment in Urban Environment Infrastructure	170.80	165.43
工业污染治理项目年完成投资总额	Investment Completed in Treatment Projects Industrial Pollution	7.91	22.39
当年完成环保验收项目环保投资总额	Investment Completed in Treatment Projects Industrial Pollution	58.39	93.33
环境污染治理投资总额相当于新疆生产总值比例(%)	Investment in Pollution Treatment Out of XJ GDP (%)	3.15	3.30
当年施工工业污染治理项目数(个)	Number of Projects in Industrial Pollution Treatment under Construction of The Year (unit)	72	83
当年竣工工业污染治理项目数(个)	Number of Projects Completed in Industrial Pollution Treatment of the Year Projects (unit)	54	79

6-6 水资源情况
Water Resource

年 份 Year	地 区 Region	水资源总量(亿立方米) Total Amount Of Water Resources (100 million cu.m)	地表水资源量 Surface Water Resources	地下水资源量 Ground Water Resources	地表水与地下水资源重复量 Duplicated Measurement Between surface Water and Groundwater	人均水资源量(立方米/人) Per Capita Water Resources (cu.m/person)
	2000	952.40	897.10	636.29	580.99	5255
	2001	1024.40	966.90	692.31	634.81	5500
	2002	1068.60	1006.00	724.85	662.25	5652
	2003	920.10	863.20	604.30	547.40	4793
	2004	855.40	809.20	502.60	456.40	4390
	2005	962.82	910.66	562.57	510.41	4789
	2006	953.12	903.84	554.13	504.85	4695
	2007	863.80	816.60	514.10	466.90	4168
	2008	802.60	759.50	518.50	475.36	3798
	2009	754.29	713.64	470.47	429.82	3517
	2010	1124.00	1063.00	624.30	563.20	5120
	2011	885.70	841.00	539.80	495.10	4035
	2012	903.20	854.20	557.00	508.00	4141
	2013	956.07	905.58	561.27	510.89	4223
乌鲁木齐市	Urumqi City	10.68	10.29	4.88	4.49	410
克拉玛依市	Karamay City	0.65	0.06	1.29	0.70	226
石河子市	Shihezi City	0.14	0.07	0.70	0.63	22
吐鲁番地区	Turpan Administrative Offices	7.81	5.94	7.02	5.15	1232
哈密地区	Hami [Kumul] Administrative Offices	11.69	9.70	7.80	5.81	1947
昌吉回族自治州	Changji Hui Autonomous Prefecture	35.36	31.27	21.32	17.23	2519
伊犁州直属县(市)	Counties (Cities) Direct Under Ili Prefecture	146.40	143.90	73.80	71.29	4961
塔城地区	Tacheng [Tarbagatai] Administrative Offices	55.85	51.82	34.41	30.39	5300
阿勒泰地区	Altay Administrative Offices	159.30	153.50	66.81	61.04	23887
博尔塔拉蒙古自治州	Bortala Mongol Autonomous Prefecture	25.33	23.19	14.92	12.78	5197
巴音郭楞蒙古自治州	Bayangol Mongol Autonomous Prefecture	129.10	122.50	70.79	64.20	9292
阿克苏地区	Aksu Administrative Offices	61.05	54.71	65.39	59.04	2515
克孜勒苏柯尔克孜自治州	Kizilsu Kirgiz Autonomous Prefecture	69.21	68.03	39.59	38.41	12176
喀什地区	Kashgar [Kaxgar] Administrative Offices	107.60	101.00	88.16	81.59	2568
和田地区	Hotan Administrative Offices	135.90	129.60	64.38	58.14	6354

6-7 供水和用水情况
Water Supply and Water Used

单位：亿立方米 (2013 年) (100 million cu.m)

年 份 Year	地 区 Region	供水总量 Water Supply	地表水 Surface Water	地下水 Ground Water	中 水 利用量 Use of Intermediate Water	用水总量 Water Used	生 产 Production
总 计	**Total**	**588.05**	**472.21**	**114.67**	**1.17**	**588.05**	**573.08**
乌鲁木齐市	Urumqi City	12.08	6.12	5.31	0.65	12.08	10.20
克拉玛依市	Karamay City	5.79	4.77	0.78	0.24	5.79	5.11
石河子市	Shihezi City	3.59	1.62	1.97		3.59	2.50
吐鲁番地区	Turpan Administrative Offices	14.24	4.85	9.37	0.02	14.24	13.86
哈密地区	Hami [Kumul] Administrative Offices	12.61	4.83	7.66	0.12	12.61	12.09
昌吉回族自治州	Changji Hui Autonomous Prefecture	43.65	25.42	18.20	0.03	43.65	42.52
伊犁州直属县(市)	Counties (Cities) Direct Under Ili Prefecture	49.31	45.30	3.99	0.02	49.31	47.68
塔城地区	Tacheng [Tarbagatai] Administrative Offices	41.39	28.61	12.76	0.02	41.39	40.39
阿勒泰地区	Altay Administrative Offices	31.48	30.95	0.46	0.07	31.48	30.89
博尔塔拉蒙古自治州	Bortala Mongol Autonomous Prefecture	15.11	8.12	6.99		15.11	14.74
巴音郭楞蒙古自治州	Bayangol Mongol Autonomous Prefecture	57.72	42.71	15.01		57.72	56.19
阿克苏地区	Aksu Administrative Offices	118.59	108.86	9.73		118.59	117.04
克孜勒苏柯尔克孜自治州	Kizilsu Kirgiz Autonomous Prefecture	10.97	10.10	0.87		10.97	10.72
喀什地区	Kashgar [Kaxgar] Administrative Offices	124.82	105.39	19.43		124.82	123.40
和田地区	Hotan Administrative Offices	46.70	44.56	2.14		46.70	45.75

年 份 Year	地 区 Region	第一产业 Primary Industry	第二产业 Secondary Industry	第三产业 Tertiary Industry	居民生活 Consumption	生态环境 Ecological Protection	人均用水量(立方米/人) Per Capita Water Used (cu.m/person)
总 计	**Total**	**557.71**	**13.81**	**1.56**	**9.14**	**5.83**	**2594**
乌鲁木齐市	Urumqi City	7.34	2.54	0.32	1.48	0.40	459
克拉玛依市	Karamay City	3.90	1.09	0.12	0.14	0.54	1995
石河子市	Shihezi City	1.73	0.74	0.03	0.50	0.59	338
吐鲁番地区	Turpan Administrative Offices	13.24	0.61	0.01	0.25	0.13	2213
哈密地区	Hami [Kumul] Administrative Offices	11.55	0.49	0.06	0.27	0.24	2071
昌吉回族自治州	Changji Hui Autonomous Prefecture	40.57	1.80	0.15	0.73	0.40	3107
伊犁州直属县(市)	Counties (Cities) Direct Under Ili Prefecture	46.45	1.13	0.10	1.23	0.40	1649
塔城地区	Tacheng [Tarbagatai] Administrative Offices	39.85	0.48	0.06	0.36	0.64	3923
阿勒泰地区	Altay Administrative Offices	30.49	0.38	0.02	0.16	0.43	4711
博尔塔拉蒙古自治州	Bortala Mongol Autonomous Prefecture	14.57	0.16	0.01	0.24	0.13	3087
巴音郭楞蒙古自治州	Bayangol Mongol Autonomous Prefecture	53.95	2.02	0.22	0.70	0.83	4103
阿克苏地区	Aksu Administrative Offices	115.55	1.33	0.15	1.14	0.41	4825
克孜勒苏柯尔克孜自治州	Kizilsu Kirgiz Autonomous Prefecture	10.58	0.11	0.03	0.17	0.08	1899
喀什地区	Kashgar [Kaxgar] Administrative Offices	122.55	0.73	0.12	1.13	0.29	2949
和田地区	Hotan Administrative Offices	45.39	0.20	0.16	0.64	0.32	2161

6-8 主要年份环保系统机构、人员数

Number of Environmental Protection Agencies and Persons Engaged in Main Years

年　份 Year	机构数 (个) Number of Agencies (unit)	人员数 (人) Total Number of Staff & Workers (person)	#科技人员 Scientific and Technical Personnel	#监测人员 Monitoring Personnel	#监察人员 Supervising and Administrative Personnel
2000	208	1965	110	654	416
2001	208	2096	109	636	420
2002	238	2386	99	692	523
2003	275	2588	107	766	671
2004	288	2694	107	763	701
2005	304	2796	120	758	790
2006	326	2968	125	777	923
2007	326	2962	77	786	955
2008	296	2962	100	812	993
2009	319	3197	103	857	998
2010	324	3237	109	936	1126
2011	335	3372	121	967	1194
2012	324	3459	111	995	1112
2013	335	3438	104	985	1042

注：本表数据从 2009 年开始不包含兵团数据。(6-15、6-16、6-17 同)
Note: The date of this table don't cover the date of XJPCC from 2009.(the same as the table of 6-15,6-16,6-17)

6-9 工业按行业重点调查工业企业废气及污染物排放情况

Emission and Treatment of Waste Water and Pollutant in Industrial Enterprises by Sector

单位：吨　　(2013 年)　　(ton)

行　业	Sector	工业废气排放量(亿立方米) Total Volume of Industrial Waste Gas Emission (100 million cu.m)	工业二氧化硫排放量 Volume of Sulphur Dioxide Emission by Industry	工业氮氧化物排放量 Volume of Nitrogen Dioxide Emission by Industry	工业烟(粉)尘排放量 Volume of Industrial Soot Emission
合　计	**Total**	**19970.87**	**727644.70**	**571599.10**	**659626.18**
黑色金属矿采选业	Mining and Processing of Ferrous Metal Ores	50.69	777.91	98.27	8414.60
有色金属矿采选业	Mining and Processing of Non-Ferrous Metal Ores	37.81	824.85	355.77	3977.02
农副产品加工业	Processing of Food from Agricultural Products	118.36	10510.60	4791.18	4620.39
造纸及纸制品业	Manufacture of Paper and Paper Products	29.72	4384.12	1112.77	904.39
石油加工、炼焦及核燃料加工业	Oil Processing, Coking and Nuclear Fuel Processing	1409.72	71929.20	52852.38	35221.05
化学原料及化学制品制造业	Raw Chemical Material and Chemical Products	1613.43	65499.83	54930.41	13396.06
非金属矿物制品业	Nonmetal Mineral Products Manufacturing	3485.48	40393.18	82484.83	105105.11
水泥行业	The Cement Industry	2580.02	15513.46	72070.23	60938.99
黑色金属冶炼及压延加工业	Smelting and Pressing of Ferrous Metals	3654.02	77999.23	32506.96	43661.06
钢铁冶炼行业	Smelting of Iron and Steel Industry	3596.01	76272.53	32189.09	41841.49
有色金属冶炼及压延加工业	Smelting and Pressing of Non-ferrous Metals	1335.06	155477.90	23654.32	16092.46
电力、热力的生产和供应业	Electricity and Thermal Production and Supply	6485.13	264107.75	297217.54	143881.93
其他行业	Ohters	1751.45	35740.13	21594.67	284352.11

6-10 工业按行业重点调查工业企业废水及污染物排放情况
Emission and Treatment of Waste Water and Pollutant in Industrial Enterprises by Sector

(2013 年)

行业	Sector	工业废水排放量（万吨） Volume Of Waste Water Discharged (10 000 tons)	工业废水中化学需氧量排放量（吨） COD Discharge From Industral WasteWater (ton)	工业废水中氨氮排放量（吨） Ammonia Nitrogen Discharge form Industrial Waste Water (ton)
合　计	**Total**	**33939.67**	**181570.76**	**11722.22**
农副食品加工业	Processing of Food from Agricultural Products	1705.75	8956.20	264.47
食品制造业	Food Manufacturing	2517.96	10490.36	534.25
酒、饮料和精制茶制造业	Processing of Food from Agricultural Products	692.88	10911.82	138.02
纺织业	Textile Industry	547.85	3253.93	110.20
造纸及纸制品业	Paper and Paper Products Manufacturing	1890.02	9656.98	151.73
石油加工、炼焦及核燃料加工业	Oil Processing, Coking and Nuclear Fuel Processing	1723.79	1764.41	358.65
化学原料及化学制品制造业	Raw Chemical Material and Chemical Products	4571.05	11031.91	8637.86
化学纤维制造业	Chemical Fiber Manufacturing	6970.16	114532.67	994.40
黑色金属冶炼及压延加工业	Smelting and Pressing of Ferrous Metals	2034.52	1715.40	111.67
电力、热力的生产和供应业	Electricity and Thermal Production and Supply	3575.50	1393.22	77.36
其他行业	Ohters	7710.19	7863.86	343.61

6-11 工业按行业重点调查工业企业固体废物产生量及处理利用情况
Production and Treatment of Waste Solid in Industrial Enterprises by Region

单位：万吨　　(2013 年)　　(10 000 ton)

行业 Sector	一般工业固体废物产生量 Volume of Industrial Solid Wastes Produced	一般工业固体废物综合利用量 Volume of Industrial Solid Wastes Utilized	一般工业固体废物贮存量 Volume of Industrial Solid Wastes in Stocks	一般工业固体废物处置量 Volume of Industrial Solid Wastes Treated	一般工业固体废物倾倒丢弃量 General Volume of Industrial Solid Wastes Dumping of Discarded (10 000 tons)
合　计 Total	**9265.37**	**4801.94**	**3558.28**	**885.19**	**25.82**
煤炭开采和洗选业 Mining and Washing of Coal	2430.04	1314.58	945.77	170.10	
黑色金属矿采选业 Processing of Ferrous Metals Ores	2382.51	341.59	1828.35	212.58	
有色金属矿采选业 Processing of Nonferrous Metals Ores	1008.75	155.11	637.27	216.36	
农副产品加工业 Processing of Food from Agricultural Products	53.18	48.83	0.68	2.52	1.18
食品制造业 Food Manufacturing	26.22	25.45		0.64	0.15
纺织业 Textile Industry	3.76	3.60	0.01	0.08	0.07
化学原料及化学制品制造业 Raw Chemical Material and Chemical Products	686.65	625.58	17.51	44.54	0.01
非金属矿物制品业 Nonmetal Mineral Products Manufacturing	281.46	246.75	1.04	33.22	0.47
黑色金属冶炼及压延加工业 Smelting and Pressing of Ferrous Metals	812.50	742.90	8.79	60.95	
电力、热力的生产和供应业 Electricity and Thermal Production and Supply	976.24	870.62	51.37	54.86	2.64
其他行业 Ohters	604.06	426.93	67.49	89.34	21.30

6-12 环境污染治理投资
Investment in the Treatment of Environment Pollution

项　　目	Item	2012	2013
环境污染治理投资总额(万元)	**Total Investment in the Treatment of Environment Pollution (10 000 yuan)**	**2370936**	**2811472**
城镇环境基础设施建设投资	Investment in Urban Environmental Infrastructure	1707970	1654315
#污水处理	Volume of Waste Water	56115	92906
垃圾处理	Volume of Garbage Disposal	41937	93177
燃　气	Gas Supply	225918	300783
集中供热	Centralized Heating	959439	722248
园林绿化	Gardening and Greening	424561	445201
工业污染源治理投资	Investment in the Treatment of Industrial Pollution	79106	223866
#工业废水治理项目	Number of Project in Industrial Waste water Treatment	37905	38658
工业废气脱硫治理项目	Number of Project in Industrial Waste Gas Treatment	25349	117483
工业废气脱硝治理项目	Number of Project in Industrial Waste Gas Treatment	9225	38934
污染物自动在线监测仪器安装项目	Number of Project Installation　Pollution	248	313
当年完成环保验收项目环保投资	Investment in the Treatment of Industrial Pollution	583860	933291
#废水治理环保投资	Investment of Pollution in Waste Water Treatment	159631	264061
废气治理环保投资	Investment of Pollution in Waste Gas Treatment	108312	273689
固体废物治理环保投资	Investment of Pollution in Solid Wastes Treatment	24524	30191
噪声治理环保投资	Investment of Pollution in Noise Treatment	15036	17113
绿化及生态环保投资	Investment of Pollution in Landscape and Greening	276357	49166
环境污染治理投资总额相当于新疆生产总值比例(%)	**Investment in the Treatment of Environmental Pollution as Percent of GDP (%)**	**3.15**	**3.30**

6-13 主要年份工业污染治理投资完成情况
Investment Completed in the Treatment of Industrial Pollution in Main Years

年 份 Year	汇总工业企业数(个) Number of Industrial Enterprises (unit)	污染治理项目本年完成投资(万元) Investment In the Treatment of Industrial Pollution (10 000 yuan)	治理废水 Treatment of Waste Water	治理废气 Treatment of Waste Gas	治理固体废物 Treatment of Solid Waste	治理噪声 Treatment of Noise Pollution	治理其他 Treatment of Other Pollution	本年施工项目数(个) Projects Under Construction (unit)	本年竣工项目数(个) Projects Completed (unit)
2000	154	22311	8528	9116	349	4109	209	203	198
2001	113	32009	25917	4886	723	66	416	113	106
2002	89	16952	5015	8241	2206	261	1229	129	85
2003	83	26509	9298	9514	4865	21	2811	104	94
2004	94	29622	12334	13114	2756	92	1327	146	110
2005	97	44008	23549	9656	371	321	10111	162	153
2006	92	45229	26876	12036	2582	32	3703	143	132
2007	90	60138	29958	23891	1676	219	4394	117	103
2008	72	68004	33123	31999	1964	270	648	120	120
2009	99	125435	22242	99849	600	170	2574	109	100
2010	66	66813	19687	46276	800		50	56	48
2011	81	231693	36028	195202			317	154	92
2012	79	79106	37905	40483			718	72	54
2013	83	223866	38658	167383	8187	38	9599	83	79

6-14 工业污染治理投资来源
Source of Investment in the Treatment of Industrial Pollution

单位：万元 (10 000 yuan)

项 目	Item	2012	2013
施工项目本年投资来源	Source of Current Investment	79106	223866
排污费补助	Pollution Charges Subsidies	890	24000
政府其他补助	Other Government Subsidies	6050	1541
企业自筹	Self-raising Funds	72166	198325
#银行贷款	Bank Loans	1500	2580

6-15 主要城市空气质量指标
Ambient Air Quality in Main Cities

单位:毫克/立方米 (2013 年) (milligram/cu.m)

城 市	City	可吸入颗粒物 (PM10) Paticulate Matters	二氧化硫 (SO_2)	二氧化氮 (NO_2)	空气质量达到及好于二级的天数(天) Days of Air Quality Equal to or Above Grade II (day)
乌鲁木齐市	Urumqi City	0.141	0.030	0.068	304
克拉玛依市	Karamay City	0.071	0.011	0.028	351
石河子市	Shihezi City	0.106	0.020	0.047	305
吐鲁番市	Turpan City	0.190	0.014	0.042	180
哈 密 市	Hami [Kumul] City	0.133	0.024	0.038	276
昌 吉 市	Changji City	0.081	0.029	0.063	322
阜 康 市	Fukang City	0.095	0.024	0.044	314
奎 屯 市	Kuytun City	0.110	0.012	0.035	294
伊 宁 市	Yining [Gulja] City	0.094	0.018	0.035	347
塔 城 市	Tacheng [Qoqek] City	0.051	0.008	0.019	363
乌 苏 市	Usu City	0.085	0.008	0.028	327
阿勒泰市	Altay City	0.043	0.010	0.012	355
博 乐 市	Bole [Bortala] City	0.056	0.006	0.014	357
库尔勒市	Korla City	0.140	0.013	0.030	271
阿克苏市	Aksu City	0.223	0.016	0.023	232
阿图什市	Artux City	0.224	0.012	0.029	174
喀 什 市	Kashgar [Kaxgar] City	0.346	0.015	0.037	76
和 田 市	Hotan City	0.319	0.034	0.032	94
五家渠市	Wujiaqu City	0.097	0.029	0.039	328

6-16 主要城市道路交通噪声监测情况
Monitoring of Urban Road Traffic Noise in Major Cities

(2013 年)

城　市	City	等效声级 dB(A) Average Noise Value dB(A)
乌鲁木齐市	Urumqi City	67.5
克拉玛依市	Karamay City	64.4
石河子市	Shihezi City	66.8
吐鲁番市	Turpan City	68.1
哈 密 市	Hami [Kumul] City	64.1
昌 吉 市	Changji City	63.9
阜 康 市	Fukang City	63.5
奎 屯 市	Kuytun City	64.6
伊 宁 市	Yining [Gulja] City	64.5
塔 城 市	Tacheng [Qoqek] City	64.4
阿勒泰市	Altay City	68.4
博 乐 市	Bole [Bortala] City	65.7
库尔勒市	Korla City	63.5
阿克苏市	Aksu City	64.4
阿图什市	Artux City	69.4
喀 什 市	Kashgar [Kaxgar] City	67.5
和 田 市	Hotan City	65.8

6-17 主要城市区域环境噪声监测情况
Monitoring of Urban Environment Noise in Major Cities under National Control Programme

(2013 年)

城　市	City	等效声级 dB(A) Average Noise Value dB(A)
乌鲁木齐市	Urumqi City	54.8
克拉玛依市	Karamay City	51.7
石河子市	Shihezi City	52.7
吐鲁番市	Turpan City	49.1
哈 密 市	Hami [Kumul] City	53.6
昌 吉 市	Changji City	51.3
阜 康 市	Fukang City	52.2
奎 屯 市	Kuytun City	51.2
伊 宁 市	Yining [Gulja] City	51.0
塔 城 市	Tacheng [Qoqek] City	50.6
阿勒泰市	Altay City	51.9
博 乐 市	Bole [Bortala] City	50.4
库尔勒市	Korla City	52.5
阿克苏市	Aksu City	51.7
阿图什市	Artux City	67.0
喀 什 市	Kashgar [Kaxgar] City	54.3
和 田 市	Hotan City	50.6

6-18 主要年份自然保护区基本情况
Basic Situation of Natural Protection in Main Years

年　份 Year	自然保护区个数 (个) Number of Nature Reserves (unit)	#国家级 Nation level	自然保护区面积 (万公顷) Area of Nature Reserves (10 000 hectares)	#国家级 Nation Level	自然保护区占辖区面积比重 (%) Percentage of Nature Reserves in the Region (%)
2000	23	5	1594.05	869.08	9.6
2001	26	7	2042.40	1105.50	12.3
2005	28	8	2183.49	1275.86	13.1
2006	28	8	2162.49	1275.86	13.0
2007	34	8	2257.60	1275.86	13.6
2008	34	8	2257.60	1275.86	13.6
2009	34	8	2257.60	1275.86	13.6
2010	34	8	2257.60	1275.86	13.6
2011	28	9	2096.00	1365.53	12.6
2012	28	9	2140.56	1365.53	12.9
2013	28	9	1972.56	1196.30	11.9

注：2011 年、2012 年、2013 年自然保护区只包含自治区及国家级自然保护区。
Note: Number of nature reserves include nature reserves of region automous levels and national levels.

6-19 各地区城市生活垃圾清运和处理情况
Collection, Transport and Disposal of Consumption Wastes in Cities by Region

(2013 年)

城　市	City	生活垃圾清运量 (万吨) Consumption Wastes Collected and Transported (10 000 tons)	生活垃圾处理量 (万吨) Disposal of Consumption Wastes Treatment (10 000 tons)	无害化处理厂数 (座) Number of Factories for Wastes Treatment (unit)	无害化处理能力 (吨/日) Treatment Capacity (ton/day)	无害化处理量 (万吨) Volume of Wastes Disposed (10 000 tons)	生活垃圾处理率 (%) Treatment Rate of Consumption Wastes (%)
总　计	**Total**	**352.34**	**329.40**	**20**	**8338**	**275.13**	**93.49**
乌鲁木齐市	Urumqi City	132.26	121.73	3	3539	121.01	92.04
克拉玛依市	Karamay City	15.82	15.82	3	450	15.65	100.00
吐鲁番市	Turpan City	7.67	6.85	1	300	6.85	89.31
哈 密 市	Hami [Kumul] City	17.30	17.10	1	350	17.10	98.84
昌 吉 市	Changji City	15.00	14.25	1	420	14.25	95.00
阜 康 市	Fukang City	3.94	3.75	1	150	3.75	95.18
伊 宁 市	Yining [Gulja] City	23.00	22.54	1	600	22.54	98.00
奎 屯 市	Kuytun City	5.31	5.20	1	600	5.20	97.93
塔 城 市	Tacheng [Qoqek] City	6.80	6.50	1	190	6.50	95.59
乌 苏 市	Usu City	4.75	4.68	1	120	4.68	98.53
阿勒泰市	Altay City	3.07	2.98	1	140	2.98	97.07
博 乐 市	Bole [Bortala] City	5.80	4.38	1	149	4.38	75.52
库尔勒市	Korla City	28.00	26.76	1	500	26.76	95.57
阿克苏市	Aksu City	13.82	12.70				91.90
阿图什市	Artux City	3.00	2.80	1	80	2.80	93.33
喀 什 市	Kashgar [Kaxgar] City	19.20	17.18	1	500	17.18	89.48
和 田 市	Hotan City	18.00	16.50				91.67
石河子市	Shihezi City	18.00	18.00				100.00
阿拉尔市	Aral City	2.98	2.74				91.95
图木舒克市	Tumxuk City	1.15					
五家渠市	Wujiaqu City	3.65	3.50	1	250	3.50	95.89
北 屯 市	Beitur City	2.11	2.05				97.16
铁门关市	Tiemenguan City	0.42	0.29				69.05
阿拉山口市	Alashankou City	1.29	1.10				85.27

注：表中无害化处理数据均为二级以上无害化处理厂数据。
Note: Data on wastes disposed are provided by secondary and above factories for wastes treatment.

6-20 造林面积
Area of Afforestation

单位:公顷 (hectare)

年份 地区 Year Region	造林总面积 Total Area of Afforestation	按造林方式分 By Approach			按林种用途分 By Function				
		人工造林 Manual Planting	飞机播种 Airplane Planting	无林地和疏林地新封 Area without Forest or of Sparse Forest	用材林 Timber Forests	经济林 By-product Forests	防护林 Protection Forests	薪炭林 Fuel Forests	特种用途林 Forests for Special Purpose
2000	64173	63793	200		1605	44564	16512	1012	480
2001	106771	106771			2149	78203	24536	1424	459
2002	216924	216924			3034	78302	134723	706	159
2003	263781	253781	10000		10152	59777	191380	2390	82
2004	176540	176540			3897	73103	96897	2638	5
2005	136990	130323	6667		3226	40523	92449	738	54
2006	97424	97424			1780	38495	56548	588	13
2007	146632	124642		21990	2991	71667	71325	589	60
2008	239951	217429		22522	8744	136046	94820	341	
2009	301438	266301		35137	9387	155503	135584	954	10
2010	199629	156964		42665	1996	104527	90546	2298	262
2011	186197	140262		45935	823	92656	89942	2356	420
2012	187321	114287		73034	3702	51435	128692	3309	183
2013	147357	99659		47698	3675	42170	98541	2948	23
乌鲁木齐市 Urumqi City	2729	2729					2729		
克拉玛依市 Karamay City	1159	1159					1159		
石河子市 Shihezi City	93	93					93		
吐鲁番地区 Turpan Administrative Offices	3994	2994		1000	7	1709	2278		
哈密地区 Hami [Kumul] Administrative Offices	5046	380		4666		7	5039		
昌吉回族自治州 Changji Hui Autonomous Prefecture	10365	8366		1999		1590	8442	333	
伊犁州直属县(市) Counties (Cities) Direct Under Ili Prefecture	18368	11034		7334	2604	3916	11848		
塔城地区 Tacheng [Tarbagatai] Administrative Offices	19403	7203		12200	627	1429	17083	245	19
阿勒泰地区 Altay Administrative Offices	16697	8496		8201		3433	12630	634	
博尔塔拉蒙古自治州 Bortala Mongol Autonomous Prefecture	5161	2828		2333		202	4739	220	
巴音郭楞蒙古自治州 Bayangol Mongol Autonomous Prefecture	14400	8268		6132		4655	9578	167	
阿克苏地区 Aksu Administrative Offices	9614	8614		1000		4599	4508	507	
克孜勒苏柯尔克孜自治州 Kizilsu Kirgiz Autonomous Prefecture	6593	4593		2000	435		5988	170	
喀什地区 Kashgar [Kaxgar] Administrative Offices	21411	20745		666	2	14721	6644	40	4
和田地区 Hotan Administrative Offices	12239	12072		167		5909	5698	632	
自治区直属单位 Autonomous regions directly under the unit	85	85					85		

6-21 林业重点工程造林面积
Area of Key Afforestation Projects

单位:公顷 (hectare)

年 份 Year	地 区 Region	造林总面积 Total Area of Afforestation	#退耕还林工程 Grain for Green Projects	#三北及长江流域等防护林工程 Project on Protection Forests in North China and Yangtze River Basin
	2001	102317	13173	
	2002	199324	113010	
	2003	235924	175314	
	2004	152967	82838	70129
	2005	133778	62457	71321
	2006	88744	38160	50584
	2007	138700	32926	105774
	2008	187318	50977	136341
	2009	270997	48120	222877
	2010	177674	38034	139640
	2011	186197	31066	107390
	2012	187321	47091	113213
	2013	116713	33460	83253
乌鲁木齐市	Urumqi City	2729	340	2389
克拉玛依市	Karamay City	667		667
石河子市	Shihezi City			
吐鲁番地区	Turpan Administrative Offices	3994	1394	2600
哈密地区	Hami [Kumul] Administrative Offices	5046	832	4214
昌吉回族自治州	Changji Hui Autonomous Prefecture	10365	2698	7667
伊犁州直属县(市)	Counties (Cities) Direct Under Ili Prefecture	17921	2714	15207
塔城地区	Tacheng [Tarbagatai] Administrative Offices	18225	3793	14432
阿勒泰地区	Altay Administrative Offices	16183	6934	9249
博尔塔拉蒙古自治州	Bortala Mongol Autonomous Prefecture	4828	3067	1761
巴音郭楞蒙古自治州	Bayangol Mongol Autonomous Prefecture	13732	3145	10587
阿克苏地区	Aksu Administrative Offices	5891	2994	2897
克孜勒苏柯尔克孜自治州	Kizilsu Kirgiz Autonomous Prefecture	6448	1321	5127
喀什地区	Kashgar [Kaxgar] Administrative Offices	4213	1656	2557
和田地区	Hotan Administrative Offices	6471	2572	3899

6-22 森林火灾情况
Forest Fires

年 份 Year	地 区 Region	森林火灾次数(次) Forest Fires (case)	一般火灾 Ordinary Fires	较大火灾 Large Fires	火场总面积(公顷) Total Area of Fires (hectare)
	2005	28	1		42.33
	2006	35	5		258.27
	2007	47	13		137.09
	2008	67	19		191.38
	2009	51	35	16	83.58
	2010	34	27	7	65.95
	2011	59	46	13	713.72
	2012	41	40	1	19.16
	2013	31	29	2	64.61
乌鲁木齐市	Urumqi City				
克拉玛依市	Karamay City				
石河子市	Shihezi City				
吐鲁番地区	Turpan Administrative Offices	1	1		1.238
哈密地区	Hami [Kumul] Administrative Offices	2	2		1.501
昌吉回族自治州	Changji Hui Autonomous Prefecture	9	9		1.069
伊犁州直属县(市)	Counties (Cities) Direct Under Ili Prefecture	12	11	1	4.600
塔城地区	Tacheng [Tarbagatai] Administrative Offices	2	2		53.400
阿勒泰地区	Altay Administrative Offices	2	2		0.001
博尔塔拉蒙古自治州	Bortala Mongol Autonomous Prefecture				
巴音郭楞蒙古自治州	Bayangol Mongol Autonomous Prefecture				
阿克苏地区	Aksu Administrative Offices	2	1	1	2.475
克孜勒苏柯尔克孜自治州	Kizilsu Kirgiz Autonomous Prefecture				
喀什地区	Kashgar [Kaxgar] Administrative Offices	1	1		0.330
和田地区	Hotan Administrative Offices				
五家渠市	Wujiaqu City				

6-22 续表 Continued

年 份 Year	地 区 Region	受灾森林总面积(公顷) Destructed Forest Area (hectare)	#天然林 Natural Forest	#人工林 Man-made Forest	经济损失(万元) Economic Loss (10 000 yuan)
	2005	11.62	10.63	0.99	12.52
	2006	94.10	78.28	1.39	9.26
	2007	75.34	31.44	39.37	19.47
	2008	122.74	58.39	65.64	145.53
	2009	72.66	8.24	49.86	52.29
	2010	43.82	17.56	15.70	5.48
	2011	150.16	114.36	35.80	1426.91
	2012	17.35	4.66	12.70	45.88
	2013	12.79	3.48	9.31	14.65
乌鲁木齐市	Urumqi City				
克拉玛依市	Karamay City				
石河子市	Shihezi City				
吐鲁番地区	Turpan Administrative Offices	0.910		0.910	
哈密地区	Hami [Kumul] Administrative Offices	1.501	1.001	0.500	
昌吉回族自治州	Changji Hui Autonomous Prefecture	1.069		1.069	0.18
伊犁州直属县(市)	Counties (Cities) Direct Under Ili Prefecture	4.600	0.010	4.590	9.47
塔城地区	Tacheng [Tarbagatai] Administrative Offices	1.907		1.907	
阿勒泰地区	Altay Administrative Offices	0.001	0.001		4.00
博尔塔拉蒙古自治州	Bortala Mongol Autonomous Prefecture				
巴音郭楞蒙古自治州	Bayangol Mongol Autonomous Prefecture				
阿克苏地区	Aksu Administrative Offices	2.475	2.475		
克孜勒苏柯尔克孜自治州	Kizilsu Kirgiz Autonomous Prefecture				
喀什地区	Kashgar [Kaxgar] Administrative Offices	0.330		0.330	1.00
和田地区	Hotan Administrative Offices				
五家渠市	Wujiaqu City				

6-23 森林病虫害防治情况
Prevention of Forest Diseases and Pests

单位：公顷 (hectare)

年 份 Year	地 区 Region	合 计 Total			森林病害 Forest Diseases		
		发生面积 Area of Occurrence	防治面积 Area of Prevention	防治率(%) Prevention Rate (%)	发生面积 Area of Occurrence	防治面积 Area of Prevention	防治率(%) Prevention Rate (%)
	2005	241713	221720	91.7	4467	3440	77.0
	2006	400127	344146	86.0	21993	19273	87.6
	2007	787087	441533	56.1	30194	23393	77.5
	2008	1066659	609457	57.1	147035	92811	63.1
	2009	990580	572735	57.8	82273	68525	83.3
	2010	1051060	570973	54.3	80820	73573	91.0
	2011	1223633	547200	45.0	73747	61240	83.0
	2012	1261386	539040	42.7	68426	57025	83.3
	2013	1403008	537534	38.3	77270	64638	83.7
乌鲁木齐市	Urumqi City	5291	5091	96.2			
吐鲁番地区	Turpan Administrative Offices	9638	2875	29.8			
哈密地区	Hami [Kumul] Administrative Offices	28914	12718	44.0	1414	1199	84.8
昌吉回族自治州	Changji Hui Autonomous Prefecture	369825	7220	2.0	950	950	100.0
伊犁州直属县(市)	Counties (Cities) Direct Under Ili Prefecture	20556	19609	95.4	3309	3237	97.8
塔城地区	Tacheng [Tarbagatai] Administrative Offices	41828	1583	3.8	502	262	52.2
阿勒泰地区	Altay Administrative Offices	53844	1012	1.9	1990		
博尔塔拉蒙古自治州	Bortala Mongol Autonomous Prefecture	137234	2799	2.0			
巴音郭楞蒙古自治州	Bayangol Mongol Autonomous Prefecture	58870	17883	30.4	211	210	99.5
阿克苏地区	Aksu Administrative Offices	161783	160308	99.1	11475	11379	99.2
克孜勒苏柯尔克孜自治州	Kizilsu Kirgiz Autonomous Prefecture	13475	9540	70.8	5521	3269	59.2
喀什地区	Kashgar [Kaxgar] Administrative Offices	315076	158976	50.5	23944	20195	84.3
和田地区	Hotan Administrative Offices	176754	132925	75.2	25544	23450	91.8
自治区林业厅	Xinjiang Forestry Bureau	9920	4995	50.4	2410	487	20.2

注：自治区林业厅数据中包括石河子市和克拉玛依市的数据。
Note: The data on Bureau of Forestry include the data of Shihezi City and Karamay City.

6-23 续表 Continued

单位：公顷 (hectare)

年 份 Year	地 区 Region	森林虫害 Forest Diseases			森林鼠害 Forest Rat Plague		
		发生面积 Area of Occurrence	防治面积 Area of Prevention	防治率(%) Prevention Rate (%)	发生面积 Area of Occurrence	防治面积 Area of Prevention	防治率(%) Prevention Rate (%)
	2005	221500	199700	89.9	21747	18580	85.4
	2006	340320	290693	85.4	37813	34180	90.4
	2007	350592	331735	94.6	406301	86405	21.3
	2008	527465	446766	84.7	392159	69880	17.8
	2009	474213	431197	90.9	434093	73013	16.8
	2010	470961	432316	91.8	499279	65084	13.0
	2011	582653	457627	79.0	567233	28333	5.0
	2012	518263	455652	87.9	674697	26363	3.9
	2013	517802	443262	85.6	807936	29634	3.7
乌鲁木齐市	Urumqi City	3011	3011	100.0	2280	2080	91.2
吐鲁番地区	Turpan Administrative Offices	3618	2875	79.5	6020		
哈密地区	Hami [Kumul] Administrative Offices	11542	10367	89.8	15958	1152	7.2
昌吉回族自治州	Changji Hui Autonomous Prefecture	5688	4845	85.2	363187	1425	0.4
伊犁州直属县(市)	Counties (Cities) Direct Under Ili Prefecture	14381	13675	95.1	2866	2697	94.1
塔城地区	Tacheng [Tarbagatai] Administrative Offices	1789	1214	67.9	39537	107	0.3
阿勒泰地区	Altay Administrative Offices	8130	1012	12.5	43724		
博尔塔拉蒙古自治州	Bortala Mongol Autonomous Prefecture	2941	2799	95.2	134293		
巴音郭楞蒙古自治州	Bayangol Mongol Autonomous Prefecture	17702	15853	89.6	40957	1820	4.4
阿克苏地区	Aksu Administrative Offices	150308	148929	99.1			
克孜勒苏柯尔克孜自治州	Kizilsu Kirgiz Autonomous Prefecture	7793	6130	78.7	161	141	87.6
喀什地区	Kashgar [Kaxgar] Administrative Offices	138236	123369	89.3	152896	15412	10.1
和田地区	Hotan Administrative Offices	146544	104809	71.5	4666	4666	100.0
自治区林业厅	Xinjiang Forestry Bureau	6119	4374	71.5	1391	134	9.6

6-24 林业系统营林固定资产投资完成情况
Completed Investment in Fixed Assets for Afforestation in Forest System

单位：万元 (10 000 yuan)

年份 Year	地区 Region	本年完成投资 Investment Completed During the Year	#国家投资 State Investment	本年新增固定资产 Newly Increased Fixed Assets
	2000	23582	11686	4542
	2001	45890	23725	12492
	2002	68861	35835	
	2003	71277	40821	27223
	2004	60631	43475	23047
	2005	80150	57680	24988
	2006	96062	82235	31047
	2007	115523	94094	33091
	2008	158416	129294	55295
	2009	193818	153538	52765
	2010	168930	142678	28725
	2011	85365	39304	41378
	2012	97849	39318	35863
	2013	130356	41129	119451
乌鲁木齐市	Urumqi City	49046	22044	49046
克拉玛依市	Karamay City	41897	300	41897
石河子市	Shihezi City	3620		3620
吐鲁番地区	Turpan Administrative Offices	2280	840	2280
哈密地区	Hami [Kumul] Administrative Offices	925	115	925
昌吉回族自治州	Changji Hui Autonomous Prefecture	1600	1600	1600
伊犁州直属县(市)	Counties (Cities) Direct Under Ili Prefecture	990	990	
塔城地区	Tacheng [Tarbagatai] Administrative Offices			
阿勒泰地区	Altay Administrative Offices	5073	340	
博尔塔拉蒙古自治州	Bortala Mongol Autonomous Prefecture	7644	6336	7644
巴音郭楞蒙古自治州	Bayangol Mongol Autonomous Prefecture	1197	1128	
阿克苏地区	Aksu Administrative Offices	12439	5436	12439
克孜勒苏柯尔克孜自治州	Kizilsu Kirgiz Autonomous Prefecture			
和田地区	Hotan Administrative Offices	3645	2000	

注：自 2011 年起固定资产投资统计范围为单项投资 500 万元以上项目，2010 年及以前年份统计范围是只要形成固定资产的投资均需统计。
Note: In 2011,Statistical range of investment in fixed assets is above of 5million yuan single investment project.Before 2010,Statistical range is the formation of the investment fixed assets required statistics.

6-25 地震灾害情况
Earthquake Disasters

年 份 Year	地 区 Region	地震次数(次) Number of Earthquakes (case)	5.0-5.9 级 5.0-5.9 Richterscale	6.0-6.9 级 6.0-6.9 Richterscale	7.0 级以上 Over 7.0 Richterscale
2005		4	3	1	
2006		2	2		
2007		1	1		
2008		4	2	1	1
2009		6	6		
2010		2	2		
2011		8	7	1	
乌恰县	Wuqia [Ulugqat] County	1	1		
托克逊县	Toksun County	1	1		
青河县	Qinghe[Qinggil]County	1	1		
阿图什-伽师交界	Artux City border on Jiashi[payzawat] County	1	1		
于田县	Yutian[Keriya] County	1	1		
精河县	Jinghe[Jing] County	1	1		
尼勒克、巩留交界	Nilka County border on Gongliu[Tokkuztara] County	1		1	
莎车县	Shache[Yarkant]County	1	1		
2012		11	8	3	
和硕县	Hoxud County	1	1		
巴里坤县	Barkol Kazak Autonomous County	1	1		
乌恰县	Wuqia [Ulugqat] County	1	1		
洛浦县	Lop County	1		1	
乌恰县	Wuqia [Ulugqat] County	1	1		
轮台县	Luntai [Bugur] County	1	1		
新源、和静交界	Xinyuan [Kunes] County border on Hejing County	1		1	
于田县	Yutian [Keriya] County	1		1	
阿图什、伽师交界	Artux City border on Jiashi [Payzawat] County	1	1		
若羌	Ruoqiang [Qarkilik] County	1	1		
若羌	Ruoqiang [Qarkilik] County	1	1		
2013		5	5		
阿图什市	Artux City	1	1		
昌吉、乌鲁木齐交界	Changji City border on Urumqi City	1	1		
乌鲁木齐市	Urumqi City	1	1		
且末县	Qiemo [Qargan] County	1	1		
柯坪县	Kalpin County	1	1		

注：本表数据由自治区地震局提供。
Note: The data in this table is Provided by theBureau of Earthquake.

6-25 续表 Continued

年 份 Year	地 区 Region	人员伤亡(人) Casualties (person)	#死亡人数 Deaths	经济损失(万元) Economic Losses (10 000 yuan)	失去住所(户) Homeless (household)
2005				16316	5823
2006				126	
2007				11060	5074
2008				38437	5702
2009				20498	4393
2010				2408	675
2011				105059	15964
乌恰县	Wuqia [Ulugqat] County				
托克逊县	Toksun County			9225	4757
青河县	Qinghe[Qinggil]County			3330	915
阿图什-伽师交界	Artux City border on Jiashi[payzawat] County			18322	1994
于田县	Yutian[Keriya] County			292	
精河县	Jinghe[Jing] County			1185	324
尼勒克、巩留交界	Nilka County border on Gongliu[Tokkuztara] County			67846	7598
莎车县	Shache[Yarkant]County			4859	376
2012				272095	25713
和硕县	Hoxud County			4208	482
巴里坤县	Barkol Kazak Autonomous County				
乌恰县	Wuqia [Ulugqat] County				
洛浦县	Lop County			52325	1751
乌恰县	Wuqia [Ulugqat] County				
轮台县	Luntai [Bugur] County			4547	578
新源、和静交界	Xinyuan [Kunes] County border on Hejing County			199032	22083
于田县	Yutian [Keriya] County			4958	573
阿图什、伽师交界	Artux City border on Jiashi [Payzawat] County				
若羌	Ruoqiang [Qarkilik] County			636	
若羌	Ruoqiang [Qarkilik] County			6388	246
2013				6696	1755
阿图什市	Artux City			2397	792
昌吉、乌鲁木齐交界	Changji City border on Urumqi City			792	193
乌鲁木齐市	Urumqi City				
且末县	Qiemo [Qargan] County				
柯坪县	Kalpin County			3507	770

主要统计指标解释

自然资源　指人类可以直接从自然界获得，并用于生产和生活的物质资源。自然资源一般可以分成可再生资源和非再生资源两大类。可再生资源指在较短时间内可以再生、可以循环利用的资源，包括土地资源、水资源、气候资源、生物资源和海洋资源等。非再生资源指在使用后不能再生的资源，包括矿产资源和地热能源。

土地资源　土地指陆地的表层部分，它主要由岩石、岩石的风化物和土壤构成。土地资源按利用类型可以分为农用地、建筑用地和未利用地。农用地包括耕地、园地、林地、牧草地和水面。建筑用地包括居民点及工矿用地、交通用地和水利设施用地。未利用地指农用地和建筑用地以外的土地，包括滩涂、荒漠、戈壁、冰川和石山等。

耕地　指种植农作物的土地，包括熟地，新开发、复垦、整理地，休闲地（含轮歇地、轮作地）；以种植农作物（含蔬菜）为主，间有零星果树或其他树木的土地；平均每年能保证收获一季的已垦滩地和海涂。耕地中包括南方宽度＜1.0米，北方宽度＜2.0 米固定的沟、渠、路和地坎（埂）；临时种植药材、草皮、花卉、苗木等的耕地，以及其他临时改变用途的耕地。

园地　指种植以采集果、叶、根、茎、汁等为主的集约经营的多年生木本和草本作物，覆盖度大于 50%和每亩株数大于合理株数 70%的土地。包括用于育苗的土地。

林地　指生长乔木、竹类、灌木的土地，及沿海生长红树林的土地。包括迹地，不包括居民点内部的绿化林木用地，铁路、公路征地范围内的林木，以及河流、沟渠的护堤林。

草地　指生长草本植物为主的土地。

矿产资源　矿产资源指由地质作用形成的，具有利用价值的，呈固态、液态、气态的自然资源，是社会生产发展的重要物质基础。目前我国已发现矿种有170多种，按其特点和用途，可分为能源矿产(如煤炭、石油、天然气、地热)、金属矿产(如铁矿、锰矿、铜矿、铅矿、铝土矿)、非金属矿产(如金刚石、石灰岩、粘土)和水气矿产(如地下水、矿泉水、二氧化碳气)四大类。其中：金属矿产按其物质成份和性质又可分为：黑色金属矿产、有色金属矿产、贵金属矿产、稀有金属矿产、稀土金属矿产、分散元素金属矿产六类。

矿产基础储量　基础储量是查明矿产资源的一部分。它能满足现行采矿和生产所需的指标要求，是控制的、探明的并通过可行性或预可行性研究认为属于经济的、边界经济的部分，用未扣除设计、采矿损失的数量表示。

平均气温　气温指空气的温度，我国一般以摄氏度为单位表示。气象观测的温度表是放在离地面约 1.5 米处通风良好的百叶箱里测量的，因此，通常说的气温指的是离地面 1.5 米处百叶箱中的温度。计算方法：月平均气温是将全月各日的平均气温相加，除以该月的天数而得。年平均气温是将 12 个月的月平均气温累加后除以 12 而得。

降水量　指从天空降落到地面的液态或固态(经融化后)水，未经蒸发、渗透、流失而在地面上积聚的深度。计算方法为：月降水量是将全月各日的降水量累加而得。年降水量是将12个月的月降水量累加而得。

全年日照时数　指太阳实际照射地面的时数，通常以小时为单位表示。其统计方法与降水量相同。

水资源总量　指当地降水形成的地表和地下产水总量，即地表径流量与降水入渗补给量之和。

地表水资源量　指河流、湖泊以及冰川等地表水体中可以逐年更新的动态水量，即天然河川径流量。

地下水资源量　指地下饱和含水层逐年更新的动态水量，即降水和地表水入渗对地下水的补给量。

地表水与地下水资源重复计算量　指地表水和地下水相互转化的部分，即天然河川径流量中的地下水排泄量和地下水补给量中来源于地表水的入渗补给量。

供水总量　指各种水源为用水户提供的包括输水损失在内的毛水量。

地表水源供水量　指地表水体工程的取水量，按蓄、引、提、调四种形式统计。从水库、塘坝中引水或提水，均属蓄水工程供水量；从河道或湖泊中自流引水的，无论有闸或无闸，均属引水工程供水量；利用扬水站从河道或湖泊中直接取水的，属提水工程供水量；跨流域调水指水资源一级区或独立流域之间的跨流域调配水量，不包括在蓄、引、提水量中。

地下水源供水量　指水井工程的开采量，按浅层谈水、深层承压水和微咸水分别统计。城市地下水源供水量包括自来水厂的开采量和工矿企业自备井的开采量。

其他水源供水量　包括污水处理再利用、集雨工程、海水淡化等水源工程的供水量。

用水总量　指各类用水户取用的包括输水损失在内的毛用水量。

农业用水　包括农田灌溉用水、林果地灌溉用水、草地灌溉用水和鱼塘补水和畜禽用水。

工业用水　指工矿企业在生产过程中用于制造、加工、冷却、空调、净化、洗涤等方面的用水，按新水取用量计，不包括企业内部的重复利用水量。

生活用水　包括城镇生活用水和农村生活用水。城镇生活用水由居民用水和公共用水(含第三产业及建筑业等用水)组成；农村生活用水指居民生活用水。

生态环境补水　仅包括人为措施供给的城镇环境用水和部分河湖、湿地补水，而不包括降水、径流自然满足的水量。

一般工业固体废物产生量　指未被列入《国家危险废物名录》或者根据国家规定的危险废物鉴别标准（GB5085）、固体废物浸出毒性浸出方法（GB5086）及固体废物浸出毒性测定方法（GB／T 15555）鉴别方法判定不具有危险特性的工业固体废物。计算公式是：

一般工业固体废物产生量=（一般工业固体废物综合利用量–其中：综合利用往年贮存量）+一般工业固体废物贮存量+（一般工业固体废物处置量–其中：处置往年贮存量）+一般工业固体废物倾倒丢弃量

一般工业固体废物综合利用量　指报告期内企业通过回收、加工、循环、交换等方式，从固体废物中提取或者使其转化为可以利用的资源、能源和其他原材料的固体废物量（包括当年利用的往年工业固体废物累计贮存量）。如用作农业肥料、生产建筑材料、筑路等。综合利用量由原产生固体废物的单位统计。

一般工业固体废物处置量　指报告期内企业将工业固体废物焚烧和用其他改变工业固体废物的物理、化学、生物特性的方法，达到减少或者消除其危险成分的活动，或者将工业固体废物最终置于符合环境保护规定要求的填埋场的活动中，所消纳固体废物的量。

一般工业固体废物贮存量　指报告期内企业以综合利用或处置为目的，将固体废物暂时贮存或堆存在专设的贮存设施或专设的集中堆存场所内的量。专设的固体废物贮存场所或贮存设施必须有防扩散、防流失、防渗漏、防止污染大气、水体的措施。

一般工业固体废物倾倒丢弃量　指报告期内企业将所产生的固体废物倾倒或者丢弃到固体废物污染防治设施、场所以外的量。

生活垃圾清运量　指报告期收集和运送到各生活垃圾处理厂(场)和生活垃圾最终消纳点的生活垃圾数量。生活垃圾指城市日常生活或为城市日常生活提供服务的活动中产生的固体废物以及法律行政规定的视为城市生活垃圾的固体废物。包括：居民生活垃圾、商业垃圾、集市贸易市场垃圾、街道清扫垃圾、公共场所垃圾和机关、学校、厂矿等单位的生活垃圾。

生活垃圾无害化处理率　指报告期生活垃圾无害化处理量与生活垃圾产生量比率。在统计上，由于生活垃圾产生量不易取得，可用清运量代替。计算公式为：

生活垃圾无害化处理率=生活垃圾无害化处理量/生活垃圾产生量×100%

森林面积　包括郁闭度0.2以上的乔木林地面积和竹林面积，国家特别规定的灌木林地面积，农田林网以及村旁、路旁、水旁、宅旁林木的覆盖面积。

人工林面积　指由人工播种、植苗或扦插造林形成的生长稳定，(一般造林3-5年后或飞机播种5-7年后)每公顷保存株数大于或等于造林设计植树株数80%或郁闭度0.20以上(含0.20)的林分面积。

森林覆盖率　以行政区域为单位的森林面积占区域土地总面积的百分比。计算公式为：

森林覆盖率(%)=森林面积／土地总面积×100%

活立木总蓄积量　指一定范围内土地上全部树木蓄积的总量，包括森林蓄积、疏林蓄积、散生木蓄积和四旁树蓄积。

森林蓄积量　指一定森林面积上存在着的林木树干部分的总材积。

造林面积　指在宜林荒山荒地、宜林沙荒地、无立木林地、疏林地和退耕地等其它宜林地上通过人工措施形成或恢复森林、林木、灌木林的过程。

人工造林　指在宜林荒山荒地、宜林沙荒地、无立木林地、疏林地和退耕地等其他宜林地上通过播种、植苗和分植来提高森林植被覆被率的技术措施。

无林地和疏林地本年新封山育林　指本年开始对具有天然下种或萌蘖能力的疏林地、灌丛地、采伐迹地、火烧迹地以及荒山荒地、沙荒地等有条件的地方采取划界封禁和人工辅助措施，使其成为森林或灌草植被的面积。

用材林　指以生产木材为主要目的的森林和林木，包括以生产竹材为主要目的的竹林。

经济林　指以生产果品，食用油料、饮料、调料，工业原料和药材为主要目的的林木。经济林是人们为了取得林木的果实、叶片、皮层、胶液等产品作为工业原料或者供食用所营造的林木，如油茶、油桐、核桃、樟树、花椒、茶、桑、果等。

防护林　指以防护为主要目的的森林、林木和灌木丛。包括水源涵养林，水土保持林，防风固沙林，农田、牧场防护林，护岸林，护路林等。

薪炭林　指以生产燃料为主要目的的林木。

特种用途林　指以国防、环境保护、科学实验等为主要目的的森林和林木。包括国防林、实验林、母树林、环境保护林、风景林，名胜古迹和革命纪念地的林木，自然保护区的森林。

三北和长江流域等重点防护林体系建设工程　三北和长江中下游地区等重点防护林体系建设工程,是我国涵盖面最大、内容最丰富的防护林体系建设工程。具体包括三北防护林四期工程、长江中下游及淮河太湖流域防护林二期工程、沿海防护林二期工程、珠江防护林二期工程、太行山绿化二期工程和平原绿化二期工程。主要解决三北地区的防沙治沙问题和其他区域各不相同的生态问题。

湿地 指天然或人工、长久或暂时性的沼泽地、泥炭地或水域地带，包括静止或流动、淡水、半咸水、咸水体，低潮时水深不超过6米的水域以及海岸地带地区的珊瑚滩和海草床、滩涂、红树林、河口、河流、淡水沼泽、沼泽森林、湖泊、盐沼及盐湖。

自然保护区 指为了保护自然环境和自然资源，促进国民经济的持续发展，将一定面积的陆地和水体划分出来，并经各级人民政府批准而进行特殊保护和管理的区域个数。根据保护对象，自然保护区分为自然生态系统类、野生生物类、自然遗迹类。风景名胜区、文物保护区不计在内。

森林火灾次数 指发生在城市市区外的一切森林、林木和林地的火灾次数。按照受害森林面积和伤亡人数，森林火灾分为一般森林火灾、较大森林火灾、重大森林火灾和特别重大森林火灾：1.一般森林火灾：受害森林面积在1公顷以下或者其他林地起火的，或者死亡1人以上3人以下的，或者重伤1人以上10人以下的；2.较大森林火灾：受害森林面积在1公顷以上100公顷以下的，或者死亡3人以上10人以下的，或者重伤10人以上50人以下的；3.重大森林火灾：受害森林面积在100公顷以上1000公顷以下的，或者死亡10人以上30人以下的，或者重伤50人以上100人以下的；4.特别重大森林火灾：受害森林面积在1000公顷以上的，或者死亡30人以上的，或者重伤100人以上的。本条所称“以上”包括本数，“以下”不包括本数。

森林病虫鼠害 指对森林、林木、林木种苗及木材、竹材形成的病害、虫害和鼠害。森林病害是指林木机体遭受真菌、细菌、病毒、寄生性种子植物和线虫等的危害，而使林木在生理机能、细胞和组织结构以及外部形态等方面发生的病理性变化。森林虫害是指林木机体遭受松毛虫、金花虫、竹蝗、金龟子、蝼蛄等各种昆虫的危害，而造成一定面积森林的生长衰弱或死亡。森林鼠害是指森林、林木、林木种苗遭受各种鼠类的危害，而造成一定程度的损失或死亡。

发生地震灾害次数 指发生形成灾害(包括人员伤亡或经济损失)的所有震级的地震次数。

Explanatory Notes on Main Statistical Indicators

Natural Resources refer to material resources that could be obtained from the nature by human being and used for production and living. Natural resources in general can be classified as renewable resources and non-renewable resources. Renewable resources refer to resources that could be renewed and recycled during a relatively short period of time, including land resource, water resource, climate resource, biology resource and marine resource. Non-renewable resources include resources that could not be renewed, such as minerals and geothermal resource.

Land Resource Land refers to the surface of the earth, consisting of mainly rocks and its weathering and earth. Land resource can be classified, by its utilization, as land for agriculture, land for construction and unused land. Land for agriculture includes cultivated land, plantation land, forestland, grassland and waters. Land for construction includes land for residential purpose, for manufacturing and mining, for transportation and for water-conservancy projects. Unused land refers to land other than land for agriculture and construction, including beaches, deserts, Gobi, glaciers and rock mountains.

Cultivated Land refers to land mainly for the regular cultivation of farm crops (including vegetables), with some fruit trees, mulberry trees and others, covers cultivated land, newly-developed land, reclaimed land, consolidated land, fallow, beach land that can guarantee one harvest per year on average. It also covers fixed ditch, canal, road and sill (ridge) with width less than 1 meter in the South and 2 meters in the North, lands planted temporarily with herbs, grass, flowers and nursery stocks, and other cultivated land with temporary change of use.

Garden Land refers to land for intensive cultivation of perennial woody plants and herbs to collect fruits, leaves, roots, stems and juice, with a covering rate over 50% and plant number per mu over 70% of rational plant number. Land for nursery is included.

Forestland refers to land for planting arbor, bamboo, bush shrub and land in coastal zones for planting mangrove. It includes slash, but not the green belts in residential area, forests requested for railway and highway, and the dike protection forest around rivers and ditches.

Pastureland refers to land mainly for the growth of herbs.

Mineral Resources refer to useful minerals, with solid state, liquid state, gaseity, due to the geological process. Minerals are important natural resources, and important material base for social development. At present, there are more than 170 types of minerals discovered in China. They can be categorized into four groups: energy producing minerals (including coal, petroleum, natural gas and terrestrial heat), metallic minerals (including iron, manganese, copper, lead and bauxite), non metallic minerals (including diamond, limestone and clay), and water/gas related minerals (including ground water, mineral water and carbon dioxide). Metallic minerals can be further classified as ferrous, non-ferrous, noble metal, rare metal, rare earth metal and dispersed metals.

Ensured Mineral Reserves refer to the actual mineral reserves, which equal to the proven mineral reserves (including industrial reserves and prospective reserves) minus extracted parts and underground losses.

Average Temperature refers to the air temperature. China uses centigrade as the unit. The thermometry used for weather observation is put in a breezy shutter, which is 1.5 meters high from the ground. Therefore, the commonly used temperature refers to the temperature in the breezy shutter 1.5 meters away from the ground. The calculation method is as follows:

Monthly average temperature is the summation of average daily temperature of one month divided by the actual days of that particular month.

Annual average temperature is the summation of monthly average of a year divided by 12 months.

Volume of Precipitation refers to the deepness of liquid state or solid state (thawed) water falling from the sky to the ground that has not been evaporated, infiltrated or run off. The calculation method is as follows:

Monthly precipitation is the summation of daily precipitation of a month.

Annual precipitation is the summation of 12 months precipitation of a year.

Annual Sunshine Hours refer to the actual hours of sun irradiating the earth, usually expressed in hours. The calculation method is the same as that of the precipitation.

Total Water Resources refers to total volume of surface water and groundwater and is measured as run-off for surface water and replenishment of groundwater with rainfall in local area.

Surface Water Resources refers to total volume of year by year renewable dynamic resources which exist in rivers, lakes, glaciers and other surface water and are the natural run-off of rivers.

Groundwater Resources refers to total volume of year by year renewable dynamic resources which exist in saturation acquifers of groundwater and are measured as replenishment of groundwater with rainfall and surface water.

Duplicated Measurement between Surface Water and Groundwater refers to mutual exchange between surface water and groundwater, i.e. run-off of rivers includes some depletion into groundwater while groundwater includes some replenishment from surface water.

Water Supply refers to gross water of various sources supplied to consumers, including losses during distribution.

Surface Water Supply refers to withdrawals by surface water supply system, broken down with storage, flow, pumping and transfer. Supply from storage projects includes withdrawals from reservoirs; supply from flow includes withdrawals from rivers and lakes with natural flows no matter if there are locks or not; supply from pumping projects includes withdrawals from rivers or lakes with pumping stations; and supply from transfer refers to water supplies transferred from first-level regions of water resources or independent river drainage areas to others, and should not be covered under supplies of storage, flow and pumping.

Groundwater Supply refers to withdrawals from supplying wells, broken down with shallow layer freshwater, deep layer freshwater and slightly brackish water. Groundwater supply for urban areas includes water mining by both waterworks and own wells of enterprises.

Other Water Supply Sources include supplies by waste-water treatment, rain collection, seawater desalinization and other water projects.

Water Use refers to gross water used by various water users, including losses during distribution.

Water Use by Agriculture includes uses of water by irrigation of farming fields, forestry and orchards, irrigation of grassland, replenishment of fishing farms and water used by animal husbandry.

Water Use by Industry refers to new withdrawals of water, excluding reuse of water within enterprises.

Water Use by Living Consumption includes use of water for living consumption in both urban and rural areas. Urban water use by living consumption is composed of household use and public use (including tertiary industry and construction). Rural water use by living consumption includes water used by households.

Water Use by Ecological and Environmental Protection includes replenishment of rivers and lakes and use for urban environment.

Common Industrial Solid Wastes Produced refers to the industrial solid wastes that are not listed in the 《National Catalogue of Hazardous Wastes》, or not regarded as hazardous according to the national hazardous waste identification standards (GB5085), solid waste-Extraction procedure for leaching toxicity (GB5086) and solid waste-Extraction procedure for leaching toxicity (GB/T 15555). The calculation formula is as followed:

Common Industrial Solid Wastes Produced = (common industrial solid wastes utilized – the proportion of utilized stock of previous years) + common industrial solid waste stock + (common industrial solid wastes disposed – the proportion of disposed stock of previous years) + common industrial solid wastes discharged.

Common Industrial Solid Wastes Comprehensively Utilized refers to volume of solid wastes from which useful materials can be extracted or which can be converted into usable resources, energy or other materials by means of reclamation, processing, recycling and exchange (including utilizing in the year the stocks of industrial solid wastes of the previous year) during the report period, e.g. being used as agricultural fertilizers, building materials or as material for paving road. Examples of such utilizations include fertilizers, building materials and road materials. The information shall be collected by the producing units of the wastes.

Common Industrial Solid Wastes Disposed refers to the quantity of industrial solid wastes which are burnt or specially disposed using other methods to alter the physical, chemical and biological properties and thus to reduce or eliminate the hazard, or placed ultimately in the sites meeting the requirements for environmental protection during the report period.

Stock of Common Industrial Solid Wastes refers to the volume of solid wastes placed in special facilities or special sites by enterprises for purposes of utilization or disposal during the report period. The sites or facilities should take measures against dispersion, loss, seepage, and air and water contamination.

Common Industrial Solid Wastes Discharged refers to the volume of industrial solid wastes dumped or discharged by producing enterprises to disposal facilities or to other sites.

Consumption Wastes Transported refers to volume of consumption wastes collected and transported to disposal factories or sites during the reference period. Consumption wastes are solid wastes produced from urban households or from service activities for urban households, and solid wastes regarded by laws and regulations as urban consumption wastes, including those from households, commercial activities, markets, cleaning of streets, public sites, offices, schools, factories, mining units and other sources.

Ratio of Consumption Wastes Treated refers to consumption wastes treated over that produced. In practical statistics, as it is difficult to estimate, the volume of consumption wastes produced is replaced with that transported. It is calculated as:

$$\text{Ratio of consumption wastes treated} = \frac{\text{consumption wastes treated}}{\text{consumption wastes produced}} \times 100\%$$

Forest Area refers to the area of trees and bamboo grow with a canopy density above 0.2 degree, the area of shrubby tree according to regulations of the government, the area of forest land inside farm land and the area of trees planted by the side of villages, farm houses and along roads and rivers.

Area of Man-made Forests refer to the area of stable growing forests, planted manually or by airplanes, with a survival rate of 80% or higher of the designed number of trees per hectare, or with a canopy density of 0.20 degree or above after 3-5 years of manual planting or 5-7 years of airplane planting.

Forest Coverage Rate Taking the administrative jurisdiction as the unit, the percentage of area of afforested land to the area of total land. The formula for calculating forest coverage rate is as follows:

$$\text{Forestry coverage rate} = \frac{\text{Area of Afforested Land}}{\text{Area of Total Land}} \times 100\%$$

Total Standing Stock Volume refers to the total stock volume of trees growing in land, including trees in forest, trees in sparse forest, scattered trees and trees planted by the side of villages, farm houses and along roads and rivers.

Stock Volume of Forest refers to total stock volume of wood growing in forest area, which shows the total size and level of forest resources of a country or a region.

Area of Afforestation refers to the total area of land suitable for afforestation, including barren hills, idle land, sand dunes, non-timber forest land, woodland and "grain for green" land, on which acres of forests, trees and shrubs are planted through manual planting.

Manual Planting refers to technical measures of sowing, planting seedlings and divided transplanting on land suitable for afforestation, including barren hills, idle land, sand dunes, non-timber forest land, woodland and "grain for green" land to increase vegetation coverage rate of forests.

No-stocked Land and Sparse Forest Land Newly Closed for Afforestation This Year refers to the area of sparse forest land, brush shrub land, stump land, burned land, barren hills, barren land, sand dunes where trees can naturally grow or sprout, which are demarcated, closed down and returned to forest, shrubbery and grass land with the assistance of special measures by men.

Timber Forests refer to forests which are mainly for the production of timber, including bamboo groves planted to harvest bamboos.

By-product Forests refer to forests that mainly produce fruits, nuts, edible oil, beverages, indigents, raw materials and medicine materials. By-product forests are planted to harvest the fruits, leaves, bark or liquid of trees, and consume them as food or raw materials for the manufacturing industry, such as tea-oil trees, tung oil trees, walnut trees, camphor trees, tea bushes, mulberry trees, fruit trees, etc.

Protection Forests refer to forests, trees and bushes planted mainly for protection or preservation purpose, including water resource conservation forests, water and soil conservation forests, windbreak and dune-fixing forests, farmland and pasture protection forests, riverside protection forests, roadside protection forests, etc.

Fuel Forests refer to forests planted mainly for fuels.

Forests for Special Purpose refer to forests planted mainly for national defence, environment protection or scientific experiments, including national defence forests, experimental forests, mother-tree forests, environment protection forests, scenery forests, trees in historical or scenic spots, forests in natural reserves.

Projects on Protection Forests in North China and Yangtze River Basin covering the widest areas in China with a rich variety of contents, these projects aim at solving the problem of sand and dust in northeastern China, northern China and northwestern China and the ecological issues in other areas. More specifically, they include phase IV of Project on North China protection forests, phase II of Project on protection forests at the middle and lower streams of Yangtze River and at the Huihe River and Taihu Lake valley, phase II of Project on coastal protection forests, phase II of Project on Pearl River protection forests, phase II Project on greenery of Taihang Mountain and phase II Projects on greenery of plains.

Wetlands refer to marshland and peat bog, whether natural or man-made, permanent or temporary; water covered areas, whether stagnant or flowing, with fresh or semi-fresh or salty water that is less than 6 meters deep at low tide; as well as coral beach, weed beach, mud beach, mangrove, river outlet, rivers, fresh-water marshland, marshland forests, lakes, salty bog and salt lakes along the coastal areas.

Natural Reserves refer to number of certain areas of land, or waters that have been set aside and put under special protection and management in order to protect natural environment and natural resources, and promote the sustainable development of national economy. They are subject to formal approval from governments of various levels. According to the protected targets, natural reserves can be divided into three categories: reserves of natural ecological system, natural reserves of wildlife species, and natural heritage of historical significance.Scenic spots and cultural preservation zones are not included.

Number of Forest Fires refers to the number of fires in forests, woods and woodland outside of the downtown areas of cities. In light of the area plagued by fires and the number of casualties, forest fires can be categorized into usual forest fires, relatively larger fires, serious forest fires and extraordinary serous forest fires: 1). Usual forest fires: the destructed forest area is less than 1 hectare, or the fire erupts in other woodland, or the number of deaths is no less than 1 but less than 3, or the number of seriously injured persons is no less than 1 but less than 10 persons. 2). Relatively larger forest fires: the destructed forest area is no less than 1 hectare but less than 100 hectares, or the number of deaths is no less than 3 but less than 10, or the number of seriously injured persons is no less than 10 but less than 50 persons. 3). Serious forest fires: the destructed forest area is no less than 100 hectares but less than 1000 hectares, or the number of deaths is no less than 10 but less than 30, or the number of seriously injured persons is no less than 50 but u less than 100 persons. 4). Extraordinary serious forest fires: the destructed forest area is no less than 1000 hectares, or the number of deaths is no less than 30, or the number of seriously injured persons is no less than 100 persons.

Forest Diseases, Pest and Rat Plagues refers to the diseases, pests and rats that plague forests, woods, seedlings and timbers, and bamboos. Forest diseases refer to the plague of fungi, bacteria, virus, parasitic seed plants and nematode suffered by wood organism, which will cause pathologic changes in trees in terms of physiology function, cells, texture and shape. Forest pest plague means wood organism is plagued by pests such as pine moth, leaf beetle, bamboo locust, cockchafer, and mole cricket that damage a certain area of forest, and slow down the growth or cause them to die. Forest rat plague means the forest, trees, seedlings are damaged by rats, resulting in a certain amount of loss or death.

Number of Earthquakes the number of earthquakes of all magnitude that cause damages (including casualties or economic losses).

7

能源生产和消费

PRODUCTION AND CONSUMPTION OF ENERGY

简要说明

本篇主要内容和资料来源

本篇包括的主要内容有能源生产、消费总量及品种构成，综合能源平衡表和主要能源品种单项平衡表，分行业、分主要能源品种的消费量，能源生产和消费弹性系数，能源加工转换效率及生活用能源消费量等。

从2006年度开始，能源生产、消费等指标需经国家审定后方可公布，因国家审定、公布各省的这部分指标数据为每年的八月份，时间在年鉴出版时间之后，为此，这部分数据采取错年上，即2013年上2012年数据。

本篇资料由新疆维吾尔自治区统计局能源与资源统计处依据能源年报整理提供。

Brief Introduction

Main Content and Source of Data

Data in this chapter cover mainly the energy production and consumption and their composition, the overall balance of energy and the balance by different types of energy, the consumption of energy by sector and by types of energy the elasticity ratio of energy production and consumption, efficiency of energy conversion and the consumption of energy for non-production uses.

Since 2006, data on production and consumption of energy are announced after NBS authorized. Time of publication is August every year. So the data on energy in 2013 Statistical Yearbook is data in 2012.

Data in this chapter are provided and processed in accordance with the statistical reporting scheme on energy by the Department of Industry and Transport of the Xinjiang Bureau of Statistics.

7-1 主要年份能源生产总量及构成
Total Production of Energy and Its Composition in Main Years

年份 Year	能源生产总量 (万吨标准煤) Total Energy Production (10 000 tons of SCE)	占能源生产总量的比重(%) Percentage of Total Energy Production (%)			
		原煤 Coal	原油 Crude Oil	天然气 Natural Gas	水风电 Hydro- Power and Wind Power
1978	1410.75	60.0	35.8	2.4	1.8
1980	1527.72	58.4	36.5	3.1	2.0
1985	2092.47	60.0	34.1	3.5	2.4
1990	2801.57	58.8	35.8	2.4	3.0
1995	4266.06	50.1	43.5	3.6	2.8
2000	5419.77	40.6	48.7	7.9	2.8
2001	5720.04	38.7	48.6	9.7	3.0
2002	6156.05	39.5	47.3	10.5	2.7
2003	6657.43	41.1	46.0	10.2	2.7
2004	7112.95	41.4	45.3	10.7	2.6
2005	8175.74	37.9	42.1	17.3	2.7
2006	9528.72	37.3	37.1	22.9	2.7
2007	10735.84	36.7	34.7	26.0	2.6
2008	12669.13	41.9	30.6	24.8	2.7
2009	13542.33	46.5	26.5	24.1	2.9
2010	14696.76	49.2	24.9	22.6	3.3
2011	16117.37	54.1	23.2	19.4	3.3
2012	17744.42	55.7	21.5	19.0	3.8

注：电力折算标准煤的系数根据当年平均发电煤耗计算，并将历史资料做了调整，下表同。

Note: The coefficient for conversion of electric power into SCE (standard coal equivalent) is calculated on the basic of the data on the average coal consumption in generating electric power in the same year. The same is as in the following tables.

7-2 主要年份能源消费总量及构成
Total Consumption of Energy and Its Composition in Main Years

年份 Year	能源消费总量 (万吨标准煤) Total Energy Consumption (10 000 tons of SCE)	占能源消费总量的比重(%) As percentage of Total Energy Consumption (%)			
		煤炭 Coal	石油 Crude Oil	天然气 Natural Gas	水风电 Hydro- Power and Wind Power
1978	979.27	72.5	21.5	3.4	2.6
1980	1026.45	71.3	21.1	4.6	3.0
1985	1410.84	72.0	19.3	5.1	3.6
1990	1924.38	69.6	22.5	3.5	4.4
1995	2733.04	66.2	23.8	5.6	4.4
2000	3316.03	63.6	23.3	8.6	4.5
2001	3496.44	60.4	21.6	13.2	4.8
2002	3622.40	62.2	20.5	12.7	4.6
2003	4064.43	60.3	21.7	13.1	4.9
2004	4784.83	61.0	20.1	15.0	3.9
2005	5506.49	56.1	26.2	13.7	4.0
2006	6047.27	56.7	24.7	14.3	4.3
2007	6575.92	57.8	23.9	14.1	4.2
2008	7069.39	61.7	20.3	13.1	4.9
2009	7525.56	65.9	16.9	12.0	5.2
2010	8290.20	65.8	15.8	12.4	5.6
2011	9926.50	67.9	14.7	12.3	5.1
2012	11831.62	68.4	14.4	11.5	5.7

7-3 主要年份分品种生活能源年消费总量

Average Annual Energy Consumption for Household by Variety in Main Years

年 份 Year	合 计 (万吨标准煤) Total (10 000 tons of SCE)	煤 炭 (万吨) Coal (10 000 tons)	煤 油 (万吨) Kerosene (10 000 tons)	液化石油气 (万吨) Liquefied Petroleum Gas (10 000 tons)	天然气 (亿立方米) Natural Gas (100 million cu.m)	热 力 (万百万千焦) Heat (10 billion kilo-joule)	电 力 (亿千瓦小时) Electricity (100 million kwh)
1980	330.44	404.10					1.70
1985	355.65	421.72	0.71	3.00			2.38
1990	428.04	479.37	0.58	5.35		160.02	4.22
1995	499.84	527.00	0.50	8.94		177.29	10.11
2000	650.91	590.00	0.75	10.89	0.13	1611.81	17.60
2001	703.97	600.00	0.67	12.31	0.46	2209.66	19.50
2002	752.10	610.00	0.10	14.22	0.32	3112.58	19.20
2003	782.21	625.04		16.62	0.60	3191.14	20.37
2004	901.88	605.00		17.00	1.00	3363.45	24.26
2005	978.54	500.79	0.55	12.96	1.92	6219.00	27.10
2006	612.66	211.00	0.55	14.10	2.60	5008.00	31.90
2007	652.36	213.00	0.42	14.53	2.70	5097.43	33.52
2008	752.73	232.20	0.35	11.60	2.89	7371.00	38.55
2009	855.56	255.00	0.35	13.50	3.90	9073.84	42.62
2010	831.13	252.00	0.34	12.30	4.60	10511.04	47.10
2011	925.38	256.00	0.34	11.42	5.71	12103.27	55.15
2012	992.04	255.00	0.35	11.25	5.79	12795.81	61.94

注：表 7-12 和 7-13 中，2006 年以前数据未按新口径进行调整。
Note: Figures in table 7-12 and 7-13 did not adjusted at new coverage, except for figures in 2006.

7-4 主要年份每人年平均生活用能源

Annual Per-Capital Energy Consumption of Households in Main Years

年 份 Year	平均每人生活消费能源 (公斤标准煤/人) Annual Per Capita Consumption for Household (kg of SCE/person)	煤 炭 (公斤) Coal (kg)	电 力 (千瓦小时) Electricity (kwh)	煤 油 (公斤) Kerosene (kg)	液化石油气 (公斤) Liquefied Petroleum Gas (kg)	天然气 (立方米) Natural Gas (cu.m)
1980	258	315	13.25			
1985	261	310	17.49	0.52	2.20	
1990	268	313	27.60	0.38	3.50	
1995	301	317	65.60	0.30	5.33	
2000	353	320	95.33	0.41	5.90	0.70
2001	375	320	103.93	0.36	6.56	2.45
2002	395	320	100.78	0.05	7.46	1.68
2003	404	323	105.33		8.59	3.10
2004	459	308	123.58		8.66	5.09
2005	487	249	134.80	0.27	6.45	9.55
2006	302	104	157.13	0.27	6.95	12.81
2007	311	102	159.99	0.20	6.93	12.89
2008	352	109	180.92	0.16	5.44	13.56
2009	396	118	197.44	0.16	6.25	18.07
2010	381	115	215.90	0.16	5.64	21.09
2011	419	116	249.69	0.15	5.17	25.85
2012	426	114	277.41	0.16	5.04	25.93

7-5 主要年份综合能源平衡表
Overall Energy Balance Sheet in Main Years

单位:万吨标准煤 (10 000 tons of SCE)

项　　目	Item	1990	2000	2005	2010	2012
可供消费的能源总量	**Total Energy Available for Consumption**	**2045.32**	**3430.05**	**5349.17**	**8290.20**	**11093.79**
一次能源生产量	Primary Energy Output	2801.57	5419.77	8175.74	14696.76	17744.42
进口量	Imports		107.39	130.80	1419.77	1536.25
外省调入量	Inflow from other Provinces (Autonomons Regions and Municipalities)	2.26	25.59	58.17	175.17	
出口量(-)	Exports (-)	4.84	31.90	60.80	19.89	19.03
本区调出量(-)	Outflow (-)	694.89	2144.79	3172.41	7825.83	8142.57
年初年末库存差额	Stock Changes in the Year	-58.78	53.99	95.71	-171.00	-25.28
能源消费总量	**Total Energy Consumption**	**1924.45**	**3316.03**	**5506.49**	**8290.20**	**11831.62**
在总量中：	Consumption by Sector					
农、林、牧、渔、水利业	Farming, Forestry, Animal Husbandry, Fishery and Water Conservancy	134.91	274.97	314.25	408.45	529.32
工　业	Industry	1095.22	1860.26	3440.83	5958.10	8894.94
建筑业	Construction	41.16	81.73	43.22	74.07	112.65
交通运输和邮电通讯业	Transportation, Post and Telecommunications Services	99.72	189.76	413.77	632.52	855.39
商业、饮食、物资供销和仓储业	Commerce, Catering Services, Materials Supply, Marketing and Storage	26.28	93.83	138.39	175.97	198.87
其　他	Others	99.12	164.57	177.51	214.67	248.41
生活消费	Residential Consumption	428.04	650.91	978.54	826.42	992.04
在总量中：	Consumption by Usage					
终端消费	End-use Consumption	1825.44	3148.77	5086.96	7240.48	10685.32
#工　业	Industry	996.27	1692.96	3021.27	5018.73	7862.93
加工转换损失量	Losses During the Process of Energy Conversion	27.90	91.25	228.26	700.56	714.80
#炼　焦	Coking	13.00	72.05	77.60	303.82	350.66
炼　油	Petroleum Refining	13.16	75.99	62.18	70.58	100.89
损失量	Energy Losses	71.05	76.05	191.27	317.21	431.51
平衡差额	**Balance**	**120.87**	**114.02**	**-157.32**		**-737.84**

注：1.村办工业包括在工业中(下同)。
2.电力、热力按等价热值折算，因此加工转换损失量中不包括发电、供热损失量。
3.进口量包括新疆飞机在国外加油量，出口量包括外国飞机在新疆的加油量。

Note: a) Data on industry includes the data of village-run industry. (The same is as in the following tables).
b) Electric power and heat are converted on the basic of equal caloric value. Therefore, losses in processing and transformation exclude losses in power generation and heating.
c) Data on imports include the petroleum consumed by the Xinjiang airplanes in refueling abroad. Data on exports include the petroleum consumed by the foreign airplanes in refueling in Xinjiang.

7-6 主要年份石油平衡表
Petroleum Balance Sheet in Main Years

单位:万吨 (10 000 tons)

项 目	Item	1990	2000	2005	2010	2012
可供量	**Total Energy Available for Consumption**	**333.19**	**616.14**	**1021.31**	**870.91**	**1166.03**
生产量	Output	701.26	1848.43	2408.32	2558.16	2670.68
进口量	Imports		75.16	91.54	993.43	1061.84
外省调入量	Inflow from other Provinces (Autonomons Regions and Municipalities)	1.44	10.85	14.85		
出口量(-)	Exports (-)	3.29	11.17	5.18	1.08	4.55
本区调出量(-)	Outflow (-)	353.59	1285.38	1525.72	2680.23	2502.91
年初年末库存差额	Stock Changes in the Year	-12.63	-21.75	37.50	0.63	-59.03
消费量	**Total Energy Consumption**	**300.16**	**527.71**	**1014.84**	**869.56**	**1166.03**
在消费量中：	Consumption by Sector					
农、林、牧、渔、水利业	Farming, Forestry, Animal Husbandry, Fishery and Water Conservancy	42.46	63.65	70.68	71.27	81.45
工 业	Industry	171.96	273.95	611.18	294.96	440.73
建筑业	Construction	16.87	32.10	15.36	23.81	28.27
交通运输和邮电通讯业	Transportation, Post and Telecommunications Services	48.30	86.89	210.00	363.79	493.67
商业、饮食、物资供销和仓储业	Commerce, Catering Services, Materials Supply, Marketing and Storage	3.66	18.78	31.91	39.55	40.80
其 他	Others	8.48	32.70	46.20	44.91	47.31
生活消费	Residential Consumption	8.43	19.64	29.51	31.27	33.80
在消费量中：	Consumption by Sector					
终端消费	Final Consumption	257.06	457.99	936.88	687.99	996.47
#工 业	Industry	128.86	204.23	533.22	193.65	351.17
中间消费(用于加工转换)	Intermediate Consumption	15.69	17.34	47.37	101.31	89.56
#发 电	Power Generation	15.69	2.10	8.65	13.31	6.04
供 热	Heating		1.24	1.04	27.43	14.25
此外：当年炼油投入量	Petroleum Refining Input	464.29	1001.32	1531.68	2182.96	2465.27
平衡差额	**Balance**	**33.03**	**88.43**	**6.47**		

注：1.生产量为原油产量。
2.进口量包括新疆飞机在国外加油量，出口量包括外国飞机在新疆的加油量。

Note: a) Data on output refer to the output of crude oil.
b) Data on imports include the petroleum consumed by the Xinjiang Airplanes in refueling abroad. Data on exports include the petroleum consumed by the foreign airplanes in refueling in Xinjiang.

7-7 主要年份电力平衡表
Electricity Balance Sheet in Main Years

单位:亿千瓦小时 (100 million kwh)

项　目	Item	1990	2000	2005	2010	2012
可供量	**Total Energy Available for Consumption**	**69.79**	**182.98**	**310.14**	**675.56**	**1151.50**
生产量	Output	69.79	182.98	310.14	679.32	1188.26
水　电	Hydropower	14.25	30.54	46.49	97.07	139.62
风　电	Wind Power	0.08	1.73	2.32	31.34	46.35
火　电	Thermal Power	55.46	150.71	261.33	550.91	1002.29
消费量	**Total Energy Consumption**	**69.79**	**182.98**	**310.14**	**675.56**	**1151.50**
在消费量中:	Consumption by Sector					
农、林、牧、渔、水利业	Farming, Forestry, Animal Husbandry, Fishery and Water Conservancy	9.16	22.30	28.72	61.12	90.66
工　业	Industry	48.86	118.85	221.67	508.54	915.28
建筑业	Construction	1.18	3.50	1.44	6.86	14.09
交通运输和邮电通讯业	Transportation, Post and Telecommunications Services	1.48	4.00	4.74	6.68	10.17
商业、饮食、物资供销和仓储业	Commerce, Catering Services, Materials Supply, Marketing and Storage	0.81	6.90	11.09	16.74	21.17
其　他	Others	4.08	9.83	15.38	28.52	38.19
生活消费	Residential Consumption	4.22	17.60	27.10	47.10	61.94
在消费量中:	Consumption by Sector					
终端消费	Final Consumption	65.74	170.86	282.42	622.31	1064.08
#工　业	Industry	44.81	106.73	193.95	455.29	827.86
输配电损失量	Losses in Transmission	4.05	12.12	27.72	53.25	87.42

7-8 分行业能源消费总量和主要能源消费量

(2012 年)

行业	Sector	能源消费总量（万吨标准煤） Total Energy Consumption (10 000 tons of SCE)	煤炭消费量（万吨） Coal Consumption (10 000 tons)	焦炭消费量（万吨） Coke Consumption (10 000 tons)
消费总量	**Total Consumption**	**11831.62**	**11867.27**	**1011.07**
农、林、牧、渔业	**Farming, Forestry, Animal Husbandry, and Fishery**	**529.32**	**103.00**	
工　业	**Industry**	**8894.94**	**11344.27**	**1011.07**
采 矿 业	**Mining and Quarrying**	**1481.25**	**715.53**	**27.82**
煤炭开采和洗选业	Mining and Washing of Coal	399.17	566.73	22.64
石油和天然气开采业	Extraction of Petroleum and Natural Gas	873.92	82.20	
黑色金属矿采选业	Mining and Processing of Ferrous Metals Ores	78.31	34.53	1.04
有色金属矿采选业	Mining and Processing of Nonferrous Metals Ores	36.98	13.11	2.16
非金属矿采选业	Mining and Processing of Non-metal Ores	17.40	13.94	1.98
开采辅助活动	Mining Support Activities	75.48	5.02	
其他采矿业	Mining of Other Ores			
制 造 业	**Manufacturing**	**6279.14**	**5632.75**	**983.25**
农副食品加工业	Processing of Food from Agricultural Products	110.70	115.87	3.35
食品制造业	Manufacture of Food	78.70	75.38	
酒、饮料和精制茶制造业	Manufacture of Wine,Beverage,Refined Tea	23.76	17.43	
烟草制品业	Manufacture of Tobacco	1.28	0.95	
纺织业	Manufacture of Textile	82.48	21.31	
纺织服装、鞋、帽制造业	Manufacture of Textile Wearing Apparel,Footware and Caps	0.44	0.31	
皮革、毛皮、羽绒及其制品业	Manufacture of Leather, Fur, Feather and Related Products	0.50	0.37	
木材加工及木、竹、藤、棕、草制品业	Timber Production, Wood, Bamboo, Cane and Grass	13.12	14.10	
家具制造业	Manufacture of Furniture	1.06	0.65	
造纸及纸制品业	Manufacture of Paper and Paper Products	29.12	32.60	
印刷和记录媒介复制业	Printing and Copying of Medium for Record	0.60		
文教、工美、体育和娱乐用品制造业	Manufacture of Articles for Culture,Art,Sport and Entertainment Activities	0.26		
石油加工、炼焦及核燃料加工业	Processing of Oil Processing, Coking and Nuclear Fuel	1406.43	2543.36	

Consumption of Total Energy and Its Main Varieties by Sector

原油消费量（万吨） Crude Oil Consumption (10 000 tons)	汽油消费量（万吨） Gasoline Consumption (10 000 tons)	煤油消费量（万吨） Kerosene Consumption (10 000 tons)	柴油消费量（万吨） Diesel Oil Consumption (10 000 tons)	燃料油消费量（万吨） Fuel Oil Consumption (10 000 tons)	天然气消费量（亿立方米） Natural Gas Consumption (100 million cu.m)	电力消费量（亿千瓦小时） Electricity Consumption (100 million kwh)
2602.85	**164.73**	**45.36**	**473.35**	**8.06**	**101.95**	**1151.50**
	9.90	**0.45**	**70.00**		**0.02**	**90.66**
2522.85	**8.01**	**0.04**	**79.71**	**8.06**	**89.75**	**915.28**
102.39	**3.51**		**55.26**	**0.04**	**55.72**	**82.82**
	0.79		14.41		0.01	24.83
102.38	1.66		1.98		54.94	37.16
	0.14		5.21		0.25	10.76
	0.10		1.32			7.38
	0.02		1.18			0.81
0.01	0.80		31.16	0.04	0.52	1.88
2420.44	**2.87**	**0.02**	**23.59**	**7.99**	**31.19**	**625.48**
	0.36		0.49		0.04	7.43
	0.20		0.45		0.10	4.92
	0.08		0.05		0.07	1.88
	0.02					0.14
	0.16		0.06		0.01	17.38
	0.01					0.05
	0.01		0.01			0.05
			0.08			1.14
	0.02		0.02			0.12
	0.03		0.04	0.01		2.25
	0.03		0.01			0.10
						0.03
2420.44	0.25	0.02	1.21	7.98	12.31	53.22

7-8 续表

行　业	Sector	能源消费总量(万吨标准煤) Total Energy Consumption (10 000 tons of SCE)	煤炭消费量(万吨) Coal Consumption (10 000 tons)	焦炭消费量(万吨) Coke Consumption (10 000 tons)
化学原料及化学制品制造业	Manufacture of Raw Chemical Material and Chemical Products	1498.64	1046.44	231.56
医药制造业	Manufacture of Medicine	7.32	7.42	
化学纤维制造业	Manufacture of Chemical Fiber	114.11	142.58	
橡胶和塑料制品业	Manufacture of Rubber and Plastics	29.58	8.36	
非金属矿物制品业	Manufacture of Non-metallic Mineral Products	819.42	723.93	1.05
黑色金属冶炼及压延加工业	Smelting and Pressing of Ferrous Metals	1326.40	765.69	736.62
有色金属冶炼及压延加工业	Smelting and Pressing of Non-ferrous Metals	638.64	9.93	5.88
金属制品业	Metal Products Manufacturing	12.59	2.65	4.74
通用设备制造业	Manufacture of General Purpose Machinery	0.96	0.31	
专用设备制造业	Manufacture of Special Purpose Machinery	3.01	0.60	0.05
汽车制造业	Manufacture of Automobile	1.41	0.03	
铁路、船舶、航空航天和其他运输设备制造业	Manufacture of Railroads,Ships,Aerospace and Other Transportation Equipment	0.04		
电气机械和器材制造业	Manufacture of Electric Equipment and Machinery	9.80	83.84	
通信设备、计算机及其他电子设备制造业	Communication Equipment, Computer and Other Electronic Equipment	62.56	15.17	
仪器仪表制造业	Manufacture of Measuring Instruments	0.05		
其他制造业	Other Manufacturing Sector	1.31		
废弃资源综合利用业	Recycling and Disposal of Waste	4.70	3.47	
金属制品、机械和设备修理业	Repair of Metal Products,Machinery and Equipment	0.15		
电力、燃气及水的生产和供应业	**Electric Power, Gas and Water Production and Supply**	**1134.56**	**4995.99**	
电力、热力的生产和供应业	Production and Distribution of Power, Steam and Hot Water	1121.11	4989.02	
燃气生产和供应业	Production and Supply of Gas	8.80	6.72	
水的生产和供应业	Production and Supply of Water	4.65	0.25	
建筑业	**Construction**	**112.65**	**25.00**	
交通运输储运业和邮政业	**Transport, Storage and Post**	**855.39**	**51.00**	
批发、零售业和住宿、餐饮业	**Wholesale and Retail Trades,Hotel**	**198.87**	**49.00**	
其他行业	**Others**	**248.41**	**40.00**	
生活消费	**Household Consumption**	**992.04**	**255.00**	

Continued

原油消费量 (万吨) Crude Oil Consumption (10 000 tons)	汽油消费量 (万吨) Gasoline Consumption (10 000 tons)	煤油消费量 (万吨) Kerosene Consumption (10 000 tons)	柴油消费量 (万吨) Diesel Oil Consumption (10 000 tons)	燃料油消费量 (万吨) Fuel Oil Consumption (10 000 tons)	天然气消费量 (亿立方米) Natural Gas Consumption (100 million cu.m)	电力消费量 (亿千瓦小时) Electricity Consumption (100 million kwh)
	0.44		3.28		17.70	190.51
	0.03		0.02		0.01	0.30
	0.04		0.07			7.78
	0.10		0.08		0.04	4.25
	0.44		11.74		0.51	67.02
	0.16		4.77		0.29	77.21
	0.11		0.68		0.02	171.20
	0.13		0.21		0.05	1.13
	0.05		0.02			0.12
	0.08		0.04			0.41
	0.01		0.06		0.03	0.08
						0.01
	0.08		0.04		0.01	1.34
	0.02		0.06			14.52
						0.01
			0.07			0.33
			0.01			0.54
	0.01		0.02			0.01
0.02	**1.63**	**0.02**	**0.86**	**0.03**	**2.84**	**206.98**
0.02	1.52	0.02	0.76	0.03	2.62	204.90
	0.06		0.08		0.21	0.95
	0.05		0.02		0.01	1.13
	3.32	**0.17**	**14.50**		**0.03**	**14.09**
80.00	**98.00**	**44.00**	**251.00**		**4.51**	**10.17**
	10.80	**0.05**	**25.00**		**1.40**	**21.17**
	20.80	**0.30**	**24.90**		**0.45**	**38.19**
	13.90	**0.35**	**8.24**		**5.79**	**61.94**

7-9 主要年份能源生产弹性系数
Elasticity Ration of Energy Production in Main Years

年 份 Year	能源生产比上年增长(%) Growth Rate of Energy Production Over Preceding Year(%)	电力生产比上年增长(%) Growth Rate of Electricity Production over Preceding Year(%)	新疆生产总值比上年增长(%) Growth Rate of Gross Domestic Product (GDP) Over Preceding Year(%)	能源生产弹性系数 Elasticity Cofficient of Energy Production	电力生产弹性系数 Elasticity Ratio of Electricity Production
1980	7.8	3.6	7.2	1.08	0.50
1985	11.6	11.5	16.9	0.69	0.68
1990	5.8	10.8	11.7	0.50	0.92
1995	7.8	13.4	9.0	0.87	1.49
2000	3.3	8.1	8.2	0.40	0.99
2001	5.5	8.0	8.1	0.68	0.99
2002	7.6	7.4	8.1	0.94	0.91
2003	8.1	10.5	10.8	0.75	0.97
2004	6.8	13.3	11.1	0.61	1.20
2005	14.9	16.6	10.9	1.37	1.52
2006	16.6	15.2	11.0	1.51	1.38
2007	12.7	16.7	12.2	1.04	1.37
2008	18.0	16.0	11.0	1.64	1.45
2009	6.9	14.3	8.1	0.85	1.77
2010	8.5	21.4	10.6	0.80	2.02
2011	9.7	28.8	12.0	0.81	2.40
2012	10.1	35.8	12.0	0.84	2.98

注：新疆生产总值增速按可比价格计算，下表同。
Note: The growth rate of GDP in Xinjiang is calculated at comparable prices and the same as in the following tables.

7-10 主要年份能源消费弹性系数
Elasticity Ration of Energy Consumption in Main Years

年 份 Year	能源消费比上年增长(%) Growth Rate of Energy Consumption Over Preceding Year(%)	电力消费比上年增长(%) Growth Rate of Electricity Consumption over Preceding Year(%)	新疆生产总值比上年增长(%) Growth Rate of Gross Domestic Product (GDP) Over Preceding Year(%)	能源消费弹性系数 Elasticity Ration of Energy Consumption	电力消费弹性系数 Elasticity Ration of Electricity Consumption
1980	4.5	3.6	7.2	0.63	0.50
1985	13.6	11.5	16.9	0.80	0.68
1990	9.3	10.8	11.7	0.79	0.92
1995	4.9	13.4	9.0	0.54	1.49
2000	3.1	8.1	8.2	0.38	0.99
2001	5.4	8.0	8.1	0.67	0.99
2002	3.6	7.4	8.1	0.44	0.91
2003	12.2	10.5	10.8	1.13	0.97
2004	17.7	13.3	11.1	1.59	1.20
2005	15.1	16.6	10.9	1.39	1.52
2006	9.8	14.8	11.0	0.89	1.35
2007	8.7	16.0	12.2	0.71	1.31
2008	7.5	16.0	11.0	0.68	1.45
2009	6.5	14.3	8.1	0.80	1.77
2010	9.7	23.3	10.6	0.92	2.20
2011	20.2	24.2	12.0	1.68	2.02
2012	19.2	37.2	11.0	1.74	3.38

7-11 主要年份能源加工转换效率
Efficiency of Energy Procession and Conversion in Main Years

单位：% (%)

年 份 Year	总效率 Total Efficiency	发 电 Electricity Generation	供 热 Heating	炼 焦 Coking	炼 油 Petroleum Refining
1980	73.9	21.2		72.0	96.9
1985	74.9	21.1		75.5	98.1
1990	73.9	20.9	69.4	85.5	98.0
1995	72.7	23.6	71.2	78.6	96.6
2000	73.6	26.6	75.0	89.4	94.7
2001	73.7	26.1	74.6	78.2	97.4
2002	73.6	26.8	73.5	83.4	96.8
2003	73.8	26.0	78.0	92.0	97.9
2004	70.2	25.9	70.3	78.8	96.2
2005	72.3	27.0	77.7	75.7	97.1
2006	74.8	27.8	76.7	85.0	97.6
2007	73.3	28.6	73.5	86.3	96.4
2008	73.8	30.0	76.6	84.8	96.6
2009	73.5	30.4	77.4	82.2	96.3
2010	74.2	32.3	76.7	80.8	96.1
2011	74.0	33.5	76.0	81.2	97.0
2012	70.8	33.9	76.2	81.9	97.2

7-12 主要年份平均每天各种能源消费量
Average Daily Energy Consumption by Type of Energy in Main Years

能源品种	Variey of Energy	1990	2000	2005	2010	2012
总计(万吨标准煤)	**Total (10 000 tons of SCE)**	**5.41**	**9.09**	**15.09**	**22.63**	**32.42**
煤炭(万吨)	Coal (10 000 tons)	5.04	7.48	10.58	22.46	32.51
焦炭(万吨)	Coke (10 000 tons)	0.16	0.20	0.50	1.78	2.77
原油(万吨)	Crude Oil (10 000 tons)	1.33	2.94	4.46	6.32	7.13
燃料油(万吨)	Fuel Oil (10 000 tons)	0.25	0.16	0.50	0.04	0.02
汽油(万吨)	Gasoline (10 000 tons)	0.20	0.28	0.29	0.36	0.45
煤油(万吨)	Kerosene (10 000 tons)	0.01	0.06	0.07	0.09	0.12
柴油(万吨)	Diesel Oil (10 000 tons)	0.24	0.43	0.83	1.00	1.30
天然气(万立方米)	Natural Gas (10 000 cu.m)	137.53	642.19	1546.85	2195.89	2793.15
电力(亿千瓦时)	Electricity (100 million kwh)	0.19	0.50	0.85	1.85	3.15

7-13 各地、州、市规模以上工业企业能源消费量
Energy Consumption of Industry above Designated Size by Prefecture, Autonomous Prefecture and City

(2012 年)

能源品种	Item	合 计 Total	乌鲁木齐市 Urumqi City	克拉玛依市 Karamay City	吐鲁番地区 Turpan Administrative Offices
原煤(吨)	Coal (ton)	94205492	19675464	3777263	4322789
洗精煤(吨)	Washed Coal(ton)	6431121	3761531		
其他洗煤(吨)	Other Washed Coal (ton)	159213	84508		
焦炭(吨)	Coke (ton)	9923981	3912223		1342472
焦炉煤气(万立方米)	Coke Oven Gas (10 000 cu.m)	219674	160950		16778
高炉煤气(万立方米)	High Oven Gas (10 000 cu.m)	1189818	1189818		
天然气(万立方米)	Natural Gas (10 000 cu.m)	895399	144382	316847	69683
原油(吨)	Coal (ton)	24827892	5702395	14090466	217187
汽油(吨)	Gasoline (ton)	42597	11752	9554	1269
煤油(吨)	Kerosene (ton)	46	12		
柴油(吨)	Diesel Oil (ton)	566638	47965	215622	43320
燃料油(吨)	Fuel Oil (ton)	80517	79280	759	79
液化石油气(吨)	Liquefied Petroleum Gas (ton)	237627	5	141961	17220
炼厂干气(吨)	Refinary Dry Gas (ton)	1214246	156121	872006	
其他石油制品(吨)	Other Oil Product (ton)	580768	447680	2937	47449
热力(百万千焦)	Heat (million KJ)	87000679	26112311	28348684	1907382
电力(万千瓦时)	Electricity (10 000 kwh)	8292647	1847770	498803	413113
其他燃料(吨标准煤)	Other (ton of SCE)	142879	13935	2307	9623
能源合计(吨标准煤)	Energy Total (ton of SCE)	151112172	38312485	30570896	6795918

能源品种	Item	塔城地区 Tacheng [Tarbagatai] Administrative Office	阿勒泰地区 Altay Administrative Offices	巴音郭楞蒙古自治州 Bayangol Mongol Autonomous Prefecture	阿克苏地区 Aksu Administrative Offices
原煤(吨)	Coal (ton)	3764310	491925	3220093	7523837
洗精煤(吨)	Washed Coal (ton)			47105	912511
其他洗煤(吨)	Other Washed Coal (ton)			16238	28842
焦炭(吨)	Coke (ton)	19622	105395	1195761	50426
焦炉煤气(万立方米)	Coke Oven Gas (10 000 cu.m)				
高炉煤气(万立方米)	High Oven Gas (10 000 cu.m)				
天然气(万立方米)	Natural Gas (10 000 cu.m)			228926	117406
原油(吨)	Coal (ton)			662867	4110464
汽油(吨)	Gasoline (ton)	1510	1186	4602	2161
煤油(吨)	Kerosene (ton)				
柴油(吨)	Diesel Oil (ton)	8112	16288	43992	21169
燃料油(吨)	Fuel Oil (ton)			108	
液化石油气(吨)	Liquefied Petroleum Gas (ton)			60753	19
炼厂干气(吨)	Refinary Dry Gas (ton)			29165	156954
其他石油制品(吨)	Other Oil Product (ton)			5270	47028
热力(百万千焦)	Heat (million KJ)	1449914	660	13765475	2904334
电力(万千瓦时)	Electricity (10 000 kwh)	188485	102461	432492	310768
其他燃料(吨标准煤)	Other (ton of SCE)			20264	33670
能源合计(吨标准煤)	Energy Total (ton of SCE)	3033157	614386	8617738	15123091

注：各地区数含兵团工业在内。
Note:Figures in different prefectures include data of XPCG enterprises.

7-13 续表 Continued

能源品种	Item	哈密地区 Hami [kumul] Administrative Offices	昌吉回族自治州 Changji Hui Autonomous Prefecture	博尔塔拉蒙古自治州 Bortala Mongol Autonomous Prefecture	伊犁州直属县(市) Counties (Cities) Direct Under Ili Prefecture
原煤(吨)	Coal (ton)	6992458	23363225	734014	5539132
洗精煤(吨)	Washed Coal (ton)		846946		863028
其他洗煤(吨)	Other Washed Coal (ton)	25141			4484
焦炭(吨)	Coke (ton)	169563	822535	40557	831784
焦炉煤气(万立方米)	Coke Oven Gas (10 000 cu.m)		14345		27601
高炉煤气(万立方米)	High Oven Gas (10 000 cu.m)				
天然气(万立方米)	Natural Gas (10 000 cu.m)		5979		114
原油(吨)	Coal (ton)		44513		
汽油(吨)	Gasoline (ton)	1767	3236	528	2756
煤油(吨)	Kerosene (ton)		2		3
柴油(吨)	Diesel Oil (ton)	58406	51785	1926	35167
燃料油(吨)	Fuel Oil (ton)		1		
液化石油气(吨)	Liquefied Petroleum Gas (ton)			6	733
炼厂干气(吨)	Refinary Dry Gas (ton)				
其他石油制品(吨)	Other Oil Product (ton)		21610	605	8179
热力(百万千焦)	Heat (million KJ)		2567129	105578	548394
电力(万千瓦时)	Electricity (10 000 kwh)	200315	823661	49117	526115
其他燃料(吨标准煤)	Other (ton of SCE)				5047
能源合计(吨标准煤)	Energy Total (ton of SCE)	5040188	19664893	632553	6740844

能源品种	Item	克孜勒苏柯尔克孜自治州 Kizilsu Kirgiz Autonomous Prefecture	喀什地区 Kashgar [kaxgar] Administrative Offices	和田地区 Hotan Administrative Offices	石河子市 Shihezi City
原煤(吨)	Coal (ton)	182115	1446181	205330	12967356
洗精煤(吨)	Washed Coal (ton)				
其他洗煤(吨)	Other Washed Coal (ton)				
焦炭(吨)	Coke (ton)	73033	101313		1259296
焦炉煤气(万立方米)	Coke Oven Gas (10 000 cu.m)				
高炉煤气(万立方米)	High Oven Gas (10 000 cu.m)				
天然气(万立方米)	Natural Gas (10 000 cu.m)	3871	3695	18	4478
原油(吨)	Coal (ton)				
汽油(吨)	Gasoline (ton)	194	698	449	936
煤油(吨)	Kerosene (ton)			5	23
柴油(吨)	Diesel Oil (ton)	4897	3856	1404	12728
燃料油(吨)	Fuel Oil (ton)				289
液化石油气(吨)	Liquefied Petroleum Gas (ton)		16914		16
炼厂干气(吨)	Refinary Dry Gas (ton)				
其他石油制品(吨)	Other Oil Product (ton)		3		6
热力(百万千焦)	Heat (million KJ)				9290818
电力(万千瓦时)	Electricity (10 000 kwh)	29231	83408	42125	2744782
其他燃料(吨标准煤)	Other (ton of SCE)		58033		
能源合计(吨标准煤)	Energy Total (ton of SCE)	296973	1380453	214671	14073926

主要统计指标解释

能源生产总量 指一定时期内，一个地区一次能源生产量的总和。该指标是观察一个地区能源生产水平、规模、构成和发展速度的总量指标。一次能源生产量包括原煤、原油、天然气、水电、核能及其他动力能(如风能、地热能等)发电量，不包括低热值燃料生产量、生物质能、太阳能等的利用和由一次能源加工转换而成的二次能源产量。

能源消费总量 指一定时期内，一个地区的各行业和居民生活消费的各种能源的总和，该指标是观察能源消费水平、构成和增长速度的总量指标。能源消费总量包括原煤和原油及其制品、天然气、电力，不包括低热值燃料、生物质能和太阳能等的利用。能源消费总量分为终端能源消费量、能源加工转换损失量和能源损失量三部分。

(1)终端能源消费量：指一定时期内，一个地区生产和生活消费的各种能源在扣除了用于加工转换二次能源消费量和损失量以后的数量。

(2)能源加工转换损失量：指一定时期内，一个地区投入加工转换的各种能源数量之和与产出各种能源产品之和的差额，该指标是观察能源在加工转换过程中损失量变化的指标。

(3)能源损失量：指一定时期内，能源在输送、分配、储存过程中发生的损失和由客观原因造成的各种损失量，不包括各种气体能源放空、放散量。

能源生产弹性系数 是研究能源生产增长速度与国民经济增长速度之间关系的指标。计算公式为：

能源生产弹性系数＝能源生产总量年平均增长速度／国民经济年平均增长速度

国民经济年平均增长速度，可根据不同的目的或需要，用国民生产总值、国内生产总值等指标来计算，本年鉴是采用国内生产总值指标计算的。

电力生产弹性系数 是研究电力生产增长速度与国民经济增长速度之间关系的指标。一般来说，电力的发展应当快于国民经济的发展，也就是说电力应超前发展。计算公式为：

电力生产弹性系数＝电力生产量年平均增长速度／国民经济年平均增长速度

能源消费弹性系数 是反映能源消费增长速度与国民经济增长速度之间比例关系的指标。计算公式为：

能源消费弹性系数＝能源消费量年平均增长速度／国民经济年平均增长速度

电力消费弹性系数 反映电力消费增长速度与国民经济增长速度之间比例关系的指标。计算公式为：

电力消费弹性系数＝电力消费量年平均增长速度／国民经济年平均增长速度

能源加工转换效率 指一定时期内，能源经过加工、转换后，产出的各种能源产品的数量与同期内投入加工转换的各种能源数量的比率。该指标是观察能源加工转换装置和生产工艺先进与落后、管理水平高低等的重要指标。计算公式为：

能源加工转换效率＝能源加工转换产出量／能源加工转换投入量×100%

单位国内生产总值能耗 指一定时期内，一个国家或地区每生产一个单位的国内生产总值所消耗的能源。计算公式为：

单位国内生产总值能耗=能源消费总量/国内生产总值

单位国内生产总值电耗 指一定时期内，一个国家或地区每生产一个单位的国内生产总值所消耗的电力。计算公式为：

单位国内生产总值电耗=全社会用电量/国内生产总值

单位工业增加值能耗 指一定时期内，一个国家或地区每生产一个单位的工业增加值所消耗的能源。计算公式为：

单位工业增加值能耗=工业能源消费量/工业增加值

Explanatory Notes on Main Statistical Indicators

Total Energy Production refers to the total production of primary energy by all energy producing enterprises in the country in a given period of time. It is a comprehensive indicator to show the level, scale, composition and pace of development of energy production of the country. The production of primary energy includes that of coal, crude oil, natural gas, hydro-power and electricity generated by nuclear energy and other means such as wind power and geothermal power. However, it does not include the production of fuels of low calorific value, bio-energy, solar energy and secondary energy converted from primary energy.

Total Energy Consumption refers to the total consumption of energy of various kinds by the production sectors and the households in the country in a given period of time. It is a comprehensive indicator to show the scale, composition and pace of increase of energy consumption. Total energy consumption includes that of coal, crude oil and their products, natural gas and electricity. However, it does not include the consumption of fuel of low calorific value, bio-energy and solar energy. Total energy consumption can be divided into three parts: end-use energy consumption; loss during the process of energy conversion; and energy loss.

(1)End-use Energy Consumption: It refers to the total energy consumption by the production sectors and the households in the country (region) in a given period of time. It does not include the consumption during the conversion of primary energy into secondary energy and the loss in the process of energy conversion.

(2)Loss During the Process of Energy Conversion: It refers to the total input of various kinds of energy for conversion, minus the total output of various kinds of energy in the country in a given period of time. It is an indicator to show the loss that occurs during the process of energy conversion.

(3)Energy Loss: It refers to the total of the loss of energy during the course of energy transport, distribution and storage and the loss caused by any objective reason in a given period of time. The loss of various kinds of gas due to gas discharges and stocktaking is not included.

Elasticity Ratio of Energy Production is an indicator to show the relationship between the growth rate of energy production and the growth rate of the national economy. The formula is:

$$\text{Elasticity Ratio of Energy Production} = \frac{\text{Average Annual Growth Rate of Energy Production}}{\text{Average Annual Growth Rate of National Economy}}$$

The average annual growth rate of the national economy can be measured by indicators such as the Gross National Product and the Gross Domestic Product, depending on the purposes or needs. The Gross Domestic Product has been used in the calculation of the ratio in this Yearbook.

Elasticity Ratio of Electricity Production is an indicator to show the relationship between the growth rate of electricity production and the growth rate of the national economy. Generally speaking, the growth rate of electricity production should be higher than that of the national economy.

Its formula is:

$$\text{Elasticity Ratio of Electricity Production} = \frac{\text{Average Annual Growth Rate of Electricity Production}}{\text{Average Annual Growth Rate of National Economy}}$$

Elasticity Ratio of Energy Consumption is an indicator to show the relationship between the growth rate of energy consumption and the growth rate of the national economy. The formula is:

$$\text{Elasticity Ratio of Energy Consumptio n} = \frac{\text{Average Annual Growth Rate of Energy Consumptio n}}{\text{Average Annual Growth Rate of National Economy}}$$

Elasticity Ratio of Electricity Consumption is an indicator to show the relationship between the growth rate of electricity consumption and the growth rate of the national economy. The formula is:

$$\text{Elasticity Ratio of Electricity Consumption} = \frac{\text{Average Annual Growth Rate of Electricity Consumption}}{\text{Average Annual Growth Rate of National Economy}}$$

Efficiency of Energy Processing and Conversion refers to the ratio of the total output of energy products of various kinds after processing and conversion to the total input of energy of various kinds for processing and conversion in the same reference period. It is an important indicator to show the current conditions of energy processing and conversion equipment, production technique and management. The formula is:

$$\text{Efficiency of Energy Processing \& Conversion} = \frac{\text{Output of Energy After Processing \& Conversion}}{\text{Input of Energy for Processing \& Conversion}} \times 100\%$$

Energy Consumption per Unit of GDP refers to the energy consumption per unit of Gross Domestic Product in a country or the Gross Regional Product in a region in the same reference period. The formula is:

$$\text{Energy Consumption per Unit of GDP} = \frac{\text{Total Energy Consumption}}{\text{Gross Domestic Product}}$$

Electricity Consumption per Unit of GDP refers to the electricity consumption per unit of Gross Domestic Product in a country or the Gross Regional Product in a region in the same reference period. The formula is:

$$\text{Electricity Consumption per Unit of GDP} = \frac{\text{Total Electricity Consumption}}{\text{Gross Domestic Product}}$$

Energy Consumption per Unit of Industrial Value-added refers to the energy consumption per unit of industrial value-added in a country or region in the same reference period. The formula is:

$$\text{Energy Consumption per Unit of Industrial Value-added} = \frac{\text{Total Energy Consumption}}{\text{Industrial Value-added}}.$$

8

财 政

GOVERNMENT FINANCE

简要说明

本篇主要内容和资料来源

本篇包括自治区地方财政收支及各地州、县(市)公共财政收支资料。

资料来源于新疆维吾尔自治区财政厅年度决算，由新疆维吾尔自治区统计局国民经济综合统计处编辑整理。

Brief Introduction

Main Content and Source of Data

The data in this chapter show the government revenue and expenditure of Xinjiang Uygur Autonomous region,and the data of public budgetary revenue and expenditure by prefecture,autonomous prefecture and city.

Data on the government revenue and expenditure come from the final state financial accounts.Data in this chapter are compiled and collected by the Division of comprehensive of the Xinjing Bureau of Statistics on the basis of data from the relative departments.

8-1 主要年份公共财政预算收支及增长速度

The General Budgetary Revenue & Expenses and Growth Rate of Local Finance in Main Years

单位：亿元 (100 million yuan)

年份 Year	公共财政预算收入 General Budgetary Revenue in Local Finance	公共财政预算支出 General Budgetary Expenditure in Local Finance	收支差额 Balance	指数(上年=100) Indices (precding year=100)	
				公共财政预算收入 General Budgetary Revenue in Local Finance	公共财政预算支出 General Budgetary Expenditure in Local Finance
1978	7.14	17.02	-9.88	196.5	153.3
1980	4.03	16.22	-12.19	73.4	95.4
1985	8.47	28.60	-20.14	117.2	122.6
1990	21.78	47.62	-25.84	118.9	114.2
1995	38.28	96.40	-58.12	133.4	135.6
2000	79.07	190.95	-111.88	110.9	114.8
2001	95.09	263.32	-168.23	120.3	137.9
2002	116.47	361.17	-244.70	122.5	137.2
2003	128.22	368.47	-240.25	110.1	102.0
2004	155.70	421.04	-265.34	121.4	114.3
2005	180.32	519.02	-338.70	115.8	123.3
2006	219.46	678.47	-459.01	121.7	130.7
2007	285.86	795.15	-509.29	130.3	117.2
2008	361.06	1059.36	-698.30	126.3	133.2
2009	388.78	1346.91	-958.13	107.7	127.1
2010	500.58	1698.91	-1198.34	128.8	126.1
2011	720.43	2284.49	-1564.05	143.9	134.5
2012	908.97	2720.07	-1811.10	126.2	119.1
2013	1128.49	3067.12	-1938.64	124.2	112.8

8-2 主要年份公共财政预算收入占新疆生产总值的比重

Ration of the General Budgetary Revenue in Local Finance to GDP of Xinjiang in Main Years

单位：亿元 (100 million yuan)

年份 Year	公共财政预算收入 General Budgetary Revenue in Local Finance	新疆生产总值 Gross Domestic Product in Xinjiang	公共财政预算收入相当于新疆生产总值的比例(%) Proportion of Local Financial Revenue to GDP of Xinjiang (%)
1978	7.14	39.07	18.27
1980	4.03	53.24	7.57
1985	8.47	112.24	7.56
1990	21.78	261.44	8.34
1995	38.28	814.85	4.70
2000	79.07	1363.56	5.80
2001	95.09	1491.60	6.37
2002	116.47	1612.65	7.22
2003	128.22	1886.35	6.79
2004	155.70	2209.09	7.05
2005	180.32	2604.14	6.92
2006	219.46	3045.26	7.21
2007	285.86	3523.16	8.11
2008	361.06	4183.21	8.63
2009	388.78	4277.05	9.09
2010	500.58	5437.47	9.21
2011	720.43	6610.05	10.90
2012	908.97	7505.31	12.11
2013	1128.49	8360.24	13.50

8-3 地方财政收支情况
Statistics on Total Government Revenue and Expenditures in Local Finance

单位：亿元 (100 million yuan)

项　目	Item	2012	2013
收入合计	**Total Revenue**	**1251.64**	**1556.55**
公共财政预算收入	General Budgetary Revenue in Local Finance	908.97	1128.49
税收收入	Taxes Revenue	698.93	826.34
增值税	Value-added Tax	100.57	119.14
营业税	Business Tax	259.30	305.67
企业所得税（含退税）	Corporate Income Tax	79.99	85.06
个人所得税	Individual Income Tax	35.89	43.10
资源税	Resources Tax	69.35	71.74
城市维护建设税	City Maintenance and Construction Tax	44.99	49.94
房产税	House Property Tax	18.82	20.56
契　税	Contract Tax	26.22	37.91
其他税收收入	Other Revenues	63.80	93.22
非税收入	Non-tax Revenues	210.04	302.15
专项收入	Special Program Receipts	89.40	162.64
行政性收费收入	Charge of Administrative and Institutional Units	42.58	45.30
罚没收入	Penalty Receipts	18.16	21.50
其他收入	Other Revenues	59.90	72.71
国有资本经营预算收入	Operation Budgetary Revenues of Stateowned Assets		1.74
基金预算收入	Fund Budgetary Revenues	342.67	426.32
支出合计	**Total Expenditures**	**3080.22**	**3519.62**
公共财政预算支出	General Budgetary Expenditure in Local Finance	2720.07	3067.12
一般公共服务	Expenditure for General Public Services	303.67	337.37
教　育	Expenditure for Education	473.86	532.67
科学技术	Expenditure for Science and Technology	33.01	39.85
文化体育与传媒	Expenditure for Culture Sports and Media	68.23	74.63
社会保障和就业	Expenditure for Social Safety Net and Employment Effort	227.79	263.17
医疗卫生	Expenditure for Medical and Health Care	145.88	160.91
节能环保	Expenditure for Environmental Protection	64.12	68.99
城乡社区事务	Expenditure for Urban and Rural Community Affairs	183.49	243.05
农林水事务	Expenditure for Agriculture, Forestry and Water Conservancy	365.39	387.42
交通运输	Expenditure for Transportation	226.47	284.22
资源勘探电力信息等事务	Expenditure for Miming and Quarrying,Electriaty and Information Technology	60.45	83.84
其他各项支出	Other Expenditures	567.71	591.00
国有资本经营预算支出	Operation Budgetary Expenditure of Stateowned Assets		2.17
基金预算支出	Fund Budgetary Expenditure	360.15	450.33

8-4 各地、州、市、县(市)公共财政预算收支
Government Revenue and Expenditures by Prefecture, Autonomous Prefecture, City and County

单位：万元 (2013 年) (10 000 yuan)

地　区	Region	收　入 Revenue	支　出 Expenditures
总　计	**Total**	**11284875**	**30671241**
自治区本级	Autonomous regional Level	2039093	8090910
乌鲁木齐市	**Urumqi City**	**3019047**	**3532024**
乌鲁木齐市本级	Urumqi City Level	1634080	1999416
#市本级	City Level	941914	1531698
开发区	Development Zone	350645	216085
高新区	High Tech Zone	341521	251633
乌鲁木齐县	Urumqi County	48162	124945
天山区	Tianshan District	252030	289111
沙依巴克区	Shayibak District	174571	206775
新市区	Xinshi District	292818	191118
水磨沟区	Shui Mogou District	211319	265453
头屯河区	Tou Tunhe District	119371	88147
米东区	Midong District	223885	271860
达坂城区	Da Bancheng District	62811	95199
昌吉回族自治州	**Changji Hui Autonomous Prefecture**	**813405**	**1688147**
昌吉州本级	Changji Prefecture Level	90501	292557
#州本级	Autonomous Prefecture Level	55470	256058
农业园区	Agricultural Zone	35031	36499
昌吉市	Changji City	259015	360706
阜康市	Fukang City	146166	205530
呼图壁县	Hutubi County	71307	172474
玛纳斯县	Manas County	71904	170045
奇台县	Qitai County	61668	191274
吉木萨尔县	Jimsar County	88463	170440
木垒哈萨克自治县	Mori Kazak Autonomous County	24381	125121
克拉玛依市	**Karamay City**	**658258**	**798114**
市本级	City Level	382915	418168
克拉玛依区	Karamay District	175857	198681
独山子区	Dushanzi District	59354	95696
白碱滩区	Bai Jiantan District	28889	60429
乌尔河区	Urhe District	11243	25140
吐鲁番地区	**Turpan Administrative Offices**	**305428**	**642070**
地区本级	Prefecture Level	55126	103433
吐鲁番市	Turpan City	61916	178241
鄯善县	Shanshan [Piqan] County	123205	215055
托克逊县	Toksun County	65181	145341

8-4 续表 1 Continued

单位：万元 (10 000 yuan)

地　区	Region	收 入 Revenue	支 出 Expenditures
哈密地区	**Hami [Kumul] Administrative Offices**	**401021**	**841539**
地区本级	Prefecture Level	40000	188265
哈密市	Hami [Kumul] City	289093	380404
巴里坤哈萨克自治县	Barkol Kazak Autonomous County	36180	183841
伊吾县	Yiwu [Araturuk] County	35748	89029
伊犁哈萨克自治州	**Ili Kazak Autonomous Prefecture**	**1356086**	**4656117**
伊犁州直属县(市)	**Counties (Cities) Direct Under Ili Prefecture**	**685397**	**2257619**
伊犁州直属县(市)本级	Counties (Cities) Direct Under Ili Prefecture Level	43539	287511
#州本级	Autonomous Prefecture Level	22543	258302
霍尔果斯口岸	Huoerguosi Port	20996	29209
伊宁市	Yining [Gulja] City	210644	369203
奎屯市	Kuytun City	164459	208973
伊宁县	Yining [Gulja] County	49532	242615
察布查尔锡伯自治县	Qapqal Xibe Autonomous County	32500	163618
霍城县	Huocheng [Korgas] County	38606	198927
巩留县	Gongliu [Tokkuztara] County	16560	139229
新源县	Xinyuan [Kunes] County	58346	180856
昭苏县	Zhaosu [Mongolkure] County	12257	156112
特克斯县	Tekes County	16286	144802
尼勒克县	Nilka County	42668	165773
塔城地区	**Tacheng [Tarbagatai] Administrative Office**	**365532**	**1195687**
地区本级	Prefecture Level	9919	102697
塔城市	Tacheng [Qoqek] City	40981	156915
乌苏市	Usu City	100077	224641
额敏县	Emin [Dorbiljin] County	32125	168487
沙湾县	Shawan County	61188	173932
托里县	Toli County	31517	135935
裕民县	Yumin [Qagantokay] County	6588	99185
和布克赛尔蒙古自治县	Hoboksar Mongol Autonomous County	83137	133895
阿勒泰地区	**Altay Administrative Offices**	**305157**	**1202811**
阿勒泰地区本级	Altay Administrative Offices Level	18895	137548
#地区本级	Administrative Offices Level	11269	124207
喀纳斯景区管理委员会	Kanas Scenit Area Management Committee	7626	13341
阿勒泰市	Altay City	46611	213477
布尔津县	Burqin County	22975	119846
富蕴县	Fuyun [Koktokay] County	111280	244392

8-4 续表 2 Continued

单位：万元 (10 000 yuan)

地　　区	Region	收入 Revenue	支出 Expenditure
福海县	Fuhai [Burultokay] County	26438	129648
哈巴河县	Habahe [Kaba] County	55001	142372
青河县	Qinghe [Qinggil] County	18292	128396
吉木乃县	Jeminay County	5665	87132
博尔塔拉蒙古自治州	**Bortala Mongol Autonomous Prefecture**	**131687**	**561160**
博尔塔拉州本级	Bortala Mongol Autonomous Prefecture Level	27209	155101
#州本级	Autonomous Prefecture Level	10551	134980
阿拉山口口岸	AlashanKon Port	16658	20121
博乐市	Bole [Bortala] City	72265	193442
精河县	Jinghe [Jing] County	24305	121112
温泉县	Wenquan [Araxang] County	7908	91505
巴音郭楞蒙古自治州	**Bayangol Mongol Autonomous Prefecture**	**684768**	**1645105**
巴音郭楞州本级	Bayangol Mongol Autonomous Prefecture Level	65211	236031
#州本级	Autonomous Prefecture Level	28633	212018
开发区	Development Zone	36578	24013
库尔勒市	Korla City	304001	406556
轮台县	Luntai [Bugur] County	77824	145318
尉犁县	Yuli [Lopnur] County	19500	115770
若羌县	Ruoqiang [Qarkilik] County	70530	124560
且末县	Qiemo [Qarqan] County	26713	117152
焉耆回族自治县	Yanqi Hui Autonomous County	26998	112797
和静县	Hejing County	69500	203171
和硕县	Hoxud County	12991	100125
博湖县	Bohu [Bagrax] County	11500	83625
阿克苏地区	**Aksu Administrative Offices**	**749053**	**1994981**
地区本级	Prefecture Level	26491	235016
阿克苏市	Aksu City	150419	273555
温宿县	Wensu [Onsu] County	35561	180918
库车县	Kuqa County	274847	391447
沙雅县	Xayar County	91079	182718
新和县	Xinhe [Toksu] County	34223	131052
拜城县	Baicheng [Bay] County	104687	205902
乌什县	Wushi [Uxturpan] County	10783	148530
阿瓦提县	Awat County	15642	168027
柯坪县	Kalpin County	5321	77816

8-4 续表 3 Continued

单位：万元 (10 000 yuan)

地　区	Region	收入 Revenue	支出 Expenditures
克孜勒苏柯尔克孜自治州	**Kizilsu Kirgiz Autonomous Prefecture**	**87565**	**763175**
州本级	Autonomous Prefecture Level	7385	146370
阿图什市	Artux City	28805	198472
阿克陶县	Akto County	21093	198219
阿合奇县	Akqi County	7201	95292
乌恰县	Wuqia [Ulugqat] County	23081	124822
喀什地区	**Kashgar [Kaxgar] Administrative Offices**	**457940**	**3248549**
地区本级	Prefecture Level	9090	212330
喀什市	Kashgar [Kaxgar] City	157487	402559
疏附县	Shufu County	24531	216449
疏勒县	Shule County	35143	198733
英吉沙县	Yengisar County	15819	198232
泽普县	Zepu [Poskam] County	21806	175290
莎车县	Shache [Yarkant] County	41571	496271
叶城县	Yecheng [Kagilik] County	39029	350512
麦盖提县	Makit County	21102	200853
岳普湖县	Yopurga County	15654	148468
伽师县	Jiashi [Payzawat] County	34507	273899
巴楚县	Bachu [Maralbexi] County	29162	271522
塔什库尔干塔吉克自治县	Taxkorgan Tajik Autonomous County	13039	103431
和田地区	**Hotan Administrative Offices**	**133314**	**1649362**
地区本级	Prefecture Level	9283	153392
和田市	Hotan City	46655	206804
和田县	Hotan County	11810	203297
墨玉县	Moyu [Karakax] County	18003	296574
皮山县	Pishan [Guma] County	12203	198311
洛浦县	Lop County	10005	184024
策勒县	Qira County	6836	138811
于田县	Yutian [Keriya] County	10520	193966
民丰县	Minfeng [Niya] County	7999	74183
自治区直辖县级市	**Municpality Country-LevelCity directly under the Central Govern-ment**	**448210**	**559988**
石河子市	Shihezi City	283125	331783
阿拉尔市	Aral City	39482	58663
图木舒克市	Tumxuk City	18678	33939
五家渠市	Wujiaqu City	92917	114764
北屯市	Beitun City	14008	20839

主要统计指标解释

地方财政收入 指国家财政参与社会产品分配所得的收入，是实现国家职能的财力保证。包括地方公共财政预算收入和基金预算收入。

公共财政预算收入 是通过一定的形式和程序，由各级财政部门组织并纳入预算管理的各项收入。

基金预算收入 是按规定收取，转入或通过当年财政安排，由财政管理并具有指定用途的政府性基金预算收入等。

税收收入 包括增值税、营业税、企业所得税、个人所得税、资源税、城市维护建设税、房产税、印花税、城镇土地使用税、土地增值税、车船税、耕地占用税、契税等。

非税收收入 包括专项收入、行政事业性收费、罚没收入和其他收入。

地方财政支出 是以国家为主体，以财政的事权为依据进行的一种财政资金分配活动，集中反映了国家的职能活动范围及其所发生的耗费，包括地方公共财政预算支出和基金预算支出。

公共财政预算支出 是各级财政部门对集中的一般预算收入有计划地分配和使用而安排的支出。

基金预算支出 是各级财政部门用基金预算收入安排的支出。

一般公共服务支出 指政府提供基本公共管理与服务的支出，包括人大事务、政协事务、政府办公厅 (室)及相关机构事务、发展与改革事务、统计信息事务、财政事务、税收事务、审计事务、海关事务、人力资源事务、纪检监察事务、人口与计划生育事务、 商贸事务、知识产权事务、工商行政管理事务、国土资源事务、 海洋管理事务、 测绘事务、地震事务、气象事务、民族事务、宗教事务、港澳台侨事务、档案事务、共产党事务、民主党派事务及工商联事务、群众团体事务、彩票事务等。

教育支出 指政府教育事务支出，包括教育行政管理、学前教育、小学教育、初中教育、普通高中教育、普通高等教育、初等职业教育、中专教育、技校教育、职业高中教育、高等职业教育、广播电视教育、留学生教育、特殊教育、干部继续教育、教育机关服务等。

科学技术支出 指用于科学技术方面的支出，包括科学技术管理事务、基础研究、应用研究、技术研究与开发、科技条件与服务、社会科学、科学技术普及、科技交流与合作等。

文化教育与传媒支出 指政府在文化、文物、体育、广播影视、新闻出版等方面的支出。

社会保障和就业支出 指政府在社会保障与就业方面的支出，包括社会保障和就业管理事务、民政管理事务、财政对社会保险基金的补助、补充全国社会保障基金、行政事业单位离退休、企业改革补助、就业补助、抚恤、退役安置、社会福利、残疾人事业、城市居民最低生活保障、其他城镇社会救济、农村社会救济、自然灾害生活救助、红十字事务等。

医疗卫生支出 指政府医疗卫生方面的支出，包括医疗卫生管理事务支出、医疗服务支出、医疗保障支出、疾病预防控制支出、卫生监督支出、妇幼保健支出、农村卫生支出等。

节能环保支出 指政府环境保护支出，包括环境保护管理事务支出、环境监测与监察支出、污染治理支出、自然生态保护支出、天然林保护工程支出、退耕还林支出、风沙荒漠治理支出、退牧还草支出、已垦草原退耕还草、能源节约利用、污染减排、可再生能源和资源综合利用等支出。

交通运输支出 指政府交通运输和邮政业方面的支出，包括公路运输支出、水路运输支出、铁路运输支出、民用航空运输支出、邮政业支出等。

城乡社区事务支出 指政府城乡社区事务支出，包括城乡社区管理事务支出、城乡社区规划与管理支出、城乡社区公共设施支出、城乡社区住宅支出、城乡社区环境卫生支出、建设市场管理与监督支出等。

农林水事务支出 指政府农林水事务支出，包括农业支出、林业支出、水利支出、扶贫支出、农业综合开发支出等。

信贷资金 指金融机构以信用方式积聚和分配的货币资金。金融机构信贷资金的来源有各项存款、金融债券、对国际金融机构负债、流通中现金、其他项目等；信贷资金的运用有各项贷款、有价证券及投资、金银占款、外汇占款、财政借款及在国际金融机构中的资产等。

存款 指企业、机关、团体或居民根据资金必须收回的原则，把货币资金存入银行或其他信贷机构保管并取得一定利息的一种信用活动形式。根据存款对象或性质的不同可划分为企业存款、财政存款、机关团体存款、城乡储蓄存款、农业存款、信托及委托类存款、其他存款等科目。它是银行信贷资金的主要来源。

贷款 指银行或其他信用机构根据资金必须归还的原则，按一定利率，为企业、个人等提供资金的一种信用活动形式。我国银行贷款分为短期贷款、委托及信托类贷款、其他类贷款等。

保险金额 指保险人承担赔偿或者给付保险金责任的最高限额。

保费 指投保人为取得保险人在约定范围内所承担赔偿责任而支付给保险人的费用。

赔款 指保险人根据保险合同的规定，向被保险人支付的赔偿保险责任损失的金额。

给付 包括死伤医疗给付和满期给付。死伤医疗给付是指保险人根据人寿保险及长期健康保险合同的规定，因被保险人在保险期内发生保险责任范围内的保险事故支付给被保险人(或受益人)的金额。满期给付是指被保险人生存期满，保险人按人寿保险合同规定支付给被保险人的满期保险金额。

Explanatory Notes on Main Statistical Indicators

Local Government Revenue refer to the revenue from participation of national finance in social product allocation. It is a financial guarantee to realize national functions, and includes local public budgetary financial revenue and fund budget revenue.

Local Public Budgetary Financial Revenue refers to the revenue organized by finance authorities at all levels in certain form and through certain procedures and involved in budgetary management.

Fund Budget Revenue refers to governmental fund budget revenues collected, transferred in or arranged by government finance the same year in accordance with regulations, governed by government finance and for specific use of purpose.

Tax Revenue includes value-added tax, business tax ,corporate income tax ,individual income tax, resource tax, urban maintenance and construction tax,house property tax,stamp tax,urban land use tax,1and value-added tax,tax on vehicles and boat operation, arable land occupation tax, deed etc.

Non-tax Revenue includes special revenues, administrative charges ,fines,and other revenues.

Local Financial Expenditure refers to a sort of allocation activity of financial funds by the state based on the position of finance.It is a concentrated reflection of the functional activity scope of the state and the expenditure incurred by it. It includes local public budgetary financial expenditure and fund budget expenditure.

Local Public Budgetary Financial Expenditure refers to the expenditure arranged by finance authorities at all levels during their planned distribution and use of the general budgetary revenue gathered.

Fund Budget Expenditure refers to the expenditure arranged by finance authorities at all level with the fund budget revenue.

Expenditure for General Public Services refers to the spending on the basic public management and services provided by governments,including the expense on affairs of people's congress,affairs of People's Political Consultative Conference. Affairs of government general offices and relative institutions, affairs of development and reform ,affairs of statistical information. affairs of finance, affairs of taxation, affairs of audit, affairs of customs affairs of human resources. affairs of disciplinc inspection and supervision, affairs of population and family Ling, affairs of commerce and trade, affairs of intellectual Planning affairs of administration for industry and commerce, affairs of land and resources, affairs of oceanic administration .affairs of surveying and mapping ,affairs of earthquake, weather affairs ,ethnic affairs, religious affairs, affairs of Hong Kong, Macao , Taiwan, and overseas Chinese, affairs of archives administration, affairs Of Chinese Communist Party. affairs of democratic parties and federation of industry and commerce, affairs of mass organizations, and affairs of lottery tickets, etc.

Expenditure for Education refers to the spending of government on education,including the expense on the administration of education pre-school education, primary education, junior high school education, senior high school education,regular higher education, primary vocational education,secondary vocational education, technical school education,vocational senior high school education and higher vocational education, radio and television education, student abroad education, special education,continuing education for management personnel, and services for education authorities, etc.

Expenditure for Science and Technology refers to the spending on science and technology(S&T), including the expense on the administration of S&T,basic research,applied research, research and development, conditions and services of S&T. popularization of social science and S&T. exchanges and cooperation of S&T. etc.

Expenditure for Cultural Education and Media refers to the spending on culture, cultural relics, sports, radio, film, television, press and publication, etc.

Expenditure for Social Security and Employment refers to the spending on social security and employment, including the expense on social security and employment administration affairs, civil affairs, budgetary subsidy on the social insurance funds, subsidy on National Social Security Fund. Retirees of administrative units and institutions, subsidy on enterprise reform, subsidy on employment effort, pension, placement of ex—service man, social welfare, the handicapped undertakings, the system of cost of living allowances for urban residents, other urban social relief, rural social relief, living relief of natural disasters, affairs of Red Cross, etc.

Expenditure for Medical Service and Health Care refers to the spending on medical service and health care including the expense on affairs of medical and health administration. medical services, medical guarantee, disease prevention and control, hcalth inspection and supervision, women and children' s health care, rural health care, etc.

Expenditure for Energy Saving and Environmental Protection refers to the spending of government on environmental protection,including the expense on administration of environmental protection. environment monitoring and supervision, pollution control, natural ecology protection, project of virgin forest protection, reforesting farmland, control of sources of dust storms, returning pastureland to grassland, returning cultivated land to grassland, energy conservation and utilization, emissions reduction, comprehensive utilization of renewable energy and resources, etc.

Expenditure for Transportation refers to the spending of government on transportation and postal services, including the expense on highway transportation, waterway transportation, railway transportation, civil aviation transportation and postal services, etc.

Expenditure for Urban and Rural Community Affairs refers to the spending of government on urban and rural community affairs, including the expense on administration of urban and rural communities, planning and management of urban and rural communities, public facilities in urban and rural communities, residential houses in urban and rural communities, sanitation in urban and rural communities, management and supervision of construction markets, etc.

Expenditure for Agriculture, Forestry and Water Conservancy Affairs refers to the spending of government on agriculture, forestry and water conservancy affairs, including the expense on agriculture affairs, forestry affairs, water conservancy affairs, poverty alleviation and comprehensive agricultural development, etc.

Credit Funds refer to the monetary funds accumulated and distributed in the means of credit by the financial institutions. The sources of credit funds include various deposits, financial bonds, liabilities to international financial institutions, currency in circulation, other items. The uses of credit funds include loans, securities and investment, position for bullion and silver purchase, position for foreign exchange purchase, advances to treasury, and assets with international financial institutions.

Deposit is a form of credit by which enterprises, institutions, organizations or households can put money into banks and other credit institutions for safekeeping and interest earning under the principle of free withdrawal. According to different depositors, deposits are divided into enterprise deposits, treasury deposits, deposits of government agencies and organizations, capital construction deposits, urban savings deposits, rural deposits and other deposits. Deposits are major sources of the credit funds of banks.

Loan is a form of credit by which banks and other credit institutions provide funds at certain interest rate to enterprises and individuals in the light of the principle of unconditional repayment. Loans from Chinese banks include short-term loan, medium-term and long-term loans, financial lease, bill financing, various money advanced, foreign loans.

Amount Insured refers to the maximum that the insurant will get for the claim of the case insured.

Premium is the fee paid by the insurant to the insurer to obtain the obligation of compensation from the insurance within the agreed terms.

Settled Claim is the compensation paid by the insurer to the insurant in accordance with the insurance contract.

Payment includes payment for death, injury or medical treatment and mature payment. Payment for death, injury or medical treatment refers to the money paid to the insurant (or the beneficiary) in accordance with the life or health insurance contract when the insurant encounters accidents within the insured period covered in the contract. Payment at maturity refers to the payment to the insurant in accordance with the life insurance contract at the end of the insured period.

新疆统计年鉴
XINJIANG STATISTICAL YEARBOOK

9

物　价

PRICE

简要说明

本篇主要内容和资料来源

本篇价格指数资料，反映生产、流通、消费与投资环节的价格变动趋势和变动幅度，主要包括居民消费价格指数、商品零售价格指数、农业生产资料价格指数、工业生产者出厂价格指数、工业生产者购进价格指数、固定资产投资价格指数。

居民消费价格指数、商品零售价格指数和农业生产资料价格指数出自国家统计局新疆调查总队消费价格调查处；工业生产者出厂价格指数、工业生产者购进价格指数、固定资产投资价格指数出自国家统计局新疆调查总队生产投资价格调查处。

Brief Introduction

Main Content and Source of Data

Data on the price indices in this chapter show the changing trend and the change rates in production, circulation, consumption and investment, including mainly consumer price indices of residents, retail price indices, price indices of agricultural means of production, purchasing price indices of farm products, producers' price indices of industrial products, purchasing price indices of raw materials, fuels and power, price indices of investment in fixed assets, and real estate price indices.

Data on the consumer price index, retail price index and price indices of agriculture production come from Division of Consumer Price of NBS Survey Office in Xinjiang; Data on the price indices of industrial products, indices of purchasing price of raw materials, fuels and power, price indices of investment in fixed assets, price indices for real estate come from Division of Consumer Price of NBS Survey Office in Xinjiang.

9-1 主要年份各种物价指数
Price Indices in Main Years

年 份 Year	居民消费价格指数 Consumer Price Index	城市居民消费价格指数 Urban Household	农村居民消费价格指数 Rural Household	商品零售价格指数 Retail Price Index
上年=100 Preceding year=100				
1978	101.2	101.4	100.3	101.4
1980	102.8	104.1	102.0	104.2
1985	107.8	109.5	106.4	108.1
1990	105.0	104.5	105.9	104.1
1995	119.7	118.4	122.5	116.7
2000	99.4	100.1	97.6	98.3
2001	104.0	104.0	103.8	102.5
2002	99.4	98.9	100.9	97.9
2003	100.4	100.5	100.2	99.2
2004	102.7	102.1	104.5	100.7
2005	100.7	100.6	101.2	99.4
2006	101.3	101.0	102.0	101.8
2007	105.5	104.6	107.2	105.1
2008	108.1	107.3	109.5	108.5
2009	100.7	100.2	102.0	100.4
2010	104.3	103.6	105.8	104.6
2011	105.9	105.5	106.8	105.1
2012	103.8	103.4	104.7	103.3
2013	103.9	103.8	104.1	103.3
1978 年=100 Year 1978 =100				
1978	100.0	100.0	100.0	100.0
1980	105.1	106.6	103.8	107.8
1985	120.9	125.6	117.9	124.2
1990	194.3	206.0	184.0	197.6
1995	392.7	422.7	364.2	381.0
2000	436.5	471.9	398.6	397.9
2001	454.0	490.8	413.8	407.8
2002	451.3	485.4	417.5	399.3
2003	453.1	487.8	418.3	396.1
2004	465.3	498.1	437.1	398.9
2005	468.6	501.1	442.3	396.5
2006	474.7	506.1	451.1	403.6
2007	500.8	529.4	483.6	424.2
2008	541.4	568.0	529.5	460.3
2009	545.2	569.1	540.1	462.1
2010	568.6	589.6	571.4	483.4
2011	602.1	622.0	610.3	508.1
2012	625.0	643.1	639.0	524.9
2013	649.7	667.7	665.6	541.9

9-2 居民消费价格分类指数
Consumer Price Indices by Category

(上年=100) (2013 年) (preceding year=100)

项　目	Item	全　区 Autonomous Region	城　市 Urban Indices	农　村 Rural Indices
居民消费价格总指数	**Consumer Price Index**	**103.9**	**103.8**	**104.1**
食　品	**Food**	**108.5**	**108.5**	**108.4**
粮　食	Grain	106.3	106.1	106.5
大　米	Rice	104.4	103.5	105.5
面　粉	Flour	107.2	107.0	107.4
粮食制品	Grain Products	106.8	107.0	105.8
其　它	Others	109.9	113.9	107.0
淀　粉	Starches and Tubers	103.8	101.6	106.7
干豆类及豆制品	Beans and Its Products	108.9	108.4	109.6
油　脂	Oil or Fat	103.4	103.6	103.3
肉禽及其制品	Meat, Poultry and Processed Products	114.9	115.0	114.7
蛋	Eggs	111.0	109.6	113.0
水产品	Aquatic Products	107.0	108.4	105.1
菜	Vegetables	105.8	105.2	106.8
鲜　菜	Fresh Vegetables	105.6	104.9	106.7
干菜及菜制品	Dried Vegetables and Vegetable Products	101.5	100.2	104.4
薯　类	Tubers	120.7	121.7	118.5
调味品	Flavoring	100.8	100.8	100.8
糖	Carbohydrate	98.7	100.1	97.2
食　糖	Sugar	95.8	97.6	94.2
糖　果	Candy	101.2	102.4	99.8
巧克力制品	Chocolate Goods	98.8	100.0	97.3
糖类小食品	Carbohydrate Products	99.7	100.2	98.9
茶及饮料	Tea and Beverages	103.9	104.0	103.7
干鲜瓜果	Dried and Fresh Melons and Fruits	102.9	104.2	100.5
鲜瓜果	Fresh Fruits	101.9	103.5	99.5
干(坚)果	Drie (nut) Fruits	105.2	105.7	103.9
糕点饼干面包	Cake and Biscuit	103.8	102.7	106.2
液体乳及乳制品	Milk and Its Products	111.1	112.6	107.6
在外用膳食品	Dining Out	108.8	107.8	112.1
主　食	Staple Food	107.2	107.3	106.6
炒　菜	Fried Dishes	103.7	101.4	111.9
地方小吃	Local Snack	120.8	121.8	116.7
其他	Others	109.7	105.6	115.6
其他食品	Other Foods	104.2	102.4	108.1
烟　酒	**Tobacco, Liquor**	**101.7**	**101.1**	**102.6**
烟　草	Tobacco	101.3	101.1	101.7
酒	Liquor	102.0	101.1	103.4
衣　着	**Clothing**	**99.8**	**99.5**	**100.6**
服　装	Garments	99.4	99.1	100.2
衣着材料	Clothing Material	101.6	100.9	102.3
棉　布	Cotton Cloth	102.2	99.9	104.2

9-2 续表 Continued

(上年=100) (preceding year=100)

项　目	Item	全　区 Autonomous Region	城　市 Urban Areas	农　村 Rural Areas
化纤布	Chemical Fiber Cloth	101.7	101.2	102.1
毛　线	Wool	100.4	101.8	98.8
其　他	Others	102.1	101.0	103.1
鞋袜帽	Footwear and Hats	100.2	100.1	100.5
鞋	Shoes	100.2	100.1	100.6
袜　子	Socks and Stockings	100.3	100.2	100.3
帽　子	Hats	99.6	99.3	100.4
衣着加工服务费	Clothing Processing	106.2	105.3	107.2
家庭设备用品及维修服务	**Household Facilities,Articles and Services**	**101.3**	**100.9**	**102.1**
耐用消费品	Durable Consumer Goods	99.6	99.2	100.4
家　具	Furniture	101.5	100.9	102.5
家庭设备	Household Facilities	98.5	98.1	99.0
室内装饰品	Interior Decorations	100.2	100.6	99.6
床上用品	Bed Articles	100.8	101.2	100.1
家庭日用杂品	Daily Use Household Articles	101.0	100.6	102.0
家庭服务及加工维修服务	Household Service and Mainteance and Renovation	109.8	108.0	113.1
医疗保健和个人用品	**Health Care and Personal Articles**	**101.4**	**101.2**	**101.7**
医疗保健	Health Cares	101.5	101.5	101.6
医疗器具及用品	Medical Instruments and Articles	99.6	100.8	97.8
中药材及中成药	Traditional Chinese Medicine	102.7	102.9	102.2
西　药	Western Medicine	101.3	101.0	102.1
保健器具及用品	Constitutional Appliances and Articles	106.2	107.4	102.0
医疗保健服务	Medical and Health Service	99.9	99.9	100.3
个人用品及服务	Personal Articles and Services	101.3	100.8	101.7
交通和通信	**Transportation and Communication**	**100.1**	**100.0**	**100.3**
交　通	Transportation	101.3	100.8	102.0
通　信	Communication	98.9	99.1	98.3
娱乐教育文化用品及服务	**Recreation, Education, Culture Articles**	**101.1**	**100.7**	**101.9**
文娱用耐用消费品及服务	Durable Consumer Goods for Cultural and Recreationl Use and Services	97.2	96.6	98.3
教　育	Education	101.4	100.9	102.3
文化娱乐	Culture and Recreation Articles	103.7	104.3	102.3
文化娱乐用品	Cultural and Recreational Articles	100.0	99.6	100.9
书报杂志	Newspapers and Magazines	104.6	106.3	101.3
文娱费	Expenditure on Culture and Recreation	106.6	107.3	104.7
旅　游	Touring and Outing	102.8	101.6	105.1
居　住	**Housing**	**103.4**	**103.9**	**102.5**
建房及装修材料	Building and Building Decoration Materials	99.1	99.1	99.1
住房租金	Renting	103.3	103.6	102.1
自有住房	Private Housing	104.8	105.5	103.6
水、电、燃料	Water, Electricity and Fuels	101.6	102.6	100.7
服务项目价格指数	**Services**	**102.9**	**102.7**	**103.4**

9-3 各市县居民消费价格分类指数

(上年=100) (2013 年)

项　目	Item	乌鲁木齐市 Urumqi City	喀什市 Kashgar [Kaxgar] City	伊宁市 Yining [Gulja] City	和田市 Hotan City	克拉玛依市 Karamay City	哈密市 Hami [Kumul] City
居民消费价格总指数	**Consumer Price Index**	**103.5**	**103.4**	**103.5**	**104.6**	**104.4**	**103.6**
食　品	**Food**	**107.5**	**107.6**	**107.3**	**109.4**	**110.8**	**108.2**
粮　食	Grain	106.5	106.0	107.7	105.3	102.4	106.3
大　米	Rice	101.8	99.5	102.6	103.8	100.6	102.0
面　粉	Flour	108.6	108.7	105.5	103.3	108.2	108.0
粮食制品	Grain Products	108.1	109.7	117.0	114.3	96.9	108.3
其　它	Others	116.9	111.9	112.2	107.8	112.9	115.5
淀　粉	Starches and Tubers	100.1	104.9	111.3	100.3	100.0	101.3
干豆类及豆制品	Beans and Its Products	105.3	107.5	106.9	107.0	110.6	106.2
油　脂	Oil or Fat	103.2	104.1	100.6	98.9	102.5	105.5
肉禽及其制品	Meat, Poultry and Their Products	115.1	113.1	116.6	116.4	113.4	116.0
蛋	Eggs	109.4	110.9	110.3	113.7	101.8	107.4
水产品	Aquatic Products	107.2	106.9	108.8	108.4	107.3	113.2
菜	Vegetables	100.1	104.1	101.5	110.0	116.2	108.4
鲜　菜	Fresh Vegetables	99.3	103.8	99.1	110.7	116.9	108.2
干菜及菜制品	Dried Vegetables and Vegetable Products	100.3	101.0	110.2	100.0	100.8	102.9
薯　类	Tubers	125.0	123.0	115.8	109.1	124.9	130.9
调味品	Flavoring	101.3	102.0	103.3	101.6	100.0	101.7
糖	Carbohydrate Products	102.3	100.0	100.0	100.4	101.1	100.3
食　糖	Sugar	102.6	91.4	94.3	97.7	104.1	98.7
糖　果	Candy	103.0	104.4	103.0	100.0	100.5	100.5
巧克力制品	Chocolate Goods	100.2	104.3	103.0	105.9	100.2	100.1
糖类小食品	Carbohydrate	100.7	94.3	100.1	105.5	100.0	105.4
茶及饮料	Tea and Beverages	101.6	110.1	101.1	103.8	113.2	103.2
干鲜瓜果	Dried and Fresh Melons and Fruits	100.7	104.7	102.8	108.2	109.9	102.5
鲜瓜果	Fresh Fruits	99.5	102.8	101.4	110.1	112.1	106.3
干(坚)果	Dried(nut)Fruits	103.3	108.7	107.0	103.2	102.2	96.9
糕点饼干面包	Cake, Cookie	103.6	103.6	101.2	101.5	99.8	106.6
液体乳及乳制品	Milk and Its Products	118.5	117.5	105.6	105.5	106.6	99.2
在外用膳食品	Dining Out	107.1	105.1	102.4	109.8	114.5	105.5
主　食	Staple Food	107.5	100.0	103.0	106.5	111.5	108.2
炒　菜	Fried Dishes	101.1	101.6	97.8	101.1	105.3	103.4
地方小吃	Local Snack	122.9	117.4	109.3	139.7	127.7	105.1
其　他	Others	104.8	104.3	105.2	109.3	100.0	106.7
其他食品	Other Foods	102.7	98.4	99.8	105.1	106.0	104.8
烟　酒	**Tobacco, Liquor**	**101.8**	**100.3**	**101.1**	**100.8**	**99.4**	**100.7**
烟　草	Tobacco	101.1	100.1	100.0	100.0	100.0	100.6
酒	Liquor	102.5	100.5	101.8	101.5	98.8	100.9
衣　着	**Clothing**	**99.5**	**98.8**	**104.6**	**98.3**	**101.2**	**101.7**
服　装	Garments	99.1	99.1	107.3	97.9	100.3	99.6
衣着材料	Clothing Material	100.7	95.1	102.3	101.3	100.9	104.3
棉　布	Cotton Cloth	100.0	83.6	100.0	102.4	101.9	100.0

Consumer Price Indices by Category in Cities and Counties

(preceding year=100)

昌吉市 Changji City	库尔勒市 Korla City	阿克苏市 Aksu City	焉耆回族自治县 Yanqi Hui Autonomous County	塔城市 Tacheng [Qoqek] City	阿勒泰市 Altay City	沙湾县 Shawan County	博乐市 Bole [Bortala] City	吐鲁番市 Turpan City	库车县 Kuqa County	阿图什市 Artux City	莎车县 Shache [Yarkant] County	奎屯市 Kuytun City	石河子市 Shihezi City
104.1	**103.4**	**103.5**	**103.4**	**103.4**	**104.0**	**103.6**	**104.3**	**104.0**	**103.2**	**103.4**	**104.6**	**103.8**	**103.0**
110.9	**108.5**	**107.7**	**107.0**	**108.3**	**107.2**	**107.7**	**108.2**	**108.3**	**106.1**	**105.7**	**111.1**	**107.3**	**106.6**
105.2	108.6	105.1	108.4	106.5	107.0	110.9	104.6	105.9	103.4	105.0	107.0	111.9	106.8
103.6	112.4	104.3	106.2	107.3	104.8	116.6	101.0	99.5	97.6	103.1	108.5	105.5	105.8
108.0	103.7	103.4	111.4	108.1	107.1	105.7	106.3	110.2	108.2	106.8	106.8	115.3	106.7
99.8	107.7	109.9	109.3	105.2	111.8	110.0	107.8	105.7	102.7	102.1	100.6	117.6	109.8
99.5	119.1	119.0	101.9	106.4	102.6	101.3	105.5	109.9	102.2	103.9	112.3	101.8	104.4
101.2	111.3	98.5	97.3	101.2	110.5	102.6	109.9	100.0	104.4	102.4	115.3	100.0	105.3
110.6	126.5	102.0	105.6	115.9	116.7	105.4	111.5	117.2	100.6	102.8	103.5	106.8	99.4
103.1	107.7	103.1	103.1	103.6	100.7	103.5	112.1	106.5	95.4	101.6	103.3	99.4	101.4
116.2	116.8	111.4	111.6	117.8	114.9	120.0	111.1	113.6	111.4	120.4	116.1	112.0	108.7
108.5	112.4	119.9	103.0	110.1	112.1	108.3	101.0	113.6	100.9	110.8	112.7	109.9	107.7
102.9	121.4	106.5	104.0	106.0	103.0	94.4	95.9	112.9	111.7	105.6	107.8	102.5	105.0
116.9	94.4	110.8	99.6	100.6	100.2	94.7	103.0	107.1	114.0	102.8	118.3	102.3	101.2
117.7	93.7	113.6	97.3	100.1	98.3	91.7	100.8	104.6	114.0	102.9	118.6	102.4	101.0
107.6	96.7	78.6	108.8	100.0	102.3	98.5	110.7	103.8	108.8	99.2	102.4	100.8	105.5
133.1	111.6	120.6	115.9	105.9	115.0	123.4	118.4	125.0	118.1	103.4	128.3	90.9	97.6
99.7	101.8	100.0	99.1	99.5	103.1	100.1	108.3	101.4	94.6	105.2	100.4	106.0	102.7
106.8	97.6	94.5	94.2	101.3	107.6	101.2	84.4	104.3	92.5	96.1	112.4	99.3	100.2
100.5	91.2	85.5	85.4	100.5	100.8	102.4	96.2	92.1	89.8	94.3	96.5	98.1	98.4
111.4	99.4	101.2	100.4	103.5	112.5	101.4	75.0	108.7	99.2	94.9	102.9	100.0	101.8
103.7	98.4	88.0	100.7	100.0	117.2	100.0	112.5	99.2	69.2	100.0	99.9	101.2	100.5
101.4	99.8	98.8	99.0	100.0	102.2	100.0	69.0	124.7	97.7	100.2	140.0	100.0	100.5
100.8	101.5	100.9	99.3	105.3	109.8	100.5	109.0	99.7	97.6	98.6	102.2	99.6	102.1
111.1	105.5	108.9	97.7	97.2	92.7	102.8	102.5	100.1	107.7	83.1	105.1	101.9	104.8
104.0	106.8	105.7	94.8	92.7	89.2	105.3	101.3	100.0	109.7	77.8	104.2	101.2	104.5
121.7	100.8	121.1	102.9	108.4	104.2	96.3	106.0	100.5	102.7	100.1	107.7	103.3	106.0
105.4	100.3	98.1	106.9	104.0	103.7	100.0	118.2	111.7	100.1	99.5	102.7	103.6	102.0
104.3	109.0	106.9	111.2	110.4	103.0	104.6	106.0	104.6	106.8	101.2	108.4	108.0	107.3
111.4	104.1	107.1	113.6	111.1	113.2	114.9	123.4	109.1	103.1	105.8	110.6	108.3	112.2
112.9	105.9	108.0	113.2	113.5	118.1	107.8	99.2	113.7	104.2	106.3	101.0	110.3	121.4
102.6	99.0	102.0	108.0	104.5	101.6	103.9	143.1	110.4	104.1	107.2	114.4	106.0	101.1
120.9	111.3	118.5	124.5	122.5	125.5	134.0	121.5	100.9	100.4	103.3	120.3	123.6	122.5
100.0	111.3	104.9	117.5	96.4	102.1	100.0	117.1	100.0	103.2	99.4	130.9	115.0	100.0
106.8	99.5	95.7	102.2	102.2	100.6	100.0	118.7	101.7	107.9	103.3	111.9	100.0	102.6
98.7	**100.1**	**102.7**	**101.4**	**101.4**	**105.2**	**100.5**	**101.6**	**100.3**	**101.7**	**102.0**	**102.5**	**102.1**	**101.1**
100.2	101.5	100.0	103.5	100.0	100.1	100.0	100.0	100.0	100.6	100.0	100.5	100.0	100.3
97.1	98.6	105.7	99.1	102.3	110.0	100.9	103.2	100.6	102.7	103.6	104.8	103.9	102.0
99.5	**95.1**	**102.5**	**102.5**	**100.1**	**100.0**	**100.7**	**104.5**	**99.0**	**99.8**	**100.6**	**100.0**	**103.3**	**102.1**
98.5	91.7	101.8	101.0	100.1	99.9	99.9	104.0	98.3	100.2	100.2	99.1	102.8	101.8
101.9	100.3	101.4	104.8	100.0	100.5	100.3	107.0	102.9	97.9	99.6	102.5	100.0	100.4
102.4	100.3	102.3	115.7	100.0	100.0	100.0	107.7	103.7	102.3	100.0	102.4	100.0	102.2

9-3 续表

(上年=100)

项　目	Item	乌鲁木齐市 Urumqi City	喀什市 Kashgar [Kaxgar] City	伊宁市 Yining [Gulja] City	和田市 Hotan City	克拉玛依市 Karamay City	哈密市 Hami [Kumul] City
化纤布	Chemical Fiber Cloth	100.0	100.0	104.1	100.0	97.5	108.1
毛　线	Wool	102.7	100.0	100.0	100.0	100.0	111.4
其　他	Others	100.0	100.0	106.0	101.8	102.6	100.0
鞋袜帽	Footgear and Hats	100.3	97.7	99.3	95.7	103.0	100.6
鞋	Shoes	100.4	97.0	99.2	92.4	103.6	100.5
袜　子	Socks and Stockings	100.0	100.0	100.2	106.9	100.0	101.0
帽　子	Hats	95.8	100.0	100.0	100.0	100.1	99.7
衣着加工服务费	Clothing Manufacturing Services	100.0	105.7	102.5	112.5	102.9	118.5
家庭设备用品及维修服务	**Household Facilities and Articles and Services**	**101.8**	**100.7**	**101.8**	**99.9**	**100.6**	**104.0**
耐用消费品	Durable Consumer Goods	99.8	100.6	100.4	98.7	99.5	98.5
家　具	Furniture	101.2	99.8	101.2	104.3	101.5	99.4
家庭设备	Household Facilities	98.9	101.1	100.0	94.5	98.0	98.0
室内装饰品	Interior Decorations	99.6	100.0	107.9	94.3	100.1	100.2
床上用品	Bed Articles	106.0	100.3	106.1	98.0	100.0	100.1
家庭日用杂品	Daily Use Household Articles	101.7	101.3	100.8	100.2	99.9	107.2
家庭服务及加工维修服务	Household Services and Maintenance and Renovation	110.9	100.4	100.0	114.1	106.9	120.4
医疗保健和个人用品	**Health Care and Personal Articles**	**102.3**	**103.4**	**101.6**	**102.1**	**101.5**	**102.0**
医疗保健	Health Cares	102.4	106.5	101.8	102.2	102.6	102.3
医疗器具及用品	Medical Appliances and Articles	99.3	99.9	101.6	102.6	101.3	98.1
中药材及中成药	Traditional Chinese Medicine	102.7	114.0	104.7	106.1	104.1	100.1
西　药	Western Medicine	101.3	104.5	101.0	101.5	103.3	103.1
保健器具及用品	Constitutional Appliances and Articles	116.0	102.3	101.2	100.7	100.0	110.7
医疗保健服务	Medical and Health Service	100.0	100.0	99.5	100.0	100.0	100.0
个人用品及服务	Personal Articles and Services	101.9	98.8	101.3	101.8	100.3	101.4
交通和通信	**Transportation and Communication**	**100.4**	**98.8**	**99.6**	**99.8**	**99.0**	**100.5**
交　通	Transportation	101.1	98.1	99.9	102.1	100.0	101.3
通　信	Communication	99.5	99.7	99.3	97.7	97.6	99.3
娱乐教育文化用品及服务	**Recreation, Education and Culture Articles and Services**	**102.7**	**99.4**	**100.0**	**99.2**	**99.3**	**98.5**
文娱用耐用消费品及服务	Durable Consumer Goods for Cultural and Recreationl Use and Services	94.3	94.7	97.8	95.7	98.8	94.9
教　育	Education	101.2	100.3	100.5	100.2	100.6	99.9
文化娱乐	Culture and Recreation Articles	109.1	105.0	101.3	100.8	99.3	99.4
文化娱乐用品	Cultural and Recreational Articles	99.1	98.9	102.5	100.7	99.3	98.5
书报杂志	Newspapers and Magazines	120.2	103.1	100.0	100.0	100.0	100.4
文娱费	Expenditure on Culture and Recreation	111.2	115.5	101.2	101.4	98.3	100.0
旅　游	Touring and Outing	104.1	94.5	99.4	95.0	98.4	99.6
居　住	**Residence**	**101.3**	**103.8**	**100.4**	**108.0**	**104.3**	**100.8**
建房及装修材料	Building and Building Decoration Materials	98.4	103.8	100.6	102.7	99.2	98.0
住房租金	Renting	102.3	104.0	100.0	105.5	102.5	102.9
自有住房	Private Housing	102.3	104.2	100.0	111.0	107.9	100.7
水、电、燃料	Water, Electricity and Fuels	102.1	100.3	102.7	100.8	100.0	99.7
服务项目价格指数	**Services**	**102.1**	**101.2**	**100.2**	**105.2**	**103.0**	**102.4**

Continued

(preceding year=100)

昌吉市 Changji City	库尔勒市 Korla City	阿克苏市 Aksu City	焉耆回族自治县 Yanqi Hui Autonomous County	塔城市 Tacheng [Qoqek] City	阿勒泰市 Altay City	沙湾县 Shawan County	博乐市 Bole [Bortala] City	吐鲁番市 Turpan City	库车县 Kuqa County	阿图什市 Artux City	莎车县 Shache [Yarkant] County	奎屯市 Kuytun City	石河子市 Shihezi City
99.4	100.0	102.4	100.0	100.0	100.0	100.9	108.2	100.0	101.2	98.0	103.7	100.0	97.8
104.1	100.5	100.0	100.0	100.0	103.2	100.0	95.2	101.5	95.6	100.0	97.7	100.0	100.1
100.0	100.3	100.0	100.0	100.0	100.0	100.0	110.9	114.5	87.4	100.0	105.3	100.0	100.0
100.3	99.1	98.0	104.3	100.0	99.1	102.2	103.3	99.2	98.0	100.0	99.5	103.9	103.1
100.3	98.8	100.7	105.6	100.0	98.9	103.4	104.1	99.5	97.7	100.0	99.1	104.9	104.2
100.8	100.8	89.2	95.8	100.0	100.0	100.0	102.5	98.1	97.4	100.0	101.7	100.0	101.0
100.0	101.7	99.3	104.9	100.0	100.0	100.0	98.5	99.0	105.2	100.0	100.0	103.4	98.0
108.3	108.4	112.8	106.0	101.0	104.2	101.8	113.2	102.7	103.0	108.3	112.2	118.2	100.0
100.7	**97.9**	**97.6**	**101.4**	**99.8**	**103.2**	**101.8**	**100.9**	**102.7**	**101.1**	**104.4**	**102.6**	**101.7**	**100.2**
99.2	95.7	100.4	102.9	99.1	100.8	100.0	97.8	102.0	103.3	100.0	99.3	102.3	100.0
100.2	100.0	101.6	103.9	100.4	102.3	100.0	99.7	109.4	108.5	100.0	99.7	105.0	100.8
98.9	93.8	99.6	102.3	98.4	99.6	100.0	96.4	99.4	98.1	100.0	99.1	100.9	99.7
103.5	101.5	96.0	98.5	100.0	100.0	100.0	101.8	99.5	97.9	99.6	100.1	101.5	100.0
101.6	98.5	83.0	100.0	100.0	102.0	100.0	101.0	106.7	92.9	100.0	100.0	104.0	99.5
100.5	99.5	97.9	99.6	100.0	104.4	105.8	106.1	99.2	97.2	99.5	102.0	100.6	100.1
108.0	102.0	100.3	101.9	102.9	114.6	100.0	100.7	110.5	108.2	128.2	116.1	100.0	101.7
101.2	**98.3**	**98.6**	**98.7**	**100.9**	**103.0**	**102.0**	**105.0**	**102.5**	**98.7**	**101.3**	**100.9**	**100.5**	**103.3**
99.7	98.5	98.5	98.6	101.4	101.7	102.8	106.4	102.8	98.4	101.4	100.7	100.3	104.5
100.0	101.9	95.9	85.8	104.6	100.0	106.4	98.2	100.4	90.0	100.0	98.6	100.7	100.3
97.8	95.2	100.7	99.9	101.7	105.6	110.1	110.1	104.2	87.6	105.1	100.1	101.0	108.5
100.0	100.1	96.7	96.9	104.6	99.9	97.6	109.5	102.8	104.6	100.2	101.8	99.9	105.2
102.1	101.3	93.8	104.7	100.1	100.0	100.0	106.2	102.3	104.0	100.0	98.6	100.0	105.4
100.0	98.9	100.0	100.0	100.1	100.0	100.1	100.0	101.8	100.2	100.0	100.0	100.0	100.0
104.1	97.9	98.8	99.0	99.5	105.3	101.0	103.0	102.0	99.1	101.1	101.3	100.8	101.2
100.1	**98.4**	**101.8**	**99.8**	**100.0**	**99.2**	**100.0**	**99.6**	**100.7**	**98.1**	**99.7**	**100.9**	**99.5**	**99.8**
101.3	99.1	100.5	99.9	99.8	99.8	100.7	101.3	103.2	100.7	101.4	102.6	100.0	100.7
98.9	97.4	104.1	99.7	100.4	98.5	99.2	97.9	97.8	93.1	97.5	98.9	99.0	98.7
100.3	**99.7**	**99.8**	**100.5**	**101.9**	**102.9**	**98.9**	**103.5**	**99.5**	**101.5**	**103.2**	**100.6**	**100.5**	**99.4**
95.6	96.0	101.9	97.6	99.8	97.7	94.9	99.0	96.9	98.1	100.0	100.2	100.0	96.2
100.4	100.1	100.9	101.7	102.4	100.0	100.7	102.1	100.9	104.2	103.7	100.5	100.0	100.0
100.8	99.9	100.4	101.1	102.4	100.4	99.7	106.6	101.1	102.9	103.0	100.5	102.0	98.7
101.8	99.8	100.6	99.9	106.5	100.2	99.3	100.7	98.5	101.1	100.2	100.0	98.4	97.3
99.8	100.0	100.4	103.8	100.0	101.0	100.0	103.8	96.7	100.7	100.0	102.4	100.0	100.0
101.2	100.0	100.1	99.7	100.0	99.8	100.0	116.1	110.8	106.6	111.9	99.2	108.5	100.0
102.7	105.1	94.4	100.0	100.7	118.2	100.0	114.0	95.9	99.1	108.6	102.2	100.9	102.4
100.8	**109.3**	**103.8**	**104.2**	**100.6**	**102.7**	**103.2**	**99.3**	**103.2**	**107.3**	**103.1**	**99.9**	**104.7**	**100.7**
101.3	98.3	100.1	100.2	97.9	99.9	100.9	104.6	95.4	100.9	99.8	95.7	102.7	101.4
100.2	115.3	105.5	100.0	100.0	105.1	105.0	103.2	100.0	103.5	103.6	100.5	100.0	100.0
101.1	113.3	104.6	108.0	101.5	103.6	104.1	97.3	106.1	111.1	104.7	100.2	106.8	100.0
99.8	100.0	100.3	99.4	100.5	100.5	99.1	98.1	100.1	98.8	100.4	102.0	106.3	105.5
101.4	**105.7**	**103.0**	**102.9**	**101.0**	**104.1**	**102.6**	**101.2**	**103.9**	**104.4**	**104.4**	**101.9**	**102.7**	**100.6**

9-4 商品零售价格分类指数
Retail Price Indices by Category

(上年=100) (2013 年) (preceding year=100)

项目	Item	全区 Autonomous Region	城市 Urban Indices	农村 Rural Indices
商品零售价格总指数	**Retail Price Index**	**103.3**	**103.3**	**103.1**
食品	**Food**	**108.2**	**108.1**	**108.4**
粮食	Grain	106.3	106.3	106.4
油脂	Oil or Fat	103.6	103.6	103.6
肉禽及其制品	Meat, Poultry and Processed Products	114.7	114.8	114.7
猪肉	Pork	103.8	103.5	104.5
牛肉	Beef	140.0	140.6	138.7
羊肉	Mutton	120.1	120.9	118.1
鸡	Chicken	104.1	102.9	107.1
鲜蛋	Fresh Eggs	111.8	110.8	114.0
水产品	Aquatic Products	107.4	108.0	105.7
鲜瓜果	Fresh Melons and Fruits	100.4	101.2	98.8
糕点、饼干、面包	Cake、Biscuit and Bread	104.2	103.3	106.7
饮料、烟酒	**Beverages, Tobacco and Liquor**	**102.0**	**101.9**	**102.4**
茶及饮料	Tea and Beverages	103.2	103.6	102.5
#饮料	Beverages	102.8	103.6	101.2
烟草	Tobacco	101.1	101.1	101.1
酒	Liquor	102.4	101.9	103.6
服装鞋帽	**Garments, Shoes and Hats**	**99.8**	**99.6**	**100.3**
服装	Garments	99.5	99.3	100.1
鞋袜帽	Footgear and Hats	100.1	99.9	100.5
#鞋	Shoes	100.2	100.1	100.6
纺织品	**Textiles**	**102.4**	**102.9**	**101.3**
棉布	Cotton Cloth	101.3	99.4	103.4
化纤布	Chemical Fiber Cloth	100.8	100.4	102.1
毛线	Wool	101.3	102.3	98.9
其他	Others	101.5	100.8	103.1
家用电器及音响器材	**Household Appliances,Music and Video Equipment**	**97.7**	**97.2**	**98.8**
家庭设备	Household Facilities	98.8	98.6	99.1
文娱用耐用消费品	Durable Consuming Goods for Entertainment	96.2	95.0	98.4
专业音像器材	Sound Apparatus	98.3	97.9	98.9

9-4 续表 Continued

(上年=100) (preceding year=100)

项　目	Item	全　区 Autonomous Region	城　市 Urban Indices	农　村 Rural Indices
文化办公用品	**Cultural and Office Goods**	**99.5**	**99.2**	**100.1**
日用品	**Articles for Daily Use**	**101.2**	**101.3**	**101.2**
日用百货	General Merchandise for Daily Use	101.0	100.9	101.3
日用杂品	Miscellaneous for Daily Use	100.4	100.2	100.9
洗涤用品	Washing and Cleaning Goods	102.7	102.7	102.6
其他日用品	Other Daily-use Goods	99.7	99.7	99.8
体育娱乐用品	**Sports and Entertainment Goods**	**99.2**	**98.8**	**100.1**
体育用品	Sports Articles	99.1	98.8	100.1
娱乐用品	Recreational Articles	99.2	98.9	100.2
交通、通信用品	**Traffic and Telecommunication Goods**	**97.3**	**97.5**	**97.0**
交通运输机械	Traffic and Transport Machinery	98.3	97.8	99.4
通信器材	Telecommunication Apparatus	96.0	96.9	94.0
家　具	**Furniture**	**101.1**	**100.6**	**102.6**
化妆品	**Cosmetics**	**103.0**	**103.5**	**101.9**
金银珠宝	**Gold and Silver Jewelry**	**94.4**	**94.8**	**93.3**
中西药品及医疗保健用品	**Chinese and Western Medicine, Medical-care and Healthy Goods**	**102.5**	**102.9**	**101.6**
医疗器具及用品	Medical-care Apparatus and Goods	98.9	99.5	97.9
中药材及中成药	Chinese Herbs and Patent Medicine	102.4	102.6	102.2
西　药	Western Medicine	101.3	101.2	101.7
保健器具及用品	Healthy Devices and Goods	110.1	112.0	102.0
书报杂志及电子出版物	**Books,Magazines and Electronic Publications**	**105.4**	**107.2**	**100.8**
教材及参考书	Texts and Reference Books	101.8	102.2	101.2
书报杂志	Newspapers and Magazines	111.3	114.5	101.1
电子音像制品	Electronic Audio and Video Products	100.3	100.6	99.7
燃　料	**Fuels**	**102.0**	**102.8**	**100.2**
煤炭及制品	Coal and Its Products	104.2	107.7	100.4
石油及制品	Oil and Its Products	101.2	101.6	100.0
建筑材料及五金电料	**Building Apparatus, Hardwares and Electrical Apparatus**	**99.6**	**99.9**	**99.0**
建筑装璜材料	Building Decoration Materials	98.4	98.7	97.9
五金电料	Hardwares and Electrical Apparatus	102.7	103.2	101.9

9-5 各市县商品零售价格分类指数

(上年=100) (2013 年)

项 目	Item	乌鲁木齐市 Urumqi City	喀什市 Kashgar [Kaxgar] City	伊宁市 Yining [Gulja] City	和田市 Hotan City	克拉玛依市 Karamay City	哈密市 Hami [Kumul] City
商品零售价格总指数	**General Retail Price Index**	**103.5**	**102.9**	**103.5**	**103.0**	**103.7**	**103.0**
食 品	**Food**	**107.7**	**107.4**	**107.4**	**109.5**	**110.5**	**108.5**
粮 食	Grain	106.4	106.1	107.6	104.0	102.4	106.1
油 脂	Oil or Fat	103.0	104.1	100.5	98.9	102.5	106.0
肉禽及其制品	Meat, Poultry and Their Products	114.8	112.9	116.6	117.6	112.7	117.3
猪 肉	Pork	104.1	102.6	104.6	101.1	104.7	103.5
牛 肉	Beef	141.7	146.1	141.5	140.7	129.0	138.2
羊 肉	Mutton	121.0	114.7	119.9	115.1	125.1	127.5
鸡	Chicken	101.7	105.7	98.8	105.5	104.6	101.8
鲜 蛋	Fresh Egg	110.2	112.6	110.9	115.1	100.3	107.7
水产品	Aquatic Products	107.2	104.6	108.7	108.6	107.3	113.4
鲜瓜果	Fresh Fruits	99.5	102.8	101.4	110.1	112.1	106.3
糕点、饼干、面包	Cake、Biscuit and Bread	103.7	104.0	101.2	101.5	99.8	106.5
饮料、烟酒	**Beverages, Tobacco and Liquor**	**101.7**	**102.0**	**101.1**	**101.4**	**104.7**	**101.6**
茶及饮料	Tea and Beverages	101.6	110.8	101.1	105.4	112.7	103.1
#饮 料	Beverages	102.0	112.9	101.2	102.3	111.7	102.5
烟 草	Tobacco	101.1	100.1	100.0	100.0	100.0	100.7
酒	Liquor	102.5	101.1	101.8	101.5	98.8	101.5
服装鞋帽	**Garments, Shoes and Hats**	**99.5**	**98.6**	**104.3**	**97.0**	**101.2**	**99.9**
服 装	Garments	99.1	99.0	107.3	97.8	100.4	99.5
鞋袜帽	Footgear and Hats	100.3	97.6	99.3	95.3	102.9	100.5
#鞋	Shoes	100.4	97.0	99.2	91.7	103.6	100.5
纺织品	**Textiles**	**104.6**	**97.2**	**103.0**	**99.6**	**100.2**	**102.5**
棉 布	Cotton Cloth	100.0	83.6	100.0	102.4	101.9	100.0
化纤布	Chemical Fiber Cloth	100.0	100.0	104.1	100.0	97.5	108.1
毛 线	Wool	102.7	100.0	100.0	100.0	100.0	111.4
其 他	Others	100.0	100.0	106.0	101.8	102.6	100.0
家用电器及音响器材	**Household Appliances, Music and Sound Apparatus**	**97.4**	**97.1**	**99.4**	**94.6**	**98.3**	**95.1**
家庭设备	Household Facilities	98.9	101.2	100.0	94.1	98.0	98.1
文娱用耐用消费品	Durable Consuming Goods for Entertainment	95.0	92.1	98.3	95.6	99.0	91.4
专业音像器材	Sound Apparatus	99.1	93.2	100.0	101.7	96.0	95.1

Retail Price Indices by Category in Cities and Counties

(preceding year=100)

昌吉市 Changji City	库尔勒市 Korla City	阿克苏市 Aksu City	焉耆回族自治县 Yanqi Hui Autonomous County	塔城市 Tacheng [Qoqek] City	阿勒泰市 Altay City	沙湾县 Shawan County	博乐市 Bole [Bortala] City	吐鲁番市 Turpan City	库车县 Kuqa County	阿图什市 Artux City	莎车县 Shache [Yarkant] County	奎屯市 Kuytun City	石河子市 Shihezi City
103.7	**101.0**	**102.6**	**102.1**	**102.8**	**102.7**	**102.7**	**103.3**	**102.7**	**101.7**	**102.1**	**104.1**	**103.2**	**103.0**
111.3	**107.1**	**108.1**	**106.3**	**108.5**	**106.9**	**107.5**	**107.5**	**108.8**	**105.4**	**105.9**	**110.7**	**106.5**	**106.8**
106.1	108.4	105.0	108.2	106.5	107.0	110.6	104.8	106.0	103.4	105.1	106.7	111.3	106.6
104.0	110.7	102.5	102.8	103.6	100.2	103.4	111.0	106.6	94.6	102.0	103.4	99.6	101.5
116.4	114.2	111.4	109.2	117.8	115.0	116.1	109.3	113.6	109.5	121.1	114.0	109.9	108.7
101.7	101.9	98.6	102.7	107.3	100.0	111.6	101.2	103.7	103.9	102.7	105.8	102.6	107.4
139.2	135.3	140.5	136.5	131.9	141.8	149.2	110.5	133.2	121.3	151.7	142.6	129.7	132.9
120.6	123.5	118.4	105.4	127.4	121.2	122.0	125.4	118.9	118.0	108.9	109.8	135.4	117.1
101.9	110.0	112.9	103.8	114.7	110.1	111.6	98.0	102.6	101.1	117.1	108.8	102.7	98.2
108.0	113.1	122.1	103.0	111.4	113.1	114.2	101.5	114.2	99.0	111.6	114.6	110.4	109.6
102.9	118.6	107.0	104.0	106.0	103.0	95.3	93.6	112.9	112.7	105.7	104.5	102.3	104.9
104.0	106.8	105.7	94.8	92.7	89.2	105.3	101.3	100.0	109.7	77.8	104.2	101.2	104.5
104.4	100.5	98.1	106.3	104.0	103.9	100.0	119.4	111.7	100.1	99.5	102.4	103.9	101.9
99.1	**99.0**	**102.6**	**101.6**	**102.1**	**105.9**	**100.3**	**103.7**	**100.0**	**100.1**	**100.6**	**102.5**	**101.3**	**101.8**
101.3	101.7	100.8	100.6	105.3	107.9	100.0	110.1	99.7	97.9	98.6	102.5	99.6	101.6
101.2	102.5	101.0	98.0	101.3	98.4	98.5	112.8	99.7	100.6	95.6	101.0	99.5	101.1
100.2	100.2	100.0	103.4	100.0	100.2	100.0	100.0	100.0	101.2	100.0	100.3	100.0	100.5
97.5	96.2	105.7	99.9	102.3	109.6	100.8	103.3	100.6	101.9	103.3	104.6	104.0	103.1
99.2	**94.8**	**99.6**	**102.3**	**100.1**	**99.5**	**101.1**	**102.7**	**98.6**	**99.6**	**100.1**	**99.4**	**103.3**	**102.4**
98.6	92.1	100.9	102.0	100.1	99.9	99.8	102.4	98.3	100.3	100.1	99.3	103.0	102.2
100.3	99.3	97.4	103.5	100.0	98.8	102.2	102.9	99.2	98.9	100.0	99.7	104.0	103.0
100.3	98.7	100.7	105.6	100.0	97.6	103.2	104.6	99.5	97.7	100.0	98.9	104.9	104.5
101.7	**98.4**	**91.5**	**102.5**	**100.0**	**102.1**	**100.1**	**104.4**	**102.7**	**95.4**	**99.7**	**101.6**	**103.6**	**99.0**
102.4	100.3	102.3	115.7	100.0	100.0	100.0	107.7	103.7	102.3	100.0	102.4	100.0	102.2
99.4	100.0	102.4	100.0	100.0	100.0	100.9	108.2	100.0	101.2	98.0	103.7	100.0	97.8
104.1	100.5	100.0	100.0	100.0	103.2	100.0	95.2	101.5	95.6	100.0	97.7	100.0	100.1
100.0	100.3	100.0	100.0	100.0	100.0	100.0	110.9	114.5	87.4	100.0	105.3	100.0	100.0
97.2	**93.1**	**100.7**	**100.5**	**99.8**	**98.7**	**97.4**	**98.0**	**97.8**	**98.0**	**100.0**	**98.8**	**100.4**	**97.7**
98.9	93.6	99.6	102.6	98.4	99.7	100.0	97.5	99.4	98.2	100.0	98.0	101.9	99.7
94.7	91.8	101.5	97.2	101.6	97.0	92.9	98.2	93.7	97.9	100.0	99.9	98.8	94.9
95.5	97.8	103.2	97.4	100.0	100.0	100.0	100.0	100.0	97.8	100.0	100.0	100.0	100.0

9-5 续表

(上年=100)

项　目	Item	乌鲁木齐市 Urumqi City	喀什市 Kashgar [Kaxgar] City	伊宁市 Yining [Gulja] City	和田市 Hotan City	克拉玛依市 Karamay City	哈密市 Hami [Kumul] City
文化办公用品	**Cultural and Office Appliances**	**98.4**	**101.3**	**100.0**	**97.6**	**98.9**	**100.2**
日用品	**Articles for Daily Use**	**101.4**	**98.3**	**102.5**	**100.4**	**100.0**	**104.8**
日用百货	General Merchandise for Daily Use	100.8	95.8	99.9	97.5	100.2	101.7
日用杂品	Miscellaneous for Daily Use	100.0	101.0	100.0	99.9	99.9	104.7
洗涤用品	Washing and Cleaning Goods	102.7	98.6	103.5	103.4	99.9	108.2
其他日用品	Other Daily-use Goods	98.8	100.3	104.9	100.6	100.1	100.3
体育娱乐用品	**Sports and Entertainment Goods**	**99.0**	**94.4**	**100.0**	**100.5**	**100.4**	**100.0**
体育用品	Sports Articles	98.5	93.1	100.2	100.3	100.8	101.0
娱乐用品	Recreational Articles	99.4	95.7	99.9	100.8	100.0	98.4
交通、通信用品	**Traffic and Telecommunication Goods**	**97.1**	**96.5**	**97.8**	**98.0**	**98.4**	**97.0**
交通运输机械	Traffic and Transport Machinery	97.0	94.8	100.3	98.7	100.0	99.4
通信器材	Telecommunication Apparatus	97.3	99.6	95.4	96.8	96.5	93.3
家　具	**Furniture**	**100.5**	**99.6**	**101.2**	**105.0**	**101.5**	**99.5**
化妆品	**Cosmetics**	**104.2**	**98.3**	**101.7**	**101.3**	**100.8**	**104.7**
金银珠宝	**Gold and Silver Jewelry**	**94.0**	**99.1**	**95.0**	**88.5**	**97.2**	**99.0**
中西药品及医疗保健用品	**Chinese and Western Medicine, Medical-care and Healthy Goods**	**103.5**	**107.4**	**102.5**	**102.5**	**103.0**	**103.0**
医疗器具及用品	Medical-care Apparatus and Goods	99.3	99.9	101.6	102.6	101.3	98.1
中药材及中成药	Chinese Herbs and Patent Medicine	102.6	114.5	104.7	106.1	104.1	100.1
西　药	Western Medicine	101.1	104.2	101.0	101.2	103.5	103.9
保健器具及用品	Healthy Devices and Goods	116.0	101.7	101.2	100.8	100.0	111.1
书报杂志及电子出版物	**Books, Magazines and Electronic Publications**	**111.0**	**101.8**	**101.2**	**102.3**	**100.0**	**100.1**
教材及参考书	Texts and Reference Books	103.1	101.9	102.8	101.1	100.0	100.0
书报杂志	Newspapers and Magazines	120.2	102.8	100.0	100.0	100.0	100.3
电子音像制品	Electronic Audio and Video Products	100.0	100.0	100.0	107.9	100.0	100.0
燃　料	**Fuels**	**103.3**	**102.1**	**101.3**	**98.7**	**99.4**	**97.0**
煤炭及制品	Coal and Its Products	120.0	101.5	105.8	92.8	100.0	92.0
石油及制品	Oil and Its Products	102.5	102.3	100.7	100.1	99.1	99.9
建筑材料及五金电料	**Building Apparatus, Hardwares and Electrical Apparatus**	**99.4**	**102.7**	**102.4**	**102.1**	**100.1**	**97.2**
建筑装璜材料	Building Decoration Materials	98.4	102.0	100.4	101.6	97.9	97.4
五金电料	Hardwares and Electrical Apparatus	102.5	105.1	109.1	103.2	103.9	96.9

Continued

(preceding year=100)

昌吉市 Changji City	库尔勒市 Korla City	阿克苏市 Aksu City	焉耆回族自治县 Yanqi Hui Autonomous County	塔城市 Tacheng [Qoqek] City	阿勒泰市 Altay City	沙湾县 Shawan County	博乐市 Bole [Bortala] City	吐鲁番市 Turpan City	库车县 Kuqa County	阿图什市 Artux City	莎车县 Shache [Yarkant] County	奎屯市 Kuytun City	石河子市 Shihezi City
99.0	**102.1**	**101.7**	**99.9**	**102.4**	**99.3**	**99.5**	**98.7**	**95.7**	**102.3**	**100.0**	**100.0**	**97.8**	**98.8**
100.8	**99.9**	**100.9**	**101.2**	**100.0**	**100.2**	**101.0**	**104.4**	**101.2**	**103.3**	**99.0**	**100.7**	**101.4**	**101.0**
101.6	100.6	101.5	102.5	100.1	100.4	101.4	101.4	102.5	103.7	100.3	100.2	100.9	100.6
102.4	96.6	101.9	99.7	100.0	99.2	102.9	105.4	98.9	98.3	100.3	102.9	102.1	100.7
98.6	101.3	107.6	101.3	100.0	101.0	100.0	107.9	101.2	110.5	97.1	100.9	101.3	101.7
104.7	100.7	93.5	100.3	100.0	100.0	100.0	100.4	101.4	97.4	100.1	99.9	102.1	100.6
102.9	**99.7**	**91.7**	**103.1**	**97.8**	**100.0**	**101.0**	**100.9**	**98.3**	**100.7**	**100.2**	**100.1**	**100.5**	**100.1**
103.1	101.7	87.4	104.8	96.0	100.0	103.2	100.9	97.8	101.2	100.4	100.0	101.2	101.3
102.8	97.1	93.4	100.8	99.4	100.0	100.0	100.9	99.4	100.2	100.0	100.1	99.9	98.7
98.3	**97.3**	**100.0**	**98.9**	**98.8**	**97.1**	**99.3**	**97.7**	**88.3**	**99.4**	**96.8**	**95.3**	**98.8**	**97.5**
99.8	100.0	99.6	100.0	97.2	98.5	100.0	99.5	99.5	101.1	100.2	100.0	100.0	99.0
96.5	91.0	100.7	98.3	102.1	95.7	98.5	95.1	81.1	97.4	93.0	91.5	97.9	95.2
100.2	**100.0**	**101.6**	**103.7**	**100.4**	**102.7**	**100.0**	**99.6**	**109.2**	**107.2**	**100.0**	**99.8**	**106.2**	**100.5**
104.9	**97.7**	**102.4**	**101.3**	**100.3**	**102.8**	**100.4**	**105.3**	**102.3**	**100.4**	**100.9**	**103.1**	**101.4**	**100.7**
96.3	**89.7**	**95.0**	**83.5**	**85.8**	**92.7**	**95.4**	**92.5**	**91.2**	**93.2**	**92.4**	**98.4**	**100.8**	**93.6**
99.6	**98.5**	**97.8**	**98.2**	**102.4**	**101.9**	**102.3**	**107.0**	**102.9**	**95.9**	**101.7**	**100.8**	**100.3**	**105.8**
100.0	101.9	95.9	85.8	104.6	100.0	106.4	98.2	100.4	90.0	100.0	98.6	100.7	100.3
97.6	95.8	100.7	99.9	101.7	104.9	110.0	108.9	104.4	87.2	104.8	100.1	101.0	108.5
100.0	99.8	96.7	96.9	104.6	99.9	96.0	107.6	102.2	102.4	100.2	101.6	99.9	104.6
102.3	101.1	93.8	104.4	100.1	100.0	100.0	107.6	102.2	101.7	100.0	98.9	100.1	104.7
99.8	**101.2**	**102.8**	**101.9**	**100.0**	**100.3**	**100.0**	**101.4**	**99.1**	**102.5**	**101.0**	**101.3**	**100.0**	**100.1**
100.1	100.0	101.5	102.6	100.0	100.0	100.1	100.2	100.8	106.1	104.8	99.9	100.0	100.0
99.8	100.0	100.4	102.2	100.0	100.9	100.0	103.4	96.7	100.7	100.0	102.5	100.0	100.0
99.4	105.5	105.8	92.6	100.0	100.0	100.0	99.7	100.0	100.0	100.0	100.0	100.0	100.3
99.1	**99.0**	**102.6**	**96.7**	**99.2**	**99.4**	**98.2**	**93.6**	**102.2**	**98.0**	**102.2**	**106.2**	**103.7**	**101.9**
97.6	98.4	110.1	92.8	97.2	98.8	98.7	78.8	104.4	96.5	107.7	118.1	100.0	102.3
99.1	99.2	100.1	99.2	99.8	99.7	97.8	100.7	100.7	99.3	100.5	100.1	105.6	101.7
101.2	**100.3**	**99.1**	**99.4**	**97.8**	**100.0**	**99.5**	**102.0**	**97.9**	**104.9**	**99.0**	**96.9**	**101.9**	**101.2**
99.6	96.1	99.3	99.3	97.6	99.9	99.2	102.9	95.6	100.8	98.5	96.0	102.2	101.2
106.9	109.0	98.4	99.7	100.9	100.1	100.0	100.0	102.7	108.6	100.0	100.3	100.6	101.3

9-6 主要年份农业生产资料价格分类指数
Price Indices for Means of Agricultural Production by Category in Main Years

(上年=100) (preceding year=100)

项　目	Item	2005	2010	2013
农业生产资料价格指数	**Price Indices for Means of Agricultural Production**	**105.3**	**103.1**	**102.6**
农用手工工具	Farm Handtools	104.9	101.0	102.4
饲料类	Forage	101.3	114.0	106.6
产品畜	Commodity Animals	89.4	127.1	112.3
半机械化农具	Semi-mechanized Farm Tools	100.9	101.7	101.0
机械化农具	Mechanized Farm Machinery	102.5	100.1	100.5
化学肥料	Chemical Fertilizer	110.2	95.3	98.3
农药及农药械	Pesticide and Its Appliances	102.8	101.7	101.0
农用机油	Oil for Farm Machinery	111.0	110.1	101.9
其他农业生产资料	Other Means of Agricultural Production	105.5	100.7	103.5
农业生产服务	Service for Agriculture Production		102.0	106.8

9-7 各市县农业生产资料价格指数
Price Indices for Means of Agricultural Production in Cities and Counties

(上年=100) (2013 年) (preceding year=100)

项　目	Item	塔城市 Kashgar [Kaxgar] City	阿勒泰市 Altay City	沙湾县 Shawan County	博乐市 Bole [Bortala] City	吐鲁番市 Turpan City	库车县 Kuqa County	阿图什市 Artux City	莎车县 Shache [Yarkant] County	焉耆回族自治县 Yanqi Hui Autonomous County
农业生产资料价格指数	**Price Indices for Means of Agricultural Production**	**101.7**	**103.7**	**102.3**	**104.0**	**102.0**	**103.8**	**101.8**	**103.0**	**100.0**
农用手工工具	Farm Handtools	100.9	101.3	104.7	110.0	110.3	103.9	100.0	96.5	101.3
饲料类	Forage	102.1	113.7	105.2	94.0	107.9	99.3	107.1	112.1	111.8
产品畜	Commodity Animals	112.4	107.0	108.8	111.5	113.6	109.7	144.3	112.4	113.4
半机械化农具	Semi-mechanized Farm Tools	99.2	100.2	104.4	101.4	100.0	104.6	100.0	100.3	100.7
机械化农具	Mechanized Farm Machinery	105.0	100.1	100.0	100.0	98.6	101.9	100.0	100.5	100.0
化学肥料	Chemical Fertilizer	94.2	97.5	102.3	103.7	99.3	102.9	94.1	97.9	91.7
农药及农药械	Pesticide and Its Appliances	100.7	103.8	100.1	100.3	102.2	103.5	102.6	97.7	104.3
农用机油	Oil for Farm Machinery	101.8	99.5	97.8	113.0	99.4	99.2	101.3	102.2	99.3
其他农业生产资料	Other Means of Agricultural Production	104.2	107.0	100.9	107.7	98.8	107.7	100.0	102.5	103.1
农业生产服务	Service for Agriculture Production	113.1	111.0	101.6	106.7	102.4	109.3	102.6	108.7	100.1

9-8 主要年份工业生产者出厂价格分类指数
Producer Price Indices for Manufactured Goods by Category in Main Years

(上年=100) (preceding year=100)

项　目	Item	2005	2010	2013
全部工业品	**Total Industrial Products**	**116.6**	**125.3**	**96.5**
按轻、重工业分	**By Light and Heavy Industry**			
轻工业	**Light Industry**	**99.6**	**108.9**	**99.6**
以农产品为原料	Using Farm Produces as Raw Materials	98.4	111.2	100.5
以非农产品为原料	Using Non-farm Produces as Raw Materials	101.9	104.6	94.6
重工业	**Heavy Industry**	**122.5**	**128.7**	**96.0**
采　掘	Mining and Quarrying	136.2	153.1	95.4
原　料	Raw Materials	114.2	114.0	96.3
加　工	Processing	104.1	105.6	96.0
按部类分	**By Sector**			
生产资料	**Means of Production**	**118.4**	**127.1**	**96.0**
采　掘	Mining and Quarrying	136.0	151.9	95.4
原　料	Raw Materials	114.3	115.1	96.3
加　工	Processing	100.4	107.3	96.3
生活资料	**Consumer Goods**	**101.3**	**104.1**	**101.5**
食　品	Food	101.7	104.4	101.7
衣　着	Clothing	96.4	101.5	101.0
一般日用品	Articles for Daily Use	101.1	101.4	100.3
耐用消费品	Durable Consumer Goods	99.2	102.3	100.3
按工业部门分	**Division of Industrial Setors**			
冶金工业	Metallurgical Industry	101.9	114.4	93.2
电力工业	Power Industry	100.9	100.7	100.1
煤炭及炼焦工业	Coal and Coking Industry	109.4	104.0	92.9
石油工业	Petroleum Industry	130.5	141.6	96.5
化学工业	Chemical Industry	106.1	112.1	93.3
机械工业	Machine Manufacturing Industry	112.4	97.4	101.3
建筑材料工业	Building Materials Industry	99.4	101.1	95.2
森林工业	Timber Industry	99.9	101.7	100.4
食品工业	Food Industry	101.1	104.9	102.2
纺织工业	Textile Industry	92.1	122.8	96.8
缝纫工业	Tailoring Industry	96.3	101.5	101.6
皮革工业	Leather Industry	100.0	101.1	106.7
造纸工业	Paper Industry	102.6	127.8	99.5
文教艺术用品工业	Cultural, Educational and Handicrafts Articles	99.7	101.1	100.1
其他工业	Other Industry	104.0	107.7	98.8

9-9 主要年份工业生产者购进价格分类指数
Purchasing Prices Indices for Raw Material, Fuels and Power by Category in Main Years

(上年=100) (preceding year=100)

项　目	Iterm	2005	2010	2013
全部原材料价格指数	Total of Raw Material	**110.7**	**123.9**	**97.8**
燃料、动力类	Fuel and Power	132.0	137.6	96.6
黑色金属材料类	Ferrous Metals	113.8	105.0	95.4
#钢　材	Rolled Steel	112.9	102.5	96.7
其　他	Others	114.9	112.3	92.5
有色金属材料及电线类	Nonferrous Metals and Wire Type	108.5	139.6	96.2
化工原料类	Raw Chemistry Material	113.0	106.8	99.1
木材及纸浆类	Timber and Paper Pulp	102.0	104.0	99.1
建筑材料及非金属类	Building Material and Non-metal Ore	103.9	103.0	97.8
其他工业原材料及半成品类	Other Industrial Raw Material and Semi-finished Category	105.5	101.1	98.5
农副产品类	Agricultural Products	91.9	118.7	102.7
纺织原料类	Textile Raw Materials	93.0	144.2	99.0

9-10 主要年份固定资产投资价格指数
Price Indices for Investment in Fixed Assets in Main Years

(上年=100) (preceding year=100)

项　目	Item	2005	2010	2013
固定资产投资价格指数	Investment in Fixed Assets	**102.8**	**104.6**	**100.5**
建筑安装工程	Construction and Installtion	**102.7**	**105.9**	**100.5**
人工费	Manpower Expenses	103.8	110.6	107.8
材料费	Material Expenses	102.3	104.8	97.0
#钢　材	Rolled Steel	101.7	104.4	93.8
木　材	Timber	102.5	104.8	102.7
水　泥	Cement	100.1	104.7	96.1
地方材料	Local Material	102.0	104.6	99.0
化工材料	Chemical Material	109.1	104.9	101.3
电　料	Electrical Wire	104.0	105.1	95.6
其他材料	Other Material	99.9	101.7	101.9
机械使用费	Expenses of Machine Use	102.3	103.3	105.9
设备工器具	Purchase of Equipment,Tools and Instruments	**104.8**	**100.4**	**99.5**
其他费用	Others	**100.0**	**105.2**	**103.5**

主要统计指标解释

居民消费价格指数 简称 CPI，是反映一定时期内城乡居民所购买的生活消费品和服务项目价格变动趋势和程度的相对数，是对城市居民消费价格指数和农村居民消费价格指数进行综合汇总计算的结果。通过该指数可以观察和分析消费品的零售价格和服务项目价格变动对城乡居民实际生活费支出的影响程度。

城市居民消费价格指数 是反映一定时期内城市居民家庭所购买的生活消费品价格和服务项目价格变动趋势和程度的相对数。通过该指数可以观察和分析消费品的零售价格和服务项目价格变动对城镇居民收入和消费支出的影响。

农村居民消费价格指数 是反映一定时期内农村居民家庭所购买的生活消费品价格和服务项目价格变动趋势和程度的相对数。该指数可以观察农村消费品的零售价格和服务项目价格变动对农村居民收入和生活消费支出的影响。

商品零售价格指数 是反映一定时期内城乡商品零售价格变动趋势和程度的相对数。商品零售价格的变动与国家的财政收入、市场供需的平衡、消费与积累的比例关系有关。因此，该指数可以从一个侧面对上述经济活动进行观察和分析。

农业生产资料价格指数 指反映一定时期内，农业生产资料价格变动趋势和程度的相对数。其编制目的是了解农业生产中物质资料投入价格的变动状况，服务于国民经济核算。1994 年以前，农业生产资料价格指数仅仅是商品零售价格指数的一个类别，此后，从商品零售价格指数中分离出来，单独编制。

工业生产者出厂价格指数 简称 PPI，是反映一定时期内全部工业产品出厂价格（工业企业产品第一次出售时的价格）总水平的变动趋势和程度的相对数，包括工业企业售给本企业以外所有单位的各种产品和直接售给居民用于生活消费的产品。该指数可以观察出厂价格变动对工业总产值及增加值的影响。

工业生产者购进价格指数 是反映工业企业作为生产投入，而从物资交易市场和能源、原材料生产企业购买原材料、燃料和动力产品时，所支付的价格水平变动趋势和程度的统计指标。是扣除工业企业物质消耗成本中的价格变动影响的重要依据。

目前，我国编制的工业生产者购进价格指数所调查的产品包括燃料动力、黑色金属、有色金属、化工、建材等九大类。

固定资产投资价格指数 是反映一定时期内固定资产投资品及取费项目的价格变动趋势和程度的相对数。固定资产投资额是由建筑安装工程投资完成额、设备工器具购置投资完成额和其他费用投资完成额三部分组成的。编制固定资产投资价格指数应首先分别编制上述三部分投资的价格指数，然后采用加权算术平均法求出固定资产投资价格总指数。

该指数可以准确地反映固定资产投资中涉及的各类投资品和取费项目价格变动趋势和变动幅度，消除按现价计算的固定资产投资指标中的价格变动因素，真实地反映固定资产投资的规模、速度、结构和效益，为国家科学地制定、检查固定资产投资计划并提高宏观调控水平，为完善国民经济核算体系提供科学的、可靠的依据。

Explanatory Notes on Main Statistical Indicators

Consumer Price Indices reflect the trend and degree of changes in prices of consumer goods and services purchased by urban and rural households during a given period.They are obtained by combining Consumer Price Indices of Urban Household and Consumer Price Indices of Rural Household. The Indices enable the observation and analysis of the degree of impact of the changes in the prices of retailed goods and services on the actual living expenses of urban and rural residents.

Consumer Price Indices of Urban Household reflect the trend and degree of changes in prices of consumer goods and services purchased by urban households during a given period. It can be used to observe and analyze the impact of price changes in consumer goods and services on urban household income and consumption expenditure.

Consumer Price Indices of Rural Household reflect the trend and degree of changes in prices of consumer goods and services purchased by rural households during a given period. It can be used to observe the impact of change in retail prices of consumer goods and service prices on rural household income and consumption expenditure on living.

Retail Price Indices reflect the trend and degree of change in retail prices of commodities during a given period. The change in retail prices of commodities is related to government revenue, the equilibrium of market supply and demand, and the ratio of consumption to accumulation. Therefore, the retail price indices are useful from an oblique perspective for observing and analyzing the changes of the above economic activities.

Price Indices for Means of Agricultural Production reflect the trend and degree of changes in the prices of the means of agricultural production during a given period. Compilation of these indices helps to understand the price changes of material input in agricultural production and facilitate the compilation of national accounts. Before 1994, price indices for means of agricultural production were a sub-category in the retail price indices for commodities, and it has been compiled separately since 1994.

Producer Price Indices for Industrial Products reflect the trend and degree of changes in general ex-factory prices of all manufactured goods during a given period, including sales of manufactured goods by an industrial enterprise to all units outside the enterprise, as well as sales of consumer goods to residents. It can be used to analyze the impact of ex-factory prices on gross output value and value-added of the industrial sector.

Purchasing Price Indices for Industrial Producers reflect changes in the level and degree of prices paid by industrial enterprises when they purchase production input such as raw materials, fuels and power from the market or from other energy or raw materials producing enterprises. These indices provide an important basis for measuring the material consumption of industrial enterprises after removing the influence of price changes.

At present, products in 9 categories, including fuels and power, ferrous metals, non-ferrous metals, chemicals, building materials, are covered in China for the survey to produce indices for purchasing' prices for industrial producers.

Price Indices for Investment in Fixed Assets reflect the trend and degree of changes in prices of investment goods and projects in fixed assets during a given period. The investment in fixed assets consists of three components, namely the investment in construction and installation, the investment in purchases of equipment and instrument, and the investment in other items. Price indices for investment in fixed assets are calculated as the weighted arithmetic mean of the price indices for the three components of investment in fixed assets.

Removing the factor of price change in the aggregates of investment at current prices, this indicator shows the changes in the prices of commodities and fees involved in the investment of fixed assets, and can be used to observe the actual size, growth, structure, and efficiency of investment in fixed assets and provides reliable and scientific data for government planning, management, decision-making, and further improving the current national accounting system.

新疆统计年鉴
XINJIANG STATISTICAL YEARBOOK

10

人民生活

PEOPLE'S LIVELIHOOD AND SOCIAL WELFARE

简要说明

本篇主要内容和资料来源

本篇资料反映新疆城乡居民生活现状以及城镇居民社会保障情况，主要包括居民家庭基本情况、家庭收入、支出情况、主要商品购买数量及支出金额、居住状况和耐用消费品的拥有量及居民社会保险情况等。

居民生活状况的数据来源于国家统计局新疆调查总队住户调查处。

居民社会保险情况数据来源于新疆维吾尔自治区人力资源和社会保障厅。

Brief Introduction

Main Content and Source of Data

Data in this chapter show the condition of people's livelihood in Xinjiang and social security in urban, including mainly basic condition of people's household, income of households, income and expenditure of the household, the quantity and the expenditure on major commodities purchased, the housing condition and the possession of the durable consumer goods and people's social securiyt, etc.

Data on the livelihood of residents are from the Department of households Survey , NBS Survey office in Xinjiang.

Data on social security in urban and rural are from Bureau of Human Resources and Social Security of Xinjiang Uygur Autonomous Region.

10-1 主要年份人民物质文化生活情况
People's Material and Cultural Living Conditions in Main Years

项　　目	Item	2000	2005	2010	2013
就 业	**Employment**				
城镇居民家庭每户就业人口(人)	Average Number of Employed Persons Per Urban Household (person)	1.55	1.48	1.54	1.42
农村居民家庭每户整半劳动力(人)	Average Number of Full/Semi Laborer Per (person)	3.06	2.92	3.14	2.81
每一农村劳动力负担人数(人)	Number of Dependents Per Laborer of Rural Household (person)	1.74	1.62	1.47	1.43
每一城镇就业者负担人数(人)	Number of Dependents Per Employee of Urban Household (person)	2.03	2.04	1.94	1.76
城镇登记失业率(%)	Registered Urban Unemployment Rate (%)	3.8	3.9	3.2	3.4
收入与支出	**Income and Expenditure**				
城镇居民家庭人均可支配收入(元)	Annual Per capita Disposable Income of Urban Household Residents (yuan)	5645	7990	13644	19874
农村居民家庭人均纯收入(元)	Annual per Capita Net Income of Rural Household (yuan)	1618	2482	4643	7296
城镇居民人均消费性支出(元)	Annual Per capita Net Income of Rural Household (yuan)	4423	6208	10197	15206
农村居民人均生活消费支出(元)	Annual per Capita Living Expencliture of Urban (yuan)	1236	1924	3458	6119
生活质量	**Annual Per capita Consumption**				
居住条件	Residence Condition				
城镇人均住房建筑面积(平方米)	Per Capita Building Space in Urban Area (sq.m)	26.75	26.02	27.25	30.61
农村人均住房面积(平方米)	Per Capita Living Space in Rural Area (sq.m)	17.25	21.23	24.00	24.57
交 通	Traffic				
城镇每百户拥有汽车(辆)	Number of Automobile per 100 Households in Urban Areas (unit)	0.82	2.81	8.63	18.18
农村每百户拥有摩托车(辆)	Number of Motor Cycles Per 100 Rural Household (unit)	18.33	45.42	62.84	78.51
通信条件	Communication Condition				
电话普及率(固定电话)(部/百人)	Telephone Popularization Rate (Fixed Telephone)(set/100 persons)	15.0	30.8	25.4	28.1
移动电话普及率(部/百人)	Popularization Rate of Mobile Telephone (set/100 persons)	4.3	26.7	63.0	167.2
城镇公用事业	Public Utilities in Urban Areas				
自来水普及率 (%)	Coverage Rate of Population with Access to Tap Water (%)	98.8	97.9	99.2	98.1
燃气普及率 (%)	Coverage Rate of Population with Access to Gas(%)	92.8	89.3	95.8	96.5

10-1 续表 Continued

项　目	Item	2000	2005	2010	2013
文化、教育和卫生	**Culture,Education and Health Care**				
文 化	Culture				
广播综合人口覆盖率 (%)	Radio Coverage Rate of Population (%)	89.77	93.14	94.90	95.68
电视综合人口覆盖率 (%)	TV Coverage Rate of Population (%)	92.15	92.78	95.28	95.95
每百户彩色电视机拥有量 (部/百户)	Number of Color TV Per 100 Household (set/100 Households)				
城 镇	Urban	102.57	105.70	105.61	98.59
农 村	Rural	31.87	61.81	89.87	96.97
居民家庭文教娱乐支出比重 (%)	Percentage of Household Expenditure on Education, Culture and Entertainment				
城 镇	Urban	13.58	11.94	9.93	10.51
农 村	Rural	3.76	3.70	4.92	5.08
教 育	Education				
各级普通学校毕业生升学率 (%)	Rate of Entering Higher School				
高中升学率	Promotion Rate from Senion Secondary Schools to Higher Education	80.46	64.84	84.59	88.69
初中升学率	Promotion Rate from Junior Secondary Schools to Senior Secondary Schools	30.30	39.13	45.40	52.53
小学升学率	Promotion Rate from Primary Schools to Junior Secondary Schools	92.01	99.33	100.53	97.60
卫 生	Public Health				
每万人有医院、卫生院床位(张)	Number of Hospital Beds per 10 000 Population (unit)	35.6	37.8	50.4	57.8
每万人有医生数(人)	Number of Doctors per 10 000 Population (person)	24.6	20.6	22.3	23.4
居民家庭医疗保健支出比重 (%)	Percentage of Resident Expenditure on Health Care				
城 镇	Urban	7.48	8.04	6.94	7.76
农 村	Rural	2.61	3.93	9.10	10.75
社会保障	Social Security				
参加城镇职工基本养老保险人数 (万人)	Number of Employees Joining Urban Basic Pension Insurance (10 000persons)	140.34	181.87	259.67	326.04
参加城镇职工基本医疗保险人数 (万人)	Number of Persons Joining Urban Basic Medical Care System (10 000persons)	88.20	211.85	296.72	358.93
参加失业保险人数 (万人)	Number of Employees Joining Unemploy ment Insurance (10 000persons)	122.10	140.82	180.29	218.52
参加工伤保险人数 (万人)	Number of Employees Joining Injury Insurance (10 000persons)		79.51	184.13	239.87
参加生育保险人数 (万人)	Number of persons Joining Maternity Insurance (10 000persons)		103.48	188.23	230.22

10-2 主要年份城乡居民家庭人均收入及指数
Per Capita Annual Income of Urban and Rural Households and the Related Index in Main Years

年 份 Year	农村居民家庭人均纯收入 Per Capita Annual Net Income of Rural Households		城镇居民家庭人均年可支配收入 Per Capita Annual Disposable Income of Urban Households	
	绝对数（元）Value (yuan)	指数(1978=100) Index	绝对数（元）Value (yuan)	指数(1978=100) Index
1978	119	100.0	319	100.0
1980	201	168.9	427	133.9
1985	394	331.1	735	230.4
1990	684	574.8	1314	411.8
1995	1137	955.5	4163	1172.3
2000	1618	1359.3	5645	1589.4
2001	1710	1437.0	6215	1749.9
2002	1863	1564.9	6554	1979.1
2003	2106	1768.3	7006	2115.7
2004	2245	1885.0	7503	2265.9
2005	2482	2084.0	7990	2412.9
2006	2737	2300.0	8871	2679.0
2007	3183	2674.8	10313	3114.5
2008	3503	2943.7	11432	3452.4
2009	3883	3263.0	12258	3701.8
2010	4643	3901.7	13644	4120.0
2011	5442	4573.1	15514	4684.4
2012	6394	5373.4	17921	5410.5
2013	7296	6131.5	19874	6230.1

注: 1992 年以前城镇居民人均年可支配收入为人均年生活费收入。
Note: Per capita disposal income of urban households before the year 1992 is Per capita annual income as life expense.

10-3 分地区城镇居民人均可支配收入
Per Capita Annual Income of Urban Households by Region

单位: 元　　(2013 年) (抽样调查　Sampled Survey)　　(yuan)

地 区	Region	收 入 Income	地 区	Region	收 入 Income
乌鲁木齐市	Urumqi City	21304	阿勒泰地区	Altay Administrative Offices	18427
克拉玛依市	Karamay City	25249	博尔塔拉蒙古自治州	Bortala Mongol Autonomous Prefecture	18863
吐鲁番地区	Turpan Administrative Offices	19943	巴音郭楞蒙古自治州	Bayangol Mongol Autonomous Prefecture	20408
哈密地区	Hami [Kumul] Administrative Offices	20865	阿克苏地区	Aksu Administrative Offices	20049
昌吉回族自治州	Changji Hui Autonomous Prefecture	20111	克孜勒苏柯尔克孜自治州	Kizilsu Kirgiz Autonomous Prefecture	17094
伊犁州直属县(市)	Counties (Cities) Direct Under Ili Prefecture	18496	喀什地区	Kashgar [Kaxgar] Administrative Offices	15454
塔城地区	Tacheng [Tarbagatai] Administrative Offices	19005	和田地区	Hotan Administrative Offices	18478

10-4 主要年份城镇居民家庭生活基本情况
Basic Living Conditions of Urban Households in Main Years

(抽样调查 Sampled Survey)

项 目	Item	2000	2005	2010	2013
调查户数（户）	**Number of Households Surveyed (household)**	**790**	**1380**	**1560**	**1360**
平均每户家庭人口(人)	**Average Household Size (person)**	**3.15**	**3.02**	**2.98**	**2.75**
平均每户就业人口(人)	**Average Number of Employed Persons Per Household (person)**	**1.55**	**1.48**	**1.54**	**1.42**
平均每户就业面（%）	**Proportion of Employment per Household (%)**	**49.21**	**49.01**	**51.68**	**56.80**
平均每一就业者负担人数(包括就业者本人)(人)	**Number of Dependents Per Employee (including the employee himself or herself) (person)**	**2.03**	**2.04**	**1.94**	**1.76**
平均每人全部年收入(元)	**Per Capita Annual Income (yuan)**	**5686.52**	**8693.67**	**15421.59**	**22387.85**
#可支配收入	Disposable Income	5644.86	7990.15	13643.77	19873.77
工资性收入	Income from Wages and Salaries	4128.29	6553.47	11327.91	15585.27
工资及补贴收入	Salary & Subsidy	4027.36	6331.74	11208.19	15131.85
其他劳动收入	Part-time Income	100.93	221.73	119.72	453.41
经营净收入	Net Business Income	230.29	522.14	1131.78	1803.48
财产性收入	Income from Porperties	38.03	54.51	151.94	152.66
转移性收入	Income from Transfer	1243.55	1563.54	2809.96	4846.44
平均每人消费性支出(元)	**Per Capita Annual Consumption Expenditures (yuan)**	**4422.92**	**6207.52**	**10197.09**	**15206.16**
平均每人消费性支出构成(%)(人均消费支出=100)	**Composition of Per Capita Annual Consumption (%)**	**100**	**100**	**100**	**100**
食 品	Food	36.38	36.37	36.23	35.01
衣 着	Clothing	13.05	13.31	14.84	13.40
家庭设备用品及服务	Household Facilities,Articles and Service	9.29	4.99	6.57	8.39
医疗保健	Health Care and Medical Service	7.48	8.04	6.94	6.43
交通通讯	Transport and Communication	7.48	12.20	12.32	7.76
教育文化娱乐服务	Education , Cultural and Recreation Services	13.58	11.94	9.93	14.54
居 住	Residence	7.76	9.21	8.81	10.51
其他商品和服务	Miscellaneous Goods and Services	4.98	3.94	4.36	3.98

10-5 城镇居民家庭基本情况
Basic Conditions of Urban Households

(2013 年) (抽样调查 Sampled Survey)

项 目	Item	全 区 Whole Region	最低收入户 Lowest Income Households	#困难户 Poor Households	低收入户 Low Income Households
调查户数(户)	Number of Households Surveyed (household)	1360	70	70	130
比重(%)	Proportion (%)		5	5	10
平均每户家庭人口(人)	Average Household Size (person)	2.75	3.34	3.57	3.24
平均每户就业人口(人)	Average Number of Employees per Household (person)	1.42	1.22	1.25	1.38
平均每户就业面(%)	Proportion of Employment per Household (%)	56.80	36.51	35.09	42.74
平均每一就业者负担人数(包括就业者本人)(人)	Number of Dependents per Employee (Including the employee himself or herself) (person)	1.76	2.74	2.85	2.34
平均每人全部年收入(元)	Per Capita Annual Income (yuan)	22387.85	7398.71	3708.83	10562.04
平均每人可支配收入(元)	Per Capita Disposable Income (yuan)	19873.77	6348.46	2808.27	9402.73
平均每人消费性支出(元)	Per Capita Annual Consumption Expenditure (yuan)	15206.16	6606.09	6449.70	9706.50

项 目	Item	中等偏下户 Lower Middle Income Households	中等收入户 Middle Income Households	中等偏上户 Upper Middle Income Households	高收入户 High Income Households	最高收入户 Highest Income Households
调查户数(户)	Number of Households Surveyed (household)	270	270	270	130	70
比重(%)	Proportion (%)	20	20	20	10	5
平均每户家庭人口(人)	Average Household Size (person)	2.98	2.78	2.51	2.22	2.01
平均每户就业人口(人)	Average Number of Employees per Household (person)	1.60	1.43	1.34	1.37	1.33
平均每户就业面(%)	Proportion of Employed Persons per Household (%)	53.88	51.61	53.24	61.63	66.18
平均每一就业者负担人数(包括就业者本人)(人)	Number of Dependents per Employee (Including the employee himself or herself) (person)	1.86	1.94	1.88	1.62	1.51
平均每人全部年收入(元)	Per Capita Annual Income (yuan)	17130.35	22672.01	29573.41	37011.70	43939.74
平均每人可支配收入(元)	Per Capita Disposable Income (yuan)	14723.90	20218.20	26488.14	33108.56	39799.63
平均每人消费性支出(元)	Per Capita Annual Consumption Expenditure (yuan)	11842.04	15713.37	18643.95	23086.79	25895.86

10-6 城镇居民家庭平均每人全年消费性支出
Per Capita Annual Living Expenditure of Urban Households

单位：元　　(2013 年) (抽样调查 Sampled Survey)　　(yuan)

项 目	Item	总平均 Total Average	最低收入户 Lowest Income Households	#困难户 Poor Households	低收入户 Low Income Households
消费性支出	**Consumption Expenditures**	**15206.16**	**6606.09**	**6449.70**	**9706.50**
食 品	Food	5323.50	2923.42	2710.08	4141.12
#粮 食	Grain	555.11	504.14	497.30	483.58
肉禽及其制品	Meat, Poultry and Processed Products	1129.30	684.27	664.70	1156.48
蛋 类	Eggs	85.93	63.18	54.63	73.10
水产品	Aquatic Products	107.51	36.13	36.33	64.57
奶及奶制品	Milk and Processed Products	246.31	179.23	164.76	185.98
衣 着	Clothing	2036.94	875.82	600.41	1201.91
#服 装	Garments	1490.38	601.87	433.54	864.14
家庭设备用品及服务	Household Appliances and Services	977.80	462.88	315.72	509.81
#耐用消费品	Durable Consumer Goods	405.46	179.51	127.18	151.74
医疗保健	Health Care and Medical Services	1179.77	602.85	1033.79	1046.25
交通通讯	Transport and Communication Services	2210.25	487.94	667.77	858.02
教育文化娱乐服务	Education , Cultural and Recreation Services	1597.99	469.90	421.42	964.54
#文化娱乐用品	Recreation Articles	293.53	74.41	86.33	175.23
居 住	Residence	1275.35	681.36	511.44	694.69
#住 房	Housing	483.76	126.00	59.71	140.96
其他商品和服务	Miscellaneous Goods and Services	604.55	101.93	189.07	290.16

项 目	Item	中等偏下户 Lower Middle Income Households	中等收入户 Middle Income Households	中等偏上户 Upper Middle Income Households	高收入户 High Income Households	最高收入户 Highest Income Households
消费性支出	**Consumption Expenditures**	**11842.04**	**15713.37**	**18643.95**	**23086.79**	**25895.86**
食 品	Food	4630.28	5382.49	6555.44	7234.11	7573.00
#粮 食	Grain	521.88	559.45	561.34	692.69	531.38
肉禽及其制品	Meat, Poultry and Processed Products	1059.25	1178.49	1224.46	1477.15	1389.60
蛋 类	Eggs	76.31	98.88	90.52	110.56	110.32
水产品	Aquatic Products	100.56	120.34	143.41	154.54	180.97
奶及奶制品	Milk and Processed Products	199.31	269.14	283.38	326.64	381.23
衣 着	Clothing	1650.64	2299.58	2342.90	2929.15	3955.62
#服 装	Garments	1205.61	1727.38	1637.18	2205.00	2863.69
家庭设备用品及服务	Household Appliances and Services	624.90	1032.45	1193.70	1584.20	1661.32
#耐用消费品	Durable Consumer Goods	199.74	441.62	451.67	839.33	711.05
医疗保健	Health Care and Medical Services	816.73	1262.83	1436.91	1504.05	2222.48
交通通讯	Transport and Communication Services	1467.57	2249.82	2755.56	3935.77	4441.68
教育文化娱乐服务	Education , Cultural and Recreation Services	1425.61	1618.53	2009.95	2829.21	2316.54
#文化娱乐用品	Recreation Articles	215.64	328.61	302.44	529.95	575.94
居 住	Residence	926.76	1297.27	1539.59	1894.88	2387.91
#住 房	Housing	280.71	463.09	589.21	743.90	1254.88
其他商品和服务	Miscellaneous Goods and Services	299.56	570.40	809.90	1175.43	1337.33

10-7 城镇居民家庭平均每人全年消费性支出构成
Composition of Per Capita Living Expenditure of Urban Households

单位：% (2013 年) (抽样调查 Sampled Survey) (%)

项目	Item	总平均 Total Average	最低收入户 Lowest Income Households	#困难户 Poor Households	低收入户 Low Income Households
消费性支出	**Consumption Expenditures**	**100.00**	**100.00**	**100.00**	**100.00**
食 品	Food	35.01	44.25	42.02	42.66
衣 着	Clothing	13.40	13.26	9.31	12.38
家庭设备用品及服务	Household Facilities, Articles and Services	6.43	7.01	4.90	5.25
医疗保健	Health Care and Medical Services	7.76	9.13	16.03	10.78
交通通讯	Transport and Communication Services	14.54	7.39	10.35	8.84
教育文化娱乐服务	Education , Cultural and Recreation Services	10.51	7.11	6.53	9.94
居 住	Residence	8.39	10.31	7.93	7.16
其他商品和服务	Miscellaneous Goods and Services	3.98	1.54	2.93	2.99

项目	Item	中等偏下户 Lower Middle Income Households	中等收入户 Middle Income Households	中等偏上户 Upper Middle Income Households	高收入户 High Income Households	最高收入户 Highest Income Households
消费性支出	**Consumption Expenditures**	**100.00**	**100.00**	**100.00**	**100.00**	**100.00**
食 品	Food	39.10	34.25	35.16	31.33	29.24
衣 着	Clothing	13.94	14.63	12.57	12.69	15.28
家庭设备用品及服务	Household Facilities, Articles and Services	5.28	6.57	6.40	6.86	6.42
医疗保健	Health Care and Medical Services	6.90	8.04	7.71	6.51	8.58
交通通讯	Transport and Communication Services	12.39	14.32	14.78	17.05	17.15
教育文化娱乐服务	Education , Cultural and Recreation Services	12.04	10.30	10.78	12.25	8.95
居 住	Residence	7.83	8.26	8.26	8.21	9.22
其他商品和服务	Miscellaneous Goods and Services	2.53	3.63	4.34	5.09	5.16

10-8 主要年份城镇居民家庭年人均购买的主要商品数量
Per Capita Annual Purchases of Major Commodities of Urban Households in Main Years

(抽样调查 Sampled Survey)

项　目	Item	2000	2005	2010	2013
粮食(千克)	Grain (kg)	81.91	88.38	89.76	102.80
鲜菜(千克)	Fresh Vegetables (kg)	90.56	109.45	96.15	101.97
食用植物油(千克)	Edible Vegetable Oil (kg)	9.69	11.01	10.94	16.40
猪肉(千克)	Pork (kg)	5.17	6.37	7.33	6.94
牛肉(千克)	Beef (kg)	3.62	3.51	3.86	5.16
羊肉(千克)	Mutton(kg)	13.06	11.99	9.87	9.03
禽类(千克)	Poultry (kg)	6.11	6.71	8.14	6.08
鲜蛋(千克)	Fresh Eggs (kg)	7.39	7.44	7.91	6.65
水产品(千克)	Aquatic Products (kg)	4.35	4.98	5.27	3.99
鲜乳品(千克)	Fresh Dairy Products (kg)	18.44	26.26	21.80	19.33
鲜瓜果(千克)	Fresh Fruits & Melons(kg)	64.31	66.99	57.36	53.24
管道天然气(立方米)	Natural Gas (cu.m)	1.93	22.12	39.68	62.66
煤炭(千克)	Coal (kg)	123.78	133.57	84.07	148.21

10-9 主要年份城镇居民家庭平均每百户年底耐用消费品拥有量
Number of Major Durable Consumer Goods Owned Per-100 Urban Households at Year-end in Main Years

项　目	Item	2000	2005	2010	2013
摩托车(辆)	Motorcycle (unit)	8.53	16.04	18.53	13.59
助力车(辆)	Aided Power Bicycle (unit)		2.29	8.60	17.19
家用汽车(辆)	Automobil (unit)	0.82	2.81	8.63	18.18
洗衣机(台)	Washing Machine (unit)	95.48	88.53	93.43	94.19
电冰箱(台)	Refrigerator (unit)	81.76	79.72	90.20	95.37
彩色电视机(台)	Color TV Set (set)	102.57	105.70	105.61	98.59
计算机(台)	Household Computer (set)	5.68	23.86	47.68	60.16
组合音响(套)	Hi-Fi Stereo Component System (set)	17.53	16.10	15.06	4.12
摄相机(架)	Pickug Camera (set)	1.02	3.12	4.57	7.45
照相机(架)	Camera (set)	33.71	37.42	26.83	32.27
其他中高档乐器(件)	Other Medium and High Grade Musical Instrument (piece)	9.09	5.97	6.54	5.40
微波炉(台)	Oven (unit)	5.39	19.68	34.84	42.49
空调器(台)	Air Conditioner (unit)	2.78	7.02	12.42	16.37
淋浴热水器(台)	Shower (unit)	47.91	59.58	74.27	80.44
消毒碗柜(台)	Disinfectant Machine (unit)		4.56	3.80	3.02
健身器材(台)	Healthy Equipment (unit)	2.35	3.89	2.65	2.24
固定电话(部)	Telephone (unit)	71.69	87.23	82.42	68.19
移动电话(部)	Mobile Phone (unit)	4.81	108.61	159.79	188.94
接入有线电视电视机(台)	Cable Tv (unit)		97.86	88.34	83.02
接入互连网计算机(台)	Internet Computer (unit)		12.43	32.20	52.43
接入互连网移动电话(台)	Internet Mobile Phone (unit)		0.52	7.89	74.88

10-10 按收入等级分城镇居民家庭平均每人全年购买商品数量
Per Capita Annual Purchases of Major Commodities of Urban Households by Level of Income

(2013 年) (抽样调查 Sampled Survey)

项目	Item	总平均 Total Average	最低收入户 Lowest Income Households	#困难户 Poor Households	低收入户 Low Income Households
粮　食(千克)	Grain (kg)	102.80	118.18	116.51	111.24
油脂类(千克)	Oil and Fats (kg)	16.44	16.86	19.47	18.33
食用植物油(千克)	Edible Vegetable Oil (kg)	16.40	16.86	19.47	18.29
肉　类(千克)	Meat (kg)	22.98	13.53	13.02	22.69
猪　肉	Pork	6.94	3.15	3.02	4.71
牛　肉	Beef	5.16	2.91	2.19	6.47
羊　肉	Mutton	9.03	6.70	7.29	10.19
禽　类(千克)	Poultry (kg)	6.08	3.32	2.15	5.81
蛋　类(千克)	Fresh Eggs (kg)	6.97	5.11	4.63	6.09
鱼　(千克)	Fish (kg)	3.99	1.50	2.00	2.74
虾　(千克)	Shrimp (kg)	0.38	0.12	0.11	0.21
鲜　菜(千克)	Fresh Vegetables (kg)	101.97	71.35	71.38	91.93
酒　类(千克)	Liquor (kg)	2.73	1.46	0.70	2.08
白　酒	Liquor	0.90	0.37	0.25	0.71
果　酒	Fruit Wine	0.16		0.01	0.18
啤　酒	Beer	1.66	1.09	0.44	1.19
鲜　果(千克)	Fresh Fruits (kg)	45.25	28.88	19.32	33.23
鲜　瓜(千克)	Fresh Melon (kg)	7.99	5.10	3.41	5.86
糕　点(千克)	Cake (kg)	3.60	2.13	1.04	2.32
鲜乳品(千克)	Fresh Dairy Products (kg)	19.33	18.26	15.36	19.57
奶　粉(千克)	Milk Powder (kg)	0.23	0.11	0.12	0.12
酸　奶(千克)	Yogurt (kg)	2.76	1.91	1.23	1.98
鞋　类(双)	Shoes (pair)	2.25	1.89	1.46	1.90
水(吨)	Water (ton)	26.26	30.50	18.20	20.79
电(度)	Electricity (kw)	326.20	212.11	223.33	303.43
煤　炭(千克)	Coal (kg)	148.21	299.63	292.10	332.12
罐装液化石油气(千克)	Liquefied Gas (kg)	5.32	17.86	9.41	5.72
管道天然气(立方米)	Gas Pipeline (cu.m)	62.66	23.34	12.70	41.15

10-10 续表 Continued

项　目	Item	中等偏下户 Lower Middle Income Households	中等收入户 Middle Income Households	中等偏上户 Upper Middle Income Households	高收入户 High Income Households	最高收入户 Highest Income Households
粮　食(千克)	Grain (kg)	92.03	100.21	97.33	114.32	92.28
油脂类(千克)	Oil and Fats (kg)	16.86	16.83	14.28	14.68	15.82
食用植物油(千克)	Edible Vegetable Oil (kg)	16.76	16.82	14.23	14.65	15.81
肉　类(千克)	Meat (kg)	22.47	23.71	25.50	30.47	27.37
猪　肉	Pork	7.50	6.45	9.04	10.42	8.66
牛　肉	Beef	5.09	5.41	5.81	5.29	6.00
羊　肉	Mutton	8.41	9.95	8.39	11.57	9.76
禽　类(千克)	Poultry (kg)	5.77	6.13	7.60	8.65	6.92
蛋　类(千克)	Fresh Eggs (kg)	6.12	7.97	7.36	8.77	8.97
鱼　(千克)	Fish (kg)	3.81	4.75	5.05	5.02	5.66
虾　(千克)	Shrimp (kg)	0.35	0.34	0.59	0.55	0.70
鲜　菜(千克)	Fresh Vegetables (kg)	99.28	105.39	109.35	122.49	137.59
酒　类(千克)	Liquor (kg)	2.32	2.77	3.47	2.76	8.75
白　酒	Liquor	0.89	0.85	1.28	0.87	1.56
果　酒	Fruit Wine	0.11	0.15	0.24	0.20	0.11
啤　酒	Beer	1.31	1.76	1.95	1.69	7.08
鲜　果(千克)	Fresh Fruits (kg)	40.47	48.91	56.14	61.11	58.80
鲜　瓜(千克)	Fresh Melon (kg)	7.14	8.63	9.91	10.78	10.38
糕　点(千克)	Cake (kg)	3.00	4.14	3.96	5.56	7.29
鲜乳品(千克)	Fresh Dairy Products (kg)	16.22	20.92	21.99	19.16	26.66
奶　粉(千克)	Milk Powder (kg)	0.15	0.28	0.31	0.35	0.07
酸　奶(千克)	Yogurt (kg)	2.09	2.32	3.58	4.68	6.80
鞋　类(双)	Shoes (pair)	2.01	2.29	2.43	2.82	3.21
水(吨)	Water (ton)	24.15	28.20	24.63	27.75	38.84
电(度)	Electricity (kw)	300.39	327.75	345.11	382.41	505.42
煤　炭(千克)	Coal (kg)	175.15	115.64	16.77	87.91	0.43
罐装液化石油气(千克)	Liquefied Gas (kg)	6.30	4.08	2.47	1.01	5.01
管道天然气(立方米)	Gas Pipeline (cu.m)	56.36	58.65	93.13	90.40	71.65

10-11 按收入等级分城镇居民家庭平均每百户年底耐用消费品拥有量
Ownership of Durable Consumer Goods Per100 Urban Households at Year-end by Level of Income

(2013 年) (抽样调查 Sampled Survey)

项　目	Item	总平均 Total Average	最低收入户 Lowest Income Households	#困难户 Poor Households	低收入户 Low Income Households
摩托车(辆)	Motorcycle(unit)	13.59	16.22	12.27	17.90
助力车(辆)	Aided Power Bicycle (unit)	17.19	36.77	32.54	25.60
家用汽车(辆)	Automobile(unit)	18.18	8.91	8.10	10.67
洗衣机(台)	Washing Machine (unit)	94.19	87.06	96.29	96.50
电冰箱(台)	Refrigerator (unit)	95.37	95.54	79.48	98.81
彩色电视机(台)	Color TV (set)	98.59	100.00	96.17	97.92
计算机(台)	Household Computer (set)	60.16	25.75	22.33	43.51
组合音响(套)	Hi-Fi Stereo Sound System (set)	4.12	0.97	0.75	2.58
摄像机(架)	Pickup Camera (set)	7.45			3.86
照相机(架)	Camera (set)	32.27	8.09	8.02	13.08
其他中高档乐器(件)	Other Medium and High Grade Musical Instrument (piece)	5.40	1.72	1.91	2.17
微波炉(台)	Microwave Oven (unit)	42.49	10.16	20.93	33.79
空调器(台)	Air Conditioner (unit)	16.37	1.29	4.95	6.20
淋浴热水器(台)	Water Heater for Shower (unit)	80.44	61.68	34.68	67.80
消毒碗柜(台)	Disinfectant Machine (unit)	3.02	1.95		3.43
健身器材(件)	Health Equipment (unit)	2.24			1.64
固定电话(部)	Fixed Telephone (unit)	68.19	41.92	48.19	63.39
移动电话(部)	Mobile Telephone (unit)	188.94	172.82	162.46	183.93
接入有线电视电视机(台)	Cable Tv (unit)	83.02	69.41	51.64	83.10
接入互连网计算机(台)	Internet Computer (unit)	52.43	24.12	17.05	32.49
接入互连网移动电话(台)	Internet Mobile Phone (unit)	74.88	56.87	64.08	61.00

项　目	Item	中等偏下户 Lower Middle Income Households	中等收入户 Middle Income Households	中等偏上户 Upper Middle Income Households	高收入户 High Income Households	最高收入户 Highest Income Households
摩托车(辆)	Motorcycle(unit)	15.87	19.53	7.10	8.68	4.81
助力车(辆)	Aided Power Bicycle (unit)	17.81	13.56	11.60	11.56	19.78
家用汽车(辆)	Automobile(unit)	18.61	16.18	20.54	27.80	23.52
洗衣机(台)	Washing Machine (unit)	93.00	95.85	96.12	95.39	87.83
电冰箱(台)	Refrigerator (unit)	94.00	96.60	97.15	97.84	91.37
彩色电视机(台)	Color TV (set)	99.15	100.29	95.72	101.47	97.63
计算机(台)	Household Computer (set)	56.17	67.79	67.64	71.25	61.84
组合音响(套)	Hi-Fi Stereo Sound System (set)	4.82	5.82	5.82	1.80	2.72
摄像机(架)	Pickup Camera (set)	7.34	6.04	12.39	9.98	8.35
照相机(架)	Camera (set)	25.97	34.70	41.10	48.02	47.87
其他中高档乐器(件)	Other Medium and High Grade Musical Instrument (piece)	6.09	6.28	7.05	5.42	2.92
微波炉(台)	Microwave Oven (unit)	37.90	44.46	51.63	47.47	61.01
空调器(台)	Air Conditioner (unit)	14.39	16.19	23.67	14.70	23.50
淋浴热水器(台)	Water Heater for Shower (unit)	78.76	84.92	91.88	87.97	83.36
消毒碗柜(台)	Disinfectant Machine (unit)	2.94	1.47	3.19	2.73	7.61
健身器材(件)	Health Equipment (unit)	3.26	2.42	1.64		6.02
固定电话(部)	Fixed Telephone (unit)	66.38	73.25	79.68	70.83	67.58
移动电话(部)	Mobile Telephone (unit)	188.64	197.75	185.41	196.68	195.30
接入有线电视电视机(台)	Cable Tv (unit)	82.64	86.23	90.35	82.68	81.09
接入互连网计算机(台)	Internet Computer (unit)	48.24	56.69	62.28	65.97	55.76
接入互连网移动电话(台)	Internet Mobile Phone (unit)	57.84	83.38	81.97	96.11	70.57

10-12 按收入等级分城镇居民家庭年末住房情况
Living Conditions of Urban Households by level of Income at Year-end

(2013 年) (抽样调查 Sampled Survey)

项 目	Item	总平均 Total Average	最低收入户 Lowest Income Households	#困难户 Poor Households	低收入户 Low Income Households
家庭居住人口数(人/户)	Number of Permanent Residents (person/household)	2.81	3.38	3.61	3.29
现住房总建筑面积(平方米/人)	Floor Space of Buildings (Sq.m/person)	30.61	23.95	23.82	30.38
现住房屋总使用面积(平方米/人)	Floor Space of Using(Sq.m/person)	22.96	17.97	17.87	22.79
房屋产权 (%)	House Ownership (%)	100.00	100.00	100.00	100.00
租赁公房	Renting of Publicly-Funded House	1.76	11.78	11.67	1.54
租赁私房	Renting of Private House	5.71	7.30	5.40	3.26
原有私房	Original Private House	11.19	28.71	44.22	32.03
房改私房	Private House Obtained from House Reform	37.42	21.71	12.10	37.66
商品房	Commercial House	42.81	29.17	25.55	24.09
其他	Others	1.11	1.32	1.06	1.42
住宅建筑式样 (%)	Architectural Style of Dwelling (%)	100.00	100.00	100.00	100.00
单栋住宅	Building	1.76	2.84	8.99	3.17
四居室	Four-Room House	1.39	4.67	3.03	3.06
三居室	Three-Room House	34.69	14.75	8.11	24.51
二居室	Two-Room House	43.50	31.66	27.43	32.04
一居室	One-Room House	6.01	6.78	13.58	2.72
普通楼房	Ordinary Multi-Storey Building	0.76	6.59		1.18
平房及其他	A Single-Storey House and Others	11.89	32.71	38.86	33.32
装修状况 (%)	Decoration Situation (%)	100.00	100.00	100.00	100.00
饮水情况 (%)	Condition of Drinking Water (%)	100.00	100.00	100.00	100.00
#自来水	Tap Water	99.42	100.00	100.00	97.45
井、河水	Well Water、River Water	0.33			1.29
用水情况 (%)	By Tap Water Facilities (%)	100.00	100.00	100.00	100.00
独用自来水	Tap Water Owner Per Household	99.56	97.74	100.00	98.71
公用自来水	Public Tap Water	0.11	2.26		
卫生设备 (%)	By Health Facilities (%)	100.00	100.00	100.00	100.00
无卫生设备	Without Toilet Room	0.81	2.12	5.00	2.00
有厕所浴室	Bathroom and Toilet Room Owned by Household	86.74	47.95	69.19	77.04
有厕所无浴室	Toilet Room Owned by Household and Without bathroom	10.37	49.93	21.36	16.22
公用	Public Toilet Room	2.08		4.45	4.74
取暖设备 (%)	By Heating Facilities (%)	100.00	100.00	100.00	100.00
无取暖设备	Without Heating Facilities	0.63		3.03	0.99
暖气	Warm Gas	99.37	100.00	96.97	99.01
炊用燃料使用情况 (%)	By Fuel Types (%)	100.00	100.00	100.00	100.00
管道天然气	Pipeline Gas	75.27	54.89	28.05	57.48
罐装液化石油气	LPG	13.12	19.98	33.79	15.56
煤炭	Coal	7.75	19.04	29.92	23.23
其他	Others	2.67	4.87	3.24	2.55
通信设备使用情况	By General Equipment Usage				
固定电话(部/百户)	Fixed Telephone (unit /100 Households)	68.19	41.92	48.19	63.39
移动电话(部/百户)	Mobile Telephone (unit /100 Households)	188.94	172.82	162.46	183.93
使用互联网(条/百户)	The use of Internet (unit /100 Households)	52.43	24.12	17.05	32.49

10-12 续表 Continued

项　　目	Item	中等偏下户 Lower Middle Income Households	中等收入户 Middle Income Households	中等偏上户 Upper Middle Income Households	高收入户 High Income Households	最高收入户 Highest Income Households
家庭居住人口数(人/户)	Number of Permanent Residents (person/household)	3.01	2.87	2.54	2.34	2.17
现住房总建筑面积(平方米/人)	Floor Space of Buildings (Sq.m/person)	26.88	29.46	32.62	37.37	42.37
现住房屋总使用面积(平方米/人)	Floor Space of Using(Sq.m/person)	20.17	22.10	24.47	28.03	31.78
房屋产权 (%)	House Ownership (%)	100.00	100.00	100.00	100.00	100.00
租赁公房	Renting of Publicly-Funded House	1.95				
租赁私房	Renting of Private House	4.48	5.96	3.61	8.11	14.67
原有私房	Original Private House	9.16	8.40	2.08	2.08	1.29
房改私房	Private House Obtained from House Reform	36.10	42.24	41.60	43.98	45.85
商品房	Commercial House	47.63	42.06	51.73	45.15	38.19
其他	Others	0.69	1.34	0.99	0.68	
住宅建筑式样 (%)	Architectural Style of Dwelling (%)	100.00	100.00	100.00	100.00	100.00
单栋住宅	Building	1.49	1.90		0.82	
四居室	Four-Room House	1.31	1.28	0.18	0.52	
三居室	Three-Room House	29.31	34.87	41.35	49.24	45.40
二居室	Two-Room House	50.54	47.68	49.22	42.56	41.43
一居室	One-Room House	6.12	5.13	5.57	4.15	13.16
普通楼房	Ordinary Multi-Storey Building		1.53			
平房及其他	A Single-Storey House and Others	11.23	7.61	3.67	2.71	
装修状况 (%)	Decoration Situation (%)	100.00	100.00	100.00	100.00	100.00
饮水情况 (%)	Condition of Drinking Water (%)	100.00	100.00	100.00	100.00	100.00
#自来水	Tap Water	99.01	99.36	100.00	100.00	100.00
井、河水	Well Water、River Water	0.99				
用水情况 (%)	By Tap Water Facilities (%)	100.00	100.00	100.00	100.00	100.00
独用自来水	Tap Water Owner Per Household	99.01	100.00	100.00	100.00	100.00
公用自来水	Public Tap Water					
卫生设备 (%)	By Health Facilities (%)	100.00	100.00	100.00	100.00	100.00
无卫生设备	Without Toilet Room	1.25				
有厕所浴室	Bathroom and Toilet Room Owned by Household	86.38	89.50	96.92	93.18	87.83
有厕所无浴室	Toilet Room Owned by Household and Without bathroom	11.05	7.06	1.79	5.51	12.17
公用	Public Toilet Room	1.32	3.45	1.28	1.31	
取暖设备 (%)	By Heating Facilities (%)	100.00	100.00	100.00	100.00	100.00
无取暖设备	Without Heating Facilities	0.99				
暖气	Warm Gas	99.01	100.00	100.00	100.00	100.00
炊用燃料使用情况 (%)	By Fuel Types (%)	100.00	100.00	100.00	100.00	100.00
管道天然气	Pipeline Gas	77.56	79.05	85.11	88.34	80.89
罐装液化石油气	LPG	11.32	13.06	11.04	8.18	6.76
煤炭	Coal	7.52	5.30	1.09	1.44	
其他	Others	2.25	1.99	2.77		9.93
通信设备使用情况	By General Equipment Usage					
固定电话(部/百户)	Fixed Telephone (unit /100 Households)	66.38	73.25	79.68	70.83	67.58
移动电话(部/百户)	Mobile Telephone (unit /100 Households)	188.64	197.75	185.41	196.68	195.30
使用互联网(条/百户)	The use of Internet (unit /100 Households)	48.24	56.69	62.28	65.97	55.76

10-13 城镇居民家庭就业情况
Employment Conditions of Urban Households

(抽样调查 Sampled Survey)

项 目	Item	2012	2013
调查户数(户)	**Number of Households Surveyed (household)**	**1460**	**1360**
平均每户家庭人口数(人)	**Average Household Size (person)**	**2.91**	**2.75**
有收入者人数	Number of Person Having Income	1.91	1.75
就业人数	Number of Person Employed	1.49	1.42
国有经济单位职工人数	Employed Person in State-owned Units	0.84	0.66
城镇集体经济单位职工人数	Employed Person in Collective-owned Units	0.03	
其他各种经济类型单位职工	Employed Person in Other Varions Economic Units	0.08	
城镇个体经营者人员数	Number of Employed Person by Himself in Town	0.18	0.24
城镇个体被雇人员数	Number of Employed Person in Town	0.30	
离退休再就业人员	Retired and Resigned Person Reemployed	0.01	0.02
其他就业人员	Person Employed in Other Way	0.04	0.49
离退休人员	Number of Retired and Resinged Person	0.39	0.29
其他有收入者人数	Number of Other Person Having Income	0.04	0.04
无收入者人数	Number of Person Having no Income	1.00	0.99

10-14 主要年份农村居民家庭基本情况
Basic Conditions of Rural Households in Main Years

(抽样调查 Sampled Survey)

项 目	Item	2000	2005	2010	2013
调查户基本情况	**Basic Situation of Households Surveyed**				
平均每户常住人口(人/户)	Average Number of Permanent Residents per Household	5.33	4.72	4.63	4.58
平均每户整半劳动力(人/户)	Average Number of Full/semi Labour Fource per Household	3.06	2.92	3.14	2.70
平均每个劳动力负担人口(含本人)	Average Number of Dependents per Labour Force (Including the laborer himself and herself)	1.74	1.62	1.47	1.43
平均每人经营耕地面积(亩)	Average Number of Management of Cultivated Land Area(Mu)	4.20	4.20	4.76	5.42
年内每户新建(购)房屋面积(平方米)	Space of Rooms per Household Newly Built Within the Year (sq.m)	2.03	6.45	3.68	8.91
年底人均居住面积(平方米)	Per Capita Net Living Rooms Space in Rural Area (sq.m)	17.25	21.13	24.00	24.57
平均每人年收入(元)	**Per Capita Annual Income(yuan)**				
总收入	Total Income	3129.35	4604.90	8806.87	14986.60
工资性收入	Income from Wages and Salaries	104.58	195.51	556.26	1311.84
家庭经营收入	Income from Household Operations	2926.75	4252.96	7795.26	12270.19
财产性收入	Income from Properties	40.42	33.87	126.53	230.09
转移性收入	Income from Transfers	57.60	122.56	328.82	1174.48
现金收入	Cash Income	2444.30	3921.17	7517.22	13935.58
工资性收入	Income from Wages and Salaries	104.46	195.51	556.26	1309.33
家庭经营收入	Income from Household Operations	2245.31	3580.44	6525.27	11326.73
财产性收入	Income from Properties	37.87	22.84	106.87	230.09
转移性收入	Income from Transfers	56.66	122.38	328.82	1069.43
平均每人年支出(元)	**Per Capita Annual Expenditures(yuan)**				
总支出	Total Expenditure	2819.77	4302.26	8241.28	14556.46
家庭经营费用支出	Expenditure for Household Operations	1198.23	1928.63	3800.24	7069.28
购置生产性固定资产	Purchase of Productive Fixed Assets	115.19	258.79	568.14	749.94
税费支出	Taxes and Fees	177.24	14.36	7.83	
生活消费支出	Expenditure on Household Consumption	1236.45	1924.41	3458.14	6119.06
转移性和财产性支出	Expenditure for Transfer and Property	92.66	176.07	406.93	591.74
现金支出	Cash Expenditure	2353.45	3855.34	7464.48	13795.05
家庭经营费用支出	Expenditure for Household Operations	1100.43	1823.95	3643.29	6907.45
购置生产性固定资产	Purchase of Productive Fixed Assets	115.19	258.79	568.14	749.94
税费支出	Taxes and Fees	177.22	14.36	7.83	
生活消费支出	Expenditure on Household Consumption	871.37	1582.17	2838.29	5519.91
转移性和财产性支出	Expenditure for Transfer and Property	89.24	176.07	406.93	591.30
平均每人年纯收入(元)	**Per Capita Annual Net Income (yuan)**	**1618.08**	**2482.15**	**4642.67**	**7296.46**
工资性收入	Income from Wages and Salaries	104.58	195.51	556.26	1311.84
家庭经营纯收入	Income from Household Business	1451.33	2140.76	3649.98	4654.48
财产性收入	Income from Properties	40.43	33.87	126.52	230.09
转移性收入	Income from Transfers	21.74	112.01	309.91	1100.05

10-15 农村居民家庭人均年总收入、纯收入和构成
Per Capita Annual Gross and Net Income and Its Composition of Rural Households

单位：元 (抽样调查 Sampled Survey) (yuan)

项目	Item	2012	2013	构成(%) Composition 2012	构成(%) Composition 2013
全年总收入	**Annual Gross Income**	**13675.26**	**14986.60**	**100**	**100**
工资性收入	Income from Wages and Salaries	1007.94	1311.84	7.37	8.75
家庭经营收入	Income from Household Operations	11473.81	12270.19	83.90	81.87
财产性收入	Income from Transfers	170.72	230.09	1.25	1.54
转移性收入	Income from Properties	1022.80	1174.48	7.48	7.84
全年总支出	**Annual Gross Expenditure**	**13541.28**	**14556.46**	**100**	**100**
#家庭经营费用支出	Expenditure for Household Business	6682.45	7069.28	49.35	48.56
生活消费支出	Expenditure for Consumption	5245.28	6119.06	38.74	42.04
全年纯收入	**Annual Net Income**	**6393.70**	**7296.46**	**100**	**100**
工资性收入	Income from Wages and Salaries	1007.94	1311.84	15.76	17.98
家庭经营纯收入	Income from Household Operations	4239.16	4654.48	66.30	63.79
财产性纯收入	Income from Transfers	170.72	230.09	2.67	3.15
转移性收入	Income from Properties	975.88	1100.05	15.26	15.08

10-16 主要年份农村居民家庭平均每人总收入和纯收入
Per Capita Annual Gross and Net Income of Rural Households in Main Years

单位：元 (抽样调查 Sampled Survey) (yuan)

项目	Item	2000	2005	2010	2013
总 收 入	**Gross Income**	**3129.35**	**4604.90**	**8806.87**	**14986.60**
基本收入	Basic Income	3031.33	4448.47	8351.52	13582.03
工资性收入	Income from Wages and Salaries	104.58	195.51	556.26	1311.84
家庭经营收入	Income from Household Operations	2926.75	4252.96	7795.26	12270.19
财产性收入	Income from Transfers	98.02	156.43	126.53	230.09
转移性收入	Income from Properties			328.82	1174.48
纯 收 入	**Net Income**	**1618.08**	**2482.15**	**4642.67**	**7296.46**
基本收入	Basic Income	1555.91	2336.27	4206.24	5966.32
工资性收入	Income from Wages and Salaries	104.58	195.51	556.26	1311.84
家庭经营纯收入	Income from Household Operations	1451.33	2140.76	3649.98	4654.48
农业收入	Farming	1109.39	1618.33	2670.60	3181.55
林业收入	Forestry	22.51	61.65	172.01	246.90
牧业收入	Animal Husbandry	171.18	245.10	469.08	617.94
渔业收入	Fishery				0.05
工业收入	Industry	6.35	18.84	34.65	32.17
建筑业收入	Construction	4.31	15.22	22.71	78.22
交通、运输和邮电业收入	Transportation, Post and Telecommunications Services	26.48	30.06	94.88	136.61
批发和零售贸易业、饮食业收入	Wholesale, Retail Trades and Catering Services	23.80	86.86	128.47	278.94
社会服务业收入	Services Trades	15.01	9.43	22.70	65.48
文教卫生业收入	Cultural, Education, Medicines and Medical Services			10.53	
其他行业收入	Others	72.30	55.27	24.36	16.61
转移性和财产性收入	Income from Transfers and Properties	62.17	145.88	436.43	1330.14

10-17 分地区农村居民家庭人均纯收入
Per Capita Net Income of Rural Households by Region

单位：元 (抽样调查 Sampled Survey) (yuan)

地 区	Region	2012	2013
总 计	**Total**	**6394**	**7296**
乌鲁木齐市	Urumqi City	10032	11496
克拉玛依市	Karamay City		
吐鲁番地区	Turpan Administrative Offices	7105	8170
哈密地区	Hami [Kumul] Administrative Offices	8389	9908
昌吉回族自治州	Changji Hui Autonomous Prefecture	11470	13014
伊犁州直属县(市)	Counties (Cities) Direct Under Ili Prefecture	7450	8503
塔城地区	Tacheng [Tarbagatai] Administrative Offices	9896	11096
阿勒泰地区	Altay Administrative Offices	6243	7267
博尔塔拉蒙古自治州	Bortala Mongol Autonomous Prefecture	9434	10636
巴音郭楞蒙古自治州	Bayangol Mongol Autonomous Prefecture	9936	11239
阿克苏地区	Aksu Administrative Offices	6891	7875
克孜勒苏柯尔克孜自治州	Kizilsu Kirgiz Autonomous Prefecture	3081	3857
喀什地区	Kashgar [Kaxgar] Administrative Offices	4708	5393
和田地区	Hotan Administrative Offices	4260	4951

10-18 主要年份农村居民家庭人均主要消费品消费量
Per Capita Consumption of Major Consumer Goods of Rural Households in Main Years

单位:千克 (抽样调查 Sampled Survey) (kg)

项 目	Item	2000	2005	2010	2013
粮食(原粮)	Grain(Unprocessed)	244.83	235.66	236.10	190.80
#小 麦	Wheat	199.83	188.38	191.28	137.52
稻 谷	Rice	15.19	19.93	23.20	32.10
豆类及豆制品	Soybeans and Processed Products	0.50	0.83	0.56	1.74
蔬 菜	Fresh Vegetable	89.24	67.89	77.72	75.77
食 油	Edible Oil	9.64	10.90	10.74	17.96
#植物油	Vegetable Oil	9.56	10.79	10.69	17.88
肉禽及制品	Meats,Poultry and Processed Products	12.41	14.31	15.38	19.13
#猪 肉	Pork	1.95	0.67	1.04	1.28
牛 肉	Beef	1.95	2.56	2.32	3.24
羊 肉	Mutton	7.03	8.99	9.18	11.04
家 禽	Poultry	1.36	1.70	2.27	3.30
蛋及制品	Eggs and Processed Products	1.20	1.00	1.92	4.15
食 糖	Sugar	0.42	0.45	0.49	0.48
酒	Liquor	1.12	1.27	1.06	1.41
水果及制品	Fruits and Processed Products	46.89	34.81	25.30	20.88
茶 叶	Tea	0.37	0.45	0.43	0.22

10-19 主要年份农村居民家庭平均每百户耐用消费品拥有量
Number of Durable Consumer Goods Owned by Per100 Rural Households in Main Years

(抽样调查 Sampled Survey)

项　目	Item	2000	2005	2010	2013
洗衣机(台)	Washing Machine (unit)	20.87	28.26	47.94	82.74
电冰箱(台)	Refrigerator (unit)	9.93	20.13	43.48	78.29
空调机(台)	Air Conditioner (unit)		0.39	0.65	1.15
抽油烟机(台)	Exhaust Fan(unit)	1.13	1.23	2.77	6.38
自行车(辆)	Bicycle (unit)	136.60	80.97	78.52	34.35
摩托车(辆)	Motorcycle (unit)	18.33	45.42	62.84	78.51
电话机(部)	Telephone(unit)	15.07	36.26	38.97	28.07
移动电话(部)	Mobile phone (unit)	0.33	21.29	84.32	167.16
彩色电视机(台)	Color TV (set)	31.87	61.81	89.87	96.97
照像机(架)	Camera (set)	2.20	3.23	3.29	2.78
微波炉(台)	Microwave Oven (unit)			1.81	5.65

10-20 农村居民人均生活消费支出及构成
Composition of Per Capita Living Expenditure of Rural Households

单位：元　(抽样调查 Sampled Survey)　(yuan)

项　目	Item	2012	2013	构成(%) Composition(%)	
				2012	2013
生活消费支出	**Expenditure for Consumption**	**5245.28**	**6119.06**	**100**	**100**
食　品	Food	1890.96	2072.00	36.05	33.86
#主　食	Staple Food	459.32	434.87	8.76	7.11
副食及其他食品	Non-staple Food and others	1149.56	1418.09	21.92	23.17
衣　着	Clothing	429.92	484.67	8.20	7.92
居　住	Residence	1298.44	1623.82	24.75	26.54
家庭设备、用品及服务	Household Facilities,Articles and Services	219.10	256.41	4.18	4.19
交通和通讯	Transport and Communications	646.37	700.11	12.32	11.44
文教娱乐用品及服务	Cultural, Education ,Recreation and Services	206.15	280.68	3.93	4.59
医疗保健	Health Care and Medical Services	444.15	593.37	8.47	9.70
其他商品和服务	Other Commodities and Services	110.20	108.01	2.10	1.77

10-21 农村居民家庭人均商品性生活消费支出
Per Capita Self-Sufficiency and Consumption on Commodity Goods of Living Expenditure in Rural Households

(抽样调查 Sampled Survey)

项 目	Item	2012		2013	
		合 计 Total	#货币性 In Money	合 计 Total	#货币性 In Money
生活消费支出合计(元/人)	**Expenditure for Consumption (yuan/person)**	**5245.28**	**4728.78**	**6119.06**	**5519.91**
食 品	Food	1890.96	1391.06	2072.00	1620.01
衣 着	Clothing	429.92	426.57	484.67	482.56
居 住	Residence	1298.44	1289.21	1623.82	1481.10
家庭设备、用品及服务	Household Appliances and Services	219.10	215.07	256.41	254.72
交通和通讯	Transportation and Communications	646.37	646.37	700.11	700.09
文教娱乐用品及服务	Cultural, Education and Recreational Articles and Services	206.15	206.15	280.68	280.51
医疗保健	Health Care and Medical Services	444.15	444.15	593.37	593.36
其他商品和服务	Other Commodities and Services	110.20	110.20	108.01	107.56
生活消费支出构成(%)	**Composition of Living Expenditures (%)**	**100**	**100**	**100**	**100**
食 品	Food	36.05	29.42	33.86	29.35
衣 着	Clothing	8.20	9.02	7.92	8.74
居 住	Residence	24.75	27.26	26.54	26.83
家庭设备、用品及服务	Household Facilities,Articles and Services	4.18	4.55	4.19	4.61
交通和通讯	Transportation and Communications	12.32	13.67	11.44	12.68
文教娱乐用品及服务	Cultural, Education and Recreational Articles and Services	3.93	4.36	4.59	5.08
医疗保健	Health Care and Medical Services	8.47	9.39	9.70	10.75
其他商品和服务	Other Commodities and Services	2.10	2.33	1.77	1.95

10-22 主要年份农村居民家庭房屋使用情况
Housing Conditions of Rural Households in Main Years

(抽样调查 Sampled Survey)

项 目	Item	2000	2005	2010	2013
本年新建(购)房屋	**Houses Newly built This Year**				
面积(平方米/人)	Per Capita Floor Space of Houses (sq.m/person)	0.38	1.37	0.73	1.94
价值(元/平方米)	Value of Houses (yuan/sq.m)	169.37	225.20	442.00	2081.57
年末住房情况	**Houses at Year-end**				
住房面积(平方米/人)	Per Capita Floor Space of Houses (sq.m/person)	17.25	21.23	24.00	25.41
住房价值(元/平方米)	Value of Houses (yuan/sq.m)	120.86	160.99	252.79	618.50
住房结构(平方米/人)	Structure of House (sq.m/person)				
#钢筋混凝土结构	Reinforced Concrete Structure	0.53	0.98	1.83	7.65
砖木结构	Brick and Wood Structure	2.75	6.48	10.95	11.95

10-23 主要年份居民住房情况
Housing Conditions of Rural Households in Main Years

年 份 Year	城镇人均使用面积(平方米) Per Capita Gross Living Space in Urban Areas (sq.m)	城镇人均建筑面积(平方米) Per Capita Floor Space of Residential Building in Urban Areas (sq.m)	农村人均居住面积(平方米) Per Capita Floor Space of Residential Building in Rural Areas (sq.m)
1985	10.70	14.27	12.75
1990	13.55	18.07	14.04
1995	16.57	22.09	16.12
1996	17.61	23.48	16.12
1997	13.62	18.16	16.13
1998	18.95	25.27	16.20
1999	19.76	26.35	16.90
2000	20.06	26.75	17.25
2001	20.60	27.47	18.04
2002	18.17	23.78	18.56
2003	17.91	23.36	18.62
2004	18.82	24.44	19.10
2005	20.15	26.02	21.23
2006	20.33	26.31	21.96
2007	20.38	27.17	22.45
2008	20.47	27.29	22.79
2009	20.42	27.16	23.45
2010	20.49	27.25	24.00
2011	21.70	28.92	26.14
2012	21.78	29.03	27.18
2013	22.96	30.61	24.57

10-24 社会保险基本情况
Basic Conditions on Social Insurance

指　　标	Item	2012	2013
基本养老保险	**Basic Endowment Insurance**		
职工基本养老保险	Employee Basic Pension Insurance		
年末参保人数(万人)	Contributors at Year-end (10 000 persons)	312.16	326.04
#参保职工	Staff and Workers	228.86	239.33
离退休人员	Number of Retirees	83.30	86.71
新型农村社会养老保险	New Rural Old-age Insurance		
年末参保人数(万人)	Contributors at Year-end (10 000 persons)	497.09	496.93
享受待遇人数（万人）	Beneficiaries at Year-end (10000 persons)	88.29	92.68
城镇居民社会养老保险	Urban Employee Basic Pension Insurance		
年末参保人数(万人)	Contributors at Year-end (10 000 persons)	31.62	33.42
享受待遇人数（万人）	Beneficiaries at Year-end (10000 persons)	5.14	5.88
基本医疗保险	**Basic Medical Care Insurance**		
职工基本医疗保险	Employee Basic Medical Care Insurance		
年末参保人数(万人)	Contributors at Year-end (10 000 persons)	342.56	358.93
城镇居民基本医疗保险	Urban Employee Basic Medical Care Insurance		
年末参保人数(万人)	Contributors at Year-end (10 000 persons)	286.59	291.41
工伤保险	**Work Injury Insurance**		
年末参保人数(万人)	Contributors at Year-end (10 000 persons)	225.95	239.87
年末享受待遇人次数（万人次）	Beneficiaries at Year-end (10 000 persons)	1.77	1.93
失业保险	**Unemployment Insurance**		
年末参保人数(万人)	Year-end Contributors (10 000 persons)	208.95	218.52
年末享受待遇人数（万人）	Beneficiaries at Year-end (10 000 persons)	4.93	5.87
生育保险	**Maternity Insurance**		
年末参保人数(万人)	Contributors at Year-end (10 000 persons)	217.96	230.22
年末享受待遇人次数（万人次）	Beneficiaries at Year-end (10000 persons)	8.09	9.81

注：基本医疗保险数据不含新型农村合作医疗。
Note: Statistics on basic endowment insuranse didn't coner data on new rural old-age insurance.

10-25 各地、州、市社会保险年末参保人数
Number of Social Insured Persons at the Year-end by Prefecture, Autonomous Prefecture and City

单位：万人 (10 000 persons)

年 份 Year	地 区 Region	基本养老保险 Basic Endowment Insurance 职工基本养老保险 Employee Basic Pension Insurance	新型农村社会养老保险 New Rural Old-age Insurance	城镇居民社会养老保险 Urban Non-employment Social Pension Insurance	基本医疗保险 Basic Medical Care Insurance 职工基本医疗保险 Employee Basic Medical Care Insurance
	2001	148.08			116.17
	2002	152.06			148.12
	2003	160.04			176.37
	2004	173.76			195.97
	2005	181.88			211.85
	2006	191.97			227.15
	2007	205.00			244.78
	2008	222.17			263.54
	2009	232.08			279.09
	2010	259.67			296.72
	2011	291.99	490.58	27.49	322.73
	2012	312.16	497.09	31.62	342.56
	2013	326.04	496.93	33.42	358.93
乌鲁木齐市	Urumqi City	107.46	10.67	1.24	111.32
克拉玛依市	Karamay City	5.41	0.11	0.09	20.33
吐鲁番地区	Turpan Administrative Offices	5.88	20.52	0.59	8.42
哈密地区	Hami [Kumul] Administrative Offices	11.02	8.29	0.29	11.62
昌吉回族自治州	Changji Hui Autonomous Prefecture	23.01	29.92	0.90	25.25
伊犁州直属县(市)	Counties (Cities) Direct Under Ili Prefecture	25.95	53.50	5.90	27.78
塔城地区	Tacheng [Tarbagatai] Administrative Offices	12.66	19.94	1.90	12.89
阿勒泰地区	Altay Administrative Offices	8.43	12.99	1.16	11.87
博尔塔拉蒙古自治州	Bortala Mongol Autonomous Prefecture	5.74	7.20	0.49	6.39
巴音郭楞蒙古自治州	Bayangol Mongol Autonomous Prefecture	23.90	20.58	1.76	28.08
阿克苏地区	Aksu Administrative Offices	12.83	64.86	3.82	18.64
克孜勒苏柯尔克孜自治州	Kizilsu Kirgiz Autonomous Prefecture	3.61	17.05	1.21	7.91
喀什地区	Kashgar [Kaxgar] Administrative Offices	15.46	138.87	10.92	25.58
和田地区	Hotan Administrative Offices	5.90	92.42	3.14	11.33

注：基本医疗保险数据不含新型农村合作医疗。
Note: Data of basic medical care insurance did not include new cooperative health care in agricultural and pastoral areas.

10-25 续表 Continued

单位：万人 (10 000 persons)

年 份 Year	地 区 Region	基本医疗保险 Basic Medical Care Insurance 城镇居民基本医疗保险 Urban Non-employment Basic Medical Insurance	工伤保险 Work Injury Insurance	失业保险 Unemployment Insurance	生育保险 Maternity Insurance
	2001		30.53	126.47	30.52
	2002		29.45	131.29	29.72
	2003		41.08	135.12	32.16
	2004		60.93	138.58	59.23
	2005		79.51	140.82	103.48
	2006		102.40	145.04	135.90
	2007		132.55	151.55	151.60
	2008	175.07	151.08	162.76	165.02
	2009	256.90	167.70	169.60	176.07
	2010	274.60	184.13	180.29	188.23
	2011	282.68	208.18	196.72	206.14
	2012	286.59	225.95	208.95	217.96
	2013	291.41	239.87	218.52	230.22
乌鲁木齐市	Urumqi City	58.57	75.02	75.14	64.25
克拉玛依市	Karamay City	7.54	18.43	7.67	17.23
吐鲁番地区	Turpan Administrative Offices	9.55	6.57	4.68	5.43
哈密地区	Hami [Kumul] Administrative Offices	9.89	10.02	7.07	6.84
昌吉回族自治州	Changji Hui Autonomous Prefecture	21.35	25.65	15.36	19.12
伊犁州直属县(市)	Counties (Cities) Direct Under Ili Prefecture	33.09	16.26	15.42	18.00
塔城地区	Tacheng [Tarbagatai] Administrative Offices	11.93	7.03	6.42	7.82
阿勒泰地区	Altay Administrative Offices	12.40	8.09	5.60	6.84
博尔塔拉蒙古自治州	Bortala Mongol Autonomous Prefecture	6.60	5.12	3.82	4.44
巴音郭楞蒙古自治州	Bayangol Mongol Autonomous Prefecture	23.52	17.44	16.83	17.13
阿克苏地区	Aksu Administrative Offices	25.03	10.87	10.06	11.80
克孜勒苏柯尔克孜自治州	Kizilsu Kirgiz Autonomous Prefecture	6.53	4.38	3.84	4.43
喀什地区	Kashgar [Kaxgar] Administrative Offices	47.20	16.33	15.58	17.44
和田地区	Hotan Administrative Offices	18.20	6.83	6.75	7.78

主要统计指标解释

一、城镇住户

城镇家庭人口 指居住在一起，经济上合在一起共同生活的家庭成员。凡计算为家庭人口的成员其全部收支都包括在本家庭中。

城镇就业面 指就业人口占家庭人口的百分比。

城镇就业者负担人数 指家庭人口与就业人口之比。

城镇家庭总收入 指家庭成员得到的工资性收入、经营净收入、财产性收入、转移性收入之和，不包括出售财物收入和借贷收入。

城镇居民家庭可支配收入 指家庭成员得到可用于最终消费支出和其它非义务性支出以及储蓄的总和，即居民家庭可以用来自由支配的收入。它是家庭总收入扣除交纳的所得税、个人交纳的社会保障支出以及记账补贴后的收入。计算公式为：

城镇居民家庭可支配收入=家庭总收入-交纳个人所得税-个人交纳的社会保障支出-记帐补贴

城镇家庭总支出 指家庭除借贷支出以外的全部实际支出。包括现金消费支出、财产性支出、转移性支出、社会保障支出、购房与建房支出。

城镇家庭现金消费支出 指家庭用于日常生活的全部现金支出，包括食品、衣着、居住、家庭设备及用品、交通通信、文教娱乐、医疗保健、其他等八大类支出。

城镇家庭服务性消费支出 指家庭用于支付社会提供的各种文化和生活方面的非商品性服务费用。

城镇家庭收入分组方法 是将所有调查户按户人均可支配收入由低到高排队，按10%，10%，20%，20%，20%，10%，10%的比例依次分成：最低收入户、较低收入户、中等偏下收入户、中等收入户、中等偏上收入户、较高收入户、最高收入户等七组。总体中最低5%的户为困难户。

恩格尔系数 指食品支出在现金消费支出中所占的比例。计算公式为：

恩格尔系数=食品支出/现金消费支出×100%

二、农村住户

农村住户 指农村常住户。农村常住户指长期(一年以上)居住在乡镇(不包括城关镇)行政管理区域内的住户，以及长期居住在城关镇所辖行政村范围内的农村住户。户口不在本地而在本地居住一年及以上的住户也包括在本地农村常住户范围内；有本地户口，但举家外出谋生一年以上的住户，无论是否保留承包耕地都不包括在本地农村住户范围内。

常住人口 指全年经常在家或在家居住6个月以上，而且经济和生活与本户连成一体的人口。外出从业人员在外居住时间虽然在6个月以上，但收入主要带回家中，经济与本户连为一体，仍视为家庭常住人口；在家居住，生活和本户连成一体的国家职工、退休人员也为家庭常住人口。但是现役军人、中专及以上(走读生除外)的在校学生、以及常年在外(不包括探亲、看病等)且已有稳定的职业与居住场所的外出从业人员，不算家庭常住人口。家庭常住人口主要作为计算农村住户平均每人收入、消费和积累水平及分析家庭人口状况的依据。

整、半劳动力 整劳动力指男子18周岁到50周岁，女子18周岁到45周岁；半劳动力指男子16周岁到17周岁，51周岁到60周岁；女子16周岁到17周岁，46周岁到55周岁，同时具有劳动能力的人。虽然在劳动年龄之内，但已丧失劳动能力的人，不应算为劳动力；超过劳动年龄，但能经常参加劳动，计入半劳动力数内。常住人口中的职工，若这些职工为劳动力，就包括在本户的整半劳动力中。

总收入 指调查期内农村住户和住户成员从各种来源渠道得到的收入总和。按收入的性质划分为工资性收入、家庭经营收入、财产性收入和转移性收入。

工资性收入 指农村住户成员受雇于单位或个人，靠出卖劳动所而获得的收入。

家庭经营收入 指农村住户以家庭为生产经营单位进行生产筹划和管理而获得的收入。农村住户家庭经营活动按行业划分为农业、林业、牧业、渔业、工业、建筑业、交通运输业邮电业、批发和零售贸易餐饮业、社会服务业、文教卫生业和其他家庭经营。

财产性收入 指金融资产或有形非生产性资产的所有者向其他机构单位提供资金或将有形非生产性资产供其支配，作为回报而从中获得的收入。

转移性收入 指农村住户和住户成员无须付出任何对应物而获得的货物、服务、资金或资产所有权等，不包括无偿提供的用于固定资本形成的资金。一般情况下，是指农村住户在二次分配中的所有收入。

现金收入 指农村住户和住户成员在调查期内得到以现金形态表现的收入。按来源分成工资性收入、家庭经营现金收入、财产性收入、转移性收入。

农村居民家庭纯收入 指农村住户当年从各个来源得到的总收入相应地扣除所发生的费用后的收入总和。计算方法：

农村居民家庭纯收入=总收入-家庭经营费用支出-税费支出-生产性固定资产折旧-赠送农村外部亲友

纯收入主要用于再生产投入和当年生活消费支出，也可用于储蓄和各种非义务性支出。“农民人均纯收入”按人口平均的纯收入水平，反映的是一个地区农村居民的平均收入水平。

总支出 指农村住户用于生产、生活和再分配的全部支出。包括家庭经营费用支出、购置生产性固定资产支出、税费支出、消费支出、财产性支出和转移性支出。

三、社会保险

城镇职工基本养老保险

1.（参保）职工人数：指报告期末按照国家法律、法规和有关政策规定参加基本养老保险并在社保经办机构已建立缴费记录档案的职工人数。包括中断缴费但未终止养老关系的职工人数，不包括只登记未建立缴费记录档案的人数。

2.（参保）离退休人员人数：指报告期末参加基本养老保险的离休、退休和退职人员的人数。

3.基金收入：指根据国家有关规定，由纳入基本养老保险范围的缴费单位和个人按照国家规定的缴费基数和缴费比例缴纳的养老保险基金，以及通过其他方式取得的形成基金来源的收入。包括单位和职工个人缴纳的基本养老保险费、基本养老保险基金利息收入、上级补助收入、下级上解收入、转移收入、财政补贴和其他收入。

4.基金支出：指按照国家政策规定的开支范围和开支标准从养老保险基金中支付给参加基本养老保险的个人的养老金、丧葬抚恤补助，以及由于保险关系转移、上下级之间调剂资金等原因而发生的支出。包括:离休金、退休金、退职金、各种补贴、医疗费、死亡丧葬补助费、抚恤救济费、社会保险经办机构管理费、补助下级支出、上解上级支出、转移支出、其他支出等。

5.基金累计结余：指截止报告期末基本养老保险基金收支相抵后的累计余额。

基本医疗保险

1.参保人数：指报告期末按国家有关规定参加相应基本医疗保险的人数。

2.基金收入：指由用人单位和个人按照国家规定的缴费基数、缴费比例或缴费标准缴纳的基本医疗保险基金，财政补助资金以及通过其他方式取得的形成基金来源的款项，包括：单位缴纳收入、个人缴纳收入、财政补助收入（含医疗救助补助个人收入）、财政补贴收入、利息收入和其他收入。

3.基金支出：指按照国家政策规定的开支范围和开支标准，从基本医疗保险基金中支付给参保人员的医疗保险待遇支出，以及其他支出。包括住院医疗费用支出、门急诊医疗费用支出、个人账户基金支出、其他支出。

4.基金累计结余：指截止报告期末基本医疗保险基金累计结余金额。

失业保险

1.参保人数：指报告期末按照国家法律、法规和有关政策规定参加了失业保险的城镇企业、事业单位的职工及地方政府规定参加失业保险的其他人员的人数。

2.基金收入：指报告期内筹集的失业保险基金的总额，包括失业保险费收入、利息收入、财政补贴收入、其他收入、转移收入、上级补助收入、下级上解收入。

3.基金支出：指报告期内为保障失业人员基本生活、促进其再就业等支出的基金总额，包括失业保险金支出、医疗补助金支出、丧葬补助金和抚恤金支出、职业培训和职业介绍补贴支出、农民合同制工人一次性生活补助支出、其他支出、转移支出、上级补助支出、下级上解支出。

4.基金累计结余：指截止报告期末失业保险基金收支相抵后的累计余额。

工伤保险

1.参加保险人数：指报告期末依据国家有关规定参加工伤保险的职工人数和有雇工的个体工商户的雇工数。

2.享受保险待遇人数：指年初至报告期末因工伤或职业病而享受工伤保险待遇的人数。为享受工伤医疗待遇中未评定等级的人数、享受伤残待遇人数以及享受因工死亡待遇人数之和。

3.基金收入：指根据国家有关规定，由参加工伤保险的单位按国家规定的缴费基数和缴费比例缴纳的工伤保险基金，以及通过其他形式取得的形成基金来源的款项。包括：单位缴纳的社会统筹基金收入、财政补贴收入、利息收入、其他收入。

4.基金支出：指按照国家政策规定的开支范围和开支标准从工伤保险基金中支付给参加工伤保险的人员及供养直系亲属工伤保险待遇支出及其他支出。包括工伤医疗费、伤残补助金、工亡补助金、护理费、丧葬补助费、工伤预防费用、职业康复费用和其他支出。

5.基金累计结余：指截止报告期末工伤保险基金累计结余金额。

生育保险

1.参保人数：指报告期末依据有关规定参加生育保险的人数。

2.基金收入：指根据国家有关规定，由参加生育保险的单位按照国家规定的缴费基数和缴费比例缴纳的生育保险基金，以及通过其他方式取得的形成基金来源的款项，包括：单位缴纳的基金收入、利息收入和其他收入。

3.基金支出：指按照国家政策规定的开支范围和开支标准，从生育保险基金中支付给参加生育保险的职工，因妊娠、分娩和计划生育手术而享受的待遇及其他支出。包括：生育津贴、医疗费用支出及其他支出。

4.基金累计结余：指截止报告期末生育保险基金累计结余金额。

Explanatory Notes on Main Statistical Indicators

I. Urban Households

Population of Urban Households refer to members of households living and sharing economically together in the urban areas. All the income and expenditure of all the members of such households are included in the income and expenditure of the household.

Proportion of Urban Employment refers to the proportion of employed population to the population of urban households.

Number of Dependents per Urban Employee refers to the ratio between number of persons in an urban household and the number of employed persons.

Total Income of Urban Households refers to the sum of wage income; net business income; income from properties; and income from transfers of members of the households. Income from selling of properties and income from borrowing are not included.

Disposable Income of Urban Households refers to the actual income at the disposal of members of the households which can be used for final consumption, other non-compulsory expenditure and savings. This equals to total income minus income tax, personal contribution to social security and subsidy for keeping diaries in being a sample household. The following formula is used:

Disposable Income of Urban Households= total household income - income tax - personal contribution to social security - subsidy for keeping diaries for a sampled household

Total Expenditure of Urban Households refers to all actual expenditure of households except expenditure on lending. It includes cash expenditure; property expenditure, transfer expenditure, social insurance expenditure and expenditure on house purchasing or house building.

Consumption Expenditure of Urban Households in Cash refers to total cash expenditure of households for consumption in daily life, including expenditure on the eight categories of food; clothing; housing; household appliances; transport and communications; education, cultural and recreational activities and medical care.

Consumption Expenditure of Urban Households on Services refers to non-commodity service expenditure of households on various kinds of cultural and living activities provided by society.

Urban Households by Income Group All households in the sample are grouped, by per capita disposable income of the household, into groups of lowest income, low income, lower middle income, middle income, upper middle income, high income and highest income, each group consisting of 10%, 10%, 20%, 20%, 20%, 10% and 10% of all households respectively. The lowest 5% of households are also referred to as poor households.

Engel's Coefficient refers to the percentage of expenditure on food to the total consumption in cash, using the following formula:

$$\text{Engel's Coefficient} = \frac{\text{expenditure on food}}{\text{total living consumption expenditure}} \times 100\%$$

II. Rural Household

Rural Households refer to usual resident households in rural areas. Usual resident households in rural areas are households residing on a long term basis(for more than one year) in the areas under the administration of township governments (not including county towns), and in the areas under the administration of villages in county towns. Households residing in the current addresses for over one year with their household registration in other places are still considered as resident households of the locality. For households with their household registration in one place but all members of the households having moved away to make a living in another place for over one year, they will not be included in the rural households of the area where they are registered, irrespective of whether they still keep their contracted land.

Usual Resident Population refers to persons staying at home regularly or for over 6 months during a year and integrated with the household economically and in terms of living. Members of the household staying away from the household for over 6 months but keeping a close economic relation with the household by sending the majority of income to the household are regarded as usual resident of the household. Government staff and workers or retirees living as close members of the household are also considered as usual resident. However, servicemen, students of secondary technical schools or schools of higher education and persons with stable jobs and residence outside the household (excluding those visiting relatives or seeking medical service) are not included as resident population of the household. Resident population is used in calculating income, consumption, accumulation on per capita basis of rural households and in analyzing composition of rural households.

Full/Semi Labour Force Full labour force refers to persons capable of work, aged 18-50 for males and 18-45 for females. Semi labour force refers to persons capable of work, aged 16-17 and 51-60 for males and 16-17 and 46-55 for females. Persons at their working ages but not capable of work are not to be included as labour force. Persons not at working ages but participating regularly in work are included in semi labour force. For staff and workers who are usual residents, are included as full or semi labour force of the household if they are in the labour force.

Total Income refers to the sum of income earned from various sources by the rural households and their members during the reference period, and is classified as income from wages and salaries, income from household operations, income from properties and income from transfers.

Income from Wages and Salaries refers to income from labour earned by the members of rural households employed by other units or individuals.

Income from Household Operations refers to income by the rural households as units of production and operation. Operations by rural households are classified according to their economic activities namely agriculture, forestry, animal husbandry, fishery, manufacturing, construction, transportation, post and telecommunications, wholesale, retail and catering, social service, culture, education, health, and other household operations.

Income from Properties refers to the income received as returns by owners of financial assets or tangible non-productive assets by providing capitals or tangible non-productive assets to other institutional units.

Income from Transfers refers to the receipt by rural households and their members of goods, services, capital or rights of assets without giving or repaying accordingly, excluding capital provided to them for the formation of fixed assets. In general, it refers to all income received by rural households through redistribution.

Cash Income refers to income received by rural households and their members in the form of cash during the reference period. It is classified, by source of income, into income from wages and salaries, cash income from household operations, income from properties and income from transfers.

Net Income of Rural Households refers to the total income of rural households from all sources minus all corresponding expenses. The formula for calculation is as follows:

Net income of rural households = total income - household operation expenses - taxes and fees-depreciation of fixed assets for production - gifts to rural relatives.

Net income is mainly used as input for reinvestment in production and as consumption expenditure of the year, and also used for savings and non-compulsory expenses of various forms. "Per capita net income of farmers" is the level of net income averaged by population, reflecting the average income level of rural population in a given area.

Total Expenditure refers to total expenses of rural households on production, consumption and redistribution, including expenditure on household operations; purchase of productive fixed assets; taxes and fees; consumption expenditure; expenses on properties; and expenses on transfers.

III Social Insurance

Basic Pension Insurance

1. Number of staff and workers covered refer to staff and workers participating in the basic pension insurance programme according to national laws, regulations and related policies at the end of the reference period, who have already had payment records in social security management agencies, including those who have interrupt payment without terminating the insurance programme. Those who have registered in the programme but with no payment records are not included.

2. Number of retirees participating in the basic pension insurance programme refer to the number of retirees participating in basic pension insurance programmes by the end of the reference period.

3. Revenue of the basic pension insurance programme refers to payments made by employers and individuals participating in the pension insurance programme in accordance with the basis and proportion stipulated in State regulations, and income from other sources that become source of pension insurance fund, including the premium paid by employers and staff and workers, interest income, subsidies from higher level agencies, income as transfer from subordinate agencies, transferred income, government financial subsidies and other income.

4. Expenditure of basic pension insurance programme refer to payment made on pensions and funeral subsidies to those retired and resigned people covered in pension insurance programmes according to related national policies on scope and standard of expenditure. Also included are expenditure which arises due to shift of the insurance relationship or adjustment of funds among agencies. More specifically, included are pensions for resigned people, pensions for retired people, pension for people quitting jobs, various subsidies, medical fees, funeral subsidies, compensation payments, management fees for social security agencies, expenses on subsidies to lower subordinates, expenses as transfer to agencies at higher level, transferred expenditure and other expenditure.

5. Balance of basic pension insurance programme refers to the balance of basic pension insurance funds at the end of the reference period after deducting expenses from revenue.

Basic Medical Care Insurance

1. Number of people participating in the insurance programme refers to people participating in the basic medical care insurance programme according to related regulations at the end of the reference period.

2. Revenue of the insurance programme refers to payments made by employers and individuals participating in the medical care insurance programme in accordance with the basis and proportion stipulated in State regulations, and income from other sources that become source of medical insurance fund, including income paid by units, individual paid income, financial assistance's income (including individual income from medicaid), financial subsidies' income, interest income and other income.

3. Expenditure of the insurance programme refers to payment made to people covered in basic medical care insurance programme within the scope and standards of expenditure according to related national policies, and medical care payment and other expenses, including medical expenses of hospital inpatients, medical expenses for outpatients and emergency patients, payment from individual accounts and other expenditure.

4. Balance of the basic medical care insurance programme refers to the balance of medical care insurance funds at the end of the reference period.

Unemployment Insurance

1. Number of people covered refers to staff and workers in urban enterprises or institutions who have participated in the unemployment insurance programme according to relevant policies and regulations, and other people who have participated according to local government regulations at the end of the reference period.

2. Revenue of the unemployment insurance programme refers to the total unemployment insurance funds raised in the reference period, including unemployment insurance premium, interest income, financial subsidies, other income, transferred income, subsidies from higher level agencies and income as transfer from subordinate agencies.

3.Expenditure of the unemployment insurance programme refers to total expenses during the reference period to guarantee the basic livelihood of unemployed people, and to encourage their re-employment. Included are unemployment relief, medical fees,funeral subsidies, compensation payments, training expenses, management fees for unemployment insurance agencies, subsidies to lower level agencies, expenses as transfer to higher level agencies, transferred expenditure and other expenditure.

4. Balance of the unemployment insurance programme refers to the balance of revenue of the programme after deducting expenses at the end of the reference period.

Work Injury Insurance

1. Number of people covered refers to staff and workers who have participated in the work injury insurance programme and number of employees in private business according to relevant national regulations at the end of the reference period.

2. Number of beneficiaries refers to number of people benefited from work injury insurance, as a result of work injury or occupational disease. It is the sum of beneficiaries from the work injury medical treatment without rating, disabilities and deaths at work places.

3. Revenue of the work injury insurance programme refers to payments made by employers participating in the work injury insurance programme in accordance with the basis and proportion stipulated in State regulations, and income from other sources that become source of work injury insurance fund, including income of social comprehensive funds paid by employers, government financial subsidies, interest income and other income.

4. Expenditure of the work injury insurance programme refers to payments made from work injury insurance funds to those who participated in the work injury insurance programme and their direct dependents within the scope and standards of expenditure according to related national policies, and other expenditure, including medical fees for work injury, injury and disability subsidies, death subsidies, nursing fees, funeral subsidies, injury prevention fees, occupational rehabilitation fees and other expenditure.

5. Balance of the work injury insurance programme refers to the balance of the work injury funds at the end of the reference period.

Maternity Insurance

1. Number of people covered refers to people who have participated in the maternity insurance programme according to relevant regulation at the end of the reference period.

2. Revenue of maternity insurance refers to payments made by employers participating in the maternity insurance programme in accordance with the basis and proportion stipulated in State regulations, and income from other sources that become source of maternity insurance fund, including income of funds paid by employers, interest income and other income.

3. Expenditure of the maternity insurance programme refers to payments made from maternity insurance funds to staff and workers who participate in the maternity insurance programme within the scope and standards of expenditure in accordance with related national policies, expenses paid for pregnancy, child delivery or surgeries related to family planning, and other expenditure, including allowance for child bearing, medical fees and other expenditure.

4. Balance of the maternity programme refers to the balance of the maternity insurance funds at the end of the reference period.

11

城市概况

GENERAL SURVEY OF CITIES

简要说明

本篇主要内容和资料来源

本篇资料反映新疆城市社会、经济发展和城市建设的基本情况。

城市概况资料主要包括城市公用事业基本情况、主要经济指标、市政设施、园林绿化、环境卫生、供水供气等。

本篇资料由新疆维吾尔自治区统计局国民经济综合统计处根据新疆维吾尔自治区建设厅和新疆维吾尔自治区统计局相关处室提供的年度数据整理。

Brief Introduction

Main Content and Source of Data

Data in this chapter show the social and economic development and the urban construction of Xinjiang.

Data on the general survey cities include the basic condition of urban public facilities, main economic indicators, civil facilities, urban greenery, environment and sanitation, supply of gas and heating, public transportation, etc.

Data on this chapter are compiled by the Department of National Accounts of the Xinjiang Bureau of Statistics according to the data of yearly statistics, which are provided by the Construction Bureau of Xinjiang Uygur Autonomous Region and related departments of Statistics Bureau of Xinjiang Uygur Autonomous Region.

11-1 城市公用事业基本情况
Basic Statistics on City Public Utilities

项　目	Item	2012	2013
城市及建筑物面积	**City Areas and Floor Space of Buildings**		
建成区面积(平方公里)	Area of Built Districts(sq.km)	960	1065
征用土地面积(平方公里)	Land Put in Requisition for State Construction Projects (sq. km)	32.4	31.8
城市人口密度(人/平方公里)	Population Density of City Districts(persons/sq.km)	4312	4361
供水、供气及供热	**Water Supply, Gas Supply and Heating**		
自来水年供水量(万立方米)	Annual Volume of Tap Water Supply (10 000 cu.m)	85851	87999
#生活用水量	Water Consumption for Residential use	30814	31664
平均每人日生活用水量(升)	Per -Capita Water Consumption for Residential Use (litre)	171	169
用水普及率(%)	Coverage Rate of Population with Access to Tap Water (%)	99.1	98.1
人工煤气供气量(万立方米)	Gaswork Gas Supply (10 000 cu.m)	2190	2090
#家庭用量	Consumption of Gaswork Gas for Residential Use	2190	2090
天然气供气量(万立方米)	Natural Gas Supply (10 000 cu.m)	262670	380880
#家庭用量	Consumption of Coal Gas for Residential Use	62431	75940
液化石油气供气量(吨)	Liquefied Petroleum Gas (ton)	73123	64973
#家庭用量	Consumption of Liquefied Gas for Residential Use	56695	52259
天然气、煤气管道长度(公里)	Length of Gas Pipelines (km)	10124	11138
燃气普及率(%)	Goverage Rate of Urban Population with Access to Gas (%)	96.6	96.5
集中供热面积(万平方米)	Area of Centralized Heating (10 000 sq.m)	21844	23452
#住 宅	Residential Buildings	15491	16913
市政工程	**Municipal Engineering**		
道路长度(公里)	Length of Roads (km)	5813	6527
平均每万人拥有 (公里)	Length of Paved Roads per 10 000 Population (km)	6.9	7.5
道路面积(万平方米)	Area of Paved Roads (10 000 sq.m)	9517	11086
平均每人拥有(平方米)	Area of Paved Roads per Population (sq.m)	11.2	12.7
下水道长度(公里)	Length of Sewer Pipelines (km)	4956	5660
平均每万人拥有 (公里)	Length of Sewer Pipelines per 10 000 Population (km)	5.8	6.5
城市绿化	**City Greening**		
建成区绿化覆盖面积(公顷)	Green Areas of Completed Area (hectare)	34428	38757
每万人建成区绿地面积(公顷)	Green Areas of Completed Area per 10 000 Population (hectare)	40.6	44.4
公园数(个)	Number of Parks and Zoos(unit)	139	150
公园面积(公顷)	Area of Parks (hectare)	3681	3778
环境卫生	**Environmental Sanitation**		
清运生活垃圾(万吨)	Volume of Garbage Disposal (10 000 tons)	353	352
清运粪便(万吨)	Volume of Disposal of Excrement and Urine (10 000 tons)	0.4	0.3
每万人拥有公共厕所(座)	Number of Public Lavatories per 10 000 Population (unit)	2.6	2.6

11-2 各城市主要经济指标

Major Economic Indicators by Cities

单位: 万元 (2013 年) (10 000 yuan)

城市名称	City	地区生产总值(当年价格) Gross Region Production (current-year price)	第一产业 Primary Industry	第二产业 Secondary Industry	#工业 Industry
乌鲁木齐市	Urumqi City	22028545	263065	8751032	7467517
克拉玛依市	Karamay City	8531091	44575	6567996	7157178
吐鲁番市	Turpan City	615190	161975	129640	84040
哈 密 市	Hami [Kumul] City	2635379	221306	1344834	873661
昌 吉 市	Changji City	2921346	356193	1419578	1189736
阜 康 市	Fukang City	1265151	230628	748190	658358
伊 宁 市	Yining [Gulja] City	1626561	66926	447454	233586
奎 屯 市	Kuytun City	1225782	59457	643837	513356
塔 城 市	Tacheng [Qoqek] City	646389	156930	150438	70318
乌 苏 市	Usu City	1698312	515224	853753	709352
阿勒泰市	Altay City	519316	75485	110050	61450
博 乐 市	Bole [Bortala] City	1508643	297761	397271	259462
库尔勒市	Korla City	6534087	369956	5112832	4624153
阿克苏市	Aksu City	1453838	110267	378130	345132
阿图什市	Artux City	343956	50166	85219	57845
喀 什 市	Kashgar [Kaxgar] City	1609523	56517	565813	412039
和 田 市	Hotan City	462375	35235	166291	74749
石河子市	Shi Hezi City	2553304	101818	1476482	1127974
阿拉尔市	Aral City				
图木舒克市	Tumxuk City				
五家渠市	Wujiaqu City				
北 屯 市	Beitun City				

城市名称	City	第三产业 Tertiary Industry	#交通运输、仓储和邮政业 Transport, Storage and Post	人均地区生产总值(元) Per Capita GDP (yuan)
乌鲁木齐市	Urumqi City	13014447	2853747	64695
克拉玛依市	Karamay City	1918520	156859	149127
吐鲁番市	Turpan City	323575	80869	22553
哈 密 市	Hami [Kumul] City	1069239	302759	55734
昌 吉 市	Changji City	1145575	193603	60609
阜 康 市	Fukang City	286333	31366	75712
伊 宁 市	Yining [Gulja] City	1112181	78548	31554
奎 屯 市	Kuytun City	522488	88012	79236
塔 城 市	Tacheng [Qoqek] City	339021	39384	38939
乌 苏 市	Usu City	329334	34368	50666
阿勒泰市	Altay City	333781	32041	27147
博 乐 市	Bole [Bortala] City	813611	110490	56455
库尔勒市	Korla City	1051299	117992	110980
阿克苏市	Aksu City	965441	92457	28954
阿图什市	Artux City	208571	20711	13292
喀 什 市	Kashgar [Kaxgar] City	987193	106031	27936
和 田 市	Hotan City	260849	17424	7840
石河子市	Shi Hezi City	975004	84623	73695
阿拉尔市	Aral City			
图木舒克市	Tumxuk City			
五家渠市	Wujiaqu City			
北 屯 市	Beitun City			

11-2 续表 Continued

单位：万元 (10 000 yuan)

城市名称	City	城镇固定资产投资总额 Investment in Fixed Assets in Urban Area	规模以上工业总产值（当年价格） Gross Industrial Output Value above Designated Size (At Current Prices)	公共财政预算收入 General Budgetary Revenue in Local Finance	公共财政预算支出 General Budgetary Expenditure in Local Finance
乌鲁木齐市	Urumqi City	7592505	24270070	3019047	3532024
克拉玛依市	Karamay City	4113706	17767731	658258	798114
吐鲁番市	Turpan City	522908	279485	61916	178241
哈 密 市	Hami [Kumul] City	2650881	2309602	289093	380404
昌 吉 市	Changji City	1512172	3041945	259015	360706
阜 康 市	Fukang City	1682684	1877443	146166	205530
伊 宁 市	Yining [Gulja] City	1529137	525303	210644	369203
奎 屯 市	Kuytun City	857637	1438111	164459	208973
塔 城 市	Tacheng [Qoqek] City	276639	98661	40981	156915
乌 苏 市	Usu City	783157	435490	100077	224641
阿勒泰市	Altay City	577168	182286	46611	213477
博 乐 市	Bole [Bortala] City	1042393	381695	72265	193442
库尔勒市	Korla City	3518861	6563661	304001	406556
阿克苏市	Aksu City	925056	1226700	150419	273555
阿图什市	Artux City	240590	142530	28805	198472
喀 什 市	Kashgar [Kaxgar] City	1155666	516197	157487	402559
和 田 市	Hotan City	510472	131520	46655	206804
石河子市	Shi Hezi City	1795613	3872288	283125	331783
阿拉尔市	Aral City	890688	360126	39482	58663
图木舒克市	Tumxuk City	491992	252146	18678	33939
五家渠市	Wujiaqu City	1770416	2251065	92917	114764
北 屯 市	Beitun City			14008	20839

城市名称	City	居民消费价格指数（上年=100） Consumer Price Index (preceding year=100)	社会消费品零售总额 Total Retail Sales of Consumer Goods	在岗职工平均货币工资（元） Average Money Wage of Staff and Workers (yuan)
乌鲁木齐市	Urumqi City	103.5	8114713	57392
克拉玛依市	Karamay City	104.4	535420	78964
吐鲁番市	Turpan City	104.0	177705	47944
哈 密 市	Hami [Kumul] City	103.6	580785	50029
昌 吉 市	Changji City	104.1	758133	50287
阜 康 市	Fukang City		251252	49843
伊 宁 市	Yining [Gulja] City	103.5	587562	43280
奎 屯 市	Kuytun City	103.8	211534	45394
塔 城 市	Tacheng [Qoqek] City	103.4	140832	42645
乌 苏 市	Usu City		122283	31970
阿勒泰市	Altay City	104.0	207764	38294
博 乐 市	Bole [Bortala] City	104.3	223335	40360
库尔勒市	Korla City	103.4	588237	54002
阿克苏市	Aksu City	103.5	538387	49210
阿图什市	Artux City	103.4	85049	42789
喀 什 市	Kashgar [Kaxgar] City	103.4	595988	48134
和 田 市	Hotan City	104.6	140922	53835
石河子市	Shi Hezi City	103.0	632734	50500
阿拉尔市	Aral City			43793
图木舒克市	Tumxuk City			46767
五家渠市	Wujiaqu City			53086
北 屯 市	Beitun City			

11-3 各城市市区设施水平
Level of Urban Public Facilities in Cities

(2013 年)

城市名称 City		城市用水普及率 (%) Coverage Rate of Urban Population with Access to Tap Water (%)	城市燃气普及率 (%) Coverage Rate of Population with Access to Gas (%)	人均城市道路面积 (平方米) Per Capital Area of Paved Roads (sq.m)	人均公园绿地面积 (平方米) Per Capital Area of Parks and Green Land (sq.m)	排水管道密度 (公里/平方公里) Density of Sewage Pipelines (km/sq.km)
总 计	**Total**	98.08	96.37	15.69	10.08	5.32
乌鲁木齐市	Urumqi City	99.95	99.83	9.57	10.05	3.46
克拉玛依市	Karamay City	100.00	100.00	26.26	10.20	6.47
吐鲁番市	Turpan City	98.65	95.29	16.09	14.80	6.12
哈 密 市	Hami [Kumul] City	100.00	95.34	14.35	8.55	10.41
昌 吉 市	Changji City	99.39	99.08	14.51	10.37	3.99
阜 康 市	Fukang City	98.90	100.00	21.34	13.75	8.83
伊 宁 市	Yining [Gulja] City	99.94	95.69	20.30	9.50	13.54
奎 屯 市	Kuytun City	91.50	79.91	13.98	7.88	9.93
塔 城 市	Tacheng [Qoqek] City	93.60	79.78	14.12	13.26	10.22
乌 苏 市	Usu City	90.36	77.51	18.31	6.22	7.30
阿勒泰市	Altay City	91.22	85.19	14.26	18.09	3.23
博 乐 市	Bole [Bortala] City	98.98	79.70	13.78	10.15	11.36
库尔勒市	Korla City	99.89	99.95	27.16	11.73	4.34
阿克苏市	Aksu City	87.85	97.23	12.01	10.45	4.95
阿图什市	Artux City	100.00	92.00	21.31	1.73	6.33
喀 什 市	Kashgar [Kaxgar] City	100.00	96.80	19.43	11.11	2.77
和 田 市	Hotan City	97.30	99.20	18.59	7.37	3.82
石河子市	Shihezi City	100.00	98.23	31.60	10.70	10.86
阿拉尔市	Alar City	85.60	88.32	26.43	9.10	3.05
图木舒克市	Tumxuk City	74.45	61.51	51.44	10.09	7.41
五家渠市	Wujiaqu City	100.00	100.00	22.26	11.32	3.99
北 屯 市	Beitun City	82.75	80.66	35.58	1.22	4.65
铁门关市	Tiemenguan City	89.60	92.00	44.00		6.90
阿拉山口市	Alashankou City	80.31		60.52	16.58	3.61

11-4 主要年份城市自来水情况
Basic Statistics on Tap Water Supply in Cities in Main Years

指 标	Item	2000	2010	2013
年末水厂生产能力(万吨/日)	Production Capacity of TapWater Supply (10 000 tons/day)	292	373	493
年末供水管道总长度(公里)	Length of Water Supply Piplines (km)	4448	6507	8142
全年供水总量(亿立方米)	Total Annual Volume of Water Supply (100 millon cu.m)	5.0	7.7	8.8
#生活用水	For Residential Use	2.5	2.6	3.2
生产用水	For Productive Use	2.0	2.1	2.5
平均每人日生活用水量(升)	Per-Capitall Daily Consumption of Tap Water for Residential Use (litre)	165.1	150.8	169.0
用水人口(万人)	Number of Residents with Access to Tap Water (10 000 persons)	418	626	693

11-5 主要年份城市市政建设情况
Statistics on City Construction in Cities in Main Years

指　标	Item	2000	2010	2013
实有道路长度(公里)	Length of Paved Roads (km)	2809	5178	6527
实有道路面积(万平方米)	Area of Paved Roads (10 000 sq.m)	3654	8323	11086
城市桥梁(座)	Number of City Bridges (unit)	253	384	424
城市下水道总长度(公里)	Length of Sewer Pipelines (km)	2008	4372	5660
城市污水日处理能力(万立方米)	Daily Disposal Capacity of Sewage (10 000 cu.m)	46	157	232
城市路灯盏数(千盏)	Number of Street Light (1 000 units)	72.9	400.1	484.3

注：城市污水日处理能力指污水处理厂处理能力，不包括其他污水处理设施处理量。
Note: The daily treatment capacity in urban area refers to the treatment capacity of a waste- water treatment plant, excluding the volume handled by other polluted-water treatment facility.

11-6 主要年份城市园林绿化情况
Basic Statistics on Parks and Green Areas in Cities in Main Years

指　标	Item	2000	2010	2013
城市园林绿地面积(公顷)	Area of Park and Green Land (hectare)	19124	37686	53562
#建成区绿地面积	Green Land of Completed Area		27773	35269
每万人建成区绿地面积(公顷)	Green Areas of Completed Area Per 10 000 Population (hectare)	53.4	35.7	44.4
建成区绿化覆盖率(%)	Green Covrage Rate of Completed Area (%)	29.1	36.4	36.4
平均每人公园绿地面积(平方米)	Per Capita Parks Green Areas (sq.m)	6.4	8.6	10.1
公园数(个)	Number of Parks and Zoos (unit)	84	131	150
公园面积(公顷)	Area of Parks (hectare)	1568	3156	3778

11-7 主要年份城市环境卫生情况
Basic Statistics on Urban Environment in Cities in Main Years

指　标	Item	2000	2010	2013
环卫专用车辆设备数量(辆)	Number of Special Vehicles for Environmental Sanitation (unit)	767	1690	4066
公共厕所(座)	Number of Public Lavatories (unit)	1684	2119	2235
每万人拥有公共厕所(座)	Number of Public Lavatories Per 10 000 Population (unit)	4.7	2.5	2.6
道路清扫面积(万平方米)	Area under Cleaning Program (10 000 sq.m)	3224	8080	12315
#机械化	Mechanization		3163	4617
清运生活垃圾(万吨)	Volum of Garbage Disposal (10 000 tons)	259	317	352
清运粪便 (万吨)	Volum of Excrement and Urine Disposal (10 000 tons)	16.0	4.0	0.3

11-8 主要年份城市煤气、液化石油气、天然气情况
Basic Statistics on Supply of Gas, Liquefied Petroleum Gas and Natural Gas in Cities in Main Years

指 标	Item	2000	2010	2013
人工煤气生产能力(万立方米/日)	Production Capacity of Gaswork Gas (10 000 cu.m/day)		49	46
管道长度(公里)	Length of Gas Pipelines (km)	385	7298	11138
人工煤气	Coal Gas		71	71
液化石油气	Liquefied Petroleum Gas		82	81
天然气	Natural Gas	385	7145	10986
全年供气总量(万立方米)	Volume of Gas Supply (10 000 cu.m)			
人工煤气	Coal Gas		1752	2090
液化石油气(吨)	Liquefied Petroleum Gas (ton)	244018	79617	64973
天然气	Natural Gas	5385	134711	380880
用气人口(万人)	Population with Access to Gas (10 000 persons)		604.37	681.58
人工煤气	Coal Gas		8.75	5.00
液化石油气	Liquefied Petroleum Gas	305.70	150.64	73.83
天然气	Natural Gas	27.00	444.98	602.75

11-9 主要年份城市集中供热情况
Basic Statistics on Heating in Cities in Main Years

指 标	Item	2000	2010	2013
供应能力	**Heating Capacity**			
蒸汽(吨/小时)	Steam (ton/hour)	1638	1376	1940
热水(兆瓦)	Hot Water (1 billion kw)	6145	18897	26997
供热总量(万吉焦)	**Quantity of Heating Supplied (10 000 gigajoules)**			
蒸 汽	Steam		1242	1021
热 水	Hot Water		16866	15308
管道长度(公里)	**Length of Heating Pipelines (km)**			
蒸 汽	Steam	250	207	150
热 水	Hot Water	2064	5912	8087
供热面积(万平方米)	**Area of Centralized Heating (10 000 sq.m)**	**5170**	**19162**	**23452**
#住 宅	Residential Buildings		13298	16913

主要统计指标解释

供水综合生产能力 指按供水设施取水、净化、送水、出厂输水干管等环节设计能力计算的综合生产能力。包括在原设计能力的基础上，经挖、革、改增加的生产能力。计算时，以四个环节中最薄弱的环节为主确定能力。

供水管道长度 指从送水泵至用户水表之间所有管道的长度。不包括新安装尚未使用、水厂内以及用户建筑物内的管道。

城市供水总量 指报告期供水企业(单位)供出的全部水量。包括有效供水量和漏损水量。

生产运营用水 指在城区范围内生产、运营的农、林、牧、渔业、工业、建筑业、交通运输业等单位在生产、运营过程中的用水。

公共服务用水 指为城区社会公共生活服务的用水。包括行政事业单位、部队营区和公共设施服务、批发零售业、住宿餐饮业以及社会服务业等单位的用水。

居民家庭用水 指城市范围内所有居民家庭的日常生活用水。包括城市居民、农民家庭、公共供水站用水。

用水普及率 指报告期末城区用水人口数与城市人口总数的比率。计算公式为：

用水普及率＝城区用水人口数（含暂住人口）／城区人口+城区暂住人口×100%

人工煤气生产能力 指报告期末人工煤气生产厂制气、净化、输送等环节的综合生产能力，不包括备用设备能力。一般按设计能力计算，当实际生产能力大于设计能力时，应按实际测定的生产能力计算。测定时应以制气、净化、输送三个环节中最薄弱的环节为主。

供气管道长度 指报告期末从气源厂压缩机的出口或门站出口至各类用户引入管之间的全部已经通气、投入使用的管道长度。不包括煤气生产厂、输配站、液化气储存站、灌瓶站、储配站、气化站、混气站、供应站等厂(站)内的管道。

城市供气总量 指报告期燃气企业(单位)向用户供应的燃气数量。包括销售量和损失量。

燃气普及率 指报告期末城区使用燃气的城市人口数与城市人口总数的比率。计算公式为：

燃气普及率＝城区用气人口（含暂住人口）／城区人口+城区暂住人口×100%

城市供热能力 指供热企业（单位）向城市热用户输送热源的设计能力。

城市供热总量 指在报告期供热企业（单位）向城市热用户输送全部蒸汽和热水的总热量。

城市供热管道长度 指从各类热源到热用户建筑物接入口之间的全部蒸汽和热水的管道长度。不包括各类热源厂内部的管道长度。

道路长度 指道路长度和与道路相通的桥梁、隧道的长度，按车行道中心线计算。

城市桥梁 指为跨越天然或人工障碍物而修建的构筑物。包括跨河桥、立交桥、人行天桥以及人行地下通道等。

城市排水管道长度 指所有排水总管、干管、支管、检查井及连接井进出口等长度之和。

城市污水日处理能力 指污水处理厂（污水处理装置）每昼夜处理污水量的设计能力。

城市绿地面积 指报告期末用作园林和绿化的各种绿地面积。包括公园绿地、生产绿地、防护绿地、附属绿地和其他绿地面积。

公园绿地 城市中向公众开放的、以游憩为主要功能，有一定的游憩设施和服务设施，同时兼有健全生态、美化景观，防灾减灾等综合作用的绿化用地。包括综合公园、社区公园、专类公园、带状公园和街旁绿地。其中综合公园、专类公园和带状公园面积之和为公园面积。

道路清扫保洁面积 指报告期末对城市道路和公共场所（主要包括城市行车道、人行道、车行隧道、人行过街地下通道、道路附属绿地、地铁站、高架路、人行过街天桥、立交桥、广场、停车场及其他设施等）进行清扫保洁的面积。一天清扫多次的，按清扫保洁面积最大的一次计算。

市容环卫专用车辆设备 指用于环境卫生作业、监察的专用车辆和设备，包括用于道路清扫、冲洗、洒水、除雪、垃圾粪便清运、市容监察以及与其配套使用的车辆和设备。

Explanatory Notes on Main Statistical Indicators

Production Capacity of Water Supply refers to the designed overall production capacity of water facilities, covering the four segments of water collection, purification, conveyance, and outflow through trunk pipelines. Increased capacity through transformation and innovation projects is included as well. The capacity is determined mainly on the weakest of the above-mentioned four segments.

Length of Water Supply Pipelines refers to the total length of all the pipelines between the water pumps and the user water meters, excluding pipelines newly installed but not used yet, pipeline in the water factory, and pipeline in the user's buildings.

Total Volume of Urban Water Supply refers to the total volume of water supplied by water-works (units) during the reference period, including both the effective water supply and loss during the water supply.

Consumption of Water for Production and Operation Use refers to water consumption in the process of production and operation by production and operation units of agriculture, forestry, animal husbandry, fisheries, industry, construction industry, and transportation industry, etc. in urban areas.

Consumption of Water for Public Service Use refers to water consumption for public service in the urban areas. It includes water consumption of administrative institutions, army camps, public facilities, wholesale and retail, accommodation and catering industry and social service industry, etc.

Consumption of Water for Households Use refers to consumption of water for daily life of all households in cities, including households of urban residents and farmers, and public water supply stations.

Coverage Rate of Urban Population with Access to Tap Water refers to the ratio of the urban population with access to tap water to the total urban population at the end of reference period. The formula is:

$$\text{Coverage of urban population with access to tap water} = \frac{\text{Urban population with access to tap water}}{\text{Urban population}} \times 100\ \%$$

Production Capacity of Gaswork Gas refers to the overall production capacity of the urban gasworks in gas generation, purification and delivery at the end of the reference period, excluding capacity of the reserved facilities. In general, it is determined by the designed capacity, and when actual production capacity is larger than the designed capacity, the capacity is determined by the actual measurement on the weakest segment in the production, purification and delivery.

Length of Gas Pipelines refers to the total length of pipelines in use between the outlet of the compressor of gas-work or outlet of gas stations and the leading pipe of users, excluding pipelines within gasworks, delivery stations, LPG storage stations, refilling stations, gas-mixing stations and supply stations.

Volume of Gas Supply refers to the total volume of gas provided to users by gas-producing enterprises (units) during the reporting period, including the volume sold and the volume lost.

Coverage Rate of Urban Population with Access to Gas refers to the ratio of the urban population with access to gas to the total urban population at the end of the reference period. Gas here includes artificial coal gas, natural gas and liquefied petroleum gas. The formula is:

$$\text{Coverage rate of urban population with access to gas} = \frac{\text{Urban population with access to gas}}{\text{Urban population}} \times 100\ \%$$

Heating Capacity in Urban Areas refers to the designed capacity of heating enterprises (units) in supplying heating energy to urban users during the reference period.

Quantity of Heat Supplied in Urban Areas refers to the total quantity of heat from steam and hot water supplied to urban users by heating enterprises (units) during the reference period.

Length of Urban Heating Pipelines refers to the total length of steam or hot water pipelines for sources of heat to the leading pipelines of the buildings of the users, excluding internal pipelines in heat generating enterprises.

Length of Paved Roads refers to the length of roads with paved surface including bridges and tunnels connected with roads. Length of the roads is measured by the central lines.

Urban Bridges refer to bridges built to cross over natural or man-made barriers, including bridges over rivers, overpasses for traffic and for pedestrians, underpasses for pedestrians, etc.

Length of Urban Sewage Pipes refers to the total length of general drainage, trunks, branch and inspection wells, connection wells, inlets and outlets, etc.

Daily Disposal Capacity of Urban Sewage refers to the designed 24-hour capacity of sewage disposal by the sewage treatment works or facilities.

Area of Urban Green Land refers to the total area occupied for green projects at the end of the reference period, including park green land, production green land, protection green land, green land attached to institutions, and other green areas.

Park Green Area refers to green areas open to the public for amusement and rest with the facilities of amusement, rest and services. Its function includes perfecting ecology, beautifying landscape, and preventing and reducing disaster. Park green areas include comprehensive park, community park, theme park, linear park and roadside green space. Total areas of comprehensive park, topic park and belt-shaped is the area of park.

Road Area Cleaned refers to the area which are regularly cleaned, as at the end of the reference period, at urban roads and public places (mainly including urban roadways, pedestrian walkways, vehicular tunnels, pedestrian underpasses, underground railway stations, lifted roads, pedestrians walk bridges, overpasses, plazas, parking lots and other facilities). If there are several times of cleaning in a day at a location, the area of that time of cleaning with the largest area cleaned will be taken.

Vehicles and Facilities Dedicated to Urban Cleanliness and Environmental Sanitation refer to vehicles and facilities dedicated for use in the operation, management and monitoring of environmental hygiene work. They include vehicles for road cleaning, washing, showering, ice removal, disposal of garbage and human wastes, cleanliness monitoring and related activities.

新疆统计年鉴
XINJIANG STATISTICAL YEARBOOK

12

农 业

AGRICULTURE

简要说明

本篇主要内容和资料来源

本篇资料反映新疆维吾尔自治区农业生产和农村经济基本情况，主要内容包括农村基层组织情况、乡村从业人员、国有农、林、牧、渔场情况、主要农业生产条件、农林牧渔业产值、主要农产品生产情况、特色农作物生产情况、乡镇企业情况等。

本篇资料除表12-10、12-11、12-12来自新疆维吾尔自治区水利厅，乡镇企业主要指标来自新疆维吾尔自治区乡镇企业局外，其余资料均由新疆维吾尔自治区统计局农村统计处提供。

Brief Introduction

Main Content and Source of Data

The data in this chapter show the basic conditions of agricultural production and rural economy in Xinjiang Uygur Autonomous Region, including mainly rural grassroots units rural population, rural employed labor force, basic conditions of township enterprises, statistic on forest products, cultivated land, gross output value farming, forest, animal husbandry and fishery, output of major farm products and condition on the township enterprises, ect.

Data on table12-10,12-11,12-12 are provided by the Xinjiang Bureau of Water Resources.the data on the township enterprises are from the Xinjiang Bureau of Township Enterprises. Others are provided by the Department of Rural statistics, Xinjiang Bureau of Statistics.

12-1 主要年份农村基层组织情况

Basic Conditions of Rural Grass-roots Unit in Main Years

指 标	Item	2000	2010	2013
乡镇政府(个)	**Number of Township and Town Governments (unit)**	**794**	**801**	**808**
#镇政府	Number of Township Governments	124	183	211
村民委员会(个)	**Number of Villager's Committees (unit)**	9378	8796	8633
乡村户数(户)	**Number of Rural Households (household)**	2008794	2551479	2759770
乡村人口(人)	**Rural Population (person)**	9131922	10737179	11410526
乡村从业人员(人)	**Number of Rural Laborers (person)**	**3540789**	**4650560**	**5599478**
按性别分	Grouped by Gender			
男	Male	1950559	2558491	3072612
女	Female	1590230	2092069	2526866
按行业分	Grouped by Sector			
农林牧渔业	Agriculture, Forestry, Animal Husbandry & Fishery	3144461	3758972	4463395
工 业	Industry	84766	161325	215227
建筑业	Construction	49126	162427	235928
交通运输、仓储和邮政业	Transportation,Storage, Postal and Telecommunication Services		145132	180012
信息传输、计算机服务和软件业	Information Transmission, Computer Service and Software Sector		13915	22169
批发与零售业	Wholesale and Retail Trades	76727	157457	186423
住宿和餐饮业	Hotels and Catering Serives	109217	106191	135028
其 他	Others	76492	145141	161296

12-2 国有农林牧渔场基本情况

Basic Conditions of State Agriculture, Forestry, Animal Husbandry and Fishery

指 标	Item	2012	2013
场数合计(个)	**Total (unit)**	**451**	**479**
农 场	Number of Farms	262	289
林 场	Number of Forest Farms	51	48
牧 场	Number of Ranch	126	131
渔 场	Number of Fishing Ground	12	11
场内户数(户)	**Number of Households on a Farm (household)**	**835021**	**854613**
#牧业户数	Number of Stock-breeding Household	71747	73473
场内人口(人)	**Farm Population (person)**	**2502030**	**2543914**
#牧业人口	Stock-breeding Population	254847	256553
场内实有从业人员(人)	**Persons Actually Engaged on a Farm (person)**	**1114625**	**1181074**
男	Male	613982	648451
女	Female	500643	532623
农 业	Employed Persons in Agriculture	764847	739828
工 业	Employed Persons in Industry	81147	107500
建筑业	Employed Persons in Construction	34506	47839
交通运输、仓储和邮政业	Transportation,Storage, Post and Telecommunications Services	40159	48715
信息传输、计算机服务和软件业	Information Transmission, Computer Service and Software Sector	1355	1572
批发与零售业	Wholesale and Retail Trades	64501	82581
住宿和餐饮业	Hotels and Catering Serives	29099	36841
其 他	Others	99011	116198

12-3 各地、州、市、县(市)农村基层组织情况

(2013 年)

地 区	Region	乡镇数(个) Number of Township and Town Govern-ments (unit)	#镇 town	村民委员会(个) Number of Villager's Committees (unit)	乡村户数(户) Number of Rural House-Holds (household)	#牧业户数 Stock-Breeding Households
总 计	**Total**	**808**	**211**	**8633**	**2759770**	**381266**
乌鲁木齐市	**Urumqi City**	**22**	**8**	**175**	**67025**	**9601**
#乌鲁木齐县	Urumqi County	6	1	41	12582	4888
克拉玛依市	**Karamay City**	**2**		**6**	**685**	**265**
吐鲁番地区	**Turpan Administrative Offices**	**25**	**8**	**175**	**111357**	**3887**
吐鲁番市	Turpan City	9	1	60	45281	2231
鄯善县	Shanshan [piqan]County	9	4	65	40087	352
托克逊县	Toksun County	7	3	50	25989	1304
哈密地区	**Hami [Kumul]Administrative Offices**	**31**	**8**	**170**	**54442**	**15208**
哈密市	Hami [Kumul]City	15	4	91	32940	7659
巴里坤哈萨克自治县	Barkol KazakAutonomous County	10	2	47	18592	6310
伊吾县	Yiwu [Araturuk]County	6	2	32	2910	1239
昌吉回族自治州	**Changji Hui Autonomous Prefecture**	**67**	**36**	**453**	**191737**	**33408**
昌吉市	Changji City	10	8	84	36001	6534
阜康市	Fukang City	6	3	60	18794	3109
呼图壁县	Hutubi County	6	5	50	21546	4216
玛纳斯县	Manas County	11	6	84	27942	4597
奇台县	Qitai County	15	6	60	35972	4816
吉木萨尔县	Jimsar County	9	6	55	29706	3093
木垒哈萨克自治县	Mori Kazak Autonomous County	10	2	60	21776	7043
伊犁哈萨克自治州	**Ili Kazak Autonomous Prefecture**	**212**	**65**	**1956**	**593571**	**99860**
伊犁州直属县(市)	**Counties (Cities) Direct Under Ili Prefecture**	**99**	**26**	**658**	**351699**	**48500**
伊宁市	Yining [Gulja]City	9	1	46	35171	675
奎屯市	Kuytun City	1		4	430	411
伊宁县	Yining [Gulja]County	18	2	130	73509	4694
察布查尔锡伯自治县	Qapqal Xibe Autonomous County	13	2	65	34076	2105
霍城县	Huocheng [korgas]County	10	5	75	57554	2707
巩留县	Gongliu [Tokkuzlara]County	8	4	53	26835	4497
新源县	Xinyuan [kunes]County	11	7	77	40063	7512
昭苏县	Zhaosu [mongolkure]County	10	1	73	29219	8708
特克斯县	Tekes County	8	3	60	22452	8253
尼勒克县	Nilka County	11	1	75	32390	8938
塔城地区	**Tacheng [Tarbagatai] Administrative Offices**	**61**	**25**	**790**	**153236**	**19707**
塔城市	Tacheng [Qoqek] City	5	1	115	20529	1619
乌苏市	Usu City	14	7	134	33209	869
额敏县	Emin [Dorbiljin] County	11	3	139	19590	1277
沙湾县	Shawan County	12	9	236	46029	1615
托里县	Toli County	7	3	66	17122	9554
裕民县	Yumin [Qagantokay] County	5	1	45	10328	2728
和布克赛尔蒙古自治县	Hoboksar Mongol Autonomous County	7	1	55	6429	2045
阿勒泰地区	**Altay Administrative Offices**	**52**	**14**	**508**	**88636**	**31653**
阿勒泰市	Altay City	10	3	102	16236	3588
布尔津县	Burqin County	7	2	63	14543	5541
富蕴县	Fuyun [Koktokay] County	10	4	74	11829	4141
福海县	Fuhai [Burultokay] County	5		62	9780	3735
哈巴河县	Habahe [Kaba] County	7	1	114	19522	7597
青河县	Qinghe [Qinggil] County	7	3	52	9641	5492
吉木乃县	Jeminay County	6	1	41	7085	1559

Basic Conditions of Rural Grass-roots Units by Prefecture, Autonomous Prefecture, City and County

乡村人口数(人) Rural Population (person)	#牧业人口数 Population Engaged in Livestocks	乡村从业人员(人) Number of Rural Laborers (person)	#男 Male	农林牧渔业 Agriculture, Forestry, Animal Husbandry & Fishery	工业 Industry	建筑业 Construction	交通仓储和邮政业 Transport, Storage, Post and Telecommunication Services	信息传输、计算机服务和软件业 Information Transmission, Computer Servcie and Software Industries	批发与零售业 Retail and Wholesale Trades	住宿和餐饮业 Hotels and Catering Serives	其他 Others
11410526	**1483926**	**5599478**	**3072612**	**4463395**	**215227**	**235928**	**180012**	**22169**	**186423**	**135028**	**161296**
223431	**29637**	**132563**	**71091**	**79014**	**10335**	**2118**	**13134**	**257**	**8551**	**9817**	**9337**
42542	15841	23323	12256	17379	107	158	1442	50	810	1024	2353
2149	**950**	**1232**	**652**	**1064**	**17**		**18**	**2**	**44**	**87**	
447210	**15286**	**268113**	**146594**	**213047**	**7972**	**7675**	**10707**	**1412**	**12625**	**8736**	**5939**
184772	9660	105806	59497	80828	2517	3063	5973	334	5964	5391	1736
164396	1308	102110	55064	86385	895	3398	3020	920	4628	2133	731
98042	4318	60197	32033	45834	4560	1214	1714	158	2033	1212	3472
183094	**55666**	**104390**	**55684**	**76694**	**4661**	**3991**	**7605**	**605**	**4197**	**2799**	**3838**
115131	25847	65643	35048	51387	2451	1462	3840	381	2735	1300	2087
60038	25252	33728	17858	20977	2090	2490	3694	214	1357	1433	1473
7925	4567	5019	2778	4330	120	39	71	10	105	66	278
688971	**117044**	**384000**	**209930**	**299014**	**17665**	**7697**	**15851**	**790**	**14514**	**11466**	**17003**
124557	21035	66452	36173	48583	3878	1594	3263	59	3589	2454	3032
64893	12025	37674	20945	25840	3020	1565	1284	44	1418	1814	2689
84679	16656	45873	24402	38281	1238	238	1980	210	1418	994	1514
97170	13249	53647	28812	39194	5696	538	2902	110	2012	1140	2055
151940	20479	80462	46216	64193	1390	1904	3403	140	2953	2796	3683
94995	9922	56711	30425	44443	1505	1258	2262	158	2119	1674	3292
70737	23678	43181	22957	38480	938	600	757	69	1005	594	738
2399823	**421763**	**1206477**	**686695**	**910814**	**59288**	**62628**	**41958**	**7236**	**48372**	**35865**	**40316**
1533250	**232821**	**736466**	**420634**	**534557**	**37621**	**47181**	**31069**	**5823**	**32828**	**24346**	**23041**
152769	3629	77137	42779	38127	6706	8908	8332	522	6279	4690	3573
1394	1327	898	489	830	17	26	8		14	3	
344906	24985	172826	102609	129460	9095	10872	5636	2418	6382	4922	4041
128587	9145	65102	37371	49892	3350	3237	1667	263	2336	1500	2857
213864	12117	126705	69399	96723	4036	5877	4705	1065	4705	5112	4482
124678	22479	43368	25586	37370	1427	1058	1432	36	1811	176	58
208439	38531	87237	50702	63132	5958	4582	3597	544	3997	2545	2882
115514	40431	47888	29630	33985	2463	4438	2136	304	2163	1028	1371
111494	41805	58420	30378	43761	2407	5012	853	441	2541	2197	1208
131605	38372	56885	31691	41277	2162	3171	2703	230	2600	2173	2569
547390	**68008**	**313891**	**177896**	**259820**	**12233**	**7930**	**6724**	**823**	**9400**	**7222**	**9739**
66095	5146	42507	22604	33862	1079	714	939	107	1555	720	3531
124047	2775	68240	40414	55048	3673	1994	992	96	2322	1852	2263
83845	5087	48336	29002	42775	1102	689	1063	119	1694	691	203
157225	5649	91905	48532	74491	4465	2236	2284	335	2599	3110	2385
61997	34812	37881	24541	31906	1332	1815	990	127	670	494	547
35182	8973	18300	9361	16116	372	294	366	21	481	333	317
18999	5566	6722	3442	5622	210	188	90	18	79	22	493
319183	**120934**	**156120**	**88165**	**116437**	**9434**	**7517**	**4165**	**590**	**6144**	**4297**	**7536**
63918	15346	33296	20178	24942	2668	1049	914	221	1190	613	1699
49982	18527	23972	13396	17418	556	1070	446	120	1141	1245	1976
44223	16211	21262	11942	12961	2161	1336	923	90	1063	382	2346
36653	17555	19422	10596	15473	656	1730	572	55	424	348	164
66333	27165	28470	15437	22132	1488	1578	479	56	1319	1065	353
40582	21711	19721	10120	14401	1899	754	801	48	862	583	373
17492	4419	9977	6496	9110	6		30		145	61	625

12-3 续表

地　区	Region	乡镇数（个） Number of Township and Town Govern-ments (unit)	#镇 town	村民委员会（个） Number of Villagers' Committees (unit)	乡村户数（户） Number of Rural House-Holds (household)	#牧业户数 Stock-Breeding Households
博尔塔拉蒙古自治州	**Bortala Mongol Autonomous Prefecture**	**14**	**5**	**223**	**58957**	**6212**
博乐市	Bole [Bortala] City	5	3	107	23647	2631
精河县	Jinghe [Jing] County	4	1	55	22502	1823
温泉县	Wenquan [Araxang] County	5	1	61	12808	1758
巴音郭楞蒙古自治州	**Bayangol Mongol Autonomous Prefecture**	**73**	**15**	**409**	**127235**	**12948**
库尔勒市	Korla City	10	1	59	19821	487
轮台县	Luntai [Bugur] County	10	3	65	18893	945
尉犁县	Yuli [Lopnur] County	7		50	13643	2018
若羌县	Ruoqiang [Qarkilik] County	5	1	26	6110	213
且末县	Qiemo [Qarqan] County	11	1	53	9236	1587
焉耆回族自治县	Yanqi Hui Autonomous County	7	3	49	20381	735
和静县	Hejing County	11	5	55	20451	4431
和硕县	Hoxud County	6		26	10380	2010
博湖县	Bohu [Bagrax] County	6	1	26	8320	522
阿克苏地区	**Aksu Administrative Offices**	**77**	**24**	**1105**	**355940**	**28930**
阿克苏市	Aksu City	6	2	122	36333	6940
温宿县	Wensu [Onsu] County	9	4	104	36193	3740
库车县	Kuqa County	14	8	210	69972	4703
沙雅县	Xayar County	10	4	150	48021	1769
新和县	Xinhe [Toksu] County	7	1	110	37625	4802
拜城县	Baicheng [Bay] County	12	2	150	39498	3500
乌什县	Wushi [Uxturpan] County	8	1	107	43522	1682
阿瓦提县	Awat County	7	2	119	36994	1052
柯坪县	Kalpin County	4		33	7782	742
克孜勒苏柯尔克孜自治州	**Kizilsu Kirgiz Autonomous Prefecture**	**35**	**4**	**243**	**100162**	**30822**
阿图什市	Artux City	7	1	75	39983	8621
阿克陶县	Akto County	13	2	111	42178	9302
阿合奇县	Akqi County	6	1	23	8725	5322
乌恰县	Wuqia [Ulugqat] County	9		34	9276	7577
喀什地区	**Kashgar [Kaxgar] Administrative Offices**	**157**	**21**	**2309**	**659710**	**105111**
喀什市	Kashgar [Kaxgar] City	9	2	124	43433	8809
疏附县	Shufu County	11	2	146	58267	5250
疏勒县	Shule County	14	2	218	58300	2810
英吉沙县	Yengisar County	13		163	53153	6025
泽普县	Zepu [Poskam] County	11	1	129	26479	1751
莎车县	Shache [Yarkant] County	28	6	491	137518	34347
叶城县	Yecheng [Kagilik] County	19	2	296	71824	12233
麦盖提县	Makit County	9		129	33655	1010
岳普湖县	Yopurga County	8	1	87	28556	5487
伽师县	Jiashi [Payzawat] County	12	1	297	77606	9990
巴楚县	Bachu [Maralbexi] County	11	3	186	64510	11611
塔什库尔干塔吉克自治县	Taxkorgan Tajik Autonomous County	12	1	43	6409	5788
和田地区	**Hotan Administrative Offices**	**91**	**16**	**1384**	**432587**	**34545**
和田市	Hotan City	8	2	111	44346	3318
和田县	Hotan County	12	2	206	63012	2974
墨玉县	Moyu [Karakax] County	16	3	364	112902	9659
皮山县	Pishan [Guma] County	16	4	169	49954	2710
洛浦县	Lop County	9	1	207	54692	4800
策勒县	Qira County	8	1	123	40368	6286
于田县	Yutian [Keriya] County	15	2	170	59164	3278
民丰县	Minfeng [Niya] County	7	1	34	8149	1520
生产建设兵团	**Xinjiang Production and Construction Group**	**2**	**1**	**25**	**6362**	**469**

Continued

乡村人口数(人) Rural Population (person)	#牧业人口数 Population Engaged in Livestocks	乡村从业人员(人) Number of Rural Laborers (person)	#男 Male	农林牧渔业 Agriculture, Forestry, Animal Husbandry & Fishery	工业 Industry	建筑业 Construction	交通仓储和邮政业 Transport, Storage, Post and Telecommunication Services	信息传输、计算机服务和软件业 Information Transmission, Computer Servcie and Software Industries	批发与零售业 Retail and Wholesale Trades	住宿和餐饮业 Hotels and Catering Serives	其他 Others
198019	**21865**	**97314**	**52119**	**70796**	**4391**	**3470**	**2981**	**273**	**4597**	**3674**	**7132**
90519	10591	47623	25209	33378	2483	2137	1877	176	2163	2014	3395
70244	6171	31461	17321	23016	895	975	707	22	1483	1132	3231
37256	5103	18230	9589	14402	1013	358	397	75	951	528	506
496883	**46297**	**253888**	**146067**	**203050**	**16644**	**6525**	**7189**	**716**	**8674**	**5910**	**5180**
75788	1372	40111	23539	32726	96	669	1295	160	3381	1390	394
75882	3107	34288	18868	31096	360	417	324	87	736	453	815
50161	8127	20741	11565	18854	58	188	384	88	422	222	525
23916	747	17312	11539	9167	5588	926	969	58	261	343	
41278	5936	18362	10700	15420	286	1136	708	68	422	213	109
78901	3143	42101	24153	30851	3972	1438	1788	40	1167	1306	1539
78665	14560	45831	25723	34201	5692	1318	862	72	1174	1444	1068
38538	7292	17346	9982	14954	174	134	382	118	628	371	585
33754	2013	17796	9998	15781	418	299	477	25	483	168	145
1538742	**104156**	**805528**	**431446**	**689387**	**13937**	**26021**	**17871**	**3630**	**20397**	**13024**	**21261**
170722	20426	72763	40755	50619	1975	6321	4846	628	3199	2953	2222
149622	13752	79774	42921	73102	908	832	705	141	1298	590	2198
312620	20634	164237	84186	132855	3892	8706	6027	1120	5128	2755	3754
202262	5920	110126	63310	96608	808	2994	507	574	2683	1724	4228
142559	14947	69639	37003	61102	402	1663	1331	444	813	902	2982
160853	13500	76030	42303	67181	1524	1611	1295	164	1849	889	1517
181216	6944	127740	65149	113773	2432	2222	1450	301	3076	1444	3042
182205	5037	87113	45681	78092	1629	1101	1371	216	1970	1498	1236
36683	2996	18106	10138	16055	367	571	339	42	381	269	82
436989	**129133**	**182151**	**100516**	**141466**	**8157**	**7698**	**6547**	**238**	**6888**	**4776**	**6381**
190167	34549	83216	47298	57793	5506	3464	4655	185	4507	3763	3343
174928	37802	74049	39272	63047	2033	3352	1211		1208	635	2563
34463	26032	9499	4845	8170	115	240	159	53	331	70	361
37431	30750	15387	9101	12456	503	642	522		842	308	114
3015398	**418062**	**1434829**	**780228**	**1207187**	**30054**	**69909**	**36696**	**3514**	**38307**	**27562**	**21600**
204511	27450	77820	46590	49162	2300	8226	5600		5600	6560	372
250575	21000	120770	65715	97780	3110	5810	3100		4750	3150	3070
290000	6860	221101	132101	200250	3200	7860	3510	261	2500	3520	
251989	28670	116346	60510	108170	930	1745	1445	97	2094	1645	220
112499	6780	36154	18154	28578	859	2030	1926	392	1385	321	663
661821	141229	254882	144060	201538	8472	20542	6794	1034	7308	2633	6561
317108	50569	190011	98203	156524	5179	11261	4488	205	4034	2638	5682
132110	4576	60831	32577	53240	1430	2220	415	96	915	315	2200
124366	29084	58931	29596	45937	1663	2686	2675	934	2115	2731	190
372076	40996	152683	78595	139408	1551	2587	3483	210	2686	2645	113
270137	35463	135115	68638	118852	1292	3997	2450	285	4731	1348	2160
28206	25385	10185	5489	7748	68	945	810		189	56	369
1756717	**122150**	**720974**	**387631**	**565250**	**41739**	**38046**	**19385**	**3496**	**18986**	**11218**	**22854**
192456	14646	71296	38574	44724	6012	4567	3150	863	4565	1967	5448
271277	10473	137382	70052	110150	17808	2518	2751	74	1515	1453	1113
490571	31332	160484	82630	118506	9990	13586	4677	401	4652	3900	4772
195043	8578	76245	40442	63534	1262	3381	2269	178	1503	768	3350
227076	15112	102556	54930	89578	1982	4924	1845	556	1388	606	1677
135293	22612	61443	32597	52133	1193	3428	844	165	1938	1039	703
219581	13860	102345	63136	80135	3230	4715	3491	1154	3025	1263	5332
25420	5537	9223	5270	6490	262	927	358	105	400	222	459
23100	**1917**	**8019**	**3959**	**6612**	**367**	**150**	**70**		**271**	**94**	**455**

12-4 各地、州、市、县(市)耕地面积

Area of Cultivated land by Prefecture, Autonomous Prefecture, City and County

单位：公顷 (2008 年) (hectare)

地区	Region	年末耕地面积 Cultivated Land at Year-end	#水浇地 #Irrigable Land	#旱地 Arid Land
总计	**Total**	**4124563.70**	**3812247.55**	**204501.81**
乌鲁木齐市	**Urumqi City**	**96950.66**	**78328.45**	**4035.06**
#乌鲁木齐县	Urumqi County	55412.44	48787.55	2206.13
克拉玛依市	**Karamay City**	**41926.31**	**41150.26**	**34.34**
石河子市	**Shihezi City**	**21886.21**	**21444.27**	
吐鲁番地区	**TurpanAdministrative Offices**	**48182.08**	**47560.93**	
吐鲁番市	Turpan City	17365.34	16883.43	
鄯善县	Shanshan [piqan]County	13707.94	13577.23	
托克逊县	Toksun County	17108.80	17100.27	
哈密地区	**Hami [Kumul]Administrative Offices**	**87087.69**	**83783.52**	**2617.09**
哈密市	Hami [Kumul]City	48101.16	47484.37	0.91
巴里坤哈萨克自治县	Barkol KazakAutonomous County	33793.67	31248.76	2494.56
伊吾县	Yiwu [Araturuk]County	5192.86	5050.39	121.62
昌吉回族自治州	**Changji Hui Autonomous Prefecture**	**629255.41**	**575551.19**	**48255.72**
昌吉市	Changji City	81216.70	79559.30	
阜康市	Fukang City	45008.84	43705.99	438.04
呼图壁县	Hutubi County	108240.93	107083.42	
玛纳斯县	Manas County	142651.23	140149.81	1646.14
奇台县	Qitai County	141463.80	125593.52	15405.67
吉木萨尔县	Jimsar County	59196.71	54743.95	4118.61
木垒哈萨克自治县	Mori Kazak Autonomous County	51477.20	24715.20	26647.26
伊犁哈萨克自治州	**Ili Kazak Autonomous Prefecture**	**1370619.63**	**1206934.23**	**147541.35**
伊犁州直属县(市)	**Counties (Cities) Direct Under Ili Prefecture**	**565724.94**	**462766.85**	**93380.19**
伊宁市	Yining [Gulja]City	13143.75	12397.65	157.73
奎屯市	Kuytun City	13830.81	13416.21	
伊宁县	Yining [Gulja]County	91060.36	87325.21	3074.98
察布查尔锡伯自治县	Qapqal Xibe Autonomous County	78010.92	67482.83	8691.95
霍城县	Huocheng [korgas]County	90103.57	86672.14	2627.72
巩留县	Gongliu [Tokkuzlara]County	42300.77	34067.58	5769.73
新源县	Xinyuan [kunes]County	69968.00	64130.84	3631.87
昭苏县	Zhaosu [mongolkure]County	89646.90	46655.06	42897.45
特克斯县	Tekes County	29857.44	23166.80	6399.81
尼勒克县	Nilka County	47802.42	27452.53	20128.95
塔城地区	**Tacheng [Tarbagatai] Administrative Offices**	**623638.56**	**574819.09**	**44346.27**
塔城市	Tacheng [Qoqek] City	116362.76	111668.61	4375.15
乌苏市	Usu City	90090.34	88675.34	
额敏县	Emin [Dorbiljin] County	147338.60	125362.73	21758.60
沙湾县	Shawan County	189499.02	186954.94	254.66
托里县	Toli County	24924.02	24791.30	70.37
裕民县	Yumin [Qagantokay] County	44247.45	26309.92	17887.49
和布克赛尔蒙古自治县	Hoboksar Mongol Autonomous County	11176.37	11056.25	
阿勒泰地区	**Altay Administrative Offices**	**181256.13**	**169348.29**	**9814.89**
阿勒泰市	Altay City	40931.04	40585.26	24.04
布尔津县	Burqin County	20584.37	16887.53	3469.38
富蕴县	Fuyun [Koktokay] County	14892.11	11654.88	2860.36
福海县	Fuhai [Burultokay] County	48402.20	47386.39	105.63
哈巴河县	Habahe [Kaba] County	31714.03	29103.31	2462.77
青河县	Qinghe [Qinggil] County	9825.27	8902.88	892.71
吉木乃县	Jeminay County	14907.11	14828.04	

12-4 续表 Continued

单位：公顷 (hectare)

地　区	Region	年末耕地面积 Cultivated Land at Year-end	#水浇地 #Irrigable Land	#旱　地 Arid Land
博尔塔拉蒙古自治州	**Bortala Mongol Autonomous Prefecture**	**135223.32**	**133774.95**	**23.79**
博乐市	Bole [Bortala] City	65574.44	64586.74	
精河县	Jinghe [Jing] County	36147.89	35728.97	23.79
温泉县	Wenquan [Araxang] County	33500.99	33459.24	
巴音郭楞蒙古自治州	**Bayangol Mongol Autonomous Prefecture**	**322556.95**	**312340.71**	
库尔勒市	Korla City	63399.62	55645.29	
轮台县	Luntai [Bugur] County	32947.41	32914.37	
尉犁县	Yuli [Lopnur] County	68263.86	67857.08	
若羌县	Ruoqiang [Qarkilik] County	7132.15	7070.05	
且末县	Qiemo [Qarqan] County	15088.73	15059.49	
焉耆回族自治县	Yanqi Hui Autonomous County	36128.76	35999.77	
和静县	Hejing County	45540.81	45088.93	
和硕县	Hoxud County	36168.43	35167.26	
博湖县	Bohu [Bagrax] County	17887.18	17538.47	
阿克苏地区	**Aksu Administrative Offices**	**614943.17**	**585562.62**	**1674.65**
阿克苏市	Aksu City	168847.83	161536.10	394.20
温宿县	Wensu [Onsu] County	78711.69	67549.42	831.61
库车县	Kuqa County	65204.00	63182.13	6.41
沙雅县	Xayar County	56653.34	56359.21	
新和县	Xinhe [Toksu] County	37933.16	34910.01	
拜城县	Baicheng [Bay] County	72601.88	71028.51	
乌什县	Wushi [Uxturpan] County	46465.29	43538.75	
阿瓦提县	Awat County	79372.13	78323.46	442.43
柯坪县	Kalpin County	9153.85	9135.03	
克孜勒苏柯尔克孜自治州	**Kizilsu Kirgiz Autonomous Prefecture**	**52859.60**	**50149.91**	**252.68**
阿图什市	Artux City	15715.38	15293.50	223.54
阿克陶县	Akto County	29250.53	27006.77	11.71
阿合奇县	Akqi County	6164.41	6140.43	
乌恰县	Wuqia [Ulugqat] County	1729.28	1709.21	17.43
喀什地区	**Kashgar [Kaxgar] Administrative Offices**	**530457.07**	**516515.12**	**66.56**
喀什市	Kashgar [Kaxgar] City	7165.97	6271.21	
疏附县	Shufu County	51747.77	48541.95	
疏勒县	Shule County	49364.21	47766.47	
英吉沙县	Yengisar County	5718.17	5537.15	60.69
泽普县	Zepu [Poskam] County	37625.15	36203.14	
莎车县	Shache [Yarkant] County	98935.41	95867.11	
叶城县	Yecheng [Kagilik] County	53928.82	52503.91	4.67
麦盖提县	Makit County	50533.09	50138.07	
岳普湖县	Yopurga County	22224.51	22149.50	
伽师县	Jiashi [Payzawat] County	52288.15	51455.31	0.54
巴楚县	Bachu [Maralbexi] County	96950.39	96108.71	0.66
塔什库尔干塔吉克自治县	Taxkorgan Tajik Autonomous County	3975.44	3972.59	
和田地区	**Hotan Administrative Offices**	**172615.60**	**159151.39**	**0.57**
和田市	Hotan City	5996.45	5300.40	
和田县	Hotan County	30130.79	27035.19	
墨玉县	Moyu [Karakax] County	34013.32	28767.52	
皮山县	Pishan [Guma] County	27499.96	27193.71	
洛浦县	Lop County	26977.43	26784.99	
策勒县	Qira County	16489.41	16046.82	0.57
于田县	Yutian [Keriya] County	27445.86	24235.45	
民丰县	Minfeng [Niya] County	4062.38	3787.31	

12-5 农、林、牧、渔业总产值

Gross Output Value of Agriculture, Forestry, Animal Husbandry and Fishery

单位：万元 (10 000 yuan)

年份 Year	地区 Region	农林牧渔业总产值 Total	农业产值 Farming	林业产值 Forestry	牧业产值 Animal Husbandry	渔业产值 Fishery	农林牧渔服务业产值 Output Value of Services for Farming, Forestry, Animal Husbandry and Fishery
	1978	191184	142460	3397	44990	337	
	1980	220135	164187	5394	50148	406	
	1985	565699	429519	25906	108598	1676	
	1990	1446535	1104742	38152	294963	8678	
	1995	4057332	3150055	56381	823351	27545	
	1996	4309617	3340735	61940	875560	31382	
	1997	4764743	3738602	64913	925923	35305	
	1998	4992355	3873616	74394	1008783	35562	
	1999	4611503	3409380	75565	1092279	34279	
	2000	4872005	3605405	83451	1145142	38007	
	2001	4968125	3488409	100847	1340236	38633	
	2002	5250446	3627669	110897	1480382	31498	
	2003	6883187	4827597	136936	1619823	32065	266766
	2004	7506792	5150018	138204	1874660	42985	300925
	2005	8310614	5958464	152851	1835206	43405	320688
	2006	8835409	6385954	171994	1890700	46945	339816
	2007	10634648	7669468	208623	2315097	70149	371311
	2008	11766907	7841922	231830	3182256	99097	411802
	2009	12976109	8986167	266451	3183730	111403	428358
	2010	18461828	13768852	352701	3757905	126663	455707
	2011	19553884	14378900	380808	4150000	141653	502523
	2012	22756726	16750000	430407	4853719	152600	570000
	2013	25388809	18061099	481323	6041994	171741	632652
乌鲁木齐市	Urumqi City	369437	163207	8824	188563	7189	1654
克拉玛依市	Karamay City	114780	37794	24570	40158	1151	11107
吐鲁番地区	Turpan Administrative Offices	667960	549998	4400	104818	550	8194
哈密地区	Hami [Kumul] Administrative Offices	463837	246652	13945	195428	2411	5401
昌吉回族自治州	Changji Hui Autonomous Prefecture	3081566	1395281	27712	1609762	19278	29533
伊犁哈萨克自治州	Ili Kazak Autonomous Prefecture	4978402	2721123	97230	2061867	26707	71475
伊犁州直属县(市)	Counties (Cities) Direct Under Ili Prefecture	2203248	1012306	68986	1073860	13920	34176
塔城地区	Tacheng [Tarbagatai] Administrative Offices	2113271	1365020	14677	703629	4296	25649
阿勒泰地区	Altay Administrative Offices	661883	343797	13567	284378	8491	11650
博尔塔拉蒙古自治州	Bortala Mongol Autonomous Prefecture	717541	535108	7314	123564	15539	36016
巴音郭楞蒙古自治州	Bayangol Mongol Autonomous Prefecture	2508033	1935320	49976	439455	14253	69029
阿克苏地区	Aksu Administrative Offices	2452633	1934465	36938	386028	16618	78584
克孜勒苏柯尔克孜自治州	Kizilsu Kirgiz Autonomous Prefecture	249615	143524	5646	86604	239	13602
喀什地区	Kashgar [Kaxgar] Administrative Offices	3886338	2702838	94308	995923	13013	80256
和田地区	Hotan Administrative Offices	1098076	727118	31098	321308	3588	14964
生产建设兵团	Xinjiang Production and Construction Group	9080395	7011738	124392	1320766	54961	568538

注：本表按当年价格计算。
Note：The number in this form is caculated by current price.

12-6 主要年份农、林、牧、渔业总产值指数

Indices of Gross Output Value of Agriculture, Forestry, Animal Husbandry and Fishery in Main Years

年 份 Year	农林牧渔业总产值 Total	#农业产值 Farming	#林业产值 Forestry	#牧业产值 Animal Husbandry	#渔业产值 Fishery
(上年=100) (preceding year=100)					
1978	113.0	118.6	108.8	105.4	106.7
1980	108.9	108.4	151.2	104.4	112.7
1985	110.9	111.5	131.3	104.6	135.1
1990	115.1	119.2	95.2	102.0	111.3
1995	107.1	107.0	88.5	109.0	127.0
1996	104.2	103.3	101.0	107.7	112.3
1997	109.5	109.6	100.5	110.2	108.6
1998	110.8	111.5	105.5	109.0	102.0
1999	104.8	103.9	100.9	108.1	106.3
2000	105.3	104.2	110.3	108.0	116.4
2001	104.5	103.9	116.1	105.8	104.2
2002	105.2	103.9	111.5	108.9	102.1
2003	106.3	105.2	120.7	108.7	101.7
2004	106.4	104.5	100.7	112.0	108.2
2005	107.4	107.0	105.8	109.0	105.3
2006	107.5	107.7	106.5	107.8	105.3
2007	108.2	108.9	108.6	106.0	115.2
2008	106.7	106.1	107.5	109.4	107.5
2009	105.1	107.8	106.5	98.5	106.9
2010	104.9	104.7	106.4	105.1	105.5
2011	106.9	108.3	105.9	102.0	107.1
2012	107.4	106.8	107.6	109.8	104.1
2013	107.2	107.1	108.1	107.8	107.8
(1978 年=100) (1978=100)					
1978	100.0	100.0	100.0	100.0	100.0
1980	115.9	115.5	158.8	111.1	120.5
1985	188.4	194.3	245.4	160.0	140.9
1990	303.7	322.6	244.4	243.7	442.4
1995	420.7	453.3	247.4	325.5	863.7
1996	438.4	468.1	249.8	350.6	970.0
1997	480.2	512.8	251.1	386.4	1053.2
1998	531.8	571.7	265.1	421.1	1073.9
1999	557.1	593.8	267.5	455.3	1141.6
2000	586.3	618.8	295.0	491.9	1328.4
2001	612.9	642.8	342.5	520.6	1384.1
2002	644.8	668.1	381.9	566.9	1413.2
2003	685.4	702.6	460.9	616.0	1437.2
2004	729.3	734.2	464.1	689.9	1555.1
2005	783.3	785.6	491.0	752.0	1637.5
2006	842.0	846.1	522.9	810.7	1724.3
2007	911.0	921.4	567.9	859.3	1986.4
2008	972.0	977.6	610.5	940.1	2135.4
2009	1021.6	1053.9	650.2	926.0	2282.7
2010	1071.7	1103.4	691.8	973.2	2408.2
2011	1145.6	1195.0	732.6	992.7	2579.2
2012	1230.4	1276.3	788.3	1090.0	2684.9
2013	1319.0	1366.9	852.2	1175.0	2894.3

12-7 各地、州、市、县(市)农林牧渔业总产值

Gross Output Value of Agriculture, Forestry, Animal Husbandry and Fishery by Prefecture, Autonomous Prefecture, City and County

单位：万元 (2013 年) (10 000 yuan)

地　区	Region	农林牧渔业总产值 Total	农业产值 Farming	林业产值 Forestry	牧业产值 Animal Husbandry	渔业产值 Fishery	农林牧渔服务业产值 Output Value of Services for Farming, Forestry, Animal Husbandary and Fishery
总　计	**Total**	**25388809**	**18061099**	**481323**	**6041994**	**171741**	**632652**
乌鲁木齐市	**Urumqi City**	**369437**	**163207**	**8824**	**188563**	**7189**	**1654**
#乌鲁木齐县	Urumqi County	96249	33496	1969	58764	420	1600
克拉玛依市	**Karamay City**	**114780**	**37794**	**24570**	**40158**	**1151**	**11107**
吐鲁番地区	**TurpanAdministrative Offices**	**667960**	**549998**	**4400**	**104818**	**550**	**8194**
吐鲁番市	Turpan City	277060	232144	2101	37768	463	4584
鄯善县	Shanshan [piqan]County	253850	215599	1222	35393	66	1570
托克逊县	Toksun County	137050	102255	1077	31657	21	2040
哈密地区	**Hami [Kumul]Administrative Offices**	**463837**	**246652**	**13945**	**195428**	**2411**	**5401**
哈密市	Hami [Kumul]City	234978	162752	5194	62379	2115	2538
巴里坤哈萨克自治县	Barkol KazakAutonomous County	158792	55354	622	101059	274	1483
伊吾县	Yiwu [Araturuk]County	70067	28546	8129	31990	22	1380
昌吉回族自治州	**Changji Hui Autonomous Prefecture**	**3081566**	**1395281**	**27712**	**1609762**	**19278**	**29533**
昌吉市	Changji City	452630	177833	4321	256411	10241	3824
阜康市	Fukang City	367827	164771	2354	198467	575	1660
呼图壁县	Hutubi County	526698	188514	4099	317532	3995	12558
玛纳斯县	Manas County	595743	346118	3413	234410	2808	8994
奇台县	Qitai County	659775	291449	5946	362104		276
吉木萨尔县	Jimsar County	263929	115343	5808	139898	1659	1221
木垒哈萨克自治县	Mori Kazak Autonomous County	214964	111253	1771	100940		1000
伊犁哈萨克自治州	**Ili Kazak Autonomous Prefecture**	**4978402**	**2721123**	**97230**	**2061867**	**26707**	**71475**
伊犁州直属县(市)	**Counties (Cities) Direct Under Ili Prefecture**	**2203248**	**1012306**	**68986**	**1073860**	**13920**	**34176**
伊宁市	Yining [Gulja]City	123160	70225	884	46974	2079	2998
奎屯市	Kuytun City	18620	9483	109	7644		1384
伊宁县	Yining [Gulja]County	425603	219244	2921	188931	8217	6290
察布查尔锡伯自治县	Qapqal Xibe Autonomous County	249098	148621	15306	80229	1210	3732
霍城县	Huocheng [korgas]County	280034	148939	3607	120769	544	6175
巩留县	Gongliu [Tokkuzlara]County	209277	105271	2637	100164	863	342
新源县	Xinyuan [kunes]County	341540	122544	38445	175230	786	4535
昭苏县	Zhaosu [mongolkure]County	195101	72936	867	119160	8	2130
特克斯县	Tekes County	150468	54310	600	94478	60	1020
尼勒克县	Nilka County	210347	60733	3610	140281	153	5570

注：本表按当年价格计算。
Note: The number in this form is caculated by current price.

12-7 续表 1 Continued

单位：万元 (10 000 yuan)

地　　区	Region	农林牧渔业总产值 Total	农业产值 Farming	林业产值 Forestry	牧业产值 Animal Husbandry	渔业产值 Fishery	农林牧渔服务业产值 Output Value of Services for Farming, Forestry, Animal Husbandary and Fishery
塔城地区	**Tacheng [Tarbagatai] Administrative Offices**	**2113271**	**1365020**	**14677**	**703629**	**4296**	**25649**
塔城市	Tacheng [Qoqek] City	298039	184085	2606	107116	670	3562
乌苏市	Usu City	537071	393238	4690	133067	973	5103
额敏县	Emin [Dorbiljin] County	313943	201411	1107	109966	174	1285
沙湾县	Shawan County	694099	469592	2673	207217	2373	12244
托里县	Toli County	97425	33967	1703	60445		1310
裕民县	Yumin [Qagantokay] County	91241	52209	1398	36759	68	807
和布克赛尔蒙古自治县	Hoboksar Mongol Autonomous County	81453	30518	500	49059	38	1338
阿勒泰地区	**Altay Administrative Offices**	**661883**	**343797**	**13567**	**284378**	**8491**	**11650**
阿勒泰市	Altay City	117046	59081	779	54784	735	1667
布尔津县	Burqin County	62952	27730	1353	31670	424	1775
富蕴县	Fuyun [Koktokay] County	108940	42906	2242	61881	444	1467
福海县	Fuhai [Burultokay] County	155954	104009	699	41406	6269	3571
哈巴河县	Habahe [Kaba] County	119471	65067	4368	48575	464	997
青河县	Qinghe [Qinggil] County	66424	32692	3767	28836	104	1025
吉木乃县	Jeminay County	31096	12311	359	17226	51	1149
博尔塔拉蒙古自治州	**Bortala Mongol Autonomous Prefecture**	**717541**	**535108**	**7314**	**123564**	**15539**	**36016**
博乐市	Bole [Bortala] City	306677	218380	1931	60716	13708	11942
精河县	Jinghe [Jing] County	303218	253999	3032	30175	946	15066
温泉县	Wenquan [Araxang] County	107646	62729	2351	32673	885	9008
巴音郭楞蒙古自治州	**Bayangol Mongol Autonomous Prefecture**	**2508033**	**1935320**	**49976**	**439455**	**14253**	**69029**
库尔勒市	Korla City	486084	407139	324	66666	1319	10636
轮台县	Luntai [Bugur] County	347795	297008	610	45981	355	3841
尉犁县	Yuli [Lopnur] County	279566	223630	4001	32517	20	19398
若羌县	Ruoqiang [Qarkilik] County	274195	260438	735	10672	6	2344
且末县	Qiemo [Qarqan] County	182275	133242	3724	36445	583	8281
焉耆回族自治县	Yanqi Hui Autonomous County	233054	118893	26611	76021	1379	10150
和静县	Hejing County	263601	131823	6794	118608	434	5942
和硕县	Hoxud County	292078	253262	2361	30173	95	6187
博湖县	Bohu [Bagrax] County	149385	109885	4816	22372	10062	2250
阿克苏地区	**Aksu Administrative Offices**	**2452633**	**1934465**	**36938**	**386028**	**16618**	**78584**
阿克苏市	Aksu City	374761	290012	1295	66883	2937	13634
温宿县	Wensu [Onsu] County	416709	316392	13789	59411	5117	22000
库车县	Kuqa County	426555	316113	4642	101671	609	3520

12-7 续表 2 Continued

单位：万元 (10 000 yuan)

地　　区	Region	农林牧渔业总产值 Total	农业产值 Farming	林业产值 Forestry	牧业产值 Animal Husbandry	渔业产值 Fishery	农林牧渔服务业产值 Output Value of Services for Farming, Forestry, Animal Husbandary and Fishery
沙雅县	Xayar County	274942	231508	5184	29791	465	7994
新和县	Xinhe [Toksu] County	247842	208501	2726	22546	400	13669
拜城县	Baicheng [Bay] County	203319	137635	5782	51212	6300	2390
乌什县	Wushi [Uxturpan] County	145956	117763	984	23046	695	3468
阿瓦提县	Awat County	310107	278924	1560	19700	95	9828
柯坪县	Kalpin County	52442	37617	976	11768		2081
克孜勒苏柯尔克孜自治州	**Kizilsu Kirgiz Autonomous Prefecture**	**249615**	**143524**	**5646**	**86604**	**239**	**13602**
阿图什市	Artux City	108300	64857	1496	36377	200	5370
阿克陶县	Akto County	106473	69512	3200	27702	39	6020
阿合奇县	Akqi County	17671	4524	611	11541		995
乌恰县	Wuqia [Ulugqat] County	17171	4631	339	10984		1217
喀什地区	**Kashgar [Kaxgar] Administrative Offices**	**3886338**	**2702838**	**94308**	**995923**	**13013**	**80256**
喀什市	Kashgar [Kaxgar] City	166386	78051	6374	76230	1131	4600
疏附县	Shufu County	334224	211129	5374	106411	1040	10270
疏勒县	Shule County	347747	225289	12000	109251	680	527
英吉沙县	Yengisar County	198710	132030	3586	56775	144	6175
泽普县	Zepu [Poskam] County	266475	194033	3053	64749	3840	800
莎车县	Shache [Yarkant] County	728562	547569	33846	122659	3647	20841
叶城县	Yecheng [Kagilik] County	570924	418320	13149	132811	1094	5550
麦盖提县	Makit County	309280	239495	4156	56999	294	8336
岳普湖县	Yopurga County	180244	114900	5825	56737	203	2579
伽师县	Jiashi [Payzawat] County	411868	274791	6528	120209	540	9800
巴楚县	Bachu [Maralbexi] County	355039	263888	417	80674	400	9660
塔什库尔干塔吉克自治县	Taxkorgan Tajik Autonomous County	16879	3343		12418		1118
和田地区	**Hotan Administrative Offices**	**1098076**	**727118**	**31098**	**321308**	**3588**	**14964**
和田市	Hotan City	93873	55311	2257	33411	775	2119
和田县	Hotan County	190276	142436	4202	40856	1286	1496
墨玉县	Moyu [Karakax] County	249284	165249	4693	75475	904	2963
皮山县	Pishan [Guma] County	132420	86607	5140	37235	36	3402
洛浦县	Lop County	135050	97067	4536	31484	258	1705
策勒县	Qira County	102483	70365	3532	28038	55	493
于田县	Yutian [Keriya] County	166225	99958	4807	59063	222	2175
民丰县	Minfeng [Niya] County	28465	10125	1931	15746	52	611
生产建设兵团	**Xinjiang Production and ConstructionGroup**	**9080395**	**7011738**	**124392**	**1320766**	**54961**	**568538**

12-8 各地、州、市、县(市)农业机械拥有量
Agricultural Machinery by Prefecture, Autonomous Prefecture, City and County

(2013 年)

地　区	Region	农业机械总动力(千瓦) Total Power of Agricultural Machinery (kw)	农用大中型拖拉机 Large and Medium Agricultural Tractors 数量(台) Number (unit)	动力(千瓦) Capacity (kw)	小型拖拉机 Small Tractors 数量(台) Number (unit)	动力(千瓦) Capacity (kw)
总　计	**Total**	**21658676**	**396951**	**12014260**	**318544**	**3982409**
乌鲁木齐市	**Urumqi City**	**307857**	**3518**	**108154**	**5520**	**66572**
#乌鲁木齐县	Urumqi County	54922	1186	28338	1123	15832
克拉玛依市	**Karamay City**	**30647**	**467**	**15470**	**96**	**1211**
吐鲁番地区	**TurpanAdministrative Offices**	**528444**	**2541**	**88163**	**8471**	**97522**
吐鲁番市	Turpan City	213005	729	24884	3216	35472
鄯善县	Shanshan [piqan]County	213507	890	31677	3211	39973
托克逊县	Toksun County	101899	921	31585	2043	22062
哈密地区	**Hami [Kumul]Administrative Offices**	**353879**	**4520**	**132730**	**9920**	**117903**
哈密市	Hami [Kumul]City	186382	2794	79054	3808	46680
巴里坤哈萨克自治县	Barkol KazakAutonomous County	134732	1365	40076	5199	59143
伊吾县	Yiwu [Araturuk]County	32766	361	13601	913	12081
昌吉回族自治州	**Changji Hui Autonomous Prefecture**	**2031392**	**21907**	**867061**	**44007**	**533903**
昌吉市	Changji City	334624	2908	157102	8690	110465
阜康市	Fukang City	164272	1614	71106	3317	35574
呼图壁县	Hutubi County	342713	4368	159247	5402	79028
玛纳斯县	Manas County	344463	5352	179493	7490	89488
奇台县	Qitai County	488673	3932	161029	10153	112094
吉木萨尔县	Jimsar County	200000	1618	66069	4374	51649
木垒哈萨克自治县	Mori Kazak Autonomous County	156647	2115	73015	4581	55605
伊犁哈萨克自治州	**Ili Kazak Autonomous Prefecture**	**4487424**	**83443**	**2605670**	**65750**	**839864**
伊犁州直属县(市)	**Counties (Cities) Direct Under Ili Prefecture**	**1678863**	**30132**	**996450**	**23021**	**290370**
伊宁市	Yining [Gulja]City	81697	1199	42518	1206	15438
奎屯市	Kuytun City	12140	304	11796	47	344
伊宁县	Yining [Gulja]County	301721	4912	183464	5476	68271
察布查尔锡伯自治县	Qapqal Xibe Autonomous County	206917	4072	138859	1620	17861
霍城县	Huocheng [korgas]County	206226	5441	128893	1955	21655
巩留县	Gongliu [Tokkuzlara]County	204582	2898	99913	5042	66694
新源县	Xinyuan [kunes]County	266370	5211	177248	1250	15859
昭苏县	Zhaosu [mongolkure]County	152958	2055	82370	2788	36877
特克斯县	Tekes County	109135	2112	60326	1306	16968
尼勒克县	Nilka County	137117	1928	71063	2331	30403
塔城地区	**Tacheng [Tarbagatai] Administrative Offices**	**2071550**	**39615**	**1231000**	**26538**	**336213**
塔城市	Tacheng [Qoqek] City	281224	5283	165037	3719	47240
乌苏市	Usu City	629989	13249	429247	8284	103550
额敏县	Emin [Dorbiljin] County	281801	3665	113495	3195	42874
沙湾县	Shawan County	592180	12976	383447	8176	101855
托里县	Toli County	100154	1396	43373	1028	12878
裕民县	Yumin [Qagantokay] County	140591	2165	70967	1570	20790
和布克赛尔蒙古自治县	Hoboksar Mongol Autonomous County	45612	881	25434	566	7027
阿勒泰地区	**Altay Administrative Offices**	**737011**	**13696**	**378219**	**16191**	**213281**
阿勒泰市	Altay City	159666	2560	73678	3900	50560
布尔津县	Burqin County	93971	1671	40237	2712	38783
富蕴县	Fuyun [Koktokay] County	114289	2662	68381	2092	30722
福海县	Fuhai [Burultokay] County	151133	3558	94803	1626	21152
哈巴河县	Habahe [Kaba] County	138107	1787	59012	4005	49529
青河县	Qinghe [Qinggil] County	55273	869	23563	1451	17560
吉木乃县	Jeminay County	24571	589	18545	405	4975

12-8 续表 1 Continued

地　　区	Region	农业机械总动力(千瓦) Total Power of Agricultural Machinery (kw)	农用大中型拖拉机 Large and Medium Agricultural Tractors		小型拖拉机 Small Tractors	
			数量(台) Number (unit)	动力(千瓦) Capacity (kw)	数量(台) Number (unit)	动力(千瓦) Capacity (kw)
博尔塔拉蒙古自治州	**Bortala Mongol Autonomous Prefecture**	**597694**	**10717**	**327942**	**13126**	**160910**
博乐市	Bole [Bortala] City	243985	4376	130907	5117	62193
精河县	Jinghe [Jing] County	229339	4635	140741	5641	69998
温泉县	Wenquan [Araxang] County	124370	1706	56294	2368	28719
巴音郭楞蒙古自治州	**Bayangol Mongol Autonomous Prefecture**	**1829818**	**38063**	**1123401**	**28261**	**359152**
库尔勒市	Korla City	471018	9027	258809	10334	136822
轮台县	Luntai [Bugur] County	165611	3643	99136	3590	43654
尉犁县	Yuli [Lopnur] County	261729	7787	234017	1425	19522
若羌县	Ruoqiang [Qarkilik] County	60893	1696	40915	252	3122
且末县	Qiemo [Qarqan] County	107288	2847	73013	1981	24698
焉耆回族自治县	Yanqi Hui Autonomous County	243768	3641	136248	3671	45679
和静县	Hejing County	204820	4356	121596	2174	28784
和硕县	Hoxud County	154000	2448	77145	1332	16633
博湖县	Bohu [Bagrax] County	160691	2618	82522	3502	40238
阿克苏地区	**Aksu Administrative Offices**	**2505456**	**51770**	**1407125**	**63707**	**809687**
阿克苏市	Aksu City	238993	4705	122484	7360	90058
温宿县	Wensu [Onsu] County	394143	9221	270454	6950	79925
库车县	Kuqa County	341586	7280	194962	8675	108429
沙雅县	Xayar County	295129	6182	188777	6889	76506
新和县	Xinhe [Toksu] County	187894	3682	108912	5108	61296
拜城县	Baicheng [Bay] County	379084	6727	175717	9322	122034
乌什县	Wushi [Uxturpan] County	249984	7132	154560	5010	73290
阿瓦提县	Awat County	375628	5930	166741	13801	190454
柯坪县	Kalpin County	43017	911	24517	592	7696
克孜勒苏柯尔克孜自治州	**Kizilsu Kirgiz Autonomous Prefecture**	**393408**	**11779**	**270452**	**5996**	**76409**
阿图什市	Artux City	119474	3033	73517	1494	18821
阿克陶县	Akto County	221823	6647	154974	4020	51042
阿合奇县	Akqi County	28024	1075	22350	155	2195
乌恰县	Wuqia [Ulugqat] County	24087	1024	19611	327	4351
喀什地区	**Kashgar [Kaxgar] Administrative Offices**	**3241110**	**99713**	**2301289**	**34698**	**430127**
喀什市	Kashgar [Kaxgar] City	91933	3295	65686	1029	12037
疏附县	Shufu County	313284	9159	185887	4905	65587
疏勒县	Shule County	375818	9976	233955	4583	55454
英吉沙县	Yengisar County	164764	5152	115181	2848	34960
泽普县	Zepu [Poskam] County	219240	7999	165856	2251	27665
莎车县	Shache [Yarkant] County	637374	19120	458822	8322	102263
叶城县	Yecheng [Kagilik] County	298908	10545	223524	2127	25312
麦盖提县	Makit County	231188	7899	192264	1821	22416
岳普湖县	Yopurga County	136837	5082	116202	1156	13943
伽师县	Jiashi [Payzawat] County	313294	9715	241181	3523	43682
巴楚县	Bachu [Maralbexi] County	434009	10661	281642	1892	23434
塔什库尔干塔吉克自治县	Taxkorgan Tajik Autonomous County	24462	1110	21088	241	3374
和田地区	**Hotan Administrative Offices**	**764312**	**22203**	**551227**	**6772**	**80822**
和田市	Hotan City	77141	2171	66926	343	4540
和田县	Hotan County	98290	2827	60523	1211	13393
墨玉县	Moyu [Karakax] County	186557	5465	136960	937	9546
皮山县	Pishan [Guma] County	80476	2783	56891	499	6436
洛浦县	Lop County	110420	3325	81557	786	9548
策勒县	Qira County	64116	1378	39678	1252	16418
于田县	Yutian [Keriya] County	119727	3557	89503	1299	15588
民丰县	Minfeng [Niya] County	27585	697	19190	445	5353
生产建设兵团	**Xinjiang Production and Construction Group**	**4587234**	**46310**	**2215576**	**32220**	**408326**

12-8 续表 2 Continued

地　区	Region	大中型拖拉机配套农具(部) Number of Large and Medium Tractor Towing Farm Machinery (unit)	小型拖拉机配套农具(部) Number of Small Tractor Towing Farm Machinery (unit)	农用排灌柴油机 Diesel Engines	
				数　量(台) Number (unit)	动　力(千瓦) Capacity (kw)
总　计	**Total**	**684422**	**628521**	**12108**	**179151**
乌鲁木齐市	**Urumqi City**	**4270**	**4769**	**5**	**33**
#乌鲁木齐县	Urumqi County	1266	2160	5	33
克拉玛依市	**Karamay City**	**897**	**170**	**1**	**15**
吐鲁番地区	**TurpanAdministrative Offices**	**4936**	**17516**	**13**	**158**
吐鲁番市	Turpan City	988	4408		
鄯善县	Shanshan [piqan]County	1855	5874		
托克逊县	Toksun County	2092	7233	13	158
哈密地区	**Hami [Kumul]Administrative Offices**	**10845**	**19734**		
哈密市	Hami [Kumul]City	6996	6451		
巴里坤哈萨克自治县	Barkol KazakAutonomous County	3162	11449		
伊吾县	Yiwu [Araturuk]County	687	1834		
昌吉回族自治州	**Changji Hui Autonomous Prefecture**	**45313**	**65181**	**130**	**2339**
昌吉市	Changji City	7310	12437		
阜康市	Fukang City	4121	4246		
呼图壁县	Hutubi County	13267	16883		
玛纳斯县	Manas County	6386	16823	15	183
奇台县	Qitai County	8448	7582		
吉木萨尔县	Jimsar County	3306	3809		
木垒哈萨克自治县	Mori Kazak Autonomous County	2475	3401	115	2156
伊犁哈萨克自治州	**Ili Kazak Autonomous Prefecture**	**180804**	**115482**	**4390**	**54641**
伊犁州直属县(市)	**Counties (Cities) Direct Under Ili Prefecture**	**56944**	**19580**	**841**	**8821**
伊宁市	Yining [Gulja]City	2773	858	30	653
奎屯市	Kuytun City	657	62		
伊宁县	Yining [Gulja]County	6518	5302	241	2329
察布查尔锡伯自治县	Qapqal Xibe Autonomous County	9380	2096	45	793
霍城县	Huocheng [korgas]County	10502	2320	219	1642
巩留县	Gongliu [Tokkuzlara]County	3882	2557	34	746
新源县	Xinyuan [kunes]County	9691	3070	79	1055
昭苏县	Zhaosu [mongolkure]County	3096	353	73	
特克斯县	Tekes County	5604	1590	8	382
尼勒克县	Nilka County	4841	1372	112	1221
塔城地区	**Tacheng [Tarbagatai] Administrative Offices**	**105844**	**83664**	**1501**	**19069**
塔城市	Tacheng [Qoqek] City	12790	11705	31	732
乌苏市	Usu City	43722	24852	1050	12084
额敏县	Emin [Dorbiljin] County	11978	10899	254	3736
沙湾县	Shawan County	28968	31411	78	973
托里县	Toli County	2156	1043	60	1283
裕民县	Yumin [Qagantokay] County	4949	3423		
和布克赛尔蒙古自治县	Hoboksar Mongol Autonomous County	1281	331	28	261
阿勒泰地区	**Altay Administrative Offices**	**18016**	**12238**	**2048**	**26751**
阿勒泰市	Altay City	3810	2040	51	601
布尔津县	Burqin County	995	2081	173	2249
富蕴县	Fuyun [Koktokay] County	3875	1210	619	8897
福海县	Fuhai [Burultokay] County	6639	2612	400	6000
哈巴河县	Habahe [Kaba] County	1070	1827	570	5274
青河县	Qinghe [Qinggil] County	1079	1528	217	3417
吉木乃县	Jeminay County	548	940	18	313

12-8 续表 3 Continued

地　区	Region	大中型拖拉机配套农具（部）Number of Large and Medium Tractor Towing Farm Machinery (unit)	小型拖拉机配套农具（部）Number of Small Tractor Towing Farm Machinery (unit)	农用排灌柴油机 Diesel Engines	
				数量（台）Number (unit)	动力（千瓦）Capacity (kw)
博尔塔拉蒙古自治州	**Bortala Mongol Autonomous Prefecture**	**15789**	**10135**	**8**	**187**
博乐市	Bole [Bortala] City	7434	3482	3	33
精河县	Jinghe [Jing] County	6242	5641		
温泉县	Wenquan [Araxang] County	2113	1012	5	154
巴音郭楞蒙古自治州	**Bayangol Mongol Autonomous Prefecture**	**63414**	**72658**	**2341**	**33203**
库尔勒市	Korla City	15204	28218	1268	13314
轮台县	Luntai [Bugur] County	4962	8410		
尉犁县	Yuli [Lopnur] County	7918	5494	750	13050
若羌县	Ruoqiang [Qarkilik] County	2688	1966	213	5719
且末县	Qiemo [Qarqan] County	4363	6546		
焉耆回族自治县	Yanqi Hui Autonomous County	11424	8482		
和静县	Hejing County	9932	5406	50	760
和硕县	Hoxud County	3937	3519	60	360
博湖县	Bohu [Bagrax] County	2986	4617		
阿克苏地区	**Aksu Administrative Offices**	**104907**	**141757**	**773**	**8556**
阿克苏市	Aksu City	18204	18325	38	558
温宿县	Wensu [Onsu] County	10005	13448	51	630
库车县	Kuqa County	20766	17656	50	670
沙雅县	Xayar County	15350	16736	560	5694
新和县	Xinhe [Toksu] County	7121	11240	14	154
拜城县	Baicheng [Bay] County	10179	19990	8	113
乌什县	Wushi [Uxturpan] County	9686	11090		
阿瓦提县	Awat County	12254	32346	52	737
柯坪县	Kalpin County	1342	926		
克孜勒苏柯尔克孜自治州	**Kizilsu Kirgiz Autonomous Prefecture**	**16834**	**9370**	**1**	**4**
阿图什市	Artux City	4908	3177		
阿克陶县	Akto County	8642	5342		
阿合奇县	Akqi County	1850	280		
乌恰县	Wuqia [Ulugqat] County	1434	571	1	4
喀什地区	**Kashgar [Kaxgar] Administrative Offices**	**139985**	**130878**	**952**	**14950**
喀什市	Kashgar [Kaxgar] City	1341	3906		
疏附县	Shufu County	6269	32065		
疏勒县	Shule County	21907	23003		
英吉沙县	Yengisar County	9815	6185		
泽普县	Zepu [Poskam] County	8020	18423	10	97
莎车县	Shache [Yarkant] County	20455	11393	396	7063
叶城县	Yecheng [Kagilik] County	20645	13950		
麦盖提县	Makit County	12974	8648	136	1999
岳普湖县	Yopurga County	8674	4151	30	264
伽师县	Jiashi [Payzawat] County	18144	6650	225	3094
巴楚县	Bachu [Maralbexi] County	10589	1846	155	2434
塔什库尔干塔吉克自治县	Taxkorgan Tajik Autonomous County	1152	658		
和田地区	**Hotan Administrative Offices**	**21019**	**14403**	**33**	**662**
和田市	Hotan City	1680	394		
和田县	Hotan County	2131	1853	14	180
墨玉县	Moyu [Karakax] County	5539	1217		
皮山县	Pishan [Guma] County	3380	2350	12	176
洛浦县	Lop County	2503	2258		
策勒县	Qira County	1143	2729	3	159
于田县	Yutian [Keriya] County	4107	3120		
民丰县	Minfeng [Niya] County	536	482	4	147
生产建设兵团	**Xinjiang Production and Construction Group**	**75409**	**26468**	**3461**	**64402**

12-9 各地、州、市、县(市)农村电气化和农田水利情况
Statistics on Water Conservancy and Electrification in Rural Areas by Prefecture, Autonomous Prefecture, City and County

(2013 年)

地 区	Region	有效灌溉面积(千公顷) Irrigated Area (1000 hectares)	化肥施用量(吨)(折纯) Consumption of Chemical Fertilizer (ton) (100% Purity)	#氮肥 Nitrogenous Fertilizer	#磷肥 Phosphate Fertilizer	#钾肥 Potash Fertilizer
总 计	**Total**	**4407.28**	**2032213**	**923506**	**509967**	**140959**
乌鲁木齐市	**Urumqi City**	**48.51**	**8961**	**5585**	**1545**	**1020**
#乌鲁木齐县	Urumqi County	13.37	1817	837	443	372
克拉玛依市	**Karamay City**	**13.70**	**3578**	**1235**	**817**	**317**
吐鲁番地区	**TurpanAdministrative Offices**	**41.23**	**25259**	**12073**	**4167**	**2877**
吐鲁番市	Turpan City	14.70	12499	5616	752	1553
鄯善县	Shanshan [piqan]County	10.67	7444	4842	730	508
托克逊县	Toksun County	15.87	5316	1615	2685	816
哈密地区	**Hami [Kumul]Administrative Offices**	**79.94**	**19910**	**9837**	**3526**	**1508**
哈密市	Hami [Kumul]City	50.98	10245	5546	2050	883
巴里坤哈萨克自治县	Barkol KazakAutonomous County	23.01	6065	3291	276	25
伊吾县	Yiwu [Araturuk]County	5.95	3600	1000	1200	600
昌吉回族自治州	**Changji Hui Autonomous Prefecture**	**461.29**	**145520**	**72454**	**36102**	**7448**
昌吉市	Changji City	92.51	31049	12584	7920	1540
阜康市	Fukang City	44.21	9949	5629	2031	104
呼图壁县	Hutubi County	76.47	34121	18809	9737	2061
玛纳斯县	Manas County	70.75	30084	13933	8936	687
奇台县	Qitai County	112.87	21732	11977	4356	686
吉木萨尔县	Jimsar County	42.87	13002	7626	1492	1490
木垒哈萨克自治县	Mori Kazak Autonomous County	21.61	5583	1896	1630	880
伊犁哈萨克自治州	**Ili Kazak Autonomous Prefecture**	**941.70**	**300481**	**124849**	**65418**	**17854**
伊犁州直属县(市)	**Counties (Cities) Direct Under Ili Prefecture**	**335.96**	**108304**	**33709**	**17387**	**5686**
伊宁市	Yining [Gulja]City	14.48	3856	1726		142
奎屯市	Kuytun City	4.68	3183	1263	1268	91
伊宁县	Yining [Gulja]County	70.07	29585	8942	4472	1476
察布查尔锡伯自治县	Qapqal Xibe Autonomous County	57.32	14830	5191	4374	1196
霍城县	Huocheng [korgas]County	46.77	12973	2639	1966	1264
巩留县	Gongliu [Tokkuzlara]County	34.81	9639	4202		
新源县	Xinyuan [kunes]County	40.28	11646	3219	1460	584
昭苏县	Zhaosu [mongolkure]County	24.76	7426	2971	1573	689
特克斯县	Tekes County	19.96	3086	710	833	
尼勒克县	Nilka County	22.82	12080	2846	1441	244
塔城地区	**Tacheng [Tarbagatai] Administrative Offices**	**408.20**	**151855**	**69195**	**35696**	**8476**
塔城市	Tacheng [Qoqek] City	85.37	23167	11640	7325	1476
乌苏市	Usu City	87.78	31731	16550	3464	1516
额敏县	Emin [Dorbiljin] County	74.32	24014	7822	6904	521
沙湾县	Shawan County	107.18	57936	27028	14964	4870
托里县	Toli County	25.30	5918	2709	1806	
裕民县	Yumin [Qagantokay] County	18.77	5312	2013	962	8
和布克赛尔蒙古自治县	Hoboksar Mongol Autonomous County	9.48	3777	1433	271	85
阿勒泰地区	**Altay Administrative Offices**	**197.54**	**40322**	**21945**	**12335**	**3692**
阿勒泰市	Altay City	32.94	5703	3528	2014	85
布尔津县	Burqin County	17.67	2315	1068	1247	
富蕴县	Fuyun [Koktokay] County	23.99	3409	2134	942	248
福海县	Fuhai [Burultokay] County	68.01	20703	9935	5926	2706
哈巴河县	Habahe [Kaba] County	32.29	3441	2475	840	126
青河县	Qinghe [Qinggil] County	14.67	3174	1828	910	431
吉木乃县	Jeminay County	7.98	1577	977	456	96

12-9 续表 1 Continued

地 区	Region	有效灌溉面积(千公顷) Irrigated Area(1000 hectares)	化肥施用量(吨)(折纯) Consumption of Chemical Fertilizer (ton) (100% Purity)	#氮肥 Nitrogenous Fertilizer	#磷肥 Phosphate Fertilizer	#钾肥 Potash Fertilizer
博尔塔拉蒙古自治州	**Bortala Mongol Autonomous Prefecture**	**143.78**	**56504**	**25575**	**16567**	**4511**
博乐市	Bole [Bortala] City	53.20	19455	8209	5834	1161
精河县	Jinghe [Jing] County	52.85	19269	9949	4798	703
温泉县	Wenquan [Araxang] County	37.73	17780	7417	5935	2647
巴音郭楞蒙古自治州	**Bayangol Mongol Autonomous Prefecture**	**257.32**	**145304**	**74519**	**39620**	**9986**
库尔勒市	Korla City	55.21	28889	15995	8621	2197
轮台县	Luntai [Bugur] County	31.87	24331	13250	4783	527
尉犁县	Yuli [Lopnur] County	40.67	28049	12331	9475	3240
若羌县	Ruoqiang [Qarkilik] County	7.27	6490	3374	1447	305
且末县	Qiemo [Qarqan] County	17.55	10029	6614	1130	71
焉耆回族自治县	Yanqi Hui Autonomous County	28.39	15064	7026	2356	1370
和静县	Hejing County	28.56	10225	4426	3977	1159
和硕县	Hoxud County	32.36	12962	6918	5196	214
博湖县	Bohu [Bagrax] County	15.45	9265	4585	2635	903
阿克苏地区	**Aksu Administrative Offices**	**514.98**	**262077**	**108555**	**90967**	**16406**
阿克苏市	Aksu City	62.53	59221	24179	25833	2134
温宿县	Wensu [Onsu] County	68.78	27302	3536	5984	5758
库车县	Kuqa County	72.58	43141	17011	13276	1227
沙雅县	Xayar County	80.00	40922	18826	17185	1637
新和县	Xinhe [Toksu] County	46.00	23215	9536	10995	1865
拜城县	Baicheng [Bay] County	56.07	18813	6554	7581	2220
乌什县	Wushi [Uxturpan] County	30.01	12791	9107	848	
阿瓦提县	Awat County	89.00	33414	18103	7710	1565
柯坪县	Kalpin County	10.01	3258	1703	1555	
克孜勒苏柯尔克孜自治州	**Kizilsu Kirgiz Autonomous Prefecture**	**40.80**	**20100**	**10008**	**7483**	**1117**
阿图什市	Artux City	12.74	10057	4863	5194	
阿克陶县	Akto County	20.99	9891	5040	2242	1117
阿合奇县	Akqi County	4.69	60	37	23	
乌恰县	Wuqia [Ulugqat] County	2.38	92	68	24	
喀什地区	**Kashgar [Kaxgar] Administrative Offices**	**577.32**	**323395**	**152351**	**107216**	**16548**
喀什市	Kashgar [Kaxgar] City	13.44	5374	2187	2187	
疏附县	Shufu County	39.33	25960	12760	11550	1375
疏勒县	Shule County	52.00	24700	12200	9000	2000
英吉沙县	Yengisar County	29.95	17867	9453	6905	214
泽普县	Zepu [Poskam] County	26.74	21638	8927	8071	2344
莎车县	Shache [Yarkant] County	112.57	76843	29745	18985	1980
叶城县	Yecheng [Kagilik] County	75.68	33102	17219	7653	4040
麦盖提县	Makit County	61.33	18045	12273	5134	64
岳普湖县	Yopurga County	35.73	35513	15974	10755	3412
伽师县	Jiashi [Payzawat] County	63.33	27249	16140	8070	599
巴楚县	Bachu [Maralbexi] County	61.91	35743	15174	18009	355
塔什库尔干塔吉克自治县	Taxkorgan Tajik Autonomous County	5.29	1361	299	897	165
和田地区	**Hotan Administrative Offices**	**169.39**	**69849**	**39082**	**19424**	**4284**
和田市	Hotan City	10.37	5781	3836	1466	320
和田县	Hotan County	24.43	9968	5290	2826	919
墨玉县	Moyu [Karakax] County	35.54	14584	6250	2778	1389
皮山县	Pishan [Guma] County	29.07	11897	7929	2843	537
洛浦县	Lop County	21.23	8833	5703	3130	
策勒县	Qira County	17.12	6574	4507	1906	100
于田县	Yutian [Keriya] County	28.31	10271	4660	3655	874
民丰县	Minfeng [Niya] County	3.30	1941	907	820	145
生产建设兵团	**Xinjiang Production and Construction Group**	**1117.34**	**651275**	**287383**	**117115**	**57083**

12-9 续表 2 Continued

地　　区	Region	乡村及村以下办水电站 Hydropower Station inVillage or Below		农村用电量(万千瓦小时)
		装机容量(万千瓦) Installed Capacity (10 000 kw)	发电量(万千瓦) Generating Capacity (10 000 kw)	Electricity Consumed in Rural Areas (10 000 kwh)
总　计	**Total**	**20.39**	**30201**	**839229**
乌鲁木齐市	**Urumqi City**			**18188**
#乌鲁木齐县	Urumqi County			789
克拉玛依市	**Karamay City**			**420**
吐鲁番地区	**TurpanAdministrative Offices**			**46268**
吐鲁番市	Turpan City			18745
鄯善县	Shanshan [piqan]County			21626
托克逊县	Toksun County			5896
哈密地区	**Hami [Kumul]Administrative Offices**			**23707**
哈密市	Hami [Kumul]City			18986
巴里坤哈萨克自治县	Barkol KazakAutonomous County			3745
伊吾县	Yiwu [Araturuk]County			976
昌吉回族自治州	**Changji Hui Autonomous Prefecture**			**92914**
昌吉市	Changji City			21146
阜康市	Fukang City			6294
呼图壁县	Hutubi County			20245
玛纳斯县	Manas County			9591
奇台县	Qitai County			25061
吉木萨尔县	Jimsar County			3672
木垒哈萨克自治县	Mori Kazak Autonomous County			6906
伊犁哈萨克自治州	**Ili Kazak Autonomous Prefecture**	**2.31**	**3586**	**85751**
伊犁州直属县(市)	**Counties (Cities) Direct Under Ili Prefecture**	**1.07**	**2222**	**33457**
伊宁市	Yining [Gulja]City			1936
奎屯市	Kuytun City			3520
伊宁县	Yining [Gulja]County	0.08	84	4116
察布查尔锡伯自治县	Qapqal Xibe Autonomous County			2496
霍城县	Huocheng [korgas]County			10952
巩留县	Gongliu [Tokkuzlara]County	0.09	350	1052
新源县	Xinyuan [kunes]County	0.39	1603	4001
昭苏县	Zhaosu [mongolkure]County	0.51	20	1152
特克斯县	Tekes County		165	917
尼勒克县	Nilka County			3315
塔城地区	**Tacheng [Tarbagatai] Administrative Offices**			**33839**
塔城市	Tacheng [Qoqek] City			6771
乌苏市	Usu City			4401
额敏县	Emin [Dorbiljin] County			2586
沙湾县	Shawan County			10244
托里县	Toli County			3890
裕民县	Yumin [Qagantokay] County			3952
和布克赛尔蒙古自治县	Hoboksar Mongol Autonomous County			1995
阿勒泰地区	**Altay Administrative Offices**	**1.24**	**1364**	**18455**
阿勒泰市	Altay City	1.00	207	859
布尔津县	Burqin County			1890
富蕴县	Fuyun [Koktokay] County	0.04	57	4045
福海县	Fuhai [Burultokay] County			2704
哈巴河县	Habahe [Kaba] County			976
青河县	Qinghe [Qinggil] County	0.20	1100	6785
吉木乃县	Jeminay County			1196

12-9 续表 3 Continued

地　　区	Region	乡村及村以下办水电站 HydroPower Station inVillage or Below 装机容量(万千瓦) Installed Capacity (10 000 kw)	发电量(万千瓦) Generating Capacity (10 000 kw)	农村用电量(万千瓦小时) Electricity Consumed in Rural Areas (10 000 kwh)
博尔塔拉蒙古自治州	**Bortala Mongol Autonomous Prefecture**	**0.52**	**1605**	**26772**
博乐市	Bole [Bortala] City	0.15	695	11139
精河县	Jinghe [Jing] County	0.37	910	12606
温泉县	Wenquan [Araxang] County			3027
巴音郭楞蒙古自治州	**Bayangol Mongol Autonomous Prefecture**			**67933**
库尔勒市	Korla City			17368
轮台县	Luntai [Bugur] County			12338
尉犁县	Yuli [Lopnur] County			6131
若羌县	Ruoqiang [Qarkilik] County			5749
且末县	Qiemo [Qarqan] County			1489
焉耆回族自治县	Yanqi Hui Autonomous County			3520
和静县	Hejing County			1527
和硕县	Hoxud County			16739
博湖县	Bohu [Bagrax] County			3072
阿克苏地区	**Aksu Administrative Offices**	**6.00**	**96**	**53732**
阿克苏市	Aksu City			4289
温宿县	Wensu [Onsu] County	6.00	96	2477
库车县	Kuqa County			9714
沙雅县	Xayar County			10721
新和县	Xinhe [Toksu] County			12456
拜城县	Baicheng [Bay] County			5006
乌什县	Wushi [Uxturpan] County			2355
阿瓦提县	Awat County			4486
柯坪县	Kalpin County			2228
克孜勒苏柯尔克孜自治州	**Kizilsu Kirgiz Autonomous Prefecture**	**0.12**	**254**	**5167**
阿图什市	Artux City	0.12	254	1842
阿克陶县	Akto County			2729
阿合奇县	Akqi County			340
乌恰县	Wuqia [Ulugqat] County			256
喀什地区	**Kashgar [Kaxgar] Administrative Offices**	**3.01**	**25**	**68323**
喀什市	Kashgar [Kaxgar] City			720
疏附县	Shufu County	3.00	25	1910
疏勒县	Shule County			1300
英吉沙县	Yengisar County			3293
泽普县	Zepu [Poskam] County			4631
莎车县	Shache [Yarkant] County			4408
叶城县	Yecheng [Kagilik] County			1336
麦盖提县	Makit County			12317
岳普湖县	Yopurga County			2678
伽师县	Jiashi [Payzawat] County			12212
巴楚县	Bachu [Maralbexi] County			23518
塔什库尔干塔吉克自治县	Taxkorgan Tajik Autonomous County	0.01		
和田地区	**Hotan Administrative Offices**	**1.47**	**2307**	**40384**
和田市	Hotan City	0.08		8506
和田县	Hotan County			6848
墨玉县	Moyu [Karakax] County	1.00	1230	6650
皮山县	Pishan [Guma] County			3002
洛浦县	Lop County	0.22	745	5380
策勒县	Qira County	0.16	332	3747
于田县	Yutian [Keriya] County			2898
民丰县	Minfeng [Niya] County	0.01		3354
生产建设兵团	**Xinjiang Production and Construction Group**	**6.96**	**22328**	**309669**

12-10 灌溉、水库和除涝、治水情况
Irrigation, Reservoirs, Flood Prevention, Water and Soil Conservation

项 目	Item	2013
灌溉面积(千公顷)	Irrigated Areas (1000 hectares)	4792.83
耕地灌溉面积	Irrigated Cultivated-land Areas	3658.80
林地灌溉面积	Irrigated Wooded-land Areas	588.25
园地灌溉面积	Irrigated Orchard Areas	264.99
牧草灌溉面积	Irrigated Pasture-land Areas	279.92
其他灌溉面积	Other Irrigated Areas	0.87
水库(座)	Number of Reservoirs (unit)	511
大型水库	Large Reservoir	19
中型水库	Medium-sized Reservoir	98
小型水库	Small Reservoir	394
塘坝(座)	Dam (unit)	343
泵站(处)	Pumping Station (unit)	429
节水灌溉面积(千公顷)	Water-saving Irrigated Areas (1000 hectares)	2058.58
#微灌面积	Micro Irrigated Area	1572.54
除涝面积(千公顷)	Areas wish Flood Prevention Measures (1000 hectares)	323.40
水土流失治理面积(千公顷)	Area of Soil Erosion under Control (1000 hectares)	812.49
#小流域综合治理面积	Area of Comprehensive Management of Small Watershed	169.76
堤防长度(公里)	Total Length of Dikes (km)	4748.57
#河堤长度	Length of Rivers	4487.33
堤防保护人口数(万人)	Dikes Protected Population (10000 people)	825.76
堤防保护耕地面积(千公顷)	Area of Land Protected by Dikes (1000 hectares)	1249.26

注: 1.大型水库库容: 1 亿立方米以上; 中型水库库容: 1 千万至 1 亿立方米;小型水库库容: 10 万至 1 千万立方米。2.本表和 12-11，12-12 表资料由水利厅提供。

Note: a) The capacity of the large reservoirs is over 100 million cubic meters, while that of the medium ones is from 10 million to 100 million cubic meters, and that of the small ones is from 100 000 to 10 million cubic meters. b) The data in the table is offered by the Bureau of Water Conservancy, together with table 12-11,12-12.

12-11 各地、州、市水利设施和节水灌溉面积
Water Conservancy Facilities and Water-saving Irrigated Area by Prefecture, Autonomous Prefecture and City

(2013 年)

地 区	Region	水库数 (座) Number of Reservoirs (unit)	泵站 (座) Pumping Seation (unit)	节水灌溉面积 (千公顷) Water-saving Irrigated Area (1 000 hectares)	水土流失治理面积 (千公顷) Area of Soil Erosion under Control (1 000 hectares)
总 计	**Total**	**511**	**429**	**2058.58**	**812.49**
乌鲁木齐市	Urumqi City	24	10	1.25	23.30
克拉玛依市	Karamay City	7	20	18.85	6.53
吐鲁番地区	Turpan Administrative Offices	15		48.72	16.19
哈密地区	Hami [Kumul]Administrative Offices	48	3	67.99	21.06
昌吉回族自治州	Changji HuiAutonomous Prefecture	85	33	304.82	50.73
伊犁州直属县(市)	Counties (Cities) Direct Under Ili Prefecture	20	16	215.51	200.14
塔城地区	Tacheng [Tarbagatai] Administrative Offices	68	7	384.65	66.27
阿勒泰地区	Altay Administrative Offices	81	189	165.04	72.74
博尔塔拉蒙古自治州	Bortala Mongol Autonomous Prefecture	6		86.59	40.50
巴音郭楞蒙古自治州	Bayangol Mongol Autonomous Prefecture	16	74	283.82	64.53
阿克苏地区	Aksu Administrative Offices	22	8	210.62	69.16
克孜勒苏柯尔克孜自治州	Kizilsu Kirgiz Autonomous Prefecture	13	2	6.64	21.92
喀什地区	Kashgar [Kaxgar] Administrative Offices	58	58	141.29	89.84
和田地区	Hotan Administrative Offices	48	9	122.79	69.59

12-12 各地、州、市农村集中式供水工程情况
Projects of Centralized Water Supply in Rural by Prefecture, Automou Prefecture and City

单位:处　(2013 年)　(unit)

地 区	Region	合 计 Total	城镇管网延伸工程 Project of Urban Pipe Network Extension	联村供水工程 Joint Village Water-supply Project	单村供水工程 Village Water-supply Project
总 计	**Total**	**2182**	**100**	**940**	**1142**
乌鲁木齐市	Urumqi City	91	4	36	51
克拉玛依市	Karamay City	2		2	
吐鲁番地区	Turpan Administrative Offices	43	1	34	8
哈密地区	Hami [Kumul]Administrative Offices	139	13	28	98
昌吉回族自治州	Changji HuiAutonomous Prefecture	514	9	62	443
伊犁州直属县(市)	Counties (Cities) Direct Under Ili Prefecture	215	15	125	75
塔城地区	Tacheng [Tarbagatai] Administrative Offices	229	4	76	149
阿勒泰地区	Altay Administrative Offices	161	12	57	92
博尔塔拉蒙古自治州	Bortala Mongol Autonomous Prefecture	165		110	55
巴音郭楞蒙古自治州	Bayangol Mongol Autonomous Prefecture	144	31	35	78
阿克苏地区	Aksu Administrative Offices	156	1	142	13
克孜勒苏柯尔克孜自治州	Kizilsu Kirgiz Autonomous Prefecture	116	3	48	65
喀什地区	Kashgar [Kaxgar] Administrative Offices	135	5	120	10
和田地区	Hotan Administrative Offices	72	2	65	5

12-13 主要年份农作物播种面积
Total Sown Areas of Farm Crops in Main Years

单位：千公顷 (1 000 hectares)

年份 Year	农作物播种面积 Total Sown Area	粮食作物播种面积 Sown Area of Grain Crops	谷物 Cereal	#水稻 Rice	#小麦 Wheat	#玉米 Corn	#大麦 Barley	豆类 Soybeans	薯类 Tubers	棉花 Cotton
1978	3021.67	2310.71	2297.44	105.59	1348.82	621.39	50.01	13.27	23.09	150.42
1980	2993.71	2162.37	2147.60	98.39	1354.83	555.79	23.24	14.77	17.55	181.22
1985	2846.63	1853.04	1844.47	74.50	1278.43	418.43	13.63	8.57	10.56	253.52
1990	2979.51	1826.61	1813.16	84.13	1180.11	442.40	42.92	13.45	10.67	435.22
1995	3051.44	1593.29	1528.62	73.38	952.58	439.16	41.58	64.67	10.34	742.90
2000	3388.76	1445.77	1353.99	78.15	838.99	382.45	33.50	91.78	22.59	1012.39
2001	3404.12	1394.96	1281.38	73.28	744.27	410.29	34.11	113.58	20.77	1129.72
2002	3478.37	1493.96	1386.81	74.96	749.74	501.93	36.45	107.15	20.65	943.97
2003	3470.28	1307.02	1202.61	67.16	626.09	454.14	38.25	104.41	23.89	1037.05
2004	3571.89	1378.61	1273.03	66.77	658.08	505.69	24.53	105.58	24.23	1127.55
2005	3728.11	1471.76	1371.89	69.07	761.84	497.64	27.42	99.87	20.51	1157.99
2006	4206.28	1465.82	1369.68	68.00	740.11	496.43	50.96	96.14	22.79	1664.43
2007	4394.25	1379.00	1300.58	70.95	634.02	528.91	55.86	78.42	33.15	1782.60
2008	4536.87	1649.97	1554.43	70.12	877.97	545.39	54.68	95.54	36.02	1668.01
2009	4710.26	1993.50	1867.77	73.49	1153.32	598.38	31.73	125.73	37.68	1409.31
2010	4758.64	1991.61	1879.36	66.93	1120.01	653.82	28.94	112.25	36.99	1460.60
2011	4983.48	2000.36	1916.10	70.59	1077.98	728.00	24.81	84.26	47.12	1638.06
2012	5136.74	2103.20	2034.45	69.23	1081.04	855.72	14.13	68.75	27.97	1720.80
2013	5212.26	2204.22	2130.28	67.29	1120.98	920.80	10.07	73.94	30.58	1718.26

年份 Year	#长绒棉 Long-Staple Cotton	油料 Oil Bearing Crops	#油菜 Rapeseeds	#胡麻 Flax	#葵花 Helianthus	甜菜 Beetroots	蔬菜 Vegetables	果用瓜 Melon	#甜瓜 Musk-melon	苜蓿 Lucerne
1978	29.05	202.13	90.90	65.49	23.68	17.67	55.12	41.95		174.90
1980	38.50	269.39	107.47	81.85	50.08	24.27	46.99	39.54		191.65
1985	26.28	294.78	89.82	81.12	111.39	15.51	54.91	53.69	27.95	132.07
1990	62.69	269.27	117.35	46.04	96.11	66.87	58.07	28.84	15.09	159.34
1995	8.35	306.70	130.11	26.75	140.10	71.10	71.54	25.15	9.72	120.25
2000	49.29	310.07	96.23	24.57	157.05	55.75	127.75	55.99	26.01	120.49
2001	67.69	217.64	72.85	17.10	99.76	85.54	125.96	58.19	26.55	165.06
2002	46.30	215.05	70.00	23.84	96.60	85.32	164.21	82.47	48.47	235.11
2003	70.13	226.38	74.48	22.30	100.07	67.31	163.84	62.45	32.82	294.13
2004	70.63	215.47	67.52	13.74	85.55	59.88	185.60	61.29	36.07	301.10
2005	73.38	185.49	59.92	17.37	84.62	69.90	176.66	70.57	36.02	275.91
2006	106.94	151.73	49.25	14.28	64.29	94.42	186.82	74.02	41.27	242.38
2007	142.53	176.47	59.48	12.32	96.41	94.02	234.88	103.40	62.81	231.36
2008	132.18	286.68	83.67	9.51	172.44	71.14	258.04	110.60	68.22	171.42
2009	82.60	270.05	76.95	12.43	155.74	63.74	262.17	143.47	86.70	165.34
2010	96.79	273.37	70.15	8.75	164.87	75.27	303.59	122.78	69.44	150.14
2011	83.87	264.28	64.47	7.83	163.65	75.43	322.61	118.85	57.78	145.29
2012	53.33	242.34	59.64	8.68	148.19	82.63	306.94	130.08	63.12	149.69
2013	38.28	221.74	43.71	8.08	145.77	65.90	296.68	136.45	66.13	184.70

注：粮食、棉花播种面积为国家审定数。
Note: Total sown areas of grain,cotton refer to the statistical data of state approved.

12-14 各地、州、市、县(市)农作物播种面积

单位：千公顷 (2013 年)

地　区	Region	农作物播种面积 Total Sown Area	粮食 Grain Crops	谷物 Cereal	#水稻 Rice	#小麦 Wheat	#玉米 Corn	豆类 Soy-beans
总　计	**Total**	**5212.26**	**2204.22**	**2130.28**	**67.29**	**1120.98**	**920.80**	**73.94**
乌鲁木齐市	**Urumqi City**	**51.53**	**19.33**	**18.62**	**6.58**	**5.97**	**4.33**	**0.71**
#乌鲁木齐县	Urumqi County	13.24	3.05	2.88		1.03	0.19	0.17
克拉玛依市	**Karamay City**	**10.99**	**1.33**	**1.33**		**0.23**	**1.10**	
吐鲁番地区	**TurpanAdministrative Offices**	**55.63**	**6.75**	**6.74**		**0.04**	**2.37**	**0.01**
吐鲁番市	Turpan City	14.70	1.05	1.05			0.67	
鄯善县	Shanshan [piqan]County	15.81	0.67	0.67		0.02	0.44	
托克逊县	Toksun County	25.13	5.04	5.03		0.02	1.26	0.01
哈密地区	**Hami [Kumul]Administrative Offices**	**66.07**	**27.45**	**26.76**		**20.60**	**2.12**	**0.69**
哈密市	Hami [Kumul]City	34.31	6.33	6.29		2.71	2.11	0.04
巴里坤哈萨克自治县	Barkol KazakAutonomous County	25.28	18.91	18.89		17.55	0.01	0.02
伊吾县	Yiwu [Araturuk]County	6.48	2.21	1.58		0.34		0.63
昌吉回族自治州	**Changji Hui Autonomous Prefecture**	**532.47**	**296.22**	**280.44**	**1.17**	**185.21**	**91.26**	**15.78**
昌吉市	Changji City	94.12	37.74	37.29	0.86	20.79	15.51	0.45
阜康市	Fukang City	50.94	27.38	25.85	0.14	16.57	8.79	1.53
呼图壁县	Hutubi County	78.41	30.07	30.06	0.17	20.39	9.32	0.01
玛纳斯县	Manas County	76.87	20.42	20.16	0.02	3.62	16.43	0.26
奇台县	Qitai County	130.90	101.50	99.97		72.56	26.12	1.53
吉木萨尔县	Jimsar County	52.20	34.59	32.50		23.48	8.67	2.09
木垒哈萨克自治县	Mori Kazak Autonomous County	49.03	44.51	34.60		27.81	6.43	9.91
伊犁哈萨克自治州	**Ili Kazak Autonomous Prefecture**	**1159.65**	**717.55**	**673.12**	**18.04**	**332.15**	**318.10**	**44.44**
伊犁州直属县(市)	**Counties (Cities) Direct Under Ili Prefecture**	**482.68**	**373.92**	**341.01**	**17.23**	**183.84**	**135.84**	**32.91**
伊宁市	Yining [Gulja]City	19.55	13.49	12.25	0.91	4.73	6.61	1.24
奎屯市	Kuytun City	4.68	2.78	2.78		2.21	0.57	
伊宁县	Yining [Gulja]County	91.80	79.34	67.25	0.09	19.43	47.74	12.08
察布查尔锡伯自治县	Qapqal Xibe Autonomous County	76.37	56.41	53.97	13.46	17.72	22.79	2.44
霍城县	Huocheng [korgas]County	47.73	31.90	30.73		12.67	18.07	1.17
巩留县	Gongliu [Tokkuzlara]County	56.83	46.84	35.25	0.27	24.00	10.97	11.59
新源县	Xinyuan [kunes]County	59.77	53.23	49.62	2.49	29.94	17.00	3.61
昭苏县	Zhaosu [mongolkure]County	54.34	36.64	36.64		36.03	0.21	
特克斯县	Tekes County	33.33	21.97	21.64		15.99	4.12	0.33
尼勒克县	Nilka County	38.31	31.33	30.87	0.01	21.13	7.76	0.46
塔城地区	**Tacheng [Tarbagatai] Administrative Offices**	**456.66**	**268.21**	**267.96**	**0.81**	**122.17**	**144.46**	**0.25**
塔城市	Tacheng [Qoqek] City	87.16	78.91	78.91		35.37	43.43	
乌苏市	Usu City	89.87	22.42	22.42	0.81	10.09	11.52	
额敏县	Emin [Dorbiljin] County	93.20	88.01	88.01		44.17	43.64	
沙湾县	Shawan County	109.52	28.32	28.08		14.02	14.06	0.25
托里县	Toli County	25.30	23.10	23.09		8.41	14.48	
裕民县	Yumin [Qagantokay] County	39.13	25.14	25.14		8.90	16.24	
和布克赛尔蒙古自治县	Hoboksar Mongol Autonomous County	12.48	2.31	2.31		1.22	1.10	
阿勒泰地区	**Altay Administrative Offices**	**220.31**	**75.42**	**64.15**		**26.14**	**37.79**	**11.27**
阿勒泰市	Altay City	32.94	9.67	7.56		1.90	5.66	2.11
布尔津县	Burqin County	26.01	8.82	7.56		1.00	6.56	1.26
富蕴县	Fuyun [Koktokay] County	27.41	13.42	12.33		5.99	6.28	1.09
福海县	Fuhai [Burultokay] County	66.17	15.33	15.31		2.34	12.97	0.01
哈巴河县	Habahe [Kaba] County	43.73	15.54	8.89		3.39	5.35	6.65
青河县	Qinghe [Qinggil] County	16.12	8.32	8.17		7.65	0.51	0.16
吉木乃县	Jeminay County	7.98	4.33	4.33		3.87	0.46	

注:全区农作物播种面积及棉花面积合计不等于地方和生产建设兵团汇总数。

Sown Areas of Farm Crops by Prefecture, Autonomous Prefecture, City and County

(1 000 hectares)

薯类 Tubers	棉花 Cotton	#长绒棉 Longstaple Cotton	油料 Oil Bearing Crops	#油菜 Rapeseeds	#胡麻 Flax	#葵花 Helianthus	甜菜 Beetroots	蔬菜 Vegetables	果用瓜 Melon	#甜瓜 Muskmelon	苜蓿 Lucerne
30.58	**1718.26**	**38.28**	**221.74**	**43.71**	**8.08**	**145.77**	**65.90**	**296.68**	**136.45**	**66.13**	**184.70**
4.54	**1.19**		**3.66**	**0.20**	**0.08**	**2.52**	**0.07**	**13.56**	**0.13**		**2.20**
3.23			0.69	0.18	0.04	0.48		3.17			1.44
	6.31		**0.09**			**0.07**	**0.14**	**0.89**	**0.57**	**0.05**	**0.53**
0.01	**21.19**		**0.29**					**6.04**	**10.89**	**8.50**	**0.23**
	4.99							3.27	3.45	1.95	
	7.10							1.54	5.98	5.26	0.07
0.01	9.10		0.29					1.23	1.46	1.29	0.16
1.06	**19.96**		**1.77**	**1.60**	**0.05**	**0.12**		**2.81**	**5.90**	**5.27**	**4.09**
0.03	19.72		1.23	1.12	0.05	0.07		1.75	3.01	2.38	0.87
1.01	0.23		0.16	0.10		0.06		1.02	0.17	0.17	2.59
0.02	0.01		0.38	0.38				0.04	2.72	2.72	0.63
7.73	**113.59**		**27.04**	**0.10**	**0.88**	**21.48**	**9.11**	**35.35**	**5.77**	**0.67**	**5.56**
0.04	39.12		2.53			2.21	1.44	6.01	3.64	0.09	0.57
0.98	0.34		4.41			4.41	1.43	10.85	0.44	0.15	0.39
0.54	32.00		0.55			0.45	0.70	6.48	0.46	0.09	2.33
0.93	41.69		2.52			2.24	0.20	4.61	0.41		1.48
2.32			9.70	0.04		7.99	5.00	3.73	0.07	0.01	0.15
2.02	0.45		5.50	0.06		3.24	0.33	3.44	0.58	0.29	0.64
0.90			1.83		0.88	0.95	0.01	0.24	0.18	0.05	
6.83	**139.64**		**116.20**	**16.28**	**2.64**	**86.74**	**16.79**	**33.60**	**5.57**	**2.70**	**46.95**
2.78	**4.57**		**34.23**	**14.74**	**2.33**	**16.86**	**13.27**	**17.26**	**1.97**	**0.01**	**13.71**
0.12			0.56	0.01		0.55	0.15	3.27	0.64		0.05
	1.84		0.04			0.04					
0.58	0.07		3.60	0.39		3.21	0.89	4.50	0.81	0.01	1.16
	0.36		1.55		0.14	1.11	0.85	1.23	0.20		5.84
0.25	2.30		3.59		0.03	3.55	3.35	3.13	0.10		
0.12			1.76	0.02		1.74	2.69	1.23	0.13		1.96
0.29			2.53	0.78	0.01	1.75	1.36	0.41	0.05		0.77
0.76			14.50	12.97	0.16	1.36	0.90	0.55			0.27
0.05			4.10	0.31	0.45	3.33	1.50	1.87	0.03	0.01	2.89
0.60			1.99	0.26	1.53	0.20	1.58	1.11	0.01		0.77
1.08	**135.07**		**16.96**	**1.25**	**0.32**	**5.15**	**3.08**	**14.96**	**0.50**	**0.10**	**4.39**
0.01			0.54	0.51		0.03	0.80	1.58	0.03		0.60
0.28	60.02		0.45			0.45	0.04	5.79	0.19	0.07	0.47
0.01			1.34	0.41	0.32	0.62	1.40	0.87			0.34
0.38	67.43		1.99			1.92	0.56	6.33	0.28	0.03	0.28
0.01	0.30		0.99	0.33		0.23		0.03			0.70
0.35			9.74				0.28	0.06			1.83
0.03	7.32		1.90			1.90		0.31			0.16
2.98			**65.01**	**0.29**		**64.72**	**0.44**	**1.38**	**3.09**	**2.58**	**28.84**
0.06			11.95			11.95	0.20	0.21	1.76	1.67	3.57
0.05			9.64			9.64		0.20	0.13	0.13	2.10
0.32			4.70			4.70		0.17	0.10	0.05	4.90
0.04			19.35			19.35	0.23	0.13	0.48	0.47	6.76
1.27			15.91			15.91		0.54	0.62	0.26	6.04
0.82			2.36	0.29		2.08	0.01	0.14			3.94
0.42			1.09			1.09		0.02			1.55

Note: Total of sown areas of farm crops and cotton areas by region do not mean that summary number of local and Production&Construction Corps.

12-14 续表

单位：千公顷

地　区	Region	农作物播种面积 Total Sown Area	粮食 Grain Crops	谷物 Cereal	#水稻 Rice	#小麦 Wheat	#玉米 Corn	豆类 Soy-beans
博尔塔拉蒙古自治州	**Bortala Mongol Autonomous Prefecture**	**144.21**	**59.86**	**59.84**	**0.11**	**12.62**	**47.12**	**0.01**
博乐市	Bole [Bortala] City	53.50	24.96	24.96	0.09	1.56	23.32	
精河县	Jinghe [Jing] County	52.99	2.45	2.45	0.02	2.14	0.28	
温泉县	Wenquan [Araxang] County	37.73	32.45	32.43		8.92	23.51	0.01
巴音郭楞蒙古自治州	**Bayangol Mongol Autonomous Prefecture**	**328.43**	**66.56**	**66.48**	**0.33**	**41.33**	**23.87**	**0.08**
库尔勒市	Korla City	61.66	1.73	1.71		1.05	0.66	0.02
轮台县	Luntai [Bugur] County	61.30	15.53	15.53		8.89	6.64	
尉犁县	Yuli [Lopnur] County	43.95	0.62	0.62		0.19	0.43	
若羌县	Ruoqiang [Qarkilik] County	11.39	3.70	3.68		2.21	1.47	0.02
且末县	Qiemo [Qarqan] County	29.13	11.34	11.31		7.86	3.43	0.03
焉耆回族自治县	Yanqi Hui Autonomous County	32.30	12.07	12.06		8.81	3.23	0.01
和静县	Hejing County	30.89	11.07	11.07		5.34	4.86	
和硕县	Hoxud County	33.89	5.74	5.74		4.01	1.68	
博湖县	Bohu [Bagrax] County	23.92	4.76	4.76	0.31	2.98	1.47	
阿克苏地区	**Aksu Administrative Offices**	**602.49**	**218.67**	**218.21**	**17.57**	**115.41**	**84.29**	**0.46**
阿克苏市	Aksu City	76.74	17.42	17.42	2.44	8.83	6.15	
温宿县	Wensu [Onsu] County	77.23	33.98	33.94	10.59	14.17	9.07	0.04
库车县	Kuqa County	94.27	36.15	36.15		22.03	14.11	
沙雅县	Xayar County	96.78	26.45	26.44		15.86	10.58	0.01
新和县	Xinhe [Toksu] County	54.03	17.66	17.66		10.67	6.99	
拜城县	Baicheng [Bay] County	56.86	37.02	36.75	1.27	15.00	19.82	0.27
乌什县	Wushi [Uxturpan] County	33.95	25.00	24.85	3.28	14.68	6.75	0.15
阿瓦提县	Awat County	101.45	20.87	20.87		11.33	9.53	
柯坪县	Kalpin County	11.18	4.12	4.12		2.84	1.29	
克孜勒苏柯尔克孜自治州	**Kizilsu Kirgiz Autonomous Prefecture**	**62.57**	**49.52**	**49.39**	**0.59**	**27.85**	**20.35**	**0.13**
阿图什市	Artux City	20.20	15.21	15.21	0.10	9.53	5.49	
阿克陶县	Akto County	34.54	28.51	28.51	0.50	14.33	13.62	
阿合奇县	Akqi County	4.69	3.68	3.60		2.60	0.59	0.09
乌恰县	Wuqia [Ulugqat] County	3.14	2.11	2.07		1.39	0.64	0.04
喀什地区	**Kashgar [Kaxgar] Administrative Offices**	**898.46**	**433.50**	**412.92**	**7.04**	**223.73**	**180.41**	**20.57**
喀什市	Kashgar [Kaxgar] City	22.26	12.45	12.45	1.16	7.16	4.13	
疏附县	Shufu County	63.77	40.29	40.29	0.20	23.96	16.13	
疏勒县	Shule County	74.85	37.47	37.47	0.15	21.15	16.17	
英吉沙县	Yengisar County	45.67	31.15	31.09		17.23	13.86	0.07
泽普县	Zepu [Poskam] County	46.49	27.40	18.73	0.27	12.33	6.13	8.67
莎车县	Shache [Yarkant] County	183.97	92.17	85.51	4.67	43.57	37.27	6.67
叶城县	Yecheng [Kagilik] County	101.58	61.23	56.29	0.60	29.65	26.04	4.94
麦盖提县	Makit County	101.59	36.34	36.11		16.82	19.29	0.23
岳普湖县	Yopurga County	48.38	16.33	16.33		9.00	7.33	
伽师县	Jiashi [Payzawat] County	81.83	43.05	43.05		23.83	19.23	
巴楚县	Bachu [Maralbexi] County	123.10	31.33	31.33		16.67	14.67	
塔什库尔干塔吉克自治县	Taxkorgan Tajik Autonomous County	4.91	4.27	4.27		2.37	0.17	
和田地区	**Hotan Administrative Offices**	**232.15**	**164.83**	**164.55**	**7.78**	**84.49**	**72.08**	**0.29**
和田市	Hotan City	18.62	14.25	14.25	0.45	8.06	5.74	
和田县	Hotan County	33.39	25.66	25.66	2.39	13.98	9.29	
墨玉县	Moyu [Karakax] County	54.69	42.65	42.65	2.13	22.39	18.13	
皮山县	Pishan [Guma] County	30.70	19.26	19.18		9.35	9.79	0.08
洛浦县	Lop County	32.54	23.93	23.93	0.01	11.81	12.12	
策勒县	Qira County	24.17	14.24	14.03		7.04	6.85	0.21
于田县	Yutian [Keriya] County	33.44	22.43	22.43	2.80	10.53	9.10	
民丰县	Minfeng [Niya] County	4.59	2.41	2.41		1.33	1.06	
生产建设兵团	**Xinjiang Production and Construction Group**	**1164.47**	**265.26**	**256.86**	**21.81**	**133.61**	**95.07**	**8.41**

Continued

(1 000 hectares)

薯类 Tubers	棉花 Cotton	#长绒棉 Longstaple Cotton	油料 Oil Bearing Crops	#油菜 Rapeseeds	#胡麻 Flax	#葵花 Helianthus	甜菜 Beetroots	蔬菜 Vegetables	果用瓜 Melon	#甜瓜 Muskmelon	苜蓿 Lucerne
0.13	**67.16**		**3.81**			**3.81**	**0.98**	**0.86**	**0.20**	**0.03**	**0.76**
0.04	27.16		0.01			0.01	0.55	0.67	0.06		0.01
	40.00						0.26	0.17	0.06	0.03	
0.10			3.80			3.80	0.17	0.02	0.09		0.75
0.50	**192.63**		**3.03**	**0.82**		**2.04**	**4.58**	**38.44**	**4.94**	**3.98**	**2.23**
0.01	57.13		0.17					1.06	0.26	0.06	0.04
	43.54							0.37	0.92	0.79	0.93
0.01	42.10		0.02	0.01			0.03	0.10	0.27	0.16	
	3.48		0.04	0.04				0.17	2.87	2.77	0.05
0.01	14.20		0.01	0.01				0.27	0.17	0.11	0.63
	6.89		0.60	0.01		0.59	2.73	5.55	0.05	0.02	0.31
0.39	4.49		1.03	0.74		0.29	0.97	10.41	0.15	0.03	
0.09	16.24		0.51	0.01		0.50	0.05	9.91	0.09	0.03	0.03
	4.57		0.67	0.01		0.66	0.81	10.60	0.16	0.02	0.22
1.89	**305.71**	**34.52**	**4.93**	**3.86**	**1.02**	**0.06**	**7.66**	**24.98**	**16.88**	**5.23**	**14.72**
	43.33	7.80					1.86	4.88	2.48	0.55	6.76
0.24	34.00		0.93	0.84	0.09		0.84	2.47	1.05	0.10	1.63
0.21	50.13		0.24	0.24			0.53	3.04	2.75	0.63	0.97
0.03	61.13		0.18	0.18			0.43	2.04	5.19	2.76	0.95
	32.87		0.03	0.03			0.27	1.64	1.14	0.39	0.43
1.32	0.10		2.82	2.15	0.61	0.06	3.04	4.10	1.71	0.16	2.57
0.09	3.07		0.74	0.42	0.32		0.32	3.77	0.67	0.18	0.14
	75.13	26.72						2.60	1.78	0.38	1.07
	5.93						0.37	0.45	0.10	0.09	0.19
0.08	**6.36**		**0.70**	**0.39**	**0.24**	**0.05**		**1.49**	**1.00**	**0.37**	**1.90**
0.01	2.11		0.05	0.01		0.01		0.41	0.26	0.23	0.72
	4.24		0.01			0.01		0.82	0.72	0.15	0.14
0.04			0.55	0.29	0.24	0.03		0.07			0.33
0.02	0.01		0.09	0.09				0.19	0.02		0.70
6.24	**205.36**		**5.07**	**1.59**	**1.43**	**1.23**		**57.60**	**62.69**	**25.97**	**37.27**
	1.52							5.62	0.72	0.09	0.29
0.53	4.33							9.14	9.00	3.33	
0.04	16.25							8.24	11.14	3.17	1.71
	5.53		0.20	0.20				2.42	4.17	1.27	2.20
2.00	7.33		0.03	0.01				2.29	1.90	0.33	1.20
1.47	44.51		1.81	1.14	0.13	0.20		12.71	8.77	3.99	5.95
2.21	7.33		1.44		0.15	0.83		9.36	1.64	0.53	8.11
	29.31		1.39	0.23	1.15			2.60	4.27	1.14	6.00
	12.67		0.20			0.20		1.71	4.57	2.43	4.60
	22.97							2.29	10.85	8.68	2.63
	53.33							1.09	5.67	1.00	4.33
	0.27							0.07			0.25
0.60	**19.57**		**4.71**	**1.52**	**1.30**	**1.18**		**11.32**	**4.48**	**2.11**	**21.50**
	1.52		0.08	0.08				1.49	0.52	0.26	0.39
0.33	2.73		0.60	0.45	0.05			1.58	0.68	0.31	1.16
0.02	4.00		0.25	0.19	0.05	0.01		1.86	1.07	0.30	4.33
0.09	1.87		0.95	0.29		0.66		1.47	0.17	0.06	6.36
0.02	2.47		1.14		1.14			1.59	0.71	0.30	2.35
0.03	2.49		0.98	0.03	0.06	0.30		1.18	0.40	0.18	3.15
0.11	4.49		0.69	0.47		0.21		2.01	0.39	0.19	2.92
0.01			0.03	0.01		0.01		0.14	0.54	0.51	0.83
6.09	**588.58**	**3.76**	**50.45**	**17.35**	**0.44**	**26.48**	**26.58**	**69.90**	**17.43**	**11.24**	**46.77**

12-15 主要年份农作物种植结构
Planting Structure of Major Farm Crops in Main Years

单位：% (%)

项　目	Item	1995	2000	2010	2013
农作物总播种面积	**Total Sown Areas of Farm Crops**	**100**	**100**	**100**	**100**
粮食作物	Grain Crops	52.21	42.66	41.85	42.29
谷　物	Cereal	50.10	39.95	39.49	40.87
稻　谷	Rice	2.40	2.31	1.41	1.29
小　麦	Wheat	31.22	24.75	23.54	21.51
玉　米	Corn	14.39	11.29	13.74	17.67
谷　子	Millet	0.02	0.04	0.02	0.01
高　粱	Jowar	0.47	0.39	0.12	0.15
其它谷物	Other Cereal	1.59	1.18	0.67	0.05
豆　类	Soybeans	2.12	2.71	2.36	1.42
#大 豆	Soja	0.94	1.85	1.56	1.13
杂 豆	Miscellaneous Beans	1.18	0.20	0.80	0.18
薯　类	Tubers	0.34	0.66	0.78	0.59
油　料	Oil-bearing Crops	10.05	9.15	5.74	4.25
#花　生	Peanuts		0.14	0.08	0.09
油菜籽	Rapeseeds	4.26	2.84	1.47	0.84
芝　麻	Sesame		0.02	0.03	0.02
胡麻籽	Benne	0.88	0.72	0.18	0.16
向日葵	Helianthus	4.59	4.63	3.46	2.80
棉　花	Cotton	24.35	29.87	30.69	32.97
麻　类	Fiber Crops	0.14	0.21	0.05	0.05
甜　菜	Beetroots	2.33	1.65	1.58	1.26
烟　叶	Tobacco	0.03	0.08	0.02	
药　材	Medicinal Materials	0.22	0.38	0.42	0.81
蔬菜、瓜类	Vegetables and Melon	3.17	5.42	8.96	8.31
#蔬 菜	Vegetables	2.34	3.77	6.38	5.69
其他农作物	Other Farm Crops	7.16	9.92	9.91	9.48
#青饲料	Succulence	3.94	3.56	1.26	1.42

12-16 主要年份农作物产品产量
Output of Major Farm Crops in Main Years

单位：万吨 (10 000 tons)

年份 Year	粮食 Grain Crops	谷物 Cereal	#水稻 Rice	#小麦 Wheat	#玉米 Corn	#大麦 Barley	豆类 Soybeans	薯类 Tubers	棉花 Cotton	#长绒棉 Long-staple Cotton
1978	370.01	367.71	27.39	180.02	134.45	5.01	2.30	22.91	5.50	1.19
1980	386.13	384.16	25.62	213.19	126.43	3.50	1.97	16.03	7.92	1.74
1985	496.65	495.16	30.63	314.52	139.38	1.93	1.49	15.14	18.78	1.40
1990	676.89	673.18	47.27	390.80	209.42	10.51	3.71	22.57	46.88	3.48
1995	730.16	716.83	48.25	381.21	266.74	12.82	13.33	26.43	93.50	1.13
1996	818.20	808.67	51.49	420.32	312.54	17.39	9.53	32.50	94.04	1.72
1997	825.34	813.07	55.27	437.60	294.31	17.92	12.27	26.73	115.00	3.10
1998	830.00	814.54	49.56	444.00	302.25	11.00	15.46	33.12	140.00	1.39
1999	838.78	821.70	54.14	423.29	323.06	8.00	17.08	46.06	140.75	1.67
2000	808.60	782.93	60.35	405.80	298.22	11.75	25.67	64.01	150.00	6.16
2001	796.00	767.53	56.79	374.14	318.41	11.86	28.47	60.02	157.00	9.71
2002	875.87	849.48	60.62	386.44	379.05	13.78	26.39	62.41	150.00	6.67
2003	801.64	774.62	50.73	335.67	366.25	14.33	27.02	71.80	160.00	10.10
2004	828.53	800.04	51.31	345.94	388.12	8.06	28.49	70.79	175.25	11.22
2005	877.21	852.00	54.18	400.71	380.36	10.23	25.22	65.86	195.70	11.87
2006	895.22	870.21	59.27	400.31	386.80	17.85	25.01	76.50	267.53	18.59
2007	867.04	846.35	62.52	359.22	396.00	24.26	20.69	101.36	290.00	25.02
2008	909.00	885.99	56.50	395.69	416.41	14.75	23.01	107.62	301.55	19.73
2009	1152.00	1119.77	58.30	630.70	439.38	14.30	32.23	126.06	252.40	11.04
2010	1150.20	1121.88	58.98	623.49	421.61	12.54	28.32	102.50	247.90	13.03
2011	1200.75	1171.64	60.64	576.64	517.67	11.06	29.11	119.75	289.77	12.16
2012	1259.83	1234.81	59.36	576.54	592.11	3.46	25.02	65.85	353.95	5.95
2013	1360.83	1339.71	59.82	622.08	649.02	4.92	21.12	80.85	351.80	5.35

年份 Year	油料 Oil bearing Crops	#油菜 Rapeseeds	#胡麻 Flax	#葵花 Helianthus	甜菜 Beetroots	蔬菜 Vegetables	果用瓜 Melons	#甜瓜 Muskmelon	苜蓿 Lucerne
1978	10.33	3.30	3.14	2.29	16.37	91.26	44.05		
1980	17.59	5.59	5.17	4.59	38.52	73.44	55.68		
1985	34.25	7.29	8.10	16.90	40.69	111.08	103.18	47.02	49.69
1990	38.96	12.17	6.32	18.17	224.37	187.42	93.38	37.75	89.29
1995	49.41	15.12	3.79	29.06	288.14	269.56	68.75	18.31	82.62
1996	30.95	10.15	3.12	16.91	354.52	301.94	67.16	17.33	75.42
1997	29.95	8.92	2.53	17.69	388.71	295.59	86.78	25.90	70.05
1998	37.52	12.32	2.53	20.82	513.12	321.79	88.32	29.45	67.56
1999	60.46	16.37	2.75	35.69	354.24	406.18	143.49	46.38	69.98
2000	60.14	14.75	3.60	35.47	292.65	527.84	151.03	51.22	76.32
2001	42.64	12.19	2.47	23.31	455.12	486.74	156.87	56.86	103.12
2002	44.37	12.90	3.69	23.26	466.81	674.96	233.40	107.49	149.93
2003	50.13	15.43	3.49	25.80	381.65	761.00	189.32	77.61	249.60
2004	44.54	12.16	2.10	21.90	344.21	919.13	186.06	92.54	273.04
2005	38.94	9.22	2.39	21.69	419.12	862.23	220.65	95.58	295.74
2006	32.82	9.73	2.52	16.17	555.53	958.04	237.28	109.98	240.15
2007	40.30	9.60	1.58	25.39	586.93	1173.99	338.67	192.63	205.47
2008	56.85	10.67	1.23	42.87	438.88	970.67	404.17	248.81	150.83
2009	63.91	15.72	1.89	41.40	418.41	1383.21	491.20	286.30	154.90
2010	66.62	15.14	1.32	44.11	486.97	1734.40	435.00	222.58	132.93
2011	66.76	15.18	1.23	45.36	518.95	1866.15	434.31	193.06	139.94
2012	59.04	11.20	1.40	41.44	577.19	1656.02	485.35	213.35	149.62
2013	60.63	11.29	1.37	41.90	476.47	1669.92	544.24	239.46	212.39

注：粮食、棉花总产量为国家审定数。
Note:Total grain output refers to the number of state approved.

12-17 各地、州、市、县(市)主要农产品产量

单位：吨 (2013 年)

地区	Region	粮食作物 Grain Crops	谷物 Cereal	#水稻 Rice	#小麦 Wheat	#玉米 Corn	豆类 Soy-beans
总 计	**Total**	**13608300**	**13397100**	**598200**	**6220800**	**6490200**	**211200**
乌鲁木齐市	**Urumqi City**	**146901**	**143787**	**60422**	**34162**	**42635**	**3114**
#乌鲁木齐县	Urumqi County	13203	12245		5067	904	958
克拉玛依市	**Karamay City**	**12543**	**12543**		**1007**	**11536**	
吐鲁番地区	**TurpanAdministrative Offices**	**35262**	**35248**		**130**	**13738**	**14**
吐鲁番市	Turpan City	5700	5700			2900	
鄯善县	Shanshan [piqan]County	2990	2990		46	2320	
托克逊县	Toksun County	26572	26558		84	8518	14
哈密地区	**Hami [Kumul]Administrative Offices**	**143675**	**141897**		**107526**	**19198**	**1778**
哈密市	Hami [Kumul]City	38379	38064		13502	19135	315
巴里坤哈萨克自治县	Barkol KazakAutonomous County	98892	98853		92399	63	39
伊吾县	Yiwu [Araturuk]County	6404	4980		1625		1424
昌吉回族自治州	**Changji Hui Autonomous Prefecture**	**2078986**	**2042403**	**8987**	**1072184**	**951141**	**36583**
昌吉市	Changji City	293142	292203	6056	117739	167808	939
阜康市	Fukang City	206069	202159	1197	112095	88193	3910
呼图壁县	Hutubi County	203578	203545	1553	112188	89026	33
玛纳斯县	Manas County	177958	177203	181	22411	154217	755
奇台县	Qitai County	736581	733189		453792	275255	3392
吉木萨尔县	Jimsar County	251006	245525		141135	102689	5481
木垒哈萨克自治县	Mori Kazak Autonomous County	210652	188579		112824	73953	22073
伊犁哈萨克自治州	**Ili Kazak Autonomous Prefecture**	**5990214**	**5869769**	**169159**	**1877752**	**3806825**	**120445**
伊犁州直属县(市)	**Counties (Cities) Direct Under Ili Prefecture**	**2975633**	**2889694**	**160985**	**1057967**	**1657034**	**85939**
伊宁市	Yining [Gulja]City	115439	111998	10412	25641	75945	3441
奎屯市	Kuytun City	14030	14030		8241	5789	
伊宁县	Yining [Gulja]County	751028	718428	396	116532	601500	32600
察布查尔锡伯自治县	Qapqal Xibe Autonomous County	479694	473594	132031	99826	241731	6100
霍城县	Huocheng [korgas]County	326012	322262		84170	238092	3750
巩留县	Gongliu [Tokkuzlara]County	300674	273739	2473	144540	126673	26935
新源县	Xinyuan [kunes]County	434369	423882	15605	184722	222631	10487
昭苏县	Zhaosu [mongolkure]County	192102	192102		189154	1600	
特克斯县	Tekes County	144812	143812		86764	52468	1000
尼勒克县	Nilka County	217473	215847	68	118377	90605	1626
塔城地区	**Tacheng [Tarbagatai] Administrative Offices**	**2456171**	**2455282**	**8174**	**681913**	**1763249**	**889**
塔城市	Tacheng [Qoqek] City	726880	726880		192828	533508	
乌苏市	Usu City	235789	235789	8174	66878	160737	
额敏县	Emin [Dorbiljin] County	784789	784789		250276	533522	
沙湾县	Shawan County	272529	271655		88233	183422	874
托里县	Toli County	181580	181565		37829	143325	15
裕民县	Yumin [Qagantokay] County	237937	237937		42031	195906	
和布克赛尔蒙古自治县	Hoboksar Mongol Autonomous County	16667	16667		3838	12829	
阿勒泰地区	**Altay Administrative Offices**	**558410**	**524793**		**137872**	**386542**	**33617**
阿勒泰市	Altay City	63413	56762		9053	47709	6651
布尔津县	Burqin County	68590	64566		4567	59999	4024
富蕴县	Fuyun [Koktokay] County	103532	101061		32434	68531	2471
福海县	Fuhai [Burultokay] County	162634	162594		10795	151788	40
哈巴河县	Habahe [Kaba] County	88037	67988		18185	49570	20049
青河县	Qinghe [Qinggil] County	46227	45845		41427	4379	382
吉木乃县	Jeminay County	25977	25977		21411	4566	

注：1.地方与生产建设兵团粮食产量合计不等于全区总计数。2.全区总计数为国家统计局审定数。

Output of Major Farm Crops by Prefecture, Autonomous Prefecture, City and County

(ton)

薯类 Tubers	棉花 Cotton	#长绒棉 Longstaple Cotton	油料 Oil Bearing Crops	#油菜 Rapeseeds	#胡麻 Flax	#葵花 Helianthus	甜菜 Beetroots	蔬菜 Vegetables	果用瓜 Melon	#甜瓜 Muskmelon	苜蓿 Lucerne
808500	**3518000**	**53467**	**606301**	**112857**	**13716**	**418966**	**4764656**	**16699242**	**5442440**	**2394597**	**2123859**
125002	**1540**		**9121**	**378**	**123**	**8049**	**3327**	**684229**	**2948**	**324**	**75866**
87338			1761	335	83	1343	120	139214	44		11190
44	**9934**		**400**			**326**	**8144**	**33655**	**23036**	**1234**	**6892**
275	**30362**		**1221**					**239342**	**305900**	**222953**	**7375**
	6735							139980	94388	42988	
	10112							50700	169426	144267	1300
275	13515		1221					48662	42086	35698	6075
45022	**37200**		**1781**	**1374**	**138**	**269**		**134157**	**202458**	**169477**	**29379**
851	36763		1209	889	138	182		83990	109578	76597	10031
43614	422		287	200		87		45820	3270	3270	15568
557	15		285	285				4347	89610	89610	3780
288059	**218207**		**87628**	**141**	**1261**	**75899**	**646649**	**1990739**	**343922**	**27406**	**69831**
1370	66638		9017			7683	112671	442867	253354	4344	4570
35500	1305		16052			16052	116094	354863	13894	7209	5587
15340	57790		1635			1185	46740	376306	21957	3085	29768
32457	91913		8866			7393	13435	354090	24496	66	19148
113740			30744	30		27817	333809	214267	2503	200	971
73389	561		16673	111		12389	23551	240513	19603	10181	9787
16263			4641		1261	3380	349	7833	8115	2321	
234841	**263872**		**289252**	**40062**	**4376**	**226091**	**1079788**	**1920278**	**212669**	**82153**	**427888**
94417	**5861**		**93770**	**36555**	**3974**	**44533**	**847349**	**827980**	**85064**	**423**	**178474**
5118	1		1493	25	3	1351	11506	214850	20466		591
	2487		130			130					
20390	84		9722	1135		8579	56771	148394	43215	273	10425
	425		9741		187	2743	57743	63456	8838		69165
8260	2864		11264		100	9389	230920	155238	3835		
3668			4625	52		4573	179495	59898	4280		9273
10945			5732	1756	18	3958	80370	26663	2955		8781
22970			35992	32110	279	3603	52892	20436			5186
1260			10794	696	598	9500	90000	84000	1047	150	65100
21806			4277	781	2789	707	87652	55470	428		9953
41375	**258011**		**29849**	**2603**	**402**	**16829**	**206379**	**1044374**	**26363**	**5245**	**32462**
320			893	813		70	55200	92076	450	175	2656
12633	114341		1550			1550	2367	446949	9996	3570	5693
			2759	887	402	1470	94378	43973			4056
14398	132702		7454			7160	36374	455747	15917	1500	2010
104	540		1941	903		587		1200			4725
13711			9260				18060	2115			12087
209	10428		5992			5992		2313			1235
99049			**165633**	**904**		**164729**	**26060**	**47924**	**101242**	**76485**	**216952**
1826			37228			37228	10640	7755	46979	46272	34795
2280			21979			21979		5900	2998	2998	15339
10638			11038			11038		5423	4022	2050	32499
1551			42494			42494	14900	5480	14015	13535	53631
44288			43130			43130		16508	33228	11630	46059
28166			6415	904		5511	520	6378			25390
10300			3349			3349		480			9239

Note:a) The region total output of grain is not equal to the sum of local and Production and Construction Groups.b) The region total data of grain refer to approvable data by NBS.

12-17 续表

单位：吨

地　　区	Region	粮食作物 Grain Crops	谷物 Cereal	#水稻 Rice	#小麦 Wheat	#玉米 Corn	豆类 Soy-beans
博尔塔拉蒙古自治州	**Bortala Mongol Autonomous Prefecture**	**728144**	**728097**	**1146**	**62806**	**664145**	**47**
博乐市	Bole [Bortala] City	336695	336695	960	6925	328810	
精河县	Jinghe [Jing] County	15696	15696	186	11754	3756	
温泉县	Wenquan [Araxang] County	375753	375706		44127	331579	47
巴音郭楞蒙古自治州	**Bayangol Mongol Autonomous Prefecture**	**462074**	**461905**	**2267**	**250459**	**207172**	**169**
库尔勒市	Korla City	7900	7870		4644	3226	30
轮台县	Luntai [Bugur] County	86520	86520		49474	37046	
尉犁县	Yuli [Lopnur] County	4400	4400		862	3532	
若羌县	Ruoqiang [Qarkilik] County	14626	14599		9779	4820	27
且末县	Qiemo [Qarqan] County	70861	70777		47778	22930	84
焉耆回族自治县	Yanqi Hui Autonomous County	96695	96667	91	57571	39005	28
和静县	Hejing County	94474	94474		34524	58192	
和硕县	Hoxud County	45526	45526		25081	20271	
博湖县	Bohu [Bagrax] County	41072	41072	2176	20746	18150	
阿克苏地区	**Aksu Administrative Offices**	**1682700**	**1681097**	**185850**	**777588**	**714594**	**1603**
阿克苏市	Aksu City	133034	133034	26115	60175	46744	
温宿县	Wensu [Onsu] County	282971	282935	114645	95661	72223	36
库车县	Kuqa County	241868	241868		150434	91392	
沙雅县	Xayar County	188077	188069		109730	78339	8
新和县	Xinhe [Toksu] County	116656	116656		72667	43989	
拜城县	Baicheng [Bay] County	353367	352469	11507	100404	238489	898
乌什县	Wushi [Uxturpan] County	198388	197727	33583	93602	69994	661
阿瓦提县	Awat County	141552	141552		77382	64170	
柯坪县	Kalpin County	26787	26787		17533	9254	
克孜勒苏柯尔克孜自治州	**Kizilsu Kirgiz Autonomous Prefecture**	**309401**	**308939**	**5101**	**164470**	**137720**	**462**
阿图什市	Artux City	91469	91469	652	55328	35113	
阿克陶县	Akto County	193627	193627	4449	91823	97214	
阿合奇县	Akqi County	14298	13947		10548	2403	351
乌恰县	Wuqia [Ulugqat] County	10007	9896		6771	2990	111
喀什地区	**Kashgar [Kaxgar] Administrative Offices**	**2800660**	**2749183**	**61870**	**1329406**	**1352563**	**51477**
喀什市	Kashgar [Kaxgar] City	77415	77415	9214	39426	28775	
疏附县	Shufu County	269968	269968	1674	145639	122655	
疏勒县	Shule County	251091	251091	1287	127157	122647	
英吉沙县	Yengisar County	200189	200049		101921	98128	140
泽普县	Zepu [Poskam] County	144502	121290	1620	76220	43450	23212
莎车县	Shache [Yarkant] County	592499	581499	42000	263258	276241	11000
叶城县	Yecheng [Kagilik] County	421183	404583	6075	177944	220564	16600
麦盖提县	Makit County	221691	221166		92468	128698	525
岳普湖县	Yopurga County	111341	111341		53604	57737	
伽师县	Jiashi [Payzawat] County	287059	287059		144093	142966	
巴楚县	Bachu [Maralbexi] County	207498	207498		99258	108240	
塔什库尔干塔吉克自治县	Taxkorgan Tajik Autonomous County	16224	16224		8418	2462	
和田地区	**Hotan Administrative Offices**	**1070093**	**1069407**	**56358**	**496381**	**516135**	**686**
和田市	Hotan City	92405	92405	3754	47465	41186	
和田县	Hotan County	150978	150978	15926	81123	53929	
墨玉县	Moyu [Karakax] County	273056	273056	16589	133469	122998	
皮山县	Pishan [Guma] County	139085	138953		54497	84301	132
洛浦县	Lop County	147146	147146	30	66486	80630	
策勒县	Qira County	99564	99010		42036	56596	554
于田县	Yutian [Keriya] County	152169	152169	20059	63573	68537	
民丰县	Minfeng [Niya] County	15690	15690		7732	7958	
生产建设兵团	**Xinjiang Production and Construction Group**	**2008126**	**1981286**	**210311**	**847743**	**877542**	**26840**

Continued

(ton)

薯 类 Tubers	棉 花 Cotton	#长绒棉 Longstaple Cotton	油 料 Oil Bearing Crops	#油 菜 Rapeseeds	#胡 麻 Flax	#葵 花 Helianthus	甜 菜 Beetroots	蔬 菜 Vegetables	果用瓜 Melon	#甜 瓜 Muskmelon	苜 蓿 Lucerne
3056	**144346**		**7225**			**7225**	**54783**	**40697**	**8408**	**755**	**4386**
1173	57439		20			20	32761	34743	2102		74
	86907						11900	5510	1756	755	
1883			7205			7205	10122	444	4550		4312
20783	**397388**		**6070**	**1171**		**4381**	**423949**	**2581469**	**108714**	**64587**	**29739**
360	114831		450					74932	7362	942	653
	91423		11	11				21986	16479	14125	11097
94	98007		115	65			1696	3307	12485	5913	15
	6415		55	52				5620	40576	37340	316
97	29294		7	7				9009	3252	1953	8360
	9545		1421	8		1413	261743	457939	2258	561	5626
17652	7403		1734	1005		729	86982	499728	10258	1400	
2580	32560		1059	13		1031	2871	832458	5159	1889	348
	7910		1218	10		1208	70657	676151	10885	464	3324
66699	**557336**	**46386**	**9698**	**7525**	**2053**	**120**	**483389**	**936759**	**446861**	**114912**	**263376**
	84702	11115					105741	324360	95760	23652	100880
7147	60182		1505	1364	141		31548	51812	30941	2350	20805
6533	90121		310	310			18271	76642	72235	15200	32027
1378	116918		300	297		3	6477	27345	81858	41034	16000
	63104		42	42			10000	46100	28492	8062	8760
47741	120		6056	4646	1293	117	286414	123780	67599	4682	57894
3900	4519		1485	866	619		19338	231851	19226	8232	2540
	126100	35271						46800	49450	10600	21600
	11570						5600	6840	1300	1100	2870
527	**10008**		**1018**	**599**	**251**	**125**		**40202**	**33615**	**14277**	**21479**
354	3400		95	28	6	18		15499	9114	8243	9124
	6597		31			31		19744	24149	6028	2714
117			708	387	245	76		1287	18	6	2800
56	11		184	184				3672	334		6841
262227	**354027**		**11272**	**2614**	**2596**	**4015**		**2789908**	**2829297**	**1226512**	**434397**
	2286							294873	28930	8974	4214
20800	7069							410051	404530	149680	
1325	26424							375918	525040	166180	20560
	8465		420	420				113921	188220	57300	21450
75000	11233		99	29				93879	81450	14000	9000
61000	69124		3110	1710	200	750		617184	395774	190124	89200
104102	12107		4872		320	3025		555243	79981	25600	94848
	55077		2531	455	2076			117000	195350	54042	72000
	21008		240			240		46817	149992	85952	34500
	41082							112635	525030	429660	39500
	99760							51033	255000	45000	45500
	392							1354			3625
13740	**35543**		**10133**	**3734**	**1913**	**3304**		**368424**	**148424**	**60124**	**256782**
	2323		266	266				63787	21407	9925	4688
9740	5246		704	450	123			51314	15601	4919	8696
145	7548		502	412	67	14		57337	31963	5981	52720
1033	3634		2689	1184		1503		33376	7237	2275	49070
880	4068		1566		1564			57066	27983	10170	73920
1085	4730		1861	39	159	643		40097	15506	6288	24776
757	7994		2510	1375		1135		61565	20333	12502	35049
100			35	8		9		3882	8394	8064	7863
275070	**1464000**	**7081**	**171482**	**55259**	**1005**	**89162**	**2165359**	**4939382**	**776188**	**409883**	**496469**

12-18 各地、州、市、县(市)农作物单位面积产量

Output of Major Farm Products Per Hectare by Prefecture, Autonomous Prefecture, City and County

单位：公斤/公顷　　(2013 年)　　(kg / hectare)

地　区	Region	粮 食 Grain	#谷 物 Cereal	#小 麦 Wheat	#玉 米 Corn	棉 花 Cotton	油 料 Oil-Bearing Crops	甜 菜 Beetroots
总　计	**Total**	**6174**	**6289**	**5549**	**7048**	**2047**	**2734**	**72301**
乌鲁木齐市	**Urumqi City**	**7601**	**7722**	**5722**	**9839**	**1300**	**2490**	**48593**
#乌鲁木齐县	Urumqi County	4323	4250	4926	4738		2541	30000
克拉玛依市	**Karamay City**	**9431**	**9431**	**4353**	**10500**	**1574**	**4626**	**60000**
吐鲁番地区	**TurpanAdministrative Offices**	**5225**	**5232**	**3679**	**5790**	**1433**	**4277**	
吐鲁番市	Turpan City	5446	5446		4337	1350		
鄯善县	Shanshan [piqan]County	4494	4494	3000	5249	1425		
托克逊县	Toksun County	5276	5285	4200	6750	1485	4277	
哈密地区	**Hami [Kumul]Administrative Offices**	**5234**	**5303**	**5220**	**9073**	**1863**	**1006**	
哈密市	Hami [Kumul]City	6062	6050	4980	9075	1864	983	
巴里坤哈萨克自治县	Barkol KazakAutonomous County	5231	5234	5265	8591	1803	1780	
伊吾县	Yiwu [Araturuk]County	2894	3152	4801		1216	750	
昌吉回族自治州	**Changji Hui Autonomous Prefecture**	**7018**	**7283**	**5789**	**10422**	**1921**	**3241**	**71018**
昌吉市	Changji City	7767	7835	5662	10818	1703	3570	78480
阜康市	Fukang City	7525	7820	6767	10038	3876	3642	80996
呼图壁县	Hutubi County	6770	6770	5501	9552	1806	2973	66771
玛纳斯县	Manas County	8714	8788	6197	9389	2205	3518	67175
奇台县	Qitai County	7257	7334	6254	10537		3169	66707
吉木萨尔县	Jimsar County	7256	7555	6012	11850	1238	3033	72242
木垒哈萨克自治县	Mori Kazak Autonomous County	4732	5450	4058	11501		2533	55105
伊犁哈萨克自治州	**Ili Kazak Autonomous Prefecture**	**8348**	**8720**	**5653**	**11968**	**1890**	**2489**	**64320**
伊犁州直属县(市)	**Counties (Cities) Direct Under Ili Prefecture**	**7958**	**8474**	**5755**	**12198**	**1281**	**2740**	**63832**
伊宁市	Yining [Gulja]City	8556	9143	5425	11483	1071	2650	75697
奎屯市	Kuytun City	5044	5044	3722	10200	1350	3000	
伊宁县	Yining [Gulja]County	9466	10682	5999	12600	1235	2697	63645
察布查尔锡伯自治县	Qapqal Xibe Autonomous County	8504	8775	5635	10605	1170	6291	68040
霍城县	Huocheng [korgas]County	10220	10486	6645	13179	1245	3141	69000
巩留县	Gongliu [Tokkuzlara]County	6420	7765	6023	11550		2625	66750
新源县	Xinyuan [kunes]County	8161	8543	6170	13096		2262	58914
昭苏县	Zhaosu [mongolkure]County	5244	5244	5250	7500		2483	58500
特克斯县	Tekes County	6590	6646	5425	12735		2633	60000
尼勒克县	Nilka County	6942	6992	5602	11674		2149	55549
塔城地区	**Tacheng [Tarbagatai] Administrative Offices**	**9158**	**9163**	**5582**	**12206**	**1910**	**1760**	**67067**
塔城市	Tacheng [Qoqek] City	9212	9212	5452	12285		1648	69000
乌苏市	Usu City	10516	10516	6630	13950	1905	3450	67500
额敏县	Emin [Dorbiljin] County	8917	8917	5666	12225		2054	67500
沙湾县	Shawan County	9622	9676	6293	13050	1968	3746	64501
托里县	Toli County	7862	7863	4496	9900	1800	1953	
裕民县	Yumin [Qagantokay] County	9466	9466	4725	12062		951	64500
和布克赛尔蒙古自治县	Hoboksar Mongol Autonomous County	7200	7200	3150	11700	1425	3150	
阿勒泰地区	**Altay Administrative Offices**	**7404**	**8181**	**5275**	**10229**		**2548**	**59771**
阿勒泰市	Altay City	6555	7506	4770	8422		3114	52500
布尔津县	Burqin County	7778	8542	4560	9150		2280	
富蕴县	Fuyun [Koktokay] County	7717	8197	5415	10907		2350	
福海县	Fuhai [Burultokay] County	10611	10618	4617	11702		2196	65735
哈巴河县	Habahe [Kaba] County	5666	7648	5365	9270		2711	
青河县	Qinghe [Qinggil] County	5554	5613	5415	8594		2714	78000
吉木乃县	Jeminay County	6003	6003	5532	9996		3060	

注：个别县(市)油料等作物种植在边角地头，未计面积，故单产偏高。

Note: The oil-bearing crop planted at the edge or margin of fields in small number of counties (cities), whose area is not calculated, thus per-unit output is relatively higher.

12-18 续表 Continued

单位：公斤/公顷 (kg/ hectare)

地　区	Region	粮食 Grain	#谷物 Cereal	#小麦 Wheat	#玉米 Corn	棉花 Cotton	油料 Oil-Bearing Crops	甜菜 Beet-roots
博尔塔拉蒙古自治州	**Bortala Mongol Autonomous Prefecture**	**12165**	**12167**	**4978**	**14096**	**2149**	**1897**	**55817**
博乐市	Bole [Bortala] City	13487	13487	4452	14100	2115	3659	59292
精河县	Jinghe [Jing] County	6419	6419	5482	13250	2173		45305
温泉县	Wenquan [Araxang] County	11580	11584	4948	14103		1895	60878
巴音郭楞蒙古自治州	**Bayangol Mongol Autonomous Prefecture**	**6942**	**6948**	**6059**	**8678**	**2063**	**2002**	**92518**
库尔勒市	Korla City	4571	4595	4431	4853	2010	2700	
轮台县	Luntai [Bugur] County	5572	5572	5567	5579	2100	3929	
尉犁县	Yuli [Lopnur] County	7082	7082	4521	8241	2328	7500	60000
若羌县	Ruoqiang [Qarkilik] County	3950	3966	4433	3268	1844	1418	
且末县	Qiemo [Qarqan] County	6247	6257	6079	6687	2063	1400	
焉耆回族自治县	Yanqi Hui Autonomous County	8014	8019	6534	12089	1386	2387	95865
和静县	Hejing County	8535	8535	6465	11970	1650	1683	90000
和硕县	Hoxud County	7937	7937	6256	12074	2005	2082	63145
博湖县	Bohu [Bagrax] County	8621	8621	6958	12355	1730	1820	87037
阿克苏地区	**Aksu Administrative Offices**	**7695**	**7704**	**6738**	**8478**	**1823**	**1966**	**63086**
阿克苏市	Aksu City	7636	7636	6812	7601	1955		56850
温宿县	Wensu [Onsu] County	8326	8335	6753	7959	1770	1620	37501
库车县	Kuqa County	6691	6691	6830	6478	1798	1306	34500
沙雅县	Xayar County	7112	7113	6920	7404	1913	1635	14924
新和县	Xinhe [Toksu] County	6607	6607	6813	6294	1920	1425	37500
拜城县	Baicheng [Bay] County	9544	9591	6692	12034	1200	2150	94215
乌什县	Wushi [Uxturpan] County	7936	7956	6376	10373	1470	2018	60901
阿瓦提县	Awat County	6784	6784	6828	6731	1678		
柯坪县	Kalpin County	6495	6495	6181	7189	1950		15000
克孜勒苏柯尔克孜自治州	**Kizilsu Kirgiz Autonomous Prefecture**	**6248**	**6255**	**5905**	**6768**	**1575**	**1450**	
阿图什市	Artux City	6012	6012	5808	6395	1609	2062	
阿克陶县	Akto County	6791	6791	6406	7135	1557	3185	
阿合奇县	Akqi County	3881	3877	4051	4050		1280	
乌恰县	Wuqia [Ulugqat] County	4746	4786	4877	4679	1650	1981	
喀什地区	**Kashgar [Kaxgar] Administrative Offices**	**6461**	**6658**	**5942**	**7497**	**1724**	**2225**	
喀什市	Kashgar [Kaxgar] City	6219	6219	5504	6975	1500		
疏附县	Shufu County	6700	6700	6078	7603	1631		
疏勒县	Shule County	6702	6702	6013	7583	1626		
英吉沙县	Yengisar County	6426	6435	5916	7080	1532	2100	
泽普县	Zepu [Poskam] County	5274	6475	6180	7084	1532	2970	
莎车县	Shache [Yarkant] County	6428	6801	6042	7413	1553	1721	
叶城县	Yecheng [Kagilik] County	6879	7188	6002	8470	1651	3383	
麦盖提县	Makit County	6100	6125	5498	6673	1879	1825	
岳普湖县	Yopurga County	6817	6817	5956	7873	1659	1200	
伽师县	Jiashi [Payzawat] County	6668	6668	6048	7436	1789		
巴楚县	Bachu [Maralbexi] County	6622	6622	5955	7380	1871		
塔什库尔干塔吉克自治县	Taxkorgan Tajik Autonomous County	3797	3797	3557	14772	1470		
和田地区	**Hotan Administrative Offices**	**6492**	**6499**	**5875**	**7161**	**1817**	**2150**	
和田市	Hotan City	6485	6485	5887	7180	1530	3303	
和田县	Hotan County	5884	5884	5803	5808	1923	1175	
墨玉县	Moyu [Karakax] County	6402	6402	5962	6783	1887	2010	
皮山县	Pishan [Guma] County	7222	7245	5830	8610	1943	2845	
洛浦县	Lop County	6149	6149	5631	6655	1650	1369	
策勒县	Qira County	6993	7056	5970	8260	1899	1908	
于田县	Yutian [Keriya] County	6783	6783	6035	7532	1779	3655	
民丰县	Minfeng [Niya] County	6505	6505	5799	7481		1058	
生产建设兵团	**Xinjiang Production and Construction Group**	**7570**	**7714**	**6345**	**9230**	**2487**	**3399**	**81477**

12-19 各地、州、市、县(市)特色农作物播种面积
Sown Areas of Characteristic Farm Crops by Prefecture,Autonomous Prefecture , City and County

单位：千公顷 (2013 年) (1000 hectares)

地　区	Region	番　茄 Tomato	工业用番　茄 Tomato in Industry	辣　椒 Peppers	工业用辣　椒 Capsicum	打瓜籽 Melon Seeds	啤酒花 Hop
总　计	**Total**	**75.46**	**56.65**	**66.37**	**44.75**	**69.76**	**2.10**
乌鲁木齐市	**Urumqi City**	**0.62**	**0.08**	**1.02**			**0.04**
#市辖区	Municipal Districts	0.60	0.08	0.63			0.04
乌鲁木齐县	Urumqi County	0.02		0.38			
克拉玛依市	**Karamay City**	**0.39**	**0.32**	**0.23**	**0.12**	**0.43**	
吐鲁番地区	**TurpanAdministrative Offices**	**0.97**		**0.34**			
吐鲁番市	Turpan City	0.37		0.08			
鄯善县	Shanshan [piqan]County	0.30		0.16			
托克逊县	Toksun County	0.31		0.10			
哈密地区	**Hami [Kumul]Administrative Offices**	**0.25**		**0.29**			
哈密市	Hami [Kumul]City	0.20		0.23			
巴里坤哈萨克自治县	Barkol KazakAutonomous County	0.05		0.05			
伊吾县	Yiwu [Araturuk]County						
昌吉回族自治州	**Changji Hui Autonomous Prefecture**	**12.87**	**11.52**	**3.90**	**1.50**	**8.10**	**0.26**
昌吉市	Changji City	3.62	3.42	0.27	0.04	0.23	0.06
阜康市	Fukang City	1.03	0.51	0.89		3.25	
呼图壁县	Hutubi County	3.00	3.00	1.21	1.16	0.45	0.09
玛纳斯县	Manas County	2.71	2.67	0.36	0.12	0.33	
奇台县	Qitai County	0.96	0.42	0.81		2.46	
吉木萨尔县	Jimsar County	1.54	1.49	0.35	0.19	0.99	0.11
木垒哈萨克自治县	Mori Kazak Autonomous County	0.01		0.01		0.38	
伊犁哈萨克自治州	**Ili Kazak Autonomous Prefecture**	**6.78**	**4.56**	**5.85**	**0.48**	**41.58**	**0.13**
伊犁州直属县(市)	**Counties (Cities) Direct Under Ili Prefecture**	**1.99**	**0.27**	**1.87**	**0.15**	**0.54**	
伊宁市	Yining [Gulja]City	0.43		0.50			
奎屯市	Kuytun City						
伊宁县	Yining [Gulja]County	0.82		0.53		0.03	
察布查尔锡伯自治县	Qapqal Xibe Autonomous County	0.11		0.25		0.03	
霍城县	Huocheng [korgas]County	0.43	0.27	0.23	0.15	0.27	
巩留县	Gongliu [Tokkuzlara]County	0.02		0.17			
新源县	Xinyuan [kunes]County	0.04		0.02		0.08	
昭苏县	Zhaosu [mongolkure]County			0.01			
特克斯县	Tekes County	0.12		0.13			
尼勒克县	Nilka County	0.02		0.04		0.13	

12-19 续表 1 Continued

单位：千公顷 (1000 hectares)

地区	Region	番茄 Tomato	工业用番茄 Tomato in Industry	辣椒 Peppers	工业用辣椒 Capsicum	打瓜籽 Melon Seeds	啤酒花 Hop
塔城地区	**Tacheng[Tarbagatai] Administrative Officess**	**4.66**	**4.29**	**3.83**	**0.33**	**8.63**	**0.13**
塔城市	Tacheng [Qoqek] City	0.12		0.06		4.70	
乌苏市	Usu City	3.54	3.52	0.06	0.04		
额敏县	Emin [Dorbiljin] County	0.47	0.41	0.05		1.20	
沙湾县	Shawan County	0.52	0.36	3.37	0.29	0.76	0.13
托里县	Toli County					0.17	
裕民县	Yumin [Qagantokay] County	0.01				1.51	
和布克赛尔蒙古自治县	Hoboksar Mongol Autonomous County	0.01		0.29		0.29	
阿勒泰地区	**Altay Administrative Offices**	**0.12**		**0.15**		**32.41**	
阿勒泰市	Altay City	0.02		0.02		2.28	
布尔津县	Burqin County	0.02		0.02		3.33	
富蕴县	Fuyun [Koktokay] County	0.01				3.03	
福海县	Fuhai [Burultokay] County	0.01		0.01		20.90	
哈巴河县	Habahe [Kaba] County	0.06		0.10		2.34	
青河县	Qinghe [Qinggil] County					0.26	
吉木乃县	Jeminay County					0.27	
博尔塔拉蒙古自治州	**Bortala Mongol Autonomous Prefecture**	**0.16**	**0.07**	**0.14**	**0.02**	**0.06**	
博乐市	Bole [Bortala] City	0.14	0.07	0.12	0.02		
精河县	Jinghe [Jing] County	0.02		0.01		0.01	
温泉县	Wenquan [Araxang] County					0.05	
巴音郭楞蒙古自治州	**Bayangol Mongol Autonomous Prefecture**	**11.08**	**10.47**	**18.58**	**17.86**	**2.74**	**0.04**
库尔勒市	Korla City	0.11		0.14			
轮台县	Luntai [Bugur] County	0.10	0.07	0.01			
尉犁县	Yuli [Lopnur] County	0.02		0.02			
若羌县	Ruoqiang [Qarkilik] County	0.02		0.02		0.53	
且末县	Qiemo [Qarqan] County	0.02		0.05	0.03		
焉耆回族自治县	Yanqi Hui Autonomous County	2.98	2.96	1.85	1.80	0.66	
和静县	Hejing County	2.35	2.13	7.49	7.25	0.74	
和硕县	Hoxud County	2.80	2.78	3.97	3.94	0.04	
博湖县	Bohu [Bagrax] County	2.68	2.54	5.02	4.84	0.77	0.04
阿克苏地区	**Aksu Administrative Offices**	**4.80**	**3.08**	**1.83**	**0.43**	**0.16**	**0.09**
阿克苏市	Aksu City	0.44		0.27			
温宿县	Wensu [Onsu] County	0.18		0.18		0.16	0.02
库车县	Kuqa County	0.39	0.03	0.10	0.04		

12-19 续表 2 Continued

单位：千公顷 (1000 hectares)

地　　区	Region	番　茄 Tomato	工业用番　茄 Tomato in Industry	辣　椒 Peppers	工业用辣　椒 Capsicum	打瓜籽 Melon Seeds	啤酒花 Hop
沙雅县	Xayar County	0.13		0.10			
新和县	Xinhe [Toksu] County	0.24		0.20			
拜城县	Baicheng [Bay] County	0.60	0.50	0.66	0.39		0.08
乌什县	Wushi [Uxturpan] County	2.55	2.55	0.09			
阿瓦提县	Awat County	0.25		0.22			
柯坪县	Kalpin County	0.01		0.01			
克孜勒苏柯尔克孜自治州	**Kizilsu Kirgiz Autonomous Prefecture**	**0.21**		**0.16**			
阿图什市	Artux City	0.04		0.02			
阿克陶县	Akto County	0.10		0.08			
阿合奇县	Akqi County	0.02		0.02			
乌恰县	Wuqia [Ulugqat] County	0.05		0.04			
喀什地区	**Kashgar [Kaxgar] Administrative Offices**	**6.07**	**0.55**	**11.21**	**5.58**	**1.01**	
喀什市	Kashgar [Kaxgar] City	0.40		0.10			
疏附县	Shufu County	1.57		1.34			
疏勒县	Shule County	0.60		0.48			
英吉沙县	Yengisar County	0.40		0.44			
泽普县	Zepu [Poskam] County	0.15		0.13	0.05		
莎车县	Shache [Yarkant] County	0.67	0.55	6.57	4.00		
叶城县	Yecheng [Kagilik] County	0.41		1.64	1.53		
麦盖提县	Makit County	0.25		0.12		1.01	
岳普湖县	Yopurga County	0.37		0.10			
伽师县	Jiashi [Payzawat] County	1.14		0.17			
巴楚县	Bachu [Maralbexi] County	0.10		0.12			
塔什库尔干塔吉克自治县	Taxkorgan Tajik Autonomous County						
和田地区	**Hotan Administrative Offices**	**1.46**		**0.40**	**0.02**	**0.02**	
和田市	Hotan City	0.08		0.04			
和田县	Hotan County	0.39		0.16	0.02		
墨玉县	Moyu [Karakax] County	0.11		0.02		0.02	
皮山县	Pishan [Guma] County	0.06		0.02			
洛浦县	Lop County	0.13		0.05			
策勒县	Qira County	0.01		0.02			
于田县	Yutian [Keriya] County	0.65		0.08			
民丰县	Minfeng [Niya] County	0.01					
生产建设兵团	**Xinjiang Production and Construction Group**	**29.82**	**26.00**	**22.44**	**18.73**	**15.65**	**1.54**

12-20 各地、州、市、县(市)特色农作物产量

Output of Characteristic Farm Crops by Prefecture,Autonomous Prefectura,City and County

单位：吨 (2013 年) (ton)

地区	Region	番茄 Tomato	工业用番茄 Tomato in Industry	辣椒 Peppers	工业用辣椒 Capsicum	枸杞 Medlar	打瓜籽 Melon Seeds	啤酒花 Hop
总计	**Total**	**6862973**	**5794319**	**2752312**	**1807625**	**34886**	**122435**	**8815**
乌鲁木齐市	**Urumqi City**	**36787**	**5114**	**49663**		**17**		**200**
#市辖区	Municipal Districts	35540	5114	34819		17		200
乌鲁木齐县	Urumqi County	1247		14844				
克拉玛依市	**Karamay City**	**22040**	**16562**	**5478**	**2675**		**857**	
吐鲁番地区	**TurpanAdministrative Offices**	**41491**		**6481**				
吐鲁番市	Turpan City	14286		1411				
鄯善县	Shanshan [piqan]County	11105		2460				
托克逊县	Toksun County	16100		2610				
哈密地区	**Hami [Kumul]Administrative Offices**	**12597**		**13211**				
哈密市	Hami [Kumul]City	10843		11600				
巴里坤哈萨克自治县	Barkol KazakAutonomous County	1638		1575				
伊吾县	Yiwu [Araturuk]County	116		36				
昌吉回族自治州	**Changji Hui Autonomous Prefecture**	**1175375**	**1074282**	**149764**	**42893**	**1310**	**17514**	**2269**
昌吉市	Changji City	320558	310283	13664	1300		290	953
阜康市	Fukang City	108663	58520	26866			7632	
呼图壁县	Hutubi County	248949	248864	28431	26550		1190	866
玛纳斯县	Manas County	281740	279698	13134	5400	1310	791	
奇台县	Qitai County	71489	37038	47332			4412	
吉木萨尔县	Jimsar County	143679	139879	19927	9600		2473	450
木垒哈萨克自治县	Mori Kazak Autonomous County	297		410	43		726	
伊犁哈萨克自治州	**Ili Kazak Autonomous Prefecture**	**621515**	**498551**	**295237**	**14597**	**3813**	**64235**	**926**
伊犁州直属县(市)	**Counties (Cities) Direct Under Ili Prefecture**	**119690**	**18524**	**92273**	**5850**		**1666**	
伊宁市	Yining [Gulja]City	37117		40678				
奎屯市	Kuytun City							
伊宁县	Yining [Gulja]County	31346		16590			83	
察布查尔锡伯自治县	Qapqal Xibe Autonomous County	7081		11644			38	
霍城县	Huocheng [korgas]County	29842	18524	8787	5850		1156	
巩留县	Gongliu [Tokkuzlara]County	1412		5000				
新源县	Xinyuan [kunes]County	3668		881			192	
昭苏县	Zhaosu [mongolkure]County	153		310				
特克斯县	Tekes County	8116		6940				
尼勒克县	Nilka County	955		1443			197	

12-20 续表 1 Continued

单位：吨 (ton)

地区	Region	番茄 Tomato	工业用番茄 Tomato in Industr	辣椒 Peppers	工业用辣椒 Capsicum	枸杞 Medlar	打瓜籽 Melon Seeds	啤酒花 Hop
塔城地区	**Tacheng[Tarbagatai] Administrative Officess**	**498084**	**480027**	**198041**	**8747**	**3341**	**10051**	**926**
塔城市	Tacheng [Qoqek] City	7350		3950			4456	
乌苏市	Usu City	402767	399966	2640	2300	960		
额敏县	Emin [Dorbiljin] County	38437	31015	825			1746	
沙湾县	Shawan County	49219	49046	188321	6447	240	1730	926
托里县	Toli County	30					208	
裕民县	Yumin [Qagantokay] County	232		170		2141	1542	
和布克赛尔蒙古自治县	Hoboksar Mongol Autonomous County	49		2135			369	
阿勒泰地区	**Altay Administrative Offices**	**3741**		**4923**		**472**	**52518**	
阿勒泰市	Altay City	599		598			4446	
布尔津县	Burqin County	85		990			4598	
富蕴县	Fuyun [Koktokay] County	432		53			6175	
福海县	Fuhai [Burultokay] County	299		106		472	32982	
哈巴河县	Habahe [Kaba] County	1981		2971			3573	
青河县	Qinghe [Qinggil] County	215		155			416	
吉木乃县	Jeminay County	130		50			328	
博尔塔拉蒙古自治州	**Bortala Mongol Autonomous Prefecture**	**11410**	**8050**	**5216**	**1526**	**20169**	**125**	
博乐市	Bole [Bortala] City	10791	8050	4778	1526	7		
精河县	Jinghe [Jing] County	588		428		20114	21	
温泉县	Wenquan [Araxang] County	31		10		48	104	
巴音郭楞蒙古自治州	**Bayangol Mongol Autonomous Prefecture**	**1124826**	**1080924**	**757595**	**727496**		**5137**	**531**
库尔勒市	Korla City	10421		10852				
轮台县	Luntai [Bugur] County	7462	6210	670				
尉犁县	Yuli [Lopnur] County	551		632				
若羌县	Ruoqiang [Qarkilik] County	780		638			600	
且末县	Qiemo [Qarqan] County	1047		1620	860			
焉耆回族自治县	Yanqi Hui Autonomous County	303899	301729	85540	83079		1563	
和静县	Hejing County	247889	235569	221418	217600		1214	
和硕县	Hoxud County	315877	313027	198285	196782		63	
博湖县	Bohu [Bagrax] County	236900	224389	237940	229175		1697	531
阿克苏地区	**Aksu Administrative Offices**	**258226**	**199423**	**48308**	**2643**		**705**	**191**
阿克苏市	Aksu City	17347		5101				
温宿县	Wensu [Onsu] County	5073		6049			705	81
库车县	Kuqa County	12330	590	5438	636			

12-20 续表 2 Continued

单位：吨 (ton)

地　区	Region	番　茄 Tomato	工业用番　茄 Tomato in Industr	辣　椒 Peppers	工业用辣　椒 Capsicum	枸　杞 Medlar	打瓜籽 Melon Seeds	啤酒花 Hop
沙雅县	Xayar County	1613		1007				
新和县	Xinhe [Toksu] County	13925		5065				
拜城县	Baicheng [Bay] County	30602	28395	17423	2007			110
乌什县	Wushi [Uxturpan] County	170438	170438	2630				
阿瓦提县	Awat County	6628		5495				
柯坪县	Kalpin County	270		100				
克孜勒苏柯尔克孜自治州	**Kizilsu Kirgiz Autonomous Prefecture**	**6868**		**3342**				
阿图什市	Artux City	2266		997				
阿克陶县	Akto County	2404		1366				
阿合奇县	Akqi County	606		293				
乌恰县	Wuqia [Ulugqat] County	1592		686				
喀什地区	**Kashgar [Kaxgar] Administrative Offices**	**307359**	**18040**	**533862**	**304100**		**456**	
喀什市	Kashgar [Kaxgar] City	23400		3837				
疏附县	Shufu County	76800		20100				
疏勒县	Shule County	20000		15200				
英吉沙县	Yengisar County	19360		20580				
泽普县	Zepu [Poskam] County	10000		6100	2100			
莎车县	Shache [Yarkant] County	30000	18040	344771	210000			
叶城县	Yecheng [Kagilik] County	41292		102400	92000			
麦盖提县	Makit County	10925		6361			456	
岳普湖县	Yopurga County	11500		2290				
伽师县	Jiashi [Payzawat] County	59270		6250				
巴楚县	Bachu [Maralbexi] County	4774		5955				
塔什库尔干塔吉克自治县	Taxkorgan Tajik Autonomous County	38		18				
和田地区	**Hotan Administrative Offices**	**59882**		**13801**	**650**		**45**	
和田市	Hotan City	4906		2063				
和田县	Hotan County	11997		6972	650			
墨玉县	Moyu [Karakax] County	2299		219			45	
皮山县	Pishan [Guma] County	3171		471				
洛浦县	Lop County	7213		1825				
策勒县	Qira County	626		787				
于田县	Yutian [Keriya] County	29232		1378				
民丰县	Minfeng [Niya] County	438		86				
生产建设兵团	**Xinjiang Production and Construction Group**	**3184597**	**2893373**	**870354**	**711045**	**9577**	**33361**	**4698**

12-21 各地、州、市林业生产情况
Condition on Forest Products by Prefecture, Autonomous Prefecture, City

单位:公顷 (2013 年) (hectare)

地区	Region	当年造林面积 Planting Area in the Current Year	用材林 Timber Forest	经济林 Economic Forest	防护林 Windbreak	薪炭林 Firewood Forest	特种用途林 Forest for Special Purpose
总计	**Total**	**164886**	**4275**	**47011**	**110629**	**2948**	**23**
乌鲁木齐市	Urumqi City	2729			2729		
克拉玛依市	Karamay City	1159			1159		
吐鲁番地区	Turpan Administrative Offices	3994	7	1709	2278		
哈密地区	Hami [Kumul]Administrative Offices	5046		7	5039		
昌吉回族自治州	Changji Hui Autonomous Prefecture	10365		1590	8442	333	
伊犁哈萨克自治州	Ili Kazak Administrative Prefecture	54468	3231	8778	41561	879	19
伊犁州直属县(市)	Counties (Cities) Direct Under Ili Prefecture	18368	2604	3916	11848		
塔城地区	Tacheng [Tarbagatai] Administrative Offices	19403	627	1429	17083	245	19
阿勒泰地区	Altay Administrative Offices	16697		3433	12630	634	
博尔塔拉蒙古自治州	Bortala Mongol Autonomous Prefecture	5161		202	4739	220	
巴音郭楞蒙古自治州	Bayangol Mongol Autonomous Prefecture	14400		4655	9578	167	
阿克苏地区	Aksu Administrative Offices	9614		4599	4508	507	
克孜勒苏柯尔克孜自治州	Kizilsu Kirgiz Autonomous Prefecture	6593	435		5988	170	
喀什地区	Kashgar [Kaxgar] Administrative Offices	21411	2	14721	6644	40	4
和田地区	Hotan Administrative Offices	12239		5909	5698	632	
生产建设兵团	Xinjiang Production and Construction Group	17529	600	4841	12088		

地区	Region	更新造林面积 Reforestation Area	四旁零星植树(万株) Four Sides Afforestation	年末实有育苗面积 Actual Sapling Breeding Area	未成林抚育作业面积 Unpaired Forest Tending Operations Area	中、幼龄林抚育面积 Young Forest Tending Area	核桃产量(吨) Walnut Output (ton)	村及村以下木材采伐量(立方米) Timber Felling Output in Village or Below (cu.m)
总计	**Total**	**2586**	**2108.37**	**31786**	**1373617**	**1106369**	**402768**	**256801**
乌鲁木齐市	Urumqi City		134.65	1318				1777
克拉玛依市	Karamay City		123.60	966	1386	8568		
吐鲁番地区	Turpan Administrative Offices	8	0.06	151		15667	600	2275
哈密地区	Hami[Kumul] Administrative Offices		1.62	74	61588	17440		586
昌吉回族自治州	Changji Hui Autonomous Prefecture		58.05	11467	17649	4569		29254
伊犁哈萨克自治州	Ili Kazak Administrative Prefecture	530	449.06	2133	216231	152196	970	66292
伊犁州直属县(市)	Counties (Cities) Direct Under Ili Prefecture	366	282.42	1549	128181	83827	970	42697
塔城地区	Tacheng [Tarbagatai] Administrative Offices	164	98.64	440	20084	21063		18584
阿勒泰地区	Altay Administrative Offices		68.00	144	67966	47306		5011
博尔塔拉蒙古自治州	Bortala Mongol Autonomous Prefecture	86	24.00	195	11585	8782	2	12094
巴音郭楞蒙古自治州	Bayangol Mongol Autonomous Prefecture	56	111.66	1040		2667	336	21476
阿克苏地区	Aksu Administrative Offices	434	29.30	645	235902	269085	141820	48296
克孜勒苏柯尔克孜自治州	Kizilsu Kirgiz Autonomous Prefecture		11.00	530	25776	8592	1315	128
喀什地区	Kashgar [Kaxgar] Administrative Offices	240	655.94	4109	434114	243310	153491	53993
和田地区	Hotan Administrative Offices	201	336.00	2392	98638	118803	93131	20630
生产建设兵团	Xinjiang Production and Construction Group	317	173.45	6419	269062	230753	11103	

12-22 各地、州、市水果种植面积
Planted Area of Fruits by Prefecture, Autonomous Prefecture, City

单位:公顷 (2013 年) (hectare)

地 区	Region	合 计 Total	苹 果 Apples	梨 Pears	葡 萄 Grapes	#无核葡萄 Seedless Grapes
总 计	**Total**	**933976**	**54966**	**69907**	**144754**	**48594**
乌鲁木齐市	Urumqi City	642	122		300	
克拉玛依市	Karamay City					
吐鲁番地区	TurpanAdministrative Offices	41824		26	31183	28631
哈密地区	Hami [Kumul] Administrative Offices	29709	34	44	3813	3057
昌吉回族自治州	Changji Hui Autonomous Prefecture	13895	2748	22	6442	7
伊犁哈萨克自治州	Ili Kazak Autonomous Prefecture	37344	16439	32	8724	3702
伊犁州直属县(市)	Counties (Cities) Direct Under Ili Prefecture	32494	15080	19	6886	3698
塔城地区	Tacheng [Tarbagatai] Administrative Offices	3470	1335	12	493	4
阿勒泰地区	Altay Administrative Offices	1381	23		1345	
博尔塔拉蒙古自治州	Bortala MongolAutonomous Prefecture	420	103	6	278	
巴音郭楞蒙古自治州	Bayangol Mongol Autonomous Prefecture	107350	304	36603	16545	
阿克苏地区	Aksu Administrative Offices	192304	14143	13632	7360	
克孜勒苏柯尔克孜自治州	Kizilsu Kirgiz Autonomous Prefecture	22033	143	18	6681	
喀什地区	Kashgar [Kaxgar] Administrative Offices	220281	4072	1309	4501	18
和田地区	Hotan Administrative Offices	69544	1135	481	10856	2941
生产建设兵团	Xinjiang Production and Construction Group	198629	15722	17734	48072	10239

地 区	Region	桃 Peaches	杏 Apricots	红 枣 Jujubes	石 榴 Pomegraniate	其 它 Others
总 计	**Total**	**10404**	**135861**	**486141**	**12222**	**19722**
乌鲁木齐市	Urumqi City	26	49	53		92
克拉玛依市	Karamay City					
吐鲁番地区	TurpanAdministrative Offices	7	2240	7927	441	
哈密地区	Hami [Kumul] Administrative Offices	17	2328	21885		1587
昌吉回族自治州	Changji Hui Autonomous Prefecture	255	2127	232		2070
伊犁哈萨克自治州	Ili Kazak Autonomous Prefecture	1360	6906	321		3563
伊犁州直属县(市)	Counties (Cities) Direct Under Ili Prefecture	1314	6896	304		1994
塔城地区	Tacheng [Tarbagatai] Administrative Offices	37	10	18		1565
阿勒泰地区	Altay Administrative Offices	9				4
博尔塔拉蒙古自治州	Bortala Mongol Autonomous Prefecture	17	12	1		3
巴音郭楞蒙古自治州	Bayangol Mongol Autonomous Prefecture	273	16136	35806		1683
阿克苏地区	Aksu Administrative Offices	139	22016	132237	104	2674
克孜勒苏柯尔克孜自治州	Kizilsu Kirgiz Autonomous Prefecture	512	10093	3123	202	1261
喀什地区	Kashgar [Kaxgar] Administrative Offices	4331	55492	138657	7625	4294
和田地区	Hotan Administrative Offices	964	13367	36915	3848	1978
生产建设兵团	Xinjiang Production and Construction Group	2503	5093	108984	2	517

12-23 各地、州、市水果产量
Output of Fruits by Prefecture, Autonomous Prefecture, City

单位：吨 (2013 年) (ton)

地　区	Region	合 计 Total	苹 果 Apples	梨 Pears	葡 萄 Grapes	#无核葡萄 Seedless Grapes
总　计	**Total**	**7826942**	**980834**	**913058**	**2239257**	**1144614**
乌鲁木齐市	Urumqi City	7886	913		4966	
克拉玛依市	Karamay City					
吐鲁番地区	TurpanAdministrative Offices	911313		279	868882	796792
哈密地区	Hami [Kumul] Administrative Offices	140090	157	395	86570	67741
昌吉回族自治州	Changji Hui Autonomous Prefecture	139699	16872	196	111785	5
伊犁哈萨克自治州	Ili Kazak Autonomous Prefecture	328172	142903	435	106450	51018
伊犁州直属县(市)	Counties (Cities) Direct Under Ili Prefecture	297977	128238	200	92936	51000
塔城地区	Tacheng [Tarbagatai] Administrative Offices	28783	14050	235	12939	18
阿勒泰地区	Altay Administrative Offices	1412	615		575	
博尔塔拉蒙古自治州	Bortala MongolAutonomous Prefecture	6417	1477	27	4689	
巴音郭楞蒙古自治州	Bayangol Mongol Autonomous Prefecture	548878	4037	283292	51933	
阿克苏地区	Aksu Administrative Offices	1655148	375391	282885	105060	
克孜勒苏柯尔克孜自治州	Kizilsu Kirgiz Autonomous Prefecture	195318	458	87	82242	
喀什地区	Kashgar [Kaxgar] Administrative Offices	1298884	101183	14869	91365	
和田地区	Hotan Administrative Offices	411748	10342	3226	182308	50941
生产建设兵团	Xinjiang Production and Construction Group	2183389	327101	327367	543007	178117

地　区	Region	桃 Peachs	杏 Apricots	红 枣 Jujubes	石 榴 Pomegranate	其 它 Others
总　计	**Total**	**150320**	**1406930**	**1993660**	**51753**	**91130**
乌鲁木齐市	Urumqi City	408	271	335		993
克拉玛依市	Karamay City					
吐鲁番地区	TurpanAdministrative Offices	190	13928	26243	1791	
哈密地区	Hami [Kumul] Administrative Offices	100	1646	51222		
昌吉回族自治州	Changji Hui Autonomous Prefecture	1788	4143	1554		3361
伊犁哈萨克自治州	Ili Kazak Autonomous Prefecture	30618	41184	1559		5023
伊犁州直属县(市)	Counties (Cities) Direct Under Ili Prefecture	29717	41098	1417		4371
塔城地区	Tacheng [Tarbagatai] Administrative Offices	734	85	142		598
阿勒泰地区	Altay Administrative Offices	167	1			54
博尔塔拉蒙古自治州	Bortala MongolAutonomous Prefecture	184	6	2		32
巴音郭楞蒙古自治州	Bayangol Mongol Autonomous Prefecture	2120	89270	109258		8968
阿克苏地区	Aksu Administrative Offices	257	319311	539738	395	32111
克孜勒苏柯尔克孜自治州	Kizilsu Kirgiz Autonomous Prefecture	487	105799	1374	956	3915
喀什地区	Kashgar [Kaxgar] Administrative Offices	58457	648827	327147	33148	23888
和田地区	Hotan Administrative Offices	7363	131853	53494	15431	7731
生产建设兵团	Xinjiang Production and Construction Group	48348	50692	881734	32	5108

12-24 主要年份牲畜饲养情况
Number of Livestock in Main Years

单位：万头(只) (10 000 heads)

年 份 Year	大牲畜年底头数 Large Animals (year-end)	牛 Cattle and Buffaloes	马 Horses	驴 Donkeys	骡 Mules	骆驼 Camels	在大牲畜中役畜 Draught Animals
1978	446.19	222.39	112.39	96.61	1.61	13.19	148.34
1980	482.55	250.65	106.89	108.88	1.72	14.41	154.86
1985	517.55	293.26	99.54	106.57	2.17	16.05	197.29
1990	575.88	338.22	104.58	112.96	2.69	17.43	209.95
1995	580.04	343.54	100.47	117.04	2.77	16.22	213.61
1996	589.41	349.78	101.16	119.36	2.76	16.34	215.05
1997	600.12	359.81	100.32	120.74	2.87	16.38	207.15
1998	606.79	364.29	100.26	123.45	2.80	15.99	205.31
1999	615.91	370.52	101.47	124.99	2.78	16.15	189.86
2000	632.93	384.98	102.57	125.94	2.74	16.70	173.37
2001	630.67	386.40	99.38	126.06	2.84	15.99	172.08
2002	654.46	414.13	99.71	122.22	2.59	15.81	169.51
2003	694.53	453.06	99.39	124.02	2.48	15.58	163.72
2004	716.56	482.30	95.78	120.82	2.36	15.30	151.49
2005	739.72	504.16	94.19	123.90	2.38	15.09	134.81
2006	736.33	502.86	92.09	124.94	2.14	14.30	145.97
2007	702.03	486.98	86.09	113.92	1.83	13.20	120.79
2008	543.41	336.00	83.85	109.25	1.45	12.86	96.56
2009	536.83	330.76	84.60	107.17	1.35	12.95	99.48
2010	536.82	330.47	85.29	106.96	1.19	12.91	108.93
2011	523.00	318.20	85.66	104.73	1.08	13.33	158.20
2012	565.77	365.93	86.84	97.97	1.06	13.97	162.00
2013	564.92	371.14	87.52	90.31	0.91	15.04	159.38

年 份 Year	猪年底头数 Hogs (year-end)	羊年底只数 Sheep and Goats (year-end)	山羊 Goats	绵羊 Sheep	牲畜出栏头数 Slanghtered Fattened Animals withina Year	#猪 Hogs	#牛 Cattle and Buffaloes	#羊 Sheep and Goats
1978	103.25	1927.34	349.63	1577.91	460.41	50.75	18.75	382.76
1980	84.62	2105.43	388.89	1716.54	584.09	67.32	24.22	477.81
1985	66.58	2431.91	394.79	2037.12	836.39	49.07	42.33	723.51
1990	89.71	2830.81	449.43	2381.38	1242.89	78.93	70.10	1070.43
1995	135.26	3009.02	471.38	2537.64	1709.93	122.32	101.20	1448.72
1996	138.18	3136.21	498.10	2638.11	1859.28	153.75	116.25	1550.65
1997	145.73	3261.81	514.60	2747.21	2096.67	173.06	125.72	1753.88
1998	169.82	3447.38	528.05	2919.33	2222.27	197.39	140.82	1837.57
1999	188.34	3592.29	555.21	3037.08	2223.89	203.87	145.95	1820.71
2000	201.53	3690.21	586.70	3103.51	2455.99	224.46	154.53	2017.36
2001	208.23	3764.88	601.14	3163.74	2633.83	246.00	179.32	2147.31
2002	219.08	3908.23	626.42	3281.81	2878.39	259.05	188.65	2363.02
2003	227.71	4104.30	657.15	3447.15	3201.99	307.74	202.23	2626.94
2004	223.08	4266.73	669.47	3597.26	3437.59	352.83	220.80	2790.53
2005	238.38	4355.50	659.75	3695.75	3756.92	358.71	249.41	3081.88
2006	243.88	4359.50	654.26	3705.24	4063.52	390.82	278.69	3317.99
2007	237.90	4083.44	608.10	3475.34	4108.28	393.70	271.76	3361.99
2008	177.00	3025.70	453.85	2571.85	3388.09	265.50	207.30	2842.30
2009	180.42	3127.50	469.13	2658.37	3135.72	254.23	210.89	2604.48
2010	171.96	3013.37	528.73	2484.64	3498.52	262.72	216.69	2947.22
2011	254.00	3016.40	489.70	2526.70	3606.61	411.94	203.90	2913.83
2012	265.43	3502.05	525.31	2976.74	3737.30	427.60	222.26	3001.24
2013	274.72	3663.22	505.54	3157.68	3862.06	439.57	230.26	3107.49

注：牲畜出栏数 1999 年以后计算口径与 1998 年以前不同。
Note: The calculating norm of cattles out of stock after 1999 was different from that prior to that in 1998.

12-25 各地、州、市、县(市)牲畜年底头数

Number of Livestock at the Year-end by Prefecture, Autonomous Prefecture, City and County

单位：万头(只) (2013 年) (10 000 heads)

地 区	Region	合 计 Total	#牛 Cattle and Buffaloes	#马 Horses	#驴 Donkeys	#猪 Hogs	#山 羊 Goats	#绵 羊 Sheep
总 计	**Total**	**4502.86**	**371.14**	**87.52**	**90.31**	**274.72**	**505.54**	**3157.68**
乌鲁木齐市	**Urumqi City**	**73.70**	**8.10**	**1.71**	**0.19**	**8.11**	**15.72**	**39.42**
#乌鲁木齐县	Urumqi County	27.74	2.86	1.27	0.08	0.07	3.57	19.81
克拉玛依市	**Karamay City**	**14.86**	**0.72**	**0.07**	**0.01**	**7.51**	**2.02**	**4.50**
吐鲁番地区	**TurpanAdministrative Offices**	**97.59**	**5.71**	**0.41**	**2.26**	**2.30**	**16.33**	**70.08**
吐鲁番市	Turpan City	32.65	2.74	0.03	0.55	1.25	6.15	21.90
鄯善县	Shanshan [piqan]County	31.05	0.51	0.11	0.62	0.99	3.08	25.55
托克逊县	Toksun County	33.89	2.46	0.27	1.09	0.06	7.10	22.63
哈密地区	**Hami [Kumul]Administrative Offices**	**115.17**	**6.40**	**1.21**	**0.67**	**11.12**	**15.67**	**79.24**
哈密市	Hami [Kumul]City	43.86	2.27	0.34	0.27	2.54	6.26	31.87
巴里坤哈萨克自治县	Barkol KazakAutonomous County	54.42	2.78	0.74	0.34	4.47	5.38	40.33
伊吾县	Yiwu [Araturuk]County	16.89	1.35	0.13	0.06	4.11	4.03	7.04
昌吉回族自治州	**Changji Hui Autonomous Prefecture**	**433.5**	**50.64**	**5.11**	**0.76**	**55.65**	**45.06**	**274.30**
昌吉市	Changji City	83.81	12.88	0.86	0.07	19.29	11.35	38.96
阜康市	Fukang City	28.29	4.33	0.41	0.03	3.61	6.42	13.39
呼图壁县	Hutubi County	55.40	9.51	1.26	0.03	5.27	7.57	31.45
玛纳斯县	Manas County	64.80	5.70	0.67	0.11	9.47	1.44	47.18
奇台县	Qitai County	93.37	9.55	0.70		8.36	7.15	67.27
吉木萨尔县	Jimsar County	57.19	6.65	0.62	0.29	8.15	5.14	36.23
木垒哈萨克自治县	Mori Kazak Autonomous County	50.64	2.02	0.59	0.23	1.50	5.99	39.82
伊犁哈萨克自治州	**Ili Kazak Autonomous Prefecture**	**1404.72**	**234.88**	**60.74**	**2.90**	**56.00**	**124.30**	**918.20**
伊犁州直属县(市)	**Counties (Cities) Direct Under Ili Prefecture**	**655.58**	**134.17**	**39.24**	**2.53**	**33.24**	**25.94**	**419.81**
伊宁市	Yining [Gulja]City	23.71	4.60	0.41	0.19	2.16	1.16	15.16
奎屯市	Kuytun City	4.12	0.16	0.01		2.52	0.09	1.34
伊宁县	Yining [Gulja]County	93.71	18.54	2.72	0.33	12.42	7.73	51.83
察布查尔锡伯自治县	Qapqal Xibe Autonomous County	43.59	7.27	1.47	0.90	2.68	3.16	28.11
霍城县	Huocheng [korgas]County	71.94	12.47	1.45	0.59	4.30	2.19	50.81
巩留县	Gongliu [Tokkuzlara]County	59.20	12.70	3.80	0.37	2.95	2.61	36.73
新源县	Xinyuan [kunes]County	101.79	24.54	8.36	0.05	2.34	2.13	64.36
昭苏县	Zhaosu [mongolkure]County	92.70	16.42	9.43	0.02	2.08	1.48	63.23
特克斯县	Tekes County	72.06	16.50	4.58	0.03	0.67	2.46	47.79
尼勒克县	Nilka County	92.76	20.97	7.01	0.05	1.12	2.93	60.45
塔城地区	**Tacheng [Tarbagatai] Administrative Offices**	**470.00**	**48.68**	**11.34**	**0.32**	**20.77**	**63.82**	**322.30**
塔城市	Tacheng [Qoqek] City	74.49	8.98	2.31	0.07	2.94	4.48	55.40
乌苏市	Usu City	81.60	4.86	0.82	0.06	4.16	12.63	58.66
额敏县	Emin [Dorbiljin] County	72.38	6.33	1.40		1.77	10.82	51.88
沙湾县	Shawan County	66.79	10.41	1.41	0.01	11.17	6.65	36.79
托里县	Toli County	63.48	7.96	2.10	0.09	0.26	9.76	42.61
裕民县	Yumin [Qagantokay] County	61.62	6.09	2.05		0.33	8.88	43.77
和布克赛尔蒙古自治县	Hoboksar Mongol Autonomous County	49.64	4.05	1.25	0.09	0.14	10.60	33.19
阿勒泰地区	**Altay Administrative Offices**	**279.14**	**52.03**	**10.16**	**0.05**	**1.99**	**34.54**	**176.09**
阿勒泰市	Altay City	50.50	12.18	1.98	0.01	0.48	3.11	32.08
布尔津县	Burqin County	33.18	8.04	1.66		0.11	3.56	19.50
富蕴县	Fuyun [Koktokay] County	61.01	7.42	2.81	0.01	0.10	8.20	41.18
福海县	Fuhai [Burultokay] County	41.61	7.16	0.64		1.08	5.80	25.84
哈巴河县	Habahe [Kaba] County	40.13	11.56	1.54		0.11	5.54	20.96
青河县	Qinghe [Qinggil] County	31.34	3.50	0.80	0.03	0.06	6.00	20.67
吉木乃县	Jeminay County	21.37	2.17	0.73		0.05	2.33	15.86

注：1.全区总计不等于地方与生产建设兵团汇总数。2.全区总计数为国家统计局审定数。
Note:a)The region total data is not equal to the sum of local and Production and Construction Groups.b)The region total data refer to approvable data of NBS.

12-25 续表 Continued

单位：万头(只) (10 000 heads)

地　区	Region	合 计 Total	#牛 Cattle and Buffaloes	#马 Horses	#驴 Donkeys	#猪 Hogs	#山羊 Goats	#绵羊 Sheep
博尔塔拉蒙古自治州	**Bortala Mongol Autonomous Prefecture**	**109.62**	**6.66**	**1.35**	**0.17**	**5.46**	**12.93**	**82.81**
博乐市	Bole [Bortala] City	37.20	2.74	0.36	0.09	2.74	3.42	27.72
精河县	Jinghe [Jing] County	36.73	1.49	0.36	0.02	1.31	6.60	26.91
温泉县	Wenquan [Araxang] County	35.69	2.43	0.63	0.06	1.41	2.91	28.18
巴音郭楞蒙古自治州	**Bayangol Mongol Autonomous Prefecture**	**344.01**	**16.64**	**3.29**	**2.67**	**34.22**	**67.09**	**219.36**
库尔勒市	Korla City	35.95	0.85	0.08	0.09	9.57	4.67	20.69
轮台县	Luntai [Bugur] County	37.80	1.34	0.02	0.69	1.45	9.57	24.72
尉犁县	Yuli [Lopnur] County	40.81	0.72	0.04	0.15	0.64	22.66	16.59
若羌县	Ruoqiang [Qarkilik] County	11.47	0.35	0.05	0.17	0.77	0.91	9.18
且末县	Qiemo [Qarqan] County	45.37	1.93	0.15	1.43	1.05	12.06	28.42
焉耆回族自治县	Yanqi Hui Autonomous County	28.22	2.47	0.11	0.08	2.49	0.60	22.47
和静县	Hejing County	97.08	7.06	2.14	0.02	3.64	9.01	75.09
和硕县	Hoxud County	26.61	1.08	0.48	0.03	4.98	6.70	13.13
博湖县	Bohu [Bagrax] County	20.70	0.84	0.22	0.01	9.63	0.91	9.07
阿克苏地区	**Aksu Administrative Offices**	**508.75**	**35.22**	**5.67**	**10.07**	**18.46**	**122.01**	**316.35**
阿克苏市	Aksu City	57.04	3.20	0.33	0.52	8.73	6.02	38.24
温宿县	Wensu [Onsu] County	67.95	3.99	1.56	1.68	2.36	14.87	43.42
库车县	Kuqa County	79.85	5.24	0.46	1.23	2.94	20.76	49.08
沙雅县	Xayar County	48.65	3.50	0.39	1.05	1.57	21.46	20.63
新和县	Xinhe [Toksu] County	26.93	2.89	0.48	1.05	0.19	1.54	20.73
拜城县	Baicheng [Bay] County	101.31	7.87	0.77	2.02	2.14	21.52	66.93
乌什县	Wushi [Uxturpan] County	61.32	5.68	1.43	1.89	0.13	20.35	31.64
阿瓦提县	Awat County	44.05	2.64	0.21	0.28	0.40	5.29	35.22
柯坪县	Kalpin County	21.65	0.21	0.04	0.35		10.20	10.46
克孜勒苏柯尔克孜自治州	**Kizilsu Kirgiz Autonomous Prefecture**	**165.72**	**15.99**	**2.79**	**2.74**	**0.67**	**35.78**	**106.86**
阿图什市	Artux City	47.50	4.35	0.31	0.84	0.41	12.84	28.43
阿克陶县	Akto County	52.81	9.48	0.14	1.37	0.16	7.74	33.76
阿合奇县	Akqi County	35.92	0.72	1.81	0.06	0.10	9.97	23.21
乌恰县	Wuqia [Ulugqat] County	29.49	1.44	0.53	0.47		5.23	21.46
喀什地区	**Kashgar [Kaxgar] Administrative Offices**	**840.16**	**87.89**	**1.70**	**44.91**	**14.9**	**43.94**	**646.29**
喀什市	Kashgar [Kaxgar] City	36.00	1.67	0.02	0.85	1.23	0.45	31.73
疏附县	Shufu County	96.50	9.82	0.09	3.32	1.77	2.97	78.47
疏勒县	Shule County	84.00	9.01	0.04	4.35	6.91	0.69	62.95
英吉沙县	Yengisar County	38.90	5.90	0.04	2.20	0.55	0.66	29.52
泽普县	Zepu [Poskam] County	40.50	5.78	0.17	2.35	0.93	1.60	29.67
莎车县	Shache [Yarkant] County	124.31	11.75	0.25	6.34	0.82	5.24	99.91
叶城县	Yecheng [Kagilik] County	122.53	16.32	0.30	6.89	0.75	6.64	91.50
麦盖提县	Makit County	59.50	7.10	0.20	2.10	0.52	5.20	44.37
岳普湖县	Yopurga County	39.80	5.17	0.13	8.02	0.17	3.36	22.93
伽师县	Jiashi [Payzawat] County	103.90	6.20	0.28	6.70	0.20	6.40	84.11
巴楚县	Bachu [Maralbexi] County	73.97	5.53	0.12	1.47	1.05	5.55	60.25
塔什库尔干塔吉克自治县	Taxkorgan Tajik Autonomous County	20.25	3.64	0.06	0.32		5.18	10.88
和田地区	**Hotan Administrative Offices**	**503.71**	**24.59**	**1.19**	**21.98**	**2.23**	**28.4**	**424.65**
和田市	Hotan City	32.71	1.77	0.05	0.48	1.49	0.61	28.29
和田县	Hotan County	79.22	5.68	0.09	4.91	0.11	2.38	65.99
墨玉县	Moyu [Karakax] County	121.59	8.92	0.22	6.65	0.04	2.26	103.47
皮山县	Pishan [Guma] County	51.99	0.97	0.15	2.46	0.13	3.21	44.98
洛浦县	Lop County	52.35	3.19	0.06	1.67	0.16	1.01	46.22
策勒县	Qira County	52.17	1.27	0.24	2.02	0.08	3.12	45.36
于田县	Yutian [Keriya] County	77.00	2.50	0.30	2.60	0.18	6.60	64.70
民丰县	Minfeng [Niya] County	36.68	0.29	0.08	1.19	0.04	9.21	25.64
生产建设兵团	**Xinjiang Production and Construction Group**	**628.86**	**39.9**	**2.28**	**0.98**	**135.21**	**45.06**	**405.04**

12-26 主要年份畜产品产量
Output of Livestock Products in Main Years

年份 Year	肉类产量(万吨) Output of Meat (10 000 tons)	#牛 Beef	#马 Horse Meat	#骆驼 Camels	#猪 Pork	#羊 Mutton	#禽兔肉 Poultry and Rabbit Meat
1978	9.65	1.85			2.48	5.32	
1980	12.70	2.20	0.60	0.05	3.29	6.48	
1985	18.37	4.23	0.86	0.15	3.09	9.97	
1990	30.46	7.08	1.18	0.18	4.93	15.75	1.22
1995	52.38	13.14	2.05	0.40	8.37	24.48	3.61
1996	60.31	15.18	2.24	0.38	10.43	26.93	4.82
1997	64.40	16.40	2.55	0.38	11.52	27.72	5.38
1998	75.19	19.19	2.82	0.47	13.60	32.49	6.16
1999	81.36	20.61	2.93	0.62	16.02	33.57	6.94
2000	90.00	22.24	3.57	0.63	17.18	37.50	7.76
2001	97.00	23.99	3.55	0.72	18.36	40.48	8.66
2002	105.44	25.90	3.65	0.68	19.70	43.06	10.38
2003	115.00	28.77	3.88	0.69	22.41	45.54	11.46
2004	128.13	30.42	4.34	0.70	24.58	52.65	13.27
2005	141.46	34.22	4.67	0.77	26.18	59.89	13.46
2006	158.21	39.25	4.80	0.90	28.78	66.99	14.92
2007	160.58	42.25	5.09	0.94	31.73	65.02	13.74
2008	114.74	32.40	4.29	0.95	22.30	45.40	7.89
2009	115.31	33.88	4.33	0.73	22.03	43.77	8.52
2010	121.74	35.47	4.67	0.78	23.05	46.95	8.71
2011	127.28	33.80	4.86	0.73	29.80	46.40	9.50
2012	134.23	36.16	4.96	0.80	30.15	48.01	10.54
2013	139.26	37.82	5.04	0.79	31.33	49.71	11.86

年份 Year	羊毛(万吨) Wool (10 000 tons)	#绵羊毛 Sheep Wool	山羊绒(吨) Cashmere (ton)	驼毛(吨) Camel Hair (ton)	牛奶(万吨) Cow Milk (10 000 tons)	羊奶(万吨) Sheep Milk (10 000 tons)	牛皮(万张) Oxhide (10 000 sheets)	羊皮(万张) Sheep Skin (10 000 sheets)	禽蛋(万吨) Poultry Eggs (10 000 tons)
1978	3.08	3.00	324	371	4.50	0.75	17.36	300.05	
1980	3.31	3.21	263	353	5.84	1.44	18.22	338.32	
1985	7.07	3.91	325	530	16.43	3.27	35.72	587.69	4.29
1990	5.09	4.93	607	656	30.81	4.83	56.76	839.69	6.30
1995	5.66	5.45	716	716	45.21	4.60	91.54	1125.72	9.51
1996	5.99	5.77	780	787	48.76	5.46	92.31	1178.39	10.33
1997	6.25	6.01	813	742	54.18	4.60	96.88	1326.69	12.16
1998	6.48	6.22	811	768	59.96	5.06	110.12	1391.77	13.34
1999	6.76	6.50	849	727	64.81	5.62	118.35	1569.50	16.68
2000	6.98	6.67	893	757	72.54	5.69	125.62	1686.03	18.53
2001	7.30	6.99	973	736	81.09	6.76	143.13	1689.24	20.37
2002	7.78	7.44	1034	824	94.87	5.84	139.87	1801.67	22.64
2003	8.21	7.84	1143	793	113.00	6.21	141.57	1692.35	23.62
2004	8.91	8.49	1228	770	133.32	6.41	150.15	1981.82	24.99
2005	9.38	8.98	1258	730	152.22	5.62	169.53	2022.61	24.99
2006	9.62	8.96	1263	746	179.81	5.60	196.97	2300.73	25.80
2007	9.34	8.92	1265	946	196.23	5.54	191.90	2409.84	28.37
2008	9.03	8.40	1157	1040	137.40	4.96	208.07	2441.52	28.92
2009	7.60	7.16	1261	578	120.88	4.27	193.52	2358.98	23.20
2010	8.69	8.40	1324	602	128.60	4.22	204.14	2403.25	24.35
2011	9.01	8.69	1261	610	130.50	3.41	221.35	2535.63	25.60
2012	9.20	8.85	1225	539	132.21	4.11	221.63	2573.07	25.89
2013	9.68	9.16	1227	616	134.99	4.20	245.20	2642.71	28.17

12-27 各地、州、市、县(市)总产肉量
Total Output of Meat by Prefecture, Autonomous Prefecture, City and County

单位：吔 (2013 年) (ton)

地区	Region	合计 Total	#牛 Beef	#马 Horse	#骆驼 Camels	#猪 Pork	#山羊 Goats	#绵羊 Sheep	#禽肉 Poultry Meat	#兔肉 Rabbit Meat
总计	**Total**	**1392626**	**378234**	**50369**	**7877**	**313259**	**54229**	**442914**	**114600**	**3990**
乌鲁木齐市	**Urumqi City**	**64735**	**18613**	**2084**	**323**	**18133**	**4409**	**13630**	**7352**	**63**
#乌鲁木齐县	Urumqi County	12314	3683	1514	215	79	770	5446	520	58
克拉玛依市	**Karamay City**	**10848**	**504**	**15**		**9040**	**192**	**562**	**535**	
吐鲁番地区	**TurpanAdministrative Offices**	**41089**	**10090**	**189**	**134**	**2638**	**3390**	**22758**	**1865**	**25**
吐鲁番市	Turpan City	20974	3750	50		1725	1454	12785	1210	
鄯善县	Shanshan [piqan]County	10746	1870	60	38	760	1042	6591	385	
托克逊县	Toksun County	9369	4470	79	96	153	894	3382	270	25
哈密地区	**Hami [Kumul]Administrative Offices**	**57747**	**8769**	**531**	**585**	**19366**	**3819**	**21526**	**2853**	**3**
哈密市	Hami [Kumul]City	27705	5491	73	166	5223	2402	11956	2244	3
巴里坤哈萨克自治县	Barkol KazakAutonomous County	21329	2521	312	283	9355	652	7565	527	
伊吾县	Yiwu [Araturuk]County	8713	757	146	136	4788	765	2005	82	
昌吉回族自治州	**Changji Hui Autonomous Prefecture**	**502551**	**87972**	**4332**	**1794**	**197589**	**10387**	**90888**	**108873**	**249**
昌吉市	Changji City	101503	19362	1068	722	42043	2767	15901	19372	208
阜康市	Fukang City	53936	10560	478	138	15347	2363	10118	14925	
呼图壁县	Hutubi County	88889	22979	1306	272	21584	912	12503	29310	21
玛纳斯县	Manas County	68609	6285	398	22	29688	342	15082	16760	6
奇台县	Qitai County	126428	14572	281	166	77213	1335	19235	13410	14
吉木萨尔县	Jimsar County	47365	11594	293	34	8041	1744	11554	14043	
木垒哈萨克自治县	Mori Kazak Autonomous County	15821	2620	508	440	3673	924	6495	1053	
伊犁哈萨克自治州	**Ili Kazak Autonomous Prefecture**	**525961**	**180568**	**35852**	**2806**	**108867**	**17807**	**134934**	**43757**	**241**
伊犁州直属县(市)	**Counties (Cities) Direct Under Ili Prefecture**	**275672**	**101948**	**25459**	**235**	**56451**	**3200**	**60822**	**26466**	**123**
伊宁市	Yining [Gulja]City	13698	4985	580	30	3676	179	2466	1690	2
奎屯市	Kuytun City	4602	60			4090	16	142	294	
伊宁县	Yining [Gulja]County	48745	21431	1680	32	11736	609	8211	4830	
察布查尔锡伯自治县	Qapqal Xibe Autonomous County	19526	6678	810		6096	359	3572	1602	42
霍城县	Huocheng [korgas]County	38319	8222	2190		10374	354	8311	8720	22
巩留县	Gongliu [Tokkuzlara]County	30514	11676	3103	30	5730	360	5047	4400	40
新源县	Xinyuan [kunes]County	41583	14906	6015		7252	350	11003	2037	13
昭苏县	Zhaosu [mongolkure]County	27424	12122	4095	15	3220	151	7215	595	3
特克斯县	Tekes County	18439	8288	1498	16	1316	319	6305	688	1
尼勒克县	Nilka County	32822	13580	5488	112	2961	503	8550	1610	

注：同 12-25 表。
Note:The same applies to 12-25 table following.

12-27 续表 1 Continued

单位：吨 (ton)

地　区	Region	合 计 Total	#牛 Beef	#马 Horse	#骆 驼 Camels	#猪 Pork	#山 羊 Goats	#绵 羊 Sheep	#禽 肉 Poultry Meat	#兔 肉 Rabbit Meat
塔城地区	**Tacheng [Tarbagatai] Administrative Offices**	**173349**	**45054**	**6985**	**1109**	**47805**	**9940**	**48880**	**13357**	**71**
塔城市	Tacheng [Qoqek] City	16237	5283	1050	100	1396	692	6131	1520	17
乌苏市	Usu City	37670	8340	1890	288	13088	3215	9197	1542	20
额敏县	Emin [Dorbiljin] County	26986	5820	1136	180	7276	1844	9268	1462	
沙湾县	Shawan County	51996	11288	705	145	23986	1043	6388	8406	34
托里县	Toli County	15494	5648	353	78	464	1518	7406	27	
裕民县	Yumin [Qagantokay] County	11495	3440	1041	174	723	448	5286	383	
和布克赛尔蒙古自治县	Hoboksar Mongol Autonomous County	13471	5235	810	144	872	1180	5204	17	
阿勒泰地区	**Altay Administrative Offices**	**76940**	**33566**	**3408**	**1462**	**4611**	**4667**	**25232**	**3934**	**47**
阿勒泰市	Altay City	17554	9645	962	396	504	454	5126	442	12
布尔津县	Burqin County	10819	4733	505	379	1310	595	2561	736	
富蕴县	Fuyun [Koktokay] County	14387	4140	720	360	270	978	6620	1273	26
福海县	Fuhai [Burultokay] County	11638	3994	247	66	2278	734	3934	383	2
哈巴河县	Habahe [Kaba] County	12490	7913	364	111	128	624	2975	368	7
青河县	Qinghe [Qinggil] County	5083	1335	306	60	88	1019	1653	622	
吉木乃县	Jeminay County	4969	1806	304	90	33	263	2363	110	
博尔塔拉蒙古自治州	**Bortala Mongol Autonomous Prefecture**	**22915**	**4174**	**529**	**66**	**6145**	**1069**	**8923**	**1950**	**26**
博乐市	Bole [Bortala] City	10495	1938	157	33	3955	216	3002	1177	1
精河县	Jinghe [Jing] County	5723	685	72	1	983	576	2860	540	6
温泉县	Wenquan [Araxang] County	6697	1551	300	32	1207	277	3061	233	19
巴音郭楞蒙古自治州	**Bayangol Mongol Autonomous Prefecture**	**93833**	**16817**	**1205**	**415**	**27621**	**6767**	**29266**	**10798**	**201**
库尔勒市	Korla City	20024	2366	2		6059	571	4461	6440	42
轮台县	Luntai [Bugur] County	9236	684	10		2789	1352	3697	641	3
尉犁县	Yuli [Lopnur] County	6193	934	13		606	2061	1853	687	15
若羌县	Ruoqiang [Qarkilik] County	2087	193	13	1	668	105	903	122	10
且末县	Qiemo [Qarqan] County	9127	1966	107	124	1251	1363	3798	131	39
焉耆回族自治县	Yanqi Hui Autonomous County	12593	4419	139		2893	132	3909	931	81
和静县	Hejing County	22487	5212	716	88	7194	399	8394	428	8
和硕县	Hoxud County	6738	592	182	186	2572	678	1537	976	
博湖县	Bohu [Bagrax] County	5348	451	23	16	3589	106	714	442	3
阿克苏地区	**Aksu Administrative Offices**	**215811**	**47811**	**3809**	**446**	**31005**	**16620**	**50041**	**54775**	**89**
阿克苏市	Aksu City	53346	10530	224		14264	1858	8805	17036	71
温宿县	Wensu [Onsu] County	23823	4530	546	17	2430	2292	6431	7226	
库车县	Kuqa County	53437	14065	1028		4543	4671	13292	8353	

12-27 续表 2 Continued

单位：吨 (ton)

地 区	Region	合 计 Total	#牛 Beef	#马 Horse	#骆 驼 Camels	#猪 Pork	#山 羊 Goats	#绵 羊 Sheep	#禽 肉 Poultry Meat	#兔 肉 Rabbit Meat
沙雅县	Xayar County	13066	2713	180		2296	1850	2333	3184	18
新和县	Xinhe [Toksu] County	8404	2431	188		203	164	2207	2870	
拜城县	Baicheng [Bay] County	24439	4800	320	15	5488	1910	7116	4194	
乌什县	Wushi [Uxturpan] County	17234	4668	1205	180	381	2560	4185	3185	
阿瓦提县	Awat County	18839	3570	70		1400	725	4533	8250	
柯坪县	Kalpin County	3223	504	48	234		590	1139	477	
克孜勒苏柯尔克孜自治州	**Kizilsu Kirgiz Autonomous Prefecture**	**39990**	**14522**	**1601**	**342**	**906**	**3287**	**14909**	**4418**	**5**
阿图什市	Artux City	15840	6210	285	45	580	1324	5396	2000	
阿克陶县	Akto County	14049	6461	65	60	177	820	4722	1744	
阿合奇县	Akqi County	4661	767	900	42	149	728	1975	100	
乌恰县	Wuqia [Ulugqat] County	5440	1084	351	195		415	2816	574	5
喀什地区	**Kashgar [Kaxgar] Administrative Offices**	**380380**	**84884**	**560**	**140**	**24000**	**3671**	**161073**	**97407**	
喀什市	Kashgar [Kaxgar] City	26816	6549			3600	111	14437	2074	
疏附县	Shufu County	37934	11696	30	10	3248	372	17302	4721	
疏勒县	Shule County	39182	9781	20	20	4392	63	14248	9463	
英吉沙县	Yengisar County	20719	7900	30	30	296	49	8071	3778	
泽普县	Zepu [Poskam] County	25526	3198	20		4720	99	7229	10020	
莎车县	Shache [Yarkant] County	57723	9935	20		2896	388	25042	19147	
叶城县	Yecheng [Kagilik] County	54034	11833	120	30	1152	507	21149	17548	
麦盖提县	Makit County	22441	4070	50		1440	328	12052	4206	
岳普湖县	Yopurga County	15669	3523	20		144	231	6109	4712	
伽师县	Jiashi [Payzawat] County	43104	5917	140		272	611	20350	13514	
巴楚县	Bachu [Maralbexi] County	32022	7336	80		1840	495	13662	8224	
塔什库尔干塔吉克自治县	Taxkorgan Tajik Autonomous County	5210	3146	30	50		417	1422		
和田地区	**Hotan Administrative Offices**	**115615**	**23664**	**649**	**391**	**2011**	**2827**	**54415**	**31570**	**88**
和田市	Hotan City	14129	2548		17	1537	63	5148	4816	
和田县	Hotan County	15380	3808	143	68	68	161	6506	4625	1
墨玉县	Moyu [Karakax] County	28244	7854	77	17	15	115	12214	7941	11
皮山县	Pishan [Guma] County	12872	1469	44	51	68	302	6084	4825	29
洛浦县	Lop County	10696	2772	11	17	60	70	5165	2600	1
策勒县	Qira County	8848	819	66	68	105	309	5997	1480	4
于田县	Yutian [Keriya] County	20277	3965	286	102	75	990	9902	4917	40
民丰县	Minfeng [Niya] County	5169	429	22	51	83	817	3399	366	2
生产建设兵团	**Xinjiang Production and Construction Group**	**337015**	**46460**	**1615**	**364**	**167083**	**6586**	**71403**	**38898**	**3218**

12-28 水产品产量和养殖面积
Output of Aquatic Products and Cultured Area

年 份 Year	地 区 Region	水产品产量(吨) Aquatic Products (ton)	#养殖产量 Cultured Output	养殖面积(公顷) Culture Area (hectare)
1985		8958	3403	32775
1990		23217	15401	68838
1995		44432	35341	72538
1996		47890	38876	79006
1997		52366	42656	75895
1998		53391	44557	67473
1999		55840	48068	70524
2000		60065	50974	69806
2001		60876	50902	63340
2002		63906	55159	62629
2003		67278	57244	67374
2004		73296	60405	74996
2005		79320	65571	76037
2006		84539	71440	76606
2007		88879	78639	77590
2008		92587	82040	73909
2009		97037	87863	73433
2010		101063	90913	73289
2011		116916	103315	74000
2012		125283	112590	71108
2013		131704	118551	70707
乌鲁木齐市	Urumqi City	6792	6792	1119
克拉玛依市	Karamay City	775	419	330
吐鲁番地区	Turpan Administrative Offices	409	409	43
哈密地区	Hami [Kumul] Administrative Offices	1212	1176	774
昌吉回族自治州	Changji Hui Autonomous Prefecture	18360	18360	3069
伊犁哈萨克自治州	Ili Kazak Autonomous Prefecture	25940	22723	19967
伊犁州直属县(市)	Counties (Cities) Direct Under Ili Prefecture	14661	14475	1257
塔城地区	Tacheng [Tarbagatai] Administrative Offices	3142	2631	2932
阿勒泰地区	Altay Administrative Offices	8137	5617	15778
博尔塔拉蒙古自治州	Bortala Mongol Autonomous Prefecture	2047	1002	1155
巴音郭楞蒙古自治州	Bayangol Mongol Autonomous Prefecture	11266	4801	2900
阿克苏地区	Aksu Administrative Offices	14606	13876	1307
克孜勒苏柯尔克孜自治州	Kizilsu Kirgiz Autonomous Prefecture	581	581	100
喀什地区	Kashgar [Kaxgar] Administrative Offices	10592	10259	8652
和田地区	Hotan Administrative Offices	2291	2051	487
生产建设兵团	Xinjiang Production and Construction Group	36833	36102	30804

12-29 乡镇企业主要指标
Main Indicators of Township Enterprises

单位：万元 (10 000 yuan)

年 份 Year	地 区 Region	企业个数（个） Number of Enterprises (unit)	从业人数（人） Employees of Enterprises (person)	总产值 Total Output Value
	1985	98826	367753	75179
	1990	144281	464027	222218
	1991	145762	472332	314765
	1992	155711	498132	402139
	1993	202274	600687	553616
	1994	250037	686425	924082
	1995	281130	745291	1319217
	1996	282733	781784	1622442
	1997	43548	355585	1219032
	1998	269048	712490	2457410
	1999	297147	749205	2736766
	2000	316524	806368	3022076
	2001	334694	824499	3316049
	2002	307963	866661	3629499
	2003	354640	880874	4119555
	2004	368553	933473	4562898
	2005	366883	954411	4994156
	2006	368724	990365	5574730
	2007	377385	1037023	4265895
	2008	378343	1063023	8629234
	2009	378983	1115703	8486719
	2010	383653	1167548	9574341
	2011	391680	1219552	12067084
	2012	398340	1271549	14102422
	2013	402951	1328364	16589649
乌鲁木齐市	Urumqi City	20111	68930	1396613
克拉玛依市	Karamay City	141	596	11602
石河子市	Shihezi City	3212	23504	208966
吐鲁番地区	Turpan Administrative Offices	21366	51245	427560
哈密地区	Hami [Kumul] Administrative Offices	10556	31880	283900
昌吉回族自治州	Changji Hui Autonomous Prefecture	39716	154025	4446946
伊犁州直属县(市)	Counties (Cities) Direct Under Ili Prefecture	52622	175822	2196386
塔城地区	Tacheng [Tarbagatai] Administrative Offices	26941	115442	1999512
阿勒泰地区	Altay Administrative Offices	25140	63224	494403
博尔塔拉蒙古自治州	Bortala Mongol Autonomous Prefecture	8945	37451	451662
巴音郭楞蒙古自治州	Bayangol Mongol Autonomous Prefecture	26075	117216	2601377
阿克苏地区	Aksu Administrative Offices	49749	145889	705477
克孜勒苏柯尔克孜自治州	Kizilsu Kirgiz Autonomous Prefecture	9468	22358	124046
喀什地区	Kashgar [Kaxgar] Administrative Offices	64700	177285	864144
和田地区	Hotan Administrative Offices	44209	143497	377055

12-29 续表 Continued

单位：万元 (10 000 yuan)

年份 Year	地区 Region	营业收入 Business Income	利润总额 Total Profits	上缴税金 Total Taxes
	1985	105072	9357	3136
	1990	249906	8614	5206
	1991	299890	25974	13747
	1992	374810	34644	16976
	1993	584089	51880	27354
	1994	957701	75439	69494
	1995	1493924	110656	76479
	1996	1927425	136410	76479
	1997	1128271	43337	48945
	1998	2455629	156578	82365
	1999	2742029	164949	93490
	2000	3071497	191764	100444
	2001	3377589	211439	108864
	2002	3739524	225723	126732
	2003	4276322	264661	137880
	2004	4757808	304998	152243
	2005	5164593	294021	164604
	2006	5806803	332070	190833
	2007	6776709	318943	228386
	2008	7548573	563293	249122
	2009	8547580	671806	271759
	2010	9596967	756277	306105
	2011	12287481	937847	374096
	2012	14250102	1083776	420174
	2013	16522535	1215432	474829
乌鲁木齐市	Urumqi City	1296817	61068	32714
克拉玛依市	Karamay City	11602	1533	638
石河子市	Shihezi City	223257	7289	2983
吐鲁番地区	Turpan Administrative Offices	404263	42831	18694
哈密地区	Hami [Kumul] Administrative Offices	260550	16520	13885
昌吉回族自治州	Changji Hui Autonomous Prefecture	4136821	285777	108531
伊犁州直属县(市)	Counties (Cities) Direct Under Ili Prefecture	2342951	182315	43147
塔城地区	Tacheng [Tarbagatai] Administrative Offices	1814163	200691	49820
阿勒泰地区	Altay Administrative Offices	561850	46661	17982
博尔塔拉蒙古自治州	Bortala Mongol Autonomous Prefecture	445698	14085	9318
巴音郭楞蒙古自治州	Bayangol Mongol Autonomous Prefecture	3028099	175239	116720
阿克苏地区	Aksu Administrative Offices	743059	54810	24490
克孜勒苏柯尔克孜自治州	Kizilsu Kirgiz Autonomous Prefecture	126505	8845	4353
喀什地区	Kashgar [Kaxgar] Administrative Offices	772615	74902	17952
和田地区	Hotan Administrative Offices	354285	42866	13602

主要统计指标解释

农林牧渔业总产值　指以货币表现的农、林、牧、渔业全部产品和对农林牧渔业生产活动进行的各种支持性服务活动的价值总量，它反映一定时期内农林牧渔业生产总规模和总成果。1957年以前的农林牧渔业总产值中包括了厩肥和农民自给性手工业(如农民自制衣服、鞋、袜，自己从事粮食初步加工等)。1958年及以后，林业中增加了村及村以下竹木采伐产值；牧业中取消了厩肥产值；副业中取消了农民自给性手工业产值，增加了村及村以下办的工业产值；渔业中增加了海洋捕捞水产品产值。1980年及以后，在副业中增加了农民家庭兼营工业商品部分的产值。从1984年起村及村以下工业产值划归工业。从1993年起取消副业，将野生动物的捕猎划入牧业，野生植物采集和农民家庭兼营商品性工业划归农业。从2003年起，执行新的国民经济行业分类标准，农林牧渔业总产值中包括了农林牧渔服务业产值。林业中增加了森林采运业产值。农业中取消了家庭兼营商品性工业产值，将野生林产品的采集划归林业。

农林牧渔业总产值的计算方法通常是按农、林、牧、渔业产品及其副产品的产量分别乘以各自单位产品价格求得；少数生产周期较长，当年没有产品或产品产量不易统计的，则采用间接方法匡算其产值；然后将四业产品产值及农林牧渔服务业产值相加即为农林牧渔业总产值。

粮食产量　指农业生产经营者日历年度内生产的全部粮食数量。按收获季节包括夏收粮食、早稻和秋收粮食，按作物品种包括谷物、薯类和豆类。其产量计算方法：谷物按脱粒后的原粮计算，豆类按去豆荚后的干豆计算；薯类(包括甘薯和马铃薯，不包括芋头和木薯)1963年以前按每4公斤鲜薯折1公斤粮食计算，从1964年开始改为按5公斤鲜薯折1公斤粮食计算。城市郊区作为蔬菜的薯类(如马铃薯等)按鲜品计算，并且不作粮食统计。1989年以前全国粮食产量数据主要靠全面报表取得，1989年开始使用抽样调查数据。

棉花产量　指全社会的产量。包括春播棉和夏播棉。产量按皮棉计算。不包括木棉。

油料产量　指全部油料作物的生产量。包括花生、油菜籽、芝麻、向日葵籽、胡麻籽(亚麻籽)和其他油料。不包括大豆、木本油料和野生油料。花生以带壳干花生计算。

水产品产量　指渔业（捕捞和养殖）生产活动的最终有效成果，包括全部海水和淡水鱼类、甲壳类（虾、蟹）、贝类、头足类、藻类和其他类渔业产品的最终产量。水产品产量是通过各级水产和统计部门逐级上报取得数据。1995 年及以前，贝类中牡蛎按鲜肉计算；蚶、蛤、蛙按 5 斤鲜品折 1 斤计算。1996 年以后则统一按鲜品计算。

猪、牛、羊肉产量　指当年出栏并已屠宰、除去头蹄下水后带骨肉(即胴体重)的重量。包括全社会范围内的产量。1996年以前为全面统计并逐级上报数据。1999年以后，国家统计局在部分地区开展了猪、牛、羊、禽等主要畜禽品种的抽样调查，并用抽样数据作为国家定案数据使用。2008年，建立了主要畜禽监测调查制度，猪、牛、羊、禽等主要畜禽数据均以抽样调查数为法定数据。

期初(末)畜禽存栏头(只)数　指报告期初(末)农村各种合作经济组织和国营农场、农民个人、机关、团体、学校、工矿企业、部队等单位以及城镇居民饲养的大牲畜、猪、羊、家禽等畜禽的存栏数。数据上报方式及数据调整情况同猪、牛、羊肉产量。

农作物播种面积　指农业生产经营者应在日历年度内收获农作物在全部土地（耕地或非耕地）上的播种或移植面积。凡是本年内收获的农作物，无论是本年还是上年播种，都算为播种面积，但不包括本年播种，下年收获的农作物面积。

有效灌溉面积　指具有一定的水源，地块比较平整，灌溉工程或设备已经配套，在一般年景下能够进行正常灌溉的耕地面积。在一般情况下，有效灌溉面积应等于灌溉工程或设备已经配备，能够进行正常灌溉的水田和水浇地面积之和。它是反映我国农田水利建设的重要指标。

农用化肥施用量　指本年内实际用于农业生产的化肥数量，包括氮肥、磷肥、钾肥和复合肥。化肥施用量要求按折纯量计算数量。折纯量是指把氮肥、磷肥、钾肥分别按含氮、含五氧化二磷、含氧化钾的百分之百成份进行折算后的数量。复合肥按其所含主要成分折算。公式为：

折纯量= 实物量×某种化肥有效成份含量的百分比

农业机械总动力　指全部农业机械动力的额定功率之和。农业机械是指用于种植业、畜牧业、渔业、农产品初加工、农用运输和农田基本建设等活动的机械及设备。农机总动力按使用能源不同分为以下四部分：

柴油发动机动力：指全部柴油发动机额定功率之和；

汽油发动机动力：指全部汽油发动机额定功率之和；

电动机动力：指全部电动机（含潜水电泵的电动机）额定功率之和；

其他机械动力：指采用柴油、汽油、电力之外的其他能源，如水力、风力、煤炭、太阳能等动力机械功率之和。这个指标的统计数据主要来源于农机部门。

Explanatory Notes on Main Statistical Indicators

Gross Output Value of Agriculture, Forestry, Animal Husbandry and Fishery refers to the total value of products of agriculture, forestry, animal husbandry and fishery, and total value of services in support of agriculture, forestry, animal husbandry and fishery activities. It reflects the total scale and results of agricultural production during a given period. Prior to 1957, China's gross agricultural output value included barnyard manure and handicraft products for self-consumption (clothes, shoes, stockings, and initial grain processing undertaken by peasants). Since 1958, cutting and felling of bamboo and trees by villages and other cooperative organizations under villages have been included in forestry; value of barnyard manure has been excluded from animal husbandry; self consumed handicrafts have not been included from sideline occupations, while the output value of industries run by villages and cooperative organizations under village has been included in sideline occupations; and the output value of fish catches by motor fishing boats has been added to fishery. Since 1980, the value of handicraft products made for sale by individuals in households has been added to sideline occupations. Since 1984, industries run by villages and under villages have been included in the sector of industry. Since 1993, the subdivision of sideline occupations has been cancelled, and the hunting of wild animals has been classified into animal husbandry, and the gathering of wild plants and commodity industry run by rural household have been included in farming. A new industrial classification of economic activities was introduced in 2003. Under the new classification, value of services to agriculture, forestry, animal husbandry and fishery is included in the gross output value of agriculture, value of wood felling and transport is included in forestry, value of industrial output by rural households is not included in agriculture.

Gross output value of agriculture is obtained by multiplying the output of each product or by-product by its price, resulting in the output value of each single item. For a small number of products, annual output of which is not available or difficult to get due to the long production (growing) process involved, the output value is estimated through an indirect approach. The sum of output values of all products of agriculture, forestry, animal husbandry and fishery and services in support to those industries is then equal to the gross output value of agriculture.

Grain Output refers to the total output of grains produced by agricultural producers within a calendar year. It includes summer grain, early rice and autumn grain if classified by harvest seasons; it covers cereal, tubers and beans if classified by type of crops. Output of cereal should be limited to husked grain only. Output of beans refers to dry beans without pods. The output of tubers (sweet potatoes and potatoes, not including taros and cassava) are converted into that of grain at the ratio 4:1, i.e. 4 kilograms of fresh tubers were equivalent to 1 kilogram of grain up to 1963. Since 1964 the ratio for conversion has been 5:1. Tubers supplied as vegetables (such as potatoes) in cities and suburbs are calculated as fresh vegetables and their output is not included in the output of grain. Data on grain production before 1989 were obtained through the Comprehensive Statistical Reporting System. Since 1989, data from sample surveys are used.

Cotton Output refers to cotton production in the whole country including cotton planted in spring and in autumn. Output is measured as the weight of ginned cotton. Ceiba is not included.

Output of Oil-bearing Crops refers to the total production of oil-bearing crops of various kinds, including peanuts (dry, in shell), rapeseeds, sesame, sunflower seeds, flax seeds, and other oil-bearing crops. Soybeans, oil-bearing woody plants, and wild oil-bearing crops are not included.

Output of Aquatic Products refers to final output actually yielded from fishing production (fishery and breeding), including all output of marine and freshwater fish, crustaceans (shrimps, crabs), shellfish, cephalopod, seaweed and other fishery products. Data on output of aquatic products are reported by aquatic product and statistical agencies level by level. Before 1995, among the shellfish, oyster was counted as fresh meat; 5 kilograms of ark shell, clams and frogs are equivalent to 1 kilogram of fresh aquatic products; they have all been counted as fresh aquatic products since 1996.

Output of Pork, Beef, and Mutton refers to the meat of slaughtered hogs, cattle, sheep and goats with head, feet, and offal taken away. Data refers to the production of the whole country. Before 1996, it was a comprehensive reporting from the lower level to the upper one. The First Agricultural Census of China in 1996 revealed some discrepancy between the production of animal products from the annual reports and that from the census. Efforts were made to adjust the output value of animal husbandry to make the figures from the annual reports consistent with the census data. Since 1999, the NBS conducted sample surveys for the major animal husbandry products, such as hogs, cattle, sheep and goats and fowls, and the data from sample surveys are used as national finalized data. In 2008, A Monitoring and Survey Program was set up on main livestock, the data on the main livestock such as hog, cattle, sheep and poultry became the official data based on the sampling survey.

Number of Livestock or Poultry in Stock at Beginning (or End) of Period refers to the total number of large animals, pigs, sheep, fowls, etc. raised by rural cooperative organizations,

State farms, rural individuals, government agencies, schools, industrial and mining enterprises, army, and urban residents at the beginning (or end) of the reference period. Data reporting system and data adjustment are the same as that in the output of pork, beef and mutton.

Sown Area of Crops refers to area of all land (cultivated or non-cultivated area) sown or transplanted with crops that are harvested within the calendar year by agricultural producers. All crops harvested within the year are counted as sown area, regardless of being sown in this year or the previous year. Crops sown this year but will be harvested in the coming year are excluded.

Effective Irrigated Area refers to area of land that are effectively irrigated, i.e. relatively level land, where there are water sources or complete sets of irrigation facilities to lift and move adequate water for irrigation purpose under normal conditions. Under normal situations, irrigated area is the sum of watered fields and irrigated fields where irrigation systems or equipment have been installed for regular irrigation purpose. It is an important indicator to reflect the farmland water conservancy construction in China.

Consumption of Chemical Fertilizers in Agriculture refers to the quantity of chemical fertilizers applied in agriculture in the year, including nitrogenous fertilizer, phosphate fertilizer, potash fertilizer, and compound fertilizer. The consumption of chemical fertilizers is calculated in terms of volume of effective components by means of converting the gross weight of the respective fertilizers into weight containing effective component (e.g. nitrogen content in nitrogenous fertilizer, phosphorous pentoxide contents in phosphate fertilizer, and potassium oxide contents in potash fertilizer). Compound fertilizer is converted in regard to its major components. The formula is:

Volume of effective component= physical quantity× effective component of certain chemical fertilizer (%)

Total Power of Agricultural Machinery refers to the total rated capacity of all agricultural machinery. Agricultural machinery refers to the machineries and equipments which are used for activities of planting, animal husbandry, fishery, primary processing of agricultural products, agricultural transport and infrastructure construction of farmland. Total power of agricultural machinery is grouped into four parts according to the energy used:

Diesel engine power refers to the total rated capacity of all diesel engines.

Gasoline engine power refers to the total rated capacity of all gasoline engines.

Motor power refers to the total rated capacity of all motors (include submersible pump motors).

Other mechanical powers refer to the total mechanical capacity of the sources of energy besides diesel, gasoline and motor power, such as hydro power, wind power, coal and solar energy.

Data are mainly from agricultural machinery agencies.

新疆统计年鉴
XINJIANG STATISTICAL YEARBOOK

13

工 业

INDUSTRY

简要说明

本篇主要内容和资料来源

本篇资料反映了新疆工业的基本情况，主要包括：按登记注册类型、轻重工业、企业规模、工业行业大类等分组的主要经济指标，指标包括：单位数、工业总产值、资产总计、负债合计、主营业务收入、主营业务成本、主营业务税金及附加、利润总额、应交增值税、总资产贡献率、资产负债率、成本费用利润率、全员劳动生产率、主要工业产品产量等。

本章还包括国有控股工业企业、大中型工业企业的主要经济指标，按工业行业大类、轻重工业、企业规模等主要分组数据。

本篇资料的统计范围：

1984年以前农村的村及村以下办工业归属农业，1984年以后划归工业。

1999年以前，工业的统计范围按隶属关系划分为乡及乡以上独立核算工业企业和非独立核算生产单位、村办工业、城镇合作工业、农村合作工业、城镇个体工业、农村个体工业六大部分（1984年以前村办工业不在工业统计范围内）。

2000年及以后，工业统计调查范围由按隶属关系划分，改变为按企业规模划分。2000年至2006年，分为全部国有及年主营业务收入在500万元及以上非国有工业企业（简称“规模以上”）和年主营业务收入在500万元以下非国有工业企业（简称“规模以下”）两部分。

2007年-2010年，分为年主营业务收入在500万元及以上法人工业企业（简称“规模以上”）和年主营业务收入在500万元以下法人工业企业和全部个体经营工业单位（简称“规模以下”）两部分。

2011年，分为年主营业务收入在2000万元及以上法人工业企业（简称“规模以上”）和年主营业务收入在2000万元以下法人工业企业和全部个体经营工业单位（简称“规模以下”）两部分。

本篇资料中工业行业分类按2011年《国民经济行业分类标准》划分；2010年以前企业大中小型划分执行《统计上大中小型企业划分办法（暂行）》标准；自2011年开始，大中小微型企业划分标准执行《国家统计局关于印发统计上大中小微型企业划分办法的通知》（国统字[2011]75号）。

本篇资料由新疆维吾尔自治区统计局工业交通统计处根据工业统计年度报表中有关资料整理提供。

Brief Introduction

Main Content and Source of Data

Data in this chapter reflect the basic condition of industrial sector including the gross industrial output and indices of industrial enterprises; Main indicator on economic and economic benefit of industrial enterprises above designated size by status of registration, light & heavy industries, size of enterprises, industrial sector. Main indicators including number of enterprises, gross industrial output value, value added of industry, total assets, total liabilities, revenue from principal business, cost of principle business, taxes and other charges on principal business, total profits, value added tax payable, ratio of total assets to industrial output value, assets liability ration, ratio of profits to cost, output of major industrial products, main economic indicator of state-owned and non-state-owned industrial enterprises.

This chapter covers main indicators on economic and economic benefit of all state-owned and non-state-owned industrial enterprises, cooperative enterprises, industrial enterprises with funds from Hong Kong, Macao and Taiwan, foreign funded industrial enterprises, and large & medium-sized enterprises.

Statistical scope of data:

Prior to 1984,the rural industry run by villages and cooperative organization under village was classified into agriculture. Since 1984,it has been grouped into industry.

Before 1999,industrial statistics covered six parts,i.e. on output of major industrial products is all industrial enterprises.

Since 2000,the scope of industrial was classificated from by type of registration to by size of enterprises.From 2000 to 2006,the scope of industrial statistics were grouped into two parts, all state-owned industrial enterprises,non-state-owned industrial enterprises with revenue from principal business over 5million yuan (or the industrial enterprises above designated size) and all industrial enterprises with revenue from principal business below 5million yuan (or the industrial enterprises below designated size)

From 2007 to 2010,the scope of indrstrial statistics were all industrial enterprises with revenue from principal business over 5million yuan (or the industrial enterprises above designated size) and all industrial enterprises with revenue from principal business below 5million yuan (or the industrial enterprises below designated size)

Since 2011, the scope of indrstrial statistics were all industrial enterprises with revenue from principal business over 20 million yuan (or the industrial enterprises above designated size) and all industrial enterprises with revenue from principal business below 20 million yuan (or the industrial enterprises below designated size)

Data by branch of industry in this chapter are based on the 2011's National Industrial Classification of all Economic Activities,and data by size of enterprise are based on the 2011's standards of Enterprises by size.

Data in this chapter are collected and compiled by the Department of Industry and transport, XBS in accordance with the annual report of industrial statistics.

13-1 主要年份工业总产值
Gross Industrial Output Value in Main Years

单位:亿元 (100 million yuan)

年　份 Year	工业总产值 Gross Industrial Output Value	国有工业 State-owned Enterprises	集体工业 Collective-owned Enterprises	其它经济类型工业 Enterprises of Other Types of Ownership
1978	33.91	30.22	3.69	
1980	40.71	36.20	4.50	0.01
1985	86.78	73.18	11.93	1.67
1990	219.92	176.52	36.72	6.68
1995	593.43	461.31	89.24	42.88
2000	1061.29	258.93	72.78	729.58
2005	2358.83	236.18	17.29	2105.36
2006	2894.88	272.06	16.14	2606.68
2007	3471.51	358.28	17.29	3095.94
2008	4639.02	387.53	15.70	4235.79
2009	4184.50	404.01	15.61	3764.88
2010	5766.51	382.00	25.54	5358.97
2011	7105.31	654.79	29.44	6421.08
2012	7886.25	713.43	20.41	7152.41
2013	9121.22	589.70	13.62	8517.89

13-2 主要年份工业总产值指数
Indices of Gross Industrial Output Value in Main Years

(1978 年=100)

年　份 Year	工业总产值 Gross Industrial Output Value	国有工业 State-owned Enterprises	集体工业 Collective-owned Enterprises	其它经济类型工业 Enterprises of Other Types of Ownership
1978	100.0	100.0	100.0	
1980	117.7	118.0	113.2	(1981 年=100)
1985	220.6	199.5	428.2	851.7
1990	380.3	326.0	915.9	2096.1
1995	670.8	506.1	2104.5	7441.5
2000	1000.4	227.3	1763.6	66265.2
2005	1821.8	218.2	388.9	160072.4
2006	2057.1	246.3	344.8	180922.4
2007	2322.8	319.9	339.3	201240.8
2008	2707.5	336.5	272.4	237624.5
2009	2942.2	353.4	289.2	259031.4
2010	3331.8	325.7	431.9	298801.3
2011	3721.3	527.1	451.7	323156.5
2012	4271.9	576.4	328.3	373388.6
2013	5152.3	479.2	234.6	464817.2

13-3 规模以上工业企业分行业工业增加值

Value-added of Industrial Enterprises above Designated Size by Sector

单位：万元 (10000 yuan)

行业	Sector	2012	2013
总计	**Total**	**27241641.4**	**29338650.4**
按行业分	**Grouped by Industrial Sector**		
煤炭开采和洗选业	Mining and Washing of Coal	1421680.7	1359334.6
石油和天然气开采业	Extraction of Petroleum and Natural Gas	12000740.1	12054715.4
黑色金属矿采选业	Mining and Processing of Ferrous Metals Ores	510977.7	714757.1
有色金属矿采选业	Mining and Processing of Nonferrous Metals Ores	411084.2	421547.8
非金属矿采选业	Mining and Processing of Nonmetal Ores	70077.1	81315.4
开采辅助活动	Mining Activities	780382.0	1042542.9
农副食品加工业	Processing of Food from Agricultural Products	490161.9	625522.4
食品制造业	Manufacture of Food	279449.2	432689.7
酒、饮料和精制茶制造业	Manufacture of Wine,Beverages and Refined Tea	370536.8	389638.8
烟草制品业	Manufacture of Tobacco	276304.7	298779.1
纺织业	Manufacture of Textile	240076.8	262426.5
纺织服装、服饰业	Manufacture of Textile Wearing Apparel, Footware and Caps	15727.3	12971.2
皮革、毛皮、羽毛(绒)及其制品业	Leather, Fur, Feather and Related Products Manufacturing	15855.5	19624.8
木材加工及木、竹、藤、棕、草制品业	Processing of Timber, Wood, Bamboo, Cane, Grass Products	16489.0	19792.1
家具制造业	Manufacture of Furniture	10222.3	5130.1
造纸及纸制品业	Manufacture of Paper and Paper Products	52812.4	70043.5
印刷业和记录媒介的复制	Printing and Copying of Medium for Record	16297.5	17810.1
文教、工美、体育和娱乐用品制造业	Manufacture of Articles for Culture,Education,Sports and Entertainment	13306.7	15891.3
石油加工、炼焦及核燃料加工业	Oil Processing, Coking and Nuclear Fuel Processing	2135694.8	3089950.5

13-3 续表 Continued

单位: 万元 (10000 yuan)

行　业	Sector	2012	2013
化学原料及化学制品制造业	Raw Chemical Material and Chemical Products	2020278.1	2002654.2
医药制造业	Manufacture of Medicine	52322.7	59820.1
化学纤维制造业	Manufacture of Chemical Fiber	128137.1	179474.8
橡胶和塑料制品业	Manufacture of Rubber Products	187141.1	223731.5
非金属矿物制品业	Manufacture of Nonmetal Mineral Products	818196.0	968058.6
黑色金属冶炼及压延加工业	Smelting and Pressing of Ferrous Metals	899757.0	592452.0
有色金属冶炼及压延加工业	Smelting and Pressing of Nonferrous Metals	564780.3	910871.0
金属制品业	Manufacture of Metal Products	88202.6	123312.2
通用设备制造业	Manufacture of General Purpose Machinery	29255.8	53311.4
专用设备制造业	Manufacture of Special Purpose Machinery	74051.7	116485.4
汽车制造业	Manufacture of Automobile	6058.5	7903.4
铁路、船舶、航空航天和其他运输设备制造业	Manufouture of Railroads,Ships,Aerospace and Other Transportation Equipment	1310.6	647.8
电气机械及器材制造业	Manufacture of Electric Equipment and Machinery	345111.3	523947.7
计算机、通信和其他电子设备制造业	Manufalture of Communication Equipment Computers and Other Electronic Equipment	472.7	514.9
仪器仪表制造业	Manufacture of Measuring Instruments	1226.7	1030.9
其他制造业	Others	-2970.9	-8599.5
废弃资源综合利用业	Recycling and Disposal of Waste	24600.6	29522.8
金属制品、机械和设备修理业	Manufacture and Repair of Metal Products and Machinery	5290.6	3741.8
电力、热力生产和供应业	Production and Supply of Electricity and Therma	2717733.4	2427749.1
燃气生产和供应业	Production and Supply of Gas	118854.7	143034.7
水的生产和供应业	Production and Supply of Water	33954.1	44502.4

13-4 规模以上工业企业主要经济指标

单位: 万元 (2013 年)

项目	Item	企业单位数(个) Number of Enterprises (unit)	#亏损企业 Loss- Suffering Enterprises	工业总产值(当年价格) Gross Industrial Output Value (At Current Prices)
总计	**Total**	**2224**	**604**	**86796304.7**
按登记注册类型分	**By Status of Registration**			
内资企业	Domestic Funded Enterprises	2145	582	85097744.2
国有企业	State-owned Enterprises	75	26	5355843.8
#中央企业	Central Enterprises	34	7	4316188.2
地方企业	Local Enterprises	41	19	1039655.6
#自治区属企业	Autonomous	14	9	679905.1
地区(州、市)属企业	Prefecture or City	6	1	93705.8
县(市)属企业	County or City	16	7	86603.0
集体企业	Collective-owned Enterprises	9	1	112444.4
#自治区属企业	Autonomous	4	1	82825.4
地区(州、市)属企业	Prefecture or City	1		3653.8
县(市)属企业	County or City	3		19050.1
镇属企业	Town	1		6915.1
乡属企业	Village			
股份合作企业	Cooperative Enterprises			
联营企业	Joint Ownership Enterprises	3		20229.1
#国有联营企业	State Joint Ownership Enterprises	1		8891.4
集体联营企业	Collective Joint Ownership Enterprises			
国有与集体联营企业	Joint State-collective Enterprises	1		8519.7
其他联营企业	Other Joint Ownership Enterprises	1		2818.0
有限责任公司	Limited Liability Corporations	1098	296	32433795.1
#国有独资公司	State Sole funded Corporations	96	32	3943743.1
其他有限责任公司	Other Limited Liability Corporations	1002	264	28490052.0
股份有限公司	Share-holding Corporations Ltd.	105	30	34466759.5
私营企业	Private Enterprises	851	228	12681447.6
#私营独资企业	Private-funded Enterprises	23	5	157169.3
私营合伙企业	Private Partnership Enterprises	7	3	54863.5
私营有限责任公司	Private Limited Liability Corporations	788	210	10342786.2
私营股份有限公司	Private Share-holding Corporations Ltd.	33	10	2126628.6
港、澳、台商投资企业	Enterprises with Funds from Hong Kong, Macao and Taiwan	30	10	465526.1
外商投资企业	Foreign Funded Enterprises	49	12	1233034.4
在总计中: 国有控股企业	Of the Total : State-owned and State-holding Enterprises	600	173	56688937.3
在总计中: 农村工业	Of the Total : Rural Industry	6	2	23563.8
按轻、重工业分	**Grouped by Light & Heavy Industry**			
轻工业	Light Industry	718	172	10618119.7
以农产品为原料	Using Farm Produces as Raw Materials	665	159	10207660.5
以非农产品为原料	Using Non-Farm Produces as Raw Materials	53	13	410459.2
重工业	Heavy Industry	1506	432	76178185.0
采掘工业	Mining and Quarrying	293	98	20967733.1
原料工业	Raw Material Industry	605	222	43879312.5
加工工业	Manufacturing Industry	608	112	11331139.4
按企业规模分	**Grouped by Size of Enterprises (New Standard)**			
大型企业	Large Enterprises	97	34	54638604.7
中型企业	Medium-sized Enterprises	325	97	13228677.2
小型企业	Small Enterprises	1627	415	18209533.3
微型企业	Min Enterprises	175	58	719489.5

Main Economic Indicators of Industrial Enterprises above Designated Size

(10 000 yuan)

工业销售产值（当年价） Sales Value of Industry Products (At Current Prices)	出口交货值 Delivery Value of Industry Export	实收资本 Total Capital Hold	资产合计 Total Assets	流动资产合计 Total Working Capitals	#产成品 Finished Product	固定资产原价 Net Value of Fixed Assets
84478025.4	**680082.0**	**39102343.3**	**143312541.5**	**43328466.1**	**4758198.2**	**104348403.5**
82879470.8	612741.5	38332191.5	140883541.4	42319678.2	4578203.5	102840842.5
5191891.5	1989.1	1339793.0	8935033.6	2089931.4	67467.9	6420205.8
4283599.5		515989.9	5833736.3	1197412.4	34545.7	4407641.9
908292.0	1989.1	823803.1	3101297.3	892519.0	32922.2	2012563.9
549751.0		544732.5	1688319.3	355291.3	15661.9	1068312.6
91765.2		52284.7	716007.9	361510.5	3410.4	459626.2
84116.2		199891.9	429175.8	50861.5	4277.3	400392.7
110901.2		10275.4	75549.0	56840.5	6140.9	24067.4
79311.5		4359.2	44934.9	34035.6	4539.4	9962.7
3618.3		272.1	737.4	614.0	105.3	396.6
21056.3		5449.1	21237.0	17572.9	1496.2	8979.8
6915.1		195.0	8639.7	4618.0		4728.3
19175.6		8556.6	45264.8	14297.5	1087.5	31489.8
7646.5		1720.0	9281.3	4695.0	762.9	1889.2
8519.7		6700.0	34096.1	8929.4		27883.3
3009.4		136.6	1887.4	673.1	324.6	1717.3
31317616.4	134984.5	13578956.0	63693000.3	19707555.0	2233760.5	38785432.1
3799151.5	1968.8	2852995.5	10368729.6	3289973.6	154443.6	6582717.1
27518464.9	133015.7	10725960.5	53324270.7	16417581.4	2079316.9	32202715.0
34308967.5	120290.2	20044775.6	48014686.1	10800292.0	1063294.6	50461150.4
11903434.3	355477.7	3341046.9	20089897.7	9642972.0	1205564.9	7095506.2
150802.4		15141.7	154779.8	69836.6	17302.5	90415.2
53160.4		4233.2	24319.4	10506.5		15216.8
9623838.4	111889.0	2711670.5	15394739.7	7158901.8	1137509.1	6060210.2
2075633.1	243588.7	610001.5	4516058.8	2403727.1	50753.3	929664.0
418163.9	39180.9	236475.5	700160.6	352834.0	78294.7	454844.4
1180390.7	28159.6	533676.3	1728839.5	655953.9	101700.0	1052716.6
55970581.5	162644.2	30233706.7	91014942.9	21010668.0	2011895.5	82045751.9
20901.2	813.9	56044.2	102622.1	13520.2	2928.3	10682.9
10103970.3	336924.3	3325682.4	14689545.0	7063341.0	1336185.7	7099173.9
9725379.7	325478.9	2906837.6	13185828.9	6442327.5	1293704.5	6430700.2
378590.6	11445.4	418844.8	1503716.1	621013.5	42481.2	668473.7
74374055.1	343157.7	35776660.9	128622996.5	36265125.1	3422012.5	97249229.6
20804597.8	4882.0	17734238.4	41238368.0	8356586.8	609228.7	44231160.9
42764311.9	167576.3	14743008.6	67675098.4	18560787.3	2178120.0	46402995.9
10805145.4	170699.4	3299413.9	19709530.1	9347751.0	634663.8	6615072.8
53769929.6	139231.5	26372936.5	83193725.8	20363732.9	1930109.0	73130431.1
12631464.8	306721.6	5624385.3	27852004.8	10140425.2	1111811.1	13624695.4
17402749.3	222317.1	6649525.3	30103062.5	12057124.1	1651949.0	16435603.2
673881.7	11811.8	455496.2	2163748.4	767183.9	64329.1	1157673.8

13-4 续表

单位：万元

项　目	Item	负债合计 Total Liabilities	#流动负债 Total Liquid Liabilities	#非流动负债 Total Non-liquid Liabilities	所有者权益合计 Total Owners' Equities
总　计	**Total**	**87797652.5**	**57554010.5**	**27637256.1**	**55347427.8**
按登记注册类型分	**By Status of Registration**				
内资企业	Domestic Funded Enterprises	86427101.6	56445134.4	27508804.1	54294157.3
国有企业	State-owned Enterprises	5331958.1	2698173.8	2232728.5	3596525.8
#中央企业	Central Enterprises	3169068.1	1968873.5	1194566.7	2658197.5
地方企业	Local Enterprises	2162890.0	729300.3	1038161.8	938328.3
#自治区属企业	Autonomous	1108767.3	298521.0	414909.0	579551.9
地区(州、市)属企业	Prefecture or City	652399.1	241749.6	410649.3	63608.8
县(市)属企业	County or City	227162.6	71470.2	155602.1	201934.5
集体企业	Collective-owned Enterprises	34975.4	33479.7	1093.7	40573.6
#自治区属企业	Autonomous	23299.6	22226.9	670.7	21635.3
地区(州、市)属企业	Prefecture or City	188.2	188.2		549.2
县(市)属企业	County or City	8441.3	8018.3	423.0	12795.7
镇属企业	Town	3046.3	3046.3		5593.4
乡属企业	Village				
股份合作企业	Cooperative Enterprises				
联营企业	Joint Ownership Enterprises	28963.0	6400.0	22563.0	16301.8
#国有联营企业	State Joint Ownership Enterprises	4543.0	4543.0		4738.3
集体联营企业	Collective Joint Ownership Enterprises				
国有与集体联营企业	Joint State-collective Enterprises	23306.7	746.7	22560.0	10789.4
其他联营企业	Other Joint Ownership Enterprises	1113.3	1110.3	3.0	774.1
有限责任公司	Limited Liability Corporations	44836153.9	30486635.6	13456887.8	18779490.0
#国有独资公司	State Sole funded Corporations	6976740.1	4435064.1	2164085.1	3386367.9
其他有限责任公司	Other Limited Liability Corporations	37859413.8	26051571.5	11292802.7	15393122.1
股份有限公司	Share-holding Corporations Ltd.	22802370.5	13417335.5	9277259.5	25178080.1
私营企业	Private Enterprises	13379864.7	9799011.3	2518271.6	6665892.1
#私营独资企业	Private-funded Enterprises	94060.3	81109.3	12746.7	60719.5
私营合伙企业	Private Partnership Enterprises	19391.3	19165.5	225.8	4928.0
私营有限责任公司	Private Limited Liability Corporations	10810393.7	7903040.2	1845491.4	4540274.6
私营股份有限公司	Private Share-holding Corporations Ltd.	2456019.4	1795696.3	659807.7	2059970.0
港、澳、台商投资企业	Enterprises with Funds from Hong Kong, Macao and Taiwan	403128.2	350667.0	31081.8	293536.2
外商投资企业	Foreign Funded Enterprises	967422.7	758209.1	97370.2	759734.3
在总计中：国有控股企业	Of the Total : State-owned and State-holding Enterprises	52101451.1	30895710.8	20131011.7	38847414.7
在总计中：农村工业	Of the Total : Rural Industry	45172.1	12352.6	32819.5	57449.8
按轻、重工业分	**Grouped by Light & Heavy Industry**				
轻工业	Light Industry	9591222.2	7558149.0	1118176.0	5081551.1
以农产品为原料	Using Farm Produces as Raw Materials	8629547.2	7165468.0	907411.0	4539557.6
以非农产品为原料	Using Non-Farm Produces as Raw Materials	961675.0	392681.0	210765.0	541993.5
重工业	Heavy Industry	78206430.3	49995861.5	26519080.1	50265876.7
采掘工业	Mining and Quarrying	21871486.6	13577154.5	8195308.9	19354201.3
原料工业	Raw Material Industry	44041339.2	27505011.7	15206774.0	23535325.7
加工工业	Manufacturing Industry	12293604.5	8913695.3	3116997.2	7376349.7
按企业规模分	**Grouped by Size of Enterprises (New Standard)**				
大型企业	Large Enterprises	48924233.6	30808003.4	17632436.7	34241827.8
中型企业	Medium-sized Enterprises	17478398.6	11759804.4	4706243.8	10306664.5
小型企业	Small Enterprises	19946510.9	14056997.5	4833900.8	10093554.2
微型企业	Min Enterprises	1448509.4	929205.2	464674.8	705381.3

Continued

(10 000 yuan)

主营业务收入 Revenue from Principal Business	主营业务成本 Cost of Principal Business	主营业务税金及附加 Taxes and Other Charges on Principal Business	营业利润 Business Profit	利润总额 Total Profit	亏损企业亏损总额 Losses Value of Loss-Suffering Enterprises	利税总额 Total Profits and Taxes	本年应交增值税 Value-added Taxes Payable	全部从业人员年平均人数(人) Annual Average Employed Persons (person)
87187056.8	**67946768.9**	**3298760.1**	**7934489.6**	**8552294.7**	**1345810.2**	**15346023.1**	**3494968.3**	**675747**
85506022.3	66606631.6	3283623.7	7809654.0	8415076.2	1313438.3	15138131.2	3439431.3	656552
5256043.9	4690426.5	183531.8	176021.4	191290.1	59060.9	577303.9	202482.0	42549
4299576.1	3799106.8	180358.1	222719.1	202622.4	12479.0	556847.4	173866.9	31879
956467.8	891319.7	3173.7	-46697.7	-11332.3	46581.9	20456.5	28615.1	10670
565907.6	535549.1	1714.9	-36906.2	-27363.1	34006.5	-9991.7	15656.5	4775
117774.6	129983.0	116.2	-22266.3	-1601.3	8187.5	-198.1	1287.0	2198
81288.2	63226.3	534.4	-896.9	-0.7	3775.3	6372.7	5839.0	1940
116042.1	104467.1	883.2	5292.6	5502.7	133.6	11656.4	5270.5	2136
81881.2	77268.6	398.1	1874.1	1770.2	133.6	5373.8	3205.5	1559
3618.3	3453.0	8.0	11.5	10.1		84.5	66.4	76
23627.5	19304.5	240.8	2275.5	2593.5		3919.6	1085.3	341
6915.1	4441.0	236.3	1131.5	1128.9		2278.5	913.3	160
17937.9	8250.5	505.2	6370.5	6392.5		8306.6	1408.9	193
7646.7	3721.1	479.1	2630.8	2632.6		4258.7	1147.0	55
7281.8	1977.0		3700.5	3699.1		3699.1		12
3009.4	2552.4	26.1	39.2	60.8		348.8	261.9	126
31434759.4	26817661.0	467290.7	1140239.2	1541672.6	665921.0	3258055.6	1249092.3	336620
3907117.7	3382493.2	37330.6	59436.1	188706.3	103137.3	444587.5	218550.6	68351
27527641.7	23435167.8	429960.1	1080803.1	1352966.3	562783.7	2813468.1	1030541.7	268269
36587186.2	25122889.9	2577830.8	5506435.0	5588831.9	407159.0	9876909.4	1710246.7	156824
12066086.3	9841824.3	53487.7	970280.7	1077694.0	179583.9	1401788.4	270606.7	117933
154945.7	109778.6	1764.5	24166.2	23809.2	1843.6	40470.4	14896.7	2097
56537.8	39991.8	242.8	6790.2	5943.1	325.5	13884.5	7698.6	721
9760593.5	8217124.8	42937.8	694801.1	794485.3	166157.4	1061516.1	224093.0	106280
2094009.3	1474929.1	8542.6	244523.2	253456.4	11257.4	285917.4	23918.4	8835
440393.4	356414.6	1134.0	11241.7	19185.8	11653.2	33108.9	12789.1	8834
1240641.1	983722.7	14002.4	113593.9	118032.7	20718.7	174783.0	42747.9	10361
58372725.4	43925957.1	3140604.5	5990803.9	6460499.5	938755.0	12257806.2	2656702.2	386644
24458.7	20821.5	64.2	4.3	685.7	659.1	1378.7	628.8	211
10296932.2	8493344.1	244119.6	584511.2	709501.2	200895.2	1233063.6	279442.8	133113
9933295.3	8194653.9	241199.6	609890.1	726068.8	159701.5	1232580.0	265311.6	122892
363636.9	298690.2	2920.0	-25378.9	-16567.6	41193.7	483.6	14131.2	10221
76890124.6	59453424.8	3054640.5	7349978.4	7842793.5	1144915.0	14112959.5	3215525.5	542634
22052688.6	12071586.0	1273503.3	5908315.8	5952425.9	200421.1	9032028.1	1806098.9	200191
43734162.1	38485850.9	1717231.4	533878.7	852349.5	862483.3	3659646.3	1090065.4	251386
11103273.9	8895987.9	63905.8	907783.9	1038018.1	82010.6	1421285.1	319361.2	91057
55820679.0	42242469.1	3074514.7	5964737.6	6187834.1	660807.3	11668338.4	2405989.6	316347
12741839.6	10205730.1	110567.0	801930.2	963185.7	327434.9	1598074.6	524321.9	170689
17925158.0	14924068.6	110528.6	1119681.4	1327261.3	333930.7	1990701.8	552911.9	182261
699380.2	574501.1	3149.8	48140.4	74013.6	23637.3	88908.3	11744.9	6450

13-5 按行业分规模以上工业企业主要经济指标

单位：万元　　　　(2013 年)

行　业	Sector	企业单位数(个) Number of Enterprises (unit)	#亏损企业 Loss- Suffering Enterprises	工业总产值(当年价格) Gross Industrial Output Value (At Current Prices)
总　计	**Total**	**2224**	**604**	**86796304.7**
煤炭开采和洗选业	Mining and Washing of Coal	121	44	2362426.8
石油和天然气开采业	Extraction of Petroleum and Natural Gas	5		13847366.9
黑色金属矿采选业	Mining and Processing of Ferrous Metals Ores	74	31	1495546.1
有色金属矿采选业	Mining and Processing of Nonferrous Metals Ores	36	9	634448.8
非金属矿采选业	Mining and Processing of Nonmetal Ores	30	13	215645.2
#采　盐	Extraction of Salt	4		44832.7
农副食品加工业	Processing of Food from Agricultural Products	306	58	3949988.6
#谷物磨制	Grain Grinding	55	7	498314.7
饲料加工	Fodder Processing	33	7	662769.9
制　糖	Sugar Making	13	8	258997.0
食品制造业	Manufacture of Food	121	34	1834795.9
#罐头制造	Manufacture of can	48	17	290461.9
酒、饮料和精制茶制造业	Manufacture of Wine,Beverages and Refined Tea	67	13	1053251.8
#酒的制造	Manufacture of Wine	49	8	668345.8
烟草制品业	Manufacture of Tobacco	1		402140.7
纺织业	Manufacture of Textile	82	32	1258401.8
#棉、化纤纺织及印染精加工	Cotton, Chemical Fiber, Dyeing, Printing and Processing	74	28	1189497.5
毛纺织和染整精加工	Wool Textile, Dyeing and Printing	3	2	32250.7
纺织服装、鞋、帽制造业	Manufacture of Textile Wearing Apparel, Footware and Caps	8	1	39577.3
皮革、毛皮、羽毛(绒)及其制品业	Leather, Fur, Feather and Related Products Manufacturing	4	1	73050.1
#皮革鞣制加工	Leather Tanning and Processing	4	1	73050.1
木材加工及木、竹、藤、棕、草制品业	Processing of Timber, Wood, Bamboo, Cane, Grass Products	12	3	84528.3
家具制造业	Manufacture of Furniture	6	2	35033.5
造纸及纸制品业	Manufacture of Paper and Paper Products	29	9	304621.7
印刷业和记录媒介的复制	Printing and Copying of Medium for Record	10	1	49586.6
石油加工、炼焦及核燃料加工业	Oil Processing, Coking and Nuclear Fuel Processing	96	33	17295757.9
#炼　焦	Coking	60	18	1314227.8
化学原料及化学制品制造业	Raw Chemical Material and Chemical Products	156	36	6163109.5
#基础化学原料制造	Basic Chemical Material	40	14	1665313.7
肥料制造	Fertilizer Making	40	7	1315021.6
合成材料制造	Manufacture of Synthetic Materials	20	6	2673021.7
医药制造业	Manufacture of Medicine	24	2	238725.3
化学纤维制造业	Manufacture of Chemical Fiber	15	6	987149.6
橡胶和塑料制品业	Manufacture of Rubber Products	106	13	1276271.4
非金属矿物制品业	Manufacture of Nonmetal Mineral Products	342	103	3888497.6
#水泥制造	Manufacture of Cement	88	44	1533572.9
黑色金属冶炼及压延加工业	Smelting and Pressing of Ferrous Metals	91	55	7281798.4
有色金属冶炼及压延加工业	Smelting and Pressing of Nonferrous Metals	49	14	5155995.8
金属制品业	Manufacture of Metal Products	76	19	1092643.7
通用设备制造业	Manufacture of General Purpose Machinery	23	5	206039.3
专用设备制造业	Manufacture of Special Purpose Machinery	27	2	539217.3
汽车制造业	Manufacture of Automobile	8	5	319610.6
电气机械及器材制造业	Manufacture of Electric Equipment and Machinery	45	5	3548593.0
计算机、通信和其他电子设备制造业	Telecom Equipment, Computer and Other Electronic Equipment	1		3341.5
仪器仪表制造业	Measuring Instruments and Machinery for Cultural Activify and Office Work	1		4594.5
金属制品、机械和设备修理业	Manufacture and Repairing of Metal Prodults,Mouhinery and Equipment	2		19166.5
电力、热力的生产和供应业	Electricity and Thermal Production and Supply	171	44	7889487.3
#电力生产和电力供应	Electricity Production and Supply	133	30	7649777.7
燃气生产和供应业	Gas Production and Supply	28	2	592173.4
水的生产和供应业	Water Production and Supply	12	6	78021.8

Main Economic Indicators of Industrial Enterprises above Designated Size by Sectors

(10 000 yuan)

工业销售产值(当年价) Sales Value of Industry Products (At Current Prices)	出口交货值 Delivery Value of Industry Export	实收资本 Total Capital Hold	资产合计 Total Assets	流动资产合计 Total Working Capitals	#产成品 Finished Product	固定资产原价 Original Value of Fixed Assets
84478025.4	**680082.0**	**39102343.3**	**143312541.5**	**43328466.1**	**4758198.2**	**104348403.5**
2337060.7		1900855.7	7867744.9	2037989.6	176630.2	3442282.1
13776199.9		13673524.9	25560382.1	2669133.5	152887.7	36869369.2
1443052.0	14.5	444981.9	2884250.1	1465930.9	187739.6	1051023.4
623248.9		395731.0	1691542.5	440989.6	48882.0	946072.4
206129.0	1681.5	74367.2	310446.8	164480.1	33250.4	123363.2
45312.1		16307.1	56406.7	32132.4	6319.5	20334.2
3726058.6	30650.6	750192.4	3655191.9	2223612.9	607860.8	1330628.8
501904.0		61812.0	329534.2	196421.0	29789.8	104357.8
655865.4		79173.2	436819.2	225155.9	34875.5	162207.2
262641.8		72847.3	363651.7	208870.4	124579.3	268593.0
1838858.0	197055.4	724239.7	2800249.5	1077611.4	190736.7	1845634.4
325133.8	167888.5	177861.4	858837.2	461835.9	133993.8	604550.3
1006045.4	3.5	364007.3	1364769.4	712401.1	82489.6	677673.4
638294.3	3.5	282321.7	1050142.8	622857.8	68581.6	426172.3
382123.7		18741.7	454809.0	236210.0	6940.0	133167.0
1187602.1	38606.7	654964.0	2536918.5	1142900.7	194015.5	1302964.5
1120662.9	27913.7	553237.7	2305040.6	1073731.7	179147.9	1199945.8
31181.2	10693.0	62748.0	104109.5	33692.6	4609.0	51144.0
37623.1	12276.7	15539.0	55618.2	36013.9	6875.9	13896.6
70794.1		6556.5	55629.1	46523.8	3935.9	11188.4
70794.1		6556.5	55629.1	46523.8	3935.9	11188.4
76424.9		21169.1	99027.9	52380.5	13271.6	46480.9
38430.7	18948.1	70158.0	327665.9	66405.9	3625.6	33821.7
284541.0	950.0	59620.0	448868.2	176548.7	28960.2	206616.2
49863.3		18526.3	92194.3	43155.0	6483.1	66878.9
17159126.6		5008834.6	10104037.5	3868096.5	622158.2	9056292.6
1253258.0		579562.7	2448559.6	951761.5	187439.5	1193739.2
6112346.6	17682.5	3086487.5	13952582.9	3265052.9	350537.6	9412995.4
1628747.9	2333.6	711834.1	4190612.3	1209411.0	90273.7	2585883.6
1315953.0		820948.5	4121030.3	723683.3	69914.9	2703517.4
2663514.1	15167.6	1398394.3	4900824.4	938723.6	159495.2	3876542.3
219268.9	6024.6	74794.2	424111.2	266098.1	35267.2	99612.4
899882.9	21280.1	177966.9	1168968.8	529885.0	141535.9	750226.8
1184211.7	16697.8	283936.6	1124781.7	678017.7	140309.2	414460.6
3706397.6	8.6	1930663.1	9558339.5	3301216.7	256640.0	4597280.0
1471641.8	8.6	1336097.4	5834000.7	1444283.7	95769.4	3064828.6
6932864.3	13003.5	1601010.8	9159745.5	3702530.5	633466.3	4745430.9
4668715.5	137063.0	1018622.2	10505555.6	3547122.5	539292.4	4394981.0
968812.9	5393.9	255197.7	977515.2	552651.6	69020.4	280236.8
187923.2	707.1	54454.2	259527.7	188766.4	16304.9	45908.0
511656.8	10804.6	83652.4	627604.0	369650.0	54761.2	233032.4
315[illegible]4.9	91.5	155478.2	380732.1	147269.4	8063.1	117834.2
3479335.4	133056.7	751783.8	7213717.0	4355822.7	104730.9	588406.6
4485.7	3824.8	1000.0	3553.5	1567.9	125.4	479.4
3900.0		3000.0	15114.7	6864.8	466.9	270.3
19087.1		1924.9	21329.4	18162.9	3013.8	5125.0
7859565.8		3592627.6	22443477.3	3574365.7	11495.5	18430679.0
7608783.9		3314815.8	20990670.9	2933088.5	7772.6	17357217.1
503142.9		164141.4	979986.6	390703.7	4094.4	610802.5
77574.6		298653.8	986355.5	315700.2	96.6	453357.2

13-5 续表

单位：万元

行　业	Sector	负债合计 Total Liabilities	#流动负债 Total Liquid Liabilities	#非流动负债 Total Non-liquid Liabilities	所有者权益合计 Total Owners' Equities
总　计	**Total**	**87797652.5**	**57554010.5**	**27637256.1**	**55347427.8**
煤炭开采和洗选业	Mining and Washing of Coal	5128486.4	3616188.0	1497739.5	2734512.7
石油和天然气开采业	Extraction of Petroleum and Natural Gas	11681604.0	5598177.1	6083426.9	13878778.1
黑色金属矿采选业	Mining and Processing of Ferrous Metals Ores	2072605.1	1847478.3	151708.3	810825.1
有色金属矿采选业	Mining and Processing of Nonferrous Metals Ores	867261.6	596619.0	269268.4	824280.7
非金属矿采选业	Mining and Processing of Nonmetal Ores	205660.7	190012.5	5976.9	104142.6
#采　盐	Extraction of Salt	17472.2	14721.6	2602.6	38934.4
农副食品加工业	Processing of Food from Agricultural Products	2368378.4	2180944.9	140775.9	1286053.9
#谷物磨制	Grain Grinding	190418.6	181484.2	7519.5	140424.0
饲料加工	Fodder Processing	185969.9	153814.4	31664.0	250848.1
制　糖	Sugar Making	212474.7	203231.1	7298.8	151177.0
食品制造业	Manufacture of Food	1975196.6	1861136.6	86267.0	849104.6
#罐头制造	Manufacture of can	787780.2	754078.8	31646.6	68874.6
酒、饮料和精制茶制造业	Manufacture of Wine,Beverages and Refined Tea	846440.4	604078.5	222200.5	490938.7
#酒的制造	Manufacture of Wine	665447.6	448337.7	210783.8	384649.5
烟草制品业	Manufacture of Tobacco	118220.0	117220.0	1000.0	336589.0
纺织业	Manufacture of Textile	1693077.1	1117137.0	158597.9	833427.0
#棉、化纤纺织及印染精加工	Cotton, Chemical Fiber, Dyeing, Printing and Processing	1587256.3	1023274.9	146639.3	707369.9
毛纺织和染整精加工	Wool Textile, Dyeing and Printing	25476.6	18031.8	7444.8	78632.9
纺织服装、鞋、帽制造业	Manufacture of Textile Wearing Apparel, Footware and Caps	42812.7	34676.2	8136.4	12805.5
皮革、毛皮、羽毛(绒)及其制品业	Leather, Fur, Feather and Related Products Manufacturing	41823.6	37634.6	4189.0	13805.5
#皮革鞣制加工	Leather Tanning and Processing	41823.6	37634.6	4189.0	13805.5
木材加工及木、竹、藤、棕、草制品业	Processing of Timber, Wood, Bamboo, Cane, Grass Products	55198.8	49056.7	6142.1	43828.9
家具制造业	Manufacture of Furniture	78771.9	62841.6	15930.3	248894.0
造纸及纸制品业	Manufacture of Paper and Paper Products	304327.4	252427.7	16968.6	144540.6
印刷业和记录媒介的复制	Printing and Copying of Medium for Record	44028.3	35317.6	8710.7	48166.0
石油加工、炼焦及核燃料加工业	Oil Processing, Coking and Nuclear Fuel Processing	4874229.3	4102044.2	722744.3	5186569.1
#炼　焦	Coking	1715691.4	1446447.5	219921.7	713441.7
化学原料及化学制品制造业	Raw Chemical Material and Chemical Products	8901846.0	4757816.5	4120815.8	5042080.9
#基础化学原料制造	Basic Chemical Material	2835861.9	1806358.8	1018648.1	1354230.4
肥料制造	Fertilizer Making	2794345.3	1464044.5	1321328.9	1318549.8
合成材料制造	Manufacture of Synthetic Material	2867121.3	1125012.8	1742108.2	2033703.0
医药制造业	Manufacture of Medicine	252145.8	197251.0	50431.5	171961.6
化学纤维制造业	Manufacture of Chemical Fiber	977390.0	736493.7	235576.7	189367.8
橡胶和塑料制品业	Manufacture of Rubber Products	630454.7	510780.1	80180.9	494280.7
非金属矿物制品业	Manufacture of Nonmetal Mineral Products	5873719.1	4294342.6	1299743.5	3634050.0
#水泥制造	Manufacture of Cement	3380931.2	2341454.3	981898.7	2426689.3
黑色金属冶炼及压延加工业	Smelting and Pressing of Ferrous Metals	7094916.1	6132364.8	951988.7	2052105.9
有色金属冶炼及压延加工业	Smelting and Pressing of Nonferrous Metals	7857500.8	5012391.8	2270860.3	2646660.1
金属制品业	Manufacture of Metal Products	633766.3	524139.9	111503.8	356609.1
通用设备制造业	Manufacture of General Purpose Machinery	191562.5	178849.7	7184.6	67358.8
专用设备制造业	Manufacture of Special Purpose Machinery	362353.2	343838.3	18323.1	265250.6
汽车制造业	Manufacture of Automobile	242291.4	221694.4	20597.0	138440.7
电气机械及器材制造业	Manufacture of Electric Equipment and Machinery	4233034.8	3251865.2	978408.8	2974532.2
计算机、通信和其他电子设备制造业	Telecom Equipment, Computer and Other Electronic Equipment	2182.2	2182.2		1371.3
仪器仪表制造业	Measuring Instruments and Machinery for Cultural Activify and Office Work	4066.9	3667.3	399.6	11047.8
金属制品、机械和设备修理业	Manufacture and Repairing of Metal Products, Machinery and Equipment	17284.0	17284.0		4045.4
电力、热力的生产和供应业	Electricity and Thermal Production and Supply	14775945.8	6647251.2	7505397.2	7653356.3
#电力生产和电力供应	Electricity Production and Supply	13644315.8	6126465.6	6907140.9	7332180.9
燃气生产和供应业	Gas Production and Supply	636947.2	395867.7	238656.2	342768.8
水的生产和供应业	Water Production and Supply	592489.0	163681.7	87029.5	393866.5

Continued

(10 000 yuan)

主营业务收入 Revenue from Principal Business	主营业务成本 Cost of Principal Business	主营业务税金及附加 Taxes and Other Charges on Principal Business	营业利润 Business Profit	利润总额 Total Profit	亏损企业亏损总额 Losses Value of Loss-Suffering Enterprises	利税总额 Total Profits and Taxes	本年应交增值税 Value-added Taxes Payable	全部从业人员年平均人数(人) Annual Average Employed Persons (person)
87187056.8	**67946768.9**	**3298760.1**	**7934489.6**	**8552294.7**	**1345810.2**	**15346023.1**	**3494968.3**	**675747**
2376752.6	1755381.5	62950.6	170881.1	142791.5	125249.5	453149.0	247406.9	57348
14946302.0	6657069.0	1130726.8	5232711.9	5283222.8		7602060.8	1188111.2	70848
1492341.5	978556.0	40734.6	266129.1	271324.5	24012.3	456964.5	144905.4	13550
634657.4	348368.0	11589.8	184850.6	182155.4	11923.3	259132.7	65387.5	8989
197024.3	125255.3	4770.3	6698.4	8331.5	9572.4	29467.2	16365.4	4757
44211.5	13353.4	3273.3	6899.4	7141.9		15180.1	4764.9	973
3866780.9	3322697.5	4586.8	246750.2	281569.3	32241.8	344343.1	58187.0	30928
520905.2	475119.0	352.7	25196.5	28521.0	1329.4	31303.9	2430.2	2802
650455.4	543372.1	539.5	50889.6	54966.7	1757.7	62528.2	7022.0	3646
288624.2	255302.1	1530.7	-9881.8	-7572.9	11857.2	10661.6	16703.8	5912
1736637.2	1396998.8	5762.0	117422.0	133538.2	55689.1	196177.6	56877.4	22798
363413.8	307332.1	1269.0	-33024.0	-27096.6	45414.8	-12974.7	12852.9	5185
999289.7	673603.1	53472.4	145821.9	153646.1	11904.0	252131.3	45012.8	12802
638219.1	387061.0	52716.5	116972.5	124048.4	9138.9	216888.8	40123.9	9816
382124.0	129865.0	169165.0	61130.0	60910.0		271882.0	41807.0	977
1330662.0	1270808.8	4247.3	-22681.0	11795.5	40822.5	42671.4	26628.6	34484
1267448.7	1215873.8	3970.8	-22662.5	11331.2	36009.7	41044.8	25742.8	31752
29333.0	28192.3	205.2	-4787.6	-3934.5	4488.2	-3145.9	583.4	1601
42537.9	34422.8	149.6	2227.3	3808.1	40.1	4489.9	532.2	1796
74131.8	70495.6	151.9	2235.6	2386.5	154.6	3722.4	1184.0	476
74131.8	70495.6	151.9	2235.6	2386.5	154.6	3722.4	1184.0	476
78683.1	65289.5	358.4	6469.5	8158.4	638.5	11577.4	3060.6	1119
39336.3	35415.0	575.7	-3983.6	-3144.1	3546.1	-1917.3	651.1	1134
277990.9	232355.1	762.7	19132.2	27682.6	7691.7	35011.7	6566.4	5147
51749.9	38555.5	219.0	1575.0	4929.7	18.0	6180.7	1032.0	1526
17566910.2	14967906.2	1648737.0	24185.8	8664.7	429090.8	2050255.9	392854.2	39823
1242840.9	1060743.7	3236.8	68892.5	71007.9	44862.2	110715.8	36471.1	14335
6270912.8	5077433.1	52713.8	432018.9	453402.4	64148.2	787280.3	281164.1	65788
1833229.3	1552848.9	5072.3	56487.2	66223.1	26679.0	105818.7	34523.3	23628
1239488.1	763093.6	29175.8	221635.8	209258.1	25449.7	351935.9	113502.0	13648
2625853.8	2306882.8	15152.6	97070.5	117384.1	9810.0	240414.9	107878.2	20740
188492.4	119858.7	1210.8	13740.8	16639.4	1145.4	28167.1	10316.9	3913
945499.8	847168.1	1467.4	20905.0	27836.8	7339.8	49233.6	19929.4	8758
1236171.5	1042561.6	3046.9	83072.6	93939.7	2720.7	118466.3	21479.7	13224
3725571.9	3169365.4	15400.1	84365.3	147399.1	89841.6	328205.8	165406.6	58330
1482770.9	1253365.8	6305.4	-248.6	44000.0	60657.8	126439.0	76133.6	26051
7425715.3	7109878.8	14758.5	-153279.5	-74267.6	146414.2	42351.8	101860.9	47067
4542123.5	4017757.6	1279.9	197594.5	213713.8	38833.5	277782.0	62788.3	32102
896183.0	808498.1	3091.4	23058.7	37708.2	7968.2	50398.7	9599.1	8377
216112.8	169263.8	513.4	28676.6	29894.2	605.2	33304.0	2896.4	2579
557638.5	468358.4	1243.1	42467.8	49034.9	1203.7	57410.3	7132.3	4025
360287.8	351338.1	690.4	-17412.7	6762.7	15388.1	9193.8	1740.7	2333
3648548.2	2893999.1	11295.2	318239.7	365655.2	744.1	438209.2	61258.8	9673
4487.9	3941.1	0.7	98.8	275.8		283.0	6.5	78
3888.2	2570.5	18.6	925.0	922.0		1075.8	135.2	26
18346.6	17481.8	61.7	61.9	111.3		872.2	699.2	440
7809168.4	6898008.7	23137.4	296524.5	457364.2	147778.0	774385.4	293883.8	56411
7504037.7	6572573.1	22721.2	360643.6	455523.2	134181.4	769122.4	290878.0	49771
595038.0	432657.1	5633.4	64409.3	82843.1	282.4	97402.9	8926.4	4588
80758.2	60625.2	461.9	-7656.5	-2630.4	12497.3	1465.9	3634.4	2744

13-6 各地、州、市、县(市)规模以上工业企业主要经济指标

单位：万元 (2013 年)

地　区	Region	企业单位数(个) Number of Enterprises (unit)	#亏损企业 Loss- Suffering Enterprises	工业总产值(当年价格) Gross Industrial Output Value (At Current Prices)
总　计	**Total**	**2224**	**605**	**86796304.7**
乌鲁木齐市	**Urumqi City**	**389**	**101**	**24270069.6**
天山区	Tianshan District	15	4	3494815.7
沙依巴克区	Shayibak District	25	7	607826.5
新市区	Xinshi District	158	45	8853312.4
水磨沟区	Shui Mogou District	17	5	210343.6
头屯河区	Tou Tunhe District	51	9	5456201.9
达坂城区	Da Bancheng District	13	2	221822.9
米东区	Midong District	105	27	5375643.4
乌鲁木齐县	Urumqi County	5	2	50103.2
克拉玛依市	**Karamay City**	**70**	**13**	**17767730.5**
独山子区	Dushanzi District	11	4	6554616.3
克拉玛依区	Karamay District	48	9	11027010.3
白碱滩区	Bai Jiantan District	9		167205.5
乌尔河区	Urhe District	2		18898.4
吐鲁番地区	**Turpan Administrative Offices**	**104**	**41**	**2779491.4**
吐鲁番市	Turpan City	28	11	279485.0
鄯善县	Shanshan [Piqan] County	42	14	1847425.0
托克逊县	Toksun County	34	16	652581.4
哈密地区	**Hami [Kumul] Administrative Offices**	**113**	**24**	**2777813.7**
哈密市	Hami [Kumul] City	83	19	2309601.5
巴里坤哈萨克自治县	Barkol Kazak Autonomous County	20	4	186671.9
伊吾县	Yiwu [Araturuk] County	10	1	281540.3
昌吉回族自治州	**Changji Hui Autonomous Prefecture**	**364**	**79**	**9074961.2**
昌吉市	Changji City	117	9	3041945.4
阜康市	Fukang City	54	27	1877442.9
呼图壁县	Hutubi County	59	11	665714.1
玛纳斯县	Manas County	62	9	1366674.6
奇台县	Qitai County	36	8	552023.8
吉木萨尔县	Jimsar County	29	12	1501636.2
木垒哈萨克自治县	Mori Kazak Autonomous County	7	3	69524.2
伊犁哈萨克自治州	**Ili Kazak Autonomous Prefecture**	**436**	**127**	**7163899.5**
伊犁州直属县(市)	**Counties (Cities) Direct Under Ili Prefecture**	**243**	**74**	**4321426.6**
伊宁市	Yining [Gulja] City	34	7	525303.1
奎屯市	Kuytun City	52	24	1438110.8
伊宁县	Yining [Gulja] County	36	12	386901.6
察布查尔锡伯自治县	Qapqal Xibe Autonomous County	17	4	211128.4
霍城县	Huocheng [Korgas] County	39	8	403263.8
巩留县	Gongliu [Tokkuztara] County	16	3	227459.4
新源县	Xinyuan [Kunes] County	19	7	709784.4
昭苏县	Zhaosu [Mongolkure] County	12	2	132559.5
特克斯县	Tekes County	6	4	50845.8
尼勒克县	Nilka County	12	3	236069.8
塔城地区	**Tacheng [Tarbagatai] Administrative Offices**	**118**	**33**	**1688509.8**
塔城市	Tacheng [Qoqek] City	6	2	98660.9
乌苏市	Usu City	20	11	435490.3
额敏县	Emin [Dorbiljin] County	12	3	110875.3

Main Economic Indicators of Industrial Enterprises above Designated Size by Prefecture, Autonomous Prefecture, City and County

(10 000 yuan)

工业销售产值(当年价) Sales Value of Industry Products (At Current Prices)	出口交货值 Delivery Value of Industry Export	实收资本 Total Capital Hold	资产合计 Total Assets	流动资产合计 Total Working Capitals	#产成品 Finished Product	固定资产原价 Original Value of Fixed Assets
84478025.4	**680082.0**	**39102343.3**	**143312541.5**	**43328466.1**	**4758198.2**	**104348403.5**
23576028.2	**313037.5**	**8282565.9**	**36005073.4**	**11026544.3**	**842414.9**	**24764250.8**
3525356.4	47003.7	421807.3	5594548.8	1131491.7	31579.3	4762975.4
520921.3		466361.3	2570379.4	622824.5	10769.8	812618.3
8515468.5	238524.2	3732928.0	15164703.8	5072960.2	333242.2	11292131.3
216994.8		66506.1	389341.7	127535.0	11230.8	433219.7
5155436.0	16145.0	1006525.6	5607084.0	2107488.6	207966.0	2849688.4
216597.1		167690.9	783766.8	132749.5	20494.4	475342.5
5378059.3	11364.6	2373339.6	5626582.0	1777997.1	224454.1	3866959.8
47194.8		47407.1	268666.9	53497.7	2678.3	271315.4
17767201.6	**5543.1**	**12310374.8**	**20617523.0**	**5830336.6**	**316522.0**	**21954226.2**
6536964.3	2419.0	2894717.2	4881855.0	1859241.1	138176.3	4764520.2
11049579.2		9395387.7	15537453.7	3850927.0	167570.8	17106096.5
164747.0	3124.1	19009.9	173298.0	107591.9	9371.6	73054.3
15911.1		1260.0	24916.3	12576.6	1403.3	10555.2
2764824.3	**11422.0**	**819158.0**	**6410214.7**	**2099184.5**	**221325.5**	**6038822.3**
312492.4	11422.0	220629.3	919869.9	361174.8	49801.5	473191.3
1812711.8		247213.6	3210301.0	1046909.4	137203.6	4240155.0
639620.1		351315.1	2280043.8	691100.3	34320.4	1325476.0
2759930.1	**1650.3**	**1604519.7**	**7279036.5**	**2334708.1**	**168465.2**	**3677615.9**
2311956.7	1650.3	1078401.2	5029785.1	2030338.0	125377.5	2201698.2
168561.0		161183.5	815247.7	171326.3	32982.5	474307.8
279412.4		364935.0	1434003.7	133043.8	10105.2	1001609.9
8549871.3	**71972.1**	**3004264.1**	**17491155.7**	**5628501.2**	**831917.4**	**7877992.5**
2952661.1	43957.2	646416.3	4471420.3	1959240.2	153781.1	1433653.4
1764648.7		857626.9	4525382.5	1070674.6	196455.1	2705296.7
635689.5	2811.3	148186.2	591230.0	246718.5	54950.0	270290.5
1161439.9	10045.2	449233.6	2045080.4	935251.0	171930.1	1100758.6
490758.7	3843.8	119168.0	824111.4	325393.7	106841.4	265719.7
1498122.4	11314.6	776623.1	4954620.1	1042339.3	132170.5	2075532.4
46551.0		7010.0	79311.0	48883.9	15789.2	26741.2
6831062.9	**42591.5**	**3141457.7**	**15191721.7**	**4955171.0**	**725062.3**	**9073775.4**
4115395.4	**19087.0**	**2033923.1**	**9293889.9**	**2954267.6**	**430181.8**	**5598464.6**
519500.7	3058.3	142317.8	950356.8	243289.7	20107.2	801769.1
1356043.2	126.4	531969.1	2980393.1	1086269.4	137072.7	1794999.9
383211.6		145192.0	751041.5	299948.3	30808.4	285513.4
196965.9		57470.0	324361.9	117268.9	17249.2	176427.0
393971.3	15902.3	166910.4	530741.0	192150.3	50144.1	323537.6
227484.1		488783.2	1293513.3	230324.7	7242.0	713140.4
635247.6		220742.9	1164787.9	564987.0	142331.4	556808.5
119859.7		17860.0	88322.6	59980.0	12227.6	32552.3
48667.8		64600.0	243761.8	52556.1	5214.3	169744.0
234443.5		198077.7	966610.0	107493.2	7784.9	743972.4
1594029.4	**23504.5**	**584475.8**	**3132555.6**	**1276100.7**	**192501.3**	**1731469.1**
98885.2		13416.9	182308.6	31329.9	858.1	197423.2
426913.3	9275.5	105394.4	761261.7	412450.1	45752.5	337399.0
100349.4	5059.7	83437.9	273504.3	125833.0	40672.0	180026.7

13-6 续表 1

单位：万元

地　　区	Region	企业单位数（个） Number of Enterprises (unit)	#亏损企业 Loss- Suffering Enterprises	工业总产值（当年价格） Gross Industrial Output Value (At Current Prices)
沙湾县	Shawan County	51	8	586844.9
托里县	Toli County	14	6	236990.5
裕民县	Yumin [Qagantokay] County			
和布克赛尔蒙古自治县	Hoboksar Mongol Autonomous County	15	3	219647.9
阿勒泰地区	**Altay Administrative Offices**	**75**	**20**	**1153963.1**
阿勒泰市	Altay City	16	5	182286.4
布尔津县	Burqin County	10	2	69633.3
富蕴县	Fuyun [Koktokay] County	18	7	478293.5
福海县	Fuhai [Burultokay] County	13	1	90737.2
哈巴河县	Habahe [Kaba] County	8	2	250066.9
青河县	Qinghe [Qinggil] County	8	3	38417.5
吉木乃县	Jeminay County	2	0	44528.3
博尔塔拉蒙古自治州	**Bortala Mongol Autonomous Prefecture**	**67**	**22**	**619076.1**
博乐市	Bole [Bortala] City	40	13	381694.8
精河县	Jinghe [Jing] County	17	8	100810.7
温泉县	Wenquan [Araxang] County	1		3003.6
巴音郭楞蒙古自治州	**Bayangol Mongol Autonomous Prefecture**	**152**	**37**	**8819230.1**
库尔勒市	Korla City	61	19	6563661.1
轮台县	Luntai [Bugur] County	16	3	458217.7
尉犁县	Yuli [Lopnur] County	5	1	36742.2
若羌县	Ruoqiang [Qarkilik] County	7	2	431649.8
且末县	Qiemo [Qarqan] County	1	1	
焉耆回族自治县	Yanqi Hui Autonomous County	12	2	94638.3
和静县	Hejing County	35	8	1161148.5
和硕县	Hoxud County	10	1	49967.4
博湖县	Bohu [Bagrax] County	5		20393.5
阿克苏地区	**Aksu Administrative Offices**	**200**	**62**	**4943443.7**
阿克苏市	Aksu City	63	20	1226700.4
温宿县	Wensu [Onsu] County	23	6	141776.7
库车县	Kuqa County	45	15	2656403.2
沙雅县	Xayar County	14	2	218414.5
新和县	Xinhe [Toksu] County	10		115496.1
拜城县	Baicheng [Bay] County	29	16	459053.1
乌什县	Wushi [Uxturpan] County	5		25530.4

Continued

(10 000 yuan)

工业销售产值(当年价) Sales Value of Industry Products (At Current Prices)	出口交货值 Delivery Value of Industry Export	实收资本 Total Capital Hold	资产合计 Total Assets	流动资产合计 Total Working Capitals	#产成品 Finished Product	固定资产原价 Original Value of Fixed Assets
549289.8	9169.3	144557.6	650334.5	346555.6	62548.6	331820.0
210940.8		67274.8	516566.3	223532.1	22828.1	252313.8
207650.9		170394.2	748580.2	136400.0	19842.0	432486.4
1121638.1		**523058.8**	**2765276.2**	**724802.7**	**102379.2**	**1743841.7**
181777.5		39932.4	365768.6	76993.5	8535.7	343696.0
69816.1		45893.3	430181.7	75633.8	1212.8	324790.8
458520.9		225945.9	905631.3	274089.8	60587.2	495045.9
82692.2		81129.2	216551.1	78733.4	11552.7	144616.1
251354.7		52040.0	353513.5	99149.8	10994.7	202397.5
33340.2		40200.0	324038.4	82979.2	7778.2	114857.9
44136.5		37918.0	169591.6	37223.2	1717.9	118437.5
561406.9	**4588.7**	**253837.0**	**1325278.0**	**475282.2**	**73858.4**	**864468.9**
343615.1	4588.7	122997.5	666711.0	263111.7	48417.4	487085.1
89108.0		71037.0	358758.5	107366.1	17187.5	197252.6
2916.9		108.0	3132.0	2050.6	45.3	1344.9
8843408.1	**99021.6**	**4629867.9**	**14078661.6**	**2498751.6**	**361444.8**	**15845030.1**
6571180.1	29276.7	4022711.2	10061021.6	1107951.3	169213.0	13277734.4
455092.9	23310.7	141358.0	759900.7	346243.8	24410.1	436072.2
38114.4	1681.6	7410.0	35913.9	23117.3	3405.1	9971.0
475312.7		61999.9	861860.6	293778.0	27064.2	581217.4
			22.5	3.4		388.6
96050.0	8140.8	22228.0	135614.8	69251.0	17601.6	93644.4
1132863.1	5975.8	356043.0	2109870.9	590196.7	94911.4	1369621.4
50089.0	16166.0	9805.7	81283.0	50806.8	13451.8	40594.8
21894.3	14470.0	8312.1	33173.6	17403.3	11387.6	35785.9
4753617.0	**181.3**	**1792510.8**	**8194681.1**	**2705693.8**	**363788.9**	**4104597.3**
1126163.4	58.3	650897.4	3115510.5	1003878.5	116759.2	1328292.8
133679.5		82828.5	402324.5	72566.0	11271.9	325010.0
2630145.5	123.0	751682.3	2600351.4	727304.7	89363.2	1474629.2
212716.7		86668.4	384282.1	153353.8	36663.3	225520.8
91887.7		16180.0	151474.0	79288.5	12058.0	62163.5
447627.5		175779.2	1357523.8	594743.0	71934.4	577787.1
20260.6		6100.0	31256.7	15208.7	5328.9	18746.3

13-6 续表 2

单位: 万元

地　　区	Region	企业单位数(个) Number of Enterprises (unit)	#亏损企业 Loss- Suffering Enterprises	工业总产值(当年价格) Gross Industrial Output Value (At Current Prices)
阿瓦提县	Awat County	9	3	60935.2
柯坪县	Kalpin County	2		39134.1
克孜勒苏柯尔克孜自治州	**Kizilsu Kirgiz Autonomous Prefecture**	**28**	**13**	**332798.4**
阿图什市	Artux City	11	3	142529.8
阿克陶县	Akto County	7	3	98743.5
阿合奇县	Akqi County	1		21143.9
乌恰县	Wuqia [Ulugqat] County	9	7	70381.2
喀什地区	**Kashgar [Kaxgar] Administrative Offices**	**89**	**32**	**1213846.4**
喀什市	Kashgar [Kaxgar] City	24	10	516197.2
疏附县	Shufu County	3	2	9946.8
疏勒县	Shule County	12	2	97691.4
英吉沙县	Yengisar County	4	1	27509.6
泽普县	Zepu [Poskam] County	6	2	23846.1
莎车县	Shache [Yarkant] County	6	2	135711.4
叶城县	Yecheng [Kagilik] County	10	2	120769.2
麦盖提县	Makit County	6	5	24612.3
岳普湖县	Yopurga County	3	1	23101.5
伽师县	Jiashi [Payzawat] County	3		138444.4
巴楚县	Bachu [Maralbexi] County	9	5	57659.9
塔什库尔干塔吉克自治县	Taxkorgan Tajik Autonomous County	3		38356.6
和田地区	**Hotan Administrative Offices**	**24**	**8**	**272454.7**
和田市	Hotan City	9	3	131520.2
和田县	Hotan County	5	1	45726.7
墨玉县	Moyu [Karakax] County	2		49975.2
皮山县	Pishan [Guma] County	1	1	3961.5
洛浦县	Lop County	5	2	31771.4
策勒县	Qira County	1	1	1656.5
于田县	Yutian [Keriya] County	1		7843.2
民丰县	Minfeng [Niya] County			
自治区直辖县级市	**Municpality Country-LevelCity directly under the Central Government**	**185**	**45**	**6735624.3**
石河子市	Shihezi City	92	30	3872287.8
阿拉尔市	Aral City	32	3	360125.6
图木舒克市	Tumxuk City	20	2	252145.6
五家渠市	Wujiaqu City	41	10	2251065.3

Continued

(10 000 yuan)

工业销售产值(当年价) Sales Value of Industry Products (At Current Prices)	出口交货值 Delivery Value of Industry Export	实收资本 Total Capital Hold	资产合计 Total Assets	流动资产合计 Total Working Capitals	#产成品 Finished Product	固定资产原价 Original Value of Fixed Assets
52542.9		21575.0	129377.9	42036.5	13300.2	86516.3
38593.2		800.0	22580.2	17314.1	7109.8	5931.3
323380.8		**258153.8**	**934373.4**	**375267.1**	**79153.9**	**527689.3**
142349.6		163721.8	408501.1	207059.2	36347.3	203045.7
95106.0		59938.0	179110.5	93758.8	31432.2	56354.1
21143.9			171875.2	6145.4		167379.4
64781.3		34494.0	174886.6	68303.7	11374.4	100910.1
1205642.1	**103147.6**	**301821.8**	**1853728.2**	**656086.4**	**85016.7**	**1424549.5**
519674.9	1914.5	106130.1	838174.4	219879.1	11175.6	858525.2
10106.8		2300.0	8219.5	6019.3	359.0	3737.3
98255.0		26210.0	121506.1	71207.5	12784.7	54432.7
27864.7		38445.0	92119.9	19748.1	1267.5	69916.3
25120.1		15200.0	49488.4	21875.2	8011.6	21729.7
130201.9	99157.4	23650.0	139079.9	67640.0	10102.4	66069.8
116495.4	2061.2	45299.0	160101.1	54307.3	11766.7	119070.5
24612.3		14107.7	66663.4	49864.1	5177.7	12490.8
16789.5		1150.0	36952.7	24361.0	7663.3	12058.3
139806.7		4000.0	107547.7	40955.7	3341.2	63936.9
60979.8		17010.0	65714.4	34928.8	8641.6	37127.2
35735.0	14.5	8320.0	168160.7	45300.3	4725.4	105454.8
273436.9		**272126.0**	**852754.6**	**173109.7**	**14846.0**	**769040.5**
130028.5		17882.8	188227.7	34438.5	1617.0	240589.5
44975.7		156351.2	404088.3	72344.2	299.1	318711.1
52969.2		26737.0	68815.1	27479.8	3820.7	49647.9
3961.5		998.0	17895.1	8739.0	37.2	9379.2
30550.2		45927.0	97994.5	22698.7	7041.5	78909.2
1656.5		630.0	3313.7	1021.6		2644.4
9295.3		23600.0	72420.2	6387.9	2030.5	69159.2
6242546.6	**26926.3**	**2427188.9**	**13013388.6**	**4561056.1**	**673426.1**	**7381234.9**
3671159.3	22336.5	1496349.1	7871584.8	2691425.3	339408.5	4500189.0
344716.5	1042.8	130071.6	581217.8	186642.2	40342.7	443489.3
236586.5		74900.7	478051.0	229809.0	36070.1	250853.6
1990084.3	3547.0	725867.5	4082535.0	1453179.6	257604.8	2186703.0

13-6 续表 3

单位: 万元

地　　区	Region	负债合计 Total Liabilities	#流动负债 Total Liquid Liabilities	#非流动负债 Total Non-liquid Liabilities	所有者权益合计 Total Owners' Equities
总　计	**Total**	**87797652.5**	**57554010.5**	**27637256.1**	**55347427.8**
乌鲁木齐市	**Urumqi City**	**21348412.3**	**14658799.9**	**6275035.9**	**14656137.1**
天山区	Tianshan District	3390909.3	2013910.8	1376960.1	2203639.5
沙依巴克区	Shayibak District	1557384.4	858351.2	414389.3	1012995.0
新市区	Xinshi District	8388184.8	5967817.1	2349451.7	6775996.0
水磨沟区	Shui Mogou District	143093.6	93453.4	45980.2	246248.1
头屯河区	Tou Tunhe District	4188518.6	3508357.2	668943.4	1418565.4
达坂城区	Da Bancheng District	487076.2	250141.5	213188.3	296690.5
米东区	Midong District	2981112.7	1841675.6	1119083.5	2645468.7
乌鲁木齐县	Urumqi County	212132.7	125093.1	87039.4	56533.9
克拉玛依市	**Karamay City**	**9204631.0**	**5829218.4**	**3374148.3**	**11389078.7**
独山子区	Dushanzi District	2046779.7	1760962.4	285817.0	2835075.2
克拉玛依区	Karamay District	7037422.7	3954119.3	3083115.5	8476218.1
白碱滩区	Bai Jiantan District	110571.4	104825.4	4669.9	62726.4
乌尔河区	Urhe District	9857.2	9311.3	545.9	15059.0
吐鲁番地区	**Turpan Administrative Offices**	**3966610.0**	**2558070.9**	**1358449.8**	**2433840.5**
吐鲁番市	Turpan City	558211.1	455618.2	100519.6	361658.3
鄯善县	Shanshan [Piqan] County	1904241.8	1121722.7	761839.3	1298944.9
托克逊县	Toksun County	1504157.1	980730.0	496090.9	773237.3
哈密地区	**Hami [Kumul] Administrative Offices**	**5190166.5**	**3602654.9**	**1541481.3**	**2070899.2**
哈密市	Hami [Kumul] City	3618719.7	2482300.3	1108785.7	1404915.4
巴里坤哈萨克自治县	Barkol Kazak Autonomous County	529590.7	373349.4	153556.4	273836.2
伊吾县	Yiwu [Araturuk] County	1041856.1	747005.2	279139.2	392147.6
昌吉回族自治州	**Changji Hui Autonomous Prefecture**	**11827799.6**	**7710721.7**	**3907430.6**	**5626006.8**
昌吉市	Changji City	2449336.2	1910257.0	533598.0	2020175.4
阜康市	Fukang City	2906942.1	1500179.9	1293157.8	1614765.0
呼图壁县	Hutubi County	384183.2	314904.7	69487.5	206844.4
玛纳斯县	Manas County	1551167.3	1185811.8	349538.2	470341.4
奇台县	Qitai County	516294.2	456039.1	53571.1	306228.8
吉木萨尔县	Jimsar County	3965088.0	2291918.7	1604899.9	983129.4
木垒哈萨克自治县	Mori Kazak Autonomous County	54788.6	51610.5	3178.1	24522.4
伊犁哈萨克自治州	**Ili Kazak Autonomous Prefecture**	**10175538.5**	**6680896.4**	**2843606.3**	**4981466.0**
伊犁州直属县(市)	**Counties (Cities) Direct Under Ili Prefecture**	**6182955.5**	**3927457.3**	**1772275.4**	**3084749.6**
伊宁市	Yining [Gulja] City	644857.9	332209.8	309627.0	305468.6
奎屯市	Kuytun City	2008360.7	1359510.9	622668.4	963371.4
伊宁县	Yining [Gulja] County	540335.8	406632.3	125858.2	210582.9
察布查尔锡伯自治县	Qapqal Xibe Autonomous County	239125.1	168274.6	30899.6	78821.1
霍城县	Huocheng [Korgas] County	306221.6	247545.2	50760.7	224520.9
巩留县	Gongliu [Tokkuztara] County	773886.0	229420.1	149128.8	519548.5
新源县	Xinyuan [Kunes] County	735553.2	697775.7	37777.5	429234.5
昭苏县	Zhaosu [Mongolkure] County	60068.1	57351.6	20.7	28254.3
特克斯县	Tekes County	187600.0	87297.6	100066.8	56131.5
尼勒克县	Nilka County	686947.1	341439.5	345467.7	268815.9
塔城地区	**Tacheng [Tarbagatai] Administrative Offices**	**2287102.0**	**1787552.9**	**464285.4**	**837149.0**
塔城市	Tacheng [Qoqek] City	133076.1	80224.9	52761.0	48860.6
乌苏市	Usu City	585919.3	571677.6	11043.7	175342.3
额敏县	Emin [Dorbiljin] County	160086.6	98444.8	61641.8	110245.7

Continued

(10 000 yuan)

主营业务收入 Revenue from Principal Business	主营业务成本 Cost of Principal Business	主营业务税金及附加 Taxes and Other Charges on Principal Business	营业利润 Business Profit	利润总额 Total Profit	亏损企业亏损总额 Losses Value of Loss-Suffering Enterprises	利税总额 Total Profits and Taxes	本年应交增值税 Value-added Taxes Payable	全部从业人员年平均人数（人） Annual Average Employed Persons (person)
87187056.8	**67946768.9**	**3298760.1**	**7934489.6**	**8552294.7**	**1345810.2**	**15346023.1**	**3494968.3**	**675747**
23642414.5	**19370866.4**	**888206.0**	**1345385.1**	**1640404.3**	**441151.8**	**3262416.2**	**733805.9**	**134302**
3523132.9	3306864.2	8391.4	126887.3	134954.5	37811.2	257047.0	113701.1	16240
616232.2	551387.5	6708.2	-20790.5	19408.6	14518.9	39133.4	13016.6	10035
8389960.5	5384747.4	455076.0	1478910.6	1620026.4	72330.5	2442707.3	367604.9	46102
217337.5	211456.9	1624.6	-22509.0	-15151.9	25563.2	-46.3	13481.0	2872
5025832.2	4761056.7	11763.5	-77311.4	3259.8	62624.7	83479.4	68456.1	21247
220248.5	151418.6	2597.4	29456.7	27493.9	6762.0	44332.9	14241.6	7112
5602589.5	4975437.7	401798.0	-177819.7	-159131.1	219890.9	384673.7	142006.8	30500
47081.2	28497.4	246.9	8561.1	9544.1	1650.4	11088.8	1297.8	194
19184444.0	**14402035.9**	**1371678.3**	**1885613.6**	**1975210.1**	**246347.7**	**4265325.4**	**918437.0**	**103763**
6651853.2	5861824.2	576598.3	-199198.6	-181368.7	194519.2	522463.5	127233.9	14778
12339958.2	8381827.7	793240.5	2068061.0	2138430.2	51828.5	3715132.6	783461.9	85552
173992.5	143588.4	1187.0	14696.9	15580.4		23475.0	6707.6	3237
18640.1	14795.6	652.5	2054.3	2568.2		4254.3	1033.6	196
2884308.8	**2134542.2**	**69511.7**	**322028.0**	**332355.3**	**31905.8**	**550745.3**	**148878.3**	**36189**
321758.2	265861.9	1283.9	7628.3	6063.3	12024.3	20107.5	12760.3	4538
1910175.6	1384385.0	61211.8	248221.9	258596.9	9094.0	432412.8	112604.1	22958
652375.0	484295.3	7016.0	66177.8	67695.1	10787.5	98225.0	23513.9	8693
2800491.2	**2249975.3**	**26596.3**	**240868.2**	**269061.6**	**57698.9**	**423412.4**	**127754.5**	**31226**
2353379.0	1953600.4	18510.0	171902.4	200204.6	31081.5	322104.7	103390.1	25714
167696.0	122215.7	3074.2	16326.8	41468.6	1424.7	63915.1	19372.3	3028
279416.2	174159.2	5012.1	52639.0	27388.4	25192.7	37392.6	4992.1	2484
8716993.3	**7386309.4**	**31335.3**	**564207.8**	**554077.2**	**123888.0**	**885955.1**	**300542.6**	**81047**
3131555.1	2562711.3	7274.5	332127.9	358910.3	5705.3	470069.5	103884.7	20744
1769805.4	1598846.4	2918.1	-18480.8	-14066.6	48605.0	17368.4	28516.9	22931
639498.4	513179.7	2664.6	79605.2	82527.5	5533.3	104320.7	19128.6	6043
1062039.8	871237.3	7099.5	73394.3	81407.2	10112.3	117874.7	29368.0	12673
509163.7	434058.5	6385.1	7323.9	10796.9	21383.2	51820.8	34638.8	4639
1558263.2	1366802.0	4729.3	88288.7	32725.6	31607.2	119008.7	81553.8	12431
46667.7	39474.2	264.2	1948.6	1776.3	941.7	5492.3	3451.8	1586
6976452.0	**5409970.7**	**241080.0**	**540356.7**	**591366.5**	**197853.3**	**1149388.8**	**316942.3**	**88392**
4227417.2	**3348441.3**	**209170.6**	**207608.9**	**240792.0**	**122267.2**	**628600.6**	**178638.0**	**51468**
534517.2	452250.7	2862.8	36728.7	38727.0	6392.5	62984.6	21394.8	7310
1426322.7	1100595.6	171500.9	19102.3	32249.5	48304.7	264349.7	60599.3	11913
383060.9	334857.4	2330.3	-8801.8	-1104.8	17439.7	16560.0	15334.5	7097
192959.3	147761.7	277.9	15496.3	16273.7	1034.3	22449.2	5897.6	1888
392035.0	317043.6	2028.3	26924.9	28091.1	9662.1	41192.0	11072.6	4557
228643.1	184233.3	461.6	-2005.8	5776.3	12077.0	13566.8	7328.9	2419
663937.7	514778.0	26995.9	66260.9	67079.7	4832.3	126771.3	32695.7	10979
119246.7	90190.9	320.2	21715.0	21892.2	1590.0	23711.3	1498.9	1025
47863.2	42318.8	568.1	-6752.8	-6852.9	7365.6	-4634.6	1650.2	1160
238831.4	164411.3	1824.6	38941.2	38660.2	13569.0	61650.3	21165.5	3120
1620402.1	**1407035.0**	**11225.6**	**61839.1**	**77409.2**	**51672.7**	**131719.3**	**43084.5**	**23618**
98738.7	99683.5	167.4	-6614.0	-5570.9	6339.1	-3344.6	2058.9	1104
461668.6	433075.6	4682.7	-16890.4	-9399.1	22233.5	7063.0	11779.4	4970
105906.2	85665.6	241.2	9407.0	9798.7	4189.3	12121.1	2081.2	1559

13-6 续表 4

单位: 万元

地　区	Region	负债合计 Total Liabilities	#流动负债 Total Liquid Liabilities	#非流动负债 Total Non-liquid Liabilities	所有者权益合计 Total Owners' Equities
沙湾县	Shawan County	472844.1	378362.9	72652.2	176406.7
托里县	Toli County	398748.9	299868.1	94820.5	114140.5
裕民县	Yumin [Qagantokay] County				
和布克赛尔蒙古自治县	Hoboksar Mongol Autonomous County	536427.0	358974.6	171366.2	212153.2
阿勒泰地区	**Altay Administrative Offices**	**1705481.0**	**965886.2**	**607045.5**	**1059567.4**
阿勒泰市	Altay City	273479.1	134903.2	138575.9	92287.5
布尔津县	Burqin County	362831.9	199214.9	128216.9	67193.8
富蕴县	Fuyun [Koktokay] County	506788.0	406745.7	100042.3	398843.3
福海县	Fuhai [Burultokay] County	121882.9	49969.0	71913.9	94668.1
哈巴河县	Habahe [Kaba] County	85984.3	53929.4	30720.7	267528.9
青河县	Qinghe [Qinggil] County	246489.3	48233.0	102441.3	77479.7
吉木乃县	Jeminay County	108025.5	72891.0	35134.5	61566.1
博尔塔拉蒙古自治州	**Bortala Mongol Autonomous Prefecture**	**996323.4**	**614499.4**	**380097.4**	**328954.3**
博乐市	Bole [Bortala] City	514643.8	323654.6	189262.7	152067.2
精河县	Jinghe [Jing] County	271897.2	197493.2	74404.0	86861.1
温泉县	Wenquan [Araxang] County	2128.6	2128.6		1003.4
巴音郭楞蒙古自治州	**Bayangol Mongol Autonomous Prefecture**	**8310913.7**	**4566070.9**	**3681160.5**	**5757427.4**
库尔勒市	Korla City	5578083.3	2504393.0	3038602.7	4482645.5
轮台县	Luntai [Bugur] County	446963.9	358167.6	78396.3	302966.3
尉犁县	Yuli [Lopnur] County	21388.1	19388.1		14525.7
若羌县	Ruoqiang [Qarkilik] County	540552.1	359037.2	168514.9	321308.4
且末县	Qiemo [Qarqan] County	22.5	469.7	-447.2	
焉耆回族自治县	Yanqi Hui Autonomous County	79903.2	75404.4	4498.6	55708.6
和静县	Hejing County	1566773.8	1176680.9	386898.4	543043.2
和硕县	Hoxud County	54464.3	50420.9	4043.4	26818.7
博湖县	Bohu [Bagrax] County	22762.5	22109.1	653.4	10411.0
阿克苏地区	**Aksu Administrative Offices**	**5219233.0**	**3598888.2**	**1494118.8**	**2950357.0**
阿克苏市	Aksu City	1800933.0	1022929.4	738814.8	1307503.2
温宿县	Wensu [Onsu] County	316036.3	179132.8	135953.3	86128.6
库车县	Kuqa County	1533192.0	1163138.4	310924.8	1048270.4
沙雅县	Xayar County	259127.6	169398.3	87973.5	125125.4
新和县	Xinhe [Toksu] County	114964.9	95998.2	5973.4	37814.5
拜城县	Baicheng [Bay] County	1065506.7	861499.7	203149.0	292016.4
乌什县	Wushi [Uxturpan] County	16208.1	14165.0	460.0	14805.0

Continued

(10 000 yuan)

主营业务收入 Revenue from Principal Business	主营业务成本 Cost of Principal Business	主营业务税金及附加 Taxes and Other Charges on Principal Business	营业利润 Business Profit	利润总额 Total Profit	亏损企业亏损总额 Losses Value of Loss-Suffering Enterprises	利税总额 Total Profits and Taxes	本年应交增值税 Value-added Taxes Payable	全部从业人员年平均人数(人) Annual Average Employed Persons (person)
547071.1	481342.9	1466.3	43785.1	48226.2	1938.5	65385.1	15692.6	6976
219683.1	181505.4	1218.7	10458.2	11305.2	14200.0	14899.8	2375.9	4800
187334.4	125762.0	3449.3	21693.2	23049.1	2772.3	35594.9	9096.5	4219
1128632.7	**654494.4**	**20683.8**	**270908.7**	**273165.3**	**23913.4**	**389068.9**	**95219.8**	**13306**
178223.8	152842.4	781.4	-3886.9	-2819.7	9073.3	7392.3	9430.6	2832
69711.6	32648.8	379.5	11581.4	13218.9	1876.0	17687.0	4088.6	681
469663.9	243329.9	14086.1	127649.4	130433.6	6341.3	198140.3	53620.6	5319
82567.4	60397.5	1108.0	12399.4	12882.6	1822.6	18315.6	4325.0	1146
251076.4	121801.2	4110.0	102220.2	98271.5	3649.8	124907.8	22526.3	2319
33204.5	22841.6	217.7	972.1	1090.8	1150.4	2537.2	1228.7	850
44185.1	20633.0	1.1	19973.1	20087.6		20088.7		159
581856.5	**506036.2**	**2554.5**	**15576.3**	**22236.9**	**17047.5**	**40818.7**	**16027.3**	**9288**
372522.7	341547.0	1963.6	-1388.8	1208.2	11694.3	13379.3	10207.5	6568
86712.1	74675.4	390.3	-1449.1	2293.7	5198.6	6499.7	3815.7	1630
2625.2	2331.5	0.3	84.2	254.6		255.2	0.3	34
9468884.7	**5569450.7**	**368866.7**	**2406835.4**	**2432878.4**	**40356.2**	**3284181.7**	**482436.6**	**55130**
6554907.7	3266993.5	321395.6	2133488.0	2113194.5	25697.1	2808961.5	374371.4	32467
456553.4	360455.2	7518.6	49922.8	52071.1	1213.7	76567.6	16977.9	3884
36925.2	28114.9	77.1	4938.6	5308.0	7.4	6153.8	768.7	314
470285.1	202581.0	27953.6	128957.4	170372.6	3849.8	242568.1	44241.9	4235
								63
96851.2	69647.9	1547.0	9135.7	8798.3	3668.1	15237.8	4892.5	1231
1771550.8	1574995.2	9698.2	76469.5	77814.1	4834.4	126281.4	38769.1	11718
55323.2	45422.9	568.7	4391.0	5465.1	94.1	7128.6	1094.8	765
25496.5	20248.5	107.9	524.0	846.3		2274.5	1320.3	453
4902613.2	**4053750.0**	**260926.2**	**223425.9**	**251791.4**	**55917.1**	**671136.1**	**158418.5**	**41461**
1213209.7	1071830.1	4442.0	45529.8	63992.2	10010.1	104844.8	36410.6	13610
138102.1	98105.0	1820.3	16406.5	15666.3	3162.1	24778.6	7292.0	2995
2672696.1	2171702.1	246975.7	96650.0	100522.6	19305.4	431960.7	84462.4	10845
217252.6	171804.3	124.3	19678.6	22583.6	1432.1	24463.0	1755.1	2375
113895.9	88715.1	213.1	23861.8	23818.8		24575.2	543.3	1429
428374.1	351680.2	5758.3	12214.3	14101.5	21532.3	45814.4	25954.6	8490
27730.6	20169.6	978.3	3226.4	3328.5		5324.2	1017.4	293

13-6 续表 5

单位: 万元

地　　区	Region	负债合计 Total Liabilities	#流动负债 Total Liquid Liabilities	#非流动负债 Total Non-liquid Liabilities	所有者权益合计 Total Owners' Equities
阿瓦提县	Awat County	94011.7	73373.7	10870.0	35366.2
柯坪县	Kalpin County	19252.7	19252.7		3327.3
克孜勒苏柯尔克孜自治州	**Kizilsu Kirgiz Autonomous Prefecture**	**653267.0**	**596229.3**	**55111.4**	**277376.6**
阿图什市	Artux City	234615.1	224012.1	10603.0	170156.5
阿克陶县	Akto County	116725.4	111319.9	3479.4	62384.8
阿合奇县	Akqi County	171875.2	171875.2		
乌恰县	Wuqia [Ulugqat] County	130051.3	89022.1	41029.0	44835.3
喀什地区	**Kashgar [Kaxgar] Administrative Offices**	**1292177.7**	**735534.7**	**533352.4**	**558349.7**
喀什市	Kashgar [Kaxgar] City	608456.3	301128.3	305804.4	229717.2
疏附县	Shufu County	4777.9	4777.9		2049.8
疏勒县	Shule County	87977.8	69802.2	18175.6	33528.3
英吉沙县	Yengisar County	52675.1	21898.4	30776.7	39444.8
泽普县	Zepu [Poskam] County	23940.4	14801.6	9138.8	24278.6
莎车县	Shache [Yarkant] County	90917.7	66531.4	24386.1	48162.2
叶城县	Yecheng [Kagilik] County	118648.4	71841.9	44659.1	41450.8
麦盖提县	Makit County	24585.7	24281.8	213.9	42077.7
岳普湖县	Yopurga County	33300.9	27676.0	5473.4	3651.6
伽师县	Jiashi [Payzawat] County	38472.9	32927.6	5545.3	69074.8
巴楚县	Bachu [Maralbexi] County	50119.5	42300.3	7612.6	15127.0
塔什库尔干塔吉克自治县	Taxkorgan Tajik Autonomous County	158305.1	57567.3	81566.5	9786.9
和田地区	**Hotan Administrative Offices**	**517035.7**	**312893.6**	**202630.1**	**334903.9**
和田市	Hotan City	160907.1	76361.0	84277.0	27320.6
和田县	Hotan County	239962.6	129353.4	110609.2	164125.6
墨玉县	Moyu [Karakax] County	20083.0	16263.4	3819.6	48732.1
皮山县	Pishan [Guma] County	7919.1	4124.8	3794.3	9161.2
洛浦县	Lop County	38442.0	37151.1	130.0	59552.5
策勒县	Qira County	2297.0	2215.0		1016.6
于田县	Yutian [Keriya] County	47424.9	47424.9		24995.3
民丰县	Minfeng [Niya] County				
自治区直辖县级市	**Municpality Country-LevelCity directly under the Central Government**	**9036299.4**	**6055278.3**	**1965642.6**	**3976924.3**
石河子市	Shihezi City	5038736.2	2628735.1	1419264.3	2832503.7
阿拉尔市	Aral City	491870.1	316190.0	156662.7	89527.7
图木舒克市	Tumxuk City	241197.0	177900.7	63296.2	236854.0
五家渠市	Wujiaqu City	3264496.1	2932452.5	326419.4	818038.9

Continued

(10 000 yuan)

主营业务收入 Revenue from Principal Business	主营业务成本 Cost of Principal Business	主营业务税金及附加 Taxes and Other Charges on Principal Business	营业利润 Business Profit	利润总额 Total Profit	亏损企业亏损总额 Losses Value of Loss-Suffering Enterprises	利税总额 Total Profits and Taxes	本年应交增值税 Value-added Taxes Payable	全部从业人员年平均人数(人) Annual Average Employed Persons (person)
51961.8	42154.2	27.3	5234.0	6291.7	475.1	7293.4	974.4	1289
39390.3	37589.4	586.9	624.5	1486.2		2081.8	8.7	135
337944.5	**274738.9**	**7033.8**	**9821.3**	**10641.2**	**8231.9**	**35253.0**	**17578.0**	**4116**
154252.3	135155.6	280.6	-54.5	625.7	5203.2	5362.7	4456.4	1815
95106.0	74162.9	4134.7	8004.9	8092.3	1335.4	21572.2	9345.2	914
21144.2	9836.7	252.4	2715.0	2757.9		3154.9	144.6	123
67442.0	55583.7	2366.1	-844.1	-834.7	1693.3	5163.2	3631.8	1264
1245743.3	**1075913.9**	**7132.7**	**49536.0**	**75413.4**	**20508.6**	**130545.1**	**47999.0**	**16400**
529460.5	504556.5	3972.3	-15029.6	7034.1	13040.5	31513.8	20507.4	7627
9508.9	6976.9	53.5	674.3	856.3	40.2	1241.1	331.3	243
118527.9	101693.6	150.9	8867.5	9021.2	722.9	9754.1	582.0	870
27230.0	20455.2	24.5	2866.2	2936.0	257.8	3195.8	235.3	449
22972.3	19939.1	55.5	413.5	576.1	668.4	1023.0	391.4	777
131122.8	112304.3	9.5	13083.2	13353.5	608.6	13512.2	149.2	961
115085.7	91731.8	843.8	2767.2	2759.0	1639.5	12186.7	8583.9	2193
39860.4	36554.3	72.4	-190.2	162.9	910.6	4601.9	4366.6	626
16938.7	15259.9	15.4	613.4	662.3	139.6	815.9	138.2	363
139950.7	95299.2	925.8	33833.1	35394.5		45283.6	8963.3	1232
59350.4	53395.5	51.1	-2692.0	-1708.9	2480.5	-1559.6	98.2	541
35735.0	17747.6	958.0	4329.4	4366.4		8976.6	3652.2	518
262866.6	**259010.2**	**874.6**	**-17919.7**	**1606.6**	**17277.7**	**12471.3**	**9990.1**	**5072**
126191.2	150113.5	215.8	-25462.8	-9765.4	13062.6	-8460.4	1089.2	2600
44600.2	31921.3	430.5	3313.0	3846.6	2994.6	9442.6	5165.5	611
48702.8	42365.0	79.3	3011.2	5154.0		7807.5	2574.2	400
3658.0	3423.8	30.7	-147.3	-147.5	147.5	200.7	317.5	155
28602.1	22067.1	70.8	450.6	1518.3	683.2	2409.7	820.6	1004
1817.0	2109.8	3.0	-389.6	-389.8	389.8	-386.8		97
9295.3	7009.7	44.5	1305.2	1390.4		1458.0	23.1	205
6155112.8	**5229880.6**	**22749.8**	**350686.4**	**396946.1**	**85326.9**	**634724.6**	**215028.7**	**68840**
3732645.0	3174702.2	17700.3	189196.3	232009.4	59849.1	373189.2	123479.5	46254
347007.5	265189.9	2309.4	48986.3	45379.4	6785.3	51423.8	3735.0	5616
230431.4	182094.5	235.0	26079.0	27363.9	2920.5	35907.2	8308.3	3197
1845028.9	1607894.0	2505.1	86424.8	92193.4	15772.0	174204.4	79505.9	13773

13-7 规模以上工业企业主要经济效益指标

单位: % (2013 年)

项　目	Item	产值利税率 Ratio of Profits and Taxes to Industrial Output Value
总　计	**Total**	**17.7**
按登记注册类型分	**Grouped by Registry Type**	
内资企业	Domestic Funded Enterprises	17.8
国有企业	State-owned Enterprises	10.8
#中央企业	Central Enterprises	12.9
地方企业	Local Enterprises	2.0
#自治区属企业	Autonomous	-1.5
地区(州、市)属企业	Prefecture or City	-0.2
县(市)属企业	County or City	7.4
集体企业	Collective-owned Enterprises	10.4
#自治区属企业	Autonomous	6.5
地区(州、市)属企业	Prefecture or City	2.3
县(市)属企业	County or City	20.6
镇属企业	Town	32.9
乡属企业	Village	
股份合作企业	Share-holding Cooperative Enterprises	
联营企业	Joint Ownership Enterprises	41.1
#国有联营企业	State Joint Ownership Enterprises	47.9
集体联营企业	Collective Joint Ownership Enterprises	
国有与集体联营企业	Joint State-collective Enterprises	43.4
其他联营企业	Other Joint Ownership Enterprises	12.4
有限责任公司	Limited Liability Corporations	10.0
#国有独资公司	State Sole funded Corporations	11.3
其他有限责任公司	Other Limited Liability Corporations	9.9
股份有限公司	Share-holding Corporations Ltd.	28.7
私营企业	Private Enterprises	11.1
#私营独资企业	Private-funded Enterprises	25.7
私营合伙企业	Private Partnership Enterprises	25.3
私营有限责任公司	Private Limited Liability Corporations	10.3
私营股份有限公司	Private Share-holding Corporations Ltd.	13.4
港、澳、台商投资企业	Enterprises with Funds from Hong Kong, Macao and Taiwan	7.1
外商投资企业	Foreign Funded Enterprises	14.2
在总计中: 国有控股企业	Of the Total: State-owned and State-holding Enterprises	21.6
在总计中: 农村工业	Of the Total: Rural Industry	5.9
按轻、重工业分	**Grouped by Light & Heavy Industry**	
轻工业	Light Industry	11.6
以农产品为原料	Using Farm Produces as Raw Materials	12.1
以非农产品为原料	Using Non-Farm Produces as Raw Materials	0.1
重工业	Heavy Industry	18.5
采掘工业	Mining and Quarrying	43.1
原料工业	Raw Materials Industry	8.3
加工工业	Manufacturing Industry	12.5
按企业规模分	**Grouped by Size of Enterprises (Old Standard)**	
大型企业	Large Enterprises	21.4
中型企业	Medium-sized Enterprises	12.1
小型企业	Small Enterprises	10.9
微型企业	Mini Enterprises	12.4

Main Indicators on Economic Efficiency of Industrial Enterprises above Designated Size

(%)

总资产贡献率 Ratio of Total Assets to Industrial Output Value	资本保值增值率 Ratio of Capital-hold and Rise	资产负债率 Assets Liability Ratio	流动资产周转次数(次/年) Number of Times of Annual TurnoverWorking Capitals (times/year)	成本费用利润率 Ratio of Profits to Industrial Cost	全员劳动生产率 Overall Labour Productivity
12.2	**111.0**	**61.3**	**2.0**	**11.3**	**43.4**
12.2	111.0	61.3	2.0	11.4	44.0
7.5	77.0	59.7	2.5	3.9	31.2
10.5	74.0	54.3	3.6	5.2	35.4
1.8	87.1	69.7	1.1	-1.1	18.5
0.5	150.0	65.7	1.6	-4.5	19.3
0.4	113.7	91.1	0.3	-1.2	13.9
4.0	37.2	52.9	1.6	-1.2	18.9
15.8	70.2	46.3	2.0	5.0	12.5
12.4	98.5	51.9	2.4	2.2	9.5
11.5	99.2	25.5	5.9	0.3	8.9
18.8	58.5	39.7	1.3	12.3	18.7
26.4	86.6	35.3	1.5	18.3	30.3
21.6	57.7	64.0	1.3	57.8	62.4
45.9	35.5	48.9	1.6	58.0	93.1
15.2	101.8	68.4	0.8	103.3	2590.2
18.5	17.9	59.0	4.5	2.1	8.9
6.8	138.7	70.4	1.6	5.1	26.4
5.8	158.0	67.3	1.2	4.9	23.8
7.0	135.0	71.0	1.7	5.2	27.0
21.9	100.7	47.5	3.4	20.1	101.5
8.3	120.4	66.6	1.3	9.8	23.2
27.3	43.5	60.8	2.2	18.5	34.1
57.5	56.1	79.7	5.4	12.0	42.0
8.3	134.7	70.2	1.4	8.7	20.8
7.3	102.0	54.4	0.9	15.2	48.6
5.8	69.6	57.6	1.2	4.4	11.6
11.7	144.1	56.0	1.9	10.4	31.6
15.0	107.5	57.2	2.8	13.3	57.7
1.8	102.2	44.0	1.8	2.8	14.2
9.7	118.3	65.3	1.5	7.4	18.5
10.7	118.9	65.4	1.5	7.9	19.2
1.1	113.4	64.0	0.6	-4.2	10.1
12.5	110.3	60.8	2.1	11.9	49.5
23.0	104.9	53.0	2.6	41.5	78.3
7.1	114.1	65.1	2.4	2.0	34.6
8.7	113.6	62.4	1.2	10.3	27.6
15.4	107.5	58.8	2.7	13.4	66.4
7.2	116.3	62.8	1.3	8.2	21.9
8.3	114.2	66.3	1.5	7.9	24.4
5.6	226.5	66.9	0.9	11.5	24.5

13-8 分行业规模以上工业企业主要经济效益指标

单位: % (2013 年)

行　业	Sector	产　值利税率 Ratio of Profits and Taxes to Industrial Output Value
总　计	**Total**	**17.7**
煤炭开采和洗选业	Mining and Washing of Coal	19.2
石油和天然气开采业	Extraction of Petroleum and Natural Gas	54.9
黑色金属矿采选业	Mining and Processing of Ferrous Metals Ores	30.6
有色金属矿采选业	Mining and Processing of Nonferrous Metals Ores	40.8
非金属矿采选业	Mining and Processing of Nonmetal Ores	13.7
#采　盐	Extraction of Salt	33.9
农副食品加工业	Processing of Food from Agricultural Products	8.7
#谷物磨制	Grain Grinding	6.3
饲料加工	Fodder Processing	9.4
制　糖	Sugar Making	4.1
食品制造业	Manufacture of Food	10.7
#罐头制造	Manufacture of can	-4.5
酒、饮料和精制茶制造业	Manufacture of Wine,Beverages and Refined Tea	23.9
#酒的制造	Manufacture of Wine	32.5
烟草制品业	Manufacture of Tobacco	67.6
纺织业	Manufacture of Textile	3.4
#棉、化纤纺织及印染精加工	Cotton, Chemical Fiber, Dyeing, Printing and Processing	3.5
毛纺织和染整精加工	Wool Textile, Dyeing and Printing	-9.8
纺织服装、鞋、帽制造业	Manufacture of Textile Wearing Apparel,Footware and Caps	11.3
皮革、毛皮、羽毛(绒)及其制品业	Leather, Fur, Feather and Related Products Manufacturing	5.1
#皮革鞣制加工	Leather Tanning and Processing	5.1
木材加工及木、竹、藤、棕、草制品业	Processing of Timber, Wood, Bamboo, Cane, Grass Products	13.7
家具制造业	Manufacture of Furniture	-5.5
造纸及纸制品业	Manufacture of Paper and Paper Products	11.5
印刷业和记录媒介的复制	Printing and Copying of Medium for Record	12.5
石油加工、炼焦及核燃料加工业	Oil Processing, Coking and Nuclear Fuel Processing	11.9
#炼　焦	Coking	8.4
化学原料及化学制品制造业	Raw Chemical Material and Chemical Products	12.8
#基础化学原料制造	Basic Chemical Material	6.4
肥料制造	Fertilizer Making	26.8
合成材料制造	Manufacture of Synthetic Materials	9.0
医药制造业	Manufacture of Medicine	11.8
化学纤维制造业	Manufacture of Chemical Fiber	5.0
橡胶制品业	Manufacture of Rubber Products	9.3
非金属矿物制品业	Manufacture of Nonmetal Mineral Products	8.4
#水泥制造	Manufacture of Cement	8.2
黑色金属冶炼及压延加工业	Smelting and Pressing of Ferrous Metals	0.6
有色金属冶炼及压延加工业	Smelting and Pressing of Nonferrous Metals	5.4
金属制品业	Manufacture of Metal Products	4.6
通用设备制造业	Manufacture of General Purpose Machinery	16.2
专用设备制造业	Manufacture of Special Purpose Machinery	10.6
汽车制造业	Manufacture of Automobile	2.9
电气机械及器材制造业	Manufacture of Electric Equipment and Machinery	12.3
计算机、通信和其他电子设备制造业	Telecom Equipment, Computer and Other Electronic Equipment	8.5
仪器仪表制造业	Measuring Instruments and Machinery for Cultunal Activify and OfficeWork	23.4
金属制品、机械和设备修理业	Manufacture of Repairing of Metal Products,Machinery and Equipment	4.6
电力、热力的生产和供应业	Electricity and Thermal Production and Supply	9.8
#电力生产和电力供应	Electricity Production and Supply	10.1
燃气生产和供应业	Gas Production and Supply	16.4
水的生产和供应业	Water Production and Supply	1.9

Main Indicators on Economic Efficiency of Industrial Enterprises above Designated Size by Sectors

(%)

总资产贡献率 Ratio of Total Assets to Industrial Output Value	资本保值增值率 Ratio of Capital-hold and Rise	资产负债率 Assets Liability Ratio	流动资产周转次数(次/年) Number of Times of Annual Turnover Working Capitals (times/year)	成本费用利润率 Ratio of Profits to Industrial Cost	全员劳动生产率 Overall Labour Productivity
12.2	**111.0**	**61.3**	**2.0**	**11.3**	**43.4**
6.9	108.6	65.2	1.2	6.6	23.7
30.9	102.8	45.7	5.6	66.0	170.2
17.6	115.4	71.9	1.0	22.3	52.8
16.4	109.2	51.3	1.4	41.1	46.9
10.5	137.9	66.2	1.2	4.5	17.1
27.3	103.1	31.0	1.4	21.0	26.2
11.2	126.0	64.8	1.7	7.7	20.2
11.3	108.2	57.8	2.7	5.7	19.6
15.8	128.2	42.6	2.9	9.1	27.2
3.9	90.7	58.4	1.4	-2.6	10.5
8.2	147.4	69.6	1.6	8.3	19.0
0.6	61.4	91.7	0.8	-7.0	8.9
19.5	122.1	64.0	1.4	19.0	30.4
21.8	122.5	63.4	1.0	26.1	31.5
59.8	106.2	26.0	1.6	40.0	305.8
2.6	98.0	66.7	1.2	0.9	7.6
2.8	94.2	68.9	1.2	0.9	7.7
-2.4	597.6	24.5	0.9	-11.8	3.3
8.8	145.9	77.0	1.2	9.3	7.2
7.6	120.5	75.2	1.6	3.3	41.2
7.6	120.5	75.2	1.6	3.3	41.2
13.1	138.3	55.7	1.5	11.4	17.7
-0.3	99.2	24.0	0.6	-7.1	4.5
9.1	137.0	67.8	1.6	10.7	13.6
7.6	116.8	47.8	1.2	10.2	11.7
21.5	101.0	48.2	4.5	0.1	77.6
6.1	117.4	70.1	1.3	6.0	21.4
7.6	106.8	63.8	1.9	7.7	30.4
4.6	70.7	67.7	1.5	3.7	19.6
10.3	132.5	67.8	1.7	20.4	52.0
7.2	131.1	58.5	2.8	4.7	32.8
8.0	111.5	59.5	0.7	9.6	15.3
6.7	110.1	83.6	1.8	2.9	20.5
11.7	110.7	56.1	1.8	8.3	16.9
5.1	111.1	61.5	1.1	4.0	16.6
4.0	98.8	58.0	1.0	2.9	16.2
2.3	108.7	77.5	2.0	-1.0	12.6
3.6	159.9	74.8	1.3	4.8	28.4
6.5	134.3	63.9	1.6	4.3	14.7
13.2	149.4	73.8	1.1	15.7	20.7
9.6	119.5	57.7	1.5	9.4	28.9
3.3	426.9	63.6	2.4	1.8	3.4
7.7	105.1	58.7	0.8	11.5	54.2
8.8	0.4	61.4	2.9	6.2	6.6
7.1	111.3	26.9	0.6	29.7	39.7
5.5	12.1	81.0	1.0	0.6	8.5
5.4	130.2	65.8	2.2	6.0	43.0
5.7	130.0	65.0	2.6	6.3	47.6
11.1	115.5	65.0	1.5	15.5	31.2
0.7	139.7	60.1	0.3	-2.9	16.2

13-9 各地、州、市、县(市)规模以上工业企业主要经济效益指标

单位: %　　(2013 年)

地　区	Region	产值利税率 Ratio of Profits and Taxes to Industrial Output Value
总　计	**Total**	**17.7**
乌鲁木齐市	**Urumqi City**	**13.4**
天山区	Tianshan District	7.4
沙依巴克区	Shayibak District	6.4
新市区	Xinshi District	27.6
水磨沟区	Shui Mogou District	
头屯河区	Tou Tunhe District	1.5
达坂城区	Da Bancheng District	20.0
米东区	Midong District	7.2
乌鲁木齐县	Urumqi County	22.1
克拉玛依市	**Karamay City**	**24.0**
独山子区	Dushanzi District	8.0
克拉玛依区	Karamay District	33.7
白碱滩区	Bai Jiantan District	14.0
乌尔河区	Urhe District	22.5
吐鲁番地区	**Turpan Administrative Offices**	**19.8**
吐鲁番市	Turpan City	7.2
鄯善县	Shanshan [Piqan] County	23.4
托克逊县	Toksun County	15.1
哈密地区	**Hami [Kumul] Administrative Offices**	**15.2**
哈密市	Hami [Kumul] City	13.9
巴里坤哈萨克自治县	Barkol Kazak Autonomous County	34.2
伊吾县	Yiwu [Araturuk] County	13.3
昌吉回族自治州	**Changji Hui Autonomous Prefecture**	**9.8**
昌吉市	Changji City	15.5
阜康市	Fukang City	0.9
呼图壁县	Hutubi County	15.7
玛纳斯县	Manas County	8.6
奇台县	Qitai County	9.4
吉木萨尔县	Jimsar County	7.9
木垒哈萨克自治县	Mori Kazak Autonomous County	7.9
伊犁哈萨克自治州	**Ili Kazak Autonomous Prefecture**	**16.0**
伊犁州直属县(市)	**Counties (Cities) Direct Under Ili Prefecture**	**14.5**
伊宁市	Yining [Gulja] City	12.0
奎屯市	Kuytun City	18.4
伊宁县	Yining [Gulja] County	4.3
察布查尔锡伯自治县	Qapqal Xibe Autonomous County	10.6
霍城县	Huocheng [Korgas] County	10.2
巩留县	Gongliu [Tokkuztara] County	6.0

Main Indicators on Economic Benefit of Industrial Enterprises above Designated Size by Prefecture, Autonomous Prefecture, City and County

(%)

总资产贡献率 Ratio of Total Assets to Industrial Output Value	资本保值增值率 Ratio of Capital-hold and Rise	资产负债率 Assets Liability Ratio	流动资产周转次数(次/年) Number of Times of Annual TurnoverWorking Capitals (times/year)	成本费用利润率 Ratio of Profits to Industrial Cost	全员劳动生产率 Overall Labour Productivity
12.2	**111.0**	**61.3**	**2.0**	**11.3**	**43.4**
10.3	**102.4**	**59.3**	**2.1**	**7.7**	**44.0**
5.8	113.1	60.6	3.1	3.9	42.0
2.4	63.2	60.6	1.0	2.9	12.2
17.2	109.5	55.3	1.7	25.7	76.9
3.0	85.7	36.8	1.7	-6.4	20.4
3.5	103.4	74.7	2.4	0.1	17.8
6.9	112.3	62.1	1.7	14.8	19.9
7.7	101.7	53.0	3.2	-3.0	31.5
6.9	107.6	79.0	0.9	26.6	127.9
21.7	**106.2**	**44.6**	**3.3**	**12.6**	**67.6**
12.1	97.7	41.9	3.6	-2.9	63.7
24.8	109.2	45.3	3.2	23.1	70.3
14.7	129.0	63.8	1.6	9.8	15.4
17.4	107.7	39.6	1.5	15.9	35.4
10.1	**107.8**	**61.9**	**1.4**	**13.6**	**37.2**
3.8	112.0	60.7	0.9	1.9	15.3
14.9	101.1	59.3	1.8	16.7	44.0
5.9	119.0	66.0	0.9	11.6	30.9
7.4	**131.6**	**71.3**	**1.2**	**10.5**	**27.0**
7.8	129.5	71.9	1.2	9.2	24.5
9.2	219.7	65.0	1.0	27.7	27.3
5.1	107.7	72.7	2.1	12.1	52.0
6.9	**126.1**	**67.6**	**1.5**	**6.7**	**28.0**
12.8	102.9	54.8	1.6	12.7	36.5
2.7	123.0	64.2	1.7	-0.8	17.3
19.9	141.3	65.0	2.6	14.8	27.5
7.2	227.8	75.8	1.1	8.3	30.8
8.0	103.6	62.6	1.6	2.2	31.7
3.6	189.5	80.0	1.5	2.2	31.5
7.6	125.0	69.1	1.0	3.9	11.8
9.2	**115.8**	**67.0**	**1.4**	**9.4**	**27.9**
8.3	**113.6**	**66.5**	**1.4**	**6.3**	**25.3**
9.1	137.4	67.9	2.2	7.7	23.5
10.0	116.1	67.4	1.3	2.6	37.1
3.9	81.8	71.9	1.3	-0.3	10.8
10.4	57.8	73.7	1.6	9.6	23.7
8.8	158.3	57.7	2.0	7.7	23.4
2.6	131.8	59.8	1.0	2.5	23.6

13-9 续表 1

单位: %

地　区	Region	产　值利税率 Ratio of Profits and Taxes to Industrial Output Value
新源县	Xinyuan [Kunes] County	17.9
昭苏县	Zhaosu [Mongolkure] County	17.9
特克斯县	Tekes County	-9.1
尼勒克县	Nilka County	26.1
塔城地区	**Tacheng [Tarbagatai] Administrative Offices**	**7.8**
塔城市	Tacheng [Qoqek] City	-3.4
乌苏市	Usu City	1.6
额敏县	Emin [Dorbiljin] County	10.9
沙湾县	Shawan County	11.1
托里县	Toli County	6.3
裕民县	Yumin [Qagantokay] County	
和布克赛尔蒙古自治县	Hoboksar Mongol Autonomous County	16.2
阿勒泰地区	**Altay Administrative Offices**	**33.7**
阿勒泰市	Altay City	4.1
布尔津县	Burqin County	25.4
富蕴县	Fuyun [Koktokay] County	41.4
福海县	Fuhai [Burultokay] County	20.2
哈巴河县	Habahe [Kaba] County	49.9
青河县	Qinghe [Qinggil] County	6.6
吉木乃县	Jeminay County	45.1
博尔塔拉蒙古自治州	**Bortala Mongol Autonomous Prefecture**	**6.6**
博乐市	Bole [Bortala] City	3.5
精河县	Jinghe [Jing] County	6.4
温泉县	Wenquan [Araxang] County	8.5
巴音郭楞蒙古自治州	**Bayangol Mongol Autonomous Prefecture**	**37.3**
库尔勒市	Korla City	42.8
轮台县	Luntai [Bugur] County	16.7
尉犁县	Yuli [Lopnur] County	16.7
若羌县	Ruoqiang [Qarkilik] County	56.2
且末县	Qiemo [Qarqan] County	
焉耆回族自治县	Yanqi Hui Autonomous County	16.1
和静县	Hejing County	10.9
和硕县	Hoxud County	14.3
博湖县	Bohu [Bagrax] County	11.2
阿克苏地区	**Aksu Administrative Offices**	**13.6**
阿克苏市	Aksu City	8.5
温宿县	Wensu [Onsu] County	17.5
库车县	Kuqa County	16.3

Continued

(%)

总资产贡献率 Ratio of Total Assets to Industrial Output Value	资本保值增值率 Ratio of Capital-hold and Rise	资产负债率 Assets Liability Ratio	流动资产周转次数(次/年) Number of Times of Annual TurnoverWorking Capitals (times/year)	成本费用利润率 Ratio of Profits to Industrial Cost	全员劳动生产率 Overall Labour Productivity
12.2	95.9	63.1	1.2	11.3	21.3
27.7	108.7	68.0	2.0	22.4	32.2
0.8	211.4	77.0	0.9	-12.3	9.5
8.0	114.6	71.1	2.2	18.9	39.7
5.9	**109.7**	**73.0**	**1.3**	**4.8**	**21.8**
-0.1	117.8	73.0	3.2	-5.3	25.2
2.7	92.5	77.0	1.1	-2.0	22.8
6.7	113.1	58.5	0.8	9.9	21.6
12.0	136.7	72.7	1.6	9.0	18.8
4.2	106.5	77.2	1.0	5.1	23.9
6.2	106.7	71.7	1.4	14.1	22.2
15.7	**128.7**	**61.7**	**1.6**	**32.3**	**49.1**
4.4	134.9	74.8	2.3	-1.5	21.1
7.3	250.1	84.3	0.9	24.7	50.7
23.1	108.5	56.0	1.7	39.1	60.7
10.6	103.9	56.3	1.0	18.4	27.5
36.0	114.5	24.3	2.5	68.0	72.5
1.5	369.6	76.1	0.4	3.1	14.0
13.3	413.4	63.7	1.2	83.2	154.3
5.1	**189.6**	**75.2**	**1.2**	**3.8**	**21.0**
3.7	120.0	77.2	1.4	0.3	16.8
3.8	190.0	75.8	0.8	2.6	23.1
11.2	100.0	68.0	1.3	10.0	19.5
25.1	**101.0**	**59.0**	**3.8**	**37.9**	**103.0**
29.7	98.8	55.4	5.9	55.4	150.0
11.5	127.0	58.8	1.3	12.8	43.5
17.9	326.6	59.6	1.6	16.8	26.8
29.4	97.7	62.7	1.6	54.8	74.1
		100.0			
12.7	120.6	58.9	1.4	10.2	23.0
8.4	105.8	74.3	3.0	4.6	22.9
10.1	129.2	67.0	1.1	10.7	17.2
8.4	91.1	68.6	1.5	3.4	12.1
9.7	**112.9**	**63.7**	**1.8**	**5.6**	**31.6**
5.0	120.8	57.8	1.2	5.4	21.6
8.7	102.5	78.6	1.9	12.9	21.3
18.1	105.0	59.0	3.7	4.3	59.3

13-9 续表 2

单位: %

地　区	Region	产值利税率 Ratio of Profits and Taxes to Industrial Output Value
沙雅县	Xayar County	11.2
新和县	Xinhe [Toksu] County	21.3
拜城县	Baicheng [Bay] County	10.0
乌什县	Wushi [Uxturpan] County	20.9
阿瓦提县	Awat County	12.0
柯坪县	Kalpin County	5.3
克孜勒苏柯尔克孜自治州	**Kizilsu Kirgiz Autonomous Prefecture**	**10.6**
阿图什市	Artux City	3.8
阿克陶县	Akto County	21.8
阿合奇县	Akqi County	14.9
乌恰县	Wuqia [Ulugqat] County	7.3
喀什地区	**Kashgar [Kaxgar] Administrative Offices**	**10.8**
喀什市	Kashgar [Kaxgar] City	6.1
疏附县	Shufu County	12.5
疏勒县	Shule County	10.0
英吉沙县	Yengisar County	11.6
泽普县	Zepu [Poskam] County	4.3
莎车县	Shache [Yarkant] County	10.0
叶城县	Yecheng [Kagilik] County	10.1
麦盖提县	Makit County	18.7
岳普湖县	Yopurga County	3.5
伽师县	Jiashi [Payzawat] County	32.7
巴楚县	Bachu [Maralbexi] County	-2.7
塔什库尔干塔吉克自治县	Taxkorgan Tajik Autonomous County	23.4
和田地区	**Hotan Administrative Offices**	**4.6**
和田市	Hotan City	-6.4
和田县	Hotan County	20.7
墨玉县	Moyu [Karakax] County	15.6
皮山县	Pishan [Guma] County	5.1
洛浦县	Lop County	7.6
策勒县	Qira County	-23.4
于田县	Yutian [Keriya] County	18.6
民丰县	Minfeng [Niya] County	
自治区直辖县级市	**Municpality Country-LevelCity directly under the Central Government**	**9.4**
石河子市	Shihezi City	9.6
阿拉尔市	Aral City	14.3
图木舒克市	Tumxuk City	14.2
五家渠市	Wujiaqu City	7.7

Continued

(%)

总资产贡献率 Ratio of Total Assets to Industrial Output Value	资本保值增值率 Ratio of Capital-hold and Rise	资产负债率 Assets Liability Ratio	流动资产周转次数(次/年) Number of Times of Annual TurnoverWorking Capitals (times/year)	成本费用利润率 Ratio of Profits to Industrial Cost	全员劳动生产率 Overall Labour Productivity
9.3	102.6	67.4	1.4	11.2	26.5
17.7	75.4	75.9	1.4	25.1	24.8
4.2	117.0	78.5	0.7	3.4	21.3
18.6	143.3	51.9	1.8	14.2	29.0
7.1	258.7	72.7	1.2	13.4	13.7
9.6	120.4	85.3	2.3	3.9	16.8
6.0	**129.2**	**69.9**	**0.9**	**3.3**	**31.6**
2.5	107.6	57.4	0.7	0.4	27.1
13.3	108.7	65.2	1.0	9.7	36.0
6.7		100.0	3.4	15.2	95.4
6.0		74.4	1.0	-1.2	28.6
9.2	**120.0**	**69.7**	**1.9**	**6.3**	**21.3**
6.0	139.1	72.6	2.4	1.3	18.7
15.8	98.1	58.1	1.6	11.6	9.3
9.7	98.6	72.4	1.7	8.2	20.1
6.1	168.3	57.2	1.4	11.9	19.2
3.5	127.3	48.4	1.1	2.5	8.2
11.6	122.8	65.4	1.9	11.2	29.1
11.1	114.2	74.1	2.1	2.4	16.9
7.9	96.1	36.9	0.8	0.4	12.7
3.0	110.9	90.1	0.7	4.0	13.1
42.2	77.8	35.8	3.4	33.4	43.6
-0.1	417.4	76.3	1.7	-2.8	34.9
8.9	153.9	94.1	0.8	14.1	42.3
3.0	**148.3**	**60.6**	**1.5**	**0.6**	**16.5**
-1.7	409.1	85.5	3.7	-6.2	11.1
4.0	110.3	59.4	0.6	8.7	45.9
11.7	97.4	29.2	1.8	11.4	34.0
2.3	98.5	44.3	0.4	-3.9	7.5
3.4	623.0	39.2	1.3	5.4	8.6
-10.5	72.3	69.3	1.8	-17.6	4.2
2.0		65.5	1.5	17.5	15.2
6.2	**141.0**	**69.4**	**1.3**	**6.8**	**25.3**
6.2	125.7	64.0	1.4	6.5	22.1
11.0	65.4	84.6	1.9	15.2	19.6
8.8	467.4	50.5	1.0	13.4	23.5
5.4	215.6	80.0	1.3	5.3	38.9

13-10 国有控股工业企业主要经济指标

单位：万元 (2013 年)

项目	Item	企业单位数(个) Number of Enterprises (unit)	#亏损企业 Loss- Suffering Enterprises	工业总产值(当年价格) Gross Industrial Output Value (At Current Prices)
总　　计	**Total**	**600**	**173**	**56688937.3**
按登记注册类型分	**Grouped by Registry Type**			
内资企业	Domestic Funded Enterprises	594	172	56582761.9
国有企业	State-owned Enterprises	75	26	5355843.8
#中央企业	Central Enterprises	34	7	4316188.2
地方企业	Local Enterprises	41	19	1039655.6
#自治区属企业	Autonomous	14	9	679905.1
地区(州、市)属企业	Prefecture or City	6	1	93705.8
县(市)属企业	County or City	16	7	86603.0
联营企业	Joint Ownership Enterprises	2		17411.1
#国有联营企业	State Joint Enterprises Ownership	1		8891.4
国有与集体联营企业	Joint State-collective OwnershipEnterprises	1		8519.7
有限责任公司	Limited Liability Corporations	457	129	19043327.5
#国有独资公司	Sole State-funded Corporations	93	30	3934863.9
其他有限责任公司	Other Limited Liability Corporations	364	99	15108463.6
股份有限公司	Share-holding Corporations Ltd.	60	17	32166179.5
港、澳、台商投资企业	Enterprises with Funds from Hongkong,Macao and Taiwan	1		5687.4
外商投资企业	Foreign Funded Enterprises	5	1	100488.0
在总计中：国有控股企业	Of the Total : State-owned and State-holding Enterprises	600	173	56688937.3
按轻、重工业分	**Grouped by Light & Heavy Industry**			
轻工业	Light Industry	156	39	2622535.7
以农产品为原料	Using Farm Produces as Raw Materials	140	32	2527495.5
以非农产品为原料	Using Non-Farm Produces as Raw Materials	16	7	95040.2
重工业	Heavy Industry	444	134	54066401.6
采掘工业	Mining and Quarrying	82	21	18168592.5
原料工业	Raw Material Industry	239	87	32593868.6
加工工业	Manufacturing Industry	123	26	3303940.5
按企业规模分	**Grouped by Size of Enterprises**			
大型企业	Large Enterprises	61	22	45881498.8
中型企业	Medium-sized Enterprises	155	49	6319015.0
小型企业	Small Enterprises	361	97	4365785.9
微型企业	Mini Enterprises	23	5	122637.6

Main Economic Indicators Efficiency of State-holding Industrial Enterprises

(10 000 yuan)

工业销售产值(当年价) Sales Value of Industry Products (At Current Prices)	出口交货值 Delivery Value of Industry Export	实收资本 Total Capital Hold	资产合计 Total Assets	流动资产合计 Total Working Capitals	#产成品 Finished Product	固定资产原价 Original Value of Fixed Assets
55970581.5	**162644.2**	**30233706.7**	**91014942.9**	**21010668.0**	**2011895.5**	**82045751.9**
55867684.7	162644.2	30056570.6	90665731.3	20937973.9	2008273.1	81821415.9
5191891.5	1989.1	1339793.0	8935033.6	2089931.4	67467.9	6420205.8
4283599.5		515989.9	5833736.3	1197412.4	34545.7	4407641.9
908292.0	1989.1	823803.1	3101297.3	892519.0	32922.2	2012563.9
549751.0		544732.5	1688319.3	355291.3	15661.9	1068312.6
91765.2		52284.7	716007.9	361510.5	3410.4	459626.2
84116.2		199891.9	429175.8	50861.5	4277.3	400392.7
16166.2		8420.0	43377.4	13624.4	762.9	29772.5
7646.5		1720.0	9281.3	4695.0	762.9	1889.2
8519.7		6700.0	34096.1	8929.4		27883.3
18603271.2	99809.2	9425058.1	39528837.4	10493788.0	1068481.4	27031657.0
3790073.6	1968.8	2831616.2	10319390.6	3279324.7	153558.6	6531885.9
14813197.6	97840.4	6593441.9	29209446.8	7214463.3	914922.8	20499771.1
32056355.8	60845.9	19283299.5	42158482.9	8340630.1	871560.9	48339780.6
5687.4		13000.0	34497.1	6684.1		34604.9
97209.4		164136.1	314714.5	66010.0	3622.4	189731.1
55970581.5	162644.2	30233706.7	91014942.9	21010668.0	2011895.5	82045751.9
2601429.3	119733.1	1188735.3	4718823.4	2236490.9	416472.9	2490298.1
2508269.5	119358.0	850626.7	3672405.4	1878940.1	409966.8	1985592.4
93159.8	375.1	338108.6	1046418.0	357550.8	6506.1	504705.7
53369152.2	42911.1	29044971.4	86296119.5	18774177.1	1595422.6	79555453.8
18073572.9		16477986.5	34900630.3	6046356.8	389951.4	41312958.2
32217698.8	28030.9	11506692.5	45837922.4	10641035.3	970688.6	35249672.1
3077880.5	14880.2	1060292.4	5557566.8	2086785.0	234782.6	2992823.5
45675851.6	73494.7	23622786.9	61855726.0	13642156.5	1099415.1	63324722.9
6080668.4	37657.2	3624397.9	15847116.7	4140746.1	519608.9	9380057.1
4094174.1	51492.3	2819411.4	12471349.1	3083310.9	390102.4	8666783.9
119887.4		167110.5	840751.1	144454.5	2769.1	674188.0

13-10 续表

单位: 万元

项　目	Item	负债合计 Total Liabilities	#流动负债 Total Liquid Liabilities	#非流动负债 Total Non-liquid Liabilities	所有者权益合计 Total Owners' Equities
总　计	**Total**	**52101451.1**	**30895710.8**	**20131011.7**	**38847414.7**
按登记注册类型分	**Grouped by Registry Type**				
内资企业	DomesticFunded Enterprises	51946000.4	30769886.7	20101385.1	38655396.4
国有企业	State-owned Enterprises	5331958.1	2698173.8	2232728.5	3596525.8
#中央企业	Central Enterprises	3169068.1	1968873.5	1194566.7	2658197.5
地方企业	Local Enterprises	2162890.0	729300.3	1038161.8	938328.3
#自治区属企业	Autonomous	1108767.3	298521.0	414909.0	579551.9
地区(州、市)属企业	Prefecture or City	652399.1	241749.6	410649.3	63608.8
县(市)属企业	County or City	227162.6	71470.2	155602.1	201934.5
联营企业	Joint Ownership Enterprises	27849.7	5289.7	22560.0	15527.7
#国有联营企业	State Joint Enterprises Ownership	4543.0	4543.0		4738.3
国有与集体联营企业	Joint State-collective OwnershipEnterprises	23306.7	746.7	22560.0	10789.4
有限责任公司	Limited Liability Corporations	26960074.6	16850968.1	9522903.2	12531989.6
#国有独资公司	Sole State-funded Corporations	6961337.5	4419661.5	2164085.1	3352431.5
其他有限责任公司	Other Limited Liability Corporations	19998737.1	12431306.6	7358818.1	9179558.1
股份有限公司	Share-holding Corporations Ltd.	19626118.0	11215455.1	8323193.4	22511353.3
港、澳、台商投资企业	Enterprises with Funds from Hongkong,Macao and Taiwan	19754.5	9954.5	9800.0	13000.0
外商投资企业	Foreign Funded Enterprises	135696.2	115869.6	19826.6	179018.3
在总计中: 国有控股企业	Of the Total : State-owned and State-holding Enterprises	52101451.1	30895710.8	20131011.7	38847414.7
按轻、重工业分	**Grouped by Light & Heavy Industry**				
轻工业	Light Industry	2908333.2	2208252.8	289995.4	1810669.9
以农产品为原料	Using Farm Produces as Raw Materials	2230807.2	1998615.7	164141.4	1441778.0
以非农产品为原料	Using Non-Farm Produces as Raw Materials	677526.0	209637.1	125854	368891.9
重工业	Heavy Industry	49193117.9	28687458.0	19841016.3	37036744.8
采掘工业	Mining and Quarrying	17811255.2	10277131.6	7524895.2	17082667.8
原料工业	Raw Material Industry	27944880.1	16094397.9	11295033.7	17833543.0
加工工业	Manufacturing Industry	3436982.6	2315928.5	1021087.4	2120534.0
按企业规模分	**Grouped by Size of Enterprises**				
大型企业	Large Enterprises	33183690.9	19863661.7	13319758.6	28644552.5
中型企业	Medium-sized Enterprises	9997075.7	6108173.3	3048948.7	5832553.2
小型企业	Small Enterprises	8326358.6	4596858.5	3495365.8	4123013.0
微型企业	Mini Enterprises	594325.9	327017.3	266938.6	247296.0

Continued

(10 000 yuan)

主营业务收入 Revenue from Principal Business	主营业务成本 Cost of Principal Business	主营业务税金及附加 Taxes and Other Charges on Principal Business	营业利润 Business Profit	利润总额 Total Profit	亏损企业亏损总额 Losses Value of Loss-Suffering Enterprises	利税总额 Total Profits and Taxes	本年应交增值税 Value-added Taxes Payable	全部从业人员年平均人数(人) Annual Average Employed Persons (person)
58372725.4	**43925957.1**	**3140604.5**	**5990803.9**	**6460499.5**	**938755.0**	**12257806.2**	**2656702.2**	**386644**
58269056.8	43853591.3	3139206.2	5976591.3	6446659.5	931444.2	12234440.9	2648575.2	385610
5256043.9	4690426.5	183531.8	176021.4	191290.1	59060.9	577303.9	202482.0	42549
4299576.1	3799106.8	180358.1	222719.1	202622.4	12479.0	556847.4	173866.9	31879
956467.8	891319.7	3173.7	-46697.7	-11332.3	46581.9	20456.5	28615.1	10670
565907.6	535549.1	1714.9	-36906.2	-27363.1	34006.5	-9991.7	15656.5	4775
117774.6	129983.0	116.2	-22266.3	-1601.3	8187.5	-198.1	1287.0	2198
81288.2	63226.3	534.4	-896.9	-0.7	3775.3	6372.7	5839.0	1940
14928.5	5698.1	479.1	6331.3	6331.7		7957.8	1147.0	67
7646.7	3721.1	479.1	2630.8	2632.6		4258.7	1147.0	55
7281.8	1977.0		3700.5	3699.1		3699.1		12
18747301.6	15954261.4	393923.9	440102.2	837902.3	475940.2	2031580.2	799754.0	209018
3898562.5	3375091.3	37309.7	59141.8	188305.2	102437.3	443856.4	218241.5	68097
14848739.1	12579170.1	356614.2	380960.4	649597.1	373502.9	1587723.8	581512.5	140921
34250782.8	23203205.3	2561271.4	5354136.4	5411135.4	396443.1	9617599.0	1645192.2	133976
5687.4	3727.3	13.9	1960.0	1044.9		1058.8		12
97981.2	68638.5	1384.4	12252.6	12795.1	7310.8	22306.5	8127.0	1022
58372725.4	43925957.1	3140604.5	5990803.9	6460499.5	938755.0	12257806.2	2656702.2	386644
2697463.4	2015283.4	207100.4	121112.2	159793.8	110245.0	495272.5	128378.3	42607
2601632.5	1927053.0	206157.8	157806.6	191340.2	71630.0	520795.6	123297.6	37908
95830.9	88230.4	942.6	-36694.4	-31546.4	38615.0	-25523.1	5080.7	4699
55675262.0	41910673.7	2933504.1	5869691.7	6300705.7	828510.0	11762533.7	2528323.9	344037
19243303.8	10063113.4	1212568.6	5577402.9	5650358.9	101499.6	8434746.5	1571819.0	155438
33203203.6	29270205.0	1681790.7	121292.8	374969.0	679856.2	2906351.4	849591.7	156580
3228754.6	2577355.3	39144.8	170996.0	275377.8	47154.2	421435.8	106913.2	32019
47748152.4	35326672.4	3058425.4	5481930.9	5722872.0	582241.0	10954364.8	2173067.4	251325
6243849.4	5125554.2	55329.7	254166.0	370977.1	240207.7	721753.4	295446.6	87896
4256852.9	3403994.0	26656.9	229389.6	317987.8	113901.1	530715.8	186071.1	46447
123870.7	69736.5	192.5	25317.4	48662.6	2405.2	50972.2	2117.1	976

13-11 分行业国有控股工业企业主要经济指标

单位: 万元 (2013 年)

行业	Sector	企业单位数(个) Number of Enterprises (unit)	#亏损企业 Loss- Suffering Enterprises	工业总产值(当年价格) Gross Industrial Output Value (At Current Prices)
总 计	**Total**	**600**	**173**	**56688937.3**
煤炭开采和洗选业	Mining and Washing of Coal	34	11	1286485.9
石油和天然气开采业	Extraction of Petroleum and Natural Gas	4		13775748.4
黑色金属矿采选业	Mining and Processing of Ferrous Metals Ores	14	3	864841.7
有色金属矿采选业	Mining and Processing of Nonferrous Metals Ores	16	3	412646.1
非金属矿采选业	Mining and Processing of Nonmetal Ores	11	3	113542.8
#采 盐	Extraction of Salt	4		44832.7
农副食品加工业	Processing of Food from Agricultural Products	59	11	1028538.2
#谷物磨制	Grain Grinding	16	3	136062.6
饲料加工	Fodder Processing	5		216664.1
制 糖	Sugar Making	11	7	236341.5
食品制造业	Manufacture of Food	33	9	388609.7
#罐头制造	Manufacture of can	14	6	114616.9
酒、饮料和精制茶制造业	Manufacture of Wine,Beverages and Refined Tea	13	2	266934.2
#酒的制造	Manufacture of Wine	11	2	261189.1
烟草制品业	Manufacture of Tobacco	1		402140.7
纺织业	Manufacture of Textile	13	6	228875.3
#棉、化纤纺织及印染精加工	Cotton, Chemical Fiber, Dyeing, Printing and Processing	12	5	212224.1
毛纺织和染整精加工	Wool Textile, Dyeing and Printing	1	1	16651.2
纺织服装、鞋、帽制造业	Manufacture of Textile Wearing Apparel,Footware and Caps	4	1	32139.7
造纸及纸制品业	Manufacture of Paper and Paper Products	5	2	55399.5
印刷业和记录媒介的复制	Printing and Copying of Medium for Record	6		29401.7
石油加工、炼焦及核燃料加工业	Oil Processing, Coking and Nuclear Fuel Processing	12	8	15174793.9
#炼 焦	Coking	5	3	249328.7
化学原料及化学制品制造业	Raw Chemical Material and Chemical Products	41	15	4143258.0
#基础化学原料制造	Basic Chemical Material	10	6	852981.5
肥料制造	Fertilizer Making	10	4	689357.2
合成材料制造	Manufacture of Synthetic Material	12	4	2516537.7
医药制造业	Manufacture of Medicine	6		71368.0
化学纤维制造业	Manufacture of Chemical Fiber	2	1	39958.5
橡胶制品业	Manufacture of Rubber Products	22	5	499375.8
非金属矿物制品业	Manufacture of Nonmetal Mineral Products	92	28	1634660.5
#水泥制造	Manufacture of Cement	43	20	907815.0
黑色金属冶炼及压延加工业	Smelting and Pressing of Ferrous Metals	15	8	5525359.0
有色金属冶炼及压延加工业	Smelting and Pressing of Nonferrous Metals	11	4	392412.6
金属制品业	Manufacture of Metal Products	6	2	359651.8
通用设备制造业	Manufacture of General Purpose Machinery	3	2	17341.0
专用设备制造业	Manufacture of Special Purpose Machinery	10	2	121856.4
汽车制造业	Manufacture of Automobile	5	3	292905.2
电气机械及器材制造业	Manufacture of Electric Equipment and Machinery	8	1	177588.0
电力、热力的生产和供应业	Electric Power and Thermal Production and Supply	133	35	7205910.6
#电力生产和电力供应	Electric Power Production and Supply	114	26	7059422.0
燃气生产和供应业	Gas Production and Supply	6	1	351065.4
水的生产和供应业	Water Production and Supply	10	5	60974.4

Main Economic Indicators of Stare-holding Industrial Enterprises by Sectors

(10 000 yuan)

工业销售产值(当年价) Sales Value of Industry Products (At Current Prices)	出口交货值 Delivery Value of Industry Export	实收资本 Total Capital Hold	资产合计 Total Assets	流动资产合计 Total Working Capitals	#产成品 Finished Product	固定资产原价 Net Value of Fixed Assets
55970581.5	**162644.2**	**30233706.7**	**91014942.9**	**21010668.0**	**2011895.5**	**82045751.9**
1312598.3		1192388.9	4339794.3	1179814.1	87412.8	1806566.7
13705689.3		13566924.9	25472761.9	2620889.9	152409.2	36809917.0
834315.8		244725.9	1679472.4	814237.9	88673.0	607541.0
399832.1		279674.1	1132523.3	242586.6	35266.9	616838.7
101764.8		32565.7	169089.5	90552.0	23359.9	64329.7
45312.1		16307.1	56406.7	32132.4	6319.5	20334.2
1004982.7		227079.2	1111961.0	637404.4	225311.7	538581.6
142085.2		25861.3	132608.1	86277.1	21435.1	36153.3
214727.6		46840.9	248449.5	106955.7	21983.1	93012.6
247451.2		66587.3	317021.7	184030.8	115063.6	244094.0
417897.7	104747.2	168526.8	768795.8	366554.8	91153.4	605040.9
148603.3	92320.3	92573.8	456902.1	245265.0	80740.2	391218.8
266584.8		157624.1	356530.5	201276.8	12227.6	170742.1
261440.8		152423.1	348868.0	197538.9	9629.3	163527.0
382123.7		18741.7	454809.0	236210.0	6940.0	133167.0
244104.0	9843.7	190233.0	431946.9	191355.1	29230.6	284595.1
227762.4		143483.5	350295.9	169501.8	27428.8	251040.1
16341.6	9843.7	46749.5	81651.0	21853.3	1801.8	33555.0
28986.1	4767.1	13559.0	42475.6	25872.8	4930.2	10854.5
54775.5		24534.4	244386.9	72195.8	4953.9	113659.5
30978.4		12418.3	65502.8	30591.2	4315.5	54938.5
15118457.2		4407769.8	7487246.7	2677492.3	384615.7	8039045.4
252585.5		133615.2	567194.6	170575.8	46161.7	408181.1
4174565.9	17559.5	1949684.8	8640550.2	1826844.0	207859.0	6383508.5
840004.9	2333.6	274100.3	1654544.7	462045.9	26122.0	987575.8
741641.8		225884.7	1950647.0	390346.5	25575.0	1501332.6
2511756.5	15167.6	1374777.3	4819597.8	902352.8	152200.9	3825772.9
60196.0	316.8	30808.6	158254.7	104853.3	15696.5	38288.2
32857.0		17000.0	88376.1	40683.4	17934.6	55739.7
470414.0	14430.5	159990.7	508353.0	305477.3	89322.5	196369.9
1601284.5	8.6	1236393.1	5762443.5	1589053.8	82876.6	2712433.1
887787.4	8.6	1020605.5	4311029.3	882142.3	35544.5	2086349.0
5345907.1	10521.1	1076788.6	6280581.9	2237025.2	278083.9	3402203.6
319735.3		115786.0	1041322.1	379606.0	87131.9	261695.0
230822.2		90049.8	204061.2	81526.4	17719.8	61624.7
13286.9		9991.0	16666.2	8320.8	459.6	2987.4
113945.7	449.7	42172.3	257000.6	130669.9	18278.7	95950.3
287629.3		136048.2	307750.8	97051.8	7172.1	100538.2
175852.3		29019.2	145967.3	104889.3	23320.6	40241.2
7178248.1		3236022.2	20203784.1	3092457.7	8331.6	16625069.0
7037396.7		3027559.4	19132237.8	2613746.7	5280.0	15854778.2
262426.7		73822.8	471123.4	210774.3	727.6	284444.5
60527.2		282406.0	926743.1	304890.3	96.6	390685.1

13-11 续表

单位：万元

行　业	Sector	负债合计 Total Liabilities	#流动负债 Total Liquid Liabilities	#非流动负债 Total Non-liquid Liabilities	所有者权益合计 Total Owners' Equities
总　计	**Total**	**52101451.1**	**30895710.8**	**20131011.7**	**38847414.7**
煤炭开采和洗选业	Mining and Washing of Coal	2852150.4	1883398.9	968561.2	1487635.3
石油和天然气开采业	Extraction of Petroleum and Natural Gas	11674343.3	5590916.4	6083426.9	13798418.6
黑色金属矿采选业	Mining and Processing of Ferrous Metals Ores	1231362.3	1118545.7	112816.6	447881.9
有色金属矿采选业	Mining and Processing of Nonferrous Metals Ores	541713.9	339290.6	202423.3	590809.4
非金属矿采选业	Mining and Processing of Nonmetal Ores	101193.1	87580.1	4574.9	67896.4
#采　盐	Extraction of Salt	17472.2	14721.6	2602.6	38934.4
农副食品加工业	Processing of Food from Agricultural Products	653872.2	581604.4	55779.3	458268.7
#谷物磨制	Grain Grinding	96314.7	89020.6	7079.2	36473.4
饲料加工	Fodder Processing	77911.0	62466.0	15444.9	170538.4
制　糖	Sugar Making	178194.5	173510.9	4598.8	138827.2
食品制造业	Manufacture of Food	636591.0	579269.1	44867.2	132204.7
#罐头制造	Manufacture of can	480321.2	451932.3	28358.0	-23419.1
酒、饮料和精制茶制造业	Manufacture of Wine,Beverages and Refined Tea	160312.1	156337.7	3974.4	196218.4
#酒的制造	Manufacture of Wine	159180.2	155268.3	3911.9	189687.8
烟草制品业	Manufacture of Tobacco	118220.0	117220.0	1000.0	336589.0
纺织业	Manufacture of Textile	253046.7	220710.2	32336.5	178900.1
#棉、化纤纺织及印染精加工	Cotton, Chemical Fiber, Dyeing, Printing and Processing	231358.2	206466.5	24891.7	118937.6
毛纺织和染整精加工	Wool Textile, Dyeing and Printing	21688.5	14243.7	7444.8	59962.5
纺织服装、鞋、帽制造业	Manufacture of Textile Wearing Apparel,Footware and Caps	37330.1	29243.6	8086.4	5145.5
造纸及纸制品业	Manufacture of Paper and Paper Products	162178.9	117547.2	9844.3	82208.0
印刷业和记录媒介的复制	Printing and Copying of Medium for Record	27307.9	22097.2	5210.7	38194.9
石油加工、炼焦及核燃料加工业	Oil Processing, Coking and Nuclear Fuel Processing	3137303.1	2573255.1	564047.9	4328932.1
#炼　焦	Coking	433011.2	328406.8	104604.4	134183.4
化学原料及化学制品制造业	Raw Chemical Material and Chemical Products	5405880.1	2550489.6	2854362.6	3234669.8
#基础化学原料制造	Basic Chemical Material	1209475.0	736530.0	472674.9	445069.6
肥料制造	Fertilizer Making	1296415.1	665086.7	630827.9	654231.9
合成材料制造	Manufacture of Synthetic Material	2823581.7	1089924.5	1733657.0	1996016.0
医药制造业	Manufacture of Medicine	78163.1	73447.6	4715.5	80091.7
化学纤维制造业	Manufacture of Chemical Fiber	112533.0	106881.8	1331.8	-24156.9
橡胶制品业	Manufacture of Rubber Products	293290.7	248903.2	42387.4	215062.2
非金属矿物制品业	Manufacture of Nonmetal Mineral Products	3068077.8	2084421.8	846433.2	2671264.9
#水泥制造	Manufacture of Cement	2257122.7	1499207.3	717954.9	2030806.0
黑色金属冶炼及压延加工业	Smelting and Pressing of Ferrous Metals	4791882.1	4060466.2	730761.8	1488699.8
有色金属冶炼及压延加工业	Smelting and Pressing of Nonferrous Metals	339096.7	243609.3	95208.3	701012.5
金属制品业	Manufacture of Metal Products	117324.3	85324.3	32000.0	86736.9
通用设备制造业	Manufacture of General Purpose Machinery	10618.5	10618.5		6047.7
专用设备制造业	Manufacture of Special Purpose Machinery	165282.6	155472.7	9809.8	91717.9
汽车制造业	Manufacture of Automobile	182071.6	161526.8	20544.8	125679.2
电气机械及器材制造业	Manufacture of Electric Equipment and Machinery	105512.4	99828.8	5683.6	40405.1
电力、热力的生产和供应业	Electric Power and Thermal Production and Supply	13348428.2	5852698.9	6981445.0	6841181.8
#电力生产和电力供应	Electric Power Production and Supply	12477333.1	5495763.5	6469136.2	6640730.7
燃气生产和供应业	Gas Production and Supply	363221.1	252930.6	110086.7	107902.3
水的生产和供应业	Water Production and Supply	568294.5	153287.2	73229.5	358448.6

Continued

(10 000 yuan)

主营业务收入 Revenue from Principal Business	主营业务成本 Cost of Principal Business	主营业务税金及附加 Taxes and Other Charges on Principal Business	营业利润 Business Profit	利润总额 Total Profit	亏损企业亏损总额 Losses Value of Loss-Suffering Enterprises	利税总额 Total Profits and Taxes	本年应交增值税 Value-added Taxes Payable	全部从业人员年平均人数（人） Annual Average Employed Persons (person)
58372725.4	**43925957.1**	**3140604.5**	**5990803.9**	**6460499.5**	**938755.0**	**12257806.2**	**2656702.2**	**386644**
1325446.9	995368.9	37334.3	76139.9	80569.3	58529.2	262823.0	144919.4	36840
14867534.4	6602040.7	1130264.8	5212145.7	5262641.5		7576706.8	1183800.5	70653
862549.4	559177.8	21528.6	184391.9	191308.7	1877.4	293362.5	80525.2	6240
404264.6	209984.2	6100.8	137929.3	133461.8	8291.8	182293.7	42731.1	5466
86998.2	46584.3	3642.4	8015.4	8004.0	3137.6	18652.7	7006.3	2691
44211.5	13353.4	3273.3	6899.4	7141.9		15180.1	4764.9	973
1059061.6	893937.0	2227.4	52176.9	56948.0	11560.4	85908.5	26733.1	11282
146421.8	131779.7	137.4	5651.4	6589.6	1082.2	6881.1	154.1	1047
213128.4	163046.1	405.0	16321.0	16607.5		19390.9	2378.4	1165
270868.9	237967.7	1304.0	-7890.3	-6645.1	10034.6	10461.0	15802.1	5185
454632.6	367629.8	2378.9	4258.2	8411.0	42536.4	31239.9	20450.0	6834
172148.3	147446.5	744.9	-35222.2	-34022.2	38158.0	-24386.1	8891.2	2465
268848.4	137956.9	30663.0	58983.8	59955.6	2490.7	114140.9	23522.3	4833
263669.8	134355.5	30624.4	58643.1	59588.7	2490.7	113555.3	23342.2	4676
382124.0	129865.0	169165.0	61130.0	60910.0		271882.0	41807.0	977
240238.3	235268.1	1239.6	-15059.3	-6238.5	12045.4	850.1	5849.0	7852
225687.4	220181.6	1072.2	-10114.6	-2032.0	7838.9	4765.1	5724.9	6941
14550.9	15086.5	167.4	-4944.7	-4206.5	4206.5	-3915.0	124.1	911
33252.2	26716.8	136.1	1108.8	2541.5	40.1	3129.3	451.7	1558
52557.9	46171.5	122.3	-4817.6	3162.0	1959.3	4594.9	1310.6	2132
30713.0	23895.7	162.6	793.4	2618.0		3383.7	603.1	1121
15468086.9	13130066.6	1629167.8	-98635.7	-118685.1	397133.3	1864172.9	353690.2	26793
242063.1	217474.8	1034.8	-10565.3	-10374.4	20951.7	-92.9	9246.7	4063
4309387.4	3527285.9	47101.8	230095.4	295311.8	49337.3	517805.9	175392.3	42340
1021171.7	905118.2	2521.9	3846.0	8279.1	16113.2	26038.6	15237.6	13122
736363.4	404895.4	28851.9	116026.4	156200.4	23419.1	230912.0	45859.7	6798
2471403.6	2160976.7	14936.0	90312.7	110130.6	9517.0	232000.5	106933.9	20253
57323.6	42083.2	224.0	5372.6	5467.5		7375.8	1684.3	1294
37982.8	32535.5	105.9	-4327.7	-985.1	997.7	684.5	1563.7	666
463126.4	408951.7	719.0	3198.1	9854.7	1277.9	22754.1	12180.4	6365
1655783.9	1400111.0	7443.1	33244.3	73217.9	47155.5	155387.9	74726.9	25665
887769.7	747017.5	4485.7	-195.4	34740.9	39903.7	83825.5	44598.9	16769
5818354.5	5554349.2	10334.6	-91647.0	-17403.1	65691.7	55552.7	62621.2	24046
326847.7	284268.0	316.9	14247.6	14468.5	10399.8	16985.2	2199.8	4868
235353.2	221715.0	464.2	-1670.4	492.7	1481.5	2800.6	1843.7	1381
10875.1	9397.4	141.5	-503.3	-296.3	332.3	739.7	894.5	370
148167.4	117092.5	693.5	10585.1	15884.4	1203.7	20873.8	4295.9	1985
277981.2	270705.6	568.3	-14764.8	9302.1	12847.7	10977.3	1106.9	1845
176164.6	159600.3	440.6	5623.4	6513.4	445.7	11209.1	4255.1	824
7193663.8	6473973.3	19783.2	204734.0	344709.1	139531.4	627905.7	263413.4	50474
7004794.3	6260031.0	19683.6	255362.3	343880.0	131860.1	624806.5	261242.9	46159
342951.5	288470.1	3820.9	-6392.7	13365.3	103.2	17564.6	378.4	2091
63978.3	50623.5	452.5	-11773.9	-6736.2	12079.0	-2867.6	3416.1	2557

13-12 各地、州、市、县(市)国有控股工业企业主要经济指标

单位：万元 (2013 年)

地区	Region	企业单位数(个) Number of Enterprises (unit)	#亏损企业 Loss- Suffering Enterprises	工业总产值(当年价格) Gross Industrial Output Value (At Current Prices)
总计	**Total**	**600**	**173**	**56688937.3**
乌鲁木齐市	**Urumqi City**	**130**	**37**	**18163543.7**
天山区	Tianshan District	12	4	3468721.6
沙依巴克区	Shayibak District	17	3	564834.3
新市区	Xinshi District	48	16	4235250.8
水磨沟区	Shui Mogou District	5	1	145082.6
头屯河区	Tou Tunhe District	15	3	4921260.3
达坂城区	Da Bancheng District	9	1	204420.3
米东区	Midong District	22	9	4588574.3
乌鲁木齐县	Urumqi County	2		35399.5
克拉玛依市	**Karamay City**	**17**	**10**	**16753514.4**
独山子区	Dushanzi District	8	4	6540811.3
克拉玛依区	Karamay District	9	6	10212703.1
白碱滩区	Bai Jiantan District			
乌尔河区	Urhe District			
吐鲁番地区	**Turpan Administrative Offices**	**27**	**9**	**1513678.8**
吐鲁番市	Turpan City	7	5	58523.8
鄯善县	Shanshan [Piqan] County	8	1	1221754.1
托克逊县	Toksun County	12	3	233400.9
哈密地区	**Hami [Kumul] Administrative Offices**	**46**	**7**	**1281916.9**
哈密市	Hami [Kumul] City	34	6	1154665.4
巴里坤哈萨克自治县	Barkol Kazak Autonomous County	10	1	110161.5
伊吾县	Yiwu [Araturuk] County	2		17090.0
昌吉回族自治州	**Changji Hui Autonomous Prefecture**	**37**	**12**	**1868873.1**
昌吉市	Changji City	10	2	420765.2
阜康市	Fukang City	11	3	1165142.5
呼图壁县	Hutubi County	5	1	105433.4
玛纳斯县	Manas County	6	2	35737.3
奇台县	Qitai County	1	1	21372.9
吉木萨尔县	Jimsar County	3	2	102986.3
木垒哈萨克自治县	Mori Kazak Autonomous County	1	1	17435.5
伊犁哈萨克自治州	**Ili Kazak Autonomous Prefecture**	**136**	**43**	**3774429.3**
伊犁州直属县(市)	**Counties (Cities) Direct Under Ili Prefecture**	**67**	**26**	**2403484.7**
伊宁市	Yining [Gulja] City	10	5	363364.5
奎屯市	Kuytun City	20	9	989248.6
伊宁县	Yining [Gulja] County	8	3	172137.0
察布查尔锡伯自治县	Qapqal Xibe Autonomous County	6	1	90989.5
霍城县	Huocheng [Korgas] County	7	3	133444.0
巩留县	Gongliu [Tokkuztara] County	3	1	104052.6
新源县	Xinyuan [Kunes] County	6	2	423652.3
昭苏县	Zhaosu [Mongolkure] County	1		10049.9
特克斯县	Tekes County	1	1	6912.3
尼勒克县	Nilka County	5	1	109634.0
塔城地区	**Tacheng [Tarbagatai] Administrative Offices**	**35**	**9**	**658727.3**
塔城市	Tacheng [Qoqek] City	2	1	86312.3
乌苏市	Usu City	4	2	67130.1
额敏县	Emin [Dorbiljin] County	7	1	78863.0

Main Economic Indicators of State-holding Industrial Enterprises by Prefecture, Autonomous Prefecture, City and County

(10 000 yuan)

工业销售产值(当年价) Sales Value of Industry Products (At Current Prices)	出口交货值 Delivery Value of Industry Export	实收资本 Total Capital Hold	资产合计 Total Assets	流动资产合计 Total Working Capitals	#产成品 Finished Product	固定资产原价 Net Value of Fixed Assets
55970581.5	**162644.2**	**30233706.7**	**91014942.9**	**21010668.0**	**2011895.5**	**82045751.9**
17713189.2	**78486.8**	**6894179.2**	**26193101.4**	**5912278.5**	**522807.5**	**21677482.9**
3495821.4	47003.7	418065.6	5571641.5	1113198.9	30817.8	4751466.6
478663.0		453361.3	2508892.6	581394.9	8218.1	780782.2
4066562.9	10293.4	2707322.0	7167746.5	1121878.3	166832.6	8823737.9
155958.3		43301.9	287023.8	69337.4	6739.2	380073.7
4681913.2	13953.0	935291.3	5135597.2	1770452.8	167015.3	2719490.1
200121.4		163973.9	759270.2	114549.1	10568.8	462524.2
4602146.6	7236.7	2127456.1	4516375.4	1101277.6	132615.7	3499207.0
32002.4		45407.1	246554.2	40189.5		260201.2
16749511.3	**1539.4**	**12130341.4**	**19563761.0**	**5218455.7**	**281261.0**	**21489096.2**
6522289.5	1539.4	2887768.1	4860845.0	1841584.1	136393.8	4757276.8
10227221.8		9242573.3	14702916.0	3376871.6	144867.2	16731819.4
1500941.1		**277171.3**	**3521568.5**	**788844.2**	**81388.7**	**4760725.1**
59395.5		92506.8	358094.8	73008.8	11454.6	259553.7
1207142.5		46098.8	2478414.0	590939.6	65394.8	3926339.8
234403.1		138565.7	685059.7	124895.8	4539.3	574831.6
1296654.3		**946358.6**	**4237228.5**	**1295325.7**	**98317.7**	**2119623.8**
1188873.6		886666.1	3546921.7	1133385.3	70954.1	1712241.4
90552.7		48292.5	604831.4	142969.3	27091.0	340569.6
17228.0		11400.0	85475.4	18971.1	272.6	66812.8
1779661.7	**34243.0**	**679338.4**	**4322095.8**	**862841.9**	**187505.5**	**3152506.8**
405810.8	22928.4	100192.7	790988.7	172175.8	18252.5	602482.3
1105488.3		503107.5	2972852.7	588520.1	130057.2	2067539.3
107833.6		16387.6	85972.8	22889.3	5981.1	77807.7
33517.0		18684.5	70046.4	19792.7	2275.7	45698.0
19141.5		1200.0	31175.3	12652.0	8464.9	27219.7
103995.0	11314.6	38766.1	351963.0	34227.5	9914.1	324725.0
3875.5		1000.0	19096.9	12584.5	12560.0	7034.8
3633553.1	**5186.1**	**2162921.2**	**9812735.9**	**2519207.6**	**321188.7**	**6389925.0**
2321725.1	**126.4**	**1455859.3**	**6115491.2**	**1557934.1**	**177257.7**	**3944275.4**
362930.4		104041.0	760578.7	123473.3	1958.3	732009.2
966952.0	126.4	339210.1	1852508.2	607176.8	36293.5	1185276.8
169276.3		97216.0	444992.1	145043.4	19799.9	187133.3
85186.1		28560.0	162168.9	21469.9	4598.0	119534.2
143716.5		62549.7	209906.2	64445.4	27279.3	134756.3
104052.6		477517.2	1180644.6	202958.9		622637.1
359198.5		150468.6	609330.3	344334.7	79693.9	209173.1
10049.9		100.0	5421.3	3814.0		2474.3
6912.3		20000.0	111648.4	1014.8		111682.7
113450.5		176196.7	778292.5	44202.9	7634.8	639598.4
613617.2	**5059.7**	**353684.7**	**1806281.8**	**554135.1**	**80274.0**	**1108977.2**
85307.1		11078.9	131575.4	11205.0	162.1	168513.9
62827.7		35147.0	307166.0	156846.0	5439.6	146580.4
69192.3	5059.7	70319.4	233556.6	104972.8	38821.1	161783.4

13-12 续表 1

单位: 万元

地　区	Region	企业单位数(个) Number of Enterprises (unit)	#亏损企业 Loss- Suffering Enterprises	工业总产值(当年价格) Gross Industrial Output Value (At Current Prices)
沙湾县	Shawan County	6		92930.9
托里县	Toli County	7	3	155833.0
裕民县	Yumin [Qagantokay] County			
和布克赛尔蒙古自治县	Hoboksar Mongol Autonomous County	9	2	177658.0
阿勒泰地区	**Altay Administrative Offices**	**34**	**8**	**712217.3**
阿勒泰市	Altay City	9	4	144068.7
布尔津县	Burqin County	9	1	67344.6
富蕴县	Fuyun [Koktokay] County	5	1	247974.9
福海县	Fuhai [Burultokay] County	4		29038.6
哈巴河县	Habahe [Kaba] County	5	2	212234.0
青河县	Qinghe [Qinggil] County	1		4934.0
吉木乃县	Jeminay County	1		6622.5
博尔塔拉蒙古自治州	**Bortala Mongol Autonomous Prefecture**	**13**	**4**	**213818.2**
博乐市	Bole [Bortala] City	8	3	172599.6
精河县	Jinghe [Jing] County	3	1	20851.5
温泉县	Wenquan [Araxang] County			
巴音郭楞蒙古自治州	**Bayangol Mongol Autonomous Prefecture**	**45**	**10**	**7035288.8**
库尔勒市	Korla City	20	7	5591712.7
轮台县	Luntai [Bugur] County			
尉犁县	Yuli [Lopnur] County	1		2874.0
若羌县	Ruoqiang [Qarkilik] County	3		411502.4
且末县	Qiemo [Qarqan] County	1		
焉耆回族自治县	Yanqi Hui Autonomous County	3		34736.9
和静县	Hejing County	13	2	966647.2
和硕县	Hoxud County	2		9577.0
博湖县	Bohu [Bagrax] County	2		15427.0
阿克苏地区	**Aksu Administrative Offices**	**53**	**17**	**3155849.5**
阿克苏市	Aksu City	18	6	632218.0
温宿县	Wensu [Onsu] County	10	2	67511.8
库车县	Kuqa County	14	5	2259375.2
沙雅县	Xayar County			
新和县	Xinhe [Toksu] County			
拜城县	Baicheng [Bay] County	8	4	186270.8
乌什县	Wushi [Uxturpan] County	2		8369.2

Continued

(10 000 yuan)

工业销售产值(当年价) Sales Value of Industry Products (At Current Prices)	出口交货值 Delivery Value of Industry Export	实收资本 Total Capital Hold	资产合计 Total Assets	流动资产合计 Total Working Capitals	#产成品 Finished Product	固定资产原价 Net Value of Fixed Assets
92678.7		26988.2	90894.1	52960.4	8378.2	68162.0
137959.1		49248.7	360387.9	123287.3	12333.3	188874.2
165652.3		160902.5	682701.8	104863.6	15139.7	375063.3
698210.8		**353377.2**	**1890962.9**	**407138.4**	**63657.0**	**1336672.4**
144008.6		23504.6	294101.7	40979.0	2505.7	317380.2
67235.1		40893.3	411341.8	72035.5	914.2	315279.8
232631.5		161218.6	559211.7	141741.9	49748.1	326536.1
28756.4		72662.7	156051.4	42137.1	1457.7	117491.0
214855.7		39480.0	295795.4	76935.8	7401.3	164166.8
4101.0		1000.0	117076.5	26894.2	1630.0	59284.9
6622.5		14618.0	57384.4	6414.9		36533.6
191258.9		**87111.9**	**562423.6**	**107958.5**	**19827.2**	**465305.6**
150640.7		31477.9	250559.5	65428.7	18542.2	250459.3
21182.5		13646.0	121448.5	9001.3	1285.0	62638.7
7103687.6	**31717.4**	**4174036.3**	**11145130.1**	**1218278.5**	**188028.3**	**14126848.0**
5625599.7	7996.6	3799563.5	8392250.1	452767.7	74384.8	12210192.0
2874.0		360.0	4155.8	1913.1	276.3	2441.6
456769.1		57899.9	746687.8	228663.1	16128.3	563381.3
			22.5	3.4		388.6
39917.5	8140.8	1988.0	42070.6	19770.3	12131.1	40868.9
947193.9		305687.8	1926387.0	495470.2	72278.9	1271767.4
10433.7	3038.6	1950.0	8210.3	5813.4	2345.8	6109.9
18088.1	12541.4	6587.1	25346.0	13877.3	10483.1	31698.3
3119129.7	**58.3**	**1207932.9**	**4863138.7**	**1128961.5**	**59971.6**	**2718433.3**
613281.6	58.3	459831.7	2220501.6	563011.5	12084.6	980177.8
65395.9		56750.5	312462.2	33948.1	2282.6	275767.8
2240541.4		620483.0	1965958.6	376286.0	29924.3	1244722.3
192461.2		57492.7	315705.8	145909.2	12606.1	187300.7
5345.1		4000.0	15241.8	7851.1	3074.0	11065.2

13-12 续表 2

单位：万元

地　　区	Region	企业单位数(个) Number of Enterprises (unit)	#亏损企业 Loss- Suffering Enterprises	工业总产值(当年价格) Gross Industrial Output Value (At Current Prices)
阿瓦提县	Awat County	1		2104.5
柯坪县	Kalpin County			
克孜勒苏柯尔克孜自治州	**Kizilsu Kirgiz Autonomous Prcfccturc**	**5**		**80236.6**
阿图什市	Artux City	3		52195.0
阿克陶县	Akto County			
阿合奇县	Akqi County	1		21143.9
乌恰县	Wuqia [Ulugqat] County	1		6897.7
喀什地区	**Kashgar [Kaxgar] Administrative Offices**	**15**	**6**	**399398.2**
喀什市	Kashgar [Kaxgar] City	7	4	330562.8
疏附县	Shufu County	1	1	1560.0
疏勒县	Shule County	2		30470.9
英吉沙县	Yengisar County			
泽普县	Zepu [Poskam] County			
莎车县	Shache [Yarkant] County	1		10451.6
叶城县	Yecheng [Kagilik] County	1		5712.2
麦盖提县	Makit County	1	1	3612.6
岳普湖县	Yopurga County			
伽师县	Jiashi [Payzawat] County			
巴楚县	Bachu [Maralbexi] County	1		4758.0
塔什库尔干塔吉克自治县	Taxkorgan Tajik Autonomous County	1		12270.1
和田地区	**Hotan Administrative Offices**	**9**	**2**	**180438.2**
和田市	Hotan City	3	1	90109.0
和田县	Hotan County	3	1	21785.1
墨玉县	Moyu [Karakax] County	2		49975.2
皮山县	Pishan [Guma] County			
洛浦县	Lop County	1		18568.9
策勒县	Qira County			
于田县	Yutian [Keriya] County			
民丰县	Minfeng [Niya] County			
自治区直辖县级市	**Municpality Country-LevelCity directly under the Central Government**	**65**	**16**	**2260541.7**
石河子市	Shihezi City	36	11	1884416.9
阿拉尔市	Aral City	12	1	139118.4
图木舒克市	Tumxuk City	10	1	189064.9
五家渠市	Wujiaqu City	7	3	47941.5

Continued

(10 000 yuan)

工业销售产值(当年价) Sales Value of Industry Products (At Current Prices)	出口交货值 Delivery Value of Industry Export	实收资本 Total Capital Hold	资产合计 Total Assets	流动资产合计 Total Working Capitals	#产成品 Finished Product	固定资产原价 Net Value of Fixed Assets
2104.5		9375.0	33268.7	1955.6		19399.5
78204.7		**110734.0**	**320078.3**	**35437.7**	**1973.5**	**291165.2**
50886.4		109734.0	140501.7	28180.8	1663.7	113698.5
21143.9			171875.2	6145.4		167379.4
6174.4		1000.0	7701.4	1111.5	309.8	10087.3
397080.3		**74312.5**	**593290.5**	**105877.5**	**10579.6**	**728087.2**
327195.5		38862.5	444467.6	60264.4	5544.9	605377.3
1720.0		1000.0	1075.5	518.0	353.0	1313.0
29856.6		12000.0	36560.1	17851.7	2357.0	21962.9
8395.8		15000.0	24781.9	7277.9	1268.7	14803.9
4825.5		3000.0	9625.5	3836.0	348.0	5115.7
8068.3		3900.0	3593.6	1570.7		3982.3
4048.6		350.0	4399.2	3775.0	708.0	1092.7
12970.0		200.0	68787.1	10783.8		74439.4
183227.4		**221450.8**	**579732.3**	**102226.1**	**4706.0**	**551477.1**
90109.0		10362.6	160233.6	14413.3		226871.6
21744.1		143351.2	280360.4	54467.1	299.1	209823.6
52969.2		26737.0	68815.1	27479.8	3820.7	49647.9
18405.1		41000.0	70323.2	5865.9	586.2	65134.0
2216775.3	**11413.2**	**1264521.3**	**5238862.9**	**1708678.0**	**233479.8**	**3534516.0**
1866812.8	11413.2	1004192.4	4374481.7	1403862.6	179414.5	2931294.3
133430.0		103185.8	356068.3	89271.3	19517.0	300589.0
175238.2		54264.9	363347.7	167863.0	30595.3	198396.3
41294.3		102878.2	144965.2	47681.1	3953.0	104236.4

13-12 续表 3

单位: 万元

地 区	Region	负债合计 Total Liabilities	#流动负债 Total Liquid Liabilities	#非流动负债 Total Non-liquid Liabilities	所有者权益合计 Total Owners' Equities
总 计	**Total**	**52101451.1**	**30895710.8**	**20131011.7**	**38847414.7**
乌鲁木齐市	**Urumqi City**	**15336188.5**	**10380564.2**	**4593850.4**	**10856912.5**
天山区	Tianshan District	3379035.6	2002066.7	1376960.1	2192605.9
沙依巴克区	Shayibak District	1510086.2	820459.5	405039.0	998806.4
新市区	Xinshi District	3708046.4	2893170.6	783906.6	3459700.1
水磨沟区	Shui Mogou District	71379.3	35824.9	35554.4	215644.5
头屯河区	Tou Tunhe District	3830440.3	3184662.3	639937.7	1305156.9
达坂城区	Da Bancheng District	472450.6	235515.9	213188.3	286819.5
米东区	Midong District	2168098.2	1099252.0	1052224.9	2348277.0
乌鲁木齐县	Urumqi County	196651.9	109612.3	87039.4	49902.2
克拉玛依市	**Karamay City**	**8646124.0**	**5304182.5**	**3341940.8**	**10896625.5**
独山子区	Dushanzi District	2038987.5	1753385.2	285602.0	2821857.4
克拉玛依区	Karamay District	6607136.5	3550797.3	3056338.8	8074768.1
白碱滩区	Bai Jiantan District				
乌尔河区	Urhe District				
吐鲁番地区	**Turpan Administrative Offices**	**2164632.2**	**1127506.3**	**1027965.9**	**1350465.7**
吐鲁番市	Turpan City	265507.4	169477.7	96029.6	92587.4
鄯善县	Shanshan [Piqan] County	1408467.1	723698.0	684769.1	1063476.4
托克逊县	Toksun County	490657.7	234330.6	247167.2	194401.9
哈密地区	**Hami [Kumul] Administrative Offices**	**3072773.6**	**1880489.1**	**1192284.2**	**1164405.1**
哈密市	Hami [Kumul] City	2538832.8	1526087.2	1012745.3	1008039.1
巴里坤哈萨克自治县	Barkol Kazak Autonomous County	467088.2	318536.6	148551.6	137743.2
伊吾县	Yiwu [Araturuk] County	66852.6	35865.3	30987.3	18622.8
昌吉回族自治州	**Changji Hui Autonomous Prefecture**	**2681890.6**	**1256652.1**	**1320700.2**	**1637936.7**
昌吉市	Changji City	449381.8	231262.0	218119.8	341606.8
阜康市	Fukang City	1966023.2	817996.0	1044104.0	1004561.1
呼图壁县	Hutubi County	71516.0	50830.9	20481.3	14456.8
玛纳斯县	Manas County	60591.5	29560.5	30704.4	9454.9
奇台县	Qitai County	25730.4	25645.8		5444.9
吉木萨尔县	Jimsar County	94690.3	87399.5	7290.7	257272.7
木垒哈萨克自治县	Mori Kazak Autonomous County	13957.4	13957.4		5139.5
伊犁哈萨克自治州	**Ili Kazak Autonomous Prefecture**	**6403294.1**	**3502923.9**	**2419359.5**	**3387588.6**
伊犁州直属县(市)	**Counties (Cities) Direct Under Ili Prefecture**	**4030427.3**	**2024389.5**	**1570663.8**	**2066322.2**
伊宁市	Yining [Gulja] City	531529.0	224849.3	306679.7	229049.5
奎屯市	Kuytun City	1131988.4	600299.4	531603.2	720519.6
伊宁县	Yining [Gulja] County	284540.7	186088.4	98452.1	160451.3
察布查尔锡伯自治县	Qapqal Xibe Autonomous County	114067.8	60805.6	13311.3	40285.4
霍城县	Huocheng [Korgas] County	139040.9	89085.1	49955.7	70865.3
巩留县	Gongliu [Tokkuztara] County	737083.7	194635.2	147111.5	443482.1
新源县	Xinyuan [Kunes] County	405844.1	405374.0	470.1	203486.2
昭苏县	Zhaosu [Mongolkure] County	3812.5	3812.5		1608.8
特克斯县	Tekes County	94468.6	16856.1	77612.5	17179.8
尼勒克县	Nilka County	588051.6	242583.9	345467.7	179394.2
塔城地区	**Tacheng [Tarbagatai] Administrative Offices**	**1226744.3**	**856917.6**	**359590.1**	**576582.3**
塔城市	Tacheng [Qoqek] City	88464.2	40043.0	48331.0	43111.2
乌苏市	Usu City	209707.8	208640.1	1067.7	97458.2
额敏县	Emin [Dorbiljin] County	140897.0	79255.2	61641.8	90916.9

Continued

(10 000 yuan)

主营业务收入 Revenue from Principal Business	主营业务成本 Cost of Principal Business	主营业务税金及附加 Taxes and Other Charges on Principal Business	营业利润 Business Profit	利润总额 Total Profit	亏损企业亏损总额 Losses Value of Loss-Suffering Enterprises	利税总额 Total Profits and Taxes	本年应交增值税 Value-added Taxes Payable	全部从业人员年平均人数(人) Annual Average Employed Persons (person)
58372725.4	**43925957.1**	**3140604.5**	**5990803.9**	**6460499.5**	**938755.0**	**12257806.2**	**2656702.2**	**386644**
17775574.9	**14581370.7**	**865127.8**	**1016706.9**	**1212839.1**	**402306.7**	**2724596.4**	**646629.5**	**91142**
3495451.2	3280997.7	8234.3	127228.9	134160.0	37811.2	254828.4	112434.1	15904
572970.2	509381.1	6571.8	-17239.5	19879.8	13753.4	37623.1	11171.5	9156
4074994.0	2028806.0	436755.3	1158007.7	1224832.9	53703.9	1970939.2	309351.0	19984
153592.2	148603.1	1444.7	-15154.2	-11207.3	19684.4	2669.8	12432.4	1604
4511770.2	4294266.2	10221.8	-91367.4	-13708.7	61424.4	56343.3	59830.2	16644
200606.2	134680.7	2467.2	30052.5	27073.3	6033.6	43329.6	13789.1	6648
4734188.5	4170153.0	399432.7	-184676.3	-179066.9	209895.8	347681.2	127315.4	21159
32002.4	14482.9		9855.2	10876.0		11181.8	305.8	43
18093228.0	**13487955.6**	**1353263.0**	**1805916.4**	**1888600.9**	**244601.8**	**4125733.8**	**883869.9**	**88897**
6633958.6	5846295.7	576512.9	-199697.3	-182194.7	194519.2	520944.6	126626.4	14426
11459269.4	7641659.9	776750.1	2005613.7	2070795.6	50082.6	3604789.2	757243.5	74471
1608462.6	**1086370.6**	**60018.2**	**225753.0**	**232951.0**	**9897.5**	**396877.1**	**103907.9**	**20929**
61092.4	49202.7	292.9	-3817.1	-5193.5	6551.8	-1487.8	3412.8	906
1314330.3	862356.7	57470.5	207824.5	216238.1	237.3	366660.6	92952.0	17592
233039.9	174811.2	2254.8	21745.6	21906.4	3108.4	31704.3	7543.1	2431
1323330.8	**1043406.6**	**16258.2**	**94765.1**	**149213.9**	**11309.1**	**251988.6**	**86516.5**	**19989**
1216411.4	975399.2	13589.9	83167.6	109272.3	10992.7	196012.8	73150.6	18392
89687.6	58148.7	2472.3	9203.0	34178.2	316.4	47399.8	10749.3	1449
17231.8	9858.7	196.0	2394.5	5763.4		8576.0	2616.6	148
1796494.4	**1555762.4**	**2463.6**	**55248.9**	**65051.1**	**20654.4**	**119642.0**	**52127.3**	**19177**
418783.0	353360.6	612.5	24042.8	32355.3	2027.5	59149.8	26182.0	3656
1100293.2	980527.0	792.5	5495.5	7489.2	9887.6	18087.9	9806.2	11769
105288.6	88157.4	408.2	6906.3	7167.5	2541.3	12185.5	4609.8	1396
36553.6	29796.4	296.0	-179.5	-547.8	2349.4	1783.9	2035.7	902
22740.8	19205.4	150.6	-300.2	-258.5	258.5	1397.8	1505.7	388
109602.8	81719.9	158.3	19966.6	19630.2	2805.3	27258.9	7470.4	616
3232.4	2995.7	45.5	-682.6	-784.8	784.8	-221.8	517.5	450
3701915.5	**2686672.6**	**215191.0**	**323028.1**	**344052.7**	**119114.7**	**769330.8**	**210087.1**	**47068**
2360331.0	**1750750.6**	**199015.5**	**125335.5**	**141834.7**	**71287.3**	**469179.2**	**128329.0**	**26103**
361084.6	304422.0	1464.0	29468.6	28728.8	6013.9	48155.7	17962.9	4830
1002578.9	701456.5	170980.6	37554.8	44771.3	25761.3	268148.6	52396.7	6300
167275.7	136926.1	1024.1	-2316.3	-244.6	6909.5	8695.9	7916.4	4247
90434.7	64161.7	115.0	8092.3	8237.5	358.8	11453.9	3101.4	764
143283.6	131903.0	553.6	-2284.2	-1793.3	6124.3	4740.5	5980.2	2065
105919.6	81266.4	426.0	-16104.9	-9053.3	9271.0	-1588.2	7039.1	596
359468.9	243599.2	23669.6	55965.5	56285.0	2569.8	102615.0	22660.4	5788
10049.9	6227.3	89.4	2982.7	2982.7		3072.1		98
6837.7	5192.4		-2807.1	-2820.2	2820.2	-2820.2		75
113397.4	75596.0	693.2	14784.1	14740.8	11458.5	26705.9	11271.9	1340
643226.8	**533009.6**	**5968.0**	**22419.2**	**28317.3**	**31770.3**	**57123.9**	**22838.6**	**12524**
84071.8	87448.5	50.5	-6416.5	-5612.0	6191.7	-3981.1	1580.4	805
91164.9	87269.7	1399.2	-9910.9	-7165.4	10777.5	773.6	6539.8	2447
74523.2	59466.5	162.6	7788.2	7339.5	2712.6	8833.5	1331.4	1088

13-12 续表 4

单位: 万元

地　区	Region	负债合计 Total Liabilities	#流动负债 Total Liquid Liabilities	#非流动负债 Total Non-liquid Liabilities	所有者权益合计 Total Owners' Equities
沙湾县	Shawan County	36732.5	26153.2	10579.3	54161.6
托里县	Toli County	267464.0	194213.5	69190.3	91711.4
裕民县	Yumin [Qagantokay] County				
和布克赛尔蒙古自治县	Hoboksar Mongol Autonomous County	483478.8	308612.6	168780.0	199223.0
阿勒泰地区	**Altay Administrative Offices**	**1146122.5**	**621616.8**	**489105.6**	**744684.1**
阿勒泰市	Altay City	227974.2	96608.3	131365.9	66127.5
布尔津县	Burqin County	346893.1	183276.1	128216.9	64292.7
富蕴县	Fuyun [Koktokay] County	305678.7	235044.1	70634.6	253533.0
福海县	Fuhai [Burultokay] County	79829.8	14129.8	65700.0	76221.6
哈巴河县	Habahe [Kaba] County	53975.9	37887.7	16088.2	241819.2
青河县	Qinghe [Qinggil] County	97438.7	20338.7	77100.0	19637.8
吉木乃县	Jeminay County	34332.1	34332.1		23052.3
博尔塔拉蒙古自治州	**Bortala Mongol Autonomous Prefecture**	**487907.9**	**186656.0**	**301251.6**	**74515.7**
博乐市	Bole [Bortala] City	244724.4	115170.3	129553.9	5835.1
精河县	Jinghe [Jing] County	104696.8	49349.8	55347.0	16751.7
温泉县	Wenquan [Araxang] County				
巴音郭楞蒙古自治州	**Bayangol Mongol Autonomous Prefecture**	**6306551.3**	**3191823.1**	**3076113.2**	**4838578.4**
库尔勒市	Korla City	4366095.9	1790899.6	2540408.8	4026153.9
轮台县	Luntai [Bugur] County				
尉犁县	Yuli [Lopnur] County	3527.9	1527.9		627.9
若羌县	Ruoqiang [Qarkilik] County	437799.4	269284.5	168514.9	308888.3
且末县	Qiemo [Qarqan] County	22.5	469.7	-447.2	
焉耆回族自治县	Yanqi Hui Autonomous County	16690.9	16220.5	470.3	25379.7
和静县	Hejing County	1460994.7	1092340.5	366826.8	465392.3
和硕县	Hoxud County	3429.4	3323.2	106.2	4780.9
博湖县	Bohu [Bagrax] County	17990.6	17757.2	233.4	7355.4
阿克苏地区	**Aksu Administrative Offices**	**2832515.1**	**1602742.4**	**1169568.4**	**2019750.2**
阿克苏市	Aksu City	1216486.3	551008.5	664535.6	998772.2
温宿县	Wensu [Onsu] County	255629.9	124322.1	131117.6	56832.2
库车县	Kuqa County	1113529.7	799073.5	255415.2	846798.9
沙雅县	Xayar County				
新和县	Xinhe [Toksu] County				
拜城县	Baicheng [Bay] County	217469.7	103838.8	113600.0	98235.9
乌什县	Wushi [Uxturpan] County	6053.8	5653.8	400.0	9188.0

Continued

(10 000 yuan)

主营业务收入 Revenue from Principal Business	主营业务成本 Cost of Principal Business	主营业务税金及附加 Taxes and Other Charges on Principal Business	营业利润 Business Profit	利润总额 Total Profit	亏损企业亏损总额 Losses Value of Loss-Suffering Enterprises	利税总额 Total Profits and Taxes	本年应交增值税 Value-added Taxes Payable	全部从业人员年平均人数(人) Annual Average Employed Persons (person)
92025.9	79096.3	266.8	4142.8	5002.3		8608.2	3339.1	1409
150357.2	120043.6	746.7	10400.7	10993.4	10130.9	13451.1	1711.0	3301
151083.8	99685.0	3342.2	16414.9	17759.5	1957.6	29438.6	8336.9	3474
698357.7	**402912.4**	**10207.5**	**175273.4**	**173900.7**	**16057.1**	**243027.7**	**58919.5**	**8441**
142267.2	126180.0	514.4	-7575.9	-6469.3	8138.8	144.8	6099.7	2168
67130.6	29714.1	305.1	13400.4	15053.5	41.4	19142.0	3783.4	583
235433.4	133217.6	5346.5	60805.1	61567.0	4227.1	91940.1	25026.6	3313
28304.0	17255.0	668.7	5213.5	5362.1		8797.0	2766.2	347
214530.0	92946.6	3351.7	100213.5	95225.7	3649.8	119821.0	21243.6	1844
4070.0	1240.0	21.1	36.0	41.0		62.1		169
6622.5	2359.1		3180.8	3120.7		3120.7		17
210292.3	**184889.7**	**858.1**	**357.4**	**922.5**	**9297.4**	**8525.5**	**6744.9**	**3770**
170313.1	161146.2	536.0	-4727.1	-4274.8	8125.8	914.2	4653.0	3306
20555.7	14358.2	294.5	743.3	856.1	1171.6	1773.5	622.9	422
7678609.7	**4118095.8**	**355165.1**	**2267547.6**	**2281685.4**	**17803.7**	**3067542.9**	**430692.4**	**36332**
5567202.5	2436145.5	318708.1	2087637.4	2059268.6	13806.1	2728764.7	350788.0	21934
2874.0	2073.6	0.5	425.2	425.2		490.7	65.0	60
449651.1	183471.7	27637.6	131334.5	172762.0		244026.8	43627.2	3475
								63
39903.2	31442.8	327.2	4442.3	4472.6		7054.1	2254.3	602
1589423.4	1441773.0	8294.3	42831.4	43803.4	3006.0	84605.8	32508.1	9764
10433.7	7935.4	96.4	1525.3	1532.1		1784.3	155.8	111
18130.2	14262.2	101.0	343.1	413.1		1808.1	1294.0	323
3132313.9	**2549996.3**	**252129.1**	**118897.3**	**131637.7**	**29573.4**	**496995.6**	**113228.8**	**18587**
613546.3	542035.7	2917.0	13304.9	24439.8	3616.5	52670.3	25313.5	7113
66517.4	41845.8	524.3	9410.1	9193.0	657.8	13824.3	4107.0	1597
2243116.8	1814439.4	244589.3	77520.7	79583.8	13391.7	392872.1	68699.0	6797
194912.0	143243.7	3201.6	16757.5	16512.6	11907.4	34426.3	14712.1	2922
12354.8	7396.3	896.9	1484.0	1488.4		2782.5	397.2	148

13-12 续表 5

单位: 万元

地　　区	Region	负债合计 Total Liabilities	#流动负债 Total Liquid Liabilities	#非流动负债 Total Non-liquid Liabilities	所有者权益合计 Total Owners' Equities
阿瓦提县	Awat County	23345.7	18845.7	4500.0	9923.0
柯坪县	Kalpin County				
克孜勒苏柯尔克孜自治州	**Kizilsu Kirgiz Autonomous Prefecture**	**202994.5**	**201882.2**	**1112.2**	**113354.3**
阿图什市	Artux City	25650.9	25047.9	603.0	111121.3
阿克陶县	Akto County				
阿合奇县	Akqi County	171875.2	171875.2		
乌恰县	Wuqia [Ulugqat] County	5468.4	4959.1	509.2	2233.0
喀什地区	**Kashgar [Kaxgar] Administrative Offices**	**469008.3**	**188772.0**	**279582.5**	**124282.5**
喀什市	Kashgar [Kaxgar] City	352984.6	156728.6	195602.2	91483.1
疏附县	Shufu County	1479.3	1479.3		-403.8
疏勒县	Shule County	22460.5	16879.3	5581.2	14099.6
英吉沙县	Yengisar County				
泽普县	Zepu [Poskam] County				
莎车县	Shache [Yarkant] County	8738.6	4738.6	4000.0	16043.3
叶城县	Yecheng [Kagilik] County	5735.3	735.3	5000.0	3890.2
麦盖提县	Makit County	119.8	119.8		3473.8
岳普湖县	Yopurga County				
伽师县	Jiashi [Payzawat] County				
巴楚县	Bachu [Maralbexi] County	5489.6	5471.1	18.5	-1090.3
塔什库尔干塔吉克自治县	Taxkorgan Tajik Autonomous County	72000.6	2620.0	69380.6	-3213.4
和田地区	**Hotan Administrative Offices**	**320061.9**	**190209.3**	**129852.6**	**259670.3**
和田市	Hotan City	136454.5	53230.7	83223.8	23779.1
和田县	Hotan County	135226.6	92417.4	42809.2	145133.7
墨玉县	Moyu [Karakax] County	20083.0	16263.4	3819.6	48732.1
皮山县	Pishan [Guma] County				
洛浦县	Lop County	28297.8	28297.8		42025.4
策勒县	Qira County				
于田县	Yutian [Keriya] County				
民丰县	Minfeng [Niya] County				
自治区直辖县级市	**Municpality Country-LevelCity directly under the Central Government**	**3114202.2**	**1842991.6**	**1252439.5**	**2124840.7**
石河子市	Shihezi City	2491266.7	1433589.5	1055649.2	1883215.0
阿拉尔市	Aral City	304993.9	206162.0	82088.9	51254.4
图木舒克市	Tumxuk City	204716.2	141419.9	63296.2	158631.5
五家渠市	Wujiaqu City	113225.4	61820.2	51405.2	31739.8

Continued

(10 000 yuan)

主营业务收入 Revenue from Principal Business	主营业务成本 Cost of Principal Business	主营业务税金及附加 Taxes and Other Charges on Principal Business	营业利润 Business Profit	利润总额 Total Profit	亏损企业亏损总额 Losses Value of Loss-Suffering Enterprises	利税总额 Total Profits and Taxes	本年应交增值税 Value-added Taxes Payable	全部从业人员年平均人数(人) Annual Average Employed Persons (person)
1866.6	1035.4		420.1	420.1		420.1		10
78374.5	**57640.5**	**396.2**	**6003.2**	**6521.8**		**7963.3**	**1045.3**	**793**
50872.3	43171.5	97.0	2468.1	2939.2		3497.2	461.0	488
21144.2	9836.7	252.4	2715.0	2757.9		3154.9	144.6	123
6358.0	4632.3	46.8	820.1	824.7		1311.2	439.7	182
407423.4	**402410.2**	**2727.6**	**-20602.6**	**-1593.0**	**10277.6**	**18010.5**	**16875.9**	**6377**
338580.6	351829.1	2502.5	-27423.0	-8841.6	10228.4	6962.0	13301.1	5171
1217.3	1325.4	4.4	-205.4	-22.4	22.4	29.0	47.0	110
29823.1	22508.0	12.8	5376.3	5383.7		5407.5	11.0	209
8342.7	6023.6	0.2	605.7	575.8		576.0		298
3940.2	3013.0	1.3	925.9	925.9		1203.0	275.8	186
8500.9	8348.1	62.9	-181.2	-26.8	26.8	1099.2	1063.1	181
4048.6	3562.8	12.8	341.4	362.4		375.2		60
12970.0	5800.2	130.7	-42.3	50.0		2358.6	2177.9	162
171221.3	**183868.4**	**399.4**	**-22748.1**	**-6117.9**	**15434.6**	**-47.2**	**5671.3**	**2731**
84040.8	110385.4	30.1	-26151.4	-11514.8	12440.0	-11031.7	453.0	1714
22746.9	19712.0	290.0	-532.5	-705.8	2994.6	2000.7	2416.5	375
48702.8	42365.0	79.3	3011.2	5154.0		7807.5	2574.2	400
15730.8	11406.0		924.6	948.7		1176.3	227.6	242
2386068.7	**1979750.7**	**16414.4**	**122234.1**	**156867.1**	**46185.3**	**271532.0**	**98250.5**	**30402**
2032853.8	1695468.9	14738.7	101543.7	130004.2	37593.4	233625.9	88883.0	25076
138533.2	116562.2	1418.4	3474.1	7566.0	4943.2	11383.1	2398.7	2682
169084.1	134266.6	230.9	16222.4	16841.6	1902.9	23869.2	6796.7	2069
45597.6	33453.0	26.4	993.9	2455.3	1745.8	2653.8	172.1	575

13-13 国有控股工业企业主要经济效益指标

单位: % (2013 年)

项 目	Item	产值利税率 Ratio of Profits and Taxes to Industrial Output Value
总 计	**Total**	**21.6**
按登记注册类型分	**By Status of Registration**	
内资企业	Domestic Funded Enterprises	21.6
国有企业	State-owned Enterprises	10.8
#中央企业	Central Enterprises	12.9
地方企业	Local Enterprises	2.0
#自治区属企业	Autonomous	-1.5
地区(州、市)属企业	Prefecture or City	-0.2
县(市)属企业	County or City	7.4
联营企业	Joint Ownership Enterprises	45.7
#国有联营企业	State Joint Enterprises Ownership	47.9
国有与集体联营企业	Joint State-collectiue Enterprises	43.4
有限责任公司	Limited Liability Corporations	10.7
#国有独资公司	Sole State-funded Corporations	11.3
其他有限责任公司	Other Limited Liability Corporations	10.5
股份有限公司	Share-holding Corporations Ltd.	29.9
港、澳、台商投资企业	Enterprises with Funds from Hongkong,Macao and Taiwan	18.6
外商投资企业	Foreign Funded Enterprises	22.2
在总计中:国有控股企业	Of the Total : State-owned and State-holding Enterprises	21.6
按轻、重工业分	**Grouped by Light & Heavy Industry**	
轻工业	Light Industry	18.9
以农产品为原料	Using Farm Produces as Raw Materials	20.6
以非农产品为原料	Using Non-Farm Produces as Raw Materials	-26.9
重工业	Heavy Industry	21.8
采掘工业	Mining and Quarrying	46.4
原料工业	Raw Materials Industry	8.9
加工工业	Manufacturing Industry	12.8
按企业规模分	**Grouped by Size of Enterprises**	
大型企业	Large Enterprises	23.9
中型企业	Medium-sized Enterprises	11.4
小型企业	Small Enterprises	12.2
微型企业	Mini Enterprises	41.6

Main Indicators on Economic Efficiency of State-holding Industrial Enterprises

(%)

总资产贡献率 Ratio of Total Assets to Industrial Output Value	资本保值增值率 Ratio of Capital-hold and Rise	资产负债率 Assets Liability Ratio	流动资产周转次数(次/年) Number of Times of Annual TurnoverWorking Capitals (times/year)	成本费用利润率 Ratio of Profits to Industrial Cost	全员劳动生产率 Overall Labour Productivity
15.0	**107.5**	**57.2**	**2.8**	**13.3**	**57.7**
15.0	107.8	57.3	2.8	13.3	57.7
7.5	77.0	59.7	2.5	3.9	31.2
10.5	74.0	54.3	3.6	5.2	35.4
1.8	87.1	69.7	1.1	-1.1	18.5
0.5	150.0	65.7	1.6	-4.5	19.3
0.4	113.7	91.1	0.3	-1.2	13.9
4.0	37.2	52.9	1.6		18.9
21.7	64.9	64.2	1.1	78.0	153.7
45.9	35.5	48.9	1.6	58.0	93.1
15.2	101.8	68.4	0.8	103.3	431.7
7.1	146.2	68.2	1.8	4.6	26.7
5.8	156.8	67.5	1.2	4.9	23.8
7.5	142.6	68.5	2.1	4.6	28.1
24.0	99.6	46.6	4.1	21.1	114.6
6.3	9.3	57.3	0.9	19.3	338.2
8.3	125.6	43.1	1.5	15.1	43.1
15.0	107.5	57.2	2.8	13.3	57.7
11.6	111.6	61.6	1.2	6.7	20.6
15.3	110.0	60.7	1.4	8.5	22.3
-1.6	118.1	64.7	0.3	-23.6	7.5
15.2	107.3	57.0	3.0	13.6	62.3
25.3	104.0	51.0	3.2	47.5	92.0
8.2	107.6	61.0	3.1	1.2	40.6
9.2	138.6	61.8	1.5	9.1	24.5
19.1	104.3	53.6	3.5	14.9	75.7
6.1	130.4	63.1	1.5	6.1	21.5
6.4	100.2	66.8	1.4	7.9	28.7
8.4	235.0	70.7	0.9	52.2	64.6

13-14 分行业国有控股工业企业主要经济效益指标

单位: % (2013 年)

行业	Sector	产值利税率 Ratio of Profits and Taxes to Industrial Output Value
总计	**Total**	**21.6**
煤炭开采和洗选业	Mining and Washing of Coal	20.4
石油和天然气开采业	Extraction of Petroleum and Natural Gas	55.0
黑色金属矿采选业	Mining and Processing of Ferrous Metals Ores	33.9
有色金属矿采选业	Mining and Processing of Nonferrous Metals Ores	44.2
非金属矿采选业	Mining and Processing of Nonmetal Ores	16.4
#采盐	Extraction of Salt	33.9
农副食品加工业	Processing of Food from Agricultural Products	8.4
#谷物磨制	Grain Grinding	5.1
饲料加工	Fodder Processing	8.9
制糖	Sugar Making	4.4
食品制造业	Manufacture of Food	8.0
#罐头制造	Manufacture of can	-21.3
酒、饮料和精制茶制造业	Manufacture of Wine,Beverages and Refined Tea	42.8
#酒的制造	Manufacture of Wine	43.5
烟草制品业	Manufacture of Tobacco	67.6
纺织业	Manufacture of Textile	0.4
#棉、化纤纺织及印染精加工	Cotton, Chemical Fiber, Dyeing, Printing and Processing	2.2
毛纺织和染整精加工	Wool Textile, Dyeing and Printing	-23.5
纺织服装、鞋、帽制造业	Manufacture of Textile Wearing Apparel, Footware and Caps	9.7
造纸及纸制品业	Manufacture of Paper and Paper Products	8.3
印刷业和记录媒介的复制	Printing and Copying of Medium for Record	11.5
石油加工、炼焦及核燃料加工业	Oil Processing, Coking and Nuclear Fuel Processing	12.3
#炼焦	Coking	
化学原料及化学制品制造业	Raw Chemical Material and Chemical Products	12.5
#基础化学原料制造	Basic Chemical Material	3.1
肥料制造	Fertilizer Making	33.5
合成材料制造	Manufacture of Synthetic Material	9.2
医药制造业	Manufacture of Medicine	10.3
化学纤维制造业	Manufacture of Chemical Fiber	1.7
橡胶制品业	Manufacture of Rubber Products	4.6
非金属矿物制品业	Manufacture of Nonmetal Mineral Products	9.5
#水泥制造	Manufacture of Cement	9.2
黑色金属冶炼及压延加工业	Smelting and Pressing of Ferrous Metals	1.0
有色金属冶炼及压延加工业	Smelting and Pressing of Nonferrous Metals	4.3
金属制品业	Manufacture of Metal Products	0.8
通用设备制造业	Manufacture of General Purpose Machinery	4.3
专用设备制造业	Manufacture of Special Purpose Machinery	17.1
汽车制造业	Manufacture of Automobile	3.7
电气机械和器材制造业	Manufacture of Electric Equipment and Machinery	6.3
电力、热力的生产和供应业	Electricity and Thermal Production and Supply	8.7
#电力生产和电力供应	Electricity Production and Supply	8.9
燃气生产和供应业	Gas Production and Supply	5.0
水的生产和供应业	Water Production and Supply	-4.7

Main Indicators on Economic Efficiency of State-holding Industrial Enterprises by Sectors

(%)

总资产贡献率 Ratio of Total Assets to Industrial Output Value	资本保值增值率 Ratio of Capital-hold and Rise	资产负债率 Assets Liability Ratio	流动资产周转次数(次/年) Number of Times of Annual TurnoverWorking Capitals (times/year)	成本费用利润率 Ratio of Profits to Industrial Cost	全员劳动生产率 Overall Labour Productivity
15.0	**107.5**	**57.2**	**2.8**	**13.3**	**57.7**
6.9	108.7	65.7	1.1	6.6	21.6
30.9	102.6	45.8	5.7	66.2	170.2
19.0	132.1	73.3	1.1	28.3	60.9
16.7	108.1	47.8	1.7	50.4	53.8
12.0	136.7	59.8	1.0	10.7	16.6
27.3	103.1	31.0	1.4	21.0	26.2
9.1	122.5	58.8	1.7	5.7	17.1
6.9	157.2	72.6	1.7	4.6	15.5
8.8	127.4	31.4	2.0	8.5	30.1
4.2	90.6	56.2	1.5	-2.4	11.4
5.7	79.9	82.8	1.2	1.9	14.0
-3.0		105.1	0.7	-17.5	3.3
32.9	127.8	45.0	1.3	33.4	33.4
33.4	129.3	45.6	1.3	34.1	34.1
59.8	106.2	26.0	1.6	40.0	305.8
0.6	91.0	58.6	1.3	-2.4	5.4
1.7	76.5	66.0	1.3	-0.8	6.0
-4.1		26.6	0.7	-22.7	1.4
8.1		87.9	1.3	7.8	6.7
3.0	126.9	66.4	0.7	5.4	4.7
5.7	125.3	41.7	1.0	8.5	12.4
26.0	98.7	41.9	5.8	-0.9	100.2
2.7	111.9	76.3	1.4	-4.1	15.0
8.3	95.4	62.6	2.4	7.3	30.1
4.2	37.4	73.1	2.2	0.8	14.7
14.0	111.8	66.5	1.9	26.5	55.3
7.1	131.7	58.6	2.7	4.7	32.9
5.5	103.5	49.4	0.5	10.7	14.0
5.3		127.3	0.9	-2.3	11.2
5.8	105.2	57.7	1.5	2.1	11.0
4.3	117.6	53.2	1.0	4.4	17.1
3.5	105.2	52.4	1.0	3.8	15.6
3.1	97.4	76.3	2.6	-0.3	15.8
2.1	100.8	32.6	0.9	4.5	21.5
2.1	133.5	57.5	2.9	0.2	17.8
4.9	160.0	63.7	1.3	-2.5	14.2
8.8	148.3	64.3	1.1	11.5	17.1
4.4	733.9	59.2	2.9	3.2	3.2
8.8	126.1	72.3	1.7	3.8	25.8
5.1	128.4	66.1	2.3	4.9	40.8
5.3	128.4	65.2	2.7	5.0	43.9
5.0	107.1	77.1	1.6	3.8	14.7
0.2	135.8	61.3	0.2	-8.6	13.7

13-15 各地、州、市、县(市)国有控股工业企业主要经济效益指标

单位: % (2013 年)

地 区	Region	产值利税率 Ratio of Profits and Taxes to Industrial Output Value
总 计	**Total**	**21.6**
乌鲁木齐市	**Urumqi City**	**15.0**
天山区	Tianshan District	7.3
沙依巴克区	Shayibak District	6.7
新市区	Xinshi District	46.5
水磨沟区	Shui Mogou District	1.8
头屯河区	Tou Tunhe District	1.1
达坂城区	Da Bancheng District	21.2
米东区	Midong District	7.6
乌鲁木齐县	Urumqi County	31.6
克拉玛依市	**Karamay City**	**24.6**
独山子区	Dushanzi District	8.0
克拉玛依区	Karamay District	35.3
白碱滩区	Bai Jiantan District	
乌尔河区	Urhe District	
吐鲁番地区	**Turpan Administrative Offices**	**26.2**
吐鲁番市	Turpan City	-2.5
鄯善县	Shanshan [Piqan] County	30.0
托克逊县	Toksun County	13.6
哈密地区	**Hami [Kumul] Administrative Offices**	**19.7**
哈密市	Hami [Kumul] City	17.0
巴里坤哈萨克自治县	Barkol Kazak Autonomous County	43.0
伊吾县	Yiwu [Araturuk] County	50.2
昌吉回族自治州	**Changji Hui Autonomous Prefecture**	**6.4**
昌吉市	Changji City	14.1
阜康市	Fukang City	1.6
呼图壁县	Hutubi County	11.6
玛纳斯县	Manas County	5.0
奇台县	Qitai County	6.5
吉木萨尔县	Jimsar County	26.5
木垒哈萨克自治县	Mori Kazak Autonomous County	-1.3
伊犁哈萨克自治州	**Ili Kazak Autonomous Prefecture**	**20.4**
伊犁州直属县(市)	**Counties (Cities) Direct Under Ili Prefecture**	**19.5**
伊宁市	Yining [Gulja] City	13.3
奎屯市	Kuytun City	27.1
伊宁县	Yining [Gulja] County	5.1
察布查尔锡伯自治县	Qapqal Xibe Autonomous County	12.6
霍城县	Huocheng [Korgas] County	3.6
巩留县	Gongliu [Tokkuztara] County	-1.5
新源县	Xinyuan [Kunes] County	24.2
昭苏县	Zhaosu [Mongolkure] County	30.6
特克斯县	Tekes County	-40.8
尼勒克县	Nilka County	24.4
塔城地区	**Tacheng [Tarbagatai] Administrative Offices**	**8.7**
塔城市	Tacheng [Qoqek] City	-4.6
乌苏市	Usu City	1.2
额敏县	Emin [Dorbiljin] County	11.2

Main Indicators on Economic Efficiency of State-holding Industrial Enterprises by Prefecture, Autonomous Prefecture, City and County

(%)

总资产贡献率 Ratio of Total Assets to Industrial Output Value	资本保值增值率 Ratio of Capital-hold and Rise	资产负债率 Assets Liability Ratio	流动资产周转次数(次/年) Number of Times of Annual TurnoverWorking Capitals (times/year)	成本费用利润率 Ratio of Profits to Industrial Cost	全员劳动生产率 Overall Labour Productivity
15.0	**107.5**	**57.2**	**2.8**	**13.3**	**57.7**
11.7	**101.1**	**58.6**	**3.0**	**7.6**	**55.1**
5.7	113.4	60.6	3.1	4.0	42.6
2.4	62.8	60.2	1.0	3.2	12.8
28.7	113.3	51.7	3.6	49.0	142.1
4.8	84.9	24.9	2.2	-6.8	34.0
3.2	103.6	74.6	2.5	-0.3	18.8
7.0	112.6	62.2	1.8	16.3	20.9
8.4	100.4	48.0	4.3	-4.0	40.8
7.5	99.6	79.8	0.8	54.8	534.3
22.1	**105.3**	**44.2**	**3.5**	**12.9**	**75.6**
12.1	97.7	41.9	3.6	-2.9	65.0
25.4	108.3	44.9	3.4	24.5	77.7
12.8	**105.8**	**61.5**	**2.0**	**18.7**	**45.4**
1.4	112.7	74.1	0.8	-8.3	18.2
16.0	100.6	56.8	2.2	22.2	48.6
7.2	141.5	71.6	1.9	10.5	32.7
7.5	**124.3**	**72.5**	**1.0**	**12.2**	**24.1**
7.0	118.7	71.6	1.1	9.7	23.0
9.7	163.3	77.2	0.6	43.6	34.1
11.7	527.7	78.2	0.9	38.4	61.5
5.4	**144.5**	**62.1**	**2.1**	**3.7**	**25.7**
10.1	84.2	56.8	2.4	8.1	36.1
3.2	145.0	66.1	1.9	0.7	22.0
17.5	84.9	83.2	4.6	7.4	21.7
5.8	101.7	86.5	1.8	-1.5	13.3
6.2	48.6	82.5	1.8	-1.1	14.1
10.3		26.9	3.2	19.2	80.8
-1.2		73.1	0.3	-19.1	9.7
9.6	**111.2**	**65.3**	**1.5**	**10.8**	**34.1**
9.4	**108.4**	**65.9**	**1.5**	**6.9**	**35.2**
9.0	144.3	69.9	2.9	8.5	29.3
16.0	106.4	61.1	1.7	5.6	62.7
3.8	81.5	63.9	1.2	-0.1	11.7
9.3	49.9	70.3	4.2	11.1	30.3
3.7	117.2	66.2	2.2	-1.2	19.6
1.4	140.5	62.4	0.5	-7.3	42.9
17.7	86.2	66.6	1.0	20.3	29.4
56.7	100.0	70.3	2.6	42.7	35.0
1.5		84.6	6.7	-26.7	33.3
5.3	100.9	75.6	2.6	14.2	49.1
4.9	**107.4**	**67.9**	**1.2**	**4.5**	**21.4**
-0.6	122.7	67.2	7.5	-6.2	30.4
1.8	91.0	68.3	0.6	-7.3	11.2
6.2	112.6	60.3	0.7	10.6	24.4

13-15 续表 1

单位: %

地　区	Region	产　值利税率 Ratio of Profits and Taxes to Industrial Output Value
沙湾县	Shawan County	9.3
托里县	Toli County	8.6
裕民县	Yumin [Qagantokay] County	
和布克赛尔蒙古自治县	Hoboksar Mongol Autonomous County	16.6
阿勒泰地区	**Altay Administrative Offices**	**34.1**
阿勒泰市	Altay City	0.1
布尔津县	Burqin County	28.4
富蕴县	Fuyun [Koktokay] County	37.1
福海县	Fuhai [Burultokay] County	30.3
哈巴河县	Habahe [Kaba] County	56.5
青河县	Qinghe [Qinggil] County	1.3
吉木乃县	Jeminay County	47.1
博尔塔拉蒙古自治州	**Bortala Mongol Autonomous Prefecture**	**4.0**
博乐市	Bole [Bortala] City	0.5
精河县	Jinghe [Jing] County	8.5
温泉县	Wenquan [Araxang] County	
巴音郭楞蒙古自治州	**Bayangol Mongol Autonomous Prefecture**	**43.6**
库尔勒市	Korla City	48.8
轮台县	Luntai [Bugur] County	
尉犁县	Yuli [Lopnur] County	17.1
若羌县	Ruoqiang [Qarkilik] County	59.3
且末县	Qiemo [Qarqan] County	
焉耆回族自治县	Yanqi Hui Autonomous County	20.3
和静县	Hejing County	8.8
和硕县	Hoxud County	18.6
博湖县	Bohu [Bagrax] County	11.7
阿克苏地区	**Aksu Administrative Offices**	**15.7**
阿克苏市	Aksu City	8.3
温宿县	Wensu [Onsu] County	20.5
库车县	Kuqa County	17.4
沙雅县	Xayar County	
新和县	Xinhe [Toksu] County	
拜城县	Baicheng [Bay] County	18.5
乌什县	Wushi [Uxturpan] County	33.2

Continued

(%)

总资产贡献率 Ratio of Total Assets to Industrial Output Value	资本保值增值率 Ratio of Capital-hold and Rise	资产负债率 Assets Liability Ratio	流动资产周转次数(次/年) Number of Times of Annual TurnoverWorking Capitals (times/year)	成本费用利润率 Ratio of Profits to Industrial Cost	全员劳动生产率 Overall Labour Productivity
10.5	106.5	40.4	1.7	5.7	13.4
5.5	113.4	74.2	1.2	7.3	27.5
5.8	109.4	70.8	1.4	13.4	23.0
14.5	**123.1**	**60.6**	**1.7**	**33.7**	**49.4**
2.6	148.2	77.5	3.5	-4.3	21.3
7.9	259.4	84.3	0.9	30.7	59.8
17.2	103.8	54.7	1.7	35.4	46.2
8.2	104.1	51.2	0.7	23.8	45.0
40.7	119.1	18.2	2.8	86.1	86.1
0.4		83.2	0.2	0.8	20.2
7.3	154.8	59.8	1.0	90.7	313.4
3.9	**120.9**	**86.8**	**1.9**	**0.4**	**20.3**
1.9	10.0	97.7	2.6	-2.4	14.8
3.7	499.2	86.2	2.3	4.2	28.7
29.3	**98.2**	**56.6**	**6.3**	**48.0**	**143.7**
34.1	97.1	52.0	12.3	71.8	213.7
11.9		84.9	1.5	17.4	16.9
34.1	92.9	58.6	2.0	59.9	89.4
		100.0			
17.5	117.0	39.7	2.0	12.5	19.3
6.9	111.4	75.8	3.2	2.8	20.9
22.6	175.5	41.8	1.8	16.9	25.0
8.8	106.3	71.0	1.3	2.3	14.1
11.9	**114.3**	**58.2**	**2.8**	**4.7**	**46.4**
4.2	121.5	54.8	1.1	4.0	23.7
7.5	112.5	81.8	2.0	15.9	25.9
21.3	104.1	56.6	6.0	4.1	83.3
12.9	134.5	68.9	1.3	9.5	27.7
19.3	122.1	39.7	1.6	15.8	29.7

13-15 续表 2

单位: %

地　区	Region	产　值利税率 Ratio of Profits and Taxes to Industrial Output Value
阿瓦提县	Awat County	20.0
柯坪县	Kalpin County	
克孜勒苏柯尔克孜自治州	**Kizilsu Kirgiz Autonomous Prefecture**	**9.9**
阿图什市	Artux City	6.7
阿克陶县	Akto County	
阿合奇县	Akqi County	14.9
乌恰县	Wuqia [Ulugqat] County	19.0
喀什地区	**Kashgar [Kaxgar] Administrative Offices**	**4.5**
喀什市	Kashgar [Kaxgar] City	2.1
疏附县	Shufu County	1.9
疏勒县	Shule County	17.7
英吉沙县	Yengisar County	
泽普县	Zepu [Poskam] County	
莎车县	Shache [Yarkant] County	5.5
叶城县	Yecheng [Kagilik] County	21.1
麦盖提县	Makit County	30.4
岳普湖县	Yopurga County	
伽师县	Jiashi [Payzawat] County	
巴楚县	Bachu [Maralbexi] County	7.9
塔什库尔干塔吉克自治县	Taxkorgan Tajik Autonomous County	19.2
和田地区	**Hotan Administrative Offices**	
和田市	Hotan City	-12.2
和田县	Hotan County	9.2
墨玉县	Moyu [Karakax] County	15.6
皮山县	Pishan [Guma] County	
洛浦县	Lop County	6.3
策勒县	Qira County	
于田县	Yutian [Keriya] County	
民丰县	Minfeng [Niya] County	
自治区直辖县级市	**Municpality Country-LevelCity directly under the Central Government**	**12.0**
石河子市	Shihezi City	12.4
阿拉尔市	Aral City	8.2
图木舒克市	Tumxuk City	12.6
五家渠市	Wujiaqu City	5.5

Continued

(%)

总资产贡献率 Ratio of Total Assets to Industrial Output Value	资本保值增值率 Ratio of Capital-hold and Rise	资产负债率 Assets Liability Ratio	流动资产周转次数(次/年) Number of Times of Annual TurnoverWorking Capitals (times/year)	成本费用利润率 Ratio of Profits to Industrial Cost	全员劳动生产率 Overall Labour Productivity
2.5		70.2	1.0	29.0	100.7
5.2	**95.8**	**63.4**	**2.2**	**9.2**	**37.3**
2.8	93.9	18.3	1.8	6.3	31.4
6.7		100.0	3.4	15.2	95.4
17.7		71.0	5.7	14.9	13.7
5.9	**189.5**	**79.1**	**3.8**	**-0.4**	**16.7**
4.1	203.0	79.4	5.6	-2.4	15.8
2.7		137.5	2.4	-1.6	3.0
15.2	227.4	61.4	1.7	22.2	35.6
4.3	106.2	35.3	1.1	7.4	7.4
14.4	90.4	59.6	1.0	24.4	13.8
30.6		3.3	5.4	-0.3	8.4
8.5		124.8	1.1	9.8	22.1
10.8		104.7	1.2	0.4	56.3
1.3	**141.9**	**55.2**	**1.7**	**-3.0**	**19.7**
-4.1	1210.2	85.2	5.8	-10.0	12.3
1.5	110.7	48.2	0.4	-2.7	40.5
11.7	97.4	29.2	1.8	11.4	34.0
2.8		40.2	2.7	6.4	16.9
7.1	**137.1**	**59.4**	**1.4**	**7.0**	**22.5**
7.2	132.4	56.9	1.4	6.8	23.1
5.5	75.1	85.7	1.6	5.5	14.2
8.1	337.5	56.3	1.0	11.0	26.8
4.1	261.0	78.1	1.0	6.2	18.2

13-16 分行业大中型工业企业主要经济指标

单位: 万元 (2013 年)

行　业	Sector	企业单位数(个) Number of Enterp-rises (unit)	#亏损企业 Loss- Suffering Enterprises	工业总产值(当年价格) Gross Industrial Output Value (At Current Prices)
总　计	**Total**	**422**	**131**	**67867281.9**
煤炭开采和洗选业	Mining and Washing of Coal	44	15	1659516.4
石油和天然气开采业	Extraction of Petroleum and Natural Gas	4		13775748.4
黑色金属矿采选业	Mining and Processing of Ferrous Metals Ores	13	1	1034033.6
有色金属矿采选业	Mining and Processing of Nonferrous Metals Ores	7	2	346291.8
非金属矿采选业	Mining and Processing of Nonmetal Ores	4		60416.5
#采　盐	Extraction of Salt	2		23653.0
农副食品加工业	Processing of Food from Agricultural Products	29	10	1116373.2
饲料加工	Fodder Processing	3		278300.8
制　糖	Sugar Making	13	8	258997.0
食品制造业	Manufacture of Food	13	3	1100703.2
#罐头制造	Manufacture of can	1	1	35510.9
酒、饮料和精制茶制造业	Manufacture of Wine,Beverages and Refined Tea	9	3	454556.3
#酒的制造	Manufacture of Wine	7	1	368424.1
烟草制品业	Manufacture of Tobacco	1		402140.7
纺织业	Manufacture of Textile	37	15	769521.2
#棉、化纤纺织及印染精加工	Cotton, Chemical Fiber, Dyeing, Printing and Processing	33	13	724928.9
毛纺织和染整精加工	Wool Textile, Dyeing and Printing	2	1	29410.9
纺织服装、鞋、帽制造业	Manufacture of Textile Wearing Apparel, Footware and Caps	2		27938.9
家具制造业	Manufacture of Furniture	1	1	5628.7
造纸及纸制品业	Manufacture of Paper and Paper Products	3		60561.0
印刷业和记录媒介的复制	Printing and Copying of Medium for Record	1		6274.3
石油加工、炼焦及核燃料加工业	Oil Processing, Coking and Nuclear Fuel Processing	26	14	15896400.3
#炼 焦	Coking	19	10	836172.2
化学原料及化学制品制造业	Raw Chemical Material and Chemical Products	43	15	5015485.3
#基础化学原料制造	Basic Chemical Material	17	8	1355291.2
肥料制造	Fertilizer Making	9	3	1082939.6
合成材料制造	Manufacture of Synthetic Material	11	4	2453501.9
医药制造业	Manufacture of Medicine	2		37119.8
化学纤维制造业	Manufacture of Chemical Fiber	8	1	829645.7
橡胶和塑料制品业	Manufacture of Rubber Products	7	1	413965.5
非金属矿物制品业	Manufacture of Nonmetal Mineral Products	38	8	1495010.2
#水泥制造	Manufacture of Cement	24	8	819283.1
黑色金属冶炼及压延加工业	Smelting and Pressing of Ferrous Metals	24	12	6139190.9
有色金属冶炼及压延加工业	Smelting and Pressing of Nonferrous Metals	21	8	4707736.5
金属制品业	Manufacture of Metal Products	5	2	415375.3
通用设备制造业	Manufacture of General Purpose Machinery	1		11783.1
专用设备制造业	Manufacture of Special Purpose Machinery	4	1	79817.5
汽车制造业	Manufacture of Automobile	3	2	264618.5
电气机械和器材制造业	Manufacture of Electric Equipment and Machinery	6		2558559.8
金属制品、机械和设备修理业	Manufacture of Metal　Products	1		16874.1
电力、热力的生产和供应业	Electricity and Thermal Production and Supply	44	14	6451589.4
#电力生产和电力供应	Electricity Production and Supply	36	12	6320641.2
燃气生产和供应业	Gas Production and Supply	3		363038.1
水的生产和供应业	Water Production and Supply	1	1	21240.4

Main Indicators of Large-scale and Medium-scale Industrial Enterprises by Sectors

(10 000 yuan)

工业销售产值(当年价) Sales Value of Industry Products (At Current Prices)	出口交货值 Delivery Value of Industry Export	实收资本 Total Capital Hold	资产合计 Total Assets	流动资产合计 Total Working Capitals	#产成品 Finished Product	固定资产原价 Original Value of Fixed Assets
66401394.4	**445953.1**	**31997321.8**	**111045730.6**	**30504158.1**	**3041920.1**	**86755126.5**
1680694.1		1572266.4	6248618.3	1510966.7	106715.5	2874317.0
13705689.3		13566924.9	25472761.9	2620889.9	152409.2	36809917.0
1010249.5		230515.7	1722723.5	964581.2	125198.0	561203.4
339870.1		236360.0	874044.5	188925.3	15052.1	461884.5
56757.8		23499.9	67126.9	33540.9	7568.6	33912.3
23937.1		14500.0	41364.4	22814.0	5198.7	15232.4
1052634.3	1985.7	248800.3	1122230.1	593590.1	220003.5	538432.4
276065.3		50840.9	262307.4	115643.2	21918.6	101451.4
262641.8		72847.3	363651.7	208870.4	124579.3	268593.0
1109423.8	56748.8	423590.5	1692347.3	534150.0	54258.6	1194546.0
63951.0	47003.7	43836.0	281567.4	162716.3	26902.4	229846.7
453882.5		210612.3	716462.1	418426.5	11663.0	314642.0
370134.6		196738.5	636511.1	402600.7	8443.1	243737.6
382123.7		18741.7	454809.0	236210.0	6940.0	133167.0
720651.2	35649.3	523278.7	1537324.3	702780.0	133252.8	838593.2
677605.2	24956.3	432350.9	1327808.0	644772.2	120278.7	755246.6
28142.7	10693.0	56049.5	95980.4	28492.2	3724.0	41210.2
23495.5	4767.1	6625.7	33635.2	18955.7	3461.6	8495.7
9537.8	8874.1	64728.0	296258.3	42898.2	1509.9	27164.6
60723.9		18265.9	226235.1	66935.5	5137.7	90294.7
7377.2		5727.4	25106.0	8823.2	2705.1	28154.9
15784837.3		4651090.8	8898094.4	3301687.5	496336.9	8548770.8
806207.3		361936.2	1873310.4	723383.2	138653.3	897977.4
5001383.3	17624.2	2587529.3	12401744.0	2533500.1	257655.3	8690616.3
1331944.1	2333.6	554524.5	3704170.5	1021163.0	62543.5	2253926.4
1095107.2		623949.7	3659155.3	502905.8	41337.4	2563683.7
2451406.9	15167.6	1364777.3	4766033.0	865675.8	149090.2	3808615.1
34473.5	316.8	10960.7	77665.9	50284.0	7560.8	22653.9
755532.5	21280.1	139966.9	973177.6	404973.4	111263.3	664769.2
364834.1	14430.5	131381.4	403081.4	232949.0	69342.5	150674.6
1394420.1		985227.1	5301236.1	1445214.2	115569.5	2139228.6
774814.4		836900.4	3910609.0	865600.1	53913.7	1614481.0
5971430.3	10521.1	1290890.4	7937943.9	2985495.4	512483.3	4301158.4
4233257.4	137063.0	904759.1	9997664.7	3325873.8	505318.7	4146967.9
313026.0		83109.8	272566.7	125114.5	13857.9	59636.0
12016.4		10000.0	33244.1	19039.7	2109.2	10644.1
73764.0	449.7	40924.0	195835.8	129887.0	14060.5	57716.2
264114.1		126970.0	276534.0	84449.9	2713.1	84742.7
2498208.3	133056.7	610642.6	6224372.2	3568249.0	63308.8	434561.4
16874.1		900.6	18533.1	15685.7	2735.2	4403.4
6439855.1		1716202.5	13573078.8	2395163.5	9002.9	11190363.7
6292197.4		1623099.2	12551014.4	1924376.6	5280.0	10461885.6
274399.4		89368.0	521824.8	243161.5	340.8	300282.7
21240.4		204532.0	580046.4	203809.4		190723.4

13-16 续表

单位: 万元

行　业	Sector	负债合计 Total Liabilities	#流动负债 Total Liquid Liabilities	#非流动负债 Total Non-liquid Liabilities
总　计	**Total**	**66402632.2**	**42567807.8**	**22338680.5**
煤炭开采和洗选业	Mining and Washing of Coal	4148021.8	2810890.1	1336941.6
石油和天然气开采业	Extraction of Petroleum and Natural Gas	11674343.3	5590916.4	6083426.9
黑色金属矿采选业	Mining and Processing of Ferrous Metals Ores	1232159.2	1174975.0	57184.1
有色金属矿采选业	Mining and Processing of Nonferrous Metals Ores	384724.0	233587.4	151136.6
非金属矿采选业	Mining and Processing of Nonmetal Ores	26730.5	26082.5	500.0
#采　盐	Extraction of Salt	11213.2	10565.2	500.0
农副食品加工业	Processing of Food from Agricultural Products	622227.9	564578.8	55698.5
饲料加工	Fodder Processing	86187.0	71026.4	15160.6
制　糖	Sugar Making	212474.7	203231.1	7298.8
食品制造业	Manufacture of Food	1194475.5	1148281.4	39786.9
#罐头制造	Manufacture of can	342393.3	318811.4	23581.9
酒、饮料和精制茶制造业	Manufacture of Wine,Beverages and Refined Tea	483664.4	286285.9	197378.5
#酒的制造	Manufacture of Wine	417023.5	219645.0	197378.5
烟草制品业	Manufacture of Tobacco	118220.0	117220.0	1000.0
纺织业	Manufacture of Textile	931661.7	777168.9	133036.9
#棉、化纤纺织及印染精加工	Cotton, Chemical Fiber, Dyeing, Printing and Processing	838052.4	695480.2	121116.3
毛纺织和染整精加工	Wool Textile, Dyeing and Printing	23247.5	15802.7	7444.8
纺织服装、鞋、帽制造业	Manufacture of Textile Wearing Apparel, Footware and Caps	23179.4	15212.7	7966.7
家具制造业	Manufacture of Furniture	53577.4	43566.9	10010.5
造纸及纸制品业	Manufacture of Paper and Paper Products	150744.5	106765.1	9414.3
印刷业和记录媒介的复制	Printing and Copying of Medium for Record	12646.3	8061.8	4584.5
石油加工、炼焦及核燃料加工业	Oil Processing, Coking and Nuclear Fuel Processing	4197205.4	3493705.5	680700.0
#炼 焦	Coking	1417907.4	1203131.4	191976.1
化学原料及化学制品制造业	Raw Chemical Material and Chemical Products	8083764.1	4113717.5	3969750.9
#基础化学原料制造	Basic Chemical Material	2589595.9	1655525.9	933799.9
肥料制造	Fertilizer Making	2576978.8	1282573.9	1294379.6
合成材料制造	Manufacture of Synthetic Material	2787732.8	1056054.5	1731678.1
医药制造业	Manufacture of Medicine	33946.3	25808.5	8137.8
化学纤维制造业	Manufacture of Chemical Fiber	816479.3	575800.5	235359.2
橡胶和塑料制品业	Manufacture of Rubber Products	243727.6	189649.5	38830.0
非金属矿物制品业	Manufacture of Nonmetal Mineral Products	3010721.7	2063215.0	817715.4
#水泥制造	Manufacture of Cement	2097169.1	1369166.0	688051.9
黑色金属冶炼及压延加工业	Smelting and Pressing of Ferrous Metals	6142719.1	5254178.3	886380.5
有色金属冶炼及压延加工业	Smelting and Pressing of Nonferrous Metals	7561814.7	4822064.5	2165780.5
金属制品业	Manufacture of Metal Products	155700.5	114238.2	41462.2
通用设备制造业	Manufacture of General Purpose Machinery	24888.8	23148.8	
专用设备制造业	Manufacture of Special Purpose Machinery	68283.2	66684.5	1598.7
汽车制造业	Manufacture of Automobile	156742.5	136197.7	20544.8
电气机械和器材制造业	Manufacture of Electric Equipment and Machinery	3487875.7	2535507.4	952368.3
金属制品、机械和设备修理业	Manufacture of Metal　Products	15867.7	15867.7	
电力、热力的生产和供应业	Electricity and Thermal Production and Supply	8687638.1	4216292.5	4073980.6
#电力生产和电力供应	Electricity Production and Supply	7834498.8	3882864.8	3554269.0
燃气生产和供应业	Gas Production and Supply	344809.7	228985.8	115823.7
水的生产和供应业	Water Production and Supply	344944.3	61924.4	283.0

Continued

(10 000 yuan)

所有者权益合计 Total Owners' Equities	主营业务收入 Revenue from Principal Business	主营业务成本 Cost of Principal Business	主营业务税金及附加 Taxes and Other Charges on Principal Business	营业利润 Business Profit	利润总额 Total Profit	亏损企业亏损总额 Losses Value of Loss-Suffering Enterprises	利税总额 Total Profits and Taxes	本年应交增值税 Value-added Taxes Payable	全部从业人员年平均人数（人） Annual Average Employed Persons (person)
44548492.3	**68562518.6**	**52448199.2**	**3185081.7**	**6766667.8**	**7151019.8**	**988242.2**	**13266413.0**	**2930311.5**	**487036**
2100588	1722939.7	1261561.4	49160.9	115952.1	91116.8	90741.2	315391.9	175114.2	47269
13798418.6	14867534.4	6602040.7	1130264.8	5212145.7	5262641.5		7576706.8	1183800.5	70653
490564	1037605.7	640850.3	30712.6	239834.4	245885.4	585.4	379621.8	103023.8	7265
489320.5	337286.7	161945.1	6423.1	134858.2	131756.8	5317.4	175910.1	37730.2	4857
40396.3	49291.9	28837.9	2146.5	8340.8	8632.3		14246.4	3467.6	2095
30151.2	23570.7	8531.3	2014.3	5616.2	5790.6		10687.3	2882.4	741
500002.2	1043445.5	879074.1	2255.9	43960.8	50105.4	18037.8	78831.6	26470.3	11975
176120.4	278846.3	207816.6	514.3	35354.4	35761.6		40476.5	4200.6	1529
151177	288624.2	255302.1	1530.7	-9881.8	-7572.9	11857.2	10661.6	16703.8	5912
497392.5	984086.3	781993.6	2296.4	81851.4	87296.4	37563.1	127628.6	38035.8	11244
-60825.9	64107.9	61830.1	159.3	-33851.5	-33199.3	33199.3	-26514.2	6525.8	1090
232797.7	450183.5	269106.5	37100.4	79171.5	83446.1	7121.3	150195.2	29648.7	7162
219487.6	367597.9	203316.7	36929.8	81877.3	85581.9	4985.5	150850.2	28338.5	6125
336589	382124.0	129865.0	169165.0	61130.0	60910.0		271882.0	41807.0	977
603909.1	858648.8	825291.1	2729.0	-24947.6	4209.3	22476.9	24188.3	17250.0	23404
488002.1	819130.8	787949.7	2509.7	-20923.0	7877.1	18049.1	26981.3	16594.5	21064
72732.9	26351.9	25332.0	193.7	-4391.0	-3652.8	4206.5	-3015.7	443.4	1421
10455.8	27647.7	22346.9	38.9	1880.7	2286.1		2379.3	54.3	1241
242680.9	9612.2	9121.3	497.9	-4119.5	-3528.3	3528.3	-3030.4		431
75490.6	56982.5	48285.9	188.0	-676.8	7245.1		8856.8	1423.7	2258
12459.7	7380.2	5446.6	93.1	-445.8	166.7		681.9	422.1	426
4673474.7	16140748.3	13741561.0	1630229.3	-71879.1	-90007.2	408794.9	1906630.7	366408.6	33900
449000.3	808433.1	732170.1	2277.7	-485.0	1603.6	38654.0	27767.0	23885.7	11047
4309827.5	5068230.3	4064445.7	47636.3	352554.0	363281.7	53729.8	659672.3	248754.3	54824
1114574.4	1525666.7	1301085.9	3977.9	30968.2	38360.6	21645.0	66882.0	24543.5	20269
1074024.3	1008198.2	579242.3	27591.1	199139.4	181653.6	22567.8	318330.4	109085.7	10871
1978300.2	2410947.4	2103779.1	14824.5	90315.1	109673.4	9517.0	230378.5	105880.6	20108
43719.6	28272.5	17836.4	218.3	375.7	1166.1		2785.6	1401.2	1030
154487.4	833801.5	743089.3	1151.1	18434.2	24398.4	4203.9	41870.7	16321.2	7153
159309.9	352924.9	314759.9	561.0	-2586.0	2456.7	462.4	13154.4	10136.7	5003
2255348.7	1400977.9	1187300.7	5092.5	46441.4	75478.4	17686.4	156949.5	76378.6	22514
1795960.5	783232.4	648504.8	3467.9	30499.6	54547.7	17686.4	102314.1	44298.5	13605
1782501.3	6456605.5	6157306.8	13444.5	-119351.3	-45942.6	102436.2	58362.9	90861.0	37843
2435668.4	4092632.0	3626616.9	644.9	169318.5	182837.4	29593.9	241867.8	58385.5	28147
116866.2	216692.4	202145.8	705.6	-2192.4	1095.8	1230.1	4755.3	2953.9	2518
8355.3	11519.0	9476.0	10.0	-43.3	54.1		151.1	87.0	335
127552.5	96514.9	74863.4	312.8	8329.1	12759.4	750.6	13271.8	199.6	1634
119791.5	254143.0	246005.1	537.0	-11427.5	12566.1	9254.6	13969.9	866.8	1465
2736496.5	2668652.5	2011758.6	9112.5	258279.0	302495.5		358723.2	47115.2	6661
2665.4	15574.1	15074.7	55.5	33.7	82.6		728.8	590.7	376
4885439.5	6390242.0	5899781.8	17049.9	170151.6	234175.4	107255.0	458858.9	207633.6	44583
4716515.4	6213545.8	5717585.4	16977.6	196613.8	227863.6	103622.3	451304.4	206463.2	41161
177015.0	359213.9	291075.1	4249.5	3577.8	24647.2		30391.6	1494.9	2376
235102.1	27145.2	26483.4	163.2	-13936.3	-11204.0	11204.0	-9412.1	1628.7	1165

13-17 分行业大中型工业企业主要经济效益指标

单位: %　　(2013 年)

行　业	Sector	产值利税率 Ratio of Profits and Taxes to Industrial Output Value
总　计	**Total**	**19.5**
煤炭开采和洗选业	Mining and Washing of Coal	19.0
石油和天然气开采业	Extraction of Petroleum and Natural Gas	55.0
黑色金属矿采选业	Mining and Processing of Ferrous Metals Ores	36.7
有色金属矿采选业	Mining and Processing of Nonferrous Metals Ores	50.8
非金属矿采选业	Mining and Processing of Nonmetal Ores	23.6
#采　盐	Extraction of Salt	45.2
农副食品加工业	Processing of Food from Agricultural Products	7.1
饲料加工	Fodder Processing	14.5
制　糖	Sugar Making	4.1
食品制造业	Manufacture of Food	11.6
#罐头制造	Manufacture of can	-74.7
酒、饮料和精制茶制造业	Manufacture of Wine,Beverages and Refined Tea	33.0
#酒的制造	Manufacture of Wine	40.9
烟草制品业	Manufacture of Tobacco	67.6
纺织业	Manufacture of Textile	3.1
#棉、化纤纺织及印染精加工	Cotton, Chemical Fiber, Dyeing, Printing and Processing	3.7
毛纺织和染整精加工	Wool Textile, Dyeing and Printing	-10.3
纺织服装、鞋、帽制造业	Manufacture of Textile Wearing Apparel, Footware and Caps	8.5
家具制造业	Manufacture of Furniture	-53.8
造纸及纸制品业	Manufacture of Paper and Paper Products	14.6
印刷业和记录媒介的复制	Printing and Copying of Medium for Record	10.9
石油加工、炼焦及核燃料加工业	Oil Processing, Coking and Nuclear Fuel Processing	12.0
#炼 焦	Coking	3.3
化学原料及化学制品制造业	Raw Chemical Material and Chemical Products	13.2
#基础化学原料制造	Basic Chemical Material	4.9
肥料制造	Fertilizer Making	29.4
合成材料制造	Manufacture of Synthetic Material	9.4
医药制造业	Manufacture of Medicine	7.5
化学纤维制造业	Manufacture of Chemical Fiber	5.0
橡胶和塑料制品业	Manufacture of Rubber Products	3.2
非金属矿物制品业	Manufacture of Nonmetal Mineral Products	10.5
#水泥制造	Manufacture of Cement	12.5
黑色金属冶炼及压延加工业	Smelting and Pressing of Ferrous Metals	1.0
有色金属冶炼及压延加工业	Smelting and Pressing of Nonferrous Metals	5.1
金属制品业	Manufacture of Metal Products	1.1
通用设备制造业	Manufacture of General Purpose Machinery	1.3
专用设备制造业	Manufacture of Special Purpose Machinery	16.6
汽车制造业	Manufacture of Automobile	5.3
电气机械和器材制造业	Manufacture of Electric Equipment and Machinery	14.0
金属制品、机械和设备修理业	Manufacture of Metal Products	4.3
电力、热力的生产和供应业	Electricity and Thermal Production and Supply	7.1
#电力生产和电力供应	Electricity Production and Supply	7.1
燃气生产和供应业	Gas Production and Supply	8.4
水的生产和供应业	Water Production and Supply	-44.3

Main Indicators on Economic Efficiency of Large-scale and Medium-scale Industrial Enterprises by Sectors

(%)

总资产贡献率 Ratio of Total Assets to ndustrial Output Value	资本保值增值率 Ratio of Capital-hold and Rise	资产负债率 Assets Liability Ratio	流动资产周转次数(次/年) Number of Times of Annual TurnoverWorking Capitals (times/year)	成本费用利润率 Ratio of Profits to Industrial Cost	全员劳动生产率 Overall Labour Productivity
13.3	**122.7**	**59.8**	**2.2**	**12.3**	**50.8**
6.3	114.9	66.4	1.1	5.8	22.0
30.9	110.2	45.8	5.7	66.2	170.2
23.7	165.8	71.5	1.1	31.3	71.8
20.8	115.8	44.0	1.8	65.9	55.8
21.5	171.0	39.8	1.5	22.7	13.8
25.9	129.1	27.1	1.0	36.8	24.5
8.5	129.8	55.4	1.8	5.0	15.4
16.3	157.6	32.9	2.4	14.7	39.1
3.9	80.1	58.4	1.4	-2.6	10.5
8.5	273.3	70.6	1.8	9.8	24.3
-7.1		121.6	0.4	-38.1	-7.6
22.0	143.8	67.5	1.1	24.3	30.4
24.8	161.2	65.5	0.9	33.4	33.8
59.8	123.0	26.0	1.6	40.0	305.8
2.6	94.9	60.6	1.2	0.5	6.4
3.2	88.6	63.1	1.3	0.9	6.7
-2.6	863.7	24.2	0.9	-12.3	3.1
8.0	206.6	68.9	1.5	8.8	7.3
-1.0	98.0	18.1	0.2	-25.4	2.0
5.0	122.0	66.6	0.9	12.3	6.4
4.1	105.0	50.4	0.8	2.0	11.4
22.6	94.3	47.2	4.9	-0.6	83.0
3.4	138.0	75.7	1.1	0.2	15.9
7.4	130.0	65.2	2.0	7.7	32.0
3.9	88.4	69.9	1.5	2.5	18.5
10.6	232.6	70.4	2.0	22.3	60.1
7.1	132.2	58.5	2.8	4.8	33.0
4.7	101.5	43.7	0.6	4.3	9.2
6.9	70.7	83.9	2.1	2.9	20.2
4.5	107.3	60.5	1.5	0.7	10.9
4.7	152.0	56.8	1.0	5.4	17.6
4.3	143.5	53.6	0.9	6.9	18.3
2.7	103.2	77.4	2.2	-0.7	13.9
3.4	483.2	75.6	1.2	4.6	28.4
3.3	123.5	57.1	1.7	0.5	7.2
1.9		74.9	0.6	0.5	6.5
7.0	135.7	34.9	0.7	14.4	13.5
5.8		56.7	3.0	4.7	4.0
7.5	110.8	56.0	0.7	13.5	62.7
5.6		85.6	1.0	0.5	8.5
4.9	161.1	64.0	2.7	3.7	38.0
5.2	162.5	62.4	3.2	3.8	39.9
7.0	230.2	66.1	1.5	7.0	19.3
-1.3	155.9	59.5	0.1	-25.4	9.9

13-18 主要工业产品产量
Output of Major Industrial Products

产品名称	Item	2012	2013
天然原油(吨)	Crude Oil (ton)	26706783	26584705
天然气(万立方米)	Natural Gas (10 000 cu.m)	2530101	2829064
铁矿石原矿量(吨)	Crudeiron Ore (ton)	33656556	38298614
铜选矿含铜量(吨)	Cuproaurite (ton)	93675	115417
硫铁矿(折含 S 35%)(吨)	Pyritel with Content of (S35%)(ton)	125250	116703
原盐(吨)	Salt (ton)	3014047	3186276
发电量(万千瓦小时)	Electricity (10 000 kwh)	11874792	16130139
#火 电	Thermalpower	9987236	13759435
水 电	Hydropower	1586205	1642613
供热量(万吉焦)	Heat Supply (10 000 gigajoules)	25531	27626
大米(吨)	Rice (ton)	241189	316869
小麦粉(万吨)	Wheate Flour (10 000 tons)	368	288
精制食用植物油(吨)	Refined Edible Oil (ton)	1554608	1740071
成品糖(吨)	Sugar (ton)	536366	467239
饲料(吨)	Forage (ton)	2331322	3112193
糖果(吨)	Candy (ton)	9884	3913
乳制品(吨)	Dairy Products (ton)	418854	443995
罐头(吨)	Canned Food (ton)	694119	670571
#番茄酱	Tomato Jam	628749	599909
味精(吨)	Mono Sodium Glutamate (ton)	16547	1214
酱油(吨)	Soy (ton)	28872	118837
方便面(吨)	Instant Noodles(ton)	62167	58473
发酵酒精(千升)	Zymolytic Alcohol (kilo-liter)	72429	112747
饮料酒(千升)	Alcohol Beverage(kilo-liter)	657637	662124
#白 酒	Liquor	87672	78320
啤 酒	Beer	505600	527844
葡萄酒	Grape Wine	53165	55903
软饮料(吨)	Soft Drink (ton)	1698214	2046347
#碳酸饮料	Carbonic Drink	109127	170413
果汁和蔬菜汁饮料	Fruit Juice and Vegetable Juice Drink	703768	930673
包装饮用水	Bottled Water	703255	791271
冷冻饮品(吨)	Ice Beverage (ton)	54112	53291

注：钢材里包括钢材生产中消耗的外购国内钢。
Note: Rolled steel contain that manufacture of steel consumed outsourcing of internal steel.

13-18 续表 1 Continued

产品名称	Item	2012	2013
卷烟(万支)	Cigarettes (10 000 pieces)	1700000	1800000
纱(吨)	Yarn (ton)	402151	434569
布(万米)	Cloth (10 000 m)	6676	7451
#棉 布	Pure Cotton Cloth	5298	6678
绒线(毛线)(吨)	Knitting Wool (ton)	545	323
呢绒(万米)	Woolen Cloth Goods (10 000 m)	332	259
服装(万件)	Garments (10 000 units)	2826	2982
轻革(平方米)	Light Leather (sq.m)	5180378	5933375
人造板(立方米)	Artificial Board (cu.m)	1360533	1451047
#胶合板	Plywood	397624	518404
纤维板	Fiberboard	532610	558938
刨花板	Chip Board	363785	337015
家具(件)	Furniture (unit)	2297670	2368535
#木制家具	WoodenFurniture	1964149	1998039
金属家具	Steal Furniture	193634	250192
纸浆(吨)	Paper Pulp (ton)	222132	193149
纸制品(吨)	Paper produces (ton)	415192	571198
#瓦楞纸箱(纸箱)	Corrugaled Case	364492	496401
机制纸及纸板(吨)	Machine-made Paper and Paperboard (ton)	410547	457449
原油加工量(吨)	Processed Crude Oil (ton)	24268959	25101903
汽油(吨)	Gasoline (ton)	2393159	2773513
溶剂油(吨)	Megilp (ton)	93023	43329
煤油(吨)	Kerosene (ton)	589508	626636
柴油(吨)	Diesel Oil (ton)	10590956	10631536
润滑油(吨)	Lubricating Oil (ton)	640838	464925
燃料油(吨)	Fuel Oil (ton)	105523	471430
石油沥青(吨)	Petroleum Bitumen (ton)	1591319	1698164
液化石油气(吨)	Liquefied Petroleum Gas (ton)	679463	650301
焦炭(吨)	Coke (ton)	14408656	20108249
#机械化焦炉生产的焦炭	Coke Turned out by Mechanized Coke Oven	10154319	13324872
煤气(万立方米)	Coal Gas (10 000 cu.m)	1445154	1390834
硫酸(折 100%)(吨)	Sulfuric Acid (ton)	389819	531812
盐酸(含量 31%以上)(吨)	Hydrochloric Acid (With Content of 31%) (ton)	301738	388429

13-18 续表 2 Continued

产品名称	Item	2012	2013
氢氧化钠(烧碱)(折 100%)(吨)	Caustic Soda (ton)	1464433	2133953
碳酸钠(纯碱)(吨)	Soda Ash (ton)	109224	67538
碳化钙(电石)(折 300 升/千克)(吨)	Calcium Carbide (ton)	3125805	4421861
合成氨(吨)	Synthetic Ammonia (ton)	1889044	1335922
农用氮、磷、钾化学肥料(折纯)(吨)	Chemical Fertilizers (ton)	3041687	3747746
#氮肥(折含 N 100%)	Nitrogen Fertilizers	2231963	2852571
#尿 素	Carbamide	2094356	2753626
磷肥(折合 P_2O_5 100%)	Phosphate Fertilizers	24564	28362
乙烯(吨)	Ethylene(ton)	1270893	1319248
涂料(吨)	Paint (ton)	104969	180542
合成洗涤剂(吨)	Synthetic Detergents (ton)	41324	48547
化学原料药(吨)	Chemical Medicine (ton)	214	1479
中成药(吨)	Traditional Chinese Medicine (ton)	4074	5106
轮胎外胎(条)	Outer Tyres (unit)	1279426	1594204
塑料制品(吨)	Plastic Produces (ton)	1399683	1866580
#塑料薄膜	Plastic Film	227371	253767
#农用薄膜	Farm Plastic Sheet	233812	235189
塑料型材(含板片材)	Plastic Moulding Material	67612	172298
塑料制管子及其附件(吨)	Plastic Pipe and Accessory (ton)	551290	729410
塑料编织袋(吨)	Woven Plastic Bag (ton)	120677	149665
泡沫塑料(吨)	Foamed Plastics (ton)	26050	53784
塑料包装箱及容器(吨)	Plastic Packing Case and Container (ton)	78463	86253
日用塑料制品(吨)	Household Plastic Products (ton)	31218	61101
水泥熟料(万吨)	Cement Chamotte (10 000 ton)	3520	3809
窑外分解窑熟料(预分解窑熟料)(万吨)	Clinker Cement (10 000 tons)	3014	3500
水泥(万吨)	Cement (10 000 tons)	4316	5410
水泥电杆(根)	Cement Electric Pole Piece (unit)	362627	390028
商品混凝土(立方米)	Commercial Concrete (cu.m)	36173219	55336530
预应力混凝土桩 (米)	Prestressed Concrete Piles (m)	6270284	2885021
砖(折标准砖)(万块)	Brick (Standard Brick) (10 000 pieces)	2226725	2644692
瓦(万片)	Tile (10 000 pieces)	14098	1038
大理石板材(平方米)	Marble Slab (sq.m)	1364368	400912
花岗石板材(平方米)	Granite Sheet (sq.m)	23250934	29144429

13-18 续表 3 Continued

产品名称	Item	2012	2013
石膏板(万平方米)	Plasterboard (sq.m)	1174	1079
平板玻璃(重量箱)	Plate Glass (weight case)	3751856	5014909
沥青和改性沥青防水卷材(平方米)	Bitumen and Rolled Waterproof Material (sq.m)	8243157	4737185
中空玻璃(平方米)	Insulating Glass (sq.m)	170845	327609
钢化玻璃(平方米)	Toughened Glass (sq.m)	262782	1217274
夹层玻璃(平方米)	Laminated Glass (sq.m)	20184	53695
日用玻璃制品(吨)	Household Glass Products (ton)	64840	58824
玻璃保温容器(万个)	Glass Attemperator (10 000 units)	1058	1032
陶质砖(平方米)	Carbonic Bricks (sq.m)	26982984	23567100
耐火材料制品(吨)	Fire Proof Material (ton)	281938	471022
石墨及碳素制品(吨)	Graphite and Carbon Products (ton)	451038	818207
玻璃纤维增强塑料制品(吨)	Glass Fibre Reinforced Plastices Products (ton)	50167	65250
生铁(吨)	Pig Iron (ton)	13283217	14311345
粗钢(吨)	Crude Steel (ton)	11382344	12767688
钢材(吨)	Rolled Steel (ton)	12898437	15129048
中小型型钢	Medium and Small Fasioned Steel	326079	140654
钢　筋	Concrete Iron	3307038	3643185
盘　条(线材)	Wire Rod	2885674	2893396
铁合金(吨)	Ferroalloy (ton)	173015	253174
铜(吨)	Copper (ton)	27054	37342
镍(吨)	Nickel (ton)	10150	10307
铝(吨)	Aluminium (ton)	970733	2462765
铝材(吨)	Aluminium Material (ton)	101841	301974
工业锅炉(蒸发量吨)	Industrial Boiler (evaporating quantity ton)	1213	2035
泵(台)	Pump (unit)	20035	15812
风机(台)	Fan (unit)	6511	5740
农作物收获机械(台)	Grop Harvesting Machinery (unit)	7686	16007
汽车(辆)	Motor Vehicles(unit)	3391	9902
#载货汽车	Trucks	3391	7837
改装汽车(辆)	Modified Truck (unit)	2942	7837
发电设备(千瓦)	Power Generating Equipment (kw)	2933000	3896114
变压器(千伏安)	Transformer (kva)	61945187	60363713
电力电缆(公里)	Electric Cable (km)	117789	202192

13-19 各地、州、市主要工业产品产量

年份 Year	地区 Region	纱（吨） Yarn (ton)	布（万米） Cloth (10 000 m)	绒线（吨） Knitting Wool (ton)	呢绒（万米） Woolen Piece Goods (10 000 m)
	1978	28008	15616	1239	189
	1980	31272	16931	1614	240
	1985	39130	21150	2396	680
	1990	101941	30017	2179	1230
	1995	244689	30460	2286	1262
	1996	208526	27186	2202	1361
	1997	247143	29862	2393	1227
	1998	220332	26719	1361	979
	1999	294378	27450	1349	798
	2000	334307	28060	1184	754
	2001	302654	25380	843	399
	2002	316095	20679	811	265
	2003	292713	15239	744	206
	2004	291386	13989	980	206
	2005	340864	14047	1118	284
	2006	357324	15415	799	327
	2007	408870	16000	637	368
	2008	397417	15302	578	412
	2009	386085	15148	533	376
	2010	415783	15069	741	326
	2011	399094	7303	444	383
	2012	402151	6676	545	332
	2013	434569	7451	323	259
乌鲁木齐市	Urumqi City	9877	359	185	
克拉玛依市	Karamay City		1		
吐鲁番地区	Turpan Administrative Offices	2424			
哈密地区	Hami [Kumul] Administrative Offices	8744			
昌吉回族自治州	Changji Hui Autonomous Prefecture	30154	160		
伊犁哈萨克自治州	Ili Kazak Autonomous Prefecture	53141	493	138	
伊犁州直属县(市)	Counties (Cities) Direct Under Ili Prefecture	38434			
塔城地区	Tacheng [Tarbagatai] Administrative Offices	14707	493	138	
阿勒泰地区	Altay Administrative Offices				
博尔塔拉蒙古自治州	Bortala Mongol Autonomous Prefecture	24839	134		
巴音郭楞蒙古自治州	Bayangol Mongol Autonomous Prefecture	24711	919		
阿克苏地区	Aksu Administrative Offices	79834			
克孜勒苏柯尔克孜自治州	Kizilsu Kirgiz Autonomous Prefecture				
喀什地区	Kashgar [Kaxgar] Administrative Offices	20867	157		
和田地区	Hotan Administrative Offices	7246			
自治区直辖县级市	Municpality Country-LevelCity directly under the Central Government	22612	2690		
石河子市	Shihezi City	107588	2540		259
阿拉尔市	Aral City	25510			
图木舒克市	Tumxuk City	3499			
五家渠市	Wujiaqu City	13522			

Output of Major Industrial Products by Prefecture, Autonomous Prefecture and City

机制纸及纸板(吨) Machine-made Paper and Paperboard (ton)	原盐(万吨) Salt (10 000 tons)	成品糖(万吨) Sugar (10 000 tons)	饮料酒(千升) Alcohol Beverage (kilo-liter)	卷烟(亿支) Cigarettes (100 million pieces)	原油(万吨) Crude Oil (10 000 tons)	天然气(万立方米) Natural gas (10 000 cu.m)	发电量(亿千瓦时) Electricity (100 million kwh)	#水电 Hydropower
19851	51.71	2.08	9336	15.05	353.05	25100	21.17	4.64
23838	38.18	4.43	17082	15.55	390.58	35298	23.58	5.25
41521	35.09	7.18	74809	40.20	499.00	54556	38.11	8.64
90857	159.00	16.84	118585	61.70	695.00	50161	69.79	14.25
180440	25.98	30.18	249481	68.05	1267.83	114821	120.43	22.82
169789	36.54	36.34	219961	67.80	1457.10	140609	136.03	24.49
161659	39.85	42.28	259015	66.05	1629.25	213006	150.58	26.97
168799	27.53	47.59	271056	60.20	1628.38	237826	157.76	28.23
180138	36.14	46.36	269453	55.00	1739.65	310600	169.30	30.06
176477	31.78	30.76	269761	52.50	1848.43	353930	182.98	30.53
193389	46.02	41.98	296187	55.20	1946.95	417429	197.62	34.10
226950	50.75	51.84	307167	60.00	2036.19	485237	212.24	34.67
233365	52.71	45.43	317260	62.50	2141.39	502942	234.62	36.20
263066	87.32	37.26	345770	70.00	2253.02	574805	266.30	37.08
289318	85.35	42.92	355275	70.00	2408.32	1066437	306.92	43.27
295338	153.21	53.79	401771	85.00	2474.74	1642099	357.15	53.43
252329	111.53	64.94	438502	100.00	2604.31	2103348	416.87	58.78
301606	153.06	53.78	486007	120.00	2715.13	2358941	489.17	73.84
355762	129.36	40.77	484936	135.00	2512.86	2453887	571.31	79.84
371032	174.67	45.10	565041	150.00	2558.16	2499096	679.33	97.07
422924	258.05	46.11	645919	160.00	2615.63	2353798	875.19	114.57
410547	301.40	53.64	657637	170.00	2670.68	2530101	1187.48	158.62
457449	318.63	46.72	662124	180.00	2658.47	2829064	1613.01	164.26
59285	10.31		138589		737.00	163978	255.40	
	0.09		4700		1160.02	304744	47.36	
	100.85		5355		171.01	104510	59.89	0.63
901	4.33		15987				73.78	0.06
132379		6.48	30717				341.77	0.66
2511	185.48	27.32	171329	180.00			247.31	75.22
2511		19.72	74384	180.00			127.78	56.08
	185.48	5.77	94334				94.74	2.80
		1.83	2611				24.79	16.35
	6.34	3.64	417				11.21	5.39
138109	8.23	6.47	33263		590.45	2255832	63.22	25.31
	3.00	2.49	35123				84.12	17.69
			145				9.65	8.96
4719		0.32	30502				26.81	13.43
			1117				12.00	11.81
48425			15090					
2338			140058				221.53	4.47
			36596				6.64	
							6.79	
68782			3136				145.51	0.62

13-19 续表

年 份 Year	地 区 Region	生 铁 (万吨) Pig Iron (10 000 tons)	粗 钢 (万吨) Crude Steel (10 000 tons)	大理石板材 (平方米) Marble Plate (sq.m.)	钢 材 (万吨) Steel Rolled (10 000 tons)
	1978	17.52	8.46		6.83
	1980	15.81	10.74		8.59
	1985	22.87	19.79		16.73
	1990	40.57	36.49	9589	28.48
	1995	69.53	70.59	34169	66.55
	1996	85.64	87.47	6420	86.70
	1997	93.82	97.21	53588	99.89
	1998	100.40	107.67	9197	116.19
	1999	101.30	105.60	7807	117.30
	2000	106.42	109.70	6294	131.26
	2001	111.73	131.83	22786	134.42
	2002	122.78	175.45	34185	173.07
	2003	144.86	204.12	117306	203.10
	2004	193.89	249.13	109663	238.52
	2005	258.66	306.54	78577	326.96
	2006	324.08	394.19	176025	411.45
	2007	394.97	447.24	119926	470.94
	2008	505.70	536.60	160011	576.62
	2009	764.62	653.32	190480	690.81
	2010	941.12	825.54	328249	891.70
	2011	1088.45	892.98	1240465	985.14
	2012	1328.32	1138.23	1364368	1289.84
	2013	1431.13	1276.77	400912	1512.90
乌鲁木齐市	Urumqi City	730.88	727.64	27007	894.82
克拉玛依市	Karamay City				11.70
吐鲁番地区	Turpan Administrative Offices	71.14	0.67		
哈密地区	Hami [Kumul] Administrative Offices	21.61			
昌吉回族自治州	Changji Hui Autonomous Prefecture	69.62	13.03		11.71
伊犁哈萨克自治州	Ili Kazak Autonomous Prefecture	208.07	205.52	94134	205.30
伊犁州直属县(市)	Counties (Cities) Direct Under Ili Prefecture	199.52	197.51	1300	199.40
塔城地区	Tacheng [Tarbagatai] Administrative Offices		8.01		5.82
阿勒泰地区	Altay Administrative Offices	8.54		92834	0.08
博尔塔拉蒙古自治州	Bortala Mongol Autonomous Prefecture	17.40			
巴音郭楞蒙古自治州	Bayangol Mongol Autonomous Prefecture	223.11	232.93	14385	232.12
阿克苏地区	Aksu Administrative Offices	2.35			58.52
克孜勒苏柯尔克孜自治州	Kizilsu Kirgiz Autonomous Prefecture	12.82		2091	
喀什地区	Kashgar [Kaxgar] Administrative Offices	17.63	43.66	2500	48.07
和田地区	Hotan Administrative Offices			39	0.01
自治区直辖县级市	Municpality Country-LevelCity directly under the Central Government	15.73	14.84	260756	11.56
石河子市	Shihezi City				4.60
阿拉尔市	Aral City				
图木舒克市	Tumxuk City				
五家渠市	Wujiaqu City	40.78	38.47		34.49

Continued

水 泥 (万吨) Cement (10 000 tons)	硫 酸 (吨) Sulfuric Acid (ton)	烧 碱 (吨) Caustic Soda (ton)	合成氨 (吨)(折纯) Synthetic Ammonia (ton)	农用氮、磷、钾化肥(吨) Farm Nitrogen Phophate and Potassium (ton)	碳化钙 (电石)(吨) Calcium Crbide (ton)	塑料制品 (吨) Plastic Products (ton)
78.15	20262	4164	33155	20276	4895	3194
90.89	19153	3542	13762	9207	4486	2051
201.05	23921	5045	85728	58080	5989	17974
285.00	47732	15063	397062	287640	15976	40958
489.88	88491	24732	492754	383279	12344	100739
562.87	76413	28008	488337	372056	15901	129059
628.00	77187	35544	581449	428711	28350	143916
728.94	64836	39614	688069	520681	28999	168372
805.83	68169	42161	896632	685587	40216	139497
895.67	71458	51831	947511	754668	51749	197756
981.29	72511	68589	884340	729034	65763	262873
1029.71	70407	93362	956732	766291	73680	230729
1128.98	85322	114110	1082601	854530	82057	314891
1212.99	114046	174445	1015630	869795	115991	388270
1241.74	126901	295917	1192001	1285346	290591	349151
1334.50	160073	423901	1303586	1290802	501283	412032
1536.77	183484	485880	1325017	1385279	711277	517069
1672.76	201993	630314	1471312	1609409	910659	653230
2049.60	300423	814393	1407674	1591027	1560762	697269
2400.96	326112	916205	1484103	1591043	1845104	830651
3171.71	361779	1315745	1775660	2335610	2784380	1041107
4315.93	389819	1464433	1889044	3041687	3125805	1399683
5410.34	531812	2133953	1335922	3747746	4421861	1866580
435.31	5914	540272	564853	633995	166415	629491
						27839
326.81	104642	81745			899687	
303.80	7408			28560		12816
678.53		675216		436570	1330955	312749
1107.60	370577	2271		643156	161107	143018
562.10	265820	2271		607622	54377	47977
371.65	25674			35534	106730	86665
173.85	79083					8376
163.42	10000					47409
319.60		3895	771069	1494307		36744
702.78	13850			313443		49305
214.55						380
485.84	19421					48187
252.13						3960
29.17				95755		435346
353.08		808034			1837448	99441
		22520		101961	26249	8330
37.72						6216
						5351

13-20 国有控股企业主要指标占全区规模以上工业比重
Percentage of Main Indicators in State-holding Enterprises to Enterprises above Designated Size

单位：万元　　(2013 年)　　(10 000 yuan)

指　标	Item	全区规模以上工业企业 Enterprises Above Designated Size	国　有控股企业 State-Holding Enterprises	比 重 (%) Percentage (%)
企业单位数(个)	Number of Enterprises(unit)	2224	600	26.98
从业人员(人)	Employed Person (person)	675747	386644	57.22
工业总产值	Gross Industrial Output Value	86796304.7	56688937.3	65.31
工业销售产值	Sales Value of Industry Products	84478025.4	55970581.5	66.25
出口交货值	Delivery Value of Industry Export	680082.0	162644.2	23.92
资产总计	Total Assets	143312541.5	91014942.9	63.51
负债合计	Total Liabilities	87797652.5	52101451.1	59.34
所有者权益	Owner's Right and Interest	55347427.8	38847414.7	70.19
实收资本	Substantial Capital	39102343.3	30233706.7	77.32
主营业务收入	Revenue from Principal Business	87187056.8	58372725.4	66.95
主营业务税金及附加	Taes and Other Charges on Principal Business	3298760.1	3140604.5	95.21
利润总额	Total Profits	8552294.7	6460499.5	75.54
利税总额	Total Profits and Tax	15346023.1	12257806.2	79.88
亏损单位数(个)	Number of Loss-suffering Enterprises (unit)	604	173	28.64
亏损企业亏损额	Losses Value of Loss-suffering	1345810.2	938755.0	69.75

13-21 重点行业主要指标占全区规模以上工业比重
Percentage of Main Indicators in Key Industrial Sectors to Xinjiang's Industry above Designated Size

(2013 年)

指　标	Item	合　计 Total	占全区比重(%) Percentage (%)
从业人员(人)	**Employed Persons (person)**	**675737**	**100.0**
石油和天然气开采业	Extraction of Petroleum and Natural Gas	70848	10.5
石油加工、炼焦及核燃料加工业	Petroleum Processing,Coking and Nuclear Fuel Processing	40192	5.9
黑色金属冶炼及压延加工业	Smelting and Pressing of Ferrous Metal	47067	7.0
电力、热力的生产和供应业	Electric Power, Thermal Power Production and Supply	56401	8.3
化学原料及化学制品制造业	Raw Chemical Material and Chemical Products	65788	9.7
纺织业	Textile Industry	34484	5.1
农副食品加工业	Processing of Food from Agricultural Products	30928	4.6
工业总产值(万元)	**Gross Industrial Output Value (10 000 yuan)**	**86799116.3**	**100.0**
石油和天然气开采业	Extraction of Petroleum and Natural Gas	13847366.9	16.0
石油加工、炼焦及核燃料加工业	Petroleum Processing,Coking and Nuclear Fuel Processing	17310573.8	19.9
黑色金属冶炼及压延加工业	Smelting and Pressing of Ferrous Metal	7281798.4	8.4
电力、热力的生产和供应业	Electric Power, Thermal Power Production and Supply	7892298.9	9.1
化学原料及化学制品制造业	Raw Chemical Material and Chemical Products	6163109.5	7.1
纺织业	Textile Industry	1258401.8	1.4
农副食品加工业	Processing of Food from Agricultural Products	3949988.6	4.6
工业销售产值(万元)	**Sales Value of Industry Products (10 000 yuan)**	**84480837.0**	**100.0**
石油和天然气开采业	Extraction of Petroleum and Natural Gas	13776199.9	16.3
石油加工、炼焦及核燃料加工业	Petroleum Processing,Coking and Nuclear Fuel Processing	17173233.2	20.3
黑色金属冶炼及压延加工业	Smelting and Pressing of Ferrous Metal	6932864.3	8.2
电力、热力的生产和供应业	Electric Power, Thermal Power Production and Supply	7862377.4	9.3
化学原料及化学制品制造业	Raw Chemical Material and Chemical Products	6112346.6	7.2
纺织业	Textile Industry	1187602.1	1.4
农副食品加工业	Processing of Food from Agricultural Products	3726058.6	4.4

注：所列行业为工业总产值百亿元以上行业。
Note: Listed sector of gross industrial output value were above ten billion sector.

13-21 续表 Continued

指　　标	Item	合　计 Total	占全区比重 (%) Percentage (%)
资产总计(万元)	**Total of Assets (10 000 yuan)**	**143312541.5**	**100.0**
石油和天然气开采业	Extraction of Petroleum and Natural Gas	25560382.1	17.8
石油加工、炼焦及核燃料加工业	Petroleum Processing,Coking and Nuclear Fuel Processing	10104037.5	7.1
黑色金属冶炼及压延加工业	Smelting and Pressing of Ferrous Metal	9159745.5	6.4
电力、热力的生产和供应业	Electric Power, Thermal Power Production and Supply	22443477.3	15.7
化学原料及化学制品制造业	Raw Chemical Material and Chemical Products	13952582.9	9.7
纺织业	Textile Industry	2536918.5	1.8
农副食品加工业	Processing of Food from Agricultural Products	3655191.9	2.6
利润总额(万元)	**Total Profits (10 000 yuan)**	**8552294.7**	**100.0**
石油和天然气开采业	Extraction of Petroleum and Natural Gas	5283222.8	61.8
石油加工、炼焦及核燃料加工业	Petroleum Processing,Coking and Nuclear Fuel Processing	8664.7	0.1
黑色金属冶炼及压延加工业	Smelting and Pressing of Ferrous Metal	-74267.6	
电力、热力的生产和供应业	Electric Power, Thermal Power Production and Supply	457364.2	5.3
化学原料及化学制品制造业	Raw Chemical Material and Chemical Products	453402.4	5.3
纺织业	Textile Industry	11795.5	0.1
农副食品加工业	Processing of Food from Agricultural Products	281569.3	3.3
利税总额(万元)	**Total Profitsand Tax (10 000 yuan)**	**15346023.1**	**100.0**
石油和天然气开采业	Extraction of Petroleum and Natural Gas	7602060.8	49.5
石油加工、炼焦及核燃料加工业	Petroleum Processing,Coking and Nuclear Fuel Processing	2050255.9	13.4
黑色金属冶炼及压延加工业	Smelting and Pressing of Ferrous Metal	42351.8	0.3
电力、热力的生产和供应业	Electric Power, Thermal Power Production and Supply	774385.4	5.0
化学原料及化学制品制造业	Raw Chemical Material and Chemical Products	787280.3	5.1
纺织业	Textile Industry	42671.4	0.3
农副食品加工业	Processing of Food from Agricultural Products	344343.1	2.2
主营业务收入(万元)	**Revenue from Principal Business (10 000 yuan)**	**87187056.8**	**100.0**
石油和天然气开采业	Extraction of Petroleum and Natural Gas	14946302	17.1
石油加工、炼焦及核燃料加工业	Petroleum Processing,Coking and Nuclear Fuel Processing	17566910.2	20.1
黑色金属冶炼及压延加工业	Smelting and Pressing of Ferrous Metal	7425715.3	8.5
化学原料及化学制品制造业	Raw Chemical Material and Chemical Products	6270912.8	7.2
电力、热力的生产和供应业	Electric Power, Thermal Power Production and Supply	7809168.4	9.0
纺织业	Textile Industry	1330662	1.5
农副食品加工业	Processing of Food from Agricultural Products	3866780.9	4.4

13-22 规模以上工业主要产品生产能力
Production Capacity of Major Industrial Products above Designated Size

产品名称	Item	2012	2013
原煤(吨)	Raw Coal (ton)	150837000	174998866
天然原油(吨)	Crude Oil (ton)	26297800	27027900
发电设备容量(万千瓦)	Generating Capacity (10 000 kw)	2135	3209
卷烟(万支)	Cigarettes (10 000 pieces)	2376000	2376000
化学纤维(吨)	Chemical Fiber (ton)	491000	578000
棉纺锭(环锭纺)(锭)	Cotton Hasp (unit)	4539522	4716267
气流纺锭(转杯纺)(头)	Airflow Hasp (unit)	56088	86644
棉布织机(台)	Calico Spinning Machine (set)	2042	2026
原油加工能力(吨)	Crude Petroleum Oil	28950000	33420000
焦炭(吨)	Coke (ton)	28941000	37212004
烧碱(折 100%)(吨)	Caustic Soda	1523100	2625000
炭化钙(电石)(折 300 升/千克)(吨)	Calcium Carbide (ton)	5013000	5353000
农用氮、磷、钾化学肥料(折纯)(吨)	Chemical Fertilizers (ton)	4670520	5130322
初级形态塑料(吨)	Primary Plastic	3991600	5845100
水泥熟料(吨)	Cement Chamotte (ton)	51113000	65752650
水泥(吨)	Cement (ton)	66765000	90091000
平板玻璃(重量箱)	Plate Glass (weight case)	5200000	7520000
生铁(吨)	Pig Iron (ton)	15026600	17702003
粗钢(吨)	Crude Steel (ton)	13359600	17928600
钢材(吨)	Rolled Steel (ton)	15461960	18990623
铁合金(吨)	Ferroalloy (ton)	230000	375200
原铝(电解铝)(吨)	Aluminium (ton)	2344700	4104700
汽车(辆)	Motor Vehicles(unit)	20000	25000

主要统计指标解释

工业　指从事自然资源的开采，对采掘品和农产品进行加工和再加工的物质生产部门。具体包括：(1)对自然资源的开采，如采矿、晒盐等(但不包括禽兽捕猎和水产捕捞)；(2)对农副产品的加工、再加工，如粮油加工、食品加工、缫丝、纺织、制革等；(3)对采掘品的加工、再加工，如炼铁、炼钢、化工生产、石油加工、机器制造、木材加工等，以及电力、自来水、煤气的生产和供应等；(4)对工业品的修理、翻新，如机器设备的修理、交通运输工具(如汽车)的修理等。

工业统计调查单位为独立核算法人工业企业。

独立核算法人工业企业指从事工业生产经营活动的单位。独立核算法人工业企业应同时具备以下条件：①依法成立，有自己的名称、组织机构和场所，能够承担民事责任；②独立拥有和使用资产，承担负债，有权与其他单位签订合同；③独立核算盈亏，并能够编制资产负债表。

国有及国有控股企业　指国有企业加上国有控股企业。国有企业(即原全民所有制工业或国营工业)指企业全部资产归国家所有，并按《中华人民共和国企业法人登记管理条例》规定登记注册的非公司制的经济组织。包括国有企业、国有独资公司和国有联营企业。1957年以前的公私合营和私营工业，后均改造为国营工业，1992年改为国有工业，这部分工业的资料不单独分列时，均包括在国有企业内。国有控股企业是对混合所有制经济的企业进行的"国有控股"分类。它是指这些企业的全部资产中国有资产(股份)相对其他所有者中的任何一个所有者占资(股)最多的企业。该分组反映了国有经济控股情况。

本篇涉及的其他企业登记注册类型的解释详见综合篇。

轻工业　指主要提供生活消费品和制作手工工具的工业。按其所使用的原料不同，可分为两大类：(1)以农产品为原料的轻工业，是指直接或间接以农产品为基本原料的轻工业。主要包括食品制造、饮料制造、烟草加工、纺织、缝纫、皮革和毛皮制作、造纸以及印刷等工业；(2)以非农产品为原料的轻工业，是指以工业品为原料的轻工业。主要包括文教体育用品、化学药品制造、合成纤维制造、日用化学制品、日用玻璃制品、日用金属制品、手工工具制造、医疗器械制造、文化和办公用机械制造等工业。

重工业　指为国民经济各部门提供物质技术基础的主要生产资料的工业。按其生产性质和产品用途，可以分为下列三类：(1)采掘(伐)工业，是指对自然资源的开采，包括石油开采、煤炭开采、金属矿开采、非金属矿开采等工业；(2)原材料工业，指向国民经济各部门提供基本材料、动力和燃料的工业。包括金属冶炼及加工、炼焦及焦炭、化学、化工原料、水泥、人造板以及电力、石油和煤炭加工等工业；(3)加工工业，是指对工业原材料进行再加工制造的工业。包括装备国民经济各部门的机械设备制造工业、金属结构、水泥制品等工业，以及为农业提供的生产资料如化肥、农药等工业。

根据上述划分原则，修理业中以重工业产品为修理作业对象的划为重工业，反之划为轻工业。

工业总产值

(1)定义：

工业总产值是工业企业在一定时期内生产的以货币形式表现的工业最终产品和提供工业性劳务活动的总价值量。它反映一定时间内工业生产的总规模和总水平。

(2)计算原则：

工业生产的原则，即凡是企业在报告期内生产的最终产品和提供的劳务，均应包括在内。其中的最终产品，不管是否在报告期内销售，只要是报告期内生产的，就应包括在内。凡不是工业生产的产品，均不得计入工业总产值。

最终产品的原则，即企业生产的成品价值必须是本企业生产的，经检验合格不需再进行任何加工的最终产品。企业对外销售的半成品也应视为最终产品计入工业总产值。而在本企业内各车间转移的半成品和在制品只能计算其期末期初差额价值。

工厂法原则，即以法人工业企业作为一个整体计算工业总产值，是其报告期内生产的最终产品和提供劳务的总价值量。

(3)内容及计算方法：

1995年全国工业普查对工业总产值(原规定)的内容及计算原则和方法做了某些修订，修订后的工业总产值(新规定)包括三项内容：即本期生产成品价值、对外加工费收入、在制品半成品期末期初差额价值三部分。

本期生产成品价值：指企业本期生产，并在报告期内不再进行加工，经检验、包装入库的全部工业成品(半成品)价值合计，包括企业生产的自制设备及提供给本企业在建工程、其他非工业部门和福利部门等单位使用的成品价值。本期生产成品价值为按自备原材料生产的产品的数量乘以本期不含增值税(销项税额)的产品实际销售平均单价计算；会计核算中按成本价格转帐的自制设备和自产自用的成品，按成本价格计算生产成品价值。生产成品价值中不包括用定货者来料加工的成品(半成品)价值。

对外加工费收入：指企业在报告期内完成的对外承接的工业品加工(包括用定货者来料加工产品)的加工费收入和对外工业修理作业所取得的加工费收入。对外加工费收入按不含增值税(销项税额)的价格计算，可根据会计"产品销售收入"科目的有关资料取得。

对于本企业对内非工业部门提供的加工修理、设备安装的劳务收入，如果企业会计核算基础较好，能取得这部分资料，而且这部分价值所占比重较大，应包括在对外加工费收入中。

自制半成品在制品期末期初差额价值：指企业报告期在制品期末减期初的差额价值，本指标一般可以从会计核算资料中取得。如果会计产品成本核算中不计算半成品、在制品的成本，则总产值中也不包括这部分价值，反之则包括。

资产总计 指企业过去的交易或者事项形成的、由企业拥有或者控制的、预期会给企业带来经济利益的资源。资产一般按流动性分为流动资产和非流动资产。其中流动资产可分为货币资金、交易性金融资产、应收票据、应收账款、预付款项、其他应收款、存货等；非流动资产可分为长期股权

投资、固定资产、无形资产及其他非流动资产等。根据会计

“资产负债表”中“资产总计”项目的期末余额数填报。

流动资产合计 资产满足以下条件之一应归为流动资产：（1）预计在一个正常营业周期中变现、出售或耗用，主要包括存货、应收账款等；（2）主要为交易目的而持有；（3）预计在资产负债表日起一年内（含一年）变现；（4）自资产负债日起一年内，交换其他资产或清偿负债的能力不受限制的现金或现金等价物。包括货币资金、应收票据、应收账款、存货等项目。根据会计“资产负债表”中“流动资产合计”项目的期末余额数填报。

固定资产原价 指固定资产的成本，包括企业在购置、自行建造、安装、改建、扩建、技术改造某项固定资产时所发生的全部支出总额。根据会计“固定资产”科目的期末借方余额填报。

累计折旧 指企业在报告期末提取的历年固定资产折旧累计数。根据会计“累计折旧”科目的期末贷方余额填报。

负债合计 指企业过去的交易或者事项形成的，预期会导致经济利益流出企业的现时义务。负债一般按偿还期长短分为流动负债和非流动负债。根据会计“资产负债表”中“负债合计”项目的期末余额数填报。

流动负债合计 负债满足下列条件之一的应归为流动负债：（1）预计在一个正常营业周期中清偿；（2）主要为交易目的而持有；（3）自资产负债表日起一年内到期应予清偿；（4）企业无权自主地将清偿推迟至资产负债表日后一年以上。包括短期借款、应付票据、应付账款、应付职工薪酬、应交税费等项目。根据会计“资产负债表”中“流动负债合计”项目的期末余额数填报。

所有者权益合计 指企业资产扣除负债后由所有者享有的剩余权益。公司的所有者权益又称股东权益。包括实收资本、资本公积、盈余公积、未分配利润等。根据会计“资产负债表”中“所有者权益合计”项目的期末余额填报。

主营业务收入 指企业确认的销售商品、提供劳务等主营业务的收入。根据会计“主营业务收入”科目的期末贷方余额填报。

主营业务成本 指企业经营主要业务所发生的成本总额。根据会计“主营业务成本”科目的期末借方余额填报。

主营业务税金及附加 指企业经营主要业务应负担的营业税、消费税、城市维护建设税、教育费附加等。根据会计“主营业务税金及附加”科目的期末借方余额填报。

利润总额 指企业在一定会计期间的经营成果，是生产经营过程中各种收入扣除各种耗费后的盈余，反映企业在报告期内实现的亏盈总额。根据会计“利润表”中“利润总额”项目的本期金额数填报。

应交增值税 指企业按税法规定，从事货物销售或提供加工、修理修配劳务等增加货物价值的活动本期应交纳的税金。计算公式为：

应交增值税=销项税额-（进项税额-进项税额转出）-出口抵减内销产品应纳税额-减免税款+出口退税

进项税额指企业在报告期内购入货物或接受应税劳务而支付的、准予从销项税额中抵扣的增值税额。

销项税额指工业企业在报告期内销售货物或提供应税劳务应收取的增值税额。

总资产贡献率 反映企业全部资产的获利能力，是企业经营业绩和管理水平的集中体现，是评价和考核企业盈利能力的核心指标。计算公式为：

总资产贡献率（%）=（利润总额+税金总额+利息支出）/ 平均资产总额*100%

公式中：税金总额为主营业务税金及附加与应交增值税之和；平均资产总额为期初期末资产之和的算术平均值。

资产负债率 该指标既反映企业经营风险的大小，也反映企业利用债权人提供的资金从事经营活动的能力。计算公式为：

资产负债率（%）=负债总额 / 资产总额 *100%

资产与负债均为报告期期末数。

流动资产周转次数 指一定时期内流动资产完成的周转次数，反映投入工业企业流动资金的周转速度。计算公式为：

流动资产周转次数=主营业务收入 / 全部流动资产平均余额

公式中：全部流动资产平均余额为期初和期末的流动资产之和的算术平均值。

成本费用利润率 反映企业投入的生产成本及费用的经济效益，同时也反映企业降低成本所取得的经济效益。计算公式为：

成本费用利润率(%)=利润总额 / 成本费用总额*100%

公式中：成本费用总额为主营业务成本、销售费用、管理费用、财务费用之和。

产品销售率 该指标反映工业产品已实现销售的程度，是分析工业产销衔接情况，研究工业产品满足社会需求的指标。计算公式为：

产品销售率(%) =工业销售产值 / 工业总产值*100%

Explanatory Notes on Main Statistical Indicators

Industry refers to the material production sector which is engaged in the extraction of natural resources and processing and reprocessing of minerals and agricultural products, including (1) extraction of natural resources, such as mining, salt production (but not including hunting and fishing); (2) processing and reprocessing of farm and sideline produces, such as rice husking, flour milling, wine making, oil pressing, silk reeling, spinning and weaving, and leather making; (3) manufacture of industrial products, such as steel making, iron smelting, chemicals manufacturing, petroleum processing, machine building, timber processing; water and gas production and electricity generation and supply; (4)repairing of industrial products such as the repairing of machinery and means of transport (including cars).

In industrial statistics surveys, the units of enquiry are corporate industrial enterprises with independent accounting systems.

Corporate industrial enterprises with independent accounting systems refer to enterprises engaging in industrial production activities, which meet the following requirements: (1) They are established legally, having their own names, organizations, location and able to take civil liability; (2) They possess and use their assets independently, assume liabilities and are entitled to sign contracts with other units; (3) They are financially independent and compile their own balance sheets.

State-owned and State-holding Enterprises refer to state-owned enterprises plus State-holding enterprises. State-owned enterprises (originally known as State-run enterprises with ownership by the whole society) are non-corporate economic entities registered in accordance with the Regulation of the People's Republic of China on the Management of Registration of Legal Enterprises, where all assets are owned by the State. Included in this category are State-owned enterprises, State-funded corporations and State-owned joint-operation enterprises. Joint State-private industries and private industries, which existed before 1957, were transformed into state-run industries since 1957, and into State-owned industries after 1992. Statistics on those enterprises are included in the State-owned industries instead of being grouped them separately. State-holding enterprises are a sub-classification of enterprises with mixed ownership, referring to enterprises where the percentage of State assets (or shares by the State) is larger than any other single share holder of the same enterprise. This sub-classification illustrates the control of the State over a particular industry.

For explanation of enterprises of other types of registration covered in this chapter, please refer to General Survey.

Light Industry refers to the industry that produces consumer goods and hand tools. It consists of two categories, depending on the materials used:

(1) Industries using farm products as raw materials. These are the branches of light industry which directly or indirectly use farm products as basic raw materials, including the manufacture of food and beverages, tobacco processing, textile, clothing, fur and leather manufacturing, paper making, printing, etc.

(2) Industries using non-farm products as raw materials. These are the branches of light industry which use manufactured goods as raw materials, including the manufacture of cultural, educational articles and sports goods, chemicals, synthetic fibre, chemical products for daily use, glass products for daily use, metal products for daily use, hand tools, medical apparatus and instruments, and the manufacture of cultural and office machinery.

Heavy Industry refers to the industry which produces capital goods, and provides various sectors of the national economy with necessary material and technical basis for production. It consists of the following three branches according to the purpose of production or the use of products:

(1) Mining, quarrying and logging industry, which refers to the industry that extracts natural resources, including extraction of petroleum, coal, metal and non-metal ores.

(2) Raw materials industry refers to the industry that provides various sectors of the national economy with raw materials, fuels and power. It includes smelting and processing of metals, coking and coke chemistry, chemical materials and building materials such as cement, plywood, and power, petroleum refining and coal dressing.

(3) Manufacturing industry which refers to the industry that processes raw materials. It includes machine-building industries which equip sectors of the national economy; industries producing metal structure and cement products; and industries producing means of agricultural production, such as chemical fertilizers and pesticides.

In accordance with the above principles of classification, the repairing trades, which are engaged primarily in repairing products of heavy industry, are classified as heavy industry while those which are engaged in repairing products of light industry are classified as light industry.

Gross Industrial Output Value

(1) Definition: Gross industrial output value is the total volume of final industrial products produced and industrial services provided during a given period in monetary terms. It reflects the total achievements and overall scale of industrial production during a given period.

(2) Principles for calculation:

Statistics on industrial production follow the principle that all final industrial products produced and industrial services provided during the reference period are to be included. The final industrial products are included as long as being produced during the reference period, no matter whether they are sold or not during the reference period. The gross industrial output value will not cover those products that are not from industrial production.

Determination of final products follows the principle that all products that are included in the calculation of gross industrial output value are the final products of the enterprise. which have been accepted through quality check and require no further processing. The intermediate products sold by enterprises are considered as the final products of the enterprise and counted into the gross industrial output value. However, for the intermediate products being transferred among workshops and the work-in-progress products, only the balance value from the beginning to the end of the period is calculated.

Gross industrial output value is calculated following the principle of factory approach, i.e. industrial enterprise with legal entity is used as a whole in calculating the gross industrial output value, which will cover the total value of final industrial products produced and industrial services provided by these enterprises during the reference period.

(3) Content and method of calculation: The old definition of gross industrial output value was modified during the 1995 National Industrial Census. The revised (new) definition of gross industrial output value consists of 3 components: value of the finished products during the reference period, income from processing for external parties, and value of change in semi-finished products between the end and the beginning of the reference period.

Value of finished products during the reference period: refers to the value of all finished (semi-finished) industrial products that are produced during the reference period without the need for further processing, checked for acceptance, packed and put into the warehouse of the enterprise, including the value of own-produced equipment and the value of products provided to the projects under construction of the enterprise, and to other non-industrial or welfare units. Value of finished products during the reference period is calculated by the quantity of products produced using own materials multiplied by the average unit prices at which products are sold (excluding value-added tax). Own-produced equipment and products produced for own use are valued at cost prices as in the case of enterprise accounting. Value of finished products does not include the value of finished products (semi-finished products) that are produced using the materials from the clients who place the orders.

Income from external processing: refers to income from contracted external processing of industrial products (including processing of industrial products using materials from the clients), and the income from industrial repairing work provided to other parties. Income from external processing is calculated using information from the item "products sales income" in the enterprise accounting at the prices with value-added tax excluded.

For income from services such as processing, repairing and installation of equipment provided to non-industrial units within the enterprise, if the accounting work of the enterprise is good enough to separate it from other records, and the share of such services is significant, it should also be included in the income from external processing.

Value of change in semi-finished products between the end and the beginning of the reference period: refers to the value of change in semi-finished products between the end and the beginning of the reference period, which generally can be obtained from accounting records of enterprises. If the enterprise accounting excludes the cost of semi-finished products, then it should not be included in the gross industrial output value, and the reverse if otherwise.

Total Assets refer to all resources that are owned or controlled by enterprises through previous trades or transactions with expectation of making economic profits. Classified by the degree of liquidity, total assets include current assets, and non-current assets. Current assets can be classified into monetary assets, trading financial assets, notes receivable, accounts receivable, advanced payments, other prepaid money and inventories. Non-current assets can be divided into long-term equity investment, fixed assets, intangible assets and other non-current assets. Data on this indicator can be obtained by the year-end figures of total assets in the Assets and Liability Table of accounting records of enterprises.

Total Current Assets refer to the assets that meet one of the following requirements: (1) expected to be cashed, sold or used in a normal operation cycle, mainly including inventory and accounts receivable; (2) be owned for trading purpose mainly; (3) expected to be cashed in one year (including one year) from the day of the Assets and Liability Table; (4) unlimited cash or cash equivalents that can be exchanged with other assets or being capable of settling debts during one year since the day of Assets and Liability Table. Included are monetary assets, notes receivable, accounts receivable and inventories. Data on this indicator can be obtained by the year-end figures of total current assets in the Assets and Liability Table of the accounting records of enterprises.

Original Value of Fixed Assets refers to the cost of fixed assets, or the total expenditure of an enterprise spent on certain fixed assets, through purchase, construction, installation, transformation, expansion or technical upgrading. It is reported according to the year-end debit balance of fixed assets of accounting records.

Accumulated Depreciation refers to the accumulated figure of fixed assets depreciation over the past years that are extracted by the enterprise at the end of the reference period. It is reported according to the year-end credit balance of accumulated depreciation of accounting records.

Total Liabilities refer to payable liabilities of enterprises that accumulated from previous trades or transactions with expectation of economic profits leaking out. In terms of payment, it can be divided into liquid liabilities and long-term liabilities. Data on this item is obtained from the year-end figures on total liabilities from the Assets and Liability Table of the accounting record of the enterprises.

Total Liquid Liabilities refer to the liabilities that meet one of the following requirements: (1) expected to be repaid in a normal operation cycle; (2) be owned for trading purpose mainly; (3) expected to be repaid in one year from the day of the Assets and Liability Table; (4) enterprise has no right to postpone the settlement of which over a year from the day of the Assets and Liability Table. Included are short-term loans, notes payable, accounts payable, employee compensations, taxes and expenses due. Data on this indicator can be obtained by the year-end figures of total liquid liabilities in the Assets and Liability Table of the accounting records of enterprises.

Total Equity refers to the residual ownership of enterprise investors by deducting total liabilities from the total assets, including the paid-in capital, accumulation of capital, operating surplus and non-distributed profits. Data are obtained from the year-end figures on "total equity" from the Assets and Liability Table of the accounting record of enterprise.

Revenue from Principal Business refers to the income confirmed of an enterprise from the principal business of selling products and providing labor services. Data on this indicator can be obtained from the year-end credit balance of "revenue from principal business" in the accounting record of enterprise.

Cost of Principal Business refers to the total cost occurred from the principal business of the enterprise. Data can be obtained from the year-end debit balance of "cost of principal business" in the accounting record of enterprise.

Tax and Extra Charges from Principal Business refer to the sales tax, consumption tax, urban maintenance and construction tax and education expenses shouldered by the enterprise from its principal business. Data are obtained from the year-end debit balance of "tax and extra charges from principal business" in the accounting record of enterprise.

Total Profits refers to the operation results in a certain accounting period, and it is the balance of various incomes minus various spendings in the course of operation, reflecting the total profits and losses of enterprises in reporting period. Data are obtained from the amount of "total profits" in the "profit table" of the accounting record of enterprise.

Value-added Tax Payable refers to the payable tax of enterprises which engaged in selling of goods or providing services that bring added value to the goods, such as processing, repairing, fitting and other activities should be paid according to Tax Law. The formula is as follows:

Value-added Tax Payable = tax on sales-(tax on purchase-transferred tax on purchase)-exports deduct tax payable on domestic sales-tax relief+the export tax rebate.

Tax on Purchase refers to the value-added tax payable by enterprises that purchase goods or receiving taxable services during the reference period and this part of the tax is allowed to be deducted from the tax on sales.

Tax on Sales refers to the value-added tax chargeable by enterprises that sell goods or provide taxable services during the reference period.

Ratio of Profits, Taxes and Interests to Average Assets reflects the profit-making capability of all assets of the enterprise and is a key indicator manifesting the performance and management and evaluating the profit-making potential of the enterprise. It is calculated as follows:

$$\text{Ratio of Profits, Taxes and Interests to Average Assets (\%)} = \frac{\text{total profits} + \text{total taxes} + \text{interest payment}}{\text{average assets}} \times 100\%$$

In the above formula, total taxes is the sum of tax and extra charges on the principal business and value-added tax payable; and average assets is the arithmetic mean of the sum of beginning assets and ending assets.

Ratio of Debts to Assets reflects both the operation risk and the capability of the enterprise in making use of the capital from the creditors. It is

$$\text{Ratio of Debts to Assets (\%)} = \frac{\text{total debts}}{\text{total assets}} \times 100\%$$

Both assets and debts are figures at the end of the reference period.

Turnover of Current Assets refers to the number of times of turnover of current assets in a given period of time, which reflects the speed of the turnover of current assets of industrial enterprises, and is calculated as follows:

$$\text{Turnover of Current Assets} = \frac{\text{sales revenue of products}}{\text{average balance of total current assets}}$$

In the above formula, average balance of total current assets refers to the arithmetic mean of the sum of current assets at the beginning and at the end of the reference period.

Ratio of Profits to Total Industrial Costs refers to the ratio of profits realized in a given period to the total costs in the same period, which reflects the economic efficiency of input cost and is calculated as follows:

$$\text{Ratio of Profits to Total Industrial Cost (\%)} = \frac{\text{total profits}}{\text{total costs}} \times 100\%$$

Total costs in the above formula are the sum of cost of principal business, marketing cost,

Sales Ratio of Products is an indicator reflecting the actual sale of industrial products, analyzing the production-selling and supply-demand relations. It is calculated as:

$$\text{Sales Ratio of Products (\%)} = \frac{\text{value of industrial sales}}{\text{gross industrial output value (current prices)}} \times 100\%$$

14

建筑业

CONSTRUCTION

简要说明

本篇主要内容和资料来源

本篇资料反映在新疆维吾尔自治区注册的建筑法人企业概况及发展情况，包括建筑业企业基本情况和生产经营情况。主要指标有企业个数、从业人员和建筑企业签定合同情况、承包工程完成情况及总产值、企业技术装备情况、房屋建筑面积、利润、税金、劳动生产率等。

根据建筑业发展的实际情况，建筑业统计范围从2002年起，由原具有建筑业资质等级四级及四级以上的独立核算的建筑业企业调整为具有施工总承包、专业承包和劳务分包的法人建筑业企业。

本篇建筑业企业统计数据是根据国家统计局制定的《建筑业统计报表制度》整理汇总的。建筑业统计数据采取全面调查的方法。资料由新疆维吾尔自治区统计局固定资产投资统计处提供。

Brief Introduction

Main Content and Source of Data

Data in this chapter show the general situation and the development of the construction in Xinjiang Uygur Autonomous Region. They cover the situation of production and management of the enterprises on construction, including the number of enterprises, number of employed persons, complete and gross output value of construction industry, value added floor space of the buildings, profits and taxes of enterprises and labor productivity, etc.

According to the development of construction industry, starting from 2002,the coverage of construction statistics has been adjusted to include all the construction enterprises of various types of ownership with qualification certificates and with independent accounting system ,instead of the original criteria that required construction enterprises of various types of ownership to have qualification certificates at or above Class 4 with independent accounting system.

Data on construction enterprises are collected in accordance with the Reporting System of Construction Statistics stipulated by the National Bureau of Statistics. Data on the construction industry are collected through comprehensive reporting system and provided by the Department of Investment in Fixed Assets Statistics, Xinjiang Bureau of Statistics.

14-1 建筑企业概况
Main Indicators on Construction Enterprises

年份 Year	地区 Region	企业个数(个) Number of Enterprises (unit)				从业人员(万人) Number of Persons Employed (10 000 persons)			
		合计 Total	国有 State-owned	集体 Collective-owned	其他 Others	合计 Total	国有 State-owned	集体 Collective-owned	其他 Others
	1985	275	117	158		25.85	19.21	6.64	
	1990	353	183	170		22.86	18.36	4.50	
	1995	928	481	432	15	35.33	26.33	8.72	0.28
	1996	886	478	386	22	24.97	18.53	6.09	0.35
	1997	650	313	312	25	30.75	20.39	8.56	1.80
	1998	682	269	348	65	22.14	14.83	6.42	0.89
	1999	711	272	344	95	19.35	13.00	4.94	1.41
	2000	690	226	293	171	26.16	17.69	4.25	4.22
	2001	594	175	152	267	25.27	14.77	2.68	7.82
	2002	730	146	109	475	23.57	8.64	1.89	13.04
	2003	776	112	77	587	20.81	6.16	1.12	13.53
	2004	932	105	51	776	33.22	7.21	0.84	25.17
	2005	881	107	43	731	34.37	8.70	0.90	24.77
	2006	914	102	39	773	33.84	8.81	0.84	24.19
	2007	967	103	35	829	37.02	9.63	0.92	26.47
	2008	998	99	32	867	42.37	11.28	0.48	30.61
	2009	993	90	28	875	48.18	12.01	0.52	35.65
	2010	1004	81	28	895	56.48	12.66	0.52	43.30
	2011	1025	89	22	914	52.73	9.89	0.40	42.44
	2012	1045	89	20	936	63.81	12.86	0.48	50.47
	2013	1123	76	19	1028	79.11	13.68	0.61	64.82
乌鲁木齐市	Urumqi City	445	34	7	404	28.84	7.19	0.27	21.38
克拉玛依市	Karamay City	64	2	2	60	3.36	0.23	0.04	3.09
吐鲁番地区	Turpan Administrative Offices	19	2		17	0.61	0.01		0.60
哈密地区	Hami [Kumul] Administrative Offices	45	2	1	42	1.48	0.39	0.01	1.08
昌吉回族自治州	Changji Hui Autonomous Prefecture	89	1	1	87	3.75	0.06	0.01	3.68
伊犁哈萨克自治州	Ili Kazak Autonomous Prefecture	133	16	6	111	11.11	1.89	0.11	9.11
伊犁州直属县(市)	Counties (Cities) Direct Under Ili Prefecture	71	7	3	61	6.43	1.21	0.08	5.14
塔城地区	Tacheng [Tarbagatai] Administrative Offices	32	4	3	25	3.40	0.45	0.03	2.92
阿勒泰地区	Altay Administrative Offices	30	5		25	1.28	0.23		1.05
博尔塔拉蒙古自治州	Bortala Mongol Autonomous Prefecture	32	2	1	29	2.59	0.50	0.17	1.92
巴音郭楞蒙古自治州	Bayangol Mongol Autonomous Prefecture	68	4	1	63	6.36	0.10		6.26
阿克苏地区	Aksu Administrative Offices	69	2		67	3.76	0.06		3.70
克孜勒苏柯尔克孜自治州	Kizilsu Kirgiz Autonomous Prefecture	22	1		21	0.67			0.67
喀什地区	Kashgar [Kaxgar] Administrative Offices	61	2		59	3.73	0.10		3.63
和田地区	Hotan Administrative Offices	20	1		19	1.55	0.21		1.34
石河子市	Shihezi City	29	4		25	7.70	2.53		5.17
阿拉尔市	Aral City	9	1		8	1.12	0.38		0.74
图木舒克市	Tumxuk City	8	1		7	1.18	0.01		1.17
五家渠市	Wujiaqu City	10	1		9	1.30	0.02		1.28

注：1.2000 年至 2002 年建筑业所有指标数据均包括克拉玛依石油管理局工业部分，2003 年起将此部分扣除(以下同)。
2.2004 年建筑业所有数据为经济普查数，企业个数及其他指标包括没有工作量或者停业企业，往年未包括(以下同)。
3.根据我区建筑特点，建筑业从业人员为年平均人数。

Note: a) All the quota indices in building sector from 2000 to 2002 include the industrial part of Karamay Oil Administration. From 2003, this part was omitted. (the same as in the following) . b) All the data in architectural sector are the statistics of economic census, enterprise numbers and other quota exclude work volume or closed enterprises except for previous years. (the same as in the following) . c)In view of the features of the construction, the number of employed persons refers to the annual average.

14-2 按登记注册类型分建筑企业总产值
Total Output Value of Construction Enterprises by Registration Status

单位：万元 (10 000 yuan)

年 份 Year	地 区 Region	合 计 Total	国有经济 State-owned Units	集体经济 Collective -owned Units	其他经济 Others Units
	1985	175165	138138	37027	
	1990	273893	220574	53319	
	1995	1070085	816396	238387	15302
	1996	1284669	977358	283776	23535
	1997	1141318	828482	288081	24755
	1998	1434787	1002235	378956	53596
	1999	1569486	1085080	365588	118818
	2000	2349506	1436653	362649	550204
	2001	2742800	1394099	252076	1096625
	2002	3136257	1270601	170319	1695337
	2003	3221502	739953	147256	2334293
	2004	3439968	910264	89189	2440515
	2005	3615674	1138005	102580	2375089
	2006	3856223	1269722	88474	2498027
	2007	4541026	1548285	97418	2895323
	2008	6292562	1879497	86431	4326634
	2009	7913768	2245048	119717	5549003
	2010	9694741	2486878	119917	7087946
	2011	13278310	3302487	104738	9871085
	2012	16331061	3670127	161626	12499308
	2013	20988887	3532297	222053	17234537
乌鲁木齐市	Urumqi City	6701059	1757994	64051	4879014
克拉玛依市	Karamay City	1494942	32026	39935	1422981
吐鲁番地区	Turpan Administrative Offices	192827	8671		184156
哈密地区	Hami [Kumul] Administrative Offices	492412	175090	16930	300392
昌吉回族自治州	Changji Hui Autonomous Prefecture	1213866	19393	24720	1169753
伊犁哈萨克自治州	Ili Kazak Autonomous Prefecture	3005035	579264	25759	2400012
伊犁州直属县(市)	Counties (Cities) Direct Under Ili Prefecture	1815525	358169	18479	1438877
塔城地区	Tacheng [Tarbagatai] Administrative Offices	779874	147593	7280	625001
阿勒泰地区	Altay Administrative Offices	409636	73502		336134
博尔塔拉蒙古自治州	Bortala Mongol Autonomous Prefecture	728718	149745	50500	528473
巴音郭楞蒙古自治州	Bayangol Mongol Autonomous Prefecture	1919766	57397	158	1862211
阿克苏地区	Aksu Administrative Offices	1122597	21212		1101385
克孜勒苏柯尔克孜自治州	Kizilsu Kirgiz Autonomous Prefecture	218806	18957		199849
喀什地区	Kashgar [Kaxgar] Administrative Offices	949565	36063		913502
和田地区	Hotan Administrative Offices	449222	81463		367759
石河子市	Shihezi City	1394211	438132		956079
阿拉尔市	Aral City	448444	151532		296912
图木舒克市	Tumxuk City	362042	510		361532
五家渠市	Wujiaqu City	295375	4848		290527

14-3 按构成分建筑企业总产值
Total Output Value of Construction Enterprises by Composition

单位：万元 (10 000 yuan)

年 份 Year	地 区 Region	总产值 Total Output Value	建筑工程 Output Value of Construction Projects	安装工程 Output Value of Installation Projects	其 他 Others
	1985	175165	154496	18042	2627
	1990	273893	241574	28211	4108
	1995	1070085	942158	106744	21183
	1996	1284669	1124271	132079	28319
	1997	1141318	1009082	105891	26345
	1998	1434787	1270483	139104	25200
	1999	1569486	1398179	146154	25153
	2000	2349506	2073166	214425	61915
	2001	2742800	2403688	279909	59203
	2002	3136257	2637362	405115	93780
	2003	3221502	2708269	336535	176698
	2004	3439968	2836668	396509	206791
	2005	3615674	2981373	487239	147062
	2006	3856223	3209192	510770	136261
	2007	4541026	3822922	564228	153876
	2008	6292562	5359129	804719	128714
	2009	7913768	6924156	867812	121800
	2010	9694741	8450628	1107006	137107
	2011	13278310	11850908	1223095	204307
	2012	16331061	14545263	1420629	365169
	2013	20988887	18887487	1691824	409576
乌鲁木齐市	Urumqi City	6701059	5897352	710944	92763
克拉玛依市	Karamay City	1494942	956444	463031	75467
吐鲁番地区	Turpan Administrative Offices	192827	115371	71526	5930
哈密地区	Hami [Kumul] Administrative Offices	492412	486321	2592	3499
昌吉回族自治州	Changji Hui Autonomous Prefecture	1213866	1055144	121064	37658
伊犁哈萨克自治州	Ili Kazak Autonomous Prefecture	3005035	2888652	103152	13231
伊犁州直属县(市)	Counties (Cities) Direct Under Ili Prefecture	1815525	1772519	36359	6647
塔城地区	Tacheng [Tarbagatai] Administrative Offices	779874	728624	47627	3623
阿勒泰地区	Altay Administrative Offices	409636	387509	19166	2961
博尔塔拉蒙古自治州	Bortala Mongol Autonomous Prefecture	728718	724465	2603	1650
巴音郭楞蒙古自治州	Bayangol Mongol Autonomous Prefecture	1919766	1756485	57986	105295
阿克苏地区	Aksu Administrative Offices	1122597	1074552	42338	5707
克孜勒苏柯尔克孜自治州	Kizilsu Kirgiz Autonomous Prefecture	218806	207573	1994	9239
喀什地区	Kashgar [Kaxgar] Administrative Offices	949565	870538	75359	3668
和田地区	Hotan Administrative Offices	449222	407686	9639	31897
石河子市	Shihezi City	1394211	1343951	26716	23544
阿拉尔市	Aral City	448444	446659	1757	28
图木舒克市	Tumxuk City	362042	360988	1054	
五家渠市	Wujiaqu City	295375	295306	69	

14-4 按行业和登记注册类型分建筑企业总产值
Total Output Value of Construction Enterprises by Registration Status and Sectors

单位：万元 (10 000 yuan)

项　目	Item	2012	2013
总　计	**Total**	**16331061**	**20988887**
#一、二级企业	First Grade and Second Grade Enterprises	13620448	16859031
#国有及国有控股	State-owned and State-holding	8290122	10277068
按登记注册类型分组	**Grouped by Registration Status**		
内资企业	Domestic Funded	16330949	20988739
国有企业	State-owned Enterprises	2644686	1842413
集体企业	Collective-owned Enterprises	161626	222053
股份合作企业	Share-holding Cooperative		
联营企业	Joint Ownership Enterprises	117	
有限责任公司	Limited Liability Corporations	9591250	13396363
国有独资公司	Sole State -funded Company	1025443	1689884
其他有限责任公司	Other Limited Liability Companies	8565808	11706479
股份有限公司	Share-holding Corporations Ltd	895952	1005564
私营企业	Private Enterprises	3020942	4522346
#私营有限责任公司	Private Limited Liability Companies	2892708	4435592
私营股份有限公司	Private Stock Limited Companies	99066	85534
其他企业	Others	16376	
港、澳、台及外商企业	Enterprises With Funds from Hong Kong, Macao , Taiwan and Foreign	112	148
#合资经营企业(港或澳、台资)	Joint-Venture	85	77
按国民经济行业分组	**Grouped by National Economic Sectors**		
房屋和土木工程建筑业	Buildings and Civil Engineering Construction	15500234	20004049
房屋工程建筑	Building Construction	11055872	14734957
土木工程建筑	Civil Engineering Construction	4444362	5269092
铁路、道路、隧道和桥梁	Railways, Roads, Tunnels and Bridges	2267180	2321076
水利和港口建筑	Water Conservancy and Seaport Construction	1140935	1726055
工矿工程建筑	Mine Project	252386	264161
架线和管道工程建筑	Cabling and Piping Project	744068	930142
其他土木工程建筑	Other Civil Engineering	39793	27658
建筑安装业	Construction and Installation	615302	699672
建筑装饰业	Building Decoration	89647	112770
其他建筑业	Others	125878	172396
按隶属关系分组	**Grouped by Subordination**		
中 央	Central Government	4973648	7069147
地 方	Local	11357413	13919740
按企业资质等级分组	**Grouped by Enterprise's Qualification**		
施工总承包	Undertaking Porjects	14975525	19373835
特　级	Special Grade	226404	255527
一　级	First Grade	6462209	7728882
二　级	Second Grade	6015910	7808391
三级及以下	Third Grade and Below	2271002	3581035
专业承包	Specialized Undertaking	1247620	1422802
一　级	First Grade	281384	321409
二　级	Second Grade	579147	627003
三级及以下	Third Grade and Below	387089	474390
劳务分包	Work Subcontractors	107916	192250

14-5 建筑企业利税总额
Total Pre-tax Profits of Construction Enterprises

单位：万元 (10 000 yuan)

年份 Year	地区 Region	利税总额合计 Total Pre-tax Profits	利润总额 Total Profits	工程结算税金及附加 Taxes and Extra Charges on Project Settlement Accounts	管理费用中的税金 Taxes in Management Expenses	产值利税率(%) Ratio of Pre-tax Profits to Output Value (%)	资金利税率(%) Ratio of Pre-tax Profits to Assets (%)
	1994	28199	5535	20195	2469	3.81	4.11
	1995	30156	2974	24916	2266	3.44	3.46
	1996	20752	-8625	26816	2561	1.97	-0.93
	1997	31970	-4347	33360	2957	2.80	2.51
	1998	37596	-5875	41162	2309	2.62	2.41
	1999	64777	13359	48995	2423	4.13	3.72
	2000	19274	-48005	64614	2665	0.82	0.63
	2001	28688	-47485	74206	1967	1.05	0.84
	2002	84833	-11089	92484	3438	2.70	2.18
	2003	169594	67146	96888	5560	5.26	5.51
	2004	174255	65037	102990	6228	5.07	5.65
	2005	165236	46909	112565	5762	4.57	4.91
	2006	177102	54570	116426	6106	4.59	4.83
	2007	221117	67796	145119	8202	4.87	5.40
	2008	328484	120146	198718	9620	5.22	6.67
	2009	422062	156541	252547	12974	5.33	7.08
	2010	536197	208372	317056	10769	5.53	7.54
	2011	725740	274797	438927	12016	5.47	7.68
	2012	928871	356595	555058	17218	5.69	8.06
	2013	1126029	421152	678809	26068	5.36	7.94
乌鲁木齐市	Urumqi City	336474	108546	222506	5422	5.02	4.90
克拉玛依市	Karamay City	77835	35818	39771	2246	5.21	4.64
吐鲁番地区	Turpan Administrative Offices	22018	15158	6659	201	11.42	13.69
哈密地区	Hami [Kumul] Administrative Offices	25750	10281	13999	1470	5.23	8.45
昌吉回族自治州	Changji Hui Autonomous Prefecture	70329	29364	39913	1052	5.79	12.65
伊犁哈萨克自治州	Ili Kazak Autonomous Prefecture	136197	36055	98563	1579	4.53	12.84
伊犁州直属县(市)	Counties (Cities) Direct Under Ili Prefecture	62922	7091	55185	646	3.47	9.93
塔城地区	Tacheng [Tarbagatai] Administrative Offices	49118	20482	28033	603	6.30	18.37
阿勒泰地区	Altay Administrative Offices	24157	8482	15345	330	5.90	15.13
博尔塔拉蒙古自治州	Bortala Mongol Autonomous Prefecture	25022	4049	20717	256	3.43	12.98
巴音郭楞蒙古自治州	Bayangol Mongol Autonomous Prefecture	143842	71120	71762	960	7.49	18.11
阿克苏地区	Aksu Administrative Offices	86912	49547	35303	2062	7.74	13.88
克孜勒苏柯尔克孜自治州	Kizilsu Kirgiz Autonomous Prefecture	9739	2347	6964	428	4.45	6.80
喀什地区	Kashgar [Kaxgar] Administrative Offices	55380	18641	35160	1579	5.83	11.13
和田地区	Hotan Administrative Offices	22956	6604	16086	266	5.11	18.92
石河子市	Shihezi City	63605	17451	37806	8348	4.56	8.65
阿拉尔市	Aral City	21185	7441	13635	109	4.72	14.49
图木舒克市	Tumxuk City	12020	1695	10302	23	3.32	7.31
五家渠市	Wujiaqu City	16765	7035	9663	67	5.68	12.63

14-6 建筑企业劳动生产率
Labor Productivity of Construction Enterprises

单位：元/人 (yuan/person)

年份 Year	地区 Region	按总产值计算的劳动生产率 Overall Labor Productivity in Terms of Total Output Value	#国有经济 State-owned Enterprises	#集体经济 Collective-owned Enterprises
	1994	29871	32616	23023
	1995	34668	38483	26617
	1996	32606	36557	25291
	1997	38808	40629	33658
	1998	47698	51465	40819
	1999	55593	61196	44235
	2000	74994	87999	48767
	2001	84666	94344	62458
	2002	86302	108857	66231
	2003	94165	98095	86190
	2004	107150	112145	107185
	2005	112214	137966	127587
	2006	121506	149550	118932
	2007	126303	134275	139988
	2008	152795	182536	168023
	2009	173714	204170	233869
	2010	176404	200435	231859
	2011	226848	284263	176207
	2012	249202	245195	286875
	2013	265325	257911	369964
乌鲁木齐市	Urumqi City	232412	244376	241152
克拉玛依市	Karamay City	443905	141396	1103177
吐鲁番地区	Turpan Administrative Offices	316731	661893	
哈密地区	Hami [Kumul] Administrative Offices	331187	447686	2143000
昌吉回族自治州	Changji Hui Autonomous Prefecture	325877	317911	1765686
伊犁哈萨克自治州	Ili Kazak Autonomous Prefecture	269708	307155	248645
伊犁州直属县(市)	Counties (Cities) Direct Under Ili Prefecture	281787	296498	249716
塔城地区	Tacheng [Tarbagatai] Administrative Offices	229645	333016	245966
阿勒泰地区	Altay Administrative Offices	314403	313175	
博尔塔拉蒙古自治州	Bortala Mongol Autonomous Prefecture	283536	300090	293605
巴音郭楞蒙古自治州	Bayangol Mongol Autonomous Prefecture	301003	564928	176000
阿克苏地区	Aksu Administrative Offices	297439	332483	
克孜勒苏柯尔克孜自治州	Kizilsu Kirgiz Autonomous Prefecture	312490	4860692	
喀什地区	Kashgar [Kaxgar] Administrative Offices	255671	331766	
和田地区	Hotan Administrative Offices	293282	396219	
石河子市	Shihezi City	181137	172888	
阿拉尔市	Aral City	400539	396369	
图木舒克市	Tumxuk City	309068	68000	
五家渠市	Wujiaqu City	229453	272360	

14-7 建筑企业技术装备情况
Number and Power of Machinery and Equipment Owned by Construction Enterprises

年份 Year	地区 Region	自有机械设备总台数(台) Number of Machinery and Equipment Owned (set)	自有机械设备总功率(万千瓦) Total Power of Equipment and Machinery Owned (10 000 kw)	自有机械设备净值(万元) Net Value of Machinery and Equipment Owned (10 000 yuan)	技术装备率(元/人) Value of Machines Per Laborer (yuan/ person)	动力装备率(千瓦/人) Power of Machines Per Laborer (kw/person)
	1985	30307	105	29308	1332	6
	1990	34806	91	46098	2511	5
	1995	55455	138	106383	4211	5
	1996	60567	129	127572	4478	5
	1997	64252	149	139617	4747	5
	1998	72606	148	164157	7415	7
	1999	73735	155	184559	9543	8
	2000	77975	182	224485	8582	7
	2001	85981	177	238142	9425	7
	2002	96116	207	442787	18996	9
	2003	100913	207	395865	11866	6
	2004	98541	239	358397	11389	8
	2005	99324	190	326360	10372	6
	2006	96674	197	348344	11187	6
	2007	103431	203	374396	10650	6
	2008	102266	230	392371	9692	6
	2009	103285	235	407809	9136	5
	2010	97562	238	383196	7145	4
	2011	98768	246	398762	6812	4
	2012	91704	242	430432	6568	4
	2013	95627	313	437656	5533	3
乌鲁木齐市	Urumqi City	30404	166	155446	5391	5
克拉玛依市	Karamay City	7128	25	50438	14977	7
吐鲁番地区	Turpan Administrative Offices	1529	4	5646	9274	5
哈密地区	Hami [Kumul] Administrative Offices	2028	5	10628	7148	2
昌吉回族自治州	Changji Hui Autonomous Prefecture	4961	11	28952	7773	1
伊犁哈萨克自治州	Ili Kazak Autonomous Prefecture	15600	27	45695	4101	2
伊犁州直属县(市)	Counties (Cities) Direct Under Ili Prefecture	8655	12	28542	4430	1
塔城地区	Tacheng [Tarbagatai] Administrative Offices	4697	11	8510	2506	3
阿勒泰地区	Altay Administrative Offices	2248	4	8643	6634	2
博尔塔拉蒙古自治州	Bortala Mongol Autonomous Prefecture	3812	6	15098	5874	2
巴音郭楞蒙古自治州	Bayangol Mongol Autonomous Prefecture	12179	24	34697	5440	3
阿克苏地区	Aksu Administrative Offices	5311	15	22072	5848	3
克孜勒苏柯尔克孜自治州	Kizilsu Kirgiz Autonomous Prefecture	348	1	4475	6391	1
喀什地区	Kashgar [Kaxgar] Administrative Offices	3419	11	16404	4417	3
和田地区	Hotan Administrative Offices	3389	2	6244	4077	
石河子市	Shihezi City	3269	9	19983	2596	1
阿拉尔市	Aral City	1105	4	18371	16409	3
图木舒克市	Tumxuk City	539	2	2680	2288	2
五家渠市	Wujiaqu City	606	1	827	642	

14-8 按登记注册类型分建筑企业技术装备情况
Number and Power of Machinery and Equipment Owned by Registration Status

(2013 年)

项　　目	Item	自有机械设备年末总台数（台） Number of Machinery and Equipment Owned Year-end (set)	自有机械设备年末总功率（千瓦） Total Power of Machinery and Equipment Owned Year-end (kw)	自有机械设备年末净值（万元） Net Value of Machinery and Equipment Owned Year-end (10 000 yuan)
总　　计	**Total**	**95627**	**3133345**	**437656**
#一、二级企业	First, Second Enterprises	77896	2800476	352467
#国有及国有控股	State-owned and State-holding	39754	1974326	202843
按登记注册类型分组	**Grouped by Registration Status**	**95627**	**3133345**	**437656**
内资企业	Domestic Funede	95627	3133345	437656
国有企业	State-owned Enterprises	14904	935120	48497
集体企业	Collective-owned Enterprises	920	23738	4457
有限责任公司	Limited Liability Corporations	54036	1416517	256915
国有独资公司	Sole State -funded Company	4388	130736	33221
其他有限责任公司	Other Limited Liability Companies	49648	1285781	223694
股份有限公司	Share-holding Corporations Ltd.	3137	288756	18423
私营企业	Private Enterprises	22630	469214	109364
#私营有限责任公司	Private Limited Liability Companies	21460	461850	107539
私营股份有限公司	Private Stock Limited Companies	1170	7364	1825
按国民经济行业分组	**Grouped by National Economic Sectors**			
房屋和土木工程建筑业	Buildings and Givil Engineering	87791	2944362	388482
房屋工程建筑	Building	62513	1278857	225665
土木工程建筑	Civil Engineering	25278	1665505	162817
铁路、道路、隧道和桥梁	Railways, Roads, Tunnels and Bridges	10594	835305	78618
水利和港口建筑	Water Conservancy and Seaport	7102	258018	41849
工矿工程建筑	Mining Project	3662	409389	15757
架线和管道工程建筑	Cabling and Piping Project	3877	160693	26385
其他土木工程建筑	Other Civil Engineering	43	2100	208
建筑安装业	Construction and Installation	6464	152461	36198
建筑装饰业	Building Decoration	827	22632	3760
其他建筑业	Others	545	13890	9216
按隶属关系分组	**Grouped by Subordination**			
中　央	Central Government	24666	1267391	146046
地　方	Local	70961	1865954	291610
按企业资质等级分组	**Grouped by Enterprise's Qualification**			
施工总承包	Undertaking Porjects	90348	2983357	401187
特　级	Special Grade	651	27870	1321
一　级	First Grade	37832	1876982	190360
二　级	Second Grade	35981	790841	138341
三　级	Third Grade	15884	287664	71165
专业承包	Specialized Undertaking	5279	149988	36469
一　级	First Grade	1988	68652	13078
二　级	Second Grade	1444	36131	9367
三　级	Third Grade	1847	45205	14024

14-9 建筑企业签订合同情况
Contracts Signed by Construction Enterprises

单位：万元 (10 000 yuan)

年份 Year	地区 Region	合同总额 Total Value Of Contracts	上年结转合同 Value from Contracts Signed In Last Year	本年新签合同 Value from New Contracts Signed In This Year
	2002	3962086	988485	2973601
	2003	4312515	1236887	3075628
	2004	4725501	1351086	3374415
	2005	4857604	1557300	3300304
	2006	5692120	1483664	4208455
	2007	7220300	1986086	5234214
	2008	9907859	2906991	7000868
	2009	12473691	3859836	8613855
	2010	15883584	5459941	10423643
	2011	21956637	6083819	15872818
	2012	27266741	9965704	17301037
	2013	34204813	11167870	23036943
乌鲁木齐市	Urumqi City	12743652	4897844	7845808
克拉玛依市	Karamay City	2805123	1298578	1506545
吐鲁番地区	Turpan Administrative Offices	319673	115453	204220
哈密地区	Hami [Kumul] Administrative Offices	705990	171278	534712
昌吉回族自治州	Changji Hui Autonomous Prefecture	1652092	401553	1250539
伊犁哈萨克自治州	Ili Kazak Autonomous Prefecture	4112827	918888	3193939
伊犁州直属县(市)	Counties (Cities) Direct Under Ili Prefecture	2489694	484834	2004860
塔城地区	Tacheng [Tarbagatai] Administrative Offices	1086863	325301	761562
阿勒泰地区	Altay Administrative Offices	536270	108753	427517
博尔塔拉蒙古自治州	Bortala Mongol Autonomous Prefecture	1037790	145490	892300
巴音郭楞蒙古自治州	Bayangol Mongol Autonomous Prefecture	2837521	784976	2052545
阿克苏地区	Aksu Administrative Offices	1967525	864828	1102697
克孜勒苏柯尔克孜自治州	Kizilsu Kirgiz Autonomous Prefecture	332645	79879	252766
喀什地区	Kashgar [Kaxgar] Administrative Offices	1491701	499767	991934
和田地区	Hotan Administrative Offices	734028	200680	533348
石河子市	Shihezi City	2103351	579053	1524298
阿拉尔市	Aral City	538038	87528	450510
图木舒克市	Tumxuk City	448964	59930	389034
五家渠市	Wujiaqu City	373893	62145	311748

注：14-9、14-10 表口径为总承包和专业承包企业。
Note:The data of the table 14-9&14-10 refer to all general construction contractors and professional contractors.

14-10 建筑企业承包工程完成情况
Completion of Contracted Projects by Construction Enterprises

单位：万元 (10 000 yuan)

年份 Year	地区 Region	直接从建设单位承揽工程完成产值 Completed Output Value of Projects Contracted Directly from Investors	自行完成施工产值 Own-Completed Output Value	分包出去工程产值 Output Value Of Out-Sourced Projects	从建设单位以外承揽工程产值 Completed Output Value of Projects Contracted From Non-investors
	2002	3141928	3048086	93842	88171
	2003	3238170	3135725	102445	85777
	2004	3443802	3377532	66270	62436
	2005	3634746	3563947	70799	51727
	2006	3856300	3775975	80325	80248
	2007	4534324	4420958	113366	120068
	2008	6309803	6128312	181492	164251
	2009	7993048	7805261	187787	108507
	2010	9723428	9503630	219798	191111
	2011	13382657	13026735	355922	251577
	2012	16409068	16042803	366265	288258
	2013	21128364	20726750	401614	262137
乌鲁木齐市	Urumqi City	6717166	6574750	142417	126307
克拉玛依市	Karamay City	1684612	1444488	240125	50458
吐鲁番地区	Turpan Administrative Offices	192827	192827		
哈密地区	Hami [Kumul] Administrative Offices	483844	483844		8567
昌吉回族自治州	Changji Hui Autonomous Prefecture	1208066	1208066		5800
伊犁哈萨克自治州	Ili Kazak Autonomous Prefecture	3000265	2995645	4620	9390
伊犁州直属县(市)	Counties (Cities) Direct Under Ili Prefecture	1813585	1813585		1940
塔城地区	Tacheng [Tarbagatai] Administrative Offices	779874	779874		
阿勒泰地区	Altay Administrative Offices	406806	402186	4620	7450
博尔塔拉蒙古自治州	Bortala Mongol Autonomous Prefecture	721899	721899		6819
巴音郭楞蒙古自治州	Bayangol Mongol Autonomous Prefecture	1919574	1909495	10079	10271
阿克苏地区	Aksu Administrative Offices	1117702	1115315	2387	7282
克孜勒苏柯尔克孜自治州	Kizilsu Kirgiz Autonomous Prefecture	218813	218146	665	659
喀什地区	Kashgar [Kaxgar] Administrative Offices	949288	947967	1321	1598
和田地区	Hotan Administrative Offices	449222	449222		
石河子市	Shihezi City	1359225	1359225		34986
阿拉尔市	Aral City	448444	448444		
图木舒克市	Tumxuk City	362042	362042		
五家渠市	Wujiaqu City	295375	295375		

14-11 建筑企业资产及资本金
Assets and Capital Principal of Construction Enterprises

单位：万元 (10 000 yuan)

年份 Year	地区 Region	资产合计 Total Assets	流动资产合计 Total of Circulating Funds	固定资产合计 Total of Fixed Assets	固定资产净值 Net Value of Fixed Assets	本年折旧 Deprecia-tion in the Year	资本金合计 Total of Principal Value	#国家资本金 National Principal
1995		939205	647608	240076	225084	18463	221212	110987
2000		3256421	1855185	1215525	1106384	65383	892851	208214
2001		3740312	2187385	1243161	1048023	82884	1055531	227457
2002		4244587	2527414	1364782	1179599	95565	1327186	227601
2003		3375330	2292828	787690	675947	61335	835618	219826
2004		3810825	2632242	825567	722019	62725	929293	225884
2005		3818087	2665404	826376	700835	72103	936389	184447
2006		4115800	2952267	796558	712740	69191	985436	202670
2007		4611598	3387459	804007	706591	76979	1095997	222967
2008		5527993	4040796	958379	862286	91915	1408249	429579
2009		6565349	4966204	1080129	960338	103188	1528701	396188
2010		7906943	6141713	1078910	939519	99050	1585475	412634
2011		10577644	8275111	1395723	1176365	119913	1960348	1948237
2012		13091083	10327841	1462446	1200685	152195	2149972	2138479
2013		16337241	12804962	1656199	1373052	193299	3569213	3553059
	乌鲁木齐市 Urumqi City	7992310	6247168	703802	618251	78175	2139359	2126967
	克拉玛依市 Karamay City	1829413	1564468	114893	111800	14072	184504	182032
	吐鲁番地区 Turpan Administrative Offices	173270	145631	15862	15217	3103	41497	41460
	哈密地区 Hami [Kumul] Administrative Offices	333405	275356	31986	29319	2758	51688	51263
	昌吉回族自治州 Changji Hui Autonomous Prefecture	678261	498477	76124	57563	7246	150517	149970
	伊犁哈萨克自治州 Ili Kazak Autonomous Prefecture	1251331	896758	206773	163637	46023	253470	253374
	伊犁州直属县(市) Counties (Cities) Direct Under Ili Prefecture	706264	521577	119478	111794	41472	129575	129575
	塔城地区 Tacheng [Tarbagatai] Administrative Offices	308146	239492	58343	27854	2564	60689	60593
	阿勒泰地区 Altay Administrative Offices	236921	135689	28952	23989	1987	63206	63206
	博尔塔拉蒙古自治州 Bortala Mongol Autonomous Prefecture	233198	146093	50010	46745	983	49573	49573
	巴音郭楞蒙古自治州 Bayangol Mongol Autonomous Prefecture	971155	720528	103058	73691	11062	203932	203932
	阿克苏地区 Aksu Administrative Offices	741395	540163	135251	86191	11982	146380	146380
	克孜勒苏柯尔克孜自治州 Kizilsu Kirgiz Autonomous Prefecture	157830	125651	22003	17531	869	34717	34582
	喀什地区 Kashgar [Kaxgar] Administrative Offices	575699	459897	43915	37815	2231	107643	107643
	和田地区 Hotan Administrative Offices	140961	99205	24732	22157	1978	50474	50474
	石河子市 Shihezi City	770350	664646	79138	70700	4005	107050	107050
	阿拉尔市 Aral City	166659	133262	20949	12905	7565	15710	15710
	图木舒克市 Tumxuk City	176169	159707	14223	4791	865	18553	18503
	五家渠市 Wujiaqu City	145835	127952	13480	4739	382	14146	14146

14-12 建筑企业负债及所有者权益
Liabilities and Owner's Equity of Construction Enterprises

单位：万元 (10 000 yuan)

年 份 Year	地 区 Region	负债合计 Total Liabilities	所有者权益 Owners' Equity
1994		540403	192618
1995		699997	239208
1996		815330	324051
1997		1018007	350659
1998		1175839	385913
1999		1325825	415026
2000		2068439	1187982
2001		2300621	1439690
2002		2717728	1526859
2003		2327382	1047948
2004		2631252	1174864
2005		2651255	1159206
2006		2886203	1220298
2007		3240248	1359137
2008		3806899	1707855
2009		4553885	1996439
2010		5798936	2089888
2011		7857731	2707722
2012		9797466	3167556
2013		12275613	4018977
乌鲁木齐市	Urumqi City	6209038	1770705
克拉玛依市	Karamay City	1522105	279274
吐鲁番地区	Turpan Administrative Offices	132288	40947
哈密地区	Hami [Kumul] Administrative Offices	253024	79884
昌吉回族自治州	Changji Hui Autonomous Prefecture	438384	238649
伊犁哈萨克自治州	Ili Kazak Autonomous Prefecture	948103	303097
伊犁州直属县(市)	Counties (Cities) Direct Under Ili Prefecture	552569	153690
塔城地区	Tacheng [Tarbagatai] Administrative Offices	219428	88587
阿勒泰地区	Altay Administrative Offices	176106	60820
博尔塔拉蒙古自治州	Bortala Mongol Autonomous Prefecture	110920	122286
巴音郭楞蒙古自治州	Bayangol Mongol Autonomous Prefecture	531801	439357
阿克苏地区	Aksu Administrative Offices	471876	269529
克孜勒苏柯尔克孜自治州	Kizilsu Kirgiz Autonomous Prefecture	115464	42231
喀什地区	Kashgar [Kaxgar] Administrative Offices	427017	148690
和田地区	Hotan Administrative Offices	86551	54409
石河子市	Shihezi City	621876	148477
阿拉尔市	Aral City	136799	29861
图木舒克市	Tumxuk City	153456	22655
五家渠市	Wujiaqu City	116911	28926

14-13 建筑企业总收入
Total Income of Construction Enterprises

单位：万元 (10 000 yuan)

年份 Year	地区 Region	企业总收入 Total Income of Enterprises	工程结算收入 Revenue of Project Settlement Accounts	#工程结算成本 Costs of Project Settlement Accounts	其他业务收入 Revenue from Other Business	#其他业务利润 Profits from Other Business
	1994	813369	714469	627830	98900	9332
	1995	898810	821713	713940	77097	9445
	1996	983170	904800	799183	78370	8765
	1997	1210813	1081666	950091	129147	17368
	1998	1454758	1346748	1193276	108010	19146
	1999	1595986	1500818	1320898	95167	14882
	2000	2659696	2514011	2252154	145686	30012
	2001	2961754	2807549	2521902	154205	34532
	2002	3360613	3199880	2854350	160733	30853
	2003	3221521	3090768	2716009	130753	21692
	2004	3395793	3276421	2900842	119372	21601
	2005	3685197	3566042	3202712	119155	23629
	2006	3766819	3643783	3255171	123036	20730
	2007	4584374	4431221	3983622	153154	22186
	2008	6382510	6225083	5635311	157427	33187
	2009	7958865	7788105	7074708	170760	39289
	2010	9849630	9610000	8752747	239630	46564
	2011	13467486	13201119	12045042	266367	39679
	2012	17359472	17075648	15598630	283824	64353
	2013	21758625	21427070	19539511	331555	25951
乌鲁木齐市	Urumqi City	7676103	7447216	6828637	228887	7671
克拉玛依市	Karamay City	1850698	1810267	1679076	40431	3281
吐鲁番地区	Turpan Administrative Offices	223492	222904	168383	588	276
哈密地区	Hami [Kumul] Administrative Offices	469885	468414	426858	1471	1089
昌吉回族自治州	Changji Hui Autonomous Prefecture	1162633	1160134	1049055	2499	1025
伊犁哈萨克自治州	Ili Kazak Autonomous Prefecture	2965110	2951535	2739306	13575	1294
伊犁州直属县(市)	Counties (Cities) Direct Under Ili Prefecture	1835948	1831261	1729362	4687	1086
塔城地区	Tacheng [Tarbagatai] Administrative Offices	720476	713638	645774	6838	250
阿勒泰地区	Altay Administrative Offices	408687	406636	364170	2051	-42
博尔塔拉蒙古自治州	Bortala Mongol Autonomous Prefecture	509542	508319	477201	1223	158
巴音郭楞蒙古自治州	Bayangol Mongol Autonomous Prefecture	1898439	1891579	1682816	6860	1410
阿克苏地区	Aksu Administrative Offices	1060553	1054956	875871	5597	1495
克孜勒苏柯尔克孜自治州	Kizilsu Kirgiz Autonomous Prefecture	181866	174818	162233	7048	714
喀什地区	Kashgar [Kaxgar] Administrative Offices	995915	992252	905763	3663	2010
和田地区	Hotan Administrative Offices	523096	521818	492452	1278	124
石河子市	Shihezi City	1273175	1264349	1180918	8826	2182
阿拉尔市	Aral City	369945	368488	339024	1457	46
图木舒克市	Tumxuk City	303839	295815	279937	8024	3048
五家渠市	Wujiaqu City	294334	294206	251981	128	128

14-14 建筑企业亏损额及从业人数
Losses and Employed Persons of Construction Enterprises

(2013 年)

项 目	Item	企业数（个） Number of Enterprises (unit)	#亏损企业个数 Number of Losssuffering Enterprises	亏损企业亏损额（万元） Amount of Total Loss (10000 yuan)	计算劳动生产率的平均人数（人） Average Number of Staff for Calculation of Labour Productivity (person)	期末从业人数（人） Employees atYear- end (person)
总 计	**Total**	**1123**	**297**	**90204**	**791060**	**361628**
#一、二级企业	First, Second Enterprises	510	117	68391	633104	269938
#国有及国有控股	State-owned and State-holding	174	34	54678	406796	150990
按登记注册类型分组	**Grouped by Registration Status**	**1123**	**297**	**90204**	**791060**	**361628**
内资企业	Domestic Funede	1120	296	90202	791051	361619
国有企业	State-owned Enterprises	38	10	37436	77234	41796
集体企业	Collective-owned Enterprises	19	3	1704	6002	3005
股份合作企业	Share-holding Cooperative					
有限责任公司	Limited Liability Corporations	469	104	30016	502412	194706
国有独资公司	Sole State -funded Company	38	11	10916	59724	23872
其他有限责任公司	Other Limited Liability Companies	431	93	19100	442688	170834
股份有限公司	Share-holding Corporations Ltd	11	2	559	38940	17374
私营企业	Private Enterprises	583	177	20487	166463	104738
#私营有限责任公司	Private Limited Liability Companies	576	175	20412	163364	102078
私营股份有限公司	Private Stock Limited Companies	6	2	75	3063	2620
港、澳、台及外商企业	Enterprises With Funds from Hong Kong, Macao , Taiwan and Foreign	3	1	2	9	9
按国民经济行业分组	**Grouped by National Economic Sectors**					
房屋和土木工程建筑业	Buildings and Givil Engineering	783	174	79632	752772	325956
房屋工程建筑	Building	553	122	23812	580779	238176
土木工程建筑	Civil Engineering	230	52	55820	171993	87780
铁路、道路、隧道和桥梁	Railways, Roads, Tunnels and Bridges	93	21	10907	74788	41224
水利和港口建筑	Water Conservancy and Seaport	47	11	2230	64282	19007
工矿工程建筑	Mining Project	19	7	39104	8300	6486
架线和管道工程建筑	Cabling and Piping Project	53	8	3417	23582	20408
其他土木工程建筑	Other Civil Engineering	18	5	162	1041	655
建筑安装业	Construction and Installation	162	49	7685	23366	19834
建筑装饰业	Building Decoration	108	50	2138	6647	6833
其他建筑业	Others	70	24	749	8275	9005
按隶属关系分组	**Grouped by Subordination**					
中 央	Central Government	78	10	42323	294773	90952
地 方	Local	1045	287	47881	496287	270676
按企业资质等级分组	**Grouped by Enterprise's Qualification**					
施工总承包	Undertaking Porjects	713	155	79612	726752	315159
特 级	Special Grade	1			9100	1867
一 级	First Grade	64	8	45553	307078	121810
二 级	Second Grade	287	49	17718	273349	116745
三 级及以下	Third Grade	361	98	16341	137225	74737
专业承包	Specialized Undertaking	310	98	10107	57195	36467
一 级	First Grade	23	5	203	12557	11201
二 级	Second Grade	89	33	4615	26013	10857
三级及以下	Third Grade	198	60	5289	18625	14409
劳务分包	Work Subcontractors	100	44	485	7113	10002

14-15 建筑企业工程施工情况
Condition of Building Works by Construction Enterprise

单位：万平方米 (10 000 sq.m)

年份 Year	地区 Region	房屋建筑施工面积 Floor Space of Buildings Under Construction	#本年新开工面积 New-opened Works for This Year	施工面积中实行投标承包面积 Space of Building and Contracting	#本年新开工面积 New-opened Works for This Year	房屋建筑竣工面积 Floor Space of Buildings Completed
	1995	1212.45	657.34	214.65	148.22	609.84
	1996	1207.45	673.17	397.83	272.22	645.89
	1997	1400.28	778.14	653.90	400.75	747.24
	1998	1662.36	1032.15	1023.88	678.42	879.67
	1999	1943.05	1068.05	1210.90	807.87	1042.51
	2000	2241.48	1448.34	1666.87	1110.04	1261.42
	2001	2659.69	1679.41	2056.30	1380.07	1467.54
	2002	2572.62	1489.38	2133.56	1274.07	1469.59
	2003	2719.22	1735.19	2411.27	1527.79	1450.80
	2004	2812.30	1791.50	2426.79	1613.19	1483.35
	2005	2767.64	1639.80	2512.79	1517.41	1429.36
	2006	2889.64	1854.91	2687.63	1751.99	1645.02
	2007	3552.36	2421.17	3299.73	2277.87	1849.64
	2008	4234.71	2862.31	3982.24	2784.92	2155.98
	2009	5151.60	3560.54	4812.84	3378.63	2517.79
	2010	6620.14	4449.78	6119.70	4235.58	2891.45
	2011	8947.71	5796.89	8318.62	5446.50	3465.49
	2012	11026.49	6247.32	9563.64	5678.19	4553.97
	2013	13096.18	7550.88	11318.17	6787.97	5775.28
乌鲁木齐市	Urumqi City	3643.96	1825.07	3342.73	1684.22	1076.59
克拉玛依市	Karamay City	212.50	107.41	157.80	85.35	96.06
吐鲁番地区	Turpan Administrative Offices	77.88	37.88	73.58	34.88	49.44
哈密地区	Hami [Kumul] Administrative Offices	416.38	330.40	355.02	286.16	172.49
昌吉回族自治州	Changji Hui Autonomous Prefecture	860.62	532.88	673.05	474.46	471.92
伊犁哈萨克自治州	Ili Kazak Autonomous Prefecture	1790.63	1155.50	1611.22	1057.13	970.57
伊犁州直属县(市)	Counties (Cities) Direct Under Ili Prefecture	1009.28	655.73	940.56	614.79	474.44
塔城地区	Tacheng [Tarbagatai] Administrative Offices	476.66	304.00	394.27	261.34	316.28
阿勒泰地区	Altay Administrative Offices	304.69	195.77	276.39	181.00	179.85
博尔塔拉蒙古自治州	Bortala Mongol Autonomous Prefecture	418.60	308.29	309.47	228.27	249.78
巴音郭楞蒙古自治州	Bayangol Mongol Autonomous Prefecture	1528.55	857.40	1118.36	741.53	711.60
阿克苏地区	Aksu Administrative Offices	970.51	578.06	896.79	487.74	426.47
克孜勒苏柯尔克孜自治州	Kizilsu Kirgiz Autonomous Prefecture	167.40	127.81	163.01	124.44	102.93
喀什地区	Kashgar [Kaxgar] Administrative Offices	983.04	496.86	705.94	434.31	464.91
和田地区	Hotan Administrative Offices	429.93	239.71	412.63	238.38	193.84
石河子市	Shihezi City	995.56	496.02	911.35	453.51	412.13
阿拉尔市	Aral City	222.05	148.58	218.49	148.58	133.68
图木舒克市	Tumxuk City	221.46	185.07	221.46	185.07	163.61
五家渠市	Wujiaqu City	157.11	123.94	147.27	123.94	79.26

注：该表口径为总承包和专业承包企业，以下同。
Note: The data of the table refer to all general construction contractors and professional contractors. (the same as in the following)

14-16 按登记注册类型分建筑企业工程施工情况
Condition of Building Works by Construction Enterprise by Registration Status

单位：万平方米 (2013 年) (10 000 sq.m)

项目	Item	房屋建筑施工面积 Floor Space of Buildings Under Construction	#本年新开工面积 New-opened Works for This Year	施工面积中实行投标承包面积 Space of Buildings and Contracting	#本年新开工面积 New-opened Works for This Year	房屋建筑竣工面积 Floor Space of Buildings Completed
总　计	**Total**	**13096.18**	**7550.88**	**11318.17**	**6787.97**	**5775.28**
#一、二级企业	First, Second Enterprises	10709.03	5885.13	9437.47	5376.91	4417.43
#国有及国有控股	State-owned and State-holding	5711.85	3071.74	5333.49	2901.04	2143.68
按登记注册类型分组	**Grouped by Registration Status**					
内资企业	Domestic Funede	13096.18	7550.88	11318.17	6787.97	5775.28
国有企业	State-owned Enterprises	717.91	402.58	695.78	389.09	312.37
集体企业	Collective-owned Enterprises	43.03	31.44	37.50	30.48	33.87
有限责任公司	Limited Liability Corporations	8862.98	4942.98	7609.94	4477.27	3858.01
国有独资公司	Sole State -funded Company	918.06	475.72	896.13	475.72	320.26
其他有限责任公司	Other Limited Liability Companies	7944.92	4467.26	6713.81	4001.55	3537.75
股份有限公司	Share-holding Corporations Ltd	359.69	204.01	317.12	197.76	127.63
私营企业	Private Enterprises	3112.57	1969.87	2657.83	1693.37	1443.40
#私营有限责任公司	Private Limited Liability Companies	3009.15	1909.41	2606.96	1658.95	1376.87
私营股份有限公司	Private Stock Limited Companies	102.87	59.91	50.87	34.42	65.98
按国民经济行业分组	**Grouped by National Economic Sectors**					
房屋和土木工程建筑业	Buildings and Givil Engineering	13036.89	7513.12	11261.48	6752.81	5757.00
房屋工程建筑	Building	12411.68	7159.36	10830.88	6493.11	5431.89
土木工程建筑	Civil Engineering	625.21	353.76	430.60	259.70	325.11
铁路、道路、隧道和桥梁	Railways, Roads, Tunnels and Bridges	206.67	116.26	111.34	71.68	124.66
水利和港口建筑	Water Conservancy and Seaport	385.21	213.52	298.27	176.38	179.72
工矿工程建筑	Mine Project	28.60	21.05	16.35	8.80	16.04
建筑安装业	Construction and Installation	57.89	36.36	55.29	33.76	16.88
其他建筑业	Others	1.40	1.40	1.40	1.40	1.40
按隶属关系分组	**Grouped by Subordination**					
中　央	Central Government	4116.81	2152.30	3943.91	2071.16	1538.64
地　方	Local	8979.37	5398.58	7374.26	4716.81	4236.64
按企业资质等级分组	**Grouped by Enterprise's Qualification**					
施工总承包	Undertaking Porjects	12485.89	7294.34	10725.80	6535.04	5656.94
特　级	Special Grade	392.64	168.56	392.64	168.56	116.32
一　级	First Grade	4310.84	2047.61	3779.30	1950.99	1519.48
二　级	Second Grade	5436.11	3434.40	4697.45	3024.16	2685.35
三级及以下	Third Grade	2346.30	1643.77	1856.41	1391.33	1335.79
专业承包	Specialized Undertaking	610.29	256.54	592.37	252.93	118.34
一　级	First Grade	10.77	1.28	10.77	1.28	9.50
二　级	Second Grade	558.67	233.28	557.31	231.92	86.78
三级及以下	Third Grade	40.85	21.98	24.29	19.73	22.06

14-17 按登记注册类型分建筑企业竣工房屋建筑面积
Floor Space of Buildings Constructed of Construction Enterprises by Registration Status

单位：平方米 (2013 年) (sq.m)

项目	Item	合计 Total	住宅用房 Residential Building	商业、居民服务业用房 Houses for Commercial and Residential Service	办公用房 Office Occupancy
总计	**Total**	**57751397**	**40676690**	**4171477**	**4039423**
#一、二级企业	First, Second Enterprises	44173169	31842961	2927466	3057092
#国有及国有控股	State-owned and State-holding	21436525	16281146	1326768	993806
按登记注册类型分组	**Grouped by Registration Status**	57751397	40676690	4171477	4039423
内资企业	Domestic Funede	57751397	40676690	4171477	4039423
#国有企业	State-owned Enterprises	3123770	2448361	240158	66638
集体企业	Collective-owned Enterprises	338629	292645	13995	18710
有限责任公司	Limited Liability Corporations	38578981	26671871	2932565	2874742
国有独资公司	Sole State -funded Company	3202355	2430641	121620	179906
其他有限责任公司	Other Limited Liability Companies	35376626	24241230	2810945	2694836
股份有限公司	Share-holding Corporations Ltd	1276224	1187735	22331	15469
私营企业	Private Enterprises	14433793	10076078	962428	1063864
私营有限责任公司	Private Limited Liability Companies	13768389	9533148	857183	1063864
私营股份有限公司	Private Stock Limited Companies	659887	537413	105245	
按国民经济行业分组	**Grouped by National Economic Sectors**				
房屋和土木工程建筑业	Buildings and Givil Engineering	57568616	40529302	4155627	4039353
房屋工程建筑	Building	54317637	37982119	4063824	3946938
土木工程建筑	Civil Engineering	3250979	2547183	91803	92415
铁路、道路、隧道和乔梁工程建筑	Railways, Roads, Tunnels and Bridges	1246546	1018028	24436	25448
水利和港口工程建筑	Water Conservancy and Seaport	1797253	1430596	44498	66967
工矿工程建筑	Mine Project	160350	86359	5000	
架线和管道工程建筑	Stringing and Pipeline Constrnction Project	46351	12200	17869	
其他土木工程建筑	Other Civil Engineerings	479			
建筑安装业	Construction and Installation	168759	147388	15850	70
其他建筑业	Others	14022			
按隶属关系分组	**Grouped by Subordination**				
中央	Central Government	15386253	11630401	918250	783897
地方	Local	42365144	29046289	3253227	3255526
按企业资质等级分组	**Grouped by Enterprise's Qualification**				
施工总承包	Undertaking Porjects	56567956	39906129	4161005	3873000
特级	Special Grade	1163184	809035	63371	9173
一级	First Grade	15194367	11038065	1238034	773463
二级	Second Grade	26852814	19234060	1616589	2151418
三级及以下	Third Grade	13357591	8824969	1243011	938946
专业承包	Specialized Undertaking	1183441	770561	10472	166423
一级	First Grade	94945	92555		
二级	Second Grade	867859	669246	9472	123038
三级及以下	Third Grade	220637	8760	1000	43385

14-17 续表 Continued

单位：平方米 (sq.m)

项　目	Item	科研、教育、医疗用房 House for Science Medical and Education	文化、体育、娱乐用房 House for Culture and Sports and Entertainment	厂房及建筑物用房 House for Plant and Buildings	仓库 Warehouses	其他 Others
总　计	**Total**	**3500005**	**490421**	**2647942**	**482034**	**1743405**
#一、二级企业	First, Second Enterprises	2705252	348567	1840480	350411	1100940
#国有及国有控股	State-owned and State-holding	740081	233977	1177850	357028	325869
按登记注册类型分组	**Grouped by Registration Status**	**3500005**	**490421**	**2647942**	**482034**	**1743405**
内资企业	Domestic Funede	3500005	490421	2647942	482034	1743405
#国有企业	State-owned Enterprises	81608	8531	128632	145742	4100
集体企业	Collective-owned Enterprises	10815	2464			
有限责任公司	Limited Liability Corporations	2640144	406897	1613557	295302	1143903
国有独资公司	Sole State -funded Company	195218	39111	99474	14437	121948
其他有限责任公司	Other Limited Liability Companies	2444926	367786	1514083	280865	1021955
股份有限公司	Share-holding Corporations Ltd	38104	4000	5456		3129
私营企业	Private Enterprises	729334	68529	900297	40990	592273
私营有限责任公司	Private Limited Liability Companies	712105	68529	900297	40990	592273
私营股份有限公司	Private Stock Limited Companies	17229				
按国民经济行业分组	**Grouped by National Economic Sectors**					
房屋和土木工程建筑业	Buildings and Givil Engineering	3499885	490421	2628589	482034	1743405
房屋工程建筑	Building	3362684	482498	2409308	481229	1589037
土木工程建筑	Civil Engineering	137201	7923	219281	805	154368
铁路、道路、隧道和桥梁工程建筑	Railways, Roads, Tunnels and Bridges	101402	4471	3500		69261
水利和港口工程建筑	Water Conservancy and Seaport	19517	3452	146311	805	85107
工矿工程建筑	Mine Project			68991		
架线和管道工程建筑	Stringing and Pipeline Constrnction Project	16282				
其他土木工程建筑	Other Civil Engineerings			479		
建筑安装业	Construction and Installation	120		5331		
其他建筑业	Others			14022		
按隶属关系分组	**Grouped by Subordination**					
中央	Central Government	445887	183156	809957	334432	280273
地方	Local	3054118	307265	1837985	147602	1463132
按企业资质等级分组	**Grouped by Enterprise's Qualification**					
施工总承包	Undertaking Porjects	3493716	489421	2423636	481034	1740015
特级	Special Grade	66004	1775	213826		
一级	First Grade	978471	225109	640937	109340	190948
二级	Second Grade	1655488	121683	924903	241071	907602
三级及以下	Third Grade	793753	140854	643970	130623	641465
专业承包	Specialized Undertaking	6289	1000	224306	1000	3390
一级	First Grade					2390
二级	Second Grade	5289		60814		
三级及以下	Third Grade	1000	1000	163492	1000	1000

主要统计指标解释

建筑业统计单位　指从事房屋、构筑物建造和设备安装活动的法人企业。建筑业法人企业应具有建筑业资质并能够独立核算，同时还应具备以下条件：①依法成立，有自己的名称、组织机构和场所，能够承担民事责任；②独立拥有和使用资产，承担负债，有权与其他单位签订合同；③独立核算盈亏，能够编制资产负债表。

建筑业总产值　是以货币形式表现的建筑业企业在一定时期内生产的建筑业产品和提供服务的总和。建筑业总产值包括：

(1)建筑工程产值：指列入建筑工程预算内的各种工程价值。

(2)安装工程产值：指设备安装工程价值，不包括被安装设备本身价值。

(3)其他产值：建筑业总产值中除建筑工程、安装工程以外的产值。包括房屋构筑物修理产值、非标准设备制造产值、总包企业向分包企业收取的管理费以及不能明确划分的施工活动所完成的产值。

a.房屋构筑物修理产值：指房屋和构筑物修理所完成的产值，但不包括被修理房屋、构筑物本身价值和生产设备的修理价值。

b.非标准设备制造产值：指加工制造没有定型的非标准生产设备的加工费和原材料价值(如化工厂、炼油厂用的各种罐、槽，矿井生产统一使用的各种漏斗、三角槽、阀门等)以及附属加工厂为本企业承建工程制作的非标准设备的价值。

建筑业增加值　指建筑业企业在报告期内以货币形式表现的建筑业生产经营活动的最终成果。

从 2004 年第一次全国经济普查开始，建筑业现价增加值按生产法和分配法(收入法)两种方法计算，以收入法的计算结果为准，即从收入的角度出发，根据生产要素在生产过程中应得的收入份额计算。具体计算方法：经济普查年度建筑业增加值按照《经济普查年度 GDP 核算方案》计算，非经济普查年度建筑业增加值按照《非经济普查年度 GDP 核算方案》计算

房屋施工面积　指在报告期内施工的全部房屋建筑面积，包括本期新开工的房屋建筑面积、上期跨入本期继续施工的房屋建筑面积、上期停缓建在本期恢复施工的房屋建筑面积、本期竣工的房屋建筑面积及本期施工后又停缓建的房屋建筑面积。

房屋竣工面积　指在报告期内房屋建筑按照设计要求已全部完工，达到住人和使用条件，经验收鉴定合格或达到竣工验收标准，可正式移交使用单位的各栋房屋建筑面积的总和。

自有机械设备年末总台数　指归本企业所有，属于本企业固定资产的生产性机械设备年末总台数。包括施工机械、生产设备、运输设备以及其他设备。

自有机械设备年末总功率　指本企业自有施工机械、生产设备、运输设备以及其他设备等列为在册固定资产的生产性机械设备年末总功率，按设定能力或查定能力计算。包括机械本身的动力和为该机械服务的单独动力设备，如电动机等。计算单位用千瓦，动力换算可按 1 马力＝0.735 千瓦折合成千瓦数。电焊机、变压器、锅炉不计算动力。

工程结算收入　指企业承包工程实现的工程价款结算收入，以及向发包单位收取的除工程价款以外的按规定列作营业收入的各种款项，如临时设施费、劳动保险费、施工机械调迁费等以及向发包单位收取的各种索赔款。

企业总收入　指与企业生产经营直接有关的各项收入，包括工程结算收入和其他业务收入。计算公式为：

企业总收入＝工程结算收入＋其他业务收入

Explanatory Notes on Main Statistical Indicators

Statistical Unit in the Construction Industry refers to a corporate enterprise engaged in the construction of buildings and structures and in the installation of equipment. A corporate construction enterprise should have qualification certificates with independent accounting system, and should meet the following 3 requirements: a) being set up in line with relevant legal basis, having its full name, organization and location, and capable of taking civil liabilities; b) independently possessing and using its assets and assuming its liabilities, and entitled to sign contracts with other institutions; and c) making independent accounts of its profits and losses, and capable of compiling its own balance sheet.

Gross Output Value of Construction refers to total of construction products and services, expressed in money terms, produced or rendered by construction and installation enterprises during a given period of time. It includes:

(1) Output value of construction projects: the value of projects covered by the project budgets;

(2) Output value of installation projects: the value of the installation of equipment, (excluding the value of the equipment to be installed);

(3) Other output values: the output value of construction industry apart from that of construction projects and installation projects. It includes: output value of repair of buildings and structures; output value of non-standard equipment manufacture-ing; overhead expenses received by contracted enterprises from the sub-contracted enterprises and the completed output value of construction activities for which there is no clear definition.

a. Output value of repair of buildings and structures: the value created through the repairs of buildings or structures. It does not include the value of buildings or structures being repaired and the value of the repair of production equipment;

b. Output value of manufactured non-standard equipment: the value of non-standard production equipment, including raw materials and manufacturing cost, made for the construction project (i.e., chemical plant; kettles or tanks used by refineries; various fillers, triangle tanks, valves used by mines). It also includes the output value of equipment manufactured by subsidiary workshops.

Value-added of Construction refers to the final result of the activities of production and operation of enterprises of the construction industry in monetary terms during the reference period.

Starting from the 2004 economic census, value-added of construction is calculated by both production approach and income approach, with the figures from the income approach as the final figures.Under the income approach,, calculation starts from the perspective of income and is based on the share of income derived from the production process by the relevant factors of production. Specifically, value-added of construction for the Census years is calculated in accordance with the Programme of Compilation of GDP and National Accounts for the Year of Economic Census, and value-added of construction for other years is calculated in accordance with the Programme of Compilation of GDP and National Accounts for the Non Economic Census Years.

Floor Space of Buildings refers to floor space of buildings under construction in the reference period, including the space of buildings for which construction has newly started; buildings for which construction has started earlier and is continuing during the reference period; and buildings for which construction has been suspended earlier but has restarted during the reference period; buildings completed during the reference period; and buildings under construction but construction has subsequently been during the reference period.

Floor Space of Buildings Completed refers to the total floor space of each building that has been completed in the reference period in accordance with the requirements of the design, up to the standard for being resided in and put into use, or has been checked and accepted by departments concerned as qualified ones or up to the standard of buildings completed and can be handed over for putting into use.

Total Number of Machinery and Equipment Owned by the End of Year refers to the number of machines and equipment owned by the enterprises, and listed as the fixed assets of the enterprises by the end of the year, including machinery and equipment for construction, production and transportation.

Total Power of Machinery and Equipment Owned by the End of Year refers to the total power of machinery and equipment owned by the enterprises,and listed as the fixed assets of the enterprises by the end of the year, including machinery and equipment for construction,production and transportation.The power of the machinery is calculated on basis of the designed or verified capacity,covering the power of the machinery/equipment and the separate power equipment serving the machinery/equipment (such as electric motors), but excluding welders, transformers and boilers.The unit used for the calculation of power is kilowatt, with horsepower converted to kilowatt by 1 horsepower=0.735 kilowatt.

Income from Settlement of Projects refers to the income received by the construction enterprise from the contracted project through settlement procedures, and other charges to the contractoree as operational costs in addition to the value of the project, such as temporary facility fee,labour insurance premium, moving cost of construction equipment,as well as various types of claims to the contractee.

Total Revenue of Enterprises refers to the sum of income from production and operation of enterprises, including income from settlement of projects and other operational income, namely:

Total Revenue of Enterprises=Income from Settlement of Projects+Other Operational Inc

15

运输和邮电

TRANSPORT, POSTAL AND TELECOMMUNICATION SERVICES

简要说明

本篇主要内容和资料来源

本篇资料反映新疆维吾尔自治区交通运输业和邮政、电信业发展的基本状况。

运输业资料主要包括：铁路、公路、民航、管道四种运输方式的线路条数、里程、总运量及周转量、货物运输平均运距、铁路运输主要技术经济指标；民用机动车辆情况。

邮政、电信业资料主要包括：邮政、电信业务完成情况，邮政、电信业务发展水平等资料。

铁路资料来自乌鲁木齐铁路局；公路资料来自新疆维吾尔自治区公路局；民航运输数据资料来自中国南方航空股份有限公司新疆分公司；电信资料来自新疆维吾尔自治区通信管理局；邮政数据来自新疆维吾尔自治区邮政公司。

本篇资料由新疆维吾尔自治区统计局工业交通统计处收集整理。

Brief Introduction

Main Content and Source of Data

Data in this chapter cover mainly the basic condition of the development of transportation, post and telecommunications in Xinjiang Uygur Autonomous Region.

Data on transport cover mainly the length of the routes of four means of railway, highways, civil aviation and pipeline. total fright traffic, total freight ton-kilometers, average transport distance of fright, principal economic and technical indicators of railway transport, possession of civil vehicles.

Data on post and telecommunication cover mainly the complete business volume of post and telecommunication services, and the development of the post and telecommunication service, ect.

Data on railways transportation come from the Urumqi Bureau of the Railway. Data on the highways come from the Bureau of Transportation. Data on the civil aviation transport come from the China Southwest Airlines, Xinjiang Branch. Data on telecommunication services come from telecommunication Bureau. Data on post are provided by the Post Bureau.

Data in this chapter are collected and compiled by the Division of Industry and Transport Statistics, Xinjiang Bureau of Statistics.

15-1 主要年份运输业基本情况
Basic Conditions of Transport in Main Years

指　标	Item	2000	2010	2013
运输线路长度(公里)	**Length of Transport Routes (km)**			
铁路营业里程	Railways in Operation	3010	4393	4911
公路里程	Highways	80875	152843	170154
民用航线里程	Total Civil Aviation Routes	152941	176992	226089
管道输油(气)里程	Petroleum and Gas Pipelines	2696	11464	11666
客运量(万人)	**Total Passenger Traffic (10 000 persons)**	**23191**	**46346**	**59024**
铁　路	Railways	1147	1523	2318
公　路	Highways	21877	44333	56000
民用航空	Civil Aviation	167	490	706
旅客周转量(亿人公里)	**Total Passenger-Kilometers (100 million passenger-km)**	**292.80**	**670.75**	**895.50**
铁　路	Railways	97.40	170.10	250.83
公　路	Highways	158.20	404.00	499.40
民用航空	Civil Aviation	37.20	96.65	145.27
货运量(万吨)	**Total Freight Traffic (10 000 tons)**	**33090.50**	**64596.70**	**83716.66**
铁　路	Railways	4199	6853	7399
公　路	Highways	27048	50448	68528
民用航空	Civil Aviation	3.50	3.70	6.66
输油(气)管道	Petroleum and Gas Pipelines	1840	7292	7783
货物周转量(亿吨公里)	**Total Freight Ton-kilometers (100 million ton-km)**	**660.88**	**2053.82**	**2490.29**
铁　路	Railways	355.00	814.03	996.71
公　路	Highways	272.90	767.14	1055.20
民用航空	Civil Aviation	0.98	0.98	1.60
输油(气)管道	Petroleum and Gas Pipelines	32.00	471.67	436.78
民用汽车拥有量(万辆)	**Possession of Civil Motor Vehicles (10 000 units)**	**37.0**	**135.9**	**243.3**
#载客汽车辆数	Buses and Cars	18.0	87.6	177.5
载货汽车辆数	Trucks	17.5	37.0	55.6
#私人汽车拥有量	Privat Vehicles	13.9	85.8	175.4

注：1.2000 年以后公路里程包括兵团数据。2.2006 年起新疆公路通车里程包含村道里程(以下同)。
Note: a) Since 2000 thc highway mileage cover the data of XJPCC. b) Length of highways include lenth of backroad since 2006.(the same as in the following table)

15-2 主要年份运输线路长度
Length of Transport Routes in Main Years

单位:公里 (km)

年 份 Year	铁路营业里程 Length of Railways in Operation	#新疆境内 Inside Xinjiang	公 路 Length of Highways	#有铺装和简易铺装路(高级次高级路面) Simple Pavement and Pavement Roads	民用航空 Length of the Civil Aviation	#新疆境内 Inside Xinjiang	管道输油(气)里程 Petrolurn and Gas Pipelines
1978	1031	796	23818	5810	4783	4783	443
1980	1103	868	21148	6390	4412	4412	443
1985	1579	1344	22232	8369	4527	4527	473
1990	1578	1343	25425	12566	36465	5159	740
1995	2038	1803	30298	19013	69789	6693	875
1996	2038	1803	31609	20461	122089	9183	928
1997	2038	1803	32053	21495	123664	9717	1373
1998	2038	1803	32762	22485	150473	9717	1955
1999	3008	2780	33484	23214	141872	9719	2496
2000	3010	2775	80875	31059	152941	9719	2696
2001	3010	2774	80947	31635	161814	9719	2965
2002	3010	2775	82929	32541	132483	9898	3153
2003	3009	2775	83633	33891	141456	9898	3008
2004	2999	2763	86824	40679	111768	8664	3003
2005	2925	2761	89531	43803	119481	8664	3003
2006	2925	2761	143736	50119	138564	9064	4631
2007	2925	2761	145219	55080	160354	11363	6793
2008	2925	2925	146652	60233	147753	10560	9455
2009	3837	3673	150683	67684	152392	10754	11235
2010	4393	4228	152843	72887	176992	9939	11464
2011	4480	4316	155150	80974	175797	9939	11077
2012	4914	4315	165909	92456	179054	11727	12843
2013	4911	4741	170154	99887	226089	11721	11666

15-3 主要年份运输线路质量
Quality of Transport Routes in Main Years

单位：公里 (km)

指 标	Item	1995	2000	2010	2013
铁路营业里程	Length of National Railways in Operation	2038	3010	4393	4741
#复线里程	Double-Tracking Length		986	1324	1834
#自动闭塞里程	Automatic Blocking Length	273	685	1408	1931
公路线路里程	Length of Highways	30298	80875	152843	170154
#水泥沥青路面	Lenth of bituminous Pavement	27982	33035	72887	99887

注：铁路上述里程是新疆境内里程。
Note: Length of railways refers to length of railway inside in Xinjiang.

15-4 主要年份客运量及周转量
Passenger Traffic and Passenger kilometers in Main Years

年 份 Year	客运量(万人) Passenger Traffic (10 000 persons)				旅客周转量(亿人公里) Passenger-Kilometers (100 million passenger-km)			
	总 计 Total	铁 路 Railways	公 路 Highways	民用航空 Civil Aviation	总 计 Total	铁 路 Railways	公 路 Highways	民用航空 Civil Aviation
1978	941	148	786	7	25.23	13.72	10.96	0.55
1980	1356	193	1152	10	30.49	18.83	10.83	0.83
1985	3728	320	3399	9	63.16	33.16	29.13	0.87
1986	4058	362	3674	22	73.87	36.40	34.00	3.74
1987	4439	377	4327	34	83.67	37.14	39.44	7.09
1988	5205	459	4698	48	99.17	42.86	46.35	9.96
1989	8740	453	8240	47	120.69	44.52	66.37	9.80
1990	9602	388	9161	53	103.80	37.96	55.11	10.73
1991	14582	383	14142	56	122.08	41.94	68.05	12.09
1992	14997	425	14490	82	138.24	44.48	75.38	18.38
1993	16352	513	15749	90	174.23	50.04	103.51	20.73
1994	17181	670	16405	106	195.58	58.08	112.50	25.00
1995	17533	672	16739	122	204.89	58.00	117.17	29.68
1996	18858	610	18110	138	218.79	57.80	128.58	32.20
1997	20237	748	19360	129	233.39	64.70	139.00	29.69
1998	21747	878	20735	134	256.90	76.90	149.60	30.40
1999	22763	1000	21618	145	270.74	81.90	157.05	31.79
2000	23191	1147	21877	167	292.80	97.40	158.20	37.20
2001	24344	932	23255	157	309.70	104.10	170.30	35.30
2002	26016	950	24883	183	330.80	106.00	185.60	39.20
2003	26972	879	25878	215	342.00	106.10	195.00	40.90
2004	29782	1023	28473	286	423.80	121.90	249.00	52.90
2005	33220	1134	31747	339	457.42	125.20	271.20	61.02
2006	34471	1272	32835	364	498.30	138.90	292.10	67.30
2007	38434	1873	36159	402	548.10	144.46	326.70	76.94
2008	42111	1311	40392	408	594.60	149.89	363.60	81.11
2009	43410	1371	41604	435	614.66	152.90	376.30	85.46
2010	46346	1523	44333	490	670.75	170.10	404.00	96.65
2011	50461	2002	47927	532	758.26	216.16	437.90	104.16
2012	55298	2162	52473	663	849.25	236.72	478.50	134.03
2013	59024	2318	56000	706	895.50	250.83	499.40	145.27

注：2013 年民航旅客吞吐量为 1987.86 万人。
Note: Air passenger handling capacity is 198786 million persons in 2013.。

15-5 主要年份货运量及货物周转量
Freight Traffic and Ton-kilometers in Main Years

年 份 Year	货运量(万吨) Freight Traffic (10 000 tons)				
	总 计 Total	铁 路 Railways	公 路 Highways	民用航空 Civil Aviation	输油(气)管道 Petroleum and Gas Pipelines
1978	6064.12	923	4843	0.12	298
1980	8422.16	884	7209	0.16	329
1990	13919.87	1691	11551	0.87	677
1995	25406.00	2733	21754	2.00	917
2000	33090.50	4199	27048	3.50	1840
2001	33589.00	3904	27751	2.00	1932
2002	34966.70	4121	28861	2.70	1982
2003	37485.20	4602	30881	2.20	2000
2004	38885.50	5083	31700	2.50	2100
2005	40600.20	5397	33000	3.20	2200
2006	43096.40	6001	34835	3.40	2256
2007	49009.62	7430	38427	3.62	3149
2008	57187.80	6120	44987	3.80	6077
2009	60162.80	6413	46787	3.80	6959
2010	64596.70	6853	50448	3.70	7292
2011	70361.90	6904	55965	3.90	7489
2012	78248.80	6933	61850	5.80	9460
2013	83716.66	7399	68528	6.66	7783

年 份 Year	货物周转量(亿吨公里) Freight Ton-kilometers (100 million ton-km)				
	总 计 Total	铁 路 Railways	公 路 Highways	民用航空(万吨公里) Civil Aviation (10 000 ton-km)	输油(气)管道 Petroleum and Gas Pipelines
1978	106.96	67.76	32.06	98.10	7.13
1980	121.14	67.27	45.89	137.80	7.97
1990	262.29	141.16	108.09	2048.00	12.84
1995	474.39	240.88	219.72	5744.00	13.22
2000	660.88	355.00	272.90	9776.00	32.00
2001	714.43	403.90	275.90	6300.00	34.00
2002	759.62	425.30	298.00	8238.00	35.50
2003	837.04	475.00	325.00	6400.00	36.40
2004	947.24	548.50	361.00	7400.00	37.00
2005	1032.75	586.90	405.00	8500.00	40.00
2006	1143.31	647.10	425.68	8921.00	69.64
2007	1264.31	678.53	468.80	9085.78	116.07
2008	1656.88	758.74	672.30	9285.43	224.91
2009	1815.81	751.09	705.90	9700.00	357.85
2010	2053.82	814.03	767.14	9837.00	471.67
2011	2199.52	857.01	852.17	9700.00	488.38
2012	2558.68	910.58	946.90	14400.00	699.76
2013	2490.29	996.71	1055.20	15999.00	436.78

15-6 主要年份货物运输平均运距
Average Transport Distance of Freight in Main Years

单位：公里 (km)

年份 Year	合计 Total	铁路 Railways	公路 Highways	民用航空 Civil Aviation	输油(气)管道 Petroleum and Gas Pipelines
1978	168	565	66	818	239
1980	139	566	64	861	242
1985	158	624	69	945	206
1990	188	835	94	2354	190
1995	187	881	101	2872	144
2000	200	845	101	2857	174
2001	211	1023	99	3150	176
2002	217	1032	103	3051	179
2003	224	865	105	2909	182
2004	244	904	114	2960	176
2005	254	901	122	2656	182
2006	265	894	122	2598	308
2007	257	913	122	2528	368
2008	289	926	149	2456	370
2009	301	873	151	2552	518
2010	317	934	152	2637	514
2011	312	935	152	2480	652
2012	327	945	153	2486	646
2013	297	958	154	2616	561

15-7 主要年份铁路运输主要财务指标
Main Financial Indicators of Railway Transport in Main Years

单位：万元 (10 000 yuan)

指标	Item	1990	1995	2000	2010	2013
运输总收入	**Total Transport Revenue**	**86686**	**192555**	**509480**	**1926749**	**2638086**
旅客票价收入	Passenger Fares	18763	33560	82121	234979	378308
货物运费收入	Freight Revenue	62516	142168	318485	1197619	1546037
运输清算收入	**Transportation Claring Revenue**	**59765**		**467142**	**1311275**	**2001165**
运输总支出	**Toatl Transport Expenditure**	**51875**	**193693**	**418497**	**1552877**	**2166464**
#工资	Wages and Salaries	11163	38429	98293	238570	421627
材料	Materials	6702	23183	36210	79181	108957
燃料	Fuel	9308	32996	74487	340960	301408
电力	Electricity	666	2433	4701	8022	83823
折旧	Depreciation	17174	13137	60859	127368	219245
营业外收支净额	**Non-operating Net Revenue or Expenditure**	**6886**	**14503**	**23236**	**-21947**	**9790**
实现利润	**Profits**	**6291**	**-12591**	**34130**	**-273121**	**-216596**
#运输利润	Transport Profits	5501	-11649	33195	-266910	-193445

注：运输总收入、旅客票价收入、货物运费收入是运送到全国范围的客、货运输收入。
Note: Revenue from transport,passenger traffic and freight traffic refer to revenue from transport to allover China.

15-8 铁路运输技术经济主要指标
Main Technical and Economic Indicators of Railway Transport

指　标	Item	2012	2013
货运机车日产量(万吨公里)	Average Daily Ton-kilometers of Freight Locomotives (10 000 ton-km)	113.9	126.5
#内燃机车	Diesel Locomotives	110.9	88.1
货运列车平均总重(吨)	Average Total Tonnage of Freight Locomotives (ton)	2846.0	2915.0
#内燃机车	Diesel Locomotives	2857.0	2534.0
货运机车日车公里(公里)	Daily Distance per Freight Locomotive (km)	550.0	554.0
客运机车日车公里(公里)	Daily Distance per Passenger Locomotive (km)	871.0	881.0
内燃机车每万吨公里耗油(公斤)	Oil Consumption of Diesel Locomotives (kg/10 000 ton-km)	28.9	33.8
货物列车出发正点率(%)	Punctuality Rate of Freight Trains at Departure (%)	98.5	98.5
货物列车运行正点率(%)	Punctuality Rate of Freight Trains in Running (%)	98.4	98.4
旅客列车出发正点率(%)	Punctuality Rate of Passenger Trains at Departure (%)	98.6	99.5
旅客列车运行正点率(%)	Punctuality Rate of Passenger Trains in Running (%)	96.8	98.2
旅客列车技术速度(公里/小时)	Technical Speed of Passenger Trains (km/hr)	70.5	73.7
旅客列车旅行速度(公里/小时)	Travelling Speed of Passenger Trains (km/hr)	62.7	64.9
客运密度(万人公里/公里)	Density of Passenger Transport (10 000 passenger-km/km)	593.7	610.5
货物列车技术速度(公里/小时)	Technical Speed of Freight Trains (km/hr)	47.2	51.3
货物列车旅行速度(公里/小时)	Running Speed of Freight Trains (km/hr)	36.3	40.4
货运密度(万吨公里/公里)	Density of Freight Transport (10 000 ton-km/km)	1998.6	2155.1
货车周转时间(天)	Turning Around Time of Freight Cars (day)	4.5	4.3
一次货物作业时间(小时)	Handling Time of Freight (hour)	17.7	17.0
货车中转停留时间(小时)	Transfer Waiting Time per Car (hour)	3.2	3.0
货车静载重(准轨)(吨)	Static Load of Freight Cars (Standard Gauge) (ton)	56.9	57.9

15-9 民用车辆拥有量
Number of Civil Vehicles

单位：辆 (unit)

指　标	Item	2012		2013	
		总　计 Total	#私　人 Private	总　计 Total	#私　人 Private
民用汽车	**Civil Vehicles**	**2110700**	**1474576**	**2433393**	**1753738**
载客汽车	Passenger Vehicles	1490810	1205254	1775178	1457477
#大　型	Large	31864	1553	30898	1296
中　型	Medium	34172	11703	31869	10489
小　型	Small	1391403	1162239	1678832	1415455
微　型	Minicar	33371	29759	33579	30237
载货汽车	Trucks	511776	211872	556103	245117
#重　型	Large	153855	14659	157730	14765
中　型	Medium	53133	13053	47910	12280
轻　型	Light	301913	181994	347866	216060
微　型	Mini	2875	2166	2597	2012
其它汽车	Others	108114	57450	102112	51144

15-10 主要年份邮电事业情况
Basic Conditions of Postal and Telecommunication Services in Main Years

指　标	Item	2000	2010	2013
邮政局营业网点(处)	**Number of Post Offices (unit)**		**1276**	**1253**
邮路长度(单程)(公里)	**Length of Postal Routes (km)**	**134109**	**75571**	**69718**
#农 村	Rural	55852	18238	56967
邮政业务总量(万元)	Business Volume of Postal Services	59370	165794	187804
电信业务总量(万元)	Business Volume of Telecommunication Services	413630	5654665	2681682
函件(万件)	Number of Letters (10 000 pieces)	7148	2926	2041
包件(万件)	Number of Parcels (10 000 pieces)	163	174	254
快递(万件)	Pieces of Express Mail Services (10 000 pieces)	124	487	5092
报刊期发数(万份)	Number of Newspapers and Magazines Circulation (10 000 copies)	535	307	353
长途电话(万分钟)	Number of Long-distance Calls (10 000 minutes)	34712	105001	1246123
固定电话年末用户(万户)	Local Telephone Subscribers at Year-end (10 000 subscribers)	191.0	547.5	544.8
#城市电话年末数	Urban Telephone Subscribers at Year-end	136.3	395.8	393.6
乡村电话年末数	Number of Rural Telephones Subscribers at Year-end	54.7	132.1	125.1
#住宅电话年末数	Residential Telephone Subscribers	149.3	346.6	331.6
移动电话年末用户(万户)	Number of Mobile Telephones Subscribers at Year-end (10 000 subscribers)	78.0	1359.8	2133.9
长途电信线路	**Telecommunication Lines**			
光缆线路长度(公里)	Length of Long Distance Optical Cable Lines (km)	10828	259307	38619
邮电通信设备	**Telecommunication Facilities**			
固定长途交换机容量(路端)	Capacity of long-distance Telephone Excharges (circuit)	102540	315982	284632
本地电话局用交换机容量(万门)	Capacity of Local Office Telephone Excharge (10 000 line)	241.7	928.2	832.3
邮电通信水平	**Level of Postal and Telecommunication Services**			
平均每百人每年发函件数(件)	Annual Arerage Number of Letters Mailed Per 100 persons (piece)	387.0	122.0	94.0
平均每百人每年订报刊数(份)	Annual Arerage Number of Newspaper Subscribed Per 100 Persons (piece)	28.9	12.6	16.2
平均每百人拥有电话机数(固定)(部)	Number of Telephone Sets Owned per 100 Persons(stable) (set)	15.0	25.4	24.4
平均每百人拥有电话机数(移动)(部)	Number of Telephone Sets Owned per 100 Persons (mobile) (set)		63.0	98.6
农村邮电通信水平	**Rural Level**			
通电话的乡(镇)比重(%)	Percentage of Townships with Telephone Communication (%)	100	100	100

注：1.2013 年快递按全口径计算，包含邮政企业和快递企业的快递业务量。2.2013 年邮政业务总量全口径计算，包含邮政企业和快递企业的业务量。
Note:a)Figures of pieces of express mail services are caculated at full standard,include volume of enterprices in postal services and pieces of express mail services.b)Figures of business volume of postal services are caculated at full standard, include volume of enterprices in postal services and pieces of express mail services.

15-11 主要年份邮电业务情况
Conditions of Postal and Telecommunication Services in Main Years

年 份 Year	邮政业务总量(万元) Business Volume of Postal Services (10000 yuan)	电信业务总量(万元) Business Volume of Telecommunication Services (10000 yuan)	函件(万件) Number of Letters (10 000 pieces)
1978			4842.7
1980			5890.8
1985			7032.6
1990	8203	8312	7380.5
1995	17322	71220	9041.8
2000	59370	413630	7148.0
2001	62265	572073	5601.0
2002	68032	878968	6814.0
2003	72007	1072831	5987.0
2004	74835	1457000	4756.7
2005	80500	1643259	4450.0
2006	94188	2195000	4129.8
2007	100498	2936000	3177.0
2008	113802	3673709	2900.0
2009	133535	4663000	2800.0
2010	165794	5654665	2926.0
2011	138398	2126602	3202.4
2012	181720	2466653	2529.0
2013	187804	2681682	2041.0

年 份 Year	快递(万件) Pieces of Express Mail Services (10 000 pieces)	报刊期发数(万份) Issue of Newspapers and Magazines (10 000 copies)	集邮业务(万枚) Stamps for Collection (10 000 pieces)	长途电话(万分钟) Length of Long-distance Calls (10 000 minutes)
1978		223.8		258.8
1980		329.6		276.5
1985		578.9		425.1
1990	…	805.7	1034.5	762.5
1995	93.6	478.1	3086.6	11705.9
2000	124.0	534.5	5766.0	34712.0
2001	147.0	358.0	5491.0	89844.0
2002	163.0	399.0	4620.0	45769.0
2003	199.0	587.3	3112.8	35554.2
2004	238.1	283.0	3141.3	62526.0
2005	266.0	293.0	2072.0	52482.0
2006	291.0	341.7	2205.1	46478.0
2007	324.0	305.0	2134.0	67660.0
2008	362.0	296.0	2335.0	42550.0
2009	412.0	296.0	2520.0	48816.0
2010	487.0	307.0	2672.0	105001.0
2011	579.0	296.4	2306.8	91298.0
2012	583.0	310.0	2253.5	14024.8
2013	5092.0	353.0	2795.4	1246123.0

注：从 1997 年起，市内电话户数统计口径有了较大调整，故农村电话户数增幅较大。

Note: Since 1997, greater adjustment has been made on the Statistic Method about the number of telephone subscribers and the number of rural subscribers has gone up by a bigger margin.

15-11 续表 Continued

年　份 Year	移动电话用户(万户) Number of Mobile Telephone Subscribers (10 000 subscribers)	国际互联网络用户(万户) Number of Subscribers of Internet Services (10 000 subscribers)	固定电话年末用户(万户) Number of Subscribers of Local Telephone at Year-end (10 000 subscribers)	#城市电话用户 Number of Urban Telephone Subscribers
1978			2.9	1.9
1980			3.2	2.1
1985			4.7	3.7
1990			8.9	7.9
1995	2.7		44.6	42.0
2000	78.0		191.0	136.3
2001	180.9	12.8	262.6	196.1
2002	297.0	17.3	337.5	238.3
2003	421.2	60.8	431.0	293.9
2004	489.7	78.0	516.7	387.0
2005	531.3	105.8	612.2	457.5
2006	671.1	123.7	706.9	533.6
2007	808.3	157.8	678.1	520.6
2008	1051.3	142.8	634.9	462.2
2009	1119.6	133.7	573.1	409.6
2010	1359.8	161.1	547.5	395.8
2011	1670.9	208.8	540.5	390.8
2012	2008.5	255.0	540.1	391.0
2013	2133.9	293.0	544.8	393.6

年　份 Year	#住宅电话 Household Fixed Telephone Subscribers	#乡村电话用户 Rural Fixed Telephone Subscribers	#住宅电话 Household Fixed Telephone Subscribers	公用电话(户) Public Telephone (subscriber)
1978		1.1		
1980		1.0		
1985		1.0		
1990	1.2	1.1		257
1995	26.0	2.6	1.2	5612
2000	101.1	54.7	48.2	70753
2001	124.3	66.5	57.8	84309
2002	179.9	79.5	73.4	166000
2003	180.0	93.5	88.6	281632
2004	194.0	108.2	103.4	432000
2005	318.9	135.2	115.4	570047
2006	369.9	154.5	131.7	668335
2007	359.6	157.5	136.1	675309
2008	310.6	150.0	126.3	597000
2009	234.6	140.8	117.2	570982
2010	237.4	132.1	109.2	529322
2011	236.8	127.5	104.9	476633
2012	234.6	126.9	102.4	436471
2013	233.3	125.1	98.3	435087

主要统计指标解释

铁路营业里程 又称营业长度，指投入客货运输营业或临时营业的线路长度。

铁路自动、半自动闭塞里程 为保证列车安全运行，在一个区间、同一时间内，一般只允许一列列车运行，这种保证列车在这个区间安全间隔运行的技术方法称为"闭塞"。自动闭塞是根据列车运行及有关闭塞分区状态，自动变换通过信号机显示而司机凭信号显示行车的闭塞方法，采用此方式的闭塞公里为自动闭塞里程。半自动闭塞是由人工办理闭塞手续，列车凭信号显示发车后，出站信号机自动关机闭塞，靠车站值班员确认列车整列到达，办理区间闭塞复原的一种闭塞方式，采用此方式的闭塞公里为半自动闭塞里程。

公路里程 指报告期末公路的实际长度。统计范围：包括城间、城乡间、乡（村）间能行驶汽车的公共道路，公路通过城镇街道的里程，公路桥梁长度、隧道长度、渡口宽度。不包括城市街道里程，断头路里程，农（林）业生产用道路里程，工（矿）企业等内部道路里程。统计原则：按已竣工验收或交付使用的实际里程计算；两条或多条公路共同经由同一路段的重复里程，只计算一次。

定期航班航线里程 指定期航班营运里程的总长度，以万公里为计算单位。航线里程的统计分为按重复距离计算和按不重复距离计算两种形式。"按重复距离计算"是指不同航线的相同航段距离可以重复累加；"按不重复距离计算"则不同航线相同航段只统计一次。

管道输油(气)里程 指油、气、成品油等各类介质实际输送距离，是反映运输管线长度的指标，也是计算周转量的依据。对于有复线和备用线的地段，原则上按单线计算管输里程。双线同时输送又不能分开计量的情况下，管输里程为双线长度之和除以2。

货(客)运量 指在一定时期内，各种运输工具实际运送的货物重量(旅客数量)。该指标是反映运输业为国民经济和人民生活服务的数量指标，也是制定和检查运输生产计划、研究运输发展规模和速度的重要指标。货运按吨计算，客运按人计算。货物不论运输距离长短、货物类别，均按实际重量统计。旅客不论行程远近或票价多少，均按一人一次客运量统计；半价票、小孩票也按一人统计。

货物(旅客)周转量 指在一定时期内，由各种运输工具运送的货物(旅客)数量与其相应运输距离的乘积之总和。该指标可以反映运输业生产的总成果，也是编制和检查运输生产计划，计算运输效率、劳动生产率以及核算运输单位成本的主要基础资料。计算货物周转量通常按发出站与到达站之间的最短距离，也就是计费距离计算。计算公式为：

货物(旅客)周转量=∑（货物（旅客）运输量×运输距离）

铁路货车平均静载重 指货物在装车时的静止装载重量。计算公式为：

货车平均静载重=货物发送吨数/装车数

铁路货运机车日产量 指在一定时期内，平均每台货运机车在一昼夜内所完成的总重吨公里数，包括载运货物的重量和车辆本身的自重。该指标从时间和牵引能力两方面反映了机车运用效率。计算公式为：

货运机车平均日产量=货运总重吨公里数/货运机车台日数

民用汽车拥有量 指报告期末，在公安交通管理部门按照《机动车注册登记工作规范》，已注册登记领有民用车辆牌照的全部汽车数量。汽车拥有量统计的主要分类：根据汽车结构分为载客汽车、载货汽车及其他汽车；根据汽车所有者不同分为个人(私人)汽车、单位汽车；根据汽车的使用性质分为营运汽车、非营运汽车；根据汽车大小规格不同，载客汽车分为大型、中型、小型和微型，载货汽车分为重型、中型、轻型和微型。

邮电业务总量 邮电业务总量 指以货币形式表现的邮电企业为社会提供各类邮电通信服务的总数量。该指标是用于观察邮电业务发展变化总趋势的综合性总量指标，分别按邮政业务总量和电信业务总量统计。邮电业务总量是以各类业务的实物量分别乘以相应的不变单价，求出各类业务的货币量加总求得。不变单价是一定时期内计算业务总量的同度量因素，是根据基年各类邮电业务量与相对应的邮电业务收入测算的平均单价。

移动电话用户 指在电信运营企业营业网点办理开户登记手续，通过移动电话交换机进入移动电话网，占用移动电话号码的各类电话用户。包括各类签约用户、智能网预付费用户、无线上网卡用户。

互联网上网人数 指过去半年内使用过互联网的6周岁及以上中国居民人数。

固定电话用户 指在电信企业营业网点办理开户登记手续并已接入固定电话网上的全部电话用户。包括普通电话用户、无线市话用户、公用电话用户、窄带综合业务数字网（N—ISDN）用户、智能网专用接入终端用户等。

城市电话用户 指按行政区划属于中央直辖市、省辖市、地级市、县级市的市区、市郊区及县城区范围内的电话用户数。包括分布在农村地区但以县团级以上建制的独立工矿区、林区、驻军的电话用户。

农村电话用户 指按行政区划属于城市范围以外的乡（镇）、村电话用户。

住宅电话用户 指私人付费或安装在居民住宅并按照私人或住宅电话用户登记注册和收费的各类电话用户。

长途电话交换机容量 指电信企业用于接入长途电话网的电话交换机的设备额定容量。

局用交换机容量 指安装在电信运营企业内用于接续本地固定电话的电话交换机容量，包括接入网设备容量（安装在电信运营企业用于连接语音用户的远端节点的设备容量）。

移动电话交换机容量 指移动电话交换机根据一定话务模型和交换机处理能力计算出来的最大同时服务用户的数量。按报告期末已割接入网正式投入使用的设备实际容量统计。

互联网宽带接入端口 指用于接入互联网用户的各类实际安装运行的接入端口的数量，包括xDSL用户接入端口、LAN接入端口、其他类型接入端口等，不包括窄带拨号接入端口。

Explanatory Notes on Main Statistical Indicators

Length of Railways in Operation refers to the total length of the trunk line for passenger and freight transportation in full operation or temporary operation.

Length of Automatic-blocking and Semi- automatic-blocking Railways Blocking is a spacing technique by which a section of the railway only allows one train to pass at a time with the aim of ensuring traffic safety. Automatic-blocking is the blocking method that signal display transforms automatically based on the state of train operation and related block partition, while the driver operates according to the signal display. The section which is blocked using the above method is called as length of automatic-blocking railways. Semi-blocking is realized manually. After the train departs based on signal display, the departure signal machine will perform automatic shutdown blocking, while the station attendant will conduct restoration of section blocking with arrival confirmation of the entire train. The section which is blocked using the above method is called as length of semi-automatic-blocking railways.

Length of Highways refers to the actual length of highways at the end of reference period. It covers public roads running vehicles among cities, city and rural areas, township (villages), highways passing through streets at small cities and towns, length of bridges and tunnels, width of ferry piers. It does not include the length of streets in cities, dead end highways, the length of streets built for agricultural (forest) production and inside factories (mines). It can only be calculated with the actual mileage having been completed, checked and accepted or put into operation. If two or more highways go the same section of the way, the length of the section is only calculated for once.

Length of Routes with Scheduled Flights refers to the total length of all routes for scheduled flights, which is calculated using million kilometres as the unit. There are usually two ways to calculate the route length: duplicated calculation and non-duplicated calculation. Duplicated calculation means that the same segment of different routes can be added duplicately, while the non-duplicated calculation allows the same segment of different routes be counted once only.

Length of Oil (Gas) Pipelines refers to the actual transport distance of oil, gas and oil products, an indicator reflecting the length of transportation routes and a reference to calculate the freight-kilometers. For those sections with double pipelines and alternate pipeline, the length will be calculated according to the length of single pipeline in principle. If the double pipelines perform the transportation at the same time and unable to be counted separately, the length of pipelines will be the length of double pipelines divided by 2.

Freight (Passenger) Traffic refers to the weight of freight (number of passenger) transported with various means within a specific period of time. This indicator reflects the service of the transport industry towards the national economy and people's living conditions, as well as an important indicator used in formulating and monitoring transport production plans and research into the scale and pace of transport development. Freight transport is calculated in tons and passenger traffic is calculated in terms of number of persons. Freight transport is calculated in terms of the actual weight of the goods and takes no account of the type of freight and distance of travel. Passenger traffic is calculated by the principle that one person can be counted only once in one trip and takes no account of the travelling distance and ticket price. The passengers who travel with a half price ticket or a child's ticket is also calculated as one person.

Freight Ton-kilometres (Passenger-kilometres) refers to the sum of the product of the volume of transported cargo (passengers) multiplied by the transport distance. It is an important indicator to reflect the achievement of the transportation industry. This is an important indicator to show the total results of the transport industry; to prepare and examine the transport plan; and to serve as the main basic data for calculating the efficiency, labour productivity and unit cost of transport. Normally, the shortest distance between the departure station and the destination station (i.e., the payable distance) is the basis in calculating the freight ton-kilometres. The formula is as follows:

$$\begin{matrix}\text{Freight to n - kilometres}\\ \text{(passenger - kilometres)}\end{matrix} = \sum \begin{matrix}\text{freight}\\ \text{(passenger)traffic}\end{matrix} \times \begin{matrix}\text{distance of}\\ \text{transportation}\end{matrix}$$

Average Static Load of Freight Cars refers to the average cargo weight when loaded onto each freight car under the static condition. For its calculation the following formula is applied:

$$\begin{matrix}\text{Average static}\\ \text{load of freight cars}\end{matrix} \text{(tons)} = \frac{\text{Tonnage of goods dispatched}}{\text{Number of freight cars loaded}}$$

Average Daily Haul of Freight Locomotives refers to the average total ton-kilometres accomplished by each freight transport locomotive over one day and night during a given period of time. It includes both the weight of the goods carried and the dead weight of the train itself. It is a comprehensive indicator reflecting the locomotive efficiency in terms of both time and the pulling force.

$$\begin{matrix}\text{Average daily haul of}\\ \text{freight transport locomotive}\\ \text{(ton - kilometre)}\end{matrix} = \frac{\text{Total ton - kilometres of freight}}{\text{Daily number of freight transport locomotive}}$$

Possession of Civil Motor Vehicles refer to the total numbers of vehicles that are registered and received vehicles license tags according to the *Work Standard for Motor Vehicles Registration* formulated by the Transport Management Office under the department of public security at the end of the reference period. They are divided into categories. According to the structure of motor vehicles, they are divided into passenger vehicles, trucks and others; according to ownership into private vehicles and vehicles for the unit's use; according to kind of usage into working vehicles and non-working vehicles; and according to size of vehicles into large passenger vehicles, medium-sized passenger vehicles, small passenger vehicles and mini passenger vehicles, heavy trucks, light-heavy trucks, light trucks and mini-trucks.

Business Volume of Post and Telecommunications refers to the total amount of postal and telecommunication services, expressed in value terms, provided by the post and telecommunications departments for society. This indicator reflects the overall results of development of postal and telecommunication services. It can be classificated as postal services and telecommunication services. Business volume of post and telecommunications is the sum of each service in kind multiplying with its correspondent unit price (constant price).

Mobile Telephone Subscribers refers to persons who have gone through registration procedures in the operation points of enterprises engaged in telecommunications and are hence connected with the mobile telephone communication network through the mobile telephone switchboards and occupy mobile phone numbers. Included are various types of subscriber, prepaid users for intelligent network and wireless network card users.

Internet Users refer to the number of Chinese citizens aged 6 and over who use the Internet in the past six months.

Local Telephone Subscribers refer to all subscribers who have gone through registration procedures in the operation points of enterprises engaged in telecommunications and are hence connected to the local telecommunications service provider through fixed line network. Included are general subscribers, wireless local telephone subscribers, public telephones subscribers, N-ISDN subscribers and intelligent network terminal subscribers.

Urban Telephone Subscribers refer to the number of telephone subscribers, located at the municipalities directly under the Central Government, cities under the jurisdiction of province, cities at prefecture level, downtown and suburb of city at county level town and county towns according to the administrative division, including subscribers in rural mineral area, forest area, military area that are at or above county level.

Rural Telephone Subscribers refer to telephone subscribers, located at the towns and villages outside the coverage of urban areas according to the administrative division.

Household Telephone Subscribers refers to all kinds of subscribers with telephone sets paid privately or installed in the dwelling units of residents, and registered as private subscribers or residence subscribers for payment.

Capacity of Long Distance Telephone Exchanges refers to the rated capacity of telephone exchanges to connect long distance telephone network by enterprises engaged in telecommunications.

Capacity of Office Telephone Exchanges refers to the capacity (measured in gate) of telephone exchanges installed in the offices of telecommunication service providers for communication between fixed telephones.It includes the capacity of access network equipment(capacity of equipment installed in the offices of telecommunication service providers for connecting distant nodes of voice users).

Capacity of Mobile Telephone Exchanges refers to the capacity of the maximum services provided to subscribers at any one time as computed based on a certain model of calls distribution and transacting capacity of the mobile telephone exchanges. It is calculated based on the actual capacity of equipments connected to network through cutover and put into operation officially at the end of the reference period.

Broadband Connection Terminals refer to the connection terminals to internet users actually installed and put into operation, including connection terminals for XDSL, connection terminals for LAN, and other types of connection terminals. N-ISDN connection terminals are not included.

新疆统计年鉴
XINJIANG STATISTICAL YEARBOOK

16

批发和零售业、住宿和餐饮业

WHOLESALE & RETAIL TRADES, HOTELS AND CATERING SERVICES

简要说明

本篇主要内容和资料来源

本篇资料反映新疆维吾尔自治区商品流通市场发展及批发和零售业、住宿和餐饮业经营情况。主要内容有社会消费品零售额；限额以上批发和零售业、住宿和餐饮业情况；限额以上批发和零售业商品销售及商品分类销售情况；限额以上批发和零售贸易企业及住宿和餐饮企业主要财务情况；亿元商品交易市场成交情况；连锁经营情况等。

限额以上批发和零售业、住宿和餐饮业统计限额标准：批发业年销售额2000万元及以上；零售业年销售额500万元及以上；餐饮业年营业额200万元及以上；住宿业为年主营业务收入200万元以上企业。

本篇资料由新疆维吾尔自治区统计局贸易外经统计处提供。

Brief Introduction

Main Content and Source of Data

Data in this chapter reflect the development of Xinjiang's circulation of domestic market and the management situation of wholesale and retail & hotels and catering services, etc. Main contents include the total retail sales, condition of wholesales & retail trades and hotels and catering services above designated size; condition of sale value of enterprises above designated size of wholesales and retail trade and sale value of trade by category of main commodities.

Criteria for wholesale and retail sale trades, hotels and catering services above designated size is defined as follows: wholesale trade has annual sales over 20 million yuan; retail sale trade have annual sale over 5 million yuan; catering services have annual income over 2 million yuan. Enterprise above designated size in accommodation refers to star-rated unit.

Data in this chapter are provided by the Division of Trade Statistics, the Xinjiang Bureau of Statistics.

16-1 主要年份国内贸易基本情况
Basic Conditions of Domestic Trade in Main Years

指　标	Item	2000	2005	2010	2013
法人企业(个)	**Number of Corporation Enterprises (unit)**	**394**	**1097**	**1449**	**1878**
批发和零售业	Wholesale and Retail Trades	370	800	1175	1557
住宿和餐饮业	Hotels and Catering Servicess	24	297	274	321
#餐饮业	Catering Services	24	65	53	77
产业活动单位(个)	**Number of Establishments (unit)**	**431**	**2396**	**4563**	**5211**
批发和零售业	Wholesale and Retail Trades	382	1998	4137	4665
住宿和餐饮业	Hotels and Catering Services	49	398	426	546
#餐饮业	Catering Services	49	96	122	163
批发和零售业	**Wholesale and Retail Trades**				
商品销售总额（亿元)	Total Sales (100 million yuan)	478.3	1182.0	4230.9	8884.7
社会消费品零售总额(亿元)	**Total Retail Sales of Consumer Goods (100 million yuan)**	**374.5**	**640.2**	**1324.5**	**2039.2**
按销售单位所在地分	By Location of Establishments				
城　镇	Urban	233.7	443.9	1181.3	1861.4
#城　区	Urban Area	65.2	95.6	945.0	1593.7
乡　村	Rural	75.6	100.7	143.2	177.8
按行业分	By Sector				
批发和零售业	Wholesale and Retail Trades	242.3	509.3	1156.6	1769.3
住宿和餐饮业	Hotels and Catering Services	38.2	92.8	167.9	269.8
其他行业	Others	94.0	38.1		

注：1.法人企业、产业活动单位统计范围为限额以上企业(单位)。2.商品销售总额、社会消费品零售总额为全口径数据。3.2008 年限额以上住宿业数据为年主营业务收入 200 万元以上企业。4.从 2010 年开始,按销售单位所在地分组由市、县、县以下调整为城镇、城区、乡村。5.从 2010 年开始,按行业分组取消其他行业。

Note: a) Scope of corporation enterprises,industrial activity units covers enterprises(units)above designated size. b) Data of total sales and total retail sales of consumer goods are those of full coverage. c) Data of hotels and catering services above designated size in 2008 are figures from enterprises of annual income over 2 million yuan. d) Since 2010,By the sales units of the group was adjusted,from city,county and under county level to town,city and country.e) Since 2010,by the sector of the group canceled oter sectors.

16-2 主要年份社会消费品零售总额
Total Retail Sales of Consumer Goods in Main Years

单位：亿元 (100 million yuan)

年 份 Year	社会消费品零售总额 Total Retail Sales of Consumer Goods	按销售单位所在地分 By Location		
		城 镇 Urban	#城 区 Urban Area	乡 村 Rural
1978	21.89	7.44	4.80	9.65
1980	29.36	11.06	6.05	12.25
1985	57.38	24.55	10.70	22.13
1990	104.30	57.17	24.27	22.86
1995	253.65	145.74	50.03	57.88
1996	295.36	171.51	55.38	68.47
1997	310.42	186.37	57.54	66.51
1998	327.52	197.89	59.89	69.74
1999	347.40	213.96	61.51	71.93
2000	374.50	233.66	65.15	75.69
2001	406.35	256.58	69.73	80.04
2002	442.88	284.74	74.32	83.82
2003	421.16	311.33	49.20	60.63
2004	563.41	385.81	85.79	91.81
2005	640.20	443.95	95.60	100.65
2006	733.20	513.12	107.68	112.40
2007	857.50	606.74	123.64	127.12
2008	1041.50	740.85	150.78	149.87
2009	1177.53	834.42	171.76	171.35
2010	1324.48	1181.27	945.03	143.21
2011	1557.09	1411.01	1165.29	146.08
2012	1798.99	1642.24	1406.67	156.75
2013	2039.15	1861.36	1593.69	177.79

年 份 Year	按行业分 By Sector		
	批发和零售业 Wholesale and Retail Trades	住宿和餐饮业 Hotels and Catering Services	其他行业 Others
1978	17.34	0.57	3.98
1980	22.95	0.94	5.47
1985	40.83	2.51	14.04
1990	72.68	6.06	25.56
1995	169.16	17.27	67.22
1996	191.14	19.44	84.78
1997	198.73	22.22	89.47
1998	206.92	27.84	92.76
1999	222.57	32.76	92.07
2000	242.29	38.21	94.00
2001	266.38	44.57	95.40
2002	296.13	53.04	93.71
2003	341.90	60.64	18.62
2004	450.65	76.22	36.54
2005	509.25	92.82	38.13
2006	582.28	111.55	39.37
2007	685.94	130.51	41.05
2008	841.65	156.49	43.36
2009	956.64	177.21	43.68
2010	1156.62	167.86	
2011	1351.36	205.73	
2012	1553.37	245.62	
2013	1769.33	269.82	

16-3 分类型、分地区限额以上批发和零售业、住宿和餐饮业基本情况

Basic Conditions of Enterprises above Designated Size in Wholesale and Retail Trades, Hotels and Catering Services by Category and Region

(2013 年)

指 标	Item	法人企业数(个) Number of Corporation Enterprises (unit)	产业活动单位数(个) Number of Establishments (unit)	从业人员数(人) Engaged Persons (person)
总 计	**Total**	**1878**	**5211**	**158001**
批发业	**Wholesale Trades**	**944**	**2580**	**64716**
内资企业	Domestic Funded Enterprises	940	2562	63900
国有企业	State-owned Enterprises	63	254	11021
集体企业	Collective-owned Enterprises	17	72	1675
股份合作企业	Cooperative Enterprises			
联营企业	Joint Ownership Enterprises	1	13	15
集体联营企业	Collective Joint Ownership Enterprises	1	13	15
有限责任公司	State Sole Funded Corporations	335	972	24844
国有独资公司	State Sole Funded Corporations	62	212	7856
其他有限责任公司	Other Limited Liability Corporations	273	760	16988
股份有限公司	Share-holding Corporations Ltd.	38	705	11531
私营企业	Private Enterprises	476	536	14814
私营独资企业	Private-funded Enterprises	1	1	5
私营合伙企业	Private Partnership Enterprises	2	2	32
私营有限责任公司	Private Limited Liability Corporations	466	524	13847
私营股份有限公司	Private Share-holding Corporation Ltd.	7	9	930
其他企业	Others	10	10	
港、澳、台商投资企业	Enterprises With Funds from Hong Kong, Macao and Taiwan	1	3	360
港、澳、台商独资经营企业	Enterprises With Sole Funds from Hong Kong, Macao and Taiwan	1	3	360
外商投资企业	Foreign Funded Enterprises	3	15	456
中外合资经营企业	Enterprises with Foreign Investment	2	5	77
外资企业	Enterprises with Sole Fund	1	9	325
零售业	**Retail Trades**	**613**	**2085**	**47878**
内资企业	Domestic Funded Enterprises	603	1982	45756
国有企业	State-owned Enterprises	27	144	2357
集体企业	Collective-owned Enterprises	2	9	85
股份合作企业	Share-holding Cooperative Enterprises	1	10	94
有限责任公司	Limited Liability Corporations	193	556	12745
国有独资公司	State Sole Funded Enterprises	7	24	154
其他有限责任公司	Other Limited Liability Corporations	186	541	12591
股份有限公司	Share-holding Corporations Ltd.	7	118	6667
私营企业	Private Enterprises	371	1156	23772
私营独资企业	Private-funded Enterprises	1	1	16
私营有限责任公司	Private Limited Liability Corporations	365	1157	23420
私营股份有限公司	Private Share-holding Corporation Ltd.	4	4	336
其他企业	Others	2	2	25
港、澳、台商投资企业	Enterprises With Funds from Hong Kong, Macao and Taiwan	5	5	563
港、澳、台商独资经营企业	Enterprises With Sole Funds from Hong Kong, Macao and Taiwan	4	6	563
外商投资企业	Foreign Funded Enterprises	5	8	1559
中外合资经营企业	Enterprises with Foreign Investment	4	6	648
外资企业	Enterprises with Sole Fund	1	4	911
住宿业	**Hotels**	**244**	**354**	**33350**
内资企业	Domestic-funded Enterprises	241	350	32779
国有企业	State-owned Enterprises	70	100	10766
集体企业	Collective-owned Enterprises	5	6	781
联营企业	Joint Ownership Enterprises	1	1	51
国有联营企业	State Joint Ownership Enterprises	1	1	51

16-3 续表 Continued

指　标	Item	法人企业数(个) Number of Corporate Enterprises (unit)	产业活动单位数(个) Number of Economic Active Unit (unit)	从业人员数(人) Engaged Persons (person)
有限责任公司	Limited Liability Corporations	79	114	12393
国有独资公司	State Sole Funded Corporations	10	10	1008
其他有限责任公司	Other Limited Liability Corporations	69	104	11385
股份有限公司	Share-holding Corporations Ltd.	6	11	981
私营企业	Private Enterprises	79	117	7767
私营独资企业	Private-funded Enterprises	10	21	274
私营合伙企业	Private Partnership Enterprises	1	2	134
私营有限责任公司	Private Limited Liability Corporations	66	91	7144
私营股份有限公司	Private Share-holding Corporation Ltd.	2	3	215
其他企业	Other Enterprises	1	1	40
港、澳、台商投资企业	Enterprises With Funds from Hong Kong, Macao and Taiwan	1	1	26
合资经营企业（港或澳、台资）	Joint-venture Enterprises (Funds from Hong Kong, Macao and Taiwan)	1	1	26
外商投资企业	Foreign Funded Enterprises	2	3	545
中外合资经营企业	Enterprises with Foreign Investment		1	411
外资企业	Enterprises with Sole Fund	2	2	134
餐饮业	**Catering Services**	**77**	**192**	**12057**
内资企业	Domestic Funded Enterprises	76	163	11157
国有企业	State-owned Enterprises	8	17	1606
集体企业	Collective-owned Enterprises	1	1	52
有限责任公司	Limited Liability Corporations	16	28	2143
国有独资公司	State Sole Funded Enterprises	1	1	51
其他有限责任公司	Other Limited Liability Corporations	15	27	2092
股份有限公司	Share-holding Corporations Ltd.	1	1	129
私营企业	Private Enterprises	49	115	7036
私营独资企业	Private-funded Enterprises	7	7	469
私营合伙企业	Private Partnership Enterprises	2	2	239
私营有限责任公司	Private limited Liability Corporations	39	105	6232
私营股份有限公司	Private Share-holding Corporation Ltd.	1	1	96
其他企业	Others	1	1	191
外商投资企业	Foreign Funded Enterprises	1	29	900
外资企业	Enterprises With Sole Fund	1	29	900
按地区分	**By Region**			
乌鲁木齐市	Urumqi City	647	1680	73915
克拉玛依市	Karamay City	70	150	7563
吐鲁番地区	Turpan Administrative Offices	33	108	1743
哈密地区	Hami [Kumul] Administrative Offices	82	224	4827
昌吉回族自治州	Changji Hui Autonomous Prefecture	82	337	5839
伊犁哈萨克自治州	Ili Kazak Autonomous Prefecture	282	639	14618
伊犁州直属县(市)	Counties (Cities) Direct Under Ili Prefecture	202	368	9972
塔城地区	Tacheng [Tarbagatai] Administrative Offices	43	134	2359
阿勒泰地区	Altay Administrative Offices	37	137	2287
博尔塔拉蒙古自治州	Bortala Mongol Autonomous Prefecture	23	63	1294
巴音郭楞蒙古自治州	Bayangol Mongol Autonomous Prefecture	136	401	11221
阿克苏地区	Aksu Administrative Offices	179	544	9489
克孜勒苏柯尔克孜自治州	Kizilsu Kirgiz Autonomous Prefecture	12	12	753
喀什地区	Kashgar [Kaxgar] Administrative Offices	95	263	8750
和田地区	Hotan Administrative Offices	16	76	1368
生产建设兵团	Production and Construction Corps	221	714	16621

16-4 分行业、分地区限额以上批发和零售业商品销售额
Total Sales Values of Enterprises above Designated Size of Wholesale and Retail Trades by Sector and Region

单位：万元 (2013 年) (10 000 yuan)

指 标	Item	销售总额 Total Sales Value	批 发 Wholesale Value	零 售 Retail Value
总 计	**Total**	**79233395**	**69827340**	**9406054**
批发业	**Wholesale Trade**	**70950607**	**69232100**	**1718507**
农、林、牧产品批发	Wholesale of Farm Produce and Livestock Products	12556793	12556218	575
谷物、豆及薯类批发	Wholesale of Grain,Bean and Potato	487020	487020	
种子批发	Wholesale of Seed	316456	316456	
棉、麻批发	Wholesale of Cotton and Liner	11695137	11694647	490
其他农牧产品批发	Wholesale of Other Farm Produce and Livestock Products	38631	38631	
食品、饮料及烟草制品批发	Wholesale of Food,Beverages and Tobaccos	3838652	3830697	7955
米、面制品及食用油批发	Wholesale of Rice, Flour and Edible Oil	279118	279054	63
糕点、糖果及糖批发	Wholesale of Pastry,Candy and Sugar	35697	34587	1109
果品、蔬菜批发	Wholesale of Fruit and Vegetable	217179	217043	136
肉、禽、蛋及水产品批发	Wholesale of Meat,Birds and Equatic Products	69850	69830	20
盐及调味品批发	Wholesale of Salt and Condiment Flavoring Material	49497	48953	543
酒、饮料及茶叶批发	Wholesale of Soft Drink and Tea Leaf	65510	65510	
烟草制品批发	Wholesale of Tobaccos	3101583	3095550	6033
其他食品批发	Wholesale of Other Food	20220	20170	50
纺织、服装及家庭用品批发	Wholesale of Textitle, Garments and Daily Consumer Articles	503497	490737	12760
纺织品、针织品及原料批发	Wholesale of Textile,Hosiery and Raw Material	137629	137629	
服装批发	Wholesale of Garment	89490	79222	10268
化妆品及卫生用品批发	Wholesale of Cosmetics and Health Aids	37117	36618	499
家用电器批发	Wholesale of Other Covenience Goods	190321	188328	1993
其他家庭用品批发	Wholesale of Culture, Sports Appliances and Equipments	48941	48941	
文化、体育用品及器材批发	Wholesale of Books	214185	199372	14812
图书批发	Wholesale of Textitle, Garments and Daily Consumer Articles	166189	151415	14775
首饰、工艺品及收藏品批发	Wholesale of wear、Jewellery、Handicraft、Collectim	3921	3883	38
其他文化用品批发	Wholesale of Other Culture Products	44075	44075	
医药及医疗器材批发	Wholesale of Medicines and Medical Appliances	760843	757603	3240
西药批发	Wholesale of Western Medicine	718415	715926	2488
中药批发	Wholesale of Chinese Medicinal Plant	33104	32353	752
医疗用品及器材批发	Wholesale of Medicine and Medical Appliances	9324	9324	
矿产品、建材及化工产品批发	Wholesale of Mineral Products, Building Material and Chemical Products	49708045	48197181	1510864
煤炭及制品批发	Wholesale of Coal and Related Products	552935	552935	
石油及制品批发	Wholesale of Petroleum and Related Products	39723451	38316583	1406869
金属及金属矿批发	Wholesale of Metal and Metal Materials	5777484	5709146	68338
建材批发	Wholesale of Building Materials	819797	811122	8675
化肥批发	Wholesale of Chemical Fertilizer	1888907	1884694	4213
农药批发	Wholesale of Pesticides	24201	24201	

16-4 续表 1 Continued

单位：万元 (10 000 yuan)

指 标	Item	销售总额 Total Sales Value	批 发 Wholesale Value	零 售 Retail Value
其他化工产品批发	Wholesale of Other Chemical Product	911072	888303	22769
机械设备、五金交电及电子产品批发	Wholesale of Machinery, Hardware and Electronic Equipments	3036633	2868408	168225
农业机械批发	Wholesale of Agriculture Machinery	197779	188208	9571
汽车批发	Wholesale of Motor Vehicles	427603	409123	18480
汽车零配件批发	Wholesale of Motor Vehicles and Parts	593022	526228	66794
摩托车及零配件批发	Wholesale of Motorcycles and Parts	10640	10640	
五金产品批发	Wholesale of Hardware	114955	114955	
电气设备批发	Wholesale of Electric Machinery	55967		55967
计算机、软件及辅助设备批发	Wholesale of Computer, Software and Assistant Appliances	120390	109242	11148
通讯及广播电视设备批发	Wholesale of Communicating and Broadcasting Television Device	28084	28050	35
其他机械设备及电子产品批发	Wholesale of Other Mechanical Equipment and Electronic Products	1488194	1481965	6229
贸易经纪与代理	Trades Broker and Agency	91355	91355	
贸易代理	Trade Agency	91355	91355	
其他批发业	Wholesales of Others	240604	240529	75
再生物资回收与批发	Recovery and Wholesale of Regeneration Material	125419	125343	75
其他未列明的批发	Wholesale of Un-listed	115186	115186	
零售业	**Retail Trades**	**8282788**	**595240**	**7687548**
综合零售	Integrated Retail	1517194	8996	1508198
百货零售	Retail of General Merchandise	1140248	4826	1135422
超级市场零售	Retail of Supermarkets	375965	4169	371796
其他综合零售	Retail of Other Integrate	981		981
食品、饮料及烟草制品专门零售	Monopoly Retail of Foods, Beverages and Tobacco	16279	1834	14445
粮油零售	Retail of Grain and Oil	3774		3774
果品、蔬菜零售	Retail of Fruite and Vegetables	1450		1450
肉、禽、蛋及水产品零售	Retail of Meat,Poultry and Eggs	198		198
营养和保健品零售	Retail of Health Products			
酒、饮料及茶叶零售	Retail of Soft Drink and Tea Leaf	6382	1834	4548
烟草制品零售	Retail of Tobaccos	4475		4475
纺织、服装及日用品专门零售	Monopoly Retail of Textile, Garments and Daily Consumer Articles	409864	16215	393649
服装零售	Retail of Garment	295593	5120	290473
化妆品及卫生用品零售	Retail of Cosmetics and Health Aids	6534		6534
钟表、眼镜零售	Retail of Timelceeper and Spectacle	12924	10585	2339
其他日用品零售	Retail of Other Covenience Goods	54187		54187
文化、体育用品及器材专门零售	Monopoly Retail of Cultural, Sports Goods and Apparatus	207909	16688	191221
文具用品零售	Retail of Stationery and Office Supplies	4235		4235
图书、报刊零售	Retail of Books,Newspapers	174407	7966	166441
珠宝首饰零售	Retail of Jewelry	29233	8722	20511

16-4 续表 2 Continued

单位：万元 (10 000 yuan)

指　标	Item	销售总额 Total Sales Value	批　发 Wholesale Value	零　售 Retail Value
照相器材零售	Retail of Photographic Materials	34		34
医药及医疗器材专门零售	Monopoly Retail of Medicine and Medical-care Apparatus	887334	151864	735470
药品零售	Retail of Medcine	883752	151865	731887
医疗用品及器材零售	Wholesale of Medical Treatment and Equipment	3583		3583
汽车、摩托车、燃料及零配件专门零售	Monopoly Retail of Car, Motor, Fuel and Parts as Well as Components	4555933	359852	4196081
汽车零售	Retail of Automobiles	3215714	129082	3086632
汽车零配件零售	Retail of Automobiles' Parts	5948		5948
摩托车及零配件零售	Retail of Motorcycle and Fittings	18377	1985	16392
机动车燃料零售	Retail of Auto Fuel	1315893	228786	1087107
家用电器及电子产品专门零售	Monopoly Retail of House Hold Electric Appliancesound Electronic Products	449843	39072	410771
家用视听设备零售	Retail of Home audio-visual equipment	233385	14481	218904
日用家电设备零售	Retail of Household Electuic Appliances	99984	4912	95072
计算机、软件及辅助设备零售	Retail of Cumputers,Software and Office Appliances	68164	12403	55761
通信设备零售	Retail of Telecommunication Equipments	48310	7276	41034
五金、家具及室内装修材料专门零售	Monopoly Retail of Hardware, Furniture and Indoor Decorating Material	201958		201958
五金零售	Retail of Hardware	9135		9135
家具零售	Retail of Living Equipment	192823		192823
货摊、无店铺及其他零售业	Non-shop and Other Retail	36474	719	35755
邮购及电视、电话零售	Distribution of Post and E-commerce	6513		6513
生活用燃料零售	Retail of Life Fuels	29960	719	29241
按地区分	**By Region**			
乌鲁木齐市	Urumqi City	48296516	42760472	5536043
克拉玛依市	Karamay City	1480220	1158390	321830
吐鲁番地区	Turpan Administrative Offices	562989	403796	159193
哈密地区	Hami [Kumul] Administrative Offices	1334251	1053105	281145
昌吉回族自治州	Changji Hui Autonomous Prefecture	1439824	1054921	384903
伊犁哈萨克自治州	Ili Kazak Autonomous Prefecture	4206242	3580942	625300
伊犁州直属县(市)	Counties (Cities) Direct Under Ili Prefecture	3195829	2724315	471514
塔城地区	Tacheng [Tarbagatai] Administrative Offices	689005	590139	98866
阿勒泰地区	Altay Administrative Offices	321408	266488	54920
博尔塔拉蒙古自治州	Bortala Mongol Autonomous Prefecture	1159015	1111135	47881
巴音郭楞蒙古自治州	Bayangol Mongol Autonomous Prefecture	2921140	2460979	460161
阿克苏地区	Aksu Administrative Offices	2890518	2316962	573555
克孜勒苏柯尔克孜自治州	Kizilsu Kirgiz Autonomous Prefecture	59394	56331	3062
喀什地区	Kashgar [Kaxgar] Administrative Offices	2014540	1673967	340573
和田地区	Hotan Administrative Offices	258188	205994	52193
生产建设兵团	Production and Construction Group	12610560	11990345	620215

16-5 限额以上餐饮企业经营情况
Operations of Enterprises above Designated Size of Catering Services

单位：万元 (2013 年) (10 000 yuan)

项　目	Item	法人企业数(个) Number of Corporation Enterprises (unit)	产业活动单位数(个) Number of Establishments (unit)	营业额 Business Revenue	#商品零售额 Retail Sales of Commodities
总　计	**Total**	**77**	**192**	**162326**	**138559**
正餐服务	Dinner	72	101	111678	88618
快餐服务	Snack	5	91	50649	49941
按地区分	**By Region**				
乌鲁木齐市	Urumqi City	23	112	101827	94175
克拉玛依市	Karamay City	1	13	5105	4810
吐鲁番地区	Turpan Administrative Offices	1	1	196	93
哈密地区	Hami [Kumul] Administrative Offices	2	2	488	424
昌吉回族自治州	Changji Hui Autonomous Prefecture	3	6	2023	1570
伊犁哈萨克自治州	Ili Kazak Autonomous Prefecture	20	22	22937	14290
伊犁州直属县(市)	Counties (Cities) Direct Under Ili Prefecture	20	22	22937	14290
巴音郭楞蒙古自治州	Bayangol Mongol Autonomous Prefecture	15	18	15329	12396
阿克苏地区	Aksu Administrative Offices	4	4	3299	2366
喀什地区	Kashgar [Kaxgar] Administrative Offices	1	1	932	738
生产建设兵团	Production and Construction Group	7	13	10190	7697

16-6 限额以上住宿企业经营情况
Operation of Enterprises above Designated Size in Hotels Services

单位：万元 (2013 年) (10 000 yuan)

项　目	Item	营业额 Business Revenue	客房收入 From Hotel Rooms	餐费收入 From Meals
总　计	**Total**	**462517**	**219811**	**188269**
按星级分	**By Stars**			
五　星	Five-Star	76691	26722	36805
四　星	Four-Star	96073	42749	37532
三　星	Three-Star	143205	71940	59092
二　星	Two-Star	57575	32133	19895
一　星	One-Star	24698	10980	11075
其　他	Others	64275	35286	23871
按行业分	**By Sector**			
旅游饭店	Tourist Hotel	413761	191984	171843
一般旅馆	Fonda	48290	27408	16409
其他住宿服务	Others	467	420	17
按地区分	**By Region**			
乌鲁木齐市	Urumqi City	248798	107883	100242
克拉玛依市	Karamay City	21707	8722	11289
吐鲁番地区	Turpan Administrative Offices	5800	3978	1683
哈密地区	Hami [Kumul] Administrative Offices	21637	8546	12050
昌吉回族自治州	Changji Hui Autonomous Prefecture	11846	5325	5623
伊犁哈萨克自治州	Ili Kazak Autonomous Prefecture	40161	21514	16483
伊犁州直属县(市)	Counties (Cities) Direct Under Ili Prefecture	19010	10588	7154
塔城地区	Tacheng [Tarbagatai] Administrative Offices	5983	2736	3027
阿勒泰地区	Altay Administrative Offices	15168	8190	6302
博尔塔拉蒙古自治州	Bortala Mongol Autonomous Prefecture	4138	2139	1884
巴音郭楞蒙古自治州	Bayangol Mongol Autonomous Prefecture	24947	12301	10880
阿克苏地区	Aksu Administrative Offices	12555	8807	3524
克孜勒苏柯尔克孜自治州	Kizilsu Kirgiz Autonomous Prefecture	1703	864	760
喀什地区	Kashgar [Kaxgar] Administrative Offices	15615	9073	5158
和田地区	Hotan Administrative Offices	2339	1764	453
生产建设兵团	Production and Construction Group	51272	28894	18241

16-6 续表 Continued

单位：万元 (10 000 yuan)

项　目	Item	商品销售收入 From Commodities	其他收入 Others	床位数（张） Number of beds (unit)
总　计	**Total**	**6789**	**47648**	**80701**
按星级分	**Classified by Star**			
五　星	Five-Star	3387	9777	5934
四　星	Four-Star	886	14906	15897
三　星	Three-Star	1775	10398	31289
二　星	Two-Star	449	5097	11032
一　星	One-Star	102	2541	2136
其　他	Others	190	4929	14413
按行业分	**By Sector**			
旅游饭店	Tourist Hotel	6519	43415	69089
一般旅馆	Fonda	270	4203	11444
其他住宿服务	Others		30	168
按地区分	**By Region**			
乌鲁木齐市	Urumqi City	4740	35933	29200
克拉玛依市	Karamay City	69	1628	2936
吐鲁番地区	Turpan Administrative Offices		139	1597
哈密地区	Hami [Kumul] Administrative Offices	172	869	2584
昌吉回族自治州	Changji Hui Autonomous Prefecture	70	827	2240
伊犁哈萨克自治州	Ili Kazak Autonomous Prefecture	478	1686	13329
伊犁州直属县(市)	Counties (Cities) Direct Under Ili Prefecture	118	1150	5669
塔城地区	Tacheng [Tarbagatai] Administrative Offices	162	58	1413
阿勒泰地区	Altay Administrative Offices	198	478	6247
博尔塔拉蒙古自治州	Bortala Mongol Autonomous Prefecture	96	19	834
巴音郭楞蒙古自治州	Bayangol Mongol Autonomous Prefecture	512	1254	5314
阿克苏地区	Aksu Administrative Offices	62	162	4366
克孜勒苏柯尔克孜自治州	Kizilsu Kirgiz Autonomous Prefecture		80	268
喀什地区	Kashgar [Kaxgar] Administrative Offices	65	1319	6291
和田地区	Hotan Administrative Offices	38	84	1152
生产建设兵团	Production and Construction Group	488	3649	10590

16-7 各地、州、市、县(市)社会消费品零售总额
Total Retail Sales of Consumer Goods by Prefecture, Autonomous Prefecture, City and County

单位：万元 (2013 年) (10 000 yuan)

地　区	Region	社会消费品零售总额 Total Retail Sales of Consumer Goods	城　镇 Urban		乡　村 Rural
				城　区 Urban Area	
总　计	**Total**	**20391521**	**18613756**	**15936938**	**1777765**
乌鲁木齐市	**Urumqi City**	**8114713**	**15936938**	**8110775**	**3938**
#乌鲁木齐县	Urumqi County	70100	66170	66170	3930
克拉玛依市	**Karamay City**	**535420**	**533650**	**533650**	**1769**
吐鲁番地区	**TurpanAdministrative Offices**	**323433**	**234829**	**130457**	**88604**
吐鲁番市	Turpan City	177705	149681	130457	28025
鄯善县	Shanshan [piqan]County	107178	66089		41089
托克逊县	Toksun County	38550	19059		19491
哈密地区	**Hami [kumul]Administrative Offices**	**649170**	**616173**	**560400**	**32998**
哈密市	Hami [kumul]City	580785	563183	560400	17603
巴里坤哈萨克自治县	Barkol KazakAutonomous County	51455	36504		14951
伊吾县	Yiwu [Araturuk]County	16930	16486		444
昌吉回族自治州	**Changji Hui Autonomous Prefecture**	**1822731**	**1650070**	**1547528**	**172661**
昌吉市	Changji City	758133	688099	598629	70034
阜康市	Fukang City	251252	229959	216887	21293
呼图壁县	Hutubi County	213601	192241	192241	21360
玛纳斯县	Manas County	234812	211331	211331	23481
奇台县	Qitai County	205979	185381	185381	20598
吉木萨尔县	Jimsar County	98770	88893	88893	9877
木垒哈萨克自治县	Mori Kazak Autonomous County	60184	54166	54166	6018
伊犁哈萨克自治州	**Ili Kazak Autonomous Prefecture**	**2652888**	**2086379**	**1350659**	**566509**
伊犁州直属县(市)	**Counties (Cities) Direct Under Ili Prefecture**	**1553804**	**1214552**	**1026804**	**339252**
伊宁市	Yining [Gulja]City	587562	554636	504558	32926
奎屯市	Kuytun City	211534	211534	211534	
伊宁县	Yining [Gulja]County	121034	71389	67316	49645
察布查尔锡伯自治县	Qapqal Xibe Autonomous County	26224	19025	14972	7199
霍城县	Huocheng [korgas]County	169600	105072	77752	64528
巩留县	Gongliu [Tokkuzlara]County	51047	34643	13323	16404
新源县	Xinyuan [kunes]County	200800	105441	54482	95359
昭苏县	Zhaosu [mongolkure]County	45403	24779	24054	20624
特克斯县	Tekes County	77000	46196	35564	30804
尼勒克县	Nilka County	63600	41837	23249	21763
塔城地区	**Tacheng [Tarbagatai] Administrative Offices**	**608555**	**433630**	**173773**	**174925**
塔城市	Tacheng [Qoqek] City	140832	94288	90654	46544
乌苏市	Usu City	122283	100523	57806	21759
额敏县	Emin [Dorbiljin] County	120606	71001	9843	49605
沙湾县	Shawan County	135792	103094		32698
裕民县	Yumin [Qagantokay] County	25095	16894		8201
和布克赛尔蒙古自治县	Hoboksar Mongol Autonomous County	28618	21362	7221	7256
托里县	Toli County	35329	26468	8250	8862
阿勒泰地区	**Altay Administrative Offices**	**490530**	**438197**	**150082**	**52332**
阿勒泰市	Altay City	207764	193562	150082	14202
布尔津县	Burqin County	103574	91149		12424
富蕴县	Fuyun [Koktokay] County	53466	44768		8698
福海县	Fuhai [Burultokay] County	50219	44443		5776
哈巴河县	Habahe [Kaba] County	40591	35983		4608
青河县	Qinghe [Qinggil] County	25046	20846		4200
吉木乃县	Jeminay County	9869	7445		2424

16-7 续表 Continued

单位：万元 (10 000 yuan)

地　　区	Region	社会消费品零售总额 Total Retail Sales of Consumer Goods	城　镇 Urban	城　区 Urban Area	乡　村 Rural
博尔塔拉蒙古自治州	**Bortala Mongol Autonomous Prefecture**	**296223**	**257153**	**159716**	**39070**
博乐市	Bole [Bortala] City	223335	208775	159716	14560
精河县	Jinghe [Jing] County	50885	32695		18190
温泉县	Wenquan [Araxang] County	22003	15683		6320
巴音郭楞蒙古自治州	**Bayangol Mongol Autonomous Prefecture**	**811872**	**756795**	**532959**	**55077**
库尔勒市	Korla City	588237	569441	532959	18796
轮台县	Luntai [Bugur] County	40500	32838		7662
尉犁县	Yuli [Lopnur] County	17996	14185		3811
若羌县	Ruoqiang [Qarkilik] County	7956	6523		1433
且末县	Qiemo [Qarqan] County	9568	8120		1449
焉耆回族自治县	Yanqi Hui Autonomous County	64788	60452		4336
和静县	Hejing County	40907	32172		8735
和硕县	Hoxud County	16685	12697		3988
博湖县	Bohu [Bagrax] County	25234	20367		4867
阿克苏地区	**Aksu Administrative Offices**	**980361**	**830866**	**439302**	**149495**
阿克苏市	Aksu City	538387	514843	437303	23544
温宿县	Wensu [Onsu] County	69301	53396		15906
库车县	Kuqa County	142891	103775	627	39115
沙雅县	Xayar County	78472	60340		18132
新和县	Xinhe [Toksu] County	32823	23348		9475
拜城县	Baicheng [Bay] County	60106	37951	1373	22155
乌什县	Wushi [Uxturpan] County	14310	6211		8099
阿瓦提县	Awat County	39509	29142		10366
柯坪县	Kalpin County	4564	1861		2703
克孜勒苏柯尔克孜自治州	**Kizilsu Kirgiz Autonomous Prefecture**	**138669**	**126869**	**124136**	**11800**
阿图什市	Artux City	85049	78891	78891	6158
阿克陶县	Akto County	30160	25731	24581	4429
阿合奇县	Akqi County	9428	9001	9001	427
乌恰县	Wuqia [Ulugqat] County	14032	13246	11663	786
喀什地区	**Kashgar [Kaxgar] Administrative Offices**	**1312985**	**1050726**	**515344**	**262260**
喀什市	Kashgar [Kaxgar] City	595988	553788	488821	42200
疏附县	Shufu County	16327	8471		7856
疏勒县	Shule County	65227	51805	25828	13423
英吉沙县	Yengisar County	42010	25737		16273
泽普县	Zepu [Poskam] County	46012	32175		13837
莎车县	Shache [Yarkant] County	127586	87683	694	39903
叶城县	Yecheng [Kagilik] County	110161	71739		38422
麦盖提县	Makit County	88821	58761		30060
岳普湖县	Yopurga County	29349	21297		8052
伽师县	Jiashi [Payzawat] County	76198	55866	1	20332
巴楚县	Bachu [Maralbexi] County	102115	72798		29317
塔什库尔干塔吉克自治县	Taxkorgan Tajik Autonomous County	13192	10607		2585
和田地区	**Hotan Administrative Offices**	**285735**	**214799**	**108915**	**70937**
和田市	Hotan City	140922	128132	70118	12790
和田县	Hotan County	17999	398		17601
墨玉县	Moyu [Karakax] County	35137	24537	17468	10600
皮山县	Pishan [Guma] County	17801	6976	480	10824
洛浦县	Lop County	18604	14124		4480
策勒县	Qira County	20920	13542		7378
于田县	Yutian [Keriya] County	25208	19559	15770	5649
民丰县	Minfeng [Niya] County	9145	7530	5079	1615
生产建设兵团	**Xinjiang Production andConstruction Group**	**3856430**	**3471285**	**2345849**	**385145**

16-8 各地、州、市、县(市)社会消费品零售总额(按行业分)

Total Retail Sales of Consumer Goods by Sector and Prefecture, Autonomous Prefecture, City and County

单位：万元　　(2013 年)　　(10 000 yuan)

地　区	Region	社会消费品零售总额 Total Retail Sales of Consumer Goods	批发和零售业 Wholesale And Retail Sale Trades	住宿和餐饮业 Hotels and Catering Services
总　计	**Total**	**20391521**	**17779616**	**2611905**
乌鲁木齐市	**Urumqi City**	**8114713**	**7260748**	**853965**
#乌鲁木齐县	Urumqi County	70100	65740	4360
克拉玛依市	**Karamay City**	**535420**	**482504**	**52916**
吐鲁番地区	**TurpanAdministrative Offices**	**323433**	**287370**	**36063**
吐鲁番市	Turpan City	177705	163868	13837
鄯善县	Shanshan [piqan]County	107178	92000	15178
托克逊县	Toksun County	38550	31502	7048
哈密地区	**Hami [kumul]Administrative Offices**	**649170**	**532485**	**116685**
哈密市	Hami [kumul]City	580785	482626	98159
巴里坤哈萨克自治县	Barkol KazakAutonomous County	51455	38757	12698
伊吾县	Yiwu [Araturuk]County	16930	11102	5828
昌吉回族自治州	**Changji Hui Autonomous Prefecture**	**1822731**	**1502521**	**320210**
昌吉市	Changji City	758133	635615	122518
阜康市	Fukang City	251252	199114	52138
呼图壁县	Hutubi County	213601	172918	40683
玛纳斯县	Manas County	234812	194506	40306
奇台县	Qitai County	205979	167345	38634
吉木萨尔县	Jimsar County	98770	82474	16296
木垒哈萨克自治县	Mori Kazak Autonomous County	60184	50549	9635
伊犁哈萨克自治州	**Ili Kazak Autonomous Prefecture**	**2652888**	**2203339**	**449549**
伊犁州直属县(市)	**Counties (Cities) Direct Under Ili Prefecture**	**1553804**	**1297406**	**256398**
伊宁市	Yining [Gulja]City	587562	491307	96255
奎屯市	Kuytun City	211534	191385	20149
伊宁县	Yining [Gulja]County	121034	109148	11886
察布查尔锡伯自治县	Qapqal Xibe Autonomous County	26224	18982	7242
霍城县	Huocheng [korgas]County	169600	138883	30717
巩留县	Gongliu [Tokkuzlara]County	51047	41146	9901
新源县	Xinyuan [kunes]County	200800	164250	36550
昭苏县	Zhaosu [mongolkure]County	45403	38306	7097
特克斯县	Tekes County	77000	65194	11806
尼勒克县	Nilka County	63600	38805	24795
塔城地区	**Tacheng [Tarbagatai] Administrative Offices**	**608555**	**511883**	**96671**
塔城市	Tacheng [Qoqek] City	140832	116012	24820
乌苏市	Usu City	122283	99131	23151
额敏县	Emin [Dorbiljin] County	120606	110482	10123
沙湾县	Shawan County	135792	113340	22453
裕民县	Yumin [Qagantokay] County	25095	19882	5213
和布克赛尔蒙古自治县	Hoboksar Mongol Autonomous County	28618	22429	6189
托里县	Toli County	35329	30607	4722
阿勒泰地区	**Altay Administrative Offices**	**490529**	**394050**	**96479**
阿勒泰市	Altay City	207764	171648	36116
布尔津县	Burqin County	103574	68494	35080
富蕴县	Fuyun [Koktokay] County	53466	44864	8602
福海县	Fuhai [Burultokay] County	50219	43478	6741
哈巴河县	Habahe [Kaba] County	40591	35983	4608
青河县	Qinghe [Qinggil] County	25046	21543	3503
吉木乃县	Jeminay County	9869	8040	1829

16-8 续表 Continued

单位：万元 (10 000 yuan)

地　区	Region	社会消费品零售总额 Total Retail Sales of Consumer Goods	批发和零售业 Wholesale And Retail Sale Trades	住宿和餐饮业 Hotels and Catering Services
博尔塔拉蒙古自治州	**Bortala Mongol Autonomous Prefecture**	**296223**	**254206**	**42017**
博乐市	Bole [Bortala] City	223335	200695	22640
精河县	Jinghe [Jing] County	50885	34788	16097
温泉县	Wenquan [Araxang] County	22003	18723	3280
巴音郭楞蒙古自治州	**Bayangol Mongol Autonomous Prefecture**	**811872**	**721269**	**90603**
库尔勒市	Korla City	588238	537361	50877
轮台县	Luntai [Bugur] County	40500	31862	8638
尉犁县	Yuli [Lopnur] County	17996	12775	5221
若羌县	Ruoqiang [Qarkilik] County	7956	5665	2291
且末县	Qiemo [Qarqan] County	9568	6848	2720
焉耆回族自治县	Yanqi Hui Autonomous County	64788	61042	3746
和静县	Hejing County	40907	34032	6875
和硕县	Hoxud County	16685	10374	6311
博湖县	Bohu [Bagrax] County	25234	21310	3924
阿克苏地区	**Aksu Administrative Offices**	**980361**	**876425**	**103936**
阿克苏市	Aksu City	538387	515492	22895
温宿县	Wensu [Onsu] County	69301	64880	4421
库车县	Kuqa County	142890	109918	32972
沙雅县	Xayar County	78472	62345	16127
新和县	Xinhe [Toksu] County	32823	25558	7265
拜城县	Baicheng [Bay] County	60106	52692	7414
乌什县	Wushi [Uxturpan] County	14310	12548	1762
阿瓦提县	Awat County	39509	29061	10448
柯坪县	Kalpin County	4564	3932	632
克孜勒苏柯尔克孜自治州	**Kizilsu Kirgiz Autonomous Prefecture**	**138669**	**121630**	**17039**
阿图什市	Artux City	85049	78147	6902
阿克陶县	Akto County	30160	25197	4963
阿合奇县	Akqi County	9428	8018	1410
乌恰县	Wuqia [Ulugqat] County	14032	10268	3764
喀什地区	**Kashgar [Kaxgar] Administrative Offices**	**1312985**	**1144655**	**168331**
喀什市	Kashgar [Kaxgar] City	595988	569690	26298
疏附县	Shufu County	16327	12885	3442
疏勒县	Shule County	65227	53199	12028
英吉沙县	Yengisar County	42010	33012	8998
泽普县	Zepu [Poskam] County	46012	36684	9328
莎车县	Shache [Yarkant] County	127586	107611	19975
叶城县	Yecheng [Kagilik] County	110161	84418	25743
麦盖提县	Makit County	88821	70610	18211
岳普湖县	Yopurga County	29349	21338	8011
伽师县	Jiashi [Payzawat] County	76198	56770	19428
巴楚县	Bachu [Maralbexi] County	102115	85812	16302
塔什库尔干塔吉克自治县	Taxkorgan Tajik Autonomous County	13192	12625	567
和田地区	**Hotan Administrative Offices**	**285735**	**250140**	**35595**
和田市	Hotan City	140922	127968	12953
和田县	Hotan County	17999	13606	4393
墨玉县	Moyu [Karakax] County	35137	31964	3173
皮山县	Pishan [Guma] County	17801	16769	1032
洛浦县	Lop County	18604	15721	2883
策勒县	Qira County	20920	16562	4358
于田县	Yutian [Keriya] County	25208	19951	5257
民丰县	Minfeng [Niya] County	9145	7598	1547
生产建设兵团	**Production and Construction Group**	**3856430**	**3209068**	**647362**

16-9 限额以上批发企业资产及负债情况
Assets and Liabilities of Enterprises above Designated Size of Wholesale Trades

单位：万元 (2013 年) (10 000 yuan)

指标	Item	资产合计 Total Assets	#流动资产 Working Capitals	#固定资产 Fixed Assets	负债合计 Total Liabilities
总 计	**Total**	**20611906**	**15973610**	**1519438**	**16920235**
按登记注册类型分	**By Type of Registration**				
内资企业	Domestic Funded Enterprises	20542739	15917277	1511063	16864217
国有企业	State-owned Enterprises	3107601	2578400	242820	2275825
集体企业	Collective-owned Enterprises	301596	251017	36060	247912
联营企业	Joint Ownership Enterprises	966	674	237	275
集体联营企业	Collective Joint Ownership Enterprises	966	674	237	275
有限责任公司	Limited Liability Corporations	8493036	6569888	680579	6829161
国有独资公司	State Sole Funded Corporations	1610602	799027	182001	1368899
其他有限责任公司	Other Limited Liability Corporations	6882433	5770861	498578	5460262
股份有限公司	Share-holding Corporations Ltd.	4646559	3257181	270473	4518709
私营企业	Private Enterprises	3968841	3246995	270785	2982320
私营独资企业	Private-funded Enterprises	1139	1107	13	556
私营合伙企业	Private Partnership Enterprises	607	172	60	527
私营有限责任公司	Private Limited Liability Corporations	3772569	3115932	233807	2826015
私营股份有限公司	Private Share-holding Corporation Ltd.	194528	129784	36905	155221
其他企业	Other Enterprises	24140	13122	10109	10015
港、澳、台商投资企业	Enterprises With Funds from Hong Kong, Macao and Taiwan	4742	3876	834	27
港、澳、台商独资经营企业	Enterprises with Sole Funds from Hong Kong, Macao and Taiwan	4742	3876	834	27
外商投资企业	Foreign Funded Enterprises	64426	52457	7541	55991
中外合资经营企业	Enterprises with Foreign Investment	11637	10211	846	3224
外资企业	Enterprises with Sole Funds	52789	42246	6695	52767
按批发行业小类分组	**By Sector of Wholesale**				
农、林、牧产品批发	Wholesale of Farm Produce and Livestock Products	5850364	4879207	523798	4857237
谷物、豆及薯类批发	Wholesale of Grain,Bean and Potato	644203	511818	85845	542704
种子批发	Wholesale of Fodder	419920	283617	70875	235614
棉、麻批发	Wholesale of Cotton and Liner	4741840	4046777	362371	4044465
其他农牧产品批发	Wholesale of Other Farm Produce and Livestoclc Products	35250	29105	3968	28177
食品、饮料及烟草制品批发	Wholesale of Food,Beverages and Tobaccos	1491397	1143978	169644	671151
米、面制品及食用油批发	Wholesale of Rice, Flour and Edible Oil	286595	231957	40345	236276
糕点、糖果及糖批发	Wholesale of Pastry,Candy and Sugar	11778	9232	187	6709
果品、蔬菜批发业	Wholesale of Fruit and Vegetable	272181	176259	55076	211130
肉、禽、蛋及水产品批发	Wholesale of Meat,Birds and Equatic Products	15934	9838	3769	12333
盐及调味品批发	Wholesale of Salt and Condiment Flavoring Material	60443	27037	5733	33494
酒、饮料及茶叶批发	Wholesale of Soft Drink and Tea Leaf	44604	35657	2574	41319
烟草制品批发	Wholesale of Tobaccos	771619	638596	50948	111926
其他食品批发	Wholesale of Other Food	28242	15403	11013	17964
纺织、服装及日用品批发	Wholesale of Textitle, Garments and Daily Consumer Articles	179831	142268	30602	166639
纺织品、针织品及原料批发	Wholesale of Textile,Hosiery and Raw Material	73674	50830	21698	70846
服装批发	Wholesale of Garment	40895	37832	534	31845
化妆品及卫生用品批发	Wholesale of Cosmetics and Health Aids	11699	10176	1428	10737
家用电器批发	Wholesale of Household Elictric Appliances	31885	23930	5407	35659
其他家庭用品批发	Wholesale of Household Goods	21679	19501	1535	17552
文化、体育用品及器材批发	Wholesale of Culture, Sports Goods and Apparatus	157936	97320	20608	101652
图书批发	Wholesale of Books	123956	67688	18203	71911

16-9 续表 Continued

单位：万元 (10 000 yuan)

指　　标	Item	资产合计 Total Assets	#流动资产 Working Capitals	#固定资产 Fixed Assets	负债合计 Total Liabilities
首饰、工艺品及收藏品批发	Wholesale of wear、Jewellery、Handicraft、Collectim	6520	5555	965	5835
其他文化用品批发	Wholesale of Other Culture Products	27460	24076	1440	23906
医药及医疗器械批发	Wholesale of Medicines and Medical Appliances	420406	362341	39498	332395
西药批发	Wholesale of Western Medicine	391716	336411	37697	308516
中药批发	Wholesale of Chinese Medicinal Plant and Chinese Patent Medicine	22064	19539	1609	18524
医疗用品及器材批发	Wholesale of Medicine and Medical Appliances	6626	6391	192	5355
矿产品、建材及化工产品批发	Wholesale of Mineral Products, Building Material and Chemical Products	10726219	7822844	638727	9422035
煤炭及制品批发	Wholesale of Coal and Related Products	1743087	1021513	15602	953190
石油及制品批发	Wholesale of Petroleum and Related Products	5285603	3600662	469058	5443552
金属及金属矿批发	Wholesale of Metal and Metal Materials	2052857	1804030	23609	1676527
建材批发	Wholesale of Building Materials	294618	274725	3869	250811
化肥批发	Wholesale of Fertilizer	1147205	947763	118099	946944
农药批发	Wholesale of Pesticides	18133	13989	1675	12883
其他化工产品批发	Wholesale of Other Chemical Product	181851	157893	6228	135624
机械设备、五金交电及电子产品批发	Wholesale of Machinery, Hardware and Electronic Equipments	1613607	1388736	81095	1223551
农业机械批发	Wholesale of Agriculture Machinery	204132	168608	22068	156303
汽车批发	Wholesale of Motor Vehicles, Motorcycles and Parts	275043	244848	10063	199066
汽车零配件批发	Retail of Automobiles' Parts	358804	322148	19173	245166
摩托车及零配件批发	Retail of Motorcycle and Fittings	2431	2396	36	1647
五金产品批发	Wholesale of Hardware and Electromic Equipment	54443	51209	633	47611
电气设备批发	Wholesale of Household Electrical Appliances	43709	43673		42701
计算机、软件及辅助设备批发	Wholesale of Computer, Software and Accessory Equipment	24936	23246	1110	14104
通讯及广播电视设备批发	Wholesale of Communicating and Broadcasting Television Device	9766	8925	330	7352
其他机械设备及电子产品批发	Wholesale of Other Mechanical Equipment and Electronic Products	640343	523683	27682	509602
贸易经纪与代理	Trades Broker and Agent	84323	70988	5842	66683
贸易代理	Trades Broker and Agency	84323	70988	5842	66683
其他批发业	Wholesales of Others	87825	65929	9622	78891
再生物资回收与批发业	Recovery and Wholesale of Regeneration Material	66393	52153	4476	65190
其他未列明的批发业	Wholesale of Un-listed	21431	13776	5146	13701
按地区分	**By Region**				
乌鲁木齐市	Urumqi City	9330233	7766915	295826	6740674
克拉玛依市	Karamay City	821075	186901	92103	414187
吐鲁番地区	Turpan Administrative Offices	153565	125318	19972	115789
哈密地区	Hami [Kumul] Administrative Offices	391455	315172	43105	302414
昌吉回族自治州	Changji Hui Autonomous Prefecture	671720	481185	86769	675684
伊犁哈萨克自治州	Ili Kazak Autonomous Prefecture	1291266	925225	121542	1345530
伊犁州直属县(市)	Counties (Cities) Direct Under Ili Prefecture	741127	577037	78159	755783
塔城地区	Tacheng [Tarbagatai] Administrative Offices	494808	316359	24345	413017
阿勒泰地区	Altay Administrative Offices	55331	31829	19038	176731
博尔塔拉蒙古自治州	Bortala Mongol Autonomous Prefecture	218644	180721	15264	188190
巴音郭楞蒙古自治州	Bayangol Mongol Autonomous Prefecture	899311	657937	146369	1013539
阿克苏地区	Aksu Administrative Offices	1353609	1130912	134642	1350520
克孜勒苏柯尔克孜自治州	Kizilsu Kirgiz Autonomous Prefecture	49683	44612	3573	37334
喀什地区	Kashgar [Kaxgar] Administrative Offices	1003041	581006	126292	881722
和田地区	Hotan Administrative Offices	39035	23920	13346	30863
生产建设兵团	Production and Construction Group	4389270	3553788	420634	3823791

16-10 限额以上零售企业资产及负债情况
Assets and Liabilities of Enterprises above Designated Size of Retail Trades

单位：万元　　(2013 年)　　(10 000 yuan)

指　标	Item	资产合计 Total Asset	#流动资产 Working Capitals	#固定资产 Fixed Asset	负债合计 Total Liabilities
总　计	**Total**	**5135791**	**3470618**	**790900**	**3988287**
按登记注册类型分	**By Status of Registration**				
内资企业	Domestic funded Enterprises	4349162	3045831	729286	3587594
国有企业	State-owned Enterprises	218907	112305	63146	106543
集体企业	Collective-owned Enterprises	4581	3289	807	3518
股份合作企业	Share-holding Cooperative Enterprises	1389	705	480	773
有限责任公司	Limited Liability Corporations	1294156	989900	167199	925749
国有独资公司	State Sole Funded Corporations	19882	14629	1420	16128
其他有限责任公司	Other Limited Liability Corporations	1274275	975271	165780	909622
股份有限公司	Share-holding Corporations Ltd.	772411	349913	237191	995444
私营企业	Private Enterprises	2056476	1588486	260455	1554651
私营独资企业	Private-funded Enterprises	405	361	8	472
私营有限责任公司	Private Limited Liability Corporations	2037622	1571434	259441	1541137
私营股份有限公司	Private Share-holding Corporation Ltd.	17625	16214	787	12450
其他企业	Others	1241	1233	8	917
港、澳、台投资企业	Enterprises With Funds from Hong Kong, Macao and Taiwan	691442	350036	46234	338979
港、澳、台商独资经营企业	Enterprises with Sole Funds from Hong Kong, Macao and Taiwan	48792	34687	7869	30267
外商投资企业	Foreign Funded Enterprises	95187	74751	15381	61714
中外合资经营企业	Enterprises with Foreign Investment	67695	53243	12667	47074
外资企业	Enterprises with Sole Fund	27493	21508	2714	14640
按零售行业小类分组	**By Sector of Retail**				
综合零售	Integrated Retail	1307700	726309	324492	1052950
百货零售	Retail of Merchandile	1128669	595855	290552	915703
超级市场零售	Retail of Supermarket	178801	130254	33940	137183
其他综合零售	Retail of other integrate	230	201		64
食品、饮料及烟草制品专门零售	Monopoly Retail of Foods, Beverages and Tobacco	38800	28869	2864	40058
粮油零售	Retail of Grain and Oil	12964	12377	575	13959
果品、蔬菜零售	Retail of Fruit and Vegetables	7241	3352	1107	5024
肉、禽、蛋及水产品零售	Retail of Meat,Poultry and Eggs	888	875	12	27
酒、饮料及茶叶零售	Retail of Soft Drink and Tea Leaf	10984	9591	802	17334
烟草制品零售	Retail of Tobauos	6724	2674	368	3715
纺织、服装及日用品专门零售	Monopoly Retail of Textile, Garments and Daily Consumer Articles	240725	141336	54293	215251
服装零售	Garment Retail	200523	123864	35161	186778
钟表、眼镜零售	Retail of Timekeeper and Spectacle	7345	6332	42	6616
其他日用品零售	Retail of Other Covenience Goods	32773	11084	19059	21856
文化、体育用品及器材专门零售业	Monopoly Retail of Cultural, Sports Appliances And Equipments	248009	150973	57084	114142
文具用品零售	Retail of Stationery and Office Supplies	2863	2841	22	1720
图书、报刊零售	Retail of Books	174945	80797	55312	80062

16-10 续表 Continued

单位：万元 (10 000 yuan)

指　　标	Item	资产合计 Total Assets	#流动资产 Working Capitals	#固定资产 Fixed Assets	负债合计 Total Liabilities
珠宝首饰零售	Retail of Jewelry	69983	67120	1747	32097
照相器材零售	Retail of Photographic Materials	219	216	3	264
医药及医疗器材专门零售	Monopoly Retail of Medicine and Medical-care Apparatus	528159	469123	37976	366115
药品零售	Retail of Medcine	527178	468207	37911	365234
医疗用品及器材零售	Wholesale of Medical Treatment and Equipment	981	916	65	882
汽车、摩托车、燃料及零配件专门零售	Monopoly Retail of Car, Motor, Fuel and Parts as Well as Components	2221173	1497282	264590	1865475
汽车零售	Retail of Car	1337225	1064942	158203	1027488
汽车零配件零售	Retail of Automobiles' Accessories	5877	4440	582	4473
摩托车及零配件零售	Retail of Motorcycle and Fittings	14472	14009	460	11581
机动车燃料零售	Retail of Auto Fuel	863599	413891	105345	821932
家用电器及电子产品专门零售	Monopoly Retail of House hold Electric Appliancesound Electronic Products	233518	223219	4002	188427
家用视听设备零售	Retail of Electric Appliances	142973	138401	857	130963
日用家电设备零售	Retail of Household Electric Equipment	40296	37531	1851	27367
计算机、软件及辅助设备零售	Retail of Cumputers,Software and Office Appliances	32580	30290	1038	17024
通讯设备零售	Retail of Telecommunication Equipments	17669	16997	256	13073
五金、家具及室内装修材料专门零售	Monopoly Retail of Hardware, Furniture and Indoor Decorating Material	281310	213557	34460	122894
五金零售	Retail of Hardware	5230	5135	95	3654
家具零售	Retail of Living equipment	276080	208422	34365	119240
货摊、无店铺及其他零售业	Retail of Storeless and others	36397	19950	11140	22976
邮购及电视、电话零售	Distribution of Post and E-commerce	4366	2709	114	4102
生活用燃料零售业	Retail of Life Fueis	32031	17242	11025	18874
按地区分	**By Region**				
乌鲁木齐市	Urumqi City	3771014	2525217	558772	2978491
克拉玛依市	Karamay City	132098	103720	15026	117451
吐鲁番地区	Turpan Administrative Offices	19347	12319	5217	15137
哈密地区	Hami [Kumul] Administrative Offices	138879	82931	21017	97086
昌吉回族自治州	Changji Hui Autonomous Prefecture	144630	102641	16818	112049
伊犁哈萨克自治州	Ili Kazak Autonomous Prefecture	247161	178879	35749	180389
伊犁州直属县(市)	Counties (Cities) Direct Under Ili Prefecture	217402	163243	25100	162162
塔城地区	Tacheng [Tarbagatai] Administrative Offices	21820	11168	7994	13116
阿勒泰地区	Altay Administrative Offices	7939	4468	2655	5111
博尔塔拉蒙古自治州	Bortala Mongol Autonomous Prefecture	9710	5365	1991	7892
巴音郭楞蒙古自治州	Bayangol Mongol Autonomous Prefecture	171859	131080	20147	142073
阿克苏地区	Aksu Administrative Offices	221021	139856	58462	174846
克孜勒苏柯尔克孜自治州	Kizilsu Kirgiz Autonomous Prefecture	4321	1757	1508	2508
喀什地区	Kashgar [Kaxgar] Administrative Offices	106637	76771	18940	78804
和田地区	Hotan Administrative Offices	12023	8916	2234	4573
生产建设兵团	Production and Construction Group	157090	101165	35021	76989

16-11 限额以上餐饮企业资产及负债情况
Assets and Liabilities of Enterprises above Designated Size of Catering Services

单位：万元 (2013 年) (10 000 yuan)

指 标	Item	资产合计 Total Asset	#流动资产 Working Capitals	#固定资产 Fixed Asset	负债合计 Total Liabilities
总 计	**Total**	**240024**	**75988**	**110746**	**159229**
按登记注册类型分	**By Status of Registration**				
内资企业	Domestic-funded Enterprises	233000	74720	109522	156008
国有企业	State – owned Enterprises	54298	9762	41215	9571
集体企业	Collective-owned Enterprises	15	9	6	43
有限责任公司	Limited Liability Corporations	50948	12073	33196	54229
国有独资公司	Enterprise with Sole Funds	3083	359	2724	172
其他有限责任公司	Other Limited Liability Corporations	47865	11714	30472	54057
股份有限公司	Share-holding Corporations Ltd.	26626	14361	2622	13579
私营企业	Private Enterprises	101057	38466	32477	78476
私营独资企业	Private-funded Enterprises	14072	5307	2852	13396
私营合伙企业	Private Partnership Enterprises	4031	2885	589	666
私营有限责任公司	Private Limited Liability Corporations	82708	30082	28982	64221
其他企业	Others	56	49	7	110
外商投资企业	Foreign Funded Enterprises	7025	1269	1224	3222
外资企业	Enterprises with Sole Fund	7025	1269	1224	3222
按餐饮行业小类分组	**By Sector of Catering**				
正餐服务	Dinner	215682	69034	101805	150800
快餐服务	Snack	24342	6954	8941	8429
按地区分	**By Region**				
乌鲁木齐市	Urumqi City	90076	24285	49311	35956
克拉玛依市	Karamay City	1199	1165	33	943
吐鲁番地区	Turpan Administrative Offices	15	9	6	43
哈密地区	Hami [Kumul] Administrative Offices	1163	758	291	921
昌吉回族自治州	Changji Hui Autonomous Prefecture	2779	1028	582	1657
伊犁哈萨克自治州直属县(市)	Ili Kazak Autonomous Prefecture	74889	14205	44729	74266
巴音郭楞蒙古自治州	Bayangol Mongol Autonomous Prefecture	19342	10843	5534	14155
阿克苏地区	Aksu Administrative Offices	17921	6438	5128	13401
喀什地区	Kashgar [Kaxgar] Administrative Offices	246	192	54	192
生产建设兵团	Production and Construction Group	32394	17065	5079	17696

16-12 限额以上住宿企业资产及负债情况
Assets and Liabilities of Enterprises above Designated Size of Accommodation Services

单位：万元 (2013 年) (10 000 yuan)

指 标	Item	资产合计 Total Assets	#流动资产 Working Capitals	#固定资产 Fixed Assets	负债合计 Total Liabilities
总 计	**Total**	**1141549**	**354731**	**453043**	**824401**
按登记注册类型分	**By Status of Registration**				
内资企业	Domestic-funded Enterprises	1136776	354216	448940	821185
国有企业	State-owned Enterprises	234309	70455	120322	116798
集体企业	Collective-owned Enterprises	46770	2492	2626	47818
联营企业	Joint Ounership Enterprises	2358	1467	891	1250
国有联营企业	State Ounership Enterprises	2358	1467	891	1250
有限责任公司	Limited Liability Corporations	548029	164781	214266	395804
国有独资公司	State Sole Funded Corporations	23145	7802	13309	17207
其他有限责任公司	Other Limited Liability Corporations	524884	156979	200958	378597
股份有限公司	Share-holding Corporations Ltd.	22856	4916	9445	14511
私营企业	Private Enterprises	282061	110027	101089	244816
私营独资企业	Private-funded Enterprises	19621	6971	11686	12819
私营合伙企业	Private Partnership Enterprises	3643	399	2847	4320
私营有限责任公司	Private Limited Liability Corporations	252995	99742	83668	225453
私营股份有限公司	Private Limited Liability Corporations	5802	2915	2888	2224
其他企业	Others	394	81	300	188
港、澳、台商投资企业	Enterprises With Funds from Hong Kong, Macao and Taiwan	509	80	419	79
合资经营企业（港或澳、台资）	Joint-venture Enterprises (Funds from Hong Kong, Macao and Taiwan)	509	80	419	79
外商投资企业	Foreign funded Enterprises	4264	435	3684	3138
外资企业	Enterprises with Sole Foreign Fund	4264	435	3684	3138
按住宿行业分组	**By Sector of**				
旅游饭店	Tourist Hotel	1058158	324081	410323	769143
一般旅馆	Ordinary Hotel	83391	30650	42720	55258
按星级等级分	**Classified by Stars**				
五 星	Five-Star	261974	85307	165210	193309
四 星	Four-Star	258352	112684	109369	188625
三 星	Three-Star	389394	102664	135146	245765
二 星	Two-Star	38387	15616	10993	22438
一 星	One-Star	652	163	289	520
其 他	Other	192789	38298	32037	173744
按地区分	**By Region**				
乌鲁木齐市	Urumqi City	448473	177508	168002	303026
克拉玛依市	Karamay City	45948	3356	41729	55631
吐鲁番地区	Turpan Administrative Offices	33466	13582	7561	30053
哈密地区	Hami [Kumul] Administrative Offices	43254	8260	24372	19471
昌吉回族自治州	Changji Hui Autonomous Prefecture	12290	5174	6383	11568
伊犁哈萨克自治州	Ili Kazak Autonomous Prefecture	136328	40447	55807	78568
伊犁州直属县(市)	Counties (Cities) Direct Under Ili Prefecture	60768	21196	19643	38608
塔城地区	Tacheng [Tarbagatai] Administrative Offices	18137	5776	8742	13610
阿勒泰地区	Altay Administrative Offices	57423	13475	27422	26349
博尔塔拉蒙古自治州	Bortala Mongol Autonomous Prefecture	6745	2785	3357	3454
巴音郭楞蒙古自治州	Bayangol Mongol Autonomous Prefecture	70992	18950	46434	63474
阿克苏地区	Aksu Administrative Offices	57782	13772	31112	46308
克孜勒苏柯尔克孜自治州	Kizilsu Kirgiz Autonomous Prefecture	6906	808	5897	3746
喀什地区	Kashgar [Kaxgar] Administrative Offices	179245	37048	13348	161437
和田地区	Hotan Administrative Offices	11412	2420	5797	3364
生产建设兵团	Production and Construction Group	88709	30622	43244	44301

16-13 限额以上批发企业主要财务指标
Main Financial Indicators of Wholesale Enterprises above Designated Size

单位：万元 (2013 年) (10 000 yuan)

指标	Item	商品销售收入 Revenue of Product Sales	商品销售成本 Cost of Product Sales	商品销售税金及附加 Sales Tax and Extra Changes	商品销售利润 Profits of Product Sales
总计	**Total**	**64340308**	**62331857**	**114135**	**1894316**
按登记注册类型分	**By Status of Registration**				
内资企业	Domesticfunded Enterprises	64274686	62271167	114090	1889429
国有企业	State-owned Enterprises	8784953	8335189	65599	384166
集体企业	Collective-owned Enterprises	419318	393083	474	25762
联营企业	Joint Ounership Enterprises	3754	3716	1	37
集体联营企业	Collective Joint Ounership Enterprises	3754	3716	1	37
有限责任公司	Limited Liability Corporations	27638239	26917901	31866	688472
国有独资公司	State Sole Funded Corporations	2938060	2774314	22469	141277
其他有限责任公司	Other Limited Liability Corporations	24700179	24143587	9398	547195
股份有限公司	Share-holding Corporations Ltd.	20445093	20026724	9729	408640
私营企业	Private Enterprises	6956419	6571341	6421	378657
私营独资企业	Private-funded Enterprises	5870	5855	1	15
私营合伙企业	Private Partnership Enterprises	2612	2476	3	133
私营有限责任公司	Private Limited Liability Corporations	6687091	6326111	6240	354739
私营股份有限公司	Private Share-holding Corporation Ltd.	260846	236898	177	23771
其他企业	Other Enterprises	26909	23214		3695
港、澳、台商投资企业	Enterprises With Funds from Hong Kong, Macao and Taiwan	6744	6329		415
港、澳、台商独资经营企业	Enterprises with Sole Funds from Hong Kong, Macao and Taiwan	6744	6329		415
外商投资企业	Foreign funded Enterprises	58879	54361	45	4473
中外合资经营企业	Enterprises with Foreign Investment	7175	6376	9	790
外资企业	Enterprises with Sole Fund	51704	47985	36	3683
按批发行业小类分组	**By Sector of Wholesale**				
农、林、牧产品批发	Wholesale of Farm Produce and Livestock Products	11287426	10901399	2749	383278
谷物、豆及薯类批发	Wholesale of Grain,Bean and Potato	487770	450951	229	36591
种子批发	Wholesale of Seed and Fodder	284261	226099	154	58009
棉、麻批发	Wholesale of Cotton and Lliner	10462822	10175087	2348	285388
其他农牧产品批发	Wholesale of Other Farm Produce and Livestoclc Products	37462	35716	17	1729
食品、饮料及烟草制品批发	Wholesale of Food,Beverages and Tobaccos	3314816	2888180	84385	342251
米、面制品及食用油批发	Wholesale of Rice, Flour and Edible Oil	263138	251357	400	11381
糕点、糖果及糖批发	Wholesale of Pastry,Candy and Sugar	17727	15477	15	2235
果品、蔬菜批发	Wholesale of Fruit and Vegetable	188057	164780	175	23102
肉、禽、蛋及水产品批发	Wholesale of Meat,Birds and Equatic Products	61613	54016	128	7470
盐及调味品批发	Wholesale of Salt and Condiment Flavoring Material	43842	33131	169	10542
酒、饮料及茶叶批发	Wholesale of Soft Drink and Tea Leaf	63682	49792	328	13563
烟草制品批发	Wholesale of Tobaccos	2656492	2301798	83125	271570
其他食品批发	Wholesale of Other Food	20264	17830	46	2388
纺织、服装及家庭用品批发	Wholesale of Textitle, Garments and Daily Consumer Articles	368237	339034	427	28776
纺织品、针织品及原料批发	Wholesale of Textile,Hosiery and Raw Material	137695	133599	26	4069
服装批发	Wholesale of Garment	81663	69035	196	12431
化妆品及卫生用品批发	Wholesale of Cosmetics and Health Aids	34508	31695	39	2775
家用电器批发	Wholesale of Electrical Appliances	70137	64465	109	5563
其他家庭用品批发	Wholesale of Other Covenience Goods	44235	40240	56	3939
文化、体育用品及器材批发	Wholesale of Culture, Sports Goods and Apparatus	153631	137870	454	15306
图书批发	Wholesale of Books	108607	95559	362	12686

16-13 续表 Continued

单位：万元 (10 000 yuan)

指　　标	Item	商品销售收入 Revenue of Product Sales	商品销售成本 Cost of Product Sales	商品销售税金及附加 Sales Tax and Extra Changes	商品销售利润 Product Sales Profits
首饰、工艺品及收藏品批发	Wholesale of wear、Jewellery、Handicraft、Collectim	3922	3639	50	234
其他文化用品批发	Wholesale of Other Culture Products	41101	38672	43	2386
医药及医疗器械批发	Wholesale of Medicines and Medical Appliances	707480	651170	940	55370
西药批发	Wholesale of Western Medicine	670318	618223	880	51215
中药批发	Wholesale of Chinese Medicinal Plant and Chinese Patent Medicine	28732	26048	46	2637
医疗用品及器材批发	Wholesale of Medicine and Medical Appliances	8430	6899	14	1518
矿产品、建材及化工产品批发	Wholesale of Mineral Products, Building Material and Chemical Products	45722516	44794052	21621	906844
煤炭及制品批发	Wholesale of Coal and Related Products	479070	412063	2470	64537
石油及制品批发	Wholesale of Petroleum and Related Products	36999060	36395760	14499	588801
金属及金属矿批发	Wholesale of Metal and Metal Materials	5133236	5008231	3225	121780
建材批发	Wholesale of Building Materials	667743	647107	460	20176
化肥批发	Wholesale of Fertilizer	1607369	1532286	310	74774
农药批发	Wholesale of Pesticides	21489	18673		2816
其他化工产品批发	Wholesale of Other Chemical Product	809588	776154	615	32820
机械设备、五金交电及电子产品批发	Wholesale of Machinery, Hardware and Electronic Equipments	2537469	2391418	2609	143442
农业机械批发	Wholesale of Agriculture Machinery	192473	185975	77	6422
汽车批发	Wholesale of Motor Vehicles	372320	346834	845	24642
汽车零配件批发	Wholesale of Motor Vehicles Parts	495584	468364	537	26683
摩托车及零配件批发	Wholesale of Motorcycles	9094	8336	20	738
五金产品批发	Wholesale of Hardware and Electromic Equipment	112893	103152	21	9720
电气设备批发	Wholesale of Electric Equipments	55967	54814	25	1128
计算机、软件及辅助设备批发	Wholesale of Computer, Software and Accessory Equipment	73618	68750	134	4735
通讯及广播电视设备批发	Wholesale of Communicating and Broadcasting Television Device	24194	23213	20	960
其他机械设备及电子产品批发	Wholesale of Other Mechanical Equipment and Electromic Products	1201327	1131981	930	68415
贸易经纪与代理	Trades Broker and Agent	89799	87416	351	2032
贸易代理	Trades Agent	89799	87416	351	2032
其他批发业	Wholesales of Others	158934	141319	598	17017
再生物资回收与批发业	Recovery and Wholesale of Regeneration Material	106653	101543	387	4723
其他未列明的批发业	Wholesale of Un-listed	52282	39776	211	12295
按地区分	**By Region**				
乌鲁木齐市	Urumqi City	39321589	38467063	41676	812850
克拉玛依市	Karamay City	1024107	943507	4145	76454
吐鲁番地区	Turpan Administrative Offices	489935	457421	3093	29421
哈密地区	Hami [Kumul] Administrative Offices	1016421	951276	5075	60070
昌吉回族自治州	Changji Hui Autonomous Prefecture	1018033	932173	8538	77322
伊犁哈萨克自治州	Ili Kazak Autonomous Prefecture	3472044	3329744	17108	125192
伊犁州直属县(市)	Counties (Cities) Direct Under Ili Prefecture	2610073	2528569	8012	73492
塔城地区	Tacheng [Tarbagatai] Administrative Offices	592621	558485	6081	28055
阿勒泰地区	Altay Administrative Offices	269350	242690	3015	23645
博尔塔拉蒙古自治州	Bortala Mongol Autonomous Prefecture	1077687	1037608	2480	37599
巴音郭楞蒙古自治州	Bayangol Mongol Autonomous Prefecture	2373777	2242038	9163	122577
阿克苏地区	Aksu Administrative Offices	2230421	2090258	8819	131344
克孜勒苏柯尔克孜自治州	Kizilsu Kirgiz Autonomous Prefecture	54475	50086	50	4340
喀什地区	Kashgar [Kaxgar] Administrative Offices	1753019	1657762	8437	86819
和田地区	Hotan Administrative Offices	212626	195733	2337	14556
生产建设兵团	Production and Construction Group	10296176	9977188	3294	315694

16-14 限额以上零售企业主要财务指标
Main Financial Indicators of Retail Enterprises above Designated Size

单位：万元　　(2013 年)　　(10 000 yuan)

指　　标	Item	商品销售收　　入 Revenue of Product Sales	商品销售成　　本 Cost of Product Sales	商品销售税金及附加 Sales Tax and Extra Changes	商品销售利　　润 Product Sales Profits
总　计	**Total**	**7414189**	**6582239**	**30586**	**801364**
按登记注册类型分	**By Status of Registration**				
内资企业	Domestic Funded Enterprises	6993559	6227032	28433	738095
国有企业	State-owned Enterprises	185848	138757	817	46275
集体企业	Collective-owned Enterprises	6620	5726	40	854
股份合作企业	Share-holding Cooperative Enterprises	1444	1289	1	154
有限责任公司	Limited Liability Corporations	2592314	2396325	6583	189405
国有独资公司	State Sole Funded Corporations	16948	12459	116	4374
其他有限责任公司	Other Limited Liability Corporations	2575366	2383867	6468	185031
股份有限公司	Share-holding Corporations Ltd.	1128285	999547	8503	120235
私营企业	Private Enterprises	3075988	2682538	12485	380964
私营独资企业	Private-funded Enterprises	506	423	2	81
私营有限责任公司	Private Limited Liability Corporations	735	651	6	78
私营股份有限公司	Private Share-holding Corporation Ltd.	3042048	2651285	12442	378321
其他企业	Others	3060	2850	3	207
港、澳、台投资企业	Enterprises With Funds from Hong Kong, Macao and Taiwan	192018	158802	692	32524
港、澳、台商独资经营企业	Enterprises with Sole Funds from Hong Kong, Macao and Taiwan	149983	131283	667	18034
外商投资企业	Foreign funded Enterprises	228612	196405	1461	30746
中外合资经营企业	Enterprises with Foreign Investment	176859	153279	1120	22460
外资企业	Enterprises with Sole Fund	51753	43126	341	8286
按零售行业小类分组	**By Sector of Retail**				
综合零售	Integrated Retail	1431307	1204474	15825	211008
百货零售	Retail of General Merchandise	1108505	923748	14438	170319
超级市场零售	Retail of Supermarket	322673	280603	1387	40683
其他综合零售	Retail of Other Integrate	129	123		6
食品、饮料及烟草制品专门零售	Monopoly Retail of Foods, Beverages and Tobacco	13816	13031	37	748
粮油零售	Retail of Grain and Oil	3250	3626		-376
果品、蔬菜零售	Retail of Fruite and Vegetables	1088	878	2	208
肉、禽、蛋及水产品零售	Retail of Meat,Poultry and Eggs	198	121		77
酒、饮料及茶叶零售	Retail of Soft Drink and Tea Leaf	5455	5034	24	398
烟草制品零售	Retail of Tobaccos	3824	3372	12	441
纺织、服装及日用品专门零售	Monopoly Retail of Textile, Garments and Daily Consumer Articles	309282	253627	3362	52294
服装零售	Garment Retail	249475	202507	2771	44197
钟表、眼镜零售	Retail of Timelceeper and Spectacle	12781	10942	67	1772
其他日用品零售	Retail of other Covenience Goods	46515	39678	524	6313
文化、体育用品及器材专门零售	Monopoly Retail of Cultural, Sports Goods And Apparatus	179137	124815	1219	53103
文具用品零售	Retail of Stationery and Office Supplies	3923	3588	6	329
图书、报刊零售业	Retail of Books	148612	111279	548	36786

16-14 续表 Continued

单位：万元 (10 000 yuan)

指　　标	Item	商品销售收　入 Revenue of Product Sales	商品销售成　本 Cost of Product Sales	商品销售税金及附加 Sales Taxes and Extra Changes	商品销售利　润 Product Sales Profits
珠宝首饰零售	Retail of Bijouterie	26568	9926	665	15977
照相器材零售	Retail of Photographic Materials	34	22	1	11
医药及医疗器材专门零售	Monopoly Retail of Medicine and Medical-care Apparatus	763511	689594	2146	71772
药品零售	Retail of Medcine	760449	687097	2135	71217
医疗用品及器材零售	Wholesale of Medical Treatment and Equipment	3062	2497	11	555
汽车、摩托车、燃料及零配件专门零售	Monopoly Retail of Car, Motor, Fuel and Parts as Well as Components	4080969	3809449	5220	266300
汽车零售	Retail of Automobiles	2931453	2735773	4132	191548
汽车零配件零售	Retail of Automobiles' Parts	6398	5508	13	877
摩托车及零配件零售	Retail of Motorcycle and Fittings	17132	15776	15	1341
机动车燃料零售	Retail of Auto Fuel	1125986	1052392	1060	72534
家用电器及电子产品专门零售	Monopoly Retail of House hold Electric Appliancesound Electronic Products	430943	386542	898	43503
家用视听设备零售	Retail of Electric Appliances	239226	213220	564	25442
日用家电设备零售	Retail of Household Elctric Appliances	90576	81030	156	9390
计算机、软件及辅助设备零售	Retail of Cumputers,Software and Office Appliances	61445	56807	99	4539
通讯设备零售	Retail of Telecommunication Equipments	39697	35485	80	4132
五金、家具及室内装修材料专门零售	Monopoly Retail of Hardware, Furniture and Indoor Decorating Material	171747	74755	1533	95460
五金零售	Retail of Hardware	8583	8112	9	463
家具零售	Retail of Living Equipment	163164	66643	1524	94997
货摊、无店铺及其他零售业	Retail of Storeless and Others	33475	25953	346	7177
邮购及电视、电话零售	Distribution of Post and E-commerce	6363	6183	13	167
生活用燃料零售	Retail of Life Fuels	27112	19770	333	7010
按地区分	**By Region**				
乌鲁木齐市	Urumqi City	5013195	4409093	22679	581424
克拉玛依市	Karamay City	241977	219478	909	21589
吐鲁番地区	Turpan Administrative Offices	22243	18465	66	3712
哈密地区	Hami [Kumul] Administrative Offices	149792	134116	281	15395
昌吉回族自治州	Changji Hui Autonomous Prefecture	223056	201740	1141	20176
伊犁哈萨克自治州	Ili Kazak Autonomous Prefecture	357322	315862	1248	40213
伊犁州直属县(市)	Counties (Cities) Direct Under Ili Prefecture	317661	283357	1062	33242
塔城地区	Tacheng [Tarbagatai] Administrative Offices	29262	23919	143	5200
阿勒泰地区	Altay Administrative Offices	10399	8586	42	1770
博尔塔拉蒙古自治州	Bortala Mongol Autonomous Prefecture	17853	15535	126	2192
巴音郭楞蒙古自治州	Bayangol Mongol Autonomous Prefecture	319430	290489	1141	27800
阿克苏地区	Aksu Administrative Offices	266199	237063	1254	27882
克孜勒苏柯尔克孜自治州	Kizilsu Kirgiz Autonomous Prefecture	4381	3613	10	757
喀什地区	Kashgar [Kaxgar] Administrative Offices	164096	147043	343	16710
和田地区	Hotan Administrative Offices	17909	14959	62	2888
生产建设兵团	Production and Construction Group	616736	574785	1324	40627

16-15 限额以上餐饮企业主要财务指标

Main Financial Indicators of Catering Enterprises above Designated Size

单位：万元 (2013 年) (10 000 yuan)

指　标	Item	主营业务收入 Revenue from Principal Business	主营业务成本 Cost of Principal Business	主营业务税金及附加 Tax and Addition of Major Business	主营业务利润 Profit From Principal Business
总　计	**Total**	**120727**	**59184**	**6319**	**55223**
按登记注册类型分	**By Status of Registration**				
内资企业	Domestic-funded Enterprises	95409	46892	4902	43615
国有企业	State – owned Enterprises	10144	6253	305	3587
集体企业	Collective-owned Enterprises	196	181	11	4
有限责任公司	Limited Liability Corporations	20867	9221	1124	10521
国有独资公司	State Sole Funded Corporations	819	429	62	328
其他有限责任公司	Other Limited Liability Corporations	20048	8792	1062	10193
股份有限公司	Share-holding Corporations Ltd	1440	316	52	1072
私营企业	Private Enterprises	61365	30513	3332	27521
私营独资企业	Private-funded Enterprises	5077	3474	317	1286
私营合伙企业	Private Partnership Enterprises	2833	1236	133	1464
私营有限责任公司	Private Limited Liability Corporations	52523	25315	2849	24359
其他企业	Others	1397	408	78	911
外商投资企业	Foreign Funded Enterprises	25318	12292	1417	11608
外资企业	Enterprises with Sole Fund	25318	12292	1417	11608
按餐饮行业小类分组	**By Sector of Catering**				
正餐服务	Dinner	78165	39806	3959	34401
快餐服务	Snack	42561	19378	2360	20823
按地区分	**By Region**				
乌鲁木齐市	Urumqi City	70981	34673	3686	32621
克拉玛依市	Karamay City	1938	969	34	935
吐鲁番地区	Turpan Administrative Offices	196	181	11	4
哈密地区	Hami [Kumul] Administrative Offices	486	141	28	317
昌吉回族自治州	Changji Hui Autonomous Prefecture	1170	1157	10	3
伊犁哈萨克自治州直属县(市)	Ili Kazak Autonomous Prefecture	22758	9331	1290	12138
巴音郭楞蒙古自治州	Bayangol Mongol Autonomous Prefecture	13713	7316	828	5569
阿克苏地区	Aksu Administrative Offices	2818	1811	242	765
喀什地区	Kashgar [Kaxgan] Administratine Offices	932	488	33	412
生产建设兵团	Production and Construction Group	5735	3118	157	2460

16-16 限额以上住宿企业主要财务指标
Main Financial Indicators of Hotels Enterprises above Designated

单位：万元　　(2013 年)　　(10 000 yuan)

指　标	Item	主营业务收入 Revenue from Principal Business	主营业务成本 Cost of Principal Business	主营业务税金及附加 Tax and Addition of Principal Business	主营业务利润 Profit From Principal Business
总　计	**Total**	**338554**	**164036**	**18668**	**155850**
按登记注册类型分	**By Status of Registration**				
内资企业	Domestic-funded Enterprises	336983	163789	18572	154622
国有企业	State-owned Enterprises	102770	51559	5595	45615
集体企业	Collective-owned Enterprises	7872	2557	385	4930
联营企业	Joint Ownership Enterprises	196	19	36	141
国有联营企业	State Joint Ownership Enterprises	196	19	36	141
有限责任公司	Limited Liability Corporations	133890	73508	7250	53133
国有独资公司	State Sole Funded Corporations	12634	4237	711	7687
其他有限责任公司	Other Limited Liability Corporations	121256	69271	6539	45446
股份有限公司	Share-holding Corporations Ltd.	6118	3729	344	2045
私营企业	Private Enterprises	85813	32231	4935	48647
私营独资企业	Private-funded Enterprises	12020	2224	711	9085
私营合伙企业	Private Partnership Enterprises	1231	311	68	852
私营有限责任公司	Private Limited Liability Corporation	70840	28256	4047	38538
私营股份有限公司	Private Share-holding Corporation Ltd.	1722	1440	109	172
其他企业	Others	324	187	27	110
港、澳、台商投资企业	Enterprises With Funds from Hong Kong, Macao and Taiwan	283	4	16	263
合资经营企业（港或澳、台资）	Joint-venture Enterprises (Funds from Hong Kong, Macao and Taiwan)	283	4	16	263
外商投资企业	Foreign Funded Enterprises	1288	243	80	965
外资企业	Enterprises with Sole Fund	1288	243	80	965
按住宿行业小类分组	**By Sector of National Economic**				
旅游饭店	Tourist Hotel	299677	138219	16276	145181
一般旅馆	Ordinary Hotel	38877	25817	2392	10669
按星级等级分	**Classified by Stars**				
五　星	Five-Star	75197	48516	3950	22731
四　星	Four-Star	92170	39158	5096	47917
三　星	Three-Star	110370	51986	6409	51975
二　星	Two-Star	18236	6118	907	11211
一　星	One-Star	209	79	20	111
其　他	Other	42371	18179	2287	21906
按地区分	**By Region**				
乌鲁木齐市	Urumqi City	164023	74262	9172	80589
克拉玛依市	Karamay City	9323	9411	522	-610
吐鲁番地区	Turpan Administrative Offices	5807	2338	491	2978
哈密地区	Hami [Kumul] Administrative Offices	23179	11429	931	10819
昌吉回族自治州	Changji Hui Autonomous Prefecture	6244	3278	323	2643
伊犁哈萨克自治州	Ili Kazak Autonomous Prefecture	36180	21064	2156	12961
伊犁州直属县(市)	Counties (Cities) Direct Under Ili Prefecture	18658	10316	1129	7213
塔城地区	Tacheng [Tarbagatai] Administrative Offices	5904	3963	384	1557
阿勒泰地区	Altay Administrative Offices	11619	6784	643	4192
博尔塔拉蒙古自治州	Bortala Mongol Autonomous Prefecture	4119	2410	211	1498
巴音郭楞蒙古自治州	Bayangol Mongol Autonomous Prefecture	24279	8609	1348	14322
阿克苏地区	Aksu Administrative Offices	10659	5189	674	4797
克孜勒苏柯尔克孜自治州	Kizilsu Kirgiz Autonomous Prefecture	1703	816	104	784
喀什地区	Kashgar [Kaxgar] Administrative Offices	18706	9762	808	8136
和田地区	Hotan Administrative Offices	2587	1457	151	979
生产建设兵团	Production and Construction Group	31745	14013	1778	15954

16-17 限额以上批发和零售业商品销售类值
Total Sales of Enterprises above Designated Size in Wholesale and Retail Trades by Category of Commodities

单位：万元 (10 000 yuan)

项目	Item	销售总额 Value		批发 Wholesale Trades		零售 Retail Trades	
		2012	2013	2012	2013	2012	2013
总计	**Total**	**55903055**	**65812894**	**48292313**	**57255102**	**7610742**	**8557792**
食品、饮料、烟酒类	Foods, Beverages, Tobacco and Liquor	4578501	4865278	4010565	4237371	567936	627907
服装、鞋帽类、针纺织品类	Garments, Shoes and Hats, Knitted Goods and Textiles	937247	1061052	169382	229903	767865	831149
化妆品类	Cosmetics	162853	171801	39726	39188	123127	132613
金银珠宝类	Gold and Silver Jewelry	231914	293380	4952	17016	226962	276364
日用品类	Commodity Categories	259894	269721	62730	56232	197164	213489
五金、电料类	Hardwares, Electrical Materials	45126	44971	34182	26329	10944	18642
体育、娱乐用品类	Sports and Recreational Articles	21438	20601	1345	1003	20093	19598
书报杂志类	Books and Newspapers	316247	340582	149004	157548	167243	183034
电子出版物及音像制品类	E-journal and Video Products	3612	3916	307	126	3305	3790
家用电器及音像器材类	Household Appliances and Video Equipments	514645	560742	201636	227949	313009	332793
中西药品类	Chinese Traditional Medicine and Western Medicines	1335187	1555867	468655	807705	866532	748162
文化办公用品类	Office Articles	269342	259993	160530	151618	108812	108375
家具类	Furnitures	168902	142838	988	601	167914	142237
通讯器材类	Communication Appliances	82007	90730	22097	15863	59910	74867
煤炭及制品类	Coal and Related Products	473298	1139459	467784	1132638	5514	6821
木材及制品类	Wood and Wooden Products	108		108			
石油及制品类	Petroleum and Related Products	27872855	29448810	26208355	27316491	1664500	2132319
化工材料及制品类	Raw Chemical Materials and Related Products	2566121	2979297	2566121	2979297		
金属材料类	Metal Materials	4441222	5892738	4441222	5892738		
建筑装潢材料类	Building and Decoration Materials	128112	178648	128103	176545	9	2103
机电产品及设备类	Mechanical and Electrical Products and Accessories	1063169	875383	1045518	858469	17651	16914
汽车类	Automobile	3244532	3550345	972235	3287159	2272297	263186
种子饲料类	Seed and Fddestuff	244854	286111	244854	286111		
棉麻类	Cotton and Hemp	6402834	11251474	6401011	11251474	1823	
其他类	Others	539035	529160	490903	474419	48132	54741

16-18 亿元以上商品交易市场总体情况
Statistics on Commodity Exchange Markets of Transaction Value over 100 Million Yuan

项　目	Item	市场数(个) Number of Markets (unit)		总摊位数(个) Number of Booths (unit)		年末出租摊位数(个) Number of Rental Booths at Year-end (unit)	
		2012	2013	2012	2013	2012	2013
总　计	**Total**	**76**	**89**	**72012**	**75293**	**66674**	**65368**
按市场类别分组	**By Market Categories**						
综合市场	**Integrated Markets**	**28**	**34**	**43123**	**36665**	**39486**	**32923**
生产资料综合市场	roduction Comprehensive Market	3	3	3752	3782	3695	3664
工业消费品综合市场	Industrial Consumable Comprehensive Markets	10	12	25980	11503	25615	10823
农产品综合市场	Farm Produce Comprehensive Markets	8	10	5779	6409	5136	5811
其他综合市场	Other Comprehensive Markets	7	9	7612	14971	5040	12625
专业市场	**Special Markets**	**48**	**55**	**28889**	**38628**	**27188**	**32445**
生产资料市场	Production Markets	9	12	6652	14382	6172	10068
农业生产用具市场	Agricultural Production Equiment Markets	1	1	548	548	296	350
农用生产资料	Agricultural Production Markets	2	2	238	238	179	179
煤炭市场	Coal and Charcoal Markets	1	1	45	60	45	34
金属材料市场	Metal Materials Markets	2	3	1113	1242	1113	1172
机械设备市场	Mechanical Equipments Markets	1	1	1000	1200	1000	1200
其他生产资料市场	Others	2	2	3708	3708	3539	3440
农产品市场	Farm Produce Markets	13	15	4888	5943	3858	4627
粮油市场	Grain and Oil Markets	1	1	181	208	106	173
肉禽蛋市场	Meat, Poultry and Eggs Markets	3	3	225	225	215	215
水产品市场	Aquatic Products Markets	1	1	500	500	500	500
蔬菜市场	Vegetables Markets	3	4	998	1910	687	1608
干鲜果市场	Dried and Fresh Melons and Fruits Markets	3	3	2554	2170	1945	1584
其他农产品市场	Others	2	3	430	930	405	547
食品、饮料及烟酒市场	Food, Beverages, Tobacco and Liquor Markets	2	2	438	438	343	374
食品饮料市场	Food and Beverages Markets	1	1	200	200	105	146
其他食品饮料及烟酒市场	Others	1	1	238	238	238	228
纺织、服装、鞋帽市场	Textiles, Clothing, Shoes and Hats Markets	12	13	12068	12457	12055	12202
服装市场	Clothing Markets	7	9	7086	7802	7073	7549
其他纺织服装鞋帽市场	Others	5	4	4982	4655	4982	4653
日用品及文化用品市场	Daily Use Articles and Cultural Goods Markets	1	1	315	360	271	272
小商品市场	Merchandise Markets	1	1	315	360	271	272
黄金、珠宝、玉器等首饰市场	Gold, Jeweller, Jade Markets	1	1	712	712	712	712
黄金、珠宝、玉器等首饰市场	Gold, Jeweller, Jade Markets	1		712	712	712	712
电器、通讯器材、电子设备市场	Electrical Appliances, Communication Appliances and Electronical Appliances Markets	3	3	1035	1058	1035	1058
计算机及辅助设备市场	Computer and Auxillary Equipments Markets	2	3	755	1058	755	1058
其他电器、通讯器材、电子设备市场市场	Others	1		280		280	
家具、五金及装饰材料市场	Furniture, Hardware and Decoration Materials Markets	3	3	1635	1058	1635	1635
家具市场	Furniture Markets	1	1	510	1058	510	510
装饰材料市场	Decoration Materials Markets	1	1	325	1635	325	325
其他装饰市场	Others	1	1	800	510	800	800
汽车、摩托车及零配件市场	Cars, Motorcycles and Spare Parts Markets	3	4	824	325	807	897
汽车市场	Cars Markets	3	4	824	800	807	897
花、鸟、鱼、虫市场	Flower, Bird, Fish and Insects Markets	1	1	322	1043	300	600
花卉市场	Flower Markets	1	1	322	1043	300	600
按营业状态分组	**By Operating State**						
常年营业	Business Year	75	88	71967	600	66629	65334
季节性营业	Seasonal Business	1	1	45	60	45	34
按经营方式分组	**By Mode of Operating**						
以批发为主	Mainly in the Wholesale	49	56	55748	56866	51071	47680
以零售为主	Mainly in the Retail	27	33	16264	18427	15603	17688
按经营环境分组	**By Operating Environment**						
露天式	Open Type	17	19	9664	10271	8954	9675
封闭式	Closed Type	54	60	60335	53355	55777	48124
其　他	Others	5	10	2013	11667	1943	7569

16-18 续表 Continued

项　　目	Item	营业面积(平方米) Operating Area (sq.m)		成交额(万元) Turnouer (100 million yuan)	
		2012	2013	2012	2013
总　计	**Total**	**6186284**	**11784038**	**9097630**	**13925190**
按市场类别分组	**By Market Categories**				
综合市场	**Integrated Markets**	**3151599**	**4599112**	**3099824**	**3675047**
生产资料综合市场	Production Comprehensive Market	463756	463756	290213	311062
工业消费品综合市场	Industrial Consumable Comprehensive Markets	1867700	988829	1562819	756603
农产品综合市场	Farm Produce Comprehensive Markets	361162	2112142	887648	1155861
其他综合市场	Other Comprehensive Markets	458981	1034385	359144	1451521
专业市场	**Special Markets**	**3034685**	**7184926**	**5997806**	**10250143**
生产资料市场	Production Markets	741679	4645429	2534830	5560463
农业生产用具市场	Agricultural Production Equiment Markets	45436	49506	15860	17860
农用生产资料	Agricultural Production Markets	56090	56090	36057	35044
煤炭市场	Coal and Charcoal Markets	2000	2550	16390	16737
金属材料市场	Metal Materials Markets	320150	342744	1705650	4123666
机械设备市场	Mechanical Equipments Markets	49000	49000	500000	600000
其他生产资料市场	Others	269003	269003	260873	309533
农产品市场	Farm Produce Markets	1090069	1242069	1502443	2852050
粮油市场	Grain and Oil Markets	10000	25000	53000	35000
肉禽蛋市场	Meat, Poultry and Eggs Markets	708671	708671	186316	166269
水产品市场	Aquatic Products Markets	100000	100000	220000	200000
蔬菜市场	Vegetables Markets	48998	125998	215489	486405
干鲜果市场	Dried and Fresh Melons and Fruits Markets	155000	145000	741282	1837643
其他农产品市场	Others	67400	137400	86356	126733
食品、饮料及烟酒市场	Food, Beverages, Tobacco and Liquor Markets	24503	24503	60782	66001
食品饮料市场	Food and Beverages Markets	7013	7013	24667	25545
其他食品饮料及烟酒市场	Others	17490	17490	36115	40456
纺织、服装、鞋帽市场	Textiles, Clothing, Shoes and Hats Markets	388507	394963	1175111	890425
服装市场	Clothing Markets	214685	241941	958542	683680
其他纺织服装鞋帽市场	Others	173822	153022	216569	206745
日用品及文化用品市场	Daily Use Articles and Cultural Goods Markets	6000	6000	11707	11130
小商品市场	Merchandise Markets	6000	6000	11707	11130
黄金、珠宝、玉器等首饰市场	Gold, Jeweller, Jade Markets	57420	57420	28361	34207
黄金、珠宝、玉器等首饰市场	Gold, Jeweller, Jade Markets	57420	57420	28361	34207
电器、通讯器材、电子设备市场	Electrical Appliances, Communication Appliances and Electronical Appliances Markets	26098	134524	58820	134524
计算机及辅助设备市场	Computer and Auxillary Equipments Markets	17098	134524	42020	134524
其他电器、通讯器材、电子设备市场市场	Others	9000		16800	
家具、五金及装饰材料市场	Furniture, Hardware and Decoration Materials Markets	212656	212656	126377	128648
家具市场	Furniture Markets	44056	44056	36420	36930
装饰材料市场	Decoration Materials Markets	70000	70000	20257	21963
其他装饰市场	Others	98600	98600	69700	69755
汽车、摩托车及零配件市场	Cars, Motorcycles and Spare Parts Markets	387753	475838	484375	507695
汽车市场	Cars Markets	387753	475838	484375	507695
花、鸟、鱼、虫市场	Flower, Bird, Fish and Insects Markets	100000	100000	15000	65000
花卉市场	Flower Markets	100000	100000	15000	65000
按营业状态分组	**By Operating State**				
常年营业	Business Year	6184284	11781488	9081240	13908453
季节性营业	Seasonal Business	2000	2550	16390	16737
按经营方式分组	**By Mode of Operating**				
以批发为主	Mainly in the Wholesale	5191885	10560864	7909383	12403159
以零售为主	Mainly in the Retail	994399	1223174	1188247	1522031
按经营环境分组	**By Operating Environment**				
露天式	Open Type	1590706	3349321	1415690	1434537
封闭式	Closed Type	4424912	4272857	7284659	7195644
其　他	Others	170666	4161860	397281	5295009

16-19 亿元以上商品交易市场成交情况(按摊位分)
Basic Statistics on Commodity Exchange Markets of Transaction Value over 100 Million Yuan (by Booths)

项　目	Item	年末出租摊位数(个) Number of Booths at Year-end (unit)		成交额(万元) Turnover (100 million yuan)	
		2012	2013	2012	2013
总　计	**Total**	**66674**	**65368**	**9097630**	**13925190**
食品、饮料、烟酒类	Food, Beverages, Tobacco and Liquor	12353	15410	2600267	4205867
粮油、食品类	Food,Grain and Oil	11329	14007	2492113	4094353
粮油类	Grain and Oil	835	1103	116821	129278
肉禽蛋类	Meat, Poultry and Eggs	1422	1478	415677	399473
水产品类	Aquatic Products	663	869	286103	272886
蔬菜类	Vegetables	4367	5342	824294	979095
干鲜果品类	Dried and Fresh Melons and Fruits	2939	4567	785805	2270533
饮料类	Beverages	593	630	61900	60850
烟酒类	Tobacco and Liquor	431	773	46254	50664
服装、鞋帽、针纺织品类	Clothing, Shoes, Hats and Textiles	14248	15094	1203758	1086741
服装类	Clothing	9973	10545	913006	776602
鞋帽类	Footwear and Hats	2447	2549	238508	196315
针纺织品类	Knitwear and Textiles	1828	2000	52244	113824
化妆品类	Cosmetics	730	710	39368	38638
金银珠宝类	Gold, Silver and Jewellery	4005	991	114704	157105
日用品类	Articles for Daily Use	2739	2985	168632	201787
洗涤用品类	Washing Articles	644	1223	75351	146207
儿童玩具类	Children Toys	246	272	7888	12715
五金、电料类	Hardware & Electrical Materials	2637	3802	120789	280865
体育、娱乐用品类	Sports & Recreational Articles	396	282	18709	10109
书报杂志类	Newspapers and Magazines	262	193	13013	11951
电子出版物及音像制品类	E-journal and Video Products	792	199	26678	7416
家用电器和音像器材类	Household Appliances and Video Equipments	1139	1317	115556	160710
中西药品类	Traditional Chinese and Western Medicine	140	260	10521	18751
西药类	Western Medicine	67	69	4539	9420
中草药及中成药类	Traditional Chinese	21	135	5010	7100
文化办公用品类	Cultural and Official Goods	1475	1761	96603	215824
家具类	Furniture	3527	3483	335091	398529
通讯器材类	Communication Appliances	490	608	22781	43773
煤炭及制品类	Coal and Related Products	192	180	19309	19110
木材及制品类	Wood and Wooden Products	716	741	18492	15858
石油及制品类	Petroleum and Related Products	1	1	27	26
化工材料及制品类	Raw Chemical Materials and Related Products	1690	1190	300765	248130
化肥类	Fertilizer	741	726	215867	221932
金属材料类	Metal Materials	2009	1731	1720917	4140248
建筑及装潢材料类	Building and Decoration Materials	5223	4617	200884	384809
机电产品及设备类	Mechanical & Electrical Products	3575	2869	649357	906308
农机类	Agricultural Machinery	252	224	50346	55313
汽车类	Automobile	1013	1140	630626	750173
种子饲料类	Seed and Feedstuff	386	426	26774	34020
棉麻类	Cotton and Hemp	20	61	383	47372
其他类	Others	6916	5317	643626	541070

16-20 各地区亿元以上商品交易市场总体情况
Basic Statistics on Commodity Exchange Markets of Transaction Value over 100 Million Yuan by Region

项　目	Item	市场数(个) Number of Markets (unit)		总摊位数(个) Number of Booths (unit)		年末出租摊位数(个) Number of Rental booths at Year-end (unit)	
		2012	2013	2012	2013	2012	2013
总　计	**Total**	**76**	**89**	**72012**	**75293**	**66674**	**65368**
乌鲁木齐市	Urumqi City	25	25	35883	33394	35201	28984
克拉玛依市	Karamay City	1	1	510	510	436	440
吐鲁番地区	Turpan Administrative Offices	1	1	650	780	650	780
哈密地区	Hami [Kumul] Administrative Offices	1	2	896	1285	896	1285
昌吉回族自治州	Changji Hui Autonomous Prefecture	2	2	3998	3998	3571	3584
伊犁哈萨克自治州直属县(市)	Ili Kazak Autonomous Prefecture	12	19	6818	9138	6272	8344
巴音郭楞蒙古自治州	Bayangol Mongol Autonomous Prefecture	9	9	8185	7930	4912	4928
阿克苏地区	Aksu Administrative Offices	5	5	2693	2798	2452	2493
喀什地区	Kashgar [Kaxgar] Administrative Offices	8	8	6551	6552	6551	6552
和田地区	Hotan Administrative Offices	2	2	2187	2187	2117	2106
生产建设兵团	Xinjiang Production and Construction Group	10	15	3641	6721	3616	5872

项　目	Item	营业面积(平方米) Operating Area (sq.m)		成交额(万元) Turnover (100 million Yuan)	
		2012	2013	2012	2013
总　计	**Total**	**6186284**	**11784038**	**9097630**	**13925190**
乌鲁木齐市	Urumqi City	3031178	6355752	6154367	5967613
克拉玛依市	Karamay City	30000	30000	69450	70780
吐鲁番地区	Turpan Administrative Offices	15000	15000	97057	128000
哈密地区	Hami [Kumul] Administrative Offices	20000	1764520	28297	69371
昌吉回族自治州	Changji Hui Autonomous Prefecture	320303	320303	123817	133808
伊犁哈萨克自治州直属县(市)	Ili Kazak Autonomous Prefecture	803891	1044557	590655	798433
巴音郭楞蒙古自治州	Bayangol Mongol Autonomous Prefecture	653164	653249	396055	443256
阿克苏地区	Aksu Administrative Offices	408000	408550	364709	380868
喀什地区	Kashgar [Kaxgar] Administrative Offices	585170	585170	776327	808061
和田地区	Hotan Administrative Offices	99859	99859	119975	121906
生产建设兵团	Production and Construction Group	219719	507078	376921	5003094

16-21 连锁批发和零售企业总体情况
Total Conditions of Chain Wholesale and Retail Enterprises

项　目 Item	合　计 Total		直营店 Straight Camp Shop		加盟店 Join in Store	
	2012	2013	2012	2013	2012	2013
连锁总店数(个) Number of Head Stores (unit)	**95**	**94**				
连锁门店总数(个) Number of Stores (unit)	3711	4020	3063	3197	648	823
年末从业人员数(人) Engaged Persons at Year-end (person)	30983	31290	28826	28971	2157	2319
年末零售营业面积(平方米) Operating Area of Retail Enterprises at Year-end (sq.m)	2919672	3411975	2812467	3291840	107205	120135
连锁门店商品购进总额(万元) Total Purchases Value of Chain Stores (100 million yuan)	6593447	7100987	6453929	6950035	139519	150952
其中:统一配送商品购进额(万元) Centralized Purchase and Delivery (100 million yuan)	5777005	6171965	5655014	6041789	121991	130176
其中:自有配送中心配送商品购进额(万元) Own Purchase and Delivery (100 million yuan)	3724544	3834394	3613481	3716825	111063	118496
非自有配送中心配送商品购进额(万元) Public Puchase and Delivery (100 million yuan)	1628702	1892279	1617774	1880656	10928	11623
商品销售额(万元) Total Sales of Commodities (100 million yuan)	7138861	7908697	6982697	7727877	156164	180820
其中:零售额(万元) Of which:Retail of value	2834992	3811884	2748425	3727374	86568	84511

16-22 连锁批发和零售企业基本情况
Basic Condition of Chain Wholesale and Retail Enterprises

项　目	Item	连锁总店数 Number of Chain Stores	门店数合计(个) Total Stores (unit)	
			2012	2013
总　计	**Total**	**94**	**3711**	**4020**
按登记注册类型分组	**by Status of Registration**			
内资企业	Domestic Funded Enterprises	93	3708	4016
国有企业	State-owned Enterprises	34	1996	2289
集体企业	Collective-owned Enterprises	1	8	8
有限责任公司	Limited Liability Corporations	18	376	382
其他有限责任公司	Other Limited Liability Corporations	18	376	382
股份有限公司	Share-holding Corporations Ltd.	9	394	387
私营企业	Private Enterprises	30	910	920
私营有限责任公司	Private-funded Enterprises	30	910	920
其他企业	Other Enterprises	1	24	30
外商投资企业	Foreign Funded Enterprises	1	3	4
外资企业	Enterprises with Sole Fund	1	3	4
按行业分组	**By Sector**			
批发业	**Wholesale**	**29**	**2192**	**2474**
食品、饮料及烟草制品批发	Special Wholesale of Food, Beverages and Tobaccos	4	24	17
医药及医疗器材批发	Wholesale of Medicines and Medical Appliances	2	7	7
矿产品、建材及化工产品批发	Wholesale of Minerals、Building Materials and Chemical Materials	23	2158	2450
其他批发	Others		3	
零售业	**Retail Trades**	**65**	**1519**	**1546**
综合零售	Integrated Retail	12	402	377
食品、饮料及烟草制品专门零售	Monopoly Retail of Foods, Beverages and Tobacco	1	6	6
纺织、服装及日用品专门零售	Monopoly Retail of Textile, Garments and Daily Consumer Articles	1	3	3
文化、体育用品及器材专门零售	Monopoly Retail of Cultural, Sports Goods and Apparatus	14	114	117
医药及医疗器材专门零售	Monopoly Retail of Medicine and Medical-care Apparatus	24	732	774
汽车、摩托车、燃料及零配件专门零售	Monopoly Retail of Car, Motor, Fuel and Parts as Well as Components	3	121	123
家用电器及电子产品专门零售	Monopoly Retail of House Hold Electric Appliancesound Electronic Products	9	87	88
五金、家具及室内装修材料专门零售	Monopoly Retail of Hardware, Furniture and Indoor Decorating Material	1	54	58
按业态分组	**By Business Categories**			
便利店	Convenience Store	1	121	133
超　市	Supermarket	4	49	62
大型超市	Hypermarket	4	20	23
百货店	Department Store	1	82	82
专业店	Specialty Store	77	2458	3616
其中：加油站	Gas Station	19	867	852
专卖店	Franchised Store	6	86	79
其　他	Other Store	1	28	25

16-22 续表 1 Continued

项　目	Item	年末从业人员数(人) Engaged Persons at Year-end (person)		年末零售营业面积(平方米) Operating Area of Retail Enterprises at Year-end (sq.m)	
		2012	2013	2012	2013
总　计	**Total**	**30983**	**31290**	**2919672**	**3411975**
按登记注册类型分组	**by Status of Registration**				
内资企业	Domestic Funded Enterprises	30135	30433	2890930	3383233
国有企业	State-owned Enterprises	9382	10154	1302616	1343579
集体企业	Collective-owned Enterprises	56	56	200	200
有限责任公司	Limited Liability Corporations	4865	4620	278583	280278
其他有限责任公司	Other Limited Liability Corporations	4865	4620	278583	280278
股份有限公司	Share-holding Corporations Ltd.	6817	6043	935547	1349768
私营企业	Private Enterprises	8892	9434	369698	406528
私营有限责任公司	Private-funded Enterprises	8892	9434	369698	406528
其他企业	Other Enterprises	123	126	4286	2880
外商投资企业	Foreign Funded Enterprises	848	857	28742	28742
外资企业	Enterprises with Sole Fund	848	857	28742	28742
按行业分组	**By Sector**				
批发业	**Wholesale**	**11903**	**12243**	**1926511**	**1973491**
食品、饮料及烟草制品批发	Special Wholesale of Food, Beverages and Tobaccos	628	508	6401	6401
医药及医疗器材批发	Wholesale of Medicines and Medical Appliances	113	125	961	961
矿产品、建材及化工产品批发	Wholesale of Minerals、Building Materials and Chemical Materiac	11021	11610	1916149	1966129
其他批发	Others	141		3000	
零售业	**Retail Trades**	**19080**	**19047**	**993161**	**1438484**
综合零售	Integrated Retail	6421	6266	294351	726107
食品、饮料及烟草制品专门零售	Monopoly Retail of Foods, Beverages and Tobacco	21	24	445	445
纺织、服装及日用品专门零售	Monopoly Retail of Textile, Garments and Daily Consumer Articles	7	7	150	200
文化、体育用品及器材专门零售	Monopoly Retail of Cultural, Sports Goods and Apparatus	1758	1689	99349	99983
医药及医疗器材专门零售	Monopoly Retail of Medicine and Medical-care Apparatus	4367	4609	100955	104575
汽车、摩托车、燃料及零配件专门零售	Monopoly Retail of Car, Motor, Fuel and Parts as Well as Components	2105	1901	253638	267207
家用电器及电子产品专门零售	Monopoly Retail of House Hold Electric Appliancesound Electronic Products	1779	1985	144532	139852
五金、家具及室内装修材料专门零售	Monopoly Retail of Hardware, Furniture and Indoor Decorating Material	2622	2566	99741	100115
按业态分组	**By Business Categories**				
便利店	Convenience Store	460	501	30000	31500
超　市	Supermarket	1937	1974	108904	526651
大型超市	Hypermarket	3327	3175	142213	159016
百货店	Department Store	96	96	3175	3175
专业店	Specialty Store	9206	22362	661633	2577664
其中：加油站	Gas Station	12388	11543	1857968	1898667
专卖店	Franchised Store	3531	3143	115643	112934
其　他	Other Store	38	39	136	1035

16-22 续表 2 Continued

项　目	Item	直营店门店数(个) Straight Camp Shop (unit)		年末从业人员数(人) Engaged Persons at Year-end (person)	
		2012	2013	2012	2013
总　计	**Total**	**3063**	**3197**	**28826**	**28971**
按登记注册类型分组	**by Status of Registration**				
内资企业	Domestic Funded Enterprises	3060	3193	27978	28114
国有企业	State-owned Enterprises	1709	1828	9253	9800
集体企业	Collective-owned Enterprises	8	8	56	56
有限责任公司	Limited Liability Corporations	327	333	4791	4546
其他有限责任公司	Other Limited Liability Corporations	327	333	4791	4546
股份有限公司	Share-holding Corporations Ltd.	394	387	6817	6043
私营企业	Private Enterprises	598	609	6938	7548
私营有限责任公司	Private-funded Enterprises	598	609	6938	7548
其他企业	Other Enterprises	24	28	123	121
外商投资企业	Foreign Funded Enterprises	3	4	848	857
外资企业	Enterprises with Sole Fund	3	4	848	857
按行业分组	**By Sector**				
批发业	**Wholesale**	**1942**	**2050**	**11809**	**11924**
食品、饮料及烟草制品批发	Special Wholesale of Food, Beverages and Tobaccos	24	17	628	508
医药及医疗器材批发	Wholesale of Medicines and Medical Appliances	7	7	113	125
矿产品、建材及化工产品批发	Wholesale of Minerals、Building Materials and Chemical Materiac	1908	2026	10927	11291
其他批发	Others	3		141	
零售业	**Retail Trades**	**1121**	**1147**	**17017**	**17047**
综合零售	Integrated Retail	204	177	4703	4652
食品、饮料及烟草制品专门零售	Monopoly Retail of Foods, Beverages and Tobacco	6	6	21	24
纺织、服装及日用品专门零售	Monopoly Retail of Textile, Garments and Daily Consumer Articles	3	3	7	7
文化、体育用品及器材专门零售	Monopoly Retail of Cultural, Sports Goods and Apparatus	114	117	1758	1689
医药及医疗器材专门零售	Monopoly Retail of Medicine and Medical-care Apparatus	532	575	4022	4223
汽车、摩托车、燃料及零配件专门零售	Monopoly Retail of Car, Motor, Fuel and Parts as Well as Components	121	123	2105	1901
家用电器及电子产品专门零售	Monopoly Retail of House Hold Electric Appliancesound Electronic Products	87	88	1779	1985
五金、家具及室内装修材料专门零售	Monopoly Retail of Hardware, Furniture and Indoor Decorating Material	54	58	2622	2566
按业态分组	**By Business Categories**				
便利店	Convenience Store	23	23	140	131
超　市	Supermarket	33	46	1748	1785
大型超市	Hypermarket	11	15	2217	2199
百货店	Department Store	16	16	17	17
专业店	Specialty Store	1999	2993	8747	21657
其中：加油站	Gas Station	867	852	12388	11543
专卖店	Franchised Store	86	79	3531	3143
其　他	Other Store	28	25	38	39

16-22 续表 3 Continued

项　目	Item	年末零售营业面积(平方米) Operating Area of Retail Enterprises at Year-end (sq.m)		加盟店门店数(个) Number of Join in Stores (unit)	
		2012	2013	2012	2013
总　计	**Total**	**2812467**	**3291840**	**648**	**823**
按登记注册类型分组	**by Status of Registration**				
内资企业	Domestic Funded Enterprises	2783725	3263098	648	823
国有企业	State-owned Enterprises	1297465	1326477	287	461
集体企业	Collective-owned Enterprises	200	200		
有限责任公司	Limited Liability Corporations	275983	277678	49	49
其他有限责任公司	Other Limited Liability Corporations	275983	277678	49	49
股份有限公司	Share-holding Corporations Ltd.	935547	1349768		
私营企业	Private Enterprises	270244	306275	312	311
私营有限责任公司	Private-funded Enterprises	270244	306275	312	311
其他企业	Other Enterprises	4286	2700		2
外商投资企业	Foreign Funded Enterprises	28742	28742		
外资企业	Enterprises with Sole Fund	28742	28742		
按行业分组	**By Sector**				
批发业	**Wholesale**	**1923528**	**1958557**	**250**	**424**
食品、饮料及烟草制品批发	Special Wholesale of Food, Beverages and Tobaccos	6401	6401		
医药及医疗器材批发	Wholesale of Medicines and Medical Appliances	961	961		
矿产品、建材及化工产品批发	Wholesale of Minerals、Building Materials and Chemical Materiac	1913166	1951195	250	424
其他批发	Others	3000			
零售业	**Retail Trades**	**888939**	**1333283**	**398**	**399**
综合零售	Integrated Retail	202737	634953	198	200
食品、饮料及烟草制品专门零售	Monopoly Retail of Foods, Beverages and Tobacco	445	445		
纺织、服装及日用品专门零售	Monopoly Retail of Textile, Garments and Daily Consumer Articles	150	200		
文化、体育用品及器材专门零售	Monopoly Retail of Cultural, Sports Goods and Apparatus	99349	99983		
医药及医疗器材专门零售	Monopoly Retail of Medicine and Medical-care Apparatus	88347	90528	200	199
汽车、摩托车、燃料及零配件专门零售	Monopoly Retail of Car, Motor, Fuel and Parts as Well as Components	253638	267207		
家用电器及电子产品专门零售	Monopoly Retail of House Hold Electric Appliancesound Electronic Products	144532	139852		
五金、家具及室内装修材料专门零售	Monopoly Retail of Hardware, Furniture and Indoor Decorating Material	99741	100115		
按业态分组	**By Business Categories**				
便利店	Convenience Store	10000	7681	98	110
超　市	Supermarket	73737	491484	16	16
大型超市	Hypermarket	108213	129016	9	8
百货店	Department Store	1007	1007	66	66
专业店	Specialty Store	645763	2548683	459	623
其中：加油站	Gas Station	1857968	1898667		
专卖店	Franchised Store	115643	112934		
其　他	Other Store	136	1035		

16-22 续表 4 Continued

项　目	Item	年末从业人员数(人) Engaged Persons at Year-end (person)		年末零售营业面积(平方米) Operating Area of Retail Enterprises at Year-end (sq.m)	
		2012	2013	2012	2013
总　计	**Total**	**2157**	**2319**	**107205**	**120135**
按登记注册类型分组	**by Status of Registration**				
内资企业	Domestic Funded Enterprises	2157	2319	107205	120135
国有企业	State-owned Enterprises	129	354	5151	17102
集体企业	Collective-owned Enterprises				
有限责任公司	Limited Liability Corporations	74	74	2600	2600
其他有限责任公司	Other Limited Liability Corporations	74	74	2600	2600
股份有限公司	Share-holding Corporations Ltd.				
私营企业	Private Enterprises	1954	1886	99454	100253
私营有限责任公司	Private-funded Enterprises	1954	1886	99454	100253
其他企业	Other Enterprises		5		180
外商投资企业	Foreign Funded Enterprises				
外资企业	Enterprises with Sole Fund				
按行业分组	**By Sector**				
批发业	**Wholesale**	**94**	**319**	**2983**	**14934**
食品、饮料及烟草制品批发	Special Wholesale of Food, Beverages and Tobaccos				
医药及医疗器材批发	Wholesale of Medicines and Medical Appliances				
矿产品、建材及化工产品批发	Wholesale of Minerals、Building Materials and Chemical Materiac	94	319	2983	14934
其他批发	Others				
零售业	**Retail Trades**	**2063**	**2000**	**104222**	**105201**
综合零售	Integrated Retail	1718	1614	91614	91154
食品、饮料及烟草制品专门零售	Monopoly Retail of Foods, Beverages and Tobacco				
纺织、服装及日用品专门零售	Monopoly Retail of Textile, Garments and Daily Consumer Articles				
文化、体育用品及器材专门零售	Monopoly Retail of Cultural, Sports Goods and Apparatus				
医药及医疗器材专门零售	Monopoly Retail of Medicine and Medical-care Apparatus	345	386	12608	14047
汽车、摩托车、燃料及零配件专门零售	Monopoly Retail of Car, Motor, Fuel and Parts as Well as Components				
家用电器及电子产品专门零售	Monopoly Retail of House Hold Electric Appliancesound Electronic Products				
五金、家具及室内装修材料专门零售	Monopoly Retail of Hardware, Furniture and Indoor Decorating Material				
按业态分组	**By Business Categories**				
便利店	Convenience Store	320	370	20000	23819
超　市	Supermarket	189	189	35167	35167
大型超市	Hypermarket	1110	976	34000	30000
百货店	Department Store	79	79	2168	2168
专业店	Specialty Store	459	705	15870	28981
其中：加油站	Gas Station				
专卖店	Franchised Store				
其　他	Other Store				

16-23 连锁住宿和餐饮企业总体情况
Total Conditions of Chain Hotels and Catering Enterprises

项 目	Item	合 计 Total		直营店 Straight Camp Shop	
		2012	2013	2012	2013
连锁总店数(个)	Number of Chain Stores (unit)	10	10		
门店总数(个)	Number of Stores (unit)	167	171	107	120
年末从业人员数(人)	Engaged Persons at Year-end (person)	5076	4406	4329	3666
年末餐饮营业面积(平方米)	Operating Area of Catering Enterprises at Year-end (sq.m)	61194	56618	54294	49518
客房数(间)	Number of Hotel Rooms (unit)	339	3492	339	3492
床位数(个)	Number of Beds (unit)	456	4617	456	4617
餐位数(位)	Number of Dining-seats (unit)	1567	17435	1253	14439
连锁门店商品购进（采购）额(万元)	Total Purchases Value of Chain Stores (100 million yuan)	18543	19208	17091	17495
其中:统一配送商品购进（采购）额(万元)	Of which:Centralized Purchase and Delivery (100 million yuan)	17603	18048	16170	16348
其中:自有配送中心配送商品购进（采购）额(万元)	Purchases Value of Its Own Distribution Center	11326	9707	9893	1700
非自有配送中心配送商品购进（采购）额(万元)	Purchases Value of Non Its Own Distribution Center	6277	8341	6277	8341
连锁门店营业额(万元)	Business Revenue of Chain Store (100 million yuan)	82467	75028	77046	68025
其中:餐费收入(万元)	Of which:From Meals (100 million yuan)	65606	59117	60714	52114
商品销售额（万元）	Total Sales of Commodities (100 million yuan)	361	313	361	313

项 目	Item	加盟店 Join in Store	
		2012	2013
连锁总店数(个)	Number of Chain Stores (unit)		
门店总数(个)	Number of Stores (unit)	60	51
年末从业人员数(人)	Engaged Persons at Year-end (person)	747	740
年末餐饮营业面积(平方米)	Operating Area of Catering Enterprises at Year-end (sq.m)	6900	7100
客房数(间)	Number of Hotel Rooms (unit)		
床位数(个)	Number of Beds (unit)		
餐位数(位)	Number of Dining-seats (unit)	314	2996
连锁门店商品购进（采购）额(万元)	Total Purchases Value of Chain Stores (100 million yuan)	1452	1713
其中:统一配送商品购进（采购）额(万元)	of which:Centralized Purchase and Delivery (100 million yuan)	1433	1700
其中:自有配送中心配送商品购进（采购）额(万元)	Purchases Value of Its Own Distribution Center	1433	8007
非自有配送中心配送商品购进（采购）额(万元)	Purchases Value of Non Its Own Distribution Center		
连锁门店营业额(万元)	Business Revenue of Chain Store (100 million yuan)	5421	7003
其中:餐费收入(万元)	of which:From Meals (100 million yuan)	4892	7003
商品销售额（万元）	Total Sales of Commodities (100 million yuan)		

16-24 连锁住宿和餐饮企业基本情况
Basic Condition of Chain Hotels and Catering Enterprises

项　目	Item	连锁总店数 Number of Head Stores (unit)	门店数合计(个) Total Stores (unit)		年末从业人员数(人) Engaged Persons at Year-end (person)	
			2012	2013	2012	2013
总　计	**Total**	**10**	**167**	**171**	**5076**	**4406**
住宿业	**Hotels**	**2**	**19**	**23**	**1617**	**1413**
按登记注册类型分组	**By Status of Registration**					
内资企业	Domestic Funded Enterprises	2	19	11	1617	1413
有限责任公司	Limited Liability Corporations	1	9	11	1077	1113
其他有限责任公司	Other Limited Liability Corporations	1	9	11	1077	1113
私营企业	Private Enterprises	1	10	12	540	300
私营有限责任公司	Private-funded Enterprises	1	10	12	540	300
行业中类分组	**By Sector**					
旅游饭店	Travel Hotels	2	19	23	1617	1413
餐饮业	**Catering Enterprises**	**8**	**148**	**148**	**3459**	**2993**
按登记注册类型分组	**By Status of Registration**					
内资企业	Domestic Funded Enterprises	7	123	123	2588	2182
有限责任公司	Limited Liability Corporations	1	3	2	165	85
其他有限责任公司	Other Limited Liability Corporations	1	3	2	165	85
股份有限公司	Share-holding Corporations Ltd.	1	36	46	1185	1046
私营企业	Private Enterprises	5	84	75	1238	1051
私营有限责任公司	Private-funded Enterprises	5	84	75	1238	1051
外商投资企业	Foreign Funded Enterprises	1	25	25	871	811
外资企业	Enterprises with Sole Fund	1	25	25	871	811
按行业分组	**By Sector**					
正餐服务	Restaurant Services	3	15	14	545	293
快餐服务	Fast Food Services	5	133	134	2914	2700

16-24 续表 1 Continued

项　目	Item	年末餐饮营业面积(平方米) Operating Area of Catering Enterprises at Year-end (sq.m)		#直营店门店数(个) Number of Straight Camp Shop (unit)	
		2012	2013	2012	2013
总　计	**Total**	**61194**	**56618**	**107**	**120**
住宿业	**Hotels**	**14400**	**16418**	**19**	**23**
按登记注册类型分组	**By Status of Registration**				
内资企业	Domestic Funded Enterprises	14400	16418	19	23
有限责任公司	Limited Liability Corporations	14000	15768	9	11
其他有限责任公司	Other Limited Liability Corporations	14000	15768	9	11
私营企业	Private Enterprises	400	650	10	12
私营有限责任公司	Private-funded Enterprises	400	650	10	12
行业中类分组	**By Sector**				
旅游饭店	Travel Hotels	14400	16418	19	23
餐饮业	**Catering Enterprises**	**46794**	**40200**	**88**	**97**
按登记注册类型分组	**By Status of Registration**				
内资企业	Domestic Funded Enterprises	36432	29838	63	72
有限责任公司	Limited Liability Corporations	3824	3795	3	2
其他有限责任公司	Other Limited Liability Corporations	3824	3795	3	2
股份有限公司	Share-holding Corporations Ltd.	19436	13486	36	46
私营企业	Private Enterprises	13172	12557	24	24
私营有限责任公司	Private-funded Enterprises	13172	12557	24	24
外商投资企业	Foreign Funded Enterprises	10362	10362	25	25
外资企业	Enterprises with Sole Fund	10362	10362	25	25
按行业分组	**By Sector**				
正餐服务	Restaurant Services	7872	7278	15	14
快餐服务	Fast Food Services	38922	32922	73	83

16-24 续表 2 Continued

项　目	Item	年末从业人员数(人) Engaged Persons at Year-end (person)		年末餐饮营业面积(平方米) Operating Area of Catering Enterprises at Year-end (sq.m)		#加盟店门店数(个) Number of Join in Store (unit)	
		2012	2013	2012	2013	2012	2013
总　计	**Total**	**4329**	**3666**	**54294**	**49518**	**60**	**51**
住宿业	**Hotels**	**1617**	**1413**	**14400**	**16418**		
按登记注册类型分组	**By Status of Registration**						
内资企业	Domestic Funded Enterprises	1617	1413	14400	16418		
有限责任公司	Limited Liability Corporations	1077	1113	14000	15768		
其他有限责任公司	Other Limited Liability Corporations	1077	1113	14000	15768		
私营企业	Private Enterprises	540	300	400	650		
私营有限责任公司	Private-funded Enterprises	540	300	400	650		
行业中类分组	**By Sector**						
旅游饭店	Travel Hotels	1617	1413	14400	16418		
餐饮业	**Catering Enterprises**	**2712**	**2253**	**39894**	**33100**	**60**	**51**
按登记注册类型分组	**By Status of Registration**						
内资企业	Domestic Funded Enterprises	1841	1442	29532	22738	60	51
有限责任公司	Limited Liability Corporations	165	85	3824	3795		
其他有限责任公司	Other Limited Liability Corporations	165	85	3824	3795		
股份有限公司	Share-holding Corporations Ltd.	1185	1046	19436	13486		
私营企业	Private Enterprises	491	311	6272	5457	60	51
私营有限责任公司	Private-funded Enterprises	491	311	6272	5457	60	51
外商投资企业	Foreign Funded Enterprises	871	811	10362	10362		
外资企业	Enterprises with Sole Fund	871	811	10362	10362		
按行业分组	**By Sector**						
正餐服务	Restaurant Services	545	293	7872	7278		
快餐服务	Fast Food Services	2167	1960	32022	25822	60	51

16-24 续表 3 Continued

项 目	Item	年末从业人员数(人) Engaged Persons at Year-end (person)		年末餐饮营业面积(平方米) Operating Area of Catering Enterprises at Year-end (sq.m)	
		2012	2013	2012	2013
总 计	**Total**	**747**	**740**	**6900**	**7100**
住宿业	**Hotels**				
按登记注册类型分组	**By Status of Registration**				
内资企业	Domestic Funded Enterprises				
有限责任公司	Limited Liability Corporations				
其他有限责任公司	Other Limited Liability Corporations				
私营企业	Private Enterprises				
私营有限责任公司	Private-funded Enterprises				
行业中类分组	**By Sector**				
旅游饭店	Travel Hotels				
餐饮业	**Catering Enterprises**	**747**	**740**	**6900**	**7100**
按登记注册类型分组	**By Status of Registration**				
内资企业	Domestic Funded Enterprises	747	740	6900	7100
有限责任公司	Limited Liability Corporations				
其他有限责任公司	Other Limited Liability Corporations				
股份有限公司	Share-holding Corporations Ltd.				
私营企业	Private Enterprises	747	740	6900	7100
私营有限责任公司	Private-funded Enterprises	747	740	6900	7100
外商投资企业	Foreign Funded Enterprises				
外资企业	Enterprises with Sole Fund				
按行业分组	**By Sector**				
正餐服务	Restaurant Services				
快餐服务	Fast Food Services	747	740	6900	7100

主要统计指标解释

批发业 指向其他批发或零售单位（含个体经营者）及其他企事业单位、机关团体等批量销售生活用品、生产资料的活动，以及从事进出口贸易和贸易经纪与代理的活动，包括拥有货物所有权，并以本单位(公司)的名义进行交易活动，也包括不拥有货物的所有权，收取佣金的商品代理、商品代售活动；还包括各类商品批发市场中固定摊位的批发活动，以及以销售为目的的收购活动。

零售业 指百货商店、超级市场、专门零售商店、品牌专卖店、售货摊等主要面向最终消费者（如居民等）的销售活动，以互联网、邮政、电话、售货机等方式的销售活动，还包括在同一地点，后面加工生产，前面销售的店铺（如面包房）；谷物、种子、饲料、牲畜、矿产品、生产用原料、化工原料、农用化工产品、机械设备（乘用车、计算机及通信设备除外）等生产资料的销售不作为零售活动；多数零售商对其销售的货物拥有所有权，但有些则是充当委托人的代理人，进行委托销售或以收取佣金的方式进行销售。

批发和零售业商品购进、销售、库存额 指各种登记注册类型的批发和零售业企业(单位)以本企业(单位)为总体的，从国内、国外市场购进的商品总量，销售和出口的商品总量、库存的商品总量等情况。该指标可以反映商品流转过程中商品的购进、销售、库存之间的比例关系和存在的问题。

商品购进额 指从本企业以外的单位和个人购进（包括从国外直接进口）作为转卖或加工后转卖的商品金额（含增值税）。商品购进包括：（1）从工农业生产者、批发和零售业企业、住宿和餐饮业企业、出版社或报社的出版发行部门和其他服务业企业购进的商品；（2）从机关团体、事业单位购进的商品；（3）从海关、市场管理部门购进的缉私和没收的商品；（4）从居民收购的废旧商品等。不包括：（1）企业为本单位自身经营用，不是作为转卖而购进的商品，如材料物资、包装物、低值易耗品、办公用品等；（2）未通过买卖行为而收入的商品，如接受其他部门移交的商品、借入的商品、收入代其他单位保管的商品、其他单位赠送的样品、加工回收的成品等；（3）经本单位介绍，由买卖双方直接结算，本单位只收取手续费的业务；（4）销售退回和买方拒付货款的商品；（5）商品溢余。

商品销售额 指对本单位以外的单位和个人出售的商品金额（包括售给本单位消费用的商品，含增值税）。商品销售包括（1）售给城乡居民和社会集团消费用的商品；（2）售给农业、工业、建筑业、服务业等国民经济各行业用于生产、经营用的商品，包括售予批发和零售业作为转卖或加工后转卖的商品；（3）对国（境）外直接出口的商品，不包括：（1）未通过买卖行为付出的商品，如随机构变动移交给其他企业单位的商品、借出的商品、归还受其他单位委托代保管的商品、付出的加工原料和赠送给其他单位的样品等；（2）经本单位介绍，由买卖双方直接结算，本单位只收取手续费的业务；（3）购货退回的商品；（4）商品损耗和损失；（5）出售本单位自用的废旧物资。

商品库存额 对于批发和零售业法人单位和个体经营户，是指报告期末取得所有权的全部商品金额（含增值税）；对于批发和零售业产业活动单位，是指报告期末实际在库且归属法人具有所有权的全部商品金额（含增值税）。库存商品包括：(1)存放在本单位(如门市部、批发站、采购站、经营处)的仓库、货场、货柜和货架中的商品；(2)挑选、整理、包装中的商品；(3)已记入购进而尚未运到本单位的商品，即发货单或银行承兑凭证已到而货未到的商品；(4)寄放他处的商品，如因购货方拒绝付款而暂时存在购货方的商品；(5)委托其他单位代销(未作销售或调出)尚未售出的商品；(6)代其他单位购进尚未交付的商品。不包括：所有权不属于本单位的商品；委托外单位加工的商品；外贸企业代理其他单位从国外进口，尚未付给订货单位的商品；代国家储备部门保管的商品。

连锁总店（总部） 指负责连锁企业资源（商号、商誉、经营模式、服务标准、管理模式等等）的开发、配置、控制或使用等功能的企业核心管理机构。连锁经营是指经营同类商品或服务，使用统一商号的若干店铺，在同一总店（总部）的管理下，采取统一采购或特许经营等方式，实现规模效益的组织形式，包括直营连锁、特许连锁和自愿连锁三种形式。其中，直营连锁是指连锁店铺由连锁公司全资或控股开设，在总部的直接控制下，开展统一经营的连锁经营形式；特许连锁是指拥有注册商标、企业标志、专利、专有技术等经营资源的企业（特许人），以合同形式将其拥有的经营资源许可其他经营者（被特许人）使用，被特许人按合同约定在统一的经营模式下开展经营，并向特许人支付特许经营费用的连锁经营形式；自愿连锁是指若干个店铺或企业自愿组合起来，在不改变各自资产所有权关系的情况下，以同一个品牌形象面对消费者，以共同进货为纽带开展的连锁经营形式。

亿元以上商品交易市场 指年成交额在亿元及以上的商品交易市场。商品交易市场是指经有关部门和组织批准设立，有固定场所、设施，有经营管理部门和监管人员，若干市场经营者入内，常年或实际开业三个月以上，集中、公开、独立地进行生活消费品、生产资料等现货商品交易以及提供相关服务的交易场所，包括各类消费品市场、生产资料市场等。

社会消费品零售总额 指企业（单位、个体户）通过交易直接售给个人、社会集团非生产、非经营用的实物商品金额，以及提供餐饮服务所取得的收入金额。个人包括城乡居民和入境人员，社会集团包括机关、社会团体、部队、学校、企事业单位、居委会或村委会等。

住宿业 指为旅行者提供短期留宿场所的活动，有些单位只提供住宿，也有些单位提供住宿、饮食、商务、娱乐一体的服务，不包括主要按月或按年长期出租房屋住所的活动。

餐饮业 指通过即时制作加工、商业销售和服务性劳动等，向消费者提供食品和消费场所及设施的服务。

营业额 指住宿和餐饮业单位在经营活动中因提供服务或销售商品等取得的收入。包括：客房收入、餐费收入、商品销售额（含增值税）和其他收入。其中，客房收入指住宿和餐饮业单位在经营活动中因提供住宿服务取得的收入。餐费收入指本单位为顾客提供就餐服务取得的收入，包括：经烹饪、调制加工后出售的各种食品，如主食、炒菜、凉拌菜等的收入。

Explanatory Notes on Main Statistical Indicators

Wholesale Trade refers to the activities of selling wholesale commodities for daily use and capital goods to enterprises of wholesale and retail trades (including self-employed individuals) and other enterprises, institutions and government organs and organizations, and the activities of engaging in import and export and acting as a trade agent. The wholesaler may have the ownership of the commodities for wholesale and trade in the name of its own (a company), and the wholesaler can act as commission agent or commodity broker without the ownership of commodities. Also included are the wholesale activities at the fixed stalls in wholesale market and the acquisition for sales purpose.

Retail Trade refers to the activities of department store, supermarket, franchised store, brand store, retail stall and on-the-spot-making-selling store selling commodities to the final consumers (residents) by any means including internet, post, telephone, sales machine. It also includes shops with sales and production localted in the same places (such as bakeries). Retail trade excludes the activities of sales of capital goods such as grain, seed, feed, livestock, mineral products, raw material for production, industrial chemicals, chemical products for agricultural use, machine and equipment (excluding vehicles, computers and communication equipment). Most retailers have the ownership of commodities to sell, but some are acting as agents or brokers to make transactions for a commission.

Purchase, Sales and Stock of Commodities by Wholesale and Retail Trades refers to the total volume of commodities purchased, total volume of sales and exports, and the stock of commodities by wholesale and retail enterprises (establishments) of different status of registration from domestic and overseas markets. This indicator reflects the relationship among purchase, sales and stock of commodities in the circulation of goods and reveals the existing problems.

Total Purchases of Commodities refers to the total value of purchases of commodities by enterprises (establishments) from other establishments or individuals (including direct import from abroad) for the purpose of re-selling, either with or without further processing of the commodities purchased. The commodities include: (1)commodities purchased from agricultural and industrial producer, wholesaler, retailer, publishing house and other service business, (2) commodities purchased from institutions and government departments, (3) confiscated goods purchased from the customs authorities or market management agencies, (4) second-hand goods and wastes purchased from residents. The commodities exclude (1)commodities purchased by enterprises (establishments) for use in their own business operation, commodities obtained without buying or selling procedures such as materials, consumable goods of low value, office appliance,etc.(2) received goods without trading, such as goods handed over from others, borrowed goods, preserved goods for others, donated goods from others, processed and retrieved goods, etc. (3)goods of direct settlement between buyer and seller with handling fees introduced by others, (4)goods returned or refused to pay by the buyer,(5)excessive goods.

Total Sales of Commodities refer to value of commodities sold by the establishments to other establishments and individuals (including goods sold for self consumption, including the value-added tax). The commodities include: (1) commodities sold to urban and rural residents and social groups for their consumption; (2) commodities sold to establishments in all industries for their production and operation, including agriculture, industry, construction, and catering services including commodities sold to wholesale and retail establishments for re-selling, with or without further processing; and (3) commodities for direct export to abroad. Excluded are (1) extended commodities without trading, such as goods handed over to other enterprises and institutions because of the change of organizations, lent goods, returned goods preserved for others, extended processing materials and samples donated to others, (2) goods of direct settlement between buyer and seller with handling fees introduced by others,(3) goods returned after purchase, (4) damaged and spoiled goods, (5) waste and used goods of self use.

Total Stock of Commodities For the legal entities and self-employed individuals engaged in wholesale and retail trade, it refers to total value (including VAT) of commodities possessed at the end of the reference period; and for wholesale and retail establishments, it refers to the value (including VAT) of all commodities actually in stock and owned by their legal persons at the end of reference period. The commodities in stock includes: (1) commodities located in storage, garages, counters, and shelves of operating places of wholesale and retail trades (such as sale stores, wholesale centres, procurement stations and operating offices); (2) commodities in the process of being selected, sorted, and packed; (3) commodities not arrived but recorded as purchase in the account, i.e. commodities not arrived but payment receipts for the commodities from the sellers or the banks arrived; (4) commodities deposited in other places rather than places mentioned above, for instance: commodities in the hold of purchasers temporarily due to the refusal of payment; (5) commodities entrusted to other units to sell but not sold yet; (6) commodities purchased for other units but not delivered yet. Commodities not included as stock are those not owned by the enterprises (units), commodities on commission for processing, imported commodities of agency of foreign trade enterprise but not yet delivered to ordering units and finally those put in stock on behalf of the state reserves units.

Chain Head Stores (headquarter) refer to the core leading stores responsible for development, allocation, administration and utilization of resources (name of stores, brand of stores, operation model, service standard, management way, etc.) of chain stores. Chain stores refers to the stores engaged in providing homogeneous commodities or services, with the central leadership of head store and guided by common policies, conduct centralized purchase and distributed selling of commodities, in order to gain better efficiency through standardized operation. The chain stores include regular chain stores, franchise chain stores and voluntary chain stores.

Regular Chain store refers to chain stores that are invested or controlled by the headquarters. They operate under direct and unified management from the headquarters.

Franchise chain store refers to the chain stores (franchisees) which are franchised with operation resources such as trade marks, names, patent and operation know-how by the franchisors in form of contract and pay the operation fees to the franchisors.

Voluntary chain store refers to the stores operate jointly on the voluntary bases while maintaining their status of independent legal entities with full ownership of their assets. They sell goods of same brand from same channel of resource to the consumers.

Large Commodity Markets with Transaction Value over 100 Million Yuan refers to the commodity markets with an annual transaction at and above 100 million. The commodity market refers to the markets approved and managed by related departments, where there are fixed sites, facilities, managers and administration offices, where there are a certain number of traders to operate for three month and above or all the year, where the commodities including the articles for daily consumption and capital goods and services are traded in a centralized, independent and open way. Such market includes markets of daily goods and market of capital goods, etc.

Total Retail Sales of Consumer Goods refers to the amount obtained by enterprises (units, self-employed individuals) through direct sales of non-production and non-business physical commodity to individuals, social institutions, and revenue from providing catering services. Individuals include rural and urban households, population from abroad, social institutions include government agencies, social organizations, military units, schools, institutions, neighbourhood (village) committees.

Hotel Services refer to the accommodation services provided to visitors. Some units may provide only accommodation while others provide a combination of accommodation, meals, business services and/or recreational facilities. It excludes activities related to the provision of long-term primary residences in facilities such as apartments typically leased on a monthly or annual basis.

Catering Services refer to the activities of providing foods, serving locations and facilities to customers through instant processing, commercial sales and service-type labor.

Business Revenue refers to revenue of hotels and catering services received from providing services or selling commodities through business activities, including income from hotels, from catering services, from selling of commodities (including VAT) and from other services. Income from hotels refers to income of hotels and catering services by providing lodging services through business activities. Income from catering services refers to income from providing catering services, including selling of cooked or prepared foods, such as staple food, cooked dishes, or cold dishes.

17

金融业

FINANCIAL INTERMEDIATION

简要说明

本篇主要内容和资料来源

本篇反映新疆金融和保险业发展情况,有以下两个部分:一是金融机构存贷等活动情况;二是保险业务情况。

金融资料来自中国人民银行乌鲁木齐中心支行金融机构信贷统计月报及年报;保险业务资料取自中国保险监督管理委员会新疆监管局保险统计年报。

本篇金融部分数据由新疆维吾尔自治区统计局国民经济综合统计处根据中国人民银行乌鲁木齐中心支行所提供的资料整理;保险部分数据由中国保险监督管理委员会新疆监管局相关部门整理提供。

Brief Introduction

Main Content and Source of Data

Data in this chapter show the development of Xinjiang's financial and insruance industries,in the following two aspects:(1)the financial activities of the deposit and loan interests;(2)the situation regarding the insurance business.

Data of finanicial come from statistics monthly and yearly sheet of crdeit funds by by the Urumqi Central Sub-branch of the People's Bank of China;Data of insruance compiled by by the China Insruance Regulatory Commission. Xinjiang Bureau.

Data of finanicial are compiled by the Department of National Accounts of the Xinjiang Bureau of Statistics according to the data of yearly statistics, which are provided by the Urumqi Central Sub-branch of the People's Bank of China;Data of insurance are compiled by the China Insruance Regulatory Commission. Xinjiang Bureau.

17-1 1978-2013 年历年金融机构各项存款和贷款年底余额
Balance of Deposits and Loans of National Banking System (1978-2013)

单位：亿元 (100 million yuan)

年 份 Year	各项存款 Total Deposits	#单位存款 Deposits by Units	#储蓄存款 Savings Deposit	各项贷款 Total Loans
1978	32.07	6.86	6.42	18.26
1979	33.44	7.03	7.21	21.19
1980	38.56	9.60	9.52	24.74
1981	45.59	12.21	12.29	28.84
1982	53.47	15.23	15.30	32.86
1983	61.94	17.95	19.01	38.85
1984	73.63	23.35	24.31	52.02
1985	82.96	29.87	29.55	72.68
1986	102.75	38.15	40.37	93.18
1987	124.93	44.13	53.25	111.14
1988	141.10	47.41	66.25	139.43
1989	167.03	52.76	83.33	173.02
1990	221.80	71.23	114.13	233.72
1991	282.21	92.78	145.01	299.59
1992	336.58	119.51	175.62	380.26
1993	397.39	129.98	220.45	467.81
1994	634.44	214.13	347.71	632.32
1995	838.42	274.24	477.18	843.38
1996	1012.47	364.51	575.79	1016.20
1997	1180.78	442.76	676.13	1215.39
1998	1336.58	461.02	759.14	1318.41
1999	1548.72	544.22	824.68	1386.78
2000	1863.48	702.21	908.55	1403.13
2001	1972.55	691.74	994.00	1584.73
2002	2225.31	705.82	1137.87	1801.15
2003	2661.65	763.49	1371.59	2099.09
2004	2959.78	832.50	1534.67	2214.66
2005	3427.48	909.45	1816.38	2272.08
2006	4040.78	1106.42	2035.63	2412.69
2007	4614.62	1452.25	2054.91	2685.00
2008	5399.34	1473.24	2550.95	2826.53
2009	6845.07	2043.54	3049.91	3782.92
2010	8870.72	2791.72	3713.47	4973.16
2011	10387.00	5573.38	4421.93	6270.21
2012	12330.89	6588.72	5281.83	7914.00
2013	14088.83	7677.24	5884.50	9840.46

注：单位存款 2010 年及以前年份为企业存款。
Note: Before 2010 the deposits of units refer to the deposits of enterprises.

17-2 金融机构和人员数
Number of Financial Institutions and Staff

单位：个、人　　　　(2013 年)　　　　(unit, person)

项 目	Item	合 计 Total		法人机构 Legal Institution		一级分行 The Branch Level	
		机 构 Institutions	人 员 Employees	机 构 Institutions	人 员 Employees	机 构 Institutions	人 员 Employees
总 计	**Total**	**3567**	**65741**	**108**	**7416**	**24**	**5675**
人民银行	**The People's Bank of China**	**69**	**3470**			**1**	**435**
银监会新疆监管局	**China Banking Regulatory Commission Xingjiang Bureau**	**44**	**898**			**1**	**146**
全国性大型银行	**Large National Bank**	**1957**	**37993**			**8**	**3561**
工商银行	Industrial and Commercial Bank	282	8569			1	739
农业银行	Agricultural Bank	360	8632			1	316
兵团分行	XPCG Branch	248	4449			1	375
中国银行	Bank of China	173	4026			1	783
建设银行	Bank of Construction	208	5556			1	699
国家开发银行	State Development Bank	2	184			1	161
交通银行	Bank of Communication	31	935			1	342
邮政储蓄银行	Postal Savings Bank	653	5642			1	146
全国性中小型银行	**Small and Medium-sized National Bank**	**177**	**5993**	**1**	**515**	**9**	**1305**
中国进出口银行	Export and Import Bank of China	1	47			1	47
农业发展银行	Agricultural Development Bank	91	2148			1	125
中信银行	China Citic Bank	8	312			1	110
光大银行	Guang Da Bank	2	130			1	112
华夏银行	Hua Xia Bank	8	313			1	152
广发银行	GuangFa Bank	3	148			1	115
招商银行	Merchants Bank	11	472			1	253
浦发银行	Shanghai PuDong Development Bank	12	402			1	218
兴业银行	Xing Ye Bank	10	513			1	173
昆仑银行	KunLun Bank	31	1508	1	515		
区域性中小型银行	**Small and Medium-sized Regional Bank**	**320**	**5263**	**25**	**2075**		
城市商业银行	City Commercial Bank	127	2565	4	1008		
农村商业银行	Rural Commercila Bank	116	1588	4	420		
村镇银行	County Bank	25	305	1	108		
农村合作银行	Rural Cooperation Bank	52	805	16	539		
外资银行	**Foreign Bank**	**2**	**85**			**1**	**77**
农村信用社	**Rural Credit Cooperative**	**991**	**11522**	**79**	**4460**		
财务公司	**Finance Company**	**1**	**13**			**1**	**13**
信托投资公司	**Trust and Investment Company**	**2**	**281**	**2**	**281**		
金融租赁公司	**Financial Leasing Company**	**1**	**85**	**1**	**85**		
资产管理公司	**Assets Management Company**	**3**	**138**			**3**	**138**

17-2 续表 Continued

单位：个、人 (unit, person)

项目	Item	二级分行 The Two Level Branch 机构 Institutions	二级分行 The Two Level Branch 人员 Employees	支行及网点 Branches and Outlets 机构 Institutions	支行及网点 Branches and Outlets 人员 Employees
总　计	**Total**	**140**	**14182**	**3295**	**38468**
人民银行	**The People's Bank of China**	**14**	**1775**	**54**	**1260**
银监会新疆监管局	**China Banking Regulatory Commission Xingjiang Bureau**	**14**	**645**	**29**	**107**
全国性大型银行	**Large National Bank**	**81**	**10245**	**1868**	**24187**
工商银行	Industrial and Commercial Bank	15	3007	266	4823
农业银行	Agricultural Bank	14	2181	345	6135
兵团分行	XPCG Branch	3	510	244	3564
中国银行	Bank of China	14	1157	158	2086
建设银行	Bank of Construction	14	2148	193	2709
国家开发银行	State Development Bank	1	23		
交通银行	Bank of Communication	3	144	27	449
邮政储蓄银行	Postal Savings Bank	17	1075	635	4421
全国性中小型银行	**Small and Medium-sized National Bank**	**23**	**1247**	**144**	**2926**
中国进出口银行	Export and Import Bank of China				
农业发展银行	Agricultural Development Bank	16	640	74	1383
中信银行	China Citic Bank			7	202
光大银行	Guang Da Bank			1	18
华夏银行	Hua Xia Bank			7	161
广发银行	GuangFa Bank	1	20	1	13
招商银行	Merchants Bank			10	219
浦发银行	Shanghai PuDong Development Bank	2	55	9	129
兴业银行	Xing Ye Bank			9	340
昆仑银行	KunLun Bank	4	532	26	461
区域性中小型银行	**Small and Medium-sized Regional Bank**	**8**	**270**	**287**	**2918**
城市商业银行	City Commercial Bank	7	232	116	1325
农村商业银行	Rural Commercila Bank	1	38	111	1130
村镇银行	County Bank			24	197
农村合作银行	Rural Cooperation Bank			36	266
外资银行	**Foreign Bank**			**1**	**8**
农村信用社	**Rural Credit Cooperative**			**912**	**7062**
财务公司	**Finance Company**				
信托投资公司	**Trust and Investment Company**				
金融租赁公司	**Financial Leasing Company**				
资产管理公司	**Assets Management Company**				

17-3 金融机构人民币信贷资金平衡表
Balance Sheet of Credit Funds of Financial Institutions

单位：亿元 (100 million yuan)

项　目	Item	2013
资金来源合计	**All Sources**	**14107.28**
各项存款	Total Deposits	14088.83
单位存款	Deposits by Enterprises	7677.24
#活期存款	Current Deposits	5267.96
定期存款	Time Deposits	1417.96
个人存款	Personal Desposits	6001.74
#储蓄存款	Savings Desposits	5884.50
其他存款	Other Desposits	409.85
中长期借款	Medium and Long-term Loans	81.68
应付及暂收款	Payable and Temporary Collection	266.63
同业往来(来源方)	Inter-bank Transactions	188.40
外汇买卖(来源方)	Foreign Exchange Trading	430.30
各项准备金	Various Preparations	250.52
所有者权益	Owner's Right and Interest	688.05
其　他	Others	-1887.13
资金运用合计	**All Uses**	**14107.28**
各项贷款	Total Loans	9840.46
#境内贷款	Domestic Loans	9836.67
短期贷款	Short-term Loans	3372.94
个人贷款及透支	Personal loans and overdrafts	760.55
#个人消费贷款	Personal Consumption Loans	59.60
单位贷款及透支	Unit loans and overdrafts	2299.01
#经营贷款	Loans to Business	2267.16
固定资产贷款	Loans to fixed Assets	30.20
银团贷款	Syndicated Loans	123.64
贸易融资	Trade finance	189.73
中长期贷款	Medium & Long-term Loans	5723.23
个人贷款	Personal loans	1437.47
#个人消费贷款	Personal Consumption Loans	993.49
单位普通贷款	Common Unit Loans	3296.30
#经营贷款	Loans to Business	663.57
固定资产贷款	Loans to fixed Assets	2632.73
普通并购贷款	Ordinary Loans	11.96
银团贷款	Syndicated Loans	949.42
贸易融资	Foreign Trades Finance	26.84
境外筹资转贷款	Overseas Financing Loans	1.25
融资租赁	Finance leasing	342.04
票据融资	Bills financing	396.24
各项垫付	The various funds	2.22
境外贷款	Foreign Loans	3.79
有价证券	Securities	489.90
股权及其他投资	Equity and other investment	298.51
应收及预付款	Account Receivable and Payment Collected in Advance	251.24
系统内资金往来(运用方)	Capital Transaction inside the System	2348.07
同业往来(运用方)	Trade Current Account	159.87
外汇买卖（运用方）	Foreign Exchang Trading	430.52
固定资产	Fixed assets	178.71
其　他	Others	110.01

17-4 大型银行信贷收支情况
Deposits and Loans of State-Owned Commercial Banks

单位：亿元 (2013 年) (100 million yuan)

项 目	Item	年末余额 Funds Sources		比年初增减数 The Beginning of Growth and Reduction
		绝对数 Absolute Value	比重(%) Proportion (%)	绝对数 Absolute Value
资金来源总计	**All Sources**	**6329.40**	**100.0**	**1616.97**
各项存款	Totai Deposits	8463.00	133.7	824.44
单位存款	Unit deposit	4184.61	66.1	450.67
个人存款	Individual deposits	4238.14	67.0	388.20
临时性存款	Temporary deposit	13.18	0.2	-2.26
其他存款	Other Deposits	27.08	0.4	-12.17
代理财政性存款	Agency financial savings	6.14	0.1	-1.11
应付及暂收款	Account Payable and Deposit Received	140.95	2.2	30.36
同业往来	Interbanks Account	146.36	2.3	52.47
外汇买卖	Foreign exchange trading	413.03	6.5	307.34
委托存款及委托投资基金（净）	Entrust deposit and entrust investment fund	0.78	…	-0.17
各项准备	Reserves	92.29	1.5	10.08
所有者权益	Creditors' Equity	124.29	2.0	35.47
其他	Others	-3057.44	-48.3	356.40
资金运用总计	**All Uses**	**6329.40**	**100.0**	**1616.97**
各项贷款	Totai Loans	5195.22	82.2	896.76
境内贷款	Domestic Loans	5191.53	82.1	893.23
短期贷款	Short-term Loans	1263.66	20.0	184.32
中长期贷款	Medium-term & Long-term Loans	3866.43	61.1	737.86
其他贷款	Others	61.44	1.0	-28.95
境外贷款	Overseas Loans	3.69	0.1	3.53
有价证券	Securities	6.93	0.1	-1.87
存放中央银行准备金存款	Reserve Deposits Leaving in Central Bank	230.10	3.6	193.14
库存现金	Storage Cash	65.87	1.0	4.43
外汇买卖	Purchase of Foreign Exchanges	413.07	6.5	307.23
其他	Others	418.21	6.6	217.28

注：大型银行包括工商银行、建设银行、农业银行、中国银行、国家开发银行、交通银行和邮政储蓄银行。
Note:Large Banks include ICBC, CCB, ABC, BOC, CDB, BOC and PSBC.

17-5 中小型银行信贷收支情况
Deposits and Loans of Stock-holding System Commercial Banks

单位：亿元 (2013 年) (100 million yuan)

项目	Item	年末余额 Funds Sources 绝对数 Absolute Value	比重(%) Proportion (%)	比年初增减数 The Beginning of Growth and Reduction 绝对数 Absolute Value
资金来源总计	**All Sources**	**4026.63**	**100.0**	**689.26**
各项存款	Totai Deposits	2180.54	54.2	423.07
单位存款	Unit deposit	1849.80	45.9	355.10
个人存款	Individual deposits	307.57	7.6	72.67
临时性存款	Temporary deposit	2.66	0.1	-0.22
其他存款	Other Deposits	20.51	0.5	-4.48
代理财政性存款	Agency financial savings	23.20	0.6	-17.97
应付及暂收款	Account Payable and Deposit Received	55.22	1.4	16.14
同业往来	Interbanks Account	851.13	21.1	277.58
外汇买卖(来源方)	Foreign exchange trading	17.27	0.4	17.20
委托存款及委托投资基金(净)	Entrust deposit and entrust investment fund	10.02	0.2	5.09
各项准备	Reserves	32.88	0.8	14.34
所有者权益	Creditors' Equity	203.77	5.1	24.69
其他	Others	652.60	16.2	-70.88
资金运用总计	**All Uses**	**4026.63**	**100.0**	**689.26**
各项贷款	Totai Loans	2225.14	55.3	459.88
境内贷款	Domestic Loans	2225.04	55.3	459.83
短期贷款	Short-term Loans	1146.45	28.5	193.79
中长期贷款	Medium-term & Long-term Loans	907.66	22.5	183.71
其他贷款	Others	170.93	4.3	82.33
境外贷款	Overseas Loans	0.10	…	0.05
有价证券	Securities	517.60	12.9	76.36
存放中央银行准备金存款	Reserve Deposits Leaving in Central Bank	324.14	8.0	64.17
库存现金	Storage Cash	4.83	0.1	0.02
外汇买卖(运用方)	Purchase of Foreign Exchanges	17.44	0.4	17.26
其他	Others	937.48	23.3	71.57

注：中小型银行包括招商银行、农业发展银行、浦东发展银行、中信银行、兴业银行、民生银行、中国进出口银行、昆仑银行、光大银行和广东发展银行。

Note:Small and Medium Banks include CMB, ADBC, SPDB, China Citic Bank,CIB,CMBC,EIBC,KLB,CEB and Guangdong Development Bank.

17-6 区域性中小型银行信贷收支情况
Deposits and Loans of Urban Commercial Banks

单位：亿元 (2013 年) (100 million yuan)

项 目	Item	年末余额 Funds Sources		比年初增减数 The Beginning of Growth and Reduction
		绝对数 Absolute Value	比重(%) Proportion (%)	绝对数 Absolute Value
资金来源总计	**All Sources**	**1619.96**	**100.0**	**456.08**
各项存款	Totai Deposits	1293.94	79.9	257.79
单位存款	Unit deposit	800.64	49.4	167.67
个人存款	Individual deposits	491.08	30.3	89.72
临时性存款	Temporary deposit	2.22	0.1	0.39
代理财政性存款	Agency financial savings	13.83	0.9	-4.05
应付及暂收款	Account Payable and Deposit Received	21.60	1.3	8.85
同业往来	Interbanks Account	109.88	6.8	40.95
委托存款及委托投资基金(净)	Entrust deposit and entrust investment fund	1.54	0.1	1.43
各项准备	Reserves	30.36	1.9	7.63
所有者权益	Creditors' Equity	131.98	8.1	35.21
其他	Others	16.83	1.0	108.27
资金运用总计	**All Uses**	**1619.96**	**100.0**	**456.08**
各项贷款	Totai Loans	909.58	56.1	264.91
境内贷款	Domestic Loans	909.58	56.1	264.91
短期贷款	Short-term Loans	384.22	23.7	124.20
中长期贷款	Medium-term & Long-term Loans	395.65	24.4	116.03
其他贷款	Others	129.71	8.0	24.68
有价证券	Securities	165.43	10.2	55.60
存放中央银行准备金存款	Reserve Deposits Leaving in Central Bank	265.12	16.4	25.81
同业往来	Intercourse between Banks	161.27	10.0	87.39
库存现金	Storage Cash	10.00	0.6	1.44
其他	Others	108.56	6.7	20.93

注：区域性中小银行包括城市商业银行、农村商业银行、农村合作银行和村镇银行。
Note:Regional Small and Medium Banks include Urban commercial Banks, Rural Commercial Banks, Rural Cooperative Banks and Town Bank.

17-7 个人消费贷款情况
Basic Conditions of Personal Consumption Loans

单位：亿元 (100 million yuan)

项　　目	Item	2012	2013
个人消费贷款	**Personal Consumption Loans**	**752.90**	**1053.09**
短期个人消费贷款	Short-term Loans for Personal Consumption	26.84	59.60
住房贷款	Housing Loans	0.93	1.16
汽车贷款	Auto Loans	0.19	0.32
其他贷款	Other Loans	13.85	21.49
个人卡透支	Personalized Card is Overdrawn	11.63	36.63
长期个人消费贷款	Long-term Loans for Personal Consumption	726.06	993.49
住房贷款	Housing Loans	626.25	867.94
汽车贷款	Auto Loans	14.79	13.03
助学贷款	Student Loans	0.67	0.62
其他贷款	Other Loans	80.52	111.90

17-8 各地区金融机构存贷款年底余额
Deposits and Loans of Financial Institution by Region

单位：亿元 (2013 年) (100 million yuan)

项　　目	Item	各项存款余额 Balance of Deposits	#单位存款 #Deposits by Units	各项贷款余额 Banlance of Loans	#中长期贷款 #Medium and Long-term
总　计	**Total**	**14088.83**	**7677.24**	**9840.46**	**5723.23**
乌鲁木齐市	Urumqi City	5611.86	3339.83	3938.42	2249.87
克拉玛依市	Karamay City	1108.41	855.77	323.81	90.16
吐鲁番地区	Turpan Administrative Offices	203.95	83.66	112.79	63.96
哈密地区	Hami [Kumul] Administrative Offices	436.02	201.28	276.14	181.39
昌吉回族自治州	Changji Hui Autonomous Prefecture	924.84	419.20	653.56	322.24
博尔塔拉蒙古自治州	Bortala Mongol Autonomous Prefecture	252.80	128.07	132.11	42.84
巴音郭楞蒙古自治州	Bayangol Mongol Autonomous Prefecture	718.13	315.16	499.46	220.35
阿克苏地区	Aksu Administrative Offices	926.48	403.53	546.00	253.64
克孜勒苏柯尔克孜自治州	Kizilsu Kirgiz Autonomous Prefecture	127.67	74.48	49.77	24.95
喀什地区	Kashgar [Kaxgar] Administrative Offices	939.96	505.85	407.16	215.62
和田地区	Hotan Administrative Offices	370.08	218.04	108.19	64.55
伊犁哈萨克自治州直属	Ili Kazak Autonomous Prefecture	992.78	472.13	632.16	361.56
塔城地区	Tacheng [Tarbagatai] Administrative Offices	429.84	171.05	246.30	85.21
阿勒泰地区	Altay Administrative Offices	309.44	167.90	154.74	84.10
石河子市	Shihezi City	459.65	152.35	293.86	89.40

17-9 主要年份国内保险业务情况
Conditions of Domestic Insurance Service in Main Years

单位：亿元 (100 million yuan)

年份 Year	承保额 Amount Insured		保费 Premium		赔款及给付 Claim and Payment	
	财产险 Property Insurance	人身险 Life Insurance	财产险 Property Insurance	人身险 Life Insurance	财产险 Property Insurance	人身险 Life Insurance
1980	4		0.01			
1985	70	2	0.40	0.01	0.15	…
1990	241	41	1.04	0.53	0.47	0.08
1995	613	168	4.59	2.06	2.38	0.41
2000	1612	1711	12.49	15.72	5.99	3.72
2001	2112	1371	14.17	19.98	7.43	4.37
2002	2283	3524	16.48	35.25	7.84	5.02
2003	5588	1362	19.12	43.06	10.36	7.10
2004	6401	1735	20.04	48.09	10.65	7.70
2005	8949	9418	20.93	51.57	12.60	7.65
2006	8333	27028	24.61	60.79	12.92	10.34
2007	12188	13081	34.67	70.95	18.78	18.64
2008	13641	17555	44.25	108.26	23.61	20.79
2009	16296	19819	51.82	104.87	26.60	21.51
2010	17431	18129	63.00	127.92	29.21	20.12
2011	23575	13649	78.51	125.11	34.24	23.24
2012	29356	12729	93.68	141.88	50.34	29.77
2013	43281	20099	113.23	160.26	62.35	44.24

17-10 保险业务经济技术指标
Economic and Technical Indicators of Insurance Service

单位：万元 (10 000 yuan)

项目	Item	保费 Premium 2012	保费 Premium 2013	赔款及给付 Claim and Payment 2012	赔款及给付 Claim and Payment 2013
财产保险业务	**Property Insurance Companies**	**936810**	**1132306**	**503434**	**623510**
企业财产险	Insurance of Enterprise Property	61255	65242	27237	29264
家庭财产险	Insurance of Family Property	7340	12102	860	843
机动车辆险	Insurance of Mobile Vehicles	604686	713265	324210	390896
工程保险	Engineering Insurance	9108	3789	4482	7256
责任保险	Insurance of Liability	38971	46339	12579	13835
信用保险	Insurance of Credit	107	223		
保证保险	Insurance of Guaranty	10228	13555	1381	1106
船舶险	Insurance of Snip	7	9		10
货物运输险	Insurance of Cargo Transportation	11968	12978	1629	2587
特殊风险保险	Special insurance against risk	763	1822	181	87
农业保险	Insurance of Agriculture	192333	262951	130884	177565
其他险	Other Insurance	45	31	-9	60
人身保险业务	**Life Insurance Companies**	**1418794**	**1602555**	**297733**	**442400**
寿　险	Life Insurance	1136769	1244000	203272	310990
健康险	Health Insurance	191851	252000	72247	103741
人身意外伤害险	Unforeseen Human Injury Insurance	90174	106555	22214	27669

17-11 新疆辖区保险机构
Number of Insurance Institutions in Xinjiang

单位：个 (2013 年) (unit)

项　目	Item	机构数 Number of Institution	总公司 Head Offices	自治区分公司 Xinjiang Branch Company
总　计	**Total**	**1714**	**1**	**28**
中国人民财产保险股份有限公司	The People's Insurance Corporation Ltd.of china	554		1
中国人寿保险股份有限公司	The Life Insurance Corporation Ltd.of China	343		1
中国大地财产保险股份有限公司	Da Di Property Insurance Corporation Ltd of China	14		1
中华联合财产保险股份有限公司	The Pacific Insurance Corporation Ltd.Property Insruance Company of China	272		1
中国太平洋财产保险股份有限公司	The Pacific Insurance Corporation Ltd., Property Insurance Company of China	22		1
中国太平洋人寿保险股份有限公司	The Pacific Insurance Corporation Ltd.,Life Insurance Company of China	31		1
中国平安财产保险股份有限公司	The Ping An Insurance Corporation Ltd., Property Insurance Company of China	56		1
中国平安人寿保险股份有限公司	The Ping An Insurance Corporation Ltd.,Life Insurance Company of China	69		1
新华人寿保险股份有限公司	Xin Hua Life Insurance Corporation Ltd.	45		1
泰康人寿保险股份有限公司	Tai Kang Life Insurance Corporation Ltd.	64		1
天安保险股份有限公司	Tian An Property Insurance Corporation Ltd.	16		1
永安财产保险股份有限公司	Yong An Property Insurance Corporation Ltd.	52		1
太平人寿保险有限公司	Taiping Life Insurance Corporation Ltd.	8		1
中银保险有限公司	Zhongyin Insurance Corporation Ltd.	1		1
生命人寿保险股份有限公司	The Life Insurance Corporation Ltd.	6		1
永诚财产保险股份有限公司	Yong chen Insurance Corporation Ltd.	4		1
平安养老保险股份有限公司	The Pingan Old-age Pension Insurance Company	2		1
合众人寿保险股份有限公司	Union Life Insurance Corporation Ltd.	12		1
中国人民健康保险股份有限公司	PICC Health Insurance Corporation Ltd.	6		1
阳光财产保险股份有限公司	Sunshine Property Insurance Corporation Ltd.	41		1
都邦财产保险股份有限公司	Du-bang Property Insurance Corporation Ltd.	1		1
渤海财产保险股份有限公司	Bohai Property Insurance Corporation Ltd.	5		1
中国人民人寿保险股份有限公司	PICC Life Insurance Corporation Ltd.of China	20		1
中国人寿财产保险股份有限公司	The Life Insurance Corporation Ltd.,Property Insurance Company	21		1
泰康养老保险股份有限公司	The Taikang Old-age Pension Insurance Company	1		1
阳光人寿保险股份有限公司	The Sun of Life Insurance Corporation Ltd.	11		1
信达财产保险股份有限公司	Xinda Property Insurance Corporation Ltd.	5		1
安邦财产保险股份有限公司	An Bang Property Insurance Corporation Ltd.	31		1
中石油专属财产保险股份有限公司	The Oil in the Exclusive Property Insurance Limited by Share Ltd.	1	1	

17-11 续表 Continued

单位：个　　(2013 年)　　(unit)

项　目	Item	地区级中心支公司 Branch Company at Prefecture Level	县级支公司 Branch Company at County Level	营业部 Business Departments	营销服务部 Marketing Departments
总　计	**Total**	**207**	**539**	**4**	**935**
中国人民财产保险股份有限公司	The People's Insurance Corporation Ltd.of china	15	98	4	436
中国人寿保险股份有限公司	The Life Insurance Corporation Ltd.of China	15	69		258
中国大地财产保险股份有限公司	Da Di Property Insurance Corporation Ltd of China	3	5		5
中华联合财产保险股份有限公司	The Pacific Insurance Corporation Ltd.Property Insruance Company of China	15	181		75
中国太平洋财产保险股份有限公司	The Pacific Insurance Corporation Ltd., Property Insurance Company of China	9	12		
中国太平洋人寿保险股份有限公司	The Pacific Insurance Corporation Ltd.,Life Insurance Company of China	8	21		1
中国平安财产保险股份有限公司	The Ping An Insurance Corporation Ltd., Property Insurance Company of China	15	36		4
中国平安人寿保险股份有限公司	The Ping An Insurance Corporation Ltd.,Life Insurance Company of China	12	16		40
新华人寿保险股份有限公司	Xin Hua Life Insurance Corporation Ltd.	10	15		19
泰康人寿保险股份有限公司	Tai Kang Life Insurance Corporation Ltd.	11	18		34
天安保险股份有限公司	Tian An Property Insurance Corporation Ltd.	8			7
永安财产保险股份有限公司	Yong An Property Insurance Corporation Ltd.	14	5		32
太平人寿保险有限公司	Taiping Life Insurance Corporation Ltd.	5	2		
中银保险有限公司	Zhongyin Insurance Corporation Ltd.				
生命人寿保险股份有限公司	The Life Insurance Corporation Ltd.	3	1		1
永诚财产保险股份有限公司	Yong chen Insurance Corporation Ltd.	2			1
平安养老保险股份有限公司	The Pingan Old-age Pension Insurance Company	1			
合众人寿保险股份有限公司	Union Life Insurance Corporation Ltd.	7	4		
中国人民健康保险股份有限公司	PICC Health Insurance Corporation Ltd.	1			4
阳光财产保险股份有限公司	Sunshine Property Insurance Corporation Ltd.	10	24		6
都邦财产保险股份有限公司	Du-bang Property Insurance Corporation Ltd.				
渤海财产保险股份有限公司	Bohai Property Insurance Corporation Ltd.	4			
中国人民人寿保险股份有限公司	PICC Life Insurance Corporation Ltd.of China	10	9		
中国人寿财产保险股份有限公司	The Life Insurance Corporation Ltd.,Property Insurance Company	10	10		
泰康养老保险股份有限公司	The Taikang Old-age Pension Insurance Company				
阳光人寿保险股份有限公司	The Sun of Life Insurance Corporation Ltd.	4	6		
信达财产保险股份有限公司	Xinda Property Insurance Corporation Ltd.	3	1		
安邦财产保险股份有限公司	An Bang Property Insurance Corporation Ltd.	12	6		12
中石油专属财产保险股份有限公司	The Oil in the Exclusive Property Insurance Limited by Share Ltd.				

17-12 新疆辖区保险事业发展情况
Statistics on Development of Insurance in Xinjiang

单位：万元 (2013 年) (10 000 yuan)

项　目	Item	承保额(亿元) Amount Insured (100 million yuan)	保　费 Premium	赔款及给付 Claim and Payment
总　计	**Total**	**63379.65**	**2734861.41**	**1065910.31**
产险公司小计	**Sub-total**	**51228.89**	**1248605.40**	**685241.00**
中国人民财产保险股份有限公司	The People's Insurance Corporation Ltd.of China	26932.86	653124.55	344397.61
中华联合财产保险股份有限公司	The Property Insurance Corporation Ltd.XPCG	10474.71	330895.09	202640.41
中国太平洋财产保险股份有限公司	The Pacific Insurance Corporation Ltd., Property Insurance Company of China	3893.29	51419.68	31113.34
中国平安财产保险股份有限公司	The Ping An Insurance Corporation Ltd., Property Insurance Company of China	6257.36	106132.27	53731.01
天安保险股份有限公司	Tian An Property Insurance Corporation Ltd.	357.25	8400.40	4886.75
永安财产保险股份有限公司	Yong An Property Insurance Corporation Ltd.	903.56	22274.21	13855.47
中国大地财产保险股份有限公司	Da Di Property Insurance Corporation Ltd.	322.16	10135.17	5018.62
安邦财产保险股份有限公司	An Bang Property Insurance Corporation Ltd.	72.21	5210.86	2540.89
阳光财产保险股份有限公司	Sunshine Property Insurance Corporation Ltd.	521.85	26075.33	14042.41
都邦财产保险股份有限公司	Du-bang Property Insurance Corporation Ltd.	173.28	1726.79	848.23
渤海财产保险股份有限公司	Bohai Property Insurance Corporation Ltd.	28.25	1852.28	1376.35
永诚财产保险股份有限公司	Yongcheng Property Insurance Corporation Ltd.	180.45	650.76	1935.54
中银财产保险股份有限公司	Zhongyin Property Insurance Corporation Ltd.	154.16	2851.39	302.83
信达财产保险股份有限公司	Xinda Property Insurance Corporation Ltd.	205.58	6673.47	1658.59
中国人寿财产保险股份有限公司	The Life Insurance Corporation Ltd.,Property Insurance Company	751.92	21180.44	6892.63
寿险公司小计	**Sub-total**	**12150.76**	**1486256.01**	**380669.31**
中国人寿保险股份有限公司	The Life Insurance Corporation Ltd.of China	5848.73	535342.96	258297.04
中国太平洋人寿保险股份有限公司	The Pacific Insurance Corporation Ltd.,Life Insurance Company of China	715.57	240150.69	18763.88
中国平安人寿保险股份有限公司	The Ping An Insurance Corporation Ltd.,Life Insurance Company of China	1294.63	209189.07	42676.70
平安养老保险股份有限公司	The Pingan Old-age Pension Insurance Company	966.91	7116.99	3314.31
新华人寿保险股份有限公司	Xin Hua Life Insurance Corporation Ltd.	514.15	188569.87	11506.87
泰康人寿保险股份有限公司	Tai Kang Life Insurance Corporation Ltd.	1019.54	114924.30	22491.40
中国人民人寿保险股份有限公司	PICC Life Insurance Corporation Ltd.of China	584.79	56838.37	2830.55
太平人寿保险有限公司	Taiping Life Insurance Corporation Ltd.	79.15	63481.21	2671.90
中国人民健康保险股份有限公司	PICC Health Insurance Corporation Ltd.	873.45	31295.29	15351.68
合众人寿保险股份有限公司	Union Life Insurance Corporation Ltd.	63.13	16541.21	1209.36
阳光人寿保险股份有限公司	The Sun of Life Insurance Corporation Ltd.	99.25	11651.48	773.18
生命人寿保险股份有限公司	The Life Insurance Corporation Ltd.	91.46	11112.07	782.44
泰康养老保险股份有限公司	The Taikang Old-age Pension Insurance Company		42.50	

17-13 各地区保险业务情况
Conditions of Insurance Service by Region

单位：万元　　(2013 年)　　(10 000 yuan)

地　区	Region	全部业务 All Insurance Business		财产保险公司业务 Property Insurance Business	
		保费收入 Premium Income	比上年增长(%) Increase Rate Over preceding year(%)	保费收入 Premium Income	比上年增长(%) Increase Rate Over preceding year(%)
总　计	**Total**	**2734861.34**	**16.1**	**1248605.35**	**21.8**
乌鲁木齐市	Urumqi City	889995.53	14.7	301804.56	14.7
昌吉回族自治州	Changji Hui Autonomous Prefecture	258547.03	13.9	130956.24	21.3
伊犁州直属县(市)	Counties (Cities) Direct Under Ili Prefecture	185059.28	24.5	99052.10	33.7
克拉玛依市	Karamay City	134460.08	4.4	50969.19	14.4
博尔塔拉蒙古自治州	Bortala Mongol Autonomous Prefecture	64433.89	12.0	30933.53	12.4
石河子市	Shihezi City	144029.69	19.9	71225.45	27.3
奎屯市	Kuytun City	72365.27	17.1	38378.17	24.4
阿勒泰地区	Altay Administrative Offices	62090.12	18.2	33510.54	30.4
塔城地区	Tacheng [Tarbagatai] Administrative Offices	97727.35	20.2	42950.65	32.3
克孜勒苏柯尔克孜自治州	Kizilsu Kirgiz Autonomous Prefecture	14284.73	22.4	10900.98	29.9
和田地区	Hotan Administrative Offices	46052.29	16.4	33017.07	22.0
喀什地区	Kashgar [Kaxgar] Administrative Offices	160041.37	17.6	105298.16	22.6
巴音郭楞蒙古自治州	Bayangol Mongol Autonomous Prefecture	230160.18	19.2	111043.28	25.9
阿克苏地区	Aksu Administrative Offices	211625.24	18.8	122399.04	26.8
吐鲁番地区	Turpan Administrative Offices	57852.85	12.3	26953.13	13.8
哈密地区	Hami [Kumul] Administrative Offices	106136.44	15.6	39213.26	19.2

地　区	Region	人寿保险公司业务 Life Insurance Business		保险密度 (元/人) Insurance Density (yuan)	保险深度 (%) Insurance Depth(%)
		保费收入 Premium Income	比上年增长(%) Increase Rate Over preceding year(%)		
总　计	**Total**	**1486255.99**	**11.7**	**1207.83**	**3.27**
乌鲁木齐市	Urumqi City	588190.97	14.6	3384.91	4.04
昌吉回族自治州	Changji Hui Autonomous Prefecture	127590.79	7.2	1840.19	2.76
伊犁州直属县(市)	Counties (Cities) Direct Under Ili Prefecture	86007.18	15.4	689.54	3.31
克拉玛依市	Karamay City	83490.89	-0.9	4633.36	1.58
博尔塔拉蒙古自治州	Bortala Mongol Autonomous Prefecture	33500.36	11.7	1313.90	2.90
石河子市	Shihezi City	72804.24	13.5	2313.36	5.64
奎屯市	Kuytun City	33987.10	9.7	2400.17	5.90
阿勒泰地区	Altay Administrative Offices	28579.58	6.5	926.03	2.94
塔城地区	Tacheng [Tarbagatai] Administrative Offices	54776.70	12.1	922.04	1.80
克孜勒苏柯尔克孜自治州	Kizilsu Kirgiz Autonomous Prefecture	3383.75	3.2	247.91	1.84
和田地区	Hotan Administrative Offices	13035.22	4.3	213.75	2.68
喀什地区	Kashgar [Kaxgar] Administrative Offices	54743.21	9.1	378.51	2.59
巴音郭楞蒙古自治州	Bayangol Mongol Autonomous Prefecture	119116.90	13.5	1639.08	2.26
阿克苏地区	Aksu Administrative Offices	89226.20	9.3	861.11	3.06
吐鲁番地区	Turpan Administrative Offices	30899.72	11.0	899.87	2.22
哈密地区	Hami [Kumul] Administrative Offices	66923.18	13.6	1744.52	3.18

注：乌鲁木齐市区数据中包含自治区本级数据。
Note:Data of Urumqi city include data of Autonomous region.

主要统计指标解释

信贷资金 指金融机构以信用方式积聚和分配的货币资金。金融机构信贷资金的来源有各项存款、金融债券、对国际金融机构负债、流通中现金、其他项目等；信贷资金的运用有各项贷款、有价证券及投资、金银占款、外汇占款、财政借款及在国际金融机构中的资产等。

存款 指企业、机关、团体或居民根据资金必须收回的原则，把货币资金存入银行或其他信贷机构保管并取得一定利息的一种信用活动形式。根据存款对象或性质的不同可划分为企业存款、财政存款、机关团体存款、城乡储蓄存款、农业存款、信托及委托类存款、其他存款等科目。它是银行信贷资金的主要来源。

贷款 指银行或其他信用机构根据资金必须归还的原则，按一定利率，为企业、个人等提供资金的一种信用活动形式。我国银行贷款分为短期贷款、委托及信托类贷款、其他类贷款等

保险金额 指保险人承担赔偿或者给付保险金责任的最高限额。

保费 指投保人为取得保险人在约定范围内所承担赔偿责任而支付给保险人的费用。

赔款 指保险人根据保险合同的规定，向被保险人支付的赔偿保险责任损失的金额。

给付 包括死伤医疗给付和满期给付。死伤医疗给付是指保险人根据人寿保险及长期健康保险合同的规定，因被保险人在保险期内发生保险责任范围内的保险事故支付给被保险人(或受益人)的金额。满期给付是指被保险人生存期满，保险人按人寿保险合同规定支付给被保险人的满期保险金额。

Explanatory Notes on Main Statistical Indicators

Credit Funds refer to the funds issued as loans by banking institutions. The sources of credit funds of the banking institutions included deposits, liabilities to international financial institutions, currency in circulation, self-owned funds and current retained profits, etc. The credit funds can be used in forms of loans, gold, foreign exchange, government debt and assets in the international financial institutions.

Deposit is a form of credit by which enterprises, institutions, organizations or households can put money into banks and other credit institutions for safekeeping and interest earning under the principle of free withdrawal. According to different depositors, deposits are divided into enterprise deposits, treasury deposits, deposits of government agencies and organizations, capital construction deposits, urban savings deposits, rural deposits and other deposits. Deposits are major sources of the credit funds of banks.

Loan is a form of credit by which banks and other credit institutions provide funds at certain interest rate to enterprises and individuals in the light of the principle of unconditional repayment. Loans from Chinese banks include circulating capital loans, fixed assets loans, loans to urban and rural individuals engaged in industrial and commercial business and agricultural loans.

Amount Insured refers to the maximum that the insurant will get for the claim of the case insured.

Premium is the fee paid by the insurant to the insurer to obtain the obligation of compensation from the insurance within the agreed terms.

Settled Claim is the compensation paid by the insurer to the insurant in accordance with the insurance contract.

Payment includes payment for death, injury or medical treatment and mature payment. Payment for death, injury or medical treatment refers to the money paid to the insurant (or the beneficiary) in accordance with the life or health insurance contract when the insurant encounters accidents within the insured period covered in the contract. Mature payment refers to the mature payment to the insurant in accordance with the life insurance contract at the end of the insured period.

新疆统计年鉴
XINJIANG STATISTICAL YEARBOOK

18

教育、科技和文化

EDUCATION,SCIENCE & TECHNOLOGY AND CULTURE

简要说明

本篇主要内容和资料来源

教育统计资料包括研究生教育(高等学校研究生教育、科研机构研究生教育)；普通高等学校本专科教育；普通中等教育(中等专业教育、技工学校、普通中学、职业高中、工读学校)；初等教育(小学)、学前教育、特殊教育(盲聋哑和弱智儿童学校等)以及教育经费来源及使用等资料。

教育部分资料由新疆维吾尔自治区教育委员会依据年报资料整理提供。

科技统计资料包括科技活动基本情况、县级以上政府部门属研究与开发机构及科技信息与文献机构人员数、重大科学技术研究成果及奖励、专利申请和批准情况、高等学校科技活动情况、企事业单位专业技术人员情况、大中型工业企业科技活动情况、各类技术合同鉴定及执行情况、技术经济合同成交情况、技术流向地域情况等。

科技统计范围包括新疆地区有科技活动的企事业单位，具体涵盖规模以上工业企业(标准见工业篇)、各级各部门所属国有独立核算的科学研究与技术开发机构及科技情报与文献机构、普通高等学校等。

科技部分资料由新疆维吾尔自治区统计局社会科技统计处根据科技年报和新疆维吾尔自治区科技厅提供资料整理。

文化部分主要包括艺术表演团体、艺术表演场所、公共图书馆、博物馆、文化馆(站)、广播、电影、电视以及文物等文化单位的机构、人员、经费和业务活动情况。

文化部分资料是由新疆维吾尔自治区统计局社会科技统计处根据部门统计报表资料加工整理而成。艺术事业、图书馆事业、群众文化事业的资料主要来自新疆维吾尔自治区文化厅；文物资料来自新疆维吾尔自治区文物局；广播、电影、电视资料来自新疆维吾尔自治区广播电视局。

Brief Introduction

Main Content and Source of Data

The data on education cover the situation on postgraduate (regular institutions of higher education,research institutions), regular institution of higher education(universities and colleges), regular secondary education, (professional secondary schools, technical schools, regular secondary school,vocational senior secondary schools,schools for juvenile delinquents);primary education (primary schools), preschool education, special education(schools for the blind, deaf-mutes and the retarded) and expenditure on education.

Statistical data on education compiled by the Statistics Bureau of Xinjiang in accordance with the data from the Bureau of Education.

Data on technology mainly include: condition of scientific and technological activities, state-owned research and development institutions and information and literature institutions at and above county level and persons engaged; the situation of science and technological achievements & prizes and patent applications, basic statistics on scientific and technological activities of high education, condition of professional scientific and technological personnel of enterprises and institutions, statistics on signing and implementing technical contracts, statistics on transaction in technical and economic contract, statistics on location of technical contract.

Statistical scope on technology include scientific and technical activities in enterprises and institution, they are mainly: industrial enterprises above designated size, state-owned research and development institutions and information and literature institutions at and above county level and persons engaged, regular institutions of high education, etc.

Data on technology compiled by the Statistics Bureau of Xinjiang in accordance with the data from the Bureau of Science &Technology.

Data on culture cover mainly the situations on institutions, personal and business activities of arts (performing groups and venues), libraries, museums, cultural centers, archives, cultural stations, broadcasting, films, televisions, news and publication.

Data on culture are collected and tabulated in accordance with the statistical reporting schemes stipulated by the Statistical Bureau of Xinjiang. Data on the causes of arts, libraries, mass culture are provided by the Xinjiang Bureau of Culture; Data on archives are from Xinjiang Bureau of Archives; Data on broadcasting, film and television are mainly from Xinjiang Bureau of Broadcasting.

18-1 主要年份各级各类学校数
Number of Schools by Level and Type in Main Years

单位: 所 (unit)

年 份 Year	普通高等学校 Regular Institutions of Higher Education	中等学校 Secondary Schools	普通中等专业学校 Specialized Secondary Schools	普通中学 Regular Secondary Schools	#高 中 Senior Secondary Schools	职业高中 Vocational Secondary Schools	技工学校 Technical Schools	小 学 Primary Schools	特殊教育学校 Special Schools
1978	10	2078	78	1997	673		10	9891	1
1980	12	2197	96	2032	720	21	48	9006	2
1981	12	2201	99	2037	689	13	52	8753	2
1982	12	2243	101	2072	663	23	47	8533	2
1983	13	2333	104	2133	744	47	49	8261	2
1984	13	2374	100	2143	790	82	49	8253	3
1985	14	2360	97	2147	794	65	51	8104	3
1986	17	2284	99	2053	796	68	64	8178	3
1987	20	2284	100	2052	819	68	64	7813	5
1988	20	2335	108	2054	809	109	64	7597	5
1989	20	2301	112	2008	797	119	62	7494	5
1990	21	2274	112	1958	766	134	70	7247	6
1991	21	2229	112	1915	752	140	62	7132	6
1992	21	2239	112	1903	715	160	64	7122	6
1993	21	2206	113	1851	650	170	72	7088	6
1994	21	2168	114	1830	586	157	67	7117	6
1995	21	2121	115	1792	554	145	69	7086	6
1996	18	2092	115	1776	536	137	64	7047	7
1997	18	2090	115	1770	531	131	74	6962	8
1998	17	2066	115	1763	517	121	67	6837	7
1999	17	2022	113	1725	488	116	68	6796	7
2000	20	2000	112	1711	484	112	65	6718	7
2001	21	2179	99	1929	472	89	62	6221	7
2002	24	2173	87	1945	507	83	58	6043	7
2003	26	2154	78	1932	500	86	58	5832	8
2004	28	2186	78	1965	498	84	59	5451	8
2005	31	2185	79	1961	503	87	58	5209	10
2006	31	2101	67	1891	486	84	59	4815	9
2007	32	2040	74	1830	454	75	61	4589	9
2008	32	1973	75	1759	444	82	57	4159	10
2009	32	1832	80	1610	413	82	60	3651	10
2010	32	1772	81	1545	385	83	63	3598	13
2011	32	1766	96	1525	368	71	74	3536	15
2012	34	1744	95	1497	366	69	83	3535	19
2013	36	1738	93	1468	366	69	108	3533	26

注：从 2006 年起，职业初中并入普通中学统计。(以下同)
Note: Number of regular secondary schools include the number of junion vocational secondary schools from 2006.(The same follows)

18-2 主要年份各级各类学校教师数
Number of Teachers by Level and Type of School in Main Years

单位：人 (person)

年份 Year	普通高等学校 Regular Institutions of Higher Education	中等学校 Secondary Schools	普通中等专业学校 Specialized Secondary Schools	普通中学 Regular Secondary Schools	#高中 Senior Secondary Schools	职业高中 Vocational Secondary Schools	技工学校 Technical Schools	小学 Primary Schools	特殊教育学校 Special Schools
1978	2458	44417	2543	41661	8064		213	82616	28
1980	3149	50056	3459	45232	9292	77	1288	89027	54
1981	3377	55547	3808	50143	10341	62	1534	94966	58
1982	3994	61518	3869	55819	11441	167	1663	105556	69
1983	4724	65096	4140	58591	12567	663	1702	104536	64
1984	5109	65703	4183	58451	13128	1194	1875	101025	56
1985	5473	69185	4554	60942	15059	1567	2122	98294	67
1986	6052	72828	5114	63631	17058	1646	2437	95473	79
1987	6789	76680	5162	66395	18510	2215	2908	93910	104
1988	6822	78449	5664	67429	19010	2319	3037	94342	106
1989	6898	77756	5989	65833	19149	2680	3254	94397	111
1990	7002	78596	6158	65814	19318	3117	3507	95060	139
1991	7269	78339	6134	64923	19488	3580	3702	95565	145
1992	7280	78403	6210	64465	19000	3769	3959	96729	154
1993	7158	77200	6271	63448	17142	3853	3628	99297	129
1994	7554	75546	6383	62087	15011	3531	3545	101863	145
1995	7687	76584	6540	62934	14434	3494	3616	106001	162
1996	7835	79424	6791	65228	14781	3685	3720	112149	114
1997	7837	82459	7089	68115	15111	3568	3687	119184	156
1998	7587	83952	7194	69845	15734	3641	3272	123308	163
1999	7516	86667	7229	72195	15673	3598	3645	126401	171
2000	7924	89211	6786	75895	16069	3104	3426	131259	183
2001	9123	93126	6842	79419	17025	2546	4319	132137	187
2002	10369	96469	6031	84714	19031	2399	3325	132435	200
2003	11237	103156	5157	89332	20976	2440	6227	132284	237
2004	12239	106839	5494	94381	22809	3079	3885	134915	257
2005	12733	112941	4993	102168	25153	1696	4084	134768	262
2006	13783	120777	4339	106975	26815	2832	6631	134718	286
2007	15096	123246	5553	108232	27970	2295	7166	133626	298
2008	15755	121898	5381	108729	28735	2586	5202	132797	313
2009	16234	125152	6086	110842	29402	2464	5760	134263	319
2010	16506	128306	6232	113990	30231	2708	5706	133963	347
2011	17256	132748	7210	116501	31258	2255	6782	135182	316
2012	17570	134900	7173	118299	32375	2347	7081	136130	452
2013	18327	137901	6778	121129	35020	2478	7516	140561	547

18-3 主要年份各级各类学校在校学生数

Number of Students Enrollment by Level and Type of School in Main Years

单位：人 (person)

年 份 Year	普通高等学校 Regular Institutions of Higher Education	中等学校 Secondary Schools	普通中等专业学校 Specialized Secondary Schools	普通中学 Regular Secondary Schools	#高 中 Senior Secondary Schools	职业高中 Vocational Secondary Schools	技工学校 Technical Schools	小 学 Primary Schools	特殊教育学校 Special Schools
1978	10229	838560	23696	806386	128376		8478	2028771	270
1980	14308	886740	42362	823161	147446	1416	19801	2055513	371
1981	16546	871359	34399	813269	155816	2065	21626	2010494	414
1982	16235	894831	24881	842757	165619	6236	20957	1985976	464
1983	16493	932761	22493	873657	175157	17909	18702	1941009	527
1984	19689	994078	28150	906862	192914	38563	20503	1962981	688
1985	26500	1054293	33251	955356	223405	41825	23861	1966306	706
1986	29928	1134562	36231	1023533	261191	47149	27649	1948151	737
1987	30145	1170333	39842	1046403	270586	53425	30663	1884884	797
1988	30747	1128662	42524	993674	265301	57180	35284	1847160	745
1989	31964	1042028	44920	893198	255151	64979	38931	1842100	730
1990	31271	1015214	45985	863118	251067	65862	40249	1857246	610
1991	31374	963948	47129	806702	246950	68460	41657	1955216	652
1992	33857	941656	52102	783130	212942	65330	41094	1980686	624
1993	39422	884083	63314	718607	166203	58509	43653	2039409	549
1994	43687	892041	73922	723596	137870	50894	43629	2105911	590
1995	44918	912597	68586	749788	141330	54122	40101	2301274	643
1996	44928	967253	72782	803856	149937	51952	38663	2301764	407
1997	46342	1045980	77837	876720	168483	54038	37385	2419700	629
1998	47464	1121675	82262	958420	183230	51458	29535	2502691	613
1999	54959	1233288	93445	1062380	189037	49871	27592	2507406	681
2000	74063	1311845	105255	1132912	198639	51270	22408	2477413	674
2001	109815	1390360	97321	1228566	225411	47673	16800	2435667	922
2002	134831	1493580	83902	1338836	272381	50787	20055	2359788	3876
2003	151256	1584700	71499	1448531	315178	45330	19340	2289066	1863
2004	168247	1676971	71324	1517948	359147	61502	26197	2218109	2549
2005	188752	1717403	86744	1587850	387763	63158	26219	2143833	4961
2006	207672	1739422	108131	1572502	402321	23488	35301	2097975	4843
2007	226012	1742947	141162	1529092	413452	31741	40952	2058884	6396
2008	241288	1722667	150715	1483550	418701	41611	46791	2012004	5574
2009	253272	1695984	147439	1444836	417139	54777	48932	1973890	5991
2010	263835	1684027	152227	1422419	419141	59593	49788	1935798	5974
2011	272818	1675169	161657	1409293	432724	60734	43485	1919457	4733
2012	284172	1651618	159069	1383886	440717	57269	51394	1900844	4909
2013	295292	1632875	160368	1366013	447540	53971	52523	1894401	5229

注：1.18-3、18-4、18-5 表中高等学校含研究生数。2.特殊教育学校 2002 年新增随班就读。(以下同)

Note: a) Institntions of higher education include the number of postgraduates with table 18-3,18-4,18-5.

b) In Special Schools for the blind,deaf, mute, new comers may follow the classes accordingly from the year 2002 (The same as follows).

18-4 主要年份各级各类学校招生数
Number of New Students Enrollment by Level and Type of School in Main Years

单位：人 (person)

年份 Year	普通高等学校 Regular Institutions of Higher Education	中等学校 Secondary Schools	普通中等专业学校 Specialized Secondary Schools	普通中学 Regular Secondary Schools	#高中 Senior Secondary Schools	职业高中 Vocational Secondary Schools	技工学校 Technical Schools	小学 Primary Schools	特殊教育学校 Special Schools
1978	4118	343088	12540	323948	68261		6600	459802	40
1980	3767	336402	14688	310931	73959	792	10531	433089	90
1981	3070	332717	9751	314200	80957	1236	7530	427439	86
1982	3809	343286	7946	323580	81738	4401	7356	435334	181
1983	5158	364291	9342	334769	85514	12336	7844	409257	40
1984	6527	377785	13433	332093	91060	23020	9239	415792	235
1985	9298	386074	13919	341123	93692	20429	10603	374643	91
1986	7941	406625	14428	358590	96858	21454	12153	359007	105
1987	8347	388507	14986	336693	88115	24118	12710	328980	189
1988	8557	358913	15067	305074	87698	23849	14923	334031	117
1989	8118	326282	15123	264271	86812	31361	15527	333392	197
1990	8034	356615	15586	297641	84567	27968	15420	335552	103
1991	8179	302489	16902	239511	77525	29354	16722	344432	15
1992	10985	334705	20611	269859	61673	27041	17194	359302	119
1993	13359	331884	26572	263683	56180	24778	16851	385535	102
1994	12099	326160	29248	259237	44552	21350	16325	400700	102
1995	12307	356814	25260	286318	58203	25643	19593	419717	165
1996	12421	366772	26311	299348	59400	23003	18110	428651	67
1997	12673	392571	27302	326494	64377	21741	17034	443238	120
1998	12880	426400	27497	365234	71302	19862	13807	429247	130
1999	19821	463579	36014	399516	69801	18828	9221	391298	175
2000	30689	486763	38866	418790	76744	20027	9080	364193	177
2001	42253	510469	26763	459878	93519	16621	7207	352975	135
2002	42808	551353	22241	501824	113366	16746	10442	346386	874
2003	44733	583033	24016	532987	126163	15378	10652	347619	369
2004	53204	606666	27990	536405	138315	27585	14686	347364	390
2005	58653	602335	34882	539922	145044	12416	15115	338539	847
2006	62395	599748	45536	522425	142853	13017	18770	337994	780
2007	68999	619218	65290	510080	146449	19201	24647	340108	1158
2008	74670	603352	62098	497579	147914	21610	22065	328647	840
2009	73904	593290	53692	489838	148869	28243	21517	318488	869
2010	79216	597621	60418	489356	153238	28767	19080	311861	1055
2011	79337	581939	60669	482450	156497	21777	17043	322436	939
2012	83732	571006	56096	469674	155276	22229	23007	331734	1137
2013	89657	575331	57447	477175	163582	21943	18766	348643	1473

18-5 主要年份各级各类学校毕业生数

Number of Graduates by Level and Type of School in Main Years

单位：人 (person)

年份 Year	普通高等学校 Regular Institutions of Higher Education	中等学校 Secondary Schools	普通中等专业学校 Specialized Secondary Schools	普通中学 Regular Secondary Schools	#高中 Senior Secondary Schools	职业高中 Vocational Secondary Schools	技工学校 Technical Schools	小学 Primary Schools	特殊教育学校 Special Schools
1978	1509	205862	8801	195542	53970		1519	388359	195
1980	814	264626	11946	246382	60370	341	5957	292515	37
1981	779	280171	17039	257478	67114	367	5287	397524	37
1982	4108	269927	17201	244853	69504	385	7488	310025	32
1983	4823	283120	11584	260906	77546	1144	9486	317227	27
1984	3426	275788	8130	257833	72191	2764	7061	295993	48
1985	3511	290077	8097	267302	68096	7424	7254	289045	73
1986	4797	296360	11551	268402	58585	8543	7864	307047	52
1987	8001	321981	10623	289556	73947	12280	9522	317820	101
1988	7792	346072	12026	311224	85718	12758	10064	288594	68
1989	6900	347719	12441	308467	86489	14650	12161	249888	57
1990	8603	343313	14260	297235	81062	17938	13880	259301	98
1991	7919	324031	15571	274913	79664	17505	16042	183350	159
1992	8402	310076	14950	260953	84518	18999	15174	268074	157
1993	7741	312284	16760	261502	78675	18558	15464	259468	104
1994	7734	250909	16206	198839	57090	18100	17764	262215	55
1995	10505	271992	18981	215756	44589	16490	20765	271227	57
1996	12272	271267	21701	215295	43478	15424	18847	279866	39
1997	10908	284580	21936	228287	37966	17181	17176	294420	71
1998	11401	313807	23090	259910	49702	18038	12769	321044	100
1999	11886	341434	25118	282486	52403	18826	15004	357801	84
2000	11220	363503	25879	308225	54985	17341	12058	371758	70
2001	16121	380946	26403	329801	59251	13881	10861	395010	104
2002	16380	410299	31598	356203	61932	15087	7411	411626	848
2003	25785	434523	31304	379269	70824	15685	8265	421443	264
2004	31013	468849	24758	420583	84418	15475	8033	417588	382
2005	37920	520798	19559	474621	103928	19492	7126	397592	714
2006	45810	541729	22515	501697	115422	5510	12007	373862	684
2007	48372	557512	25735	515494	127129	5943	10340	361921	716
2008	57076	557655	32537	507098	135240	6454	11566	349300	859
2009	60092	554905	41866	492259	137290	8883	11897	339836	935
2010	66903	547288	44478	473216	135706	14442	15152	334362	728
2011	67219	526007	47371	457944	129478	10256	10436	327704	652
2012	68664	529246	45833	454590	135089	16677	12146	321020	522
2013	74758	530205	50028	451275	139843	17257	11645	321294	680

18-6 主要年份研究生数
Number of Postgraduates in Main Years

单位：人 (person)

年份 Year	招生数 New Enrollment	在校学生数 Total Enrollment	攻读博士学位 Working for Doctor's Degree	攻读硕士学位 Working for Master's Degree	毕业生数 Graduates	攻读博士学位 Working for Doctor's Degree	攻读硕士学位 Working for Master's Degree
1978	16	16		16			
1980	15	66		66			
1985	120	179		174	21		21
1990	73	256	3	253	112		112
1995	180	509	14	295	91		91
2000	544	1196	48	1148	235	5	230
2001	827	1749	80	1669	277	8	269
2002	1104	2495	112	2383	355	11	344
2003	1664	3629	186	3443	521	18	503
2004	2336	5120	283	4837	832	30	802
2005	2902	6938	415	6523	1066	35	1031
2006	3147	8421	489	7932	1628	90	1538
2007	3491	9623	549	9074	2244	110	2134
2008	3523	10317	595	9722	2786	132	2654
2009	4189	11635	653	10982	3021	121	2900
2010	4595	12675	713	11962	3360	158	3202
2011	4972	14099	840	13259	3421	133	3288
2012	5701	15456	844	14612	4073	159	3914
2013	6222	16867	1129	15738	4775	172	4603

18-7 高等学校基本情况
Basic Statistics on Institutions of Higher Education

单位：人 (2013 年) (person)

项目	Item	学校数(所) Schools (unit)	毕业生数 Graduates	招生数 New Enrollment	在校学生数 Total Enrollment	教职工数 Staff and Teachers	#专任教师 Full-time Teachers
总计	**Total**		**69983**	**83435**	**278425**	**33031**	**21027**
普通高等学校	Regular Institutions of Higher Education	36	69983	83435	278425	28781	18327
本科院校	Universities with Full Undergraduate Courses	13	40176	47557	177428	18608	11528
专科院校	Universities with Specialized Courses	23	29807	35878	100997	10173	6799
高职学校	Colleges with Specialized Courses	19	26566	31444	89043	8540	5828
综合大学	Multiversity	8	17576	19784	69806	8018	5134
理工院校	Science Engineering	13	20177	26408	70994	6745	4451
农业院校	Agriculture	5	10678	12480	46074	3899	2554
医药院校	Medicine	4	4904	4764	20114	2382	1416
师范院校	Normal Institutions	5	10623	12982	46392	4801	2999
财经学院	Economics and Finance	2	3614	4051	15938	1638	1045
政法院校	Politics & Law	2	1629	1918	5340	718	371
体育院校	Sport	1		133	187	146	92
艺术院校	Art	1	782	915	3580	434	265
成人高等学校	Ordinary Class for Adult Higher Education					4250	2700

注：在分类院校中含 5 所独立学院。
Note: Five independently established colleges are included in the number of classification of colleges and universities.

18-8 中等专业学校基本情况
Basic Statistics on Specialized Secondary Schools

单位：人 (2013 年) (person)

项　目	Item	毕业生数 Graduates	招生数 New Student Enrollment	在校学生数 Student Enrollment	专业课教师 Teachers of Various Subjects
总　计	**Total**	**74860**	**83893**	**229294**	**5501**
农林牧渔类	Agriculture	14154	8718	32304	673
资源环境类	Resource and Environment	724	483	2013	37
能源与新能源类	Energy	2089	1775	5170	151
土木水利类	Civil and Hydraulic Engineering	4541	6381	15744	225
加工制造类	Processing and Manufacturing	5912	6878	19651	444
石油化工类	Petroleum and Chemical	2807	2775	8126	123
轻纺食品类	Textile and Food	2654	3530	7802	144
交通运输类	Transportation and Communication	5214	11295	24878	172
信息技术类	Information Technologies	3824	5330	12328	417
医药卫生类	Medcine and Health	11931	9243	32581	481
休闲保健类	Recreation and Health Care	618	1047	2421	27
财经商贸类	Economics and Finance	3141	3968	9188	319
旅游服务类	Trades and Tourism	2687	4462	10791	186
文化艺术类	Culture Arts and Physical Education	5613	7801	17969	534
体育与健身类	Sports and Fitness	1033	1216	3457	180
教育类	Teacher Training	6428	7515	21353	941
司法服务类	Justice and Services	643	955	2062	69
公共管理与服务类	Scoial and Public Affairs	369	217	754	51
其　他	Others	478	304	702	327

18-9 普通中学和其他学校基本情况
Basic Statistics on Regular Secondary Schools and Other Schools

单位：人 (2013 年) (person)

项　目	Item	学校数(所) Schools (unit)	毕业生数 Graduates	招生数 New Enrollment	在校学生数 Total Enrollment	教职工数 Staff and Teachers	#专任教师 Full-time Teachers
普通中学	Regular Secondary Schools	1468	451275	477175	1366013	136704	121129
高　中	Senior Secondary Schools	366	139843	163582	447540		35020
初　中	Junior Secondary Schools	1102	311432	313593	918473		86109
职业高中	Vocational Secondary Schools	69	17257	21943	53971	3253	2478
技工学校	Technical Shools	108	11645	18766	52523	10520	7516
小　学	Primary Schools	3533	321294	348643	1894401	154884	140561
特殊教育学校	Special Schools	26	680	1473	5229	660	547

18-10 各类成人教育情况
Basic Statistics on Adult Education by Type

单位：人 (2013 年) (person)

项 目	Item	学校数(所) Schools (unit)	毕业生数 Graduates	在校学生数 Total Enrollment	教职工数 Staff and Teachers	#专任教师 Full-time Teachers
成人高等教育	Institutions of Higher Education for Adults	7	1676	5823	4250	2700
职工高等学校	Istitutions of Higher Education for Employees	1	13	377	111	82
教育学院	Pedagogical Colleges	4	485	1637	870	682
广播电视大学	Radio and TV Universities	2	1178	3809	3269	1936
成人中等教育	Secondary Schools for Adults	18	7575	14955	1073	775
成人中学	Secondary Schools for Adults	10	3114	32349	298	197
成人技术培训学校	Technical adult college	2155	1557140	1815568	4958	2418
成人初等学校	Primary Schools for Adults	809	63992	72304	1625	597
#扫盲班	Literacy Courses		50700	66936	1362	513

18-11 主要年份教育发展水平
Development Level of Education in Main Years

年 份 Year	各类学校在校生占全区人口比重(%) Students as Percentage of Total Population (%)	平均每万人口中(人) Number of Students per 10 000 Population (person)			大中小学生各占普通学校学生总数的比重(%) Students of Different Level as Percentage of Total Students(%)		
		大学生 University and College Students	中学生 Secondary School students	小学生 Primary School Students	大学生 University and College Students	中学生 Secondary School Students	小学生 Primary School Students
1978	23.34	8.30	654.00	1645.38	0.36	28.02	70.50
1980	23.04	11.15	641.47	1601.82	0.48	27.80	69.52
1985	22.39	19.47	701.88	1444.60	0.87	31.35	64.52
1990	18.99	20.45	564.44	1208.01	1.08	29.72	63.94
1995	19.61	26.84	453.23	1330.61	1.38	23.00	70.60
2000	22.84	41.05	638.26	1395.72	1.82	27.93	61.09
2001	20.98	58.53	654.84	1298.22	2.79	31.21	61.87
2002	23.14	70.04	702.72	1238.61	3.21	31.87	56.18
2003	22.53	76.33	749.00	1183.62	3.39	33.25	52.54
2004	21.91	83.09	773.23	1129.89	4.18	38.92	56.90
2005	21.96	90.44	766.67	1066.40	4.70	39.86	55.44
2006	21.78	97.20	767.07	1023.40	5.10	40.64	54.26
2007	21.21	103.20	729.77	982.65	5.69	40.19	54.12
2008	20.68	108.44	696.24	911.60	6.20	39.81	54.00
2009	20.57	111.94	669.33	914.42	6.60	39.47	53.93
2010	20.62	115.13	652.09	887.34	6.96	39.41	53.63
2011	20.65	117.14	638.06	869.04	7.21	39.28	53.51
2012	20.48	120.35	619.80	851.34	7.56	38.94	53.49
2013	20.41	122.96	603.28	836.64	7.87	38.6	53.53

18-12 主要年份各级学校教师负担学生数
Student-teacher Ratio by Level of School in Main Years

单位：人 (person)

年 份 Year	高等学校 University and College		普通中学 Secondary Schools		小 学 Primary Schools	
	教师数 Number of Teachers	平均每个教师负担学生数 Student-Teacher Ratio	教师数 Number of Teachers	平均每个教师负担学生数 Student-Teacher Ratio	教师数 Number of Teachers	平均每个教师负担学生数 Student-Teacher Ratio
1978	2458	4.16	41661	19.36	82616	24.56
1980	3149	4.54	45232	18.20	89027	23.09
1985	5473	4.84	60942	15.68	98294	20.00
1990	7002	4.47	65814	13.12	95060	19.54
1995	7687	5.78	62934	11.91	106001	20.77
2000	7924	9.34	75895	14.92	131259	18.87
2005	12733	14.82	101701	15.16	134768	15.91
2006	13783	15.07	106975	14.70	134718	15.57
2007	15096	14.33	108232	14.13	133626	15.41
2008	15755	14.66	108729	13.64	132797	15.15
2009	16234	14.88	110842	13.04	134263	14.70
2010	16506	15.22	113990	12.48	133963	14.45
2011	17256	14.99	116501	12.10	135182	14.20
2012	17570	15.29	118299	11.70	136130	13.96
2013	18327	15.19	121129	11.28	140561	13.48

18-13 主要年份各级学校女学生和女教师数
Number of Female Students and Teachers by Level of School in Main Years

单位：人 (person)

项 目	Item	2000	2010	2012	2013
女学生	**Number of Female Students**	**1889552**	**1911185**	**1891395**	**1852920**
高等学校	Institutions of Higher Education	38419	136071	149116	127104
中等专业学校	Specialized Secondary Schools	49892	82554	86008	82572
普通中学	Regular Secondary Schools	568060	718438	22536	20265
职业高中	Vocational Secondary Schools	23670	26234	13655	13954
技工学校	Technical Shools	8740	13228	703294	693650
小 学	Primary Schools	1200513	932296	914822	913207
特殊教育学校	Special Schools for the Blind, Mute and Deaf	258	2364	1964	2168
女学生占学生总数的比重(%)	**Percentage of Female Students to Total Students (%)**	**48.9**	**49.3**	**49.2**	**48.6**
女教师	**Number of Female Teachers**	**134563**	**178259**	**187720**	**194123**
高等学校	Institutions of Higher Education	3192	8362	9044	9566
中等专业学校	Specialized Secondary Schools	3408	3421	4027	3840
普通中学	Regular Secondary Schools	40030	67901	1289	1375
职业高中	Vocational Secondary Schools	1601	1458	4698	3758
技工学校	Technical Schools	1264	3937	72125	74821
小 学	Primary Schools	84944	92917	96208	100306
特殊教育学校	Special Schools for the Blind, Mute and Deaf	124	263	329	457
女教师占教师总数的比重(%)	**Percentage of Female Teachers to Total Teachers (%)**	**58.9**	**63.1**	**64.9**	**65.3**

18-14 主要年份初中毕业生和小学生升学率及小学学龄儿童入学率

Percentage of Graduates of Junior Secondary Schools and Primary Schools Entering Higher Level Schools, Enrollment Rate of School-age Children in Main Years

单位：人、% (person,%)

年份 Year	初中毕业生升高中情况 Student of Graduates of Junior Secondary Schools Entering Senior Secondary Schools			小学毕业生升初中情况 Student of Graduates of Primary Schools Entering Junior Secondary Schools			小学学龄儿童入学情况 Student of School-Age Children Enrolled		
	初中毕业生数 Graduates of Junior Secondary Schools	高中招生数 Students Entering Senior Secondary Schools	升学率 Percentage of Graduates of Junior Secondary Schools Entering Senior Secondary Schools	小学毕业生数 Graduates of Primary Schools	初中招生数 Students Entering Junior Secondary Schools	升学率 Percentage of Graduates of Primary Schools Entering Junior Secondary Schools	学龄儿童数 School-Age Children	已入学学龄儿童数 School-Age Children Enrolled in Schools	入学率 Enrollment Rate
1978	141572	68261	48.22	788359	255687	88.67	1541148	1480400	96.00
1980	186012	73989	39.76	292515	236432	80.83	1637610	1548653	94.57
1985	199206	93692	47.03	289045	247431	85.60	1645055	1569328	95.40
1990	216173	84567	39.12	259301	213074	82.17	1502163	1465325	97.50
1995	171167	58203	34.00	271227	228115	84.10	2036541	1976120	97.03
2000	253240	76744	30.30	371758	342046	92.01	2313890	2245190	97.03
2005	370693	145044	39.13	397592	394878	99.33	2007742	1981569	98.70
2006	386275	142853	36.98	373862	379572	101.53	1957604	1941068	99.15
2007	388365	146449	37.71	361921	363631	100.47	1930074	1916265	99.28
2008	371858	147914	39.78	349300	349665	100.10	1865105	1856800	99.55
2009	354969	148869	41.94	339836	340969	100.33	1839775	1829016	99.41
2010	337510	153238	45.40	334362	336118	100.53	1801872	1797853	99.78
2011	328466	156497	47.64	327704	325953	99.47	1785583	1780729	99.73
2012	319501	155276	48.60	321020	314398	97.94	1767028	1763249	99.79
2013	311432	163582	52.53	321294	313593	97.60	1756979	1753563	99.81

18-15 主要年份各级各类学校少数民族在校学生数

Number of Students Enrollment of Minority Nationalities by Level and Type of School in Main Years

单位：人 (person)

年份 Year	高等学校 Institutions of Higher Education	中等学校 Secondary Schools	中等专业学校 Specialized Secondary Schools	职业高中 Vocational Secondary Schools	技工学校 Technical Schools	普通中学 Regular Secondary Schools	#高中 Senior Secondary Schools	#初中 Junior Secondary Schools	小学（万人） Primary Schools (10 000 persons)
1978	7890	310987	10807			300180	38837	261343	106.58
1980	6455	311213	22263	592	4514	283844	50340	233504	101.73
1985	13996	346833	17888	4915	7649	316381	71199	245182	116.43
1990	17542	439140	23897	13577	13685	387981	94579	293402	126.78
1995	24125	477379	33264	20013	16040	408012	52570	355492	157.84
2000	31989	834390	62572	34992	12260	724566	91843	632723	171.44
2005	75744	993338	32698	54773	13371	892501	152244	740257	136.94
2006	77627	975346	36393	13216	18002	907735	149963	757772	132.94
2007	81978	958643	55224	19181	20476	863762	156478	707284	131.32
2008	85942	935350	62337	28387	23396	821230	160238	660992	130.44
2009	91243	927939	66502	41666	24466	795305	160720	634585	130.31
2010	94708	933338	75924	49388	24894	783132	162687	620445	129.37
2011	102358	940729	82524	54357	21743	782105	173913	608192	129.25
2012	106893	939713	85099	50841	25697	778076	185331	592745	130.10
2013	116256	956057	86810	53971	26261	789015	198588	590427	132.21

18-16 各地、州、市各级各类学校数
Number of Schools by Level, Type and by Prefecture, Autonomous Prefecture and City

单位：所 (2013 年) (unit)

地区	Region	普通高等学校 Regular Institutions of Higher Education	中等职业学校 Specialized Secondary Schools	#中等师范学校 Teacher Training Secondary Schools
总计	**Total**	**36**	**180**	**11**
乌鲁木齐市	Urumqi City	20	31	
克拉玛依市	Karamay City	1	3	1
吐鲁番地区	Turpan Administrative Offices		3	
哈密地区	Hami [Kumul] Administrative Offices		5	1
昌吉回族自治州	Changji Hui Autonomous Prefecture	3	8	
伊犁哈萨克自治州	Ili Kazak Autonomous Prefecture	3	40	3
伊犁州直属县(市)	Counties (Cities) Direct Under Ili Prefecture	3	20	1
塔城地区	Tacheng [Tarbagatai] Administrative Offices		10	1
阿勒泰地区	Altay Administrative Offices		10	1
博尔塔拉蒙古自治州	Bortala Mongol Autonomous Prefecture		1	
巴音郭楞蒙古自治州	Bayangol Mongol Autonomous Prefecture	1	8	1
阿克苏地区	Aksu Administrative Offices	1	8	
克孜勒苏柯尔克孜自治州	Kizilsu Kirgiz Autonomous Prefecture		9	1
喀什地区	Kashgar [Kaxgar] Administrative Offices	1	27	1
和田地区	Hotan Administrative Offices	2	11	1
生产建设兵团	Production and Construction Group	3	24	1
自治区直辖县级市	Municpality Country-LevelCity directly under the Central Govern-ment	1	2	1
石河子市	Shihezi City	1	2	1
阿拉尔市	Aral City			

地区	Region	普通中学 Regular Secondary Schools	#高中 Senior Secondary Schools	小学 Primary Schools	特殊教育学校 Special Schools
总计	**Total**	**1468**	**366**	**3533**	**26**
乌鲁木齐市	Urumqi City	134	52	138	4
克拉玛依市	Karamay City	18	14	28	1
吐鲁番地区	Turpan Administrative Offices	52	11	80	
哈密地区	Hami [Kumul] Administrative Offices	41	12	52	1
昌吉回族自治州	Changji Hui Autonomous Prefecture	46	18	101	1
伊犁哈萨克自治州	Ili Kazak Autonomous Prefecture	294	64	559	7
伊犁州直属县(市)	Counties (Cities) Direct Under Ili Prefecture	177	32	370	5
塔城地区	Tacheng [Tarbagatai] Administrative Offices	78	21	102	1
阿勒泰地区	Altay Administrative Offices	39	11	87	1
博尔塔拉蒙古自治州	Bortala Mongol Autonomous Prefecture	31	9	24	1
巴音郭楞蒙古自治州	Bayangol Mongol Autonomous Prefecture	60	21	97	1
阿克苏地区	Aksu Administrative Offices	143	41	601	1
克孜勒苏柯尔克孜自治州	Kizilsu Kirgiz Autonomous Prefecture	36	10	178	1
喀什地区	Kashgar [Kaxgar] Administrative Offices	204	47	951	5
和田地区	Hotan Administrative Offices	152	18	663	2
生产建设兵团	Production and Construction Group	243	46	55	
自治区直辖县级市	Municpality Country-LevelCity directly under the Central Govern-ment	14	3	6	1
石河子市	Shihezi City	13	3	6	1
阿拉尔市	Aral City	1			

18-17 各地、州、市各级各类学校教职工数
Number of Teachers and Staff by Level and Type of School and by Prefecture, Autonomous Prefecture and City

单位：人 (2013 年) (person)

地　区	Region	普通高等学校 Regular Institutions of Higher Education	中等职业学校 Specialized Secondary Schools
总　计	**Total**	**28781**	**14095**
乌鲁木齐市	Urumqi City	18002	3819
克拉玛依市	Karamay City	558	564
吐鲁番地区	Turpan Administrative Offices		308
哈密地区	Hami [Kumul] Administrative Offices		609
昌吉回族自治州	Changji Hui Autonomous Prefecture	1591	699
伊犁哈萨克自治州	Ili Kazak Autonomous Prefecture	1785	2138
伊犁州直属县(市)	Counties (Cities) Direct Under Ili Prefecture	1785	973
塔城地区	Tacheng [Tarbagatai] Administrative Offices		621
阿勒泰地区	Altay Administrative Offices		544
博尔塔拉蒙古自治州	Bortala Mongol Autonomous Prefecture		174
巴音郭楞蒙古自治州	Bayangol Mongol Autonomous Prefecture	582	457
阿克苏地区	Aksu Administrative Offices	433	465
克孜勒苏柯尔克孜自治州	Kizilsu Kirgiz Autonomous Prefecture		406
喀什地区	Kashgar [Kaxgar] Administrative Offices	935	2054
和田地区	Hotan Administrative Offices	631	553
生产建设兵团	Production and Construction Group	3866	1750
自治区直辖县级市	Municpality Country-LevelCity directly under the Central Govern-ment	398	99
石河子市	Shihezi City	398	99
阿拉尔市	Aral City		

地　区	Region	普通中学 Regular Secondary Schools	小　学 Primary Schools	特殊教育学　校 Special Schools
总　计	**Total**	**136704**	**154884**	**660**
乌鲁木齐市	Urumqi City	12700	10676	186
克拉玛依市	Karamay City	2823	2116	10
吐鲁番地区	Turpan Administrative Offices	3690	4737	
哈密地区	Hami [Kumul] Administrative Offices	3443	3922	50
昌吉回族自治州	Changji Hui Autonomous Prefecture	7336	7665	53
伊犁哈萨克自治州	Ili Kazak Autonomous Prefecture	25169	34726	68
伊犁州直属县(市)	Counties (Cities) Direct Under Ili Prefecture	14398	20698	25
塔城地区	Tacheng [Tarbagatai] Administrative Offices	6680	8200	43
阿勒泰地区	Altay Administrative Offices	4091	5828	
博尔塔拉蒙古自治州	Bortala Mongol Autonomous Prefecture	2739	3611	2
巴音郭楞蒙古自治州	Bayangol Mongol Autonomous Prefecture	7381	9615	55
阿克苏地区	Aksu Administrative Offices	12870	14910	36
克孜勒苏柯尔克孜自治州	Kizilsu Kirgiz Autonomous Prefecture	4404	6554	
喀什地区	Kashgar [Kaxgar] Administrative Offices	24557	29217	103
和田地区	Hotan Administrative Offices	11303	12682	74
生产建设兵团	Production and Construction Group	16907	13718	
自治区直辖县级市	Municpality Country-LevelCity directly under the Central Govern-ment	1382	735	23
石河子市	Shihezi City	1361	691	23
阿拉尔市	Aral City	21	44	

18-18 各地、州、市各级各类学校教师数
Number of Teachers by Level and Type of School and by Prefecture, Autonomous Prefecture and City

单位：人　　(2013 年)　　(person)

地区	Region	普通高等学校 Regular Institutions of Higher Education	中等职业学校 Specialized Secondary Schools
总　计	**Total**	**18327**	**10031**
乌鲁木齐市	Urumqi City	11032	2359
克拉玛依市	Karamay City	292	298
吐鲁番地区	Turpan Administrative Offices		231
哈密地区	Hami [Kumul] Administrative Offices		463
昌吉回族自治州	Changji Hui Autonomous Prefecture	1144	571
伊犁哈萨克自治州	Ili Kazak Autonomous Prefecture	1099	1541
伊犁州直属县(市)	Counties (Cities) Direct Under Ili Prefecture	1099	711
塔城地区	Tacheng [Tarbagatai] Administrative Offices		427
阿勒泰地区	Altay Administrative Offices		403
博尔塔拉蒙古自治州	Bortala Mongol Autonomous Prefecture		111
巴音郭楞蒙古自治州	Bayangol Mongol Autonomous Prefecture	478	363
阿克苏地区	Aksu Administrative Offices	336	404
克孜勒苏柯尔克孜自治州	Kizilsu Kirgiz Autonomous Prefecture		346
喀什地区	Kashgar [Kaxgar] Administrative Offices	725	1632
和田地区	Hotan Administrative Offices	363	463
生产建设兵团	Production and Construction Group	2543	1186
自治区直辖县级市	Municpality Country-LevelCity directly under the Central Govern-ment	315	63
石河子市	Shihezi City	315	63
阿拉尔市	Aral City		

地区	Region	普通中学 Regular Secondary Schools	#高　中 Senior Secondary Schools	小　学 Primary Schools	特殊教育学校 Special Schools
总　计	**Total**	**121129**	**35020**	**140561**	**547**
乌鲁木齐市	Urumqi City	10643	4033	9738	135
克拉玛依市	Karamay City	2418	945	1895	8
吐鲁番地区	Turpan Administrative Offices	3330	878	4465	
哈密地区	Hami [Kumul] Administrative Offices	2985	1196	3466	35
昌吉回族自治州	Changji Hui Autonomous Prefecture	6281	2296	7254	50
伊犁哈萨克自治州	Ili Kazak Autonomous Prefecture	22223	7212	30896	60
伊犁州直属县(市)	Counties (Cities) Direct Under Ili Prefecture	12983	3906	18856	21
塔城地区	Tacheng [Tarbagatai] Administrative Offices	5631	2092	6854	39
阿勒泰地区	Altay Administrative Offices	3609	1214	5186	
博尔塔拉蒙古自治州	Bortala Mongol Autonomous Prefecture	2388	780	3268	2
巴音郭楞蒙古自治州	Bayangol Mongol Autonomous Prefecture	6521	2431	8716	51
阿克苏地区	Aksu Administrative Offices	11647	2895	14014	28
克孜勒苏柯尔克孜自治州	Kizilsu Kirgiz Autonomous Prefecture	4140	1271	6035	
喀什地区	Kashgar [Kaxgar] Administrative Offices	22712	4762	26593	88
和田地区	Hotan Administrative Offices	10509	1475	11594	70
生产建设兵团	Production and Construction Group	14113	4249	11955	
自治区直辖县级市	Municpality Country-LevelCity directly under the Central Govern-ment	1219	597	672	20
石河子市	Shihezi City	1198	597	632	20
阿拉尔市	Aral City	21		40	

18-19 各地、州、市各级各类学校在校学生数
Number of Students Enrollment by Level and Type of School and by Prefecture, Autonomous Prefecture and City

单位：人 (2013 年) (person)

地　区	Region	普通高等学校 Regular Institutions of Higher Education	中等职业学校 Specialized Secondary Schools
总　计	**Total**	**278425**	**229294**
乌鲁木齐市	Urumqi City	165090	69623
克拉玛依市	Karamay City	4488	688
吐鲁番地区	Turpan Administrative Offices		3721
哈密地区	Hami [Kumul] Administrative Offices		3835
昌吉回族自治州	Changji Hui Autonomous Prefecture	22824	13250
伊犁哈萨克自治州	Ili Kazak Autonomous Prefecture	15458	21248
伊犁州直属县(市)	Counties (Cities) Direct Under Ili Prefecture	15458	12802
塔城地区	Tacheng [Tarbagatai] Administrative Offices		3432
阿勒泰地区	Altay Administrative Offices		5014
博尔塔拉蒙古自治州	Bortala Mongol Autonomous Prefecture		1122
巴音郭楞蒙古自治州	Bayangol Mongol Autonomous Prefecture	4457	11460
阿克苏地区	Aksu Administrative Offices	3010	11509
克孜勒苏柯尔克孜自治州	Kizilsu Kirgiz Autonomous Prefecture		2707
喀什地区	Kashgar [Kaxgar] Administrative Offices	11736	30882
和田地区	Hotan Administrative Offices	5944	19357
生产建设兵团	Production and Construction Group	39063	37887
自治区直辖县级市	Municpality Country-LevelCity directly under the Central Govern-ment	6355	2005
石河子市	Shihezi City	6355	2005
阿拉尔市	Aral City		

地　区	Region	普通中学 Regular Secondary Schools	#高　中 Senior Secondary Schools	小　学 Primary Schools	特殊教育学校 Special Schools
总　计	**Total**	**1366013**	**447540**	**1894401**	**5229**
乌鲁木齐市	Urumqi City	153059	59862	186289	633
克拉玛依市	Karamay City	25239	9588	22726	65
吐鲁番地区	Turpan Administrative Offices	31997	10102	51504	102
哈密地区	Hami [Kumul] Administrative Offices	32452	14143	32711	241
昌吉回族自治州	Changji Hui Autonomous Prefecture	77489	31170	78360	179
伊犁哈萨克自治州	Ili Kazak Autonomous Prefecture	240468	91079	338667	1076
伊犁州直属县(市)	Counties (Cities) Direct Under Ili Prefecture	149568	52955	222065	711
塔城地区	Tacheng [Tarbagatai] Administrative Offices	58997	24732	69392	203
阿勒泰地区	Altay Administrative Offices	31903	13392	47210	162
博尔塔拉蒙古自治州	Bortala Mongol Autonomous Prefecture	21339	9176	27315	71
巴音郭楞蒙古自治州	Bayangol Mongol Autonomous Prefecture	70623	27760	100842	229
阿克苏地区	Aksu Administrative Offices	141231	38918	218487	365
克孜勒苏柯尔克孜自治州	Kizilsu Kirgiz Autonomous Prefecture	34929	12132	57457	82
喀什地区	Kashgar [Kaxgar] Administrative Offices	252775	60305	414655	988
和田地区	Hotan Administrative Offices	111947	16547	185980	901
生产建设兵团	Production and Construction Group	152926	57143	167150	248
自治区直辖县级市	Municpality Country-LevelCity directly under the Central Govern-ment	19539	9615	12258	49
石河子市	Shihezi City	19425	9615	11959	49
阿拉尔市	Aral City	114		299	

18-20 各地、州、市各级各类学校招生数
Number of New Students Enrollment by Level and Type of School and by Prefecture, Autonomous Prefecture and City

单位：人 (2013 年) (person)

地 区	Region	普通高等学校 Regular Institutions of Higher Education	中等职业学校 Specialized Secondary Schools
总 计	**Total**	**83435**	**83893**
乌鲁木齐市	Urumqi City	49416	23599
克拉玛依市	Karamay City	1719	203
吐鲁番地区	Turpan Administrative Offices		1327
哈密地区	Hami [Kumul] Administrative Offices		1326
昌吉回族自治州	Changji Hui Autonomous Prefecture	7490	4664
伊犁哈萨克自治州	Ili Kazak Autonomous Prefecture	4725	7345
伊犁州直属县(市)	Counties (Cities) Direct Under Ili Prefecture	4725	4799
塔城地区	Tacheng [Tarbagatai] Administrative Offices		1249
阿勒泰地区	Altay Administrative Offices		1297
博尔塔拉蒙古自治州	Bortala Mongol Autonomous Prefecture		699
巴音郭楞蒙古自治州	Bayangol Mongol Autonomous Prefecture	1642	3623
阿克苏地区	Aksu Administrative Offices	1260	5506
克孜勒苏柯尔克孜自治州	Kizilsu Kirgiz Autonomous Prefecture		742
喀什地区	Kashgar [Kaxgar] Administrative Offices	2895	13813
和田地区	Hotan Administrative Offices	2044	6582
生产建设兵团	Production and Construction Group	9811	13491
自治区直辖县级市	Municpality Country-LevelCity directly under the Central Govern-ment	2433	973
石河子市	Shihezi City	2433	973
阿拉尔市	Aral City		

地 区	Region	普通中学 Regular Secondary Schools	#高 中 Senior Secondary Schools	小 学 Primary Schools	特殊教育学校 Special Schools
总 计	**Total**	**477175**	**163582**	**348643**	**1473**
乌鲁木齐市	Urumqi City	52714	20552	34968	149
克拉玛依市	Karamay City	8700	3297	4082	10
吐鲁番地区	Turpan Administrative Offices	11375	3799	10240	24
哈密地区	Hami [Kumul] Administrative Offices	10976	4933	5936	32
昌吉回族自治州	Changji Hui Autonomous Prefecture	25502	10366	13222	31
伊犁哈萨克自治州	IliKazak Autonomous Prefecture	82985	31905	62822	385
伊犁州直属县(市)	Counties (Cities) Direct Under Ili Prefecture	51943	19149	42143	312
塔城地区	Tacheng [Tarbagatai] Administrative Offices	19833	8288	12396	33
阿勒泰地区	Altay Administrative Offices	11209	4468	8283	40
博尔塔拉蒙古自治州	Bortala Mongol Autonomous Prefecture	7314	2968	5004	3
巴音郭楞蒙古自治州	Bayangol Mongol Autonomous Prefecture	24389	9748	20352	58
阿克苏地区	Aksu Administrative Offices	50175	15289	42529	41
克孜勒苏柯尔克孜自治州	Kizilsu Kirgiz Autonomous Prefecture	12272	4089	10112	42
喀什地区	Kashgar [Kaxgar] Administrative Offices	93032	25675	76283	410
和田地区	Hotan Administrative Offices	40047	8965	32854	228
生产建设兵团	Production and Construction Group	51107	18803	28178	39
自治区直辖县级市	Municpality Country-LevelCity directly under the Central Govern-ment	6587	3193	2061	21
石河子市	Shihezi City	6539	3193	2023	21
阿拉尔市	Aral City	48		38	

18-21 各地、州、市各级各类学校毕业生数
Number of Graduates by Level and Type of School and by Prefecture, Autonomous Prefecture and City

单位：人 (2013 年) (person)

地区	Region	普通高等学校 Regular Institutions of Higher Education	中等职业学校 Specialized Secondary Schools
总计	**Total**	**69983**	**74860**
乌鲁木齐市	Urumqi City	40782	22676
克拉玛依市	Karamay City	1288	245
吐鲁番地区	Turpan Administrative Offices		726
哈密地区	Hami [Kumul] Administrative Offices		1005
昌吉回族自治州	Changji Hui Autonomous Prefecture	6323	3828
伊犁哈萨克自治州	Ili Kazak Autonomous Prefecture	3529	6477
伊犁州直属县(市)	Counties (Cities) Direct Under Ili Prefecture	3529	3667
塔城地区	Tacheng [Tarbagatai] Administrative Offices		766
阿勒泰地区	Altay Administrative Offices		2044
博尔塔拉蒙古自治州	Bortala Mongol Autonomous Prefecture		224
巴音郭楞蒙古自治州	Bayangol Mongol Autonomous Prefecture	1483	4515
阿克苏地区	Aksu Administrative Offices	1075	4389
克孜勒苏柯尔克孜自治州	Kizilsu Kirgiz Autonomous Prefecture		535
喀什地区	Kashgar [Kaxgar] Administrative Offices	2612	8087
和田地区	Hotan Administrative Offices	1510	8902
生产建设兵团	Production and Construction Group	9338	12477
自治区直辖县级市	Municpality Country-LevelCity directly under the Central Govern-ment	2043	774
石河子市	Shihezi City	2043	774
阿拉尔市	Aral City		

地区	Region	普通中学 Regular Secondary Schools	#高中 Senior Secondary Schools	小学 Primary Schools	特殊教育学校 Special Schools
总计	**Total**	**451275**	**139843**	**321294**	**680**
乌鲁木齐市	Urumqi City	47710	17986	30367	137
克拉玛依市	Karamay City	8116	3151	4094	2
吐鲁番地区	Turpan Administrative Offices	10592	3405	8457	24
哈密地区	Hami [Kumul] Administrative Offices	10518	4343	5885	15
昌吉回族自治州	Changji Hui Autonomous Prefecture	27128	11439	14202	42
伊犁哈萨克自治州	Ili Kazak Autonomous Prefecture	79181	29038	52545	63
伊犁州直属县(市)	Counties (Cities) Direct Under Ili Prefecture	48548	16242	33288	23
塔城地区	Tacheng [Tarbagatai] Administrative Offices	20185	8460	11850	21
阿勒泰地区	Altay Administrative Offices	10448	4336	7407	19
博尔塔拉蒙古自治州	Bortala Mongol Autonomous Prefecture	7381	3242	4598	5
巴音郭楞蒙古自治州	Bayangol Mongol Autonomous Prefecture	23002	9395	15152	49
阿克苏地区	Aksu Administrative Offices	43331	10859	35956	19
克孜勒苏柯尔克孜自治州	Kizilsu Kirgiz Autonomous Prefecture	11232	3573	8643	4
喀什地区	Kashgar [Kaxgar] Administrative Offices	82886	16356	70621	115
和田地区	Hotan Administrative Offices	38064	3860	34167	108
生产建设兵团	Production and Construction Group	55873	20016	34277	83
自治区直辖县级市	Municpality Country-LevelCity directly under the Central Govern-ment	6261	3180	2330	14
石河子市	Shihezi City	6223	3180	2278	14
阿拉尔市	Aral City	38		52	

18-22 各类学校教育经费情况
Educational Funds in Various Schools

单位：万元 (2013 年) (10 000 yuan)

指标	Item	合计 Total	国家财政性教育经费 Government Appropriation for Education	#预算内教育经费 Budgetary Education Expense	民办学校中举办者投入 Investor Derotion	社会捐资 Donations	事业收入 Income from Undertakings	其他 Others
总计	**Total**	**6026351**	**5540886**	**5126510**	**1413**	**13687**	**299414**	**170950**
高等学校	**Institutions of Higher Education**	**763656**	**548254**	**533782**		**1714**	**141604**	**72085**
普通高等学校	Regular Institutions of Higher Education	705693	508748	494721		195	126326	70424
普通高等本科学校	Universities with Full Undergraduate Course	528325	385699	379134		91	88282	54253
普通高职高专学校	Regular Institutions of Specialized Course	177368	123050	115587		104	38044	16170
#:高等职业学校	Universities With High Vocational Course	169023	115787	108325		104	37124	16008
成人高等学校	Institutions of Higher Education for Adults	57963	39505	39060		1519	15278	1661
中等职业学校	**Vocational Secondary Schools**	**398177**	**336098**	**301565**		**5710**	**26331**	**30038**
中等专业学校	Specialized Secondary Schools	255714	217168	205204		247	18556	19743
职业高中	Vocational Senior Secondary Schools	98108	86820	65459		5453	1780	4056
#:农村	Rural Areas	374	367	363			7	
技工学校	Technical Schools	31328	21605	21200		10	4755	4959
成人中等专业学校	Specialized Secondary Schools for Adults	13028	10506	9701			1241	1281
中学	**Secondary Schools**	**2030205**	**1927736**	**1753692**	**36**	**3162**	**69830**	**29442**
普通中学	Regular Secondary Schools	2029903	1927437	1753393	36	3162	69827	29442
普通高中	Regular Senior Secondary Schools	656668	572108	500441	29	1478	64709	18345
#:农村	Rural Areas	27316	26496	18650		323	313	184
普通初中	Regular Junior Secondary Schools	1373235	1355329	1252952	7	1684	5118	11097
#:农村	Rural Areas	689517	683064	646561		1421	420	4612
成人中学	Secondary Schools for Adults	302	299	299			3	
小学	**Primary Schools**	**1986650**	**1969705**	**1859606**	**327**	**2075**	**4103**	**10440**
#普通小学	Regular Primary Schools	1986623	1969679	1859579	327	2075	4103	10440
#农村	Rural Areas	1228916	1221309	1177066		1826	847	4935
特殊教育	**Special Education**	**12216**	**11854**	**10848**		**1**	**82**	**279**
#特殊教育学校	Special Education Schools	12037	11675	10668		1	82	279
幼儿园	**Kindergartens**	**318258**	**266262**	**252577**	**1051**	**599**	**45654**	**4692**
#农村	Rural Areas	136395	131554	126404	106	470	3460	805
教育行政单位	**Education Administrative Unit**	**190355**	**172605**	**156913**		**181**	**1186**	**16383**
教育事业单位	**Education Institution**	**126771**	**116164**	**89228**		**176**	**7477**	**2955**
其他	**Others**	**200063**	**192208**	**168300**		**70**	**3148**	**4637**

补充资料：其他收入中联合办学(班)收入 2351.3 万元。
Other income (class) income 23513000 yuan. comed from Joint school .
注：本表按隶属关系填列。 Note: Data in The table according to the membership listed.

18-23 科技活动基本情况
Basic Statistics on Scientific and Technological Activities

指　　标	Item	2011	2012
研究与试验发展(R&D)投入情况	**Statistics on R&D Input**		
R&D 人员折合全时当量(人·年)	**Full-time Equivalent of Rearch and Development Personnel (person.year)**	**15440**	**15671**
#基础研究	Basic Research	1926	2673
应用研究	Applied Research	4283	4317
试验发展	Experimental Development	9231	8678
R&D 经费支出(万元)	**Expenditure on R&D (10000 yuan)**	330030	397289
#基础研究	Basic Research	20890	31797
应用研究	Applied Research	65632	74796
试验发展	Experimental Development	243509	290696
#日常性支出	Daily Expenditure	286961	349534
资产性支出	Capital Expenditure	43069	47755
#政府资金	Government Funds	88065	106678
企业资金	Self-raised Funds by Enterprises	229449	278170
研究与试验发展经费支出相当于新疆生产总值比例(%)	**Proportion of Expenditure on R&D to GDP of Xinjiang**	**0.50**	**0.52**
科技产出及成果情况	**Statistics on S&T Outputs and Results**		
发表科技论文(篇)	Scientific Papers Issued (pieces)	20018	20382
出版科技著作(种)	Publication on Science and Technology (kind)	428	446
专利申请受理数(件)	Number of Patents Application Accepted (piece)	1872	2364
#发明专利	Inventions	619	739
专利申请授权数(件)	Number of Patents Application Granted (piece)	232	332
#发明专利	Inventions	124	187

18-24 县级以上政府部门属研究与开发机构及科技信息与文献机构数、人员数
State-owned Research and Development Institutions and Information and Literature Institutions at and above County Level and Persons Engaged

(2013 年)

指　　标	Item	合　计 Total	自然科学技术领域 Field of Natural Sciences and Technology	社会、人文科学技术领域 Field of Social Sciences and Humanities	科技信息和文献机构 Scientific-technical Information and Document Institutions
机构数(个)	**Institutions (unit)**	**111**	**97**	**6**	**8**
科技活动人员(人)	**Personal Engaged in Scientific and Technological Activities (person)**	**6912**	**6278**	**401**	**233**
#大学本科及以上学历	University Graduate or above	4774	4317	280	177
研究与试验发展全时人员(人·年)	**Full-time Equivalent of Rearch and Development Personnel (person.year)**	**3225**	**2908**	**276**	**41**
科技活动收入(万元)	**Sources of Funds for S&T(10 000 yuan)**	**171137.1**	**158866.5**	**7219.7**	**5050.9**
#政府拨款	Government Funds	148045.3	138923.8	4599.2	4522.3
科技经费内部支出额(万元)	**Internal Expenditures on Scientific and Technological Activities (10 000 yuan)**	**155780.1**	**145671.8**	**4914.6**	**5193.7**
#劳务费	Service Fees	52182.7	47165.6	2441.7	2575.4
固定资产购建费	Purchases or Construction of Fixed Assets	25668.4	25050.4	193.3	424.7
研究与发展经费支出(万元)	**Expenditure on Research and Development**	**82250.7**	**78719.8**	**2506.7**	**1024.2**
#基础研究	Basic Research	13725.0	12111.3	1613.7	
应用研究	Applied Research	29226.4	27327.0	875.2	1024.2
试验发展	Experimental Development	39299.3	39281.5	17.8	

18-25 重大科学技术研究成果及奖励数
Number of Major Achievements in Scientific and Technological Research and Awarded Prizes

单位：项 (item)

年 份 Year	自治区级重大科技成果 Number of Major Achievements in Science and Technology of Autonomous Region	奖励情况 Awarded Prizes					
		国家级 National	自治区级 Autonomous Regional	一等奖 Frist Class Awards	二等奖 Second Class Awards	三等奖 Third Class Awards	四等奖 Fourth Class Awards
1978 年以前	1551	88	610				
1980-1985	1173	16	356	5	31	102	218
1990	444	3	129		18	56	55
1995	218	3	137	4	26	53	54
2000	250	2	90	5	18	67	
2001	285	6	92	4	23	65	
2002	207	5	99	5	30	64	
2003	232	3	111	8	34	69	
2004	218	4	108	4	33	71	
2005	225	3	101	6	27	68	
2006	212	3	107	8	37	62	
2007	220	8	118	10	42	66	
2008	69	8	108	9	40	59	
2009	166	12					
2010	228	9	130	15	47	68	
2011	205	6	121	14	46	61	
2012	236	6	126	15	45	66	
2013	257	5	150	21	62	67	

18-26 专利申请和批准数
Number of Patent Applications Examined and Approved

单位：件 (case)

年 份 Year	申 请 数 Number of Patent Applications Examined				批 准 数 Number of Patent Applications Granted				代理机构（个） Agency (unit)
	合 计 Total	发 明 Inventions	实用新型 Utility Models	外观设计 Designs	合 计 Total	发 明 Inventions	实用新型 Utility Models	外观设计 Designs	
1990	250	38	203	9	139	3	135	1	5
1995	609	92	467	50	312	11	285	16	6
2000	1088	179	699	210	717	66	475	176	7
2001	1088	189	683	216	755	90	522	143	5
2002	1239	216	779	244	627	61	407	159	4
2003	1472	253	940	279	751	75	520	156	5
2004	1492	272	870	350	792	75	530	187	5
2005	1851	320	1117	414	921	88	537	296	5
2006	2256	381	1166	709	1187	107	805	275	5
2007	2270	476	1255	539	1534	90	1035	409	5
2008	2412	482	1408	522	1493	82	1100	311	6
2009	2872	662	1865	345	1867	120	1261	486	6
2010	3560	914	2272	374	2562	189	2012	361	6
2011	4736	1273	2732	731	2642	302	1974	366	6
2012	7044	1679	3375	1990	3440	451	2383	606	6
2013	8224	2081	4620	1523	4998	540	3244	1214	6

18-27 高等学校科技活动情况
Basic Statistics on Higher Education for Science and Technology Activities

指 标	Item	2012	2013
高等学校研发(R&D)情况	**Statistics on R&D of Higher Education**		
有 R&D 活动的单位数	Number of Enterprises hawing R&D Activities		
#理工农医	Natural Sciences & Technology	29	30
#人文社科	Social Sciences & Humanities	20	25
研究机构(个)	Number of Institutions(unit)	75	75
研究与试验发展(R&D)投入情况	**Statistics on R&D Input**		
R&D 人员折合全时当量(人·年)	Full-time Equivalent of R&D Personnel (man-years)	3554	3692
#基础研究	Basic Research	1923	2057
应用研究	Applied Research	1549	1558
试验发展	Experimental Development	82	76
R&D 经费支出(万元)	Expenditure on R&D(10 000 yuan)	26834	32640
#基础研究	Basic Research	14533	15092
应用研究	Applied Research	11603	16336
试验发展	Experimental Development	698	1212
#日常性支出	Daily Expenditure	23612	28742
资产性支出	Capital Expenditure	3223	3899
#政府资金	Government Funds	22957	27175
企业资金	Self-raised Funds by Enterprises	2963	3742
R&D 项目(课题)情况	**Statistics on R&D Topics**		
R&D 项目(课题)数(项)	R&D Projects (item)	5343	5793
R&D 项目(课题)人员全时当量(人年)	Participants (man-years)	3551	3689
R&D 项目(课题)经费支出(万元)	Expenditure (10000 yuan)	22218	27916
科技产出及成果情况	**Statistics on S&T Outputs and Results**		
发表科技论文(篇)	Scientific Papers Issued (piece)	12219	12326
出版科技著作(种)	Publication on Science and Technology (kind)	261	204
专利申请受理数(件)	Number of Patents Applications Accepted (piece)	180	230
#发明专利	Inventions	121	151
专利申请授权数(件)	Number of Patents Applications Granted (piece)	124	121
#发明专利	Inventions	74	60

18-28 主要年份企事业单位主要专业技术人员数
Number of Main Scientific and Technical Personnel in Enterprises and Institutions in Main Years

单位：人 (person)

年 份 Year	合 计 Total	工程技术人员 Engineering	农业技术人员 Agriculture	卫生技术人员 Health Care	科学研究人员 Scientific Researcn	教学人员 Teaching
1978. 6 月末	85063	22198	13141	31741	3042	14941
1985	158709	51636	20730	57559	3416	25368
1990	241524	92383	25089	71906	4326	47820
2000	368262	58576	27764	62338	2409	217175
2001	385129	59913	30043	65585	2492	227096
2002	387726	58011	31867	65364	2337	230147
2003	385705	57506	30808	65622	2236	229533
2004	398318	55421	32831	68604	2928	238534
2005	402404	51915	32744	67945	2451	247349
2006	412977	52702	34131	68231	2460	255453
2007	411590	50680	33859	69101	2453	255497
2008	414277	49175	31799	71104	2261	259938
2009	411628	47525	30126	72827	2518	258632
2010	407651	47734	28433	77357	2071	252056
2011	421372	47357	27921	80290	6728	259076
2012	454975	47755	30422	85615	2224	288959
2013	446213	47967	30607	83161	2856	281622

注：1.1991 年起专业技术人员包括企事业单位(不含行政机关)人员数,教学人员包括社会和自然科技领域及小学教师人数。
2.1996 年后数据不包括中央单位的专业技术人员数，故人员减少较多。

Note: a) The Specialezed and technical personnel include those who work in enterprises and institutions (excluding administrative organs), teaching Staff, those work in social and nature scientific fields as well as elementary school teachers since 1991.
b) After 1996, the data exclude the figure of professionals with national establishments stationed to Xinjiang and thus the number of staff is reduced a lot.

18-29 主要年份企事业单位主要专业技术人员比重
Proportion of Scientific and Technical Personnel in Enterprises and Institutions in Main Years

单位：% (%)

年 份 Year	合 计 Total	工程技术 Engineering	农业技术 Agriculture	卫生技术 Health Care	科学研究 Scientific Research	教 学 Teaching
1978. 6 月末	100	26.10	15.45	37.31	3.58	17.56
1985	100	32.54	13.06	36.27	2.15	15.98
1990	100	38.25	10.39	29.77	1.79	19.80
2000	100	15.91	7.54	16.93	0.65	58.97
2001	100	15.55	7.80	17.03	0.65	58.97
2002	100	14.96	8.22	16.86	0.60	59.36
2003	100	14.91	7.99	17.01	0.58	59.51
2004	100	13.91	8.24	17.22	0.74	59.89
2005	100	12.90	8.14	16.89	0.61	61.46
2006	100	12.76	8.26	16.52	0.60	61.86
2007	100	12.31	8.22	16.79	0.60	62.08
2008	100	11.87	7.68	17.16	0.55	62.74
2009	100	11.55	7.32	17.69	0.61	62.83
2010	100	11.71	6.97	18.98	0.51	61.83
2011	100	11.24	6.63	19.05	1.60	61.48
2012	100	10.50	6.68	18.82	0.49	63.51
2013	100	10.75	6.86	18.64	0.64	63.11

18-30 规模以上工业企业科技活动情况

(2012 年)

项　目	Item	企业数(个) Nnmber of Industrial Enterprises (unit)	#有研究与试验发展活动的企业数 Number of Enterprises Having R&D Activities	企业办科技机构(个) R&D Institution
总　计	**Total**	**1859**	**119**	**91**
按企业规模分	**Grouped by Size of Enterprises**			
大型企业	Large Enterprises	84	29	22
中型企业	Medium-sized Enterprises	312	43	29
小型企业	Small Enterprises	1373	46	40
微型企业	Mini Enterprises	90	1	
按登记注册类型分	**Grouped by Ownership**			
内资企业	Domestic-funded Enterprises	1782	117	90
国有企业	State-owned Enterprises	119	13	9
有限责任公司	Limited Liability Corporations	838	56	41
#国有独资公司	State Sole funded Corporations	55	6	4
其他有限责任公司	Other Limited Liability Corporations	783	50	37
股份有限责任公司	Share-holding Corporations Ltd	86	28	23
私营企业	Private Enterprises	695	19	17
私营有限责任公司	Private Limited Liability Corporations	624	16	14
私营股份有限公司	Private Stock Ltd. Co.	31	3	3
其他企业	Other Enterprises	18	1	
港澳台商投资企业	Enterprises With Funds from Hong Kong, Macao and Taiwan	27	1	1
#合资经营企业(港或澳、台资)	Joint-ventures Enterprises	16	1	1
外商投资企业	Foreign Funded Enterprises	50	1	
#其他外资投资企业	Other Foreign Funded Enterprises	1	1	
按工业行业大类分	**Grouped by Sector**			
采矿业	Mining and Quarrying	242	16	14
#煤炭开采和洗选业	Coal Extracting and Dressing	108	4	2
石油和天然气开采业	Petroleum and Natural Gas Extraction	5	3	5
黑色金属矿采选业	Processing of Ferrous Metals Ores	54	1	1
有色金属矿采选业	Processing of Nonferrous Metals Ores	31	3	2
开采辅助活动	Mining Activities	23	5	4
制造业	Manufacturing	1452	100	75
#农副食品加工业	Processing of Food from Agricultural Products	269	10	5
食品制造业	Food Manufacturing	104	7	4
酒、饮料和精制茶制造业	Manufacture of Wine,Beverages and Refined Tea	55	3	3
纺织业	Textile Industry	76	5	4

Basic Statistics on Science and Technology Activities of Industrial Enterprises above Designated Size

研究与试验发展人员数(人) Number of R&D Persons	研究人员 Research personal	研究与试验发展人员折合全时当量(人·年) Full-time Equivalent of R&D personnel	研究人员 Research personal	研究与试验发展经费(万元) Expenditure on R&D	其 中 Of which		
					基础研究 Basic Research	应用研究 Applied Research	试验发展 Experimental Development
9188	**4609**	**6199.5**	**3019.0**	**273354.2**		**32337.0**	**241017.2**
6351	3604	4651.9	2476.6	231995		27651.7	204343.3
1965	707	928.1	336.4	23717.9		4290.3	19427.6
868	297	618.6	205.5	17566.8		395.0	17171.8
4	1	0.7	0.2	74.5			74.5
8962	4534	6162.1	3006.2	273077.2		32076.0	241001.2
929	487	577.9	330.0	12475.3			12475.3
2234	832	1505.2	550.2	50135.1		2128.4	48006.7
197	74	89.6	33.9	987.0		209.9	777.1
2037	758	1415.5	516.3	49148.1		1918.5	47229.6
5227	3033	3832.7	2029.5	199065.6		29947.6	169118.0
566	176	245.2	95.3	11001.2			11001.2
210	91	133.6	65.6	7020.1			7020.1
356	85	111.7	29.8	3981.1			3981.1
6	6	1.1	1.1	400.0			400.0
18	6	18.0	6.0	261.0		261.0	
18	6	18.0	6.0	261.0		261.0	
208	69	19.3	6.4	16.0			16.0
208	69	19.3	6.4	16.0			16.0
4145	3112	2717.3	2049.7	139585.2		29808.6	109776.6
196	99	73.2	30.2	1316.8		209.9	1106.9
3065	2503	1888.1	1577.2	129128		27226.9	101901.1
29	29	26.9	26.9	1200.0			1200.0
68	35	42.9	25.2	171.4			171.4
787	446	686.3	390.3	7769.0		2371.8	5397.2
4871	1429	3420.4	943.4	130257.8		2528.4	127729.4
172	73	64.7	32.1	3301.1			3301.1
379	94	84.4	22.9	4921.2			4921.2
156	62	118.2	30.8	1763.4			1763.4
368	123	107.6	28.0	2286.7			2286.7

18-30 续表 1

(2012 年)

项　　目	Item	企业数(个) Nnmber of Industrial Enterprises (unit)	#有研究与试验发展活动的企业数 Number of Enterprises Having R & D Activities	科技机构(个) Number of Scientific Technological Agencies (unit)
纺织服装、服饰业	Manufacture of Textile Wearing Apparel, Footware and Caps	6	2	1
造纸及纸制品业	Paper and Paper Products Manufacturing	25	2	3
石油加工、炼焦及核燃料加工业	Oil Processing, Coking and Nuclear Fuel Processing	87	8	4
化学原料及化学制品制造业	Raw Chemical Material and Chemical Products	129	23	16
医药制造业	Medicine Manufacturing	22	3	4
化学纤维制造业	Chemical Fiber Manufacturing	12	1	
橡胶和塑料制品业	Rubber and Plastic Products Manufacturing	87	7	9
非金属矿物制品业	Nonmetal Mineral Products Manufacturing	278	8	5
黑色金属冶炼及压延加工业	Manufacture and Processing of Ferrous Metals	72	2	2
有色金属冶炼及压延加工业	Manufalture and Processing of Non-ferrous Metals	36	2	1
金属制品业	Metal Products Manufacturing	63		2
通用设备制造业	General Purpose Machinery Manufacturing	21	1	
专用设备制造业	Special Purpose Machinery Manufacturing	21	6	4
汽车制造业	Manufacture of Automobile	7	4	3
电气机械及器材制造业	Electric Equipment and Machinery Manufacturing	37	6	5
电力、燃气及水的生产和供应业	Production and Suppoly of Electric Power,Gas and Water	165	3	2
#电力、热力的生产和供应业	Electric Power and Thermal Production and Supply	131	3	2
按企业所在地区划分	**Grouped by Region**			
乌鲁木齐市	Urumqi City	350	32	26
克拉玛依市	Karamay City	64	19	16
吐鲁番地区	Turpan Administrative Offices	78	3	4
哈密地区	Hami [Kumul] Administrative Offices	93	2	1
昌吉回族自治州	Changji Hui Autonomous Prefecture	311	13	10
伊犁州直属县(市)	Counties (Cities) Direct Under Ili Prefecture	198	7	9
塔城地区	Tacheng [Tarbagatai] Administrative Offices	89		1
阿勒泰地区	Altay Administrative Offices	57	3	2
博尔塔拉蒙古自治州	Bortala Mongol Autonomous Prefecture	41	1	
巴音郭楞蒙古自治州	Bayangol Mongol Autonomous Prefecture	132	9	4
阿克苏地区	Aksu Administrative Offices	170	5	3
克孜勒苏柯尔克孜自治州	Kizilsu Kirgiz Autonomous Prefecture	21		
喀什地区	Kashgar [Kaxgar] Administrative Offices	78	1	
和田地区	Hotan Administrative Offices	18	1	1
自治区直辖县级市	Municpality Country-LevelCity directly under the Central Govern-ment	159	23	14

Continued

研究与试验发展人员数(人) Number of R&D Persons	研究人员 Research personal	研究与试验发展人员折合全时当量(人·年) Full-time Equivalent of R&D personnel	研究人员 Research personal	研究与试验发展经费(万元) Expenditure on R&D	其中 Of which 基础研究 Basic Research	应用研究 Applied Research	试验发展 Experimental Development
46	7	16.7	3.7	665.5			665.5
32	20	9.2	5.6	139.7			139.7
380	133	313.8	111.5	10076.1			10076.1
1194	312	837.8	225.8	13129.2		475.9	12653.3
74	18	66.7	16.0	2210.6			2210.6
8	4	0.3	0.1	9.2			9.2
189	56	151.4	45.7	4771.5			4771.5
222	74	140.6	40.3	4550.2		1918.5	2631.7
196	166	162.5	144.1	22620.8			22620.8
520	42	520.0	42.0	22749.5			22749.5
16	5	14.2	4.4	392.3		134.0	258.3
200	91	190.1	85.1	3608.6			3608.6
213	77	124.0	35.2	1636.9			1636.9
506	72	498.4	70.0	31425.3			31425.3
172	68	61.7	25.5	3511.2			3511.2
172	68	61.7	25.5	3511.2			3511.2
1753	563	1302.1	404.4	59560.6		261.0	59299.6
3428	2217	2106.8	1256.1	100215.2		4955.3	95259.9
660	610	611.1	564.8	26895.2		24777.4	2117.8
106	59	20.3	10.8	335.8		209.9	125.9
1048	234	692.9	103.6	33136.7			33136.7
184	50	149.6	37.8	5149.8			5149.8
46	12	7.1	2.2	199.1			199.1
10	9	6.4	5.7	10.0			10.0
807	533	681.2	475.4	28197.1		214.9	27982.2
46	22	32.4	15.5	2886.3		1918.5	967.8
40	25	37.0	23.1	7.5			7.5
10	3	8.9	2.7	40.5			40.5
1050	272	543.7	116.4	16720.4			16720.4

18-30 续表 2

(2012 年)

项　目	Item	其　中 Of which	
		政府资金 Government Appropriation Funds	企业资金 Self-raised Funds by Enterprises
总　计	**Total**	**9213.3**	**262949.2**
按企业规模分	**Grouped by Size of Enterprises**		
大型企业	Large Enterprises	5825.3	226039.3
中型企业	Medium-sized Enterprises	1563.1	21938.4
小型企业	Small Enterprises	1824.9	14897.0
微型企业	Mini Enterprises		74.5
按登记注册类型分	**Grouped by Ownership**		
内资企业	Domestic-funded Enterprises	9163.3	262869.9
国有企业	State-owned Enterprises	174.4	12300.9
有限责任公司	Limited Liability Corporations	3050.6	46589.8
#国有独资公司	State Sole funded Corporations	68.7	918.3
其他有限责任公司	Other Limited Liability Corporations	2981.9	45671.5
股份有限责任公司	Share-holding Corporations Ltd	5217.8	193621.5
私营企业	Private Enterprises	670.5	10007.7
私营有限责任公司	Private Limited Liability Corporations	560.5	6136.6
私营股份有限公司	Private Stock Ltd. Co.	110.0	3871.1
其他企业	Other Enterprises	50.0	350.0
港澳台商投资企业	Enterprises With Funds from Hong Kong, Macao and Taiwan	50.0	63.3
#合资经营企业(港或澳、台资)	Joint-ventures Enterprises	50.0	63.3
外商投资企业	Foreign Funded Enterprises		16.0
#其他外资投资企业	Other Foreign Funded Enterprises		16.0
按工业行业大类分	**Grouped by Sector**		
采矿业	Mining and Quarrying	3296.5	136169.2
#煤炭开采和洗选业	Coal Extracting and Dressing	10.6	1306.2
石油和天然气开采业	Petroleum and Natural Gas Extraction	2917.7	126090.8
黑色金属矿采选业	Processing of Ferrous Metals Ores	25.0	1175.0
有色金属矿采选业	Processing of Nonferrous Metals Ores		171.4
开采辅助活动	Mining Activities	343.2	7425.8
制造业	Manufacturing	5892.9	123292.7
#农副食品加工业	Processing of Food from Agricultural Products	389.1	2809.6
食品制造业	Food Manufacturing	258.0	4158.6
酒、饮料和精制茶制造业	Manufacture of Wine,Beverages and Refined Tea	133.9	1629.5
纺织业	Textile Industry	188.9	2097.8

Continued

研究与试验发展项目数(项) R&D Projects (unit)	新产品开发项目数(项) New Projects (unit)	专利申请数(件) Patent Applications (piece)	发明专利(件) Invention Patents (piece)	有效发明专利数(件) Number of Patents In Force (piece)	发表科技论文(篇) Pulish Scientific Papers (article)
930	**819**	**1768**	**376**	**467**	**1796**
640	429	1135	177	228	1610
198	246	244	66	121	126
91	143	388	132	118	60
1	1	1	1		
926	819	1766	375	460	1794
84	47	261	61	56	237
167	172	808	139	126	326
10	6	9	1	3	6
157	166	799	138	123	320
538	416	465	109	198	1221
136	181	200	66	80	10
27	62	139	47	66	10
109	119	61	19	14	
1	3	32			
3		2	1	7	2
3		2	1	7	2
1					
1					
428	287	474	67	59	959
7	5	12	2	1	30
357	249	252	24	25	731
1					
4		2	1		6
59	33	208	40	33	192
466	518	1215	288	397	716
14	22	47	12	29	25
109	108	62	28	10	14
8	8	2	2		6
9	18	5	3	3	6

18-30 续表 3

(2012 年)

项　　目	Item	其　中 Of which	
		政府资金 Government Appropriation Funds	企业资金 Self-raised Funds by Enterprises
纺织服装、服饰业	Manufacture of Textile Wearing Apparel, Footware and Caps	212.5	453.0
造纸及纸制品业	Paper and Paper Products Manufacturing		139.7
石油加工、炼焦及核燃料加工业	Oil Processing, Coking and Nuclear Fuel Processing	916.2	9159.9
化学原料及化学制品制造业	Raw Chemical Material and Chemical Products	758.5	12126.1
医药制造业	Medicine Manufacturing	603.3	1607.3
化学纤维制造业	Chemical Fiber Manufacturing		9.2
橡胶和塑料制品业	Rubber and Plastic Products Manufacturing	145.8	4625.7
非金属矿物制品业	Nonmetal Mineral Products Manufacturing	220.5	4109.1
黑色金属冶炼及压延加工业	Manufacture and Processing of Ferrous Metals	28.3	22592.5
有色金属冶炼及压延加工业	Manufalture and Processing of Non-ferrous Metals	750.0	21999.5
金属制品业	Metal Products Manufacturing		
通用设备制造业	General Purpose Machinery Manufacturing	86.0	306.3
专用设备制造业	Special Purpose Machinery Manufacturing	618.0	2990.6
汽车制造业	Manufacture of Automobile		1636.9
电气机械及器材制造业	Electric Equipment and Machinery Manufacturing	583.9	30841.4
电力、燃气及水的生产和供应业	Production and Suppoly of Electric Power,Gas and Water	23.9	3487.3
#电力、热力的生产和供应业	Electric Power and Thermal Production and Supply	23.9	3487.3
按企业所在地区划分	**Grouped by Region**		
乌鲁木齐市	Urumqi City	2226.9	57062.8
克拉玛依市	Karamay City	2039.8	98175.4
吐鲁番地区	Turpan Administrative Offices	536.3	26239.4
哈密地区	Hami [Kumul] Administrative Offices		335.8
昌吉回族自治州	Changji Hui Autonomous Prefecture	1469.1	31581.6
伊犁州直属县(市)	Counties (Cities) Direct Under Ili Prefecture	359.1	4765.7
塔城地区	Tacheng [Tarbagatai] Administrative Offices		
阿勒泰地区	Altay Administrative Offices	18.7	180.4
博尔塔拉蒙古自治州	Bortala Mongol Autonomous Prefecture	7.0	3.0
巴音郭楞蒙古自治州	Bayangol Mongol Autonomous Prefecture	1522.2	26191.1
阿克苏地区	Aksu Administrative Offices	17.7	2868.6
克孜勒苏柯尔克孜自治州	Kizilsu Kirgiz Autonomous Prefecture		
喀什地区	Kashgar [Kaxgar] Administrative Offices		7.5
和田地区	Hotan Administrative Offices		40.5
自治区直辖县级市	Municpality Country-LevelCity directly under the Central Govern-ment	1016.5	15497.4

Continued

研究与试验发展项目数(项) R&D Projects (unit)	新产品开发项目数(项) New Projects (unit)	专利申请数(件) Patent Applications (piece)	发明专利(件) Invention Patents (piece)	有效发明专利数(件) Number of Patents In Force (piece)	发表科技论文(篇) Pulish Scientific Papers (article)
3	3	5			2
2	23	14	5	6	2
38	60	60	28	131	303
73	55	169	53	57	41
10	23	4	2	12	7
1	1				
26	58	99	19	13	29
18	17	33	12	20	13
14	13	486	48	11	150
61	3	53	27	32	53
	5	23	9	11	6
6	7	21	6	11	3
20	28	40	12	18	39
14	14	10	1	23	1
40	52	82	21	10	16
36	14	79	21	11	121
36	14	79	21	11	121
176	147	890	194	233	488
368	357	432	83	118	754
51	2	42	8	7	33
3	1				
139	149	141	21	27	5
19	19	40	11	4	13
	1	1	1		
4	2	2	1		6
1					
78	61	115	23	27	377
6	13	25	5	17	73
1		14	4	1	1
1					
83	67	66	25	33	46

18-31 各类技术合同签定及执行情况

Statistics on Signing and Implementing Technical Contracts by Type

单位：项、万元 (item,10 000 yuan)

项　目	Item	合同数 Number of Contracts		合同金额 Contract Amount		#技术交易额 Transaction Value in Technical Market	
		2012	2013	2012	2013	2012	2013
总　计	**Total**	**1532**	**983**	**54910.48**	**29653.08**	**53326.15**	**28370.11**
技术开发合同	Technology Development	323	222	21269.51	14910.80	20792.04	13686.17
技术转让合同	Technology Transfer	62	79	4541.55	1991.43	4073.80	1969.70
技术咨询合同	Technology Consultation	524	290	8980.15	4412.78	8847.15	4376.78
技术服务合同	Technology Service	623	392	20119.27	8338.07	19613.16	8337.47

18-32 各级技术计划项目进入技术市场情况

Statistics on Projects for Technical Plan Entering Technical Market by Level

单位：项、万元 (2013 年) (item,10 000 yuan)

项　目	Item	合　计 Total		国家计划 National Plans		部门计划 Department Plans	
		项　数 Number of Items	金　额 Values	项　数 Number of Items	金　额 Values	项　数 Number of Items	金　额 Values
总　计	**Total**	**983**	**29653.08**	**3**	**116**	**6**	**102.35**
事业法人	Institntion Legal Person	510	8242.43	1	66		
企业法人	Business Entity	473	21410.64	2	50	6	102.35

项　目	Item	省、自治区计划 单列市计划 Provinces, Municipality Plans		地、市、县计划 Area City and County Plans		计划外 Out of Plan	
		项　数 Number of Items	金　额 Values	项　数 Number of Items	金　额 Values	项　数 Number of Items	金　额 Values
总　计	**Total**	**21**	**1928.11**	**16**	**1061.30**	**937**	**26445.31**
事业法人	Institntion Legal Person	7	383.20	1	30.00	501	7763.23
企业法人	Business Entity	14	1544.91	15	1031.30	436	18682.08

18-33 技术流向地域情况
Statistics on Location of Technical Contract

单位：项、万元　　(2013 年)　　(item, 10 000 yuan)

地　区 Region	合同类别合计 Contracts of Classification Total		技术开发 Technology Development		技术转让 Technology Transfer		技术咨询 Technology Consultation		技术服务 Technology Service	
	项　数 Number of Items	金　额 Values	项　数 Number of Items	金　额 Values	项　数 Number of Items	金　额 Values	项　数 Number of Items	金　额 Values	项　数 Number of Items	金　额 Values
总　计 Total	**983**	**29653.08**	**222**	**14910.80**	**79**	**1991.43**	**290**	**4412.78**	**392**	**8338.07**
北　京 Beijing	8	202.35	2	98.18	1	45.14	2	10.50	3	48.53
天　津 Tianjing	2	19.80					1	15.00	1	4.80
河　北 Hebei	6	69.88			2	36.00			4	33.88
山　西 Shanxi	1	18.00			1	18.00				
辽　宁 Liaoning	4	66.80	2	63.00			1	3.00	1	0.80
吉　林 Jilin	2	283.50	2	283.50						
上　海 Shanghai	2	20.45	2	20.45						
江　苏 Jiangsu	2	25.00	1	5.00	1	20.00				
浙　江 Zhejiang	2	814.25	1	799.78					1	14.46
安　徽 Aanhui	4	155.43			1	121.83			3	33.60
山　东 Shandong	2	395.00	2	395.00						
湖　南 Hunan	1	18.00			1	18.00				
广　东 Guangdong	3	537.23	2	487.23					1	40.00
四　川 Sichuan	4	19.30	1	4.80	1	4.20			2	10.30
云　南 Yunnan	1	6.00							1	6.00
西　藏 Xizang	1	18.00					1	18.00		
陕　西 Shanxi	9	195.32	1	28.80	2	36.11	5	117.00	1	13.42
甘　肃 Gansu	1	28.00	1	28.00						
青海 Qinghai	1	6.00			1	6.00				
新　疆 Xinjiang	927	26764.77	205	12697.06	68	1686.15	280	4249.28	374	8132.28

18-34 技术经济合同成交情况
Statistics on Transaction in Technical and Economic Contract

单位：项、万元 (2013 年) (item, 10 000 yuan)

卖方类别 Classification of Sellers / 买方类别 Classification of Buyers		合 计 Total		#事业法人 Institntion Legal Person		#企业法人 Business Entity	
		项 数 Number of Items	金 额 Values Number	项 数 of Items	金 额 Values Number	项 数 of Items	金 额 Values
总　计	**Total**	**983**	**29653.08**	**510**	**8242.43**	**473**	**21410.64**
机关法人	Government Agency Legal Person	116	5281.04	11	593.64	105	4687.40
事业法人	Institntion Legal Person	122	2897.28	56	538.95	66	2358.34
社团法人	Corporation Aggregate	1	8.00			1	8.00
企业法人	Business Entity	734	21050.94	442	6798.54	292	14252.40
其他组织	Others	10	415.81	1	311.31	9	104.50

18-35 主要年份文化产业基本情况
Basic Statistics on Culture in Main Years

项　目	Item	2005	2010	2013
文化产业机构数(个)	**Number of Culture Institutions (unit)**	**11777**	**9430**	**4874**
文化部门	Culture Departments	2404	1826	33
其他部门	Other Departments	9373	7604	4841
文化产业人员数(人)	**Number of Person in Culture (person)**	**34001**	**37711**	**33602**
文化部门	Culture Departments	11515	13310	8818
其他部门	Other Departments	22486	24401	24784
各类文化艺术事业单位数(个)	**Number of Institutions on Various Culture and Art (unit)**			
文化馆	Cultural Centers	110	112	116
公共图书馆	Public Libraries	94	103	106
博物馆	Museums	28	71	76
艺术表演场所	Art Performance Places	47	15	15
艺术表演团体	Art Performance Troupes	89	132	108

18-36 文化艺术、文物事业机构和人员情况

Number of Institutions and Personnel in Culture, Art and Cultural Relics

(2013 年)

项 目	Item	机构数（个） Number of Institutions (unit)	从业人员数（人） Number of Persons Engaged (person)
艺术事业	**Art Institutions**	**163**	**5460**
艺术表演团体	Art Performance Troupes	108	5005
#话剧、儿童剧、滑稽剧团	Drama, Children Plays and Comedy Troupes	4	265
歌剧、舞剧、歌舞剧团	Opera, Ballet and Dance Troupes	2	187
歌舞团、轻音乐团	Song and Dance Troupe, Light Music Troupe	35	2011
文工团、文宣队、乌兰牧骑	Cultural and Performance Troupes and Ulanmuchi (equestrain art troupes)	57	2101
戏曲剧团	Local Opera Troupes	6	214
#京 剧	Local Beijing Opera Troupes	2	86
曲艺、杂技、木偶、皮影团	Recitation and Ballad Troupes, Acrobatics and Circus Troupes, Puppet Show Troupes and Shadow Play Troupes	4	227
艺术表演场所	Art Centers	15	320
#剧场、影剧院	Theaters and Music Halls	15	320
艺术创作机构	Art Creation Institutions	40	135
图书馆事业	**Libraries**	**106**	**1065**
群众文化事业	**Mass Culture**	**1260**	**4156**
文化馆	Cultural Centers	116	1371
文化站	Cultural Stations	1144	2785
#乡镇文化站	Township Cultural Stations	1144	2785
艺术教育事业	**Art Education**	**2**	**149**
艺术科研机构	**Art Research Institutions**	**2**	**48**
文化市场经营单位	**Entertainment Operators**	**4841**	**24784**
文化娱乐业	Entertainment Operators	2458	16818
文化市场其他经营单位	Cultural Market Operators	2383	7966
其他文化事业	**Other Cultural Units**	**10**	**129**
文物事业合计	**Cultural Relics**	**163**	**1495**
文物机构	Historical Relics Agency	86	355
文物保护管理机构	Agency of Historical Relics Preservation	83	185
文物科研机构	Scientific and Research Historical Relics Agency	2	104
其他文物机构	Other Historical Relics Agency	1	66
博物馆	Museums	76	1112
#历史类	History Museum	29	382
文物商店	Cultural Relics Store	1	28

18-37 电影、电视、广播事业基本情况
Basic Statistics on Feature Film, Television and Broadcasting

项　　目	Item	2012	2013
电影制片厂(个)	**Number of Film Studios (unit)**	**1**	**1**
广播电台(座)	**Number of Broadcasting Stations (unit)**	**6**	**6**
中短波发射台及转播台(座)	Transmission and Relaying Stations of MW&SW (unit)	64	66
中短波广播发射功率(千瓦)	Power of MW & SW Transmitters (kw)	2886	2898
调频发射台及转播台(座)	FM Transmission and Relaying Stations (unit)	961	679
调频发射功率(千瓦)	Power of FM Transmitters (kw)	521.8	558.6
节目(套)	Program (set)	159	161
制作广播节目(小时)	Production of Broadcasting (hour)	288223	280777
#新闻资讯类节目	News Programs	58932	59022
专题服务类节目	Feature Programs	91908	92336
综艺类节目	Variety Show	82531	78485
广播剧类节目	Radio Play	8304	8027
广告类节目	Advertisement Programs	22084	21538
其他类节目	Other Programs	24464	21367
广播人口覆盖率((%)	Listener Rate (%)	95.34	95.68
电视台(座)	**Number of Television Stations (unit)**	**8**	**8**
广播电视台(座)	**Radio and TV Stations (unit)**	**88**	**88**
#县级广播电视台(座)	Radio and TV Station at County-Level (unit)	80	80
电视发射台及转播台(座)	TV Transmission Stations and Relaying Stations (unit)	883	550
电视发射机功率(千瓦)	Power of TV Transmitters (kw)	935.62	926.19
节目(套)	Program (set)	198	192
制作电视节目(小时)	Production of TV Programs (hour)	92503	93097
#新闻资讯类节目	News Programs	32173	33624
专题服务类节目	Feature Programs	19808	20204
综艺类节目	Variety Show	10250	11747
影视剧类节目	Film and TV Play Programs	7454	4394
广告类节目	Advertisement Programs	16058	18136
其他类节目	Other Programs	6760	4992
电视人口覆盖率(%)	Viewer Rate (%)	95.62	95.95
有线电视用户(万户)	Numbe of Users of CATV (10 000 households)	216.81	199.50
#数字电视用户	Number of users Digital TV	200.28	186.36
农村直播卫星用户(万户)	Numbe of Users of Rural Live Statellite(10 000 households)	121.55	256.44

主要统计指标解释

普通高等学校 指通过国家普通高等教育招生考试，招收高中毕业生为主要培养对象，实施高等学历教育的全日制大学、独立设置的学院、独立学院和高等专科学校、高等职业学校及其他机构。

大学、独立设置的学院主要实施本科及本科层次以上的教育。独立学院主要实施本科层次的教育。高等专科学校、高等职业学校实施专科层次的教育。其他机构是指承担国家普通招生计划任务不计校数的机构，包括普通高等学校分校、大专班等。

小学学龄儿童净入学率 指调查范围内已入小学学习的学龄儿童占校内外学龄儿童总数的比重。计算公式为：

小学学龄儿童净入学率=已入学的小学学龄儿童数/校内外小学学龄儿童总数*100%

国家财政性教育经费 包括公共财政预算教育经费，各级政府征收用于教育的税费，企业办学中的企业拨款，校办产业和社会服务收入用于教育的经费，其他属于国家财政性教育经费。

公共财政预算教育经费 指中央、地方各级财政或上级主管部门在本年度内安排，并划拨到各级各类学校、教育行政单位、教育事业单位，列入国家预算支出科目的教育经费。包括教育事业费拨款、科研拨款、基本建设拨款和其他拨款。

研究与试验发展(R&D) 指在科学技术领域，为增加知识总量、以及运用这些知识去创造新的应用进行的系统的创造性的活动，包括基础研究、应用研究、试验发展三类活动。国际上通常采用R&D 活动的规模和强度指标反映一国的科技实力和核心竞争力。

基础研究 指为了获得关于现象和可观察事实的基本原理的新知识(揭示客观事物的本质、运动规律，获得新发现、新学说)而进行的实验性或理论性研究，它不以任何专门或特定的应用或使用为目的。其成果以科学论文和科学著作为主要形式。用来反映知识的原始创新能力。

应用研究 指为获得新知识而进行的创造性研究，主要针对某一特定的目的或目标。应用研究是为了确定基础研究成果可能的用途，或是为达到预定的目标探索应采取的新方法(原理性)或新途径。其成果形式以科学论文、专著、原理性模型或发明专利为主。用来反映对基础研究成果应用途径的探索。

试验发展 指利用从基础研究、应用研究和实际经验所获得的现有知识，为产生新的产品、材料和装置，建立新的工艺、系统和服务，以及对已产生和建立的上述各项作实质性的改进而进行的系统性工作。其成果形式主要是专利、专有技术、具有新产品基本特征的产品原型或具有新装置基本特征的原始样机等。在社会科学领域，试验发展是指把通过基础研究、应用研究获得的知识转变成可以实施的计划(包括为进行检验和评估实施示范项目)的过程。人文科学领域没有对应的试验发展活动。主要反映将科研成果转化为技术和产品的能力，是科技推动经济社会发展的物化成果。

R&D 人员 指参与研究与试验发展项目研究、管理和辅助工作的人员，包括项目(课题)组人员，企业科技行政管理人员和直接为项目(课题)活动提供服务的辅助人员。反映投入从事拥有自主知识产权的研究开发活动的人力规模。

R&D 人员全时当量 指全时人员数加非全时人员按工作量折算为全时人员数的总和。例如：有两个全时人员和三个非全时人员(工作时间分别为 20%、30%和 70%)，则全时当量为 2+0.2+0.3+0.7=3.2 人年。为国际上比较科技人力投入而制定的可比指标。

R&D 经费支出合计 指调查单位用于内部开展 R&D 活动（基础研究、应用研究和试验发展）的实际支出。包括用于 R&D 项目（课题）活动的直接支出，以及间接用于 R&D 活动的管理费、服务费、与 R&D 有关的基本建设支出以及外协加工费等。不包括生产性活动支出、归还贷款支出以及与外单位合作或委托外单位进行 R&D 活动而转拨给对方的经费支出。

R&D 经费支出中政府资金 指 R&D 经费内部支出中来自各级政府部门的各类资金，包括财政科学技术拨款、科学基金、教育等部门事业费以及政府部门预算外资金的实际支出。

R&D 经费支出中企业资金 指 R&D 经费内部支出中来自本企业的自有资金和接受其他企业委托而获得的经费，以及科研院所、高校等事业单位从企业获得的资金的实际支出。

新产品 指采用新技术原理、新设计构思研制、生产的全新产品，或在结构、材质、工艺等某一方面比原有产品有明显改进，从而显著提高了产品性能或扩大了使用功能的产品。既包括政府有关部门认定并在有效期内的新产品，也包括企业自行研制开发，未经政府有关部门认定，从投产之日起一年之内的新产品。用来反映科技产出及对经济增长的直接贡献。

专利 是专利权的简称，是对发明人的发明创造经审查合格后，由专利局依据专利法授予发明人和设计人对该项发明创造享有的专有权。包括发明、实用新型和外观设计。反映拥有自主知识产权的科技和设计成果情况。

发明(专利) 指对产品、方法或者其改进所提出的新的技术方案。是国际通行的反映拥有自主知识产权技术的核心指标。

实用新型(专利) 指对产品的形状、构造或者其结合所提出的适于实用的新的技术方案。反映具有一定技术含量的技术成果情况。

外观设计(专利) 指对产品的形状、图案、色彩或者其结合所作出的富有美感并适于工业上应用的新设计。反映拥有自主知识产权的外观设计成果情况。

文化及相关产业 指为社会公众提供文化、娱乐产品和服务的活动以及与这些活动有关联的活动的集合。根据提供文化、娱乐产品和服务活动的属性特点，划分为公益性文化活动和经营性文化活动两大类。

文化及相关产业是第三产业的重要组成部分。是在我国《国民经济行业分类》基础上的派生分类，有文化服务和相关文化服务两大类：

文化服务 主要指新闻服务，出版发行和版权服务，广播、电视、电影服务，文化艺术服务，网络文化服务，文化休闲娱乐服务，其他文化服务。

艺术表演团体 指由文化部门主办或实行行业管理（经文化行政部门审批或已申报登记并领取相关许可证），专门从事表演艺术等活动的各类专业艺术表演团体，含民间职业剧团。不包括群众业余文艺表演团体。

艺术表演场馆 指由文化部门主办或实行行业管理（经文化市场行政部门审批或已申报登记并领取相关许可证），有观众席、舞台、灯光设备，公开售票、专供文艺团体演出的文化活动场所。

文化市场经营机构 经文化市场行政部门审批或已申报登记并领取相关许可证的、从事文化经营和文化服务活动的机构。

广播/电视节目综合人口覆盖率 指根据原国家广电总局制定的《广播电视人口覆盖率统计技术标准和方法》进行统计调查的，在对象区内能接收到由中央、省、地市或县通过无线、有线或卫星等各种技术方式转播的各级广播/电视节目的人口数占全国总人口数的百分比。

Explanatory Notes on Main Statistical Indicators

Regular Institutions of Higher Education refer to educational establishments recruiting graduates from senior secondary schools as the main target through National Matriculation TEST. They include full-time universities, independently established colleges, colleges, and institutions of higher professional education, institutions of higher vocational education and others.

Universities and independently established colleges primarily provide undergraduate and above courses; colleges mainly impart undergraduate courses, institutions of higher professional education and institutions of higher vocational education primarily provide professional trainings; and others refer to educational establishments, which are responsible for enrolling higher education students under the State Plan but not enumerated in the total number of schools, including: branch schools of universities and colleges and junior colleges.

Net Enrolment Ratio of Primary Schools refers to the proportion of school age children enrolled at schools to the total number of school age children both in and outside schools (including retarded children, but excluding blind, deaf and mute children). The formula is:

$$\text{Net Enrolment Ratio of Primary Schools} = \frac{\text{Total Primary School - age Children at Schools}}{\text{Total Primary School - age Children Whether or Not Attending School}} \times 100\ \%$$

Government Appropriation for Education refers to the public budgetary fund for education, taxes and fees collected by governments at all levels that are used for education purpose, enterprise appropriation for enterprise-run schools, income from school-run enterprises and social services that are used for education purpose and other national appropriations for education.

Public Budgetary Fund for Education refers to education funding from the central and local financial departments and supervision departments that is planned to be allocated to various schools, education administration institutions and education institutions within the reference year, which is within the State budgetary expenditure, including: appropriated funds for education, science and research, capital construction and others.

Research and Development (R&D) refers to systematic and creative activities in the field of science and technology aiming at increasing the knowledge and using the knowledge for new application. R&D includes 3 categories of activities: basic research, applied research and experimentation for development. The scale and intensity of R&D are widely used internationally to reflect the strength of S&T and the core competitiveness of a country in the world.

Basic Research refers to empirical or theoretical research aiming at obtaining new knowledge on the fundamental principles regarding phenomena or observable facts to reveal the intrinsic nature and underlying laws and to acquire new discoveries or new theories. Basic research takes no specific or designated application as the aim of the research. Results of basic research are mainly released or disseminated in the form of scientific papers or monographs. This indicator reflects the innovation capacity for original knowledge.

Applied Research refers to creative research aiming at obtaining new knowledge on a specific objective or target. Purpose of the applied research is to identify the possible uses of results from basic research, or to explore new (fundamental) methods or new approaches. Results of applied research are expressed in the form of scientific papers, monographs, fundamental models or invention patents. This indicator reflects the exploration of ways to apply the results of basic research.

Experiments and Development refer to systematic activities aiming at using the knowledge from basic and applied researches or from practical experience to develop new products, materials and equipment, to establish new production process, systems and services, or to make substantial improvement on the existing products, process or services. Results of experiment and development activities are embodied in patents, exclusive technology, and monotype of new products or equipment. In social sciences, experiment and development activities refer to the process of converting the knowledge from basic or applied researches into feasible programmes (including conduct of demonstration projects for assessment and evaluation). There are no experiment and development activities in the science of humanities. This indicator reflects the capability of transferring the results of S&T into technique and products, and measures the realization of S&T in spearheading the economic and social development.

R&D Personnel refers to persons engaged in research, management and supporting activities of R&D, including persons in the project teams, persons engaged in the management of S&T activities of enterprises and supporting staff providing direct service to the research projects. This indicator reflects the size of personnel engaged in R&D activities with independent intellectual property.

Full-time Equivalent of R&D Personnel refers to the sum of the full-time persons and the full-time equivalent of part-time persons converted by workload. For instance, if there are 2 full-time persons and 3 part-time workers (20%, 30% and 70% of working hours respectively on R&D activities), the full-time equivalent are 2+0.2+0.3+0.7=3.2 person-years. This is an internationally comparable indicator of S&T manpower input.

Total Expenditure of Funds on R&D refers to the real expenditure of surveyed units on their own R&D activities (basic research, application study, test and development) including direct expenditure on R&D activities, indirect expenditure of management and services on R&D activities, expenditure on capital construction and material processing by others. Excluding the expenditure on production activities, return of loan, and fees transferred to cooperated and entrusted agencies on R&D activities.

Expenditure of Government Funds on R&D refers to the expenditure of funds on R&D activities from government agencies at different levels, including appropriate funds on science and technology from financial departments, scientific funds, operating expenses from education departments and the real expenditure of extra budgetary funds from government agencies.

Expenditure of Funds of Enterprises on R&D refers to the expenditure of funds on R&D activities from self-raised funds of enterprises and funds from other enterprises through entrustment, and the expenditure of funds of institutions, such as institution of scientific research and universities, from enterprises.

New Products refer to brand new products produced with new technology and new design, or products that represent noticeable improvement in terms of structure, material, or production process for improving significantly the character or function of the older versions. They include new products certified by relevant government agencies within the period of certification, as well as new products designed and produced by enterprises within a year without certification by government agencies. This indicator reflects the direct contribution of S&T output to economic growth.

Patent is an abbreviation for the patent right and refers to the exclusive right of ownership by the inventors or designers for the creation or inventions, given from the patent offices after due process of assessment and approval in accordance with the Patent Law. Patents are granted for inventions, utility models and designs. This indicator reflects the achievements of S&T and design with independent intellectual property.

Patented Inventions refer to new technical proposals to the products or methods or their modifications. This is universal core indicator reflecting the technologies with independent intellectual property.

Patented Utility Models refer to the practical and new technical proposals on the shape and structure of the product or the combination of both. This indicator reflects the condition of technological results with certain technical content.

Designs refer to the aesthetics and industrially applicable new designs for the shape, pattern and colour of the product, or their combinations. This indicator reflects the appearance design achievements with independent intellectual property.

Culture and Related Industries refer to the aggregate of activities, providing the mass with culture goods, amusement goods and services. According to the characteristics of culture goods, amusement goods and services, they can be classified into two categories, or nonprofit cultural activities and profit cultural activities.

Culture and related industries is the important component of the tertiary industry. These are the derivative sector from the Industrial Classification of the National Economy and are composed of two categories of culture services and related cultural services.

Culture services mainly include news services, publishing and copyright services, radio, television, film, arts, network, recreation, and other cultural services

Arts Performance Troupes refer to the various professional performing arts groups, which sponsored by the cultural sectors or guided by the cultural society (approved by the cultural market administration, or registered and permitted with the relative certificate), including non-governmental troupes. The mass amateur arts performance troupes are not included.

Arts Performance Places refer to the various sites for cultural activities, which sponsored by the cultural sectors or guided by the cultural society (approved by the cultural market administration, or registered and permitted with the relative certificate), with the facility of auditorium, stage, and lighting, and selling tickets in public.

Cultural Market Operating Units refer to the units dealing in culture and cultural services, which registered and permitted with the relative certificate by cultural market administration.

The Population Coverage Rate of Radio/Television refers to the percentage of the whole country's population who can receive radio/television programmes transmitted by national, provincial, municipal or county stations through wireless, cable or satellite techniques, according to Statistical Standard and Method on Television and Radio Coverage of Population established by the former State Administration of Broadcasting, Film and Television.

19

卫生及其他

PUBLIC HEALTH AND OTHERS

简要说明

本篇主要内容和资料来源

本篇资料主要包括卫生事业、民政事业、公安机关案件受理处治情况、安全生产情况、道路交通事故和火灾事故等内容，除卫生事业外其他部门数据由新疆维吾尔自治区统计局社会科技处与综合处根据有关部门资料整理。

卫生部门资料是由新疆维吾尔自治区卫生厅依据年报资料整理提供。民政部分资料由新疆维吾尔自治区民政厅提供，治安、刑事案件资料由新疆维吾尔自治区公安厅提供，安全生产情况来自新疆维吾尔自治区安全生产监督管理局，道路交通事故和火灾事故分别由新疆维吾尔自治区公安交通管理局和新疆维吾尔自治区消防总队提供。

Brief Introduction

Main Content and Source of Data

Data in this chapter mainly include the development of public health, sports, civil affairs, labor and society protection, offense cases against public order handled by public Security organs, traffic accidents and fires. These statistics are provided by Department of Population and Social Science &Technology in Statistics Bureau of Xinjiang according to the data from the related Department of Statistics Bureau.

Data on public health are from the Bureau of Public Health, these statistics are according to the data of yearly statistics; increased the data of condition of village clinic and basic condition of institution on new cooperative health care of agricultural and pastoral areas; Data on civil affairs and labor protection are provided respectively by the Bureau of Civil Affairs and the Bureau of Labor and Social Security. Data on public security, statistics on procuratorial, legal and judicial affairs are provided by the Bureau of Public Security. Data on production safety are come from Xinjiang Administration of Work Safety. Data on traffic accident and fire are respectively provided by the Xinjiang Traffic Management Bureau and the Xinjiang Fire Department.

19-1 卫生机构、床位、人员数

Number of Health Institutions, Beds and Persons Engaged by Type of Institutons

(2013 年)

项　目	Item	机构数(个) Number of Institutions (unit)	实有床位数(张) Beds (unit)	在岗职工合计(人) Total Number of Medical Personnel (person)	卫生技术人员小计 Medical Technical Personnel	执业(助理)医师 Licensed Assistant Doctor	执业医师 Licensed Doctors	注册护士 Registered Nurses	药剂人员 Pharmacist
总　计	**Total**	**18663**	**137325**	**189578**	**145851**	**53020**	**43582**	**56578**	**6923**
按经济类型分	**Grouped by Economic Type**								
公　立	Public	12326	122571	161807	123792	42680	34726	48885	5847
国　有	State-owned	9126	119843	152551	119986	41132	33589	47424	5696
集　体	Collective-owned	3200	2728	9256	3806	1548	1137	1461	151
民　营	Non-public	6337	14754	27771	22059	10340	8856	7693	1076
联　营	Joint Ownership	30	112	175	132	54	47	47	12
私　营	Private	5499	12789	23628	19473	9300	7950	6670	925
其　他	Others	808	1853	3968	2454	986	859	976	139
按设置主办单位分	**Grouped by sponsors**								
政府办	Run by Government	8318	116220	145451	113570	38109	30915	45077	5336
社会办	Run by Society	5021	8127	20044	12133	5309	4445	4607	642
个人办	Run by Private	5324	12978	24083	20148	9602	8222	6894	945
按市县分	**Guouped by Ctiy and County**								
市	City	7146	80376	117008	94620	35271	31541	38444	4515
县	County	11517	56949	72570	51231	17749	12041	18134	2408
按城乡分	**Grouped by Rural and Urban**								
城　市	Urban	2106	35307	56658	45296	17290	16203	19235	2118
农　村	Rural	16557	102018	132920	100555	35730	27379	37343	4805
按营利性质分	**Grouped by Profit**								
非营利性	Non-profit	13371	123996	156009	118115	40559	33113	48699	5892
营利性	Profit	4784	13329	23520	19853	9292	8004	6937	932
其　他	Others	508		10049	7883	3169	2465	942	99
按机构分	**Grouped By Organizations**								
医　院	Total Number of Hospitals	860	107897	117690	96061	31709	27989	41756	5120
综合医院	Comprehensive Hospitals	667	83136	96357	79320	25908	22925	35127	3801
中医医院	Hospitals of Traditional Chinese Medicine	51	7170	6996	5678	2171	2033	2188	448
中西医结合医院	TCM and Western Medicine Hospital	4	542	580	438	107	72	171	24
民族医院	Hospitals for Nationalities	46	7253	5356	4390	1508	1095	1385	556
专科医院	Specialist Hospitals	92	9796	8401	6235	2015	1864	2885	291

注：1.本表人员合计中包括乡村医生 13005 人和卫生员 1333 人；
　　2.不含乡镇卫生院在村卫生室工作的执业(助理)医师、注册护士数。

Note: a). Total data in this table included 13005 doctors and 1333 medical personels.
　　b). Total data in this table didn't include licensed doctors and registered nurses in county health centers.

19-1 续表 1 Continued

项目	Item	技师(士) Technician (artificer)	检验人员 Laboratory Technicians	其他 Others	见习医师 Intern Doctor	其他技术人员 Other Technicians	管理人员 Administrative Personnel	工勤人员 Logistics Workers
总计	**Total**	**8659**	**5903**	**20671**	**5011**	**7807**	**7179**	**14403**
按经济类型分	**Grouped by Economic Type**							
公立	Public	7573	5234	18807	4536	6853	6111	12431
国有	State-owned	7417	5126	18317	4407	6697	5830	12117
集体	Collective-owned	156	108	490	129	156	281	314
民营	Non-public	1086	669	1864	475	954	1068	1972
联营	Joint Ownership	8	7	11	2	4	9	15
私营	Private	938	564	1640	418	767	885	1621
其他	Others	140	98	213	55	183	174	336
按设置主办单位分	**Grouped by sponsors**							
政府办	Run by Government	7022	4874	18026	4331	6446	5450	11495
社会办	Run by Society	674	449	901	258	558	834	1238
个人办	Run by Private	963	580	1744	422	803	895	1670
按市县分	**Guouped by Ctiy and County**							
市	City	5503	3810	10887	3033	4930	4854	10003
县	County	3156	2093	9784	1978	2877	2325	4400
按城乡分	**Grouped by Rural and Urban**							
城市	Urban	2427	1695	4226	1280	2413	2696	6253
农村	Rural	6232	4208	16445	3731	5394	4483	8150
按营利性质分	**Grouped by Profit**							
非营利性	Non-profit	6511	4219	16454	4517	6462	5434	11795
营利性	Profit	967	595	1725	438	798	958	1776
其他	Others	1181	1089	2492	56	547	787	832
按机构分	**Grouped By Organizations**							
医院	Total Number of Hospitals	5690	3529	11786	3756	5648	5071	28
综合医院	Comprehensive Hospitals	4742	2913	9742	3275	4356	4167	348
中医医院	Hospitals of Traditional Chinese Medicine	312	221	559	112	475	306	140
中西医结合医院	TCM and Western Medicine Hospital	21	9	115	47	2	46	51
民族医院	Hospitals for Nationalities	245	153	696	142	363	141	
专科医院	Specialist Hospitals	370	233	674	180	452	411	70

19-1 续表 2 Continued

项　目	Item	机构数(个) Number of Institutions (unit)	实有床位数(张) Beds (unit)	在岗职工合计(人) Total Number of Medical Personnel (person)	卫生技术人员小计 Medical Technical Personnel	执业(助理)医师 Lecensed Assistant Doctor	执业医师 Lecensed Doctors	注册护士 Registered Nurses	药剂人员 Pharmacist
口腔医院	Nonnasality Hospitals	4	42	266	213	117	111	71	4
眼科医院	Ophthalmology Hospitals	7	200	296	185	58	50	86	15
耳鼻喉科医院	Otolaryngology Hospitals	2	150	227	166	64	58	61	15
肿瘤医院	Tumour Hospital	1	1470	2120	1592	445	445	766	46
心血管病医院	Cardiovascular Hospitals	1	257	588	356	109	106	193	17
胸科医院	Chest Hospital	1	516	545	455	134	132	194	19
妇产(科)医院	Hospitals for Gynaecology and Obsterics	17	545	627	478	175	155	208	24
儿童医院	Children Hospital	1	30	54	34	11	5	14	4
精神病医院	Mental Hospitals	13	3996	1750	1310	345	314	743	61
传染病医院	Infectous Diseases Hospitals	4	790	514	377	131	117	164	20
皮肤病医院	Skin disease hospital	3	124	94	74	29	24	32	6
结核病医院	Tubercuiosis Hospitals	1	486	171	150	59	54	66	6
职业病医院		1							
骨科医院	Hospital of Orthopedics	4	125	118	91	20	15	29	8
康复医院	Recovery Hospitals	3	168	87	68	40	38	17	3
整形外科医院	Plastic surgical holpital	1	50	44	28	18	14	7	2
美容医院		1	20	35	20	8	4	10	1
其他专科医院	Other Specialist Hospitals	27	827	865	638	252	222	224	40
基层医疗卫生机构	Basic Medical Institutions	17190	26373	57226	38140	16535	11847	12504	1544
社区卫生服务中心(站)	Community Health Service Center	794	2951	8297	7137	2951	2496	2741	454
社区卫生服务中心	Community Health Service Center	181	2502	5109	4300	1624	1313	1618	298
社区卫生服务站	Community Health Service Station	613	449	3188	2837	1327	1183	1123	156
卫生院	Total Number of Public Health Center	924	22992	21459	18312	5929	2924	5664	781
乡镇卫生院	Public Health Center in Township and Towns	924	22992	21459	18312	5929	2924	5664	781
中心卫生院	Public Health Center in Rural Area	138	4795	4070	3519	1124	594	1102	157
乡卫生院	Public Health Center in Township	786	18197	17389	14793	4805	2330	4562	624
村卫生室	Village Clinics	10567		15727	1389	1061	576	328	
门诊部	Outpatients Department	278	430	1956	1730	899	778	523	89
综合门诊部	Comprehensive Department	212	397	1491	1349	661	588	432	74
中医门诊部	Department of Traditional Chinese Medicine	4	5	21	16	7	7	4	2
中西医结合门诊部	TCM and Western Medicine Department	5	5	15	14	5	5	4	1
民族医门诊部	Department for Nationalities	5		47	39	22	13	6	3
专科门诊部	Specialist Department	52	23	382	312	204	165	77	9
诊所.卫生所.医务室	Clinics, Health Centers	4627		9787	9572	5695	5073	3248	220
诊所	Clinics	3968		8378	8211	4896	4472	2844	184
卫生所、医务室	Health Centers, Health Rooms	650		1397	1349	798	601	395	36

19-1 续表 3 Continued

项目	Item	技师(士) Technician (artificer)	检验人员 Laboratory Technicians	其他 Others	见习医师 Intern Doctor	其他技术人员 Other Technicians	管理人员 Administrative Personnel	工勤人员 Logistics Workers
口腔医院	Nonnasality Hospitals	5	2	16	8	9	21	5
眼科医院	Ophthalmology Hospitals	9	9	17	7	20	17	268
耳鼻喉科医院	Otolaryngology Hospitals	11	6	15	8	10	23	87
肿瘤医院	Tumour Hospital	72	31	263	61	115	65	12
心血管病医院	Cardiovascular Hospitals	16	12	21	11	47	45	9
胸科医院	Chest Hospital	16	15	92	3	34	5	
妇产(科)医院	Hospitals for Gynaecology and Obsterics	40	25	31	12	28	51	17
儿童医院	Children Hospital	5	4			4	11	7
精神病医院	Mental Hospitals	62	41	99	30	99	73	14
传染病医院	Infectous Diseases Hospitals	33	17	29		32	18	10
皮肤病医院	Skin disease hospital	7	5				8	140
结核病医院	Tubercuiosis Hospitals	11	9	8	8	6	6	
职业病医院								392
骨科医院	Hospital of Orthopedics	6	3	28	28	4	6	283
康复医院	Recovery Hospitals	5	3	3		6	6	109
整形外科医院	Plastic surgical holpital	1	1				2	1501
美容医院		1	1			3	2	
其他专科医院	Other Specialist Hospitals	70	49	52	4	35	52	1501
基层医疗卫生机构	Basic Medical Institutions	1490	1071	6067	1150	1401	1013	1214
社区卫生服务中心(站)	Community Health Service Center	380	266	611	140	353	415	
社区卫生服务中心	Community Health Service Center	280	190	480	119	254	272	226
社区卫生服务站	Community Health Service Station	100	76	131	21	99	143	142
卫生院	Total Number of Public Health Center	967	698	4971	924	1048	598	5
乡镇卫生院	Public Health Center in Township and Towns	967	698	4971	924	1048	598	8
中心卫生院	Public Health Center in Rural Area	210	143	926	242	167	97	70
乡卫生院	Public Health Center in Township	757	555	4045	682	881	501	215
村卫生室	Village Clinics							167
门诊部	Outpatients Department	97	69	122	19			48
综合门诊部	Comprehensive Department	82	59	100	16			
中医门诊部	Department of Traditional Chinese Medicine			3				1087
中西医结合门诊部	TCM and Western Medicine Department	2	1	2				563
民族医门诊部	Department for Nationalities	3	1	5				69
专科门诊部	Specialist Department	10	8	12	3			107
诊所.卫生所.医务室	Clinics, Health Centers	46	38	363	67			115
诊所	Clinics	32	24	255	58			220
卫生所、医务室	Health Centers, Health Rooms	14	14	106	9			52

19-1 续表 4 Continued

项 目	Item	机构数(个) Number of Institutions (unit)	实有床位数(张) Beds (unit)	在岗职工合计(人) Total Number of Medical Personnel (person)	卫生技术人员小计 Medical Technical Personnel	执业(助理)医师 Lecensed Assistant Doctor	执业医师 Lecensed Doctors	注册护士 Registered Nurses	药剂人员 Pharmacist
护理站	Nursing Department	9		12	12	1		9	
专业公共卫生机构	Specialized Public Health Institution	605	2679	14364	11495	4719	3698	2250	250
疾病预防控制中心	Center for Disease Control and Prevetion	229		6296	4960	2626	2059	532	68
自治区属	Autonoumous Areas	1		439	314	185	183	3	
区辖市(地区)属	District Municipal	14		1255	1002	513	457	72	14
地辖市属	administer the municipal	26		1140	892	484	398	66	12
县属	County	76		2134	1615	769	542	196	33
其他	Others	112		1328	1137	675	479	195	9
专科疾病防治院(所、站)	Specialized Disease Prevention &Treatment Institution	5	99	100	56	30	18	10	2
专科疾病防治院	Specialized Disease Prevention &Treatment Centers	1	15	27	24	14	10	2	1
其他	Others	1	15	27	24	14	10	2	1
专科疾病防治所(站、中心)	Specialized Disease Prevention&Treatment Stations	4	84	73	32	16	8	8	1
药物戒毒所(中心)	The drug detoxificatio Center	3	84	73	32	16	8	8	1
其他	Others	1							
妇幼保健院(所、站)	Women and Children Care Agencies	92	2530	4131	3476	1489	1186	1254	147
区辖市(地区)属	District Municipal	5	504	844	750	247	238	334	26
地辖市属	administer the municipal	19	667	1314	1110	508	429	416	51
县属	County	64	1319	1832	1489	667	462	459	65
其他	Others	4	40	141	127	67	57	45	5
妇幼保健院	Women and Children Care Hospitals	39	1755	2656	2282	937	812	903	104
妇幼保健所	Women and Children Care Center	5		118	97	55	41	18	1
妇幼保健站	Women and Children Care Stations	48	775	1357	1097	497	333	333	42
急救中心(站)	Urgent Care Center	5	50	142	105	42	38	52	3
采供血机构	Blood transfusion services	21		575	391	59	50	137	3
卫生监督所(中心)	Health Inspection Institution (center)	159		1712	1501				
自治区属	Autonoumous Areas	1		76	65				
区辖市(地区)属	District Municipal	14		312	276				
地辖市属	administer the municipal	27		388	357				
县属	County	68		619	536				
其他	Others	49		317	267				
计划生育技术服务机构	The family planning technical service institutions	94		1408	1006	473	347	265	27
其他卫生机构	Others	8	376	298	155	57	48	68	9
疗养院	Sanatoriums	4	376	240	130	46	39	60	8
卫生监督检验(监测、检测)所(站)	Health Inspection Institution (center)	1		7	7	2	2	3	
其他	Others	3		51	18	9	7	5	1

19-1 续表 5 Continued

项　　目	Item	技师(士) Technician (artificer)	检验人员 Laboratory Technicians	其　他 Others	见习医师 Intern Doctor	其他技术人员 Other Technicians	管理人员 Administrative Personnel	工勤人员 Logistics Workers
护理站	Nursing Department			2				
专业公共卫生机构	Specialized Public Health Institution	1469	1296	2807	100	739	1043	
疾病预防控制中心	Center for Disease Control and Prevetion	929	859	805	46	328	445	
自治区属	Autonoumous Areas	81	79	45		39	17	
区辖市(地区)属	District Municipal	257	248	146	9	67	79	
地辖市属	administer the municipal	191	177	139	5	49	84	
县属	County	307	264	310	8	121	178	
其他	Others	93	91	165	24	52	87	
专科疾病防治院(所、站)	Specialized Disease Prevention &Treatment Institution	6	4	8	8	3	41	
专科疾病防治院	Specialized Disease Prevention &Treatment Centers	1		6	6	3		
其他	Others	1		6	6	3		
专科疾病防治所(站、中心)	Specialized Disease Prevention&Treatment Stations	5	4	2	2		41	
药物戒毒所(中心)	The drug detoxificatio Center	5	4	2	2		41	3
其他	Others							118
妇幼保健院(所、站)	Women and Children Care Agencies	278	201	308	36	192	219	117
区辖市(地区)属	District Municipal	59	41	84		36	27	17
地辖市属	administer the municipal	95	64	40		68	73	79
县属	County	117	89	181	36	82	114	82
其他	Others	7	7	3		6	5	11
妇幼保健院	Women and Children Care Hospitals	174	123	164	18	126	130	15
妇幼保健所	Women and Children Care Center	11	10	12		3	9	14
妇幼保健站	Women and Children Care Stations	93	68	132	18	63	80	35
急救中心(站)	Urgent Care Center	6	3	2		12	8	102
采供血机构	Blood transfusion services	146	144	46	3	45	60	72
卫生监督所(中心)	Health Inspection Institution (center)			1501		3	126	66
自治区属	Autonoumous Areas			65				
区辖市(地区)属	District Municipal			276			21	
地辖市属	administer the municipal			357			17	
县属	County			536		3	45	
其他	Others			267			43	
计划生育技术服务机构	The family planning technical service institutions	104	85	137	7	156	144	6
其他卫生机构	Others	10	7	11	5	19	52	
疗养院	Sanatoriums	8	6	8	5	4	40	
卫生监督检验(监测、检测)所(站)	Health Inspection Institution (center)	2	1					
其他	Others			3		15	12	

19-2 主要年份卫生机构数(不含村卫生室)
Number of Health Institutions in Main Years(Excluding Village Clinics)

单位：个 (unit)

年 份 Year	合 计 Total	医院、卫生院 Hospitals And Township Hospitals	#医院 Hospitals	疗养院 Sanit-arium	门诊部 Clinics	专科防治所、站 Specialized Prevention & Treatment Centers or Stations	疾病防控中心 Sanitation and Antiepide-mic Agencies	妇幼保健所、站 Maternity and Child Care Centers	社区卫生服务中心(站) Health Service Center for Community	卫生监督所(中心) Research Institutes of Medical Science	其他卫生机构 Other Institutions	诊所、医务保健室、医务室 Clinics Health Care Room Infirmary
1978	2581	806	204	2	1609	1	104	12			47	
1980	2818	884	270	4	1756	4	102	12			56	
1985	3320	947	389	5	2125	2	139	27			75	
1990	3945	1049	435	6	2536	13	191	59			91	
1995	3932	1292	507	8	2247	16	216	69			84	
2000	7314	1352	522	8	154	16	210	74			96	5404
2005	8087	1516	685	6	224	8	197	88	46	30	113	5859
2006	8175	1560	699	6	220	7	211	92	62	49	83	5885
2007	7465	1629	756	7	240	7	214	87	250	112	30	4889
2008	6739	1629	741	4	217	6	213	89	264	121	31	4165
2009	7288	1669	763	5	221	5	214	90	405	128	30	4521
2010	7650	1712	802	4	259	4	221	90	641	133	31	4555
2011	7587	1742	820	4	247	4	216	90	683	128	30	4443
2012	7820	1759	836	4	278	5	224	91	744	158	32	4525
2013	8096	1784	860	4	278	5	229	92	794	159	124	4627

注：1.2002 年起卫生部新制度规定持有"医疗执业许可证"所有卫生机构算为一个机构,兵团连队卫生室统计到卫生所中,所以卫生机构总数增加。2.从 2007 年开始卫生部门实行网络直报。

Note: a) From 2002, in line with new regulations of ministry of public health,all the health institutions that have medical service permit shall be counted as one and health care rooms shall be counted in health clinics,therefore the total number of health institutions increased.
b) Since 2007, health care institution have carried out direct network report.

19-3 主要年份卫生人员数(不含村卫生室)
Number of Persons Engaged in Health Institutions in Main Years (Excluding Village Clinics)

单位：人 (person)

年 份 Year	合 计 Total	#卫生技术人员 Medical Technical Personnel	#医 生 Doctors	执业医师 Lecensed Doctors	执业助理医 师 Lecensed Assistant Doctor	#注 册 护 士 Registered Nurses	平均每万人医生数 Number of Doctors per 10 000 Population
1978	66252	51050	16898	7368	9530	10765	13.70
1980	74627	57949	20614	10092	10522	12077	16.06
1985	88460	68961	25721	13330	12391	17136	18.90
1990	102053	79853	33683	24967	8716	23386	22.03
1995	116856	92028	39636	30038	9598	26350	23.86
2000	122064	98093	45402	34892	10510	30850	24.55
2005	117165	96266	41426	32563	8863	30657	20.61
2006	121400	99839	42775	33988	8787	32119	20.87
2007	127621	104671	43551	34838	8713	34662	20.79
2008	130174	106853	43456	35320	8136	36084	20.39
2009	138344	114521	45616	37223	8393	40425	21.13
2010	149069	122860	48166	39301	8865	44238	22.25
2011	155701	129354	48618	39763	8855	48422	22.49
2012	150083	135401	49558	40834	8724	52141	22.63
2013	159513	144462	51959	43006	8953	56250	23.39

注：2002 年以前执业医师为中医师、西医师、中西医结合医师，执业助理医师为中医士、西医士、中西医结合医士，注册护士为护师、护士。(以下同)

Note: Prior to 2002,doctors with license were doctors trained in western medicine,assistant doctors are practioners with secondary western medical education,and registered nurses are master nurses and nurses (The following is the same as below) .

19-4 主要年份卫生机构床位数
Number of Sick-Beds in Health Institutions in Main Years

单位：张 (unit)

年份 Year	合计 Total	医院卫生院 Hospitals And Health Centers	#医院 Hospitals	社区服务中心(站) Sanitarium	其他卫生机构 Other Health Institutions	每万人医院、卫生院床位数 Number of Hospital Beds per 10 000 Population
1978	57647	39179	25514		18468	31.78
1980	61075	47236	32944		13839	36.81
1985	60930	55298	42486		5632	40.63
1990	67414	60707	47924		6707	39.70
1995	72955	66696	53336		6259	40.15
2000	70542	65916	52438		4626	35.64
2005	79753	76002	63013	209	3542	37.81
2006	83722	80090	65589	445	3187	39.07
2007	90329	87131	71496	343	2855	41.59
2008	96852	93253	76321	843	2756	43.76
2009	107193	102620	83776	1851	2722	47.54
2010	116230	109851	89871	3588	2791	50.36
2011	125391	118781	97436	3691	2919	53.93
2012	131542	125064	103074	3084	3394	56.01
2013	137325	130889	107897	2951	3485	57.75

19-5 2000-2013 年历年分市县医院床位和专业卫生技术人员数
Hospital Beds and Medical Technical Personnel by City and County Areas(2000-2013)

年 份 Year	医院床位(张) Number of Hospital Beds (unit)		专业卫生技术人员(人) Number of Medical Technical Personnel (person)		#执业医师、执业助理医师 Lecensed Doctors & Assistant Doctors		#注册护士 Registered Nurses	
	市 City	县 County	市 City	县 County	市 City	县 County	市 City	县 County
2000	38398	27518	44115	31138	18408	13225	16805	9918
2001	38323	27685	44113	31055	18811	13271	16714	10105
2002	38700	26178	41850	27932	16689	10578	15965	8840
2003	42880	26915	44678	28228	17883	10916	17015	9087
2004	46300	27722	46956	28552	19207	10583	17185	9054
2005	50238	29515	54188	31132	23191	12323	18240	9289
2006	52275	31125	56701	32178	24033	13049	19365	9538
2007	54595	32536	68546	36125	28896	14655	24174	10488
2008	57242	36011	69292	37561	28215	15241	24976	11108
2009	58373	25403	54356	19490	20044	7242	22453	6979
2010	61157	28714	56706	21500	20953	7637	23777	8037
2011	65905	31531	61309	22893	21481	7881	26559	8964
2012	70217	32857	65326	24184	22081	8105	28960	9715
2013	71935	35962	69353	26708	23284	8425	30579	11177

19-6 2000-2013 年历年分市县卫生院床位和专业卫生技术人员数
Hospital Beds and Medical Technical Personnel by City and County Areas(2000-2013)

年 份 Year	卫生院床位(张) Number of Hospital Beds (unit)		专业卫生技术人员(人) Number of Medical Technical Personnel (person)		#执业医师、执业助理医师 Lecensed Doctors & Assistant Doctors		#注册护士 Registered Nurses	
	市 City	县 County	市 City	县 County	市 City	县 County	市 City	县 County
2000	2138	11119	3442	13131	1622	6299	1021	3756
2001	2141	11247	3602	13129	1782	6300	1095	3808
2002	2180	9991	4021	11215	1611	4370	970	2829
2003	2471	10147	3645	10901	1364	4227	946	2950
2004	2351	10479	3703	10936	1429	3963	992	2746
2005	5061	11679	10345	13646	5004	5704	2056	3024
2006	4732	13079	10930	14105	5370	6048	2207	3213
2007	2832	12803	18725	18220	9548	8000	4771	4182
2008	3037	13895	17745	19239	8888	8446	4710	4626
2009	3313	15531	3684	12578	1595	4435	1161	3527
2010	3383	16597	3641	13240	1536	4381	1180	3741
2011	3674	17671	3672	13653	1538	4334	1195	4097
2012	3768	18222	3694	14037	1466	4407	1241	4301
2013	3757	19235	3670	14642	1427	4502	1216	4448

19-7 各地、州、市卫生机构、床位和人员数

年 份 Year	地 区 Region	机构数 (个) Number of Institutions (unit)	床位数 (张) Beds (unit)	在岗职工合计 (人) Total Number of Medical Personnel (person)
	2005	8087	79753	117165
	2006	8175	83722	121400
	2007	7465	90329	127621
	2008	6739	96852	130174
	2009	7288	107193	138344
	2010	7650	116230	149069
	2011	17412	125391	167828
	2012	18320	131542	177085
	2013	18663	137325	189578
乌鲁木齐市	Urumqi City	1769	26989	43862
克拉玛依市	Karamay City	92	1652	3796
吐鲁番地区	Turpan Administrative Offices	411	2904	4364
哈密地区	Hami [Kumul] Administrative Offices	502	3630	5724
昌吉回族自治州	Changji Hui Autonomous Prefecture	1498	9870	13872
伊犁哈萨克自治州	Ili Kazak Autonomous Prefecture	4197	25074	35697
伊犁州直属县(市)	Counties (Cities) Direct Under Ili Prefecture	2121	16294	20963
塔城地区	Tacheng [Tarbagatai] Administrative Offices	1308	5140	8774
阿勒泰地区	Altay Administrative Offices	768	3640	5960
博尔塔拉蒙古自治州	Bortala Mongol Autonomous Prefecture	672	2905	4616
巴音郭楞蒙古自治州	Bayangol Mongol Autonomous Prefecture	1278	8868	12469
阿克苏地区	Aksu Administrative Offices	1606	13382	13454
克孜勒苏柯尔克孜自治州	Kizilsu Kirgiz Autonomous Prefecture	348	3111	4228
喀什地区	Kashgar [Kaxgar] Administrative Offices	3498	19511	23949
和田地区	Hotan Administrative Offices	1770	12474	13214
自治区直辖县级市	Municpality Country-LevelCity directly under the Central Govern-ment	1022	6955	10333
石河子市	Shihezi City	739	5318	7810
阿拉尔市	Aral City	190	590	997
图木舒克市	Tumxuk City	2	179	198
五家渠市	Wujiaqu City	91	868	1335

注：1.本表 2013 年数据含乡村医生 13005 人和卫生员 1333 人。
2.不含乡镇卫生院在村卫生室工作的执业(助理)医师、注册护士数。

Number of Health Institutions, Beds and Personnel by Prefecture, Autonomous Prefecture and City

卫生技术人员 Medical Technical Personnel	其他技术人员 Other Technicians	管理人员 Administrative Personnel	工勤人员 Logistics Workers	平均每万人床位数(张) Number of Beds per 10 000 Population (unit)
96266	4626	6330	9943	39.71
99839	5168	6258	10135	39.07
104671	5276	7143	10531	43.11
106853	5694	6419	11208	45.45
114521	6111	6453	11259	49.66
122860	6979	7089	12141	53.28
130604	6904	6837	12606	56.93
136691	6972	6631	13935	58.91
145851	7807	7179	14403	60.59
34303	1857	2168	5325	102.65
3057	174	190	373	56.93
3495	188	163	263	45.17
4914	229	146	261	59.66
11423	626	378	806	70.25
28089	1642	1284	2157	53.17
16770	927	780	1325	54.58
6706	426	282	531	48.50
4613	289	222	301	54.29
3647	120	254	364	59.24
10482	571	385	504	63.15
9757	608	459	818	54.45
3288	159	100	207	53.99
17226	591	1002	1469	46.14
7592	639	295	1266	57.90
8578	403	355	590	65.38
6496	323	282	491	85.42
760	25	28	47	31.70
183	6	6	3	10.91
1146	49	39	49	95.38

Note: a).Total data in this table included 13005 doctors and 1333 medical personnel.
b).Total data in this table didn't include licensed doctors and registered nurses in tounship in county health Centers.

19-8 各地、州、市卫生技术人员数

单位:人

年 份 Year	地 区 Region	卫生技术人员合计 Number of Medical Technical Personnel	执业医师 Doctors with License	执业助理医 师 Licensed Assistant Doctor
	2005	96266	32563	8863
	2006	99839	33988	8787
	2007	104671	34838	8713
	2008	106853	35320	8136
	2009	114521	37223	8393
	2010	122860	39301	8865
	2011	130604	40265	9265
	2012	136691	41358	9182
	2013	145851	43582	9438
乌鲁木齐市	Urumqi City	34303	12692	656
克拉玛依市	Karamay City	3057	1105	34
吐鲁番地区	Turpan Administrative Offices	3495	1108	246
哈密地区	Hami [Kumul] Administrative Offices	4914	1533	293
昌吉回族自治州	Changji Hui Autonomous Prefecture	11423	3382	774
伊犁哈萨克自治州	Ili Kazak Autonomous Prefecture	28089	8267	2226
伊犁州直属县(市)	Counties (Cities) Direct Under Ili Prefecture	16770	4980	1247
塔城地区	Tacheng [Tarbagatai] Administrative Offices	6706	1866	574
阿勒泰地区	Altay Administrative Offices	4613	1421	405
博尔塔拉蒙古自治州	Bortala Mongol Autonomous Prefecture	3647	1111	346
巴音郭楞蒙古自治州	Bayangol Mongol Autonomous Prefecture	10482	2984	769
阿克苏地区	Aksu Administrative Offices	9757	2540	794
克孜勒苏柯尔克孜自治州	Kizilsu Kirgiz Autonomous Prefecture	3288	829	347
喀什地区	Kashgar [Kaxgar] Administrative Offices	17226	3716	1710
和田地区	Hotan Administrative Offices	7592	1669	748
自治区直辖县级市	Municpality Country-LevelCity directly under the Central Govern-ment	8578	2646	495
石河子市	Shihezi City	6496	2117	355
阿拉尔市	Aral City	760	155	73
图木舒克市	Tumxuk City	183	34	12
五家渠市	Wujiaqu City	1146	343	55

注：1.本表人员合计中包括乡村医生 13005 人和卫生员 1333 人。
2.不含乡镇卫生院在村卫生室工作的执业(助理)医师、注册护士数。

Number of Medical Technical Personnel by Prefecture, Autonomous Prefecture and City

(person)

注册护士 Registered Nurses	药剂人员 Pharmacist	技师(士) Technician (artificer)	检验人员 Laboratory Technicians	其他 Others	平均每万人医生数 Number of Doctors per 10 000 Population
30657	5848	4773		13562	20.61
32119	5948	4980		14017	20.87
34662	5647	6701	4746	14110	20.79
36084	5721	6876	4803	14716	20.39
40425	5989	7164	4977	15327	21.13
44238	6364	7742	5301	16350	22.25
48760	6483	7726	5391	18105	22.49
52449	6557	7984	5539	19161	22.63
56578	6923	8659	5903	20671	23.39
14476	1616	1759	1260	3104	50.77
1239	197	177	128	305	39.25
1388	168	245	160	340	21.06
2041	257	244	188	546	30.01
4486	620	665	446	1496	29.58
10748	1161	1845	1275	3842	22.25
6277	732	1178	833	2356	20.86
2681	262	414	257	909	23.02
1790	167	253	185	577	27.23
1347	184	203	153	456	29.71
4051	418	614	410	1646	26.73
3866	460	611	401	1486	13.57
1163	152	172	114	625	20.41
5764	863	1148	767	4025	12.83
2308	498	469	280	1900	11.22
3701	329	507	321	900	29.53
2785	256	384	237	599	39.70
330	27	46	31	129	12.25
90	5	10	8	32	2.80
500	41	67	45	140	43.73

Note: a). Total data in this table included 13005 doctors and 1333 medical personels.
b). Total data in this table didn't include licensed doctors and registered nurses in county health centers.

19-9 社区卫生服务中心(站)工作量
Medical Services in Health Service Centers for Community

年 份 Year	社区卫生服务中心 Health Service Centers for Community				社区卫生服务站诊疗人次(万人) Health Service Stations for Community (10 000 patients)
	诊疗人次（万人次） Visits (10 000 patient-times)	入院人数(万人) Inpatients (10 000 patients)	病床使用率(%) Utilization Rate (%)	平均住院日(日) Average Stay Days (day)	
2002	76.84	0.16	53.86	10.16	34.41
2003	88.10	0.60	89.51	16.13	33.75
2004	85.62	0.03	36.42	10.00	82.67
2005	67.04	0.03	16.71	11.08	152.68
2006	107.49	0.35	11.71	6.94	179.32
2007	105.73	0.24	59.77	11.70	109.22
2008	156.05	0.94	51.68	11.30	121.92
2009	232.95	2.36	49.93	9.90	207.23
2010	298.47	4.24	61.07	10.40	355.78
2011	323.93	4.37	53.51	9.80	351.28
2012	330.09	4.85	50.32	7.60	341.43
2013	410.08	4.32	50.85	8.80	359.09

19-10 乡村卫生室基本情况
Basic Conditions of Country Health Room

(2013 年)

项 目	Item	合 计 Total	中 医 Traditional Chinese Medicine	西 医 Western Medicine	中西医结合 Combination Traditional and Western Medicine
机构数(个)	Number of Institutions(unit)	10567	86	9119	1362
执业(助理)医师(人)	Lecensed (Assistant) Doctors (person)	1061	24	930	107
注册护士(人)	Registered Nurses(person)	328	4	310	14
乡村医生和卫生员(人)	Country Doctor and Assistant Nurse(person)	14338	105	12270	1963
乡村医生	Country Doctor	13005	97	11069	1839
卫生员	Assistant Nurse	1333	8	1201	124
诊疗人次数(万人次)	Number of Patients Treated(10 000 patient-times)	945.97	13.22	781.71	151.04
#出 诊	Out-call	76.64	0.70	61.43	14.51

19-11 新型农牧区合作医疗基本情况

Basic Statistics on New Cooperative Health Care in Agricultural and Pastoral Areas

项 目	Item	2012	2013
开展县(市)数(个)	Number of Counties(citys) to Carry Out(unit)	89	89
覆盖农牧业人口数(万人)	Population Coverage of Agriculture and Animal Husbandry(10 000 persons)	1081.61	1104.59
参合农牧业人口数(万人)	Livestok Population Parameters(10 000 persons)	1078.30	1102.68
参合率(%)	Ratio of Participation(%)	99.70	99.80
当年筹集基金(万元)	Paise Funds This Year(10 000 yuan)	339771.84	409910.45
#中央补助	Central Subsidy	165111.00	204304.00
自治区补助	Autonpmous Region Subsidy	87090.00	97383.00
地方补助	Local Subsidy	31048.10	38784.07
个人缴费	Individual Pay	54131.77	65886.60
当年人均筹集资金(元/人·年)	Annual per Capita Raise Funds(yuan/persons.year)	320.33	368.51
当年基金支出(万元)	Expenditure of Fund This Yesr(10 000 yuan)	318926.04	422383.60
当年基金使用率(%)	Ratio of Fund Utilization This Yesr(%)	93.86	103.04
当年补偿受益人次(万人次)	Benefit of Compensation Population this Year(10 000 person-times)	1389.99	1810.26
住 院	Inpatients	234.52	224.82
门 诊	Out-patient Services	948.47	1502.66
体 检	Physical Examination	19.77	10.28
其 他	Others	187.24	57.28
当年总体受益率(%)	Ratio of Total Benefit(%)	128.91	164.17
住院受益率	Benefit Ratio of be in Hospital	21.75	20.39
门诊受益率	Benefit Ratio of out-patient Services	87.96	136.27
当年总补偿比(%)	Total Compensation Ratio(%)	55.67	60.50
#住院平均补偿比	Average Compensation Ratio of be in Hospital	55.04	60.17
新农合管理机构实有人数(人)	Number of Employed Persons in Institution on New Cooperative Health Care of Agriculturial and Pastoral Areas(person)	1248	1278
新农合管理机构经费收入(万元)	Income of Institution on New Cooperative Health Care of Agriculturial and Pastoral Areas(10 000 yuan)	6660.40	8284.90
新农合管理机构经费支出(万元)	Expenditure of Institution on New Cooperative Health Care of Agriculturial and Pastoral Areas(10 000 yuan)	6501.82	8342.61
每实有人员管理参合人数(人)	Number of Participated Persons by per Practical Employed Persons(person)	14900	15003

19-12 医疗卫生机构门诊服务情况
Basic Conditions of Outpatient service medical and health institutions

(2013 年)

项　目	Item	总诊疗人次数(万人次) Number of Visits(10000 times)	门、急诊 Outpatients with Emergency Treatment 小计 Total	门诊 Outpatients	急诊 Emergency Treatment	家庭卫生服务人次数 Vistits
总　计	**Total**	**9381.95**	**9045.17**	**8691.90**	**353.27**	**27.25**
医　院	Hospitals	4550.05	4422.29	4116.77	305.52	8.45
综合医院	General Hospital	3798.09	3686.42	3403.14	283.28	8.12
中医医院	Hospital Specialized in Traditional Chinese Medicine	421.16	418.62	403.64	14.98	0.04
中西医结合医院	Hospital Specialized in Combination Of Traditional Chinese and Western Medicine Medicine	22.17	22.06	21.98	0.08	
民族医院	National Hospital	154.76	143.98	138.54	5.44	0.25
专科医院	Specialized Hospital	153.87	151.22	149.47	1.75	0.04
基层医疗卫生机构	Basic Medical Institutions	4514.25	4316.13	4276.87	39.25	17.36
社区卫生服务中心(站)	Health Service Center for Community	769.18	749.89	740.22	9.68	9.26
卫生院	Health Center	1541.69	1485.97	1456.39	29.58	8.10
村卫生室	Village Clinics	945.97	869.34	869.34		
门诊部	Out-patients Department	119.25	113.43	113.43		
诊所.卫生所.医务室	Clinics Health Care Room Infirmary	1138.16	1097.50	1097.50		
专业公共卫生机构	Specialized Public Health Institution	314.84	303.96	295.46	8.49	1.44
专科疾病防治院(所、站)	Specialized Disease Prevention & Treatment Institute	3.27	3.27	2.66	0.61	
妇幼保健院(所、站)	Hospitals for Maternity and Child Care	305.71	294.83	292.80	2.02	1.44
内：妇幼保健院	Women and Children Care Agencies	193.96	188.59	187.03	1.57	0.67
急救中心(站)	Emergency center	5.85	5.85		5.85	
其他机构	Other Institutions	2.81	2.80	2.80		
疗养院	Sanatorium	2.81	2.80	2.80		

项　目	Item	观察室留观病例数(万人) Cases in Observation Room(10000 persons)	健康检查人数(万人) Number of Health Examinations (10000 persons)	急诊病死率(%) Fatality Rate among Emergency Admissions(%)	观察室病死率(%) Fatality Rate in Observation Room (%)
总　计	**Total**	**73.52**	**590.51**	**0.13**	**0.11**
医　院	Hospitals	48.11	312.38	0.15	0.17
综合医院	General Hospital	39.65	283.18	0.15	0.20
中医医院	Hospital Specialized in Traditional Chinese Medicine	7.89	16.49	0.19	
中西医结合医院	Hospital Specialized in Combination Of Traditional Chinese and Western Medicine Medicine	0.02	0.03		
民族医院	National Hospital	0.27	4.29	0.03	0.33
专科医院	Specialized Hospital	0.28	8.38	0.55	
基层医疗卫生机构	Basic Medical Institutions	24.07	226.95	0.03	0.01
社区卫生服务中心(站)	Health Service Center for Community	18.71	65.34	0.10	0.01
卫生院	Health Center	5.36	161.62	0.01	0.01
村卫生室	Village Clinics				
门诊部	Out-patients Department				
诊所.卫生所.医务室	Clinics Health Care Room Infirmary				
专业公共卫生机构	Specialized Public Health Institution	1.35	51.02		
专科疾病防治院(所、站)	Specialized Disease Prevention & Treatment Institute		0.04		
妇幼保健院(所、站)	Hospitals for Maternity and Child Care	1.35	50.98		
内：妇幼保健院	Women and Children Care Agencies	0.99	27.59		
急救中心(站)	Emergency center				
其他机构	Other Institutions		0.16		
疗养院	Sanatorium		0.16		

19-13 医疗卫生机构住院服务情况
Basic Conditions of Service in medical and health institutions

(2013 年)

项　目	Item	入院人数(人) Number of Inpatients (Person)	出院人数(人) Patients Discharged (Person)
总　计	**Total**	**4640490**	**4619993**
医　院	Hospitals	3616321	3599653
综合医院	General Hospital	3020478	3009162
中医医院	Hospital Specialized in Traditional Chinese Medicine	254909	252891
中西医结合医院	Hospital Specialized in Combination Of Traditional Chinese and Western Medicine Medicine	11099	11116
民族医院	National Hospital	182495	180146
专科医院	Specialized Hospital	147340	146338
基层医疗卫生机构	Basic Medical Institutions	927992	925169
社区卫生服务中心(站)	Health Service Center for Community	48827	52999
卫生院	Health Center	875630	868635
门诊部	Village Clinics	3535	3535
专业公共卫生机构	Specialized Public Health Institution	94874	93880
专科疾病防治院(所、站)	Specialized Disease Prevention & Treatment Institute	2860	1020
妇幼保健院(所、站)	Hospitals for Maternity and Child Care	92014	92860
内：妇幼保健院	Women and Children Care Agencies	64734	66447
其他机构	Other Institutions	1303	1291
疗养院	Sanatorium	1303	1291

项　目	Item	住院病人手术人次数(人次) Surgical Operation of Hospitalized (person-times)	每百门急诊的入院人数(人) Inpatients per 100 Outpatient and Emergency Visits (person)	入院病人死亡率(%) Inpatient mortality (%)
总　计	**Total**	**745666**	**6.67**	**0.29**
医　院	Hospitals	719039	8.18	0.36
综合医院	General Hospital	644184	8.19	0.39
中医医院	Hospital Specialized in Traditional Chinese Medicine	36823	6.09	0.11
中西医结合医院	Hospital Specialized in Combination Of Traditional Chinese and Western Medicine Medicine	50	5.03	1.84
民族医院	National Hospital	7861	12.68	0.03
专科医院	Specialized Hospital	30121	9.74	0.48
基层医疗卫生机构	Basic Medical Institutions		4.13	0.02
社区卫生服务中心(站)	Health Service Center for Community		0.65	0.23
卫生院	Health Center		5.89	0.01
门诊部	Village Clinics			
专业公共卫生机构	Specialized Public Health Institution	26627	3.18	0.03
专科疾病防治院(所、站)	Specialized Disease Prevention & Treatment Institute		8.73	
妇幼保健院(所、站)	Hospitals for Maternity and Child Care	26627	3.12	0.03
内：妇幼保健院	Women and Children Care Agencies	23797	3.43	0.04
其他机构	Other Institutions		4.66	0.23
疗养院	Sanatorium		4.66	0.23

19-14 医疗卫生机构门诊病人人均医疗费用
The per capita medical expenses of patients hospitalized in the medical and health institutions

(2013 年)

项 目	Item	门诊病人次均诊疗费用(元) The per Capita Medical Expenses of Outpatient	挂号费 Registered Fee	诊察费 Diagnostic Fee	检查费 Inspection Fee	化验费 Laboratory Fee
总 计	**Total**	**117.9**	**0.6**	**1.4**	**23.8**	**11.3**
医 院	Hospitals	181.4	1.0	2.2	40.5	17.9
综合医院	General Hospital	177.2	1.0	2.2	42.5	18.6
中医医院	Hospital Specialized in Traditional Chinese Medicine	213.1	1.0	1.9	29.2	11.7
中西医结合医院	Hospital Specialized in Combination Of Traditional Chinese and Western Medicine Medicine	193.0	0.1	0.3	3.0	2.8
民族医院	National Hospital	104.3	0.8	1.2	16.6	5.0
专科医院	Specialized Hospital	273.5	1.3	5.9	49.6	32.9
基层医疗卫生机构	Basic Medical Institutions	36.8	0.2		2.5	1.5
社区卫生服务中心(站)	Health Service Center for Community	83.6	0.2		4.4	2.6
社区卫生服务中心	Health Service Center for Community	108.1	0.3		6.8	3.9
社区卫生服务站	Health Service Center for Community	55.7	0.1		1.8	1.0
卫生院	Total Number of Public Health Center	36.2	0.4		3.7	2.1
街道卫生院	Public Health Center in Neighbourhood					
乡镇卫生院	Public Health Center in Township and Towns	36.2	0.4		3.7	2.1
中心卫生院	Public Health Center in Rural Area	35.5	0.2		4.7	2.4
乡卫生院	Public Health Center in Township	36.4	0.4		3.4	2.0
门诊部	Village Clinics	89.6				
护理站	Nursing Hospital	47.1				
专业公共卫生机构	Specialized Public Health Institution	112.9	0.7	6.1	22.5	27.6
专科疾病防治院(所、站)	Specialized Disease Prevention & Treatment Institute	100.2	3.9	2.7	4.1	7.8
妇幼保健院(所、站)	Hospitals for Maternity and Child Care	115.2	0.7	6.2	23.1	28.4
内：妇幼保健院	Women and Children Care Agencies	139.0	0.7	8.8	26.5	34.6
其他机构	Other Institutions	299.2		0.1	1.8	1.8
疗养院	Sanatorium	299.2		0.1	1.8	1.8

项 目	Item	治疗费 Treatment Costs	手术费 Operation Fee	卫生材料费 Sanitary Materials Fee	药 费 Expenses for Medicine	药事服务费 Pharmaceutical Service Fee
总 计	**Total**	**9.8**	**2.0**	**2.3**	**60.5**	**0.5**
医 院	Hospitals	15.5	3.3	3.7	91.0	0.8
综合医院	General Hospital	13.6	2.9	4.0	85.8	0.9
中医医院	Hospital Specialized in Traditional Chinese Medicine	14.6	1.8	2.2	148.3	0.1
中西医结合医院	Hospital Specialized in Combination Of Traditional Chinese and Western Medicine Medicine	107.3	1.1	0.5	75.9	1.0
民族医院	National Hospital	8.3	0.5	1.0	67.8	0.2
专科医院	Specialized Hospital	59.0	19.5	6.0	87.0	0.9
基层医疗卫生机构	Basic Medical Institutions	2.7	0.2	0.5	23.6	
社区卫生服务中心(站)	Health Service Center for Community	5.4	0.5	1.2	64.9	
社区卫生服务中心	Health Service Center for Community	7.5	0.8	1.6	82.0	
社区卫生服务站	Health Service Center for Community	3.1	0.2	0.7	45.3	
卫生院	Total Number of Public Health Center	3.6	0.3	0.5	22.1	
街道卫生院	Public Health Center in Neighbourhood					
乡镇卫生院	Public Health Center in Township and Towns	3.6	0.3	0.5	22.1	
中心卫生院	Public Health Center in Rural Area	4.0	0.1	0.5	20.7	
乡卫生院	Public Health Center in Township	3.5	0.3	0.5	22.5	
门诊部	Village Clinics					
护理站	Nursing Hospital	28.6		1.3	17.2	
专业公共卫生机构	Specialized Public Health Institution	7.9	3.7	2.8	33.8	0.5
专科疾病防治院(所、站)	Specialized Disease Prevention & Treatment Institute	65.2			16.4	
妇幼保健院(所、站)	Hospitals for Maternity and Child Care	7.4	3.8	2.8	34.7	0.5
内：妇幼保健院	Women and Children Care Agencies	8.5	4.6	3.6	41.2	0.4
其他机构	Other Institutions	24.1	21.3	0.2	249.9	
疗养院	Sanatorium	24.1	21.3	0.2	249.9	

19-15 医疗卫生机构住院病人人均医疗费用
The per capita medical expenses of patients hospitalized in the medical and health institutions

(2013 年)

项目	Item	合计 Total	床位费 Bed Fee	检查费 Inspection Fee
总计	**Total**	**4646.6**	**147.5**	**537.0**
医院	Hospitals	5641.9	170.7	658.6
综合医院	General Hospital	5480.0	159.7	637.9
中医医院	Hospital Specialized in Traditional Chinese Medicine	6795.8	174.0	784.6
中西医结合医院	Hospital Specialized in Combination Of Traditional Chinese and Western Medicine Medicine	6268.9	478.9	1407.4
民族医院	National Hospital	2844.5	145.2	252.3
专科医院	Specialized Hospital	10372.0	398.4	1309.8
基层医疗卫生机构	Basic Medical Institutions	979.8	48.6	101.7
社区卫生服务中心(站)	Health Service Center for Community	2097.3	87.9	204.1
社区卫生服务中心	Health Service Center for Community	2362.9	103.8	234.2
社区卫生服务站	Health Service Center for Community	979.5	20.7	77.6
卫生院	Total Number of Public Health Center	915.6	46.4	95.8
乡镇卫生院	Public Health Center in Township and Towns	915.6	46.4	95.8
中心卫生院	Public Health Center in Rural Area	973.1	50.9	101.4
乡卫生院	Public Health Center in Township	898.0	45.0	94.1
专业公共卫生机构	Specialized Public Health Institution	2563.6	215.2	165.6
专科疾病防治院(所、站)	Specialized Disease Prevention & Treatment Institute	931.4	117.6	117.6
妇幼保健院(所、站)	Hospitals for Maternity and Child Care	2581.5	216.3	166.2
内：妇幼保健院	Women and Children Care Agencies	3083.2	275.1	213.8
其他机构	Other Institutions	8913.2	1509.7	210.7
疗养院	Sanatorium	8913.2	1509.7	210.7

项目	Item	化验费 Laboratory Fee	治疗费 Treatment Costs	手术费 Operation Fee	药费 Expenses for Medicine
总计	**Total**	**592.1**	**567.3**	**281.3**	**1763.6**
医院	Hospitals	725.2	687.9	348.1	2115.8
综合医院	General Hospital	723.9	585.2	365.2	2058.7
中医医院	Hospital Specialized in Traditional Chinese Medicine	808.0	1504.2	281.7	2134.3
中西医结合医院	Hospital Specialized in Combination Of Traditional Chinese and Western Medicine Medicine	849.1	951.0	9.1	2421.9
民族医院	National Hospital	300.0	563.1	35.0	1282.4
专科医院	Specialized Hospital	1123.8	1523.5	521.5	4260.3
基层医疗卫生机构	Basic Medical Institutions	94.4	114.9	11.8	516.9
社区卫生服务中心(站)	Health Service Center for Community	207.6	256.1	79.2	924.9
社区卫生服务中心	Health Service Center for Community	230.2	276.3	94.2	1029.5
社区卫生服务站	Health Service Center for Community	112.7	171.0	15.9	484.8
卫生院	Total Number of Public Health Center	87.8	106.7	7.7	494.1
乡镇卫生院	Public Health Center in Township and Towns	87.8	106.7	7.7	494.1
中心卫生院	Public Health Center in Rural Area	102.3	108.7	2.7	529.9
乡卫生院	Public Health Center in Township	83.4	106.1	9.2	483.2
专业公共卫生机构	Specialized Public Health Institution	397.0	355.8	384.0	545.3
专科疾病防治院(所、站)	Specialized Disease Prevention & Treatment Institute	127.5	245.1		205.9
妇幼保健院(所、站)	Hospitals for Maternity and Child Care	400.0	357.0	388.2	549.0
内：妇幼保健院	Women and Children Care Agencies	504.4	421.1	482.6	615.2
其他机构	Other Institutions	334.6	3727.3		1623.5
疗养院	Sanatorium	334.6	3727.3		1623.5

19-16 法定报告传染病发病及死亡情况
Confirmed Incidence and Death from Infectious Diseases

项　目	Item	发病率（1/10 万）Disease Incidence (1/100 000)		死亡率（1/10 万）Death Rate (1/100 000)	
		2012	2013	2012	2013
总　计	**Total**	**624.4794**	**618.9861**	**3.1557**	**3.8831**
鼠　疫	The Plague				
霍　乱	Cholera				
传染性非典	SARS				
艾滋病	AIDS	11.0925	8.0214	2.3362	2.6156
肝　炎	Viral Hepatitis	273.1557	262.4172	0.1041	0.0537
脊　灰	Epidemic Cerebrospinal Meningitis				
人禽流感	Highly Pathogenic Bird Flu				
甲型 H1N1 流感	A(H1N1) Flu	0.7968	0.5867	0.0045	0.0045
麻　疹	Measles	2.6441	4.1159	0.0091	0.0134
出血热	Hemorrhage Fever	0.0045			
狂犬病	Hydrophobia				
乙　脑	Encephalitis B		0.0045		
登革热	Dengue Fever		0.0045		
炭　疽	Anthrax	0.1313	0.0985		
痢　疾	Dysentery	33.0194	35.1087		6.3275
肺结核	Plumonary Tuberculosis	181.1651	172.7308	0.6384	1.1152
伤寒+副伤寒	Typhoid	1.1817	1.7422		
流 脑	Encephalitis B	0.1177	0.2956	0.0181	0.0134
百 日 咳	Pertussis	3.4726	3.4726		
白 喉	Diphtheria				
新生儿破伤风	Newborn Baby Tetanus	0.1463	0.1692	0.0061	0.0091
猩 红 热	Scarlet Fever	10.0285	7.8243		
布鲁氏菌病	Brucellosis	9.7976	17.5073	0.0045	
淋 病	Gonorrhea	10.1236	9.3964		
梅 毒	Syphilis	87.4857	97.5465	0.0272	0.0358
钩 体 病	Leptospirosis	0.0045			
血吸虫病	Schistosomiasis	0.0091	0.0090		
疟　疾	Malaria	0.0317	0.0269	0.0045	0.0045

注: 1.2012 年度按发病日期统计中，涉及与艾滋病相关的发病数/率的计算，包括既往已报告 HIV 感染者转化为艾滋病病例。2.新生儿破伤风死亡率单位为千分率。

Note: The unit of incidence disease rate and death rate of newborn baby tetanus is 1‰.

19-17 城市前十位疾病死亡原因及构成

Death Causes and Percentage of 10 Major Diseases in Urban Areas

(2013 年)

疾病死亡原因	Cause of Death	死亡总人数 (人) Total Deaths (person)	占死亡总人数的比重 (%) Percentage to Total Deaths (%)
死因合计	**Total**	**8370**	**100**
循环系统	Circulatory System	3180	37.99
肿　瘤	Malignant Tumour	2202	26.31
呼吸系统	Diseases of the Respiratory System	1025	12.25
损伤和中毒外部原因	Trauma and Toxicosis	434	5.19
传染病和寄生虫病合计	Infections and Parasitic Diseases	283	3.38
消化系统	Diseases of the Digestive System	281	3.36
内分泌、营养和代谢	Endocrine, Nutritional and Metabolic	184	2.20
其它疾病	Others	167	2.00
神经系统疾病	Diseases of the Nervous System	149	1.78
起源于围生期的某些情况	Perinatal Factors	109	1.30
除以上其他疾病	In Addition to the above Other Diseases	356	4.25

注：统计范围包括乌鲁木齐市及辖区资料。
Note: Statistics in data covers Urumqi and its Districts.

19-18 安全生产情况

Basic Statistics on Work Safety

单位：人 (person)

项　目	Item	2012	2013
亿元新疆生产总值生产安全事故死亡人数	Mortality Rate of Work Safety Accident Average 100 Billion Yuan GDP	0.31	0.26
工矿商贸企业就业人员生产安全事故十万人死亡人数	Mortality Rate of Work Safety Accident of Employment in Industrial & Mining and Commercial & Tradal Enterprises Average 100 000 Persons	6.20	5.40
煤矿百万吨死亡人数	Mortality Rate of Coal Procuction Average 1 Million Tons	0.39	0.39
道路交通万车死亡人数	Mortality Rate of Highway Traffic Accident Average 10 000 Vehicles	5.10	4.70

19-19 社会福利事业单位基本情况
Basic Statistics on Social Welfare Institutions

(2013 年)

指　标	Item	院　数(个) Number of Homes (unit)	工作人员数(人) Number of Persons Engaged (person)	床位数(张) Number of Beds (unit)	年末收养人数(人) Number of Persons Housed (person)	#女　性 Female
总　计	**Total**	**600**	**4957**	**53442**	**32612**	**7791**
社会福利院	Social Welfare Homes	31	711	8086	5126	1078
儿童福利院	Children Welfare Homes	49	593	6782	4598	1409
光荣院	Homes for Disabled Veterans	10	68	459	316	53
社会福利医院	Psychopathy Welfare Homes	8	930	2380	2251	648
城镇老年性福利机构	Urban Elderly Welfare Units	117	1212	15003	8087	1315
农村老年性福利机构	Rural Elderly Welfare Units	371	1369	20390	12047	3254
荣誉军人康复医院	Recuperative Hospital for Soldiers with Honour	1	35	80	9	
其他收养性机构	Other Residential Institutions	13	39	262	178	34

19-20 社会福利事业、企业单位数和工作人员数
Number of Social Welfare Institutions and Enterprises and Persons Engaged

(2013 年)

项　目	Item	机构数(个) Number of Institutions or Enterprises (unit)	工作人员数(人) Number of Persons Engaged (person)
收养性福利事业单位	Adopting Social Welfare Institutions	672	5308
工商部门登记	Administravie Office of Industry and Commerce	1	26
编制部门登记	Organization Department	270	3020
民政部门登记	Civil Administration Department	230	1614
未登记	Un-register	171	648
社会福利企业	Social Welfare Enterprises	140	11483
优抚安置事业单位	Administration Agencies for Martyrs	43	446
救助类单位	Salvaged Deparement	71	443
殡葬服务事业单位	Funeral and Interment Institutions	151	817
福利彩票发行单位	Welfare Lottery-Ticked Issuance Unit	23	239
社区服务中心	Community Service Institutions	238	1106

19-21 社会救济情况
Basic Statistics on Social Relief Funds

指 标	Item	2013
城镇居民最低生活保障人数(人)	**Number of Persons Receiving Lowest Cost-of-living in Urban Area (person)**	**823435**
按人员性质分类	**By Ruahty of Staff**	
#女性	Female	378707
#残疾人	Disabled Person	57155
#三无人员	Three Non Person	28919
按人员年龄分类	**By Aged of Staff**	
成年人	Adult	
老年人	Old Folks	106557
在职人员	Full Employed Staff and Workers	10065
灵活就业人员	Flexible Employed Persons	131426
登记失业人员	Registered Employed Persons	116237
未登记失业人员	Unregistered Employed Persons	191903
未成年人	Minors	
在校生	Enrollment	173296
其他未成年人	Others	93951
城镇居民最低生活保障家庭数(户)	**Number of Family Receiving Lowest Cost-of-living in Urban Area (household)**	**357108**
农村最低生活保障人数(人)	**Number of Persons Receiving Lowest Cost-of-living in Rural Area (person)**	**1348235**
#女性	Female	549047
#老年人	Old Folks	381813
#未成年人	Minors	260816
#残疾人	Disabled Person	92749
农村最低生活保障家庭数(户)	**Number of Family Receiving Lowest Cost-of-living in Rural Area (household)**	**582078**

19-22 主要年份工会组织情况
Basic Statistics on Trades Unions in Main Years

年 份 Year	工会基层组织个数(个) Number of Grassroots Unions (unit)	全区已建工会组织的基本单位职工与会员人数(万人) Membership and Number of Staff and Workers in Grassroots Unions (10 000 persons)				专职工会干部(万人) Number of Full-time Personnel of Unions (10 000 persons)
		职工人数 Number of Staff and Workers	#女 Female	会员人数 Number of Membership	#女 Female	
1980	3255	84.20	30.25	67.13	20.42	0.48
1990	10685	231.48	90.64	196.58	76.97	0.79
1995	14457	271.43	114.13	254.49	104.97	1.19
2000	13016	211.73	90.80	200.80	84.93	0.59
2001	18219	234.84	100.71	215.31	91.07	0.73
2002	20806	236.58	99.65	220.85	93.11	0.49
2003	11263	230.24	93.43	220.55	87.05	0.45
2004	11979	224.52	94.49	219.35	90.62	0.48
2005	11721	232.78	97.50	232.03	97.20	0.41
2006	13163	302.05	130.12	263.80	115.64	0.69
2007	15040	323.37	139.45	289.65	124.23	0.60
2008	16880	337.80	147.31	308.81	134.71	0.55
2009	17849	351.69	146.56	326.91	136.48	0.70
2010	19668	371.23	153.55	342.07	147.54	0.60
2011	21023	386.47	159.54	355.78	150.67	0.72
2012	22682	393.94	165.98	371.14	157.39	1.07
2013	24517	387.40	157.40	373.30	153.94	0.72

19-23 残疾人事业基本情况
Basic Information of People with Disabilities

项　目	Item	2012	2013
康　复	**Rehabilitation**		
白内障复明	Sight-restoring of Cataract Surgery		
白内障复明手术(万例)	Sight-restoring of Cataract Surgeries (10 000 cases)	1.26	1.36
低视力配用助视器(人)	Vision-aids Provided for Individuds with Low-vision (person)	1415	6163
聋儿康复	Rehabilitation of Children With Hearing Disability		
年收训聋儿(人)	Hearing and Speech Training (person)	195	220
聋儿入普幼普小率(%)	Enrollment Rate to General Infant School or Elementary School (%)	24.1	40.0
培训家长(人)	Parents Trained (person)	1510	449
精神病防治康复	Prevention and Treatment of Psychiatric Diseases		
开展精神病防治康复工作市县数(个)	Number of Counties Carried on the Works (unit)	68	69
综合防治康复精神病人数(万人)	Number of Psychosis Sicks Synthetically Prevented, Cured and Rehabilitated (10 000 persons)	1.60	1.56
监护率(%)	Guardianship Rate (%)	63.90	66.60
显好率(%)	Rate of Getting Better (%)	51.22	50.00
社会参与率(%)	Social Participation Rate (%)	34.36	32.60
肇事率(%)	Violent Everds Rate (%)	0.08	
救济贫困患者数(人)	Number of Poor Sufferer Relieved (person)	4634	4820
用品用具供应件数(万件)	Number of Appliances Supplied (10 000 units)	1.59	3.78
康复训练与服务	Rehabilitation Training and Service		
肢体残疾康复训练数(人)	Rehabilitation Training of Body Disabilities (person)	5136	4972
智力残疾儿童康复训练数(人)	Rehabilitation Training of Mental Disabilities Children (person)	1398	2165
教　育	**Education**		
未入学适龄残疾儿童(万人)	Number of Uneducated Children (10 000 persons)	0.37	0.42
残疾人中等职业学校(班)	Secondary Vocational Schools for PWDS		
残联系统办	Run by Institution of Disabled Person's	1	1
教育部门办	Run by Education	1	1
在校学生(万人)	Number of Enrollments (10 000 persons)	0.0584	0.0530

19-23 续表 Continued

项　目	Item	2012	2013
就　业	**Employment**		
城镇残疾人就业状况(万人)	Employment of Urban Handicappeds (10 000 persons)		
当年安排就业	Persons Employed in the Year	0.41	0.55
按比例就业	Employment by Quota Scheme	0.15	0.18
集中就业	Employment at Welfare Enterprises	0.10	0.19
个体就业	Individual Employment	0.11	0.18
未安排就业	Unemployment	1.43	1.62
农村残疾人就业状况(万人)	Employment of Rural Handicapped (10 000 persons)		
就　业	Employed	21.60	22.98
未就业	Unemployed	4.30	3.81
残疾人就业服务机构(个)	Number of Institutions Engaging in Handicappeds Employment (unit)		
省	Provinces	1	1
地	Prefectures	14	14
市(含县级市)	Cities (Cities at County Level)	16	16
县	County	68	68
市辖区	Districts under the Jurisdiction of Cities	11	11
实施分散按比例就业的地区数(个)	Number of Regions Implemented the Policy of the Disperse Employment by Proportion (unit)		
省	Provinces	1	1
地	Prefectures	14	14
市(含县级市)	Cities (Cities at County Level)	16	16
县	County	68	68
市辖区	Districts under the Jurisdiction of Cities	11	11
残联组织建设	**Organization of Association for the Handicapped**		
残疾人工作者(万人)	Number of Workers for the Handicappeds (10 000 persons)	0.31	0.28

19-24 历届全区人民代表大会代表人数
Number of Deputies to all the Previous People's Congresses of Xinjiang

项 目 Item	第一届 (1954) First Congress	第二届 (1959) Second Congress	第三届 (1964) Third Congress	第四届 (1975) Fourth Congress	第五届 (1978) Fifth Congress	第六届 (1983) Sixth Congress	第七届 (1988) Seventh Congress	第八届 (1993) Eighth Congress	第九届 (1998) Ninth Congress	第十届 (2003) Tenth Congress	第十一届 (2008) Eleventh Congress	第十二届 (2013) Twelfth Congress
代表总数(人) Total Number of All Deputies (person)	**376**	**386**	**453**	**809**	**672**	**550**	**550**	**542**	**550**	**550**	**550**	**550**
#中国共产党党员 Deputies from the Communist Party of China	178		240			374	357	381	396	396	352	356
占总数比重(%) Percentage to Total (%)	47.3		53.0			68.0	64.9	70.3	72.0	72.0	64.0	64.7
#少数民族 Deputies from National Minorities	331		383	510	430	357	363	355	363	363	363	364
占总数比重(%) Percentage to Total(%)	88.0		84.5	63.8	64.0	64.9	66.0	65.5	66.0	66.0	66.0	66.2
#妇 女 Female Deputies	52	61	89	200	146	17	126	123	135	135	143	139
占总数比重(%) Percentage to Total(%)	13.8	15.8	19.6	24.7	21.7	21.3	22.9	22.7	24.5	24.5	26.0	25.3

19-25 历届全区政治协商会议委员人数
Number of Deputies to all the Previous People's Political Consultative Conferences of Xinjiang

项 目 Item	第一届 (1954) First Congress	第二届 (1959) Second Congress	第三届 (1964) Third Congress	第四届 (1978) Fourth Congress	第五届 (1983) Fifth Congress	第六届 (1988) Sixth Congress	第七届 (1993) Seventh Congress	第八届 (1998) Eighth Congress	第九届 (2003) Ninth Congress	第十届 (2008) Tenth Congress	第十一届 (2013) Eleventh Congress
委员总数(人) Total Number of All Deputies (person)	**141**	**275**	**303**	**407**	**441**	**429**	**416**	**444**	**470**	**515**	**529**
#中国共产党党员 Deputies from the Communist Party of China	28	57	65	149	158	157	161	183	196	225	261
占总数比重(%) Percentage to Total(%)	19.9	20.7	21.5	36.6	35.8	36.6	38.7	41.2	41.7	43.7	49.3
#少数民族 Deputies from National Minorities	121	196	205	221	253	245	204	246	246	263	258
占总数比重(%) Percentage to Total(%)	85.8	71.3	67.7	54.3	57.4	57.0	49.0	55.4	52.3	51.1	48.8
#妇 女 Female Deputies	10	28	28	40	49	63	66	82	95	125	139
占总数比重(%) Percentage to Total(%)	7.1	10.2	9.2	9.8	11.1	14.7	15.9	18.5	20.2	24.3	26.3

19-26 主要年份律师、公证、调解工作基本情况
Basic Statistics on Lawyers, Notarization and Mediation in Main Years

项目	Item	1995	2000	2005	2010	2013
律师工作	**Lawyers**					
律师事务所(个)	Number of Law Offices (unit)	169	227	243	318	371
律师(人)	Number of Lawyers (person)	1705	2414	2088	2900	3733
#专职律师(人)	Full-time Lawyers (person)	1209	1508	1987	2704	3454
兼职律师(人)	Part-time Lawyers (person)	336	418	101	114	118
聘请担任常年法律顾问的单位(处)	Number of Units with Permanent Legal Advisors (unit)	2560	2613	2663	3858	5491
民事诉讼代理(件)	Agent of Civil Cases (case)	6380	16165	23389	38822	34357
刑事辩护及代理(件)	Defender and Agent of Criminal Cases (case)	5850	5826	7716	8510	8746
非诉讼法律事务(件)	Agent of Non-Litigious Legal Affairs (case)	5357	4810	7066	2450	4637
解答法律咨询(万件)	Agent of Legal Advisory Services (10 000 cases)	4.21	7.45	8.14	10.13	11.24
代写法律事务文书(万件)	Agent of Legal Documents Written on Behalf of Clients (10 000 cases)	1.06	1.94	3.00	2.16	2.34
公证工作	**Notarization**					
公证处(个)	Number of Notary Offices (unit)	126	131	126	125	125
公证员(人)	Notaries (person)	266	332	457	416	435
办理公证文书(万件)	Number of Notarized Document (10 000 cases)	10.11	18.85	18.05	30.93	37.82
人民调解工作	**Number of People's Mediation**					
人民调解委员会(个)	Number of People's Mediation Committees (unit)	19045	22294	15852	14157	13704
调解人员(万人)	Number of Mediators (10 000 persons)	12.04	10.04	7.86	7.62	6.70
调解民间纠纷(万件)	Number of Civil Disputes Mediated (10 000 cases)	9.18	8.09	6.83	17.21	23.88

19-27 调解民间纠纷分类
Number of Civil Disputes Mediated by Type

(2013 年)

项　目	Item	调解纠纷(件) Civil Disputes (case)	各类纠纷所占比重(%) Percentage (%)
总　计	**Total**	**238751**	**100**
婚姻家庭	Marriage and Family	59258	24.82
合　同	Contract	15298	6.41
劳　动	Labor	12857	5.39
村务管理	Village-affair Management	2067	0.87
土　地	Land	17773	7.44
征地拆迁	Requisitioned Land Demolition	1144	0.48
房屋宅基地	Housing and Housing Sites	6380	2.67
计划生育	Family Planning	238	0.10
邻　里	Neighbour	51997	21.78
损害赔偿	Compensation for Damages	17431	7.30
环境保护	Environment Protection	817	0.34
道路交通事故	Road Traffic Accidents	12383	5.19
物　业	Property Management	4483	1.88
医　疗	Medical Treatment	320	0.13
生产经营	Production and Operation	7406	3.10
其　他	Others	28899	12.10

19-28 火灾事故发生情况
Basic Statistics on Fire Accidents

(2013 年)

指　标	Item	合　计 Total	按事故发生程度分 By Serious Dgree of Fires			
			特　大 Extraordinarily Serious	重　大 Serious	较　大 Comparatively Serious	一　般 Ordinary
发生起数(起)	Fires (case)	11909				11909
死亡(人)	Death (person)	32				32
受伤(人)	Injuries (person)	26				26
损失折款(万元)	Losses Converted into Cash (10 000 yuan)	8685.69				8685.69
平均每起事故损失(元)	Average Loss per Fire (yuan)	7293.38				7293.38

19-29 2011-2013 年历年交通事故发生情况
Basic Statistics on Traffic Accidents (2011-2013)

指　标	Item	2011	2012	2013
发生起数(起)	Traffic Accidents (case)	5182	4942	8923
死亡(人)	Death (person)	1992	1932	1828
受伤(人)	Injuries (person)	5903	5422	5632
损失折款(万元)	Losses Converted into Cash (10 000 yuan)	1036	1233	1316
平均每起事故损失(元)	Average Loss per Fire (yuan)	2000	2494	2673

19-30 公安机关受理查处治安案件情况
Offense Cases Against Public Order Handled by Public Security Organs

单位：起　　(2013 年)　　(case)

案件类别	Category of Cases	受理 Number of Cases Accepted to be Treated	查处 Number of Cases Investigated and Treated
总　计	**Total**	**117371**	**112143**
扰乱公共秩序	Disturbing Work or Public Order	5369	5342
扰乱单位秩序	Disturbing Business Orders	600	594
扰乱公共场所秩序	Disturbing the Orders in Public Places	569	465
寻衅滋事	Causing Quarrels and Making Troubles	668	679
其　他	Others	3532	3604
妨害公共安全	Disorderly Cordnct	550	531
非法携带枪支、弹药、管制刀具	Violation of Firearms Control Regulations	153	149
盗窃、损毁公共设施	Stealing and Damaging Public Facilities	80	73
其　他	Others	317	309
侵犯他人人身权利、财产权利	Offences Against, Citizens'Personal and Property Rights	82585	77559
侮辱、诽谤、诬告陷害	Insult, Slander and Circumvention	709	662
殴打他人	Beating Other Body	59202	56616
故意伤害	Wilfully Injuring Others	2638	2493
盗　窃	Stealing Property	12596	10901
诈　骗	Swindling, Seizing and Extorting Property	904	743
抢　夺	Robbery and Snatch	175	159
敲诈勒索	Extertion and Blackmail	42	34
其　他	Others	6319	5951
妨害社会管理	Disorderly Social Management	28867	28711
阻碍执行职务	Obstructing Government Workers in Performing Their Duties	742	723
违反旅馆业管理	Violating the Hotel Management Regulations	2749	2744
违反房屋出租管理	Violating the Rent Control Regulations	6502	6495
卖淫、嫖娼	Prostitution or Going Whoring	918	914
赌博或为赌博提供条件	Gambling	1842	1818
毒品违法活动	Illegal Drug Related Action	10977	10926
其　他	Others	5137	5091

19-31 2008-2013 年历年刑事案件中青少年犯罪情况
Juvenile Delinquency Among Criminal Cases(2008-2013)

单位：人　　(person)

年份 Year	刑事罪犯总数 Offenders	#青少年罪犯 Young Offenders	不满 18 岁 Less than 18	18 岁至 25 岁 Between 18 to 25	青少年罪犯占刑事罪犯 (%) Percentage to Total (%)
2008	37222	18317	5899	12418	49.20
2009	33121	15989	4538	11451	48.27
2010	29257	13299	4012	9287	45.45
2011	29690	12627	3697	8930	42.53
2012	30775	12738	3613	9125	41.39
2013	28981	11290	3215	8075	39.96

主要统计指标解释

医疗卫生机构 指从卫生行政部门取得《医疗机构执业许可证》、《计划生育技术服务许可证》，或从民政、工商行政、机构编制管理部门取得法人单位登记证书，为社会提供医疗保健、疾病控制、卫生监督服务或从事医学科研和医学在职培训等工作的单位。医疗卫生机构包括医院、基层医疗卫生机构、专业公共卫生机构、其他医疗卫生机构。

医院 包括综合医院、中医医院、中西医结合医院、民族医院、各类专科医院和护理院，不包括专科疾病防治院、妇幼保健院和疗养院。

基层医疗卫生机构 包括社区卫生服务中心、社区卫生服务站、街道卫生院、乡镇卫生院、村卫生室、门诊部、诊所(医务室)。

专业公共卫生机构 包括疾病预防控制中心、专科疾病防治机构、妇幼保健机构(含妇幼保健计划生育服务中心)、健康教育机构、急救中心(站)、采供血机构、卫生监督机构、取得《医疗机构执业许可证》或《计划生育技术服务许可证》的计划生育技术服务机构。

其他医疗卫生机构 包括疗养院、临床检验中心、医学科研机构、医学在职教育机构、医学考试中心、农村改水中心、人才交流中心、统计信息中心等卫生事业单位。

卫生人员 指在医院、基层医疗卫生机构、专业公共卫生机构及其他医疗卫生机构工作的职工，包括卫生技术人员、乡村医生和卫生员、其他技术人员、管理人员和工勤人员。一律按支付年底工资的在岗职工统计，包括各类聘任人员(含合同工)及返聘本单位半年以上人员，不包括临时工、离退休人员、退职人员、离开本单位仍保留劳动关系人员、本单位返聘和临聘不足半年人员。

卫生技术人员 包括执业医师、执业助理医师、注册护士、药师(士)、检验技师(士)、影像技师、卫生监督员和见习医(药、护、技)师(士)等卫生专业人员。不包括从事管理工作的卫生技术人员(如院长、副院长、党委书记等)。

执业医师 指《医师执业证》“级别”为“执业医师”且实际从事医疗、预防保健工作的人员，不包括实际从事管理工作的执业医师。执业医师类别分为临床、中医、口腔和公共卫生四类。

执业助理医师 指《医师执业证》“级别”为“执业助理医师”且实际从事医疗、预防保健工作的人员，不包括实际从事管理工作的执业助理医师。执业助理医师类别分为临床、中医、口腔和公共卫生四类。

每万人口执业(助理)医师 每万人口执业(助理)医师=(执业医师数+执业助理医师数)/人口数×10000。人口数系年末常住人口。

每万人口卫生技术人员 每万人口卫生技术人员=卫生技术人员数/人口数×10000。人口数系年末常住人口。

每万人口医疗卫生机构床位 每万人口医疗卫生机构床位=医疗卫生机构床位/人口数×10000。人口数系年末常住人口。

甲乙类法定报告传染病发病率 是指某年某地区每10万人口中甲、乙类法定报告传染病发病数。即甲乙类法定报告传染病发病率=甲、乙类法定报告传染病发病人数/人口数×100000。

甲乙类法定报告传染病死亡率 是指某年某地区每10万人口中甲、乙类法定报告传染病死亡情况。即甲乙类法定报告传染病死亡率=甲、乙类法定报告传染病死亡人数/人口数×100000。

甲乙类法定报告传染病病死率 是指某年某地区甲、乙类法定报告传染病死亡人数与发病人数之比。即甲乙类法定报告传染病病死率=甲、乙类法定报告传染病死亡人数/发病人数×100%。

参加新农合人数 指根据本地新农合实施方案到年内新农合筹资截止时已缴纳新农合资金的人口数。

新农合当年基金支出 指本年度实际从新农合基金帐户中支出用于新农合补偿的资金。

新农合补偿支出受益人次 指年内新农合参合人员因病就医获得补偿的人次数，包括住院、家庭帐户形式、门诊、特殊病种大额门诊、住院正常分娩、体检和其他补偿人次之和。

新农合本年度筹资总额 指为本年度筹集的、实际进入新农合专用帐户的基金数额。包括本年度中央及地方财政配套资金、农民个人交纳资金（含民政部门及其他相关部门代缴的救助资金）、新农合基金本年度产生的全部利息收入及其他渠道实际筹集到的新农合基金额。筹资数额以进入新农合专用帐户的基金数额为准，不含上年结转额资金。

卫生总费用 指一个国家或地区在一定时期内，为开展卫生服务活动从全社会筹集的卫生资源的货币总额，按来源法核算。它反映一定经济条件下，政府、社会和居民个人对卫生保健的重视程度和费用负担水平，以及卫生筹资模式的主要特征和卫生筹资的公平性合理性。

政府卫生支出 指各级政府用于医疗卫生服务、医疗保障补助、卫生和医疗保险行政管理、人口与计划生育事务支出等各项事业的经费。

社会卫生支出　指政府支出外的社会各界对卫生事业的资金投入。包括社会医疗保障支出、商业健康保险费、社会办医支出、社会捐赠援助、行政事业性收费收入等。

个人现金卫生支出　指城乡居民在接受各类医疗卫生服务时的现金支付，包括享受多种医疗保险制度的居民就医时自付的费用。可分为城镇居民、农村居民个人现金卫生支出，反映城乡居民医疗卫生费用的负担程度。

人均卫生费用　即某年卫生总费用与同期平均人口数之比。

社会福利事业单位　指集中收养社会孤老、残、幼的机构，包括由民政部门管理的社会福利院、儿童福利院、精神病人福利院和城镇集体举办的福利院及农村集体举办的敬老院以及优抚医院和具有收养能力的社区服务中心等。该指标主要反映我国在社会福利性单位投入的水平。

社会福利事业单位收养人数　包括民政部门管理和城镇、农村集体举办的社会福利事业单位中收养的老人、少年儿童、缺乏生活自理能力的残疾人员和精神病人。该指标主要反映收养性社会福利单位的收养能力。

社会福利企业　指以集中安置有一定劳动能力的残疾人员就业为目（残疾职工占生产人员 10%以上）、带有社会福利性质的企业总称。主要包括福利工厂、假肢厂和其他福利企业。

城市居民最低生活保障人数　指在报告期末家庭平均收入在当地规定的最低生活保障线以下的城镇居民数。包括“三无”对象，失业人员和在职、下岗、退休人员等。

农村居民最低生活保障人数　指报告期末在建立农村最低生活保障制度的地区，得到当地政府或集体给予最低生活保障的农业人口家庭人数。

综合防治康复精神病人数　指在开展精神病防治康复工作地区，采取不同形式，接受综合性防治康复措施、开放式管理的精神病人数。该指标主要反映精神病患者接受治疗康复情况。

监护率　指通过监护小组、家庭病床、工疗站、社会就业以及精神卫生机构，接受社会化、综合性、开放式治疗与康复的精神病人占经调查摸底、登记在册的精神病人数的百分比。该指标主要反映对精神病患者落实治疗康复措施的情况。

社会参与率　指生活能自理，并参加生产劳动和社会生活的精神病人数占监护精神病人数的百分比。该指标主要反映精神病人康复状况和参与社会的情况。

未入学学龄残疾儿童少年　指截止到本年度 12 月 31 日，《义务教育法》规定的入学年龄段(6-14 周岁或 7-15 周岁)内的，因各种原因未能入学的各类残疾儿童少年。

律师　指依法取得律师执业证书，担任法律顾问，民事(刑事、行政)案件代理人、刑事案件辩护人、办理非诉讼业务，解答法律询问，代写法律事务文书等，为社会提供法律服务的人员。

公证人员　指在公证处工作的人员总称，包括公证处主任、副主任、公证员、公证员助理(助理公证员)和其他从事辅助性工作的人员。

公证文书　指公证处根据当事人申请，依照事实和法律，按照法定程序制作的，具有法律效力的司法证明文书。

调解员　指在人民调解委员会担负调解民间纠纷工作的人员，包括调解委员会的委员和调解小组的调解员。该指标主要反映从事人民调解工作的人员数量。

调解民间纠纷　指调解委员会按照法律规定，根据自愿原则，用说服教育的方法调解民间发生的有关民事权利和义务争执的件数，包括调解成功数和调解未成功数。该指标主要反映人民调解委员会的工作量。

特大交通事故　指一次造成死亡 3 人以上，或者重伤 11 人以上，或者死亡 1 人，同时重伤 8 人以上，或者死亡 2 人，同时重伤 5 人以上，或者财产损失 6 万元以上的交通事故。

重大交通事故　指一次造成死亡 1 至 2 人，或者重伤 3 人以上 10 人以下，或者财产损失 3 万元以上不足 6 万元的交通事故。

特大火灾　指造成 30 人以上死亡，或者 100 人以上重伤，或者 1 亿元以上直接财产损失的火灾。

重大火灾　指造成 10 人以上 30 人以下死亡，或者 50 人以上 100 人以下重伤，或者 5000 万元以上 1 亿元以下直接财产损失的火灾。

较大火灾　指造成 3 人以上 10 人以下死亡，或者 10 人以上 50 人以下重伤，或者 1000 万元以上 5000 万元以下直接财产损失的火灾。

一般火灾　指造成3人以下死亡，或者10人以下重伤，或者1000万元以下直接财产损失的火灾。

Explanatory Notes on Main Statistical Indicators

Medical and Health Care Institutions refer to the units which have been qualified the Certification of Health Care Institution, certification of family planning technical service by the administration of public health, or qualified the Certification of Corporate Unit by the civil affairs, administration for industry and commerce, commission office for public sector reform, and engaging in medical care, disease prevention and control, health supervision and inspection, medicine research and on-job training, etc., including: hospitals, health care institutions at grass-root level, specialized public health institutions, and other medical and health care institutions.

Hospitals include general hospitals, hospitals specialized in traditional Chinese medicine, hospitals of integrated traditional Chinese and western medicine, ethnic hospitals, specialized hospitals and nursing hospitals, excluding specialized disease prevention and treatment institutes, maternal and child health care hospitals and convalescent hospitals.

Health Care Institutions at Grass-root Level include community health service centers, urban health centers, township health centers, village clinics, outpatient departments and clinics (health centers).

Specialized Public Health Institutions include centers for disease control and prevention, specialized disease prevention and treatment institutions, women and children care agencies(including women and children health care family planning service center), health education institutions, first aid centers, blood gathering and supplying institutions, health supervision and inspection agencies, and family planning technical service centers that obtained the Certification of Health Care Institution or certification of family planning technical service centers.

Other Medical and Health Care Institutions include sanatoriums, clinical laboratory centers, medicinal scientific research institutions, on-job training institutions, medical examination centers, rural water improvement centers, talent exchange centers, and statistical information centers, etc.

Health Care Employees refer to all employees engaged in the health care institutions, such as hospitals, health care institutions at grass-root level, specialized public health institutions, and other medical and health care institutions, including medical technical personnel, village doctors and assistants, other technical personnel, managerial and service staff. The data is based on the year end payroll, including personnel hired (including contract labor) and re-employed after retirement by the institution for over half a year and excluding temporary workers, retired personnel, resigned personnel, personnel who have left the institution but kept the contract relation and personnel who are re-employed after retirement or temporarily employed for less than half a year.

Medical Technical Personnel refer to the professional staff engaged in health care, including licensed doctors, licensed assistant doctors, registered nurses, pharmacists, laboratory technicians, imaging staff, health care supervisors and intern doctors, pharmacists, nurses, and technical personnel, excluding the medical technical personnel engaged in managerial job(e.g. president, vice president and secretary of the party committee etc).

Licensed Doctors refer to the medical workers who have obtained the licenses of qualified doctors and are employed in medical treatment, disease prevention or healthcare institutions, excluding the licensed doctors engaged in management job. The licensed doctors are divided into 4 categories: clinician, Chinese medicine physicians, dentist and public health physicians.

Licensed Assistant Doctors refer to the medical workers who have obtained the licenses of qualified assistant doctors and are employed in medical treatment, disease prevention or healthcare institutions, excluding the licensed assistant doctors engaged in management job. The classification of licensed assistant doctors is clinician, Chinese medicine, dentist and public health.

Number of Licensed (Assistant) Doctors per 10000 Population The formula is:

Number of Licensed Doctors per 10000 Population = (Number of Licensed Doctors + Number of Licensed Assistant Doctors) / Population *10000

The population is the figure of usual population at year-end.

Number of Medical Technical Personnel per 10000 Population The formula is:

Number of Medical Technical Personnel per 10000 Population = Number of Medical Technical Personnel / Population *10000

The population is the figure of usual population at year-end.

Number of Beds of Medical and Health Care Institutions per 10000 Population the formula is:

Number of Beds of Medical and Health Care Institutions per 10000 Population = Number of Beds of Medical and Health Care Institutions / Population *10000

The population is the figure of usual population at year-end.

Incidence Rate of A and B Type of Notifiable Infectious Diseases refer to the incidence cases notifiable class A and class B infectious diseases per 100 thousand population in the reference region in the reference year. The formula is:

Incidence Rate of A and B Type of Notifiable Infectious Diseases = Incidence Cases Notifiable Class A and Class B Infectious Diseases / Population *100000

Death Rate of A and B Type of Notifiable Infectious Diseases refer to the death cases notifiable class A and class B infectious diseases per 100 thousand population in the reference region in the reference year. The formula is:

Death Rate of A and B Type of Notifiable Infectious Diseases= Death Cases Notifiable Class A and Class B Infectious Diseases / Population *100000

Mortality Rate of A and B Type Notifiable Infectious Diseases refer to the ratio of death cases notifiable class A and class B infectious diseases to the incidence cases in the reference region in the reference year. The formula is:

Mortality Rate of A and B Type Notifiable Infectious Diseases = Death Cases Notifiable Class A and Class B Infectious Diseases / Incidence Cases *100%

Number of Persons Participated in the New Rural Cooperative Medical System refers to the number of persons who have given payment to the new cooperative medical system by the deadline of fundraising during the year according to the implementation plan of the new system.

Expenditure of Funds for the New Rural Cooperative Medical System This Year refers to expenditures on compensation funds for the new rural cooperative medical system from the fund account of new cooperative medical system this year.

Persons Benefited from the Compensation Expenditure of New Rural Cooperative Medical System refers to the number of persons participated in the new system who have been compensated for medical treatment in the year, including hospitalization, family account form, out-patient, large special diseases out-patient, normal childbirth in hospital, medical examination and other compensations.

Funds Raised for the New Rural Cooperative Medical System this Year refers to the amount of funds raised this year and put into the special new rural cooperative medical account, including the matching funds of central and local governments, paid money by farmers (including relief funds paid by the civil affairs department and other relevant departments), all the interest income generated this year of the funds and funds actually raised from other channels this year. The amount of funding equals to the funds entering into the special new rural cooperative medical account, excluding the carry-over funds from the previous year.

Total Expenditure on Public Health refers to the total monetary value of health resources in a country or a region collected by the whole society for public health based on source approach. It reflects the attention and affordability of the government, society and individual for public health and the major characteristics, justice and rationality of the health fund-raising model under certain economic circumstance.

Government Expenditure on Public Health refers to the expenditure of the governments at all levels on medical and health care services, medical subsidies, health administration and health insurance management, and undertakings of family planning etc.

Social Expenditure on Public Health refers to all inputs of society except the government in public health including the expenditures on social medical security, commercial health insurance, private expenditure on operation of medical and health care, social donation and contribution, and income from administrative fees etc.

Individual Cash Expenditure on Health refers to expenditure in cash on various health services by rural and urban residents, including self payments of residents within the system of multi-medical insurance. It can be categorized as cash expenditure on health by urban and rural residents and reflects their affordability of public health.

Average Expenditure on Health refers to the ratio of total expenditure on health in a year to the average population.

Social Welfare Institutions refer to institutions taking care of old pople without children, handicapped people and orphans. They include social welfare institutions run by civil affairs departments, children welfare institutions, social welfare institutions for mental patients, collective-owned old peoples homes in rural areas, convalescent homes and community service centers with the capaCity of receiving those people. This indicator reflects the input in social welfare institutions.

Number of People Taken in by Social Welfare Institutions refers to the number of old people, children, totally dependent handicapped people and mental patients taken in by social welfare institutions run by civil affairs departments and those run by collective units in urban and rural areas. This indicator reflects the cap a City of social welfare institutions.

Social Welfare Enterprises refer to those welfare-oriented enterprises employing a significant number of handicapped people with certain labour ability (handicapped employees shall exceed 10% of the production staff). They can be categorized as welfare factories, artificial limb plants and other welfare enterprises. They can be in the form of state ownership, collective ownership or other kinds of ownership.

Number of Urban Residents Entitled to Minimum Living Allowances refers to the number of those whose average family income is below a minimum local standard by the end of the reporting period, including both the employed and unemployed, laid off and retired, and those jobless people without stable residence or valid IDs.

Number of Rural Residents Entitled to Minimum Living Allowances refers to the number of those receiving the minimum living allowances from the local government or community in the rural areas where this allowances system is in place as of the end of the reference period.

Number of Mental Patients under Integrated Prevention and Rehabilitation Program refers to mental disease patients receiving integrated prevention and rehabilitation treatment of various forms under open environment in areas with mental disease rehabilitation programs. This indicator reflects the condition of metal patients receiving rehabilitation treatment.

Supervision Rate refers to the percentage of patients among the total number of registered mental disease patients, who participate in social integrated and open treatment and rehabilitation programs through various forms such as supervision groups, family treatment, employment or guidance from psychiatric institutions. This indicator reflects the implementation of various measures aimed at rehabilitating those metal patients.

Social Participation Rate of Mental Patients refers to proportion of mental disease patients who are able to manage their daily life and participate in economic activities to the total number of mental disease patients under supervision. This indicator reflects the condition of recovery of those metal patient sand their participation in social activities.

Handicapped School-age Children without School Attendance refers to the number of handicapped children of the school age in accordance with the Law on Compulsory Education (6 to 14 years old or 7 to 15 years old) who fail to attend any schools for various reasons as of December 31 of the current year.

Lawyers are certified legal workers according to law, and who are employed by legal counseling firms to act as legal advisers, agents in criminal or civil lawsuits, or defenders in criminal lawsuits, or to handle non-litigious legal affairs, to advise on matters of law or to write legal papers for others, and provide service to the public.

Notary Personnel refers to people working for notary offices including: directors, deputy direct or, notaries, assistant notaries, and other people providing assistance.

Notary Documents refer to the judicatory notary documents drawn up by the request of the party and are in accordance with facts and laws and following certain legal proceedings. According to usage and locality, the notary documents are divided into following 4 types: domestic notary documents, domestic economic notary documents, foreign-related civil notary documents and foreign-related economic notary documents.

Mediators refer to workers on peoples mediation committees responsible for mediating in civil disputes and cases of slight infraction of the law. They include members of the mediation committees and mediators of mediation groups. This indicator reflects the number of people engaged in meditation.

Mediation of Civil Disputes refers to number of cases made by mediation committees in mediating in civil disputes concerning civil rights and duties through persuasion and education in accordance witht he provisions of lawona voluntary basis, so as to solve disputes by helping the parties involved come to an agreement and understanding, including those unsuccessful ones. This indicator reflects the workload of the mediation committees.

Extraordinarily Serious Traffic Accident refers to an accident which has caused three or more deaths; or over 11 serious injuries; or one death and over 8 serious injuries; or two deaths and over 5 serious injuries; or a loss over 60 thousand yuan.

Serious Traffic Accident refers to an accident which has caused one or two deaths; or three to ten serious injuries; or a loss over 30 thousand yuan to 60 thousand yuan.

Extraordinarily Serious Fire Case refers to a case which has caused over 30 deaths; or over 100 serious injuries; or a direct property loss over 100 million yuan.

Serious Fire Case refers to a case which has caused over 10 to 30 deaths; or over 50 to 100 serious injuries; or a direct property loss over 50 million to 100 million yuan.

Comparatively Serious Fire Case refers to a case which has caused over three to ten deaths; or over 10 to 50 serious injuries; or a direct property loss over 10 million to 50 million yuan.

Ordinary Fire Case refers to a case which has caused less than three deaths; or less than 10 serious injuries; or a direct property loss less than 10 million yuan.

新疆统计年鉴
XINJIANG STATISTICAL YEARBOOK

20

各地州市主要经济指标排序

RANKING OF MAIN ECONOMIC INDICATORS BY PREFECTURE, AUTONOMOUS PREFECTURE, CITY AND COUNTY OF XINJIANG

简要说明

本篇主要内容和资料来源

本篇反映2013年新疆各地州(市)主要经济指标排序情况。

本篇资料由新疆维吾尔自治区统计局国民经济综合统计处根据新疆维吾尔自治区统计局各相关专业处提供资料整理。

Brief Introduction

Main Content and Source of Data

Data in this chapter mainly include main social economic statistics by prefecture, autonomous prefecture, city and county in 2013.

Data on this chapter are compiled by the Department of Comprehensive Statistic, XBS according to the data provided by the related department of Statistics Bureau of Xinjiang Uygur Autonomous Region.

20-1 各地、州、市生产总值
Gross Regional Product by Prefecture, Autonomous Prefecture and City

单位：万元 (2013 年) (10 000 yuan)

地区	Region	地区生产总值 Gross Regional Product	位次 Rank	第一产业增加值 Primary Industry	位次 Rank
乌鲁木齐市	Urumqi city	22028545	1	263065	12
克拉玛依市	Karamay city	8531091	4	50093	15
石河子市	Shihezi city	2553304	11	115764	14
吐鲁番地区	Turpan Administrative Offices	2608927	10	397772	10
哈密地区	Hami [Kumul] Administrative Offices	3339310	9	373130	11
昌吉回族自治州	Changji Hui Autonomous Prefecture	9373116	3	2387831	1
伊犁哈萨克自治州	Ili Kazak Autonomous Prefecture	14350077		3914568	
伊犁州直属县(市)	Counties (Cities) Direct Under Ili Prefecture	6811619	6	1616612	6
塔城地区	Tacheng [Tarbagatai] Administrative Offices	5429094	8	1885001	4
阿勒泰地区	Altay Administrative Offices	2109364	13	412955	9
博尔塔拉蒙古自治州	Bortala Mongol Autonomous Prefecture	2221707	12	602552	7
巴音郭楞蒙古自治州	Bayangol Mongol Autonomous Prefecture	10169959	2	1766244	5
阿克苏地区	Aksu Administrative Offices	6926045	5	2202847	2
克孜勒苏柯尔克孜自治州	Kizilsu Kirgiz Autonomous Prefecture	778395	15	123806	13
喀什地区	Kashgar [Kaxgar] Administrative Offices	6173033	7	1913001	3
和田地区	Hotan Administrative Offices	1716493	14	531147	8

地区	Region	第二产业增加值 Secondary Industry	位次 Rank	第三产业增加值 Tertiary Industry	位次 Rank	人均地区生产总值(元) Per-capital GDP (yuan)	位次 Rank
乌鲁木齐市	Urumqi city	8751032	1	13014448	1	64695	4
克拉玛依市	Karamay city	7390278	2	1090720	9	149127	1
石河子市	Shihezi city	1476482	11	961058	11	73695	2
吐鲁番地区	Turpan Administrative Offices	1585763	10	625392	14	41473	8
哈密地区	Hami [Kumul] Administrative Offices	1722402	9	1243778	8	55622	6
昌吉回族自治州	Changji Hui Autonomous Prefecture	4514582	4	2470703	4	58479	5
伊犁哈萨克自治州	Ili Kazak Autonomous Prefecture	5272107		5163402		30328	
伊犁州直属县(市)	Counties (Cities) Direct Under Ili Prefecture	2319909	5	2875098	2	24567	12
塔城地区	Tacheng [Tarbagatai] Administrative Offices	1980362	7	1563731	7	40587	9
阿勒泰地	Altay Administrative Offices	971836	12	724573	13	33945	10
博尔塔拉蒙古自治州	Bortala Mongol Autonomous Prefecture	575415	13	1043740	10	45579	7
巴音郭楞蒙古自治州	Bayangol Mongol Autonomous Prefecture	6402135	3	2001580	6	72492	3
阿克苏地区	Aksu Administrative Offices	2183366	6	2539832	3	28535	11
克孜勒苏柯尔克孜自治州	Kizilsu Kirgiz Autonomous Prefecture	253804	15	400785	15	13694	14
喀什地区	Kashgar [Kaxgar] Administrative Offices	1850058	8	2409974	5	16076	13
和田地区	Hotan Administrative Offices	337711	14	847635	12	8025	15

20-2 各地、州、市人口状况

Population Status by Prefecture, Autonomous Prefecture and City

单位：万人 (2013 年) (10 000 persons)

地　区	Region	总人口 Total Population	位次 Rank	城镇人口 Urban Population	位次 Rank
乌鲁木齐市	Urumqi City	262.93	3	256.68	1
克拉玛依市	Karamay City	29.02	15	29.02	15
石河子市	Shihezi City	62.26	11	62.26	9
吐鲁番地区	Turpan Administrative Offices	64.29	10	46.38	11
哈密地区	Hami [Kumul] Administrative Offices	60.84	12	53.89	10
昌吉回族自治州	Changji Hui Autonomous Prefecture	140.50	6	121.24	5
伊犁哈萨克自治州	Ili Kazak Autonomous Prefecture	471.57		284.34	
伊犁州直属县(市)	Counties (Cities) Direct Under Ili Prefecture	298.53	2	166.25	2
塔城地区	Tacheng [Tarbagatai] Administrative Offices	105.99	8	79.84	7
阿勒泰地区	Altay Administrative Offices	67.05	9	38.25	13
博尔塔拉蒙古自治州	Bortala Mongol Autonomous Prefecture	49.04	14	39.38	12
巴音郭楞蒙古自治州	Bayangol Mongol Autonomous Prefecture	140.42	7	110.77	6
阿克苏地区	Aksu Administrative Offices	245.76	4	157.65	4
克孜勒苏柯尔克孜自治州	Kizilsu Kirgiz Autonomous Prefecture	57.62	13	33.98	14
喀什地区	Kashgar [Kaxgar] Administrative Offices	422.82	1	160.31	3
和田地区	Hotan Administrative Offices	215.45	5	75.74	8

地　区	Region	乡村人口 Rural Population	位次 Rank	人口自然增长率(‰) Natural Growth Rate (‰)	位次 Rank
乌鲁木齐市	Urumqi City	6.25	13	6.89	12
克拉玛依市	Karamay City			6.79	13
石河子市	Shihezi City			1.07	15
吐鲁番地区	Turpan Administrative Offices	17.91	10	19.17	2
哈密地区	Hami [Kumul] Administrative Offices	6.95	12	6.48	14
昌吉回族自治州	Changji Hui Autonomous Prefecture	19.26	9	14.38	5
伊犁哈萨克自治州	Ili Kazak Autonomous Prefecture	187.23		12.37	
伊犁州直属县(市)	Counties (Cities) Direct Under Ili Prefecture	132.28	3	14.37	6
塔城地区	Tacheng [Tarbagatai] Administrative Offices	26.15	7	7.87	11
阿勒泰地区	Altay Administrative Offices	28.80	6	10.88	8
博尔塔拉蒙古自治州	Bortala Mongol Autonomous Prefecture	9.66	11	8.17	10
巴音郭楞蒙古自治州	Bayangol Mongol Autonomous Prefecture	29.65	5	9.54	9
阿克苏地区	Aksu Administrative Offices	88.11	4	12.43	7
克孜勒苏柯尔克孜自治州	Kizilsu Kirgiz Autonomous Prefecture	23.64	8	23.68	1
喀什地区	Kashgar [Kaxgar] Administrative Offices	262.51	1	18.11	4
和田地区	Hotan Administrative Offices	139.71	2	19.07	3

注：城镇、乡村人口按公安年报口径计算。

Note: The urban and rural population in Prefecture, Autonomous Prefecture and City are calculated on the annals of public security.

20-3 各地、州、市全社会固定资产投资
Total Investment in Fixed Assets by Prefecture, Autonomous Prefecture and City

单位：万元　　(2013 年)　　(10 000 yuan)

地　区	Region	合 计 Total	位 次 Rank	建筑工程 Construction Works	位 次 Rank
乌鲁木齐市	Urumqi City	10559221	1	6902877	1
克拉玛依市	Karamay City	4564651	7	2882900	7
石河子市	Shihezi City	2088010	12	843268	14
吐鲁番地区	Turpan Administrative Offices	2360493	11	1211391	13
哈密地区	Hami [Kumul] Administrative Offices	4435424	8	2206865	9
昌吉回族自治州	Changji Hui Autonomous Prefecture	10400162	2	5213037	4
伊犁哈萨克自治州	Ili Kazak Autonomous Prefecture	13314554		8830544	
伊犁州直属县(市)	Counties (Cities) Direct Under Ili Prefecture	7062821	4	4417606	5
塔城地区	Tacheng [Tarbagatai] Administrative Offices	3584137	9	2650733	8
阿勒泰地区	Altay Administrative Offices	2667596	10	1762205	10
博尔塔拉蒙古自治州	Bortala Mongol Autonomous Prefecture	2050059	13	1449072	12
巴音郭楞蒙古自治州	Bayangol Mongol Autonomous Prefecture	7238110	3	5440503	2
阿克苏地区	Aksu Administrative Offices	4903854	6	3116544	6
克孜勒苏柯尔克孜自治州	Kizilsu Kirgiz Autonomous Prefecture	911218	15	729503	15
喀什地区	Kashgar [Kaxgar] Administrative Offices	6582883	5	5226558	3
和田地区	Hotan Administrative Offices	1890891	14	1758518	11

地　区	Region	安装工程 Installation Works	位 次 Rank	设备工具器具购置 Purchase of Equipment and Instruments	位 次 Rank	其他费用 Others	位 次 Rank
乌鲁木齐市	Urumqi City	846418	2	1827040	2	982886	1
克拉玛依市	Karamay City	533025	5	679572	9	469154	4
石河子市	Shi Hezi City	230255	9	812408	8	202079	8
吐鲁番地区	Turpan Administrative Offices	177471	11	846343	7	125288	12
哈密地区	Hami [Kumul] Administrative Offices	381867	8	1681873	3	164819	10
昌吉回族自治州	Changji Hui Autonomous Prefecture	919606	1	3755896	1	511623	3
伊犁哈萨克自治州	Ili Kazak Autonomous Prefecture	880943		2391559		1211508	
伊犁州直属县(市)	Counties (Cities) Direct Under Ili Prefecture	603152	4	1227843	4	814220	2
塔城地区	Tacheng [Tarbagatai] Administrative Offices	190922	10	503680	12	238802	7
阿勒泰地区	Altay Administrative Offices	86869	12	660036	11	158486	11
博尔塔拉蒙古自治州	Bortala Mongol Autonomous Prefecture	75846	13	412616	13	112525	13
巴音郭楞蒙古自治州	Bayangol Mongol Autonomous Prefecture	494854	6	1062566	5	240187	6
阿克苏地区	Aksu Administrative Offices	604761	3	911524	6	271025	5
克孜勒苏柯尔克孜自治州	Kizilsu Kirgiz Autonomous Prefecture	49675	14	121009	14	11031	15
喀什地区	Kashgar [Kaxgar] Administrative Offices	481896	7	677882	10	196547	9
和田地区	Hotan Administrative Offices	41643	15	42612	15	48118	14

20-4 各地、州、市农林牧渔业总产值

Gross Output Value of Farming, Forestry, Animal Husbandry and Fishery by Prefecture, Autonomous Prefecture and City

单位：万元 (2013 年) (10 000 yuan)

地　区	Region	农林牧渔业总产值 Total	位次 Rank	农业 Farming	位次 Rank	林业 Forestry	位次 Rank
乌鲁木齐市	Urumqi City	369437	12	163207	12	8824	11
克拉玛依市	Karamay City	114780	14	37794	14	24570	7
吐鲁番地区	Turpan Administrative Offices	667960	9	549998	8	4400	14
哈密地区	Hami [Kumul] Administrative Offices	463837	11	246652	11	13945	9
昌吉回族自治州	Changji Hui Autonomous Prefecture	3081566	2	1395281	4	27712	6
伊犁哈萨克自治州	Ili Kazak Autonomous Prefecture	4978402		2721123		97230	
伊犁州直属县(市)	Counties (Cities) Direct Under Ili Prefecture	2203248	5	1012306	6	68986	2
塔城地区	Tacheng [Tarbagatai] Administrative Offices	2113271	6	1365020	5	14677	8
阿勒泰地区	Altay Administrative Offices	661883	10	343797	10	13567	10
博尔塔拉蒙古自治州	Bortala Mongol Autonomous Prefecture	717541	8	535108	9	7314	12
巴音郭楞蒙古自治州	Bayangol Mongol Autonomous Prefecture	2508033	3	1935320	2	49976	3
阿克苏地区	Aksu Administrative Offices	2452633	4	1934465	3	36938	4
克孜勒苏柯尔克孜自治州	Kizilsu Kirgiz Autonomous Prefecture	249615	13	143524	13	5646	13
喀什地区	Kashgar [Kaxgar] Administrative Offices	3886338	1	2702838	1	94308	1
和田地区	Hotan Administrative Offices	1098076	7	727118	7	31098	5

地　区	Region	牧业 Animal Husbandry	位次 Rank	渔业 Fishery	位次 Rank	农林牧渔服务业 Farming, Forestry, Animal Husbandary and Fishery	位次 Rank
乌鲁木齐市	Urumqi City	188563	10	7189	8	1654	14
克拉玛依市	Karamay City	40158	14	1151	12	11107	11
吐鲁番地区	Turpan Administrative Offices	104818	12	550	13	8194	12
哈密地区	Hami [Kumul] Administrative Offices	195428	9	2411	11	5401	13
昌吉回族自治州	Changji Hui Autonomous Prefecture	1609762	1	19278	1	29533	6
伊犁哈萨克自治州	Ili Kazak Autonomous Prefecture	2061867		26707		71475	
伊犁州直属县(市)	Counties (Cities) Direct Under Ili Prefecture	1073860	2	13920	5	34176	5
塔城地区	Tacheng [Tarbagatai] Administrative Offices	703629	4	4296	9	25649	7
阿勒泰地区	Altay Administrative Offices	284378	8	8491	7	11650	10
博尔塔拉蒙古自治州	Bortala Mongol Autonomous Prefecture	123564	11	15539	3	36016	4
巴音郭楞蒙古自治州	Bayangol Mongol Autonomous Prefecture	439455	5	14253	4	69029	3
阿克苏地区	Aksu Administrative Offices	386028	6	16618	2	78584	2
克孜勒苏柯尔克孜自治州	Kizilsu Kirgiz Autonomous Prefecture	86604	13	239	14	13602	9
喀什地区	Kashgar [Kaxgar] Administrative Offices	995923	3	13013	6	80256	1
和田地区	Hotan Administrative Offices	321308	7	3588	10	14964	8

注：本表按当年价格计算。
Notes：The number in this table is computed at current price.

20-5 各地、州、市主要农产品产量
Yield of Major Farm Crops by Prefecture, Autonomous Prefecture and City

单位：吨 (2013 年) (ton)

地 区	Region	粮 食 Grain	位 次 Rank	棉 花 Cotton	位 次 Rank
乌鲁木齐市	Urumqi City	146901	11	1540	13
克拉玛依市	Karamay City	12543	14	9934	11
吐鲁番地区	Turpan Administrative Offices	35262	13	30362	9
哈密地区	Hami [Kumul] Administrative Offices	143675	12	37200	7
昌吉回族自治州	Changji Hui Autonomous Prefecture	2078986	4	218207	5
伊犁哈萨克自治州	Ili Kazak Autonomous Prefecture	5990214		263872	
伊犁州直属县(市)	Counties (Cities) Direct Under Ili Prefecture	2975633	1	5861	12
塔城地区	Tacheng [Tarbagatai] Administrative Offices	2456171	3	258011	4
阿勒泰地区	Altay Administrative Offices	558410	8		
博尔塔拉蒙古自治州	Bortala Mongol Autonomous Prefecture	728144	7	144346	6
巴音郭楞蒙古自治州	Bayangol Mongol Autonomous Prefecture	462074	9	397388	2
阿克苏地区	Aksu Administrative Offices	1682700	5	557336	1
克孜勒苏柯尔克孜自治州	Kizilsu Kirgiz Autonomous Prefecture	309401	10	10008	10
喀什地区	Kashgar [Kaxgar] Administrative Offices	2800660	2	354027	3
和田地区	Hotan Administrative Offices	1070093	6	35543	8

地 区	Region	油 料 Oil Bearing Crops	位 次 Rank	甜 菜 Beetroots	位 次 Rank
乌鲁木齐市	Urumqi City	9121	8	3327	9
克拉玛依市	Karamay City	400	14	8144	8
吐鲁番地区	Turpan Administrative Offices	1221	12		
哈密地区	Hami [Kumul] Administrative Offices	1781	11		
昌吉回族自治州	Changji Hui Autonomous Prefecture	87628	3	646649	2
伊犁哈萨克自治州	Ili Kazak Autonomous Prefecture	289252		1079788	
伊犁州直属县(市)	Counties (Cities) Direct Under Ili Prefecture	93770	2	847349	1
塔城地区	Tacheng [Tarbagatai] Administrative Offices	29849	4	206379	5
阿勒泰地区	Altay Administrative Offices	165633	1	26060	7
博尔塔拉蒙古自治州	Bortala Mongol Autonomous Prefecture	7225	9	54783	6
巴音郭楞蒙古自治州	Bayangol Mongol Autonomous Prefecture	6070	10	423949	4
阿克苏地区	Aksu Administrative Offices	9698	7	483389	3
克孜勒苏柯尔克孜自治州	Kizilsu Kirgiz Autonomous Prefecture	1018	13		
喀什地区	Kashgar [Kaxgar] Administrative Offices	11272	5		
和田地区	Hotan Administrative Offices	10133	6		

20-6 各地、州、市规模以上工业企业主要经济指标
Main Indicators on Economic of Industrial Enterprises above Designated Size by Prefecture, Autonomous Prefecture and City

单位：% (2013 年) (%)

地区	Region	工业总产值(万元) Gross Industrial Output Value (10 000 yuan)	位次 Rank	工业销售产值(万元) Sales Value of Industry Products (10 000 yuan)	位次 Rank
乌鲁木齐市	Urumqi City	24270070	1	23576028	1
克拉玛依市	Karamay City	17767731	2	17767202	2
石河子市	Shihezi City	3872288	7	3671159	7
吐鲁番地区	Turpan Administrative Offices	2779491	8	2764824	8
哈密地区	Hami [Kumul] Administrative Offices	2777814	9	2759930	9
昌吉回族自治州	Changji Hui Autonomous Prefecture	9074961	3	8549871	4
伊犁哈萨克自治州	Ili Kazak Autonomous Prefecture	7163900		6831063	
伊犁州直属县(市)	Counties (Cities) Direct Under Ili Prefecture	4321427	6	4115395	6
塔城地区	Tacheng [Tarbagatai] Administrative Offices	1688510	10	1594029	10
阿勒泰地区	Altay Administrative Offices	1153963	12	1121638	12
博尔塔拉蒙古自治州	Bortala Mongol Autonomous Prefecture	619076	13	561407	13
巴音郭楞蒙古自治州	Bayangol Mongol Autonomous Prefecture	8819230	4	8843408	3
阿克苏地区	Aksu Administrative Offices	4943444	5	4753617	5
克孜勒苏柯尔克孜自治州	Kizilsu Kirgiz Autonomous Prefecture	332798	14	323381	14
喀什地区	Kashgar [Kaxgar] Administrative Offices	1213846	11	1205642	11
和田地区	Hotan Administrative Offices	272455	15	273437	15

地区	Region	总资产贡献率 Ratio of Total Assets to Industrial OutputValue	位次 Rank	资本保值增值率 Ratio of Capital Holding And Rise	位次 Rank
乌鲁木齐市	Urumqi City	10.3	4	102.4	14
克拉玛依市	Karamay City	21.7	2	106.2	13
石河子市	Shihezi City	6.2	11	125.7	7
吐鲁番地区	Turpan Administrative Offices	10.1	5	107.8	12
哈密地区	Hami [Kumul] Administrative Offices	7.4	9	131.6	3
昌吉回族自治州	Changji Hui Autonomous Prefecture	6.9	10	126.1	6
伊犁哈萨克自治州	Ili Kazak Autonomous Prefecture	9.2		115.8	
伊犁州直属县(市)	Counties (Cities) Direct Under Ili Prefecture	8.3	8	113.6	9
塔城地区	Tacheng [Tarbagatai] Administrative Offices	5.9	13	109.7	11
阿勒泰地区	Altay Administrative Offices	15.7	3	128.7	5
博尔塔拉蒙古自治州	Bortala Mongol Autonomous Prefecture	5.1	14	189.6	1
巴音郭楞蒙古自治州	Bayangol Mongol Autonomous Prefecture	25.1	1	101.0	15
阿克苏地区	Aksu Administrative Offices	9.7	6	112.9	10
克孜勒苏柯尔克孜自治州	Kizilsu Kirgiz Autonomous Prefecture	6.0	12	129.2	4
喀什地区	Kashgar [Kaxgar] Administrative Offices	9.2	7	120.0	8
和田地区	Hotan Administrative Offices	3.0	15	148.3	2

20-6 续表 Continued

单位：% (%)

地　区	Region	资产负债率 Assets Liability Ratio	位次 Rank	成本费用利润率 Ratio of Profits to Industrial Cost	位次 Rank
乌鲁木齐市	Urumqi City	59.3	13	7.7	6
克拉玛依市	Karamay City	44.6	15	12.6	4
石河子市	Shihezi City	64.0	8	6.5	8
吐鲁番地区	Turpan Administrative Offices	61.9	10	13.6	3
哈密地区	Hami [Kumul] Administrative Offices	71.3	3	10.5	5
昌吉回族自治州	Changji Hui Autonomous Prefecture	67.6	6	6.7	7
伊犁哈萨克自治州	Ili Kazak Autonomous Prefecture	67.0		9.4	
伊犁州直属县(市)	Counties (Cities) Direct Under Ili Prefecture	66.5	7	6.3	9
塔城地区	Tacheng [Tarbagatai] Administrative Offices	73.0	2	4.8	12
阿勒泰地区	Altay Administrative Offices	61.7	11	32.3	2
博尔塔拉蒙古自治州	Bortala Mongol Autonomous Prefecture	75.2	1	3.8	13
巴音郭楞蒙古自治州	Bayangol Mongol Autonomous Prefecture	59.0	14	37.9	1
阿克苏地区	Aksu Administrative Offices	63.7	9	5.6	11
克孜勒苏柯尔克孜自治州	Kizilsu Kirgiz Autonomous Prefecture	69.9	4	3.3	14
喀什地区	Kashgar [Kaxgar] Administrative Offices	69.7	5	6.3	9
和田地区	Hotan Administrative Offices	60.6	12	0.6	15

地　区	Region	产值利税率 Ratio of Profits and Taxes to Industrial Output Value	位次 Rank	流动资产周转次数(次/年) Number of Times of Annual TurnoverWorking Capitals (times/year)	位次 Rank
乌鲁木齐市	Urumqi City	13.4	8	2.1	3
克拉玛依市	Karamay City	24.0	3	3.3	2
石河子市	Shihezi City	9.6	12	1.4	9
吐鲁番地区	Turpan Administrative Offices	19.8	4	1.4	9
哈密地区	Hami [Kumul] Administrative Offices	15.2	5	1.2	13
昌吉回族自治州	Changji Hui Autonomous Prefecture	9.8	11	1.5	7
伊犁哈萨克自治州	Ili Kazak Autonomous Prefecture	16.0		1.4	
伊犁州直属县(市)	Counties (Cities) Direct Under Ili Prefecture	14.5	6	1.4	9
塔城地区	Tacheng [Tarbagatai] Administrative Offices	7.8	13	1.3	12
阿勒泰地区	Altay Administrative Offices	33.7	2	1.6	6
博尔塔拉蒙古自治州	Bortala Mongol Autonomous Prefecture	6.6	14	1.2	13
巴音郭楞蒙古自治州	Bayangol Mongol Autonomous Prefecture	37.3	1	3.8	1
阿克苏地区	Aksu Administrative Offices	13.6	7	1.8	5
克孜勒苏柯尔克孜自治州	Kizilsu Kirgiz Autonomous Prefecture	10.6	10	0.9	15
喀什地区	Kashgar [Kaxgar] Administrative Offices	10.8	9	1.9	4
和田地区	Hotan Administrative Offices	4.6	15	1.5	7

20-7 各地、州、市主要工业产品产量

Output of Major Industrial Products by Prefecture, Autonomous Prefecture and City

(2013 年)

地　区	Region	纱 (吨) Yarn (ton)	位 次 Rank	布 (万米) Cloth (10 000 m)	位 次 Rank	呢 绒 (万米) Woolen Piece Goods (10 000 m)	位 次 Rank
乌鲁木齐市	Urumqi City	9877	9	359	4		
克拉玛依市	Karamay City			1	8		
石河子市	Shihezi City	107588	1	2540	1	259	1
吐鲁番地区	Turpan Administrative Offices	2424	12				
哈密地区	Hami [Kumul] Administrative Offices	8744	10				
昌吉回族自治州	Changji Hui Autonomous Prefecture	30154	4	160	5		
伊犁哈萨克自治州	Ili Kazak Autonomous Prefecture	53141		493			
伊犁州直属县(市)	Counties (Cities) Direct Under Ili Prefecture	38434	3				
塔城地区	Tacheng [Tarbagatai] Administrative Offices	14707	8	493	3		
阿勒泰地区	Altay Administrative Offices						
博尔塔拉蒙古自治州	Bortala Mongol Autonomous Prefecture	24839	5	134	7		
巴音郭楞蒙古自治州	Bayangol Mongol Autonomous Prefecture	24711	6	919	2		
阿克苏地区	Aksu Administrative Offices	79834	2				
克孜勒苏柯尔克孜自治州	Kizilsu Kirgiz Autonomous Prefecture						
喀什地区	Kashgar [Kaxgar] Administrative Offices	20867	7	157	6		
和田地区	Hotan Administrative Offices	7246	11				

地　区	Region	成品糖 (万吨) Sugar (10 000 tons)	位 次 Rank	饮料酒 (千升) Alcohol Beverage (kilo-liter)	位 次 Rank	塑料制品 (吨) Plastic Products (ton)	位 次 Rank
乌鲁木齐市	Urumqi City			138589	2	629491	1
克拉玛依市	Karamay City			4700	11	27839	10
石河子市	Shihezi City			140058	1	99441	3
吐鲁番地区	Turpan Administrative Offices			5355	10		
哈密地区	Hami [Kumul] Administrative Offices			15987	9	12816	11
昌吉回族自治州	Changji Hui Autonomous Prefecture	6.48	2	30717	7	312749	2
伊犁哈萨克自治州	Ili Kazak Autonomous Prefecture	27.32		171329		143018	
伊犁州直属县(市)	Counties (Cities) Direct Under Ili Prefecture	19.72	1	74384	4	47977	7
塔城地区	Tacheng [Tarbagatai] Administrative Offices	5.77	4	94334	3	86665	4
阿勒泰地区	Altay Administrative Offices	1.83	7	2611	12	8376	12
博尔塔拉蒙古自治州	Bortala Mongol Autonomous Prefecture	3.64	5	417	14	47409	8
巴音郭楞蒙古自治州	Bayangol Mongol Autonomous Prefecture	6.47	3	33263	6	36744	9
阿克苏地区	Aksu Administrative Offices	2.49	6	35123	5	49305	5
克孜勒苏柯尔克孜自治州	Kizilsu Kirgiz Autonomous Prefecture			145	15	380	14
喀什地区	Kashgar [Kaxgar] Administrative Offices	0.32	8	30502	8	48187	6
和田地区	Hotan Administrative Offices			1117	13	3960	13

20-7 续表 Continued

地　区	Region	机制纸及纸板(吨) Machine-made Paper and Paper board (ton)	位次 Rank	粗钢(万吨) Crude Steel (10 000 tons)	位次 Rank	钢材(万吨) Steel Rolled (10 000 tons)	位次 Rank
乌鲁木齐市	Urumqi City	59285	3	727.64	1	894.82	1
克拉玛依市	Karamay City					11.70	7
石河子市	Shihezi City	2338	6			4.60	9
吐鲁番地区	Turpan Administrative Offices			0.67	7		
哈密地区	Hami [Kumul] Administrative Offices	901	7				
昌吉回族自治州	Changji Hui Autonomous Prefecture	132379	2	13.03	5	11.71	6
伊犁哈萨克自治州	Ili Kazak Autonomous Prefecture	2511		205.52		205.30	
伊犁州直属县(市)	Counties (Cities) Direct Under Ili Prefecture	2511	5	197.51	3	199.40	3
塔城地区	Tacheng [Tarbagatai] Administrative Offices			8.01	6	5.82	8
阿勒泰地区	Altay Administrative Offices					0.08	10
博尔塔拉蒙古自治州	Bortala Mongol Autonomous Prefecture						
巴音郭楞蒙古自治州	Bayangol Mongol Autonomous Prefecture	138109	1	232.93	2	232.12	2
阿克苏地区	Aksu Administrative Offices					58.52	4
克孜勒苏柯尔克孜自治州	Kizilsu Kirgiz Autonomous Prefecture						
喀什地区	Kashgar [Kaxgar] Administrative Offices	4719	4	43.66	4	48.07	5
和田地区	Hotan Administrative Offices					0.01	11

地　区	Region	水泥(万吨) Cement (10 000 tons)	位次 Rank	生铁(万吨) Pig Iron (10 000 tons)	位次 Rank	农用化肥(吨) Chemical Fertilizers (ton)	位次 Rank
乌鲁木齐市	Urumqi City	435.31	5	730.88	1	633995	2
克拉玛依市	Karamay City						
石河子市	Shihezi City	353.08	7	4.60	11	95755	6
吐鲁番地区	Turpan Administrative Offices	326.81	8	71.14	4		
哈密地区	Hami [Kumul] Administrative Offices	303.80	10	21.61	6	28560	8
昌吉回族自治州	Changji Hui Autonomous Prefecture	678.53	2	69.62	5	436570	4
伊犁哈萨克自治州	Ili Kazak Autonomous Prefecture	1107.60		208.07		643156	
伊犁州直属县(市)	Counties (Cities) Direct Under Ili Prefecture	562.10	3	199.52	3	607622	3
塔城地区	Tacheng [Tarbagatai] Administrative Offices	371.65	6			35534	7
阿勒泰地区	Altay Administrative Offices	173.85	13	8.54	10		
博尔塔拉蒙古自治州	Bortala Mongol Autonomous Prefecture	163.42	14	17.40	8		
巴音郭楞蒙古自治州	Bayangol Mongol Autonomous Prefecture	319.60	9	223.11	2	1494307	1
阿克苏地区	Aksu Administrative Offices	702.78	1	2.35	12	313443	5
克孜勒苏柯尔克孜自治州	Kizilsu Kirgiz Autonomous Prefecture	214.55	12	12.82	9		
喀什地区	Kashgar [Kaxgar] Administrative Offices	485.84	4	17.63	7		
和田地区	Hotan Administrative Offices	252.13	11				

20-8 各地、州、市社会消费品零售总额

Total Retail Sales of Consumer Goods by Prefecture, Autonomous Prefecture and City

单位：万元 (2013 年) (10 000 yuan)

地　区	Region	社会消费品零售总额 Total Retail Sales of Consumer Goods	位次 Rank	城镇 Urban	位次 Rank
乌鲁木齐市	Urumqi City	8114713	1	15936938	1
克拉玛依市	Karamay City	535420	9	533650	8
吐鲁番地区	Turpan Administrative Offices	323433	11	234829	12
哈密地区	Hami [Kumul] Administrative Offices	649170	7	616173	7
昌吉回族自治州	Changji Hui Autonomous Prefecture	1822731	2	1650070	2
伊犁哈萨克自治州	Ili Kazak Autonomous Prefecture	2652888		2086379	
伊犁州直属县(市)	Counties (Cities) Direct Under Ili Prefecture	1553804	3	1214552	3
塔城地区	Tacheng [Tarbagatai] Administrative Offices	608555	8	433630	10
阿勒泰地区	Altay Administrative Offices	490530	10	438197	9
博尔塔拉蒙古自治州	Bortala Mongol Autonomous Prefecture	296223	12	257153	11
巴音郭楞蒙古自治州	Bayangol Mongol Autonomous Prefecture	811872	6	756795	6
阿克苏地区	Aksu Administrative Offices	980361	5	830866	5
克孜勒苏柯尔克孜自治州	Kizilsu Kirgiz Autonomous Prefecture	138669	14	126869	14
喀什地区	Kashgar [Kaxgar] Administrative Offices	1312985	4	1050726	4
和田地区	Hotan Administrative Offices	285735	13	214799	13

地　区	Region	城区 Urban Area	位次 Rank	乡村 Rural	位次 Rank
乌鲁木齐市	Urumqi City	8110775	1	3938	13
克拉玛依市	Karamay City	533650	5	1769	14
吐鲁番地区	Turpan Administrative Offices	130457	12	88604	6
哈密地区	Hami [Kumul] Administrative Offices	560400	4	32998	11
昌吉回族自治州	Changji Hui Autonomous Prefecture	1547528	2	172661	4
伊犁哈萨克自治州	Ili Kazak Autonomous Prefecture	1350659		566509	
伊犁州直属县(市)	Counties (Cities) Direct Under Ili Prefecture	1026804	3	339252	1
塔城地区	Tacheng [Tarbagatai] Administrative Offices	173773	9	174925	3
阿勒泰地区	Altay Administrative Offices	150082	11	52332	9
博尔塔拉蒙古自治州	Bortala Mongol Autonomous Prefecture	159716	10	39070	10
巴音郭楞蒙古自治州	Bayangol Mongol Autonomous Prefecture	532959	6	55077	8
阿克苏地区	Aksu Administrative Offices	439302	8	149495	5
克孜勒苏柯尔克孜自治州	Kizilsu Kirgiz Autonomous Prefecture	124136	13	11800	12
喀什地区	Kashgar [Kaxgar] Administrative Offices	515344	7	262260	2
和田地区	Hotan Administrative Offices	108915	14	70937	7

20-9 各地、州、市海关进出口总额

Total Value of Imports and Exports by Prefecture, Autonomous Prefecture and City

单位：万美元 (2013 年) (USD 10 000)

地 区	Region	进出口总额 Total Imports and Exports	位次 Rank	出口额 Exports	位次 Rank	进口额 Imports	位次 Rank
乌鲁木齐市	Urumqi City	779766	1	639936	1	139830	2
克拉玛依市	Karamay City	77846	9	21346	11	56500	4
石河子市	Shihezi City	149700	6	146005	5	3695	8
吐鲁番地区	Turpan Administrative Offices	9274	13	8339	13	935	14
哈密地区	Hami [Kumul] Administrative Offices	8159	14	2685	14	5474	6
昌吉回族自治州	Changji Hui Autonomous Prefecture	157655	5	145737	6	11918	5
伊犁哈萨克自治州	Ili Administrative Offices	981094		792749		188345	
伊犁州直属县(市)	Counties (Cities) Direct Under Ili Prefecture	750372	2	568855	2	181517	1
塔城地区	Tacheng [Tarbagatai] Administrative Offices	119832	7	116040	7	3792	7
阿勒泰地区	Altay Administrative Offices	110890	8	107854	8	3036	9
博尔塔拉蒙古自治州	Bortala Mongol Autonomous Prefecture	269842	3	156315	4	113527	3
巴音郭楞蒙古自治州	Bayangol Mongol Autonomous Prefecture	19023	12	16101	12	2922	10
阿克苏地区	Aksu Administrative Offices	58448	10	57184	9	1264	13
克孜勒苏柯尔克孜自治州	Kizilsu Kirgiz Autonomous Prefecture	43180	11	40364	10	2816	11
喀什地区	Kashgar [Kaxgar] Administrative Offices	200939	4	199171	3	1768	12
和田地区	Hotan Administrative Offices	1265	15	1048	15	217	15

20-10 各地、州、市在岗职工工资总额和平均工资

Total Wages of Employed Staff and Workers and Average Wage by Prefecture, Autonomous Prefecture and City

(2013 年)

地 区	Region	在岗职工工资总额(万元) Total Wages of Staff and Workers (10 000 yuan)	位次 Rank	在岗职工平均货币工资(元) Average of Staff and Workers Wage (yuan)	位次 Rank
乌鲁木齐市	Urumqi City	4649082	1	57392	2
克拉玛依市	Karamay City	1364369	2	78964	1
石河子市	Shihezi City	769626	9	50500	5
吐鲁番地区	Turpan Administrative Offices	435435	12	56683	3
哈密地区	Hami [Kumul] Administrative Offices	470778	11	48894	7
昌吉回族自治州	Changji Hui Autonomous Prefecture	1221230	4	48164	8
伊犁哈萨克自治州	Ili Kazak Autonomous Prefecture	2655092		38785	
伊犁州直属县(市)	Counties (Cities) Direct Under Ili Prefecture	1362855	3	41658	12
塔城地区	Tacheng [Tarbagatai] Administrative Offices	874833	8	36764	14
阿勒泰地区	Altay Administrative Offices	417404	13	34940	15
博尔塔拉蒙古自治州	Bortala Mongol Autonomous Prefecture	385834	14	37605	13
巴音郭楞蒙古自治州	Bayangol Mongol Autonomous Prefecture	1194435	5	49049	6
阿克苏地区	Aksu Administrative Offices	996144	7	44683	11
克孜勒苏柯尔克孜自治州	Kizilsu Kirgiz Autonomous Prefecture	203798	15	45202	10
喀什地区	Kashgar [Kaxgar] Administrative Offices	1100631	6	46390	9
和田地区	Hotan Administrative Offices	491064	10	51059	4

20-11 各地、州、市公共财政预算收支
The General Budgetary Revenue and Expenditures of Local Finance by Prefecture, Autonomous Prefecture and City

单位：万元 (2013 年) (10 000 yuan)

地　区	Region	公共财政预算收入 Local Financial Revenue	位次 Rank	公共财政预算支出 Local Financial Expenditure	位次 Rank
乌鲁木齐市	Urumqi City	3019047	1	3532024	1
克拉玛依市	Karamay City	658258	6	798114	11
石河子市	Shihezi City	283125	12	331783	15
吐鲁番地区	Turpan Administrative Offices	305428	10	642070	13
哈密地区	Hami [Kumul] Administrative Offices	401021	8	841539	10
昌吉回族自治州	Changji Hui Autonomous Prefecture	813405	2	1688147	5
伊犁哈萨克自治州	Ili Kazak Autonomous Prefecture	1356086		4656117	
伊犁州直属县(市)	Counties (Cities) Direct Under Ili Prefecture	685397	4	2257619	3
塔城地区	Tacheng [Tarbagatai] Administrative Offices	365532	9	1195687	9
阿勒泰地区	Altay Administrative Offices	305157	11	1202811	8
博尔塔拉蒙古自治州	Bortala Mongol Autonomous Prefecture	131687	14	561160	14
巴音郭楞蒙古自治州	Bayangol Mongol Autonomous Prefecture	684768	5	1645105	7
阿克苏地区	Aksu Administrative Offices	749053	3	1994981	4
克孜勒苏柯尔克孜自治州	Kizilsu Kirgiz Autonomous Prefecture	87565	15	763175	12
喀什地区	Kashgar [Kaxgar] Administrative Offices	457940	7	3248549	2
和田地区	Hotan Administrative Offices	133314	13	1649362	6

20-12 分城镇居民消费价格指数和商品零售价格指数
General Retail Price and Consumer Price Index by City/County

(上年=100) (2013 年)(抽样调查) (Sampled Survey) (preceding year=100)

地　区	Region	商品零售价格指数 General Retail Price Index	位次 Rank	居民消费价格指数 General Consumer Price Index	位次 Rank
乌鲁木齐市	Urumqi City	103.5	4	103.5	11
喀什市	Kashgar [Kaxgar] City	102.9	11	103.4	14
伊宁市	Yining [Gulja] City	103.5	4	103.5	11
和田市	Hotan City	103.0	8	104.6	1
克拉玛依市	Karamay City	103.7	2	104.4	3
哈密市	Hami [Kumul] City	103.0	8	103.6	9
昌吉市	Changji City	103.7	2	104.1	5
库尔勒市	Korla City	101.0	20	103.4	14
阿克苏市	Aksu City	102.6	16	103.5	11
焉耆回族自治县	Yanqi Hui Autonomous County	102.1	17	103.4	14
塔城市	Tacheng [Qoqek] City	102.8	12	103.4	14
阿勒泰市	Altay City	102.7	13	104.0	6
乌苏市	Usu City	102.7	13	103.6	9
博乐市	Bole [Bortala] City	103.3	6	104.3	4
吐鲁番市	Turpan City	102.7	13	104.0	6
库车县	Kuqa County	101.7	19	103.2	19
阿图什市	Artux City	102.1	17	103.4	14
莎车县	Shache [Yarkant] County	104.1	1	104.6	1
奎屯市	Kuytun City	103.2	7	103.8	8
石河子市	Shihezi City	103.0	8	103.0	20

20-13 各地、州、市各类学校在校学生数
Number of Students Enrollment by Type of School and by Prefecture, Autonomous Prefecture and City

单位：人 (2013 年) (person)

地区	Region	普通高等学校 Regular Institutions of Higher Education	位次 Rank	中等职业学校 Specialized Secondary Schools	位次 Rank
乌鲁木齐市	Urumqi City	165090	1	69623	1
克拉玛依市	Karamay City	4488	7	688	15
石河子市	Shihezi City	6355	5	2005	13
吐鲁番地区	Turpan Administrative Offices			3721	10
哈密地区	Hami [Kumul] Administrative Offices			3835	9
昌吉回族自治州	Changji Hui Autonomous Prefecture	22824	2	13250	4
伊犁哈萨克自治州	Ili Kazak Autonomous Prefecture	15458		21248	
伊犁州直属县(市)	Counties (Cities) Direct Under Ili Prefecture	15458	3	12802	5
塔城地区	Tacheng [Tarbagatai] Administrative Offices			3432	11
阿勒泰地区	Altay Administrative Offices			5014	8
博尔塔拉蒙古自治州	Bortala Mongol Autonomous Prefecture			1122	14
巴音郭楞蒙古自治州	Bayangol Mongol Autonomous Prefecture	4457	8	11460	7
阿克苏地区	Aksu Administrative Offices	3010	9	11509	6
克孜勒苏柯尔克孜自治州	Kizilsu Kirgiz Autonomous Prefecture			2707	12
喀什地区	Kashgar [Kaxgar] Administrative Offices	11736	4	30882	2
和田地区	Hotan Administrative Offices	5944	6	19357	3

地区	Region	普通中学 Regular Secondary Schools	位次 Rank	小学 Primary Schools	位次 Rank
乌鲁木齐市	Urumqi City	153059	2	186289	4
克拉玛依市	Karamay City	25239	13	22726	14
石河子市	Shihezi City	19425	15	11959	15
吐鲁番地区	Turpan Administrative Offices	31997	11	51504	10
哈密地区	Hami [Kumul] Administrative Offices	32452	10	32711	12
昌吉回族自治州	Changji Hui Autonomous Prefecture	77489	6	78360	7
伊犁哈萨克自治州	Ili Kazak Autonomous Prefecture	240468		338667	
伊犁州直属县(市)	Counties (Cities) Direct Under Ili Prefecture	149568	3	222065	2
塔城地区	Tacheng [Tarbagatai] Administrative Offices	58997	8	69392	8
阿勒泰地区	Altay Administrative Offices	31903	12	47210	11
博尔塔拉蒙古自治州	Bortala Mongol Autonomous Prefecture	21339	14	27315	13
巴音郭楞蒙古自治州	Bayangol Mongol Autonomous Prefecture	70623	7	100842	6
阿克苏地区	Aksu Administrative Offices	141231	4	218487	3
克孜勒苏柯尔克孜自治州	Kizilsu Kirgiz Autonomous Prefecture	34929	9	57457	9
喀什地区	Kashgar [Kaxgar] Administrative Offices	252775	1	414655	1
和田地区	Hotan Administrative Offices	111947	5	185980	5

20-14 各地、州、市每万人口医院床位数和医生数
Number of Doctors and Hospital Beds Per 10 000 Population by Prefecture, Autonomous Prefecture and City

(2013 年)

地　区	Region	每万人床位数(张) Number of Beds per 10 000 Population (unit)	位 次 Rank	平均每万人医生数(人) Number of Doctors Per 10 000 Population (person)	位 次 Rank
乌鲁木齐市	Urumqi City	102.65	1	50.77	1
克拉玛依市	Karamay City	56.93	8	39.25	3
石河子市	Shihezi City	85.42	2	39.70	2
吐鲁番地区	Turpan Administrative Offices	45.17	15	21.06	10
哈密地区	Hami [Kumul] Administrative Offices	59.66	5	30.01	4
昌吉回族自治州	Changji Hui Autonomous Prefecture	70.25	3	29.58	6
伊犁哈萨克自治州	Ili Kazak Autonomous Prefecture	53.17		22.25	
伊犁州直属县(市)	Counties (Cities) Direct Under Ili Prefecture	54.58	9	20.86	11
塔城地区	Tacheng [Tarbagatai] Administrative Offices	48.50	13	23.02	9
阿勒泰地区	Altay Administrative Offices	54.29	11	27.23	7
博尔塔拉蒙古自治州	Bortala Mongol Autonomous Prefecture	59.24	6	29.71	5
巴音郭楞蒙古自治州	Bayangol Mongol Autonomous Prefecture	63.15	4	26.73	8
阿克苏地区	Aksu Administrative Offices	54.45	10	13.57	13
克孜勒苏柯尔克孜自治州	Kizilsu Kirgiz Autonomous Prefecture	53.99	12	20.41	12
喀什地区	Kashgar [Kaxgar] Administrative Offices	46.14	14	12.83	14
和田地区	Hotan Administrative Offices	57.90	7	11.22	15

20-15 各地、州、市卫生技术人员和医生数
Medical Technical Personnel and Doctors by Prefecture, Autonomous Prefecture and City

单位：人　　(2013 年)　　(person)

地　区	Region	卫生技术人员 Medical Technical Personnel	位 次 Rank	执业医师 Doctors with Licence	位 次 Rank	执业助理医师 Assistant Doctors with Licence	位 次 Rank
乌鲁木齐市	Urumqi City	34303	1	12692	1	656	7
克拉玛依市	Karamay City	3057	15	1105	14	34	15
石河子市	Shihezi City	6496	9	2117	7	355	10
吐鲁番地区	Turpan Administrative Offices	3495	13	1108	13	246	14
哈密地区	Hami [Kumul] Administrative Offices	4914	10	1533	10	293	13
昌吉回族自治州	Changji Hui Autonomous Prefecture	11423	4	3382	4	774	4
伊犁哈萨克自治州	Ili Kazak Autonomous Prefecture	28089		8267		2226	
伊犁州直属县(市)	Counties (Cities) Direct Under Ili Prefecture	16770	3	4980	2	1247	2
塔城地区	Tacheng [Tarbagatai] Administrative Offices	6706	8	1866	8	574	8
阿勒泰地区	Altay Administrative Offices	4613	11	1421	11	405	9
博尔塔拉蒙古自治州	Bortala Mongol Autonomous Prefecture	3647	12	1111	12	346	12
巴音郭楞蒙古自治州	Bayangol Mongol Autonomous Prefecture	10482	5	2984	5	769	5
阿克苏地区	Aksu Administrative Offices	9757	6	2540	6	794	3
克孜勒苏柯尔克孜自治州	Kizilsu Kirgiz Autonomous Prefecture	3288	14	829	15	347	11
喀什地区	Kashgar [Kaxgar] Administrative Offices	17226	2	3716	3	1710	1
和田地区	Hotan Administrative Offices	7592	7	1669	9	748	6

附录

各省市区主要经济指标排序

RANKING OF MAIN ECONOMIC INDICATORS BY REGION

各省市区主要经济指标排序
Ranking of Main Economic Indicators by Region

(2013 年)

省市区	Region	地区生产总值(亿元) Gross Regional Product (100 million yuan)	位次 Rank	地区生产总值比上年增长(%) Increase Rate of Gross Region Production over the previous year(%)	位次 Rank
全国	**China**	**568845.20**		**107.7**	
北京	Beijing	19500.56	13	107.7	30
天津	Tianjin	14370.16	19	112.5	1
河北	Hebei	28301.41	6	108.2	27
山西	Shanxi	12602.24	23	108.9	23
内蒙古	Inner Mongolia	16832.38	15	109.0	21
辽宁	Liaoning	27077.65	7	108.7	24
吉林	Jilin	12981.46	21	108.3	26
黑龙江	Heilongjiang	14382.93	17	108.0	29
上海	Shanghai	21602.12	12	107.7	30
江苏	Jiangsu	59161.75	2	109.6	19
浙江	Zhejiang	37568.49	4	108.2	27
安徽	Anhui	19038.87	14	110.4	11
福建	Fujian	21759.64	11	111.0	6
江西	Jiangxi	14338.50	20	110.1	13
山东	Shandong	54684.33	3	109.6	19
河南	Henan	32155.86	5	109.0	21
湖北	Hubei	24668.49	9	110.1	13
湖南	Hunan	24501.67	10	110.1	13
广东	Guangdong	62163.97	1	108.5	25
广西	Guangxi	14378.00	18	110.2	12
海南	Hainan	3146.46	28	109.9	17
重庆	Chongqing	12656.69	22	112.3	3
四川	Sichuan	26260.77	8	110.0	16
贵州	Guizhou	8006.79	26	112.5	1
云南	Yunnan	11720.91	24	112.1	4
西藏	Tibet	807.67	31	112.1	4
陕西	Shanxi	16045.21	16	111.0	6
甘肃	Gansu	6268.01	27	110.8	9
青海	Qinghai	2101.05	30	110.8	9
宁夏	Ningxia	2565.06	29	109.8	18
新疆	Xinjiang	8360.24	25	111.0	6

续表 1

省市区	Region	第一产业增加值(亿元) Value Added of the Primary Industry (100 million yuan)	位次 Rank	第二产业增加值(亿元) Value Added of the Secondary Industry (100 million yuan)	位次 Rank	第三产业增加值(亿元) Value Added of the Tertiary Industry (100 million yuan)	位次 Rank
全 国	**China**	**56957.00**		**249684.00**		**262203.80**	
北 京	Beijing	161.83	29	4352.30	24	14986.43	5
天 津	Tianjin	188.45	28	7276.68	17	6905.03	14
河 北	Hebei	3500.42	4	14762.10	6	10038.89	9
山 西	Shanxi	773.81	24	6792.68	20	5035.75	21
内蒙古	Inner Mongolia	1599.41	17	9084.19	13	6148.78	16
辽 宁	Liaoning	2321.63	12	14269.46	7	10486.56	7
吉 林	Jilin	1509.34	19	6858.23	19	4613.89	24
黑龙江	Heilongjiang	2516.79	9	5918.22	22	5947.92	17
上 海	Shanghai	129.28	30	8027.77	15	13445.07	6
江 苏	Jiangsu	3646.08	3	29094.03	2	26421.64	2
浙 江	Zhejiang	1784.62	15	18446.65	4	17337.22	4
安 徽	Anhui	2348.09	10	10403.96	12	6286.82	15
福 建	Fujian	1936.31	13	11315.30	11	8508.03	13
江 西	Jiangxi	1636.49	16	7671.38	16	5030.63	22
山 东	Shandong	4742.63	1	27422.47	3	22519.23	3
河 南	Henan	4058.98	2	17806.39	5	10290.49	8
湖 北	Hubei	3098.16	7	12171.56	9	9398.77	11
湖 南	Hunan	3099.23	6	11517.35	10	9885.09	10
广 东	Guangdong	3047.51	8	29427.49	1	29688.97	1
广 西	Guangxi	2343.57	11	6863.04	18	5171.39	20
海 南	Hainan	756.47	25	871.29	30	1518.70	28
重 庆	Chongqing	1016.77	22	6397.92	21	5242.00	19
四 川	Sichuan	3425.61	5	13579.03	8	9256.13	12
贵 州	Guizhou	1029.05	21	3243.70	26	3734.04	25
云 南	Yunnan	1895.34	14	4927.82	23	4897.75	23
西 藏	Tibet	86.82	31	292.92	31	427.93	31
陕 西	Shaanxi	1526.05	18	8911.64	14	5607.52	18
甘 肃	Gansu	879.37	23	2821.04	27	2567.60	27
青 海	Qinghai	207.59	27	1204.31	29	689.15	30
宁 夏	Ningxia	222.98	26	1264.96	28	1077.12	29
新 疆	Xinjiang	1468.30	20	3776.98	25	3114.96	26

Continued

第一产业占GDP比重(%) Composition of Primary Industry Product to GDP(%)	位次 Rank	第二产业占GDP比重(%) Composition of Secondary Industry Product to GDP(%)	位次 Rank	第三产业占GDP比重(%) Composition of Tertiary Industrial Product to GDP(%)	位次 Rank
10.0		**43.9**		**46.1**	
0.8	30	22.3	31	76.9	1
1.3	29	50.6	13	48.1	5
12.4	12	52.2	10	35.5	25
6.1	26	53.9	6	40.0	17
9.5	18	54.0	5	36.5	22
8.6	23	52.7	9	38.7	19
11.6	14	52.8	8	35.5	24
17.5	2	41.1	26	41.4	13
0.6	31	37.2	28	62.2	2
6.2	25	49.2	18	44.7	9
4.8	28	49.1	19	46.1	8
12.3	13	54.6	4	33.0	29
8.9	20	52.0	11	39.1	18
11.4	15	53.5	7	35.1	27
8.7	21	50.1	15	41.2	14
12.6	9	55.4	3	32.0	31
12.6	9	49.3	16	38.1	20
12.6	9	47.0	22	40.3	16
4.9	27	47.3	21	47.8	6
16.3	4	47.7	20	36.0	23
24.0	1	27.7	30	48.3	4
8.0	24	50.5	14	41.4	12
13.0	7	51.7	12	35.2	26
12.9	8	40.5	27	46.6	7
16.2	5	42.0	25	41.8	11
10.7	16	36.3	29	53.0	3
9.5	18	55.5	2	34.9	28
14.0	6	45.0	24	41.0	15
9.9	17	57.3	1	32.8	30
8.7	21	49.3	17	42.0	10
17.6	3	45.2	23	37.2	21

续表 2

省市区	Region	人均地区生产总值(元) Per Capita GDP (yuan)	位 次 Rank	总人口(万人) Total Population (10 000 persons)	位 次 Rank
全 国	**China**	**41908**		**136072**	
北 京	Beijing	93213	2	2115	26
天 津	Tianjin	99607	1	1472	27
河 北	Hebei	38716	16	7333	6
山 西	Shanxi	34813	22	3630	18
内蒙古	Inner Mongolia	67498	6	2498	23
辽 宁	Liaoning	61686	7	4390	14
吉 林	Jilin	47191	11	2751	21
黑龙江	Heilongjiang	37509	17	3835	15
上 海	Shanghai	90092	3	2415	24
江 苏	Jiangsu	74607	4	7939	5
浙 江	Zhejiang	68462	5	5498	10
安 徽	Anhui	31684	26	6030	8
福 建	Fujian	57856	9	3774	16
江 西	Jiangxi	31771	25	4522	13
山 东	Shandong	56323	10	9733	2
河 南	Henan	34174	23	9413	3
湖 北	Hubei	42613	14	5799	9
湖 南	Hunan	36763	19	6691	7
广 东	Guangdong	58540	8	10644	1
广 西	Guangxi	30588	27	4719	11
海 南	Hainan	35317	21	895	28
重 庆	Chongqing	42795	12	2970	20
四 川	Sichuan	32454	24	8107	4
贵 州	Guizhou	22922	31	3502	19
云 南	Yunnan	25083	29	4687	12
西 藏	Tibet	26068	28	312	31
陕 西	Shaanxi	42692	13	3764	17
甘 肃	Gansu	24296	30	2582	22
青 海	Qinghai	36510	20	578	30
宁 夏	Ningxia	39420	15	654	29
新 疆	Xinjiang	37181	18	2264	25

Continued

全社会固定资产投资（亿元）Total Investment in Fixed Assets in the Whole Country (100 million yuan)	位 次 Rank	居民消费价格指数 Consumer Price Index	位 次 Rank	城镇居民人均可支配收入(元) Per Capita Annual Disposable Income of Urban households (yuan)	位 次 Rank	城镇居民人均消费性支出(元) Per Capita Annual Living Expenditures for Consumption (yuan)	位 次 Rank
447074.4		**102.6**		**26955.1**		**18022.6**	
6847.1	25	103.3	5	40321.0	2	26274.9	2
9130.3	22	103.1	8	32293.6	6	21711.9	5
23194.2	5	103.0	11	22580.3	19	13640.6	28
11031.9	18	103.1	8	22455.6	20	13166.2	30
14215.5	14	103.2	6	25496.7	10	19249.1	8
25107.7	4	102.4	24	25578.2	9	18029.7	9
10133.5	20	102.9	13	22274.6	23	15932.3	15
12126.0	16	102.2	29	19597.0	29	14161.7	24
5647.8	27	102.3	26	43851.4	1	28155.0	1
36373.8	2	102.3	26	32537.5	5	20371.5	6
20777.1	7	102.3	26	37850.8	3	23257.2	4
18621.6	10	102.4	24	23114.2	15	16285.2	14
15327.4	12	102.5	19	30816.4	7	20092.7	7
12866.1	15	102.5	19	21872.7	24	13850.5	26
36789.1	1	102.2	29	28264.1	8	17112.2	11
26220.9	3	102.9	13	22398.0	21	14822.0	23
19307.3	9	102.8	15	22906.4	17	15749.5	17
17846.3	11	102.5	19	23414.0	12	15887.1	16
22307.8	6	102.5	19	33090.0	4	24133.3	3
11907.7	17	102.2	29	23305.4	13	15417.6	19
2697.4	28	102.8	15	22928.9	16	15593.0	18
10429.6	19	102.7	18	25216.1	11	17813.9	10
20325.2	8	102.8	15	22367.6	22	16343.5	13
7373.6	24	102.5	19	20667.1	26	13702.9	27
9968.3	21	103.1	8	23235.5	14	15156.1	22
876.0	31	103.6	3	20023.4	27	12231.9	31
14867.3	13	103.0	11	22858.4	18	16679.7	12
6527.9	26	103.2	6	18964.8	31	14020.7	25
2361.1	30	103.9	1	19498.5	30	13539.5	29
2651.1	29	103.4	4	21833.3	25	15321.1	20
8148.4	23	103.9	1	19873.8	28	15206.2	21

续表 3

省市区	Region	农民人均纯收入(元) Annual Per Capita Disposable Income of Rural Households (yuan)	位次 Rank	#工资性收入(元) Income from Wages and Salaries (yuan)	位次 Rank	农民人均生活消费支出(元) Annual Per Capita Living Expenditure of Rural Households (yuan)	位次 Rank
全　国	**China**	**8895.9**		**4025.4**		**6625.5**	
北　京	Beijing	18337.5	2	12034.9	2	13553.2	2
天　津	Tianjin	15841.0	4	9091.5	4	10155.0	4
河　北	Hebei	9101.9	12	5236.7	7	6134.1	17
山　西	Shanxi	7153.5	23	4041.1	14	5812.7	20
内蒙古	Inner Mongolia	8595.7	15	1694.6	29	7268.3	10
辽　宁	Liaoning	10522.7	9	4209.4	12	7159.0	11
吉　林	Jilin	9621.2	11	1813.2	27	7379.7	9
黑龙江	Heilongjiang	9634.1	10	1991.4	26	6813.6	12
上　海	Shanghai	19595.0	1	12239.4	1	14234.7	1
江　苏	Jiangsu	13597.8	5	7608.5	5	9909.8	5
浙　江	Zhejiang	16106.0	3	9204.3	3	11760.2	3
安　徽	Anhui	8097.9	20	3733.5	16	5724.5	22
福　建	Fujian	11184.2	7	5193.9	8	8151.2	7
江　西	Jiangxi	8781.5	14	4422.1	11	5653.6	24
山　东	Shandong	10619.9	8	5127.2	9	7392.7	8
河　南	Henan	8475.3	16	3581.6	17	5627.7	25
湖　北	Hubei	8867.0	13	3868.2	15	6279.5	16
湖　南	Hunan	8372.1	17	4595.6	10	6609.5	13
广　东	Guangdong	11669.3	6	7072.4	6	8343.5	6
广　西	Guangxi	6790.9	25	2712.3	22	5205.6	27
海　南	Hainan	8342.6	18	3001.5	20	5465.6	26
重　庆	Chongqing	8332.0	19	4089.2	13	5796.4	21
四　川	Sichuan	7895.3	21	3542.8	18	6308.5	15
贵　州	Guizhou	5434.0	30	2572.6	23	4740.2	30
云　南	Yunnan	6141.3	29	1729.2	28	4743.6	29
西　藏	Tibet	6578.2	26	1475.3	30	3574.0	31
陕　西	Shaanxi	6502.6	27	3151.2	19	5724.2	23
甘　肃	Gansu	5107.8	31	2203.4	25	4849.6	28
青　海	Qinghai	6196.4	28	2347.5	24	6060.2	19
宁　夏	Ningxia	6931.0	24	2878.4	21	6489.7	14
新　疆	Xinjiang	7296.5	22	1311.8	31	6119.1	18

注：现金收支为不含储蓄借贷后的现金收支。

Continued

农林牧渔业总产值(亿元) Gross Output Value of Farming, Forestry, Animal Husbandry and Fishery (100 million yuan)	位次 Rank	农林牧渔业总产值比上年增长(%) Output Value Increase Rate in 2013 over 2012 of Farming,Forestry, Animal Husbandry and Fishery(%)	位次 Rank	粮食产量(万吨) Grain (10 000 tons)	位次 Rank	棉花产量(万吨) Cotton (10 000 tons)	位次 Rank	油料产量(万吨) Oil bearing Crops (10 000 tons)	位次 Rank
96995.3		**4.0**		**60193.5**		**629.9**		**3517.0**	
421.8	27	2.1	29	96.10	30	0.02	23	1.0	30
412.4	28	3.8	20	174.70	27	4.8	12	0.6	31
5832.9	4	3.3	25	3365.00	7	45.7	4	151.1	8
1447.0	24	4.5	13	1312.80	18	3.1	13	19.5	24
2699.5	16	4.7	9	2773.00	10	0.2	18	158.1	7
4349.7	10	4.1	18	2195.60	12	0.1	20	113.6	11
2670.6	17	3.5	22	3551.00	4	0.6	16	84.0	14
4633.3	9	4.7	9	6004.10	1			19.0	25
323.5	29	-2.9	31	114.20	28	0.4	17	1.5	29
6158.0	3	2.6	27	3423.00	5	20.9	6	150.4	9
2837.4	15	0.4	30	733.90	23	2.8	14	37.8	21
4009.2	11	3.4	24	3279.60	8	25.1	5	225.4	5
3282.0	13	4.5	13	664.40	24	0.01	24	28.8	23
2578.4	18	4.5	13	2116.10	13	13.1	9	119.3	10
8750.0	1	3.8	20	4528.20	3	62.1	2	349.6	2
7198.1	2	4.4	16	5713.70	2	19.0	8	589.1	1
5160.6	6	5.6	5	2501.30	11	46.0	3	333.2	3
5043.6	7	2.7	26	2925.80	9	19.8	7	224.4	6
4946.8	8	2.2	28	1315.90	17			101.0	12
3755.2	12	4.4	16	1521.80	15	0.2	18	57.2	19
1144.9	25	6.2	3	190.90	26			10.9	27
1513.7	23	4.6	12	1148.10	20	0.01	24	53.1	20
5620.3	5	3.5	22	3387.10	6	1.3	15	290.4	4
1663.0	21	6.0	4	1030.00	22	0.1	20	91.5	13
3056.0	14	7.0	2	1824.00	14	0.04	22	60.7	16
128.0	31	4.0	19	95.80	31			6.4	28
2562.5	19	4.8	8	1215.80	19	5.8	11	59.5	18
1517.7	22	4.9	7	1138.90	21	7.1	10	69.7	15
310.3	30	5.6	5	102.40	29			32.6	22
430.0	26	4.7	9	373.40	25			16.8	26
2538.9	20	7.2	1	1360.83	16	351.8	1	60.6	17

Note: The cash income and expenditure refer to the one absent of deposit loan.

续表 4

省市区	Region	工业增加值(亿元) Value-added of Industry (100 million yuan)	位 次 Rank	天然气(亿立方米) Natural Gas (100 million cu. m)	位 次 Rank	原 油(万吨) Crude Oil (10 000 tons)	位 次 Rank
全 国	**China**	**210689.4**		**1170.5**		**20946.9**	
北 京	Beijing	3536.9	24	5.8	12		
天 津	Tianjin	6678.6	16	18.7	9	3044.53	3
河 北	Hebei	13194.8	6	15.6	10	591.01	9
山 西	Shanxi	6033.0	19	31.6	7		
内蒙古	Inner Mongolia	7944.4	13	0.2	21		
辽 宁	Liaoning	12510.3	7	7.6	11	1001.01	7
吉 林	Jilin	6033.4	18	23.7	8	620.29	8
黑龙江	Heilongjiang	5090.3	22	35.0	6	4000.98	1
上 海	Shanghai	7236.7	15	2.3	16	7.24	18
江 苏	Jiangsu	25612.2	2	0.5	19	201.46	12
浙 江	Zhejiang	16368.4	4				
安 徽	Anhui	8928.0	12				
福 建	Fujian	9455.0	11				
江 西	Jiangxi	6434.4	17				
山 东	Shandong	24222.2	3	5.1	13	2765.55	4
河 南	Henan	15960.6	5	4.9	14	476.51	10
湖 北	Hubei	10531.4	9	3.1	15	80.08	13
湖 南	Hunan	10001.0	10				
广 东	Guangdong	27426.3	1	75.3	4	1291.78	6
广 西	Guangxi	5749.7	20			43.68	15
海 南	Hainan	551.1	30	1.7	17	26.46	16
重 庆	Chongqing	5249.7	21	1.7	17		
四 川	Sichuan	11578.6	8	214.3	3	22.36	17
贵 州	Guizhou	2686.5	26	0.5	19		
云 南	Yunnan	3767.6	23				
西 藏	Tibet	61.2	31				
陕 西	Shaanxi	7507.3	14	371.6	1	3688.04	2
甘 肃	Gansu	2225.2	27	0.2	21	72.81	14
青 海	Qinghai	970.5	28	68.1	5	214.5	11
宁 夏	Ningxia	944.5	29			6.08	19
新 疆	Xinjiang	3035.3	25	282.9	2	2658.47	5

Continued

社会消费品零售总额(亿元) Total Retail Sales of Consumer Goods (100 million yuan)	位 次 Rank	社会消费品零售总额比上年增长(%) Increase Rate in 2013 over 2012 of Total Retail Sales of Consumer Goods(%)	位 次 Rank	进出口总 额(亿美元) Total Value of Imports and Exports (USD 100 million)	位 次 Rank	#出口总额(亿美元) Total Exports (USD 100 million)	位 次 Rank
237809.9		**13.1**		**41596.9**		**22093.7**	
8375.1	11	8.7	30	4291.3	4	631.1	8
4470.4	23	14.0	3	1285.1	8	490.1	9
10516.7	9	13.6	20	549.0	13	309.6	13
5139.3	17	14.0	3	157.9	24	80.0	23
5114.2	19	11.8	29	120.0	26	40.9	27
10581.4	7	13.7	18	1144.9	9	645.4	7
5426.4	16	13.7	18	258.6	20	67.6	25
6251.2	15	13.8	14	388.8	15	162.3	19
8052.0	13	8.6	31	4412.2	3	2041.8	4
20796.5	3	13.4	23	5508.1	2	3288.1	2
15225.5	4	12.0	28	3357.9	5	2487.5	3
6542.4	14	14.0	3	455.6	14	282.5	14
8275.3	12	14.0	3	1693.3	7	1064.8	6
4576.1	22	13.6	20	367.5	16	281.7	15
22294.8	2	13.4	23	2665.6	6	1341.9	5
12426.6	5	13.8	15	599.5	12	359.9	12
10885.9	6	13.8	15	363.8	17	228.4	16
9018.6	10	13.8	15	251.7	22	148.2	21
25453.9	1	12.2	27	10915.9	1	6363.7	1
5133.1	18	13.6	20	328.3	18	186.9	18
992.9	28	14.0	3	149.8	25	37.1	28
4599.8	21	14.0	3	687.0	10	468.0	10
10561.4	8	13.9	13	645.7	11	419.5	11
2366.2	25	14.0	3	82.9	28	68.9	24
4004.6	24	14.0	3	257.9	21	159.4	20
293.2	31	15.2	1	33.2	29	32.7	29
4999.5	20	14.0	3	201.3	23	102.3	22
2173.8	26	14.0	3	102.3	27	46.8	26
544.1	30	14.3	2	14.0	31	8.5	31
610.5	29	12.5	26	32.2	30	25.5	30
2039.2	27	13.4	23	275.6	19	222.7	17

续表 5 Continued

省市区	Region	公共财政预算收入 General Budgetary Revenue in Local Finance	位次 Rank	金融机构各项存款 Deposits of Financial Institutions	位次 Rank	金融机构各项贷款 Loans of Financial Institutions	位次 Rank
全国	**China**	**68969.13**		**1043847**		**718962**	
北京	Beijing	3661.10	6	87991	2	40507	5
天津	Tianjin	2078.30	13	22685	17	19453	13
河北	Hebei	2293.48	10	39221	8	23966	10
山西	Shanxi	1700.20	18	26105	15	14888	19
内蒙古	Inner Mongolia	1719.54	17	15206	23	12944	22
辽宁	Liaoning	3341.80	7	38668	9	27944	8
吉林	Jilin	1156.96	25	14781	24	10697	24
黑龙江	Heilongjiang	1277.40	23	18132	22	11359	23
上海	Shanghai	4109.51	4	65037	5	39749	6
江苏	Jiangsu	6568.50	2	85604	3	61837	3
浙江	Zhejiang	3797.00	5	71987	4	62598	2
安徽	Anhui	2075.10	14	26739	14	19089	14
福建	Fujian	2118.67	12	28044	12	24488	9
江西	Jiangxi	1620.20	20	19435	20	12953	21
山东	Shandong	4560.00	3	62078	6	44761	4
河南	Henan	2413.06	9	37049	10	23101	11
湖北	Hubei	2189.98	11	32636	11	20797	12
湖南	Hunan	2023.61	15	26757	13	17775	15
广东	Guangdong	7075.54	1	114855	1	68493	1
广西	Guangxi	1316.84	22	18267	21	13653	20
海南	Hainan	480.52	29	5887	28	3989	28
重庆	Chongqing	1692.92	19	22202	18	17382	16
四川	Sichuan	2781.10	8	47667	7	29543	7
贵州	Guizhou	1206.00	24	13265	26	10104	25
云南	Yunnan	1610.69	21	20712	19	15812	18
西藏	Tibet	95.00	31	2499	31	1076	31
陕西	Shaanxi	1747.24	16	25577	16	16220	17
甘肃	Gansu	590.20	27	12030	27	8430	27
青海	Qinghai	368.56	30	4103	29	3398	30
宁夏	Ningxia	528.22	28	3868	30	3910	29
新疆	Xinjiang	1128.49	26	14089	25	9840	26

中国统计出版社最新图书简目

(仅供参考,以最后出书为准)

统计资料

综合类: 中国统计年鉴　中国统计摘要　中国发展报告
国际资料类: 国际统计年鉴　金砖国家联合统计手册　世界能源资源年鉴
区域资料类: 中国区域经济统计年鉴　中国县域统计年鉴　中国城市统计年鉴　中国农村统计年鉴　中国地区经济监测报告
经贸与投资类:中国贸易外经统计年鉴　中国对外直接投资统计公报　中国商品交易市场统计年鉴　大中型批发零售和住宿餐饮企业统计年鉴　中国零售和餐饮连锁企业统计年鉴
住户与物价类:中国住户调查年鉴　中国价格统计年鉴　中国农产品价格调查年鉴　全国农产品成本收益资料汇编
资源与环境类:中国环境统计年鉴　中国能源统计年鉴
产业类: 中国工业统计年鉴　中国建筑业统计年鉴　中国房地产统计年鉴　中国第三产业统计年鉴　中国证券期货统计年鉴
科技类: 中国科技统计年鉴　中国高技术产业统计年鉴　工业企业科技活动资料
人口与就业类:中国劳动统计年鉴　中国人口和就业统计年鉴　中国人才资源统计报告
社会与文化类:中国社会统计年鉴　中国文化及相关产业统计年鉴
公共管理类: 中国民政统计年鉴　中国民族统计年鉴　中国乡镇街道行政区域简册

省级综合统计年鉴系列

北京 天津 河北 山西 内蒙古　辽宁 吉林 黑龙江 上海 江苏　浙江 安徽 福建 江西 山东
河南 湖北 湖南 广东 广西 海南　重庆 四川 贵州 云南 西藏 陕西　甘肃 青海 宁夏 新疆
新疆生产建设兵团

市(县)级综合统计年鉴系列

天津滨海新区 石家庄 唐山 邯郸　太原 大同 阳泉 长治 晋城 朔州　晋中 运城 忻州 临汾 呼和浩特
鄂尔多斯 包头 沈阳 大连 长春　吉林市 四平 哈尔滨 黑龙江垦区　上海浦东新区 南京 无锡 徐州
常州 苏州 南通 连云港 淮安 盐城　扬州 镇江 泰州 宿迁 江阴 丹阳　杭州 宁波 温州 嘉兴 绍兴 金华
衢州 舟山 台州 合肥 福州 厦门　宁德 福州经济技术开发区 南昌　济南 青岛 郑州 洛阳 平顶山
三门峡 南阳 武汉 十堰 荆州 宜昌　荆门 咸宁 长沙 广州 深圳 惠州　东莞 南宁 柳州 桂林 来宾 海口
三亚 成都 贵阳 昆明 西安 兰州　庆阳 银川 乌鲁木齐

调查年鉴系列

山西 内蒙古 吉林 辽宁 上海　福建 湖北 广西 重庆 四川 云南　甘肃 宁夏 新疆 南宁 桂林

"十二五"规划教材

统计学（经济管理类专业本科适用，单薇 等）　抽样调查理论与方法（冯士雍 等）
贝叶斯统计（茆诗松 等）　统计学（黄良文 等）　试验设计（茆诗松 等）
统计学：从数据到结论（吴喜之）　医学统计学（于浩）　统计学（经济、管理类专业基础教材，张小斐）
概率论与数理统计三十三讲（魏振军）　概率论与数理统计三十三：学习指导与习题解答（魏振军）
非参数统计（吴喜之 等）　统计学：经济与管理中的数据分析（李慧云 等）
卫生管理统计学（新编医学院校基础课教材，尚磊）　医院统计学（新编医学院校基础课教材，徐天和 等）
社会统计学（蒋萍 等）　现代金融投资统计分析（李腊生 等）
国民经济核算初级教程（经济类、统计类、管理类专业适用，蒋萍 等）

重点图书

新中国 65 年　新编英汉汉英统计大词典　中华医学统计百科全书
挑大学选专业 2014—考研择校指南　挑大学选专业 2014—高考志愿填报指南

[illegible]

[illegible]

[illegible]

《新疆统计年鉴——2013》特邀编委

（排名不分先后）

新疆维吾尔自治区经济和信息化委员会	胡开江
新疆维吾尔自治区信息中心	赵若平
新疆维吾尔自治区教育厅	赵德忠　吐尔逊·伊不拉音
新疆生产建设兵团第一师阿拉尔市	邹跃斌　王新民
和田地区行政公署	艾则孜·木莎
新疆生产建设兵团第八师石河子市	孙长青
克拉玛依市统计局	王朝晖
中共阿图什市委员会	申海涛
中共伊宁市委员会	李宁平　阿不力克木·努兰别克
博乐市人民政府	刘　强　莎　茹
哈密市人民政府办公室	莫合买提·尼亚孜
中共乌苏市委员会	梁　浩　马依山·扎合帕尔
阿克苏地区发展和改革委员会	周春阳
霍城县人民政府	葛　国　热夏提·木沙江
中共乌鲁木齐县委员会	陈　钢
中共伊宁县委员会	张继生　阿不都克尤木·吐达洪
察布查尔锡伯自治区县人民政府	王春光
尼勒克县人民政府	周立新　努尔卡·卡那甫
新和县人民政府	马国强　艾买尔江·依明
富蕴县人民政府	祁崇江　叶尔江
巴里坤哈萨克自治县人民政府	韩雪峰　叶尔江·胡思满
伊吾县人民政府办公室	
中共新疆生产建设兵团第一师委员会党校	蒲必明
新疆准东经济技术开发区管理委员会	要建军　肖仁俊
新汶矿业集团(伊犁)能源开发有限责任公司	王贯东
新疆天富电力(集团)有限责任公司	赵　磊　刘　伟
新疆伊珠葡萄酒有限公司	邹新山
中华联合财产保险股份有限公司新疆分公司	梁英辉

努力开创新型工业化和信息化发展新局面

自治区经济和信息化委员会

自治区经信委党组书记、主任胡开江在 2013 年自治区经济和信息化工作会议上讲话。

胡开江主任（右一）在新疆机械研究院股份有限公司调研。

哈密新世纪纺织服装公司向自治区经信委赠送锦旗。

2013 年，自治区经济和信息化委员会在自治区党委、人民政府的坚强领导下，认真贯彻落实党的十八大、十八届三中全会和自治区党委八届四次、八届六次全委（扩大）会议精神，牢牢把握“稳中求进、进中求变”的总要求，按照“新春好开局、实干促落实”的工作部署，启动实施“千百亿工程”，扎实推进信息化发展战略，深入开展党的群众路线教育实践活动，班子成员作风建设有了新的转变，服务能力有了新的提高，为推进新疆跨越式发展和长治久安做出了新的贡献。

助推新型工业化发展迈上新水平，充分发挥新型工业化第一推动力的作用，积极构建符合新疆实际的现代产业体系，加快推进重大项目建设，疆电东送第二通道、八钢拜城、新疆梅花氨基酸等一批具有行业代表性的重点项目建成投产运行。实施创新驱动发展战略，技术创新体系建设取得新进展。注重科学规划，园区发展步伐加快。全疆自治区级以上园区达到 81 家，园区产业聚集效应进一步凸显。2013 年，全区规模以上工业企业 2102 家，比 2012 年增加 143 家，增长 7.3%，实现工业增加值 2895.95 亿元，增长 12.9%；工业增速创近 3 年来新高，居全国第 7 位。

开启信息化发展新局面。落实两化深度融合专项行动计划，培育“数字企业”3000 家。扎实推进“天山云计划”，乌鲁木齐、克拉玛依云计算产业园区建设顺利推进，促进总投资 200 亿元的中兴能源新疆云计算绿色数据中心项目落地，电子政务、电子商务、物联网得到了广泛应用，全区信息化水平进一步提升。

促进产业惠民政策取得新成效。扎实推进“民生工业促进计划”，推广伊犁民生坊、木垒民族刺绣产业园的示范经验，带动全疆民生产业共同发展。落实中央“千方百计把就业搞上去”的要求，对南疆三地州一批稍加扶持就能增加就业的中小微企业给予大力支持。

克拉玛依云计算产业园启动建设

新疆维吾尔自治区信息中心
新疆维吾尔自治区电子政务外网管理中心

自治区信息中心主任、自治区电子政务外网管理中心主任赵若平。

自治区发展改革委主任、援疆办主任张春林莅临我中心检查指导工作。

中心成立于1988年，是隶属于自治区发展和改革委员会管理的副厅级事业单位，核定事业编制85名，专业技术人员占75%，其中高级、中级专业技术人才占50%以上。主要职责是承担全区经济信息资源开发利用的规划和管理，为自治区党委、人民政府及经济综合管理部门宏观经济决策提供信息服务；承担全区电子政务外网规划、建设、运行、维护及相关管理工作；为党政机关、事业单位提供信息化技术支持与服务。

近年来，在自治区党委、人民政府和自治区发改委党组的正确领导下，我中心紧紧围绕“五个服务”理念，拓宽工作思路，创新机制模式，各项工作取得积极进展。2010–2012年先后荣获“自治区级文明单位”、“巾帼文明岗”、“自治区级青年文明号”、“自治区级模范职工之家”等荣誉称号，2013年在自治区文明单位“零基启动”评选中，再次荣获“自治区文明单位”荣誉称号。

在自治区党委、人民政府的高度重视和正确领导下，自治区电子政务外网一期建设项目于2009年正式启动，经过多方共同努力，我区电子政务外网建设和应用工作取得突破性进展，建成了上联国家、下联14个地（州市）和97个县（市、区、口岸、管委会）、横联近100个区级政务部门和单位的纵横向网络，承载了政法委、发改委、审计厅、安监局等部门多项纵向业务应用，为满足各级政务部门社会管理和公共服务的需要，促进政府监管能力和服务水平的提高奠定了良好的基础。一期建设项目于2013年8月顺利通过了自治区发改委组织的竣工验收。我区电子政务外网建设和应用工作也得到了国家的积极肯定；2010–2013年连续四年荣获国家电子政务外网管理中心的通报表彰，我中心作为后发赶超的典型，多项工作进入了全国前列。

在今后的发展中，我中心将紧紧围绕自治区党委、人民政府和发改委的中心工作，认真贯彻落实十八届三中全会和自治区党委八届六次全委会议精神，按照《新疆维吾尔自治区电子政务外网“十二五”发展规划》确定的目标，开拓创新，狠抓落实，努力践行新疆效率，为推动新疆跨越式发展和长治久安做出更大的贡献。

自治区发展改革委主任、援疆办主任张春林及自治区发展改革委党组副书记、发展改革委副主任牛晓萍莅临我中心检查指导工作。

自治区电子政务外网一期建设项目竣工验收会议。

自治区区直机关工会工委领导为自治区信息中心“自治区模范职工之家”授牌。

新疆维吾尔自治区教育厅

近年来，自治区牢固树立“教育立区、人才强区”理念，坚持教育优先发展，大力发展学前教育，巩固提高九年义务教育，加快发展高中阶段教育，积极发展高等教育，有效推进双语教育，加强教师队伍建设，加强学校党建和德育思政工作，加大扶持南疆三地州等边远贫困地区教育力度，不断优化教育结构、提高教育质量、增强办学效益，各级各类学校持续保持稳定。2013 年，全区有各类学校 9124 所，在校学生 462.16 万人，其中少数民族占 63.5%。各类学校有教职工 38.77 万人，其中专任教师 32.47 万人，少数民族专任教师占 55.5%。学前三年毛入园率达到 70.3%，初中毕业升入高中阶段升学率达到 88.7%，高中阶段毛入学率达到 79.0%，高等教育毛入学率达到 29.2%。全区每万人口拥有的普通高校、普通中专、普通高中、初中、小学在校生分别为 123 人、71 人、198 人、406 人、837 人。全区主要劳动年龄人口平均受教育年限为 9 年。

多年来，自治区教育工委、教育厅在建设服务型、创新型、节约型、法治型和谐机关方面起到了“排头兵”的作用，曾连续三年在自治区绩效考核中荣获第一名，2013 年，在自治区精神文明单位复验中高票通过，并被自治区有关部门评选为 “自治区保密工作先进单位”、“自治区涉密文件管理优秀单位”、“2010-2012 年度密级文件清退工作优秀单位”、“自治区计划生育工作先进单位”、“自治区档案工作优秀单位”、“亚欧博览会特别贡献奖” 及党委、政府和教育部信息报送先进单位等。

2014 年，自治区教育工作将全面贯彻党的十八大、十八届三中全会、第二次中央新疆工作座谈会和自治区党委八届七次全委（扩大）会议精神，深化教育综合改革，按照以改革推动发展、提高质量、促进公平、增强活力的总体思路，紧紧围绕社会稳定和长治久安抓发展，推进教育事业科学跨越、后发赶超，切实办好人民满意的教育。

农村义务教育保障机制的全面建立，确保了我区“两基”工作的巩固和提高，此图为克州一寄宿制学校学生高兴的领到免费教材。

奥什国立大学孔子学院揭牌仪式。

中国工程院院士、新疆大学信息科学与工程学院教授吾守尔·斯拉木在给研究生上课。

职业院校学生在实训基地学习。

自治区教育工委、教育厅2014年度工作会议。

师市党委书记、政委邹跃斌(右一)慰问新疆美丰职工。

师市党委副书记、师长、阿拉尔市市长王新民(右一)看望师退休老干部。

第一师阿拉尔市

“两个力争、两个率先”目标　大力推进“三化”进程

第一师阿拉尔市位于天山南麓,塔克拉玛干大沙漠北缘,与阿克苏地区五县一市接壤,行政区划面积6930平方公里,现拥有1个县级直辖市,1个垦区中心建制镇、1个国家级经济技术开发区、14个农牧团场、2个农场、3个处、1个少数民族牧业乡和731家企业、事业单位,全社会总人口31万人。

第一师阿拉尔市是一支具有光荣革命传统的老部队,其前身是中国工农红军二方面军第六军团,抗日战争时期为八路军一二零师三五九旅,解放战争时期改编为人民解放军第一野战军第一兵团二军第五师,1953年改编为新疆军区农业建设第一师。“生在井冈山,长在南泥湾,转战数万里,屯垦在天山”是第一师阿拉尔市光辉历程的真实写照。

“十二五”以来,在党中央、自治区、兵团党委的正确领导下,第一师阿拉尔市坚持贯彻落实中央新疆工作座谈会精神,紧紧抓住中央支持、全国援助的历史机遇,大力实施城镇崛起、工业振兴、创新引领、民生保障四大战略,以转方式调机构为主线、以推“三化”保民生为重点,促进经济和社会实现同步发展。

在城镇化建设方面,师市在“一河两岸、一轴三组团”的总体框架下,实施“北联、南扩、中提升”工程,城市中心区扩大到55平方公里;团场城镇以实现人的全面发展、满足人的方便快捷为要求,形成了“一团一品,风格各异”的规划特色。突出抓好城镇基础设施、公共服务设施和绿化美化亮化建设,使城镇功能进一步提升,整体城镇化率达到63%。

在新型工业化建设中,师市完成了基本面的布局,初步构建了“三酸两碱”的循环化工产业链。构建了从纺纱到织布整个棉花全产业链,国家级经济技术开发区成功挂牌;硝基复合肥作为兵团第一家天然气化工项目顺利投产;青松建化迈出了向化工领域拓展、整合兵团水泥的重要步伐。

在农业现代化建设中,师市出台相关优惠政策,引导规范奶牛养殖、油脂、棉纤维和塑料等行业协会运行,延伸棉业、果业、乳业和农资等产业链条,提升了农产品加工转化率。大力推广棉花机采,机采棉面积达到110多万亩,平均采净率达到了95.82%;实施品牌战略,“天山雪米”荣获第11届国际农产品展览会金奖。

2013年,师市实现生产总值200.17亿元。其中第一产业增加值103.43亿元;第二产业增加值58.05亿元;第三产业增加值38.69亿元;三次产业结构为51.7:29:19.3;人均生产总值65831元,城镇居民人均可支配收入23263元,团场农牧工人均纯收入16968元。

在农业现代化建设中，师市出台相关优惠政策，大力推广棉花机采，机采棉面积达到110多万亩，平均采净率达到了95.82%。

在新型工业化建设中，青松建化迈出了向化工领域拓展、整合兵团水泥的重要步伐。

在城镇化建设上，突出抓好城镇基础设施、公共服务设施和绿化美化亮化建设。

世界玉都 丝路名城 和田

地委书记闫国灿在皮山县藏桂乡为民服务中心调研。

观摩于田县先拜巴扎镇初级中学。

电网

和田地区位于新疆维吾尔自治区最南端，南枕昆仑山与西藏自治区相连，北部深入塔克拉玛干沙漠腹地与阿克苏地区阿瓦提县接壤，东部与巴音郭楞蒙古自治州且末县毗连，西南越喀喇昆仑山与印度、巴基斯坦实际控制的克什米尔地区毗邻，边境线长 210 公里，总面积 24.81 万平方公里，辖 7 县 1 市，91 个乡镇，13 个街道办事处，1388 个行政村，116 个社区，总人口 215.45 万人，其中维吾尔族占 96.4%、汉族占 3.4%、其他民族占 0.2%，有维吾尔、汉、回、塔吉克、柯尔克孜等 22 个民族成份。

和田地区资源丰富，光热充足，是自治区重要的粮食和特色林果基地。能源矿产资源品种多、储量大，具有巨大的开发潜力，已发现矿种占全疆的 44.2%；气、煤、金刚石、玉石矿、铜、铁及各种有色金属矿藏较为可观。和田有几千年遗留下来的古代文明，许许多多的人文遗事和古代景观、佛教文化遗址引人注目，境内古文化遗迹众多。独特的自然风光，浓郁的民族风情，丰富的旅游特色产品等吸引了大量的国内外旅客，丝绸、地毯、和田玉闻名中外，维吾尔医医药、阿胶、大芸、核桃、石榴、安迪尔甜瓜、山药、杏、红枣、玫瑰系列产品等在全疆乃至全国都独具特色。

近年来，全地区各族人民保持和发扬和田的优良传统，忘我工作，同心同德、奋力拼搏，各项事业发展不断创新。特别是中央新疆工作座谈会以来，和田地区紧紧抓住国家大力支持和援疆省市对口支援的有利机遇，坚持发展与稳定并重，改革与创新同行，全面推进“三化”建设，重点改善民生，综合实力增强。农牧业现代化发展势头良好，防沙治沙绿色生态工程建设富有成效，各项强农惠农政策全面落实，粮食喜获丰收，特色林果继续保持快速发展，畜禽养殖业提质增效，农村面貌发生显著变化，农牧民生产生活水平大幅提高；新型工业化扎实推进，一批能源、建材企业相继建成投产，农副产品加工业、民族传统手工业逐步壮大，企业集群活力初显；新型城镇化建设进程不

和田机场

和田玉

断加快，城乡面貌明显改善；民生保障力度空前，为百姓谋福祉，让生活更舒心，各族人民群众的幸福感得到提升；稳定是第一责任的认识进一步强化，社会治安防控体系建设和社会管理能力不断增强，社会的安全感、满意度明显提升，社会政治大局持续稳定。

2013 年，全地区生产总值 170.99 亿元，比上年增长 11.6%；全社会固定资产投资 177.59 亿元，增长 21.7%；公共财政预算收入 13.33 亿元，增长 19.2%；招商引资到位资金 37.12 亿元，增长 28.6%；社会消费品零售总额 28.57 亿元，增长 11.5%；农牧民人均纯收入 4542 元，增长 16.6%；城镇居民人均可支配收入 18478.2 元，增长 12.4%。

金戈铁马闻征鼓，只争朝夕启新程。和田地区各族干部群众将紧密团结在以习近平同志为总书记的党中央周围，在自治区党委、人民政府的坚强领导下，坚信只有努力才能改变，只要努力就能改变，先行先试、勇于担当、勇于创新、锐意进取、扎实工作，在新的起点上建设和谐稳定繁荣发展的美好和田，为实现与全国同步进入小康社会而努力奋斗。

大芸

和田地毯

艾德莱斯

大漠胡杨

大芸

打造“丝绸之路经济带”上的魅力之都

——第八师石河子市建设新亮点

习近平总书记在2013年访问中亚四国期间，提出了共同打造“丝绸之路经济带”的战略构想。第一次中央新疆工作座谈会召开以来，八师石河子市党委认真贯彻落实中央重大决策部署，抢抓全国对口援疆的重大机遇，坚持以城镇化建设为载体，新型工业化建设为支撑、农业现代化建设为基础，不断壮大经济实力，呈现出经济发展质量和效益的持续提升，结构优化的良好态势，社会经济发展的前进步伐明显加快，为打造“丝绸之路经济带”重要区域奠定了坚实的基础。

天业巨龙

美不胜收

走进石河子国家级经济技术开发区

一 综合实力明显增强

第八师石河子市生产总值由 2009 年的 143.23 亿元增加到 2013 年的 332.02 亿元，年均增长 16.9%。固定资产投资由 85 亿元增加到 299.47 亿元，累计投入 950 亿元，年均增长 41.1%。城镇居民人均可支配收入由 13300 元增加到 23292 元，年均增长 15.0%。团场农牧工家庭人均纯收入由 8915 元增加到 15916 元，年均增长 15.6%。

二 城镇化建设快速推进

八师石河子市加大城市建设的投入力度，四年累计投入资金 40 多亿元，重点用于涉及民生的老旧小区改造、城市基础设施、市政工程、公共服务设施、居民文化休闲游乐场所建设和环境治理，公共服务和社会管理精细化、科学化水平不断提升。石河子市已成为西北五省唯一的“全国社区管理和服务创新实验区”。

三 产业结构调整和转型升级步伐明显加快

八师石河子市充分发挥农业生产集约化、规模化程度较高，农机装备和现代农业技术推广水平较好等优势，以农业产业化为抓手，积极推进全国节水灌溉示范基地、全国农业机械化推广基地、全国现代农业生产基地“三大基地”建设。

八师石河子市依托新疆丰富的矿产资源和垦区优质农产品资源优势，把新型工业化作为经济发展的第一推动力。四年来，工业增长速度均保持在 20%以上，以化工、新材料、纺织、食品、电力能源等为支柱的新型工业化产业体系初步形成。

八师石河子市坚持把加快服务业发展作为促进产业优化升级的突破口，重点建设便民服务体系、支持物流、综合市场体系等服务业的发展，全面提升消费环境和城市现代服务业体系，通过招商引资，建设了一批现代服务业项目，发展后劲明显增强。

四 招商引资注入新的活力

八师石河子市坚持以存量引增量、以资源引投资、以环境引客商、以市场引项目，加大招商引资力度，借助外力加快发展。2013 年，累计实现招商引资到位资金 203 亿元，增长 49%。师市国有企业在各类资本市场直接融资 75 亿元。八师石河子市把科技创新作为推动科学发展的不竭动力，扎实推进全国创新型城市试点工作，承担了 15 项国家“863”项目课题和国家科技支撑计划课题。四年来，鉴定验收科技成果 196 项，其中 2 项国际领先、3 项国际先进、43 项国内领先；建设国家和兵团创新型试点企业 18 家，国家高新技术企业 19 家。国家级石河子高新技术产业开发区获国务院批准，成为兵团第一个高新区。

天业工业园

"戈壁明珠"石油城

克拉玛依市

"是塞北却似江南,无渔舟而有晚唱。妩媚千姿,可比绿野将萌;风情万种,最是华灯初上。"摘自易中天《克拉玛依赋》。

克拉玛依,坐落在新疆准噶尔盆地西北缘,下辖克拉玛依、独山子、白碱滩、乌尔禾四个行政区,总面积7700多平方公里,居住着汉、维吾尔、哈萨克等38个民族,人口40余万。

依油而始、因油而兴的克拉玛依从未停止探索可持续、跨越式发展的脚步,尤其是在经济全球化的今天,克拉玛依的发展,与区域、全国乃至世界紧密联系在一起。克拉玛依着眼于城市的可持续发展,根据国际、国内发展形势和新疆的发展部署,结合克拉玛依的工业基础优势、石油技术人才聚集优势、位于中亚油气富集区中心的区位优势及"克拉玛依"的城市品牌优势,提出了立足中国西部、面向中亚,把克拉玛依打造成为世界石油城的战略构想。围绕实现这一战略构想,明确了建设油气生产、炼油化工、技术服务、机械制造、石油储备、工程教育"六大基地",做大做强油气核心产业;发展金融、信息、旅游"三大新兴产业",促进城市经济多元化发展;打造高品质城市和最安全城市"两个平台",构建城市发展支撑体系的战略目标。随着打造世界石油城战略的实施,克拉玛依已进入了一个新的大发展的历史机遇期,经济和社会各项事业实现快速发展,城市面貌日新月异,呈现出蓬勃的生命力和可持续发展的美好前景。2013年,克拉玛依市实现地区生产总值853.5亿元,经济总量继续位居各地州市前列。随着经济的不断发展,人民生活水平也有了较大提高。2013年,城镇居民人均可支配收入25248元,农牧民人均纯收入15595元。

美丽的克拉玛依是一座处处焕发着勃勃生机与活力的朝阳城市。作为北疆区域的重要城市,也有着迷人的风景,"中国最瑰丽的雅丹"和"中国最值得外国人去的50个地方"——世界魔鬼城、世界地质奇观——黑油山、新中国"第一口油井"、中国唯一在荒漠中建成的国家4A级景区——克拉玛依河,让过往游客在饱览戈壁美景、石油工业奇观之余,感受着现代城市迷人的魅力。北疆各著名旅游胜地环为一线,宛如一枚贝壳,而克拉玛依恰好点缀在她的中心。伴随着克拉玛依通用航空产业的快速发展与推进,一座贯通南北疆,连接中东部大中城市,辐射中亚、俄罗斯的旅游、交通、休闲中心城市正离克拉玛依越来越近。

克拉玛依,一座走进您心灵的城市,一座为梦想而加油的城市,热情欢迎各界有识之士前来旅游、兴业,与我们共创造美好的明天。

魔鬼城景区

建设美丽和谐的阿图什

阿图什市是新疆克孜勒苏柯尔克孜自治州的首府，位于天山南麓，塔里木盆地西缘，西北与吉尔吉斯斯坦共和国接壤，全市总面积1.55万平方公里，边境线长88.3公里，市境东西长约241公里，南北宽约136公里。乌－喀铁路、阿喀高速、喀伊高速公路穿境而过，距乌鲁木齐市铁路里程1553公里，公路里程1430公里，距伊尔克斯坦口岸190公里，距吐尔尕特口岸150公里，距托帕口岸60公里，距喀什飞机场35公里，有着“五口通八国、一路连欧亚”的独特区位优势。

阿图什市于1986年撤县建市，辖6乡1镇，75个行政村，2个街道办事处，16个社区和1个工业园区。全市有维、柯、汉等11个常住民族，总人口26.38万人（不含流动人口）。其中维吾尔族20.94万人，占79.6%；柯尔克孜族3万人，占11.4%；汉族2.3万人，占8.7%。

2013年，阿图什市地区生产总值完成33.8亿元，同比增长16%；全社会固定资产投资完成30.5亿元，增长21.8%；地方财政收入完成4.15亿元，增长36%，其中公共财政预算收入完成2.88亿元，增长44%；招商引资到位资金24.11亿元，增长15%；社会消费品零售总额8.4亿元，增长13%；城镇居民人均可支配收入18350元，增长12%；农牧民人均纯收入4350元，增长24%；城镇登记失业率为1.69%，人口自然增长率为13.1‰。

阿图什市成矿条件好，资源十分丰富，是国家确定的16个重点金属成矿区带之一的天山成矿带横穿阿图什市，重点矿区主要分布在哈拉峻乡和吐古买提乡，初步发现的矿种有铅锌、铜、金、钼、铌、钒、锡、钛、铁、石灰石、花岗岩、大理石、石膏、萤石、砂石、粘土等32种矿产资源。具有资源优势的矿种有铅锌、钒、钛、磁、铁、盐、水泥用石灰岩矿等。

阿图什境内有天门、大峡谷、怪柳林、怪石山等神奇独特的自然景观；骑仕大观园等维吾尔特色民居和民风民俗独具特色；同时，阿图什市是伊斯兰教在新疆的发源地，境内有喀拉汗王朝遗址、莫尔佛塔、汉代佛窟“三仙洞”等名胜古迹和文化遗产。作为全国日照排名第二的阿图什市，素有“中国木纳格葡萄之乡”、“无花果之乡”的美称，木纳格葡萄曾多次荣获国家优质鲜食葡萄金奖，木纳格葡萄、无花果、石榴、胡安纳杏等特色果品深受国内外市场的青睐。

阿图什市正以得天独厚的资源优势显示出广阔的发展前景，市委、市人民政府将以最优惠的政策、最优质的服务、最宽松的环境为企业发展保驾护航，真诚欢迎社会各界朋友到阿图什市观光、旅游、考察、投资，阿图什市各族人民群众愿与您携手共创美好的明天、共创美好的未来。

克州党委常委、市委书记申海涛在轻工业园区调研。

市委副书记沈立新（援疆干部）、市委常委、副市长肖建明（援疆干部）参加市医院师带徒签约仪式。

江苏昆山援建阿图什市第一中学。

天山北坡西部中心城市

——伊宁市

伊犁州党委书记黄三平、伊宁市市委书记李宁平在王蒙书屋调研。

伊宁市市长阿布力克木·努兰别克（右）在霍尔果斯开发区伊宁园区调研。

伊宁市第二届民俗文化旅游节 "欢乐家园·纳格尔之声"文艺演出。

伊宁市是伊犁哈萨克自治州的首府城市，是伊犁河谷的政治、经济、文化、交通中心，是新丝绸之路经济的主要支点，是伊犁河谷的物资交流中心和商品集散地，是连接霍尔果斯口岸、都拉塔口岸、木扎尔特口岸的新疆天山北坡西部中心城市，是祖国西部最大的沿边开放城市。伊宁市横亘伊犁河谷中部，雄踞伊犁河北岸，连接 312 国道最西端，东连伊宁县，西接霍城县，南与察布查尔锡伯自治县隔河相望，北靠天山支脉科古尔琴山。

全市总面积 675.5 平方公里，市辖 8 乡、1 镇、1 场、8 个街道办事处。2013 年末，37 个民族总人口 535668 人，其中维吾尔族 258913 人、汉族 192871 人、哈萨克族 25375 人、回族 38893 人，较上年分别增长 3.2%、5.7%、2.3%和 2.9%。维、汉、哈、回人口占总人口的比重分别为 48.3%、36%、4.7%和 7.3%。

2013 年，全市预计实现生产总值 164 亿元，较上年增长 16%。其中第二产业增加值 43.9 亿元，增长 21%；第三产业增加值 113.2 亿元，增长 14.8%。三次产业结构比为 4.2:26.8:69.0，呈现"三二一"型的发展态势。按全市常住人口计算，人均 GDP 达到 31813 元（折合 5218 美元），较上年增长 13%。

伊宁市气候宜人，物产丰富，自然条件得天独厚。土地热量和水资源条件较为优越，适宜种植小麦、水稻、玉米、油菜、蔬菜、瓜果等多种农作物和经济作物。伊宁市矿产资源丰富，有煤、石油、金、银、铜、铁、镍、铅、锰、铀、云母、水晶、石棉、石膏等。

生态伊宁

伊宁市苏拉宫工业园

伊宁市是被誉为祖国西部边陲塞外江南的一座花园城市。北倚天山雪峰，南临悠然西去的伊犁河，四周是美丽的西部大地——一望无际的草原和神秘的森林。市内既有宽敞大道和现代建筑群，又有小巷深处绿荫流水的维吾尔人家。街市上各种民族特色产品琳琅满目，有民族英雄林则徐纪念馆、拜吐拉清真寺、伊宁回族大寺、三区革命烈士陵园、伊犁哈萨克自治州文化博物馆、汉宾乡果园八角凉亭、汉家公主纪念馆、喀赞奇民俗旅游等景区。

伊宁市下苏拉宫安居富民工程

伊宁市地缘优势突出，对外开放条件优越，是新疆乃至全国向西开放的重要商埠。1989 年元月，伊宁市被国务院确定为开放城市，1992 年又被确定为沿边进一步开放城市，并在市区内设立国家级边境经济合作区。在 2010 年 5 月的新疆中央经济工作会议上，国家提出了成立霍尔果斯特殊经济开发区，随后伊宁园区 35 平方公里正式成为霍尔果斯特殊经济开发区的重要组成部分，并提出了“建设天山北坡西部中心城市”、“打造百万人口城市”的奋斗目标。

喀赞其民俗旅游区

伊宁市是新疆西部交通枢纽，被国家列为全国公路交通枢纽之一。现形成以铁路航空公路为主的立体交通网络。伊宁客运站规模新疆第二。伊宁火车站是新疆第二大火车站，全疆唯一按空港理念设计的车站。伊宁机场是中国 28 个中型机场，70 个主要机场之一，客流量连续十年排在新疆前三甲，每天都有数千人进出伊宁空港，同时争取开通与欧亚城市的国际通航航线。

伊宁各族青少年放飞梦想

西来之异境　世外之灵壤

塞外明珠——博乐市

中央政治局委员、自治区党委书记张春贤(左五)调研博乐市城市建设情况,自治州党委常委、市委书记刘强(右一)、市委副书记、市长莎茹(右五)一起陪同。

博尔塔拉大桥

博乐市位于新疆西北部,北与哈萨克斯坦共和国接壤,距离新疆首府乌鲁木齐市524公里。博乐市是博尔塔拉蒙古自治州首府,是全州政治、经济、文化中心,也是中国西部的重要沿边开放城市,辖区内有中国唯一的公路、铁路和管道运输并举的国家一类开放口岸阿拉山口口岸,为中国连接中亚和欧洲各国及向西开放国际贸易大通道的前沿。博乐市居住着蒙古族、汉族、维吾尔族、哈萨克族等31个民族,总人口26.37万。

博乐市历史悠久,山水雄奇,历来就是一个多民族聚居地,是"丝绸之路"北道上的重镇之一。1920年设博乐县,1985年撤县建市,1989年被国务院列为对外开放城市,1990年被国务院批准为沿边进一步对外开放城市,1990年境内的阿拉山口经批准对外开放,1992年经国务院批准建立博乐国家级边境经济合作区。先后荣获西部大开发新疆县域经济增长最快县市之一、全国科技进步先进市、全国科普工作先进市、全国民政工作先进市、全国文化工作先进市、全国双拥模范城、中国优秀旅游城市、自治区卫生红旗城市、自治区文明城市、自治区平安县市等多项国家级及自治区级荣誉称号。

博乐市是一个以农牧业为主的县级市,现有耕地4.53万公顷、宜农荒地近8000公顷、草场44.95万公顷,森林覆盖率8.5%,以种植棉花、玉米、小麦、甜菜为主,是新疆重要的优质棉生产基地;盛产绿色牛羊肉、禽、蛋、奶等畜禽产品,是新疆三大养禽基地之一。非金属矿产资源丰富,主要有石灰岩、花岗岩、大理石、珍珠岩等,其中石灰岩矿总储量高达3.5亿吨,是新疆最大的优质石灰岩生产加工基地。商业服务网点遍布

全市，金融保险、房地产、信息服务、社区家政等现代服务业发展势头良好，商贸流通、餐饮、交通运输等传统服务业繁荣活跃，拥有非常便捷的公路、铁路、航空交通网络。体育文化生活丰富，“那达慕”草原节已成为新疆的三大旅游节之一，环赛里木湖公路自行车赛成为中国重要体育赛事。文教、卫生事业蓬勃发展，教学设施完善、师资力量雄厚；卫生设备齐全，卫生机构、卫生技术人员布局合理，形成了遍布城乡、防治结合的医疗、卫生防疫网络。博乐旅游资源丰富独特，境内有新疆海拔最高、面积最大的高山湖泊——国家AAAA级风景名胜区赛里木湖；有山水清秀、气候宜人的避暑胜地－国家级森林公园哈日图热格；有以奇石闻名的亚洲最大怪石群落——国家级风景名胜区怪石峪；有山深林幽、风景如画的夏尔希里自然保护区；有省级文物保护单位——达勒特古城遗址……自然风光雄奇壮丽，边塞文化粗犷豪放、民族风俗淳朴浓郁、异域风情惹人心醉，被誉为“西来之异境，世外之灵壤”。

北京桥

清河桥

永隆广场双子楼鸟瞰图

夏尔西里

赛里木湖

哈密市 开拓创新谋发展

地委委员、市委书记黄建昆

市委副书记、市长莫合买提·尼亚孜

哈密石油基地全景

哈密市是哈密瓜的故乡，以盛产哈密瓜闻名于世。哈密雄踞新疆东部，是古丝绸之路重镇，素有“西域咽喉”、“新疆门户”之称，历史和战略地位突出，文化底蕴厚重，民族风情浓郁，人文、历史、自然景观星罗棋布。雄伟的天山山脉横贯全境，形成迥然不同的两个气温带，让人深切感观到“一日游四季，十里不同天”的气候特点。独特的地域特点和气候条件，使“哈密瓜、大枣、奇石”成为哈密市对外宣传的三张名片。

哈密市域面积8.56万平方公里，东西长约404公里，南北宽约322公里，约占全疆总面积的5.14%。城市规划区面积1005平方公里。下辖18个乡(镇)，5个街道办事处，91个行政村，47个居委会。总人口48.02万人，其中，城镇人口32.94万人，城镇化率达到68.6%。有维、汉、哈、回等37个民族，其中：维吾尔族10.05万人，汉族34.21万人，哈萨克族1.47万人，回族1.78万人。

哈密市矿产资源非常丰富，被确定为新疆副中心城市、一级综合交通枢纽、新型工业化主战场、重要增长极，是全国十大资源集中区之一，已探明矿产86种，发现矿产地1000多处，占全疆探明矿产的60%以上，目前已开采的32种。哈密年日照时数达3170–3380小时，是全国日照时数充裕的地区之一；哈密市拥有预测资源量22.1亿吨位居全疆第一位的铁矿，预测资源量1584万金属吨位居全疆第一位，仅次于镍都金川的镍矿，具有可大规模开采的铁矿、铜镍矿、钼矿等黑色、有色金属矿和花岗岩、白云石、红柱石、石英石、石灰石等非金属矿产资源。

哈密市区位优势十分明显，是集公路、铁路、航空于一体的“东联、西出、南通、北拓”的现代交通枢纽中心，是新疆7座被确定为国家公路运输枢纽城市之一。连霍高速、京新高速横穿全境，兰新第二双线、哈密—罗布泊等多条铁路已开工建设或即将开工建设，哈密市至乌鲁木齐、北京、上海、广州、郑州、西安、库尔勒航线的开通，缩短了哈密通向全国融入世界的距离，形成了三维一体的运输体系。

随着国家新能源战略的实施，哈密市依托丰富的风能、太阳能资源、风力发电、光伏发电及与其配套的装备制造业，迎来了更大的发展机遇。目前，围绕“疆电东送”战略的实施及哈密——郑州±800特高压直流输电线路建设、750千伏输

哈密市全民健身广场

哈密机场

富民安居房

风力发电

变电工程，哈密市以神华国能哈密煤电有限公 4×660MW 电网建设项目、国电哈密能源开发有限公司大南湖 2×660MW 建设项目、国投哈密发电有限公司 2×660MW 电厂建设项目等项目为依托，着力提高煤电生产规模；以东南部风区 200 万 MW，十三间房风场 35 万 MW 为龙头，以石城子 14 万 MW、29 万 MW 太阳能光伏并网发电项目为引领，进一步打造光电产业发展示范基地。风电装备制造业也从无到有并不断壮大，截止 2013 年末，已引进风电装备制造企业 10 家。

近年来，哈密市以全面建成小康社会为目标，依托资源发展优势，坚定不移地实施优势资源转化战略、大企业大集团战略，坚定不移地实施“工业强市”发展战略，新型工业化着眼产业完善和产业创新，推动产业优化升级，加快推进煤电冶材、风电、光电、煤电、煤炭生产交易及外运、制造业、特色农业、现代物流业“八大”基地建设，延伸“九大产业链”，形成新型工业化产业格局。

2013 年，哈密市国民经济总体攀升，实现生产总值 263.54 亿元，按可比价计算，比上年增长 20.9%；地方规模以上工业增加值 53.79 亿元，增长 31.2%；全社会固定资产投资总额 450.79 亿元，增长 50.4%；社会消费品零售总额 58.08 亿元，增长 17.1%；地方财政收入完成 54.25 亿元，增长 30.9%；城镇居民人均可支配收入 21128 元，增长 13.2%；农村居民人均纯收入 10697 元，增长 17.7%。

光伏发电

疆电东送——电力高速公路。

哈密市胜拓石材有限公司石板材全自动石材磨光生产线。

绚丽多彩的哈密市夜景。

国网能源哈密 2×30 万千瓦电厂

乌苏市

自治区党委常委哈尼巴提·沙布开（前排左三）在我市调研。

地委书记张博(右二)在乌苏市调研经济社会发展情况。

地委副书记、行署专员沙尔合提·阿汗(前排右一)在我市调研。

乌苏，民国以前称库尔喀喇乌苏，源于明末据有此地的和硕特蒙古语；“库尔”，积雪；“喀喇”，黑色；“乌苏”，水也，意为“积雪之地的黑水”。西汉神爵二年（前 60 年），汉宣帝置西域都护府，如今乌苏地区随西域隶属于祖国版图；公元七世纪，唐政府在此设 4 个守捉；乾隆二十六年（1761 年）清廷派兵驻防，正式设治，隶属乌鲁木齐办事大臣管辖；乾隆四十六年（1781 年）改为通知直隶厅；民国 2 年（1913 年）改厅为县，省去库尔喀喇，定名为乌苏；1996 年 7 月撤县建市。

乌苏市地处准噶尔盆地西南缘、天山北麓，东与克拉玛依市、沙湾县毗连，南与尼勒克县相望，西与精河县为邻，北与托里县接壤，位于北纬 43° 29′ ~45° 27′ 、东经 82° 58′ ~85° 16′ 之间，东西长 180 千米，南北宽 220 千米，土地总面积 14300 平方千米。地势南高北低，依次为高山、中低山、丘陵、平原、沙漠 5 个地形带，自西向东绵延 140 多千米，最高海拔 5500 米，市区海拔 440 ~ 530 米，农区海拔 220 ~ 1600 米。与奎屯、独山子构成北疆地区“金三角”，是自治区天山北坡经济带优先发展县市之一，经国务院批准的对外开放城市，是通往伊宁市、博乐市、霍尔果斯口岸、阿拉山口口岸的重要门户，距自治州首府伊宁市公路里程 420 千米。2013 年辖 10 镇、7 乡。年末总人口 231401 人（少数民族 84989 人），其中农村人口 148747 万人；人口出生率 11.39‰，自然增长率 7.86‰。耕地面积 87782 公顷，粮食播种面积 22422 公顷，经济作物播种面积 65359.9 公顷。

境内有奎屯河、四棵树河、古尔图河 3 条主要河流，年总径流量 12.5 亿立方米。矿产资源有煤、铁、铜、沙金、石油、铅、石灰石、石膏、膨润土、花岗岩等。野生动物主要有熊、鹿、黄羊、雪鸡、雪豹、旱獭等。北部荒漠属国家级准原始梭梭林自然保护区。主要旅游景点有天山山脉的大南沟冰达坂、哈布勒根冰达坂、白杨沟泥火山群景观、古尔图天鹅湖、待甫僧生态园（国家 AAA 级）、巴音沟乌拉斯台景区、南山温泉、准原始梭梭林、苏木喇嘛庙、春秋岩画、乌孙土墩墓葬等。属北温带大陆性干旱气候。

2013 年，全市生产总值 1433023 万元，其中第一产业增加值 305012 万元、第二产业增加值 864585 万元、第三产业增加值 263426 万元。

农林牧渔及其服务业总产值 537071 万元，其中农业产值 393238 万元、林业产值 4690 万元、牧业产值 133067 万元、渔业产值 973 万元、服务业产值 5103 万元。主要农产品产量：粮食 235789 吨，棉花 114341 吨，油料 1550 吨，番茄 456199 吨，甜菜 2367 吨，薯类 12633 吨，枸杞 960 吨，蔬菜 90750 吨，瓜果 9996 吨。牲畜存栏 81.6 万头（只）。肉类总产 37670 吨，

伊犁哈萨克自治州第十七届阿肯阿依特斯文化旅游节上展示哈萨克族传统美食。

央视《过年七天乐》栏目组来乌苏拍摄专场。

市委书记梁浩(前排右二)深入乡场镇检查指导农业生产工作。

市委副书记、市长马依山·扎合帕尔(左三)调研吉尔格勒德水利工程建设。

羊毛 1556 吨,山羊绒 35000 千克,禽蛋 3610 吨,牛奶 22760 吨。年末农牧业机械总动力 62.99 万千瓦。

工业总产值 1339082 万元,比上年增长 33.3%;工业增加值 720184 万元(规模以上企业工业增加值 606703 万元)。主要工业产品产量:原煤 221 万吨,发电 355541 万千瓦·时,啤酒 92896 千升,面粉 102444 吨,食用植物油 96655 吨,果葡糖浆 19850 吨,番茄酱 43590 万吨,淀粉 44150 吨。建筑业实现增加值 14.44 亿元,建筑企业房屋施工面积 111.8 万平方米。

全社会固定资产投资 720834 万元。完成邮政业务收入 1661 万元,电信业务收入 15295 万元。年末固定电话用户 4.44 万户,移动电话用户 16.66 万户,计算机互联网用户 2.9 万户。社会消费品零售总额 12.01 亿元。进出口贸易总额 7.8 亿美元,其中出口额 7.79 亿美元、进口额 110.12 万美元。接待旅游者 49.62 万人次,旅游业收入 3.01 亿元。地方财政收入 118981 万元,地方财政支出 243545 万元。年末城乡居民储蓄存款余额 646722 万元。

全市有各类专业技术职务人员 4912 人,其中中级以上 2545 人。有中等专业学校 1 所,在校学生 555 人(少数民族 220 人);普通中学 26 所,在校学生 13235 人(少数民族 4357 人);小学 14 所,在校学生 16529 人(少数民族 7854 人);各类教师 3175 人(少数民族 1423 人)。全年教育基建投资 11008.87 万元。科技项目 1 项成果获自治区科技进步奖,5 项成果获塔城地区科技进步奖。

全市有市直医疗卫生机构 4 家,3 个社区卫生服务中心,10 个社区卫生服务站,20 个乡(场)镇卫生院,141 个村卫生室,市、乡、村三级新农合定点医疗机构 165 家,专业公共卫生机构 2 个。有医务人员 1778 人,其中卫生专业技术人员 1556 人(含乡村医生 141 人),市乡两级医疗机构共开放床位 1368 张。年内在国际、全国或自治区举办的重大体育比赛中获 2 枚金牌、1 枚银牌、2 枚铜牌。

全年城镇居民人均可支配收入 120121.9 元,人均消费性支出 55645 元,农村居民人均纯收入 14568 元。在职职工年均货币工资 29778 元。新增就业人员 5800 人,城镇登记失业率 2.3%。截至年底,全市参加城镇失业保险 13819 人,参加基本养老保险 19572 人,城镇职工参加基本医疗保险 29030 人。参加新型农村合作医疗 120753 人,参合率 91.6%。参加新型农村养老保险 41421 人(含已退休 10873 人),领取养老保险待遇 19572 人。城镇居民中有 8558 人得到政府最低生活保障救济。

乌苏市九莲泉水景公园喷泉。

乌苏啤酒节,人潮涌动。

乌苏啤酒自动化生产线。

聚力长治久安　奋力谱写发展改革新篇章

阿克苏地区发展和改革委员会

地委书记窦万贵同志在地委扩大会议上作重要讲话。

地委副书记、行署专员麦尔丹·木盖提调研柯坪县农村经济发展情况。

地委副书记、纪检委书记、政法委书记贠书霞参加民生项目开工剪裁。

自治区发改委主任、援疆办主任张春林来我委调研。

阿克苏地区发展和改革委员会是综合研究制定阿克苏地区经济和社会发展战略、规划和政策，进行总量平衡、结构调整，指导经济体制改革，主管重点项目和固定资产投资的宏观调控部门。2013 年以来，面对复杂多变的经济形势，阿克苏地区发展和改革委员会在地委、行署的坚强领导下，认真贯彻落实十八届三中全会精神及地委（扩大）会议精神，以“三干两努力”的工作状态，用“新疆精神”提升“新疆效率”，在变化变革中求新创新，认真落实民生建设年、“跨越奋进”四大工程、“四化”、“94122”工程等一系列部署，解放思想、改革开放、凝聚力量、攻坚克难，发展改革各项工作取得了新的进展、新的成效、新的突破，实现了贯彻落实党的十八大精神的良好开局。

宏观经济调控力度持续增强。预计实现地方生产总值 516.8 亿元，增长 12.5%，三次产业结构调整为 22.6:35.3:42.1。实现公共财政预算收入 74.9 亿元，增长 3.8%。全社会消费品零售总额 98.03 亿元，增长 14.5%。农牧民人均纯收入 9657 元，增长 16.8%；城镇居民人均可支配收入 20758 元，增长 14%。

重点项目建设有力推进。地区 139 个重点项目累计完成投资 270.47 亿元，完成年度计划 244.09 亿元的 110.80%。浙能阿克苏纺织工业城 2×35 万千瓦热电联产项目获国家发改委路条，乌什亚曼苏水电站开工建设，柯坪、乌什、阿瓦提等县（市）7 个光伏发电项目并网发电、10 个光伏发电项目获得自治区发改委核准，18 个光伏发电项目获得自治区发改委“路条”。

对口援阿工作稳步推进。实施民生援疆项目 86 个（含一师），完工项目 79 个，累计完成投资 40.28 亿元，完成年度投资计划任务 104.9%，浙江援疆资金 9.29 亿元。浙江企业与阿克苏地区共达成产业合作项目 100 个，协议资金 687 亿元，实际到位资金 100 亿元，89 个项目已经开工建设，50 个项目建成或部分建成投产，创造就业岗位 5932 个。实施人才援疆项目 392 个，投入援疆资金 4.13 亿元，培训培养各类干部人才 29600 人。

面对新形势、新任务、新要求，阿克苏地区发展和改革委员会将继续深入贯彻落实党的十八届三中全会精神，牢牢把握建设“丝绸之路经济带”、浙江对口援疆重大战略机遇，坚持变化变革、敢于担当，紧紧围绕社会稳定长治久安抓发展，促改革，惠民生，大力实施“富民强区，长治久安”战略，加快转变经济发展方式，坚持资源开发、生态环境可持续，强力推进“五化”，强投资、保增长、调结构、提质量、促和谐，以党的群众路线教育实践活动为抓手，努力完成发展改革工作的各项目标任务，为地区社会稳定长治久安和跨越式发展而努力奋斗。

华锦化肥有限公司一角

八钢南疆钢铁基地轧钢生产线

克孜尔千佛洞

塞外明珠

霍城县

发展中的霍城

我们的生活充满阳光

霍城县因霍尔果斯河得名，简称“霍城”，北依天山与博尔塔拉蒙古自治州温泉县、博乐市毗连；南濒伊犁河与察布查尔县隔水相望；东与伊宁县、伊宁市毗邻；西以霍尔果斯河为界与哈萨克斯坦国接壤。总面积5720平方千米。距自治州首府伊宁市公路里程45千米。县辖13个乡镇（中心）、清水河经济技术开发区（清水河镇）。境内驻有新疆生产建设兵团农四师所属5个团场、4个师直属企业及霍尔果斯口岸管委会、“一关两检”、69348部队等20多个县团级单位。年末总人口41.3万人（含生产建设兵团农四师驻县人口），其中农村人口26.11万人；人口出生率13.75‰，人口自然增长率10.87‰。耕地面积（不含生产建设兵团农四师）61.33万亩，粮食作物种植面积46.2万亩，经济作物种植面积15.13万亩。

境内野生动植物品种繁多。野生动物有马鹿、黄羊、野猪、狐狸、熊、豹、狼、野兔、旱獭、野鸡、天鹅等。野生植物有野苹果、野杏、野山楂、野麻、野核桃等。其中四爪陆龟、野生樱桃李是世界珍奇动物和稀有树种。矿产资源丰富，已发现的矿藏有煤、铁、金、铜、铅、锌、金、银、石灰石、大理石、磷等33种，占新疆已知138种矿产的23.9%，其中探明矿种为发现矿种的6.6%，尤其是煤储量最为丰富，已探明储量17亿吨。

三中心全景图

霍城县历史悠久，有元朝时中亚政治、经济中心和东西方交通的枢纽阿力麻里城遗址；有清代新疆军事、政治中心伊犁将军府遗址；有元朝察合台汗国首府阿力玛力城旧址、成吉思汗七世孙吐虎鲁克·铁木尔汗麻扎；有景色秀丽、曾经是元、清时期新疆最大的道教活动场所大西沟福寿山汉庙及气势雄浑的惠远钟鼓楼。境内的可克达拉是著名歌曲《草原之夜》的诞生地。邱处机、祁韵士、洪亮吉、林则徐、徐松、谢彬、袁鹰等历史文化名人都曾驻留霍城，留下传诵久远的妙文佳句。雪山峡谷、草原湖泊、长河大漠、历史文化、民族风情，赋予霍城县浓郁的西部特色。主要旅游景点有赛里木湖、惠远将军府、萨尔布拉克怪榆沟、三道河图开沙漠、大西沟福寿山庙。著名地方产品有红地球葡萄、油桃、蟠桃、红富士苹果等。属大陆干燥性气候。

萨河治理

2013年，完成生产总值89.6亿元，比上年增长16%，完成固定资产投资4.9亿元，增长38.2%，完成地方财政收入81553万元，增长81.2%，社会消费品零售总额13.86亿元，增长15.0%，城镇居民人均可支配收入16399元，增长13%，农牧民人均纯收入10994元，比上年增加1397元，增长14.6%。进出口贸易总额达3500万美元。全年接待旅游人数100万人次，旅游综合收入达4亿元。广播覆盖率98%，电视人口覆盖率97%，有线电视用户2万户。全县有医疗卫生机构20所，学校70所。

丰收的薰衣草

蓬勃发展的

乌鲁木齐县

自治区党委副书记、自治区主席努尔·白克力视察冬运会场馆。

自治区党委常委、市委书记朱海仑来我县调研。

自治区政协主席努尔兰·阿不都满金在我县植树。

县委书记陈钢、县长李伟参观亚博会企业。

乌鲁木齐南部燃气供热工程开工奠基。

新农村建设

天山大峡谷获国家 5A 级景区。

叼羊

美丽的菊花台

乌鲁木齐县地处准噶尔盆地南缘的天山北麓，是首府乌鲁木齐市唯一的市辖县。清光绪 12 年（1886 年）设置迪化县。1953 年 11 月 20 日经国务院批准改迪化县为乌鲁木齐县。为顺应城市总体发展的需要，从 2000 年 8 月以来，乌鲁木齐县先后进行四次行政区划调整。目前，县辖 1 镇 5 乡 41 个行政村，行政区域面积 4141 平方公里，总户数 18126 户，总人口 56165 人。

乌鲁木齐县旅游资源总量大、类型多、品种优、分布相对集中，旅游资源占全市旅游资源的 60%以上。目前，全县有规模大小不等的旅游风景区（点）15 处，其中国家 AAAAA 级旅游景区 1 处（天山大峡谷）、国家 AAAA 级旅游景区 1 处（苜蓿台生态公园）、国家 AAA 级旅游景区 1 处（东白杨沟旅游风景区），AA 级旅游景点 3 处，国家级森林公园 1 处，自治区级森林公园 1 处，全国农业旅游示范点 2 处，S 级以上旅游滑雪场 5 处，各类度假村 80 余处。

在 2014 年初召开的县委十二届五次全委（扩大）会议上，确定全县工作的总体要求是：深入贯彻党的十八届三中全会精神，全面落实区、市党委全委（扩大）会议精神，紧紧抓住历史机遇，坚持“生态立县、旅游兴县、和谐稳县、富民强县”的总体战略，以 2016 年全国冬运会在乌鲁木齐县举办为发展契机，以县域总规划实施为基础，以天山大峡谷国家 5A 级景区提档升级为抓手，以农牧民旧村居改造为着力点，以全力推进南山旅游产业基地建设、创建国家旅游度假区为目标，解放思想、创新变革，敢于担当、务求实效，为建设好我们的“幸福家园”和首府“美丽大花园”，打造南山旅游产业基地，与首府一道率先全面建成小康社会而奋发努力。

静影沉璧——照壁山天鹅湖风光

伊宁县

自治区党委副书记、人民政府主席努尔·白克力在伊宁县吐鲁番于孜乡看望群众。

自治区政协主席努尔兰·阿不都满金在伊宁县调研。

自治州党委书记黄三平在伊宁县调研指导工作。

江苏南通援建的县人民医院建成投入使用。

伊宁县地处伊犁河谷中部，全县总面积6153平方公里，辖20个乡镇(场),141个村(队),6个社区，总人口44.8万。伊宁县物产资源丰富，尤其以杏花、杏子被广大宾朋而熟知，素有"塞外杏乡"的美誉。

2013年，全县实现生产总值63.7亿元，增长13.1%;地方固定资产投资79亿元，增长11.6%;公共财政预算收入4.95亿元，增长27%;社会消费品零售总额12.1亿元，增长16%;招商引资到位资金52亿元;城镇居民人均可支配收入1.6万元，增长15.2%。外贸进出口总额440万美元，增长38%。

全县工业企业111家，全年实现乡及乡以上工业增加值10.48亿元，增长17.2%。煤化工、矿产品加工、新型建材、能源、农副产品加工五大产业格局基本形成。努力提高农牧民收入，出台强农惠农一号文件，县财政拿出7000万元支持现代农牧业发展，落实粮食种植102万亩，牲畜存栏达到百万头(只),农牧民人均增收1100元，人均纯收入达到10424元。大力改善城乡面貌，乡村规划实现全覆盖，一大批城市道路、住房、供水、供热等项目建成投入使用，城市功能日趋完善，人居环境焕然一新。第七批援疆工作顺利完成，三年来，南通市累计在伊宁县投入援助资金3.9亿元，援建了县人民医院、文化艺术中心等46个民生项目，引进了新月湾建材市场、中石油铁路专用线等11个产业项目，有力地助推了伊宁县经济社会发展。

新疆庆华循环经济工业园区

县委书记张继生

县委副书记、县长阿不都克尤木·吐达洪

第四届新疆伊犁杏花旅游节开幕式。

第四届新疆伊犁杏花旅游节活动。

第七届国际男篮邀请赛。

新汶集团泰山阳光新型陶瓷生产线。

伊宁县多浪农场 5000 亩高效节水工程。

冬季农村富余劳动力大培训学员展示学习到的技能。

冬季农村富余劳动力大培训学员汽修技能竞赛。

南通医疗队为灾区人民献爱心义诊活动。

现代农业科技示范园无土栽培技术。

伊犁河谷一颗璀璨的明珠

察布查尔锡伯自治县

县委书记王奕文在抗击雪灾一线

县长王春光(左二)查看设施大棚受灾情况

察布查尔,锡伯语为“粮仓”之意,是全国唯一以锡伯族为主体的多民族聚居的自治县,距伊犁哈萨克自治州首府伊宁市15公里,与哈萨克斯坦国边境线长73.4公里,有国家批准开放的一类陆路口岸—都拉塔口岸,区位优势十分突出。全县总面积4485平方公里,总人口19.8万人,由25个主要民族组成,其中锡伯族人口2.06万人,少数民族人口占总人口的72%。县辖13个乡镇、2个国营农场,县内驻有兵团农四师67团、68团、69团,伊犁州林业局平原林场和天山西部林业局山区林场等单位。

绚丽的锡伯风情。完整保留、延续了锡伯族语言、文字和传统风俗习惯。近年来,察布查尔县抓紧抢救、深入挖掘、系统整理、大力弘扬锡伯文化。锡伯民族博物院完成提升改造,被誉为国内一流的县级博物院。搜集整理锡伯族濒临灭绝的非物质文化遗产项目108个,“西迁节”、“贝伦舞”、“弓箭制作技艺”、“锡伯刺绣”等5个被列入国家级名录,还有18个被列入自治区级名录;中国首部锡伯族民俗数字电影《箭乡少女》拍摄完成,在中央电视台电影频道播映。启动实施国家锡伯族传统文化生态保护区建设项目。

丰富的矿产资源。目前初步探明的有煤、石灰石、铀、金、铜、铁、铅、锌、锰、重晶石、冰洲石、花岗岩等21个矿种,已开发利用13种。境内煤田已探明煤炭精查储量303亿吨,是新疆四大煤电煤化工产业基地之一伊犁矿区主战场。自治区级园区伊南工业园区占地160平方公里,现有伊泰、中电投、新汶、中煤、华电、国能等中国500强企业投资,已有煤基多联产、煤制天然气、煤制烯烃等一批项目落地建设,投资总额超3000亿元人民币。

怡人的自然环境。年水径流量166亿立方米,可利用水资源20亿立方米。全县现有灌溉面积138.83万亩。伊犁河流域水土开发将新增150万亩,适合重大项目用地和现代化、集约化、规模化发展。全县天然草场面积300万亩,林地面积156万亩,森林覆盖率12%;全年有效光照时数2846小时,无霜期177天,积温3800℃,年平均降水量222毫米。适宜种植各类农作物,是发展绿色有机食品原料的天然理想之地。

县域经济快速发展。第一次中央新疆工作座谈会四年来,察布查尔县县委、县人民政府变化变革、敢于担当、务求实效,科学判断县域经济形势,强势推进“九个坚定不移”的发展战略,各项工作在较短时间内实现较大突破。与2009年相比,2012年全县生产总值翻一番,地方公共财政预算收入翻一番半,地方规模以上工业企业增加值翻一番,全社会固定资产投资翻两番,招商引资翻三番。

2013年,全县完成生产总值41.93亿元,增长20%;乡及乡以上工业增加值5.7亿元,增长41.9%;地方公共财政预算收入3.25亿元,增长25%;全社会固定资产投资80亿元,增长21.2%;城镇居民家庭人均可支配收入16310元,增长16%;农牧民人均纯收入增加1316元,接近万元。

民生投入大幅增加。2010年以来,察布查尔县民生支出28.82亿元,占公共财政总支出的77.6%。28类136项重点民生工程全部落实。累计投入7.48亿元,稳定脱贫19203人。建成安居富民房16040套、牧民定居房1510套,实现牧民定居1070户。投

有机水稻基地。

伊泰伊犁540万吨年煤制液体燃料（一期180万吨）项目。

标准化养殖场。

全国青少年射箭比赛。

薰衣草基地。

资13437万元建成廉租房、公租房1983套。出台城乡居民大病医疗、脑瘫儿童、困难群众临时救助等11项惠民政策深得民心，惠及各族群众3.3万人。财政投入教育经费8.8亿元，占财政预算支出23.7%。实施普通高中免费教育、学前四年免费教育、贫困大学生资助工程等政策。争取项目资金2.7亿元，新建、改建校舍15万平方米，18526名学生纳入自治区义务教育学校学生营养改善计划。锡伯文教材编写工作全面启动，城乡义务教育呈现特色化、标准化发展，县乡村三级卫生服务网络体系进一步完善。投资6047万元的县综合体育馆完成主体工程。投入3.77亿元，新建、改扩建道路56.2公里，供排水、供热管网107.4公里。在全疆率先建成城际、城区、城乡、乡村"四位一体"公共交通体系。全力打造伊犁州最低物价区，建立县域价格监测体系，恩格尔系数始终保持在0.4左右，居民消费价格总水平涨幅始终控制在2%以下。

热情的"箭乡"人民真诚欢迎五湖四海的宾朋前来观光旅游，期待有识之士来投资兴业，同全县人民群众一道，共同建设民生、宜居、人文、幸福的察布查尔。

甜蜜、多彩、宜居 尼勒克县

县委书记周立新

县委副书记、县长努尔卡·卡那甫

这是一座古老而又年轻的希望之城，是一座甜蜜和谐宜居的园林之城。在这里，您可以与三千多年的历史不期而遇；在这里，您可以与西域多姿多彩的民族风情对接；在这里，您还可以踏遍山山水水，追流云，问明月，听蒙古长调………

这里就是伊犁河谷熠熠生辉的璀璨明珠——尼勒克。尼勒克，意为"新生命、希望"，地处新疆北部中天山西段、伊犁河谷东北腹地，距省会乌鲁木齐市516公里、首府伊宁市112公里，县域G218、S315、X779和G217、S316、S242、X774线相互贯通。全县辖13个乡(镇)场，东西长243公里，南北宽70公里，总面积10053平方公里，地貌特征呈柳叶状。全县18.99万人，由哈、汉、维、回、蒙等32个民族构成，其中哈萨克族8.7万人，占总人口的45.8%。

尼勒克县凭借得天独厚的自然资源优势，打造了别具特色的"四张名片"(即蜜蜂之都、岫玉之城、柯绣之乡、百里画廊)，也是伊犁河谷矿产资源、水能资源、旅游资源、生态资源和畜牧资源较为富集之地，更是中国特有蜜蜂物种-新疆黑蜂的保护区和能源化工的集聚区。现已发现煤、铁、铜等矿产22种，已建成瑞祥焦化、伊力特煤化工2家百万吨煤焦化项目、国电平煤、国投宝地2个120万吨煤矿技改项目、松湖铁矿100万吨铁选矿厂、南方矿业一期日处理2000吨及宝马矿业日处理1000吨铜选厂，建成了年产值8亿元、增加值4亿元的"一园两区"产业集聚基地；境内喀什河是伊犁河第二大支流，年径流量38.5亿立方米，建成首条横贯天山的750千伏输变电站，外输电为780万度/天；有雪山、云杉、草原、高山平湖、温泉、湿地古杨、民俗古迹等七大独具特色的旅游资源，形成以喀什河景观为主线和东部唐布拉风景区、中部吉林台亲水游乐区、西部喀什河谷湿地古杨风景区的"一线三区"旅游发展格局；有着千万亩优质草场、百万亩饲草基地、百万头只牲畜的巨大潜力，农业产业化经营面积达到27万亩。目前，农业和畜牧业万亩科技示范园初见成效，黑蜂产业园效益明显，沿S315线打造的万亩生态林初具规模。

中小企业创业基地（绿农产业园）——创业综合服务中心。

县城全貌

近年来，县委、政府紧密团结各族人民群众，抢抓中央新疆工作座谈会、对口援疆、全面深化改革及建设“丝绸之路经济带”的历史机遇，坚持以现代文化为引领，以富民强县为目标，围绕保障和改善民生这个核心，大力培育煤电煤化工、有色金属冶炼加工、现代农牧业和文化旅游四大产业，推进新型工业化、农牧业现代化、新型城镇化、现代服务产业化、基础设施配套化进程，大力实施生态立县、工业强县、畜牧大县、旅游名县、文化兴县五大战略，努力构建“甜蜜、多彩、宜居”的尼勒克。2013 年全县完成生产总值 40.9 亿元，同比增长 13%，其中第一、二、三产业增加值分别为 12.4 亿元、20.8 亿元、7.7 亿元，分别增长 8.1%、15.7%、11.2%。三次产业结构比为 30.3:50.8:18.9。全社会固定资产投资 57 亿元，增长 26.7%；公共财政预算收入 4.27 亿元，增长 18.1%；社会消费品零售总额 6.36 亿元，增长 14.8%；城镇居民人均可支配收入 15858 元，增长 12.7%，农牧民人均纯收入 10003 元，较上年同期增加 1580 元；旅游收入 11354.4 万元，增长 52.1%。

回顾往昔，旧城换新颜；展望未来，豪情绘蓝图。尼勒克人用真诚和热情欢迎国内外有识之士和各界宾朋，莅临考察指导，观光旅游，投资兴业，共谋发展。

蜜蜂之都

岫玉之城

柯绣之乡

国家 AAAA 级湿地古杨旅游风景区

新和县

新和县位于天山南麓，塔里木盆地北缘，东与库车县相望，南与沙雅县相连，西与温宿县相交，北与拜城县相邻，全县总面积8223平方公里，耕地面积76万亩；辖六乡两镇一个农场，110个行政村、6个社区，总人口17万人，是一个以维吾尔族为主体的多民族聚居县。

新和历史悠久、人文荟萃，在这块美丽神奇的土地上孕育了灿烂的龟兹文化，是古“龟兹国”繁锦之区，享有“汉唐重镇”、“班超府治”、“龟兹故里”的美誉。境内有托乎拉艾肯石窟、唐柘厥关、它乾城、玉奇喀特古城、通古孜巴什古城等宝贵历史文化遗产54处。非物质文化遗产——木卡姆艺术、民族乐器制作技艺等都彰显出新和县独具特色的艺术魅力，塔什艾日克乡被文化部授予“中国民间艺术之乡”称号。2009年10月，新和县境内面积达10万亩的“汉唐屯田遗址”被授予“大世界吉尼斯”之最。

新和县县委书记马国强

新和县县委副书记、县长艾买尔江依明

新和县有山地、绿洲、戈壁、沙漠四种地貌特征，属温带大陆性气候，昼夜温差大，无霜期长，日照充足，地下水资源丰富，得天独厚的水、土、光、热资源造就了新和“水果之乡”的美名。新和是传统的农业灌溉生产区，是国家优质棉生产基地，也是自治区粮食生产基地之一。全县年产优质皮棉6.5万吨，棉纺、种子产业发展潜力巨大；以红枣、核桃为主的特色林果面积达40万亩，红枣、核桃等产品远销国内外。境内石油、天然气储量丰富，天然气地质储量656.28亿立方米、凝析油及原油地质储量2600万吨，境内英买力、羊塔克、玉东三个区域为“西气东输”主气源地，已布探井135口，年产天然气22.74亿立方米、凝析油加原油55.05万吨。盐、石膏、铜等矿产资源尚待勘探开发。国道314线、库阿高速、南疆铁路横贯全境，龟兹机场毗邻县城，西气东输管道穿城而过，各种交通形态齐备，交通十分便利。

上级领导视察新和县便民服务中心“一站式”行政服务大厅。

近年来，新和县在自治区党委、人民政府及地委、行署的坚强领导下，坚持以“三个代表”重要思想为指导，以科学发展观统领全局，紧紧围绕跨越式发展和长治久安两大历史使命，团结带领全县各族干部群众全力推动经济社会各项事业快速健康可持续发展。2013年，全县实现生产总值28.1亿元，增长10%。第一产业实现增加值11.4亿元，增长8.7%；第二产业实现增加值5.8亿元，增长18.5%；第三产业实现增加值10.9亿元，增长7.1%。完成全社会固定资产投资22亿元，增长9.7%；完成地方公共财政预算收入3.4亿元；社会消费品零售总额3.3亿元，增长14.7%；城镇居民人均可支配收入19813元，增长13.2%；农民人均纯收入10027元（不含农场），增长16.2%。

西气东输主气源地新和英买力油气田

美丽富饶的富蕴县

富蕴县县委书记祁崇江

富蕴县县长叶尔江·卡孜木

宏泰铸铁厂一角。

富蕴县地处新疆维吾尔自治区北部，阿勒泰地区东端，额尔齐斯河上游，总面积3.22万平方公里。是新疆矿业基础较好的少数县(市)之一。目前共发展矿种四大种，92个品种，尤以黄金，宝石，有色金属闻名遐迩。有色金属，稀有金属储量居全国之首。10种矿产储量居全国前十位，全疆前列的有：铁、铜、钼、铅、锌。

县域内的水系主要是额尔齐斯河和乌伦古河两大水系。额尔齐斯河是我国唯一流入北冰洋的河流，正常流量为107.31KM3/S，年径流量为33.81亿KM3。乌伦古河为内流河，富蕴段属于中上游，多年平均径流量为9.7亿KM3。富蕴县野生动物种类繁多，有100余种。有林地面积505.06万亩，森林面积420万亩。可可托海景区成功创建为5A级风景名胜区，跻身全疆5个5A级景区之一。县辖6乡4镇，74个行政村。2013年，全县总人口9.67万人，由汉族、哈萨克族等26个民族组成，其中哈萨克族人口7.05万人，占总人口的72.91%；汉族人口2.12万人，占总人口的21.92%；全县总人口中，非农业人口3.96万人，占40.95%。

2013年，完成生产总值48.37亿元，同比增长11.7%。销售收入500万元以上工业企业增加值完成28.87亿元，增长22.7%。全社会固定资产投资完成60.93亿元，增长37.3%。地方财政收入11.63亿元，增长21.65%；地方财政支出25.14亿元，增长25.5%。金融机构存款余额32.35亿元，增长9.4%，贷款余额18.80亿元，增长34.5%。农牧民人均纯收入8739元，增长18.3%。全年共接待游客109万人次，增长23.2%，实现旅游总收入8.4亿元，增长28.1%。

金昊铁业有限公司生产车间

可可托海景区国家地质公园

钟山冬韵

巴里坤哈萨克自治县

书记韩雪峰(右二) 在三塘湖能源综合基地调研

书记韩雪峰(右二) 在三塘湖能源综合基地调研

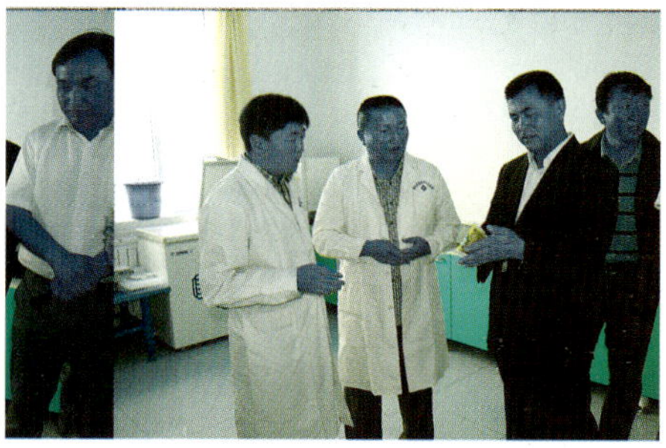

县长叶尔江(右三)调研哈萨克医事业发展

巴里坤哈萨克自治县成立于1954年9月30日,地处新疆东北部,东邻伊吾县,南接哈密市,西毗昌吉州木垒哈萨克自治县,北与蒙古国接壤,是全国三个哈萨克自治县之一,也是国家扶贫开发工作重点县,是新疆典型的边境县、高寒县、易灾县,2006年被国家确定为五类地区。境内中蒙边界线长313.4公里,设有国家一类季节性开放口岸——老爷庙口岸,是新疆与蒙古国发展边贸的重要开放口岸之一。

巴里坤县行政区划总面积3.84万平方公里,其中山地、戈壁2.55万平方公里,占全县总面积的66%。县域总人

现代畜牧

特色养殖

机械化收割

口10.24 万人，由汉、哈、维、蒙等 13 个民族构成，其中哈萨克族占 35%。县辖 15 个乡镇场区、46 个行政村、12 个自然村、6 个社区。境内驻有 69330 部队、兵团十三师红山农场和哈密地区伊吾马场。

巴里坤地形特征为“三山夹两盆”，有“新疆缩影”之称。巴里坤属温带大陆性冷凉干旱气候区，平均海拔 1650 米，冬季严寒，夏季凉爽，光照充足，四季不分明。年均气温 1℃，极端最高气温 35℃，极端最低气温 -43.6℃，无霜期 98-104 天，年降水量仅 200 毫米左右，蒸发量 1638 毫米。

巴里坤县经济以资源型工业、农牧业和旅游业为主。主要农产品有马铃薯、大路菜、大麦、小麦、晚熟哈密瓜、牛羊肉、驼奶等，其中巴里坤“力坤”牌牛羊肉、马铃薯获得了国家“绿色食品”认证；主要工业产品有煤炭、风电、芒硝、硫化碱、原油、黄金等。

2013 年，实现县域生产总值 43 亿元，同比增长 18%，其中一产 9.2 亿元，增长 7%；二产 22.4 亿元，增长 24%；三产 11.4 亿元，增长 16%。完成全社会固定资产投资 56.35 亿元，增长 40%；地方财政收入 3.86 亿元，同比增长 27%；社会消费品零售总额 5 亿元，增长 16%。城镇居民人均可支配收入 1.88 万元，增长 16.1%。农村居民人均纯收入 8444 元，增加 1432 元。

文化

大路菜喜获丰收

定居兴牧

煤炭

风电

田园彩城　梦幻伊吾

县委书记王跃斌慰问宗教人士。

县长牙合甫·排都拉慰问驻伊官兵。

淖毛湖哈密瓜丰收。

千人木卡姆。

伊吾县位于新疆东北部、天山北麓东段，县境东西长 215 公里，南北宽 175 公里，总面积 19519 平方公里，与蒙古国相邻，国境线长 274 公里，年无霜期最长 175 天，最短仅 80 天。“伊吾”是隋唐前哈密古地名，汉称伊吾卢，隋唐设伊吾郡，指以哈密为中心及周边地区。今之伊吾，于 1929 年废哈密王设哈密、宜禾、伊吾三县后转借得名。

伊吾县资源禀赋条件优越，煤炭、石油等在自治区乃至国家都有一定的战略地位，其中煤炭主要为 41 号长焰煤，挥发份 48.4%，灰分 7.4%，低温干溜焦油产率 8.2-19.11%，属副油、特副油煤，十分适合发展煤化工产业。光、热、风等可再生能源也十分丰富，70 米高风功率密度为 547-687W/m^2，该风电场风功率密度等级超过 3 级，日照天数大于 6 小时的天数在 300 天左右，年平均日照时数达 3253.6 小时以上，同时，伊吾县拥有草原秀色、民俗风情、冰川雪山、大漠胡杨等极具新疆特点的旅游资源，“伊吾维吾尔刺绣”获得新疆礼物大赛铜奖，伊吾木卡姆代表新疆参加全国少数民族非物质文化遗产展演活动，是新疆旅游业发展的缩影。

伊吾区位优势十分突出，随着红柳河——淖毛湖——三塘湖铁路、“山北捷道”、淖毛湖——甘肃柳沟矿产资源道路的贯通，伊吾将成为新疆的门户县，进出疆的桥头堡，带动物流、人流、资金流、信息流的迅速扩张，为伊吾跨越式发展奠定了坚实的基础。

近年来，伊吾县委、县人民政府团结和带领全县各族干部群众，坚持以科学发展观统领全局，紧紧围绕“六个率先”的发展目标，大力实施“六大战略”，积极培育“八大产业”，努力打造“五大基地”，加快推进“五化”同步建设，以发展为第一要务，以改革为第一动力，以稳定为第一责任，把伊吾建设成新疆东联西出的门户强县，环东天山经济圈重要的经济增长极。

2013 年，全县完成地区生产总值 28.5 亿元，同比增长 39%；完成地方财政收入 3.88 亿元，同比增长 55%，完成年初计划的 111%；城镇居民人均可支配收入 24367 元，同比增长 15%；农牧民人均纯收入达到 11122 元，同比增长 22%；全社会固定资产投资 83.8 亿元，同比增长 45%。三次产业比例达到 14:65:21，第二产业在经济总量中的比重大幅提高。招商引资实际到位资金 93 亿元，同比增长 35%，全年共接待游客 65 万人次，同比增长 30.5%，实现旅游收入 1.24 亿元，同比增长33.3%。

站在新起点　谋划新未来

中共新疆生产建设兵团第一师委员会党校

常务副校长　蒲必明

中共新疆生产建设兵团第一师委员会党校始建于1960年5月，原系中国人民解放军二军五师干训队，“文革”期间停办，1984年恢复。党校（行政学院）在师党委的直接领导下，是培训轮训师市党员领导干部的主渠道主阵地，是党的理论研究机构，是师市党委的重要工作部门。党校实行校委制，校领导3人，在职人员32人，其中高级职称7人，中级职称7人，研究生7人，离退休人员44人。

一师党校始终围绕师市党委的中心工作，按照培养“靠得住、有本事、留得下、用得上”的人才为目标，充分发挥主渠道作用，坚持改革创新，突出办学特色，全面提升教学科研、管理和后勤服务工作水平，在干部培训、理论研究等方面取得了一定成效。2013年，共举办各类培训班43个，培训各级干部4467人。其中主体班11个415人，培训规模和培训层次实现了新突破，首次对副处级及团场基层副连级以上干部进行了大规模的培训，实现了干部教育培训的全覆盖；在科研水平上得到提升，发表论文27篇，其中省部级8篇，地市级19篇。参加兵师举办的各类研讨会，送选论文31篇次。由解素梅撰写的《一师阿拉尔市少数民族聚居团场跨越式发展的思考》获国家统战部三等奖。在《塔里木报》刊登理论专刊9期，发表论文27篇；在教学上采取缺需与补学相结合、分类与分层相结合、传统方式与创新方式相结合的形式推进教学模式改革，坚持“走出去，请进来”的办学理念，外请专家教授及师市领导50人次进行专题授课，组织教师参加疆内外培训学习30余人次，通过一系列行之有效的教学方式方法，使干部教育培训质量有所提高。

2012年争取了中组部加强新疆基层政权建设项目，建设一师阿拉尔市党委党校，占地92亩，建筑面积19212，总投入8248万元，2014年下半年将投入使用并实现整体向阿拉尔搬迁。新校区建成后，拥有容纳500人和200人的报告厅各1个，配套有多媒体教学设施的标准教室15个，电教室4个，可一次性容纳350人住宿，1500人培训，成为兵团南疆培训中心。

多年来，第一师党委党校始终本着“立党育人、求真创新”的校训精神，坚持开展精神文明创建活动，自2008年以来，先后被授予阿克苏地区级文明单位、安全文明小区、“花园式单位”、“无烟单位”、卫生红旗单位和兵团级文明单位等称号，并连续多年保持师级文明单位荣誉称号，现已成为兵团一类党校。

领导关怀，倍受鼓舞。

上门走访，征求意见。

学习焦裕禄同志先进事迹交流会。

理论宣传的阵地，党性锻炼的熔炉。

新疆准东经济技术开发区

昌吉州副州长、新疆准东经济技术开发区党工委书记要建军

新疆准东经济技术开发区党工委副书记、管委会主任肖仁俊

新疆准东经济技术开发区(以下简称准东)位于昌吉州境内,是自治区推进优势资源转换战略,依托准东煤田规划建设的大型煤电煤化工产业示范区,是国家规划建设的第十四个大型煤炭基地重要组成部分,是“西气东输”、“疆电外送”的重要基地。煤田东西长 220 公里,南北宽 60 公里,总面积 1.3 万平方公里。煤炭资源预测储量 3900 亿吨,占全疆储量(2.19 万亿吨)17.8%、全国储量(5.56 万亿吨)7%。

2012 年,准东经国务院批准设立为国家级经济技术开发区,标志着准东产业发展进入了新的阶段,将成为新疆经济发展最快、最具成长潜力的区域之一。同时,自治区批准实施《新疆准东经济技术开发区总体规划》,明确了准东经济开发区主要以煤炭、煤电、煤电冶、现代煤化工为主的产业发展定位,通过努力将建设成为世界级煤炭资源综合利用产业聚集区、国家战略型能源开发综合改革试验区。

在区、州党委、人民政府的正确领导下,以党的十八大精神为统领,牢固树立和落实科学发展观,大力弘扬“开拓、创新、坚守、奉献”的准东精神,加快推进准东开发建设。截止 2013 年底,准东入驻企业集团 78 家,计划投资超过 8000 亿元;累计完成投资 1090 亿元,其中工业项目 969 亿元,基础设施 121 亿元。开发区基础设施完善,公路、铁路、供水、供电、通讯五大骨干基础设施一期工程完工投运,二期全面开始建设。产业项目扎实推进,促进准东快速发展,生态绿化和环境整治工作全面实施,坚定不移地推进准东快速崛起,为昌吉州乃至新疆经济快速发展做出新的贡献。

湖北宜化 30 万吨 PVC。

神火铝业。

乌准铁路准东站。

新汶矿业集团(伊犁)能源开发有限责任公司

董事长、党委书记亓会平

总经理(法人代表)王贯东

山东能源是国有独资大型企业集团,由新汶矿业集团有限责任公司(以下简称“新矿集团”)等6家集团组成,位列世界500强373位、中国煤炭工业100强前三甲。

新矿集团建企于1956年,是一家以国有资产为主体、多种所有制并存,以煤为主、多种产业共同发展的大型企业集团,企业信贷信誉AAA级。2013年,原煤产量4665万吨,营业收入724亿元,资产总额951亿元。先后荣获全国资源综合利用先进单位、全国煤炭行业节能减排先进单位、中国煤炭工业优秀企业管理奖、全国企业文化优秀奖,全国煤炭行业企业文化建设示范基地等荣誉称号,被国家发改委等六部委确定为国家第一批循环经济试点企业,在2010年7月党中央、国务院召开的西部大开发工作会议上被授予“国家西部大开发突出贡献集体”,2013年荣获全国“五一”劳动奖状。

新矿集团紧紧抓住国家深入实施“西部大开发”的战略机遇,于2004年进驻开发新疆西部“塞外江南”伊犁河谷。煤田分布在伊犁河南、北两岸,由伊南、伊北两个煤田组成。伊南煤田位于察布查尔县南部,面积338 km^2;伊北煤田位于霍城县东南部,伊宁市北部及伊宁县境内,面积113.4 km^2,已探明煤炭储量129.6亿吨。该煤田煤种以长焰煤为主,低灰、特低硫、中高发热量,挥发分高、化学活性强,是动力、气化、液化的优质原料。

2005年7月,注册成立新汶矿业集团(伊犁)能源开发有限责任公司(以下简称“伊犁能源”),是新矿集团的全资子公司,全面负责新矿集团在疆煤炭资源的开发、转化项目建设,属省级文明单位。先后被授予自治区“双百”优强企业,连续三年被授予“党风廉政建设先进单位”、“宣传思想工作先进单位”。

经过近年来的艰辛探索和艰苦创业,累计投资154亿元,构建形成了以煤炭生产为基础、资源转化为主导、机械制造为支撑、商贸物流为引擎的“四大产业”发展格局。

全球最大的煤化工单体工程施工现场。

伊犁四矿办公楼

昭苏煤矿外景

新天煤化20亿立方米煤制天然气项目建设场景。

伊犁一矿南工厂

新疆天富电力(集团)有限责任公司

兵团政委车俊在天富调研。

自治区常委哈尼巴提·沙布开在天富调研。

徐志新政委、张广新副师长在天富调研。

盛焉江师长来天富调研。

新疆天富电力(集团)有限责任公司由原石河子电力工业公司改制组建而成，于2002年2月4日正式在石河子市工商局注册为国有独资公司,注册资本10.4亿元。其中控股子公司天富能源股份有限公司于2002年2月28日在上海证券交易所发行上市。

公司主营发电、供电、供热、供天然气及煤炭生产、销售,担负着石河子垦区的电、热、气集中统一经营及大部分煤炭的生产经营管理,也是新疆唯一一家热电联产,水火电并举,发、供、调一体化的能源工业企业。

截止2013年底,公司资产总额206亿元。2013年,实现利润总额3.56亿元,完成工业总产值45.60亿元,完成工业增加值15.91亿元,年末从业人数8116人。年供电量85亿千瓦时,供热量1755万吉焦,供天然气6728万立方,全年生产原煤76万吨。

作为师市能源基础企业,公司将“统一规范、安全环保”作为企业的中长期发展指导思想。着力实现企业主业特色更加凸显,经营结构日趋完善的产业,重点发展电热产业、煤矿产业、燃气产业、房地产业、节能环保、现代物流等六大产业。奋力打造“三百”企业,即以2012年为基期,到2015年末实现产值倍增;到2016年末实现总产值100亿元,同时企业净资产100亿元,为打造百年天富奠定坚实的基础。

安全工作现场会

查看维稳装备。

220KV 环网启动仪式。

天富集团业余党校揭牌。

慰问一线职工。

参观煤矿井下紧急避险系统。

天富 1×12MW 垃圾发电项目锅炉钢架起吊。

公司在发展经济的同时，企业文化建设取得了丰硕成果。近几年，公司先后荣获全国“绿化模范单位”、全国“安康杯竞赛优秀企业”、全国“职工体育先进单位”和“学习型组织”优秀单位、全国电力系统十大“学习型企业”、兵团“屯垦戍边先进单位”、师市“创建四好领导班子”先进集体等荣誉称号。

从 2010 年至现在，天富已投入运行的总装机容量达 156.9 万千瓦，在天富过去 50 年全部装机规模 56.2 万千瓦基础上净增 100 万千瓦。

“十二五”期间，公司主要围绕师市的发展，不断提升煤、电、网的支撑力，做大增强基础产业，满足师市经济和社会发展的需要。“十二五”末，发电装机容量力争达到 400 万千瓦。重点建设石河子化工新材料产业园区天富发电厂一期 2×660MW 工程、南热电厂二期 2×330MW 热电联产扩建工程、天河热电厂一期 2×330MW 热电联产工程、东热电厂 2×135MW 热电联产技改工程、热电厂 2×135MW 热电联产技改工程。

在电网建设方面，在现有 110KV 输电网络的基础上，完成 220KV 骨干网架结构。2013 年 12 月 30 日，覆盖石河子垦区的 220 千伏环形电网联通投运，这也是兵团首个 220 千伏大环网。提前两年在石河子城区、工业园区内部以及城区与团场外围形成不完全双环网。2020 年进一步实现双环网结构。

站在新的起点上，天富人将以争创一流的进取之心，埋头苦干的工作作风，百折不挠的意志品格，实现天富电力的科学发展、跨越发展。

拆除小机组电厂。

天富第二届和谐小康家庭颁奖。

天富民兵迅速集结。

鲜花丛中的电厂

幸福的微笑脸。

新疆伊珠葡萄酒有限公司企业概况

原兵团司令员华士飞来公司参观指导工作。

公司新一届领导班子检查生产现场。

澳大利亚旺马库钠瓦拉葡萄酒业总裁来厂参观考察。

新疆伊珠葡萄酒有限公司，原名新疆伊犁葡萄酒厂，国有独资企业，隶属新疆兵团农四师七十团。是新疆伊犁哈萨克自治州最早生产葡萄酒系列产品的厂家，也是自治区和兵团最早生产干葡萄酒、冰葡萄酒的重点企业之一。六十年代初开始种植各种酿酒葡萄，1964 年建厂开始酿造葡萄酒，1984 年扩建。

厂区北距伊宁市 24 公里，紧靠 218 国道，位于伊宁县境内，年有效积温 3178℃–4100℃，日照 2820 小时，地理坐标：北纬 43° 49′ –43° 53′ 与世界生产葡萄酒的法国波尔多地区，生产冰酒的加拿大安大略省纬度基本相一致。这里光照充足，昼夜温差大，土壤有机含量高，是我国种植酿酒葡萄和冰葡萄的最佳产区。

20 世纪六十年代末，企业先后引进十余种世界优质酿酒葡萄品种：雷司令、晚红蜜、赤霞珠、品丽珠、梅鹿辄、蛇龙珠、法国兰等，现已发展优质无污染葡萄基地 6000 余亩，近期计划将葡萄基地发展到一万亩。公司设有原料部，负责葡萄基地的管理和对种植户的技术指导，

经过四十多年的发展，现厂区占地 4 万平方米，年生产各种葡萄酒 3500 吨，现有员工 83 人。产品主要有“伊珠”冰酒、干酒、甜酒、饮料四大系列 51 个品种。目前，公司自主研发设计的的伊珠 15.5 度、12 度冰酒、伊珠 2001、2003 世纪干红、伊珠桃红、纯红葡萄酒，伊珠葡萄庄园酒 7 款瓶贴外观设计获得国家专利。

近几年，投资引进了法国、意大利先进葡萄酒生产设备，加大科技投入和技术创新力度，不断提高产品品质。2004 年，在厂技术人员的努力下，成功研发出了高档冰红、冰白葡萄酒，达到国内先进技术水平，填补了新疆自治区空白。

公司产品以其选料精良、浓香悦人、绵甜爽口、风味独特而畅销天山南北，并远销北京、上海、广州、福建、江苏、浙江、甘肃兰州、陕西西安、苏州、湖南、四川、深圳等十余个省市。多次获国家、自治区荣誉。2006 年 2 月，新疆伊珠葡萄酒有限公司被中国特产之乡推荐暨宣传活动组织委员会定为“中国冰葡萄酒之乡”；2006 年 4 月，“伊珠冰红、冰白葡萄酒”同获第二届亚洲葡萄酒质量大赛金奖；2006 年 9 月冰葡萄酒产业化开发被国家科学技术部星火计划办公室列入星火计划项目；2006 年 10 月荣获“新疆特色产品(上海)交易会最佳畅销产品奖”；2007 年 9 月，“伊珠”冰红、冰白葡萄酒被授予“新疆名牌产品”称号；2008 年 7 月，“伊珠”品牌被自治区命名为“新疆著名商标”。为纪念改革开放 30 周年，公司被国家农业部乡镇企业局授予“全国优秀乡镇企业开拓创新奖”；2009 年“伊珠”干红葡萄酒荣获新疆名牌产品，同时干酒和冰酒通过了有机食品转换认证。2010 年，“伊珠”精制干红葡萄酒在烟台国际葡萄酒质量大赛上，从来自世界各地的 180 多款葡萄酒中脱颖而出，荣获银奖。2011 年，伊珠冰酒荣获新疆名牌产品称号。2012 年获得首届新疆品牌节“雪莲花银奖”。

投资 600 多万元新建不锈钢发酵罐

公司员工包装干葡萄酒生产现场

采摘葡萄

中华联合财产保险股份有限公司
CHINA UNITED PROPERTY INSURANCE COMPANY LIMITED

新疆分公司（简介）

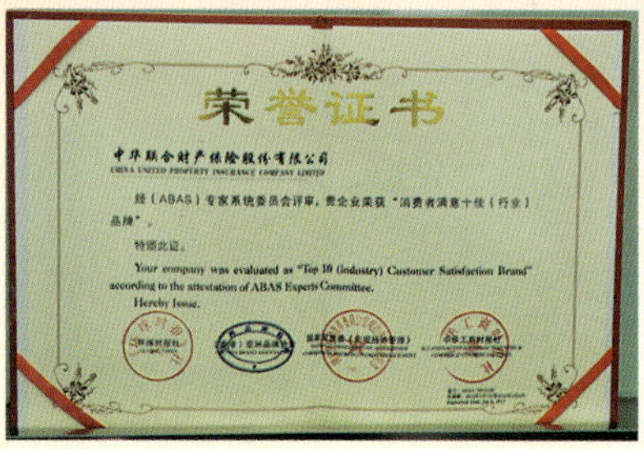

中华联合财产保险股份有限公司创立于1986年7月15日，是新中国之后我国成立的第二家国有保险公司，也是目前全国唯一一家以"中华"冠名的全国性保险公司。截至2013年底，公司已在全国设立了25家分公司，208家中心支公司，1186家支公司，706家营销服务部，获批分公司营业总部1家，机构总计2126家，员工35103人，形成了比较完整的营销服务网络，建立了一支高素质的保险经营与营销专业队伍。2013年，公司实现保费收入297.45亿元，位居国内财险市场第五位，各项主要经营指标名列行业前茅。

新疆是总公司的发源地，新疆分公司于2011年2月24日成立，是在原新疆区各地州机构的组织架构上新设立的省级分公司，新疆分公司所属各级机构共有289家，机构网络遍布天山南北、乡镇团场。自新疆分公司成立以来，广大干部员工充分发扬"敬业、责任、争先、奉献"的八字精神，同心协力，积极进取，为着力打造国内领先、专业化的综合保险金融集团而努力拼搏。公司现保费规模位居全公司首位，当地财险市场位居第二。

公司始终践行"服务至上、创造价值"对客户负责的服务宗旨，本着效益为先、专业经营的思想理念，不断提升公司核心竞争力，勇于承担社会责任。通过诚信服务赢得市场，通过提供全方位的保险保障服务于社会经济发展大局，得到了社会各界的广泛认可。